FOREWORD

Insolvency law, with its blend of the principled and the pragmatic, of the domestic and the cross-border, continues to fascinate. At one end of the spectrum the Supreme Court wrestles with the theory of "modified universalism" and with the true nature of decisions in insolvency proceedings: and at the other lesser mortals struggle with the consequences of filing the wrong form. In every case a clear, workable answer has to be provided promptly; and an answer which not only addresses the immediate problem but which takes into account the consequences for the system as a whole.

So an overview is essential. Another edition of this book, with its focus upon those cases that establish or develop principles, and its insightful commentary on matters of doubt, is most welcome. What is even more welcome is the proposal that the text will be updated on-line on a quarterly basis. Such careful and contemporary work enables the advocates to argue the cases well, and provides the decision maker with an invaluable tool when judgments have to be given with little time for reflection and often after limited argument.

I draw particular attention to the strong connection that the editorial team has with Leeds. Andrew Keay is Professor of Corporate and Commercial Law and Gerard McCormack Professor of International Business Law at the University of Leeds. Louis Doyle practices from Kings Chambers at Leeds (as well as Manchester and Birmingham). It is only right that the regional centres of excellence should be given the prominence they deserve. Indeed, an assiduous reader of the reports will soon discover how many significant cases were decided out of London.

A Foreword such as this also provides an opportunity to remind the reader of the unsung but significant leadership role played by the jurisdiction's only truly specialist insolvency judges, the Registrars. Their decisions take their rightful place in this work.

I commend this book to you.

Alastair Norris
Vice-Chancellor of the County Palatine
February 2014

PREFACE

The first and second editions of this book were published in 2005 and 2007. Since the appearance of the third edition in 2009 we have stalled the publication of this fourth edition more than once in the hope of being able to include a treatment of what we anticipated would be an over-hauled version of the Insolvency Rules. Five years on we can hold off no longer, that overhaul having reached the stage of the draft version of the new Rules (available on the Insolvency Service's website under the heading 'Insolvency Rules 2015') presently under consultation.

As with previous editions we have sought to update (and at certain points re-write) our annotations and commentary to include all of the relevant case-law and the legislative amendments whilst being economical with decisions that, whilst reported, add nothing new beyond the application of established principles to their own particular facts.

With the publication of this fourth edition comes a sea change in the way the text will be updated and made available online. With immediate effect the text will be available as part of Jordans' Insolvency Law Online service, *www.jordanpublishing.co.uk*. That online version of the book will be updated on an ongoing six-monthly basis. It is our hope that the fifth edition of the text will appear in 2016 and will feature annotations and commentary on the new version of the Insolvency Rules.

We have been assisted in the production of this edition not only by our friend and colleague Gerry McCormack (who continues to have primary responsibility for the cross-border material) but also by Holly Doyle, Simon Passfield and Stefan Ramel, all barristers at Guildhall Chambers, Bristol. We are grateful to each for his or her input and assistance.

We also extend our thanks to our publishers, Jordan Publishing, especially Mary Kenny and Kate Hather, for their customary patience and profes-sionalism in bringing this edition to print.

Finally, we thank the Honourable Mr Justice Norris for the benefit of his Foreword. The Vice-Chancellor's role in the development of the law of insolvency in recent years, especially that relating to administrations under Schedule B1 of the 1986 Act, will be well known to readers and is apparent from cases referred to in the pages that follow.

As with previous editions, we welcome and are grateful for the feedback we receive with a view to improving the text.

We have sought to deal with the law as it stood at 1 November 2013 subject to the inclusion of a number of subsequent developments.

Responsibility for the work, including any errors, rests with us alone.

LOUIS DOYLE   ANDREW KEAY

Kings Chambers   Centre for Business Law and Practice
Manchester, Leeds & Birmingham   School of Law
and   University of Leeds
9, Stone Buildings   *and*
Lincoln's Inn   King's Chambers
ldoyle@kingschambers.com   Manchester, Leeds & Birmingham
ldoyle@9stonebuildings.com   *and*
                                              9, Stone Buildings
                                                    Lincoln's Inn

February 2014

CONTENTS

Table of Cases

References are to page numbers.

Table of Cases

Table of Cases

Table of Cases

Table of Cases

Table of Cases

Table of Statutes

References are to page numbers.

Table of Statutory Instruments

References are to page numbers.

Table of International Legislation

References are to page numbers.

Table of SIPs and Dear IPs

References are to page numbers.

Introduction to the Insolvency Legislation

Our starting point in this book is the Insolvency Act 1986. The need for this legislation resulted from the work done by the Insolvency Law Review Committee and contained in its Report, titled *Insolvency Law and Practice* (Cmnd 8558) – known as 'the Cork Report' – handed down in 1982. The Cork Report made many recommendations and a good number of them were taken up by the Government. From the earliest times, and at the time of the Cork Committee's work, UK insolvency law was provided for mainly in two pieces of legislation: the Bankruptcy Act for personal insolvency and the Companies Act for corporate insolvency. The Committee advocated unified legislation, something that already existed in the United States.

The Insolvency Act 1986 represented a major reform of insolvency law in the UK. The process that led to the advent of this legislation began with the enactment of the Insolvency Act 1985. It provided for the bankruptcy of individuals and partly for the insolvency of companies, but the Companies Act 1985 still governed aspects of corporate insolvency.[1] The Insolvency Act became law on 30 October 1985, but few of its provisions became operative. The Government had decided to put forward a fresh Insolvency Bill. This latter Bill, to become the Insolvency Act 1986, was to act as a consolidating statute in relation to most of the Insolvency Act 1985[2] and to the parts of the Companies Act 1985 which covered corporate insolvency, so giving us unified legislation.[3] At the same time the Government decided to consolidate the law as it related to company director disqualification, and so the Company Directors' Disqualification Act 1986 was enacted. This legislation and the Insolvency Act began to operate from 29 December 1986. Contemporaneously, the Insolvency Rules 1986 came into force. While personal and corporate insolvency are now contained within the four corners of the same statute, the statute does not provide for a unified system per se. This is because, in the main, separate procedures and rules are maintained for the two forms of insolvency.

There have been a number of pieces of insolvency legislation enacted subsequent to the advent of the Insolvency Act 1986, both primary and secondary. The Insolvency Act 2000 is of particular note, although the biggest change came with the enactment of the Enterprise Act 2002. Part 10 of that legislation introduced a number of critical changes to both corporate and personal insolvency. Other legislation has been enacted, like the Enterprise Act 2002, that is not dedicated to insolvency law, but amends the Insolvency Act 1986 in some way. Another piece of legislation that is of importance and was introduced very recently is the Insolvency Rules 2005.

---

[1]   For example, winding up in ss 501–650 and 659–674.
[2]   For example, ss 12–14, 16, 17 and Sch 2 were consolidated into the Company Directors' Disqualification Act 1986.
[3]   Sections 467–650 and 659–674.

Insolvency Act 1986

As explained in the Preface and Introduction, this legislation was a result of a comprehensive review of UK insolvency law and practice undertaken by the Cork Committee from 1977 until 1982. The Insolvency Act 1986 ('the Act') represents the first time that the UK had had unified insolvency legislation. Until this legislation was enacted, personal insolvency was covered by the various Bankruptcy Acts and corporate insolvency was covered by the various Companies Acts. But besides covering insolvent companies the legislation also deals with the liquidation and receivership of solvent companies. While the legislation is unified to a certain extent, there are significant parts that are devoted to either companies or individuals. The same level of unification as the Americans have was not achieved.

The legislation is divided broadly into three Groups of Parts. The first Group addresses corporate insolvency (ss 1–251, inclusive of a definition Part). The second group deals with personal insolvency, including bankruptcy. It covers ss 252–385, again including a Part addressing interpretation issues. The third Group (ss 386–444) deals with miscellaneous matters, including important aspects relevant to the administration of insolvency practice, and many of the provisions cover both personal and corporate insolvency regimes. The major elements of the legislation are Parts. The larger Parts are then divided into Chapters. The two largest Parts are Part IV dealing with liquidation, and Part IX dealing with bankruptcy, although as a result of changes brought about by the enactment of the Enterprise Act 2002 the Part addressing administrations is quite large. The Schedules to the Act are more important than schedules attached to many statutes. Of particular importance is the aforementioned Sch B1, which houses most of the provisions that deal with administrations.

As one might expect, the statute is long and quite complex in places. The legislation covers the following corporate insolvency regimes: company voluntary arrangements, administrations, receiverships, provisional liquidations, and liquidations. The following personal insolvency regimes are covered: individual insolvency arrangements, interim receiverships and bankruptcies.

Until the advent of the Enterprise Act 2002 the Act was only amended in relatively minor ways. But the Enterprise Act has seen some extensive changes. These are addressed in the *Introduction to the Enterprise Act*, found later in the book. Provisions in the Enterprise Act that addressed corporate insolvency became operative from 15 September 2003, and the personal insolvency provisions from 1 April 2004.

Insolvency Act 1986

General note—As explained in the Preface and Introduction, this legislation was a result of a comprehensive review of UK insolvency law and practice undertaken by the Cork Committee from 1977 until 1982. The Insolvency Act 1986 ('the Act') represents the first time that the UK had had unified insolvency legislation. Until this legislation was enacted, personal insolvency was covered by the various Bankruptcy Acts and corporate insolvency was covered by the various Companies Acts. But besides covering insolvent companies the legislation also deals with the liquidation and receivership of solvent companies. While the legislation is unified to a certain extent, there are significant parts that are devoted to either companies or individuals. The same level of unification as the Americans have was not achieved.

The legislation is divided broadly into three Groups of Parts. The first Group addresses corporate insolvency (ss 1–251, inclusive of a definition Part). The second group deals with personal insolvency, including bankruptcy. It covers ss 252–385, again including a Part addressing interpretation issues. The third Group (ss 386–444) deals with miscellaneous matters, including important aspects relevant to the administration of insolvency practice, and many of the provisions cover both personal and corporate insolvency regimes. The major elements of the legislation are Parts. The larger Parts are then divided into Chapters. The two largest Parts are Part IV dealing with liquidation, and Part IX dealing with bankruptcy, although as a result of changes brought about by the enactment of the Enterprise Act 2002 the Part addressing administrations is quite large. The Schedules to the Act are more important than schedules attached to many statutes. Of particular importance is the aforementioned Sch B1, which houses most of the provisions that deal with administrations.

As one might expect, the statute is long and quite complex in places. The legislation covers the following corporate insolvency regimes: company voluntary arrangements, administrations, receiverships, provisional liquidations, and liquidations. The following personal insolvency regimes are covered: individual insolvency arrangements, interim receiverships and bankruptcies.

Until the advent of the Enterprise Act 2002 the Act was only amended in relatively minor ways. But the Enterprise Act has seen some extensive changes. These are addressed in the *Introduction to the Enterprise Act*, found later in the book. Provisions in the Enterprise Act that addressed corporate insolvency became operative from 15 September 2003, and the personal insolvency provisions from 1 April 2004.

ARRANGEMENT OF SECTIONS

FIRST GROUP OF PARTS
COMPANY INSOLVENCY; COMPANIES WINDING UP

PART I
COMPANY VOLUNTARY ARRANGEMENTS

The proposal

PART IV
WINDING UP OF COMPANIES REGISTERED UNDER THE COMPANIES ACTS

Chapter I
Preliminary

Introductory

Contributories

Chapter II
Voluntary Winding Up (Introductory and General) Resolutions for, and Commencement of, Voluntary Winding Up

Consequences of resolution to wind up

Declaration of solvency

Chapter III
Members' Voluntary Winding Up

PART VIII
INDIVIDUAL VOLUNTARY ARRANGEMENTS

Chapter I
Bankruptcy Petitions; Bankruptcy Orders

Preliminary

Creditor's petition

Debtor's petition

Chapter IV
Administration by Trustee
Preliminary

Chapter VII
Bankruptcy Offences

Power of court in bankruptcy

PART X
INDIVIDUAL INSOLVENCY: GENERAL PROVISIONS

PART XI
INTERPRETATION FOR SECOND GROUP OF PARTS

THIRD GROUP OF PARTS
MISCELLANEOUS MATTERS BEARING ON BOTH COMPANY AND INDIVIDUAL INSOLVENCY; GENERAL INTERPRETATION; FINAL PROVISIONS

PART XII
PREFERENTIAL DEBTS IN COMPANY AND INDIVIDUAL INSOLVENCY

PART XV
SUBORDINATE LEGISLATION

PART XVI
PROVISIONS AGAINST DEBT AVOIDANCE (ENGLAND AND WALES ONLY)

PART XVII
MISCELLANEOUS AND GENERAL

FIRST GROUP OF PARTS
COMPANY INSOLVENCY; COMPANIES WINDING UP

PART I
COMPANY VOLUNTARY ARRANGEMENTS

Introductory note to company voluntary arrangements—Company voluntary arrangements (CVAs) were a creation of the 1986 Act. This new mechanism followed observations made in paras 400–403 of the Cork Committee Report to the effect that company law was deficient in failing to provide a relatively straightforward mechanism by which a company might reach a binding arrangement with its unsecured creditors. Although schemes of compromise or arrangement were available under ss 206–208 of the Companies Act 1948, ss 425–427 of the Companies Act 1985 and remain available under ss 895-901 of the Companies Act 2006, such schemes are often perceived as being unattractive on account of the relatively complex procedure associated with implementation.

Section 1(1) defines a voluntary arrangement (VA) as either a composition by a company in satisfaction of its debts or a scheme of arrangement of its affairs. The difference between a composition and a scheme is discussed in the notes to s 1. It should be understood, however, that, strictly, there is no requirement for a company to be insolvent under any provision in Part I as a pre-requisite of a company proposing a CVA. In practice, however, a CVA might only conceivably have any practical use to a solvent company where that company has real grounds for anticipating its impending and unavoidable liquidation or, possibly, pursuant to a re-structuring.

CVAs have not been the success that was first anticipated following the implementation of the 1986 Act. There are a number of possible reasons for this, although the lack of popularity in usage of the moratorium-backed CVA under the Insolvency Act 2000 suggests that any previous lack of such protection was hardly one of them. There can be little doubt that both the former and present administration regimes offer, relatively speaking, an attractive mechanism for rescue or asset value maximisation, although it has to be said that CVAs are commonly used as an exit route from a wide variety of administrations. Furthermore, notwithstanding what might appear to a company and its directors to be the draw of a contractual based procedure, it remains that the stakes in some CVAs are very high, in that a failure to adhere to an approved proposal runs the risk of a default winding-up petition being presented by the supervisor of the arrangement, with the net consequence that a company and its creditors might find itself in a worse position than if it had entered into administration or even, in some cases, liquidation. These observations apart, there is no doubt that the CVA is an appropriate mechanism in the right case. The use of the procedure relies on qualified and experienced insolvency practitioners, and now turn-around specialists, who are able to diagnose particular difficulties in an ailing company to which the CVA procedure lends itself.

The key feature of a CVA lies in the ability of a company and a requisite majority of its creditors – on which see r 5.23(1) – to bind a dissentient minority in the way of what amounts to a form of statutory binding. In this sense a CVA has more than a passing resemblance to a scheme of arrangement: see *Re NFU Development Trust* [1972] 1 WLR 1548. Section 6(1)(a) and (b) allows for a creditor to challenge either the approval of a CVA as a material irregularity or the 'effect' of the arrangement as being unfairly prejudicial. Those matters are discussed in the notes to those provisions.

A CVA does not constitute an 'agreement' for the purposes of s 203 of the Employment Rights Act 1996: *Re Britannia Heat Transfer Ltd* [2007] BCC 195 (HHJ Norris QC sitting as a judge of the High Court).

The proposal

1 Those who may propose an arrangement

(1) The directors of a company (other than one which is in administration or being wound up) may make a proposal under this Part to the company and to its creditors for a composition in satisfaction of its debts or a scheme of arrangement of its affairs (from here on referred to, in either case, as a 'voluntary arrangement').

(2) A proposal under this Part is one which provides for some person ('the nominee') to act in relation to the voluntary arrangement either as trustee or otherwise for the purpose of supervising its implementation; and the nominee must be a person who is qualified to act as an insolvency practitioner or authorised to act as nominee, in relation to the voluntary arrangement.

(3) Such a proposal may also be made—

(a) where the company is in administration, by the administrator, and

(b) where the company is being wound up, by the liquidator.

(4) In this Part 'company' means—

(a) a company registered under the Companies Act 2006 in England and Wales or Scotland;

(b) a company incorporated in an EEA State other than the United Kingdom; or

(c) a company not incorporated in an EEA State but having its centre of main interests in a member State other than Denmark.

(5) In subsection (4), in relation to a company, 'centre of main interests' has the same meaning as in the EC Regulation and, in the absence of proof to the contrary, is presumed to be the place of its registered office (within the meaning of that Regulation).

(6) If a company incorporated outside the United Kingdom has a principal place of business in Northern Ireland, no proposal under this Part shall be made in relation to it unless it also has a principal place of business in England and Wales or Scotland (or both in England and Wales or Scotland).

Amendments—Insolvency Act 2000, s 2, Sch 2, paras 1, 2; Enterprise Act 2002, s 248(3), Sch 17, paras 9, 10; SI 2002/1240; SI 2005/879; SI 2009/1941.

General note—Despite its heading, this provision touches on a wide range of issues which, for convenience, are considered here.

Section 1(1)

Eligible applicants—Other than where a company is in administration (ie under the former Part II or under the new Sch B1) or a company is being wound up compulsorily or voluntarily – in which case the office-holder may put a proposal under s 1(3) – 1(1) envisages only the directors of a company making a proposal to the company and its creditors for what is commonly termed a CVA. There is no provision for a proposal to be put by either the members or creditors of a company, or any other person.

The Independent Regulator may direct an NHS foundation trust to have recourse to a CVA by virtue of s 53 of the National Health Service Act 2006. Pursuant to s 113 of the Banking Act 2009, a bank liquidator may also propose a CVA.

The scope of the term 'creditor'—Whilst the legislation provides no definition of the word 'creditor' (a term employed both in s 1(1) and in r 1.17(1) on voting rights) the term extends not only to unliquidated debts (given specific language to that effect in r 1.17(3)) but also to future or contingently payable debts: *Re Cancol Ltd* [1996] 1 All ER 37 (Knox J, future payments of rents to fall due under an existing lease) applying to CVAs the reasoning applied by the Court of Appeal in *Doorbar v Alltime Securities Ltd (No 2)* [1995] BCC 1, 149, affirming Knox J at first instance [1994] BCC 728, in relation to individual voluntary arrangements.

Unliquidated debts—Rule 1.17(3) provides that a creditor voting in respect of an unliquidated amount or any debt whose value is not ascertained shall, for voting purposes only, have his debt valued at £1 unless the chairman agrees to put a higher value on it. For further illustrations on the treatment of such creditor claims see *Beverley Group plc v McClue* [1995] BCC 751 (Knox J); *Re Sweatfield Ltd* [1997] BCC 744 (His Honour Judge Weeks QC); *Re Wisepark Ltd* [1994] BCC 221 (untaxed (ie unassessed) litigation costs not a debt for CVA purposes) and *County Bookshops Ltd v Grove* [2002] BPIR 772 (Neuberger J, contractual instalment payments which had not fallen due as at date of CVA admitted to arrangement as contingent debts) and *Leighton Contracting (Qatar) WLL v Simms* [2011] EWHC 1735 (Ch), [2011] BPIR 1395.

Disputed debts—In the case of disputed debts the proper course under r 1.17A(4) is for the chairman to mark the claims objected to and allow the creditor to vote for the full amount, on which see *Re A Debtor (No 222 of 1990) ex parte Bank of Ireland* [1992] BCLC 137 at 144F–144H (Harman J).

Contingent debts—The decision of David Richards J in *Re Federal-Mogul Aftermarket UK Ltd* [2008] EWHC 1099 (Ch), [2008] BPIR 846 includes valuable guidance on the application of the so-called 'hindsight principle' – that is, in valuing a contingent debt it is necessary to take into account everything which has actually happened between the date of valuation and the date on which the contingent liability is actually calculated – as explained by Lord Hoffmann in *Stein v Blake* [1996] 1 AC 243 at 252E–252F.

Court control over the admission of creditor's proof—The court has jurisdiction to direct that a creditor be admitted to proof in an arrangement: *Re FMS Financial Management Services Ltd* (1989) 5 BCC 191 (Hoffmann J (as he then was), joint administrators proposing CVA directed to admit to proof shareholders with prima facie good claim against the company for misrepresentation). It should be noted that the standing of *FMS*, an ex tempore judgment upon an appearance by administrators only without reference to authority, is, to use the words of HHJ Pelling QC, sitting as a High Court judge in *Re Beloit Walmsley Ltd* [2008] BPIR 1445 at [20], 'seriously circumscribed'. Certainly in *Re Alpa Lighting Ltd* [1997] BPIR 341 at 347A–347B Nourse LJ had distinguished *FMS* on the basis that in *FMS* no amendment of the CVA had been sought and that it was unnecessary to go into the question of whether the admission of a new class of creditors to an arrangement amounted to such an amendment.

The effect of an arrangement on third parties—Although a CVA is capable either expressly or by necessary implication of varying the relationship between a creditor of the company and a third party (eg so as to release a co-debtor or security which is not itself a party to the arrangement), an arrangement will ordinarily be construed as reserving the rights of creditors against third parties: see *March Estates plc v Gunmark* [1996] 2 BCLC 1 at 5H–6G (Lightman J) and the cases cited therein: see also *Lombard NatWest Factors Ltd v Koutrouzas* [2002] EWHC 1084 (QB), [2003] BPIR 444 (surety not released by individual voluntary arrangement (IVA) of co-surety where guarantee expressly provided that guarantee would not be affected by indulgence granted to co-surety). For an unsuccessful attempt at materially affecting the rights of third parties, see *Re Sixty UK Ltd (In Administration and Company Voluntary Arrangement); Mourant & Co Trustees Ltd and Mourant Property Trustees Ltd v Sixty UK Ltd (In Administration), Hollis and O'Reilly* [2010] EWHC 1890 (Ch) [2010] BPIR 1264 which was a CVA which failed on the grounds of unfair prejudice (cf *Prudential Assurance Co Ltd v PRG Powerhouse Ltd* [2007] EWHC 1002 (Ch), [2007] BPIR 839). Construction of an arrangement term purporting to modify third party rights is not a matter of general principle and depends on the surrounding circumstances and account being taken not only of the express words employed in the arrangement but also any terms which may be properly implied: *Johnson v Davies* [1998] 2 BCLC 252 at 259B–259D (Chadwick LJ). For further general guidance on the construction of voluntary arrangements see the notes under that heading to s 5(2)(b) below.

'Composition' and 'scheme of arrangement'—The distinction between the terms 'composition' and 'scheme of arrangement' was considered by the Court of Appeal in *Commissioners of Inland Revenue v Adams* [2001] 1 BCLC 222 at 230G–231F (Mummery LJ), affirming the decision of Nicholas Warren QC, sitting as he then was as a deputy High Court judge, at [1999] 2 BCLC 730. A composition is an arrangement to pay a sum in lieu of a larger debt or other obligation, or forbearance to sue for the full amount being exchanged for a money payment or other consideration. A scheme of arrangement, on the other hand, involves something less than the release or discharge of creditor debts (as on a composition) and might include nothing more than a moratorium on the enforcement of creditor claims so as to suspend the date for repayment of such debts, with or without the payment of a dividend in the interim: see *March Estates plc v Gunmark* [1996] 2 BCLC 1 at

5A–5G (Lightman J). Accordingly, the approved proposal in *Adams*, which imposed a moratorium on the prosecution of creditor claims for a three year period with no prospect of a dividend to preferential or unsecured creditors, constituted a scheme of arrangement so as to amount to a voluntary arrangement within s 1(1). A scheme of arrangement which amounts to nothing more than a moratorium on creditor claims, even if capable of being brought within the definition of a voluntary arrangement, will not usually be of great attraction to a debtor for the simple reason that arrangement creditors will be free to pursue their claims against the debtor on the cessation of the moratorium. In practice, therefore, a debtor might seek to obtain the fuller advantage of a composition by offering a dividend, even a very small dividend, to creditors in consideration for the discharge in full of creditor claims.

Proposals which do not amount to a composition or a scheme of arrangement—If a proposal is put to creditors which amounts to neither a composition nor a moratorium, then the original proposal remains a nullity such that the proposal is not capable of being saved by modifications introduced at the first statutory meeting of creditors, even where the creditors support such modifications: *Commissioners of Inland Revenue v Bland* [2003] BPIR 1274 (Lloyd J, as he then was, original IVA proposal which offered nothing to creditors successfully challenged by Revenue under s 262 notwithstanding modifications introduced to provide for dividend). The same considerations as apply to IVAs apply to CVAs: *Bland* at [39].

Section 1(2)

Implementation—A valid proposal is implemented on it being approved under s 4(1) at a creditors' meeting summoned under s 3 by the requisite majority of creditors as provided for in r 1.19(1). Thereafter, the nominee – or any person appointed in his stead under s 2(4) or s 4(2) – is known as the supervisor of the voluntary arrangement: see s 7(2) and the notes thereto.

Qualifications of the nominee—In addition to the observations as to the nature of a voluntary arrangement in the notes to s 1(1) above, s 1(2) imposes a requirement that, so as to constitute a proposal, a proposed CVA must provide for a person who is qualified to act as an insolvency practitioner 'in relation to the voluntary arrangement either as trustee or otherwise for the purpose of supervising its implementation'.

The phrase 'act as an insolvency practitioner' is defined in s 388: see also s 419. By virtue of Insolvency Act 2000, s 4 certain persons who are not licensed insolvency practitioners (commonly termed turnaround specialists) may also be authorised under s 389A to act as nominees (and supervisors) in relation to CVAs.

Identity of the nominee—In practice the nominee is invariably the same individual who takes office subsequently as supervisor, although s 4(2) provides that a modification to the proposal replacing the nominee with another individual (who will then take office as supervisor) may be approved by creditors at the meeting summoned to consider the proposal. The nominee may also be replaced by the court under s 2(4) on prescribed grounds.

'to act … either as trustee or otherwise for the purpose of supervising its implementation'—In *Re Leisure Study Group Ltd* [1994] 2 BCLC 65 at 68A Harman J suggested that a nominee acting in relation to a voluntary arrangement would so act as a trustee. In *Re Bradley-Hole (a Bankrupt)* [1995] 4 All ER 865 Rimer J adopted the same reasoning in relation to the status of the supervisor of an approved arrangement to whom assets had been transferred by the debtor. Harman J's decision in *Leisure Study* was approved by the Court of Appeal in *Re N T Gallagher & Son Ltd, Shierson and another v Tomlinson and another* [2002] EWCA Civ 404 [2002] 2 BCLC 133 (at para 32). Given this approach, it is one view that it would not appear to matter whether the proposal provides expressly that a nominee is to hold arrangement assets as trustee. The words 'or otherwise' would appear to catch any action by a nominee other than in his capacity as a trustee of the proposed arrangement assets; although the use of the words 'or otherwise' might also refer to a nominee who is not a trustee but who will nonetheless supervise the implementation of the voluntary arrangement.

Proposal by administrator or liquidator—Under the former Part II of the Act relating to administration orders, a CVA – in contrast with the other purposes identified in s 8(3) – constituted a common 'exit route' by which assets could be distributed to creditors in the administration. Although a CVA will continue to be used as an exit route by administrators appointed under Sch B1 of the Act, it should be noted that an administrator is now empowered by para 65 of Sch B1 to make distributions to creditors, subject to court permission where the distribution is to an unsecured creditor.

CVA proposals by liquidators are rare in practice.

Role of the nominee—The legislation confers no powers on a nominee in relation to the company or the assets of the company subject to the proposed CVA. In practice, the nominee will usually play a significant role in assisting the directors of the company in the drafting of the proposal, although the proposal itself remains that of the directors (or an office-holder under s 1(3)). The nominee is not, however, the agent of the debtor: *Re A Debtor (No 222 of 1990) ex parte Bank of Ireland (No 2)* [1993] BCLC 233 at 235D (Harman J).

The involvement of the nominee in the proposal process must be tempered with the fundamental requirement for the nominee to retain objectivity in the discharge of his function and in the preparation of his report to the court under s 2(2).

SIP 3 identifies best practice in relation to voluntary arrangements; Paragraph 2.2 provides that 'In dealing with a VA the member should bear in mind his overriding duty to ensure a fair balance between the interests of the company/debtor, the creditors and any other parties involved. In considering whether to accept appointment as either nominee or supervisor the member should have regard to the ethical guidelines of his authorising body.' The Insolvency Service's Dear IP Letter of March 1995 suggests that practitioners pose the following questions in relation to a proposed arrangement: (1) Is it feasible? (2) Is it fair to the creditors? (3) Is it an acceptable alternative to formal insolvency? (4) Is it fit to be considered by the creditors? (5) Is it fair to the debtor? The loss of professional objectivity plainly carries with it the risk of professional criticism and sanction. In addition, where a nominee falls significantly below the standards required of a licensed insolvency practitioner the court may, on an application under s 262, require the nominee to pay all or part of the costs of any proceedings arising out of the inadequate discharge of his duties, including his conduct as chairman of the creditors' meeting: *Re A Debtor (No 222 of 1990) ex parte Bank of Ireland (No 2)* [1993] BCLC 233 (Harman J) and see also the decision of Andrew Simmonds QC in *Tradition (UK) Ltd v Ahmed and Other* [2008] EWHC 3448 (Ch), [2009] BPIR 626 for an unsuccessful attempt at making the nominee liable for all of the costs of an application to challenge a voluntary arrangement – the decision of Andrew Simmonds QC contains a useful analysis of the principles to be applied when determining whether a proposed nominee should be liable for costs. This is the case even where the application could have been pursued by way of an appeal under r 1.17A(3), in relation to which r 1.17A(7) provides that a chairman of a creditors' meeting may not be personally liable for the costs of such an appeal. It is vitally important, therefore, that a nominee (or supervisor) maintains his objectivity throughout, remaining, in effect, between the debtor and his creditors, and is not seen to take up the debtor's cause where a creditor raises a legitimate complaint.

Duties of the nominee—For commentary see the notes to s 2(2) below.

The status of arrangement assets in a winding up or bankruptcy—In *Re NT Gallagher & Son Ltd, Shierson v Tomlinson* [2002] 2 BCLC 133, [2002] EWCA Civ 404 Peter Gibson LJ, giving the judgment of the court also comprising Ward and Dyson LJJ, considered the issue of whether arrangement assets held on a trust for CVA creditors survived liquidation and whether the arrangement creditors were entitled to prove in an ensuing liquidation. The guidance provided in the *Gallagher* judgment was much needed given the eleven hardly reconcilable first instance decisions considered in the judgment. At para [54] the following conclusions were identified:

'(1) Where a CVA or IVA provide for money or other assets to be paid to or transferred or held for the benefit of CVA or IVA creditors, this will create a trust of those moneys or assets for those creditors. (2) The effect of the liquidation of the company or the bankruptcy of the debtor on a trust created by the CVA or IVA will depend on the provision of the CVA or IVA relating thereto. (3) If the CVA or IVA provides what is to happen on liquidation or bankruptcy (or a failure of the CVA or IVA), effect must be given thereto. (4) If the CVA or IVA does not so provide, the trust will continue notwithstanding the liquidation, bankruptcy or failure and must take effect according to its terms. (5) The CVA or IVA creditors can prove in the liquidation or bankruptcy for so much of their debt as remains after payment of what has been or will be recovered under the trust.'

For the purposes of conclusion (1) it should be noted that the Court of Appeal approved of the concession by counsel for the CVA supervisors, by reference to the decision of Harman J in *Re Leisure Study Group Ltd* [1994] 2 BCLC 65, to the effect that the supervisors were trustees of the assets in their hands notwithstanding the absence of an express trust having been created by the CVA. The combined effects of conclusions (3) and (4) is that arrangement assets will remain ring-fenced for arrangement creditors on a liquidation or bankruptcy or failure of the arrangement unless the arrangement itself specifically provides that the arrangement assets are to be treated differently, most obviously by way of falling into the liquidation or bankruptcy for the benefit of liquidation or bankruptcy creditors. The justification for what might be termed the default rule on ring-fencing in conclusions (3) and (4) appears in para [50] of the judgment which provided, following an observation that the general law leaves trusts of assets not held for a company unaffected by its liquidation:

'Further, as a matter of policy, in the absence of any provision in the CVA as to what should happen to trust assets on liquidation of the company, the court should prefer a default rule which furthers rather than hinders what might be taken to be the statutory purpose of Part I of the Act. Parliament plainly intended to encourage companies and creditors to enter into CVAs so as to provide creditors with a means of recovering what they are owed without recourse to the more expensive means provided by winding up or administration, thereby giving many companies the opportunity to continue to trade.'

Precisely the same rationale justifies the operation of the default rule on ring-fencing in IVAs under Part VIII, which were introduced as a means of avoiding the consequences of bankruptcy, subject to approval by a requisite majority of creditors.

Section 1(4)

The meaning of the term 'company'—Since 1 October 2009, the term 'company' is defined by reference to the Companies Act 2006 (see the Companies Act 2006 (Consequential Amendments, Transitional Provisions and Savings) Order 2009 (SI 2009/1942).

Section 1(4) was originally introduced with effect from 31 May 2002 by reg 4 of the Insolvency Act 1986 (Amendment) (No 2) Regulations 2002 (SI 2002/1240) and had the effect of extending the scope of the statutory definition. However, following the confusion caused by the decision in *Re The Salvage Association* [2003] BCC 504 (Blackburne J) as to whether the EC Regulation permitted an unincorporated entity to avail itself of a CVA, s 1(4) was amended with effect from 13 April 2005 by the Insolvency Act 1986 (Amendment) Regulations 2005 (SI 2005/879) so as to limit the scope of Part I to companies as defined in s 735(1) of the Companies Act 1985 and certain overseas companies. The provision was amended again with effect from 1 October 2009, as described above.

Article 3(1) of the EC Regulation—Voluntary arrangements under insolvency legislation are expressly included in Annex A of the EC Regulation on Insolvency Proceedings 2000 as 'insolvency proceedings' within the meaning of Art 2(a) for the purposes of the Regulation. Although Art 3(1) refers to the 'courts' of a Member State having jurisdiction to open main insolvency proceedings, the term, in line with Art 2(d) of the Regulation and para 66 of the Virgos-Schmit Report's commentary on the earlier draft EC Bankruptcy Convention, includes not only the judiciary but also a person or body empowered by national law to make decisions in the course of those proceedings, such as meetings of members and creditors in a CVA.

A CVA may be proposed in relation to a company incorporated outside the European Community if the company's centre of main interests can be shown to be within the United Kingdom: *Re BRAC Rent-a-Car International Inc* [2003] 1 WLR 1421 (Lloyd J, administration order made in respect of Delaware incorporated company) and to similar effect see *Daisytek-ISA Ltd* [2003] BCC 562 (His Honour Judge McGonigal sitting as a judge of the High Court).

The decisions in *Salvage Association* and *Rent-a-Car* were preceded by that of Lawrence Collins J in *Re Television Trade Rentals Ltd* [2002] BCC 807 where orders (which were not retrospective) were granted in favour of the provisional liquidators of two Isle of Man registered companies with strong English trading connections in response to a letter of request by the Isle of Man court asking the English court to direct and declare that Part I of the 1986 Act, which had no equivalent in the Isle of Man, should apply to the companies pursuant to s 426. It would now appear that, subject to the revised scope of s 1(4) and a debtor company establishing eligibility to make a proposal under s 1 and centre of main interests within the United Kingdom, a non-EC incorporated corporation need not have recourse to s 426 in pursuing a CVA.

1A Moratorium

(1) Where the directors of an eligible company intend to make a proposal for a voluntary arrangement, they may take steps to obtain a moratorium for the company.

(2) The provisions of Schedule A1 to this Act have effect with respect to—

    (a)   companies eligible for a moratorium under this section,

    (b)   the procedure for obtaining such a moratorium,

    (c)   the effects of such a moratorium, and

    (d)   the procedure applicable (in place of sections 2 to 6 and 7) in relation to the approval and implementation of a voluntary arrangement where such a moratorium is or has been in force.

Amendments—Inserted by Insolvency Act 2000, s 1, Sch 1, paras 1, 2.

General note—This provision was brought into effect from 1 January 2003 by virtue of the Insolvency Act 2000 Commencement (No 3) and Transitional (Provisions) Order 2002 (SI 2002/2711) and allows for the obtaining of a moratorium protecting the company and its assets from creditor action pending implementation of a proposal by the company's directors.

The detailed provisions governing eligibility and the nature of and procedure for obtaining the moratorium appear in Sch A1. The moratorium is not available where a company is in administration, administrative receivership, liquidation, provisional liquidation, CVA or where the company has obtained a moratorium in the preceding twelve-month period.

Pursuant to paragraph 3(2) of Sch A1, a CVA with a moratorium may be proposed in relation to a company which satisfies 2 or more of the requirements for being a small company as specified in s 382(3) of the Companies Act 2006. Those requirements are that the company has a turnover of not more than £6.5 million, or a balance sheet total of not more than £3.26 million or not more than 50 employees. Sch A1 contains detailed provisions for determining the precice moment in time when the requirements must be met.

In practice, CVAs with the protection of a moratorium are rare, not least on account of the relative convenience of the new administration regime under Sch B1.

2 Procedure where nominee is not the liquidator or administrator

(1) This section applies where the nominee under section 1 is not the liquidator or administrator of the company and the directors do not propose to take steps to obtain a moratorium under section 1A for the company.

(2) The nominee shall, within 28 days (or such longer period as the court may allow) after he is given notice of the proposal for a voluntary arrangement, submit a report to the court stating—

(a) whether, in his opinion, the proposed voluntary arrangement has a reasonable prospect of being approved and implemented,

(aa) whether, in his opinion, meetings of the company and of its creditors should be summoned to consider the proposal, and

(b) if in his opinion such meetings should be summoned, the date on which, and time and place at which, he proposes the meetings should be held.

(3) For the purpose of enabling the nominee to prepare his report, the person intending to make the proposal shall submit to the nominee—

(a) a document setting out the terms of the proposed voluntary arrangement, and

(b) a statement of the company's affairs containing—

    (i) such particulars of its creditors and of its debts and other liabilities and of its assets as may be prescribed, and

    (ii) such other information as may be prescribed.

(4) The court may—

(a) on an application made by the person intending to make the proposal, in a case where the nominee has failed to submit the report required by this section or has died, or

(b) on an application made by that person or the nominee, in a case where it is impracticable or inappropriate for the nominee to continue to act as such,

direct that the nominee be replaced as such by another person qualified to act as an insolvency practitioner, or authorised to act as nominee, in relation to the voluntary arrangement.

Amendments—Insolvency Act 2000, s 2, Sch 2, paras 1, 3.

General note—The detailed procedural rules governing the preparation and contents of CVA proposals together with the preparation of the proposal and the nominee's report to the court as set out in rr 1.2–1.9.

Section 2(1)

Scope of provision—Section 2 applies either where the CVA proposal is made by the directors under s 1(1) (but not where it is proposed to take steps to obtain a moratorium under s 1A) or where (far less commonly) an administrator or liquidator proposing an arrangement under s 1(3) nominates an individual other than himself as nominee.

Section 2(2)

The viability of the proposal and the duties of the nominee in reporting to the court—In *Re A Debtor (No 222 of 1990) ex parte Bank of Ireland and Others (No 2)* [1993] BCLC 233 at 234E–234G Harman J, in the course of a judgment heavily critical of a nominee, expressed the following view:

'In my judgment, the nominee both in making his report and in acting as chairman of the meeting is to be taken as having a duty (arising from the requirement in the statute that he shall report his own opinion to the court) to exercise a professional independent judgment. The fact that judgment is required to be that of a licensed insolvency practitioner emphasises the fact that the court is to receive a report from a qualified person skilled and experienced in these matters, who is exercising his own professional functions in judging whether the matter is, in his opinion, fit to go forward.'

The substance of the judgment in *Bank of Ireland* is reflected in the guidance in SIP 3 and was referred to in the Dear IP Letter of March 1995 noted under the heading 'Role of the nominee' to s 1(2) above.

In *Greystoke v Hamilton-Smith* [1997] BPIR 24 at 28B–28F Lindsay J made reference to the Dear IP Letter of March 1995 as representing 'a fair view in general terms of responsibilities which the legislation casts upon a nominee.' The judge, however, went on to express the view that a nominee cannot be expected in every case to have verified personally every figure and to have tested every part of the proposal where, for example, financial resources preclude such enquiries. Lindsay J did, nonetheless, consider that a nominee has an obligation to satisfy himself of three specific matters, 'at least in those cases where the fullness or candour of the debtor's information has properly come into question', namely (1) that the debtor's true position as to assets and liabilities does not appear to him in any material respect to differ substantially from that as it is to be represented to creditors, (2) that the debtor's proposal to creditors has a real prospect of being implemented in the way it is to be represented that it will be (bearing in mind that a measure of modification to proposals is possible under s 258), and (3) that the information provides a basis for the view that no already manifest yet unavoidable prospective unfairness in relation to the nominee's functions of admitting or rejecting claims to vote and agreeing values for voting purposes is present. In each particular case, therefore, it is submitted that the question of further enquiry or investigation by the nominee remains a judgment call for the nominee, whose decision must be capable of being justified, objectively speaking, in those circumstances which are known or ought to be known to him. His Lordship also considered but rejected the proposition that the arrangement must appear to offer a reasonable prospect of a better recovery than bankruptcy (or liquidation).

Having identified the above three minimum steps, Lindsay J went on in *Greystoke* (at 28H–29A) to qualify his view with the proviso that the steps which it is reasonable for a nominee to take in satisfying himself of the matters identified will, amongst a host of variables particular to any case, include the availability of funds to meet the expense entailed in such further enquiries. That view is consistent with the approach adopted subsequently by His Honour Judge Cooke, sitting as a judge of the High Court in *Pitt v Mond* [2001] BPIR 624 at 640F–641B, to the effect that, whilst a nominee is entitled to rely on information provided to him by a debtor, he is under a duty to investigate further any fact or matter which appears to him to be doubtful, but only by the taking of such steps as are reasonable on the facts of the case. This scope for limited enquiry is reflected in the best practice guidance in SIP 3, para 5(d). Any limitation imposed by a lack of funds, however, should not obviate the court being made aware by the nominee of any concerns on his part in relation to the three basic minimum points identified by Lindsay J in *Greystoke* (above). SIP 3, para 6.2 specifically provides that 'If the nominee cannot satisfy himself that the above three conditions [in *Greystoke*] are met but still recommends that a meeting should be held, he should explain in his comments the basis on which he is making that recommendation and qualify his comments so that the fact that the conditions are not met is conspicuously brought to the attention of the court.' As such, a nominee would be obliged, at least as a matter of best practice, and almost certainly as a matter of law, to bring to the court's attention the nature of his concerns and the reasons (eg lack of funding) for his being unable to assuage those concerns.

For further cases involving claims against nominees see *Heritage Joinery (a firm) v Krasner* [1999] BPIR 683; *Harmony Carpets v Chaffin-Laird* [2000] BPIR 61 (Rattee J); and *Prosser v Castle Sanderson (a firm)* [2002] BPIR 1163 (Mummery, Clarke and Hale LJJ, insolvency practitioner did not owe duty of care to debtor as nominee or chairman of creditors' meeting, but did owe such a duty in his capacity as the debtor's adviser during the short adjournment of the creditors' meeting) and *Tradition (UK) Ltd v Ahmed and Other* [2008] EWHC 3448 (Ch), [2009] BPIR 626.

'Whether … the proposed voluntary arrangement has a reasonable prospect of being approved and implemented'—This requirement in s 2(2)(a) differs from that in s 2(2)(aa) in that the latter requires consideration of whether meetings of the company and its creditors should be summoned (which brings into play the 'serious and viable' test considered under the next heading), whereas the former provision requires the nominee to express a view not only as to whether the proposal has a reasonable prospect of being approved by creditors but also, it is submitted, whether the approved arrangement is capable of being implemented as envisaged by the proposal.

The formation of an opinion on the prospects of approval must, it is submitted, involve a consideration of the likely attitude of the debtor's unsecured creditors to the proposal. This was in fact the view adopted by the court in *Tradition (UK) Ltd v Ahmed and Other* [2008] EWHC 3448 (Ch), [2009] BPIR 626 in the context of an IVA (see para 226 of the judgment), although in that case, the Court questionned to some extent whether spending time and effort trying to predict the outcome of the creditors' meeting would be a productive exercise given that known creditors may not vote, unknown creditors may emerge and in either case a creditor may change their mind. It is suggested that it may be sufficient for a nominee to be satisfied that the proposal has the support of at least one creditor or a group of creditors of a substantial size (see para 229). SIP 3, para 6.3(f) indicates that, as a matter of best practice, the nominee's report will normally include 'information on the attitude of any major unsecured creditor which may affect the approval of the arrangement by creditors'. It is submitted that s 2(2)(a) does not of itself impose an obligation on the nominee to make contact with creditors for the purpose of taking soundings, although a nominee may well regard such a step as prudent in a particular case. Equally, the nominee may, in the absence of suspicion, rely upon representations made to him by the directors as to the likely attitude of any particular creditor. In many cases, however, neither the directors nor the nominee will be in a position to express an opinion as to the likely position of creditors, other than where the proposal is plainly derisory in terms of any proposed dividend.

The question of implementation involves the nominee making an informed assessment as to the viability of the proposal on its terms. It is submitted that any mechanism within the proposal for the post-approval modification of the arrangement will usually constitute a factor affecting implementation.

There is no authority on the meaning of the term 'reasonable prospect' in the present context. It is suggested that this threshold test is relatively low and, by definition, will not be met only where there is no reasonable prospect of the proposal being both approved and – just as importantly and perhaps rather more stringently – implemented.

'Whether ... meetings of the company and its creditors should be summoned to consider the proposal': the 'serious and viable' test—In *Cooper v Fearnley* [1997] BPIR 20 at 21B–21C Aldous J, as he then was, considered, in the context of an appeal against the decision of a deputy district judge to refuse the making of an interim order in relation to a proposed individual voluntary arrangement, that a proposal must be 'serious and viable'. That yardstick was adopted by Sir Richard Scott V-C in *Hook v Jewson Ltd* [1997] BPIR 100 at 105D and is now well established.

The serious and viable threshold requires not merely that a proposal is seriously made or is made bona fide; rather, the proposal must have both substance and be one which should seriously be considered by the creditors or, alternatively, be capable of serious consideration by creditors, even if there were serious and well-founded doubts and questions over the proposal itself: *Shah v Cooper* [2003] BPIR 1018 (Deputy Registrar Schekerdemian). The fact that a proposal offers only a modest projected dividend to creditors is a relevant factor, but need not of itself mean that the proposal is not serious and viable, since the matter can be left for approval or rejection by creditors: *Knowles v Coutts* [1998] BPIR 96 at 99E–100F (proposal of 1.4 pence in the pound) and *National Westminster Bank plc v Scher* [1998] BPIR 224 (proposed dividend of 0.06 pence in the pound).

For best practice guidance see SIP 3, para 6. For a case in which Blackburne J regarded the proposal as 'an essay in make-believe' see *Davidson v Stanley* [2004] EWHC 2595 (Ch), [2005] BPIR 279, an IVA case.

Section 2(3)

'a document setting out the terms of the proposed voluntary arrangement'—The proposal, as distinct from the statement of the company's affairs, provides the basis for the conduct of the voluntary arrangement. The detailed information which must appear in the directors' proposal is prescribed in r 1.3. Best practice guidance appears in SIP 3, paras 2 and 5.

A proposal does not extend, for the purposes of s 4, to an agreement or other understanding between a third party and creditors where the distribution to those creditors is to be made from funds advanced by the third party: *IRC v Wimbledon Football Club Ltd* [2004] EWCA Civ 44, [2005] 1 BCLC 66 at [59] (Neuberger LJ).

In practice, it will frequently be necessary to supplement that information prescribed by r 1.3 with further details so as to enable the nominee to report to the court and for the purpose of enabling creditors to make an informed assessment of what is proposed. For example, in the case of a 'trading' arrangement the directors will usually wish to provide something akin to a business plan which extends beyond the very general and which identifies the company's strategy and objectives through ongoing trading.

A proposal will also commonly include certain procedural and administrative provisions which allow for the operation of the arrangement itself. Such provisions commonly include an express statement of the supervisor's powers, together with an indication of whether the supervisor is deemed to act as agent for the company in the exercise of those powers, given the absence of any statutory provision providing for such agency. It is also common for arrangements to provide for the treatment of disputed, contingent and/or prospective debts, the status of claims asserted against the company which are not known to exist at the time of the proposal together with a facility for the subsequent modification of the arrangement by, typically, 75% of creditors voting on any modification, given that an arrangement may only be modified with the unanimous approval of all creditors in the absence of such a provision: *Raja v Rubin* [1999] 3 WLR 606, CA; and see *Re Alpa Lighting Ltd, Mills v Samuels* [1997] BPIR 341, CA (court has no jurisdiction to direct modifications to approved proposal).

The 28-day period in s 2(2) runs from the date from which the directors' proposal is received by him: r 1.4(3).

The directors' proposal may be amended at any time prior to the delivery of the nominee's report to the court under s 2(2): r 1.3(3).

The Appendix to SIP 3 suggests that a proposal should include sections covering six key areas and also identifies other matters which should be considered in order to facilitate the practical implementation of a proposal.

'a statement of the company's affairs'—The statement of the company's affairs must be delivered to the nominee at the same time as delivery of the directors' proposal: r 1.5(1). In any event, in practice, both documents are almost always delivered together.

The statement of affairs must include those particulars prescribed by r 1.5(2) and must supplement or amplify those particulars already given in the directors' proposal 'so far as is necessary for clarifying the state of the company's affairs'.

Best practice guidance on the preparation of the statement of affairs and the obtaining of additional information by the nominee appears in SIP 3, para 4.

A mis-statement of the amount of the assets and liabilities of the debtor may be actionable by an aggrieved creditor as a material irregularity within the meaning of s 6(1)(b) with the potential for revocation of approval of the arrangement.

False representations etc—For the criminal consequences of an offer of a company falsely or fraudulently obtaining the approval of the members of creditors to a CVA proposal see s 6A.

Section 2(4)(a)

Scope of provision—This provision allows for the replacement (and not merely the removal) of the nominee by the court whether the nominee has died or failed to submit his report to the court within the extendable 28-day period stipulated in s 2(2). Applications to replace a nominee in default of his reporting obligations will be rare since, in cases where the nominee is unwilling to vacate office voluntarily, the debtor is properly entitled to abort the process and to proceed with an alternative nominee. In those circumstances it is submitted that the original nominee would not, on being given notice of the company's position, fall within the definition of 'nominee' in s 1(2) and would therefore have no obligation to report to the court under s 2(2).

Section 2(4)(b)

'in a case where it is impracticable or inappropriate for the nominee to continue to act as such'—The observations in the preceding note apply equally here. Alternatively, the person intending to make the proposal or the nominee may make application if, say, the nominee is subject to geographical relocation or is professionally embarrassed.

If an application is made to replace a nominee on professional grounds, then the proposed replacement nominee should, as a matter of good practice, confirm to the court that his appointment does not conflict with any statement of professional ethics or professional guidelines which apply to him.

3 Summoning of meetings

(1) Where the nominee under section 1 is not the liquidator or administrator, and it has been reported to the court that such meetings as are mentioned in section 2(2) should be summoned, the person making the report shall (unless the court otherwise directs) summon those meetings for the time, date and place proposed in the report.

(2) Where the nominee is the liquidator or administrator, he shall summon meetings of the company and of its creditors to consider the proposal for such a time, date and place as he thinks fit.

(3) The persons to be summoned to a creditors' meeting under this section are every creditor of the company of whose claim and address the person summoning the meeting is aware.

General note—For the detailed procedural rules governing the summoning of meetings, see rr 1.9 and 1.13–1.16.

Failure to give notice of a creditors' meeting to a person so entitled is capable of having serious practical consequences, since a person not properly summoned may challenge the arrangement on the 'material irregularity' grounds in s 6(1)(b).

For best practice on the summoning of meetings see SIP 3, para 7.1.

Section 3(1)

Scope of provision—If the nominee files a positive report for the purposes of s 2(2)(a) and (aa), then he is under an obligation to summon meetings of the company and of its creditors, subject to contrary order of the court, in accordance with his proposals under s 2(2)(b). In practice, a positive report will not usually elicit any response from the court such that the nominee will proceed to summon the meetings as a matter of course in accordance with his proposals. The subsection appears to anticipate that a contrary order of the court may be made of the court's own volition or following an application by any party with a genuine interest in the business of the proposed meetings of the company or its creditors.

Timing of the meetings of the company and creditors—Rules 1.9(1) and 1.9(2) provide that the meetings of the company and its creditors must be held not less than 14, nor more than 28 days from the date on which the nominee's report is filed in court under r 1.7. The reference to 14 days' notice is to 14 days' clear notice being given to a creditor; there is no scope for arguing for 'substantial compliance' with the provision where less than 14 days' clear notice has been given: *Mytre Investments Ltd v Reynolds (No 2)* [1996] BPIR 464 at 468H–470H. This point is relevant to the question of whether a creditor can be said to have had notice of a creditors' meeting 'in accordance with the rules' under s 5(2)(b).

Section 3(2)

Scope of provision—The procedure under s 2 has no application where the nominee is the liquidator or administrator, in which case the office-holder proceeds directly to the summoning of meetings of the company and its creditors without notification to the court. The absence of court involvement would explain the absence of any provision allowing for a contrary order of the court in the summoning of meetings.

For the summoning of meetings where the nominee is liquidator or administrator of the company see r 1.11.

Section 3(3)

Scope of provision—The most obvious source of information regarding the identity of the creditors of the company is the statement of affairs submitted to the nominee under s 2(3)(b) (where that section applies) or produced for or provided to a liquidator under s 99(1) or 131(1) or an administrator under s 22(1) (Part II) or para 47(1) of Sch B1. Plainly the nominee should not rely blindly on the list of creditors particularised in the statement of affairs if he has reason to believe that other creditors may exist, given that the subsection is based on the nominee's state of knowledge.

For the binding effect of a CVA on persons entitled to notice of the creditors' meeting in accordance with the rules see s 5(2)(b) and the notes thereto.

Consideration and implementation of proposal

4 Decisions of meetings

(1) The meetings summoned under section 3 shall decide whether to approve the proposed voluntary arrangement (with or without modifications).

(2) The modifications may include one conferring the functions proposed to be conferred on the nominee on another person qualified to act as an insolvency practitioner or authorised to act as nominee, in relation to the voluntary arrangement.

But they shall not include any modification by virtue of which the proposal ceases to be a proposal such as is mentioned in section 1.

(3) A meeting so summoned shall not approve any proposal or modification which affects the right of a secured creditor of the company to enforce his security, except with the concurrence of the creditor concerned.

(4) Subject as follows, a meeting so summoned shall not approve any proposal or modification under which—

    (a)   any preferential debt of the company is to be paid otherwise than in priority to such of its debts as are not preferential debts, or

    (b)   a preferential creditor of the company is to be paid an amount in respect of a preferential debt that bears to that debt a smaller proportion than is borne to another preferential debt by the amount that is to be paid in respect of that other debt.

However, the meeting may approve such a proposal or modification with the concurrence of the preferential creditor concerned.

(5) Subject as above, each of the meetings shall be conducted in accordance with the rules.

(6) After the conclusion of either meeting in accordance with the rules, the chairman of the meeting shall report the result of the meeting to the court, and, immediately after reporting to the court, shall give notice of the result of the meeting to such persons as may be prescribed.

(7) References in this section to preferential debts and preferential creditors are to be read in accordance with section 386 in Part XII of this Act.

Amendments—Insolvency Act 2000, s 2, Sch 2, paras 1, 4.

General note—For the procedural rules governing meetings of the company and its creditors see rr 1.13–1.21.

For the purposes of s 4, a 'proposal' does not extend to an agreement or other understanding between a third party and creditors where the money from which a distribution is to be made is from the third party's 'free money', being money which is not advanced at the cost of the debtor company: *IRC v Wimbledon Football Club Ltd* [2004] EWCA Civ 55, [2005] 1 BCLC 66 at [59] (Neuberger LJ).

Section 4(1)

Scope of provision—The decisions of the meetings of the company and its creditors are, notwithstanding the heading to s 4, referred to in the sub-heading as a single decision. This accords with s 4A(2) by which a decision of the creditors' meeting overrides a contrary decision of the members' meeting subject to the standing of a member to apply to court under s 4A(3).

'with or without modifications'—Whilst it appears implicit that the meetings of the company and its creditors must each consider identical forms of the proposed voluntary arrangement, whether or not in modified form, note that s 4A(2) provides that approval under s 4(1) requires only the approval of the creditors' meeting.

In practice, proposed modifications, particularly those introduced at the last moment, can create difficulties and may prompt the chairman to consider adjourning the creditors' meeting, even for a short time, under r 1.21 where creditors require time to consider their respective positions.

Where modifications are introduced, it is prudent to include a provision of a kind frequently required as a condition of support for a proposal by Crown creditors to the effect that any modification is deemed to override any term in the original proposal where an inconsistency arises between the two.

Section 4(2)

Scope of provision—Any modification altering the identity of the nominee squares with s 1(2) in that the amendment will not deprive the CVA proposal of its status as such.

'... any modification by virtue of which the proposal ceases to be a proposal ...'—Section 4(2) imposed no limitation on the extent of the modifications which may be proposed. In practice, such modifications are common enough and may be insisted upon by a significant creditor or creditors as the price for their support of the proposal, subject to the standing of an eligible applicant making application to the court complaining of unfair prejudice or material irregularity under s 6(1). In theory, therefore, there is no good reason why the proposal should not be modified extensively at the meetings stage, provided that the modifications do not fall within the scope of challenge under s 6(1).

The specific limitation imposed prevents the proposal being modified so as to deprive it of its status as a composition or a scheme of arrangement such that, if approved, the proposal would not constitute a voluntary arrangement as defined in s 1(1).

No requirement for consent to modifications—There is no requirement for a company or its directors to agree to modifications to a proposal as submitted by creditors, or even the members of the company or the chairman of the meeting, in contrast to the position in an IVA where the debtor's consent is required under s 258(2).

Section 4(3)

Scope of provision—A proposal or modified proposal is incapable of affecting the rights of a secured creditor 'to enforce his security' other than with the 'concurrence' of the secured creditor. For the definition of 'secured creditor' and of 'security' see s 248. Schedule A1 provides no definition of the term 'security' where a CVA is coupled with a moratorium; it is submitted, however, that there is no good reason why the term should have any meaning other than that attributed by s 248.

'... to enforce his security ...'—The prohibition in s 4(3) does not safeguard the rights of a non-concurring secured creditor generally, but only the rights of such a creditor 'to enforce his security'. In *Razzaq v Pala* [1998] BCC 66 Lightman J confirmed (in the context of the former s 11(3)(c)) that the term 'security' does not include a landlord's right of re-entry as Lightman J had previously held to be the case, albeit without full argument on the point, in *March Estates plc v Gunmark Ltd* [1996] BPIR 439. The adoption of Lightman J's approach in *Razzaq* by the House of Lords in *Re Park Air Services plc* [1999] 2 WLR 396 confirms that a landlord's right of re-entry does not constitute security for the performance of lease covenants including, most obviously, a covenant for the payment of rent reserved. It follows that a CVA may affect the right of a landlord to exercise his right of re-entry under a lease without the concurrence of the landlord, subject to the standing of the landlord to challenge such a decision as unfairly prejudicial under s 6(1)(a). A voluntary arrangement is capable of modifying a landlord's right as a creditor in relation to reserved rent, including arrears and/or future rent: *Re Cancol Ltd* [1996] 1 All ER 37. In *Re Naeem (a Bankrupt)* [1990] 1 WLR 48 at 50 Hoffmann J (as he then was) rejected a landlord's complaint of unfair prejudice and held that, in keeping with the modification of the claims of other creditors, the right of the landlord to forfeit under a lease should operate for the recovery of rent as modified by the arrangement and not the landlord's original claim. The decision in *Re Naeem*, it is submitted, is consistent with that in *Razzaq*. See also *Re Cotswold Co Ltd* [2009] EWHC 1151 (Ch), [2009] 2 BCLC 371.

It is suggested that there are at least two obvious reasons why the reasoning of Hoffmann J in *Re Naeem*, as it applies to the modification of a landlord's claim for rent, would not apply to a debt due to a creditor secured by a mortgage or charge. First, a mortgagee or chargee obtains an immediate proprietary interest by way of security in the debtor's property, which encumbrance the debtor is only able to discharge through payment in full of the underlying indebtedness. A landlord, on the other hand, obtains no such proprietary interest in the debtor's property, but enjoys instead proprietary remedies (forfeiture, re-entry etc) which are exercisable in relation to the leased property. Secondly, it is extremely unlikely that Parliament could have intended to allow for the modification of the security rights of a non-concurring mortgage or charge-holder under the terms of a voluntary arrangement where the same rights would be unaffected by the process of liquidation or administration.

'... except with the concurrence of the creditor concerned ...'—The word 'concurrence', it is suggested, would allow for the passive acquiescence of a secured creditor as something distinct from the pro-active approval on the part of the creditor which would otherwise have been required if the word 'consent' had been employed in the provision. As such, it would appear that a secured creditor will be bound by any modification to his security rights, in terms of the enforcement of such rights, merely by virtue of that creditor being entitled to vote at the creditors' meeting within the meaning of s 5(2)(b) and doing nothing, but not, it would appear, if the secured creditor did not have actual notice of the meeting since, in those circumstances, he could not be said to have concurred with the modification approved.

A secured creditor is not automatically deemed to have waived its security rights through the acceptance of a dividend under a voluntary arrangement: *Whitehead v Household Mortgage Corporation* [2002] EWCA Civ 1657; compare *Khan v Permayer* [2001] BPIR 95.

Section 4(4)

Scope of provision—This subsection prohibits the variation of the priority status afforded to preferential debts and the treatment of any preferential debt vis-à-vis other preferential debts other than with the concurrence of the preferential creditor concerned.

For the meaning of 'preferential debts' and 'preferential creditors' see s 4(7). On the term 'concurrence' see the note to s 4(3) above.

Section 4(4)(a) and (b)

Scope of provision—A decision under s 4(1) cannot take away the priority afforded to preferential debts by statute. Neither is a voluntary arrangement capable of modifying the claim of a single preferential creditor such that the reduction in that preferential creditor's claim would be greater than the reduction suffered by any other preferential creditor.

Section 4(5)

Scope of provision—See rr 1.13–1.21. Note also rr 1.22–1.24, which relate to implementation of the arrangement.

Section 4(6)

Scope of provision—Rule 1.13(3) and (4) provide that the creditors' meeting is to be held in advance of the company meeting and the meetings must be held within five business days of each other. In practice, the creditors' meeting is usually held immediately prior to the company meeting. Those rules envisage that there is no purpose in a meeting of members if the creditors have rejected the proposal. It is also implicit in r 1.14(1) and (2) and in r 1.24(1), that the chairman of both meetings will be the same person. Despite the suggestion in the wording to the subsection that a separate report should be prepared in respect of each of the meetings of the company and its creditors, the wording in r 1.24(1), which accords with common practice, indicates that a single report of the meetings is to be prepared by the chairman. Rule 1.24(2) prescribes the contents of the report, which must be filed with the court under r 1.24(3) within four business days of the meetings being held. If the arrangement is approved, then the supervisor must also send a copy of the chairman's report to the Registrar of Companies: r 1.24(5). The chairman must also send a notice of the result of each of the meetings – but not necessarily a copy of the chairman's report – to all those persons who were sent notice of each of the meetings summoned under s 3, and he must do so as soon as reasonably practicable.

The filing of the chairman's report with the court amounts to a reporting obligation only and has no substantive consequence. The CVA comes into being as a consequence of approval under s 4A alone; the court is not involved in the ongoing conduct of the arrangement in the absence of an application to it.

Section 4(7)

Scope of provision—The 'relevant date' for the assessment of preferential debts is the date on which the voluntary arrangement takes effect or, if the company is in administration, the date on which it entered administration: s 387(2). The fact that the company is in receivership will not affect the relevant date for the assessment of preferential debts in a company voluntary arrangement.

4A Approval of arrangement

(1) This section applies to a decision, under section 4, with respect to the approval of a proposed voluntary arrangement.

(2) The decision has effect if, in accordance with the rules—

    (a)   it has been taken by both meetings summoned under section 3, or

    (b)   (subject to any order made under subsection (4)) it has been taken by the creditors' meeting summoned under that section.

(3) If the decision taken by the creditors' meeting differs from that taken by the company meeting, a member of the company may apply to the court.

(4) An application under subsection (3) shall not be made after the end of the period of 28 days beginning with—

    (a)   the day on which the decision was taken by the creditors' meeting, or

    (b)   where the decision of the company meeting was taken on a later day, that day.

(5) Where a member of a regulated company, within the meaning given by paragraph 44 of Schedule A1, applies to the court under subsection (3), the Financial Services Authority is entitled to be heard on the application.

(6) On an application under subsection (3), the court may—

    (a)   order the decision of the company meeting to have effect instead of the decision of the creditors' meeting, or

    (b)   make such other order as it thinks fit.

Amendments—Inserted by Insolvency Act 2000, s 2, Sch 2, paras 1, 5.

General note—These new provisions were introduced, with effect from 1 January 2003, by Insolvency Act 2000, s 2 and Sch 2 thereto. Save for s 4A(5) the provisions confirm that, in effect, only the requisite support of the creditors' meeting is required to approved a proposed CVA, subject to the standing of a member of the company to apply to the court under s 4A(3) for relief under s 4A(6) where the meeting of the company does not approve the proposal. A new r 1.22A which imposes requirements for the giving of notice of any order made under s 4A(6) was introduced by para 14 of the Schedule to the Insolvency (Amendment) (No 2) Rules 2002 (SI 2002/2712).

Section 4A(1)

Scope of provision—The scope of s 4A is limited to the decision under s 4(1) to approve the proposed CVA, with or without modifications. The provisions have no wider scope.

The date on which a voluntary arrangement takes effect, or any associated moratorium comes into force, amounts to the 'effective date' for the purposes of s 233(4) (supplies of gas, water, electricity, etc to company).

Section 4A(2)(a) and (b)

Scope of provision—Subject to any contrary order under s 4A(4) the decision under s 4(1) requires only the approval of the creditors' meeting.

'... in accordance with the rules ...'—A decision under s 4(1) can only have effect if the meeting of the company and the creditors' meeting have been summoned under s 3 in accordance with rr 1.9 and 1.13, although it is arguable from the wording of s 4A(2)(b) that only the creditors' meeting need actually be summoned in accordance with s 3 and the applicable rule.

Section 4A(3)

Scope of provision—To make application to court under this subsection a member of a company need establish no other grounds than the fact of the creditors' meeting having made a decision for s 4(1) purposes which differs from that of the company meeting. Whilst the court has the broadest powers under s 4A(6) on such an application, it is difficult to envisage circumstances in which those powers might properly be exercised. If the creditors' meeting has approved a proposed CVA without the support of the company meeting, then it is far from clear on what basis the court might interfere, at least where the company is insolvent, by allowing the decision of the company meeting to override that of the creditors' meeting so as, in effect, to withdraw the approval provided for in s 4A(2)(b). Equally, the court's interference by order under s 4A(6) is unlikely to be justified in a case where the creditors' meeting has not given its approval to the proposal, at least, again, where the company is insolvent.

An application under s 4A(3) does not apparently require proof that the CVA prejudices the interests of a creditor, member or contributory or that there has been some material irregularity at, or in relation to, the meeting of the company or the creditors' meeting. Proof of either such matter, however, is required on an application under s 6(1) by a member eligible under s 6(2)(a). The absence of either such ground in an application under s 4A(3), it is submitted, can only militate against the making of an order under s 4A(6) where the decision of the creditors' meeting has been validly resolved at a meeting convened in accordance with s 3 and the rules thereto.

Section 4A(4)

Scope of provision—For the purposes of s 4A(4)(b) a company meeting must be held within seven days of the creditors' meeting: r 1.13(4).

Extension by the court of the seven-day period?—Based on the reasoning of Lloyd J in *Re Bournemouth & Boscombe AFC Co Ltd* [1998] BPIR 183 at 186A–186D in relation to very similar wording in s 6(3), the 28-day time limit prescribed in this subsection will not be capable of extension by the court. In *Re Beloit Walmsley Ltd* [2008] EWHC 1888 (Ch), [2008] BPIR 1445 at [29] HHJ Pelling QC, sitting as a judge of the High Court, confirmed that the reasoning in the *Bournemouth* case, which had been decided by reference to the formerly operative RSC Ord 3, r 5, continued to apply following the implementation of CPR r 3.2(1).

Section 4A(5)

Scope of provision—The term 'regulated company' is defined in para 44(18) of Sch A1.

Section 4A(6)

Scope of provision—The court has an unfettered discretion in terms of the scope of any order it may make. See, however, the notes to s 4A(3) above.

For the procedure following the making of an order under s 4A(6) see r 1.22A.

5 Effect of approval

(1) This section applies where a decision approving a voluntary arrangement has effect under section 4A.

(2) The voluntary arrangement—

    (a)   takes effect as if made by the company at the creditors' meeting, and

    (b)   binds every person who in accordance with the rules—

        (i)   was entitled to vote at that meeting (whether or not he was present or represented at it), or

        (ii)   would have been so entitled if he had had notice of it,

as if he were a party to the voluntary arrangement.

(2A) If—

    (a)   when the arrangement ceases to have effect any amount payable under the arrangement to a person bound by virtue of subsection (2)(b)(ii) has not been paid, and

    (b)   the arrangement did not come to an end prematurely,

the company shall at that time become liable to pay to that person the amount payable under the arrangement.

(3) Subject as follows, if the company is being wound up or is in administration, the court may do one or both of the following, namely—

    (a)   by order stay or sist all proceedings in the winding up or provide for the appointment of the administrator to cease to have effect;

    (b)   give such directions with respect to the conduct of the winding up or the administration as it thinks appropriate for facilitating the implementation of the voluntary arrangement.

(4) The court shall not make an order under subsection (3)(a)—

    (a)   at any time before the end of the period of 28 days beginning with the first day on which each of the reports required by section 4(6) has been made to the court, or

(b)   at any time when an application under the next section or an appeal in respect of such an application is pending, or at any time in the period within which such an appeal may be brought.

(5) Where the company is in energy administration, the court shall not make an order or give a direction under subsection (3) unless—

(a)   the court has given the Secretary of State or the Gas and Electricity Markets Authority a reasonable opportunity of making representations to it about the proposed order or direction; and

(b)   the order or direction is consistent with the objective of the energy administration.

(6) In subsection (5) 'in energy administration' and 'objective of the energy administration' are to be construed in accordance with Schedule B1 to this Act, as applied by Part 1 of Schedule 20 to the Energy Act 2004.

Amendments—Insolvency Act 2000, ss 2, 15(1), Sch 2, paras 1, 6, Sch 5; Enterprise Act 2002, s 248(3), Sch 17, paras 9, 11; Energy Act 2004, s 159(1), Sch 20, Pt 4, para 43.

General note—Taken together, these provisions, together with s 4A, identify the meeting of creditors as the key event for the bringing of the arrangement into effect. An approved arrangement remains in force until either revoked by way of a modification validly approved by creditors or until the making of any order setting aside the arrangement under s 6.

Section 5(1)

Scope of provision—Section 5 applies only where s 4A(1) has effect. The application of the section is not affected by the fact of an application to court under s 4A(3) or s 6(1), subject to any order of the court.

Section 5(2)

Scope of provision—This is a deeming provision, which provides for the binding nature of the CVA. The effect of the arrangement taking effect as if made by the company operates so as to bind the company to the arrangement.

Section 5(2)(a)

Scope of provision—The word 'made' replaced the word 'approved' by amendment under Sch 5 of the Insolvency Act 2000. The earlier version of s 5(2) was considered by the Court in *Wood v Heart Hospital* [2009] BPIR 1538.

Section 5(2)(b)

The meaning of 'notice'—This new provision was inserted by Insolvency Act 2000, s 2 and Sch 2 thereto and represents a significant change from the previous position. Formerly, it had been held that a creditor must have actual notice of the creditors' meeting so as to be bound by the arrangement. In particular, the court had rejected the operation of a doctrine of deemed notice: see *Re a Debtor (No 64 of 1992)* [1994] BCC 55, and *Skipton Building Society v Collins* [1998] BPIR 267 (Jonathan Parker J). The court had, however, been prepared to find that proper notice had been given where it had been obtained from a third party, as in *Beverley Group plc v McClue* [1995] 2 BCLC 407 (Knox J). The new provision does away with the requirement for actual notice. Instead, s 5(2)(b) binds two classes of person (see below) as party to the CVA on the assumption that any such person would have been entitled to vote at the creditors' meeting. In this regard, r 1.17(1) (entitlement to vote) must be read in light of s 5(2)(b) to the extent that the former provision refers to 'every creditor who has notice of the creditors' meeting'; s 5(2)(b) suggests that those words must be interpreted as meaning every creditor who has notice or would have been entitled to have had notice of the creditors' meeting.

The two classes of person within s 5(2)(b)—The two classes of person bound by s 5(2)(b) are (i) every person entitled to vote at the creditors' meeting (ie who had notice of the meeting, irrespective of whether or not he was present or represented), or (ii) any person who would have been entitled to have had such notice (ie irrespective of whether such notice was received or otherwise communicated). Class (i) will not extend to a person who is not entitled to vote at the creditors' meeting: *RA Securities Ltd v Mercantile Credit Co Ltd* [1994] BCC 598 at 600H (Jacob J, as he then was); and see also *Burford Midland Properties Ltd v Marley Extrusions Ltd* [1994] BCC 604 (His Honour Judge Roger Cooke sitting as a High Court judge). Class (ii) will catch both creditors who are not known to the nominee summoning the creditors' meeting and also creditors who are known but to whom notice is not given through, say, an administrative oversight or even a deliberate omission.

Failure to give notice as ground for alleging unfair prejudice/material irregularity under s 6—The fact of a creditor being bound by an arrangement under s 5(2)(b) in circumstances where that creditor can establish, as a matter of fact, that it had not been given notice of the creditors' meeting is capable of founding an application alleging material irregularity and/or, possibly, unfair prejudice under s 6(1), but only where that creditor would have been capable of affecting or influencing the outcome of the creditors' meeting.

Unliquidated, future or contingent debts, co-debtors and third parties—For the treatment of unliquidated, future or contingent debts in a CVA and the position of co-debtors and third parties, see the notes to s 1(1) above.

The effect of an arrangement on assignees—Subject to an effective contrary term within an arrangement, the assignee of a contractual right which is modified by an arrangement prior to assignment acquires only the benefit of that right as modified by the arrangement. In the context of leases it is well established that an assignee may reach agreement with his landlord to alter the terms on which the assignee holds the estate so as to bind an original tenant: *Baynton v Morgan* (1888) 22 QBD 741, and see *Centrovincial Estates plc v Bulk Storage Ltd* (1983) 46 PCR 393. Whether or not future rent under a lease falls within the scope of the arrangement as a prospective debt will depend on the particular terms and construction of the arrangement.

Single creditor with a claim within and a claim outside of the arrangement—One problem which may arise in relation to s 5(2)(b) concerns the position where a creditor maintains two separate claims against the debtor where one of the claims does not fall plainly within the scope of the arrangement. The decision on Knox J in *Doorbar v Alltime Securities Ltd* [1994] BCC 994 involved claims by a landlord in respect of arrears and interest for a liquidated sum together with a further claim for the aggregate of rent prospectively payable until the end of the contractual term of the lease disregarding possible upward rent reviews. At 1000E of his judgment Knox J opined that a creditor entitled to vote in respect of one debt was not bound by an approved arrangement in respect of a different debt if (as was the case on the facts of *Doorbar*) the creditor was not entitled to vote in respect of that different debt. That position appears to have been assumed in the judgment of the Court of Appeal given by Peter Gibson LJ: see [1995] BCC 1149 at 1155C. That view, as expressed, however, runs contrary to the decision of Rimer J in *Re Bradley-Hole (a Bankrupt)* [1995] BCC 418 at 434B–434C which held that a creditor is bound by an arrangement in respect of both debts where one carried an entitlement to vote and the other did not. This problem is probably now more apparent than real following the Court of Appeal's decision in *Doorbar* and the finding (at 1157E) that a chairman is entitled to place an estimated minimum value on an unliquidated debt for voting purposes, on which see now the express wording in r 1.17(3) and the notes to that provision. Where a creditor disagrees with that minimum value it can hardly be said that the creditor has no entitlement to vote for the purposes of s 5(2)(b).

Where the chairman declines to admit a claim for unliquidated damages and attributes to it only a nominal value, in circumstances where the same creditor is admitted to the arrangement for a liquidated sum relating to a separate debt so as to be bound by it in respect of the liquidated debt, any entitlement to pursue the unliquidated claim outside of the terms of the arrangement will depend on a construction of the terms of the CVA. In *Sea Voyager Maritime Inc v Bielecki (tla Hughes Hooker & Co)* [1999] 1 BCLC 133 at 150–151, Richard McCombe QC, sitting as he then was as a deputy High Court judge, held that it was implicit in the terms of that particular arrangement that those bound by it were prevented from commencing or pursuing proceedings outside of the arrangement. No such bar was held to have been implied in the less elaborately drawn CVA considered by Rimer J in *Alman v Approach Housing Ltd* [2001] BPIR 203. Ultimately, the implication of a term into a CVA turns on whether the term is necessary to give efficacy to the arrangement; although such terms will not be implied lightly: see *Johnson v Davies* [1999] Ch 117 at 128G–128H (Chadwick LJ).

Single creditor pursuing only part of single debt in arrangement—What of the position where a single creditor seeks to be bound only in respect of part of that debt? It is submitted that that possibility now seems doubtful, given the revised wording in s 5(2)(b)(i).

In *Re C J Hoare* [1997] BPIR 683 Edward Nugee QC, sitting as a deputy High Court judge, held (at 695D), following the decision of the Court of Appeal in *Doorbar v Alltime Securities Ltd* and adopting the approach of Knox J in *Re Cancol Ltd* [1996] 1 All ER 37, that it is not open to a creditor to put an estimated figure on his debts which is stated as being subject to verification and possible amendment, only to claim later that he is owed some other debt which was not included in the original figure and in respect of which he is not bound by the arrangement. Whilst the deputy judge accepted the possibility of a distinction being drawn between two separate debts arising out of the same claim (at 694G), it now seems unlikely, given the amended forms of s 5(2) (and s 260(2) applicable to individual voluntary arrangements), that a single debt might be divided so as to allow part of it to be pursued outside of the arrangement other than where the terms of the arrangement expressly provide for such an outcome.

The court's approach to the construction of voluntary arrangements—The judgment of Blackburne J in *Welsby v Brelec Installations Ltd* [2000] 2 BCLC 576 concerned in part the construction of certain express terms employed in a CVA for the purpose of determining if and when there had been 'failure' for the purposes of that arrangement. The following passage (at 585I–586B), it is submitted, will be of general assistance in construing the express terms of a voluntary arrangement:

> 'An arrangement is usually put together with some haste. Modifications to it are frequently made at the statutory meeting of creditors with little time to reflect on how they relate to the other terms of the debtor's proposal. Quite often, as this case demonstrates, the resulting terms are clumsily worded. The arrangement ought therefore to be construed in a practical fashion. Otherwise there is a risk that careless drafting coupled with a too-literal approach to its construction will serve to frustrate rather than achieve the purpose of the arrangement. The underlying purpose in most arrangements – and certainly this one – is to provide the arrangement creditors with a means of debt recovery which avoids the need to have recourse to the formal and more expensive mechanisms of winding up or administration (or bankruptcy in the case of an individual) and, if the arrangement is successful, to give the debtor the chance to continue trading in the longer term.'

Accordingly, it is submitted, so far as the interpretation of express terms in a voluntary arrangement is concerned, the court is not constrained by the ordinary rules on contractual interpretation, on which see the judgment of Hoffmann LJ (as he then was) in *Investor Compensation Scheme v West Bromwich Building Society* [1998] 1 WLR 896. Rather, the court has a very broad hand in terms of construction and should be guided principally by what the court identifies as the underlying purpose of the arrangement, as opposed to the rather more selective approach to evidence in the ordinary course of contractual interpretation.

For a case adopting the *Welsby* approach to construction of a CVA, which involved reconciliation of terms as to a CVA providing for failure and termination through the issue of a certificate of non-compliance or an abort certificate so as to determine the destination of CVA trust assets see *Re Zebra Industrial Projects Ltd* [2005] BPIR 1022 (John Martin QC, sitting as a deputy High Court judge).

It is necessary, in construing specific terms of a CVA, to analyse such terms carefully. However, in undertaking that analysis, it must be borne in mind that the CVA must be read as a whole, and further that specific terms must not be analysed so closely as to overlook the overall commercial context or the practical consequences: see *Tucker and Spratt (Joint Supervisors of Energy Holdings (No 3) (In Liquidation) v Gold Fields Mining LLC* [2009] EWCA Civ 173, [2009] BPIR 704.

The implication of terms into an arrangement—As regards terms implied into a voluntary arrangement, given that an arrangement is ordinarily a lengthy and complex document and has the effect by statutory force under s 5(2) (and s 260(2) in an IVA) of binding all creditors entitled to notice of it, it is perhaps not surprising that the court will be very slow to imply a term unless it is absolutely necessary to give efficacy to an arrangement. In the words of Chadwick LJ in *Johnson v Davies* [1999] Ch 117 at 138A–138B, in the context of a case which considered whether an arrangement was capable of releasing a co-debtor from liability:

'Under Part VIII [in the case of an IVA] of the 1986 Act, the discharge of the debtor depends entirely on the terms of the arrangement. One must look at the arrangement, and nothing else, in order to find the terms (if any) under which the debtor is discharged. This is emphasised by the words in s 260(2) [or s 5(2)] of the 1986 Act ...'

In *El Ajou v Stern* [2006] EWHC 3067 (Ch), [2007] BPIR 693 at [31]–[34] Kitchin J accepted that an IVA was subject to an implied term that creditors subject to the IVA would take no steps to enforce their claim against the debtor since such a term was necessary to give business efficacy to the arrangement, mindful of the comments of Chadwick LJ in *Johnson* at 128F–128G to the effect that such a term must be implied if an arrangement is to work as intended. Kitchin J could not, however, find any basis for implying a term prohibiting a creditor from pursuit of a claim to judgment following discharge of the interim order imposing a stay. A similar conclusion was reached by Rimer J in *Alman v Approach Housing Ltd* [2001] BCLC 530 (a CVA case) where the arrangement contained no machinery for the determination of disputed claims.

In *Re Hellard and Goldfarb* [2007] BPIR 1322 HHJ Norris QC, sitting as a judge of the High Court, was prepared to imply a term (by way of a direction to that effect) that supervisors of a CVA were entitled to drawn remuneration from arrangement assets on a time cost basis where a cap on fees had been reached and where a further meeting to seek sanction for the drawing of further fees in accordance with the terms of the CVA had been inquorate upon nobody attending.

Section 5(2A)

Scope of provision—This provision was inserted by Insolvency Act 2000, s 2 and Sch 2 thereto. Its effect is such that, where an arrangement does not end prematurely, a creditor who is bound by an arrangement, but has not had notice of it by virtue of s 5(2)(b)(ii), is entitled to any sum due to him under the arrangement to the extent that that creditor has not already been paid. The provision does not, however, confer any entitlement to vote on such a creditor.

For the meaning of the term 'comes to an end prematurely' see s 7B.

Section 5(3) and (4)

Scope of provision—These provisions are largely self-explanatory and are designed, subject to the constraints imposed by s 5(4), to enable the court to stay winding-up proceedings or, apparently, to discharge the appointment of an administrator for the purpose of 'facilitating the implementation of the voluntary arrangement'. For cases under the equivalent s 147(1) see *Re Lowston* [1991] BCLC 570, ChD (Harman J) and the authorities therein.

The provisions do not identify the parties eligible to make an application for an order under s 5(3). Procedurally, an application should be made in any winding-up or administration proceedings. It is submitted that such an application may be made by any party with an interest in the CVA, which would include the company itself, the nominee or supervisor, a liquidator or administrator, a member of the company or a creditor, whether or not an arrangement creditor. In Scotland it has been held that the burden rests on the applicant in satisfying the court that an order should be made and that the court must consider the rights and interests of all who may be affected by the decision: *Re McGruther v Seoble* [2004] SC 514 at [16]–[18].

For the discharge of the remuneration etc of a liquidator or administrator where a voluntary arrangement is approved see r 1.23(2)–(6).

6 Challenge of decisions

(1) Subject to this section, an application to the court may be made, by any of the persons specified below, on one or both of the following grounds, namely—

    (a)   that a voluntary arrangement which has effect under section 4A unfairly prejudices the interests of a creditor, member or contributory of the company;

    (b)   that there has been some material irregularity at or in relation to either of the meetings.

(2) The persons who may apply under subsection (1) are—

    (a)   a person entitled, in accordance with the rules, to vote at either of the meetings;

    (aa)   a person who would have been entitled, in accordance with the rules, to vote at the creditors' meeting if he had had notice of it

    (b)   the nominee or any person who has replaced him under section 2(4) or 4(2); and

    (c)   if the company is being wound up or is in administration, the liquidator or administrator.

(2A) Subject to this section, where a voluntary arrangement in relation to a company in energy administration is approved at the meetings summoned under section 3, an application to the court may be made—

    (a)   by the Secretary of State, or

    (b)   with the consent of the Secretary of State, by the Gas and Electricity Markets Authority,

on the ground that the voluntary arrangement is not consistent with the achievement of the objective of the energy administration.

(3) An application under this section shall not be made—

    (a)   after the end of the period of 28 days beginning with the first day on which each of the reports required by section 4(6) has been made to the court, or

    (b)   in the case of a person who was not given notice of the creditors' meeting, after the end of the period of 28 days beginning with the day on which he became aware that the meeting had taken place,

but (subject to that) an application made by a person within subsection (2)(aa) on the ground that the voluntary arrangement prejudices his interests may be made after the arrangement has ceased to have effect, unless it came to an end prematurely.

(4) Where on such an application the court is satisfied as to either of the grounds mentioned in subsection (1) or, in the case of an application under subsection (2A), as to the ground mentioned in that subsection, it may do one or both of the following, namely—

(a) revoke or suspend any decision approving the voluntary arrangement which has effect under section 4A or, in a case falling within subsection (1)(b), any decision taken by the meeting in question which has effect under that section;

(b) give a direction to any person for the summoning of further meetings to consider any revised proposal the person who made the original proposal may make or, in a case falling within subsection (1)(b), a further company or (as the case may be) creditors' meeting to reconsider the original proposal.

(5) Where at any time after giving a direction under subsection (4)(b) for the summoning of meetings to consider a revised proposal the court is satisfied that the person who made the original proposal does not intend to submit a revised proposal, the court shall revoke the direction and revoke or suspend any decision approving the voluntary arrangement which has effect under section 4A.

(6) In a case where the court, on an application under this section with respect to any meeting—

(a) gives a direction under subsection (4)(b), or

(b) revokes or suspends an approval under subsection (4)(a) or (5),

the court may give such supplemental directions as it thinks fit and, in particular, directions with respect to things done under the voluntary arrangement since it took effect.

(7) Except in pursuance of the preceding provisions of this section, a decision taken at a meeting summoned under section 3 is not invalidated by any irregularity at or in relation to the meeting.

(8) In this section 'in energy administration' and 'objective of the energy administration' are to be construed in accordance with Schedule B1 to this Act, as applied by Part 1 of Schedule 20 to the Energy Act 2004.

Amendments—Insolvency Act 2000, s 2, Sch 2, paras 1, 7; Enterprise Act 2002, s 248(3), Sch 17, paras 9, 12; Energy Act 2004, s 159(1), Sch 20, Pt 4, para 44.

General note—This section allows for an application to court by any of the applicants within s 6(2) on either or both of the grounds identified in s 6(1), either of which may extend to breach of a substantive statutory prohibition: *IRC v Wimbledon Football Club Ltd* [2004] EWCA Civ 655, [2005] 1 BCLC 66 at [37] (Neuberger LJ). The use of the words 'an application to the court may be made' in s 6(1) together with the reference to 'a voluntary arrangement which has effect' in s 6(1)(a) (to which s 6(1)(b) implicitly makes reference) strongly suggests that an application may only be made once an arrangement has actually been approved by creditors, such that no grounds are available for an application in respect of prospective or anticipated unfair prejudice or material irregularity prior to approval of the arrangement.

The court has wide powers under s 6(4)–(6) to tailor its order to the circumstances of the case, including the revocation of the approval of the voluntary arrangement or directions for the summoning of further meetings to consider either the original proposal or any revised proposal with which the debtor seeks to proceed. Many of the reported first instance decisions on applications under s 6 (and its equivalent in s 262 in relation to individual voluntary arrangements) are of very limited assistance in terms of general application, given that the grounds in s 6(1), and any order or direction made by the court, necessarily depend on the particular facts of each case.

Save for s 6, an application to court may also be available under s 4A(3): see the notes to that subsection. A creditor or member of the company may also appeal the chairman's decision on the admission of any creditor claim for voting purposes under r 1.17A(3). The 28-day time limit imposed by s 6(3), which is not extendable by the court, is of considerable practical significance, since it is doubtful that the court retains any inherent jurisdiction to revoke or otherwise stay a voluntary arrangement, given the specific terms in which s 6 is drafted.

Section 6(1)(a)

Scope of provision—The language of the subsection requires that the unfair prejudice complained of must be caused by the voluntary arrangement, and not merely the voluntary arrangement itself taking effect through statutory force under s 4A.

In *Re A Debtor (No 222 of 1990) ex parte Bank of Ireland* [1992] BCLC 137 at 145C–145G Harman J (in considering the virtually identical provisions in s 262(1)) considered that subsection (a) 'plainly looks at the arrangement itself and requires consideration of whether it prejudices the creditor, presumably because of some differential treatment, some restriction upon the creditors or some advantage to another creditor so that there is an unfair prejudice by reason of the voluntary arrangement itself': see also *Re A Debtor (No 87 of 1993) (No 2)* [1996] 1 BCLC 63 at 86 (Rimer J) in which, having cited and relied upon the above passage, counsel for the claimant was forced to abandon an argument to the effect that the court may embark upon consideration of the overall merits of the arrangement on an unfair prejudice complaint and to accept that there is no relevant prejudice to any creditor if each creditor under the scheme is put in the same position as the other creditors and suffers no discriminatory treatment as a consequence. Subsection (b), on the other hand, 'seems plainly to divide the matter into events occurring at the meeting which are wrong, which are irregularities, and matters in relation to the voluntary arrangement which could be unfairly prejudicial.' Accordingly, a wrong decision at a meeting to exclude or prohibit a vote gives rise to a complaint of material irregularity and not unfair prejudice.

To similar effect, in *Peck v Craighead* [1995] 1 BCLC 337 Martin Mann QC, sitting as a deputy High Court judge, observed at 343E that 'Irregularity involving unlawfulness at a meeting of creditors is conceptually different from unfair prejudice which predicates unfairness inherent in a proposal or modification which otherwise lawfully affects a creditor's interest.'

'... unfairly prejudices the interests of the creditor, member or contributory of the company'—The term 'unfairly prejudicial' is also employed in s 994 of the Companies Act 2006, which together with its predecessors ss 459, 460 of the Companies Act 1985 and the Companies Acts of 1948 and 1980, have given rise to a plethora of reported case law. The term 'unfairly prejudicial' is, however, employed in a very different context in s 994 of the 2006 Act, in that it relates to the conduct of the management of a company. As a consequence, authorities on s 994 and its predecessors are unlikely to be of any assistance in the present context, on which see the comments in *Doorbar v Alltime Securities Ltd* [1995] BCC 1149 at 1159A (Peter Gibson LJ).

The meaning and scope of unfair prejudice—In the context of voluntary arrangements, the Court of Appeal appears to have addressed the test applicable to unfair prejudice in *Cadbury Schweppes plc v Somji* [2001] 1 WLR 615 to the extent that Robert Walker LJ referred to the 'fairly strong line of first instance authority' which is 'uniformly in favour of limiting the effect of the provisions to unfairness brought about by the terms of the [arrangement] itself'. At least two key principles are clear enough from decisions at first instance. First, the unfair prejudice must result from the arrangement itself: *Re A Debtor (No 222 of 1990) ex parte Bank of Ireland*. Secondly, whether the interests of an applicant are unfairly prejudiced requires the court to consider all the circumstances of the case: *Re A Debtor (No 101 of 1999)* [2001] 1 BCLC 54 at 63D (Ferris J). It is not sufficient that an applicant establishes mere prejudice resulting from the arrangement; rather, the prejudice must be unfair. The judgment of Lightman J at first instance in *IRC v Wimbledon Football Club Ltd* [2004] EWCA Civ 655, [2005] 1 BCLC 66 also contains very useful guidance on the issue of unfair prejudice. In particular (at [18]) 'the unfair prejudice must have been caused by the terms of the arrangement' and (at [23]) 'the question of fairness of the arrangement requires consideration of all of the circumstances and in particular the alternatives available and the practical consequences of a decision to confirm or reject the arrangement'.

In *Doorbar v Alltime Securities Ltd* [1995] BCC 1149 the Court of Appeal upheld a finding of Knox J at first instance to the effect that a landlord, who was precluded from petitioning for bankruptcy of the debtor on the arrangement taking effect, with the consequence that the landlord could not rely on a clause in the lease which required that the debtor and his wife would take a new lease on the debtor's bankruptcy, was prejudiced by the arrangement, but not unfairly prejudiced. The taking into account of all relevant circumstances required the court to balance the prejudice to the landlord in having its rights against the debtor's wife restricted on the one hand, and the prejudice to the general body of creditors in being prevented from having the benefits of any voluntary arrangement (which included future payments of rent) under the lease on the other. Accordingly, the court would not exercise its discretion in interfering with the arrangement.

Differential treatment of creditors which is not assented to by a creditor who considers that he has been less favourably treated than other creditors may give cause for an inquiry, but does not of itself necessarily establish unfair prejudice in that there may well be an explanation justifying such differential treatment. In *Re A Debtor (No 101 of 1999)* [2001] 1 BCLC 54 Ferris J overturned the decision of the judge below who had failed to consider all of the circumstances of the case in this regard. At a meeting of creditors various friends of the debtor, with a collective claim of £440,000, approved an arrangement whereby a sum of £20,000 would be introduced by a third party, which sum, subject to costs and expenses of £5,000, would leave some £15,000 in discharge of the Crown's debt of £77,000 whilst doing nothing to modify the total indebtedness due to the debtor's friends. The use of the friends' voting power to achieve a differential treatment for the Crown, whilst at the same time preserving their rights and remedies in full, was held to constitute unfair prejudice. The court was, however, prepared to allow the debtor a direction (under s 262(4)(b)) for the summoning of a further meeting of creditors to consider a revised proposal.

In considering unfair prejudice it is not for the court to speculate as to whether the terms proposed were the best that could have been achieved. Unless the court can be satisfied that such alternatives would certainly have been on offer the comparison must be between the proposed compromise and no compromise at all as at the date of the vote on the arrangement: *SISU Capital Fund Ltd v Tucker* [2006] BPIR 154 at [73].

Cases on unfair prejudice—For further cases on unfair prejudice see *Cadbury Schweppes plc v Somji* [2001] 1 WLR 615, CA (secret deal with two creditors inducing their support of a voluntary arrangement not unfairly prejudicial but a fraud on creditors); *National Westminster Bank plc v Scher* [1998] BPIR 224 (John Martin QC, sitting as a deputy High Court judge, no unfair prejudice to two bank creditors prevented from enforcing rights against debtor's wife under terms of arrangement where wife had no separate assets or income); *Sea Voyager Maritime Inc v Bielecki (t/a Hughes Hooker & Co)* [1999] 1 BCLC 133 (Richard McCombe QC (as he then was), creditor unfairly prejudiced by arrangement which prevented creditor from proceeding to judgment against debtor with consequence that creditor unable to make recovery from debtor's insurers under the Third Parties (Rights Against Insurers) Act 1930); *Re Naeem (a Bankrupt) (No 18 of 1988)* [1990] 1 WLR 48 (Hoffmann J (as he then was), arrangement reducing debtor's liability for rent for which landlord retained usual enforcement remedies prejudicial but not unfairly prejudicial to landlord); and *Re Cancol Ltd* [1995] BCC 1133 (Knox J, no unfair prejudice to landlord under terms of arrangement providing for landlord to be paid either rent in full whilst debtor occupied premises or a dividend on premises being vacated where landlord not deprived of right of forfeiture on rent ceasing to be paid in full). A creditor may also apply to court alleging unfair prejudice where an arrangement has the effect of releasing a co-debtor against whom that creditor would otherwise have a right of action: *Johnson v Davies* [1998] 3 WLR 1299 at 1317B (Chadwick LJ). In *Prudential Assurance Co Ltd v PRG Powerhouse Ltd* [2007] EWHC 1002 (Ch), [2007] BCC 500 Etherton J held that, whilst each case must turn on its own facts, the landlords of properties occupied by the company had been unfairly prejudiced by the terms of a CVA which operated to release the company's parent from guarantees given to the landlords. *Mourant & Co Trustees Limited & Anor v Sixty UK Limited (in administration) & Ors* [2010] EWHC 1890 (Ch), [2010] BPIR 1264 was another attempt at guarantee stripping which also failed. The judge (Henderson J), after undertaking both a vertical and a horizontal comparison, concluded that the voluntary arrangement did unfairly prejudice the interests of the applicant landlords whose guarantees had been stripped. The judge, somewhat emphatically, stated: 'This is, in my view, a CVA that should never have seen the light of day …' although he also went on to observe 'I do not say that it is necessarily impossible to propose a fair CVA of this type but the greatest care is needed to ensure fairness to the [minority creditors who are to be deprived of valuable contractual rights], both in the substance of what is proposed and in the procedure that is adopted'. In *HM Revenue and Customs v Portsmouth City Football Club Limited (in administration) & Ors* [2010] EWHC 2013 (Ch) [2010] BPIR 1123, HMRC sought to challenge a voluntary arrangement on the grounds that it (in particular in upholding the so-called football creditors rule) was unfairly prejudicial. Mann J, who had an eye on the commercial realities, rejected the challenge. *Child Maintenance and Enforcement Commission v Beesley and Whyman* [2010] EWCA Civ 1344 (Ch), [2011] BPIR 608 was a case in which CMEC brought a challenge in the context of an individual voluntary arrangement and in which the Court of Appeal considered CMEC's alternative contention that the voluntary arrangement was unfairly prejudicial. Both at first instance in that case, and on appeal, the Court concluded that the voluntary arrangement was unfairly prejudicial to CMEC.

Unfair prejudice based on lower projected dividend than in bankruptcy?—It is submitted that an allegation that the interests of a creditor are unfairly prejudiced on the sole ground that the approved arrangement will produce a lower return to a class of creditors than that projected on liquidation (or bankruptcy) will be bound to fail since an arrangement cannot unfairly prejudice the interests of a creditor where the modification of a creditor's entitlement comes about through the operation of an arrangement with statutory force consequent upon the approval of the prescribed requisite majority of creditors.

Section 6(1)(b)

The meaning and scope of material irregularity—Section 6(7) expressly provides that, in the absence of an application under s 6, the mere fact of an irregularity at, or in relation to, either the company meeting or the meeting of creditors does not of itself invalidate any decision in relation to the arrangement. To obtain a remedy under s 6 an applicant must establish not only an irregularity, but also the fact of its materiality: *Re Sweatfield Ltd* [1997] BCC 744 at 750E (His Honour Judge Weeks QC, sitting as a High Court judge).

Perhaps the most obvious form of material irregularity in relation to meetings concerns the assertion and treatment of voting rights. In *Doorbar v Alltime Securities Ltd* [1995] BCC 1149 at 1158D–1158H the Court of Appeal, upholding the decision of Knox J below, rejected an allegation of material irregularity by a landlord in circumstances where the chairman of the creditors' meeting had placed a minimum value of one year's rent on the landlord's claim in making allowance for the possibility that the landlord would exercise its power of re-entry and, in so doing, had rejected the landlord's claim for the aggregate of the whole of the future rent under the lease. Given that the chairman's approach was entirely reasonable, and that the landlord would only have had 25% or more of the voting power of the meeting if the estimated value of its claim was increased threefold, there could be no material irregularity.

In *Commissioners of Inland Revenue v Duce* [1999] BPIR 189 Hazel Williamson QC, sitting as a deputy High Court judge, considered an allegation of material irregularity by the Inland Revenue where a debtor had failed to disclose the fact that a significant creditor supporting approval of the arrangement had taken assignment of the debt from a company in which the debtor had a substantial interest and where the debtor had failed to identify accurately the creditor which was to purchase the debtor's property for full market value less £90,000 so as to produce funds in full and final settlement of all creditor claims. The deputy judge took the view that the judge below had erred in principle in failing to undertake a balancing exercise which took full account of the circumstances of the case, namely the seriousness and heinousness of the irregularity on the one hand, and the likely attitude of the other creditors on the other. On the basis that creditors ought to be given the opportunity to reconsider an arrangement with knowledge of the proper facts, the deputy judge directed the re-convening of the creditors' meeting and overturned the decision of the judge below which had revoked approval of the arrangement and directed that no further meeting of creditors should be convened.

Material irregularity may also arise by virtue of a meeting failing to acknowledge the security rights of a creditor whose consent would otherwise be required for the modification of such rights. For example, in *Peck v Craighead* [1995] 1 BCLC 337 Martin Mann QC, sitting as a deputy High Court judge, found material irregularity (under s 262(1)(b) in the context of an individual voluntary arrangement) where the meeting of creditors had approved an arrangement which envisaged the sale of chattels which had been used by the debtors, but over which the complainant creditor had obtained a writ of fi fa and walking possession pursuant to a consent judgment. Given that the complainant creditor had not consented to the modification of what amounted to its rights as a secured creditor, the deputy judge held that the approval constituted a material irregularity, as a consequence of which the complainant creditor's execution could proceed notwithstanding the approval of the arrangement.

As a general principle in material irregularity cases, where the irregularity is based on some omission from information provided to a creditors' meeting, the following formulation appears in the judgment of the Court of Appeal in *Somji v Cadbury Schweppes plc* [2001] 1 BCLC 498 at [25]: '[the question is] whether, had the truth been told, it would be likely to have made a material difference to the way in which the creditors would have assessed the term of the proposed [arrangement]'. For an application of that test see *Re Trident Fashions plc (in administration) (No 2)* [2004] EWHC 293 (Ch), [2004] 2 BCLC 35 (Lewison J).

It is plainly arguable that an application may be made under s 6(1)(b) by a creditor who is bound by an arrangement through the operation of s 5(2)(b) where the creditor would have been entitled at the creditors' meeting but did not have notice of it in circumstances where that creditor could have affected or influenced the outcome of the meeting: see, for example, *Tager v Westpac Banking Corp* [1997] 1 BCLC 313 at 325F–325G (His Honour Judge Weeks QC, sitting as a High Court judge).

For a finding of material irregularity resulting in the revocation of the approval of an individual voluntary arrangement, see *Re Cardona* [1997] BCC 697, where the chairman of the creditors' meeting wrongly refused to allow the Inland Revenue, being the debtor's largest creditor, to withdraw a proxy form lodged for the purposes of a creditors' meeting, which was adjourned, and to lodge a second proxy for the purposes of the re-convened meeting.

For an unsuccessful allegation of material irregularity which was based on fundamental misunderstandings on the part of the secured creditor as to the effect of the CVA and unsubstantiated allegations of irregularities at the creditors' meeting and the counting of votes see *Swindon Town Properties Ltd v Swindon Town Football Co Ltd* [2003] BPIR 253 (Hart J). A challenge based on an alleged material irregularity succeeded in Re *Gatnom Capital & Finance Ltd; Macaria Investments Ltd v (1) Sanders (2) Gatnom Capital & Finance Ltd* [2010] EWHC 3353 (Ch) [2011] BPIR 1013. In that case, Roth J accepted the applicant's contention that two land contracts were shams, and accordingly, creditors under those contracts who had been allowed to vote at the creditor's meeting should not have been allowed to vote. The same amounted to a material irregularity.

Section 6(1)(b) is sufficiently broad to extend to a material irregularity in a debtor's proposal or statement of affairs: *Re A Debtor (No 87 of 1993) (No 2)* [1996] BCL 80 at 107C–108E (Rimer J), an IVA case. That case, which resulted in the court revoking the arrangement, involved an application by four creditors of the debtor alleging that the debtor's proposal was dishonest and misleading in that it falsely disclosed a non-existent asset, it failed to disclose all of the debtor's assets, and made false representation with regard to those assets and liabilities which had been disclosed by the debtor.

It is submitted that a finding of material irregularity involves a finding of fact alone and is in no way dependent on any finding of fault.

Paragraph 4.1 at SIP 3 advises that a mis-statement of the amount of the assets and liabilities in the debtor's statement of affairs is capable of constituting a material irregularity.

Section 6(2)

Scope of provision—For the standing of the FSA to apply and be heard on applications under s 6 (and s 262 in the case of an IVA) see ss 356 and 357 of the Financial Services and Markets Act 2000.

Eligible applicants—Categories (a) and (aa) are clear enough by reference to the two grounds in s 6(1).

It appears that either the nominee (or his replacement) or a liquidator or administrator has standing to make application under s 6(1)(a), although such an application may only proceed on the basis of alleged unfair prejudice to the interests of a creditor, member or contributory and, as such, and in the absence of an application by either such party, such applications are unlikely. More obviously plausible are applications under s 6(1)(b), since these are not restricted to prejudice to the interests of a creditor's member or contributory. A nominee, for example, may consider an application if the effect of the decision of the meetings is to inhibit the discharge of his function under s 1(2) or, given that no standing to apply is conferred on the company itself or its directors, to challenge a decision which approves a modified proposal where the consent of the directors has not been forthcoming to such modifications.

Procedure on a s 6(2) application—Care must be taken in naming the respondents to an application under s 6(1). In *Re Naeem (a Bankrupt) (No 18 of 1988)* [1990] 1 WLR 48, a case involving an unsuccessful allegation of unfairly prejudicial conduct in the context of an individual voluntary arrangement, Hoffmann J (as he then was) indicated that the applicant had been wrong to join the nominee and two creditors as respondents to the application. His Lordship also held that a nominee should not be ordered to pay the costs of a successful application in the absence of actual misconduct on the nominee's part. Hoffmann J did comment, however, that convenience may dictate giving the nominee notice of the application in such a case. In the words of Hoffmann J in *Naeem* (at 51), 'If there had been some personal conduct on the part of the nominee which would justify an order for costs against him, that could be done.'

It is suggested that it will usually be appropriate to join the nominee, and possibly one or more creditors, to an application alleging material irregularity at or in relation to a meeting at which the nominee and/or such creditors have played a part.

For further discussion on costs, see *Re A Debtor (No 222 of 1990) ex parte Bank of Ireland* [1992] BCLC 137 and *(No 2)* [1993] BCLC 233 (Harman J); and *Harmony Carpets v Chaffin-Laird* [2000] BPIR 61 (Rattee J, no order for costs against nominee of individual voluntary arrangement notwithstanding criticisms of nominee in reporting to court on the basis that it was not clear, had proper reports been made, that the court would have declined to allow meetings of creditors to take place such that the complainant would still have incurred the costs of challenging the decision of the meeting). For the possibility of obtaining costs against non-parties, see *Re Gatnom Capital & Finance Ltd; Macaria Investments Ltd v (1) Sanders (2) Gatnom Capital & Finance Ltd (3) Omatov (No 2)* [2011] EWHC 3716 (Ch), [2012] BPIR 299.

For further general guidance on procedure see the notes to rr 7.1, 7.2 and 7.10(2).

Section 6(3)

'**... shall not be made ... after the end of the period of 28 days ...**'—These words are not a common formulation for the computation of time under statute although they do correspond with the formulation employed in s 5(4)(a). The 28-day period begins with and includes the dates specified in s 6(3)(a) and (b). In the case of s 6(3)(a) the reference to 'the reports' envisages separate reports being filed for the purposes of s 4(6), although in practice the chairman of the company meeting and the meeting of creditors will usually file a single report at the same time. If separate reports were filed at different times, then it would follow that two differing 28-day periods would come into effect, one affecting the standing of creditors and the other applying to applications by members of contributories of the company.

The 28-day period cannot be extended by the court: *Re Bournemouth & Boscombe Athletic Football Club Co Ltd* [1998] BPIR 183 (Lloyd J, as he then was) (this proposition was also accepted without comment in the Court of Appeal in *Tucker and Spratt (Joint Supervisors of Energy Holdings (No 3) (In Liquidation) v Gold Fields Mining LLC* [2009] EWCA Civ 173, [2009] BPIR 704 and was applied by Registrar Jaques in *Wood v Heart Hospital* [2009] BPIR 1538). Neither is it appropriate to allow an application out of time to be joined with a live s 6 application made within the 28-day period since such a course would serve to defeat the purpose of the stipulated limitation period. If a proposal has been approved, but can nonetheless be shown to have been invalid then, at least where the proposal is advanced bona fide and approved and implemented accordingly, and in particular where the invalidity is overlooked by all concerned up to the time of approval and expiration of the 28-day period, the arrangement should be treated as valid notwithstanding the infringement giving rise to the apparent invalidity: *IRC v Wimbledon Football Club Ltd* [2004] EWCA Civ 655, [2005] 1 BCLC 66 at [38] (Neuberger LJ). Technically, but without any real substantive justification, the position in CVAs differs from that in IVAs, in relation to which the 28-day period in s 262(3) is capable of extension under s 376 (time limits): *Tager v Westpac Banking Corp* [1997] 1 BCLC 313 (His Honour Judge Weeks QC). There is no equivalent to s 376 applicable to Part I. In the context of IVAs His Honour Judge Weeks QC held in *Tager* (at 325D) that the factors relevant to the exercise of discretion and extending time are the length of delay, the reasons for the delay, the apparent merits of the underlying application and the prejudice to each side other than the inevitable prejudice inherent in re-opening the question of approval of the arrangement. The conclusion of His Honour Judge Weeks QC in extending was approved of by Carnwath J in *Plant v Plant* [1998] 1 BCLC 38. In *Warley Continental Services Ltd (in liquidation) v Johal* (2002) *The Times*, October 28 His Honour Judge Norris QC, sitting as a High Court judge, also identified the conduct of the parties as being of potential significance in a wide range of cases; an extension of time in that case was refused, given the unjustifiable and significant delay in making the application, notwithstanding the obvious merits of the case.

Section 6(4)

Remedies and relief on a s 6(2) application—Whilst the discretion of the court in making an order under this subsection appears unfettered through the use of the word 'may', the court has a positive duty to act in setting aside an arrangement where the arrangement is in clear conflict with a statutory provision (see below). In other cases the court would be perfectly entitled in the exercise of its discretion to refuse to make any order if the practical effect of, most obviously, setting aside an arrangement would be to harm the interests of the creditors of the debtor generally, say where the purpose of the arrangement was all but complete, even where the court was satisfied as to the fact of unfair prejudice and/or material irregularity.

The scope of any such order made is defined in fairly restrictive terms by s 6(4)(a) and (b) which do not read as being mutually exclusive in that the court may make an order suspending the decision under (a) whilst at the same time providing directions under (b). In particular, the court has no power to direct the modification of a proposal or that any particular modification should be considered by any further meeting, since the formulation of the proposal remains at all times entirely a matter for the party making the proposal.

The court's discretion in granting relief—The exercise of the court's powers under s 6(4) – upon which the powers in s 6(5) and s 6(6) are dependent – is discretionary. However, where an approved arrangement conflicts with a clear statutory prohibition, which goes to the substance of the proposal and has resulted in clear prejudice, the court must revoke the arrangement save, possibly, in the most exceptional circumstances: *IRC v Wimbledon Football Club Ltd* [2004] EWCA Civ 655, [2005] 1 BCLC 66 at [39] (Neuberger LJ). *IRC v Wimbledon* involved an unsuccessful challenge to an arrangement by the Inland Revenue, which complained of a breach of s 4(4)(a) on the grounds that so-called football creditors would receive 100 pence in the pound, whereas the Revenue would receive only 30. The application and appeal by the Revenue failed, since the football creditors were to be discharged by third party monies such that there was no infringement of s 4(4)(a). Another example of interference with statutory provisions might include an arrangement which purported to vary and undermine the statutory trust created in favour of the Law Society under Sch 6 of the Solicitors Act 1974 following a Law Society intervention into a solicitors' practice.

Section 6(4)(a)

Scope of provision—If an arrangement is revoked or suspended then, in the absence of some contrary supplemental direction under s 6(6), there is nothing to prevent a fresh proposal being formulated and advanced, even, it would appear, a proposal in identical terms to that revoked or suspended.

Section 6(4)(b)

Scope of provision—The provision for the giving of a direction 'to any person' for the summoning of further meetings is probably designed to allow for summoning by a person other than the incumbent nominee where the court forms the view that future conduct by that individual is inappropriate although in those circumstances further steps would be required to replace the nominee for the purposes of s 1(2). In the absence of grounds for concern, the court's direction will be to the incumbent nominee.

The court will not ordinarily be inclined to direct the summoning of further meetings to consider any revised proposal if it is satisfied on evidence before it that a sufficient number of creditors in value will vote against, so as to defeat, approval of the proposal. Even where such a direction is given, the court must revoke the direction under s 6(5) if satisfied that the party making the original proposal does not intend to proceed with a revised proposal.

Section 6(6)

Scope of provision—Although the court may tailor any supplemental directions to complement any order under s 6(4) or (5), this provision addresses in particular the interim period between the approval of an arrangement and the making of any such order, given that an arrangement remains valid pending the making of such an order.

Section 6(7)

Scope of provision—See the note to s 6(1)(b).

6A False representations, etc

(1) If, for the purpose of obtaining the approval of the members or creditors of a company to a proposal for a voluntary arrangement, a person who is an officer of the company—

    (a)   makes any false representation, or
    (b)   fraudulently does, or omits to do, anything,

he commits an offence.

(2) Subsection (1) applies even if the proposal is not approved.

(3) For purposes of this section 'officer' includes a shadow director.

(4) A person guilty of an offence under this section is liable to imprisonment or a fine, or both.

Amendments—Inserted by Insolvency Act 2000, s 2, Sch 2, paras 1, 8.

General note—These new provisions were effective from 1 January 2003 on implementation under s 2 of the Insolvency Act 2000 and para 8 of Sch 2 thereto; the formerly operative r 1.30 was revoked by the Insolvency (Amendment) (No 2) Rules 2002 (SI 2002/2712). In practice, a proposal will typically include a declaration that the directors had been made aware of s 6A. Some proposals also include a statement of truth of a kind employed in witness statements and statements of case under the Civil Procedure Rules 1998 which verifies the deponent's belief as to the matters of fact represented in the proposal.

Section 6A(1)

Scope of provision—The actus reus of the offence includes the making of a false representation or, alternatively, the fraudulent commission, or omission, of anything for the purpose of obtaining the approval of the members or creditors of a company to a proposal.

For a criminal prosecution for fraudulent representation in the context of an IVA proposal see *R v Dawson* (unreported, 29 June 2001). The scope of s 6A has been extended to the obtaining of a moratorium in connection with a CVA by para 42 of Sch A1. The wording of the subsection, it is suggested, does not extend to obtaining approval for the modification to the terms of a subsisting arrangement.

Section 6A(2)

Scope of provision—The fact that a proposal is not approved has no bearing on the committing of an offence under s 6A(1), which requires only proof of the acts or omissions within its scope 'for the purpose' of obtaining approval of the arrangement.

Section 6A(3)

Scope of provision—For the terms 'officer' and 'shadow director' see the note to s 206(3).

Section 6A(4)

Scope of provision—On penalties see s 430 and Sch 10.

7 Implementation of proposal

(1) This section applies where a voluntary arrangement has effect under section 4A.

(2) The person who is for the time being carrying out in relation to the voluntary arrangement the functions conferred—

    (a)   on the nominee by virtue of the approval given at one or both of the meetings summoned under section 3, or

    (b)   by virtue of section 2(4) or 4(2) on a person other than the nominee,

shall be known as the supervisor of the voluntary arrangement.

(3) If any of the company's creditors or any other person is dissatisfied by any act, omission or decision of the supervisor, he may apply to the court; and on the application the court may—

    (a)   confirm, reverse or modify any act or decision of the supervisor,

    (b)   give him directions, or

    (c)   make such other order as it thinks fit.

(4) The supervisor—

    (a)   may apply to the court for directions in relation to any particular matter arising under the voluntary arrangement, and

    (b)   is included among the persons who may apply to the court for the winding up of the company or for an administration order to be made in relation to it.

(5) The court may, whenever—

    (a)   it is expedient to appoint a person to carry out the functions of the supervisor, and

    (b)   it is inexpedient, difficult or impracticable for an appointment to be made without the assistance of the court,

make an order appointing a person who is qualified to act as an insolvency practitioner or authorised to act as supervisor, in relation to the voluntary arrangement, either in substitution for the existing supervisor or to fill a vacancy.

(6) The power conferred by subsection (5) is exercisable so as to increase the number of persons exercising the functions of supervisor or, where there is more than one person exercising those functions, so as to replace one or more of those persons.

Amendments—Insolvency Act 2000, s 2, Sch 2, paras 1, 9.

General note—These provisions provide for the automatic appointment of the supervisor following approval of the voluntary arrangement (under s 7(2)) and for the making of applications to court in the event of dissatisfaction with the conduct of the supervisor (under s 7(3)) or where the supervisor requires the assistance of the court in relation to the voluntary arrangement or seeks a winding-up order against the company (under s 7(4)). Very similar provisions in relation to IVAs appear in s 263.

Best practice guidance on the implementation of a voluntary arrangement following the meeting of creditors and the conclusion/termination of the arrangement appears in paras 8 and 9 of SIP 3. The supervisor is expected to keep creditors abreast of developments in the conduct of the arrangement. In particular para 8.1 of SIP 3 provides:

'If actual events suggest a deviation from the terms of the arrangement, the supervisor should take appropriate action. Such action should correspond to further detailed provisions of the proposal. If he is authorised to exercise discretion in any area, and that discretion is exercised, the supervisor should explain the circumstances to creditors (and members in a CVA) at the next available opportunity.'

Despite the heading to s 7, its provisions provide no specific guidance on the implementation of the proposal itself. Detailed procedural rules do, however, appear in rr 1.22–1.29. In addition, the terms of the arrangement itself will dictate the method of implementation on a case-by-case basis. Rule 1.55 also contains new rules on time recording which a supervisor must comply with.

On the declaration of payment of dividends see rr 11.1–11.13.

In practice, it is common to find that the terms of a CVA import the provisions in rr 4.73–4.94, which provide a procedure for proof and quantification of claims for dividend purposes in liquidation; for the equivalent rules in bankruptcy see rr 6.96–6.114.

Appleyard Ltd v Ritecrown Ltd [2007] EWHC 3515 (Ch) [2009] BPIR 235 is a case in which Lewison J considered the scope of the supervisor's duty. He stated (at para 38): 'The primary duty of the supervisor is to implement the CVA in accordance with the Insolvency Act, the Insolvency Rules, and the terms of the proposals as modified. Any power or discretion given to him under those proposals is in my judgment to be exercised for that purpose, and that purpose only, and not for a collateral purpose. It is common ground that as an officer of the court the supervisor must also act reasonably'.

Section 7(1)

Scope of provision—For guidance see the notes to s 4A.

Section 7(2)

Scope of provision—The nominee, or his replacement, becomes known as the supervisor of the voluntary arrangement automatically by force of this provision on the arrangement coming into effect under s 4A.

The circumstances in which the nominee does not become supervisor are specified in ss 2(4) and 4(2). The first arises where the court has appointed a replacement nominee because the original nominee failed to submit his report to the court in accordance with s 2(2). The second situation arises where the proposal has been modified so as to confer the functions of the nominee on another appropriately qualified person.

The consequence of the supervisor's appointment is that the person so appointed becomes entitled, indeed obliged, to discharge his functions and exercise his powers under and in accordance with the arrangement.

Section 7(3)

Scope of provision—This subsection is concerned only with complaints directed against a supervisor; it has no bearing on whether a creditor is able to sustain a claim against a company, notwithstanding the approval of the voluntary arrangement, on which see the notes to s 5(2)(b).

Provided that the court is not minded to strike out an underlying claim on the basis that it is bound to fail, s 7(3) will permit an application seeking declaratory relief against a company in CVA as to the existence and quantum of a debt, and as against the supervisors of the CVA as regards admission of the debt to the CVA, without contravention of s 11(3)(d) (now para 43(6) of Sch B1) where the company in CVA is also in administration since ss 7 and 11 have different purposes and do not conflict: *Holdenhurst Securities plc v Cohen* [2001] 1 BCLC 460 at [11]–[17] (Laddie J).

'... any other person ...'—This term will, it is submitted, extend to any person capable of establishing to the court that he has a sufficient interest in the voluntary arrangement. This might include the directors of the company or, alternatively, a person with a beneficial interest in the arrangement assets: see *Port v Auger* [1994] 1 WLR 862 at 873–874 (Harman J, considering similar wording in s 303).

'... is dissatisfied ...'—This phrase also appears in s 263(3) in relation to IVAs, as it does in s 303(1) in relation to complaints made against a trustee-in-bankruptcy. The term is to be contrasted with 'is aggrieved by', which applies to complaints made against a liquidator under s 168(5) in a compulsory liquidation and which also appeared in the former s 80 of the Bankruptcy Act 1914 in relation to trustees-in-bankruptcy. In *Re Dennis Michael Cooke* [1999] BPIR 881 Stanley Burnton QC, sitting as he then was as a deputy High Court judge, considered (at 883F–883G), in the context of an application under s 303, that the term 'dissatisfied' is certainly no narrower than 'aggrieved', and is arguably wider and should not be given a restricted interpretation so as to include a person who has a genuine grievance against the actions of the office-holder, but not merely busybody interfering in things which do not concern him. That interpretation, it is submitted, would apply equally in the context of the present provision.

'... by any act, omission or decision of the supervisor ...'—The subsection, for no obvious reason, distinguishes a 'decision' from an 'act' or 'omission'. The scope of the conduct capable of falling within these words is plainly broad, but will only include conduct on the part of the supervisor acting as such, including such conduct undertaken on his behalf, say by a member of the supervisor's staff.

Does s 7(3) preclude the existence of a private right of action outside of the provision in favour of a creditor?—In *King v Anthony* [1999] BPIR 73 the Court of Appeal (Nourse, Schiemann and Brooke LJJ) held (in the judgment of Brooke LJ at 78H–79B), in relation to the identical provision in s 263(3) applicable to IVAs, that a creditor had no private right of action allowing for complaint to be made against a supervisor, since s 263(3) provided an effective means of enforcing the duties of a supervisor. Furthermore, Part VIII of the 1986 Act constitutes a self-contained statutory scheme which in s 263(3) provides expressly for the court to give appropriate directions to a supervisor, thereby allowing the court to maintain control over the performance of its officer. This issue had arisen in that case in the context of a claim by a supervisor against two debtors who had served a defence and counterclaim which alleged a private law remedy against the supervisor which sounded in damages and which constituted a set-off against the supervisor's claim. Based on its construction of s 263 the Court of Appeal upheld the decision of the judge below in striking out the defence and counterclaim.

There is every reason why the reasoning in *King v Anthony* should apply to claims brought against the supervisor of a CVA in that s 7(3) specifically lends itself to the enforcement of the duties of a CVA supervisor, just as Part I of the 1986 Act constitutes a self-contained statutory scheme for the regulation of CVAs and, in particular, nominees and supervisors.

Is a private law remedy available against a nominee?—Section 7(3) applies only to a supervisor. *King v Anthony*, therefore, cannot operate so as to limit any private law remedy available against a nominee, as opposed to a supervisor. It would appear to follow from the reasoning in *King v Anthony* that misconduct by a nominee which constitutes unfair prejudice and/or material irregularity within the meaning of s 6(1)(a) and/or (b) is actionable only under these provisions and will not be open to a private law remedy. However, to the extent that any breach of the nominee's duties – on which see the notes to s 2(2) – falls outside s 6(1), that conduct would appear actionable by way of a private law remedy, say in a claim for breach of duty and/or negligence.

Section 7(4)(a)

'... **directions in relation to any particular matter arising under the voluntary arrangement** ...'—There is no authority which deals with the scope of s 7(4)(a), most likely because the court will usually be willing to respond to a genuine request for assistance by a supervisor in connection with any specific (or 'particular') matter which arises under – seemingly, in connection with or caused by – the CVA. The objective of the provision, it is submitted, is to afford a supervisor easy access to court for the resolution of such genuine difficulties. Whilst plainly drafted more broadly in scope than s 7(3), the s 7(4)(a) facility should not be employed for the purpose of seeking the court's approval or 'rubber stamp' – which will most likely be refused in any case – where the substance of the particular matter raised amounts to a commercial decision for the office-holder personally. Neither, it is submitted, is an application for directions appropriate where the application constitutes an obvious attempt on the part of the supervisor to avoid alternative and plainly more appropriate proceedings.

The Court of Appeal has held that the court has no jurisdiction to give directions modifying the terms of an approved arrangement since the power to give directions in relation to an arrangement is something very different from a power to amend an arrangement: *Re Alpa Lighting Ltd* [1997] BPIR 341 and see the note 'Control over the admission of creditor's proof' to s 1(1). There have been a number of recent cases in which supervisors have made applications for directions under s 7(4). For instance *Re Federal-Mogul Aftermarket Ltd* [2008] BPIR 846, *Re Energy Holdings (No 3) Ltd* [2010] BPIR 1339 and *TXU Europe Group Plc* [2011] EWHC 2072 (Ch), [2012] BPIR 463.

Section 7(4)(b)

Petition by supervisor for winding up—In the absence of the supervisor of a CVA appearing within the classes of person eligible to petition for the winding up of a company within s 124(1), this provision expressly provides such standing.

In practice, the provisions of a CVA will commonly require a supervisor either to petition or to consider petitioning for winding up in the event of one or more specified defaults. The supervisor of a CVA does not necessarily lose standing to petition under this provision by virtue of the fact that an arrangement is no longer functioning (as in a trading arrangement) as originally envisaged. In *Re Arthur Rathbone Kitchens Ltd* [1997] 2 BCLC 280 Roger Kaye QC, sitting as deputy High Court judge, rejected submissions to the effect that a supervisor could not petition for winding up under s 7(4)(b) if the CVA was not still on foot so as to deprive the supervisor of locus standi as 'supervisor' within the meaning of s 7(2). The deputy judge identified that, on the particular terms of the CVA, the arrangement had not terminated, although the company was in default, at the time of the presentation of the supervisor's petition. Neither does a supervisor lose standing to petition on the expiration of a fixed-term arrangement, provided that, at the time of presentation of the petition, the supervisor was still 'carrying out in relation to the voluntary arrangement the functions' conferred on the supervisor by virtue of s 7(2) (or s 263(2) in an IVA): *Harris v Gross* [2001] BPIR 586 (His Honour Judge Maddocks sitting as a High Court judge, bankruptcy orders made on petitions presented by IVA supervisor one month after expiration of four-year fixed term interlocking IVAs in respect of ongoing defaults committed during the term of the fixed period of the arrangements).

A CVA supervisor's winding-up petition is treated as if it were a contributories' petition under r 4.7(9), for the consequences of which see rr 4.22–4.24.

Application by supervisor for administration order—The supervisor of a CVA is not identified in para 12(1) of Sch B1 as a person having standing to apply to the court for the making of an administration order. It is plain, however, that a supervisor has such standing from s 7(4)(b) and from para 12(5) of Sch B1, which provides that para 12(1) is without prejudice to s 7(4)(b). Rule 2.2(4) provides that an application for an administration order by the supervisor of a CVA is to be treated as if it were an application by the company.

7A Prosecution of delinquent officers of company

(1) This section applies where a moratorium under section 1A has been obtained for a company or the approval of a voluntary arrangement in relation to a company has taken effect under section 4A or paragraph 36 of Schedule A1.

(2) If it appears to the nominee or supervisor that any past or present officer of the company has been guilty of any offence in connection with the moratorium or, as the case may be, voluntary arrangement for which he is criminally liable, the nominee or supervisor shall forthwith—

  (a) report the matter to the appropriate authority, and
  (b) provide the appropriate authority with such information and give the authority such access to and facilities for inspecting and taking copies of documents (being information or documents in the possession or under the control of the nominee or supervisor and relating to the matter in question) as the authority requires.

In this subsection, 'the appropriate authority' means—

  (i) in the case of a company registered in England and Wales, the Secretary of State, and
  (ii) in the case of a company registered in Scotland, the Lord Advocate.

(3) Where a report is made to the Secretary of State under subsection (2), he may, for the purpose of investigating the matter reported to him and such other matters relating to the affairs of the company as appear to him to require investigation, exercise any of the powers which are exercisable by inspectors appointed under section 431 or 432 of the Companies Act 1985 to investigate a company's affairs.

(4) For the purpose of such an investigation any obligation imposed on a person by any provision of the Companies Acts to produce documents or give information to, or otherwise to assist, inspectors so appointed is to be regarded as an obligation similarly to assist the Secretary of State in his investigation.

(5) An answer given by a person to a question put to him in exercise of the powers conferred by subsection (3) may be used in evidence against him.

(6) However, in criminal proceedings in which that person is charged with an offence to which this subsection applies—

  (a) no evidence relating to the answer may be adduced, and
  (b) no question relating to it may be asked,

by or on behalf of the prosecution, unless evidence relating to it is adduced, or a question relating to it is asked, in the proceedings by or on behalf of that person.

(7) Subsection (6) applies to any offence other than—

(a) an offence under section 2 or 5 of the Perjury Act 1911 (false statements made on oath otherwise than in judicial proceedings or made otherwise than on oath), or

(b) an offence under section 44(1) or (2) of the Criminal Law (Consolidation) (Scotland) Act 1995 (false statements made on oath or otherwise than on oath).

(8) Where a prosecuting authority institutes criminal proceedings following any report under subsection (2), the nominee or supervisor, and every officer and agent of the company past and present (other than the defendant or defender), shall give the authority all assistance in connection with the prosecution which he is reasonably able to give.

For this purpose—

'agent' includes any banker or solicitor of the company and any person employed by the company as auditor, whether that person is or is not an officer of the company,

'prosecuting authority' means the Director of Public Prosecutions, the Lord Advocate or the Secretary of State.

(9) The court may, on the application of the prosecuting authority, direct any person referred to in subsection (8) to comply with that subsection if he has failed to do so.

Amendments—Inserted by Insolvency Act 2000, s 2, Sch 2, paras 1, 10. Amended by SI 2009/1941.

7B Arrangements coming to an end prematurely

For the purposes of this Part, a voluntary arrangement the approval of which has taken effect under section 4A or paragraph 36 of Schedule A1 comes to an end prematurely if, when it ceases to have effect, it has not been fully implemented in respect of all persons bound by the arrangement by virtue of section 5(2)(b)(i) or, as the case may be, paragraph 37(2)(b)(i) of Schedule A1.

Amendments—Inserted by Insolvency Act 2000, s 2, Sch 2, paras 1, 10.

PART II
ADMINISTRATION

General comment on Part II—With effect from 15 September 2003 a new statutory regime in Sch B1 of the 1986 Act governing administration of companies came into effect and replaced the provisions in Part II (being ss 8–27). That new regime amounts to a remodelled, streamlined mechanism, which is outlined in the introductory note to Sch B1. For those undertakings to which the former Part II continues to apply, see the notes under that heading to para 10 of Sch B1.

8 Administration

Schedule B1 to this Act (which makes provision about the administration of companies) shall have effect.

9–27   (*Repealed*)

PART III
RECEIVERSHIP

General introduction to receivership—Receivership is a formal method of debt enforcement which can be traced back to Elizabethan times and which allows a secured creditor to enforce his security through the appointment of a receiver, or more commonly a receiver and manager, over the assets of the debtor with a view to recouping monies due to him.

The administrative receiver (being an individual appointed, most commonly, by a financial institution over the whole or substantially the whole of the company's assets and undertakings pursuant to a 'global' floating charge which in practice is invariably supplemented by one or more fixed charges over specific assets) was a creation of the 1986 Act. Administrative receivership was, by its nature, mutually exclusive with the procedure of administration introduced under Part II of the 1986 Act. With the passage of time it became increasingly difficult to characterise administrative receivership as a rescue mechanism in common with the other procedures under the 1986 Act and which were increasingly referred to as constituent parts of the so-called 'rescue culture'. That position was not helped by the heavy reliance of the banks on the administrative receivership procedure following the property collapse and economic slump in the UK in the early 1990s. In perhaps the most far-reaching amendment to the insolvency legislation since the implementation of the 1986 Act, a new s 72A, introduced by s 250 of the Enterprise Act 2002 and effective from 15 September 2003, effectively abolished administrative receivership from that date. The abolition, however, was not without its provisos, and concessions reached with the banks in the course of the Enterprise Bill making its way through Parliament. First, s 72A has no effect on floating charge security created prior to 15 September 2003 and compliant with s 29(2), with the consequence that an administrative receiver will be capable of appointment pursuant to such security so long as that security remains enforceable. Secondly, by virtue of s 176A(9), the charge-holder enforcing floating charge security created prior to 15 September 2003 enjoys not only freedom from the prescribed-part provisions in s 176A but also benefits from the abolition of Crown preference. Thirdly, those excepted cases provided for in ss 72B to 72H allow for the appointment of an administrative receiver in relation to such undertakings, irrespective of the date of the creation of the requisite floating charge under s 29(2).

There is no doubt that s 72A represents a major statutory shift against the interests of secured creditors. Those secured rights will continue to subsist in the new form of administration under Sch B1, although that regime precludes the appointment of an administrator, even one appointed by the holder of a qualifying floating charge under para 14, other than an office-holder who acts in the interests of the creditors of a company in general. This is a matter discussed further in the notes to para 3 of Sch B1.

Notwithstanding the implementation of Sch B1, it remains the case that administrative receivership will continue to have a role to play as a debt enforcement mechanism so long as s 29(2) compliant security created before 15 September 2003 remains enforceable, and so long as such debenture holders opt for receivership in preference to administration. In this regard it is interesting to note that in Australia, where receivership has continued to be available alongside an administration procedure closely related to Sch B1, the banks have, for the most part, embraced the new administration regime.

Section 72A has no effect on the appointment of receivers pursuant to security which is either fixed in nature or which is floating but less extensive than the s 29(2) threshold.

Chapter I

Receivers and Managers (England and Wales)

Preliminary and general provisions

28 Extent of this Chapter

(1) In this Chapter 'company' means a company registered under the Companies Act 2006 in England and Wales or Scotland.

(2) This Chapter does not apply to receivers appointed under Chapter 2 of this Part (Scotland).

Amendments—SI 2009/1941.

General note—Chapter I, comprising ss 28–49, applies only to receivers and managers appointed under the law of England and Wales. Chapter II, comprising ss 50–71, governs receivers appointed under Scottish law.

Jurisdiction—In practice it is usual for standard form debentures to provide that the debenture itself and any receiver appointed pursuant to its terms is to be construed in accordance with and governed by the law of a specified jurisdiction.

'Administrative receiver'—For the scope of the term 'administrative receiver' and the scope of its application to a foreign company see the notes to s 29(2) below.

Building societies—Chapter I also applies to building societies subject to certain modifications provided for in Sch 15A and the Building Societies Act 1997, s 39.

29 Definitions

(1) It is hereby declared that, except where the context otherwise requires—

    (a)   any reference in this Act to a receiver or manager of the property of a company, or to a receiver of it, includes a receiver or manager, or (as the case may be) a receiver of part only of that property and a receiver only of the income arising from the property or from part of it; and

    (b)   any reference in this Act to the appointment of a receiver or manager under powers contained in an instrument includes an appointment made under powers which, by virtue of any enactment, are implied in and have effect as if contained in an instrument.

(2) In this Chapter 'administrative receiver' means—

    (a)   a receiver or manager of the whole (or substantially the whole) of a company's property appointed by or on behalf of the holders of any debentures of the company secured by a charge which, as created, was a floating charge, or by such a charge and one or more other securities; or

    (b)   a person who would be such a receiver or manager but for the appointment of some other person as the receiver of part of the company's property.

Amendments—SI 2009/1941.

General note—This definition provision defines the scope of a receiver and manager (in s 29(1)) as distinct from the statutorily created receiver and manager known as the administrative receiver (as defined in s 29(2)). Sections 42–49 apply only to administrative receivers, as does s 2 of the Insolvency Act 1994.

Qualification to act—A person who acts as an administrative receiver of a company acts in relation to it as an insolvency practitioner and must be qualified to act as such on pain of criminal sanction: see ss 388(1), 389(1) and 390(1). A receiver and manager within s 29(1) (such as an LPA receiver) need not be qualified to act as an insolvency practitioner in relation to a company.

Administrative receivers and other receivers and managers distinguished—An administrative receiver may also be distinguished from an ordinary receiver and manager in other respects. An administrative receiver has conferred on him the investigatory and related powers in ss 234–236. Further, his powers derive from Sch 1, which is implied into the debenture pursuant to which the administrative receiver is appointed, subject to contrary provision therein: see s 42(1). In addition, an administrative receiver may apply for an order for sale under s 43 where charged property is subject to security ranking in priority to that pursuant to which he is appointed. Furthermore, unlike an ordinary receiver and manager who may be removed by his appointor at any time, an administrative receiver may only be removed by order of the court under s 45.

A receiver and manager appointed under s 51 (Scotland) may also be an administrative receiver, on which see the definitions in s 251.

Section 29(1)

Scope of provision—Save where the context otherwise requires, the term receiver and manager in the legislation will catch an LPA receiver (ie a receiver and manager appointed under a fixed charge, on which consider the effect of *Meadrealm Ltd v Transcontinental Golf Construction* (unreported) 29 November 1991, ChD (Vinelott J), noted under s 29(2)(a) below, and a receiver appointed in respect of part only of the company's property (ie less than 'substantially the whole' of the company's property, on which see s 29(2)(a) and the notes thereto below)).

Section 29(2)(a)

Scope of provision—Despite a number of anomalies, there is no reported judgment which includes a detailed analysis of the ambiguous terminology employed in this provision.

'... receiver or manager ...'—Although the wording envisages the appointment of a receiver 'or' manager, in practice appointees invariably take office as both.

'... the whole or substantially the whole of the company's property ...'—The term 'the whole or substantially the whole of the company's property' is open to a number of possible interpretations. Reference to 'substantially the whole' necessitates some objective criteria by which that element of the company's property may be adjudged to amount to such in comparison with that element of the company's property to which the appointment does not extend (ie that part other than substantially the whole). The most obvious objective criterion which, it is suggested, is also entirely appropriate and workable for these purposes, is the financial value of the relevant property subject to the floating charge security as at the date of the appointment, as valued, not by the appointing debenture-holder, but by the company itself, say by reference to the company's most recent financial statements or audited accounts, provided those sources include objective and credible values.

'... a company ...'—The term 'company' in the context of s 29(2) might at first be taken as a company which is formed and registered under the Companies Act 1985 or former Companies Acts, subject to contrary intention based on the definition in s 251 and its reference to Part XXVI of the Companies Act 1985 which refers to s 735(1) and (4) of the Companies Act 1985. Whilst this definition would not extend to foreign companies, in *Re International Bulk Commodities Ltd* [1993] Ch 77 at 85C–87C Mummery J (as he then was) identified such a contrary intention in s 29(2) such that the term 'company' for s 29(2) purposes extends to any corporation incorporated abroad which can be wound up as an unregistered company under s 221(1). It followed that the receiver and manager appointed under the English form of a debenture to a foreign company in that case constituted an administrative receiver capable of exercising the Sch 1 statutory powers implied into the debenture by virtue of s 42(1). This reasoning, it is suggested, is correct despite having been doubted in *Re Devon and Somerset Farmers Ltd* [1993] BCC 410, where it was held that a receiver and manager appointed to an industrial and provident society is incapable of constituting an administrative receiver because such an unregistered company falls outside the definition of the term 'company' (see above) for s 29(2) purposes. In *Devon and Somerset*

Farmers His Honour Judge Hague QC, sitting as a High Court judge, distinguished *International Bulk Commodities* as being restricted to foreign companies and not concerned with English unregistered companies.

A limited liability partnership is capable of creating a floating charge over its assets and can, therefore, be subject to the appointment of an administrative receiver.

'... appointed by or on behalf of the holders of any debentures of the company ...'—The reference to 'appointed by or on behalf of the holders of any debentures of the company' excludes court appointed receivers from the definition of the term 'administrative receiver'; a court appointment on the application of the holder of a debenture cannot, it is suggested, at least not realistically be argued to be made 'on behalf of' the applicant.

'... secured by a charge which, as created, was a floating charge ...'—The key element of the phrase 'secured by a charge which, as created, was a floating charge, or by such a charge in one or more other securities' is the reference to a prerequisite floating charge as defined in s 251. The reference to 'one or more other securities' covers the common scenario where an appointing debenture-holder holds one or more fixed charges over specific property in addition to a 'global' floating charge which will convert to a fixed equitable charge on crystallisation. More importantly, however, the reference to a floating charge on either side of the word 'or' in the above phrase denotes that the floating charge must be a global security which extends at least to substantially the whole of the company's property. Consistent with this approach, a receiver appointed under a fixed charge or charges has been held not to amount to an administrative receiver, even where the appointing debenture-holder held, but made no appointment pursuant to, a global floating charge: *Meadrealm Ltd v Transcontinental Golf Construction Ltd* (unreported) 29 November 1991 (Vinelott J).

'Lightweight' floating charges—The floating charge pursuant to which an administrative receiver is appointed need not catch any assets on creation or subsequently, so as to amount to a so-called 'lightweight' floating charge: *Re Croftbell Ltd* [1990] BCLC 844.

Section 29(2)(b)

Scope of provision—This provision preserves the status of an administrative receiver where a receiver and manager (within s 29(1)) is previously appointed over part only of a company's property where the residual part over which that appointment is not made amounts to less than substantially the whole of the company's property.

Section 29(2)(b), it is suggested, precludes the contemporaneous appointment of two or more administrative receivers (ie other than as joint appointees).

30 Disqualification of a body corporate from acting as a receiver

A body corporate is not qualified for appointment as receiver of the property of a company, and any body corporate which acts as such a receiver is liable to a fine.

General note—This provision continues the bar on corporate receivers (ie appointed in or out of court) as was previously provided for in the now repealed s 366 of the Companies Act 1948 and s 489 of the Companies Act 1985. The appointment of a corporate receiver is a nullity: *Portman Building Society v Gallwey* [1955] 1 WLR 96 at 100 (Wynn Parry J).

Any body corporate acting as receiver of the property of a company is liable to a fine as prescribed in s 430 and in Sch 10.

For the more general bar on bodies corporate being qualified to act as insolvency practitioners and related criminal sanctions see ss 389(1) and 390(1).

31 Disqualification of bankrupt or person in respect of whom a debt relief order is made

(1) A person commits an offence if he acts as receiver or manager of the property of a company on behalf of debenture holders while—

    (a)   he is an undischarged bankrupt,

    (aa) a moratorium period under a debt relief order applies in relation to him, or

    (b)   a bankruptcy restrictions order or a debt relief restrictions order is in force in respect of him.

(2) A person guilty of an offence under subsection (1) shall be liable to imprisonment, a fine or both.

(3) This section does not apply to a receiver or manager acting under an appointment made by the court.

Amendments—Enterprise Act 2002, s 257(3), Sch 21, para 1; Tribunals, Courts and Enforcement Act 2007, s 108(3), Sch 20, Pt 1, paras 1, 2.

General note—This provision, introduced by Sch 21 of the Enterprise Act 2002 and effective from 1 April 2004, continues the bar on an undischarged bankrupt, but not a discharged bankrupt, acting as a receiver or manager of the property of a company. In addition, however, the bar now extends to persons subject to a bankruptcy restriction undertaking. Although s 31(3) envisages the possibility of such a barred person from being appointed as a court appointed receiver or manager, in practice the court will be very unlikely to accede to such an application.

    A substantively similar prohibition appeared previously in the now repealed s 367 of the Companies Act 1948 and s 490 of the Companies Act 1985. Such appointment would appear to be a nullity, based on the reasoning of Wynn Parry J in *Portman Building Society v Gallwey* [1955] 1 All ER 227 at 230B–230D.

    Any person acting in contravention of s 31 is liable to imprisonment or a fine as prescribed in s 430 and Sch 10.

    A person disqualified from acting as a company director is also disqualified from acting as an insolvency practitioner: see s 1(1)(b) of the Company Directors Disqualification Act 1986.

32 Power for court to appoint official receiver

Where application is made to the court to appoint a receiver on behalf of the debenture holders or other creditors of a company which is being wound up by the court, the official receiver may be appointed.

General note—Applications under this provision are very rare in practice but might conceivably arise where a defect within a debenture precludes the appointment of a receiver and manager in circumstances where an incumbent liquidator disputes the validity of the security comprised in the debenture where the secured assets are in need of immediate protection or management; in these circumstances, however, any prospective applicant might well prefer an appointee of his own choice other than the official receiver.

    Sections 399–401 deal with the appointment, functions and status of official receivers as office-holders under the legislation.

Receivers and managers appointed out of court

33 Time from which appointment is effective

(1) The appointment of a person as a receiver or manager of a company's property under powers contained in an instrument—

    (a)   is of no effect unless it is accepted by that person before the end of the business day next following that on which the instrument of appointment is received by him or on his behalf, and

(b)   subject to this, is deemed to be made at the time at which the instrument of appointment is so received.

(2) This section applies to the appointment of two or more persons as joint receivers or managers of a company's property under powers contained in an instrument, subject to such modifications as may be prescribed by the rules.

General note—This provision requires acceptance by an appointee or appointees within a relatively stringent timescale as a pre-condition of the effective appointment of a receiver and/or manager out of court. In practice, an appointor will invariably confirm willingness to act with an appointee prior to offering appointment.

The timing of an effective appointment is relevant because the most common event of external intervention giving rise to the crystallisation of a floating charge is the out of court appointment of a receiver and manager, on which see *Evans v Rival Granite Quarries Ltd* [1910] 2 KB 979 at 1000–1001 (Buckley LJ). In the absence of specific provision in a debenture there is no requirement for notification of appointment of a receiver and manager to the chargor or any other third party for the purpose of effecting crystallisation of a floating charge. Crystallisation of a floating charge confers priority in favour of the charge-holder over secured assets over which execution has been levied but not completed by way of payment of monies over to the execution creditor: *Re Standard Manufacturing Co Ltd* [1891] 1 Ch 627, CA; *Re Opera Ltd* [1891] 3 Ch 260; and see, though on unusual facts, *Robinson v Burnell's Bakery* [1904] 2 KB 624.

Section 33 and its associated formalities, noted below, are not dependent on the taking of possession of charged assets by a receiver, which would in any case be unnecessary, given that the execution of a debenture allowing for the appointment of a receiver can be taken as a surrender by the chargor company of those powers assumed by a receiver on appointment: *Alberta Paper Co Ltd v Metropolitan Graphics Ltd* (1983) 49 CBR (2d) 63.

Effective appointment of a receiver and manager is not in itself confirmatory of the substantive validity of the appointment.

Procedure on appointment—For the formalities on acceptance and confirmation of appointment see rr 3.1 and 3.2 and the notes thereto which, despite the misleading heading to those provisions, apply to appointments of all out-of-court receivers, including administrative receivers, for confirmation of which see r 0.3(2) of the Insolvency Rules 1986 (SI 1986/1925). For the notification of the appointment of a receiver and manager see also s 39.

The legislation does not prescribe any statutory form for confirmation or evidencing of the appointment of a receiver or manager. A debenture may, however, and commonly will, prescribe formalities necessary on the effecting of an appointment. It is useful for the instrument of appointment to confirm compliance with such formalities such as the obtaining of any prescribed consent or the service of a demand on the chargor company prior to appointment.

On the validity of an office-holder's acts notwithstanding defects in appointment, nomination or qualifications, see s 232 and the notes thereto.

Section 33(1)(a) and (b)

Scope of provision—Provided that acceptance of appointment is effected within the period prescribed by s 33(1)(a), s 33(1)(b) deems appointment to have been effected at the time of receipt of the instrument or offer of appointment.

'Business day'—For the meaning of 'business day' in s 33(1)(a) see s 251.

Instrument of appointment executed in anticipation of appointment—There is nothing objectionable in an instrument of appointment being executed, signed and dated in readiness for the possible future appointment of a receiver: *Windsor Refrigerator Co Ltd v Branch Nominees Ltd* [1961] Ch 375 at 397 (Harman LJ).

Section 33(2)

Scope of provision—In the case of a joint appointment – usually, in practice, partners in the same firm – r 3.1(1) provides that each joint appointee must accept appointment as if each were a sole appointee, consequent upon which any such appointment will be effective from the time at which the instrument of appointment was received by or on behalf of all the appointees.

On joint appointments see also s 231 (appointment to office of two or more persons) and the discussion in *Re Melson Velcrete Pty Ltd* (1996) 14 ACLC 778 on the joint, several and joint, and several roles of multiple receivers.

34 Liability for invalid appointment

Where the appointment of a person as the receiver or manager of a company's property under powers contained in an instrument is discovered to be invalid (whether by virtue of the invalidity of the instrument or otherwise), the court may order the person by whom or on whose behalf the appointment was made to indemnify the person appointed against any liability which arises solely by reason of the invalidity of the appointment.

General note—This provision confers a discretion on the court to order that the appointor of a person as receiver or manager of a company's property indemnifies the appointee in respect of any liability arising 'solely' by reason of the invalidity of his appointment.

The tort of unlawful interference with contractual relations does not arise where a board of directors is replaced by an invalidly appointed receiver who then takes charge of a company's contractual relations; neither does English law recognise a tort of conversion of a chose in action: *OBG v Allan & Others* [2007] UKHL 1, [2008] 1 AC 1. Procedurally, the proper course in assessing liability consequent on the defective appointment of a receiver is the provision of directions for the taking of an inquiry.

Quite apart from s 34 it is a well established principle that a debenture holder may rely on any circumstance, existing at the time of the appointment of the receivers, which would justify their appointment notwithstanding that that circumstance was not being expressly relied on by the debenture holder at the time the appointment was made: *Byblos Bank SAL v Al-Khudairy* (1986) 2 BCC 99, 549 at 99, 564 (Nicholls LJ).

Invalid and defective appointments distinguished—A distinction is drawn between invalidity in appointment under this provision, say where there is no power to appoint or no substantive appointment (on which see *Morris v Kanssen* [1946] AC 459), and mere defects in the formalities or procedure by which appointment is effected, which defects may be cured by s 232, by which the actions of an improperly appointed receiver may also remain valid: *OBG v Allan & Others*.

'... any liability ...'—The reference to 'any liability' appears wide enough to cover liabilities flowing solely from the invalidity of the appointment and which are incurred by the appointee either to the company itself, save for wrongful interference with goods or conversion, or to a third party with whom the appointee has had dealings as receiver. However, it is doubtful that any such liability will arise 'solely' from any invalidity in appointment where the liability is incurred by the appointee contracting with personal liability as receiver on the basis of an indemnity from the company's assets (which indemnity would be lost by virtue of the invalidity of the appointment).

The exercise of the court's discretion under this provision will depend on the extent to which the appointor and appointee can each be shown to have been aware of the invalidity of the appointment or capable of establishing such invalidity on reasonable investigation.

Invalidly appointed receiver: agent of appointor?—In the case of an invalidly appointed receiver, quite apart from s 34, the appointor will be vicariously liable for the acts of his agent, the purported receiver, where the purported receiver acts on the instructions or directions of his appointor: *Standard Chartered Bank v Walker* [1982] 1 WLR 1410 at 1416A, CA. Section 34 itself, however, it is suggested, does not preclude the existence of such an agency relationship; compare the reasoning of Walton J in *Bank of Baroda v Panessar* [1986] 3 All ER 564 to opposite effect. However, neither does the mere fact of appointment automatically trigger an agency relationship between appointor and appointee in the usual absence of a provision to such effect in the debenture: *National Bank of Greece v Pinios* [1990] 1 AC 637 at 648–649 (Lloyd LJ).

Indemnities beyond s 34—The statutory indemnity provided for in s 34 is also discrete from any indemnity which may be claimed by a receiver who incurs liability to the chargor company or any third party in the course of acting on the instructions of his appointor: *Re B Johnson & Co (Builders) Ltd* [1955] Ch 634 at 647–648 (Evershed MR).

Where there are concerns over the validity of an appointment, a prospective appointee may seek a contractual indemnity, usually in the form of a deed, from his appointor to cover consequential liabilities as a condition of his appointment. The provision of indemnities very much varies in practice. An indemnity will ordinarily only protect a receiver from liability arising from invalidity in the debenture or in the form of appointment. The provision of an indemnity in respect of a receiver's acts or omissions, certainly by an institutional lender, is usually commercially inconceivable.

For examples of invalid appointment see *Heald v O'Connor* [1971] 1 WLR 497 (mortgagor guaranteed loan in contravention of the predecessor to s 151 of the Companies Act 1985 rendering unlawful the giving of financial assistance by a company for the acquisition of its shares) and *Ford & Carter v Midland Bank plc* (1979) 129 NLJ 543, HL (no subsisting debt for which debenture holder bank could make demand).

35 Application to court for directions

(1) A receiver or manager of the property of a company appointed under powers contained in an instrument, or the persons by whom or on whose behalf a receiver or manager has been so appointed, may apply to the court for directions in relation to any particular matter arising in connection with the performance of the functions of the receiver or manager.

(2) On such an application, the court may give such directions, or may make such order declaring the rights of persons before the court or otherwise, as it thinks just.

General note—This provision provides a useful facility for the resolution of disputes within the scope of s 35(1) on the application of a receiver or manager or his appointor. Appointors were not afforded such a facility in the earlier legislation. It is very doubtful that the court retains some inherent jurisdiction to entertain applications by persons outside the scope of s 35(1), not only because of the specific and express scope of s 35(1), but also because appointments covered by s 35 are effected out of court and remain a matter of contract between the chargor company and chargee creditor. Such a wide-ranging jurisdiction would also be inconsistent with the fact that a receiver appointed out of court is not subject to the control of the court under the rule in *Ex parte James* (1874) 9 Ch App 609.

The court should not be troubled with matters of commercial judgment, which remain the sole professional responsibility of the office-holder: *Re T & D Industries* [2000] 1 WLR 646 (Neuberger J, as he then was, in the context of a directions application in an old-style administration: the court should not be seen as a 'bomb shelter' in the face of what amounts essentially to a commercial decision on the part of the office-holder).

Section 35(1)

Eligible applicants—The scope of applicants under this provision is limited to a receiver 'or' manager of the property of the company, including an administrative receiver. Alternatively, the application may be made by the person or persons by whom or on whose behalf the appointment 'has' been made, being, most commonly, the appointor under a debenture or, less commonly, trustees under a debenture trust stock deed or those for whom such trustees act. The provision therefore does not extend to ordinary creditors, or a creditor who may be entitled to effect appointment of a receiver or manager outside the scope of s 29(2). The FSA has standing to be heard on an application in an appropriate case: FMSA 2000, s 363(2).

The scope of a s 35 application—The scope of the directions which may be sought extends to any 'matter arising in connection with the performance of [the receiver's] functions'. This confers on the court a very broad jurisdiction and will include, for example, issues concerning the nature or priority of security under which a receiver is accountable or whether funds available for payment of preferential claims may be employed in ongoing trading. The provision also extends to disputes concerning a receiver's or manager's remuneration: *Re Therm-a-Stor Ltd* [1996] 2 BCLC 400 (Laddie J, as he then was); and see *Mumms v Perkins* [2002] BPIR 120 (Evans-Lombe J) and the notes to s 36 below.

Whilst a strict construction of the wording in s 35(1) would appear to preclude an application by a receiver or his appointor to consider the validity of the receiver's appointment, say where validity is disputed by others, such a conclusion, it is suggested, is doubtful and at odds with both the apparent purpose of the provision and the very practical requirement for the speedy resolution of any such issue, given the receiver's recourse to company assets in respect of his remuneration and the statutory indemnity in his favour under s 34. This purposive approach to s 35(1) would also bring the provision in line with the substance of the court's approach in *Re Wood and Martin Ltd* [1971] 1 All ER 732 at 736C–736E (Megarry J) to s 352 of the Companies Act 1948 (now s 651 of the Companies Act 1985) which, whilst being drafted very differently to s 35, was held to allow an invalidly appointed liquidator to seek a declaration that the dissolution of the company was void as a 'person interested', albeit not as 'liquidator'.

Section 35(2)

Remedies and relief on a s 35 application—The court enjoys an unfettered discretion in resolving the dispute or issue before it. This includes the making of orders, which affect not only those before the court, on which see r 7.47(1) (review of the court's decisions) and CPR, r 40.9 (applications to vary or set aside by non-parties). The court may also give such directions or other form of relief as it thinks just. In the context of the application the court may consider making costs orders which regulate the extent to which the costs of any particular party may or may not be claimed as an expense of the receivership.

Costs on a s 35 application—There is no fixed practice in the Companies Court as to the proper order on costs in cases where a receiver issues an application to determine questions arising in the course of the receivership. In hostile cases involving, say, ownership of property, costs will normally follow the event. On the other hand, the court will usually consider meeting the costs of a representative respondent, who is joined into the proceedings to argue a point on behalf of a class, out of the assets of the company: *Re Westdock Realisations Ltd* (1988) 4 BCC 192 at 197–198 (Browne-Wilkinson V-C). An office-holder will usually be awarded his costs from the assets of the company as an expense of his office, save where some exceptional circumstances justify the draconian consequence of an order that such costs should constitute a personal liability of the office-holder.

36 Court's power to fix remuneration

(1) The court may, on an application made by the liquidator of a company, by order fix the amount to be paid by way of remuneration to a person who, under powers contained in an instrument, has been appointed receiver or manager of the company's property.

(2) The court's power under subsection (1), where no previous order has been made with respect thereto under the subsection—

    (a)   extends to fixing the remuneration for any period before the making of the order or the application for it,

(b) is exercisable notwithstanding that the receiver or manager has died or ceased to act before the making of the order or the application, and

(c) where the receiver or manager has been paid or has retained for his remuneration for any period before the making of the order any amount in excess of that so fixed for that period, extends to requiring him or his personal representatives to account for the excess or such part of it as may be specified in the order.

But the power conferred by paragraph (c) shall not be exercised as respects any period before the making of the application for the order under this section, unless in the court's opinion there are special circumstances making it proper for the power to be exercised.

(3) The court may from time to time on an application made either by the liquidator or by the receiver or manager, vary or amend an order made under subsection (1).

General note—A receiver's right to remuneration, costs, disbursements etc will usually be provided for expressly in a well-drawn debenture. Such contractual provisions may also provide for remuneration on a time-cost basis, with or without stipulations being made as to specific rates, or as a percentage of recoveries. Section 109 of the Law of Property Act 1925 is either varied or, more commonly, excluded.

Section 36(1) repeats s 371(1) of the Companies Act 1948 and confers a limited right on a liquidator – and only a liquidator – to apply to the court to fix the amount to be paid by way of remuneration to a person appointed out of court as receiver or manager of a company's property. Where, however, such an order has been made, an application to vary or amend the order may be made under s 36(3) by either the liquidator 'or' by the receiver or manager.

The absence of a large number of reported cases on s 36(1) applications has nothing at all to do with any perceived sense of courtesy between insolvency practitioners. On the contrary, a liquidator who has credible evidence of the drawing of excessive remuneration by a receiver will need very good reasons for justifying inaction to creditors. In practice, however, any such claim, for very obvious reasons, may well be capable of compromise between liquidator and receiver without the need for resolution by the court.

Section 36(1)

Scope of provision—Section 36(1) is limited to the fixing of remuneration only and makes no mention of costs, disbursements etc.

The reference to appointment under powers in an instrument in s 36(1) precludes an application relating to a receiver appointed either under statutory powers or by the court (on which see RSC Ord 30, r 3 within CPR, Sch 1).

The provisions in s 36 are distinct from the standing of a mortgagor to apply to the court for the fixing of an account between mortgagor and mortgagee, the scope of which extends beyond remuneration, and on which see *Parker-Tweedale v Dunbar Bank plc (No 2)* [1990] 2 All ER 588 at 591 (Nourse LJ) and generally *Gomba Holdings Ltd v Minories Finance Ltd (No 2)* [1992] 4 All ER 588 (Scott LJ).

Irrespective of s 36, there appears to be no English authority for the proposition that a receiver may apply to the court for an increase in the remuneration to which the receiver is entitled under the debenture pursuant to which he is appointed. However, in *Odessa Promotions Pty Ltd (in liquidation)* (1979) ACLC 49-253 the Supreme Court of Victoria refused to allow receivers to claim scale rates agreed with their appointing debenture-holder following appointment, where those scale rates were in excess of the 5% of all gross monies recovered rate as expressly provided for in the debenture, on the basis that no statutory power existed for such provision to be made.

In *Re Delberry Ltd* [2008] EWHC 925 (Ch), [2008] BPIR 1277, Terence Mowschenson QC (sitting as a deputy judge of the High Court) held that it was not was not improper for a liquidator to use s 236 to gather information to determine whether to make an application under s 36.

The court's approach to an application under s 36(1)—Section 36(1) allows the court to interfere with the contractual rights of the receiver and mortgagee and involves the court in the exercise of two separate and unfettered discretions. First, the court has a discretion as to whether to interfere at all. Interference, however, should be confined to cases in which the remuneration claimed can be seen on its face, or after only preliminary inquiry, to be excessive rather than the application taking the form of a routine assessment by the court of a receiver's remuneration: *Re Potters Oils Ltd (No 2)* [1986] 1 All ER 890 at 895H (Hoffmann J (as he then was), application by liquidator under s 371 of the Companies Act 1948 dismissed where sum claimed not unreasonable by comparison with official receiver's statutory fees and in any case less than maximum stipulated in debenture). The second discretion, once a decision has been made to fix remuneration, is as to the quantum of such remuneration.

In *Mumms v Perkins* [2002] BPIR 120, applying *Potters Oils*, Evans-Lombe J allowed on appeal a receiver's claim for remuneration equating to 4.2% of the value of assets realised following an application by the debenture-holder under s 35, complaining that the fee in the region of £11,000 claimed by the receiver exceeded an estimate of £3,000 to £4,000 given by telephone prior to appointment. Evans-Lombe J noted in particular that the debenture itself allowed for a remuneration on a time-cost basis, that the conduct of the receivership had largely involved unusual work by way of transferring assets in specie, and that much of the work was conducted by a senior manager.

Part V of the *Practice Direction: Insolvency Proceedings* has no application to an administrative receiver or a non-administrative receiver or manager as appointee. However, the Practice Direction and in particular the objective and guiding principles identified in para 20.2 thereof will, it is submitted, apply on an application by a liquidator under s 36(1). For earlier guidance on office-holders' remuneration generally see *Mirror Group Newspapers plc v Maxwell (No 2)* [1998] 1 BCLC 638 (Ferris J) and the report on taxation (now assessment) of Chief Taxing Master Hurst at [1999] BCC 694. The Chief Taxing Master allowed £659,260 of £744,289 remuneration claimed and indicated (at 681E) that 'The correct viewpoint to be taken by a taxing officer in considering whether any step was reasonable was that of a sensible solicitor considering what, in the light of his then knowledge, was reasonable in the interests of his client ... in assessments on either the standard or indemnity basis.' For further guidance see SIP 9.

Section 36(2)

Scope of provision—These powers appear exercisable only in the course of an application under s 36(1). Once an order is made under that provision the court's power is restricted to variation or amendment under s 36(3).

The original form of s 36(2)(a) appeared in s 309 of the Companies Act 1929, which applied only to remuneration claimed after the date of the order.

The meaning of 'special circumstances' in s 36(2)(c) remains unclear; the provision appears to anticipate that a receiver or manager or his personal representatives will only be required to account for pre-order remuneration paid or retained where some exceptional factor, such as remuneration having been drawn on a plainly excessive or exorbitant basis, is at play.

Section 36(3)

Scope of provision—In practice only a material change in circumstances will warrant an application for variation or amendment under this provision which, it is suggested, is not intended as an appeal mechanism from any order made under s 36(1).

37 Liability for contracts etc

(1) A receiver or manager appointed under powers contained in an instrument (other than an administrative receiver) is, to the same extent as if he had been appointed by order of the court—

    (a)   personally liable on any contract entered into by him in the performance of his functions (except in so far as the contract otherwise provides) and on any contract of employment adopted by him in the performance of those functions, and

(b)   entitled in respect of that liability to indemnity out of the assets.

(2) For the purposes of subsection (1)(a), the receiver or manager is not to be taken to have adopted a contract of employment by reason of anything done or omitted to be done within 14 days after his appointment.

(3) Subsection (1) does not limit any right to indemnity which the receiver or manager would have apart from it, nor limit his liability on contracts entered into without authority, nor confer any right to indemnity in respect of that liability.

(4) Where at any time the receiver or manager so appointed vacates office—

(a)   his remuneration and any expenses properly incurred by him, and

(b)   any indemnity to which he is entitled out of the assets of the company,

shall be charged on and paid out of any property of the company which is in his custody or under his control at that time in priority to any charge or other security held by the person by or on whose behalf he was appointed.

General note—These provisions apply to non-administrative receivers. Very similar provisions relating to administrative receivers appear in certain parts of s 44, although those provisions, in contrast to s 37, provide expressly – in s 44(1)(a) – that an administrative receiver is the deemed agent of a company until the company's liquidation.

The personal liability imposed and the corresponding indemnity provided by these provisions arises 'to the same extent as if [the receiver or manager] had been appointed by order of the court' and applies only to contractual liability. Section 37(3) makes clear, however, that this statutory liability and indemnity will not limit or vary the personal liability of a receiver who enters into a contract without authority, in which circumstances no corresponding indemnity will arise in the receiver's favour. Conversely, and notwithstanding these provisions, a receiver will remain entitled to an indemnity from the company's assets under the terms of any contractual indemnity obtained from his appointing debenture-holder, although in practice the provision of such indemnities by institutional lenders remains a matter for individual cases and is uncommon. Private lenders may be more open to providing a suitable indemnity as a pre-condition of an appointee taking office. In New Zealand it has been held that failure to advise a receiver to obtain such an indemnity may form a basis for a negligence claim by a receiver against an advising solicitor: *RA Price Securities Ltd v Henderson* [1989] 2 NZLR 257, NZCA.

A prospective receiver should always ensure that he has in place professional indemnity insurance of an appropriate level to cover the risk of his own negligence and that of his subordinates.

Section 37 is not concerned with the effects of a receiver causing a company to terminate a subsisting contract with the company in receivership, on which see *Re Newdigate Colliery Ltd* [1912] 1 Ch 468 and *Airline Airspares Ltd v Handley Page Ltd* [1970] Ch 193.

Section 37(1)(a)

Scope of provision—The wording of this subparagraph plainly envisages a receiver contracting out of personal liability on contracts – including employment contracts – entered into by him 'in the performance of his functions'. Such contracting out is usual practice.

Implying an exclusion of personal liability—The exclusion of personal liability in practice is frequently not a matter of express agreement but one which is communicated by words endorsed to that effect on the company's notepaper and documents. In *Hill Samuel & Co Ltd v Laing* (1988) 4 BCC 9 the Court of Session in Scotland considered a receiver's claim that express wording in a bank debenture excluded the receiver from personal liability on a loan contract to the bank. In rejecting the view of Cross J, expressed obiter at first instance in *Lawson v Hosemaster Co Ltd* [1965] 1 WLR 1399 at 1410–1411, to the effect that the exclusion of personal liability requires express provision, Lord Cullen indicated (at 20–22) that such exclusion is capable of being implied. This approach accords with the common practice in receiverships.

The adoption by a non-administrative receiver of contracts and contracts of employment—A receiver does not incur personal liability on an existing contract between the company and a third party, other than a contract of employment, as considered below: *Re Atlantic Computer Systems plc* [1990] BCC 859 at 866C–866E (Nicholls LJ).

The question of whether a contract of employment has been 'adopted' by a receiver is one of fact and is considered further in the note to s 37(2) below. Following the House of Lords' decision in *Re Paramount Airways Ltd (No 3), Powdrill v Watson* [1994] BCC 172 (also considered below) the amending legislation in s 2 of the Insolvency Act 1994 was not extended to non-administrative receivers. There is no good reason why it should not have been.

It follows that a non-administrative receiver may have no option but to terminate subsisting contracts of employment within the 14-day period provided for in s 37(1)(b), with the possible hope of re-negotiating fresh contracts of employment, in the absence of sufficient assets or a contractual indemnity to meet such liabilities as would otherwise be incurred by the non-administrative receiver personally. One practical alternative, albeit one requiring some speed within the 14-day period in s 37(2), is to seek to contract out of such liabilities by express agreement with employees, a possibility which is not excluded by the present provisions and which is hardly in conflict with public policy. In *Powdrill* Dillon LJ resiled from expressing a view on the possibility of contracting out, despite arguments before the Court of Appeal on the point: see [1994] BCC 172 at 180C–180D. The point was neither an issue in, nor discussed on, the subsequent appeal to the House of Lords.

Section 37(1)(b)

Scope of provision—The statutory indemnity provided by s 37(1)(b) is only as good as the extent to which a company's assets are capable of meeting those liabilities under s 37(1)(a) to which the indemnity relates.

The priority of the receiver's claim for remuneration and expenses—In practice, a well-drawn standard form debenture will ordinarily include an express contractual provision to the effect that a receiver's remuneration and expenses are to be met out of receipts and realisations in priority to the sums secured by the debenture. Even in the absence of such an express provision, a receiver enjoys such priority over the claims of the appointing debenture-holder and preferential creditors, but only from company assets which are not subject to the security of a prior-ranking debenture-holder: *Re Glyncorrwg Colliery Co Ltd* [1956] Ch 951.

Section 37(2)

The 'adoption' of a contract of employment by a receiver—In *Re Paramount Airways Ltd (No 3), Powdrill v Watson* [1995] BCC 319 at 335A Lord Browne-Wilkinson considered that adoption in the context of this subsection arises as a matter of fact if a receiver causes or allows a company to continue a contract of employment for more than 14 days after his appointment by virtue of his not taking steps to terminate or repudiate such a contract. Accordingly, correspondence of the so-called *Specialised Mouldings*-type, as commonly employed previously by receivers and administrators as a means of excluding personal liability on employment contracts by unilateral notice, is of no effect in law. The judgment in *Paramount* lends weight to the view that a contract of employment is capable of termination through a repudiatory act notwithstanding the absence of acceptance of the repudiatory act by the other party, an exception to the general rule to the contrary in contract law.

Section 37(3)

Scope of provision—See the General note above and the note to s 37(1)(b) above for the limits on the scope of this indemnity.

Section 37(4)

Scope of provision—The statutory charge created by this provision in respect of remuneration, expenses and the receiver's indemnity is triggered only on the receiver's vacation from office. Despite its wording, however, this provision will not prevent the receiver drawing his remuneration and expenses and claiming on any indemnity during the course of the receivership, such that the charge may only catch outstanding claims on vacation: see *Powdrill v Watson* [1994] BCC 172 at 180F–180H (Dillon LJ); and see *Re Salmet International Ltd* [2001] BCC 796 at 803B–803H (Blackburne J) on very similar wording to the same effect in administrations under the former s 19(4) and (5).

The priority of the s 37(4) statutory charge—The statutory charge secures priority for the receiver only over the security of his appointor. In *Choudhri v Palta* [1992] BCC 787 the Court of Appeal held, in a case involving a court appointed receiver and without addressing s 37 or s 44 specifically, but in making note of s 43, that the court has no jurisdiction to order that a charge, created in that case by order of the court, securing a receiver's remuneration and costs should stand in priority to any prior ranking security. It is submitted that there is no good reason why the position should be different in the case of a non-administrative receiver. For the position of an administrative receiver see s 43 and the notes thereto.

'... remuneration ...'—On the term 'remuneration' in s 37(4)(a) see the notes to s 36. Whether expenses are 'properly incurred' is an issue capable of confirmation by a receiver or his appointor under s 35, or challenged by a liquidator under s 112 or s 168(3) on an application to the court for directions.

'... any indemnity ...'—The reference to 'any indemnity' in s 37(4)(b) extends the charge to both the statutory indemnity in s 37(1)(b) and any contractual indemnity existing in favour of the receiver.

38 Receivership accounts to be delivered to registrar

(1) Except in the case of an administrative receiver, every receiver or manager of a company's property who has been appointed under powers contained in an instrument shall deliver to the registrar of companies for registration the requisite accounts of his receipts and payments.

(2) The accounts shall be delivered within one month (or such longer period as the registrar may allow) after the expiration of 12 months from the date of his appointment and of every subsequent period of 6 months, and also within one month after he ceases to act as receiver or manager.

(3) ...

(4) ...

(5) A receiver or manager who makes default in complying with this section is liable to a fine and, for continued contravention, to a daily default fine.

Amendments—SI 2013/1947.

General note—This provision imposes an obligation on non-administrative receivers to file abstracts of receipts and payments with the Registrar of Companies on a periodical basis. The obligation is enforceable under s 41. The analogous obligations imposed on an administrative receiver are provided for in r 3.32.

There is no provision which envisages a non-administrative receiver convening a meeting of creditors as in an administrative receivership under s 48.

The nature and scope of the receiver's duty to provide information—In *Gomba Holdings UK Ltd v Homan* [1986] 3 All ER 95 at 99E–99H Hoffmann J (as he then was) held that a receiver's duty to provide accounts or other information to a debtor company extended beyond the statutory obligations to account (then contained in ss 497 and 499 of the Companies Act 1985) and included an equitable duty to the company to provide information subject to the company 'demonstrating a "need to know" for the purpose of enabling the board to exercise its residual rights [on which see the note to s 42 below] or perform its duties'. Thus, 'A board which demonstrates a *bona fide* intention and ability to redeem is entitled not merely to a redemption statement showing how much is still owing but also to reasonable information about the nature of the assets remaining in the hands of the receivers. On the other hand, comfortably with the principles I have discussed, I think that the receiver's duty to provide such information must be subordinated to his primary duty not to do anything which may prejudice the interests of the debenture-holder.' Notwithstanding Hoffmann J's reference here to the board of a company, there is no good reason, it is submitted, why this equitable duty should not also be enforceable by a liquidator.

Notwithstanding s 38(2), a receiver is under a general duty to account to the company at the end of the receivership: *Smiths Ltd v Middleton* [1979] 3 All ER 842 (Blackett-Ord V-C).

Section 38(2), (3)(b)

Scope of provision—This obligation triggers where an incumbent receiver or manager 'ceases to act', which will extend to his removal or vacation from office as well as the closure of the receivership.

Section 38(3)

Scope of provision—For building societies see para 25, Sch 15A as inserted by s 6 and Sch 6 of the Building Societies Act 1997.

Section 38(5)

Scope of provision—On penalties see s 430 and Sch 10.

Provisions applicable to every receivership

39 Notification that receiver or manager appointed

(1) Where a receiver or manager of the property of a company has been appointed –

   (a)   every invoice, order for goods or services, business letter or order form (whether in hard copy, electronic or any other form) issued by or on behalf of the company or the receiver or manager or the liquidator of the company; and
   (b)   all the company's websites,

must contain a statement that a receiver or manager has been appointed.

(2) If default is made in complying with this section, the company and any of the following persons, who knowingly and wilfully authorises or permits the default, namely, any officer of the company, any liquidator of the company and any receiver or manager, is liable to a fine.

Amendments—SI 2008/1897.

General note—In addition to the obligations in s 39(1), an administrative receiver must also comply with the notice and advertisement obligations in s 46(1).

The appointor of a receiver or manager (including an administrative receiver) must give notice to the Registrar of Companies within seven days of the appointment: Companies Act 1985, s 405(1). The appointment is then entered on the company's register of charges.

Railway companies and building societies—The enforcement of security against the assets of a railway company is subject to advance notice requirements imposed by the Railways Act 1993, s 62(7). For building societies see para 25, Sch 15A as inserted by the Building Societies Act 1997, s 6 and Sch 6.

40 Payment of debts out of assets subject to floating charge

(1) The following applies, in the case of a company, where a receiver is appointed on behalf of the holders of any debentures of the company secured by a charge which, as created, was a floating charge.

(2) If the company is not at the time in course of being wound up, its preferential debts (within the meaning given to that expression by section 386 in Part XII) shall be paid out of the assets coming to the hands of the receiver in priority to any claims for principal or interest in respect of the debentures.

(3) Payments made under this section shall be recouped, as far as may be, out of the assets of the company available for payment of general creditors.

General note—Section 40 is of considerable practical importance, in that practitioners must be alive to the risk of trading on floating charge realisations, given the obligations imposed by these provisions. The relevance of preferential claims is now very much reduced, on which see the note to s 40(2). Preferential claims are considered in some detail in Sch 6 and the notes thereto.

The application of s 40 to receivership has the same effect as the Companies Act 1985, s 196 (as amended by the Insolvency Act 1986, s 439(1) and Sch 13) has on a debenture-holder taking possession: *Re H & K (Medway) Ltd* [1997] BCC 853 at 857H (Neuberger J, as he then was).

The operation of this provision depends very much on the categorisation by the office-holder of security as fixed or floating, on which see the note on floating charges in s 251. The allocation of receivership expenses between fixed and floating charge accounts is also of great practical relevance, since receivership expenses take in priority to preferential claims and floating charge claims.

Section 40(1)

Scope of provision—The combined effect of this provision and s 40(2) is to afford preferential creditors priority over the claims of holders of any charge which, as created, was a floating charge in contrast to the position under the previous legislation. The priority point, therefore, is not concerned with the timing or the fact of the crystallisation of the floating charge.

'... which, as created, was a floating charge'—Under the earlier legislation, in which a floating charge was not defined as in this provision, a floating charge holder could avoid the priority afforded to preferential claims by crystallising the floating charge so that the charge was fixed at the relevant date for the assessment of preferential liabilities. The technique employed in the drafting of this subsection is also employed in s 175(2)(b) and s 251, to which reference should also be made.

Section 40(2)

Scope of provision—The scope of preferential debts was much reduced by the abolition of Crown debts by operation of s 251 of the Enterprise Act 2002, effective from 15 September 2003. Contributions to occupational pension schemes and state pension schemes and certain employee entitlements as identified in Categories 4 and 5 respectively to Sch 6 of the 1986 Act remain preferential. Despite the effective date of the provisions of the 2002 Act, the virtual abolition of preferential debts will also apply to the appointment of administrative receivers pursuant to security created prior to 15 September 2002.

An administrative receiver appointed pursuant to security on or after 15 September 2003 will also fall subject to the obligation to make available a prescribed part of the company's net property under s 176A, although a receiver appointed pursuant to security created prior to that date will not.

'... **a company** ...'—See here the note under this heading to s 29(2)(a). The term does not catch an industrial and provident society: *Re Devon and Somerset Farmers Ltd* [1993] BCC 410.

'... **in the course of being wound up** ...'—A company is 'in the course of being wound up' once a winding-up order has been made against it or a resolution for winding up has been passed: *Re Christionette International Ltd* [1982] 3 All ER 225 at 231F (Vinelott J). Once a company goes into liquidation, the operation of s 40 is not entirely superseded by s 175(2) whilst the receiver remains in office: see *Re Pearl Maintenance Services Ltd* [1995] BCC 675 as noted under the heading 'in priority to any claims for principal or interest' below.

Priority of preferential and secured claims and the receiver's claims for remuneration, costs and expenses where company being wound up—In *Re Leyland DAF Ltd, Buchler v Talbot* [2004] 2 AC 298 the House of Lords provided much-needed clarification on the interplay between s 40 and s 175(2)(b), being the current re-enactment of a provision which could be traced back to s 4 of the Companies Act 1883 (and further in bankruptcy), which confers priority on preferential claims over what s 175(2)(b) now terms '... the assets of the company available for payment of general creditors', which are now perhaps more conveniently labelled 'the company's free assets'. In overruling the decision of the Court of Appeal in *Re Barleycorn Enterprises Ltd* [1970] Ch 465 their Lordships were of the opinion in *Buchler* that, whilst s 175(2)(b) amounted to an incursion on the proprietary rights of debenture-holders by way of making provision for the payment of preferential debts out of property subject to a floating charge and in priority to the claims of the charge holder, neither s 175(2)(b) nor any of its statutory predecessors had the effect of authorising the liquidator's costs and expenses of a winding up to be paid out of the assets subject to a floating charge in priority to the claims of the charge holder. The decision in *Buchler* had potentially far-reaching (and unhelpful) implications and has been reversed by way of s 1282 of the Companies Act 2006.

'... **assets coming to the hands of the receiver** ...'—This is a term which does not extend to property subject to a fixed charge, which takes free of this provision, subject to any deed of priority providing otherwise: *Re Lewis Merthyr Consolidated Collieries* [1929] 1 Ch 498 at 511 (Lord Hanworth MR) and 512 (Lawrence LJ) and see also on this point the explanation by Chadwick J, as he then was, in *Re Portbase (Clothing) Ltd* [1993] BCC 96 at 101E.

Application of fixed charge surplus where debenture-holder discharged in full—Where a debenture-holder is discharged in full, any fixed charge surplus is payable to the company (or its liquidator) and does not fall subject to any floating charge and is not therefore subject to any preferential claims which would otherwise bite on floating charge assets: *Re GL Saunders* [1986] 1 WLR 215.

Consequences of a receiver's breach of the positive duty imposed by s 40(2)—Section 40(2) imposes a positive duty on a receiver to account to preferential creditors from available assets coming into his hands. Breach of this statutory duty renders the receiver personally liable in damages for resultant loss or, arguably, in tort: *Westminster City Council v Traby* [1936] 2 All ER 21 (Farwell J); *Westminster Corpn v Haste* [1950] Ch 442 at 447 (Danckwerts J).

In *IRC v Goldblatt* [1972] Ch 498, when monies were paid over by a receiver to the company in the knowledge that the company would pay over the monies to the debenture-holder with notice of the receiver's statutory duty in satisfaction of the debenture-holder's claim, Goff J held that the debenture-holder held the monies on constructive trust for the preferential creditor, although it must be doubtful, it is submitted, that notice is relevant to such a claim where damages are sought on a restitutionary basis. Where a claim is brought against a receiver by a creditor in such circumstances, the receiver will be entitled to an indemnity from the debenture-holder: see *Westminster City Council v Traby*.

For an unsuccessful restitutionary claim against a charge holder following a payment by administrative receivers in contravention of s 40 see *Re BHT (UK) Ltd, Duckworth v Nat West Finance Ltd* [2004] BCC 301.

'**... in priority to any claims for principal or interest ...**'—Whilst it might be argued that the term 'in priority to any claims for principal or interest' points to the positive duty imposed by s 40(2) ceasing once claims of floating charge holders have been met in full, a contrary view was reached by Carnwath J in *Re Pearl Maintenance Services Ltd* [1995] BCC 657 at 663C–664B. Notwithstanding appointment by a debenture-holder, the duty imposed by s 40(2) is capable of a separate life of its own which is not brought to an end on discharge of a debt secured by a floating charge. Until vacation of office, the receiver remains under a duty to meet preferential claims so far as possible out of floating charge assets.

'**... the debentures ...**'—The reference to 'the debentures' at the end of this subsection is a reference back to 'any debentures of the company secured by a charge which, as created, was a floating charge' in s 40(1) and, as such, is not merely a reference to any debenture or debentures pursuant to which a receiver has been appointed: *Re H & K (Medway) Ltd* [1997] BCC 853 at 857D–858F. The statutory duty imposed on the receiver and manager extends to all such debentures. In *Medway* Neuberger J, as he then was, departed from the decision in *Griffiths v Yorkshire Bank plc* [1994] 1 WLR 1427, in which Morritt J, as he then was, in considering s 196 of the Companies Act 1985 in its earlier form, had construed the term 'the debentures' in the narrower sense. Neuberger J noted, however, that Morritt J had not heard submissions on behalf of preferential creditors and that the report of the decision in *Griffiths* was doubtful.

Building societies—These provisions are inapplicable to building societies: see para 27, Sch 15A as inserted by the Building Societies Act 1997, s 39 and Sch 6.

Section 40(3)

Scope of provision—The receiver's right of recoupment from assets which would otherwise become available to unsecured creditors under this subsection is only triggered once payment to preferential creditors is made from floating charge assets pursuant to s 40(2).

41 Enforcement of duty to make returns

(1) If a receiver or manager of a company's property—

    (a)   having made default in filing, delivering or making any return, account or other document, or in giving any notice, which a receiver or manager is by law required to file, deliver, make or give, fails to make good the default within 14 days after the service on him of a notice requiring him to do so, or

    (b)   having been appointed under powers contained in an instrument, has, after being required at any time by the liquidator of the company to do so, failed to render proper accounts of his receipts and payments and to vouch them and pay over to the liquidator the amount properly payable to him,

the court may, on an application made for the purpose, make an order directing the receiver or manager (as the case may be) to make good the default within such time as may be specified in the order.

(2) In the case of the default mentioned in subsection (1)(a), application to the court may be made by any member or creditor of the company or by the registrar of companies; and in the case of the default mentioned in subsection (1)(b), the application shall be made by the liquidator.

In either case the court's order may provide that all costs of and incidental to the application shall be borne by the receiver or manager, as the case may be.

(3) Nothing in this section prejudices the operation of any enactment imposing penalties on receivers in respect of any such default as is mentioned in subsection (1).

General note—These enforcement provisions are not restricted to the obligations prescribed by s 38.

Section 41(1)(a)

Scope of provision—No form is prescribed for a notice under s 41(1)(a).

Section 41(1)(b)

Scope of provision—This provision extends beyond the accounts etc identified in s 41(1)(a) and permits a liquidator specifically, following a request for such information by or on his behalf, to seek an order requiring not only the rendering and vouching of proper receipts and payments accounts but also payment of the account properly due to the liquidator. For a receiver's duty to account see s 38 and the notes thereto.

Section 41(2)

Scope of provision—Although the court would in any case have jurisdiction to make an order against the receiver or manager personally, this subsection confirms that the court should positively consider the making of such an order. A direction within an order precluding the receiver from recouping such costs from the assets of the company will prevent those costs being borne ultimately by the company's unsecured creditors.

For the standing of the FSA to apply for an enforcement order see FMSA 2000, s 363(3).

Administrative receivers: general

42 General powers

(1) The powers conferred on the administrative receiver of a company by the debentures by virtue of which he was appointed are deemed to include (except in so far as they are inconsistent with any of the provisions of those debentures) the powers specified in Schedule 1 to this Act.

(2) In the application of Schedule 1 to the administrative receiver of a company—

    (a)   the words 'he' and 'him' refer to the administrative receiver, and

    (b)   references to the property of the company are to the property of which he is or, but for the appointment of some other person as the receiver of part of the company's property, would be the receiver or manager.

(3) A person dealing with the administrative receiver in good faith and for value is not concerned to inquire whether the receiver is acting within his powers.

General note—In addition to the powers identified in the note to s 42(1) below, an administrative receiver, like a non-administrative receiver, will, in his capacity as an agent, and subject to contrary provision in the debenture pursuant to which he is appointed, enjoy implied authority to do all those things necessary for or incidental to the effective exercise of his express authority in the ordinary course. For the nature of the agency of an administrative receiver see the note to s 44(1) below.

Notably, s 43 confers an additional power to dispose of property subject to prior or equal ranking security, which is unique to an administrative receiver, but similar to a less extensive power available to an administrator under para 70(1) of Sch B1. An administrative receiver is also empowered to require continued supply of utilities (s 233) and delivery up of property (s 234).

Section 42(1)

Scope of provision—The technique adopted by the legislation here is to imply into the contractual debenture pursuant to which an administrative receiver is appointed those express powers in Sch 1, save to the extent that the debenture provides to the contrary. In practice, standard form debentures commonly provide such express powers, in any case, which will be effective on the appointment of a non-administrative receiver whose powers do not derive from Sch 1 but are dictated by the debenture itself. For further commentary on the nature of the Sch 1 powers and for the effect of liquidation on the exercise of a receiver's powers, see the notes to s 44(1) below.

The liability of receivers for costs in proceedings brought by a company in receivership—Where receivers cause a company to bring proceedings there is no general rule that the receivers should be personally liable for the costs of the successful party; the normal expectation is that the successful party would and should seek an order for security for costs against the company in receivership: *Dolphin Quays Developments Ltd v Mills* [2008] EWCA Civ 385, [2008] 1 WLR 1829 (Mummery, Lawrence Collins LJJ and Munby J upholding the decision of Morritt C to the effect that neither the appointing bank nor the receivers was a real party to the proceedings, which involved the enforcement of a contractual claim, and that there were no exceptional circumstances taking the case out of the ordinary run of cases to justify the imposition of a personal costs order).

The residual status and powers of directors in receivership—The appointment of an administrative receiver or, indeed, any receiver, does not displace the directors from office. Rather, the directors remain in office, although their powers as such are effective only to the extent that the same powers are not assumed by the administrative receiver either by virtue of the Sch 1 powers or by virtue of the appointing debenture-holder's security encompassing property, such as a cause of action, which would otherwise be available to the company: *Newhart v Co-operative Commercial Bank* [1978] QB 814 at 819 (Shaw LJ). It is suggested that, in order to avoid an unhelpful and unintended confusion of interests between the company and receiver/debenture-holder, the directors may assume a right to exercise a power or control of an asset available to an administrative receiver only on the receiver, as agent of the debenture-holder, giving a clear and unambiguous indication of his consent to such a course. In some cases, most obviously involving a cause of action caught by a debenture-holder's security, it may be necessary for the debenture-holder to re-assign the asset to the company so as to allow for its pursuit or realisation by the company acting by its directors.

In *Newhart* Shaw LJ was mindful of the potential embarrassment to a receiver seeking to enforce causes of action against his appointing debenture-holder and perceived no difficulty in such claims being pursued by the company itself: see, for example, *Watts v Midland Bank* [1986] 2 BCC 98, 961 (Peter Gibson J, as he then was) (no reason why a company should not sue a receiver in respect of an improper exercise of powers). In *Tudor Grange Holdings Ltd v Citibank* [1992] Ch 53 Browne-Wilkinson V-C doubted the reasoning in *Newhart* and identified s 35 as a mechanism by which a receiver might avoid embarrassment by seeking directions as to the proper course to be taken by him in a case involving his appointor. Whilst bound by *Newhart*, the Vice-Chancellor took the view that any claim by the company acting by its directors would be liable to be struck out in the absence of a complete indemnity from the directors for the costs of the proposed action. It should be noted that it is only the provision of such an indemnity which guards against the risk of the dissipation of company assets to the cost of the debenture-holder and/or the company's unsecured creditors, a point underpinning the reasoning of Keane J in the Irish High Court in *Lascomme Ltd v United Dominions Trust* [1994] ILRM 224 in reconciling the decision in *Newhart* with that in *Tudor Grange*.

Section 42(3)

Scope of provision—Whilst the third party is not required to inquire as to whether a receiver is acting within his powers, this provision is predicated on the assumption that the receiver is validly appointed. No protection is afforded to a third party dealing with a receiver who is never validly appointed. For the distinction between an invalid appointment and one subject to procedural defects, see ss 34 and 232 and the notes thereto.

43 Power to dispose of charged property etc

(1) Where, on an application by the administrative receiver, the court is satisfied that the disposal (with or without other assets) of any relevant property which is subject to a security would be likely to promote a more advantageous realisation of the company's assets than would otherwise be effected, the court may by order authorise the administrative receiver to dispose of the property as if it were not subject to the security.

(2) Subsection (1) does not apply in the case of any security held by the person by or on whose behalf the administrative receiver was appointed, or of any security to which a security so held has priority.

(3) It shall be a condition of an order under this section that—

(a) the net proceeds of the disposal, and
(b) where those proceeds are less than such amount as may be determined by the court to be the net amount which would be realised on a sale of the property in the open market by a willing vendor, such sums as may be required to make good the deficiency,

shall be applied towards discharging the sums secured by the security.

(4) Where a condition imposed in pursuance of subsection (3) relates to two or more securities, that condition shall require the net proceeds of the disposal and, where paragraph (b) of that subsection applies, the sums mentioned in that paragraph to be applied towards discharging the sums secured by those securities in the order of their priorities.

(5) A copy of an order under this section shall, within 14 days of the making of the order, be sent by the administrative receiver to the registrar of companies.

(6) If the administrative receiver without reasonable excuse fails to comply with subsection (5), he is liable to a fine and, for continued contravention, to a daily default fine.

(7) In this section 'relevant property', in relation to the administrative receiver, means the property of which he is or, but for the appointment of some other person as the receiver of part of the company's property, would be the receiver or manager.

Amendments—SI 2009/1941.

General note—It is, of course, open to a debenture-holder to sell property subject to its security, without the requirement for a court order, either as mortgagee-in-possession or by way of its receiver, so as to override the interests of subsequent mortgagees. The detailed provisions dealing with a mortgagee's power of sale appear in ss 101–107 of the Law of

Property Act 1925. Where there are several mortgagees interested in the same land, a prior mortgagee holds any surplus proceeds on trust for later mortgagees of whose incumbrances the prior mortgagee has notice, subject to the payment of the expenses of sale: *Thorne v Heard and Marsh* [1895] AC 495, and see s 105 of the Law of Property Act 1925. However, no such power exists in relation to a security interest ranking in priority or equal to that of a mortgagee wishing to realise its security. So as to facilitate rescue schemes and to avoid the potentially obstructive fetter of such security, s 43, in accordance with a recommendation of the Cork Committee in its review (at paras 1510–1513), provides an additional power to an administrative receiver to seek the authority of the court for a sale of such property charged in favour of a prior ranking mortgagee as if the property were not subject to such security. Although the above commentary refers to interests in land, s 43 has general application to security interests held over property in any form.

Section 43 has no application in Scotland: s 440(2)(a).

For the non-application of this provision to so-called market charges within the meaning of s 173 of the Companies Act 1989, see s 175 of the Companies Act 1985 and the Financial Markets and Insolvency Regulations 1991 (SI 1991/880, 1995/586 and 1998/27).

Procedure—For procedure see r 3.31.

Section 43(1)

Scope of provision—The phrase 'with or without other assets' envisages the possibility of certain parts of the charged property being subject to prior or equal security where a composite sale, typically of a business as a going concern (on which see paras 2, 15 and 16 of Sch 1), is envisaged.

The term 'likely' should, it is suggested, be construed in accordance with the relatively low threshold of the 'real prospect' test laid down by Hoffmann J (as he then was) in *Re Harris Simons Construction Ltd* [1989] 1 WLR 368 in relation to the former administration order regime under s 8(1)(b).

Section 43(2)

Scope of provision—No application is necessary where, for example, an administrative receiver is appointed under a floating charge (and, usually, accompanying fixed charges in the same debenture) where the appointing debenture-holder itself also holds prior ranking security pursuant to which the appointment is not made.

Section 43(3)

Scope of provision—These conditions (and those in s 43(4) below) must be taken as binding by statutory force on a debenture-holder, even if not incorporated – as they should be – in the court's order following a s 43 application.

'**... net proceeds ...**'—The reference to 'net proceeds' in s 43(3)(a) allows for the costs of realisation in favour of the appointing debenture-holder.

'**... where those proceeds are less than such amount as may be determined by the court ...**'—The practical effect of s 43(3)(b) is that, where the proceeds are less than the amount specified by the court on the hearing of the application, the shortfall must be paid to the prior or equal ranking security holder by, and from the assets available to, the appointing debenture-holder – and seemingly from it in any case if those funds are insufficient – in priority to any preferential claims and those of any other creditors.

Where the net realisation figure assessed by the court is higher than the actual open-market value, s 43(3)(b) dictates that the prior or equal ranking security holder stands to benefit from any windfall in terms of the potential consequent shortfall to be made good by the appointing debenture-holder. In these circumstances an application may be made for a revision by the court of its assessment of the net realisation figure prior to sale. The provisions in s 43(3) do not envisage any such application being made following sale.

Section 43 application coinciding with dispute as to validity of security—Where an application coincides with a dispute as to the validity of a prior ranking security or the competing priority of securities there is, it is submitted, every good reason why the court should not entertain a s 43 application and should instead make an order pursuant to s 43(1) or s 35 or the court's inherent jurisdiction to the effect that the proceeds of sale are to be held as directed by the court, or as agreed between the parties, pending resolution of the dispute: compare the contrary and, with respect, doubtful view of His Honour Judge O'Donoghue in *Re Newman Shopfitters (Cleveland) Ltd* [1991] BCLC 407 in relation to an administration case under the former s 15(2).

Section 43(4)

Scope of provision—This provision is a logical extension of s 43(3) where there are two or more prior or equal ranking securities.

Section 43(5) and (6)

Scope of provision—For the penalties in relation to these administrative provisions see s 430 and Sch 10.

Section 43(7)

Scope of provision—This provision defines the term 'relevant property' as employed in s 43(1). For further explanation see the notes to s 29(2).

44 Agency and liability for contracts

(1) The administrative receiver of a company—

(a) is deemed to be the company's agent, unless and until the company goes into liquidation;

(b) is personally liable on any contract entered into by him in the carrying out of his functions (except in so far as the contract otherwise provides) and, to the extent of any qualifying liability, on any contract of employment adopted by him in the carrying out of those functions; and

(c) is entitled in respect of that liability to an indemnity out of the assets of the company.

(2) For the purposes of subsection (1)(b) the administrative receiver is not to be taken to have adopted a contract of employment by reason of anything done or omitted to be done within 14 days after his appointment.

(2A) For the purposes of subsection (1)(b), a liability under a contract of employment is a qualifying liability if—

(a) it is a liability to pay a sum by way of wages or salary or contribution to an occupational pension scheme,

(b) it is incurred while the administrative receiver is in office, and

(c) it is in respect of services rendered wholly or partly after the adoption of the contract.

(2B) Where a sum payable in respect of a liability which is a qualifying liability for the purposes of subsection (1)(b) is payable in respect of services rendered partly before and partly after the adoption of the contract, liability under subsection (1)(b) shall only extend to so much of the sum as is payable in respect of services rendered after the adoption of the contract.

(2C) For the purposes of subsections (2A) and (2B)—

(a) wages or salary payable in respect of a period of holiday or absence from work through sickness or other good cause are deemed to be wages or (as the case may be) salary in respect of services rendered in that period, and

(b) a sum payable in lieu of holiday is deemed to be wages or (as the case may be) salary in respect of services rendered in the period by reference to which the holiday entitlement arose.

(2D) In subsection (2C)(a), the reference to wages or salary payable in respect of a period of holiday includes any sums which, if they had been paid, would have been treated for the purposes of the enactments relating to social security as earnings in respect of that period.

(3) This section does not limit any right to indemnity which the administrative receiver would have apart from it, nor limit his liability on contracts entered into or adopted without authority, nor confer any right to indemnity in respect of that liability.

Amendments—Insolvency Act 1994, s 2.

General note—Section 44 applies to administrative receivers only. Sections 44(1)(b) and (c) and 44(2) mirror those provisions in ss 37(1)(a) and (b) and 37(2) in relation to non-administrative receivers. Administrative receivers alone, however, are afforded the protection of the 'qualifying liability' regime provided for in ss 44(1)(b) and 44(2A)–(2D) as modified and inserted by s 2(1), (3) and (4) of the Insolvency Act 1994. Those new provisions limit the personal liability of an administrative receiver for services rendered wholly or in part after adoption of a contract for such services on or after 15 March 1994 and were introduced by Parliament in response to the decision of the Court of Appeal in *Re Paramount Airways Ltd (No 3), Powdrill v Watson* [1993] BCC 662.

Section 44(1)(a)

Scope of provision—The deeming of an administrative receiver as agent of a company until liquidation is consistent with an express term to such effect commonly found in practice in debenture documents. This deemed agency, however, is unusual in nature since it does not operate for the benefit of the company – which itself has no power to determine the agency relationship or to control the function of the administrative receiver – but, rather, serves to protect the appointing debenture-holder's security: *Gomba Holdings UK Ltd v Minories Finance Ltd* [1989] 1 All ER 261 at 263 (Fox LJ). The deeming of the administrative receiver as agent of the company also serves to insulate his appointing debenture-holder from liability for the acts or commissions of the receiver. The debenture-holder is, however, at risk of incurring such liability if the acts or omissions of the receiver can be shown to have been undertaken on the instructions of the debenture-holder, in which case the receiver will amount to the de facto agent of the debenture-holder notwithstanding s 44(1)(a): *American Express International Banking Corp v Hurley* [1985] 3 All ER 564 at 571F–571J (Mann J).

The receiver's duties to the company in receivership are subordinate to the duties owed to the appointing debenture-holder—The receiver's position is dual-faceted in terms of the duties owed contemporaneously by him to the company and to his appointing debenture-holder. It is well established that the receiver's duties to the company over the assets of which he is appointed are subordinate to the receiver's primary duties owed to his appointing debenture-holder: *Downsview Nominees Ltd v First City Corp Ltd* [1993] AC 295 (Lord Templeman).

Termination of the receiver's agency consequent upon liquidation—An administrative receiver may cause a company to enter into contractual and other liabilities or, alternatively, the receiver may enter into such liabilities personally as agent of the company. Liquidation has the effect of terminating the power of the receiver to act as agent and to cause the company to commit to such liabilities, in addition to bringing to an end the indemnity out of the company's assets in favour of the receiver under s 44(1)(c). The fact of liquidation, however, does nothing to terminate the receivership itself or the standing of the receiver to exercise in rem security rights, in the name of the appointing debenture-holder as mortgagee or chargee or in the name of the company, for the benefit of the debenture-holder: *Sowman v David Samuel Trust Ltd* [1978] 1 All ER 616 (Goulding J) and the later decision in *Barrows v Chief Land Registra* (1977) *The Times*, October 20 (receiver entitled to exercise power of sale in debenture in conveying legal estate in the name of company in receivership following winding up).

The duties of a receiver in carrying on the business of a company—A receiver will incur no liability to the company, or, indeed, to a junior ranking secured creditor, a guarantor or any other party with an interest in the equity of redemption if he acts in good faith and (a) in exercising his powers of management he tries to bring about a situation in which interests on the secured debt can be paid and the debt itself repaid, and (b) in carrying on the business constituted by the charged assets (there being no such obligation imposed on the receiver) all reasonable steps are taken by him to carry on the business profitably: *Medforth v Blake* [1999] 3 All ER 97 at 110J–111J (Sir Richard Scott V-C). For a more recent summary of the nature and extent of the duties owed by a receiver, and by a mortgagee-in-possession, see the judgment of the Court of Appeal in *Silven Properties Ltd v Royal Bank of Scotland plc* [2004] 1 BCLC 359 (Lightman J delivering judgment, Aldous and Tuckey LJJ agreeing).

The duties of a receiver as regards the timing and method of sale of property under his control—In *Bell v Long* [2008] EWHC 1273 (Ch), [2008] 2 BCLC 706 Patten J held that administrative receivers were entitled to sell four properties as a portfolio at a discount on their individual valuations since such a sale guaranteed realisation as opposed to the uncertainties of a longer marketing period in uncertain market conditions. Whilst a receiver is effectively in the same position as a mortgagee and owes duties to those with an interest in the equity of redemption, the receiver is not trustee of the power to sell for the mortgagor and is therefore entitled to choose the time for sale, even if that course later turns out to have been disadvantageous to the mortgagor. Notably, Patten J identified that the characterisation of the receiver's duty as a duty to obtain the best price reasonably obtainable at the time of sale is not an accurate or adequate description of the duty as an absolute test of liability regardless of the circumstances prevailing at the time of the decision to market and sell.

Liability of the receiver for rates—In *Re Beck Foods Ltd, Boston BC v Rees* [2002] BPIR 665 the Court of Appeal (Pill and Jonathan Parker LJJ) confirmed that the management and carrying on of a business by a receiver does not bring to an end the rateable occupation of a property by the company so as to make the receiver personally liable as the rateable occupier. That decision is consistent with the earlier judgment of the Court of Appeal in *Ratford v Northavon District Council* [1987] QB 357, and in particular the judgment of Slade LJ at 374E and 376E, which had held that the fact of a receiver entering into a company's premises for the purpose of managing and carrying on its business did not of itself bring about the cessation of the company's rateable occupation. The position is not affected by the fact of the company going into liquidation during the course of the receivership. In *Beck* the company had been placed into creditor's voluntary liquidation less than three months after the appointment of the receivers, following which part of the company's business was continued by the receivers at the company's premises until the eventual sale of all of the assets some seven months later; the liquidation, which had been brought about by the receivers themselves for the purpose of protecting the interests of unsecured creditors, involved no change in the day-to-day conduct of the business which was monitored by the receivers by way of a weekly site visit. It is submitted that a receiver may incur liability for rateable occupation if, as a matter of fact, the receiver can be said to have taken possession and gone into occupation of the premises; in those circumstances a receiver will be personally liable for rates if he has lost his position as agent of the company through liquidation, subject to any indemnity in his favour from his appointor. It is further submitted that, based on the reasoning in both *Beck* and *Ratford*, a receiver will not incur a liability for rates if premises are actually unoccupied, on which see *Bannister v Islington London Borough Council* (1971) LGR 239 and *Re Sobam BV* [1996] BCC 351. An administrative receiver cannot be required by a rating authority to exercise any power or discretion to pay rates; neither are such rates payable as an expense of the receivership: *Brown v City of London Corporation* [1996] 1 WLR 1070.

Administrative receiver as shadow director?—It is inconceivable that an administrative receiver would fall within the definition of 'shadow director' in s 251 and s 744 of the Companies Act 1985 by virtue of his deemed agency for the company alone, though the point might be arguable where the administrative receiver acts beyond the scope of his office.

Section 44(1)(b)

Scope of provision—This provision provides that an administrative receiver is personally liable on a contract entered into by him in two distinct scenarios. First, personal liability arises where the administrative receiver enters into a contract, save to the extent that the contract provides to the contrary, most obviously by identifying the principal company – and not the administrative receiver – as the contracting party. The administrative receiver's powers to cause the company to enter into such a contract terminate on liquidation: see s 44(1)(a) above. The commentary on the contracting out of personal liability by a receiver in the notes to s 37(1)(a) above applies equally to an administrative receiver. The second scenario in which an administrative receiver incurs personal liability on a contract arises where a contract of employment is 'adopted by him', in which case his liability is capped to the extent that the liability amounts to a 'qualifying liability' as defined and provided for in s 44(2A)–(2D).

The concept of 'qualifying liability'—The introduction of the concept of capping the administrative receiver's liabilities to the extent of one or more qualifying liabilities in the modifications and amendments introduced by the Insolvency Act 1994 followed from the decision of the Court of Appeal in *Re Paramount Airways Ltd (No 3), Powdrill v Watson* [1993] BCC 662, which had dealt a body blow to the idea of corporate rescue in rejecting any legal basis for the common (former) practice by which administrative receivers (and administrators) had written to employees within the 14-day period provided for in s 44(2) giving unilateral notice in standard form that an employee's contract of employment would be continued as previously but that the administrative receiver (or administrator) was not to be taken as adopting a contract and, as such, assumed no personal liability on the contract of employment. That practice had been followed by office-holders based on an unreported decision of Harman J (which had never been reduced to writing) in *Re Specialised Mouldings Ltd* (Chancery Division, 13 February 1987) which, on an application by an administrative receiver for directions under s 35, had held that such letters were effective in avoiding adoption notwithstanding the continuation of any affected contract of employment in fact beyond the s 44(2) 14-day period. As such, *Specialised Mouldings* letters had had the effect of protecting office-holders from the effects of the decision in *Nicoll v Cutts* [1985] BCLC 322.

The true meaning of adoption—In *Paramount* the Court of Appeal had upheld the decision of Evans-Lombe J at first instance to the effect that adoption by an office-holder was a question of fact which was determined by any act or acquiescence after the 14-day statutory period and which was indicative of the office-holder's intention to treat the contract as being on foot. In addition, the Court of Appeal held that a continuing contract which had been adopted by an office-holder was only capable of being adopted in its entirety.

The appeal from the decision of the Court of Appeal in *Paramount* was consolidated with appeals from the decisions of Lightman J in *Re Leyland DAF Ltd (No 2)* and *Re Ferranti International plc* [1994] BCC 654. On appeal, the House of Lords held that adoption may only apply to a contract as a whole and requires conduct amounting to an election as a matter of fact on the part of the office-holder to treat the continued employment as a separate liability in the receivership (or administration), although that conduct may apparently involve nothing more than a failure on the part of the office-holder to terminate or repudiate a contract of employment within the statutory 14-day period: see [1995] 2 AC 394 at 448, 449, 450 and 452 (Lord Brown-Wilkinson).

In *Re Antal International Ltd (in administration)* [2003] 2 BCLC 406 the court was asked to determine whether administrators had adopted contracts of employment where the administrators had genuinely but erroneously believed that employees were employed by a French subsidiary where, on discovering that the French subsidiary did not exist, the administrators had taken all necessary steps to terminate the employment contracts in accordance with French law. Neuberger J (as he then was) held that the contracts of employment had not been adopted on the basis that there was no evidence of conduct on the part of the administrators capable of constituting an election to carry on the contracts.

Can an office-holder contract out of adoption?—It is suggested that there is no good reason why, in principle, an administrative receiver should not seek to contract out of the consequences of adoption of a contract of employment. Such express contracting-out would, however, it is further submitted, require the express agreement of employees and might be seen as less likely in any case, given the reduction of the receiver's liabilities by way of the introduction of the scheme of qualifying liabilities.

For the notification of proposed redundancies to a trades union or employee representative see s 188 of the Trade Union and Labour Relations (Consolidation) Act 1992.

'… in the carrying out of his functions …'—Both scenarios in which an administrative receiver may incur personal liability on a contract, as discussed above in the note to s 44(1)(b), assume the contract had been entered into by an administrative receiver 'in the carrying out of his functions'. It is very difficult to see how an administrative receiver might incur personal liability other than in the carrying out of his functions other than where an office-holder intentionally incurs a liability which is not in any way incidental to the preservation and/or realisation of secured assets; in such circumstances the administrative receiver will not have the benefit of the indemnity in s 44(1)(c).

Section 44(2)

Scope of provision—On adoption of a contract of employment see the notes to s 44(1)(b) above.

Section 44(2A)–(2D)

Scope of provision—These provisions elaborate on the term 'qualifying liability' in s 44(1)(b). Essentially, qualifying liabilities are limited to those restricted classes incurred under the adopted contract of employment whilst the administrative receiver is in office.

Statutory compensation for unfair dismissal will not amount to a qualifying liability, since such liability does not accrue under a contract of employment: *Re Paramount (No 3)* [1994] 2 BCLC 118 at 132E.

Whether or not a particular liability amounts to a qualifying liability is a question determined on the particular facts of the case based on all surrounding circumstances which are known or ought to have been known to the parties: *Re A Company (No 005174 of 1999)* [2000] 1 WLR 502 at 508 (Neuberger J, as he then was).

Section 44(3)

Scope of provision—The commentary and the notes to s 37(1)(b), s 37(3) and the general note to s 37 apply equally to this provision.

45 Vacation of office

(1) An administrative receiver of a company may at any time be removed from office by order of the court (but not otherwise) and may resign his office by giving notice of his resignation in the prescribed manner to such persons as may be prescribed.

(2) An administrative receiver shall vacate office if he ceases to be qualified to act as an insolvency practitioner in relation to the company.

(3) Where at any time an administrative receiver vacates office—

    (a)   his remuneration and any expenses properly incurred by him, and

    (b)   any indemnity to which he is entitled out of the assets of the company, shall be charged on and paid out of any property of the company which is in his custody or under his control at that time in priority to any security held by the person by or on whose behalf he was appointed.

(4) Where an administrative receiver vacates office otherwise than by death, he shall, within 14 days after his vacation of office, send a notice to that effect to the registrar of companies.

(5) If an administrative receiver without reasonable excuse fails to comply with subsection (4), he is liable to a fine and, for continued contravention, to a daily default fine.

General note—An administrative receiver will hold office until his resignation or removal by the court under s 45(1) or, alternatively, in the event of his ceasing to be qualified to act as an insolvency practitioner in relation to a company under s 45(2), on his death (on which see r 3.34) or on his vacating office on completion of the receivership (on which see r 3.35). Unlike a non-administrative receiver, an administrative receiver may not be removed by his appointing debenture-holder. The logic in this apparently harsh rule lies in preventing interference by the debenture-holder with the statutory obligations imposed on his appointee, perhaps most obviously the discharge of senior-ranking secured debt and the payment of preferential debts under s 40.

The receiver's duty to cease acting—As regards vacating office on completion of the receivership, the decision of His Honour Judge Roger Cooke, sitting as a judge of the High Court, in *Rottenberg v Monjack* [1992] BCC 688, is authority for the proposition that a cause of action arises in favour of a company in respect of any breach on the part of a receiver of his duty to cease acting where the receiver has in his hands sufficient funds to discharge the total debt under the security pursuant to which he was appointed in addition to his remuneration and all possible claims which could be made against him. For an Australian authority to similar effect see *Expo International Pty Ltd v Chant* [1979] 2 NSWLR 820. The duty to cease acting is not, however, triggered where there remains outstanding a contingent liability due to the debenture-holder: *Re Rudd & Son Ltd* (1986) BCC 98, 955, CA.

The duty to vacate is not affected by the views of the receivers or the appointing debenture-holder as to the merits of handing control of the company back to its directors and, furthermore, operates irrespective of the liquidation of the company. An insolvency practitioner will act in breach of the duty to vacate if he fails to vacate office on the sole basis of an objectively unsustainable outstanding claim under the security of the debenture pursuant to which he was appointed.

Procedure—On procedure see rr 3.33–3.35.

Form 3.7 is prescribed for giving notice of death to the Registrar of Companies.

On an application to remove an administrative receiver under s 45(1) notice should ordinarily be given to the appointee.

Section 45(1)

Scope of provision—Where an incumbent office-holder will not resign voluntarily, any application under this provision to remove him will usually be combative.

Eligible applicants under s 45(1)—The provisions give no guidance as to the eligible applicants or the appropriate test applicable to a removal application. It is suggested that, as a first step, the court will only entertain an application by an individual with a sufficient interest in the receivership. Such persons might include the appointee's professional body, a co-appointee, the appointing debenture-holder, the holder of other security affected by the receivership or a liquidator. However, it is doubtful that a minority shareholder or an unsecured creditor for a relatively small sum will be able to establish sufficient interest in the absence of some exceptional circumstances: see *Walker Morris (a firm) v Khalastchi* [2001] 1 BCLC 1. As a second step, it is suggested, the court must be satisfied that cause can be shown justifying removal. It is suggested that there is good reason that that test should require proof to the standard applicable to removal of liquidators, on which see the notes to ss 108 and 172. Commonwealth authority suggests that the court will usually intervene by removing an office-holder where he is guilty of a flagrant breach of duty jeopardising the debenture-holder's security: see *Re Neon Signs (Australasia) Ltd* [1965] VR 125.

Replacement following removal of a receiver—On removal, a debenture-holder will usually wish to appoint a replacement office-holder of its choice although the court might appoint a receiver, if only to hold the proverbial ring, where a replacement cannot be appointed for any reason. In *Re A & C Supplies Ltd* [1998] 1 BCLC 603 at 609F Blackburne J, in the context of a contested block appointment transfer application, held that the court has no jurisdiction to appoint an administrative receiver.

Section 45(2)

Scope of provision—For the meaning of being qualified to act as an insolvency practitioner in relation to a company see ss 389–391.

Section 45(3)

Scope of provision—This provision is in identical form to s 37(4), on which see the notes to that section.

Section 45(4) and (5)

Scope of provision—The ongoing daily default fine previously imposed by s 45(5) was abolished by Schs 16 and 24 of the Companies Act 1989.
   For penalties see s 430 and Sch 10.

Administrative receivers: ascertainment and investigation of company's affairs

46 Information to be given by administrative receiver

(1) Where an administrative receiver is appointed, he shall—

   (a)   forthwith send to the company and publish in the prescribed manner a notice of his appointment, and
   (b)   within 28 days after his appointment, unless the court otherwise directs, send such a notice to all the creditors of the company (so far as he is aware of their addresses).

(2) This section and the next do not apply in relation to the appointment of an administrative receiver to act—

   (a)   with an existing administrative receiver, or
   (b)   in place of an administrative receiver dying or ceasing to act,

except that, where they apply to an administrative receiver who dies or ceases to act before they have been fully complied with, the references in this section and the next to the administrative receiver include (subject to the next subsection) his successor and any continuing administrative receiver.

(3) If the company is being wound up, this section and the next apply notwithstanding that the administrative receiver and the liquidator are the same person, but with any necessary modifications arising from that fact.

(4) If the administrative receiver without reasonable excuse fails to comply with this section, he is liable to a fine and, for continued contravention, to a daily default fine.

General note—These administrative provisions provide for the publicising of the appointment of an administrative receiver and should be read with rr 3.1 and 3.2. Whilst criminal sanctions are imposed in default, non-compliance with these formalities, however significant the consequence, will not affect the validity of an appointment.

Section 46(1)

The extent of the duty to give notice—Save for the general duty to give notice within 28 days in the manner described in s 46(1)(b) an administrative receiver is under no obligation to bring the fact of his appointment to the attention of any particular creditor or any other party.

'... unless the court otherwise directs ...'—These words in s 46(1)(b) suggest that an appointee sending notice to creditors outside the 28-day period without court permission will, whatever the reasons for default, incur liability for the criminal sanctions in s 46(4). An application to the court will be by way of originating application with witness statement in support and should name the appointing debenture-holder as respondent.

Procedure—For the contents of the notice and advertisement see r 3.2.

Quite apart from the provisions in s 46, a person appointing a receiver and manager of the property of a company under any powers contained in an instrument (including statutorily implied powers in an instrument) must, within seven days from the date of the appointment, give notice of the fact of the appointment to the Registrar of Companies, who is then obliged to register the fact on the company's register of charges: Companies Act 1985, s 405, and see s 401 for the register.

Section 39 obligations—An administrative receiver is also bound to comply with the obligations in s 39 relating to statements and invoices and the like.

Section 46(4)

Penalties—See s 430 and Sch 10.

47 Statement of affairs to be submitted

(1) Where an administrative receiver is appointed, he shall forthwith require some or all of the persons mentioned below to make out and submit to him a statement in the prescribed form as to the affairs of the company.

(2) A statement submitted under this section shall be verified by a statement of truth by the persons required to submit it and shall show—

    (a)   particulars of the company's assets, debts and liabilities;
    (b)   the names and addresses of its creditors;
    (c)   the securities held by them respectively;
    (d)   the dates when the securities were respectively given; and
    (e)   such further or other information as may be prescribed.

(3) The persons referred to in subsection (1) are—

    (a)   those who are or have been officers of the company;
    (b)   those who have taken part in the company's formation at any time within one year before the date of the appointment of the administrative receiver;
    (c)   those who are in the company's employment, or have been in its employment within that year, and are in the administrative receiver's opinion capable of giving the information required;

(d)   those who are or have been within that year officers of or in the employment of a company which is, or within that year was, an officer of the company.

In this subsection 'employment' includes employment under a contract for services.

(4) Where any persons are required under this section to submit a statement of affairs to the administrative receiver, they shall do so (subject to the next subsection) before the end of the period of 21 days beginning with the day after that on which the prescribed notice of the requirement is given to them by the administrative receiver.

(5) The administrative receiver, if he thinks fit, may—

(a)   at any time release a person from an obligation imposed on him under subsection (1) or (2), or
(b)   either when giving notice under subsection (4) or subsequently, extend the period so mentioned;

and where the administrative receiver has refused to exercise a power conferred by this subsection, the court, if it thinks fit, may exercise it.

(6) If a person without reasonable excuse fails to comply with any obligation imposed under this section, he is liable to a fine and, for continued contravention, to a daily default fine.

Amendments—SI 2010/18.

General note—These provisions stipulate the requirements for the preparation and submission of a statement of affairs to the administrative receiver. The failure to comply with the obligation to deliver up a statement of affairs is a matter within Sch 1 of the Company Directors Disqualification Act 1986 in determining the unfitness of a company director on an application for a disqualification order.

Procedure—Detailed procedural provisions appear in rr 3.3–3.8.

Section 47(1) and (4)

Scope of provision—The administrative receiver is under an obligation – through use of the word 'shall' – to require submission to him of the statement of affairs 'forthwith' – and not within, say, a reasonable time – following his appointment. The prescribed form of the statement of affairs is in Form 3.2. By s 47(2) the recipients of the prescribed form are afforded 21 days from receipt to submit the completed document; the word 'given' connotes actual receipt.

Subject to s 47(5), provided that the administrative receiver discharges his obligation to require submission of the statement of affairs, by way of the imposition of that requirement on one or more of the individuals in s 47(3), the receiver has a discretion as to which specific individuals are made subject to the s 47(2) obligation.

Under r 3.4(2) an administrative receiver may also require any one of those persons mentioned in s 47(3) to submit an affidavit of concurrence stating that the deponent concurs in the statement of affairs submitted to him.

Enforcement of the obligation by the receiver—The obligation to submit a statement of affairs is enforceable by the administrative receiver under r 7.20(1)(a) and (2)(b).

Section 47(2)

Scope of provision—The swearing of the statement of affairs renders a deponent liable to prosecution under s 5 of the Perjury Act 1911 for false or misleading statements.

Section 47(3)

Scope of provision—Section 47(3)(c) will extend to employment under a contract for services.

Section 47(4)

Scope of provision—See the note to s 47(1) above.
  For the recovery by a 'deponent' under r 3.3(2) of his expenses in making the statement of affairs and supporting affidavit see r 3.7.

Section 47(5)

Scope of provision—An administrative receiver may either release an individual from the obligation under s 47(1) or (2) (ie irrespective of whether a s 47(4) notice has been served) or, alternatively, extend the 21-day period in s 47(4). This provision anticipates that an application to the court for the same relief, which would be in the form of an originating application with witness statement or affidavit in support, may only be made following a refusal by the administrative receiver of such release or extension of time.

Procedure—For procedure on the release from duty to submit the statement of affairs or for the extension of time see r 3.6.

Section 47(6)

Penalties—See s 430 and Sch 10.

48 Report by administrative receiver

(1) Where an administrative receiver is appointed, he shall, within 3 months (or such longer period as the court may allow) after his appointment, send to the registrar of companies, to any trustees for secured creditors of the company and (so far as he is aware of their addresses) to all such creditors a report as to the following matters, namely—

(a)   the events leading up to his appointment, so far as he is aware of them;

(b)   the disposal or proposed disposal by him of any property of the company and the carrying on or proposed carrying on by him of any business of the company;

(c)   the amounts of principal and interest payable to the debenture holders by whom or on whose behalf he was appointed and the amounts payable to preferential creditors; and

(d)   the amount (if any) likely to be available for the payment of other creditors.

(2) The administrative receiver shall also, within 3 months (or such longer period as the court may allow) after his appointment, either—

(a)   send a copy of the report (so far as he is aware of their addresses) to all unsecured creditors of the company; or

(b)   publish in the prescribed manner a notice stating an address to which unsecured creditors of the company should write for copies of the report to be sent to them free of charge,

and (in either case), unless the court otherwise directs, lay a copy of the report before a meeting of the company's unsecured creditors summoned for the purpose on not less than 14 days' notice.

(3) The court shall not give a direction under subsection (2) unless—

(a)   the report states the intention of the administrative receiver to apply for the direction, and

(b)   a copy of the report is sent to the persons mentioned in paragraph (a) of that subsection, or a notice is published as mentioned in paragraph (b) of that subsection, not less than 14 days before the hearing of the application.

(4) Where the company has gone or goes into liquidation, the administrative receiver—

(a)   shall, within 7 days after his compliance with subsection (1) or, if later, the nomination or appointment of the liquidator, send a copy of the report to the liquidator, and

(b)   where he does so within the time limited for compliance with subsection (2), is not required to comply with that subsection.

(5) A report under this section shall include a summary of the statement of affairs made out and submitted to the administrative receiver under section 47 and of his comments (if any) upon it.

(6) Nothing in this section is to be taken as requiring any such report to include any information the disclosure of which would seriously prejudice the carrying out by the administrative receiver of his functions.

(7) Section 46(2) applies for the purposes of this section also.

(8) If the administrative receiver without reasonable excuse fails to comply with this section, he is liable to a fine and, for continued contravention, to a daily default fine.

General note—The detailed requirements of this section are largely prescriptive and provide for the provision of specific information by an administrative receiver within the extendable three-month period following the receiver's appointment, as provided for in s 48(1), subject to the facility for the limiting of disclosure under s 48(6). In practice, the provision of information by an administrative receiver commonly amounts to little more than a formalistic disclosure exercise with little practical consequence. Save that the meeting of creditors convened under s 48(2) may establish a creditors' committee, which may require information of the administrative receiver under s 49, the creditors' meeting itself is not concerned with the approval of proposals, but merely receives the report provided by the administrative receiver.

The equitable duty to account as an agent and the receiver's duty as a fiduciary—Quite apart from the requirements under s 48 a receiver, including an administrative receiver, is under an equitable duty to the company, as its agent and as a fiduciary, to account for his conduct of the receivership. As a basic principle, this duty will ordinarily require the receiver to keep full accounts and to produce those accounts to the company on being required to do so: *Smith v Middleton* [1979] 3 All ER 842 (Blackett-Ord V-C). However, the scope of the duty is variable, depending upon the nature of the receivership and, in particular, two specific factors. First, the right of the company to require information is dependent on the company being able to establish that the information sought is necessary for the purpose of enabling the directors to discharge any of the residual obligations remaining on them, most obviously the filing of accounts or the redemption of the debenture-holder's security: *Gomba Holdings (UK) Ltd v Homan, Same v Johnson Matthey Bankers* [1986] 1 WLR 1301 (Hoffmann J, as he then was). Secondly, given his primary duty to his appointing debenture-holder (on which see the notes to s 44(1)(a)) the receiver may refuse to disclose information if he is of the objectively reasonable subjective view that such disclosure would be prejudicial to the interests of the debenture-holder in realising his security: *Gomba Holdings*.

Whistle-blowing obligation—An administrative receiver is subject to a so-called whistle-blowing duty to the Financial Services Authority by virtue of s 364 of the FSMA 2000.

Procedure—On procedure see rr 3.8–3.15.

Section 48(1) and (4)

Scope of provision—The parties to whom the administrative receiver must submit a report include not only those listed in s 48(1) but also, by virtue of s 48(4), any liquidator of the company and, if appropriate, the Financial Services Authority by virtue of FSMA 2000, s 363(4).

Section 48(2)

Scope of provision—Section 48(2) places an obligation on the administrative receiver to summon a meeting of unsecured creditors on not less than 14 days' notice within 3 months of his appointment. That obligation is subject to two provisos. First, an application may be made to the court extending the 3-month period. Secondly, the court may direct that the meeting of creditors be dispensed with, although such applications in practice are rare. The subsection gives no indication as to the parties eligible to make an application under either of the grounds identified, although in practice such applications would ordinarily be made by the administrative receiver or, possibly, by his appointing debenture-holder.

See also the general note above.

Quorum—The quorum for the meeting is one creditor present in person or by proxy and being entitled to vote: r 12.4A. The former r 3.13, which required a meeting of creditors to have at least three creditors – or all of the creditors if less than three in number – present in person or by proxy was revoked by the Insolvency (Amendment) Rules 1987.

Procedure for summoning of creditors' meeting—See r 3.9.

Chairman of the creditors' meeting—See r 3.10.

Voting rights at the creditors' meeting—For voting rights see r 3.11.

Resolutions at the creditors' meeting—Resolutions by a simple majority in value of those present and voting in person or by proxy: see r 3.15(1).

Section 48(6)

'… any information the disclosure of which would seriously prejudice the carrying out … of his functions'—The most obvious examples of such information are price-sensitive information where the viability of the company's business might be damaged by the disclosure of such information to creditors and/or business competitors or details of offers received by the administrative receiver to date for the whole or part of the company's undertaking where such disclosure might prejudice the making of what would otherwise be a significantly more competitive bid.

For procedure on the application to court see r 3.5.

Section 48(7)

Scope of provision—The obligations imposed by this section do not apply to an administrative receiver who is appointed to act with an administrative receiver or, save to the extent that an outgoing administrative receiver has failed to comply with his obligations under the section, an administrative receiver appointed to replace one who has died or ceased to act as such.

Section 48(8)

Scope of provision—For penalties see s 430 and Sch 10.

49 Committee of creditors

(1) Where a meeting of creditors is summoned under section 48, the meeting may, if it thinks fit, establish a committee ('the creditors' committee') to exercise the functions conferred on it by or under this Act.

(2) If such a committee is established, the committee may, on giving not less than 7 days' notice, require the administrative receiver to attend before it at any reasonable time and furnish it with such information relating to the carrying out by him of his functions as it may reasonably require.

General note—The practical significance of the creditors' committee very much depends upon the level of interest on the part of creditors in the conduct and outcome of the administrative receivership. In some cases, as s 49(1) envisages, the meeting of creditors summoned under s 48 may not see fit even to establish a creditors' committee.

In contrast to the largely administrative function of the creditors' meeting convened under s 48, there is a real power in the creditors' committee in the terms of s 49(2), on which see the notes below. Conversely, however, the creditors' committee 'shall assist the administrative receiver in discharging his functions, and act in relation to him in such manner as may be agreed from time to time': r 3.18(1).

Procedure—For procedure and formalities in relation to the creditors' committee see rr 3.16–3.30A. Rule 3.30A, as inserted by the Insolvency (Amendment) Rules 1987, provides that the acts of the creditors' committee are valid notwithstanding any defect in the appointment, election or qualifications of any member of the committee or any committee-member's representative or in the formalities of its establishment.

Section 49(1)

Scope of provision—Despite the apparent suggestion that there may be functions conferred on the creditors' committee by the 1986 Act, in fact the only functions provided for are in the very general terms of r 3.18(1) which appears in substance in the general note above. That provision does, however, envisage that specific functions on the part of the creditors' committee may be agreed between the committee and the administrative receiver from time to time.

The administrative receiver shall call a first meeting of the creditors' committee not later than three months after its establishment and thereafter in accordance with the request or direction of the committee itself in accordance with r 3.18.

For the position of the Financial Services Authority in relation to the creditors' committee see FSMA 2000, s 363(5).

Chairman of the creditors' committee—See r 3.19.

Quorum—See r 3.20.

Section 49(2)

'... as it may reasonably require'—The limit on information to be furnished by the administrative receiver by reference to the words 'reasonably require' guards, it is submitted, against two scenarios. First, it cannot be envisaged that the committee might require the administrative receiver to disclose something to it, which the administrative receiver would not be required to disclose in his report to creditors under s 48(6) on the grounds that such disclosure would seriously prejudice the carrying out by the administrative receiver of his functions. Secondly, the sub-provision protects the administrative receiver from vexatious, irrelevant or disproportionate (in terms of time and expense as against perceived benefit) requests for information.

Chapter II

Receivers (Scotland)

50 Extent of this chapter

This Chapter extends to Scotland only.

51 Power to appoint receiver

(1) It is competent under the law of Scotland for the holder of a floating charge over all or any part of the property (including uncalled capital), which may from time to time be comprised in the property and undertaking of an incorporated company (whether a company registered under the Companies Act 2006 or not)—

- (a)   which the Court of Session has jurisdiction to wind up; or
- (b)   where paragraph (a) does not apply, in respect of which a court of a member state other than the United Kingdom has under the EU Regulation jurisdiction to open insolvency proceedings,

to appoint a receiver of such part of the property of the company as is subject to the charge.

(2) It is competent under the law of Scotland for the court, on the application of the holder of such a floating charge, to appoint a receiver of such part of the property of the company as is subject to the charge.

(2ZA) But, in relation to a company mentioned in subsection (1)(b), a receiver may be appointed under subsection (1) or (2) only in respect of property situated in Scotland.

(2A) Subsections (1) and (2) are subject to section 72A.

(3) The following are disqualified from being appointed as receiver—

- (a)   a body corporate;
- (b)   an undischarged bankrupt;
- (ba)   a person subject to a bankruptcy restrictions order; and
- (c)   a firm according to the law of Scotland.

(4) A body corporate or a firm according to the law of Scotland which acts as a receiver is liable to a fine.

(5) An undischarged bankrupt or a person subject to a bankruptcy restrictions order who so acts is liable to imprisonment or a fine, or both.

(6) In this section, 'receiver' includes joint receivers; and

'bankruptcy restrictions order' means—
- (a)   a bankruptcy restrictions order made under section 56A of the Bankruptcy (Scotland) Act 1985 (c 66);
- (b)   a bankruptcy restrictions undertaking entered into under section 56G of that Act;
- (c)   a bankruptcy restrictions order made under paragraph 1 of Schedule 4A to this Act; or

(d)   a bankruptcy restrictions undertaking entered into under paragraph 7 of that Schedule.

'the EU Regulation' is the Regulation of the Council of the European Union published as Council Regulation (EC) No 1346/2000 on insolvency proceedings;

'court' is to be construed in accordance with Article 2(d) of the EU Regulation;

'insolvency proceedings' is to be construed in accordance with Article 2(a) of the EU Regulation.

Amendments—Enterprise Act 2002, s 248(3), Sch 17, paras 9, 13; Bankruptcy and Diligence etc (Scotland) Act 2007, s 3; SI 2009/1941; SSI 2011/140.

52 Circumstances justifying appointment

(1) A receiver may be appointed under section 51(1) by the holder of the floating charge on the occurrence of any event which, by the provisions of the instrument creating the charge, entitles the holder of the charge to make that appointment and, in so far as not otherwise provided for by the instrument, on the occurrence of any of the following events, namely—

(a)   the expiry of a period of 21 days after the making of a demand for payment of the whole or any part of the principal sum secured by the charge, without payment having been made;

(b)   the expiry of a period of 2 months during the whole of which interest due and payable under the charge has been in arrears;

(c)   the making of an order or the passing of a resolution to wind up the company;

(d)   the appointment of a receiver by virtue of any other floating charge created by the company.

(2) A receiver may be appointed by the court under section 51(2) on the occurrence of any event which, by the provisions of the instrument creating the floating charge, entitles the holder of the charge to make that appointment and, in so far as not otherwise provided for by the instrument, on the occurrence of any of the following events, namely—

(a)   where the court, on the application of the holder of the charge, pronounces itself satisfied that the position of the holder of the charge is likely to be prejudiced if no such appointment is made;

(b)   any of the events referred to in paragraphs (a) to (c) of subsection (1).

53 Mode of appointment by holder of charge

(1) The appointment of a receiver by the holder of the floating charge under section 51(1) shall be by means of an instrument subscribed in accordance with the Requirements of Writing (Scotland) Act 1995 ('the instrument of appointment'), a copy (certified in the prescribed manner to be a correct copy) whereof shall be delivered by or on behalf of the person making the appointment to the registrar of companies for registration within 7 days of its execution and shall be accompanied by a notice in the prescribed form.

(2) If any person without reasonable excuse makes default in complying with the requirements of subsection (1), he is liable to a fine and, for continued contravention, to a daily default fine.

(3) (*Repealed*)

(4) If the receiver is to be appointed by the holders of a series of secured debentures, the instrument may be executed on behalf of the holders of the floating charge by any person authorised by resolution of the debenture-holders to execute the instrument.

(5) On receipt of the certified copy of the instrument of appointment in accordance with subsection (1), the registrar shall, on payment of the prescribed fee, enter the particulars of the appointment in the register.

(6) The appointment of a person as a receiver by an instrument of appointment in accordance with subsection (1)—

(a)   is of no effect unless it is accepted by that person before the end of the business day next following that on which the instrument of appointment is received by him or on his behalf, and

(b)   subject to paragraph (a), is deemed to be made on the day on and at the time at which the instrument of appointment is so received, as evidenced by a written docquet by that person or on his behalf;

and this subsection applies to the appointment of joint receivers subject to such modifications as may be prescribed.

(7) On the appointment of a receiver under this section, the floating charge by virtue of which he was appointed attaches to the property then subject to the charge; and such attachment has effect as if the charge was a fixed security over the property to which it has attached.

Amendments—Law Reform (Miscellaneous Provisions) (Scotland) Act 1990, s 74, Sch 8, para 35, Sch 9; Requirements of Writing (Scotland) Act 1995, s 14(1), Sch 4, para 58; SI 2013/600.

54 Appointment by court

(1) Application for the appointment of a receiver by the court under section 51(2) shall be by petition to the court, which shall be served on the company.

(2) On such an application, the court shall, if it thinks fit, issue an interlocutor making the appointment of the receiver.

(3) A copy (certified by the clerk of the court to be a correct copy) of the court's interlocutor making the appointment shall be delivered by or on behalf of the petitioner to the registrar of companies for registration, accompanied by a notice in the prescribed form, within 7 days of the date of the interlocutor or such longer period as the court may allow.

If any person without reasonable excuse makes default in complying with the requirements of this subsection, he is liable to a fine and, for continued contravention, to a daily default fine.

(4) On receipt of the certified copy interlocutor in accordance with subsection (3), the registrar shall, on payment of the prescribed fee, enter the particulars of the appointment in the register.

(5) The receiver is to be regarded as having been appointed on the date of his being appointed by the court.

(6) On the appointment of a receiver under this section, the floating charge by virtue of which he was appointed attaches to the property then subject to the charge; and such attachment has effect as if the charge were a fixed security over the property to which it has attached.

(7) In making rules of court for the purposes of this section, the Court of Session shall have regard to the need for special provision for cases which appear to the court to require to be dealt with as a matter of urgency.

Amendments—SI 2013/600.

55 Power of receiver

(1) Subject to the next subsection, a receiver has in relation to such part of the property of the company as is attached by the floating charge by virtue of which he was appointed, the powers, if any, given to him by the instrument creating that charge.

(2) In addition, the receiver has under this Chapter the powers as respects that property (in so far as these are not inconsistent with any provision contained in that instrument) which are specified in Schedule 2 to this Act.

(3) Subsections (1) and (2) apply—

    (a) subject to the rights of any person who has effectually executed diligence on all or any part of the property of the company prior to the appointment of the receiver, and

    (b) subject to the rights of any person who holds over all or any part of the property of the company a fixed security or floating charge having priority over, or ranking pari passu with, the floating charge by virtue of which the receiver was appointed.

(4) A person dealing with a receiver in good faith and for value is not concerned to enquire whether the receiver is acting within his powers.

56 Precedence among receivers

(1) Where there are two or more floating charges subsisting over all or any part of the property of the company, a receiver may be appointed under this Chapter by virtue of each such charge; but a receiver appointed by, or on the application of, the holder of a floating charge having priority of ranking over any other floating charge by virtue of which a receiver has been appointed has the powers given to a receiver by section 55 and Schedule 2 to the exclusion of any other receiver.

(2) Where two or more floating charges rank with one another equally, and two or more receivers have been appointed by virtue of such charges, the receivers so appointed are deemed to have been appointed as joint receivers.

(3) Receivers appointed, or deemed to have been appointed, as joint receivers shall act jointly unless the instrument of appointment or respective instruments of appointment otherwise provide.

(4) Subject to subsection (5) below, the powers of a receiver appointed by, or on the application of, the holder of a floating charge are suspended by, and as from the date of, the appointment of a receiver by, or on the application of, the holder of a floating charge having priority of ranking over that charge to such extent as may be necessary to enable the receiver second mentioned to exercise his powers under section 55 and Schedule 2; and any powers so suspended take effect again when the floating charge having priority of ranking ceases to attach to the property then subject to the charge, whether such cessation is by virtue of section 62(6) or otherwise.

(5) The suspension of the powers of a receiver under subsection (4) does not have the effect of requiring him to release any part of the property (including any letters or documents) of the company from his control until he receives from the receiver superseding him a valid indemnity (subject to the limit of the value of such part of the property of the company as is subject to the charge by virtue of which he was appointed) in respect of any expenses, charges and liabilities he may have incurred in the performance of his functions as receiver.

(6) The suspension of the powers of a receiver under subsection (4) does not cause the floating charge by virtue of which he was appointed to cease to attach to the property to which it attached by virtue of section 53(7) or 54(6).

(7) Nothing in this section prevents the same receiver being appointed by virtue of two or more floating charges.

57 Agency and liability of receiver for contracts

(1) A receiver is deemed to be the agent of the company in relation to such property of the company as is attached by the floating charge by virtue of which he was appointed.

(1A) Without prejudice to subsection (1), a receiver is deemed to be the agent of the company in relation to any contract of employment adopted by him in the carrying out of his functions.

(2) A receiver (including a receiver whose powers are subsequently suspended under section 56) is personally liable on any contract entered into by him in the performance of his functions, except in so far as the contract otherwise provides, and, to the extent of any qualifying liability, on any contract of employment adopted by him in the carrying out of those functions.

(2A) For the purposes of subsection (2), a liability under a contract of employment is a qualifying liability if—

    (a)   it is a liability to pay a sum by way of wages or salary or contribution to an occupational pension scheme,

    (b)   it is incurred while the receiver is in office, and

(c)   it is in respect of services rendered wholly or partly after the adoption of the contract.

(2B) Where a sum payable in respect of a liability which is a qualifying liability for the purposes of subsection (2) is payable in respect of services rendered partly before and partly after the adoption of the contract, liability under that subsection shall only extend to so much of the sum as is payable in respect of services rendered after the adoption of the contract.

(2C) For the purposes of subsections (2A) and (2B)—

(a)   wages or salary payable in respect of a period of holiday or absence from work through sickness or other good cause are deemed to be wages or (as the case may be) salary in respect of services rendered in that period, and

(b)   a sum payable in lieu of holiday is deemed to be wages or (as the case may be) salary in respect of services rendered in the period by reference to which the holiday entitlement arose.

(2D) In subsection (2C)(a), the reference to wages or salary payable in respect of a period of holiday includes any sums which, if they had been paid, would have been treated for the purposes of the enactments relating to social security as earnings in respect of that period.

(3) A receiver who is personally liable by virtue of subsection (2) is entitled to be indemnified out of the property in respect of which he was appointed.

(4) Any contract entered into by or on behalf of the company prior to the appointment of a receiver continues in force (subject to its terms) notwithstanding that appointment, but the receiver does not by virtue only of his appointment incur any personal liability on any such contract.

(5) For the purposes of subsection (2), a receiver is not to be taken to have adopted a contract of employment by reason of anything done or omitted to be done within 14 days after his appointment.

(6) This section does not limit any right to indemnity which the receiver would have apart from it, nor limit his liability on contracts entered into or adopted without authority, nor confer any right to indemnity in respect of that liability.

(7) Any contract entered into by a receiver in the performance of his functions continues in force (subject to its terms) although the powers of the receiver are subsequently suspended under section 56.

Amendments—Insolvency Act 1994, s 3.

58 Remuneration of receiver

(1) The remuneration to be paid to a receiver is to be determined by agreement between the receiver and the holder of the floating charge by virtue of which he was appointed.

(2) Where the remuneration to be paid to the receiver has not been determined under subsection (1), or where it has been so determined but is

disputed by any of the persons mentioned in paragraphs (a) to (d) below, it may be fixed instead by the Auditor of the Court of Session on application made to him by—

    (a)   the receiver;

    (b)   the holder of any floating charge or fixed security over all or any part of the property of the company;

    (c)   the company; or

    (d)   the liquidator of the company.

(3) Where the receiver has been paid or has retained for his remuneration for any period before the remuneration has been fixed by the Auditor of the Court of Session under subsection (2) any amount in excess of the remuneration so fixed for that period, the receiver or his personal representatives shall account for the excess.

59 Priority of debts

(1) Where a receiver is appointed and the company is not at the time of the appointment in course of being wound up, the debts which fall under subsection (2) of this section shall be paid out of any assets coming to the hands of the receiver in priority to any claim for principal or interest by the holder of the floating charge by virtue of which the receiver was appointed.

(2) Debts falling under this subsection are preferential debts (within the meaning given by section 386 in Part XII) which, by the end of a period of 6 months after advertisement by the receiver for claims in the Edinburgh Gazette and in a newspaper circulating in the district where the company carries on business either—

    (i)   have been intimated to him, or

    (ii)   have become known to him.

(3) Any payments made under this section shall be recouped as far as may be out of the assets of the company available for payment of ordinary creditors.

60 Distribution of moneys

(1) Subject to the next section, and to the rights of any of the following categories of persons (which rights shall, except to the extent otherwise provided in any instrument, have the following order of priority), namely—

    (a)   the holder of any fixed security which is over property subject to the floating charge and which ranks prior to, or pari passu with, the floating charge;

    (b)   all persons who have effectually executed diligence on any part of the property of the company which is subject to the charge by virtue of which the receiver was appointed;

    (c)   creditors in respect of all liabilities, charges and expenses incurred by or on behalf of the receiver;

    (d)   the receiver in respect of his liabilities, expenses and remuneration, and any indemnity to which he is entitled out of the property of the company; and

(e)   the preferential creditors entitled to payment under section 59,

the receiver shall pay moneys received by him to the holder of the floating charge by virtue of which the receiver was appointed in or towards satisfaction of the debt secured by the floating charge.

(2) Any balance of moneys remaining after the provisions of subsection (1) and section 61 below have been satisfied shall be paid in accordance with their respective rights and interests to the following persons, as the case may require—

(a)   any other receiver;

(b)   the holder of a fixed security which is over property subject to the floating charge;

(c)   the company or its liquidator, as the case may be.

(3) Where any question arises as to the person entitled to a payment under this section, or where a receipt or a discharge of a security cannot be obtained in respect of any such payment, the receiver shall consign the amount of such payment in any joint stock bank of issue in Scotland in name of the Accountant of Court for behoof of the person or persons entitled thereto.

61 Disposal of interest in property

(1) Where the receiver sells or disposes, or is desirous of selling or disposing, of any property or interest in property of the company which is subject to the floating charge by virtue of which the receiver was appointed and which is—

(a)   subject to any security or interest of, or burden or encumbrance in favour of, a creditor the ranking of which is prior to, or pari passu with, or postponed to the floating charge, or

(b)   property or an interest in property affected or attached by effectual diligence executed by any person,

and the receiver is unable to obtain the consent of such creditor or, as the case may be, such person to such a sale or disposal, the receiver may apply to the court for authority to sell or dispose of the property or interest in property free of such security, interest, burden, encumbrance or diligence.

(1A) For the purposes of subsection (1) above, an inhibition which takes effect after the creation of the floating charge by virtue of which the receiver was appointed is not an effectual diligence.

(2) Subject to the next subsection, on such an application the court may, if it thinks fit, authorise the sale or disposal of the property or interest in question free of such security, interest, burden, encumbrance or diligence, and such authorisation may be on such terms or conditions as the court thinks fit.

(3) In the case of an application where a fixed security over the property or interest in question which ranks prior to the floating charge has not been met or provided for in full, the court shall not authorise the sale or disposal of the property or interest in question unless it is satisfied that the sale or

disposal would be likely to provide a more advantageous realisation of the company's assets than would otherwise be effected.

(4) It shall be a condition of an authorisation to which subsection (3) applies that—

> (a) the net proceeds of the disposal, and
> (b) where those proceeds are less than such amount as may be determined by the court to be the net amount which would be realised on a sale of the property or interest in the open market by a willing seller, such sums as may be required to make good the deficiency,

shall be applied towards discharging the sums secured by the fixed security.

(5) Where a condition imposed in pursuance of subsection (4) relates to two or more such fixed securities, that condition shall require the net proceeds of the disposal and, where paragraph (b) of that subsection applies, the sums mentioned in that paragraph to be applied towards discharging the sums secured by those fixed securities in the order of their priorities.

(6) A copy of an authorisation under subsection (2) shall, within 14 days of the granting of the authorisation, be sent by the receiver to the registrar of companies.

(7) If the receiver without reasonable excuse fails to comply with subsection (6), he is liable to a fine and, for continued contravention, to a daily default fine.

(8) Where any sale or disposal is effected in accordance with the authorisation of the court under subsection (2), the receiver shall grant to the purchaser or disponee an appropriate document of transfer or conveyance of the property or interest in question, and that document has the effect, or, where recording, intimation or registration of that document is a legal requirement for completion of title to the property or interest, then that recording, intimation or registration (as the case may be) has the effect, of—

> (a) disencumbering the property or interest of the security, interest, burden or encumbrance affecting it, and
> (b) freeing the property or interest from the diligence executed upon it.

(9) Nothing in this section prejudices the right of any creditor of the company to rank for his debt in the winding up of the company.

Amendments—Bankruptcy and Diligence etc (Scotland) Act 2007, s 155(1), (2); SI 2009/1941.

62 Cessation of appointment of receiver

(1) A receiver may be removed from office by the court under subsection (3) below and may resign his office by giving notice of his resignation in the prescribed manner to such persons as may be prescribed.

(2) A receiver shall vacate office if he ceases to be qualified to act as an insolvency practitioner in relation to the company.

(3) Subject to the next subsection, a receiver may, on application to the court by the holder of the floating charge by virtue of which he was appointed, be removed by the court on cause shown.

(4) Where at any time a receiver vacates office—

    (a)   his remuneration and any expenses properly incurred by him, and

    (b)   any indemnity to which he is entitled out of the property of the company,

shall be paid out of the property of the company which is subject to the floating charge and shall have priority as provided for in section 60(1).

(5) When a receiver ceases to act as such otherwise than by death he shall, and, when a receiver is removed by the court, the holder of the floating charge by virtue of which he was appointed shall, within 14 days of the cessation or removal (as the case may be) give the registrar of companies notice to that effect, and the registrar shall enter the notice in the register.

If the receiver or the holder of the floating charge (as the case may require) makes default in complying with the requirements of this subsection, he is liable to a fine and, for continued contravention, to a daily default fine.

(6) If by the expiry of a period of one month following upon the removal of the receiver or his ceasing to act as such no other receiver has been appointed, the floating charge by virtue of which the receiver was appointed—

    (a)   thereupon ceases to attach to the property then subject to the charge, and

    (b)   again subsists as a floating charge;

and for the purposes of calculating the period of one month under this subsection no account shall be taken of any period during which the company is in administration under Part II of this Act.

Amendments—SI 2003/2096; SI 2013/600.

63 Powers of court

(1) The court on the application of—

    (a)   the holder of a floating charge by virtue of which a receiver was appointed, or

    (b)   a receiver appointed under section 51,

may give directions to the receiver in respect of any matter arising in connection with the performance by him of his functions.

(2) Where the appointment of a person as a receiver by the holder of a floating charge is discovered to be invalid (whether by virtue of the invalidity of the instrument or otherwise), the court may order the holder of

the floating charge to indemnify the person appointed against any liability which arises solely by reason of the invalidity of the appointment.

64 Notification that receiver appointed

(1) Where a receiver has been appointed—

(a) every invoice, order for goods or services, business letter or order form (whether in hard copy, electronic or any other form) issued by or on behalf of the company or the receiver or the liquidator of the company; and

(b) all the company's websites,

must contain a statement that a receiver has been appointed.

(2) If default is made in complying with the requirements of this section, the company and any of the following persons who knowingly and wilfully authorises or permits the default, namely any officer of the company, any liquidator of the company and any receiver, is liable to a fine.

Amendments—SI 2008/1897.

65 Information to be given by receiver

(1) Where a receiver is appointed, he shall—

(a) forthwith send to the company and publish notice of his appointment, and

(b) within 28 days after his appointment, unless the court otherwise directs, send such notice to all the creditors of the company (so far as he is aware of their addresses).

(2) This section and the next do not apply in relation to the appointment of a receiver to act—

(a) with an existing receiver, or

(b) in place of a receiver who has died or ceased to act,

except that, where they apply to a receiver who dies or ceases to act before they have been fully complied with, the references in this section and the next to the receiver include (subject to subsection (3) of this section) his successor and any continuing receiver.

(3) If the company is being wound up, this section and the next apply notwithstanding that the receiver and the liquidator are the same person, but with any necessary modifications arising from that fact.

(4) If a person without reasonable excuse fails to comply with this section, he is liable to a fine and, for continued contravention, to a daily default fine.

66 Company's statement of affairs

(1) Where a receiver of a company is appointed, the receiver shall forthwith require some or all of the persons mentioned in subsection (3) below to make out and submit to him a statement in the prescribed form as to the affairs of the company.

(2) A statement submitted under this section shall be verified by affidavit by the persons required to submit it and shall show—

    (a)   particulars of the company's assets, debts and liabilities;
    (b)   the names and addresses of its creditors;
    (c)   the securities held by them respectively;
    (d)   the dates when the securities were respectively given; and
    (e)   such further or other information as may be prescribed.

(3) The persons referred to in subsection (1) are—

    (a)   those who are or have been officers of the company;
    (b)   those who have taken part in the company's formation at any time within one year before the date of the appointment of the receiver;
    (c)   those who are in the company's employment or have been in its employment within that year, and are in the receiver's opinion capable of giving the information required;
    (d)   those who are or have been within that year officers of or in the employment of a company which is, or within that year was, an officer of the company.

In this subsection 'employment' includes employment under a contract for services.

(4) Where any persons are required under this section to submit a statement of affairs to the receiver they shall do so (subject to the next subsection) before the end of the period of 21 days beginning with the day after that on which the prescribed notice of the requirement is given to them by the receiver.

(5) The receiver, if he thinks fit, may—

    (a)   at any time release a person from an obligation imposed on him under subsection (1) or (2), or
    (b)   either when giving the notice mentioned in subsection (4) or subsequently extend the period so mentioned,

and where the receiver has refused to exercise a power conferred by this subsection, the court, if it thinks fit, may exercise it.

(6) If a person without reasonable excuse fails to comply with any obligation imposed under this section, he is liable to a fine and, for continued contravention to a daily default fine.

67 Report by receiver

(1) Where a receiver is appointed under section 51, he shall within 3 months (or such longer period as the court may allow) after his appointment, send to the registrar of companies, to the holder of the floating charge by virtue of which he was appointed and to any trustees for secured creditors of the company and (so far as he is aware of their addresses) to all such creditors a report as to the following matters, namely—

    (a)   the events leading up to his appointment, so far as he is aware of them;

> (b) the disposal or proposed disposal by him of any property of the company and the carrying on or proposed carrying on by him of any business of the company;
>
> (c) the amounts of principal and interest payable to the holder of the floating charge by virtue of which he was appointed and the amounts payable to preferential creditors; and
>
> (d) the amount (if any) likely to be available for the payment of other creditors.

(2) The receiver shall also, within 3 months (or such longer period as the court may allow) after his appointment, either—

> (a) send a copy of the report (so far as he is aware of their addresses) to all unsecured creditors of the company, or
>
> (b) publish in the prescribed manner a notice stating an address to which unsecured creditors of the company should write for copies of the report to be sent to them free of charge,

and (in either case), unless the court otherwise directs, lay a copy of the report before a meeting of the company's unsecured creditors summoned for the purpose on not less than 14 days' notice.

(3) The court shall not give a direction under subsection (2) unless—

> (a) the report states the intention of the receiver to apply for the direction, and
>
> (b) a copy of the report is sent to the persons mentioned in paragraph (a) of that subsection, or a notice is published as mentioned in paragraph (b) of that subsection, not less than 14 days before the hearing of the application.

(4) Where the company has gone or goes into liquidation, the receiver—

> (a) shall, within 7 days after his compliance with subsection (1) or, if later, the nomination or appointment of the liquidator, send a copy of the report to the liquidator, and
>
> (b) where he does so within the time limited for compliance with subsection (2), is not required to comply with that subsection.

(5) A report under this section shall include a summary of the statement of affairs made out and submitted under section 66 and of his comments (if any) on it.

(6) Nothing in this section shall be taken as requiring any such report to include any information the disclosure of which would seriously prejudice the carrying out by the receiver of his functions.

(7) Section 65(2) applies for the purposes of this section also.

(8) If a person without reasonable excuse fails to comply with this section, he is liable to a fine and, for continued contravention, to a daily default fine.

(9) In this section 'secured creditor', in relation to a company, means a creditor of the company who holds in respect of his debt a security over property of the company, and 'unsecured creditor' shall be construed accordingly.

68 Committee of creditors

(1) Where a meeting of creditors is summoned under section 67, the meeting may, if it thinks fit, establish a committee ('the creditors' committee') to exercise the functions conferred on it by or under this Act.

(2) If such a committee is established, the committee may on giving not less than 7 days' notice require the receiver to attend before it at any reasonable time and furnish it with such information relating to the carrying out by him of his functions as it may reasonably require.

69 Enforcement of receiver's duty to make returns etc

(1) If any receiver—

   (a)   having made default in filing, delivering or making any return, account or other document, or in giving any notice, which a receiver is by law required to file, deliver, make or give, fails to make good the default within 14 days after the service on him of a notice requiring him to do so; or

   (b)   has, after being required at any time by the liquidator of the company so to do, failed to render proper accounts of his receipts and payments and to vouch the same and to pay over to the liquidator the amount properly payable to him,

the court may, on an application made for the purpose, make an order directing the receiver to make good the default within such time as may be specified in the order.

(2) In the case of any such default as is mentioned in subsection (1)(a), an application for the purposes of this section may be made by any member or creditor of the company or by the registrar of companies; and, in the case of any such default as is mentioned in subsection (1)(b), the application shall be made by the liquidator; and, in either case, the order may provide that all expenses of and incidental to the application shall be borne by the receiver.

(3) Nothing in this section prejudices the operation of any enactments imposing penalties on receivers in respect of any such default as is mentioned in subsection (1).

70 Interpretation for Chapter II

(1) In this Chapter, unless the contrary intention appears, the following expressions have the following meanings respectively assigned to them—

   'company' means an incorporated company (whether or not a company registered under the Companies Act 2006) which the Court of Session has jurisdiction to wind up;

   'fixed security', in relation to any property of a company, means any security, other than a floating charge or a charge having the nature of a floating charge, which on the winding up of the company in Scotland would be treated as an effective security over that property, and (without prejudice to that generality) includes a security over that property, being a heritable security within the meaning of the Conveyancing and Feudal Reform (Scotland) Act 1970;

'instrument of appointment' has the meaning given by section 53(1);

'prescribed' means prescribed by regulations made under this Chapter by the Secretary of State;

'receiver' means a receiver of such part of the property of the company as is subject to the floating charge by virtue of which he has been appointed under section 51;

'the register' has the meaning given by section 1080 of the Companies Act 2006;

'secured debenture' means a bond, debenture, debenture stock or other security which, either itself or by reference to any other instrument, creates a floating charge over all or any part of the property of the company, but does not include a security which creates no charge other than a fixed security; and

'series of secured debentures' means two or more secured debentures created as a series by the company in such a manner that the holders thereof are entitled pari passu to the benefit of the floating charge.

(2) Where a floating charge, secured debenture or series of secured debentures has been created by the company, then, except where the context otherwise requires, any reference in this Chapter to the holder of the floating charge shall—

    (a)   where the floating charge, secured debenture or series of secured debentures provides for a receiver to be appointed by any person or body, be construed as a reference to that person or body;

    (b)   where, in the case of a series of secured debentures, no such provision has been made therein but—

        (i)   there are trustees acting for the debenture-holders under and in accordance with a trust deed, be construed as a reference to those trustees, and

        (ii)   where no such trustees are acting, be construed as a reference to—

            (aa)   a majority in nominal value of those present or represented by proxy and voting at a meeting of debenture-holders at which the holders of at least one-third in nominal value of the outstanding debentures of the series are present or so represented, or

            (bb)   where no such meeting is held, the holders of at least one-half in nominal value of the outstanding debentures of the series.

(3) Any reference in this Chapter to a floating charge, secured debenture, series of secured debentures or instrument creating a charge includes, except where the context otherwise requires, a reference to that floating charge, debenture, series of debentures or instrument as varied by any instrument.

(4) References in this Chapter to the instrument by which a floating charge was created are, in the case of a floating charge created by words in a bond or other written acknowledgement, references to the bond or, as the case may be, the other written acknowledgement.

Amendments—SI 2009/1941; SI 2013/600.

71 Prescription of forms etc; regulations

(1) The notice referred to in section 62(5), and the notice referred to in section 65(1)(a) shall be in such form as may be prescribed.

(2) Any power conferred by this Chapter on the Secretary of State to make regulations is exercisable by statutory instrument; and a statutory instrument made in the exercise of the power so conferred to prescribe a fee is subject to annulment in pursuance of a resolution of either House of Parliament.

Chapter III

Receivers' Powers in Great Britain as a Whole

72 Cross-border operation of receivership provisions

(1) A receiver appointed under the law of either part of Great Britain in respect of the whole or any part of any property or undertaking of a company and in consequence of the company having created a charge which, as created, was a floating charge may exercise his powers in the other part of Great Britain so far as their exercise is not inconsistent with the law applicable there.

(2) In subsection (1) 'receiver' includes a manager and a person who is appointed both receiver and manager.

Chapter IV

Prohibition of Appointment of Administrative Receiver

72A Floating charge holder not to appoint administrative receiver

(1) The holder of a qualifying floating charge in respect of a company's property may not appoint an administrative receiver of the company.

(2) In Scotland, the holder of a qualifying floating charge in respect of a company's property may not appoint or apply to the court for the appointment of a receiver who on appointment would be an administrative receiver of property of the company.

(3) In subsections (1) and (2)—

'holder of a qualifying floating charge in respect of a company's property' has the same meaning as in paragraph 14 of Schedule B1 to this Act, and
'administrative receiver' has the meaning given by section 251.

(4) This section applies—

    (a)   to a floating charge created on or after a date appointed by the Secretary of State by order made by statutory instrument, and

> (b) in spite of any provision of an agreement or instrument which purports to empower a person to appoint an administrative receiver (by whatever name).

(5) An order under subsection (4)(a) may—

> (a) make provision which applies generally or only for a specified purpose;
> (b) make different provision for different purposes;
> (c) make transitional provision.

(6) This section is subject to the exceptions specified in sections 72B to 72GA.

Amendments—Inserted by Enterprise Act 2002, s 250(1). Amended by SI 2003/1832.

General note—On ss 72A–72H see the commentary in the General introduction to receivership preceding s 28.

72B First exception: capital market

(1) Section 72A does not prevent the appointment of an administrative receiver in pursuance of an agreement which is or forms part of a capital market arrangement if—

> (a) a party incurs or, when the agreement was entered into was expected to incur, a debt of at least £50 million under the arrangement, and
> (b) the arrangement involves the issue of a capital market investment.

(2) In subsection (1)—

> 'capital market arrangement' means an arrangement of a kind described in paragraph 1 of Schedule 2A, and
> 'capital market investment' means an investment of a kind described in paragraph 2 or 3 of that Schedule.

Amendments—Inserted by Enterprise Act 2002, s 250(1).

General note—On ss 72A–72H see the commentary in the General introduction to receivership preceding s 28.

72C Second exception: public-private partnership

(1) Section 72A does not prevent the appointment of an administrative receiver of a project company of a project which—

> (a) is a public-private partnership project, and
> (b) includes step-in rights.

(2) In this section 'public-private partnership project' means a project—

> (a) the resources for which are provided partly by one or more public bodies and partly by one or more private persons, or
> (b) which is designed wholly or mainly for the purpose of assisting a public body to discharge a function.

(3) In this section—

'step-in rights' has the meaning given by paragraph 6 of Schedule 2A, and

'project company' has the meaning given by paragraph 7 of that Schedule.

Amendments—Inserted by Enterprise Act 2002, s 250(1).

General note—On ss 72A–72H see the commentary in the General introduction to receivership preceding s 28.

72D Third exception: utilities

(1) Section 72A does not prevent the appointment of an administrative receiver of a project company of a project which—

(a)   is a utility project, and

(b)   includes step-in rights.

(2) In this section—

(a)   'utility project' means a project designed wholly or mainly for the purpose of a regulated business,

(b)   'regulated business' means a business of a kind listed in paragraph 10 of Schedule 2A,

(c)   'step-in rights' has the meaning given by paragraph 6 of that Schedule, and

(d)   'project company' has the meaning given by paragraph 7 of that Schedule.

Amendments—Inserted by Enterprise Act 2002, s 250(1).

General note—On ss 72A–72H see the commentary in the General introduction to receivership preceding s 28.

72DA Exception in respect of urban regeneration projects

(1) Section 72A does not prevent the appointment of an administrative receiver of a project company of a project which—

(a)   is designed wholly or mainly to develop land which at the commencement of the project is wholly or partly in a designated disadvantaged area outside Northern Ireland, and

(b)   includes step-in rights.

(2) In subsection (1) 'develop' means to carry out—

(a)   building operations,

(b)   any operation for the removal of substances or waste from land and the levelling of the surface of the land, or

(c)   engineering operations in connection with the activities mentioned in paragraph (a) or (b).

(3) In this section—

'building' includes any structure or erection, and any part of a building as so defined, but does not include plant and machinery comprised in a building,

'building operations' includes—

    (a)   demolition of buildings,

    (b)   filling in of trenches,

    (c)   rebuilding,

    (d)   structural alterations of, or additions to, buildings and

    (e)   other operations normally undertaken by a person carrying on business as a builder,

'designated disadvantaged area' means an area designated as a disadvantaged area under section 92 of the Finance Act 2001,

'engineering operations' includes the formation and laying out of means of access to highways,

'project company' has the meaning given by paragraph 7 of Schedule 2A,

'step-in rights' has the meaning given by paragraph 6 of that Schedule,

'substance' means any natural or artificial substance whether in solid or liquid form or in the form of a gas or vapour, and

'waste' includes any waste materials, spoil, refuse or other matter deposited on land.

Amendments—Inserted by SI 2003/1832.

General note—On ss 72A–72H see the commentary in the General introduction to receivership preceding s 28.

72E Fourth exception: project finance

(1) Section 72A does not prevent the appointment of an administrative receiver of a project company of a project which—

    (a)   is a financed project, and

    (b)   includes step-in rights.

(2) In this section—

    (a)   a project is 'financed' if under an agreement relating to the project a project company incurs, or when the agreement is entered into is expected to incur, a debt of at least £50 million for the purposes of carrying out the project,

    (b)   'project company' has the meaning given by paragraph 7 of Schedule 2A, and

    (c)   'step-in rights' has the meaning given by paragraph 6 of that Schedule.

Amendments—Inserted by Enterprise Act 2002, s 250(1).

General note—On ss 72A–72H see the commentary in the General introduction to receivership preceding s 28.

'Step-in rights'—In *Cabvision Ltd v Feetum* [2006] BCC 341 at [93] the Court of Appeal (Jonathan Parker LJ, Sir Peter Gibson and Ward LJ agreeing) identified a number of propositions regarding the meaning and scope of para 6 of Sch 2A which could be stated with 'some degree of confidence' despite the concerns expressed over the state of the drafting of the provisions.

72F Fifth exception: financial market

Section 72A does not prevent the appointment of an administrative receiver of a company by virtue of—

(a)   a market charge within the meaning of section 173 of the Companies Act 1989,

(b)   a system-charge within the meaning of the Financial Markets and Insolvency Regulations 1996,

(c)   a collateral security charge within the meaning of the Financial Markets and Insolvency (Settlement Finality) Regulations 1999.

Amendments—Inserted by Enterprise Act 2002, s 250(1).

General note—On ss 72A–72H see the commentary in the General introduction to receivership preceding s 28.

72G Sixth exception: social landlords

Section 72A does not prevent the appointment of an administrative receiver of a company which is—

(a)   a private registered provider of social housing, or

(b)   registered as a social landlord under Part I of the Housing Act 1996 or under Part 2 of the Housing (Scotland) Act 2010 (asp 17).

Amendments—Inserted by Enterprise Act 2002, s 250(1); SI 2010/866; SI 2012/700.

General note—On ss 72A–72H see the commentary in the General introduction to receivership preceding s 28.

72GA Exception in relation to protected railway companies etc

Section 72A does not prevent the appointment of an administrative receiver of—

(a)   a company holding an appointment under Chapter I of Part II of the Water Industry Act 1991,

(b)   a protected railway company within the meaning of section 59 of the Railways Act 1993 (including that section as it has effect by virtue of section 19 of the Channel Tunnel Rail Link Act 1996, or

(c)   a licence company within the meaning of section 26 of the Transport Act 2000.

Amendments—Inserted by SI 2003/1832.

General note—On ss 72A–72H see the commentary in the General introduction to receivership preceding s 28.

72H Sections 72A to 72G: supplementary

(1) Schedule 2A (which supplements sections 72B to 72G) shall have effect.

(2) The Secretary of State may by order—

(a)   insert into this Act provision creating an additional exception to section 72A(1) or (2);

(b)   provide for a provision of this Act which creates an exception to section 72A(1) or (2) to cease to have effect;

(c)   amend section 72A in consequence of provision made under paragraph (a) or (b);

(d)   amend any of sections 72B to 72G;

(e)   amend Schedule 2A.

(3) An order under subsection (2) must be made by statutory instrument.

(4) An order under subsection (2) may make—

(a)   provision which applies generally or only for a specified purpose;

(b)   different provision for different purposes;

(c)   consequential or supplementary provision;

(d)   transitional provision.

(5) An order under subsection (2)—

(a)   in the case of an order under subsection (2)(e), shall be subject to annulment in pursuance of a resolution of either House of Parliament,

(b)   in the case of an order under subsection (2)(d) varying the sum specified in section 72B(1)(a) or 72E(2)(a) (whether or not the order also makes consequential or transitional provision), shall be subject to annulment in pursuance of a resolution of either House of Parliament, and

(c)   in the case of any other order under subsection (2)(a) to (d), may not be made unless a draft has been laid before and approved by resolution of each House of Parliament.

Amendments—Inserted by Enterprise Act 2002, s 250(1).

General note—On ss 72A–72H see the commentary in the General introduction to receivership preceding s 28.

PART IV
WINDING UP OF COMPANIES REGISTERED UNDER THE COMPANIES ACTS

General comment on Part IV—This Part deals with the winding up of the vast majority of companies in England and Wales, and Scotland, namely those that are registered pursuant to the Companies Acts. The next Part (Part V) of the Act deals with the winding up of unregistered companies. This latter category covers oversea companies and other companies the liquidation of which is not dealt with in separate legislation. Some specialist companies are wound up under specific legislation, e g building societies (Building Societies Act 1986). Companies in Northern Ireland are wound up pursuant to the Companies (Northern Ireland) Order 1986, although such companies may be wound up as unregistered companies under s 221(1) if they have a principal place of business in Great Britain: *Re a Company (No 007946 of 1993)* [1994] Ch 198. Insolvent partnerships are able to be wound up as unregistered companies due to the operation of the Insolvent Partnerships Order 1994 (SI 1994/2421).

Winding up involves the administration of the affairs of a company so as to prepare it for corporate death, i e dissolution.

Chapter I

Preliminary

Introductory

73 Scheme of this Part

(1) This Part applies to the winding up of a company registered under the Companies Act 2006 in England and Wales or Scotland.

(2) The winding up may be either—

    (a)   voluntary (see Chapters 2 to 5), or

    (b)   by the court (see Chapter 6).

(3) This Chapter and Chapters 7 to 10 relate to winding up generally, except where otherwise stated.

Amendments—SI 2009/1941.

General note—The provision identifies two forms of liquidation – voluntary winding up and winding up by the court, with the latter being more usually referred to as compulsory winding up. The former is initiated by the company, and is brought about by a resolution for winding up passed by the company in general meeting (s 84(1)). If the company is solvent, the liquidator is appointed by the members and such liquidations are known as 'members' voluntary liquidations'. It might seem strange that companies that are solvent at the point of winding up are dealt with pursuant to the Insolvency Act, but it is probably efficient and convenient to have all companies that are wound up regulated by the same statute. Notwithstanding that some companies are solvent when they are wound up either voluntarily or by the court, the vast majority of companies that are liquidated each year are insolvent to varying degrees.

Compulsory liquidations are commenced by a court order. See Chapter VI of this Part.

A company—This term is not defined in the Act, but s 251 provides that 'any expression for whose interpretation provision is made by Part XXVI of the Companies Act 1985, other than an expression defined above in this section, is to be construed in accordance with that provision.' 'Company' is defined in ss 1(1) and 1171 of the Companies Act 2006 as a company formed and registered under that statute, or an existing company (s 735(1)(a)). Section 735(1)(b) provides that an existing company is a company formed and registered pursuant to the former Companies Acts, but does not include a company registered under the Joint Stock Companies Acts, the Companies Act 1862 or the Companies (Consolidation) Act 1908 in what was, when the legislation was passed, Ireland. 'The former Companies Acts' are defined to mean the Joint Stock Companies Acts, the Companies Act 1862 or the Companies (Consolidation) Act 1908, the Companies Act 1929 and the Companies Acts 1948 to 1983 (s 735(1)(c)). In relation to existing companies, s 675(1) of the Companies Act 1985 provides that in its application to existing companies the Companies Act applies just as if they had been formed and registered pursuant to Part I of the legislation. The upshot from all of this is that no matter under which legislation a company was registered, it is to be viewed in the same manner for the purposes of the Companies Act 1985, and can be wound up under the Insolvency Act as a company registered in England and Wales or Scotland.

Contributories

74 Liability as contributories of present and past members

(1) When a company is wound up, every present and past member is liable to contribute to its assets to any amount sufficient for payment of its debts

and liabilities, and the expenses of the winding up, and for the adjustment of the rights of the contributories among themselves.

(2) This is subject as follows—

(a) a past member is not liable to contribute if he has ceased to be a member for one year or more before the commencement of the winding up;

(b) a past member is not liable to contribute in respect of any debt or liability of the company contracted after he ceased to be a member;

(c) a past member is not liable to contribute, unless it appears to the court that the existing members are unable to satisfy the contributions required to be made by them;

(d) in the case of a company limited by shares, no contribution is required from any member exceeding the amount (if any) unpaid on the shares in respect of which he is liable as a present or past member;

(e) nothing in the Companies Acts or this Act invalidates any provision contained in a policy of insurance or other contract whereby the liability of individual members on the policy or contract is restricted, or whereby the funds of the company are alone made liable in respect of the policy or contract;

(f) a sum due to any member of the company (in his character of a member) by way of dividends, profits or otherwise is not deemed to be a debt of the company, payable to that member in a case of competition between himself and any other creditor not a member of the company, but any such sum may be taken into account for the purpose of the final adjustment of the rights of the contributories among themselves.

(3) In the case of a company limited by guarantee, no contribution is required from any member exceeding the amount undertaken to be contributed by him to the company's assets in the event of its being wound up; but if it is a company with a share capital, every member of it is liable (in addition to the amount so undertaken to be contributed to the assets), to contribute to the extent of any sums unpaid on shares held by him.

Amendments—SI 2009/1941.

Contributory—'Contributory' is a term that is defined in s 79. It involves any member or past member who is liable to contribute to the assets of a company on winding up. This seems to indicate that one is only a contributory if at the point of winding up, one is liable to make payment to the company. However, this would mean that a fully paid up shareholder was not a contributory, and yet it has been settled for many years that such a shareholder is a contributory: *Re Anglesea Colliery Co* (1866) 1 Ch App 555; *Re Phoenix Oil & Transport Co* [1958] Ch 560. A person or company who owes a debt to the company is not a contributory (*Re European Society Arbitration Acts* (1878) 8 Ch D 679 at 708), but treated as owing a debt to the company. The law acknowledges that there is a distinction to be made between the status of being a contributory, and a liability to contribute to the assets. Being a contributory means essentially that one is part of the membership of the company, and this status can exist before winding up, while having a liability to contribute only occurs when the winding up commences. There are two kinds of persons who, though not registered as members of the company, are, according to ss 81 and 82, to be regarded as contributories, namely the personal representatives of a deceased contributory and the trustee of a bankrupt contributory. See the comments accompanying ss 81 and 82, which specifically deal with these kinds of contributories.

The sums that are recovered from contributories are deposited in a fund that will be used to repay creditors (*Webb v Whiffin* (1872) LR 5 HL 711), provided that there are sufficient funds following the payment of the costs and expenses of the liquidation.

Section 74 first provides that all present and past members are liable to contribute to its assets to the extent of paying off debts and liabilities and meeting the expenses of winding up, as well as providing for the adjustment of rights amongst the contributories. Then the section states that certain persons are effectively exempt from payment or their contribution is limited. This restriction on liability recognises the concept of limited liability, namely that members are only liable in a limited liability company to pay what is unpaid on their shares.

The liquidator is charged with the job of recovering contributions from the members in winding up. First, the liquidator will ascertain or identify those who are liable to contribute, and this is achieved by what is known as 'settling the list of contributories'. The obligation is, according to s 148, something that falls to the court, but r 4.196 provides that the liquidator is to discharge this court duty as a delegate of the court. After the completion of the settling, the liquidator makes and enforces calls on as many of those persons listed (to the full extent of their liability) as is necessary in order to discharge the debts of the company or to adjust the rights of contributories. Adjustment occurs in order to have losses evenly distributed amongst all the members. See the comments attaching to s 148.

If the articles permit shares to be paid for in instalments, this arrangement will cease if liquidation intervenes before the date on which the instalments become due and payable: *Re Cordova Union Gold Co* [1891] 2 Ch 580.

Past members—Their liability is limited in various ways by s 74(2)(a)–(c). The obligation of past members to contribute is further restricted to the amount left unpaid by the present members on the shares that they once held.

Past members are those who have ceased for any reason, perhaps because of death, transfer, or forfeiture, to be members: *Re National Bank of Wales; Taylor, Phillips and Rickards' Case* [1897] 1 Ch 298 at 307.

In the character of a member—According to s 74(2)(f), in circumstances where a member is liable to pay a sum to the liquidator, then that member is unable to prove in the liquidation, in competition with other creditors who are not members of the company, for any amount owed to the member 'in his character of a member'. This phrase has caused problems for the courts. Sums due 'in his character of a member' will include sums owed as dividends, profits or otherwise, but they will not include claims that might have depended on membership of the company, and where membership was not the foundation of the cause of action: *Soden v British and Commonwealth Holdings plc* [1998] AC 298, [1997] 2 WLR 206, [1997] BCC 952, HL. So damages that emanate from a claim against the company for misrepresentation after the purchase of shares from a third party is not a claim in the character of a member (*Soden*). In delivering the leading speech in *Soden*, Lord Browne-Wilkinson said ([1997] BCC 952 at 956) that:

> '[I]n the absence of any contrary indication sums due to a member "in his character of a member" are only those sums the right to which is based by way of cause of action on the statutory contract [between the members and the company and provided by s 14 of the Companies Act 1985 (now s 33 of the Companies Act 2006)].'

However, where members purchased the shares by subscription from the company and had a claim for misrepresentation, the claim would be one in the character of a member: *Re Addlestone Linoleum Co* (1887) 37 Ch D 191; *Webb Distributors (Aust) Pty Ltd v The State of Victoria* (1993) 11 ACLC 1178, (1993) 11 ACSR 731, Aust HC. The advent of s 111A of the Companies Act 1985 (now Companies Act 2006, s 655 when it comes into force on 1 October 2009 (Companies Act 2006 (Commencement No 8, Transitional Provisions and Savings) Order 2008)) might well mean that these cases would now be decided differently on the relevant point.

According to *Soden*, loans made by a member to the company, sums due to a member under a contract for the sale of goods by the member to the company, and arrears of remuneration due to a member in his or her capacity as a director would not be affected by s 74(2)(f), so members with these sorts of claims could line up for payment with the creditors of the company: [1997] BCC 952 at 955. *Soden* provides that there was not a 'members come last' principle in a winding up, for a member with an independent claim is in no worse position than a creditor; it is only in considering the rights of a member *qua* member that his or her rights are placed last.

Any amount owed in the character of a member may be taken into account for the purpose of the final adjustment of the rights of contributories amongst each other.

75   (*Repealed*)

76 Liability of past directors and shareholders

(1) This section applies where a company is being wound up and—

    (a)   it has under Chapter 5 of Part 18 of the Companies Act 2006 (acquisition by limited company of its own shares: redemption or purchase by private company out of capital) made a payment out of capital in respect of the redemption or purchase of any of its own shares (the payment being referred to below as 'the relevant payment'), and

    (b)   the aggregate amount of the company's assets and the amounts paid by way of contribution to its assets (apart from this section) is not sufficient for payment of its debts and liabilities, and the expenses of the winding up.

(2) If the winding up commenced within one year of the date on which the relevant payment was made, then—

    (a)   the person from whom the shares were redeemed or purchased, and

    (b)   the directors who signed the statement made in accordance with section 714(1) to (3) of the Companies Act 2006 for purposes of the redemption or purchase (except a director who shows that he had reasonable grounds for forming the opinion set out in the statement),

are, so as to enable that insufficiency to be met, liable to contribute to the following extent to the company's assets.

(3) A person from whom any of the shares were redeemed or purchased is liable to contribute an amount not exceeding so much of the relevant payment as was made by the company in respect of his shares; and the directors are jointly and severally liable with that person to contribute that amount.

(4) A person who has contributed any amount to the assets in pursuance of this section may apply to the court for an order directing any other person jointly and severally liable in respect of that amount to pay him such amount as the court thinks just and equitable.

(5) Section 74 does not apply in relation to liability accruing by virtue of this section.

(6) (*Repealed*)

Amendments—SI 2009/1941; SI 2011/1265.

General note—Here the legislature is concerned that the company will have been divested of capital, which could have been used to pay creditors, in order to pay the seller of the shares. Hence, it is a measure that is designed to protect the unsecured creditors, who will have recourse to the company's capital on liquidation.

77 Limited company formerly unlimited

(1) This section applies in the case of a company being wound up which was at some former time registered as unlimited but has re-registered as a limited company.

(2) Notwithstanding section 74(2)(a) above, a past member of the company who was a member of it at the time of re-registration, if the winding up commences within the period of 3 years beginning with the day on which the company was re-registered, is liable to contribute to the assets of the company in respect of debts and liabilities contracted before that time.

(3) If no persons who were members of the company at that time are existing members of it, a person who at that time was a present or past member is liable to contribute as above notwithstanding that the existing members have satisfied the contributions required to be made by them.

This applies subject to section 74(2)(a) above and to subsection (2) of this section, but notwithstanding section 74(2)(c).

(4) Notwithstanding section 74(2)(d) and (3), there is no limit on the amount which a person who, at that time, was a past or present member of the company is liable to contribute as above.

Amendments—SI 2009/1941.

General note—This constitutes a qualification to the restriction on the liability of a past member in s 74(2)(a). In the circumstance set out in the section a past member can be liable for up to three years since he or she ceased to be a member.

78 Unlimited company formerly limited

(1) This section applies in the case of a company being wound up which was at some former time registered as limited but has been re-registered as unlimited.

(2) A person who, at the time when the application for the company to be re-registered was lodged, was a past member of the company and did not after that again become a member of it is not liable to contribute to the assets of the company more than he would have been liable to contribute had the company not been re-registered.

Amendments—SI 2009/1941.

General note—Where the change of a company's status is from public company to unlimited company, pursuant to s 102 of the Companies Act 2006, then past members at the time of the change (who did not again become members of the company) are protected in that they are not liable to contribute more than what they would have been liable to contribute had the company not changed status.

79 Meaning of 'contributory'

(1) In this Act the expression 'contributory' means every person liable to contribute to the assets of a company in the event of its being wound up, and f with respect to the personal representatives, to the heirs and legatees or the purposes of all proceedings for determining, and all proceedings prior to the final determination of, the persons who are to be deemed contributories, includes any person alleged to be a contributory.

(2) The reference in subsection (1) to persons liable to contribute to the assets does not include a person so liable by virtue of a declaration by the court under section 213 (imputed responsibility for company's fraudulent trading) or section 214 (wrongful trading) in Chapter X of this Part.

(3) A reference in a company's articles to a contributory does not (unless the context requires) include a person who is a contributory only by virtue of section 76.

Amendments—SI 2009/1941.

General note—See the notes accompanying s 74.

80 Nature of contributory's liability

The liability of a contributory creates a debt (in England and Wales in the nature of an ordinary contract debt) accruing due from him at the time when his liability commenced, but payable at the times when calls are made for enforcing the liability.

Amendments—SI 2009/1941.

General note—If a person is liable as a contributory, then this creates a debt, a specialty debt (in England and Wales) owed to the company, and payable at the time when calls are made for the enforcing of the liability. The limitation period for specialty debts is 12 years.

81 Contributories in case of death of a member

(1) If a contributory dies either before or after he has been placed on the list of contributories, his personal representatives, and the heirs and legatees of heritage of his heritable estate in Scotland, are liable in a due course of administration to contribute to the assets of the company in discharge of his liability and are contributories accordingly.

(2) Where the personal representatives are placed on the list of contributories, the heirs or legatees of heritage need not be added, but they may be added as and when the court thinks fit.

(3) If in England and Wales the personal representatives make default in paying any money ordered to be paid by them, proceedings may be taken for administering the estate of the deceased contributory and for compelling payment out of it of the money due.

General note—This provision (and s 82) constitutes an exception to the rule that the group of contributories consists of members present or past.

The executors of the estate of a deceased member do not become personally liable unless they agree to be registered as members: *Re City of Glasgow Bank; Buchan's Case* (1879) 4 App Cas 583; *Re Cheshire Banking Co; Duff's Executors Case* (1885) 32 Ch D 301.

It might be thought that, as the death of a member terminates his or her membership of the company (*Permanent Trustee Co v Palmer* (1929) 42 CLR 277 at 283), the estate of a member dying before winding up would be liable only as a past member. But it is settled that, while the name of the deceased member remains on the register of members, the deceased's estate is a member of the company and so the liability is that of a present member: *Re Agriculturist Cattle Insurance Co; Baird's Case* (1870) 5 Ch App 725 at 735.

82 Effect of contributory's bankruptcy

(1) The following applies if a contributory becomes bankrupt, either before or after he has been placed on the list of contributories.

(2) His trustee in bankruptcy represents him for all purposes of the winding up, and is a contributory accordingly.

(3) The trustee may be called on to admit to proof against the bankrupt's estate, or otherwise allow to be paid out of the bankrupt's assets in due course of law, any money due from the bankrupt in respect of his liability to contribute to the company's assets.

(4) There may be proved against the bankrupt's estate the estimated value of his liability to future calls as well as calls already made.

General note—If the trustee in bankruptcy of a member is registered in place of the bankrupt member, the trustee becomes personally liable unless he or she disclaims the shares. It is unusual for the trustee to be registered if the shares are of no value. In a liquidation it is the trustee and not the bankrupt who is the contributory. Hence, the trustee represents the bankrupt for all the purposes of winding up and the liquidator is entitled to prove against the bankrupt estate.

83 Companies registered but not formed under the Companies Act 2006

(1) The following applies in the event of a company being wound up which is registered but not formed under the Companies Act 2006.

(2) Every person is a contributory, in respect of the company's debts and liabilities contracted before registration, who is liable—

(a) to pay, or contribute to the payment of, any debt or liability so contracted, or

(b) to pay, or contribute to the payment of, any sum for the adjustment of the rights of the members among themselves in respect of any such debt or liability, or

(c) to pay, or contribute to the amount of, the expenses of winding up the company, so far as relates to the debts or liabilities above-mentioned.

(3) Every contributory is liable to contribute to the assets of the company, in the course of the winding up, all sums due from him in respect of any such liability.

(4) In the event of the death, bankruptcy or insolvency of any contributory, provisions of this Act, with respect to the personal representatives, to the

heirs and legatees of heritage of the heritable estate in Scotland of deceased contributories and to the trustees of bankrupt or insolvent contributories respectively, apply.

Amendments—SI 2009/1941.

General note—This relates to companies covered by s 1040 of the Companies Act 2006, namely those that have not been registered under the Companies Act, but which are entitled to become so registered. An example is a company formed pursuant to an Act of Parliament (s 1040(1)(b)).

Chapter II

Voluntary Winding Up (Introductory and General) Resolutions for, and Commencement of, Voluntary Winding Up

84 Circumstances in which company may be wound up voluntarily

(1) A company may be wound up voluntarily—

    (a)   when the period (if any) fixed for the duration of the company by the articles expires, or the event (if any) occurs, on the occurrence of which the articles provide that the company is to be dissolved, and the company in general meeting has passed a resolution requiring it to be wound up voluntarily;

    (b)   if the company resolves by special resolution that it be wound up voluntarily;

    (c)   *(repealed)*

(2) In this Act the expression 'a resolution for voluntary winding up' means a resolution passed under either of the paragraphs of subsection (1).

(2A) Before a company passes a resolution for voluntary winding up it must give written notice of the resolution to the holder of any qualifying floating charge to which section 72A applies.

(2B) Where notice is given under subsection (2A) a resolution for voluntary winding up may be passed only—

    (a)   after the end of the period of five business days beginning with the day on which the notice was given, or

    (b)   if the person to whom the notice was given has consented in writing to the passing of the resolution.

(3) Chapter 3 of Part 3 of the Companies Act 2006 (resoloutions affecting a company's constitution) applies to a resoloution under paragraph (a) of subsection (1) as well as a special resoloution under paragraph (b).

(4) This section has effect subject to section 43 of the Commonhold and Leasehold Reform Act 2002.

Amendments—Commonhold and Leasehold Reform Act 2002, s 68, Sch 5, para 6; SI 2003/2096; SI 2007/2194.

General note—Voluntary liquidation manifests the policy of allowing the creditors and contributories in winding up to manage what essentially are their own affairs: *Re Wear Engine Works Co* (1875) 10 Ch App 188 at 191. As the section provides, no application to court is necessary in order to initiate this form of winding up, and the liquidator is appointed by, and answerable to, the creditors or contributories who exercise some degree of control over what he or she does in administering the winding up. There is no court involvement in the liquidation process except on certain occasions when court involvement is necessary, such as when: there is a need for the determination of questions arising in winding up and an application is made under s 112(1); some disagreement occurs amongst those persons who are interested in the winding up; or the liquidator has commenced proceedings in order to recover property disposed of, or obtained improperly, the commencement of the winding up.

A voluntary winding up commences with the passing by the members of one of the three kinds of resolutions set out in s 84(1). The usual company law rules regulating the calling and conduct of company meetings apply in relation to matters such as notice, quorum, voting and procedure.

Members may call the meeting, but usually it is convened by the board of directors, and is valid only if issued with the authority of the directors: *Re Haycraft Gold Reduction Co* [1900] 2 Ch 230; *Re State of Wyoming Syndicate* [1901] 2 Ch 431.

With private companies, a resolution may be passed without the need for a general meeting being held. To do this all the members who are entitled to vote on the resolution must sign a document containing a statement that they support the resolution that is stated in the document (Companies Act 2006, ss 288, 289 (and note the procedure for circulation of the document under ss 290–295)).

The resolution sometimes includes a further resolution to appoint a liquidator. If not, then a separate resolution can be passed after the resolution to wind up has been passed, and this second resolution can be passed without notice: *Bethell v Trench Tubeless Tyres Co* [1900] 1 Ch 408.

A resolution to wind up cannot be passed during the time in which a company is in administration (Sch B1, para 42(2)). Also, a resolution to wind up cannot be passed during the period between the presentation of an application for an administration order and either the making of an administration order or dismissal of the application (Sch B1, para 44(5)). The same paragraph covers the situation where an administration order has been made, but has not taken effect.

Australasian authority provides that the members are not able to revoke a resolution to wind up (*Ross v PJ Heringa Pty Ltd* [1970] NZLR 170; *Dean-Willcocks v Payee (Buildings) Pty Ltd* (unreported, NSW Sup Ct, Young J, 1 September 1994)); application for a court order terminating the winding up would have to be made by the company: *Dean-Willcocks*.

See A Keay *McPherson's Law of Company Liquidation* (Sweet and Maxwell, 3rd edn, 2013) at 42–45 for further explanation of the practice and procedure prior to, and, at the meeting.

The section is subject to the Commonhold and Leasehold Reform Act 2002 and this provides in s 43 for the winding up of commonhold associations (private companies limited by guarantee).

Resolution—An ordinary resolution merely requires a simple majority of the members attending the meeting for it to be passed. Special resolutions require a majority of not less than three-fourths (Companies Act 2006, s 283). 14 days' notice of the meeting is required (Companies Act 2006, s 307(1), (2)) (21 days for an annual general meeting of public companies) for whatever resolution is required at the meeting. The members can agree to a shorter notice period (Companies Act 2006, s 307(4)).

Copy of resolution filed—The liquidator is obliged to file with the registrar of companies a copy of the resolution within 15 days, or else the liquidator is liable for a fine (Companies Act 2006, s 30(1), (2), (4)).

For a detailed and integrated discussion of voluntary liquidation, see A Keay *McPherson's Law of Company Liquidation* (Sweet and Maxwell, 3rd edn, 2013) at 42–45.

85 Notice of resolution to wind up

(1) When a company has passed a resolution for voluntary winding up, it shall, within 14 days after the passing of the resolution, give notice of the resolution by advertisement in the Gazette.

(2) If default is made in complying with this section, the company and every officer of it who is in default is liable to a fine and, for continued contravention, to a daily default fine.

For purposes of this subsection the liquidator is deemed an officer of the company.

86 Commencement of winding up

A voluntary winding up is deemed to commence at the time of the passing of the resolution for voluntary winding up.

General note—The date of the commencement of a winding up is a critical point, as a number of provisions of the Act refer to this time. For instance, the date of commencement terminates the power of the company to dispose of its property (s 127), it fixes the status and liability of contributories, and it deprives creditors of their ordinary remedies against the company (s 128(1)). The time of the commencement in voluntary winding up is to be contrasted with the commencement of a compulsory winding up. In the latter case, while a company is not actually in winding up until a court order is made to that effect, a winding up is nevertheless deemed to have commenced at the time of the presentation of the petition, if an order is made subsequently (s 129(2)).

If an administrator of a company should move from administration to creditors' winding up under para 83 of Sch B1, then the commencement date under s 86 will be, according to para 83, as if the reference to the time of the passing of the resolution for voluntary winding up were a reference to the beginning of the date of registration of the notice under para 83(3), that is when the administrator sends a notice to the registrar of companies that para 83 is to apply.

Consequences of resolution to wind up

87 Effect on business and status of company

(1) In case of a voluntary winding up, the company shall from the commencement of the winding up cease to carry on its business, except so far as may be required for its beneficial winding up.

(2) However, the corporate state and corporate powers of the company, notwithstanding anything to the contrary in its articles, continue until the company is dissolved.

General note—This provision details an important effect that the advent of liquidation has on the company and clarifies the fact that the company continues to exist as a corporate entity.

Ceasing business—A liquidator in a voluntary liquidation is empowered to carry on the company's business so far as is necessary for its beneficial disposal: *Re Great Eastern Electric Co Ltd* [1941] 1 Ch 241. A person wishing to impugn the decision to carry on the business on the basis that it is not beneficial for the company has the onus of proving it: *The Hire Purchase Furnishing Co Ltd v Richens* (1887) 20 QBD 387, CA.

Corporate state and powers—A voluntary liquidation does not affect the corporate personality of the company (*Reigate v Union Manufacturing Co* [1918] 1 KB 592 at 606), which remains a separate entity from the members who comprise it (*Ditcham v Miller* (1931) 100 LJPC 177), and the company's powers are not limited by the fact that it has gone into liquidation: *Re Woking Urban District Council Act* [1914] 1 Ch 300.

88 Avoidance of share transfers etc after winding-up resolution

Any transfer of shares, not being a transfer made to or with the sanction of the liquidator, and any alteration in the status of the company's members, made after the commencement of a voluntary winding up, is void.

General note—This provision is aimed at preventing shareholders from evading liability as contributories by transferring, after winding up has commenced, shares to someone who is impecunious (*Rudge v Bowman* (1865) LR 3 QB 659 at 695; *Re National Bank of Wales* [1896] 2 Ch 851 at 857, 858), but courts have, on occasions, even refused to approve transfers in the case of solvent companies, for instance where it was done for speculative purposes: *Re Onward Building Society* [1891] 2 QB 463.

The transferring of shares is not the only way that a shareholder might seek to evade liability to contribute, and so Parliament probably had this in mind when it provided in this section that no alteration in the status of a member of the company should be valid if it occurs after winding up has commenced.

If agreement was reached in relation to a transfer of shares before winding up, and the transfer has not been registered by the time of winding up because of the failure of the directors of the company to act, the court will order the liquidator to register it: *Re Joint Stock Discount Co* (1869) 4 Ch App 768.

Sanction of the liquidator—If the liquidator refuses to sanction the transfer, an application could be made to the court under s 112.

Declaration of solvency

89 Statutory declaration of solvency

(1) Where it is proposed to wind up a company voluntarily, the directors (or, in the case of a company having more than two directors, the majority of them) may at a directors' meeting make a statutory declaration to the effect that they have made a full inquiry into the company's affairs and that, having done so, they have formed the opinion that the company will be able to pay its debts in full, together with interest at the official rate (as defined in section 251), within such period, not exceeding 12 months from the commencement of the winding up, as may be specified in the declaration.

(2) Such a declaration by the directors has no effect for purposes of this Act unless—

(a) it is made within the 5 weeks immediately preceding the date of the passing of the resolution for winding up, or on that date but before the passing of the resolution, and

(b) it embodies a statement of the company's assets and liabilities as at the latest practicable date before the making of the declaration.

(3) The declaration shall be delivered to the registrar of companies before the expiration of 15 days immediately following the date on which the resolution for winding up is passed.

(4) A director making a declaration under this section without having reasonable grounds for the opinion that the company will be able to pay its debts in full, together with interest at the official rate, within the period specified is liable to imprisonment or a fine, or both.

(5) If the company is wound up in pursuance of a resolution passed within 5 weeks after the making of the declaration, and its debts (together with interest at the official rate) are not paid or provided for in full within the period specified, it is to be presumed (unless the contrary is shown) that the director did not have reasonable grounds for his opinion.

(6) If a declaration required by subsection (3) to be delivered to the registrar is not so delivered within the time prescribed by that subsection, the company and every officer in default is liable to a fine and, for continued contravention, to a daily default fine.

General note—This is a critical section in the voluntary winding-up process. Unless a declaration of solvency can be made by the directors, the liquidation of a company must proceed as a creditors' voluntary liquidation; for a members' voluntary liquidation of a company, there must be this declaration of solvency. The two forms of voluntary liquidation are referred to in s 90.

The section deters directors from acting imprudently in making a declaration. First, s 89(5) provides that they have the burden of overcoming a presumption that they did not have reasonable grounds for the opinion that is expressed in the statement. Second, civil and criminal consequences might flow from a breach of the section.

A statutory declaration—While the declaration is often referred to as a declaration of solvency, the directors do not have to state that the company is, or will be, solvent. The directors must, in the declaration, state when, in their view, the company's debts, in a period not exceeding 12 months, will be paid in full. The declaration is only effective if made either within five weeks immediately preceding the date of the passing of the resolution for voluntary winding up, or on that date, but before the passing of the resolution, and it includes a statement of the company's assets and liabilities as at the latest practicable date before the declaration is made. The time period set for the compilation of the statement is designed, obviously, to ensure that the statement shows, as much as possible, the current state of the company's affairs.

If, after a statement has been made, errors and omissions are found, it will not prevent the statement from being a statement within the terms of the section: *De Courcy v Clement* [1971] Ch 693, [1971] 1 All ER 681; *Re New Millenium Experience Co Ltd* [2003] EWHC 1823, [2004] 1 BCLC 19 at [107], [111].

If the company is the subject of a petition for winding up, following a voluntary winding up it is then that the statement is likely to be scrutinised, as in *Re Leading Guides International Ltd (in liquidation)* [1998] 1 BCLC 620.

Penalty—Directors who breach the section may be subject to a civil penalty (having to pay the company's debts) and a criminal penalty (a fine or imprisonment or both). The fine is unlimited and the term of imprisonment could be anything up to two years if the prosecution is tried on indictment (Sch 10): see the comments of Harman J in *Re Surplus Properties (Huddersfield) Ltd* [1984] 1 BCLC 89 at 91.

90 Distinction between 'members' and 'creditors' voluntary winding up

A winding up in the case of which a directors' statutory declaration under section 89 has been made is a 'members' voluntary winding up'; and a winding up in the case of which such a declaration has not been made is a 'creditors' voluntary winding up'.

General note—This sets out the distinction between the two forms of voluntary liquidation. Sections 91–96 cover members' voluntary liquidation and ss 97–106 address creditors' voluntary liquidation. Then ss 107–116 are provisions that apply to both forms.

Chapter III

Members' Voluntary Winding Up

91 Appointment of liquidator

(1) In a members' voluntary winding up, the company in general meeting shall appoint one or more liquidators for the purpose of winding up the company's affairs and distributing its assets.

(2) On the appointment of a liquidator all the powers of the directors cease, except so far as the company in general meeting or the liquidator sanctions their continuance.

General note—This provision deals exclusively with members' voluntary winding up. Creditors do not become involved in this form of winding up because they have no financial interest in the outcome of the liquidation, as the company will be able to pay all its debts in full (provided that the statutory declaration in s 89 is correct).

See A Keay *McPherson's Law of Company Liquidation* (Sweet and Maxwell, 3rd edn, 2013) at 40–45 for further discussion concerning the members' voluntary winding up process.

Appointing a liquidator—The members' meeting appoints the liquidator (who consents) by resolution. This appointment can be part of the resolution to wind up. If this does not occur, then the liquidator can be appointed by ordinary resolution, and such a resolution can be put and passed without notice after the resolution to wind up has been passed: *Bethell v Trench Tubeless Tyres Co* [1900] 1 Ch 408. The members may appoint more than one liquidator (*Bethell*), although this would be unusual. Where more than one liquidator is appointed, the resolution should state whether the liquidators are to exercise their powers and duties jointly or separately (see s 231(2)). Anyone who is nominated as a liquidator must be qualified to act as an insolvency practitioner pursuant to ss 388 and 389.

Directors' powers—While the powers of directors terminate on winding up, the office of a director does not come to an end, because the Act permits directors to exercise certain powers in some circumstances after the commencement of winding up. There is judicial authority that supports such a view (*Midland Counties District Bank Ltd v Attwood* [1905] 1 Ch 357), as does s 114.

92 Power to fill vacancy in office of liquidator

(1) If a vacancy occurs by death, resignation or otherwise in the office of liquidator appointed by the company, the company in general meeting may, subject to any arrangement with its creditors, fill the vacancy.

(2) For that purpose a general meeting may be convened by any contributory or, if there were more liquidators than one, by the continuing liquidators.

(3) The meeting shall be held in manner provided by this Act or by the articles, or in such manner as may, on application by any contributory or by the continuing liquidators, be determined by the court.

Arrangement with the creditors—Given the fact that this is a members' voluntary liquidation, it is hard to see why the reference to the creditors has any relevance.

This Act—The reference to 'this Act' is undoubtedly meant to be a reference to the companies legislation, and not to the Insolvency Act, as the latter makes no provision for the convening of meetings. Part 13 of the Companies Act 2006 now covers the convening of meetings for companies.

92A Progress report to company at year's end (England and Wales)

(1) Subject to sections 96 and 102, in the event of the winding up of a company registered in England and Wales continuing for more than one year, the liquidator must—

    (a)   for each prescribed period produce a progress report relating to the prescribed matters; and

    (b)   within such period commencing with the end of the period referred to in paragraph (a) as may be prescribed send a copy of the progress report to—

        (i)   the members of the company; and

        (ii)   such other persons as may be prescribed.

(2) A liquidator who fails to comply with this section is liable to a fine.

Amendments—Inserted by SI 2010/18.

93 General company meeting at each year's end (Scotland)

(1) Subject to sections 96 and 102, in the event of the winding up of a company registered in Scotland continuing for more than one year, the liquidator shall summon a general meeting of the company at the end of the first year from the commencement of the winding up, and of each succeeding year, or at the first convenient date within 3 months from the end of the year or such longer period as the Secretary of State may allow.

(2) The liquidator shall lay before the meeting an account of his acts and dealings, and of the conduct of the winding up, during the preceding year.

(3) If the liquidator fails to comply with this section, he is liable to a fine.

Amendments—SI 2010/18.

94 Final meeting prior to dissolution

(1) As soon as the company's affairs are fully wound up, the liquidator shall make up an account of the winding up, showing how it has been conducted and the company's property has been disposed of, and thereupon shall call a general meeting of the company for the purpose of laying before it the account, and giving an explanation of it.

(2) The meeting shall be called by advertisement in the Gazette, specifying its time, place and object and published at least one month before the meeting.

(3) Within one week after the meeting, the liquidator shall send to the registrar of companies a copy of the account, and shall make a return to him of the holding of the meeting and of its date.

(4) If the copy is not sent or the return is not made in accordance with subsection (3), the liquidator is liable to a fine and, for continued contravention, to a daily default fine.

(5) If a quorum is not present at the meeting, the liquidator shall, in lieu of the return mentioned above, make a return that the meeting was duly

summoned and that no quorum was present; and upon such a return being made, the provisions of subsection (3) as to making of the return are deemed complied with.

(6) If the liquidator fails to call a general meeting of the company as required by subsection (1), he is liable to a fine.

General note—At the end of three months from the registration of the return of the liquidator's final account and return stating that the final meeting has been held, the company is automatically dissolved (s 201(1), (2)). See the comments accompanying s 201, which deals with dissolution.

Section 94 is essentially the same as s 106, which covers creditors' voluntary liquidations. See the notes accompanying that section.

See r 4.126.

95 Effect of company's insolvency

(1) This section applies where the liquidator is of the opinion that the company will be unable to pay its debts in full (together with interest at the official rate) within the period stated in the directors' declaration under section 89.

(2) In the case of the winding up of a company registered in Scotland, the liquidator shall—

(a) summon a meeting of creditors for a day not later than the 28th day after the day on which he formed that opinion;

(b) send notices of the creditors' meeting to the creditors by post not less than 7 days before the day on which that meeting is to be held;

(c) cause notice of the creditors' meeting to be advertised once in the Gazette and once at least in 2 newspapers circulating in the relevant locality (that is to say the locality in which the company's principal place of business in Great Britain was situated during the relevant period); and

(d) during the period before the day on which the creditors' meeting is to be held, furnish creditors free of charge with such information concerning the affairs of the company as they may reasonably require;

and the notice of the creditors' meeting shall state the duty imposed by paragraph (d) above.

(2A) In the case of the winding up of a company registered in England and Wales, the liquidator—

(a) shall summon a meeting of creditors for a day not later than the 28th day after the day on which he formed that opinion;

(b) shall send notices of the creditors' meeting to the creditors not less than 7 days before the day on which that meeting is to be held;

(c) shall cause notice of the creditors' meeting to be advertised once in the Gazette;

(d) may cause notice of the meeting to be advertised in such other manner as he thinks fit; and

(e)   shall during the period before the day on which the creditors' meeting is to be held, furnish creditors free of charge with such information concerning the affairs of the company as they may reasonably require;

and the notice of the creditors' meeting shall state the duty imposed by paragraph (e) above.

(3) The liquidator shall also—

(a)   make out a statement in the prescribed form as to the affairs of the company;
(b)   lay that statement before the creditors' meeting; and
(c)   attend and preside at that meeting.

(4) The statement as to the affairs of the company shall show—

(a)   particulars of the company's assets, debts and liabilities:
(b)   the names and addresses of the company's creditors;
(c)   the securities held by them respectively;
(d)   the dates when the securities were respectively given; and
(e)   such further or other information as may be prescribed.

(4A) The statement as to the affairs of the company shall be verified by the liquidator—

(a)   in the case of a winding up of a company registered in England and Wales, by a statement of truth; and
(b)   in the case of a winding up of a company registered in Scotland, by affidavit.

(5) Where the company's principal place of business in Great Britain was situated in different localities at different times during the relevant period, the duty imposed by subsection (2)(c) applies separately in relation to each of those localities.

(6) Where the company had no place of business in Great Britain during the relevant period, references in subsections (2)(c) and (5) to the company's principal place of business in Great Britain are replaced by references to its registered office.

(7) In this section 'the relevant period' means the period of 6 months immediately preceding the day on which were sent the notices summoning the company meeting at which it was resolved that the company be wound up voluntarily.

(8) If the liquidator without reasonable excuse fails to comply with this section, he is liable to a fine.

Amendments—SI 2009/864; SI 2010/18.

General note—If the situation provided for in this section occurs, then from the time of the creditors' meeting held under the section, the Insolvency Act applies as if the statutory declaration had not been made and the creditors' meeting and the company meeting at which it was resolved that the company be wound up were the meetings referred to in s 98, and hence the liquidation proceeds as a creditors' voluntary winding up (s 96). Any appointment made or liquidation committee established by a members' meeting held under s 95 is deemed to have been made or established by a meeting held in accordance with s 98 (s 102).

The details that the liquidator has to supply to creditors is equivalent to what the directors have to provide in their statement of affairs prepared for the creditors' meeting under s 99.

In general see rr 4.51, 52(1), 53A, 56.

Creditors' meeting—In making a decision about the fixing of a venue for the meeting the liquidator must consider the convenience of creditors (r 4.60(1)). The meeting must commence between 10.00 am and 4.00 pm on a business day, unless the court orders otherwise (r 4.60(2)).

Statement of affairs—See rr 4.34–4.34A, 4.38.

96 Conversion to creditors' voluntary winding up

As from the day on which the creditors' meeting is held under section 95, this Act has effect as if—

(a) the directors' declaration under section 89 had not been made; and

(b) the creditors' meeting and the company meeting at which it was resolved that the company be wound up voluntarily were the meetings mentioned in section 98 in the next Chapter;

and accordingly the winding up becomes a creditors' voluntary winding up.

General note—This section makes it clear that the liquidation that began as a members' voluntary is converted into a creditors' voluntary liquidation. All that has been done up until and including the creditors' meeting referred in to in s 95 are deemed equivalent to initiating a creditors' voluntary liquidation. See the comments in relation to s 95.

The creditors at their meeting are entitled to change liquidators if they so wish.

Chapter IV

Creditors' Voluntary Winding Up

97 Application of this Chapter

(1) Subject as follows, this Chapter applies in relation to a creditors' voluntary winding up.

(2) Sections 98 and 99 do not apply where, under section 96 in Chapter III, a members' voluntary winding up has become a creditors' voluntary winding up.

General note—A creditors' voluntary liquidation is regarded as a collective proceeding that is covered by the EC Regulation on Insolvency Proceedings (Art 1(1)). Annexes A and B to the EC Regulation both refer to creditors' voluntary winding up in relation to the UK.

Pursuant to Art 3 of the EC Regulation on Insolvency Proceedings, a foreign company that has its centre of main interests in the UK may be wound up by way of a creditors' voluntary winding up: *Re TXU Europe German Finance BV* [2005] BCC 90.

See the comments under the heading of 'Voluntary Liquidation' in relation to s 221.

98 Meeting of creditors

(1) In the case of the winding up of a company registered in Scotland, the company shall—

(a)   cause a meeting of its creditors to be summoned for a day not later than the 14th day after the day on which there is to be held the company meeting at which the resolution for voluntary winding up is to be proposed;

(b)   cause the notices of the creditors' meeting to be sent by post to the creditors not less than 7 days before the day on which that meeting is to be held; and

(c)   cause notice of the creditors' meeting to be advertised once in the Gazette and once at least in two newspapers circulating in the relevant locality (that is to say the locality in which the company's principal place of business in Great Britain was situated during the relevant period).

(1A) In the case of the winding up of a company registered in England and Wales, the company—

(a)   shall cause a meeting of its creditors to be summoned for a day not later than the 14th day after the day on which there is to be held the company meeting at which the resolution for voluntary winding up is to be proposed;

(b)   shall cause the notices of the creditors' meeting to be sent to the creditors not less than 7 days before the day on which that meeting is to be held;

(c)   shall cause notice of the creditors' meeting to be advertised once in the Gazette; and

(d)   may cause notice of the meeting to be advertised in such other manner as the directors think fit.

(2) The notice of the creditors' meeting shall state either—

(a)   the name and address of a person qualified to act as an insolvency practitioner in relation to the company who, during the period before the day on which that meeting is to be held, will furnish creditors free of charge with such information concerning the company's affairs as they may reasonably require; or

(b)   a place in the relevant locality where, on the two business days falling next before the day on which that meeting is to be held, a list of the names and addresses of the company's creditors will be available for inspection free of charge.

(3) Where the company's principal place of business in Great Britain was situated in different localities at different times during the relevant period, the duties imposed by subsections (1)(c) and (2)(b) above apply separately in relation to each of those localities.

(4) Where the company had no place of business in Great Britain during the relevant period, references in subsection (1)(c) and (3) to the company's principal place of business in Great Britain are replaced by references to its registered office.

(5) In this section 'the relevant period' means the period of 6 months immediately preceding the day on which were sent the notices summoning the company meeting at which it was resolved that the company be wound up voluntarily.

(6) If the company without reasonable excuse fails to comply with subsection (1), (1A) or (2), it is guilty of an offence and liable to a fine.

Amendments—SI 2009/864; SI 2010/18.

General note—The meeting of creditors will follow a members' meeting that has resolved that the company wind up and where the directors have not made a statutory declaration referred to in s 89. Many of the provisions in this section are identical to s 95. This is to be expected, as s 95 is the instrument which is used to provide for the conversion of a members' voluntary liquidation into a creditors' voluntary liquidation.

For a resolution at the creditors' meeting to be passed, a majority, according to value, of the creditors' present and voting, in person or by proxy, must be in favour (r 4.63(1)).

The costs associated with the convening of the meeting of creditors may be made out of the company's assets before or after the commencement of winding up (r 4.62(1); see r 4.62(2)–(4)).

Notice to creditors—It has been made clear by a revised version of Statement of Insolvency Practice 8 (issued by the Association of Business Recovery Professionals) that seven clear days' notice needs to be given to creditors, and that this means that the date of the sending of the notice and the date of the meeting cannot be taken into account in the calculation of the seven days; this is consistent with the Civil Practice Rules (CPR, r 2.8(2), (3)), which are incorporated by r 12.9(1) of the Insolvency Rules. See Lincoln, Donnelly and Briggs 'Notice of the Section 98 Creditors' Meeting' (2002) 15 *Insolvency Intelligence* 36.

The failure to notify a creditor concerning the meeting may invalidate the meeting unless the court otherwise orders: see *FV Saxton & Sons Ltd v R Miles (Confectioners) Ltd* [1983] 2 All ER 1025.

The meeting, while it does not have to be held for up to 14 days from the time of the members' meeting, is often held on the same day, perhaps being scheduled for an hour to two after the expected completion time for the members' meeting.

See rr 4.51, 4.52(1), 4.53, 4.53A, 4.56, 4.62.

99 Directors to lay statement of affairs before creditors

(1) The directors of the company shall—

(a) make out a statement in the prescribed form as to the affairs of the company;

(b) cause that statement to be laid before the creditors' meeting under section 98; and

(c) appoint one of their number to preside at that meeting; and it is the duty of the director so appointed to attend the meeting and preside over it.

(2) The statement as to the affairs of the company shall show—

(a) particulars of the company's assets, debts and liabilities;

(b) the names and addresses of the company's creditors;

(c) the securities held by them respectively;

(d) the dates when the securities were respectively given; and

(e) such further or other information as may by prescribed.

(2A) The statement as to the affairs of the company shall be verified by some or all of the directors—

(a) in the case of a winding up of a company registered in England and Wales, by a statement of truth; and

(b) in the case of a winding up of a company registered in Scotland, by affidavit.

(3) If—

    (a)   the directors without reasonable excuse fail to comply with subsection (1), (2) or (2A); or

    (b)   any director without reasonable excuse fails to comply with subsection (1), so far as requiring him to attend and preside at the creditors' meeting,

the directors are or (as the case may be) the director is guilty of an offence and liable to a fine.

Amendments—SI 2010/18.

General note—In circumstances where a liquidator has been nominated at a members' meeting prior to the holding of the creditors' meeting under s 98, the directors are required to provide the liquidator with a copy of the statement of affairs (r 4.34A).

If the correct procedure is not adopted as far as the convening of the creditors' meeting is concerned, then the liquidator, within seven days of the date on which he or she was nominated as liquidator, or whenever he or she first becomes aware of the default (whichever is the later), is required to apply to the court for directions as to how the default can be remedied (s 166(5)).

At the meeting of creditors, the director who is presiding at the meeting or another person who is aware of the company's affairs will present a written or oral report that will update the statement of affairs, which has already been prepared, by indicating any material transactions affecting the company and occurring between the date of the making of the statement and the date of the meeting (r 4.53B(1)).

If a liquidator was previously nominated by the members, then he or she must attend the meeting of creditors and report on any exercise of the liquidator's powers during the period between the members' meeting and the creditors' meeting (s 166(4)).

Director presiding—If the director, who is nominated by the company's board to attend the creditors' meeting and preside at it, is absent, then it appears that the persons who are entitled to attend the meeting are able to appoint someone to preside: *Re Salcombe Hotel Development Co Ltd* (1989) 5 BCC 807.

Statement of affairs—See rr 4.34, 4.34A, 4.38.

100 Appointment of liquidator

(1) The creditors and the company at their respective meetings mentioned in section 98 may nominate a person to be liquidator for the purpose of winding up the company's affairs and distributing its assets.

(2) The liquidator shall be the person nominated by the creditors or, where no person has been so nominated, the person (if any) nominated by the company.

(3) In the case of different persons being nominated, any director, member or creditor of the company may, within 7 days after the date on which the nomination was made by the creditors, apply to the court for an order either—

    (a)   directing that the person nominated as liquidator by the company shall be liquidator instead of or jointly with the person nominated by the creditors, or

    (b)   appointing some other person to be liquidator instead of the person nominated by the creditors.

General note—The meeting of creditors may nominate a person(s) to act as liquidator. It is likely that in some cases, particularly where the person nominated, effectively, by the directors of the insolvent company to act as liquidator, is not to the liking of the creditors and so the creditors will appoint. This is especially the case if it is likely that the liquidator will need to investigate the conduct of the directors and there is concern that the liquidator is too close to the directors: see *Re Palmer Marine Surveys Ltd* [1986] BCLC 106. This, however, is not as likely now since the introduction in the Act of a strict regime for the appointment of insolvency practitioners. If the person nominated by the creditors is different from the nominee of the members, the creditors' nomination prevails over the members' nomination, although any director, member or creditor may apply to court, within seven days of the nomination of a liquidator by the creditors' meeting, for a direction either that the company's nominee shall be liquidator either jointly with or instead of the person nominated by the creditors, or appointing someone else as liquidator instead of the person nominated by the creditors. See r 4.63.

Once the position of liquidator is determined, any subsequent vacancies in the office of liquidator may be filled by the creditors (s 104).

Anyone who is nominated as a liquidator must be qualified to act as an insolvency practitioner pursuant to ss 388 and 389.

101 Appointment of liquidation committee

(1) The creditors at the meeting to be held under section 98 or at any subsequent meeting may, if they think fit, appoint a committee ('the liquidation committee') of not more than 5 persons to exercise the functions conferred on it by or under this Act.

(2) If such a committee is appointed, the company may, either at the meeting at which the resolution for voluntary winding up is passed or at any time subsequently in general meeting, appoint such number of persons as they think fit to act as members of the committee, not exceeding 5.

(3) However, the creditors may, if they think fit, resolve that all or any of the persons so appointed by the company ought not to be members of the liquidation committee; and if the creditors so resolve—

  (a) the persons mentioned in the resolution are not then, unless the court otherwise directs, qualified to act as members of the committee; and

  (b) on any application to the court under this provision the court may, if it thinks fit, appoint other persons to act as such members in place of the persons mentioned in the resolution.

(4) In Scotland, the liquidation committee has, in addition to the powers and duties conferred and imposed on it by this Act, such of the powers and duties of commissioners on a bankrupt estate as may be conferred and imposed on liquidation committees by the rules.

General note—The liquidation committee is designed to enable the creditors to have some control over the administration of the liquidation. It also can be a body from which the liquidator can seek advice and gauge the opinions of some of the major creditors. The equivalent provision for compulsory liquidations is s 141.

It has been held in Australia that if it is clear that creditors will not receive full payment from the winding up, then providing that all other matters are equal all members of the committee should represent creditors, but if all creditors will be paid in full, then contributories should have fair representation on the committee: *Re James; In re Cowra Processors Pty Ltd* (1995) 15 ACLC 1582.

In a creditors' voluntary winding up, the committee must have three members before it can be established (r 4.152(2)).

See rr 4.151–172A and the notes accompanying those rules.

See the notes accompanying s 141.

See A Keay *McPherson's Law of Company Liquidation* (Sweet and Maxwell, 3rd edn, 2013) at 500–512 for a detailed discussion of the liquidation committee.

102 Creditors' meeting where winding up converted under s 96

Where, in the case of a winding up which was, under section 96 in Chapter III, converted to a creditors' voluntary winding up, a creditors' meeting is held in accordance with section 95, any appointment made or committee established by that meeting is deemed to have been made or established by a meeting held in accordance with section 98 in this Chapter.

103 Cesser of directors' powers

On the appointment of a liquidator, all the powers of the directors cease, except so far as the liquidation committee (or, if there is no such committee, the creditors) sanction their continuance.

General note—See the note under 'Directors' powers' in relation to s 91.

104 Vacancy in office of liquidator

If a vacancy occurs, by death, resignation or otherwise, in the office of a liquidator (other than a liquidator appointed by, or by the direction of, the court), the creditors may fill the vacancy.

General note—Where there is a need to fill a vacancy, a meeting of creditors may be convened by any creditor, or where there was more than one liquidator the meeting may be convened by the liquidator(s) who intend(s) to continue in office (r 4.101A).

104A Progress report to company and creditors at year's end (England and Wales)

(1) If the winding up of a company registered in England and Wales continues for more than one year, the liquidator must—

    (a)   for each prescribed period produce a progress report relating to the prescribed matters; and

    (b)   within such period commencing with the end of the period referred to in paragraph (a) as may be prescribed send a copy of the progress report to—

        (i)   the members and creditors of the company; and

        (ii) such other persons as may be prescribed.

(2) A liquidator who fails to comply with this section is liable to a fine.

Amendments—Inserted by SI 2010/18.

105 Meetings of company and creditors at each year's end (Scotland)

(1) If the winding up of a company registered in Scotland continues for more than one year, the liquidator shall summon a general meeting of the company and a meeting of the creditors at the end of the first year from the

commencement of the winding up, and of each succeeding year, or at the first convenient date within 3 months from the end of the year or such longer period as the Secretary of State may allow.

(2) The liquidator shall lay before each of the meetings an account of his acts and dealings and of the conduct of the winding up during the preceding year.

(3) If the liquidator fails to comply with this section, he is liable to a fine.

(4) Where under section 96 a members' voluntary winding up has become a creditors' voluntary winding up, and the creditors' meeting under section 95 is held 3 months or less before the end of the first year from the commencement of the winding up, the liquidator is not required by this section to summon a meeting of creditors at the end of that year.

Amendments—SI 2010/18.

General note—This is equivalent to the meetings prescribed by s 93 for members' voluntary windings up. In this latter case only a report to members has to be given.

Creditors' meeting—No meeting of creditors is required to be held in a liquidation that has converted from a members' to a creditors' voluntary liquidation where the s 95 meeting was held three months or less before the end of the first year from the commencement of the winding up. To require a meeting could well be pointless and would incur unnecessary costs.

106 Final meeting prior to dissolution

(1) As soon as the company's affairs are fully wound up, the liquidator shall make up an account of the winding up, showing how it has been conducted and the company's property has been disposed of, and thereupon shall call a general meeting of the company and a meeting of the creditors for the purpose of laying the account before the meetings and giving an explanation of it.

(2) Each such meeting shall be called by advertisement in the Gazette specifying the time, place and object of the meeting, and published at least one month before it.

(3) Within one week after the date of the meetings (or, if they are not held on the same date, after the date of the later one) the liquidator shall send to the registrar of companies a copy of the account, and shall make a return to him of the holding of the meetings and of their dates.

(4) If the copy is not sent or the return is not made in accordance with subsection (3), the liquidator is liable to a fine and, for continued contravention, to a daily default fine.

(5) However, if a quorum is not present at either such meeting, the liquidator shall, in lieu of the return required by subsection (3), make a return that the meeting was duly summoned and that no quorum was present; and upon such return being made the provisions of that subsection as to the making of the return are, in respect of that meeting, deemed complied with.

(6) If the liquidator fails to call a general meeting of the company or a meeting of the creditors as required by this section, he is liable to a fine.

General note—The provision is, excepting the need here for a creditors' meeting, the same as s 94. See r 4.126 and the notes relating to s 94.

The affairs are fully wound up—It has been held that a company's affairs are able to be regarded as fully wound up in situations where there is property still retained by the liquidator, but all that can be done has been done: *Re London & Caledonian Marine Insurance Co* (1879) 11 Ch D 140 at 143; *Re Wilmott Trading Ltd (in liquidation) (No 1 and 2)*; sub nom *Henry v Environmental Agency (No 2)* [1999] 2 BCLC 541, [2000] BCC 321 (the continued holding of a waste management licence).

See r 4.126.

Chapter V

Provisions Applying to Both Kinds of Voluntary Winding Up

107 Distribution of company's property

Subject to the provisions of this Act as to preferential payments, the company's property in a voluntary winding up shall on the winding up be applied in satisfaction of the company's liabilities pari passu and, subject to that application, shall (unless the articles otherwise provide) be distributed among the members according to their rights and interests in the company.

General note—This provision embraces what is often regarded as the most fundamental principle of insolvency law, namely the pari passu principle (*Re Western Welsh International System Buildings Ltd* (1985) 1 BCC 99, 296 at 99, 297). The principle can be traced back to the bankruptcy statute of 1570 (13 Eliz c 7).

The implementation of the pari passu principle is made subject to the payment of preferential payments, which includes the costs and expenses of winding up (s 115) and preferential debts covered in s 386 and Sch 6. Besides such payments, the pari passu principle is pushed aside and made subject to other arrangements, such as set-off. The reason for permitting set-off in liquidations and bankruptcy is 'to do substantial justice between the parties, where a debt is really due from the debtor to his estate' (*Forster v Wilson* (1843) 12 M & W 191 at 204, 152 ER 1165 at 1171). See *Stein v Blake* [1993] BCLC 1478, [1993] BCC 587. See also notes to rule 4.90.

In distributing company funds a liquidator will normally apply the funds generally in the following way:

- costs and expenses of winding up (s 115);
- preferential debts (s 175(1), ss 386, 387 and Sch 6);
- any preferential charge on goods distrained that arises pursuant to s 176(3);
- general body of ordinary unsecured creditors;
- post-liquidation interest on debts (s 189);
- deferred creditors – mentioned in s 74(2)(f);
- any balance is divided amongst the contributories pursuant to the memorandum and articles.

Because of the many exceptions to the pari passu rule, demonstrated, in part, by the above hierarchy, it is highly questionable whether the rule is as important as many assert. However, when it comes to case authority, the courts do focus on the rule and many have maintained the fundamental importance of it to insolvency law (e g *Re HIH Casualty and General Insurance Ltd* [2005] EWHC 2125 (Ch)); *Re Courts plc* [2008] EWHC 2339 (Ch); *Re Nortel GmbH* [2011] EWCA Civ 1124; *Revenue and Customs Commissioners v Football League Ltd* [2012] EWHC 1372 (Ch)). The rule effectively only applies to the general body of unsecured creditors who have no right to preferential treatment. But having said, that there might be other exceptions, such as set-off, which will also affect the application of the rule as far as the general unsecured creditors are concerned.

Of course, a company that is in liquidation might be subject to a floating charge. The question that has arisen in this context is whether a liquidator is entitled to pay liquidation expenses from the property subject to the charge before paying the preferential debts. Except where a receiver has been appointed over the assets covered by a floating charge and had made distributions to the chargeholder before the advent of winding up, the law was, until recently, that a liquidator was able to have recourse to the assets subject to floating charges, whether the charge crystallised by reason of, and immediately after the commencement of winding up, or before the commencement of winding up: *Re Barleycorn Enterprises Ltd* [1970] Ch 465 at 474, CA; *Re Portbase (Clothing) Ltd* [1993] Ch 388, [1993] BCC 96; *Re Leyland DAF Ltd* [2002] 1 BCLC 571, CA. But in *Buchler v Talbot* [2004] UKHL 9, [2004] 2 AC 298, [2004] 2 WLR 582, [2004] 1 BCLC 281, a decision of the House of Lords when hearing an appeal in the *Leyland DAF* litigation, it was held that this previous position was, in fact, incorrect. Their Lordships stated that liquidation expenses are not to be paid out of assets subject to the charge. It was wrong to permit a liquidator to make such an incursion into the chargeholder's rights. Their Lordships noted that where a company is in both administrative receivership and liquidation, its assets are comprised in two different funds. One fund involved some assets that were subject to a floating charge and the other fund involved assets that were just subject to the liquidation. Generally each fund bears its own costs and, as the chargeholder has no interest in the liquidation, he or she should not have to contribute towards the liquidation expenses (at [30] and [31]). See R Mokal 'Liquidation Expenses and Floating Charges – The Separate Funds Fallacy' [2004] LMCLQ 387; H Rajak 'Liquidation Expenses Versus a Claim Secured by a Floating Charge' (2005) 18 *Insolvency Intelligence* 97.

The Government has now overturned the decision in *Buchler* by legislation. Section 176ZA was introduced through the Companies Act 2006 (s 1282) and came into force on 6 April 2008, together with some new rules. The amendment does not have retrospective effect. See s 176ZA and rr 4.218A–4.218E, as well as the notes accompanying the section and the rules.

If the liquidator does not pay the preferential debts, a receiver acting for the chargeholder will be required to pay out those debts before making distributions to the chargeholder (s 40).

Preferential debts are now not as important a concern as they once were. Since the corporate insolvency provisions of the Enterprise Act 2002 became operational from 15 September 2003, the main preferential debts are likely to be the wages and leave entitlements of the employees of the company. Previously, the Crown was entitled to claim certain debts owed to it as preferential (e g VAT payments) and these often constituted large sums that had to be paid before the floating chargeholder and the unsecured creditors were paid.

Attempts have been made from time to time to circumvent the statutory order set out above. But English courts have generally been set against such action: *Re Buckingham International plc (No 2)* [1998] BCC 943, [1998] 2 BCLC 369. They have, for the most part, frowned on debt subordination schemes, where one debtor seeks, other than through security-taking, to push himself or herself into a priority position on the basis that it is against public policy to contract out of the pari passu rule: see *British Eagle International Air Lines Ltd v Compagnie Nationale Air France* [1975] 1 WLR 758. Yet in *Re Maxwell Communications Corporation plc (No 3)* [1993] BCC 369, Vinelott J recognised several policy matters which favoured refraining from preventing the contracting out of the statutory scheme by way of subordination agreement. His Lordship favoured permitting a liquidator to distribute according to an agreement entered into before liquidation whereby it is agreed, for some reason, that an unsecured creditor's debt ranks ahead of other unsecured creditors, providing that to do so would not adversely affect any creditor not a party to the agreement, ie creditors not involved in the subordination agreement would receive less under that agreement than would have been received if distributions had been made according to the statutory scheme. Recently in *International Air Transport Association v Ansett Australia Holdings Ltd* [2008] HCA 3, [2008] BPIR 57 the Australian High Court considered the clearing house rules that were the subject of the *British Eagle* decision. For further discussion, see E Ferran 'Recent Developments in Unsecured Debt Subordination' in B A K Rider (ed) *The Realm of Company Law* (Kluwer Law International, 1998).

Anti-deprivation—The notion that it is contrary to public policy to contract out of the pari passu principle overlaps with the anti-deprivation rule, both of which are sub-rules of the general rule that parties are not permitted to contract out of the insolvency legislation: *Belmont Park Investments Pty Ltd v BNY Corporate Trustee Services Pty Ltd* [2011] UKSC 38, [2011] BPIR 1223. The anti-deprivation rule is aimed at preventing attempts to withdraw assets from the creditors in an insolvency regime such as liquidation so as to reduce the size of the insolvent estate. Such action would, of course, reduce the dividends received by creditors. The rule only applies where there is a deliberate intention to evade the insolvency laws: *Belmont Park* at [78]–[79].There is some overlap with the pari passu principle, but it is separate from it and aimed at a different mischief (*Belmont Park* at [1]). It applies only if the deprivation is triggered by an insolvency proceeding, and the deprivation must be of an asset of the debtor which would otherwise be available to creditors (*Revenue and Customs Commissioners v Football League Ltd* [2012] EWHC 1372 (Ch) at [67]). The Court of Appeal in *Lomas v JFB Firth Rixson Inc* [2012] EWCA Civ 419 stated that: 'The anti-deprivation principle therefore protects the value of the estate from attempts to evade the insolvency laws and, as a consequence, facilitates the application of the pari passu rule. But their areas of operation are distinct and it is clear that the pari passu rule is only engaged in respect of assets of the estate as at the commencement of the bankruptcy or liquidation' (at [97]). Pari passu deals with the situation where the assets which form the insolvent estate have been identified, and it ensures that the assets identified are distributed according to the statutory scheme.

To be void a provision in a contract had to be interpreted as a deliberate attempt to evade the insolvency laws, although the intention did not have to be subjective. However, contractual provisions which are commercially justifiable may be upheld even if they did offend the anti-deprivation rule (*Lomas v JFB Firth Rixson Inc* [2012] EWCA Civ 419). If it were established that the contract was entered into because of commercial reasons and not to evade the insolvency laws, that would be taken into account in determining whether there had been a breach of the rule. The rule does not apply to commercial transactions entered into in good faith where it was not the predominant or one of the main purposes of the parties to deprive creditors of a company's property on liquidation: *Belmont Park Investments Pty Ltd v BNY Corporate Trustee Services Pty Ltd* at [75], [102], [104]. See, R Calnan, 'Anti-deprivation: a missed opportunity' (2011) 9 JIBFL 531; R Cole, 'Anti-deprivation: a rule of 'purgatorial complexity' (2011) CRI 149 (Oct); T Cleary, 'Perpetuating Uncertainty: The Anti-Deprivation Principle and Contractual Rights in the Post-Lehman World' (2011) 20 IRR 185.

Distributed among the members—After all the property of the company has been got in and realised, and there has been a distribution to creditors so that all the debts and liabilities, including the costs of winding up, have been paid or provided for, the liquidator may proceed to distribute any surplus among the members of the company. The rights of sharing in the surplus may be prescribed in the company's constitution, but if not then the distribution will be on the basis of equality. To do all of this the liquidator may have to adjust the rights of the contributories inter se, and this will be done by making calls on those who have paid less on their shares than other members in order to ensure that losses are evenly distributed among all the members of the company.

See A Keay *McPherson's Law of Company Liquidation* (Sweet and Maxwell, 3rd edn, 2013), chs 13 and 14.

108 Appointment or removal of liquidator by the court

(1) If from any cause whatever there is no liquidator acting, the court may appoint a liquidator.

(2) The court may, on cause shown, remove a liquidator and appoint another.

General note—The provision entitles a court to do two things: appoint a liquidator where none is acting; and remove a liquidator. The former can also be done by the members in a members' voluntary liquidation (s 92) or the creditors in a creditors' voluntary liquidation (s 104). The latter can also be done, in a creditors' voluntary liquidation, by a general meeting of the creditors (s 171(2)(b)) and, in a members' voluntary winding up, by the general meeting of the company (ie the members) (s 171(2)(a)).

It seems a little strange that the court is given the power to remove liquidators in voluntary liquidations by both s 108 and s 171. The difference between the two provisions is that only the former sets out any reason, namely there has to be 'cause shown'. It is, however, unlikely that a court would remove under s 171 unless a cause was shown. Therefore, one wonders why two provisions should continue to exist.

No liquidator acting—It can be said that there is no liquidator acting in the situation where the liquidator is not performing his or her function: *Clements v Udal* [2001] BCC 658, [2002] 2 BCLC 606, [2001] BPIR 454.

Appoint a liquidator—If a liquidator has been appointed under this section, then a meeting of the creditors (in a creditors' voluntary) or a meeting of members (in a members' voluntary) is to be summoned for the purpose of replacing the liquidator only if he or she thinks fit or the court so directs (s 171(3)). Alternatively, a meeting may be summoned if the meeting is requested in accordance with the Rules, in the case of a members' voluntary, by members representing not less than one half of the total voting rights of all the members who have, at the date of the request, a right to vote at the meeting and, in the case of a creditors' voluntary, by not less than one half in value of the company's creditors (s 171(3)).

In cases involving the withdrawal of a liquidator's authority to act, which terminates the liquidator's office automatically, the Secretary of State for Trade and Industry (now Business Enterprise and Regulatory Reform) has been permitted to apply for the appointment of a new liquidator: *Re Bridgend Goldsmiths Ltd* [1995] 2 BCLC 208.

Where appropriate, courts are able to appoint additional liquidators on a temporary basis: *Clements v Udal* [2001] BCC 658, [2002] 2 BCLC 606, [2001] BPIR 454.

Removal—An application to the court for removal is to be in accordance with Form 4.39 (r 4.120(1)). The court, if it thinks that no sufficient cause is shown for the application to remove, may dismiss it, but this is not to be done unless the applicant has had the chance to attend court for an ex parte hearing of which seven days' notice has been given (r 4.120(2)). See r 4.120.

Where a person is aggrieved by a decision which the liquidator has taken, he or she should apply pursuant to s 112 for a review of the decision, rather than seeking removal of the liquidator.

Applications should not be made ex parte, except in circumstances where either the need for relief was so urgent that it was not possible to notify the defendant of the proposed application or the kind of relief sought meant that it was inappropriate to notify because that would risk making any relief granted nugatory (*Clements v Udal* [2001] BCC 658, [2002] 2 BCLC 606, [2001] BPIR 454).

A court will not remove a liquidator simply because it disagrees with a decision which he or she has taken: *Re Shruth Ltd* [2005] EWHC 1293 (Ch), [2005] BPIR 1455, [2006] 1 BCLC 294 at [40].

On cause shown—The equivalent provision for a compulsory liquidation is said to be s 172(2) (*Re Sankey Furniture Ltd* [1995] 2 BCLC 594 at 597), although this latter provision is worded differently and includes no reference to 'on cause shown'. Notwithstanding this, r 4.119(2), together with past case law, indicates that the same criterion applies, ie that a cause must be shown for removal to be ordered.

The words of the section are very wide and it is not appropriate either to limit the cause for which removal is the correct remedy (*Re Keypak Homecare Ltd* (1987) 3 BCC 558 at 564) or to lay down the circumstances that would establish the grounds for removal (*AMP Enterprises Ltd v Hoffman*; sub nom *AMP Music Box Enterprises Ltd v Hoffman* [2002] EWHC 1899 (Ch), [2002] BCC 996, [2003] 1 BCLC 319, [2003] BPIR 11): and see *Re Buildlead Ltd (No 2)* [2004] EWHC 2443 (Ch), [2004] BPIR 1139, [2005] BCC 138. Simply, the applicant must establish good grounds for the removal: *AMP Enterprises Ltd v Hoffman*. The difficult task for a court is to effect a balance between the requirement for liquidators to be efficient, vigorous and unbiased in their conduct of liquidations, as against the fact that courts must be careful before they remove liquidators who have generally been effective and honest: *AMP Enterprises Ltd v Hoffman*; *Re Buildlead Ltd (No 2)* [2004] EWHC 2443 (Ch), [2004] BPIR 1139, [2005] BCC 138.

It is not necessary for an applicant for a removal to establish misconduct or personal unfitness on the part of the liquidator, or that he or she has a personal grievance against the liquidator. Cause can be that there is an unavoidable interruption in the ability of the liquidator to do his or her job (*Re Parkdawn Ltd* (unreported) 15 June 1993, per Harman J; *Re Sankey Furniture Ltd* [1995] 2 BCLC 594 at 602), such as where the liquidator is experiencing ill health: *Re Sankey Furniture Ltd*. Courts have to take into account all the circumstances: *Re Marseilles Extension Railway and Land Co* (1867) LR 4 Eq 692. In an Australian decision, the Queensland Supreme Court ordered removal because the liquidator had given personal advice to the directors at a conference that occurred before liquidation: *Re Club Superstores Ltd* (1993) 10 ACSR 730. The advice included advising on the effect of a winding up on the interests of the directors, and this raised the possibility of a conflict, even though the advice was given without charge and was delivered with no ulterior or improper motives.

It appears that if a court is satisfied on the evidence before it that it is against the interest of the liquidation, and this includes all those who have some interest in the company being liquidated, that a liquidator should remain in post, then the court has the power to remove the liquidator: *Re Adam Eyton Ltd* (1887) 36 Ch D 299; *Re Edennote Ltd* [1996] 2 BCLC 389; *Re Pinstripe Farming Co Ltd* [1996] BCC 913. Clearly, the courts are not limited in what they consider, and it is wrong for a court to seek to limit or define the kind of cause which is required for removal: *Re Keypak Homecare Ltd* (1987) 3 BCC 558. In some cases it may well be appropriate to remove a liquidator even though there is nothing that can be said against him or her as an individual (*Re Adam Eyton Ltd*), or where no particular breaches are identified: *Re Buildlead Ltd (No 2)* [2004] EWHC 2443 (Ch), [2004] BPIR 1139, [2005] BCC 138. For instance, a liquidator might be removed, and replaced, if he or she resides and practices a considerable distance from where the company operated and where its offices and facilities are to be found, because of the additional expense and inconvenience that this might precipitate for the winding up: *Northbuild Constructions Pty Ltd v ACN 103 753 484 Pty Ltd* [2008] QSC 182 (Qld S Ct). Liquidators may be removed for unfitness on the basis of their personal standing (although private immorality is not sufficient for removal: *Re Urmston Grange Steam Ship Co* (1901) 17 TLR 553); their personal conduct (such as relations with the directors); or in the conduct of the particular liquidation (*Re Keypak Homecare Ltd* at 564). Liquidators have, in removing a liquidator, taken into account the fact that a considerable number of creditors are opposed to the liquidator remaining in office (*Re Adam Eyton Ltd*), or the fact that the creditors have lost faith in the liquidator, and this loss of faith is reasonable in the circumstances: *Re Edennote Ltd* [1996] 2 BCLC 389, CA; *Re Buildlead Ltd (No 2)*. But the wishes of creditors are certainly not decisive (*Re Mercantile Finance & Agency Co* (1894) 13 NZLR 472; *Re Edennote Ltd* [1996] 2 BCLC 389 at 398), as removal is a very serious matter for the liquidator and that fact requires to be taken into consideration so as to be fair to the liquidator: *Re Adam Eyton & Co* (1887) 36 Ch D 299 at 306. Thus, the courts will have regard to the impact of removal of a liquidator on his or her professional standing and reputation (*Re Edennote Ltd* at 398), but will not refrain from ordering removal just because such an action would redound to the point of discrediting the liquidator: *AMP Enterprises Ltd v Hoffman*; sub nom *AMP Music Box Enterprises Ltd v Hoffman* [2002] EWHC 1899 (Ch), [2002] BCC 996, [2003] 1 BCLC 319, [2003] BPIR 11. But even if removal may lead to the discredit of a liquidator, courts should not fail to remove in appropriate cases (*AMP Enterprises Ltd v Hoffman*). Notwithstanding this, removal of a professional is not to be undertaken lightly (*Hobbs v Gibson* [2010] EWHC 3676 (Ch) at [47]), and those who submit that a liquidator should be removed are under a duty to establish at least a prima facie case that this is for the general advantage of the persons interested in the winding up (*Re Mercantile Finance & Agency Co* (1894) 13 NZLR 472).

The courts will be careful that they do not encourage applications by disgruntled creditors: *AMP Enterprises Ltd v Hoffman*.

In *Re Keypak Homecare Ltd* (1987) 3 BCC 558 the liquidator was removed because he had been too relaxed in his conduct of the liquidation, and the creditors were justified in thinking that the liquidator would fail to pursue proceedings against the directors with the necessary vigour. If a liquidator fails to carry out his or her duties, that constitutes a cause for removal: *Re Ryder Installations Ltd* [1966] 1 WLR 524. The courts are likely to consider whether there is a possibility that the liquidator will not act impartially or objectively in relation to the company's affairs: *Re Lowestoft Traffic Services Ltd* (1986) 2 BCC 98, 945, [1986] BCLC 81; *Re Magnus Consultants Ltd* [1995] 1 BCLC 203. Courts will remove liquidators where their independence (*Re Zirceram Ltd* [2000] 1 BCLC 751 at 760; *HM Customs and Excise v Allen* [2003] BPIR 830) or fiduciary position (*Re Queensland Stations Pty Ltd (in liquidation)* (1991) 9 ACLC 1341) is compromised, such as where there is a conflict of interest (*Re Charterlands Goldfields Ltd* (1909) 26 TLR 182; *Re Corbenstoke Ltd (No 2)* (1989) 5 BCC 767, [1990] BCLC 60) or where the liquidator fails to act in an efficient manner within a reasonable period of time: *Re Buildlead Ltd (No 2)* [2004] EWHC 2443 (Ch), [2004] BPIR 1139, [2005] BCC 138. In *SISU Capital Fund Ltd v Tucker* [2005] EWHC 2170 (Ch), [2006] BCC 463 at [96], it was acknowledged that there are likely to be more conflicts in large insolvencies as there are so few accounting firms competent to deal with them. In that case Warren J pointed to a number of cases where the courts suggested that conflicts can often be managed (eg at [112]). Subsequently, Norris J stated in *Re Kimberly Scott Services Ltd* [2011] EWHC 1563 (Ch), [2012] BPIR 135, [2012] BCC 205 that removal would not occur where any conflicts of interest could be managed by way of applications to court for directions. One way to manage a conflict situation was to appoint an additional liquidator from a firm that is different from the firm to which the existing liquidator belongs: *Re York Gas Ltd* [2010] EWHC 2275 (Ch), [2011] BCC 447.

Instances of removal include the following circumstances: the liquidator trying to prevent misfeasance proceedings from being commenced against him or her (*Re Sir John Moore Gold Mining Co* (1879) 12 Ch D 326); the liquidator has been closely associated with promoters or directors whose conduct required investigation (*Re Charterlands Goldfields Ltd)*; the liquidator has demonstrated a propensity to prefer one person's interests over those of another (*Re City & County Investment Co* (1877) 25 WR 342; *Re Rubber & Produce Investment Trust* [1915] 1 Ch 382); the liquidator has taken action or failed to act because of personal animosity toward some of those interested in the winding up (*Re London Flats Ltd* [1969] 1 WLR 711); the liquidator is guilty of being dilatory in dealing with creditors' claims: *Re AMF International Ltd* [1995] BCC 439; the liquidator was previously the administrator of the company and this was undesirable: *Hobbs v Gibson* [2011] EWHC 3676. Liquidators were removed where they were connected professionally with a former liquidator (removed by the court on the liquidator's own application). The court did this because it had removed the former liquidator on the basis of his alleged ill health, yet the real reason why he wished to be removed was that he was insolvent: *HM Customs and Excise v Allen* [2003] BPIR 830.

A liquidator should not be removed simply because he or she is the choice of a creditor(s) who is concerned to see the claims of the company pursued by the liquidator: *Fielding v Seery* [2004] BCC 315 at 322.

Misconduct or unfitness may be constituted by some breach of duty (*Re Scotch Granite Co* (1868) 17 LT 538; *Re Baron Cigarette Machine Co* (1912) 28 TLR 294) or appearance of partiality on the part of the liquidator (*Re London Flats Ltd* [1969] 1 WLR 711), but it also seems to be enough for removal if one can show that winding up can be conducted more cheaply (*Re Tavistock Ironworks & Co* (1871) 24 LT 605; *Re Association of Land Financiers* (1878) 10 Ch D 269) or more effectively (*Re Montratier Asphalte Co* (1874) 22 WR 527) by a different liquidator who can be appointed following removal.

It will be hard for an applicant for removal to discharge the burden of proof if the liquidator has become conversant with the business and affairs of the company (*Re Civil Service & General Stores Ltd* [1884] WN 158; *Re Urmston Grange Steam Ship Co* (1909) 17 TLR 553), or the process of winding up has almost reached completion: *Re Llynvi & Tondu Co* (1889) 6 TLR 11. In some Australian cases courts have been of the opinion they should be less ready to discharge a liquidator towards the end of a winding up: *Advance Housing Pty Ltd (in liquidation) v Newcastle Classic Developments Pty Ltd* (1994) 14 ACSR 230 at 237; *Wood v Targett* (1997) 23 ACSR 291. The fact that removal of a liquidator could lead to disruption and extra cost should be considered: *AMP Enterprises Ltd v Hoffman*; sub nom *AMP Music Box Enterprises Ltd v Hoffman* [2002] EWHC 1899 (Ch), [2002] BCC 996, [2003] 1 BCLC 319, [2003] BPIR 11. One Australian appellate court has indicated that courts should be cautious in removing a liquidator where it seems possible that the applicant is trying to avoid the consequences of some wrongdoing by attacking the liquidator and seeking his or her removal: *Re Biposo Pty Ltd; Condon v Rogers* (1995) 120 FLR 399 at 403.

Applicants—The section gives no indication as to who may apply for removal, and it is likely that it will depend very much on the circumstances of each case. A person who applies for removal must demonstrate both that he or she is entitled to make the application and that he or she is a proper person to make the application: *Deloitte Touche AG v Johnson* [1999] BCC 992, PC. A creditor is entitled to apply (*HM Customs and Excise v Allen* [2003] BPIR 830). It has been held in Australia, in *Re Greight Pty Ltd (in liquidation)* [2006] FCA 17, Aust Fed Ct, that a person who is a possible creditor of the company may apply.

It is probably correct to say that a contributory who is fully paid up is not entitled to apply for removal, because in *Re Corbenstoke Ltd (No 2)* (1989) 5 BCC 767, [1990] BCLC 60 it was said (at 771; 61–62) that only someone who has an interest in the outcome of a liquidation can apply for removal, and if a company is insolvent then a contributory has no such interest: see also *Deloitte and Touche AG v Johnson* [1999] BCC 992. Defendants to a legal action commenced by the liquidator, such as the former auditors of the company in liquidation, were not able to bring proceedings for the removal of the liquidator for they were deemed to be strangers to the liquidation: *Deloitte and Touche AG v Johnson*.

A liquidator whose authorisation to act as a liquidator has been suspended may apply for an order of removal: *Re AJ Adams (Builders) Ltd* [1991] BCC 62. In similar circumstances, an application by the Insolvency Practitioners' Association, a recognised professional body for the accrediting of practitioners under the Act and Rules, was allowed to apply (*Re Stella Metals Ltd (in liquidation)* [1997] BCC 626), because it was held to be appropriate for the Insolvency Practitioners' Association to bring such an application. The courts have even permitted an insolvency practitioner (with the support of the Secretary of State for Trade and Industry (now Business Enterprise and Regulatory Reform)) to apply under this provision for the liquidator to be removed and replaced where the liquidator is no longer authorised to act: *Re a Licence-holder* [1997] BCC 666.

If a liquidator is removed then in Scotland he or she cannot retain from the company's assets any assets as security for costs, but in England and Wales the courts have a discretion to permit him or her to do so: *Re Echelon Wealth Management Ltd* [2011] CSOH 87; 2011 SCLR 678.

See rr 4.120 and 4.143 concerning the removal of a liquidator in creditors' voluntary liquidations and members' voluntary liquidations respectively. Also, see rr 4.103 and 140 concerning the appointment of a liquidator under s 108.

109 Notice by liquidator of his appointment

(1) The liquidator shall, within 14 days after his appointment, publish in the Gazette and deliver to the registrar of companies for registration a notice of his appointment in the form prescribed by statutory instrument made by the Secretary of State.

(2) If the liquidator fails to comply with this section, he is liable to a fine and, for continued contravention, to a daily default fine.

110 Acceptance of shares etc as consideration for sale of company property

(1) This section applies, in the case of a company proposed to be, or being, wound up voluntarily, where the whole or part of the company's business or property is proposed to be transferred or sold—

    (a)   to another company ('the transferee company'), whether or not the latter is a company registered under the Companies Act 2006, or

    (b)   to a limited liability partnership (the 'transferee limited liability partnership').

(2) With the requisite sanction, the liquidator of the company being, or proposed to be, wound up ('the transferor company') may receive, in compensation or part compensation for the transfer or sale—

    (a)   in the case of the transferee company, shares, policies or other like interests in the transferee company for distribution among the members of the transferor company, or

    (b)   in the case of the transferee limited liability partnership, membership in the transferee limited liability partnership for distribution among the members of the transferor company.

(3) The sanction requisite under subsection (2) is—

    (a)   in the case of a members' voluntary winding up, that of a special resolution of the company, conferring either a general authority on the liquidator or an authority in respect of any particular arrangement, and

    (b)   in the case of a creditors' voluntary winding up, that of either the court or the liquidation committee.

(4) Alternatively to subsection (2), the liquidator may (with that sanction) enter into any other arrangement whereby the members of the transferor company may—

    (a)   in the case of the transferee company, in lieu of receiving cash, shares, policies or other like interests (or in addition thereto) participate in the profits of, or receive any other benefit from, the transferee company, or

    (b)   in the case of the transferee limited liability partnership, in lieu of receiving cash or membership (or in addition thereto), participate in some other way in the profits of, or receive any other benefit from, the transferee limited liability partnership.

(5) A sale or arrangement in pursuance of this section is binding on members of the transferor company.

(6) A special resolution is not invalid for purposes of this section by reason that it is passed before or concurrently with a resolution for voluntary winding up or for appointing liquidators; but, if an order is made within a year for winding up the company by the court, the special resolution is not valid unless sanctioned by the court.

Amendments—SI 2001/1090; SI 2009/1941.

General note—This provision deals with a relatively infrequent occurrence, namely where a company in liquidation is subject to a scheme of reorganisation. The company's business is sold by the liquidator to another company and in return either the liquidator will distribute to the members, in a members' voluntary liquidation, shares or other securities in the company buying the business of the former company, or the members will be able to participate in the profits of the company buying the business. Certain tax advantages can be obtained from a reorganisation under this provision, such as a reorganisation would not be a distribution within s 209 of the Income and Corporation Taxes Act 1988 (R Richards and J Tribe 'Members' Liquidations' (2005) 26 Co Law 132 at 133).

The provision may also apply to a creditors' voluntary liquidation (see s 110(3)(b)), but it is hard to envisage the circumstances where this will occur, as the company will be insolvent and the creditors will not receive full payment of their debts. Perhaps the only situation where this might occur is where the company in creditors' voluntary liquidation is eventually found to be solvent.

If a company has more than one class of shares, the company can only decide on the nature of consideration to be accepted, and it is not able to decide, given a statutory majority, the mode of distribution of the consideration accepted as between the various classes of shareholders: *Griffith v Padget* (1877) 5 Ch D 894.

The courts are willing to assist by exercising their equitable jurisdiction where the correct order required by a scheme entered into to take advantage of section 110 has not been adhered to because of a mistake: *Manuplastics Ltd v BPSW19 Ltd* [2011] EWHC 3853 (Ch), [2012] BCC 368.

111 Dissent from arrangement under s 110

(1) This section applies in the case of a voluntary winding up where, for the purposes of section 110(2) or (4), there has been passed a special resolution of the transferor company providing the sanction requisite for the liquidator under that section.

(2) If a member of the transferor company who did not vote in favour of the special resolution expresses his dissent from it in writing, addressed to the liquidator and left at the company's registered office within 7 days after the passing of the resolution, he may require the liquidator either to abstain from carrying the resolution into effect or to purchase his interest at a price to be determined by agreement or by arbitration under this section.

(3) If the liquidator elects to purchase the member's interest, the purchase money must be paid before the company is dissolved and be raised by the liquidator in such manner as may be determined by special resolution.

(4) For purposes of an arbitration under this section, the provisions of the Companies Clauses Consolidation Act 1845 or, in the case of a winding up in Scotland, the Companies Clauses Consolidation (Scotland) Act 1845 with respect to the settlement of disputes by arbitration are incorporated with this Act, and—

(a) in the construction of those provisions this Act is deemed the special Act and 'the company' means the transferor company, and

(b) any appointment by the incorporated provisions directed to be made under the hand of the secretary or any two of the directors may be made in writing by the liquidator (or, if there is more than one liquidator, then any two or more of them).

General note—Any attempt to circumvent the thrust of the provision, such as requiring in the company's constitution that dissenting members must accept a scheme, set out in the constitution, for providing compensation to members, will not be enforced: *Bisgood v Henderson's Transvaal Estates* [1908] 1 Ch 743, CA. Due to the need for the shares of dissenters to be bought, a scheme under the s 895 of the Companies Act 2006 procedure might be easier and less expensive, although the process under this provision is not quick and inexpensive.

112 Reference of questions to court

(1) The liquidator or any contributory or creditor may apply to the court to determine any question arising in the winding up of a company, or to exercise, as respects the enforcing of calls or any other matter, all or any of the powers which the court might exercise if the company were being wound up by the court.

(2) The court, if satisfied that the determination of the question or the required exercise of power will be just and beneficial, may accede wholly or partially to the application on such terms and conditions as it thinks fit, or may make such other order on the application as it thinks just.

(3) A copy of an order made by virtue of this section staying the proceedings in the winding up shall forthwith be forwarded by the company,

or otherwise as may be prescribed, to the registrar of companies, who shall enter it in his records relating to the company.

General note—While it is not mandatory to have any court involvement in a voluntary liquidation, it might be necessary at some point during the course of a voluntary liquidation for the liquidator to obtain a court order or direction on a given matter. As this provision enables the court in voluntary winding up to exercise all or any of the powers which it might exercise if the company were being wound up by the court, and because of the liberal interpretation of the section (*Re Campbell Coverings Ltd* [1953] Ch 488), there is not a lot of difference between compulsory and creditors' voluntary liquidations. For instance, public examinations can be initiated in relation to voluntary liquidations through the agency of s 112 (*Re Campbell Coverings Ltd (No 2)* [1954] Ch 225; *Re Serene Shoes Ltd* [1958] 1 WLR 1087; *Bishopsgate Investment Management Ltd (in prov liq) v Maxwell* [1992] Ch 1 at 24 and 46, [1992] BCC 222 at 232 and 249, CA), even though public examinations are only allowed under s 131 in compulsory liquidations. But the section cannot be used as an alternative basis for a creditor instigating the private examination process, where this process might not be available and it would give a liquidator of a voluntary liquidation more powers than a liquidator in a compulsory liquidation: *Re James McHale Automobiles Ltd* [1997] 1 BCLC 273, [1997] BCC 202. An application can be made under 112 in a voluntary liquidation whereby a court can exercise the power set out in s 167(3) allowing the court to control the exercise of powers by a liquidator: *Cooper v PRG Powerhouse Ltd* [2008] EWHC 498 (Ch).

Often an application under s 112 will be made by a liquidator seeking directions concerning an issue of importance in the winding-up process. For instance, in *Re Harvard Securities Ltd (in liquidation)* [1997] 2 BCLC 369 the liquidator needed guidance as to who were the beneficial owners of shares, and the liquidator in *Re Agrimarche Ltd* [2010] EWHC 1655 (Ch), had the need of directions concerning the valuation of call options held by the company. In *Whitehouse v Wilson* [2006] EWCA Civ 1688, [2007] BPIR 230, [2007] BCC 596, a liquidator in a creditors' voluntary liquidation applied for the sanction of the court in relation to his decision to compromise his misfeasance claim against a director An application can be made by a liquidator of more than one company in a group where the subject matter is common to all of the companies: *Re William Pickles plc (in liquidation)* [1996] 1 BCLC 681, [1996] BCC 408. Liquidators can apply under s 112 for directions whether and to what extent a debenture grants a valid and enforceable fixed charge of the assets of the company: *Re Double S Printers Ltd (in liquidation)* [1999] BCC 303.

Where a company has sufficient funds and the matter can be best dealt with pursuant to ordinary litigation, a court might well decline to hear any application for directions: *Re Stetzel Thompson & Co Ltd* (1988) 4 BCC 74.

The court has a discretion as to whether it will make an order under s 112, with the conditions governing its exercise being set out in s 112(2). But it has been said that an application under s 112 will only be entertained where its purpose is a legitimate purpose of winding up: *IRC v Mills* [2003] EWHC 2022 (Ch). Directions should only be provided for where it is just and beneficial and it will be of advantage in the liquidation: *S & D International (in liq) v MIG Property Services Pty Ltd* [2010] VSC 336.

For recent applications under s 112, see *Re Spectrum Plus Ltd* [2003] EWHC 9 (Ch) and *Tombs v Moulinex SA* [2004] EWHC 454 (Ch). In the former the liquidators sought directions concerning the fate of book debts, and the question was whether the charge covering the book debts was a fixed or floating charge (this litigation has since been finalised with a decision of the House of Lords: *National Westminster Bank plc v Spectrum Plus Ltd* [2005] UKHL 41). In *Tombs v Moulinex SA*, involving a members' voluntary, the liquidators were seeking directions on the possible distribution of funds remaining under their control. In this case there was some possibility of future consumer actions against the company as a result of products that it had sold. The court does have jurisdiction to order distribution in a members' voluntary notwithstanding the existence of future creditors emerging: *Re R-R Realisations Ltd* [1980] 1 WLR 805. In *Re Sunwing Vacations Inc* [2011] EWHC 1544 (Ch), [2011] BPIR 1524 there was an application by a creditor that the liquidator disclose company documents to the applicant (the provision in compulsory liquidation is s 155).

In *Re Anglican Insurance Ltd* [2008] NSWSC 41 SC (NSW), the New South Wales Supreme Court, in dealing with the Australian equivalent of s 112 of the Insolvency Act, said that it could not make orders affecting the rights of outsider, and it was not the task of the court to determine the rights and liabilities arising from the company's transactions entered into before the commencement of liquidation.

Any application that is made under the section should be made to the court which has jurisdiction to wind up the company ('the court' – s 1156 as incorporated by s 251 of the Insolvency Act).

See the notes related to s 117.

'Creditor'—This includes a secured creditor: *Re Alfred Priestman & Co* (1929) [1936] 2 All ER 1340.

Stay on proceedings against the company—In compulsory liquidations there is a specific statutory provision, namely s 130(2), that prohibits, automatically, the initiation or prosecution of proceedings against the company unless leave is obtained from the courts. There is no corresponding provision in voluntary liquidations, but it is has always been the practice for the court, upon application by the liquidator under s 112(1), to exercise its power in s 130(2) of staying actions and proceedings after commencement of voluntary winding up: *Freeman v General Publishing Co* [1894] 2 QB 380; *Anglo-Baltic & Mediterranean Bank v Barber* [1924] 2 KB 410; *Re Dicksmith (Manufacturing) Ltd (in liquidation)* [1999] 2 BCLC 686. The liquidator has the onus of establishing that there are special reasons for making the stay: *Re Roundwood Colliery Co* [1897] 1 Ch 373 at 381; *Currie v Consolidated Kent Collieries Corp* [1906] 1 KB 134.

To ensure the implementation of the principle of rateable division of assets, there is a trend in the courts for stays to be ordered in relation to execution proceedings, on the application of the liquidator under s 112, where voluntary liquidation has commenced (*Re Poole Firebrick & Blue Clay Co* (1873) 17 Eq 268; *Re Thurso New Gas Co* (1889) 42 Ch D 486; *Westbury v Twigg* [1892] 1 QB 770), so that through s 112 the court's powers under s 128 are applied in a creditors' voluntary winding up. However, this is not the case with members' voluntary windings up. It has been held that this practice would not be followed in a members' voluntary winding up, as it could be assumed that the company was able to pay its debt in full: *Gerard v Worth of Paris, Ltd* [1936] 2 All ER 905, CA.

See the notes related to s 130 for a discussion of the principles that apply when a court is faced with an application for leave to commence, or continue with, an action.

Stay on winding-up proceedings—The section can be used in a voluntary liquidation to obtain a stay of the liquidation proceedings (*Re Serene Shoes Ltd* [1958] 1 WLR 1087, [1958] 3 All ER 316; *Re Calgary and Edmonton Land Co Ltd* [1975] 1 All ER 1046, [1975] 1 WLR 355), just as one can with compulsory liquidations under s 147: *Re South Barrule Slate Quarry Co* (1869) 8 Eq 688; *Re J Burrows (Leeds) Ltd (in liquidation)* (1982) 126 SJ 227.

See s 147 and the notes accompanying that section.

113 Court's power to control proceedings (Scotland)

If the court, on the application of the liquidator in the winding up of a company registered in Scotland, so directs, no action or proceeding shall be proceeded with or commenced against the company except by leave of the court and subject to such terms as the court may impose.

114 No liquidator appointed or nominated by company

(1) This section applies where, in the case of a voluntary winding up, no liquidator has been appointed or nominated by the company.

(2) The powers of the directors shall not be exercised, except with the sanction of the court or (in the case of a creditors' voluntary winding up) so far as may be necessary to secure compliance with sections 98 (creditors' meeting) and 99 (statement of affairs), during the period before the appointment or nomination of a liquidator of the company.

(3) Subsection (2) does not apply in relation to the powers of the directors—

(a) to dispose of perishable goods and other goods the value of which is likely to diminish if they are not immediately disposed of, and

(b) to do all such other things as may be necessary for the protection of the company's assets.

(4) If the directors of the company without reasonable excuse fail to comply with this section, they are liable to a fine.

General note—This provision covers the period from the time of the resolution to wind up to the appointment of the liquidator. It is aimed at ensuring, inter alia, that the assets of the company are protected from dissipation during the interim period between the resolution to wind up and the appointment of a liquidator. The provision is designed to encourage the early appointment of a liquidator. It was introduced in the 1986 Act, together with s 166, to proscribe what was known as 'centrebinding'. This process derived its name from the case of *Re Centrebind Ltd* [1967] 1 WLR 377, [1966] 3 All ER 889. See the notes accompanying s 166 for more discussion.

This provision restricts the powers that the directors can exercise. The directors have to exercise some powers and their office does not end. For instance, one of their number has to preside at the creditors' meeting held under s 98 (as mentioned in s 114(2)).

115 Expenses of voluntary winding up

All expenses properly incurred in the winding up, including the remuneration of the liquidator, are payable out of the company's assets in priority to all other claims.

General note—In general terms the expenses of the winding up are paid out of the company's assets before any other unsecured creditors (see notes accompanying s 107). The kinds of expenses that can be claimed are detailed in r 4.218, which also sets out the order of priority as far as payment occurs if there are insufficient assets to pay all expenses. This order may be varied by the courts under a combination of ss 112 and 156. However, the courts will not be quick to vary the priority order, as they are generally content to adopt the order of priorities in r 4.218(1): *Re Grey Marlin Ltd* [2000] 1 WLR 370, [2000] 2 BCLC 658. Rule 4.220 expressly provides for a re-ordering of the priorities set out in rr 4.218 and 4.219 by a court.

'Incurred in the winding up'—This does not encompass any expenses incurred prior to the making of the resolution to wind up unless they directly related to the obtaining of the resolution or were required by legislation (*Re WF Fearman Ltd (No 2)* (1988) 4 BCC 141 (costs of the preparation of a petition for an administration order – presented after the winding-up petition – were permitted, but no other costs); *Re Sandwell Copiers Ltd* (1988) 4 BCC 227 (an accountant could not claim his fees out of the funds held in the liquidation for collecting company debts prior to a commencement of the winding up)).

See the note relating to s 156.

116 Saving for certain rights

The voluntary winding up of a company does not bar the right of any creditor or contributory to have it wound up by the court; but in the case of an application by a contributory the court must be satisfied that the rights of the contributories will be prejudiced by a voluntary winding up.

General note—When confronted with a petition by a creditor, the general issue that a court must consider is whether it is preferable for the creditors that a winding-up order is made or the voluntary winding continues: *Re Fitness Centre (South East) Ltd* [1986] BCLC 518, (1986) 2 BCC 99, 535; *Re Rhine Film Corp (UK) Ltd* (1986) 2 BCC 98, 949.

An order will not be made unless the court is satisfied that the voluntary winding up cannot be continued having regard to the interests of the members and creditors. It has been held that where a declaration of solvency had been completed then it was proper to hear the views of contributories on a petition for a winding up by the court: *Re Surplus Properties (Huddersfield) Ltd* [1984] BCLC 89 at 91.

If a creditor has a concern over the identity of the liquidator of a creditors' voluntary winding up, the creditor should not petition for a compulsory winding up, but rather apply for removal of the liquidator: *Re Inside Sports Ltd* [2000] BCC 40 at 42.

It appears that a creditor petitioning for an order must demonstrate that it would be detrimental to the interests of creditors if voluntary liquidation were to continue: *Re Riviera Pearls Ltd* [1962] 1 WLR 722; *Re Medisco Equipment Ltd* [1983] BCLC 305, (1983) 1 BCC 98, 944; *Re Magnus Consultants Ltd* [1995] BCLC 203. To secure an order, it is unnecessary for the liquidator's probity or competence to be challenged: *Re Lowestoft Traffic Services Ltd* (1986) 2 BCC 98, 945, [1986] BCLC 81; *Re Palmer Marine Surveys Ltd* [1986] 1 WLR 573, [1986] BCLC 106, (1986) 1 BCC 99, 557; *Re Falcon RJ Development Ltd* [1987] BCLC 437, (1987) 3 BCC 146.

An order would not be made against the wishes of the majority as they had the largest stake in the company (*Re JD Swain Ltd* [1965] 1 WLR 909 at 913, 915, 916, [1965] 1 All ER 761 at 764, 765, 766, CA; *Re Zirceram Ltd* [2000] 1 BCLC 751 at 758) unless good reason was given for the court deciding to refrain from accepting the wishes of the majority. But in taking into account the wishes of the majority, the views of outside creditors will be given greater weight than those who are also members: *Re Medisco Equipment Ltd* [1983] BCLC 305, (1983) 1 BCC 98, 944; *Re H J Tomkins Ltd* [1990] BCLC 76. It has been said that it would not be right to refuse a winding-up order if the refusal would lead to the majority of creditors who are substantial and independent having a justified strong feeling of grievance that they had been unfairly denied the chance of having an independent liquidator being given the conduct of the winding up: *Re Falcon RJ Development Ltd* [1987] BCLC 437, (1987) 3 BCC 146; *Re Palmer Marine Surveys Ltd* [1986] 1 WLR 573, [1986] BCLC 106, (1986) 1 BCC 99, 557; *Re MCH Services Ltd* [1987] BCLC 535, (1987) 3 BCC 179. Furthermore, in arriving at a decision, the courts must consider: the quantity and the quality of debts owed by the company; and connections between any particular creditor with the company which may indicate any motivation for the creditor voting one way or the other: *Re Inside Sports Ltd* [2000] BCC 40 at 41.

Courts will exercise their discretion and order a winding up, on the basis of fairness and commercial morality, when they feel that the circumstances of the company warrant special scrutiny and to ensure that the creditors' interests were not prejudiced: *Re Zirceram Ltd* [2000] 1 BCLC 751 at 758. Courts have made orders where: the creditors lack confidence in the liquidator, and the latter is perceived as not being impartial (*Re Palmer Marine Surveys Ltd* [1986] 1 WLR 573, [1986] BCLC 106, (1986) 1 BCC 99, 557; *Re Roselmar Properties Ltd (No 2)* (1986) 2 BCC 99, 157; *Re Pinstripe Farming Co Ltd* [1996] 2 BCLC 295, [1996] BCC 913; *Re Zirceram Ltd* [2000] 1 BCLC 751 at 760); the liquidator has admitted into proof inflated or non-substantiated claims against the company (*Re Magnus Consultants Ltd* [1995] 1 BCLC 203; *Re Gordon & Breach Science Publishers Ltd* [1995] 2 BCLC 189, [1995] BCC 261); the liquidator had transferred company assets to associated companies for inadequate consideration (*Re Palmer Marine Surveys Ltd*); there have been inordinate delays in the winding up (*Re Hewitt Branson (Tools) Co Ltd* [1990] BCC 354); and there is a need for an urgent and quick investigation of the company's affairs (*Re William Thorpe & Son Ltd* (1988) 5 BCC 156).

It has been said that a factor in a decision to order a compulsory winding up could be the fact that the liquidator in a voluntary liquidation had not progressed far: *Souster v Carman Construction Co Ltd* [2000] BPIR 371 at 380. It is less likely that a court will make an order where the voluntary liquidation is nearly finalised and the liquidator undertakes to complete the winding up promptly: *Re J Russell Electronics Ltd* [1968] 1 WLR 1252, [1968] 2 All ER 559.

At the hearing of the petition: the incumbent liquidator is entitled (*Re Medisco Equipment* [1983] BCLC 305, (1983) 1 BCC 98, 944), and is probably advised, to appear by counsel; the liquidator may merely give evidence of the current state of the liquidation; and the liquidator should remain independent and refrain from expressing a view as to the desirability of a compulsory winding-up order: *Re Medisco Equipment Ltd* [1983] BCLC 305, (1983) 1 BCC 98, 944; *Re Arthur Rathbone Kitchens Ltd* [1997] 2 BCLC 280; *Souster v Carman Construction Co Ltd* [2000] BPIR 371. If he or she appears, the liquidator would be allowed the costs of doing so (*Re Roselmar Properties Ltd (No 2)* (1986) 2 BCC 99, 157), unless he or she adopts a less than independent approach, where the court may decide not to allow his or her costs out of the company's property: *Re Roselmar Properties Ltd (No 2); Re Pinstripe Farming Co Ltd* [1996] 2 BCLC 295.

The official receiver is given specific power by s 124(5) to petition for a winding-up order in relation to a company that is in voluntary liquidation.

'Creditor'—Any creditor of the company, whether a pre- or post-voluntary liquidation creditor, may petition: *Re Bank of South Australia (No 2)* [1985] 1 Ch 578; *Re Greenwood and Co* [1900] 2 QB 306.

'Petition by contributory'—The same issues that apply when a creditor petitions apply when a contributory petitions: *Re Internet Investment Corporation Ltd* [2009] EWHC 2744 (Ch), [2010] 1 BCLC 458

For further discussion, see A Keay *McPherson's Law of Company Liquidation* (Sweet and Maxwell, 3rd edn, 2013) at 186–193.

Chapter VI

Winding Up by the Court Jurisdiction (England and Wales)

117 High Court and county court jurisdiction

(1) The High Court has jurisdiction to wind up any company registered in England and Wales.

(2) Where the amount of a company's share capital paid up or credited as paid up does not exceed £120,000, then (subject to this section) the county court of the district in which the company's registered office is situated has concurrent jurisdiction with the High Court to wind up the company.

(3) The money sum for the time being specified in subsection (2) is subject to increase or reduction by order under section 416 in Part XV.

(4) The Lord Chancellor may, with the concurrence of the Lord Chief Justice, by order in a statutory instrument exclude a county court from having winding-up jurisdiction, and for the purposes of that jurisdiction may attach its district, or any part thereof, to any other county court, and may by statutory instrument revoke or vary any such order.

In exercising the powers of this section, the Lord Chancellor shall provide that a county court is not to have winding-up jurisdiction unless it has for the time being jurisdiction for the purposes of Parts VIII to XI of this Act (individual insolvency).

(5) Every court in England and Wales having winding-up jurisdiction has for the purposes of that jurisdiction all the powers of the High Court; and every prescribed officer of the court shall perform any duties which an officer of the High Court may discharge by order of a judge of that court or otherwise in relation to winding up.

(6) For the purposes of this section, a company's 'registered office' is the place which has longest been its registered office during the 6 months immediately preceding the presentation of the petition for winding up.

(7) This section is subject to Article 3 of the EC Regulation (jurisdiction under EC Regulation).

(8) The Lord Chief Justice may nominate a judicial office holder (as defined in section 109(4) of the Constitutional Reform Act 2005) to exercise his functions under this section.

Amendments—SI 2002/1240; Constitutional Reform Act 2005, s 15(1), Sch 4, Pt 1, paras 185, 186(1).

General note—Where a company has have been registered in Scotland, it must be wound up in Scotland (see s 120), while a company that is registered in Northern Ireland may be wound up by the High Court of England and Wales as an unregistered company if it has a principal place of business in England or Wales: *Re Normandy Marketing Ltd* [1994] Ch 198, [1993] BCC 879.

It is stated in s 117(5) that every court which has a winding-up jurisdiction has all of the powers of the High Court, and as a result a county court is able, while hearing proceedings in relation to the winding up, to resolve issues where the value of the assets or the claim is in excess of its normal jurisdictional limit: *Re F & E Stanton Ltd* [1928] 1 KB 464. In the case of voluntary liquidation, where an application needs to be made to a court (such as pursuant to s 112), then the court to which the application is made is to the court which has jurisdiction to wind up the company (s 1156 of the Companies Act 2006 as incorporated by s 251 of the Insolvency Act).

The jurisdiction of the High Court is exercised by judges who are members of the Companies Court, in London and at district registries, but all of the High Court judges are able to exercise jurisdiction in relation to an application that is in some way incidental to a liquidation: *Fabric Sales Ltd v Eratex Ltd* [1984] 1 WLR 863 at 865.

While taking proceedings in county courts may be more convenient, the practice tends to be to use the High Court more than the county courts.

The Court of Appeal is only able to hear appeals relating to petitions for winding-up orders, and it does not have the power to hear petitions at first instance: *Re Dunraven Adare Coal & Iron Co* (1875) 33 LT 371.

Where appropriate, hearings may be held in private: *Banco Nacional de Cuba v Cosmos Trading Corp* [2000] 1 BCLC 813 at 816, CA.

The provision is subject to Art 3 of the EC Regulation on Insolvency Proceedings. The article provides that where the centre of a debtor's main interests is in a Member State of the EU, that State will have jurisdiction to open insolvency proceedings and the place where a company has its registered office is presumed to be the centre of the company's main interests. Proceedings cannot be commenced in another Member State unless the company has an establishment in that State's territory. In *Telia AB v Hillcourt (Docklands) Ltd* [2003] BCC 856) the court took the view that winding-up proceedings could not be brought in England and Wales against a Swedish company as the company had no establishment in the jurisdiction. It was held that the existence of business premises was not sufficient to provide the company with an establishment here, for the purposes of Art 3. In a case where proceedings have been opened in the Member State, being the location of the registered office, then any proceedings commenced elsewhere in the EU will be regarded as secondary proceedings. See the notes relating to Art 3 of the EC Regulation.

118 Proceedings taken in wrong court

(1) Nothing in section 117 invalidates a proceeding by reason of its being taken in the wrong court.

(2) The winding up of a company by the court in England and Wales, or any proceedings in the winding up, may be retained in the court in which the proceedings were commenced, although it may not be the court in which they ought to have been commenced.

General note—In such circumstances the court may make one of three orders: that the proceedings be transferred to the correct court; that the proceedings continue in the court; or that the proceedings be struck out (r 7.12).

119 Proceedings in county court; case stated for High Court

(1) If any question arises in any winding-up proceedings in a county court which all the parties to the proceedings, or which one of them and the judge of the court, desire to have determined in the first instance in the High Court, the judge shall state the facts in the form of a special case for the opinion of the High Court.

(2) Thereupon the special case and the proceedings (or such of them as may be required) shall be transmitted to the High Court for the purposes of the determination.

General note—See rr 7.11–7.14 and the notes attaching thereto.

Jurisdiction (Scotland)

120 Court of Session and sheriff court jurisdiction

(1) The Court of Session has jurisdiction to wind up any company registered in Scotland.

(2) When the Court of Session is in vacation, the jurisdiction conferred on that court by this section may (subject to the provisions of this Part) be exercised by the judge acting as vacation judge

(3) Where the amount of a company's share capital paid up or credited as paid up does not exceed £120,000, the sheriff court of the sheriffdom in which the company's registered office is situated has concurrent jurisdiction with the Court of Session to wind up the company; but—

    (a) the Court of Session may, if it thinks expedient having regard to the amount of the company's assets to do so—
        (i) remit to a sheriff court any petition presented to the Court of Session for winding up such a company, or
        (ii) require such a petition presented to a sheriff court to be remitted to the Court of Session; and

    (b) the Court of Session may require any such petition as above-mentioned presented to one sheriff court to be remitted to another sheriff court; and

    (c) in a winding up in the sheriff court the sheriff may submit a stated case for the opinion of the Court of Session on any question of law arising in that winding up.

(4) For purposes of this section, the expression 'registered office' means the place which has longest been the company's registered office during the 6 months immediately preceding the presentation of the petition for winding up.

(5) The money sum for the time being specified in subsection (3) is subject to increase or reduction by order under section 416 in Part XV.

(6) This section is subject to Article 3 of the EC Regulation (jurisdiction under EC Regulation).

Amendments—Court of Session Act 1988, s 52(2), Sch 2, Pt I; SI 2002/1240.

121 Power to remit winding up to Lord Ordinary

(1) The Court of Session may, by Act of Sederunt, make provision for the taking of proceedings in a winding up before one of the Lords Ordinary; and, where provision is so made, the Lord Ordinary has, for the purposes of the winding up, all the powers and jurisdiction of the court.

(2) However, the Lord Ordinary may report to the Inner House any matter which may arise in the course of a winding up.

Grounds and effect of winding-up petition

122 Circumstances in which company may be wound up by the court

(1) A company may be wound up by the court if—

(a) the company has by special resolution resolved that the company be wound up by the court,

(b) being a public company which was registered as such on its original incorporation, the company has not been issued with a trading certificate under section 761 of the Companies Act 2006 (requirement as to minimum share capital) and more than a year has expired since it was so registered,

(c) it is an old public company, within the meaning of Schedule 3 to the Companies Act 2006 (Consequential Amendments, Transitional Provisions and Savings) Order 2009,

(d) the company does not commence its business within a year from its incorporation or suspends its business for a whole year,

(e) *(repealed)*

(f) the company is unable to pay its debts,

(fa) at the time at which a moratorium for the company under section 1A comes to an end, no voluntary arrangement approved under Part I has effect in relation to the company,

(g) the court is of the opinion that it is just and equitable that the company should be wound up.

(2) In Scotland, a company which the Court of Session has jurisdiction to wind up may be wound up by the Court if there is subsisting a floating charge over property comprised in the company's property and undertaking, and the court is satisfied that the security of the creditor entitled to the benefit of the floating charge is in jeopardy.

For this purpose a creditor's security is deemed to be in jeopardy if the Court is satisfied that events have occurred or are about to occur which render it unreasonable in the creditor's interests that the company should retain power to dispose of the property which is subject to the floating charge.

Amendments—SI 1992/1699; Insolvency Act 2000, s 1, Sch 1, paras 1, 6; SI 2008/948; SI 2009/1941; SI 2011/1265.

General note—This provision, together with s 125, makes it clear that the court has a discretion as to whether it orders the winding up of a company. The section sets out the circumstances when an order may be made.

Only one of the grounds set out in this section makes insolvency the basis for a winding-up order (s 122(1)(f)), but this ground is by far the most frequent ground relied on by a winding-up petition. It must always be remembered that the Act does not deal exclusively with issues of insolvency, as can be seen from the fact that it encompasses members' voluntary windings up. Solvent companies are wound up under the Act.

Section 122(1)(a)

Where there is a special resolution—As a company can be wound up pursuant to the voluntary liquidation process if a special resolution to wind up is passed, it is difficult to envisage circumstances where the members are going to prefer the more complicated and expensive compulsory form of winding up. A possible reason is where it is felt that it is desirable that the official receiver's investigative powers are exercised under ss 132–133.

The courts have a discretion whether or not to make a winding-up order or not under this ground. Generally speaking the court's discretion should be exercised in favour of making an order: *Hillig v Darkinjung Pty Ltd* [2006] NSWSC 137, (2006) 205 FLR 450 (S Ct (NSW)).

Section 122(1)(b)

Public company not meeting share capital requirements—Here the company is a public company which was registered on or after 22 December 1980, being the date on which a new definition of 'public company' came into operation (Companies Act 1980 (Commencement No 2) Order 1980 (SI 1980/1785)), and which has not, for more than a year since its registration, been issued with a certificate of compliance with the share capital requirements.

Section 122(1)(c)

An old public company—This applies where the company is an old public company which failed to re-register as either a public or a private company by 22 March 1982. Section 8 of the Companies Act 1980 required public companies (known as 'old public companies') to re-register as either public or private companies (see s 1 of the Companies Consolidation (Consequential Provisions) Act 1985 for the definition of 'old public company').

Section 122(1)(d)

Company does not commence business—Originally, this ground was designed essentially to enable shareholders to have a way of recovering their investment from a company which fails to carry on its intended business. To succeed, the petitioner must establish that the company had no intention of carrying on business: *Re Middlesborough Assembly Rooms* (1879) 14 Ch D 104. Even if the petitioner is able to do this, the court retains a discretion whether or not to make an order (*Re Metropolitan Rly Warehousing Co* (1867) 36 LJ Ch 227, (1867) 17 LT 108), and in exercising this discretion the courts will take into account the wishes of the majority of the shareholders: *Re Tomlin Patent Horse Shoe Co* (1886) 55 LT 314.

'Business'—At one stage this was taken to refer to the business specified in the objects' clause of the company's memorandum. Now, with the abolition (virtually) of the ultra vires rule and courts taking a liberal view on objects' clauses, it is probable that courts will interpret the term 'business' far more broadly.

'Commencement'—For the commencement of a business the company must 'actually set to work' (*Re South Luipaard's Vlei Gold Mines Co* (1897) 13 TLR 504), and this does not include merely allotting shares (*Re South Luipaard's*), making calls, or holding board meetings: *Re Capital Fire Insurance Association* (1882) 21 Ch D 209. Action which involves making arrangements which are necessary before starting business may be sufficient for a commencement: *Re Petersburgh & Viborg Gas Co* (1874) WN 1996.

'Suspension'—Suspension occurs where the business is abandoned either with the deliberate intention of abandoning it (*Re Madrid & Valencia Ry Co* (1850) 19 LJ Ch 260), or because of inability to proceed: *Re Middlesborough Assembly Rooms Co* (1879) 14 Ch D 104; *Re Tomlin Patent Horse Shoe Co* (1886) 55 LT 314.

Section 122(1)(e)

Reduced below two—This exempts private companies that have less than two members as they are entitled to have just one member (Companies (Single Member Private Limited Companies) Regulations 1992 (SI 1992/1699)).

Section 122(1)(f)

The company is unable to pay its debts—This is the main ground upon which companies are liquidated. Companies falling into this category are insolvent.

The meaning of 'unable to pay its debts' is explained in s 123. See the notes relating to that section.

Section 122(1)(g)

Just and equitable—Following the previous ground, this is the next most popular ground under section 122 for founding a winding-up petition. Ordinarily this ground will be relied on by a contributory of the company. Most frequently it is invoked in relation to quasi-partnerships where there has been a breakdown in the relations between the controllers. It is, together with s 994 of the Companies Act 2006, the ground on which the majority of contributories' petitions rely where contributories are dissatisfied with the way in which the company is being run or they feel that the controllers of companies have acted improperly and unfairly towards them. But creditors do have the right to rely on the just and equitable ground (*Re Dollar Land Holdings plc* [1993] BCC 823, [1994] 1 BCLC 404; *Bell Group Finance Pty Ltd (in liquidation) v Bell Group (UK) Holdings Ltd* [1996] BCC 505, [1996] 1 BCLC 304; *Morrice v Brae Hotel (Shetland) Ltd* [1997] BCC 670), provided that the creditor is able to establish that he or she has the necessary standing to bring the proceedings: *Morrice v Brae Hotel (Shetland) Ltd.* A creditor is not entitled to rely on the ground where the bases for the petition are public interest reasons, as Parliament has determined that where such reasons exist the Secretary of State for Business Enterprise and Regulatory Reform should present a petition under s 124A: *Re Millennium Advanced Technology Ltd* [2004] EWHC 711, (Ch) at [33], [2004] 1 BCLC 77 at 85.

Courts have a wide discretion in deciding whether to make an order or not, but s 125(2) provides that winding up is only to be ordered by the court if it is of the view that there is no alternative remedy available to the petitioner and he or she is not acting unreasonably in seeking winding up. One alternative is to bring an action under s 994 of the Companies Act 2006 (unfair prejudice ground). Another alternative is where there is an offer to purchase shares at a reasonable value: *Re Cyracuse Ltd* [2001] 1 BCLC 187, [2001] BCC 806. It is possible that where there is an alternative remedy, a petition will be struck out: *Re a Company* [1997] 1 BCLC 479.

As mentioned above, parties may seek a winding-up order or a remedy under s 994 of the Companies Act 2006 in the alternative. It might be thought to be a bit of a gamble to do this now, as the courts have, on occasions, struck out such petitions and, in fact, *Practice Direction No 1 of 1990* [1990] BCC 292 stated that the two should not be included as a matter of course. It indicates that it is undesirable to ask as a matter of course for a winding-up order unless that is either the specific relief that the petitioner is seeking or it is the only relief to which he or she is entitled. Notwithstanding this, it has been said that courts will accept, on occasions, that the pleading of an alternative remedy is allowed (*Re Copeland and Craddock Ltd* [1997] BCC 294), and this is likely to be where it is unclear on the facts whether unfairly prejudicial conduct under s 994 can be made out: *Re RA Noble & Sons Ltd* [1997] BCC 294. Of importance in making any decisions on this score is the recent judicial comment that the just and equitable ground does not provide a wider basis for granting relief, with the result that if conduct was not sufficient to obtain an order under s 994, then a court would not grant a winding-up order on the basis of s 122(1)(g), for the jurisdiction to wind up is not more extensive than that under s 994: *Re Guidezone Ltd* [2001] BCC 692. But winding up is only permitted pursuant to a claim under the just and equitable ground, and not pursuant to a claim under s 994.

It has been made clear in the leading case that there should be flexibility with this ground and courts should refrain from setting down categories into which petitioners have to bring themselves: *Ebrahimi v Westbourne Galleries Ltd* [1973] AC 360, HL. Most cases have involved closely-held companies that are, substantially, in the nature of a partnership, whose members are unable to co-operate in the conduct of its affairs: *Ebrahimi v Westbourne Galleries Ltd.*

It has been held that a petitioner must come with clean hands, and if he or she does not do so then his or her relevant misconduct could mean that relief will be denied: *Ebrahimi v Westbourne Galleries Ltd.* However, in a recent Australian case it was said that while the actions of the applicant for a winding-up order on this ground should be an important consideration for the court when deciding whether or not to grant the order, unclean hands would not constitute an absolute bar to an applicant in a winding-up application, as in many instances both parties will come with unclean hands: *Pham Thai Duc v PTS Australian Distributor Pty Ltd* [2005] NSWSC 98 (New South Wales Supreme Court).

Courts will only order winding up on the petition of a contributory if he or she is endeavouring to protect his or her position as a member, for a member is not permitted to obtain a winding-up order under s 122(1)(f) to protect a wider range of interests than could be protected under s 994 of the Companies Act 2006: *Re JE Cade & Son Ltd* [1991] BCC 360 at 377.

In *Sea Management Singapore Pte Ltd v Professional Service Brokers Ltd* [2012] CIV-2011-404-5315, the New Zealand High Court stated that the petitioner has the onus of establishing that it is either impracticable or inequitable to be limited to remedies in any shareholders' agreement.

It has been held in New Zealand that the court would not regard the possible impact on a shareholder who was not involved directly in the circumstances that led to the breakdown of confidence as a sufficient reason to deny a winding-up order (*Jenkins v Supscaf Ltd* [2006] 3 NZLR 264, NZHC).

A *Practice Direction* ([1999] BCC 741 at 744) makes it incumbent on the petitioner to state whether he or she is willing to consent to a validating order under s 127. The problem for the company is that once a petition has been presented it can be restricted in its dealings. See the notes attached to s 127.

At one time it was thought that this ground was to be construed in the light of other grounds, namely those now contained in s 122(1)(a)–(f), but clearly this ground is now regarded as being independent of the other grounds in s 122(1): *Loch v John Blackwood Ltd* [1924] AC 783 at 788–790; *Davis & Co (Australia) Ltd* [1936] 1 All ER 299; *Ebrahimi v Westbourne Galleries Ltd* [1973] AC 360.

If a controlling shareholder causes a company to oppose unreasonably a petition for a winding-up order on this ground, he or she might be held liable personally for the costs: *Cassegrain v CTK Engineering Pty Ltd* [2005] NSWSC 495 (NSW Sup Ct).

See A Keay *McPherson's Law of Company Liquidation* (Sweet and Maxwell, 3rd edn, 2013) at 244–259.

123 Definition of inability to pay debts

(1) A company is deemed unable to pay its debts—

    (a) if a creditor (by assignment or otherwise) to whom the company is indebted in a sum exceeding £750 then due has served on the company, by leaving it at the company's registered office, a written demand (in the prescribed form) requiring the company to pay the sum so due and the company has for 3 weeks thereafter neglected to pay the sum or to secure or compound for it to the reasonable satisfaction of the creditor, or

    (b) if, in England and Wales, execution or other process issued on a judgment, decree or order of any court in favour of a creditor of the company is returned unsatisfied in whole or in part, or

    (c) if, in Scotland, the induciae of a charge for payment on an extract decree, or an extract registered bond, or an extract registered protest, have expired without payment being made, or

    (d) if, in Northern Ireland, a certificate of unenforceability has been granted in respect of a judgment against the company, or

(e)   if it is proved to the satisfaction of the court that the company is unable to pay its debts as they fall due.

(2) A company is also deemed unable to pay its debts if it is proved to the satisfaction of the court that the value of the company's assets is less than the amount of its liabilities, taking into account its contingent and prospective liabilities.

(3) The money sum for the time being specified in subsection (1)(a) is subject to increase or reduction by order under section 416 in Part XV.

General note—The provision details six instances where a company will be deemed to be unable to pay its debts. Where any of these can be established, a court will presume the company to be insolvent, and the onus is then on the company to prove that it is able to pay its debts.

The fact that a creditor is able to establish that the company is unable to pay its debts does not mean that a winding-up order will be made automatically: the court has an unfettered discretion (s 125(1)). The company might be able to establish positively that it is solvent. After saying that, a court may still make a winding-up order if the assets of the company are greater than liabilities, and if the company does not dispute the fact that it owes money to the creditor who has requested payment, because non-payment gives rise to a legitimate suspicion of inability to pay: *Cornhill Insurance plc v Improvement Services Ltd* [1986] 1 WLR 114, [1986] 2 BCC 98, 942. But it might be necessary to be able to prove first that any sum owed has been demanded from the company: *Re a Company (No 006798 of 1995)* [1996] 2 BCLC 48, [1996] BCC 395.

Petitioners must be able to establish that the company is unable to pay its debts at the time of the hearing as well as when the petition was presented: *Re Fildes Bros Ltd* [1970] 1 WLR 592.

Written demand—This demand is referred to as a 'statutory demand' in winding-up proceedings (r 4.4(2)), and is a procedure that dates back to the Companies Act 1862. There is no limit to the life of a demand nor any time specified in which a petition, when it is founded on the non-compliance with a demand, is to be presented. But one would think that the court may take the view that reliance on the failure to comply with a demand served many months or even weeks before the presentation of the petition would not be appropriate, as the company's situation might have changed in that time.

There seems nothing to prohibit a creditor using the non-compliance with a statutory demand to found a petition even where the demand was served by another creditor, as the only effect of a failure to comply is to lead to the presumption of insolvency: *Re Island of Anglesea Coal Co* (1861) 4 LT 684. Yet to do so the creditor would surely have to establish that in excess of £750 was owed and that the creditor had demanded payment in some way.

The company must be given a complete three-week period in which to comply, and a petition should not be presented until a full 21 days have elapsed.

The non-compliance with a statutory demand only provides a presumption that the company is unable to pay its debts. So, the company might be able to present evidence, besides arguing that the debt on which the petition is founded is disputed, that rebuts the presumption of insolvency. To rebut the presumption a company that wishes to establish the fact of solvency must adduce evidence for that purpose. Once that is done then the judge will decide whether the evidence is relevant, followed by a determination as to whether the evidence is admissible. Then the judge will assess the probative value of the evidence. That assessment is inductive. Finally the judge will decide whether the claimed solvency is probable or more probable than not: *Deputy Commissioner of Taxation v De Simeone Consulting Pty Ltd* [2007] FCA 548 at [12] (Aust Fed Ct).

See rr 4.4–4.6 and the notes attached to those rules for the form of, and practice concerning demands.

Creditor—To be able to invoke s 123(1)(a), the person who serves a statutory demand must be a creditor owed in excess of £750. The meaning of creditor is discussed under 'Creditor' in the notes attached to s 124.

A person who is the creditor by assignment may serve a demand, but an equitable assignee is not able to, as it must be served by the person who holds the legal title to the debt: *Re Steel Wing Co* [1921] 1 Ch 349 at 356.

Creditors who serve a demand on a company may be held liable for the costs of the company if it applies successfully for an order restraining the presentation of a petition on the basis of a dispute over the debt relied on in the demand: *Cannon Screen Entertainment Ltd v Handmade Films (Distributors) Ltd* (1989) 5 BCC 207 at 209.

Where a company has been served with a demand and the company wishes to resist the demand, the appropriate course of action is to apply for an injunction to prevent the creditor from either presenting a petition or advertising a petition that is presented.

See r 13.12 and the notes relating to it.

The debt—A debt must be due, and must be payable to the one serving the demand at that time, so this rules out contingent (it has been held that while a contingent debt is a debt for the purposes of winding up, such a debt could not be used as the basis for a statutory demand until the relevant contingency had happened (*JSF Finance and Current Exchange Co Ltd v Akma Solutions Inc* [2001] 2 BCLC 307, [2002] BPIR 621) and prospective debts, as well as unliquidated sums.

It has been held that a claim for money had and received, whilst restitutionary, is able to be treated as a debt due for the purposes of a provision like s 123: *OPC Managed Rehab Ltd v Accident Compensation Corporation* [2006] 1 NZLR 778, NZCA.

In circumstances where the debt is owed in a foreign currency then, as there is no express provision requiring conversion, the creditor may make the demand in the foreign currency, or the creditor may convert the amount into pounds sterling: *Re a Debtor (No 51/SD/91)* [1992] 1 WLR 1294, [1993] 2 All ER 40. If the debt is converted into pounds sterling it would appear that the creditor is not obliged to state the rate of exchange or the date of conversion (*Re a Debtor (No 51/SD/91)*), which might appear to be unfair to the company.

In *HMRC v Earley* [2011] EWHC1783 (Ch), [2011] BPIR 1590, it was held that the amount of an assessment of tax was a debt and it was liquidated and ascertained.

See r 13.12 and the notes relating to it.

The demand—See rr 4.4–4.6 and the accompanying notes concerning the elements of a demand.

At one time demands were construed very strictly by the courts and minor mistakes would invalidate them for the purposes of s 123. But now, as with demands relied on in bankruptcy petitions, the courts have exhibited a more liberal approach. For instance, in *Re a Debtor (No 1 of 1987)* [1988] 1 All ER 959, the court refused to set aside a defective demand served on an individual debtor even though it was perplexing. On appeal the decision was affirmed ([1989] 1 WLR 271, [1989] 2 All ER 46, CA) and Nicholls LJ said that while the demand may have been confusing for the debtor, it was not confusing enough to set aside the demand. Where there is a defective demand, but no prejudice to the debtor and no indication that the debtor would have complied with a demand, which was not defective, the demand should not be regarded as fatally flawed: *Re a Debtor (No 1 of 1987)* [1987] 1 WLR 271 at 279. If a demand overstates the amount owed by a debtor to a creditor, it has been held that the demand is not necessarily invalid, as the debtor could have avoided the presumption of insolvency by paying what he or she admitted was owing and taking issue with the demand as far as the balance was concerned: *Re A Debtor (No 490/SD/91)* [1992] 1 WLR 507, [1992] 2 All ER 664, [1993] BCLC 164 – following *Re a Debtor (No 1 of 1987)* [1989] 1 WLR 271, [1989] 2 All ER 46, CA. But all of this should not be seen as a signal to creditors and their advisers that they can be slipshod in their preparation of demands: *Re a Debtor (No 1 of 1987)* [1989] 2 All ER 46 at 51.

See Milman 'Statutory Demands in the Courts: A Retreat from Formalism in Bankruptcy Law' [1994] Conv 289.

There is no English authority that determines whether the insertion in the demand of a wrong name for the company is defective. There is divergence of opinion in Australia, but the stronger view is that the court will make an allowance for minor errors (*Transfloors Pty Ltd v SWF Hoists & Industrial Equipment Pty Ltd* (1985) 3 ACLC 66) or for errors which do not frustrate the purpose of the provisions or do not deprive a party of a right (*Pro Image Production (Vic) Pty Ltd v Catalyst Television Productions Pty Ltd* (1988) 6 ACLC 888; *Hornet Aviation Pty Ltd v Ansett Australia Ltd* (1995) 13 ACLC 613). But there is an opposite view, namely that the use of the wrong company name is a defect which makes the demand invalid: *B&M Quality Constructions Pty Ltd v WG Brady Pty Ltd* (1994) 12 ACLC 970; *Re Scandon Pty Ltd* (1996) 14 ACLC 124.

There is Australian authority to the effect that a multiple number of creditors are unable to serve a single demand on one company – it is a defect which would cause a substantial injustice: *First Line Distribution Pty Ltd v Whiley* (1995) 13 ACLC 1216 at 1220. Australian authority also provides that a valid demand can claim a portion of the debt owed to the creditor: *Commonwealth Bank of Australia v Garuda Aviation Pty Ltd* [2013] WASCA 61.

Service—The creditor has the obligation to do all that he or she can reasonably do to bring the demand to the notice of the company. Unlike bankruptcy, where the creditor is required, if practicable, to serve the demand personally (r 6.3(2); *Practice Direction: Insolvency Proceedings* [1999] BPIR 441, [2000] BCC 92 at para 11.1), there is no indication in the Insolvency Act or Rules as to what constitutes effective service on companies.

While it has been said that service by post does not constitute leaving the demand at the company's registered office (something required by the provision) (*Re a Company* [1985] BCLC 37), judges are willing to accept service by post provided that it can be proved that the demand had arrived at the office. If that can be established, then the view is that the demand has been left at the office by the postal worker who delivered it: *Re a Company No 008790 of 1990* [1991] BCLC 561. So the consequence of this is that where a company denies receipt of a demand by post, a creditor is not going to be able to rely on the demand, even if proof of posting could be adduced.

It has been held that 'leaving it at the registered office' does not mean serving the company at its registered office by telex (*Re a Company* [1985] BCLC 37); however, it is thought that if the company admitted receiving the telex or fax, then, on the basis of the approach in *Re a Company No 008790 of 1990*, the demand would be effective.

It was held in the Australian case of *R & R Consultants Pty Ltd v Commissioner of Taxation* [2006] NSWSC 1152, (2006) 204 FLR 149 (NSW S Ct) that the service of a photocopy of a signed statutory demand that is in the prescribed form is valid, but it is highly debatable whether a court in England or Wales would take the same view.

For further discussion, see Keay 'The Service of Statutory Demands on Companies' [2003] *Insolvency Lawyer* 148.

Neglected to pay—This phrase does not mean fail to pay, but a failure to pay without a reasonable excuse: *Re London and Paris Banking Corp* (1875) 19 Eq 444; *Mann v Goldstein* [1968] 1 WLR 1091; *Re Lympne Investments Ltd* [1972] 1 WLR 523, [1972] 2 All ER 385; *Re a Company (No 033729 of 1982)* [1984] 3 All ER 78, [1984] 1 WLR 1090; *Re a Company (No 006273 of 1992)* [1992] BCC 794. As a consequence, where a company refuses to pay on the basis that it believes that the debt claimed is not actually owing, ie there is a genuine dispute, then the company cannot be said to be presumed insolvent: *Re Lympne Investments Ltd* [1972] 1 WLR 523 at 527, [1972] 2 All ER 385 at 389. For a discussion as to a genuine dispute concerning a debt, see the notes accompanying s 125.

Secure or compound to the reasonable satisfaction of the creditor—A bankruptcy provision, s 383(2), states that the securing of a debt involves the giving of a mortgage, charge, lien or other security over the property of the debtor: see *Re a Debtor (No 310 of 1988)* [1989] 1 WLR 271, [1989] 2 All ER 42.

A compounding of the debt occurs when the creditor and the debtor company come to some arrangement which reasonably satisfies the creditor. The test of whether an offer is reasonable and should be accepted by a creditor is objective and depends on whether a reasonable hypothetical creditor in the position of the petitioning creditor, and in the light of the actual history of the dealings between the creditor and the debtor, could have reached the conclusion that the petitioning creditor reached: *Re a Debtor (No 32 of 1993)* [1995] 1 All ER 628; *HM Customs and Excise v Dougall* [2001] BPIR 269. There may be a range of reasonable positions that the hypothetical reasonable creditor could take and a rejection of an offer by the petitioner is only to be regarded as unreasonable if the refusal is beyond the range of reasonable responses to it: *HM Customs and Excise v Dougall* [2001] BPIR 269 at 272. The court has to look at the position as at the date of the hearing: *HMRC v Garwood* [2012] BPIR 575. The debtor must be full, frank and open with the creditor and provide all the information that a creditor needs in order to make an informed decision: *HM Customs and Excise v Dougall*. Where a creditor has a very rigid policy of rejecting offers that could tell against it, but coherent in-house policies adopted by a creditor were not necessarily wrong. A creditor is not obliged to be patient or generous and could be concerned about its own interests. In this regard the costs implications for a creditor were a highly material consideration: *HMRC v Garwood* [2012] BPIR 575. If a reasonable offer to compound is accepted, the creditor cannot renege on the arrangement: *Kema Plastics Pty Ltd v Mulford Plastics Pty Ltd* [1981] ACLC 33, 225.

In *Re a Debtor (No 32 of 1993)* [1995] 1 All ER 628 an offer by a debtor of £15,000 in full settlement of a debt over £33,000 was held to be an offer to compound for a debt.

Unsatisfied execution—It is not possible to petition for winding up on the basis of unsatisfied execution if the sheriff is unable to gain access to the company's premises, as that would merely be a failure to levy execution and not a case of execution not being satisfied: *Re A Debtor (No 340 of 1992); The Debtor v First National Commercial Bank plc* [1994] 3 All ER 269, [1994] 2 BCLC 171, [1993] TLR 402 (affirmed on appeal in [1996] 2 All ER 211). If a petitioner did seek to do so then this would be a serious defect within the meaning of r 7.55: *Re A Debtor (No 340 of 1992)*. Petitioning creditors have to satisfy the words of s 123(1)(b) strictly (*Re A Debtor (No 340 of 1992)*) and the court is not able to waive parts of the paragraph: *Re A Debtor (No 340 of 1992)*.

Courts may go behind any return in order to determine whether the execution was in fact unsatisfied. Also, they may even investigate the judgment on which proceedings were based: *Re Railway Finance Co* (1866) 14 WR 785; *Eberhardt v Mair* [1995] 1 WLR 1180. See the notes under the heading 'Judgment obtained in relation to petition debt' found under s 125.

See the comments accompanying s 268.

Unable to pay debts as they fall due—This provides for a cash flow test of insolvency, and tends to be the ground relied on most frequently now by petitioning creditors in practice. Companies that are covered by this phrase are those that are unable to meet current demands (*Re Capital Annuities Ltd* [1979] 1 WLR 170), irrespective of whether the company is possessed of assets which, if realised, would enable it to discharge its liabilities in full. It has been held that where a debt is due, an invoice has been sent and the debt is not disputed, if the company fails to pay then that is evidence of inability to pay: *Taylor's Industrial Flooring Ltd v M & H Plant Hire (Manchester) Ltd* [1990] BCLC 216, [1990] BCC 44, CA. But it has been said that if the creditor has not made a demand for payment prior to petitioning courts should be less ready to infer inability of a company to pay its debts: *Mac Plant Services Ltd v Contract Lifting Services (Scotland) Ltd* [2008] CSOH 158, 2009 SC 125 at [68].

Debts are usually regarded as liquidated claims, namely claims for amounts that are able to be ascertained or readily ascertained: *Stooke or Taylor* (1880) 5 QBD 565 at 575.

An important issue is whether future debts are to be taken into account in determining ability to pay, or are we limited to a consideration of debts presently due? Whilst old authority has held that contingent and prospective debts cannot be taken into consideration: *Re London & Manchester Industrial Association* (1875) 1 Ch D 466 at 472, they dealt with differently worded legislation, and the answer to the question now appears to be 'yes,' according to Briggs J in *Re Cheyne Finance plc* [2007] EWHC 2402 (Ch), [2008] 1 BCLC 741, [2008] BCC 182, because the words 'as they fall due' invite considerations of futurity (the words were regarded as synonymous with 'become due' which in Australia has led courts to look to future debts in assessing ability to pay within the equivalent of s 123(1)(e) (at [53])). His Lordship said that the fact that s 123(2) required one to consider contingent and prospective liabilities in determining solvency under that provision, did not mean that prospective liabilities could not be taken into account under s 123(1)(e). *Re Cheyne Finance* does not resolve the issue of how far in the future must the debt be due. Briggs J specifically indicated that a debt coming due in six months would be able to be taken into account. In *New Cap Reinsurance Corporation Ltd (in liq) v A E Grant* [2008] NSWSC 1015 at [44] the Court said that one looks to the reasonably immediate future, which is what Briggs J probably did. Briggs J approved of the view of the New South Wales Court of Appeal in *Lewis v Doran* [2005] NSWCA 243, (2005) 219 ALR 555 at [103] that how far one goes into the future depends on the kind of business conducted by the company and, if known, the company's future liabilities. The approach adopted in *Re Cheyne Finance* permits flexibility but does introduce a fair amount of uncertainty. In *BNY Corporate Trustee Services Limited v Eurosail-UK 2007-3BL Plc* [2013] UKSC 28, [2013] 1 WLR 1408 at [37] the Supreme Court confirmed the approach taken by Briggs J in *Cheyne* accepting the fact that the cash flow test is concerned both with due debts and with debts falling due from time to time in the 'reasonably near' future (which will depend on all the circumstances, but especially on the nature of the company's business). The Court said that beyond the reasonably near future any attempt to apply a cash flow test is completely speculative, and a comparison of present assets with present and future liabilities (discounted for contingencies and deferment) is the only sensible way to proceed, even though it is far from an exact science. In *Re Casa Estates (UK) Ltd* [2013] EWHC 2371 (Ch) at [34] Warren J said that balance sheet insolvency is not irrelevant to a company's ability to pay debts as they fall due. His Lordship did not think that the judgments in the *BNY Corporate Trustee Services Limited v Eurosail-UK 2007-3BL PLC* case suggested a rigid demarcation between cash flow and balance sheet insolvency. His Lordship had earlier said that anticpated income and outgoings over the reasonably near future cannot be taken into account (at [29], but that might not rule out what was said in the Australian case of *Sandell Porter* (1966) 115 CLR 666, (1966) 40 ALJR 71 that a company can rely upon money which might be obtained from the sale of assets or upon loan money where the loan was granted because security could be taken against he company's assets.

The UK Supreme Court in *BNY Corporate Trustee Services Ltd v Eurosail–UK 2007-3BL plc* said in obiter that s 123(1)(e) 'does not treat proof of a single specific default by a company as conclusive of the general issue of its inability to pay its debts.' The Court said that the scope of s 123(1)(e) is wider than a single debt (at [25]).

An issue that does not appear to have been decided in England is whether a claim for unliquidated damages is to be taken into account in deciding the quantum of the debts of the company. This is probably because the answer is relatively straightforward. At the time one is determining whether the company is unable to pay, for the purposes of s 123, the claim has yet to be decided on and, therefore, the amount of the claim could not be taken into account. This is despite the fact that r 13.12(1)(b) provides that 'debt' means, inter alia, 'any debt or liability to which the company may become subject after that date by reason of any obligation incurred before that date.' This latter provision is referring to someone proving in a winding up and cannot be applied to a decision concerning the solvency of a company under s 123. The New South Wales Court of Appeal in *Box Valley Pty Ltd v Kidd* [2006] NSWCA 26, (2006) 24 ACLC 471, stated that even if it was highly probable that a claim would lead to a liability to pay damages it could not be considered as a debt in determining inability to pay. The type of claim envisaged in this paragraph cannot, of course, be classified as a prospective debt as there is no certainty that it will be due in the future.

There has been significant uncertainty as to whether the fact that a creditor grants the debtor company some forbearance in requiring payment of a debt (such as an extension of time to pay) that is due can be regarded as meaning that that debt has not fallen due for the purposes of determining the debtor's solvency. In Australia there is a divergence of opinion, with cases such as *Carrier Air Conditioning Pty Ltd v Kurda* (1993) 11 ACSR 247 (SA S Ct) taking the view that forbearance should not be taken into account in determining whether a debt has fallen due, while other cases, such as *Re Newark Pty Ltd* [1993] 1 Qd R 409, (1991) 6 ACSR 255 (Qld S Ct (Full Ct)) and, much more recently, *Tru Floor Service Pty Ltd v Jenkins (No 2)* [2006] FCA 632 (Aust Fed Ct) have adopted a more liberal line and held that forbearance might be considered. An obiter comment of Warren J in *Re Casa Estates (UK) Ltd* [2013] EWHC 2371 (Ch) at [75] suggests that his Lordship would agree with the approach taken in *Carrier Air Conditioning Pty Ltd v Kurda*.

In determining whether a company is able to pay its debts, the courts must take into account what current revenue the company has as well as what the company can procure by realising assets within a relatively short time: *Re Capital Annuities Ltd* [1979] 1 WLR 170 at 182, 188. As mentioned above, a company is not limited to its own cash on hand in determining whether it has the ability to pay its debts. A company can rely upon money which might be obtained from the sale of assets or upon loan money where the loan was granted because security could be taken against he company's assets: *Sandell v Porter* (1966) 115 CLR 666, (1966) 40 ALJR 71; *Lewis v Doran* [2005] NSWCA 243, (2005) 219 ALR 555, NSWCA. Where the sale of a major asset is near enough to certain, the funds that will be realised may be taken into account: *Cuthbertson & Richards Sawmills Pty Ltd v Thomas* (1998) 28 ACSR 310 at 319. But a hope or expectation that the company will obtain future assets would not be able to be taken into account unless there was a right to hold that hope or expectation: *Byblos Bank SAL v Al Khudhairy* [1987] BCLC 232; *BNY Corporate Trustee Services Ltd v Eurosail–UK 2007-3BL plc* [2010] EWHC 2005 (Ch) at [35]. It has been held in Australia that property could not be taken into account when it would take six months to realise it and debts were falling due within a month: *Hall v Poolman* [2007] NSWSC 1330, (2007) 215 FLR 243, [2008] BPIR 892 at [187].

Other Australian authority has held that a debtor could not rely on realising assets which would involve a cessation or breaking up of its business: *Re Timbatec Pty Ltd* (1974) 24 FLR 30 at 36–37. Other Australian authority has stated that a court might take into account the fact that the company is able to obtain funds under an unsecured loan provided that the court was convinced that the third party lender was clearly willing to extend funds to the company: *Lewis v Doran* [2004] NSWSC 608, (2005) 50 ACSR 175 at [113] (NSW S Ct) and accepted on appeal in *Lewis v Doran* [2005] NSWCA 243, (2005) 219 ALR 555, NSW CA. Recently, in *Leveraged Equities Ltd v Hilldale Australia Pty Ltd* [2008] NSWSC 190 it was said that the promised provision of a loan which would enable the company to pay its debts could be taken into account in determining whether the company was insolvent or not. There are indications that the judgment of Warren J in *Re Casa Estates (UK) Ltd* [2013] EWHC 2371 (Ch) at [35] supports that approach.

In a situation where one company in a corporate group had recourse to the assets of another company in the group and such a recourse did not cause the second company to become insolvent or involves merely delaying the inevitable insolvency of the first, this would be taken into account in determining whether the first company was able to pay its debts as they fall due: *Hall v Poolman* [2007] NSWSC 1330, (2007) 215 FLR 243, [2008] BPIR 892, NSW S Ct.

Recently, it has been held in the Australian case of *Austin Australia Pty Ltd v De Martin & Gasparini Pty Ltd* [2007] NSWSC 1238, NSW S Ct. that the following might be taken into account in order to determine whether a company is unable to pay its debts: a history of dishonoured cheques; suppliers insisting on cash on delivery; the issuing of post-dated cheques; the issuing of rounded cheques (suggesting part payment of debts); special arrangements with creditors; inability to produce timely audited accounts; non-payment of workers' compensation premiums, VAT, pension payments and group tax; demands from bankers to reduce amount owing on overdraft; receipt of letters of demand and court processes.

In *Leveraged Equities Ltd v Hilldale Australia Pty Ltd* [2008] NSWSC 190 it was said that the promised provision of a loan which would enable the company to pay its debts could be taken into account in determining whether the company was insolvent or not.

Generally, determining whether a company is cash flow insolvent is a question of fact, that may be established by a receiver for debenture-holders taking possession of all of the company's assets: *Re Lyric Club* (1892) 36 Sol Jo 801. Indicators of cash flow insolvency are that: the company has a large number of outstanding debts and unsatisfied judgments (*Re Tweeds Garages Ltd* [1962] Ch 406); the company or its solicitors have admitted that the company is unable to pay (*Re Great Northern Copper Co* (1869) 20 LT 264); or the absence of assets on which execution can be levied: *Re Flagstaff Silver Mining Co of Utah* (1875) 20 Eq 268; *Re Yate Colleries Co* [1883] WN 171; *Re Douglas Griggs Engineering Ltd* [1963] Ch 19. An Australian decision has indicated that the question of inability to pay debts is a question of commercial reality having regard to the facts of the particular case: *Lewis v Doran* (2004) NSWSC 608, (2005) 50 ACSR 175, NSW S Ct.

For further discussion, see RM Goode *Principles of Corporate Insolvency Law* (Sweet and Maxwell, 4th edn, 2011) at 121–129; K Baird and P Sidle 'Cash Flow Insolvency' (2008) 21 *Insolvency Intelligence* 40.

Value of assets less than liabilities—Section 123(2) provides for a balance sheet test of insolvency.

In determining insolvency on this basis a court is able to take into account contingent and prospective liabilities, but not contingent and prospective assets: *Byblos Bank SAL v Al-Khudhairy* (1986) 2 BCC 99, 549, CA; *BNY Corporate Trustee Services Ltd v Eurosail-UK 2007-3BL plc* [2010] EWHC 2005 (Ch) at [35] (affirmed on appeal – [2011] EWCA Civ 227, [2011] BCC 399 and [2013] UKSC 28, [2013] 1 WLR 1408). 'Liabilities' is a broader term than 'debts' (*Re A Debtor (No 17 of 1966)* [1967] Ch 590, [1967] 1 All ER 668) and is defined for the purposes of winding up in r 13.12(4). Rule 13.12(3) states that it is immaterial whether the liability is present or future, whether it is certain or contingent, or whether its amount is fixed or liquidated, or is capable of being ascertained by fixed rules or as a matter of opinion. See the comments relating to 'Contingent or prospective creditors' in relation to s 124.

The starting point in relation to a company is that if its immediate liabilities are in excess of the assets the company is insolvent: *Re Casa Estates (UK) Ltd* [2013] EWHC 2371 (Ch) at [81] (the evidential burden would fall on the company to demonstrate why it can, notwithstanding its balance sheet, reasonably be expected to meet its liabilities). But, while this test seems to be quite simple to apply, it has been made clear in the *BNY Corporate Trustee Services Ltd v Eurosail–UK 2007-3BL plc* litigation [2010] EWHC 2005 (Ch) by Sir Andrew Morritt C and by the Court of Appeal on appeal (affirming the judgment at first instance ([2011] EWCA Civ 227, [2011] BCC 399) and the Supreme Court on appeal from the Court of Appeal ([2013] UKSC 28)) that this is not always the case. In the Supreme Court it was indicated that employing the balance sheet test did not simply involve computing the asset value and that of the liabilities and comparing them, without allowing some discount to take account of deferment and contingencies. The Court of Appeal said that it would be impractical as well as undesirable for a company to be deemed balance sheet insolvent every time its liabilities exceeded its assets. The provision does not call for an annual balance sheet in order to provide a snapshot of the affairs of the company at any specific time (as is the usual reason for accounting reasons). So, a company's audited accounts that show a net liability will not be conclusive evidence of insolvency for s 123(2) purposes. The court must look at the company's finances from a commercial and overall perspective and consider the facts of each case; the fact that there are temporary imbalances will not mean that insolvency is to be concluded. The courts will look at whether it is clear in practical terms that because of incurable deficiencies in assets it will not be able to meet future or prospective liabilities (*BNY Corporate Trustee Services Ltd v Eurosail–UK 2007-3BL plc* [2011] EWCA Civ 227, [2011] BCC 399 at [48]). The Supreme Court did not appear to demur to these views and in fact expressly endorsed aspects (at [38]). It did reject Lord Neuberger's 'end of the road' test, namely a company is to be seen as insolvent if it has reached the end of the road of put up the shutters. The Supreme Court did say that whether or not the balance sheet test was satisfied relied on the evidence of the company's circumstances in any given case (at [38]). The Court accepted the fact that the more distant a liability is the more difficult it is to establish it (at [42]).

In *BNY Corporate Trustee Services Ltd v Eurosail–UK 2007-3 BL plc* [2013] UKSC 28, [2013] 1 WLR 1408 at [48] the Supreme Court, affirming the decision of the Court of Appeal, said that for the purposes of the 'balance-sheet' test the ability of a company to meet liabilities, both prospective and contingent, is to be determined on the balance of probabilities with the burden of proof on the party asserting balance-sheet insolvency.

What 'taking account' means must be considered in the context of the overall question of whether the company is to be deemed to be insolvent because the amount of its liabilities exceeds the value of its assets. 'This will involve consideration of the relevant facts of the case, including when the prospective liability falls due, whether it is payable in sterling or some other currency, what assets will be available to meet it and what if any provision is made for the allocation of losses in relation to those assets': *BNY Corporate Trustee Services Ltd v Eurosail–UK 2007-3BL plc* [2010] EWHC 2005 (Ch) at [35] per Sir Andrew Morritt C. The Court of Appeal affirmed the judgment of Morritt C and these decisions appear to provide courts with greater discretion than was once thought when dealing with this test. While the Supreme court disapproved of some of the things that the Court of Appeal said this seems correct.

A court may only take into account the assets of the company held at that time; so assets which are expected to be received in the future by the company or funds that it has on loan are both excluded from being taken into account: *Byblos Bank SAL v Al-Khudairy* (1986) 2 BCC 99, 549 at 99, 562 and 99, 563.

For further discussion, see RM Goode *Principles of Corporate Insolvency Law* (Sweet and Maxwell, 4th edn, 2011) at 129–147; P Walton '"Inability to pay debts": Beyond the Point of No Return' [2013] JBL 160; P Walton '*BNY Corporate Trustee Services Ltd v Eurosail–UK 2007-3BL plc* – from the point of no return to crystal ball gazing' (2013) 26 Insol Intel 124; A Keay *McPherson's Law of Company Liquidation* (3rd edn Sweet and Maxwell, 2013) at 98-119.

124 Application for winding up

(1) Subject to the provisions of this section, an application to the court for the winding up of a company shall be by petition presented either by the company, or the directors, or by any creditor or creditors (including any contingent or prospective creditor or creditors), contributory or

contributories, or by a liquidator (within the meaning of Article 2(b) of the EC Regulation) appointed in proceedings by virtue of Article 3(1) of the EC Regulation or a temporary administrator (within the meaning of Article 38 of the EC Regulation) or by the designated officer for a magistrates' court in the exercise of the power conferred by section 87A of the Magistrates' Courts Act 1980 (enforcement of fines imposed on companies), or by all or any of those parties, together or separately.

(2) Except as mentioned below, a contributory is not entitled to present a winding-up petition unless either—

(a)   the number of members is reduced below 2, or

(b)   the shares in respect of which he is a contributory, or some of them, either were originally allotted to him, or have been held by him, and registered in his name, for at least 6 months during the 18 months before the commencement of the winding up, or have devolved on him through the death of a former holder.

(3) A person who is liable under section 76 to contribute to a company's assets in the event of its being wound up may petition on either of the grounds set out in section 122(1)(f) and (g), and subsection (2) above does not then apply; but unless the person is a contributory otherwise than under section 76, he may not in his character as contributory petition on any other ground.

(3A) A winding-up petition on the ground set out in section 122(1)(fa) may only be presented by one or more creditors.

(4) A winding-up petition may be presented by the Secretary of State—

(a)   if the ground of the petition is that in section 122(1)(b) or (c), or

(b)   in a case falling within section 124A or 124B below.

(4AA) A winding up petition may be presented by the Financial Conduct Authority in a case falling within section 124C(1) or (2).

(4A) A winding-up petition may be presented by the Regulator of Community Interest Companies in a case falling within section 50 of the Companies (Audit, Investigations and Community Enterprise) Act 2004.

(5) Where a company is being wound up voluntarily in England and Wales, a winding-up petition may be presented by the official receiver attached to the court as well as by any other person authorised in that behalf under the other provisions of this section; but the court shall not make a winding-up order on the petition unless it is satisfied that the voluntary winding up cannot be continued with due regard to the interests of the creditors or contributories.

Amendments— Criminal Justice Act 1988, s 62(2)(b); Companies Act 1989, s 60(2); Access to Justice Act 1999, s 90, Sch 13, para 133; Insolvency Act 2000, s 1, Sch 1, paras 1, 7; SI 2002/1240; Courts Act 2003, s 109(1), Sch 8, para 294; SI 2004/2326; Companies (Audit, Investigations and Community Enterprise) Act 2004, s 50(3); SI 2006/2078; SI 2009/1941; SI 2013/496.

General note—This provision sets out who is entitled to present a petition for winding up. But it must be noted that there are pieces of legislation that give other parties the right to present petitions. These are, for example Charities Act 2006, s 113 (Attorney-General);

Building Societies Act 1986, s 37(1)(a) (Financial Services Authority); Credit Unions Act 1979, s 20(2) (Financial Services Authority); Agricultural Marketing Act 1958, s 2 (Minister for Agriculture); Companies (Audit, Investigations and Community Enterprise) Act 2004, s 50 (Regulator of Community Interest Companies).

In very exceptional circumstances a court may order winding up on its own motion: *Lancefield v Lancefield* [2002] BPIR 1108 (a case actually dealing with an insolvent partnership); *Re Marches Credit Union Ltd* [2013] EWHC 1731 (Ch) (this involved an entity that was an Industrial and Provident Society and winding up was ordered on a public interest basis).

The petition—The petition is not to contain matters of evidence: *Re Rica Gold Washing Co* (1879) 11 Ch D 36 at 43. It does not have to be signed by the petitioner: *Re Testro Bros Consolidated Ltd* [1965] VR 18, Vic S Ct. A petitioner can only rely, at the hearing, on the grounds set out in the petition (*Re Fildes Bros Ltd* [1970] 1 WLR 592; *Re Armvent Ltd* [1975] 1 WLR 1679), and if a petition fails to provide a ground for winding up, or states one that is not covered by the Act, then, unless the court allows amendment of the petition, it will be dismissed: *Re Wear Engine Works Co* (1875) 10 Ch App 188. Leave can be granted to amend a petition to enable reliance to be placed on a post-petition debt, and this is despite the fact that otherwise the petition would have been liable to be struck out: *Re Richbell Strategic Holdings Ltd* [1997] 2 BCLC 429.

As a petition is not an action on a judgment for the purposes of s 24 of the Limitation Act 1980, a petitioner is not required to present a petition within six years of the judgment on which the petition relies: *Ridgeway Motors (Isleworth) Ltd v Altis Ltd* [2004] EWHC 1535 (Ch), [2004] BPIR 1323, [2005] BCC 496 (disagreeing with *Jelly v All Type Roofing Co* [1997] BCC 465, sub nom *Re A Debtor* [1997] Ch 310 which involved a bankruptcy petition).

A petition is not to be classified as a claim or counterclaim in law, although it is a species of legal proceedings: *Best Beat Ltd v Rossall* [2006] EWHC 1494 (Comm), [2006] BPIR 1357. See rr 4.7–4.14 and the comments accompanying those rules.

Company—Applications by companies to have themselves wound up by the court are rather rare (e g *Re Winis Trading Pty Ltd* (1984) 3 ACLC 39), probably because where it is thought proper for the company to wind up, a resolution to wind up will be obtained, and voluntary liquidation will ensue. However, this requires an extraordinary or special resolution, and for some reason or other this might not be possible as a three-fourths majority of shareholders able to vote and voting must support a resolution. It might be possible, however, to secure an ordinary resolution, sufficient for the company to apply for a winding-up order.

If the directors were to present a petition in the name of the company, but without securing the necessary vote in support, the court might adjourn the petition and permit the company meeting to ratify what the directors had done: *Re Galway and Salthill Tramways Co* [1918] IR 62.

Where a company presents a petition, it may rely on any ground contained in s 122(1): *Re Langham Skating Rink Co* (1877) 5 Ch D 669; *Smith v Duke of Manchester* (1883) 24 Ch D 611; *Re Emmadart Ltd* [1979] Ch 540, [1979] 1 All ER 599.

If a petition is presented by an administrative receiver or supervisor of a company voluntary arrangement, then it is done in the name of the company. Where an administrator presents a petition, the petition should be expressed to be the petition of the company by its administrator (r 4.7(7)(a)).

Directors—The reference to 'directors' means all of the directors and not one or a majority of them can petition; consequently, absent a proper board resolution, all of the directors must agree to the presentation of the petition: *Re Instrumentation Electrical Services Ltd* (1988) 4 BCC 301. All directors are bound by a proper resolution for the winding up of the company passed by the board, and one director may present a petition on behalf of all: *Re Equiticorp International plc* [1989] 1 WLR 1010, (1989) 5 BCC 599. For a recent example, see *Re Minrealm Ltd* [2007] EWHC 3078 (Ch) (petition brought by directors – majority supported it and passed a board resolution to wind up).

If a director were to petition, such action could be regarded as an abuse of process and liability for costs may be imposed on him or her: *Re a Company (No 003689 of 1998)* (1998) *The Times*, October 7.

Creditor—The petitioner must be a person to whom the company owes a debt, which has not been paid at the date of the presentation of the petition (*Re William Hockley Ltd* [1962] 1 WLR 555), and so there must be a debtor-creditor relationship.

Where a court had delivered a judgment in favour of the petitioner then the petitioner is a creditor for the purposes of winding up even if the judgment is subject to an appeal: *El Ajou v Dollar Land (Manhattan) Ltd* [2005] EWHC 2861 (Ch), [2007] BCC 953.

A debt may be defined as a sum payable by one person to another in respect of a liquidated sum in money. See r 13.12 and its definition of 'debt' for winding up purposes, as well as the notes accompanying that rule. While r 13.12(4) states that liability means liability to pay money or money's worth, including any liability under an enactment, any liability for breach of trust, any liability in contract, tort or bailment, and any liability arising out of any obligation to make restitution, a person with an unliquidated claim in tort or contract is not able to present a petition: *Re Pen-y-van Colliery Co* (1877) Ch D 477; *Re Milford Docks Co* (1883) 23 Ch D 292.

There is Australian authority to the effect that a creditor, to whom the company is jointly and severally liable with another person, can apply for a winding-up order: *Re Buildmat (Aust) Pty Ltd* (1981) 5 ACLR 459. A creditor by subrogation is entitled to petition: *Re National Permanent Building Society* (1869) 5 Ch App 309. Any debt owed must be a valid debt and a person who claims a debt resulting from an illegal transaction is not able to petition: *Re South Wales Atlantic Steamship Co* (1875) 2 Ch D 763. The executor of a creditor of the company is able to petition as a creditor provided that probate was granted prior to when the petition is heard: *Re Masonic and General Life Assurance Co* (1885) 32 Ch D 373. A person who has obtained an order for costs against a company can petition for a winding-up order on the basis of being a creditor.

While an equitable assignee of a debt is not able to serve a demand under s 123(1)(a), he or she is entitled to petition for winding up on the basis of the debt: *Re Steel Wing Co* [1921] 1 Ch 349 at 356.

If a creditor's claim, at the time of presentation of a petition, is statute-barred, he or she is not able to be classified as a 'creditor' for winding up purposes: *Re Karnose Property Trust Ltd* (1989) 5 BCC 14; *Re Joshua Shaw & Sons Ltd* (1989) 5 BCC 188. But if a creditor's claim became statute-barred after the presentation of the petition and before the hearing of the petition, the creditor still has standing to obtain a winding up order: *Motor Terms Co Pty Ltd v Liberty Insurance Ltd* (1967) 116 CLR 177, HCA.

Where a petitioner has standing as a creditor at the time of the presentation of the petition, but is not a creditor at the time of the hearing of the petition, the court has a discretion whether or not to make a winding-up order: *Australian Beverage Distributors Pty Ltd v The Redrock Co Pty Ltd* [2007] NSWSC 966, [2007] 213 FLR 450 at [33], [34].

Secured creditor—It has been said that a secured creditor is a creditor, even following the appointment of a receiver (*Re Portsmouth Borough (Kingston Fratton and Southsea) Tramways Co* [1892] Ch 362), and so it is assumed that such a creditor, whether the debt is fully or partly secured, may petition: (*Masri Apartments Pty Ltd v Perpetual Nominees Ltd* (2004) 214 ALR 338, [2004] NSWCA 471, NSW CA). This seems to be supported by the fact that in *Re Lafayette Electronics Europe Ltd* [2006] EWHC 1006 (Ch), [2007] BCC 890 at [7], H H Judge Norris QC indicated that he was not convinced that a secured creditor was unable to present a petition. Subsequently Mann J in *Re Sushinho Ltd* [2011] All ER (D) 52 had unreservedly accepted that a secured creditor may petition. It has been held in Australia that it is not incumbent on the creditor to realise its security prior to, or instead of, petitioning: *Re Alexander's Securities (No 2)* [1983] 2 Qd R 597.

Contingent or prospective creditors—A contingent creditor is 'a person towards whom, under an existing obligation, the company may or will become subject to a present liability on the happening of some future event or at some future date': *Re William Hockley Ltd* [1962] 1 WLR 555 at 558, although Arden LJ (in obiter) felt that this would be a future or prospective liability: *R v Bimingham City Council* [2005] EWCA Civ 1824, [2006] 1 WLR 2380 at [24].

It has been explained that a prospective creditor is one who is owed a debt which will certainly become due in the future, either on some determined date or some date which will be determined by reference to future events (*Stonegate Securities Ltd v Gregory* [1980] 1 Ch 576 at 579), and will include a claim that is unable to be disputed and involves unliquidated damages which remain to be quantified: *Re Dollar Land Holdings Ltd* [1994] BCLC 404.

While a contingent debt is a debt for the purposes of winding up, such a debt could not be used as the basis for a statutory demand and a subsequent petition, until the relevant contingency had happened: *JSF Finance and Current Exchange Co Ltd v Akma Solutions Inc* [2001] 2 BCLC 307, [2002] BPIR 621.

It must be noted that what is a contingent liability will depend on the circumstances and context: *R v Birmingham City Council* [2005] EWCA Civ 1824, [2006] 1 WLR 2380 at [21].

The judgment of Lord Neuberger in *Re Nortel GmbH* [2013] UKSC 52, [2013] 3 WLR 504 appears to be of some assistance in understanding contingent liabilities. His Lordship was focusing on r 13.12(1)(b) of the Rules in his judgment. He said that in determining whether it can be said that an obligation involved a liability which arose 'by reason of any obligation incurred before' the insolvency event, such as liquidation, ordinarily for a company to have incurred a liability it must have taken, or been subjected to, 'some step or combination of steps which (a) had some legal effect (such as putting it under some legal duty or into some legal relationship), and which (b) resulted in it being vulnerable to the specific liability in question, such that there would be a real prospect of that liability being incurred. If these two requirements are satisfied, it is also, I think, relevant to consider (c) whether it would be consistent with the regime under which the liability is imposed to conclude that the step or combination of steps gave rise to an obligation under rule 13.12(1)(b)' (at [77]).

Contributory—See the notes accompanying s 74 for a discussion of who is a contributory.

No provision in the memorandum or the articles can prohibit a contributory from presenting a petition, because the legislation specifically permits contributories to be able to do so: *Re Peveril Gold Mines Ltd* [1898] 1 Ch 122. Nor can the right of a contributory to petition be removed by contract: *A Best Floor Sanding Pty Ltd v Skyer Australia Pty Ltd* [1999] VSC 170, Vic S C (approved in *Exeter City AFC Ltd v Football Conference Ltd* [2004] BCC 498).

Restrictions—The right of a contributory to petition is restricted by s 124(2), although s 124(3) exempts some contributories that would ordinarily fall within s 124(2). Section 124(2) applies where the company is a public or unlimited company. The condition in that subsection that one must have held the shares for at least six months is designed to prevent a person from obtaining a share in a company with the aim of presenting a petition: *Re a Company* [1894] 2 Ch 349. The restriction in s 124(2) applies to a trustee in bankruptcy of a member: *Re HL Bolton Engineering Co Ltd* [1956] Ch 577, [1956] 1 All ER 799; *Taylor v Glenrinnes Farms Ltd* [1994] 2 BCLC 522.

Section 124(3) provides an exemption and a limitation. A contributory, because of s 76, is entitled to petition, but he or she must do so under either s 122(1)(f) or s 122(1)(g).

A further restriction is contained in s 125(2). See the notes relating to s 125, and particularly under the heading 'Restrictions on making an order on the petition of a contributory' for details.

A general rule, formulated at common law, also restricts which contributories are entitled to petition. The rule is that a contributory must demonstrate a tangible interest in the company if he or she is to petition: *Re Rica Gold Washing Co* (1879) 11 Ch D 36; *Re Chesterfield Catering Co Ltd* [1977] Ch 373; *Re Greenhaven Motors Ltd* [1997] BCC 547; *O'Connor v Atlantis Fisheries Ltd* 1998 SCLR 401. With insolvent companies, fully paid-up shareholders are normally unable to show a tangible interest, as they are only entitled to share in the assets of such companies after both the creditors have been paid in full and the costs of winding up have been paid. A member who only holds partly paid up shares has a tangible interest in that he or she may be able to stop the company incurring more debts and thus make him or her potentially liable for greater sums. It has been recognised that there can be exceptions to the general rule: *Re Rica Gold Washing Co* at 43; *Re Chesterfield Catering Co Ltd* at 380; *The Charit-Email Technology Partnership LLP v Vermillion International Investments Limited* [2009] EWHC 388 (Ch), [2009] BPIR 762. An example is *Re a Company (No 007936 of 1994)* [1995] BCC 705 where a contributory was allowed to petition in circumstances where he could not ascertain whether he had a tangible interest in the company because the company failed to provide proper access to financial details.

A contributory who is in arrears with calls on his or her shares is not able to petition unless he or she agrees to pay the arrears to the company or into court, or consents to adhere to any order which the court determines should be made in relation to the calls: *Re Crystal Reef Gold Mining Co* [1892] 1 Ch 408.

Secretary of State—The Secretary of State for Business Innovation and Skills is the political head of the Department of Business Innovation and Skills, which has the function of regulating the formation, management and insolvency of companies. In this capacity (s)he is given the power to petition for winding up. The provision under which the Secretary of State most often petitions is s 124A.

Official receiver—The official receiver is entitled to petition for a winding-up order where a company is in voluntary liquidation. See notes relating to s 116 for discussion of when a court is likely to order a court winding up of a company that is in voluntary liquidation. There is more likely to be a petition filed by the official receiver where there is a need for careful investigation of the affairs of the company.

124A Petition for winding up on grounds of public interest

(1) Where it appears to the Secretary of State from—

    (a)   any report made or information obtained under Part XIV (except section 448A) of the Companies Act 1985 (company investigations, &c.),

    (b)   any report made by inspectors under—

        (i)   section 167, 168, 169 or 284 of the Financial Services and Markets Act 2000, or

        (ii)   where the company is an open-ended investment company (within the meaning of that Act), regulations made as a result of section 262(2)(k) of that Act;

    (bb)   any information or documents obtained under section 165, 171, 172, 173 or 175 of that Act,

    (c)   any information obtained under section 2 of the Criminal Justice Act 1987 or section 52 of the Criminal Justice (Scotland) Act 1987 (fraud investigations), or

    (d)   any information obtained under section 83 of the Companies Act 1989 (powers exercisable for purpose of assisting overseas regulatory authorities),

that it is expedient in the public interest that a company should be wound up, he may present a petition for it to be wound up if the court thinks it just and equitable for it to be so.

(2) This section does not apply if the company is already being wound up by the court.

Amendments—Inserted by Companies Act 1989, s 60(3). Amended by SI 2001/3649; Companies (Audit, Investigations and Community Enterprise Act 2004, s 25(1), Sch 2, Pt 3, para 27.

General note—The Secretary of State (formerly of Trade and Industry, but now Secretary of State for Business Innovations and Skills) intervenes by petitioning for a winding-up order under this provision in order to safeguard the public from the activities of the company. Hence, petitions presented under this provision are known commonly as 'public interest petitions': *Re a Company (No 007816 of 1994)* [1997] 2 BCLC 685 at 687, CA; *Re Titan International Inc* [1998] 1 BCLC 102 at 107, CA; *Re Delfin International (SA) Ltd* [2000] 1 BCLC 71.

It has been held that only the Secretary of State is entitled to present a petition under this section as (s)he has been identified by Parliament as the guardian of the public interest: *Re Millenium Advanced Technology Ltd* [2004] EWHC 711 (Ch) at [33]. It was further stated that Parliament's intention was that the Secretary of State should act as a filter as to what is in the public interest. Anyone concerned about the activities of a company being against the public interest should bring these concerns to the attention of the Secretary of State: *Millenium Advanced Technology* at [38].

Often the Secretary of State will, following presentation of the petition, file an application for the appointment of a provisional liquidator (e g *Re a Company (No 007070 of 1996)* [1997] 2 BCLC 139), and this is frequently done because of the need for an early and rigorous examination of the affairs of a company. For comments on provisional liquidation, see the notes relating to s 135. But courts are slow to appoint a provisional liquidator unless there is a good prima facie case for saying that a winding-up order would be made: *Re Treasure Traders Corporation Ltd* [2005] EWHC 2774 (Ch).

A company that is associated with another company, against which a winding-up order is made under this ground, will not suffer the same fate, merely because of the association, where it is carrying on its own discrete business: *Re Tag World Services Ltd* [2008] EWHC 1866 (Ch).

It has been held in obiter comments that s 124A petitions are neither within the EC Regulation on Insolvency Proceedings nor the Brussels Convention on Jurisdiction and Enforcement of Judgments in Civil and Commercial Matters: *Re Marann Brooks CSV Ltd* [2003] BCC 239.

Orders might be made under this section against companies that are in voluntary liquidation (*Re ForceSun Ltd* [2002] 2 BCLC 302; *Re Alpha Club (UK) Ltd* [2002] 2 BCLC 612) or in administration (para 40(2)(a) of Sch B1).

While the Secretary of State is empowered to petition for the winding up of a company pursuant to s 124A of a company that is registered outside of Great Britain, provided that the company has a principal place of business in England or Wales (*Re Normandy Marketing Ltd* [1994] Ch 198 at 204, [1993] BCC 879 at 883), (s)he must satisfy the court that a real or sufficient connection between the company and the jurisdiction of the English and Welsh courts exists: *Re Real Estate Development Co Ltd* [1991] BCLC 210; *Re Titan International plc* [1998] 1 BCLC 102 at 107.

If a company has gone some way to rectifying concerns that the Secretary of State had with its business and affairs and at the time of the hearing there were no grounds for winding up then an order would not be given. Matters had to be looked at as at the time of the hearing of the petition and as a whole. By that time in this case the company had responded to the concerns identified by the Secretary of State. There is no rule of law or binding principle of discretion that past misconduct or past misconduct which was sufficiently serious led inevitably to winding up: *Secretary of State for Business Enterprise and Regulatory Reform v Amway (UK) Ltd* [2009] EWCA Civ 32, [2009] BCC 781.

An application to appoint a provisional liquidator should not be used instead of a winding-up petition under s 124A where the latter was appropriate: *The Commisioners for HMRC v Rochdale Drinks Distributors Ltd* [2011] EWCA Civ 1116.

Grounds—The expression 'in the public interest' is of the widest import, and the Secretary of State is not limited, in presenting petitions, to cases where illegal activity is alleged: *Re SHV Senator Hanseatische Verwaltungs Gesellschaft mbH* [1997] BCC 112 at 119, CA. It is desirable, although not essential, that a petition alleges intentional and dishonest deceit of the public: *Secretary of State for Trade and Industry v Travel Time (UK) Ltd* [2000] BCC 792, sub nom *Re a Company (No 5669 of 1998)* [2000] 1 BCLC 427. It has been held in Australia that it could be in the public interest to wind up a company even where it had no current trading activity: *ASIC v Kingsley Brown Properties Pty Ltd* [2005] VSC 506.

While companies against which petitions are presented are often insolvent, it is not a prerequisite to such proceedings (*Re Marann Brooks CSV Ltd* [2003] BCC 239), as insolvency itself is not a ground for granting a winding-up order under this section (*Re SHV Senator Hanseatische Verwaltungs Gesellschaft mbH* [1997] BCC 112, CA); more must be demonstrated than insolvency in obtaining an order, namely that the order sought is in the public interest. Nevertheless, the reasons why, and the circumstances in which, a company has become insolvent might be highly pertinent to the granting of an order: *Re UK-Euro Group plc* [2006] EWHC 2102 (Ch), [2007] 1 BCLC 812. In Australia the fact that a company is insolvent has been held to be a factor in making a winding-up order on that jurisdiction's equivalent provision: *Macquarie Bank Ltd v TM Investments Pty Ltd* [2005] NSWSC 608. One would think that in some cases permitting an insolvent company to continue in business would be against the public interest. Clearly there are situations where it is in the public interest that a solvent company be wound up: *Re a Company (No 007923 of 1994)* [1995]

BCC 634 at 637. Companies may be wound up on the basis of the section where they have been guilty of conduct that is below the generally accepted standards of commercial behaviour: *Re Marann Brooks CSV Ltd.*

Petitions have been presented for a variety of reasons, such as: the company never had, during its existence, a sufficient paid up capital to finance its activities (*In re Rubin, Rosen and Associated Ltd* [1975] 1 WLR 122); the company has committed serious breaches of the Companies Act (*Re Allied Produce Co Ltd* [1967] 1 WLR 1469); the affairs of the company were being conducted fraudulently (*In re Golden Chemical Products Ltd* [1976] 1 Ch 300); the company has engaged in making fraudulent misrepresentations (*Re Secure & Provide plc* [1992] BCC 405; *Re a Company (No 5669 of 1998)* [2000] 1 BCLC 427); the company has been party to a conspiracy to defraud customers (*Re Highfield Commodities Ltd* [1985] 1 WLR 149, [1984] BCLC 623, (1984) 1 BCC 99, 277); the company's records were inadequately maintained and members of the public had been misled (*Re Walter L Jacob Ltd* (1989) 5 BCC 244); the company had no authorisation to conduct investment business pursuant to the Financial Services Act 1986 (legislation now repealed) and had made statements in promotional literature that were misleading and contrary to that legislation (*Re Market Wizard Systems (UK) Ltd* [1998] 2 BCLC 282); the company had been carrying on an insurance business without authorisation (*Re a Company (No 007816 of 1994)* [1997] 2 BCLC 685); the company was delivering unordered goods to consumers and impersonating bona fide suppliers (*Re Forcesun Ltd* [2002] 2 BCLC 302); the company was conducting a pyramid selling scheme and a breach of the Lotteries and Amusements Act 1976 (*Re Alpha Club (UK) Ltd* [2002] 2 BCLC 612); and the company was taking advance fees and not doing the work agreed to be done: *Re Marann Brooks CSV Ltd* [2003] BCC 239. Petitions in some of these cases were not successful. Often petitions are based on several grounds. An instance is *Re Atlantic Properties Ltd* [2006] EWHC 610 (Ch), where an order was made because the company had failed to comply with an order for disclosure of documents under s 447 of the Companies Act 1985, it had failed to keep proper financial records and it was insolvent.

As a prerequisite to the presenting of a petition, the Secretary of State must be, according to the section, of the opinion that it is expedient in the public interest that the company should be wound up: *Re Walter L Jacob Ltd* (1989) 5 BCC 244 at 250–251, CA. It is permissible to petition where the Secretary of State has not formed the necessary opinion, but a senior officer in the Department of Business Enterprise and Regulatory Reform, has done so: In *Re Golden Chemical Products Ltd* [1976] 1 Ch 300.

The decision-making process—When hearing a petition, a court will examine the evidence presented and submissions made to it and undertake a balancing exercise, weighing the factors which constitute reasons for the making of a winding-up order as against those factors which are reasons for not winding up the company: *Re Walter L Jacob Ltd* (1989) 5 BCC 244 at 250, CA; *Re Market Wizard Systems (UK) Ltd* [1998] 2 BCLC 282 at 285; *Secretary of State for Trade and Industry v Leyton Housing Trustees Ltd* [2000] 2 BCLC 808 at 810; *Secretary of State for Business Enterprise and Regulatory Reform v Art IT plc* [2008] All ER(D) 237 (Jan). In their deliberations, courts will consider the views of creditors opposing the petition: In *Re Rubin, Rosen and Associated Ltd* [1975] 1 WLR 122 at 128–129. An order will not be made unless a court is convinced that there is a reasonable prospect that the public interest will be fostered by a winding up: *Re Titan International plc* [1998] 1 BCLC 102 at 107, CA. A judge has complete discretion whether or not to make a winding–up order: *Secretary of State for Trade and Industry v Bell Davies Trading Ltd* [2005] BCC 564, [2004] EWCA Civ 1066; *Secretary of State for Business Enterprise and Regulatory Reform v Amway (UK) Ltd* [2009] EWCA Civ 32, [2009] BCC 781. In *Secretary of State for Business Enterprise and Regulatory Reform v Amway (UK) Ltd* [2008] EWHC 1054 (Ch) Norris J said that a court was entitled to make an order simply because the company was managing its business in a way that was not consistent with the generally accepted minimum standards of commercial behaviour. In *Secretary of State for Business Enterprise and Regulatory Reform v Art IT* [2008] All ER (D) 237 (Jan) the court balanced the various factors involved and ordered winding up as the company had: failed to file accounts; issued a misleading advertisement claiming the company was being floated on the AIM when it was not; and failed to comply with company investigators. In making a decision the judge is permitted to consider past misconduct, but it should not be seen as conclusive and a judge could take into account changed circumstances and accept undertakings of a company that indicated its intention to improve the situation, even where the Secretary of State had declined to accept such undertakings, although a court would only do so in rare cases: *Secretary of State for Business Enterprise and Regulatory Reform v Amway (UK) Ltd* [2009] EWCA Civ 32, [2009] BCC 781.

The wrongdoing that is alleged to found a petition does not have to have been carried out by the directing mind of the company: *Secretary of State for Business Enterprise and Regulatory Reform v Amway (UK) Ltd* [2008] EWHC 1054 (Ch).

Opposing a petition—The company is naturally entitled to oppose a petition. But can a contributory of the company do so? The answer appears to be in the affirmative if the contributory can establish that the company is solvent: *Re Rodencroft Ltd*, sub nom *Allso v Secretary of State for Trade and Industry* [2004] BCC 631, [2004] EWHC 862 (Ch).

The inter-relationship and consequences of s 124A(2) and s 129(2) (commencement of winding up)—Other than in the circumstances prescribed in s 129(1) and (2), the winding up of a company is deemed to commence at the time of the presentation of a winding-up petition. Read literally, and, it is submitted, reasonably and objectively, s 124A can have no application where such a winding-up petition is extant. The point is significant since it goes to jurisdiction and is not a matter for the court's discretion. If that analysis is correct then it would appear to follow that s 124A cannot engage in the face of a winding-up petition though the provision would be capable of being engaged upon such a petition being dismissed subject to s 129(1) and (2). To the extent that any order has been made under s 124A(1) in the face of an extant winding-up petition then that order, and, apparently, any consequences following from it, would appear capable of being challenged on the footing that the order amounts to a nullity in the absence of the court having any jurisdiction to make it.

Undertakings—Companies that are the subject of public interest petitions might be willing to offer undertakings, usually to cease to continue the activity that is the subject of the Secretary of State's concerns, and courts have the discretion whether or not to accept an undertaking as to future conduct: *Secretary of State for Business Enterprise and Regulatory Reform v Amway (UK) Ltd* [2008] EWHC 1054 (Ch). But undertakings offered have been refused by judges: *Re Equity & Provident Ltd* [2002] 2 BCLC 78. In *Re Bamford Publishers Ltd* ((unreported) 2 June 1977, but considered by the Vice-Chancellor in *Re The Supporting Link Ltd* [2004] EWHC 523 (Ch)), Brightman J adverted to the problem with undertakings, namely that it is not the function of either the court or the Department of Business Innovation and Skills to police undertakings. A judge hearing a public interest petition is entitled to: dismiss the petition where undertakings have been given by the company (the judge being satisfied that the offending activity had ceased or the Secretary of State had accepted the undertakings); dismiss, in unusual circumstances, the petition on the giving of undertakings, even if the Secretary of State was opposed to this; or refuse to accept undertakings and make a winding-up order if, for instance, the judge was not satisfied that the ones giving the undertakings were trustworthy: *Secretary of State for Trade and Industry v Bell Davies Trading Ltd* [2005] BCC 564, [2004] EWCA Civ 1066. If an undertaking is given by a company, it is not entitled to appeal against it: *Secretary of State for Trade and Industry v Bell Davies Trading Ltd*.

Costs—If the Secretary of State obtains a winding-up order, the Department of Business Enterprise and Regulatory Reform will, usually, be awarded costs against the company (*Re Xyllyx plc (No 2)* [1992] BCLC 378 at 385), although the courts have awarded the costs against a director of the company personally where he or she is in control of the company's affairs and had acted in his or her interests rather than the interests of the company: *Re Aurum Marketing Ltd* [2000] 2 BCLC 645 at 650, CA; *Re Northwest Holdings plc* [2000] BCC 731 (upheld on appeal to the Court of Appeal – [2001] 1 BCLC 468, [2002] BCC 441); *Secretary of State for Trade and Industry v Liquid Acquisitions Ltd* [2003] 1 BCLC 375. It was clear that it was not the normal rule that directors should be made to pay the costs of the company, even if they knew that the company would not be able to pay any costs if the defence failed *Re Northwest Holdings plc* [2001] EWCA Civ 67, [2001] 1 BCLC 468, [2002] BCC 441 at [33], CA (dismissing an appeal from Hart J) and a director should not be liable for costs where he or she had a bona fide belief that the company had an arguable defence and it was in the company's interests that the defence be advanced: *Re Northwest Holdings plc* at [33]–[34].

If the petition fails, costs may be awarded against the Department for Business Enterprise and Regulatory Reform (*Re Secure & Provide plc* [1992] BCC 405 at 415), but this is not an automatic result, because the court needs to undertake a balancing exercise: *Re Xyllyx plc (No 2)*.

See Keay 'Public Interest Petitions' (1999) 20 *Company Lawyer* 296; Finch 'Public interest liquidation: PIL or Placebo?' [2002] *Insolvency Lawyer* 157; A Keay *McPherson's Law of Company Liquidation* (3rd edn, Sweet and Maxwell, 2013) at 281–297.

124B Petition for winding up of SE

(1) Where—

    (a)   an SE whose registered office is in Great Britain is not in compliance with Article 7 of Council Regulation (EC) No 2157/2001 on the Statute for a European company (the 'EC Regulation') (location of head office and registered office), and

    (b)   it appears to the Secretary of State that the SE should be wound up, he may present a petition for it to be wound up if the court thinks it is just and equitable for it to be so.

(2) This section does not apply if the SE is already being wound up by the court.

(3) In this section 'SE' has the same meaning as in the EC Regulation.

Amendments—Inserted by SI 2004/2326.

General note—This section mirrors s 124A as far as the new European company (Societas Europea) is concerned.

124C Petition for winding up of SCE

(1) Where, in the case of an SCE whose registered office is in Great Britain—

    (a)   there has been such a breach as is mentioned in Article 73 (1) of Council Regulation (EC) No 1435/2003 on the Statute for a European Cooperative Society (SCE) (the 'European Cooperative Society Regulation') (winding up by the court or other competent authority), and

    (b)   it appears to the Financial Conduct Authority that the SCE should be wound up,

the Authority may present a petition for the SCE to be wound up if the court thinks it is just and equitable for it to be so.

(2) Where, in the case of an SCE whose registered office is in Great Britain—

    (a)   the SCE is not in compliance with Article 6 of the European Cooperative Society Regulation (location of head office and registered office, and

    (b)   it appears to the Financial Conduct Authority that the SCE should be wound up,

the Authority may present a petition for the SCE to be wound up if the court thinks it is just and equitable for it to be so

(3) This section does not apply it the SCE is already wound up by the court.

(4) In this section 'SCE' has the same meaning as in the European Cooperative Society Regulation.

Amendments—Inserted by SI 2006/2078; SI 2013/496.

General note—This section mirrors s 124A as far as a European Cooperative Society is concerned.

125 Powers of court on hearing of petition

(1) On hearing a winding-up petition the court may dismiss it, or adjourn the hearing conditionally or unconditionally, or make an interim order, or any other order that it thinks fit; but the court shall not refuse to make a winding-up order on the ground only that the company's assets have been mortgaged to an amount equal to or in excess of those assets, or that the company has no assets.

(2) If the petition is presented by members of the company as contributories on the ground that it is just and equitable that the company should be wound up, the court, if it is of opinion—

    (a)   that the petitioners are entitled to relief either by winding up the company or by some other means, and

    (b)   that in the absence of any other remedy it would be just and equitable that the company should be wound up,

shall make a winding-up order; but this does not apply if the court is also of the opinion both that some other remedy is available to the petitioners and that they are acting unreasonably in seeking to have the company wound up instead of pursuing that other remedy.

General note—The courts are granted an unfettered discretion and they can make any of the orders contemplated by s 125(1). This is subject to the proviso that the court shall not refuse to make a winding-up order only because the company's assets have been mortgaged to the value of the assets, or in excess of the assets, or where the company has no assets.

    As far as the hearing of petitions presented in relation to companies in voluntary liquidation is concerned, see s 116 and the notes relating to it.

Discretion—While the court has a discretion as to whether or not to make a winding-up order, the general approach is that a petitioner who can prove that a debt is unpaid and that the company is insolvent is entitled to a winding-up order *ex debito justitiae*: *Re Western of Canada Oil* (1873) 17 Eq 1; *Re Demaglass Holdings Ltd* [2001] 2 BCLC 633. In this context this is taken to mean that, pursuant to settled practice, the court can exercise its discretion in only one way, namely by granting the order sought: *Re Pritchard* [1963] Ch 502 at 521. But, as indicated above, it is now settled that the rights of a creditor are always subject to the overriding discretion which the court has, and found in s 125(1): *Re P & J MacRae Ltd* [1961] 1 WLR 229 at 238, so that the court is never bound to make an order, even where there is proof that a ground for winding up exists, but has a discretion to decide whether or not it will do so. Notwithstanding this, the power of the court to deny an order is exercised in accordance with principles which are relatively well defined. Courts tend only to refuse orders in the following cases: (1) the petitioner's debt amounts to less than £750 – this is despite the fact that no minimum level is set for a winding-up order, (2) the debt is bona fide disputed by the company, (3) the petition constitutes an abuse of process, (4) the company has paid or tendered payment of the petitioner's debt, (5) winding up is opposed by other creditors, (6) the company is in the process of being wound up voluntarily; and (7) the

English and Welsh courts are not the most appropriate jurisdiction for the issues to be resolved (see A Keay *McPherson's Law of Company Liquidation* (3rd edn, Sweet and Maxwell, 2013) at 140-193).

Courts will not usually exercise their discretion against petitioners who have ulterior motives in initiating the proceedings, such as ill-will towards the company: *Bryanston Finance Ltd v De Vries (No 2)* [1976] 1 Ch 63. But, in *HM Commissioners of Customs and Excise v Anglo Overseas Ltd* [2005] BPIR 137, [2004] EWHC 2198 (Ch), Lewison J did say that the circumstances under which the petition was presented were a relevant consideration in deciding whether to make a winding-up order, although this case, it must be noted, did involve somewhat unusual facts.

Where a petitioner has standing as a creditor at the time of the presentation of the petition, but is not a creditor at the time of the hearing of the petition, Australian authority has stated that the court has a discretion whether or not to make a winding-up order: *Australian Beverage Distributors Pty Ltd v The Redrock Co Pty Ltd* [2007] NSWSC 966, [2007] 213 FLR 450 at [33], [34].

Amount of the debt relied on in the petition—While there is no minimum amount that must be owed before a court will order winding up, courts have, traditionally, been wary about making an order where the amount owed is less than £750. The reason for this is that the courts do not wish to see winding up used as an avenue for the collection of small debts (*Re Fancy Dress Balls Co* [1899] WN 109) and this accords with the approach taken in Australia, for instance:*South East Water v Kitoria Pty Ltd* (1996) 14 ACLC 1328. However, the courts may take a different view where the debtor company reduces the amount of the debt below £750 after the presentation of a petition, but before its hearing, in an effort to prevent winding up. In *Lilley v American Express Europe Ltd* [2000] BPIR 70, a bankruptcy case, it was held that the court retained jurisdiction to make a bankruptcy order even where the debtor had reduced the outstanding petition debt to beneath the bankruptcy level by the time of the hearing of the petition, and a bankruptcy order might well be made where it was clear that the debtor was 'playing cat and mouse with the petitioner' (at 74–75). See the comments accompanying s 267, where the latter case is discussed in more detail.

Debt relied on in the petition is disputed—There is a rule of practice only, and not a rule of law (*Re Claybridge Shipping Co SA* [1997] 1 BCLC 572, CA; *Re UOC Corp*; *Alipour v Ary* [1997] 1 WLR 534), that a winding-up order will not be made on a petition founded on a disputed debt. Nevertheless, the courts retain a discretion to make a winding-up order (*Parmalat Capital Finance Ltd v Food Holdings Ltd (in liq)* [2008] UKPC 23, [2008] BPIR 641 at [9]). However, the rule of practice is extremely well established in English law. It provides that the company must be able to establish that the debt is bona fide disputed, and the dispute is based on some substantial ground: *Mann v Goldstein* [1968] 1 WLR 1091 at 1098–1099; *Re Richbell Strategic Holdings Ltd* [1997] 2 BCLC 429; *Re UOC Corp; Alipour v Ary* [1997] 1 WLR 534, [1997] BCC 377, CA (it is noted that in *ICS Incorporation Ltd v Michael Wilson Partners Ltd* [2005] EWHC 404 (Ch), [2005] BPIR 804 the judge preferred 'substantial dispute' to 'bona fide dispute' since the latter might turn on issues of credibility of witnesses). In the Court of Appeal decision in *Re The Arena Corporation Ltd* [2004] BPIR 415 at 433 it was said that bona fide disputed on substantial grounds was synonymous with a case that is real and not frivolous. In the Court of Appeal in *Abbey National v JSF Finance* [2006] EWCA Civ 328 at [46] it was said that substantial grounds had to be established. Later in *Argentum Lex Wealth Management Ltd v Giannotti* [2011] EWCA Civ 1341 it was said that the test of substantial grounds was not very different from the test for granting judicial review applications in the administrative court or granting permission to appeal to the Court of Appeal, and what must exist is a realistic prospect of success ([17]). If a court holds that a debt on which the petition is founded is disputed the petition will be struck out: *Re a Company (No 0013734 of 1991)* [1993] BCLC 59; *Re Claybridge Shipping Co SA* [1997] 1 BCLC 572, CA. The rationale for this is that a winding-up petition is not to be used for the improper purpose of compelling a solvent company to pay a disputed debt which would certainly be discharged as soon as the company's liability was clearly shown to exist (*Re Imperial Silver Quarries* (1868) 14 WR 1220; *Re Imperial Hydropathic Hotel Co* (1882) 49 LT 147 at 150) and where irreparable damage could be caused to the company: *Cadiz Waterworks Company v Barnett* (1874) LR 19 Eq 182. The legal reason for the striking out of the petition is that a creditor whose debt is disputed lacks the qualification necessary to be a petitioner: *Mann v Goldstein* [1968] 1 WLR 1091; *Re Selectmove Ltd* [1994] BCLC 349.

The courts have indicated that the winding-up process should not be used as a method of debt collection where there was a dispute: *Hammonds (A Firm) v Pro-Fit USA Ltd* [2007] EWHC 1998 (Ch) at [27]ff; *Re GBI Investments Ltd* [2010] EWHC 37 (Ch), [2010] BPIR 356 at [80].

A company which claims to dispute a debt has a duty 'to bring forward a prima facie case which satisfies the court that there is something to be tried' (*Re Great Britain Mutual Life Assurance Society* (1880) 26 Ch D 246 at 253 per Jessel MR), and it is not sufficient if the company has a mere honest belief that payment to the petitioner is not due: *Taylor's Industrial Flooring Ltd v M & H Plant Hire (Manchester) Ltd* [1990] BCLC 216, [1990] BCC 44, CA. But where there is a substantial dispute, courts are likely to refuse to make a winding-up order even where the defence of the company to the claim in the petition is 'shadowy': *ICS Incorporation Ltd v Michael Wilson Partners Ltd* [2005] EWHC 404 (Ch), [2005] BPIR 804 at [12].

In seeking to determine whether there is a dispute on substantial grounds, a court should consider the witness statements and other documentary evidence: *Mac Plant Services Ltd v Contract Lifting Services (Scotland) Ltd* [2008] CSOH 158, 2009 SC 125 at [9]. If a not insignificant period has elapsed between presentation of the petition and the hearing of it a court should not be required to look not just at the circumstances that exist at the time of the hearing, but also the circumstances as they existed at the time of presentation: *Mac Plant Services Ltd v Contract Lifting Services (Scotland) Ltd* [2008] CSOH 158, 2009 SC 125 at [64].

Courts may, although they do so infrequently, ascertain, where they feel that it is appropriate, what is the true position between the company and the petitioner where a dispute is alleged, namely determining whether the company does in fact owe the debt relied on in the petition: *Brinds Ltd v Offshore Oil NL* [1985] 2 BCC 98, 916 (PC); *Re Janeash Ltd* [1990] BCC 250; *Corben v What Music Holdings Ltd* (unreported) 16 July 2003 (EWHC, Hart J). It has been said that the Companies Court may determine what the position is between the petitioner and the company and make a winding-up order where there was an unusual and extreme set of facts justifying an exception to the normal rule: *Re The Arena Corporation Ltd* [2004] BPIR 415 at 432. Factors that are relevant in determining that there are exceptional circumstances are: the company is insolvent absent the petition debt; the company is not going to suffer any prejudice; the petitioner has no adequate alternative remedy to liquidation: *Re GBI Investments Ltd* [2010] EWHC 37 (Ch), [2010] BPIR 356 at [160]–[163].

Where only part of the debt is disputed and the amount that is not in dispute exceeds £750, then a court should order a winding up: *Re Tweeds Garages Ltd* [1962] Ch 406; *Taylor's Industrial Flooring Ltd v M & H Plant Hire (Manchester) Ltd* [1990] BCLC 216, [1990] BCC 44, CA; *Mac Plant services Ltd v Contract Lifting Services (Scotland) Ltd* [2008] CSOH 158, 2009 SC 125 at [10].

Where a court had delivered a judgment in favour of the petitioner then the petitioner is a creditor for the purposes of winding up even if the judgment is subject to an appeal: *El Ajou v Dollar Land (Manhattan) Ltd* [2005] EWHC 2861 (Ch), [2007] BCC 953.

In *Parmalat Capital Finance Ltd v Food Holdings Ltd (in liq)* [2008] UKPC 23 at [9] the Privy Council (in a case on appeal from the Cayman Islands) emphasised the fact that the courts retain a discretion whether or not to make a winding-up order even where there is a substantial dispute.

The kind of dispute—While, generally, courts in England and Wales will strike out a petition based on a disputed debt, there is case law to the effect that the court still has a discretion as to whether a winding-up order is to be made: *Brinds Ltd v Offshore Oil NL* [1985] 2 BCC 98, 916 at 98, 921; *Parmalat Capital Finance Ltd v Food Holdings Ltd (in liq)* [2008] UKPC 23, [2008] BPIR 641 at [9]. But in *Re Bayoil SA* [1998] BCC 988, [1999] 1 BCLC 62 the Court of Appeal said that where a company disputes a petition on substantial grounds then whether or not there should be a dismissal of the petition is not, at any rate initially, a matter for the discretion of the court (at 990, 66). The upshot is that the principle that a dispute over a debt founding the petition will lead to dismissal tends to be applied generally, except in special circumstances. Whether or not there is a dispute on substantial grounds is a matter to be decided in each case. The kind of dispute that is contemplated is one which involves substantially disputed questions of fact which demand the taking of viva voce evidence: *Re Lympne Investments Ltd* [1972] 2 All ER 385 at 389. A company must demonstrate that the dispute is genuine and bona fide, both in the sense that it must be honestly believed to exist by those who allege it (*Stonegate Securities Ltd v Gregory* [1980] Ch 576 at 580, [1980] 1 All ER 241 at 243–244, CA), and in the sense that the belief must be based on reasonable (*Stonegate Securities Ltd v Gregory*) or substantial grounds (*Re Welsh Brick Industries Ltd* [1946] 2 All ER 197 at 198; *Taylor's Industrial Flooring Ltd v M & H Plant Hire (Manchester) Ltd* [1990] BCLC 216, [1990] BCC 44, CA; *Re a Company (No 0010656 of 1990)* [1991] BCLC 464 at 466). But it has been said that the courts will be wary of a company which seeks to raise objections to a petition in order to allow them to submit that a disputed debt exists where the objections are not able to be determined on affidavit evidence and without cross-examination (*Re a Company (No 006685 of 1996)* [1997] 1 BCLC 639, [1997] BCC 830). Courts might be willing to accept, although thus far they have not considered it, that they are not required to find that a company had no triable defence before they can order winding up, as this kind of approach has been adopted in relation to cases involving applications to restrain the advertising of a petition: *Re a Company (No 0160 of 2004)* [2004] All ER (D) 352 (Feb), Lawtel, Document No. AC9200675 at [28].

A dispute will not be viewed as substantial if it has no rational prospect of success: *Re a Company (No 0012209 of 1991)* [1992] 1 WLR 351, [1992] 2 All ER 797, [1992] BCLC 865; *Angel Group Ltd v British Gas Trading Ltd* [2012] EWHC 2702 (Ch).

A dispute will not be viewed as substantial if it has no rational prospect of success: *Re a Company (No 0012209 of 1991)* [1992] 1 WLR 351, [1992] 2 All ER 797, [1992] BCLC 865; *Angel Group Ltd v British Gas Trading Ltd* [2012] EWHC 2702 (Ch).A company might succeed on the basis of a dispute where the petitioner is an assignee of a debt and no notice of the assignment had been given to the company by the date of the presentation of the petition: *Re a Company (No 003624 of 2002)* [2002] All ER (D) 274. The relevant test is whether any notice relied upon is brought to the company's notice with reasonable certainty: *Denny, Gasquet and Metcalfe v Conklin* [1913] 3 KB 177 at 180; *Mitchell McFarlane & Partners Ltd v Foremans Ltd* 2002 WL 31784665, Lawtel (Ch D, Mr N Strauss, 18 December 2002).

See r 6.5 and the discussion relating to that rule, and especially that under the heading '… on grounds which appear to the court to be substantial'.

Set-off or cross-claim—The company might argue that the debt relied on in the petition is not owed because it has a set-off or cross-claim which equals or exceeds the amount of the petitioner's debt, and which could be pleaded in response to a claim for that debt if the petitioner were to bring proceedings to recover it. If, when a cross-claim is taken into account, there is a significant amount owed to the petitioner, the petition will be allowed to proceed: *Alexander Sheridan Ltd v Beaujersey Ltd* [2004] EWHC 2072 (Ch) at [59]. While neither a set-off nor a cross-claim is a complete answer to a petition (*Re Douglas Griggs Engineering Ltd* [1963] 1 Ch 19; *Re FSA Business Software Ltd* [1990] BCC 465; *Re Leasing and Finance Services Ltd* [1991] BCC 29), where it can be shown that the alleged set-off or cross-claim is genuine and based on a substantial ground, the court can refuse to make a winding-up order in the exercise of its discretion: *Re LHF Wools Ltd* [1970] Ch 27, [1969] 3 All ER 882, CA; In *Re Bayoil SA* [1998] BCC 988, [1999] 1 BCLC 62, CA; *MCI WorldCom Ltd v Primus Telecommunications Ltd* [2002] EWHC 2436 (Ch), [2003] 1 BCLC 330. It is necessary for a company, in addition to establishing the fact that the cross-claim is genuine and serious, to show that the cross-claim was one which the company had been unable to litigate and it is greater than the claim of the petitioning creditor: *Re Bayoil SA* [1998] BCC 988, [1999] 1 BCLC 62, CA; *Ashworth v Newnote Ltd* [2007] EWCA Civ 794, [2007] BPIR 1012 at [35], CA. In the latter case the Court of Appeal added that the cross-claim, in order to resist the petition, might raise a genuine triable issue and this means the same as a real prospect of success on the claim (at [33]–[35]). Where the company delays in taking action in relation to an alleged cross-claim, it must demonstrate a good reason for the delay (In *Re Bayoil SA*), although more recently it has been held that a company is not precluded from relying on a cross-claim because it could reasonably have litigated the cross-claim before the petition was presented: *Montgomery v Wanda Modes Ltd* [2002] 1 BCLC 289; *Denis Rye Ltd v Bolsover District Council* [2009] EWCA (Civ) 372, [2009] BPIR 778. But in deciding whether a cross-claim is genuine and serious the fact that the company had not sought to litigate the cross-claim or that there were reasons it had not done so might persuade a court that the cross-claim was not sufficiently serious or genuine (*Denis Rye Ltd v Bolsover District Council* [2009] EWCA (Civ) 372, [2009] BPIR 778, [2010] BCC 248). In bankruptcy it has been said that any delay in alleging a cross-claim might lead to the inference that the allegation is not made in good faith, but to stave off bankruptcy: *Re a Debtor (No 554/SD/98)* [2000] 1 BCLC 103, CA. Certainly courts might be averse to restraining a petition where a cross-claim is asserted late in the day and where it might be seen as a ploy to stave off liquidation: *Southern Cross Group plc v Deka Immobilien Investment* [2005] BPIR 1010.Courts have a discretion as to whether to order winding up where there is a genuine and serious cross-claim (In *Re Bayoil SA* at 990; 66), but if a court has determined that a genuine and serious cross-claim exists, then it has been held that ordinarily the court should strike out the petition. It is only if special circumstances exist that a court has a real discretion and may wind up the company: *Re Bayoil SA* at 993; 70. In *Morrside Investments Ltd v DAG Construction Ltd* (unreported, 1 November 2007, ChD, Warren J) it was said that dismissal of a petition where there is a genuine and substantial dispute is not a rule of law, but a practice that applies save where exceptional circumstances exist. For an example of a case where there were special circumstances, and a court refused to dismiss a petition, see *Atlantic & General Information Investment Trust Ltd v Richbell Information Services Inc* [2000] 2 BCLC 779.

Where the claim in the petition is substantiated, but the company has a cross-claim pending in another court, the court hearing the petition has a discretion whether or not to order winding up: *Re FSA Business Software Ltd* [1990] BCC 465 at 470. It has been held that where a disputed cross-claim exists, yet the company is unable to dispute that some money is owed by it to the petitioner, a court may make a winding-up order. In such a case the company's claim must be equal to or exceed the creditor's claim for it to escape a winding-up order: *Re Pendigo Ltd* [1996] BCC 608, [1996] 2 BCLC 64; *Re Bayoil SA* [1998] BCC 988, [1999] 1 BCLC 62, CA; *Re Greenacre Publishing Ltd* [2000] BCC 11.

It should be noted that in Scotland it has been indicated that where a company that is the subject of a petition presented by a creditor has claims against the petitioner, an order might still be made if there are other major creditors that have not been paid: *Innes, petitioner* (P158/04 (OH), Lady Paton, 16 March 2004). The court said that while a creditor must demonstrate some debt owed to him or her, the terms of s 122(1)(f) and s 123(1)(e) permit a court to take a general and overall view of the company's financial position, 'rather than a view restricted to the company's standing and relationship with one creditor' (at [18]). This appears to accord with the view expressed in Australia in several cases: e g *National Mutual Life Association of Australasia Ltd v Oasis Developments Pty Ltd* (1983) 1 ACLC 1263.

While a set-off must exist between the creditor and the debtor in the same right, this is not the case with a cross-claim: *Hurst v Bennett* [2001] 2 BCLC 290, CA at [52] per Peter Gibson LJ. A cross-claim, unlike a set-off, would not need to have any procedural or juridical relationship to the debt claimed in the petition, but is a claim by the company against the creditor: *Popely v Popely* [2004] EWCA Civ 463 at [113].

Any cross-claim relied upon by the company must be against the petitioner, and not against a subsidiary company of the petitioner: *Tottenham Hotspur plc v Edennote plc* [1994] BCC 681.

See r 6.5 and the discussion relating to that rule, and especially that under the heading '... the debtor appears to have a counterclaim'.

Judgment obtained in relation to petition debt—Where the petition is based on an unpaid judgment debt or costs, a petition may succeed even if the company has lodged an appeal (*Re Amalgamated Properties of Rhodesia Ltd* [1917] 2 Ch 115; also, see *El Ajou v Dollar Land (Manhattan) Ltd* [2005] EWHC 2861 (Ch), [2007] BCC 953) against the judgment or award. The company should seek both a stay of execution of the judgment pending determination of the appeal and an adjournment of the winding-up petition. In the opposite situation, where the petition is based on a judgment debt, and the judgment has since been overturned, the petition will be struck out notwithstanding the fact that the petitioner has appealed: *Re Anglo-Bavarian Steel Ball Co* [1899] WN 80.

If the company submits that a judgment which has produced the debt upon which the petition is based was obtained by fraud or collusion, the petition will be ordered to stand over (*Bowes v Hope Life Insurance Society* (1865) 11 HLC 389; 11 ER 1383) until the company establishes, by means of evidence (*Re Universal Stock Exchange Co* [1884] WN 251), or in proceedings taken to challenge the judgment (*Bowes v Hope Life Insurance Society*), that the judgment was obtained improperly.

Courts have a discretion to go behind the judgment relied on by the creditor where there is a possibility of fraud, collusion or miscarriage of justice so as to ensure that injustice is not done (*Ex parte Kibble* (1875) LR 10 Ch App 373 at 378, CA; *Eberhardt v Mair* [1995] 1 WLR 1180 at 1186; *Re Menastar Finance Ltd* [2003] BCC 404; *Denis Rye Ltd v Bolsover District Council* [2009] EWCA (Civ) 372, [2009] BPIR 778), and the court is not limited to the evidence that was presented at the original hearing of the petitioner's claim: *Re Treka Mines Ltd* [1960] 1 WLR 1273; *Re Menastar Finance Ltd.*

Costs—If a petition succeeds then costs will usually be awarded to the petitioner and to be paid out of the funds of the company. Occasionally a court might actually award costs against a non-party. This will usually be the directors of the company. To be liable a non-party must have been guilty of some bad faith or impropriety: *Metalloy Supplies Ltd v MA (UK) Ltd* [1997] 1 WLR 1613. A director of a company that was wound up was held liable for costs in *Gatnom Capital v Sanders and Others* [2011] EWHC 3716 (Ch) at [9]-[15], because he was the only director, he was the guiding force behind the company's conduct in the proceedings, which was improper, he funded the defence to the winding-up proceedings, he acted improperly, and at all relevant times the company was insolvent.

If a petition is dismissed on the basis that there is a substantial dispute on genuine grounds, a court is likely to award indemnity costs against the petitioner: *Re a Company (No 0012209 of 1991)* [1992] 1 WLR 351, [1992] 2 All ER 797, [1992] BCLC 865; *Re a Company (No 2507 of 2003)* [2003] 2 BCLC 346; see also *TJ Ross (Joiners) Ltd v High Range Developments Ltd* 2000 SCLR 161, save in exceptional circumstances: *Re Sykes & Sons Ltd* [2012] EWHC 1005 (Ch). In ascertaining whether there are exceptional circumstances to disregard the general rule, courts were entitled to take into account the parties' communications prior to the presentation of the petition: *Re Sykes & Sons Ltd* [2012] EWHC 1005 (Ch). In this case the petitioner had given the company every reasonable opportunity to explain the basis of its dispute and the company had not done so in any meaningful way and so this warranted departing from the general rule on costs. Where the petitioner has given the debtor company significant notice of the petitioner's intention to advertise the petition, giving the company time in which to give notice of its intention to apply for an injunction to prevent advertising, the petitioner might be ordered only to pay the company's costs on the standard basis: *Re Realstar Ltd* [2007] All ER (D) 171 (Aug).

The company may take proceedings against the petitioner for damages for malicious prosecution: *Quartz Hill Gold Mining v Eyre* (1883) 11 QBD 674; *Partizan Ltd v OJ Kenny & Co Ltd* [1998] 1 BCLC 157. Malice could involve improper motive in the presenting of a petition as well as ill-will or spite. Reliance on legal advice by a petitioner makes it almost impossible to establish malice: *Jacob v Vockrodt* [2007] EWHC 2403 (QB), [2007] BPIR 1568.

See Keay 'Claims for Malicious Presentation: The Peril Lurking on the Sidelines for Petitioning Creditors' [2001] *Insolvency Lawyer* 136.

See Galatopoulos 'Cross-Claims, Winding up and Judicial Discretion: An Overview' [1999] *Insolvency Lawyer* 240; Keay 'Disputing Debts Relied On By Petitioning Creditors Seeking Winding-up orders' (2001) 22 *Company Lawyer* 40; S Lee 'The Court's Jurisdiction to Restrain a Creditor from Presenting a Winding Up Petition Where a Cross-Claim Exists' (2010) 69 CLJ 113 for more detailed discussions of the whole issue of disputing a petition debt.

Abuse of process—The court has an inherent power to prevent abuse of its process, and may, in its discretion, grant an injunction to restrain the presentation, and advertisement, of a petition (*Stonegate Securities Ltd v Gregory* [1980] 1 All ER 241) or dismiss it with costs (*Re Doreen Boards Ltd* [1996] 1 BCLC 501) in circumstances other than where the debt founding the petition is disputed. These are: if the proceedings are bound to fail because the petitioner will not be able to establish that he or she is a creditor and, therefore, obtain the necessary standing to petition, or an inability to prove that the company is unable to pay its debts (*Pacific Communications Rentals Pty Ltd v Walker* (1994) 12 ACSR 287 at 288–289; 12 ACLC 5 at 6); the petition is presented to achieve some improper purpose: *Re a Company (No 004601 of 1997)* [1998] 2 BCLC 111. It is an improper use of the winding-up process if the aim is to put improper pressure on the company to settle liabilities that were not those on which the petition was based: *Re a Company (No 004601 of 1997)* [1998] 2 BCLC 111.

For a recent discussion of this matter, see the Privy Council's decision in *Ebbvale Ltd v Hosking* [2013] UKPC 1, [2013] 2 BCLC 204, [2013] BPIR 219.

Creditor opposition to the petition—The other creditors of the company that is the subject of a petition may, on occasions, oppose the making of a winding-up order sought by the

181

petitioning creditor. The right to have an order belongs to the creditors as a class, rather than being a right just belonging to the petitioner, so all creditors are entitled to be consulted on the desirability of such a course: *Re Crigglestone Coal Co* [1906] 2 Ch 327 at 332. The courts will be more concerned with the opposition of unsecured as opposed to secured creditor opposition: *Re Crigglestone Coal Co; Re Demaglass Holdings Ltd* [2001] 2 BCLC 633. The court is empowered by s 195(1) to have regard to the wishes of the creditors, as proved to it by any sufficient evidence, and if necessary to direct that meetings be held for the purpose of ascertaining those wishes.

It is incumbent on the court to balance the right of an unpaid creditor to a winding-up order in relation to an insolvent company, as against the fact that the majority in value of creditors may wish the company to continue: *Re Demaglass Holdings Ltd* [2001] 2 BCLC 633. The court may, in exercising its discretion, decide to refrain from making an order because of the attitude of the majority of creditors in number and value, and the fact that the creditors can demonstrate good reasons for their opposition to the order: *Re P & J Macrae Ltd* [1961] 1 WLR 229; *Re JD Swain Ltd* [1965] 1 WLR 909 at 914–915, CA; *Re Demaglass Holdings Ltd* [2001] 2 BCLC 633. But even then, the court might overlook the opposition if the petitioner can demonstrate the fact that special circumstances exist warranting the making of an order: *Re P & J Macrae Ltd; Re ABC Coupler & Engineering Co* [1961] 1 WLR 243, CA. The court will also take into account whether the petitioning creditor is seeking to gain an unfair advantage vis à vis the other creditors: *Re Leigh Estates (UK) Ltd* [1994] BCC 292.

It must be noted that the court will take cognisance of the nature of the creditors who oppose the order, as well as the quality of their debts: *Re P & J Macrae Ltd*. The court will not disregard totally the views of creditors with vested interests in the company, such as the directors of the company and creditors who are associated with the company (*Re Medisco Equipment Ltd* [1983] BCLC 305, (1983) 1 BCC 98, 944), but they will carry far less weight at the point where a court looks at which view has the majority support (*Re HJ Tompkins Ltd* [1990] BCLC 76; *Re Demaglass Holdings Ltd* [2001] 2 BCLC 633), and they may well be discounted: *Re Lummus Agricultural Services Ltd* [1999] BCC 953 at 958.

Where creditors oppose the winding up, but a court decides to make a winding-up order, the creditors may be granted their costs out of the company's assets if their views were entitled to be put forward in the circumstances: *Re William Thorpe & Son Ltd* (1988) 5 BCC 156.

For a discussion both of what might be good reasons for opposing the petition and what might constitute special circumstances in favour of the petitioner where a majority is against an order, see A Keay *McPherson's Law of Company Liquidation* (3rd edn, Sweet and Maxwell, 2013) at 183-186.

Adjourn—The general practice, in the past, has been, where the debt relied on in the petition is disputed at the winding-up hearing, to dismiss the petition (*Re Martin Wallis & Co* (1893) 37 Sol Jo 822; *Re Meaford Manufacturing Co* (1919) 46 OLR 252), but the court has on a few occasions exercised the power to adjourn in order to allow the petitioner to bring an action to establish the debt relied on (*Re Catholic Publishing Co* (1864) 33 LJ Ch 325; *Brinds Ltd v Offshore Oil NL* (1986) 2 BCC 98, 916, PC), or to enable the company to take proceedings to have a judgment set aside for fraud: *Bowes v Hope Life Insurance Society Ltd* (1865) 11 HLC 389, (1865) 11 ER 1383. Sometimes where the dispute can be resolved without a great deal of time and the taking of evidence, the court has indicated that it might determine the dispute on the hearing of the petition: *Re King's Cross Industrial Dwellings Co* (1870) 11 Eq 149; *Re Welsh Brick Industries Ltd* [1946] 2 All ER 197; *Brinds Ltd v Offshore Oil NL* (1986) 2 BCC 98, 916, PC.

Where the majority of creditors oppose the making of a winding-up order, the court will grant an adjournment ordinarily if there is a good reason to do so, such as being able to sell company stock for a higher price while the company was trading compared with if it was in liquidation: *Re Demaglass Holdings Ltd* [2001] 2 BCLC 633.

The court may well grant an adjournment if the application is not in order, for instance advertisement has not occurred. It is the practice of the High Court to grant only one adjournment to permit the application to be put in order. More than one adjournment will not usually be able to be secured merely because the petitioner is negotiating with the company. Nevertheless, if the application is in order the court will listen to an application for an adjournment to permit negotiating to take place (of for payment to be arranged) (Chief Registrar Baister 'The hearing of the petition' (2008) CRI 115 at 115).

Courts have tended to be against the granting of adjournments, either for long or indefinite periods, or on a repeated basis (*Re Boston Timber Fabrications Ltd* [1984] BCLC 328 at 333, CA), whether the application for adjournment has or has not been opposed: *Practice Note* [1977] 1 WLR 1066, [1977] 3 All ER 64. The courts will not be willing to order adjournments one after another even if the parties all agree: *Re a Company (No 001573 of 1983)* [1983] BCLC 492; *Re Pleatfine Ltd* [1983] BCLC 102. But short adjournments are often granted so as to permit the petition to be re-advertised, to enable further affidavits to be filed, to have a meeting of creditors to ascertain their wishes concerning the petition (under s 195), to provide a chance for creditors to obtain advice, or to give an opportunity for a compromise to be reached, settling a scheme of arrangement or proposing a company voluntary arrangement: *Re Piccadilly Property Management Ltd* [1999] 2 BCLC 145, [2000] BCC 44. Having said all of that, courts will stand over petitions where there are sufficiently exceptional circumstances: *MHMH Ltd v Carwood Barker Holdings Ltd* [2004] EWHC 3174 (Ch).

There is Australian authority to the effect that the principles that are to guide a court when hearing an application for an adjournment, are the same as those when exercising its discretion on whether to make a winding-up order: *Re Airfast Services Pty Ltd* (1976) 2 ACLR 1; *Re DTX Australia Ltd* (1987) 5 ACLC 343 at 350.

Courts might allow an adjournment of a petition where the company is not legally represented and the matters that surround it are complex: *Henry Butcher International Ltd v K G Engineering* [2004] EWCA Civ 1597.

'The ground only that ... the company has no assets'—At one stage the courts would not make a winding-up order against a company that held no assets which could be made available for the payment of debts: *Re Chapel House Colliery Co* (1883) 24 Ch D 259. But this led to abuse and to the introduction of the relevant words in s 125(1). It must be noted that the use of the word 'only' in s 125(1) indicates that the intention of Parliament was not to prevent the court from taking into account the total absence of property as one of the factors that might lead it to refuse the order. See *Bell Group Finance Pty Ltd v Bell Group (UK) Holdings Ltd* [1996] BCC 505, [1996] BCLC 304 for a case where Chadwick J acknowledged that the company had no assets, but said that that was not a sufficient reason for not making a winding-up order. A liquidator might always be able to recover money and assets by invoking some provisions, such as those known as the adjustment provisions (ss 238–245), or taking legal action against directors for breach of their duties, fraudulent trading or wrongful trading.

Restrictions on making an order on the petition of a contributory—Section 125(2) provides that where a contributory presents a petition on the basis of s 122(1)(g) (the just and equitable ground) the court should not make an order, even if the petitioner is entitled to the relief, if it is of the opinion that some remedy other than winding up is available to contributories and they are acting unreasonably in seeking a winding-up order rather than pursuing their other remedy. This is so even if, in the absence of any other remedy, the court is of the opinion that the company should be wound up. 'Other remedy' here means other causes of action available under the general law or statute, or even an offer to purchase the members' shares: *Re a Company* [1983] 1 WLR 927, [1983] 2 All ER 854; *Re a Company* [1987] BCLC 562 at 571; *Re Cyracuse Ltd* [2001] 1 BCLC 187, [2001] BCC 806. The corollary of the foregoing is that if the other remedy is not viable then a contributory would not be acting unreasonably in seeking a winding-up order: *Alesi v Original Australian Art Co Pty Ltd* (1989) 7 ACLC 595 at 597. Judges, in taking into account whether a member has some other remedy available to him or her, will not restrict themselves only to considering remedies that result either from a member's legal rights or from the company's constitution: *Re a Company* [1983] 1 WLR 927, [1983] 2 All ER 854. Critically, anyone resisting the petition must establish two distinct elements, namely that some other remedy was available to the petitioner, *and* that the petitioner is unreasonable in seeking winding up rather than pursuing the other remedy: *Re Cyracuse Ltd* [2001] 1 BCLC 187, [2001] BCC 806.

See the notes under 'Just and equitable' in relation to s 122.

Costs—The court has a wide jurisdiction, under s 51(1) of the Senior Courts Act 1981, in awarding costs: *Cannon Screen Entertainment Ltd v Handmade Films (Distributors) Ltd* (1988) 5 BCC 207; *Re Ryan Developments Ltd* [2002] EWHC 1121 (Ch), [2002] 2 BCLC 792. If a petitioner succeeds in obtaining a winding-up order, then usually the petitioner is entitled to his or her reasonable costs of, and in connection with the petition: *Re Ryan Developments Ltd*. If a debt is paid after winding-up proceedings have been instituted, normally the petitioner will be seen as having succeeded and will be entitled to costs of, and in connection with, the petition (*Re Donald Fisher (Ealing) Ltd* [2001] All ER (D) 278; *Re Ryan Developments Ltd*), including the costs associated with being heard on any application by the company to stay the winding-up petition: *Re Ryan Developments Ltd*. A court is entitled to take account of the conduct of the parties both before and after proceedings have been instituted as well as during the course of proceedings: Frank Saul (Fashions) Ltd v HMRC (unreported, 18 May 2012, ChD, Vos J)

A court may, if it deems it appropriate, order that some person other than the company or the petitioner pay the costs personally (*Re a Company (No 006798 of 1995)* [1996] 2 BCLC 48, [1996] BCC 395), eg the directors of the company: *Re Brackland Magazines Ltd* [1994] 1 BCLC 190, *sub nom Gamlestaden plc v Brackland Magazines Ltd* [1993] BCC 194 (directors had improperly caused the company and the petitioner to incur costs in relation to a petition). But the courts will not make orders for costs as a matter of course against directors of one person companies unless they have acted improperly: *Taylor v Pace Developments Ltd* [1991] BCC 406, CA.

Winding-up order—If the court decides to make the order it will, after doing so, make a declaration concerning the applicability of the EC Regulation on Insolvency Proceedings and whether the proceedings were main, territorial or secondary. The decision it makes in this regard could have effects on other litigation commenced subsequently in the EU (except for Denmark).

Review or rescission of winding-up order—See r 7.47 and the notes accompanying it.

126 Power to stay or restrain proceedings against company

(1) At any time after the presentation of a winding-up petition, and before a winding-up order has been made, the company, or any creditor or contributory, may—

> (a) where any action or proceeding against the company is pending in the High Court or Court of Appeal in England and Wales or Northern Ireland, apply to the court in which the action or proceeding is pending for a stay of proceedings therein, and
>
> (b) where any other action or proceeding is pending against the company, apply to the court having jurisdiction to wind up the company to restrain further proceedings in the action or proceeding;

and the court to which application is so made may (as the case may be) stay, sist or restrain the proceedings accordingly on such terms as it thinks fit.

(2) In the case of a company registered but not formed under the Companies Act 2006, where the application to stay, sist or restrain is by a creditor, this section extends to actions and proceedings against any contributory of the company.

Amendments—SI 2009/1941.

General note—Probably, the aims of this provision are, as with the analogous provision in s 130(2), to prevent a company (which is possibly going to enter liquidation) from having its assets wasted in litigation, and to make sure that there is a distribution of company assets according to the statutory scheme, should liquidation eventuate: *Bowkett v Fuller United Electic Works Ltd* [1923] 1 KB 160.

127 Avoidance of property dispositions etc

(1) In a winding up by the court, any disposition of the company's property, and any transfer of shares, or alteration in the status of the company's members, made after the commencement of the winding up is, unless the court otherwise orders, void.

(2) This section has no effect in respect of anything done by an administrator of a company while a winding-up petition is suspended under paragraph 40 of Schedule B1.

Amendments—Enterprise Act 2002, s 248(3), Sch 17, paras 9, 15.

General note—Following presentation of a winding-up petition, the rendering void of any disposition of a company's property (and those other matters relating to share transfer and the alteration of the company' membership) is triggered on the making of a winding-up order against the company. This effect may be stopped by a court order validating dispositions. The scope of the provision in rendering dispositions etc void involves a 'relation back' to the commencement of the winding up (being the presentation of the petition or any earlier resolution to wind up the company) as defined in s 129. It has been said that the purpose of the 'relation back' is in seeking to preserve the pari passu principle of distribution in the period in which a winding-up petition is pending: *Re Wiltshire Iron Co* (1868) 3 Ch App 443 at 447. A similar statement by Lightman J in *Coutts & Co v Stock* [2000] 1 BCLC 183 at 186 ('part of the statutory scheme') was approved by the Court of Appeal in *Hollicourt (Contracts) Ltd v Bank of Ireland Ltd* [2001] 2 WLR 294 at 296. The provision as cast, however, is far broader in scope than is necessary for achieving this purpose alone and will render void all post-petition dispositions, including not only dispositions which are harmful to the company but also those involved in bona fide transactions, transactions entered into in the ordinary course of the company's business, payments into and out of the company's bank account and transactions which operate significantly to the benefit of the company through an increase in its net assets. So as to avoid the prejudicial consequences of s 127, it is imperative that a contrary order of the type mentioned in the provision, commonly termed a validating order, is obtained. Dispositions of property to a company against which a winding-up petition has been presented are not caught by s 127.

The provision does not in itself provide the liquidator with any cause of action against the directors of the company which has made the disposition: *Phillips v McGregor-Paterson* [2009] EWHC 2385 (Ch), [2010] BPIR 239 at [35].

Section 127 is expressly disapplied in the case of certain financial market transactions prescribed in Companies Act 1989, ss 164(3), 173(3)–(5). Similar exemptions applicable to financial and security settlements and associated security arrangements are provided for in the Financial Markets and Insolvency (Settlement Finality) Regulations 1999 (SI 1999/2979).

See, for a detailed discussion of s 127, A Keay *McPherson's Law of Company Liquidation* (3rd edn, Sweet and Maxwell, 2013) at 341-364.

'Commencement of the winding up'—For the most part, the commencement of winding up will be the date of the presentation of the petition to wind up, but in some cases it can be earlier than that. For example, if the company passed a resolution to wind up before the presentation of the petition, then commencement will be, if a winding-up order is eventually made, the date of the resolution (s 129(1)) and, of course, this makes the period during which dispositions may be set aside longer.

'Void'—'Void' means void for all purposes related to or incidental to the administration of the winding up: *National Acceptance Corp Pty Ltd v Benson* (1988) 12 NSWLR 213 at 229, (1988) 6 ACLC 685 at 689, NSWCA; *Monds v Hammond and Suddards* [1996] 2 BCLC 470 at 474.

Disposition—The term 'disposition' is not defined in the legislation but must be attributed the widest possible meaning, given the unlimited wording employed in the provision and its underlying purpose. What is needed for s 127 to operate is a disposition amounting to an alienation of the company's property: *Mersey Steel & Iron Co Ltd v Naylor* (1884) 9 App Cas 434 at 440. The term will, therefore, include not only all forms of dealing by the company in its tangible and intangible property but also, for example, a surrender of a company's contractual rights or the taking of any other step by the company conferring value on a third party, such as the conferring of the benefit of a lien. While the term is wide, in Australia 'disposition' has been held not to catch the abandonment by a company of an alleged claim for damages: *Re Mal Bower's Macquarie Electrical Centre Pty Ltd (in liquidation)* [1974] 1 NSWLR 254. The assumption of liabilities by a company is also not within s 127, as it does not involve a disposition of the company's property: *Coutts & Co v Stock* [2000] 1 BCLC 183. A disposition which is effected by a company pursuant to a court order will nevertheless apparently fall within s 127: *Re Flint* [1993] Ch 319 (transfer of a husband's interest in matrimonial home to wife pursuant to an order under Matrimonial Causes Act 1973, s 24 and analogous to s 284(1) of the Insolvency Act, applicable in bankruptcy); reference should be made here to the observations on the judgment in *Flint* in the note with the same heading as here and under s 284 (but it must be noted that s 284 is in different terms to s 127 and so one cannot approach this section with the assumption that it is designed to achieve the same outcome as s 127, and one cannot necessarily apply a case decided under one section to the other section: *Pettit v Novakovic* [2007] BPIR 1643, [2007] BCC 462).

Post-petition payments made under what is now termed a third party debt order would fall within s 127.

In *Hollicourt (Contracts) Ltd v Bank of Ireland* [2001] 2 WLR 290 the Court of Appeal (Mummery LJ delivering the judgment of the court) departed from its earlier decision in *Re Gray's Inn Construction Ltd* [1980] 1 WLR 711 (Buckley LJ with whom Goff LJ and Sir David Cairns agreed) so as to hold that, whilst a payment out of a company's bank account constitutes a disposition of the company's property in favour of the creditor, such a payment does not involve a disposition in favour of the bank. On a payment out of a bank account a bank acts merely as the company's agent such that the avoidance of the disposition in favour of the creditor does not affect the validity of any intermediate, related transaction, most commonly the bank honouring the cheque tendered by the company to its customer, irrespective of whether the company's account is in credit or overdrawn: *Hollicourt* at 299–300. Approving the decision in *Coutts & Co v Stock* [2000] 1 BCLC 183 to similar effect, the Court of Appeal in *Hollicourt* identified not only (a) that *Re Gray's Inn* concerned payments into an overdrawn bank account but also (b) that certain observations in the judgment of Buckley LJ relied on a questionable concession by counsel for the bank to the effect that payments from the account in discharge of pre-liquidation debts amounted to dispositions of property unless, properly analysed, the payments did not amount to dispositions of property but operated to do no more than increase the company's liability on its overdraft to the bank. Despite *Hollicourt*, it might be argued, though it is thought to be doubtful, that a claim for breach of duty remains against a bank which honours payments from a company's bank account following advertisement of a winding-up petition, given the statement in *Hollicourt* to the effect that the case is restricted to s 127 without discounting the possibility of alternative lines of argument.

A payment made into a bank account which is in credit has been held not to amount to a disposition within s 127: *Re Barn Crown Ltd* [1994] 4 All ER 42. The analysis in that case (at 45) to the effect that payment on the collected cheque involves nothing more than an adjustment in favour of the company on the statement of account between the company and its bank misses the fact of the transfer of funds from the company to its bank (ie the funds collected by the bank on the cheque) in consideration for the bank's promise of repayment in accordance with the terms of the account: see also *Gray's Inn* at 818. A payment made into a bank account which is in overdraft amounts to a disposition of the company's property by way of the transfer of funds collected by the bank on the cheque in reduction of the company's indebtedness to the bank.

A disposition by X of Y Ltd's property, held by X on behalf of Y Ltd, may be set aside under s 127 even though the disposition of the property is not directly made by Y Ltd, as the central factor in s 127 is the disposition of company property: *Re J Leslie Engineers Co Ltd (in liquidation)* [1976] 2 All ER 85 at 89. If the petitioner is paid out by the company, and another creditor successfully applies to be substituted as the petitioner, and that new petitioner obtains a winding-up order, the original petitioner will have to repay the sum received less his or her reasonable costs in bringing the petition: *Re Bostels Ltd* [1968] Ch 346; *Re Western Welsh International System Buildings Ltd* (1985) 1 BCC 99, 296.

The South Australian Supreme Court has held that a payment into court is not a disposition, despite the fact that the company does not retain any legal interest in the money. A disposition will only exist where the company has a beneficial interest in the money at the time of payment out: *Pilmer v HIH Casualty Insurance Ltd* (2004) 90 SASR 465.

'The company's property'—The term 'the company's property' means property that is legally or beneficially owned by the company. The term will not catch property which is taken out of the ownership of the company under the security of a third party; accordingly the court's validation will not be required for the enforcement of fixed or floating security or the realisation of assets by a mortgagee, whether as mortgagee-in-possession or through the appointment of a receiver (*Sowman v David Samuel Trust Ltd* [1978] 1 WLR 22); neither will s 127 catch the vesting of property under an after-acquired property provision within contractual security. To similar effect, in *Re French's Wine Bar Ltd* (1987) 3 BCC 173 it was held that s 127 did not prevent completion of an unconditional contract for the sale of leasehold property, since the property had passed in equity on exchange of contracts prior to the presentation of the winding-up petition.

Where a petitioning creditor's debt is to be discharged from company funds, it will be necessary to obtain a validating order in respect of the disposition to avoid subsequent recovery by a liquidator if a supporting creditor is to be substituted on discharge of the debt: *Re Liverpool Civil Service Association* (1874) 9 Ch App 511.

Transfer of shares—The section does not affect the parties to the transfer as far as their liability to each other; the transfer is void 'so far as regards any effect to be given to it by the company':*In Re Onward v Building Society* (1891) 2 QB 463 at 475 per Lord Esher (our emphasis). 'Whether or not a transfer will be approved or not is dependent on whether it would be beneficial to the company' (*Onward Building Society* per Bowen LJ at 481) and would it 'benefit the creditors' (*Onward Building Society* per Bowen LJ at 482). The considerations that are relevant to whether a disposition of property ought to be approved are quite different from those that apply to a transfer of shares, and this is especially the case where the shares are fully paid up and so no calls can be made on them: *Carringbush Corporation Pty Ltd v ASIC* [2008] FCA 474 at [29].

Validating orders—The section makes no mention of the parties eligible to apply for a validating order, although the company respondent to a winding-up petition is in practice the most common applicant. An application by a shareholder, whose legitimate concern could be shown to be that there would be a share devaluation if there was a failure to validate a particular transaction, has been permitted: *Re Argentum Reductions (UK) Ltd* [1975] 1 WLR 186 at 190–191. There is no good reason why the court should not entertain an application by any party able to establish a legitimate interest in the validation. In practice, other than the company and a shareholder (see above) this might conceivably include any of the company's directors (if the company itself will not apply), or the other party to any potentially void disposition. In practice, the obvious difficulty facing parties other than the company is provision of the financial information necessary to support such an application. Certainly, in Australia, reluctance to grant an order has been expressed in the absence of evidence from the company itself as to the benefit of the proposed disposition: *Re Pacific Coast Fisheries Pty* (1980) 5 ACLR 354.

The applicant for a validating order has the onus of showing why a validating order should be made: *Re Rushcutters Court Pty Ltd (No 2)* (1978) ACLC 29, 965.

The granting of validating orders has developed upon what are now well settled principles, although the court has a broad, unfettered discretion: In *Re Tramways Building & Construction Co Ltd* [1988] 1 Ch 293; *Denney v John Hudson & Co Ltd* [1992] BCLC 901, sub nom *Re SA & D Wright Ltd* [1992] BCC 503 at 506, CA. Because of the discretion, an exhaustive consideration of authority at first instance is of very little practical assistance, since the cases involve the application of these principles to the particular facts of each case, though for examples of cases where orders have been refused, see *Re J Leslie Engineers Co Ltd* [1976] 1 WLR 292 (the proposed transaction promised no benefit to creditors), *Re Rafidain Bank* [1992] BCC 376 (there was an absence of benefit to creditors generally). In *Richbell Information Services Inc v Atlantic General Investments Ltd* [1999] BCC 871 an order facilitating litigation funding for a company to recover was granted. For a highly pragmatic approach, see *Re Dewrum Ltd* [2002] BCC 57, in which Neuberger J granted a bank's application for validation only of a charge granted to it by A on the same day that the said property had been transferred to A by Dewrum Ltd against which a winding-up petition had been presented on the basis that the bank sought a limited validation in respect of the charge to which Dewrum Ltd was not party, and the need to do justice between the parties.

Wherever practicable, an application should be made to seek prospective validation of a transaction; the court's discretion is less likely to be exercised favourably where validation is sought retrospectively, particularly where there is any period of unexplained delay. But the court should be cautious on prospective applications of pre-empting the work of a liquidator and should not ordinarily grant a validating order where the subsequent making of a winding-up order is inevitable: *Re Bransfield Engineering Ltd* (1985) 1 BCC 99, 409 at 99, 411.

There is no reason in principle why a validating order should not be sought in respect of only a part of a transaction, although in Australia, some reluctance has been expressed at acceding to applications to validate parts only of a transaction: see *Jardio Holdings Pty Ltd v Dorcon Construction Pty Ltd* (1984) 2 ACLC 574.

Re Gray's Inn Construction Ltd [1980] 1 WLR 711 remains the leading authority on the issue of validation, and in the Court of Appeal in *Re SA & D Wright* [1992] BCC 503, *sub nom Denney v John Hudson & Co Ltd* [1992] BCLC 901 Fox LJ (with whom Russell and Staughton LJJ agreed) identified (at 504–505) the following principles as having been approved in *Re Gray's Inn Construction Ltd (references are to pages in the report of the latter case)*:

(1) The discretion vested in the court by s 127 is entirely at large, subject to the general principles which apply to any kind of discretion, and subject also to limitation that the discretion must be exercised in the context of the liquidation provisions of the statute (at 717).

(2) The basic principle of law governing the liquidation of insolvent estates is that the assets of the insolvent at the time of the commencement of the liquidation will be distributed pari passu among the insolvent's unsecured creditors as at the date of the liquidation. In a company's compulsory liquidation this is achieved by s 127 (at 717).

(3) There are occasions, however, when it may be beneficial not only for the company but also for the unsecured creditors, that the company should be able to dispose of some of its property during the period after the petition has been presented, but before the winding-up order has been made. Thus, it may sometimes be beneficial to the company and its creditors that the company should be able to continue the business in its ordinary course (at 717).

(4) In considering whether to make a validating order, the court must always do its best to ensure that the interests of the unsecured creditors will not be prejudiced (at 717).

(5) The desirability of the company being able to carry on its business is likely to be more speculative and will be likely to depend on whether a sale of a company's business is more beneficial than a realisation of individual assets (at 717).

(6) The court should not validate any transaction or series of transactions which might result in one or more pre-liquidation creditors being paid in full at the expense of other creditors, who will only receive a dividend, in the absence of special circumstances making such a course desirable in the interests of the creditors generally. If, for example, it were in the interests of the creditors generally that the company's business should be carried on, and this could only be achieved by paying for goods already supplied to the company when the petition is presented but not yet paid for, the court might exercise its discretion to validate payments for those goods (at 718).

(7) A disposition carried out in good faith in the ordinary course of business at a time when the parties were unaware that a petition had been presented would usually be validated by the court unless there is ground for thinking that the transaction may involve an attempt to prefer the disponee – in which case the transaction would not be validated (at 718).

(8) Despite the strength of the principle of securing pari passu distribution, the principle has no application to post-liquidation creditors; for example, the sale of an asset at full market value after the presentation of the petition. That is because such a transaction involves no dissipation of the company's assets for it does not reduce the value of its assets (at 719).

For a validation order, the applicant needs to establish that either the company is solvent or that the order will be for the benefit of company creditors: *Re McGuinness Bros (UK) Ltd* (1987) 3 BCC 571 at 574; *Re Fairway Graphics Ltd* [1991] BCLC 468 at 468. Despite the need for creditor benefit, there may be exceptional cases where a validation order is granted on other grounds such as in allowing a company to make payment to enable its solicitors to raise bona fide grounds of opposition to a winding-up petition presented against it; see, by analogy, *Rio Properties v Al-Midani* [2003] BPIR 128 at 135–139.

The solvency of a company does not preclude the making of a validating order. Such an order will be more easily obtained where solvency can be demonstrated, although the court will entertain objections by parties with a legitimate interest: *Re Burton & Deakin Ltd* [1977] 1 WLR 390. A validation order might be made where a creditor who has benefited from a disposition and has changed its position as a result of the disposition, in circumstances where the creditor did not know and could not have known of the existence of the petition (because the petition had not been advertised): *Re Tain Construction Ltd* [2003] 2 BCLC 374 at [41] (where the change of position argument failed). But the change of position defence could not be relied on if the respondent knows at the time of the change of position that the disposition was invalid, as the respondent would not be acting in good faith (*Tain* at [43]).

It has been held that as the making of a validation order is squarely in the discretion of the court, the court would consider all evidence placed before it, from whatever source (including from people who did not have locus standi), if it was relevant to the exercise of the discretion: *Re Rescupine Ltd* [2003] 1 BCLC 661. While there is a broad discretion it has been said that an order will only be made where there was no serious risk to the creditors or where the court was satisfied that the company's position and hence the position of the creditors would be improved by the transaction being validated: *RC Brewery Ltd v Revenue and Customs Commissioners* [2013] EWHC 1184 (Ch).

The consequence of failing to obtain a validating order—A claim for recovery of property disposed of without the protection of a validating order constitutes a statutory cause of action which is created automatically on the making of a winding-up order, and not the election of a liquidator. The method of recovery is not prescribed in the legislation and remains a matter of general law, which would allow for trading on equitable principles: *Re J Leslie Engineers Co Ltd* [1976] 2 All ER 85 at 89. A claim to recover property will ordinarily be pursued by way of relief consequent upon an application for a declaration that the disposition pursued is void under s 127. The claim is available to the liquidator only (*Campbell v Michael Mount PPB* (1996) 14 ACLC 218), although in *Mond v Hammond Suddards* [1996] 2 BCLC 470 at 473 it was said that s 127 imposes no limit on who is able to bring a claim; with respect, this appears to be misconceived in that it ignores the class nature of liquidation. No other English authority seems to adopt such a wide view as that in *Mond*, although in *Power v Brown* [2009] EWHC 9 (Ch) Gabriel Moss QC (sitting as a deputy judge of the High Court) appeared to accept what Judge Kolbert had said, and the learned deputy judge in *Power* said in that in an appropriate case s 284 (the bankruptcy equivalent of s 127) could be relied on by parties other than the bankruptcy trustee (at [20], [21]). One must always bear in mind that s 284 is different from s 127. A liquidator may not assign a claim under s 127: *Re Ayala Holdings Ltd (No 2)* [1996] 1 BCLC 467.

A recovery made in respect of a void disposition under s 127 enures for the benefit of the company in liquidation since the property recovered remained at all times, notwithstanding any purported disposition, the property of the company. As such, the property will remain subject to any security existing at the date of the winding-up order.

Where a liquidator is unable to recover a void disposition, then a prima facie claim for damages equating to the loss suffered by the company as a consequence of the disposition, less any partial recovery made, will be available to the liquidator against the company's directors in misfeasance proceedings under s 212: *Re Neath Harbour Smelting and Rolling Works Co* [1887] WN 87.

Practice and procedure—The liquidator will seek a declaration that a disposition is void and in the same proceedings the company or a third party will usually seek an order validating the disposition.

Notwithstanding the decision in *Hollicourt (Contracts) Ltd v Bank of Ireland* [2001] 2 WLR 290, which suggests that a bank will not face a potential recovery claim under s 127 by a liquidator, it is usual practice for a clearing bank to freeze a customer company's accounts on advertisement of a winding-up petition. On a validation order being granted to the bank's satisfaction, the bank will usually operate a new account having 'ruled off' liability on the old account.

An application for a validating order must be supported in particular with sufficient and credible up-to-date financial information and supporting documentation as to allow the court to make an informed assessment of the company's position, the necessity of any payment proposed, the benefit and/or any accompanying detriment accruing to the company for the purposes of the general principles set out above. The scrutiny to which such information is subjected by the court is likely to be more exacting where the company proposes ongoing trading and seeks multiple or repeat validations. For examples of the exercise of the jurisdiction see (on the particular facts in each) *Re a Company (No 007523 of 1986)* [1987] BCLC 2001 (validation refused where the company was involved in loss-making and the trend was apparently irreversible, though note the possibility of reduced loss through the proposed transaction) and *Richbell Information Service Inc v Atlantic General Investments Trust Ltd* [1999] BCC 871 (inappropriate to validate disposition in absence of petitioning creditor's consent where disposition contrary to petitioner's contractual rights).

See *Practice Note: Validation Orders (Sections 127 and 284 of the Insolvency Act 1986)* [2007] BPIR 94, [2007] BCC 91.

Procedure and forms—An application for a validating order is usually made on notice but often, by necessity, on short notice to the petitioning creditor. For a liquidator's application to recover on a void disposition, see the procedural note to r 7.2. Section 127 is applicable in the winding up of a foreign company in England and Wales: *Re Sugar Properties (Deriseley Wood) Ltd* (1987) 3 BCC 88.

Although an application for a validation order should be made to a district judge or registrar, and only made to the judge where the application is urgent and no district judge or registrar is available or where it is complex or raises new or controversial points of law or is estimated to last for longer than 30 minutes: *Practice Note: Validation Orders (Sections 127 and 284 of the Insolvency Act 1986)* [2007] BPIR 94, [2007] BCC 91 at [3]. An application under s 127 should only be made in the winding-up proceedings established on presentation of the winding-up petition. For the transfer of proceedings between county courts and within the High Court see CPR, r 30.2 and Insolvency Rules 1986, r 7.51 (and the notes applying to the latter); for transfers between the county court and the High Court see r 7.11 of the Insolvency Rules 1986 and the accompanying notes.

'anything done by an administrator of a company while a winding-up petition is suspended'—This was introduced by the Enterprise Act 2002. For a discussion, see the comments accompanying para 40 of Sch B1. Also, see *Re J Smiths Haulage Ltd* [2007] BCC 135, where an administrator was appointed subsequent to the presentation of a petition to wind up and disposed of company property without knowledge of the petition. It was said that such a disposition was not be void under s 127 as the effect of the administrator's appointment was to suspend the petition (para 40(1)(b)), and s 127(2) confirms this.

128 Avoidance of attachments etc

(1) Where a company registered in England and Wales is being wound up by the court, any attachment, sequestration, distress or execution put in force against the estate or effects of the company after the commencement of the winding up is void.

(2) This section, so far as relates to any estate or effects of the company situated in England and Wales, applies in the case of a company registered in Scotland as it applies in the case of a company registered in England and Wales.

General note—This provision denies creditors their ordinary remedies against the company, to ensure that an insolvent company's property shall, once in liquidation, be applied in satisfaction of creditors according to the statutory scheme. This denial commences when the company enters liquidation, although it could be effected after the presentation of the winding-up petition, if a stay on proceedings under s 126 is obtained.

See s 183 and the notes relating to that section for further consideration of execution and attachment. See s 112 and the General note under that section for the position with respect to voluntary liquidations.

'**Attachment**'—Attachment encompasses the process by which a judgment creditor obtains a garnishee order attaching a debt that is owed by a third party to the debtor company. An attachment does not occur when the garnishee order is obtained (*Re Stanhope Silkstone Collieries Co* (1879) 11 Ch D 100), but only when it is served on the garnishee: *Re National United Investments Corp* [1901] 1 Ch 950; *Sedgwick Collins & Co v Rossia Insurance Co* [1926] 1 KB 1.

'**Sequestration**'—This term has no particular technical meaning, and it means 'the detention of property by a court so as to permit the answering of a demand which is made': *Re Australian Direct Steam Navigation Co* (1875) 20 Eq 325 at 326.

'**Distress**'—This is an extra-judicial process used mainly in order to enforce the payment of arrears of rent that is owed pursuant to a lease, or payment of outstanding instalments of principal and interest owing under a mortgage or mortgage debenture which either expressly grants the right to distrain or includes a provision in terms of which the mortgagor attorns the tenant to the mortgagee. 'Distrain' in the context of the renting of land is a right to resort to the chattels on the land occupied by the tenant: *Re Coal Consumers' Association* [1876] 4 Ch D 625 at 629–630. This process is due to be abolished when Part 3 of the Tribunals, Courts and Enforcement Act 2007 comes into force.

For further discussion, see Walton 'Landlord's Distress: Past Its Use By Date?' [2000] Conv 508.

Distress is to be distinguished from the other remedies referred to in s 128(1) in that it can be used against the property of third parties which is found upon the demised premises.

'**Execution**'—This has been referred to as 'the process for enforcing or giving effect to the judgment of the court': *Re Overseas Aviation Engineering Ltd* [1963] Ch 24 at 39.

'**Put in force**'—What this constitutes depends on the remedy involved. It may take the form of legal, equitable or statutory execution. The form of execution can determine when it is actually put in force. For instance, where execution is levied on the company's goods under a writ of fi fa, the execution is put in force when the goods are seized by the sheriff: *Re London & Devon Biscuit Co* (1871) 12 Eq 190. With attachment, service on the garnishee is the critical issue: *Re Stanhope Silkstone Collieries Co* (1879) 11 Ch D 160; *Croshaw v Lyndhurst Ship Co* [1897] 2 Ch 154.

All forms of execution have been put in force when proceedings have led to the creditor obtaining a charge over the property with the result that the creditor is made secured: *Croshaw v Lyndhurst Ship Co* [1897] 2 Ch 154.

Leave to proceed—While s 128 makes no mention of any right of a creditor to seek and obtain leave to proceed, it has been held that the courts may give leave to a creditor to proceed with execution where it has been instigated, but not put in force, when winding up commenced: *Re Lancashire Cotton Spinning Co* (1887) 35 Ch D 656.

Commencement of winding up

129 Commencement of winding up by the court

(1) If, before the presentation of a petition for the winding up of a company by the court, a resolution has been passed by the company for voluntary winding up, the winding up of the company is deemed to have commenced at the time of the passing of the resolution; and unless the court, on proof of fraud or mistake, directs otherwise, all proceedings taken in the voluntary winding up are deemed to have been validly taken.

(1A) Where the court makes a winding-up order by virtue of paragraph 13(1)(e) of Schedule B1, the winding up is deemed to commence on the making of the order.

(2) In any other case, the winding up of a company by the court is deemed to commence at the time of the presentation of the petition for winding up.

Amendments—Enterprise Act 2002, s 248(3), Sch 17, paras 9, 16.

General note—This provision states that voluntary liquidations commence at the time when the company resolves to wind up, whereas a compulsory liquidation commences not with the making of the winding-up order, but with the presentation of the petition on which the winding-up order is subsequently made. However, where a winding-up order is made in relation to a company that was in voluntary liquidation at the time of the making of the order, then the winding up is said to commence at the time of the resolution to wind up. So, while the commencement of winding up in voluntary liquidation is the time when winding up actually begins, in compulsory liquidation there is an artificial date for the commencement. Commencement in this latter form of winding up relates back to the point when the winding up proceedings were initiated.

Subsection (1A) was introduced by the Enterprise Act 2002 and effectively means that if a court decides to make a winding-up order when hearing an application for an administration order, the date of the winding-up order is the commencement of winding up, and, therefore, there is no back-dating.

The commencement of winding up is of significant importance: for example, it brings to an end the power of the company to dispose of its property (s 127) and it is the time from which the status and liability of contributories is determined. But while it is the point of time that is crucial for determining many things in a liquidation, the actual date when the liquidation commences is used for a few matters: for instance, an automatic stay applies from the time of the actual winding up (s 130(2)) and the time from which the Limitation Act 1980 runs, as far as determining when proceedings have to be brought by or against the company, is the date of any winding-up order: *Re General Rolling Stock Co* (1872) 7 Ch App 646; *Re Cases of Taff Wells Ltd* [1992] Ch 179, [1992] BCLC 11, [1991] BCC 582. The limitation period ceases to run during the period in which a company is in liquidation: *Re General Rolling Stock Co* (1872) 7 Ch App 646; *Financial Services Compensation Scheme Ltd v Larnell (Insurances) Ltd* [2005] EWCA Civ 1408, [2006] BPIR 1370 at [18]. However, there are exceptions to the principle enunciated in *Re General Rolling Stock Co*. These exceptions are discussed in *Financial Services Compensation Scheme Ltd v Larnell (Insurances) Ltd*.

130 Consequences of winding-up order

(1) On the making of a winding-up order, a copy of the order must forthwith be forwarded by the company (or otherwise as may be prescribed) to the registrar of companies, who shall enter it in his records relating to the company.

(2) When a winding-up order has been made or a provisional liquidator has been appointed, no action or proceeding shall be proceeded with or commenced against the company or its property, except by leave of the court and subject to such terms as the court may impose.

(3) When an order has been made for winding up a company registered but not formed under the Companies Act 2006, no action or proceeding shall be commenced or proceeded with against the company or its property or any contributory of the company, in respect of any debt of the company, except by leave of the court, and subject to such terms as the court may impose.

(4) An order for winding up a company operates in favour of all the creditors and of all contributories of the company as if made on the joint petition of a creditor and of a contributory.

Amendments—SI 2009/1941.

General note—This provision states some of the major effects of compulsory winding up. The fact that a company is subject to winding up is something that the public is not expected to be aware of until official notification has occurred. This occurs when the registrar of companies places a notice in the *London Gazette* informing the world that he or she has received a copy of a winding-up order made against the company concerned (Companies Act 2006, ss 1077(1) and 1078(2); also, see s 1116 the difficulty is that the making of the winding-up order is made retrospective and can affect parties who have no notice of the fact that winding-up proceedings are on foot against the company, but deal with the company before a winding-up order is made.

Section 130(2) enforces an automatic stay on all legal proceedings, and it has effect all over the United Kingdom (In *Re International Pulp and Paper Co* (1876) 3 Ch D 594), but while the provision can apply to a winding up of a foreign company in England, it does not apply to a foreign insolvency proceeding: *Mazur Media Ltd v Mazur Media GmbH* [2004] BPIR 1253. The provision is designed to ensure that liquidators are not required to defend a significant body of litigation instituted by disaffected creditors, thereby dissipating the company's funds: In *Re David Lloyd & Co* (1877) 6 Ch D 339. Such a result would impact on all creditors. The right of the creditors to claim a remedy through the courts is replaced with a right to lodge a proof of debt in the company's liquidation and obtain a share of the company's funds. This process should, generally, be far less expensive than litigation. It must not be forgotten that the prohibition in s 130(2) is also directed equally at actions that are being taken, or might be taken, by shareholders and others.

The imposition of the stay supports the notion that winding up ought to be seen as an orderly, effective process that prima facie treats creditors equally (but see the notes to s 107).

As s 130(4) indicates, the winding-up order operates in relation to all creditors and all contributories. This demonstrates the collective nature of the winding-up process and so where the petitioner is a creditor, he or she obtains the order as a representative of all of the creditors. In some ways this provision is the benefit given to creditors for having their right to initiate or continue legal proceedings stayed by s 130(2).

'Action or proceeding'—There is not a critical difference between these two terms. 'Action' is a generic term and the Judicature Act 1925 provides that it means 'a civil proceeding' (s 225).

The latter term has been held to include any kind of action (*Re Keystone Knitting Mills' Trade Mark* [1929] 1 Ch 92 at 102), and should be interpreted widely: *Langley Constructions (Brixham) Ltd v Wells* [1969] 1 WLR 503 at 509. See the commentary attaching to para 43 of Sch B1.

As far as specific kinds of proceedings are concerned, it has been held that the following fall within s 130(2) (not exhaustive): counterclaims (*Langley Constructions*); proceedings for recovery of a statutory penalty (*Re Briton Medical & General Life Assurance Association* (1886) 32 Ch D 503); the process directed against the property of a company such as levying execution (*Re Artistic Colour Printing Co* (1880) 14 Ch D 502 at 505); distress (*Re Exhall Coal Mining Co* (1864) 4 De GJ & S 377; *Re Lancashire Cotton Spinning Co* (1887) 35 Ch D 656 at 661); enforcing a garnishee order (*Re Herbert Berry Associates Ltd* [1977] 1 WLR 617); criminal prosecutions (*R v Dickson* [1991] BCC 719); and arbitration proceedings (*A Straume (UK) Ltd v Bradlor Developments Ltd* (1999) *The Times*, August 13).But applying for security for costs against the company (*BPM Pty Ltd v HPM Pty Ltd* (1996) 14 ACLC 857) is not a proceeding within s 130(2), nor is the lodging of an appeal if it was the company that initiated proceedings either before or after entry into liquidation, and the defendant wishes to appeal against the judgment given in favour of the company (*Humber & Co v John Griffiths Cycle Co* (1901) 85 LT 141, HL).

Leave—Where an action or proceeding falls within s 130(2), leave of the court to initiate or continue proceedings is necessary. The provision does not state when leave will be given; rather the courts have an unfettered discretion as to when they will grant leave: *Re Aro Co Ltd* [1980] Ch 196; *New Cap Reinsurance Corp Ltd v HIH Casualty and General Insurance Ltd* [2002] 2 BCLC 228, [2002] BPIR 809, CA.

There has not been significant examination in the UK as to when leave will be granted. It has been said that courts are to do what is right and fair in all of the circumstances (*Re Aro Co Ltd* [1980] Ch 196; *Re Exchange Securities & Commodities Ltd* [1983] BCLC 186 at 195; *New Cap Reinsurance Corp Ltd v HIH Casualty and General Insurance Ltd* [2002] 2 BCLC 228, [2002] BPIR 809, CA).

A court is not required to, nor should it, investigate the merits of proposed or existing proceedings, except to satisfy itself that there was a genuine claim: *Bourne v Charit-Email Technology Partnership LLP* [2010] EWHC 1901 (Ch), [2010] 1 BCLC 210. The court in this case said that the resources available to the liquidator should be taken into account in making a decision. The court is to be cautious in placing a liquidator under the burden of having to deal with difficult and time-consuming litigation.

Some types of claims will find the favour of the court as far as leave is concerned. Where a person is seeking to claim from the company what is in effect his or her own property, leave to proceed will be granted as a formality (*Re David Lloyd & Co* (1877) 6 Ch D 339; *Re Lineas Navieras Boliviarnas SAM* [1995] BCC 666), because of the fact that a liquidation should not deprive a person from having his or her property (*Re David Lloyd & Co* at 344); such property is not, of course, available for distribution among the general body of creditors. For instance, proceedings will be allowed by a mortgagee for the enforcement of security: *Re David Lloyd & Co.* In *Edwards and Smith v Flightline Ltd* [2003] EWCA Civ 63 the court at first instance had granted leave to the applicant (F) to continue an action on the basis that it had a secured interest in funds in a joint bank account which would make it a secured creditor in relation to any judgment obtained. But the Court of Appeal allowed an appeal against this ruling because it held that there were no security rights in favour of F.

The question of expedience and convenience might be a major factor (*Re Queensland Mercantile Agency Co* (1888) 58 LT 878), and leave will be withheld where the action raises issues which could be dealt with in the liquidation as conveniently as in other proceedings and with both less delay and expense: *Re Exchange Securities & Commodities Ltd* [1983] BCLC 186 at 196. So, where there are proceedings which are aimed primarily against persons other than the company, and the company is a party only as a formality, the courts normally give leave: *McEwan v London, Bombay & Mediterranean Bank* (1886) 15 LT 495; *Hall v Old Talargoch Lead Mining Co* (1876) 3 Ch D 749; *Re Rio Grande du Sol Steamship Co* (1877) 5 Ch D 282. Courts will tend to grant leave where there are claims likely to be more difficult or more expensive if handled by way of the proving of claims process in a liquidation, rather than by the normal litigious process: *Thames Plate Glass Co v Land & Sea Telegraph Co* (1871) 6 Ch App 643; *Re Joseph Pease & Co* [1873] WN 127. Also, leave is far more likely in situations where the claim is for declaratory and injunctive relief (*Wyley v Exhall Gold Mining Co* (1864) 33 Beav 538; 55 ER 478), or other equitable relief, such as for specific performance or rescission of a contract (*Re Coregrange Ltd* [1984] BCLC 453), which cannot be adjudicated on in the winding-up process very easily.

A court might be swayed such that it will refrain from granting leave if the liquidator indicates that he or she would admit a proof of debt lodged by the applicant for leave as a contingent debt: *Swaby v Lift Capital Partners Pty Ltd* [2009] FCA 749.

Leave may be granted retrospectively, ie after proceedings have been issued against a company in liquidation (*Re Saunders* [1997] Ch 60, [1997] BCC 83; *Bristol & West Building Society v Alexander* [1997] BPIR 358, [1998] 1 BCLC 485, *Re Linkrealm Ltd* [1998] BCC 478, *Adorian v Commissioner of Police of the Metropolis* [2009] EWCA Civ 18, [2009] 1 WLR 1859, *Bank of Scotland v Breytenbach* [2012] BPIR 1; *Re Colliers International UK plc* [2012] EWHC 2942 (Ch).), and there is Australian authority to the effect that simply delaying in applying for leave will not, in itself, prevent leave being granted: *Ex parte Walker* (1982) 6 ACLR 423.

The granting of leave by a court might be subject to certain conditions, which may be seen as limiting the interference with the winding-up process: *Oceanic Life Ltd v Insurance and Retirement Services Pty Ltd (in liquidation)* (1993) 11 ACLC 1157 at 1159. One condition that might be specified is the requirement on the part of the applicant for leave to give an undertaking that judgment will not be enforced without obtaining further leave of the court: *Hazell v Currie* (1867) WN 68; *Re Marine Investment Co* (1868) 17 LT 535.

If a claim is to be brought against a liquidator, in a compulsory liquidation, in his or her personal capacity and when he or she was carrying out his or her duties as a liquidator, then according to several Australian authorities leave of the court is needed to bring proceedings during the period of the company's liquidation: eg *Armitage v Gainsborough Properties Pty Ltd* [2011] VSC 419 at [34] and [42].

Making leave a requirement has been held, in relation to other legislation, not to infringe Article 6 of the European Convention for the Protection of Human Rights for if an applicant for leave had an arguable case leave would be granted: *Seal v Chief Constable of South Wales Police* [2007] UKHL 31, [2007] BPIR 1396.

See the notes under the heading, 'The scope of s 285(3) and the principles governing permission to proceed' in relation to s 285.

Investigation procedures

131 Company's statement of affairs

(1) Where the court has made a winding-up order or appointed a provisional liquidator, the official receiver may require some or all of the persons mentioned in subsection (3) below to make out and submit to him a statement in the prescribed form as to the affairs of the company.

(2) The statement shall show—

    (a)   particulars of the company's assets, debts and liabilities;
    (b)   the names and addresses of the company's creditors;
    (c)   the securities held by them respectively;
    (d)   the dates when the securities were respectively given; and
    (e)   such further or other information as may be prescribed or as the official receiver may require.

(2A) The statement shall be verified by the persons required to submit it—

    (a)   in the case of an appointment of a provisional liquidator or a winding up by the court in England and Wales, by a statement of truth; and
    (b)   in the case of an appointment of a provisional liquidator or a winding up by the court in Scotland, by affidavit.

(3) The persons referred to in subsection (1) are—

    (a)   those who are or have been officers of the company;
    (b)   those who have taken part in the formation of the company at any time within one year before the relevant date;
    (c)   those who are in the company's employment, or have been in its employment within that year, and are in the official receiver's opinion capable of giving the information required;
    (d)   those who are or have been within that year officers of, or in the employment of, a company which is, or within that year was, an officer of the company.

(4) Where any persons are required under this section to submit a statement of affairs to the official receiver, they shall do so (subject to the next subsection) before the end of the period of 21 days beginning with the day after that on which the prescribed notice of the requirement is given to them by the official receiver.

(5) The official receiver, if he thinks fit, may—

    (a)   at any time release a person from an obligation imposed on him under subsection (1) or (2) above; or
    (b)   either when giving the notice mentioned in subsection (4) or subsequently, extend the period so mentioned;

and where the official receiver has refused to exercise a power conferred by this subsection, the court, if it thinks fit, may exercise it.

(6) In this section—

'employment' includes employment under a contract for services; and
'the relevant date' means—

       (a)   in a case where a provisional liquidator is appointed, the date of his appointment; and

       (b)   in a case where no such appointment is made, the date of the winding-up order.

(7) If a person without reasonable excuse fails to comply with any obligation imposed under this section, he is liable to a fine and, for continued contravention, to a daily default fine.

(8) In the application of this section to Scotland references to the official receiver are to the liquidator or, in a case where a provisional liquidator is appointed, the provisional liquidator.

Amendments—SI 2010/18.

General note—In the course of investigating a compulsory winding up, the official receiver may, on the making of a winding-up order, require, by notice, some or all of the persons referred to in s 131(3) to make out and submit to him or her a statement of affairs of the company (s 131(1)). The notice under s 131 is to be in Form 4.16 (Sch 4 of the Rules).

Statement of affairs—The official receiver may, if he or she chooses, call for a statement of affairs. The statement of affairs will be of assistance usually to the official receiver in discovering the assets of the company, in deciding whether to apply for an examination of officers and others in relation to the company's affairs, and to ascertain who are the creditors if the official receiver decides to summon a creditors' meeting under s 136(5). The statement will be filed in court and is open to inspection (r 7.28). The statement can be used in subsequent civil proceedings, but it cannot be used in any criminal proceedings, save those mentioned in s 433(3). For further details, see the notes accompanying s 433. If, in preparing a statement of affairs, a former or present officer of the company were to make a material omission, he or she commits an offence (s 210(1)).

'Officer'—This term is not specifically defined by the Act. It will include those persons mentioned in s 1173 of the Companies Act 2006 (incorporated by s 251), namely directors, managers and secretaries. In s 206, the term includes shadow directors (s 206(3)), which is itself defined in s 251, but it might well be argued that as no specific reference is made to a shadow director being an officer, the section did not intend to include such persons as officers. It is highly unlikely that a person who acted as liquidator of a company, the liquidation of which was converted from voluntary to compulsory, would be classified as an officer, because there are cases in the Act where the legislature refers to officers and liquidators separately (eg s 235).

Failure to submit—If there is non-compliance with the official receiver's requirement, then the official receiver may apply to the court, pursuant to r 7.20, asking it to make such orders as are necessary to require persons to fulfil their obligations: *Re Wallace Smith Trust Co Ltd* [1992] BCC 707. It is more appropriate that such action is taken, rather than seeking a public examination under s 133: *Re Wallace Smith Trust Co Ltd.*

Report—Where the official receiver has required a statement of affairs and a statement has been filed, the official receiver must send out to creditors and contributories a report, unless he or she has previously reported. See r 4.45.

See rr 4.31–4.33 and 4.35–4.37 and the comments thereto.

132 Investigation by official receiver

(1) Where a winding-up order is made by the court in England and Wales, it is the duty of the official receiver to investigate—

(a)   if the company has failed, the causes of the failure; and
(b)   generally, the promotion, formation, business, dealings and affairs of the company,

and to make such report (if any) to the court as he thinks fit.

(2) The report is, in any proceedings, prima facie evidence of the facts stated in it.

General note—While the official receiver is obliged to investigate the causes of the failure of a company and generally the promotion, formation, business, dealings and affairs of a company in liquidation, he or she is given a discretion as to whether to make a report. It is likely that the report of the official receiver made pursuant to s 132 will be absolutely privileged, such that a libel action could not be sustained against the official receiver for any comments made in the report. The reason for saying this is that it was held that a report made under s 530 of the Companies Act 1985, a predecessor of s 132, could not lead to liability for defamation: *Bottomley v Brougham* [1908] KB 584. In addition, it is likely that the official receiver could not be sued in relation to any negligent misstatements contained in the report, as he or she is immune from legal suit in respect of statements that are made in the capacity of official receiver and made in relation to the liquidation proceedings: *Mond v Hyde* [1999] QB 1097, CA.

133 Public examination of officers

(1) Where a company is being wound up by the court, the official receiver or, in Scotland, the liquidator may at any time before the dissolution of the company apply to the court for the public examination of any person who—

(a)   is or has been an officer of the company; or
(b)   has acted as liquidator or administrator of the company or as receiver or manager or, in Scotland, receiver of its property; or
(c)   not being a person falling within paragraph (a) or (b), is or has been concerned, or has taken part, in the promotion, formation or management of the company.

(2) Unless the court otherwise orders, the official receiver or, in Scotland, the liquidator shall make an application under subsection (1) if he is requested in accordance with the rules to do so by—

(a)   one-half, in value, of the company's creditors; or
(b)   three-quarters, in value, of the company's contributories.

(3) On an application under subsection (1), the court shall direct that a public examination of the person to whom the application relates shall be held on a day appointed by the court; and that person shall attend on that day and be publicly examined as to the promotion, formation or management of the company or as to the conduct of its business and affairs, or his conduct or dealings in relation to the company.

(4) The following may take part in the public examination of a person under this section and may question that person concerning the matters mentioned in subsection (3), namely—

(a)   the official receiver;
(b)   the liquidator of the company;

(c)   any person who has been appointed as special manager of the company's property or business;

(d)   any creditor of the company who has tendered a proof or, in Scotland, submitted a claim in the winding up;

(e)   any contributory of the company.

General note—The examination of insolvents has a long lineage, going back to the Act of 1604 (1 Jac 1 c 15). The first examination provision in liquidation law was introduced in s 15 of the Joint Stock Companies Winding Up Act 1844. The first public examination procedure was provided for in s 8 of the Companies (Winding Up) Act 1890. But until s 133 was introduced, public examinations had fallen into relative disuse. Reference can be had to the notes accompanying s 236 (private examinations) for further details.

Public examinations can be employed in any compulsory liquidation, but they are generally only utilised in insolvent liquidations.

Public examinations are not to be used if the only purpose is to force the examinee to co-operate with the official receiver. Where non-compliance occurs it is appropriate for the official receiver to apply to the court pursuant to r 7.20 seeking such orders as are necessary to enforce the obligations involved: *Re Wallace Smith Trust Co Ltd* [1992] BCC 707. Nevertheless, a public examination might be a legitimate way of obtaining the information that an officer should provide in the statement of affairs under s 131: *Re Wallace Smith Trust Co Ltd* [1992] BCC 707.

See rr 4.211–4.217 and the notes relating to them.

Reference should also be made to the notes accompanying s 236 (private examinations) and s 290 (bankruptcy). For a more detailed discussion of public examinations, see A Keay *McPherson's Law of Company Liquidation* (3rd edn, Sweet and Maxwell, 2013) at 952–963.

Purpose—The section was designed to fulfil the purposes enumerated in the Cork Report, namely:

'(a) to form the basis of reports, which the Official Receiver may have to submit to the Department concerning the affairs of the company; for example concerning possible offences by officers of the company and others, (b) to obtain material information for the administration of the estate which cannot as well be obtained privately; and (c) to give publicity, for the information of creditors and the community at large, to the salient facts and unusual features connected with the company's failure' (*Re Seagull Manufacturing Co Ltd (in liquidation)* [1993] BCLC 1139 at 1145, CA per Peter Gibson LJ).

Voluntary liquidation—While s 133 falls within that part of the Act that is devoted to compulsory liquidation, applications for examinations are able to be made in voluntary liquidations by way of s 112: *Bishopsgate Investment Management Ltd (in provisional liquidation) v Maxwell* [1992] Ch 1 at 24 and 46, [1992] BCC 222 at 232 and 249, CA. Having said that, it is likely to be uncommon for applications to be made in voluntary liquidations.

The examinees—Subsection (1) provides that the range of persons who might be subjected to an examination is broad, and includes a liquidator of the company. This enables, for instance, the official receiver, where a voluntary liquidation has been converted to a compulsory liquidation, to examine the liquidator who administered the voluntary liquidation.

As far as costs and expenses of examinees go, see rr 4.217 and 7.41 and the notes accompanying them.

Section 133(1)(a)

'Officer'—There are a number of definitions of 'officer' in the Act (eg ss 206(3), 208(3), 210(3) and 211(2)), as well as a definition in the Companies Act 2006, s 1173. The latter section includes directors, managers and secretaries. 'Director' is explained in CA 2006, s 250 as including any person occupying the position of director by whatever name called.

Applications for an examination—The official receiver has a discretion as to whether to apply for an examination, save where he or she is requested to do so by those acting in accordance with the rules (see r 4.213) and mentioned in s 133(2). The official receiver may, if of the opinion that the request of the creditors or the contributories is an unreasonable one in the circumstances, apply to the court for an order relieving the official receiver from the obligation to make the application (r 4.213(5)). If no such application is made by the official receiver, he or she is obliged, within 28 days of receiving the request from the creditors or contributories, to make the application as required by s 133(2) (r 4.213(4)). For details concerning the procedure relating to requests by creditors and contributories, see r 4.213.

An application may be made ex parte if supported simply by evidence in the form of a report by the official receiver to the court (r 4.214(4)). Query whether it may be argued that an ex parte hearing is not consistent with Art 6 of the European Convention on Human Rights (applied by the Human Rights Act 1998), which gives persons the right to a fair hearing.

The court has no discretion as to whether it will order an examination, for it must direct that an examination of the person mentioned in the application be held on an appointed date (s 133(3)). However, it must not be thought that the function of the court is to act as 'a rubber stamp' to the application of the official receiver, for the court must be satisfied that the company is being wound up by the court and that the proposed examinee falls within one of the categories contained in s 133(1): *Jeeves v Official Receiver* [2003] EWCA Civ 1246, [2003] BCC 912, sub nom *Casterbridge Properties Ltd (in liquidation)* [2004] 1 BCLC 96, CA. But, it has been said that it would only be in an exceptional case where the court could gauge, at the time of the application, that there were no questions that could be put to the prospective examinee at the examination hearing or that the examination would not serve a useful purpose: *Jeeves v Official Receiver*. Simon Brown LJ in a form of postscript in *Jeeves* (at [59]) was of the view that it would be very rare for a court to be in a position to say that an examination would serve no useful purpose, as the court could not be alive to the detailed circumstances of the case.

Application to set aside an order—Once an order has been made and served, the person named as the examinee may apply for the rescission of the order (r 7.47(1)): *Jeeves v Official Receiver* [2003] EWCA Civ 1246, [2004] 1 WLR 602, [2003] BCC 912, sub nom *Casterbridge Properties Ltd (in liquidation) (No 2)* [2004] 1 BCLC 96, CA. The applicant for rescission has the onus of establishing that the order should not have been made: *Re Casterbridge Properties Ltd (in liquidation) (No 2)* [2002] BCC 453, [2002] BPIR 428, ChD. A court may rescind any order of examination where it is satisfied that the person to whom the order is directed is not a person within s 133(1)(c) (see r 4.211(4)), or the examination would serve no useful purpose: *Re Casterbridge Properties Ltd*. If there was a real risk that the examinee would be liable to some sanction in a foreign jurisdiction, if he or she answered questions at a public examination, then the order might be set aside as being unduly oppressive, especially where some other way was available by which the information sought by the official receiver could be obtained: *Re Mid-East Trading Ltd* [1998] BCC 726; *Re Casterbridge Properties Ltd (in liquidation)* [2003] EWHC 1731, [2003] BCC 724, ChD.

Examinations—The procedure and issues relating to the conducting of an examination are discussed in notes relating to r 4.211 et seq. Importantly, an examinee is not able to rely on the privilege against self-incrimination in relation to any question put to him or her (*Re Jeffery S Levitt Ltd* [1992] BCC 137 (affirmed by the Court of Appeal [1992] BCC 202); *Bishopsgate Investment Management Ltd (in provisional liquidation) v Maxwell* [1992] Ch 1, [1992] 2 All ER 856, [1992] BCLC 475, [1992] BCC 222, CA), no matter whether the examination relates to a compulsory or a voluntary liquidation. Any refusal to answer a question, on the basis of self-incrimination, is a contempt of court: *Bishopsgate Investment Management Ltd*. The self-incriminating answers of an examinee cannot be used in evidence in criminal proceedings, save those mentioned in s 433(3).

An examinee should be entitled at the examination to raise particular questions or areas of inquiry to which he or she could take objection: *Jeeves v Official Receiver* [2003] EWCA Civ 1246, [2003] BCC 912, sub nom *Casterbridge Properties Ltd (in liquidation) (No 2)* [2004] 1 BCLC 96.

The court's function is to ensure that there is fair play between the person being examined and those questioning the examinee: *Re Mondelphous Engineering Associates (No 2) Ltd (in liquidation)* (1989) 7 ACLC 220. While the court that orders an examination may give a direction as to the hearing, a judge presiding at the examination has a broad discretion to allow or disallow questions (r 4.215(1)): *Re Richbell Strategic Holdings Ltd (in liquidation) (No 2)* [2000] 2 BCLC 794. Questions asked only for reasons of malevolence, and not bona fide for the benefit of the creditors, contributories or the public, may be disallowed by a court: *Re London & Globe Finance Co* [1902] WN 16. Examinees are required to provide the best answers that they can to questions: *Re Richbell Strategic Holdings Ltd*. Where the company whose affairs are being examined is involved in multiple intra-group transactions, relevant questions concerning other companies in the same group may be allowed: *Re Richbell Strategic Holdings Ltd*.

It is likely that statements are able to be used in relation to civil proceedings because while the examinee is compelled to answer questions, and this might be seen as an interference with the examinee's right to privacy under Art 8 of the European Convention on Human Rights, this interference may well be seen as justified in achieving a legitimate aim (see Simmons and Smith 'The Human Rights Act 1998: the practical impact on insolvency' (2000) IL & P 167 at 171).

The procedure to be followed at a hearing is detailed in r 4.215.

The effect of non-compliance with an order to attend an examination is considered in the next section.

Examinees out of the jurisdiction—Courts are empowered to order the service of an order of examination on a person who is outside the jurisdiction and resident abroad, whether or not that person is a British subject (r 12.12): *Re Seagull Manufacturing Co Ltd (in liquidation)* [1993] Ch 345, [1993] BCC 241, CA (affirming [1992] Ch 128, [1991] BCC 550). This represents an exception to the customary approach of not applying statutes outside of the jurisdiction unless they contain express wording to that effect. But, on application to set aside the order for examination, the court may consider and find that it is not appropriate to permit the examination of the respondent who is resident in a foreign jurisdiction if he or she would be liable to some sanction in that jurisdiction as a result of answering questions at an examination: *Jeeves v Official Receiver* [2003] EWCA Civ 1246, [2003] BCC 912, sub nom *Casterbridge Properties Ltd (in liquidation) (No 2)* [2004] 1 BCLC 96, CA.

An examination would be rescinded where it was clear that the order would not be enforceable out of the jurisdiction: *Re Casterbridge Properties Ltd (in liquidation) (No 2)* [2002] BCC 453, [2002] BPIR 428.

134 Enforcement of s 133

(1) If a person without reasonable excuse fails at any time to attend his public examination under section 133, he is guilty of a contempt of court and liable to be punished accordingly.

(2) In a case where a person without reasonable excuse fails at any time to attend his examination under section 133 or there are reasonable grounds for believing that a person has absconded, or is about to abscond, with a view to avoiding or delaying his examination under that section, the court may cause a warrant to be issued to a constable or prescribed officer of the court—

    (a)   for the arrest of that person; and

    (b)   for the seizure of any books, papers, records, money or goods in that person's possession.

(3) In such a case the court may authorise the person arrested under the warrant to be kept in custody, and anything seized under such a warrant to be held, in accordance with the rules, until such time as the court may order.

General note—This section is to be considered with s 133 in that it provides enforcement of s 133 if an examinee fails to attend an examination. Rule 7.22 should be read with s 134.

Warrant for arrest—If the examinee appeals against the making of an arrest warrant, and fails, then he or she is close to contempt and may be ordered to pay, on an indemnity basis, the costs of the official receiver: *Re Avatar Communications Ltd* (1988) 4 BCC 473.

Appointment of liquidator

135 Appointment and powers of provisional liquidator

(1) Subject to the provisions of this section, the court may, at any time after the presentation of a winding-up petition, appoint a liquidator provisionally.

(2) In England and Wales, the appointment of a provisional liquidator may be made at any time before the making of a winding-up order; and either the official receiver or any other fit person may be appointed.

(3) In Scotland, such an appointment may be made at any time before the first appointment of liquidators.

(4) The provisional liquidator shall carry out such functions as the court may confer on him.

(5) When a liquidator is provisionally appointed by the court, his powers may be limited by the order appointing him.

General note—A court can, by the appointment of a provisional liquidator, give interim control of the company to a liquidator, from the time of the appointment until the final determination of the winding-up petition: *Re Forrester & Lamego Ltd* [1997] 2 BCLC 155 at 158. The court has a wide and unfettered discretion whether or not to appoint a provisional liquidator: *Re Union Accident Insurance Co Ltd* [1972] 1 All ER 1105 at 1109. The courts have, in recent years, been more flexible in appointing provisional liquidators: *Smith v UIC Insurance Co Ltd* [2001] BCC 11 at 20–21; *Re Namco Ltd* [2003] BPIR 1170.

The main reason for the filing of an application for the appointment of a provisional liquidator is that there is a concern that the assets and affairs of the company are in jeopardy, pending the hearing of the winding-up petition: *Re Namco Ltd* [2003] BPIR 1170 at 1174. Specifically, there can be concern that the directors and/or shareholders might dissipate the assets, disadvantaging the creditors should the company eventually be wound up. 'Dissipation' in this regard does not just mean the directors and/or others making away with the assets, it can also refer to the fact that there is a serious risk that the assets may not continue to be available to the company: *The Commisioners for HMRC v Rochdale Drinks Distributors Ltd* [2011] EWCA Civ 1116 at [99]. This could be where, notwithstanding the presentation of a petition, the directors contine to trade a loss-making company without securing an order under s 127: ibid. A provisional liquidator is appointed to preserve the status quo (*Re Dry Docks Corporation of London* (1888) 39 Ch D 306; *Re Namco Ltd* [2003] BPIR 1170 at 1173), but on occasions it might be appropriate for the provisional liquidator to wind down the company's business so as to reduce costs: *Re Union Accident Insurance Co Ltd* [1972] 1 All ER 1105. In *Re London Authorities Ltd* (unreported, 16 December 2009, Philip Marshall QC, ChD) the court gave the provisional liquidators permission to make a payment so as to acquire retrospective insurance.

The power provided for in this section has been referred to as a draconian power (*Re Forrester & Lamego Ltd* [1997] 2 BCLC 155 at 158) as it involves a serious intrusion into the affairs of the company, and it can often paralyse the company: *Re London, Hamburg & Continental Exchange Bank, Emmerson's Case* [1866] LR 2 Eq 231 at 237. So, if there are other adequate ways of preserving the status quo, they should be considered first: *Constantinidis v JGL Trading Pty Ltd* (1995) 17 ACSR 625 at 635, 647.

In hearing an application for the appointment of a provisional liquidator the court should first determine whether the applicant is likely to obtain a winding-up order on the hearing of the petition: *The Commisioners for HMRC v Rochdale Drinks Distributors Ltd* [2011] EWCA Civ 1116 at [77], [78]. In this respect John Randall QC (sitting as a deputy judge of the High Court) in *Re SED Essex Ltd* ([2013] EWHC 1583 (Ch) at [8]) said that a company has a burden to show a good arguable case where the evidential burden has switched to it (after the applicant has laid down a basis for an appointment), the company then has to make out a sufficiently strong case to negate such likelihood. Second, if it is likely then the court must consider whether in the circumstances of the case it is right for a provisional liquidator to be appointed: *Re Union Accident Insurance Co Ltd* [1972] 1 All ER 1105 at 1110 and approved by the Court of Appeal in *The Commisioners for HMRC v Rochdale Drinks Distributors Ltd* at [77]. In arriving at its decision on the second point the court should take into account the prejudice which the applicant may suffer if there is no appointment or the company may suffer if it is: ibid at [109].

While it has been held that applications may be made ex parte (eg *Re a Company (No 007070 of 1996)* [1997] 2 BCLC 139 at 142), normally an order will not be made on an ex parte application as the company should be served with notice of the application, except where this is not practicable: *Re London and Manchester Industrial Association* (1875) 1 Ch D 466, such as in the circumstances where there is no time to give notice before the appointment is required to prevent the threatened wrongful act: *The Commisioners for HMRC v Rochdale Drinks Distributors Ltd* [2011] EWCA Civ 1116 at [111], or either the effect of giving notice would enable the directors or others to take steps to defeat the purpose behind the appointment: *The Commisioners for HMRC v Rochdale Drinks Distributors Ltd* [2011] EWCA Civ 1116 at [111]. In this case the Court said that any notice is better than nothing: *The Commisioners for HMRC v Rochdale Drinks Distributors Ltd* [2011] EWCA Civ 1116 at [111].

In exceptional circumstances an appointment will be made where a petition for winding up has been presented against a company that is in voluntary liquidation: *Securities and Investments Board v Lancashire and Yorkshire Portfolio Management Ltd* [1992] BCC 381; *Re a Company (No 007070 of 1996)* [1997] 2 BCLC 139; *Re Pinstripe Farming Co Ltd* [1996] 2 BCLC 295, [1996] BCC 913.

The appointment of a provisional liquidator does not affect the company's legal position. It does not mean that any contracts of the company are terminated, unless there is some provision in the contract itself to this effect: *BCCI v Malik* [1996] BCC 15 at 17. The appointment does mean that there is an automatic stay on the commencement and prosecution of legal proceedings, unless the leave of the court is obtained (s 130(2)). Also, in order to ensure that the provisional liquidator is placed in control of the company's affairs, the authority of any agent of the company appointed by or on the behalf of the directors is revoked: *Pacific & General Insurance Ltd (in liquidation) v Home & Overseas Insurance Co Ltd* [1997] BCC 400.

The provisional liquidator may require some or all of the persons referred to in s 131(3) to make out and submit a statement of affairs of the company (s 131(1)), as well as require any persons who have in their possession or control company property etc to pay, deliver, convey, surrender or transfer the property etc of the company to the provisional liquidator (s 234(2)).

The notion of appointing a provisional liquidator is analogous to the appointment of an interim receiver when a bankruptcy petition has been presented: eg *Re Baars* [2003] BPIR 523.

In regard to a provisional liquidator being liable to pay third party costs in relation to legal proceedings under s 51 of the Supreme Court Act 1981, a provisional liquidator is seen as being closer to a liquiadtor than a director and so a court would be less inclined to make an order under s 51: *Apex Frozen Foods Ltd v Ali* [2007] EWHC 469 (Ch), [2007] BPIR 1437.

The principle which enables rent falling due during liquidation to be treated as if it were a liquidation expense if the property is retained for the benefit of the liquidation, applies to provisional liquidation (see the notes to rule 4.218): *MK Airlines Property Ltd (in administration) v Katz* (unreported) (Mr N Strauss QC, 16 May 2012, ChD).

It is notable that a provisional liquidator is now a liquidator for the purposes of art 2(b) of the EU Regulation on Insolvency Proceedings (see Annex C to the Regulation).

The procedure and practice is detailed in rr 4.25–4.29. See those rules and the notes relating to them.

Hearing—Ordinarily, the hearing should be in public (*Practice Direction: Insolvency Proceedings* [1999] BPIR 441, [2000] BCC 92 at para 5.1(4)). But, given the fact that appointments may have significant ramifications for a company, applications are made to a Companies Court judge, who may, if he or she thinks fit, direct that the hearing be heard in camera: *Practice Direction No 3 of 1996* [1997] 1 WLR 3, [1996] 4 All ER 1024, [1997] BCC 218, [1997] 1 BCLC 130.

Grounds—As no grounds are specified in the section (and the relevant rule, r 4.25(4) merely refers to sufficient grounds) and the courts have a wide discretion, it is not possible to identify with any certainty what grounds will suffice for an order: *ASC v Solomon* (1996) 19 ACSR 73. Often an order will be made because of a number of factors: *Commonwealth v Hendon Industrial Park Pty Ltd* (1995) 17 ACSR 358. There have been several grounds that have been relied on successfully on a number of occasions.

Urgency—Appointments often are required to be made on the basis of urgency: eg *Re Hammersmith Town Hall Company* (1877) 6 Ch D 112. Because of this, courts might not require strict adherence to the relevant procedure. In *Re WF Fearman Ltd* (1987) 4 BCC 139 an application for an appointment was heard in circumstances where there was no application in writing and the usual procedural requirements had not been followed, and yet the appointment was made.

Other grounds—These include: danger to assets (*Re Marseilles Extension Railway and Land Co* [1867] WN 68; *Re a Company (No 003102 of 1991)* [1991] BCLC 539); deadlock in company affairs because of disputes between shareholders or directors; the affairs of the company are in jeopardy because of the directors (*Re Brackland Magazines Ltd*, sub nom *Gamlestaden plc v Brackland Magazines Ltd* [1994] 1 BCLC 190, [1993] BCC 194; *Re Club Mediterranean Pty Ltd* (1975) 11 SASR 481); a need for a speedy and careful investigation of the company's affairs: *Re a Company (No 007070 of 1996)* [1997] 2 BCLC 139; where there is real concern over the integrity of the management of the company and as to the quality of the accounting and record-keeping function of management: *The Commisioners for HMRC v Rochdale Drinks Distributors Ltd* [2011] EWCA Civ 1116 at [100]. In *Re SED Essex Ltd* [2013] EWHC 1583 (Ch) at [16] John Randall QC (sitting as a deputy judge of the High Court) said that in determining whether there should be an appointment or retention of provisional liquidators in office the factors a court should consider include whether there are real questions as to the integrity of the management of the company and/or as to the quality of the company's accounting and record keeping function, whether there is any real risk of dissipation of the company's assets and/or any real need to take steps to preserve them, whether there is any real risk that the company's books and records will be destroyed and/ or any real need for steps to be taken to ensure that they are properly preserved and maintained, whether there is any real need for steps to be taken to facilitate immediate inquiries into the conduct of the Company's management and affairs and/or to investigate and consider possible claims against directors (eg for fraudulent or wrongful trading), whether or not the Company has a realistic prospect of obtaining a validation order under s 127 of the Act.

A provisional liquidator has been appointed when the court is of the view that the company's affairs are in a chaotic state and a danger to the public interest: *ASIC v Tax Returns Australia Dot Com Pty Ltd* [2010] FCA 715.

Applicants—These are enumerated in r 4.25. The most frequent applicants are creditors and the Secretary of State for Business Enterprise and Regulatory Reform, the latter where (s)he is seeking to wind up the company under s 124A. But contributories have been successful. For a recent example, see *Re Beppler and Jacobson* [2012] EWHC 3648 (Ch), [2012] All ER (D) (Dec).

'Any other fit person'—While the official receiver will often be appointed as the provisional liquidator, s 135(2) provides that it could also be any other fit person. This designation is a reference to a licensed insolvency practitioner who is qualified to act in relation to the company (s 390): for an example, see *In Re Grey Marlin Ltd* [1999] 2 BCLC 658. This accords with the decision of the Court of Appeal in *Gibson Dunn & Crutcher v Rio Properties Inc* [2004] EWCA Civ 1043 where it held, in relation to the appointment of an interim receiver in bankruptcy, that someone other than the official receiver could be appointed. Where an insolvency practitioner is appointed, he or she must fulfil the same qualities that generally apply to the appointment of liquidators. This will involve avoiding the appointment of persons who have associations with the applicant and the company. The court will want someone who is independent: *Levy v Napier* 1962 SC 468 at 475, 478. See the notes relating to s 108.

Order—The court has a discretion as to what orders are made besides the actual appointment, and wide powers can be conferred in the order (eg *Re BCCI* [1992] BCC 83; *Smith v UIC Insurance Co Ltd* [2001] BCC 11), such as those powers mentioned in Sch 4 relating to liquidators: *Re Hawk Insurance Co Ltd* [2001] BCC 57. In determining the powers that the court will bestow on the liquidator the court has to decide whether, based on the evidence, the powers were ultimately necessary to the liquidator to perform his or her mandate: *Moodliar v Hendricks* 2011 (2) SA 199.

It is often the case that the order indicates the property over which the appointee will have power. On limited occasions, the order may specify that the provisional liquidator shall have some of the powers of a permanent liquidator, including the power of settling a list of contributories, making calls and admitting and rejecting creditors' proofs of debt: *Re English Bank of the River Plate* [1892] 1 Ch 391. The order is to state what functions the provisional liquidator is to carry out (r 4.26(1)). Courts may grant liquidators the power, in unusual circumstances, to circulate material about creditors of the company to other creditors: *Equitas Ltd v Jacob* [2005] EWHC 1440 (Ch), [2005] BPIR 1312.

Remuneration—The general principles are discussed in *Re Independent Insurance Company Ltd (No 1)* [2003] BPIR 562. Also, see the notes accompanying r 4.30.

For further details, see Husband 'Application by a petitioning company for the appointment of a provisional liquidator' (2000) 16 IL & P 3; A Keay *McPherson's Law of Company Liquidation* (3rd edn, Sweet and Maxwell, 2013), ch 6.

See rr 4.25–4.31 and the accompanying notes.

136 Functions of official receiver in relation to office of liquidator

(1) The following provisions of this section have effect, subject to section 140 below, on a winding-up order being made by the court in England and Wales.

(2) The official receiver, by virtue of his office, becomes the liquidator of the company and continues in office until another person becomes liquidator under the provisions of this Part.

(3) The official receiver is, by virtue of his office, the liquidator during any vacancy.

(4) At any time when he is the liquidator of the company, the official receiver may summon separate meetings of the company's creditors and contributories for the purpose of choosing a person to be liquidator of the company in place of the official receiver.

(5) It is the duty of the official receiver—

    (a)   as soon as practicable in the period of 12 weeks beginning with the day on which the winding-up order was made, to decide whether to exercise his power under subsection (4) to summon meetings, and

    (b)   if in pursuance of paragraph (a) he decides not to exercise that power, to give notice of his decision, before the end of that period, to the court and to the company's creditors and contributories, and

    (c)   (whether or not he has decided to exercise that power) to exercise his power to summon meetings under subsection (4) if he is at any time requested, in accordance with the rules, to do so by one-quarter, in value, of the company's creditors; and accordingly, where the duty imposed by paragraph (c) arises before the official receiver has performed a duty imposed by paragraph (a) or (b), he is not required to perform the latter duty.

(6) A notice given under subsection (5)(b) to the company's creditors shall contain an explanation of the creditors' power under subsection (5)(c) to require the official receiver to summon meetings of the company's creditors and contributories.

General note—It is necessary to read the section in light of s 137.

While in most cases the official receiver becomes the liquidator on the making of a winding-up order, there are two exceptions to this. First, in the case where a winding-up order immediately follows the discharge of an administration order. Here the court may appoint the person who occupied the position of administrator as liquidator (s 140(1)). Second, where a winding-up order is made when there is a supervisor of a company voluntary arrangement in post. In such a case a court may appoint the supervisor as liquidator at the time of the making of the winding-up order (s 140(2)). In each of these situations the insolvency practitioner who was acting as either the administrator or the supervisor would be aware of the affairs of the company, and it would be sensible for him or her to continue to administer the affairs of the company.

See rr 4.43–4.50 and 4.107.

Meetings of creditors and contributories—This is covered by s 139.

See r 4.50.

It is likely that the official receiver will not convene meetings if the value of assets is not high enough for a private insolvency practitioner to be appointed as the liquidator (Insolvency Service's Guide, 'Trustees and Liquidators in Bankruptcies and Compulsory Liquidations at p 1).

137 Appointment by Secretary of State

(1) In a winding up by the court in England and Wales the official receiver may, at any time when he is the liquidator of the company, apply to the Secretary of State for the appointment of a person as liquidator in his place.

(2) If meetings are held in pursuance of a decision under section 136(5)(a), but no person is chosen to be liquidator as a result of those meetings, it is the duty of the official receiver to decide whether to refer the need for an appointment to the Secretary of State.

(3) On an application under subsection (1), or a reference made in pursuance of a decision under subsection (2), the Secretary of State shall either make an appointment or decline to make one.

(4) Where a liquidator has been appointed by the Secretary of State under subsection (3), the liquidator shall give notice of his appointment to the company's creditors or, if the court so allows, shall advertise his appointment in accordance with the directions of the court.

(5) In that notice or advertisement the liquidator shall—

    (a)   state whether he proposes to summon a general meeting of the company's creditors under section 141 below for the purpose of determining (together with any meeting of contributories) whether a liquidation committee should be established under that section, and

    (b)   if he does not propose to summon such a meeting, set out the power of the company's creditors under that section to require him to summon one.

'Apply for the appointment of a person as liquidator'—This is a right that is able to be exercised instead of convening a creditors' meeting under s 136.

Appointment – Since the introduction of the Regional and Trustee/Liquidator Units, in addition to the sort of cases in which an official receiver will act as liquidator of last resort (ie, those cases in which either there are no assets, or the assets are such that their value is minimal or they are long-term), The Insolvency Service is retaining those asset realisation cases that are not overly complicated, and which will result in a distribution to creditors rather than seeking to appoint an insolvency practitioner ('IP'). However, if creditors have sought the appointment of an IP, Chapter 17 of the Insolvency Service's Technical Manual provides for the procedure that should be adhered to.

Guidelines concerning how the official receiver should act and when an appointment might be made, as a matter of policy, have been provided by the Department of Business Innovation and Skills and they are available at:

http://www.insolvencydirect.bis.gov.uk/freedomofinformation/index.htm

The following is taken from the guidelines:

The Insolvency Practitioner Unit ('IPU'), Birmingham acts on behalf of the Secretary of State in making such appointments.

Although not required to do so, as a matter of policy (and subject to certain exceptions) the creditors' views must have been sought in appropriate cases prior to an application for an appointment being made and their wishes, where possible, complied with.

If there is the possibility of any dispute or conflict then there is a strong presumption that a meeting of creditors should be held. The official receiver is expected to provide specific justification for an appointment under s 137 rather than by a creditors' meeting and to confirm that the major creditors have been consulted. Exceptionally, if an urgent appointment is required and creditors are unavailable or cannot immediately deal with the query, an appointment may be made at the discretion of IPU.

The guidelines divide cases into those situations that require agreement in principle of an appointment from the IPU before a submission of application should be made, and those situations where agreement in principle is not needed.

Examples of the former are:

- All cases in which there is actual or potential public interest, and this is regardless of the age of the estate;
- Cases where there is, or could be perceived by any parties involved in the insolvency to be, a potential conflict of interest between the Insolvency Practitioner's duties to the insolvent estate and other matters;
- Cases where there is contention or dispute, either relating directly to the appointment of an Insolvency Practitioner ('IP') or to the case generally;
- Cases where the proposed IP is not the next IP on the official receiver's rota, except in situations where the appointment of the IP has been agreed by the majority in value of creditors; or the IP has previously acted as compulsory liquidator for the company in question and obtained his or her release; new assets have come to light or existing assets have increased in value and it would be beneficial to the estate to reappoint the same liquidator.

Examples of cases where an appointment can be sought where no agreement in principle is needed:

- a notice of no meeting and the official receiver's report to creditors has already been issued and sent to creditors, there is good reason for the assets not having been dealt with earlier and the majority of creditors have approved the appointment;
- there is no known creditor or public interest, a notice of no meeting has already been issued and sent to creditors and a creditor has requested the appointment of a particular IP who has agreed to take the case;
- a meeting of creditors has been held but no appointment was made;
- there is a charge, no surplus is expected for unsecured creditors, and the charge holder is unwilling to appoint a receiver or take action itself;
- the available assets of whatever description are, in the opinion of the official receiver, unlikely to attract a nomination at a meeting.

As far as the IP to be appointed as liquidator is concerned, the official receiver has to ensure, before an application is made for an appointment, the proposed IP is willing to act and is qualified to act, the official receiver should not do or say anything that might lead the proposed IP to believe he or she will be appointed until the appointment has been agreed by the Secretary of State, the official receiver has a duty to provide the proposed IP with complete and accurate information about the insolvent's estate and any other matters relevant to the administration of the case.

Applications for joint appointments may be made when requested by the creditors or where the circumstances of the case warrant it or where there is unlikely to be a negative effect in terms of costs. It is unlikely that the last factor will be satisfied where the proposed joint appointees are from the same firm.

If the Secretary of State declines to make an appointment, then that is tantamount to the official receiver being directed to remain in office as liquidator.

See r 4.104.

138 Appointment of liquidator in Scotland

(1) Where a winding-up order is made by the court in Scotland, a liquidator shall be appointed by the court at the time when the order is made.

(2) The liquidator so appointed (here referred to as 'the interim liquidator') continues in office until another person becomes liquidator in his place under this section or the next.

(3) The interim liquidator shall (subject to the next subsection) as soon as practicable in the period of 28 days beginning with the day on which the winding-up order was made or such longer period as the court may allow, summon separate meetings of the company's creditors and contributories for the purpose of choosing a person (who may be the person who is the interim liquidator) to be liquidator of the company in place of the interim liquidator.

(4) If it appears to the interim liquidator, in any case where a company is being wound up on grounds including its inability to pay its debts, that it would be inappropriate to summon under subsection (3) a meeting of the company's contributories, he may summon only a meeting of the company's creditors for the purpose mentioned in that subsection.

(5) If one or more meetings are held in pursuance of this section but no person is appointed or nominated by the meeting or meetings, the interim liquidator shall make a report to the court which shall appoint either the interim liquidator or some other person to be liquidator of the company.

(6) A person who becomes liquidator of the company in place of the interim liquidator shall, unless he is appointed by the court, forthwith notify the court of that fact.

139 Choice of liquidator at meetings of creditors and contributories

(1) This section applies where a company is being wound up by the court and separate meetings of the company's creditors and contributories are summoned for the purpose of choosing a person to be liquidator of the company.

(2) The creditors and the contributories at their respective meetings may nominate a person to be liquidator.

(3) The liquidator shall be the person nominated by the creditors or, where no person has been so nominated, the person (if any) nominated by the contributories.

(4) In the case of different persons being nominated, any contributory or creditor may, within 7 days after the date on which the nomination was made by the creditors, apply to the court for an order either—

    (a)   appointing the person nominated as liquidator by the contributories to be a liquidator instead of, or jointly with, the person nominated by the creditors; or

    (b)   appointing some other person to be liquidator instead of the person nominated by the creditors.

General note—This is analogous to s 100, which deals with the appointment of a liquidator in a creditors' voluntary liquidation.

The creditors will usually nominate a liquidator and that nomination will normally prevail.

See the notes under 'Secretary of State shall make an appointment or decline to make one' in s 137 relating to the fact that creditors do not seem to have the right to convene a meeting to consider the appointee.

The court must not issue the order of appointment prescribed unless and until the appointee files in court a statement to the effect that he or she is a licensed insolvency practitioner, duly qualified to act as the liquidator and that he or she consents to acting as the liquidator (r 4.102(1), (2)).

See rr 4.100 and 4.102.

140 Appointment by the court following administration or voluntary arrangement

(1) Where a winding-up order is made immediately upon the appointment of an administrator ceasing to have effect, the court may appoint as liquidator of the company the person whose appointment as administrator has ceased to have effect.

(2) Where a winding-up order is made at a time when there is a supervisor of a voluntary arrangement approved in relation to the company under Part I, the court may appoint as liquidator of the company the person who is the supervisor at the time when the winding-up order is made.

(3) Where the court makes an appointment under this section, the official receiver does not become the liquidator as otherwise provided by section 136(2), and he has no duty under section 136(5)(a) or (b) in respect of the summoning of creditors' or contributories' meetings.

Amendments—Enterprise Act 2002, s 248(3), Sch 17, paras 9, 17.

General note—The section grants to the court a discretionary power to by-pass the normal procedure for the appointment of liquidators prescribed by ss 136 and 139: *Re Exchange Travel (Holdings) Ltd* [1992] BCC 954 at 958–959. Section 140 provides two instances where the official receiver might not become the liquidator of a company following the making of a winding-up order. These exceptions exist probably because it is sensible and cost-effective to allow the insolvency practitioner who has acted either as the administrator of the company or the supervisor of a company voluntary arrangement to continue to administer the company's affairs, as he or she will be aware of the issues that need addressing, know the company's background and will not have to do some of the things that a liquidator, coming fresh to the company, would have to do.

The court might decide to invoke s 140 even where there is a question mark against the administrator or supervisor. In *Re Charnley Davies Business Services Ltd* (1987) 3 BCC 408 the court appointed the person who was the former administrator despite pending proceedings against the administrator, alleging irregularities on his part while acting as administrator. The reasons for this decision were somewhat pragmatic, namely, taking into account the time lapse in appointing the official receiver, and the fact that there was no other nominee: *Re Charnley Davies* at 412.

The court must not issue the order of appointment unless and until the appointee files in court a statement to the effect that he or she is an insolvency practitioner, duly qualified to act as the liquidator and that he or she consents to acting as the liquidator (r 4.102(1), (2)).

If an administration order is discharged and followed by a compulsory winding up, with the administrator being appointed liquidator under this section, then any creditors' committee established for the administration becomes the liquidation committee and is deemed to have been established pursuant to s 140 (r 4.174(1)), unless that committee has fewer than three members (r 4.174(2)).

It has been held in *Re Firepower Operations Pty Ltd (No2)* [2008] FCA 1228 by the Australian Federal Court that in considering whether to appoint to the position of liquidator the incumbent administrator or another practitioner, the court may take into account the relative funding capabilities of each.

There is other Australian authority to the effect that a court is able to appoint a single liquidator to deal with the liquidation of more than one company in a corporate group in the situation where a number of companies in the group occupied debtor/creditor relationships in respect of one another: *ASIC v Westpoint Corporation Pty Ltd* [2006] FCA 135, Aust Fed Ct. One assumes that this would be subject to the rider that the liquidator would not be placed potentially in a conflict of interest situation (*Re City & County Investment Co* (1877) 25 WR 342; *Re Greight Pty Ltd (in liquidation)* [2006] FCA 17, Aust Fed Ct).

See the notes under 'Secretary of State shall make an appointment or decline to make one' in s 137 relating to the fact that creditors do not seem to have the right to convene a meeting to consider the appointee.

Liquidation committees

141 Liquidation committee (England and Wales)

(1) Where a winding-up order has been made by the court in England and Wales and separate meetings of creditors and contributories have been summoned for the purpose of choosing a person to be liquidator, those meetings may establish a committee ('the liquidation committee') to exercise the functions conferred on it by or under this Act.

(2) The liquidator (not being the official receiver) may at any time, if he thinks fit, summon separate general meetings of the company's creditors and contributories for the purpose of determining whether such a committee should be established and, if it is so determined, of establishing it.

The liquidator (not being the official receiver) shall summon such a meeting if he is requested, in accordance with the rules, to do so by one-tenth, in value, of the company's creditors.

(3) Where meetings are summoned under this section, or for the purpose of choosing a person to be liquidator, and either the meeting of creditors or the meeting of contributories decides that a liquidation committee should be established, but the other meeting does not so decide or decides that a

committee should not be established, the committee shall be established in accordance with the rules, unless the court otherwise orders.

(4) The liquidation committee is not to be able or required to carry out its functions at any time when the official receiver is liquidator; but at any such time its functions are vested in the Secretary of State except to the extent that the rules otherwise provide.

(5) Where there is for the time being no liquidation committee, and the liquidator is a person other than the official receiver, the functions of such a committee are vested in the Secretary of State except to the extent that the rules otherwise provide.

General note—This is the compulsory winding up equivalent to s 101 that applies to creditors' voluntary liquidations. Liquidation committees are consultative rather than administrative or supervisory bodies. Australian authority indicates that they have an oversight role on behalf of the creditors: *Southern Cross Airlines Holdings Ltd v Arthur Anderson & Co* (1998) 16 ACLC 485 at 462.

A liquidation committee may be formed by way of three different routes: where meetings of creditors and contributories have been called for the purpose of appointing a liquidator, the meetings may decide that a liquidation committee should be set up; a liquidator, who is not the official receiver, may at any time convene separate meetings of the creditors and contributories for the purpose of deciding whether a liquidation committee should be established; a liquidator, who is not the official receiver, must summon a meeting where he or she is requested by 10 per cent in value of the creditors of the company. The latter two situations might occur where the liquidator has been appointed by court order under s 140.

The members of the committee are in a fiduciary position in relation to the creditors and contributories (*Re Geiger* [1915] 1 KB 439 at 447; *Re Bulmer* [1937] Ch 499 at 502), and as a consequence they are not permitted either to obtain a profit from their office, or to allow their private interests to conflict with their duties as committee members. Members must seek the approval of the court to benefit from their positions, and this must be obtained before any transaction is entered into that leads to a profit for a committee member: *Re Gallard* [1896] 1 QB 68 at 72–73; *Re FT Hawkins & Co* [1952] Ch 881 at 884.

The court is not empowered to remove a member of the committee, but it may direct the liquidator to convene a meeting of the creditors and contributories for them to consider removal (*Re Radford & Bright Ltd* [1901] 1 Ch D 272).

For the powers and functions of the committee, see s 167 and the notes relating to that section. Besides the powers and functions contained in s 167, the committee is obliged to review at intervals the adequacy of the liquidator's security (r 12.8). Although the duties in s 167 and r 12.8 focus on the supervisory nature of the committee, in practice the committee tends to function more in a consultative capacity. Notwithstanding the wide powers and functions of the committee, members do not have the right to inspect, or ask the liquidator questions about documents that might be conveyed between the liquidator and the Department of Business Enterprise and Regulatory Reform relating to the possible disqualification of directors of the company: *Re W&A Glaser Ltd* [1994] BCC 199 at 205.

Where a committee will not sanction a course of action for which the liquidator needs sanction, the liquidator is entitled to apply to the court for approval, and while the court will consider the opinion of the committee, it is able to overrule the committee's decision: *Re Northern Assurance Co Ltd* (1915) 113 LT 989.

Section 141(2)

Such a meeting—The relevant subsection is rather odd. It is not clear whether 'such a meeting' in the second part of the subsection is meant to be a reference to the creditors' meeting only or whether it refers to separate meetings of the creditors and contributories. The first interpretation is supported by the fact that the reference is to the singular and the summoning of the meeting can be precipitated by a portion of the creditors. However, the latter interpretation has merit in that the words used are 'such a meeting', suggesting that this refers to something just mentioned, namely the separate meetings of creditors and contributories. Furthermore, the whole section envisages meetings of both the creditors and contributories. It is submitted respectfully that the use of the singular is an error and that the intended reference is to meetings of creditors and contributories.

Composition of committee—Rule 4.152(1) provides that in a compulsory winding up, where a committee is established, other than by the contributories where the creditors make no decision on the issue, the committee is to consist of at least three, and not more than five creditors, elected by the creditors pursuant to s 141.

While a court is not granted any express power to interfere with the composition of a committee that has been established in line with the requirements in the Act and Rules, the court is to ensure that no creditor or class of creditors with a substantial interest is excluded from the representation which it wishes to have: *Re Radford & Bright Ltd* [1901] 1 Ch D 272 at 277.

Remuneration—No provision in the Act or Rules provides for remuneration of the committee members. Court approval has to be obtained before a member receives any remuneration (r 4.170). Such approval is likely to be rare, and might only be granted where the member(s) has rendered special services in the course of liquidation: *Re Security Directors Pty Ltd (in liquidation)* (1997) 24 ACSR 558, Vic S Ct).

No committee—In such a case the Secretary of State has the functions of a committee vested in him or her. Dear IP No 43, January 1999 sets out the guidelines for requests for sanction.

But the Secretary of State is not able to provide retrospective sanctioning of proceedings already commenced under one of the provisions set out in para 3A of Part 1 of Sch 4 pursuant to r 4.184 unless the proceedings had to be commenced urgently and ratification was sought without undue delay: *Gresham International Ltd v Moonie* [2009] EWHC 1093 (Ch), [2010] BPIR 122, [2009] 2 BCLC 256.

Generally, see rr 4.151–4.172A and the notes accompanying those rules.

142 Liquidation committee (Scotland)

(1) Where a winding-up order has been made by the court in Scotland and separate meetings of creditors and contributories have been summoned for the purpose of choosing a person to be liquidator or, under section 138(4), only a meeting of creditors has been summoned for that purpose, those meetings or (as the case may be) that meeting may establish a committee ('the liquidation committee') to exercise the functions conferred on it by or under this Act.

(2) The liquidator may at any time, if he thinks fit, summon separate general meetings of the company's creditors and contributories for the purpose of determining whether such a committee should be established and, if it is so determined, of establishing it.

(3) The liquidator, if appointed by the court otherwise than under section 139(4)(a), is required to summon meetings under subsection (2) if he is requested, in accordance with the rules, to do so by one-tenth, in value, of the company's creditors.

(4) Where meetings are summoned under this section, or for the purpose of choosing a person to be liquidator, and either the meeting of creditors or the meeting of contributories decides that a liquidation committee should be established, but the other meeting does not so decide or decides that a committee should not be established, the committee shall be established in accordance with the rules, unless the court otherwise orders.

(5) Where in the case of any winding up there is for the time being no liquidation committee, the functions of such a committee are vested in the court except to the extent that the rules otherwise provide.

(6) In addition to the powers and duties conferred and imposed on it by this Act, a liquidation committee has such of the powers and duties of commissioners in a sequestration as may be conferred and imposed on such committees by the rules.

The liquidator's functions

143 General functions in winding up by the court

(1) The functions of the liquidator of a company which is being wound up by the court are to secure that the assets of the company are got in, realised and distributed to the company's creditors and, if there is a surplus, to the persons entitled to it.

(2) It is the duty of the liquidator of a company which is being wound up by the court in England and Wales, if he is not the official receiver—

    (a)   to furnish the official receiver with such information,

    (b)   to produce to the official receiver, and permit inspection by the official receiver of, such books, papers and other records, and

    (c)   to give the official receiver such other assistance,

as the official receiver may reasonably require for the purposes of carrying out his functions in relation to the winding up.

General note—This provision sets out in general terms the functions that must be completed by a liquidator. How the liquidator actually carries out the functions contained in the section is, generally, left to his or her judgment and discretion. However, some matters (eg the making of calls on contributories and dealing with claims by creditors) are specifically addressed by the Act and the Rules. In discharging his or her functions the liquidator is acting as a fiduciary whose obligations are owed to the company and the body of creditors (*Knowles v Scott* [1891] 1 Ch 717 at 723; *Re Home & Colonial Insurance Co* [1930] 1 Ch 102 at 125, 133), and as a consequence the liquidator is required to act honestly, with due care, and with such a degree of diligence that will ensure that the winding up will be completed within a reasonable time frame, though what is reasonable will depend very much on the circumstances of the company in question: *Re House Property & Investment Co* [1954] Ch 576 at 612.

    See s 212 and r 7.20 and the notes relating to that section and rule.

    For a detailed discussion of the functions, duties and powers of liquidators, see A Keay *McPherson's Law of Company Liquidation* (3rd edn, Sweet and Maxwell, 2013) at 451–460 and 517–600.

144 Custody of company's property

(1) When a winding-up order has been made, or where a provisional liquidator has been appointed, the liquidator or the provisional liquidator (as the case may be) shall take into his custody or under his control all the property and things in action to which the company is or appears to be entitled.

(2) In a winding up by the court in Scotland, if and so long as there is no liquidator, all the property of the company is deemed to be in the custody of the court.

General note—This is a wide duty placed on the liquidator, for he or she must collect or control all of the company's property, including property to which the company appears to be entitled. It is likely that a liquidator will take charge of any property over which ownership rights are in doubt and then negotiate with anyone who appears to have a claim to the property.

'Assets are got in'—The liquidator might make use of s 234 to assist in the collection of assets. See the notes accompanying that section.

Where any property of the company has been seized in execution, the liquidator should serve notice on the sheriff requiring delivery of the property to the liquidator together with any money seized or received in part satisfaction of the execution (s 184).

'Realised'—In order to do this the liquidator is authorised by para 6 of Sch 4 to sell or otherwise dispose of all or any part of the property of the company. If the liquidator realises property that is subject to mortgages or charges, or other securities, he or she may deduct a reasonable sum from the proceeds in order to meet the cost of realisation before paying the proceeds to the extent of the principal debt and any outstanding interest due to the secured creditor: *Re Marine Mansions Co* (1867) 4 Eq 601; *Buchler v Talbot* [2004] UKHL 9, [2004] 2 AC 298, [2004] 2 WLR 582, [2004] 1 BCLC 281.

The realisation of the assets of the company should be carried out in the most efficient way, so as to obtain the highest possible price for the assets, and the winding up should not be unnecessarily protracted.

'Distributed to the company's creditors'—Reference should be had to the notes accompanying s 107. Also, see A Keay *McPherson's Law of Company Liquidation* (3rd edn, Sweet and Maxwell, 2013), ch 13.

Distributed a surplus to the persons entitled—In a compulsory liquidation, this is a very unlikely occurrence, save where the winding up is made pursuant to s 122(1)(g)).

See the notes accompanying s 107 and A Keay *McPherson's Law of Company Liquidation* (3rd edn, Sweet and Maxwell, 2013), ch 14.

'Property'—This is defined very broadly in s 436.

145 Vesting of company property in liquidator

(1) When a company is being wound up by the court, the court may on the application of the liquidator by order direct that all or any part of the property of whatsoever description belonging to the company or held by trustees on its behalf shall vest in the liquidator by his official name; and thereupon the property to which the order relates vests accordingly.

(2) The liquidator may, after giving such indemnity (if any) as the court may direct, bring or defend in his official name any action or other legal proceeding which relates to that property or which it is necessary to bring or defend for the purpose of effectually winding up the company and recovering its property.

General note—On winding up, while the company is divested of the beneficial interest in its property, the legal title remains in the company: *Ayerst v C & K (Constructions) Ltd* [1976] AC 107, HL. While the Privy Council has endorsed this view (*Cambridge Gas Transport Corporation v Official Committee of Unsecured Creditors of Navigator Holdings plc* [2006] UKPC 26), a majority of the Australian High Court (Kirby J dissenting) has declined to follow *Ayerst* and has held that on winding up there is not a change in beneficial ownership of company assets: *Commissioner of Taxation v Linter Australia Ltd (in liquidation)* [2005] HCA 20. See Mokal, 'What Liquidation Does For Secured Creditors, And What It Does For You' (2008) 71 MLR 699 for an interesting discussion of some aspects of the case law and the relevant concepts involved.

Unlike with bankruptcy, where a bankruptcy order vests the bankrupt's property in the trustee in bankruptcy (s 306), a winding-up order does not have that effect, and company property continues to belong to the company: *John Mackintosh & Sons Ltd v Baker's Bargain*

Stores (Seaford) Ltd [1965] 1 WLR 1182. Notwithstanding that, liquidators may apply for and obtain an order vesting in them all of any portion of the property of the company, in which case it vests in liquidators in their official capacity: *Graham v Edge* (1888) 23 QBD 683. Section 145(2) permits liquidators to bring and defend legal proceedings in respect of vested property in their own official name, namely 'X as the liquidator of ABC Ltd'.

Applications for vesting orders are extremely uncommon, probably because the liquidator is given wide powers by the Act in Sch 4.

146 Duty to summon final meeting

(1) Subject to the next subsection, if it appears to the liquidator of a company which is being wound by the court that the winding up of the company is for practical purposes complete and the liquidator is not the official receiver, the liquidator shall summon a final general meeting of the company's creditors which—

  (a)   shall receive the liquidator's report of the winding up, and
  (b)   shall determine whether the liquidator should have his release under section 174 in Chapter VII of this Part.

(2) The liquidator may, if he thinks fit, give the notice summoning the final general meeting at the same time as giving notice of any final distribution of the company's property but, if summoned for an earlier date, that meeting shall be adjourned (and, if necessary, further adjourned) until a date on which the liquidator is able to report to the meeting that the winding up of the company is for practical purposes complete.

(3) In the carrying out of his functions in the winding up it is the duty of the liquidator to retain sufficient sums from the company's property to cover the expenses of summoning and holding the meeting required by this section.

General note— This is the compulsory winding-up equivalent of the provision covering creditors' voluntary winding up (s 106) and the provision covering members' voluntary winding up (s 94). See the notes accompanying these sections. Also, see r 4.125.

The official receiver, where he or she is the liquidator, will apply to the Secretary of State for release (s 174(3)).

General powers of court

147 Power to stay or sist winding up

(1) The court may at any time after an order for winding up, on the application either of the liquidator or the official receiver or any creditor or contributory, and on proof to the satisfaction of the court that all proceedings in the winding up ought to be stayed or sisted, make an order staying or sisting the proceedings, either altogether or for a limited time, on such terms and conditions as the court thinks fit.

(2) The court may, before making an order, require the official receiver to furnish to it a report with respect to any facts or matters which are in his opinion relevant to the application.

(3) A copy of every order made under this section shall forthwith be forwarded by the company, or otherwise as may be prescribed, to the registrar of companies, who shall enter it in his records relating to the company.

General note—An application for an order staying proceedings in relation to the winding up may be made by the court at any time after a winding-up order has been made.

A stay has been granted where the winding-up order was fundamentally defective: *Re Intermain Properties Ltd* [1986] BCLC 265. But the correct procedure now would be to seek rescission of the order under r 7.47(1), provided that action can be taken within seven days of the making of the winding-up order (r 7.47(4)).

If the company or some other party seeks to challenge a winding-up order, the proper procedure in general is to appeal, pursuant to r 7.47(2): *Re St Nazaire Co* (1879) 12 Ch D 88. Normally an application under this section to obtain an order staying proceedings is not sought (*Re A & BC Chewing Gum Ltd* [1975] 1 All ER 1017), except where the appeal cannot be heard swiftly.

It is not possible to challenge the making of the winding-up order at the hearing of the application for a stay: *Re Empire Builders Ltd* (1919) 88 LJ Ch 459.

As the language of the section indicates, the court has a discretion (*Re Telescriptor Syndicate Ltd* [1903] 2 Ch 174 at 180) whether or not to stay proceedings, and while there are no rigid rules (*Re Calgary and Edmonton Land Co Ltd* [1975] 1 All ER 1046 at 1051), the courts operate within certain principles, many of which derive from those used when considering applications for annulments in bankruptcy: *Re Telescriptor Syndicate Ltd.* The applicant for a stay does not have to show special circumstances, but the court must base its decision to order a stay on some valid reason: *Aetna Properties Ltd (in liquidation) v GA Listing & Maintenance Pty Ltd* (1994) 13 ACSR 422. If a court is in doubt, a stay will not be ordered: *Re Calgary and Edmonton Land Co Ltd* [1975] 1 All ER 1046, [1975] 1 WLR 355; *Re Lowston Ltd* [1991] BCLC 570.

At a hearing for a stay, the applicant has to make out a clear case why a stay should be granted (*Re Telescriptor Syndicate Ltd* [1903] 2 Ch 174; *Re Calgary & Edmonton Land Co Ltd* [1975] 1 All ER 1046, [1975] 1 WLR 355) and the interests of the liquidator, the creditors and the members are taken into account by the court: *Re Calgary & Edmonton Land Co Ltd.* Also, the court will decide whether a stay would prejudice commercial morality and the public interest: *In Re Hester* (1889) 22 QBD 632 at 634, 636 and in the appeal at 640, 641; *Re Izod* [1897] 1 QB 241 at 255; *Re Telescriptor Syndicate Ltd* [1903] 2 Ch 174 at 180. In making a decision, the following may be considered: directors have failed to assist the official receiver; an investigation is warranted as far as aspects of the promotion, formation or demise of the company are concerned; and the business affairs of the company require investigation: *Re Telescriptor Syndicate Ltd.*

If the court finds that there has been misfeasance or improper activities in the life of the company, it will reject an application for a stay: *Re Calgary and Edmonton Land Co Ltd* [1975] 1 All ER 1046, [1975] 1 WLR 355.

Before ordering a stay the court will want to be assured that the liquidator's position is protected as far as his or her remuneration and expenses are concerned: *Re Calgary and Edmonton Land Co Ltd.*

'All proceedings'—The court has no power to stay only part of the proceedings (*Re European Assurance Society* [1872] WN 85), although it may attach terms and conditions to the order.

The effect of the stay—Where a perpetual stay is ordered, the winding–up process terminates, and the company can thereupon resume the conduct of its business and affairs as if no winding up ever existed. In such a case, the liquidator is entitled to a discharge.

If the stay is in respect of a compulsory winding up that was initiated subsequent to a voluntary one, the voluntary liquidation will proceed unless it is stayed: *Re Bristol Victoria Potteries Co Ltd* (1872) 20 WR 569.

'Such terms and conditions as the court thinks fit'—The court has, pursuant to this part of the provision, ordered that: dissenting shareholders should be allowed to retire from the company and be paid the value of their shares (*Re South Barrule Slate Quarry Co* (1869) 8 Eq 688; *Re Steamship 'Chigwell' Ltd* (1888) 4 TLR 308); any creditor has liberty to apply within a certain period to have the stay set aside: *Re Baxters' Ltd* [1898] WN 600.

148 Settlement of list of contributories and application of assets

(1) As soon as may be after making a winding-up order, the court shall settle a list of contributories, with power to rectify the register of members in all cases where rectification is required, and shall cause the company's assets to be collected, and applied in discharge of its liabilities.

(2) If it appears to the court that it will not be necessary to make calls on or adjust the rights of contributories, the court may dispense with the settlement of a list of contributories.

(3) In settling the list, the court shall distinguish between persons who are contributories in their own right and persons who are contributories as being representatives of or liable for the debts of others.

Amendments—SI 2009/1941.

General note—The provision enables duties given to the court under this section to be delegated to the liquidator, who exercises them in a quasi-judicial capacity (*Re Westaway's Garages Ltd* [1942] Ch 356 at 364), pursuant to the rules. See rr 4.195–4.201. Section 165(4)(a) gives the liquidator in a voluntary liquidation the power of the court to settle a list of contributories.

The liquidator must follow the settling process and has no right to apply to the court for a declaration that a contributory ought to be placed on the list: *Re Nathan Newman & Co* (1887) 35 Ch D 1.

For the procedure of settling a list, see rr 4.195–4.201 and the related notes.

'Settle'—The liquidator is permitted to regard the register of members as prima facie evidence concerning membership, and of the existence of an unpaid liability, but it is not conclusive. The list may well reflect the register completely, but the liquidator is certainly not bound by the register: *Isaacs' Case* [1892] 2 Ch 158; *Re J N 2 Ltd* [1978] 1 WLR 187.

The word 'settle' here involves the considering of the matter of who is a member and who is to contribute, as well as the determination of questions: *Re Murray Engineering Co* [1925] SASR 330 at 333.

Notwithstanding the fact that the Rules do not so require, two lists of contributories are often compiled, namely the A list and the B list. The A list includes all those who were members of the company at the time winding up commenced and who have not since died, become bankrupt or transferred their shares, and the personal representatives and trustees in bankruptcy respectively of members who have died or become bankrupt subsequent to the commencement of the winding up. The B list, which does not have to be compiled until the liquidator ascertains that the A list contributories will not be able to satisfy the contribution payments that they are liable to pay, includes all remaining contributories.

'Contributories'—See the comments accompanying s 74 concerning the meaning of the term and the extent of their liability.

Dispensing with the list—This would occur where all shares are fully paid up. As to whether it would occur in other situations, it will depend on the facts, but it should only be done following careful consideration: *Re Phoenix Oil and Transport Co Ltd* [1958] Ch 560.

While there is no corresponding provision to s 148(2) for voluntary winding up, it can be assumed that as the liquidation in a voluntary liquidation is given the power of the court to settle a list, he or she would also have the power, in the appropriate case, to dispense with settling a list.

149 Debts due from contributory to company

(1) The court may, at any time after making a winding-up order, make an order on any contributory for the time being on the list of contributories to pay, in manner directed by the order, any money due from him (or from the

estate of the person who he represents) to the company, exclusive of any money payable by him or the estate by virtue of any call.

(2) The court in making such an order may—

(a) in the case of an unlimited company, allow to the contributory by way of set-off any money due to him or the estate which he represents from the company on any independent dealing or contract with the company, but not any money due to him as a member of the company in respect of any dividend or profit, and

(b) in the case of a limited company, make to any director or manager whose liability is unlimited or to his estate the like allowance.

(3) In the case of any company, whether limited or unlimited, when all the creditors are paid in full (together with interest at the official rate), any money due on any account whatever to a contributory from the company may be allowed to him by way of set-off against any subsequent call.

Amendments—SI 2009/1941.

General note—While the provision does not state it expressly, it has been held that the money owed by a contributory and covered by this section only includes sums owed by a member in his or her capacity as a member: *Re Marlborough Club Co* (1868) LR 5 Eq 365; *Re Brisbane Puntowners' Association* (1893) 5 QLJ 54.

Set-off—Where a liquidator is seeking to enforce a liability to contribute to the assets of a company in winding up, the contributory is not entitled to set-off against that liability amounts which are due from the company to that contributory: *Re Overend, Gurney & Co; Grissell's Case* (1866) 1 Ch App 528; *Re General Works Co; Gill's Case* (1879) 12 Ch D 755. But set-off may be permitted by a court either in the circumstances set out in s 149(2) or s 149(3), ie when all the company's creditors have been paid in full or the company is an unlimited one, although s 149(2) does not allow set-off in relation to dividends or profits due to a member in his or her position as a member of an unlimited company.

150 Power to make calls

(1) The court may, at any time after making a winding-up order, and either before or after it has ascertained the sufficiency of the company's assets, make calls on all or any of the contributories for the time being settled on the list of the contributories to the extent of their liability, for payment of any money which the court considers necessary to satisfy the company's debts and liabilities, and the expenses of winding up, and for the adjustment of the rights of the contributories among themselves, and make an order for payment of any calls so made.

(2) In making a call the court may take into consideration the probability that some of the contributories may partly or wholly fail to pay it.

General note—The provision vests the power to make calls on contributories, but this power can be delegated to the liquidator pursuant to a combination of s 160(1)(d) and rr 4.195 and 4.202. The liquidator must seek the approval of the court, save where a liquidation committee exists (r 4.203) or special leave has been granted by the court (s 160(2)).

A liquidator will always have to make calls on contributories where the contributories' liability has not become due and payable prior to winding up. If a contributory fails to pay, the liquidator may need to obtain an order of the court ('a balance order') under r 4.205(2) enforcing the payment of the call.

When winding up commences, if sums are already due from a contributory to the company, such as calls previously made by the company, the liquidator may either make and, with court approval, enforce a call in respect of the sum already payable, or the existing right to payment may be enforced instead as a debt due to the company: *Westmoreland Green & Blue Slate Co v Feilden* [1891] 3 Ch 15.

It is not incumbent on the liquidator to wait, before making calls, until it has been ascertained that the existing assets of the company are insufficient for this purpose, and the liquidator, in determining whether a call should be made, is permitted to take into account the probability that some of the contributories may partly or wholly fail to pay the call.

151 Payment into bank of money due to company

(1) The court may order any contributory, purchaser or other person from whom money is due to the company to pay the amount due into the Bank of England (or any branch of it) to the account of the liquidator instead of to the liquidator, and such an order may be enforced in the same manner as if it had directed payment to the liquidator.

(2) All money and securities paid or delivered into the Bank of England (or branch) in the event of a winding up by the court are subject in all respects to the orders of the court.

152 Order on contributory to be conclusive evidence

(1) An order made by the court on a contributory is conclusive evidence that the money (if any) thereby appearing to be due or ordered to be paid is due, but subject to any right of appeal.

(2) All other pertinent matters stated in the order are to be taken as truly stated as against all persons and in all proceedings except proceedings in Scotland against the heritable estate of a deceased contributory; and in that case the order is only prima facie evidence for the purpose of charging his heritable estate, unless his heirs or legatees of heritage were on the list of contributories at the time of the order being made.

General note—As s 152(1) provides that an order is conclusive evidence of money being due on an order of the court for payment of calls in winding up, contributories will struggle to challenge successfully the validity of proceedings taken prior to the making of the call, particularly if the contributory has been cognisant of the existence of a defect from the very beginning, but has only raised it for the first time when proceedings are initiated: *Re Katoomba Coal & Slate Co; North's Case* (1892) 18 LR (NSW) Eq 70.

153 Power to exclude creditors not proving in time

The court may fix a time or times within which creditors are to prove their debts or claims or to be excluded from the benefit of any distribution made before those debts are proved.

General note—So as to ensure that all the liabilities of the company are proved in winding up within a reasonable time, the liquidator will fix a date for the proving of debts. The power to fix the date is delegated to the liquidator by the court under s 160(1).

Where a creditor does not prove within the time fixed by a liquidator, he or she is unable to participate in a distribution that has been made before proving (*Butler v Broadhead* [1975] Ch 97), but the creditor may be paid from any assets that remain or come into the liquidator's hands after the distribution (r 4.182(2)).

154 Adjustment of rights of contributories

The court shall adjust the rights of the contributories among themselves and distribute any surplus among the persons entitled to it.

General note—The amount to be paid by a contributory may be varied because, after the making of calls, the court may need to adjust, under this section, the rights of contributories among themselves. The equivalent for voluntary liquidation is s 165(5). Adjustment occurs in order to provide a result whereby contributories bear the loss of capital equally. Whether equal loss is to be implemented will depend on the articles.

The liquidator is not permitted to make a distribution. He or she may only distribute it after obtaining special leave from the court. The liquidator must apply to the court for an order under r 4.221. A list of persons to whom it is intended to return capital must accompany the application (r 4.221(2)). If an order is made then the liquidator is sent a sealed copy of the order and he or she is to follow the procedures set out in r 4.222 (r 4.221(4)). In the Australian case of *Re RH Trevan Pty Ltd* [2013] NSWSC 1445 it was held that the purpose of the equivalent provision was to ensure that the liquidator took all necessary steps to verify the fact that there was a surplus and that members' entitlements have been ascertained.

155 Inspection of books by creditors etc

(1) The court may, at any time after making a winding-up order, make such order for inspection of the company's books and papers by creditors and contributories as the court thinks just; and any books and papers in the company's possession may be inspected by creditors and contributories accordingly, but not further or otherwise.

(2) Nothing in this section excludes or restricts any statutory rights of a government department or person acting under the authority of a government department.

(3) For the purposes of subsection (2) above, references to a government department shall be construed as including references to any part of the Scottish Administration.

Amendments—SI 1999/1820.

General note—Before liquidation, some of a company's books, such as the register of charges (Companies Act 2006, s 877 are open to inspection by the members and creditors without a fee. On liquidation this right of inspection ends, with outsiders having no right to inspect (*Re Kent Coalfields Syndicate* [1898] 1 QB 754), and there is Australian authority (*IACS Pty Ltd v Australian Flower Exports Pty Ltd* (1993) 10 ACSR 769) to the effect that the liquidator cannot permit inspection. The right to inspect for creditors and contributories depends on this section. The court has power to make an order for inspection of any books and papers in the possession of the company, but does not cover the case where the papers are in the possession of some third party (*Re North Brazilian Sugar Factories* (1887) 35 Ch D 83 (no order where books relating to formerly held property of the company in liquidation were in the possession of a company to whom the company in liquidation had transferred its property)). It is permissible for copies to be taken of documents inspected: *Re Arauco Co* [1899] WN 134; *Re Gold Coast Syndicate Ltd* [1904] WN 72.

The predominance of authority seems to indicate that inspection exists for the purpose of the winding up and not, for example, for the benefit of individual shareholders or creditors (to enable them, for instance, to obtain information that might assist in bringing actions against directors of the company): *Re North Brazilian Sugar Factories* (1887) 35 Ch D 83; *Re DPR Futures Ltd* [1989] 1 WLR 778, (1989) 5 BCC 603; *IRC v Mills* [2003] EWHC 2022 (Ch). But, in *Re Sunwing Vacations Inc* [2011] EWHC 1544 (Ch), [2011] BPIR 1524, Morgan J was willing to make an order of disclosure (under s 112 as the company was in voluntary liquidation) because he was persuaded that if the applicants (who were creditors of the company in liquidation) obtained the information from the liquidator then they would be able to succeed against a third party, and if this occurred then the applicants' claim against the company in liquidation would be reduced (at [17] His Lordship saw this as an order that was being made for the purpose of the winding up (at [18]). The fact was that the benefit for the company would be indirect, but that sufficed as far as Morgan J was concerned (at [19]).

In several Australian cases creditors have been able to obtain orders for inspection for the purpose of furthering their own interests rather than benefiting the winding up: *Re MMC Pty Ltd (in liquidation)* (1992) 10 ACLC 365 (creditors were able to inspect in circumstances where their purpose was to assist in the preparation of their own action against the directors); *Re BPTC Ltd* (1992) 7 ACSR 291, on appeal (1993) 12 ACSR 181 (inspection was sought to enable the furtherance of proceedings against the company's insurers); *IACS Pty Ltd v Australian Flower Exports Pty Ltd* (1993) 11 ACLC 618, although an appellate court in Australia has counselled against the use of the power to inspect being overly extended: *Worthley v England* (1994) 14 ACSR 407 at 427–428.

As the section suggests, only books and papers in the possession of the company can be inspected, therefore ruling out any books or papers of the company which are held by others.

156 Payment of expenses of winding up

The court may, in the event of the assets being insufficient to satisfy the liabilities, make an order as to the payment out of the assets of the expenses incurred in the winding up in such order of priority as the court thinks just.

General note—Rule 4.220 expressly provides for a re-ordering of the priorities set out in rr 4.218 and 4.219 by a court.

This section provides for the re-ordering of priorities established in r 4.218: *Digital Equipment Co Ltd v Bower* [2004] BCC 509.

The court has an unfettered discretion, although the courts are not quick to vary the priority order, as they are generally content to adopt the order of priorities in r 4.218(1): *Re Grey Marlin Ltd* [2000] 1 WLR 370, [1999] 4 All ER 429. Courts are able to include the costs of successful litigation against the liquidator in any decision to alter the order of priority.

Courts will only give a liquidator priority for his or her remuneration over liquidation expenses that would normally rank ahead of it, where there are exceptional circumstances: *Re Linda Marie Ltd (in liquidation)* (1988) 4 BCC 463 at 472.

It is arguable whether adverse costs orders can be the subject of re-ordering. This matter depends on whether r 23 of Insolvency (Amendment) (No 2) Rules 2002, which provides that litigation expenses of liquidators incurred in relation to post 1 January 2003 liquidations will fall within the priorities in r 4.218(1)(a), was intended to include adverse costs orders or not. See the General note to r 4.218.

Reference should be had to the notes to s 107 as far as assets covered by floating charges are concerned.

The expenses of a provisional liquidator in performing his or her functions should, where the provisional liquidation is followed by a liquidation, be paid out before other expenses that are referred to in r 4.218(1)(a) where there are insufficient assets to cover all liquidation expenses: *In Re Grey Marlin Ltd* [2000] 2 BCLC 658 at 665.

157 Attendance at company meetings (Scotland)

In the winding up by the court of a company registered in Scotland, the court has power to require the attendance of any officer of the company at any meeting of creditors or of contributories, or of a liquidation committee, for the purpose of giving information as to the trade, dealings, affairs or property of the company.

158 Power to arrest absconding contributory

The court, at any time either before or after making a winding-up order, on proof of probable cause for believing that a contributory is about to quit the United Kingdom or otherwise to abscond or to remove or conceal any of his property for the purpose of evading payment of calls, may cause the contributory to be arrested and his books and papers and moveable personal property to be seized and him and them to be kept safely until such time as the court may order.

159 Powers of court to be cumulative

Powers conferred on the court by this Act are in addition to, and not in restriction of, any existing powers of instituting proceedings against a contributory or debtor of the company, or the estate of any contributory or debtor, for the recovery of any call or other sums.

Amendments—SI 2009/1941.

160 Delegation of powers to liquidator (England and Wales)

(1) Provision may be made by rules for enabling or requiring all or any of the powers and duties conferred and imposed on the court in England and Wales in respect of the following matters—

    (a)   the holding and conducting of meetings to ascertain the wishes of creditors and contributories,

    (b)   the settling of lists of contributories and the rectifying of the register of members where required, and the collection and application of the assets,

    (c)   the payment, delivery, conveyance, surrender or transfer of money, property, books or papers to the liquidator,

    (d)   the making of calls,

    (e)   the fixing of a time within which debts and claims must be proved,

to be exercised or performed by the liquidator as an officer of the court, and subject to the court's control.

(2) But the liquidator shall not, without the special leave of the court, rectify the register of members, and shall not make any call without either that special leave or the sanction of the liquidation committee.

Amendments—SI 2009/1941.

General note—In relation to the exercise of powers by the liquidator, see r 4.54 in respect of the calling of meetings, rr 4.195–4.201 in respect of the settling of the list of contributories, r 4.196 in respect of rectifying the register of members, r 4.185 in respect of enforcing delivery of company property, rr 4.202–4.205 in respect of the making of calls, and s 153 in respect of fixing the time in which to prove debts.

Enforcement of, and appeal from, orders

161 Orders for calls on contributories (Scotland)

(1) In Scotland, where an order, interlocutor or decree has been made for winding up a company by the court, it is competent to the court, on production by the liquidators of a list certified by them of the names of the contributories liable in payment of any calls, and of the amount due by each contributory, and of the date when that amount became due, to pronounce forthwith a decree against those contributories for payment of the sums so certified to be due, with interest from that date until payment (at 5 per cent per annum) in the same way and to the same effect as if they had severally consented to registration for execution, on a charge of 6 days, of a legal obligation to pay those calls and interest.

(2) The decree may be extracted immediately, and no suspension of it is competent, except on caution or consignation, unless with special leave of the court.

162 Appeals from orders in Scotland

(1) Subject to the provisions of this section and to rules of court, an appeal from any order or decision made or given in the winding up of a company by the court in Scotland under this Act lies in the same manner and subject to the same conditions as an appeal from an order or decision of the court in cases within its ordinary jurisdiction.

(2) In regard to orders or judgments pronounced by the judge acting as vacation judge—

    (a)   none of the orders specified in Part I of Schedule 3 to this Act are subject to review, reduction, suspension or stay of execution, and

    (b)   every other order or judgment (except as mentioned below) may be submitted to review by the Inner House by reclaiming motion enrolled within 14 days from the date of the order or judgment.

(3) However, an order being one of those specified in Part II of that Schedule shall, from the date of the order and notwithstanding that it has been submitted to review as above, be carried out and receive effect until the Inner House have disposed of the matter.

(4) In regard to orders or judgments pronounced in Scotland by a Lord Ordinary before whom proceedings in a winding up are being taken, any such order or judgment may be submitted to review by the Inner House by reclaiming motion enrolled within 14 days from its date; but should it not be so submitted to review during session, the provisions of this section in regard to orders or judgments pronounced by the judge acting as vacation judge apply.

(5) Nothing in this section affects provisions of the Companies Acts or this Act in reference to decrees in Scotland for payment of calls in the winding up of companies, whether voluntary or by the court.

Amendments—Court of Session Act 1988, s 52(2), Sch 2, Pt I; SI 2009/1941.

Chapter VII

Liquidators

Preliminary

163 Style and title of liquidators

The liquidator of a company shall be described—

    (a)   where a person other than the official receiver is liquidator, by the style of 'the liquidator' of the particular company, or

    (b)   where the official receiver is liquidator, by the style of 'the official receiver and liquidator' of the particular company;

and in neither case shall he be described by an individual name.

164 Corrupt inducement affecting appointment

A person who gives, or agrees or offers to give, to any member or creditor of a company any valuable consideration with a view to securing his own appointment or nomination, or to securing or preventing the appointment or nomination of some person other than himself, as the company's liquidator is liable to a fine.

Liquidator's powers and duties

165 Voluntary winding up

(1) This section has effect where a company is being wound up voluntarily, but subject to section 166 below in the case of a creditors' voluntary winding up.

(2) The liquidator may—

    (a)   in the case of a members' voluntary winding up, with the sanction of an special resolution resolution of the company, and

    (b)   in the case of a creditors' voluntary winding up, with the sanction of the court or the liquidation committee (or, if there is no such committee, a meeting of the company's creditors),

exercise any of the powers specified in Part I of Schedule 4 to this Act (payment of debts, compromise of claims, etc).

(3) The liquidator may, without sanction, exercise either of the powers specified in Part II of that Schedule (institution and defence of proceedings; carrying on the business of the company) and any of the general powers specified in Part III of that Schedule.

(4) The liquidator may—

    (a)   exercise the court's power of settling a list of contributories

> (which list is prima facie evidence of the liability of the persons named in it to be contributories),
>
> (b)   exercise the court's power of making calls,
>
> (c)   summon general meetings of the company for the purpose of obtaining its sanction by special resolution or for any other purpose he may think fit.

(5) The liquidator shall pay the company's debts and adjust the rights of the contributories among themselves.

(6) Where the liquidator in exercise of the powers conferred on him by this Act disposes of any property of the company to a person who is connected with the company (within the meaning of section 249 in Part VII), he shall, if there is for the time being a liquidation committee, give notice to the committee of that exercise of his powers.

Amendments—Amended by SI 2007/2194.

General note—This section must be considered in conjunction with Sch 4 to the Act where the detailed powers of a liquidator are enumerated. While the liquidator of a members' voluntary liquidation requires the sanction of an extraordinary resolution of the members and the liquidator of a creditors' voluntary liquidation requires the sanction of the liquidation committee (or the creditors' meeting where no committee exists) before powers in Part I of Sch 4 may be exercised, no sanction is needed for the powers in either Parts II or III.

Settle a list of contributories—The court's power to do this is delegated to the liquidator. Interestingly, provision of a delegation of the power to liquidators in compulsory liquidations is by way of the Rules (see r 4.195).

Section 165(6)

'A person who is connected with the company'—Where any property is disposed of to such a person, notice must be given to any liquidation committee, if one exists. The expression 'connected with the company' is defined in s 249 to include a director of the company, an associate of a director or an associate of the company. 'Associate' is then defined broadly in s 435. See the notes relating to these sections for further details. Parliament obviously is concerned that if property is to go to connected persons, then the liquidation committee should be given forewarning so as to thwart possible improper dealings. See the unusual facts in the Australian case of *Re ACN 003 671 387* [2004] NSWSC 368, where the judge permitted the sale of shares in companies being wound up by a liquidator to the trustee of a service trust. The liquidator was a partner in an accounting firm and the service trust involved was the firm's service trust.

166 Creditors' voluntary winding up

(1) This section applies where, in the case of a creditors' voluntary winding up, a liquidator has been nominated by the company.

(1A) The exercise by the liquidator of the power specified in paragraph 6 of Schedule 4 to this Act (power to sell any of the company's property) shall not be challengeable on the ground of any prior inhibition.

(2) The powers conferred on the liquidator by section 165 shall not be exercised, except with the sanction of the court, during the period before the holding of the creditors' meeting under section 98 in Chapter IV.

(3) Subsection (2) does not apply in relation to the power of the liquidator—

    (a)   to take into his custody or under his control all the property to which the company is or appears to be entitled;

    (b)   to dispose of perishable goods and other goods the value of which is likely to diminish if they are not immediately disposed of; and

    (c)   to do all such other things as may be necessary for the protection of the company's assets.

(4) The liquidator shall attend the creditors' meeting held under section 98 and shall report to the meeting on any exercise by him of his powers (whether or not under this section or under section 112 or 165).

(5) If default is made—

    (a)   by the company in complying with subsection (1), (1A) or (2) of section 98, or

    (b)   by the directors in complying with subsection (1), (2) or (2A) of section 99,

the liquidator shall, within 7 days of the relevant day, apply to the court for directions as to the manner in which that default is to be remedied.

(6) 'The relevant day' means the day on which the liquidator was nominated by the company or the day on which he first became aware of the default, whichever is the later.

(7) If the liquidator without reasonable excuse fails to comply with this section, he is liable to a fine.

Amendments—Bankruptcy and Diligence etc (Scotland) Act 2007, s 155(1), (3); SI 2009/864, SI 2010/18.

General note—This provision has limited operation. It applies only to companies in creditors' voluntary liquidation where the liquidator was appointed by the members, and only in relation to the period between the liquidator's appointment and the holding of the creditors' meeting under s 98.

In the period covered by the section, the liquidator is not to exercise the powers referred to in s 165 without the sanction of the court. This provision, together with s 114, was introduced to prevent the practice of 'centrebinding'. This process derived its name from the case of *Re Centrebind Ltd* [1967] 1 WLR 377, [1966] 3 All ER 889. Subsequent to this case, some companies appointed unscrupulous liquidators who delayed the holding of the creditors' meeting until after the assets of the company were disposed of at a very low price to a company which was connected with the members of the company, and the creditors could take no action whatsoever.

For a discussion of the application of this rule in relation to actions of liquidators in CVLs before the creditors' meeting, see *Re Aardvark TMC Ltd* (unrep but noted and discussed in [2013] CRI 105). In this case Arnold J said that s 166(2) does not apply to the power to disclaim, but this appears to be at odds with *Re Business Dream Ltd* [2011] EWHC 2860 (Ch), [2012] BCC 115.

'Apply to the court for directions'—If the company fails to adopt the correct procedure for the calling of the creditors' meeting, then the liquidator is required by s 166(5) to apply to the court for directions as to how the default can be remedied. In *Re Salcombe Hotel Development Co Ltd* (1989) 5 BCC 807 it was said that this subsection is directory and not mandatory and, consequently, it is not incumbent on liquidators to seek directions in cases where there is no need for directions. Yet the language of the provision, and especially the inclusion of the word 'shall' seems to suggest that liquidators must apply for directions. The fact that a liquidator is subject to a penalty for non-compliance under s 166(7) might cause liquidators to err on the side of caution and to apply for directions. More recently, in *Re Stockley Construction Company Ltd* (unreported) 26 June 2000 (but noted at (2000) 16 IL & P 218) Laddie J emphasised the fact that the liquidators had acted quite properly in seeking directions under s 166(5) where the liquidators were unable to obtain a commitment from a director to attend the adjourned meeting of the creditors, as required by s 99(1)(c).

167 Winding up by the court

(1) Where a company is being wound up by the court, the liquidator may—

(a) with the sanction of the court or the liquidation committee, exercise any of the powers specified in Parts I and II of Schedule 4 to this Act (payment of debts; compromise of claims, etc; institution and defence of proceedings; carrying on of the business of the company), and

(b) with or without that sanction, exercise any of the general powers specified in Part III of at Schedule.

(2) Where the liquidator (not being the official receiver), in exercise of the powers conferred on him by this Act—

(a) disposes of any property of the company to a person who is connected with the company (within the meaning of section 249 in part VII), or

(b) employs a solicitor to assist him in the carrying out of his functions,

he shall, if there is for the time being a liquidation committee, give notice to the committee of that exercise of his powers.

(3) The exercise by the liquidator in a winding up by the court of the powers conferred by this section is subject to the control of the court, and any creditor or contributory may apply to the court with respect to any exercise or proposed exercise of any of those powers.

General note—A liquidator of a company in compulsory liquidation is required to obtain sanction before he or she exercises certain powers. Powers in Part III of Sch 4 may be exercised without approval, but not Parts I and II. Approval can be obtained from either the court or the liquidation committee.

The provision only applies to court winding up, but in voluntary liquidations an application may be brought under s 112 so as to enable a liquidator to obtain court sanction as it is entitled to control the exercise of a liquidator's powers: *Cooper v PRG Powerhouse Ltd* [2008] EWHC 498 (Ch).

Sanction of the court—In making its decision, the court can always seek the wishes of the creditors and contributories (s 195(1)(a)), and although the court is not bound by those views (*Re Bank of Credit and Commerce International SA (No 2)* [1992] BCC 715, [1993] BCLC 1490; *Re Greenhaven Motors Ltd* [1999] BCC 463, [1999] 1 BCLC 635, CA), they should normally be accepted, save in exceptional circumstances: *Re Bank of Credit and Commerce International SA (No 2)*. If the application relates to whether or not a compromise should be sanctioned, the court could ignore the wishes of those contributories who have no realistic prospect of a distribution: *Re Barings plc (in liquidation) (No 7)* [2002] BPIR 653, [2002] 1 BCLC 401. Creditors and contributories have standing to be heard if a liquidator makes an application to the court for approval: *Re Greenhaven Motors Ltd* [1999] BCC 463, [1999] 1 BCLC 635, CA.

For an application to the court for retrospective sanctioning of the institution of proceedings, where a sanction is needed under para 3A of Part 1 of Sch 4, see *Gresham International Ltd v Moonie* [2009] EWHC 1093 (Ch), [2010] BPIR 122, [2009] 2 BCLC 256 and the notes accompanying para 3A of Part 1 of Sch 4.

See Sch 4 and the notes relating to it.

168 Supplementary powers (England and Wales)

(1) This section applies in the case of a company which is being wound up by the court in England and Wales.

(2) The liquidator may summon general meetings of the creditors or contributories for the purpose of ascertaining their wishes; and it is his duty to summon meetings at such times as the creditors or contributories by resolution (either at the meeting appointing the liquidator or otherwise) may direct, or whenever requested in writing to do so by one-tenth in value of the creditors or contributories (as the case may be).

(3) The liquidator may apply to the court (in the prescribed manner) for directions in relation to any particular matter arising in the winding up.

(4) Subject to the provisions of this Act, the liquidator shall use his own discretion in the management of the assets and their distribution among the creditors.

(5) If any person is aggrieved by an act or decision of the liquidator, that person may apply to the court; and the court may confirm, reverse or modify the act or decision complained of, and make such order in the case as it thinks just.

(5A) Where at any time after a winding-up petition has been presented to the court against any person (including an insolvent partnership or other body which may be wound up under Part V of the Act as an unregistered company), whether by virtue of the provisions of the Insolvent Partnerships Order 1994 or not, the attention of the court is drawn to the fact that the person in question is a member of an insolvent partnership, the court may make an order as to the future conduct of the insolvency proceedings and any such order may apply any provisions of that Order with any necessary modifications.

(5B) Any order or directions under subsection (5A) may be made or given on the application of the official receiver, any responsible insolvency practitioner, the trustee of the partnership or any other interested person and may include provisions as to the administration of the joint estate of the partnership, and in particular how it and the separate estate of any member are to be administered.

(5C) Where the court makes an order for the winding up of an insolvent partnership under—

    (a)   section 72(1)(a) of the Financial Services Act 1986;
    (b)   section 92(1)(a) of the Banking Act 1987; or
    (c)   section 367(3)(a) of the Financial Services and Markets Act 2000,

the court may make an order as to the future conduct of the winding up proceedings, and any such order may apply any provisions of the Insolvent Partnerships Order 1994 with any necessary modifications.

Amendments—SI 1994/2421; SI 2002/1555.

General note—The Act protects creditors and contributories. This section is one of the group of provisions that seek to achieve that objective. The section does so by providing creditors and contributories with the right to request the liquidator to call meetings, or they can apply to the court to have decisions of liquidators reviewed. The section also protects, or at least aids, liquidators in that they are permitted to seek directions from the courts.

Meetings of creditors or contributories—While a liquidator must call meetings when they are requisitioned properly, a court can override the duty of a liquidator to call meetings by directing him or her not to call the meetings: *Re Barings plc* [2001] 2 BCLC 159 at 171.
  See r 4.57.

Directions—The role of s 168(3) is to provide a procedure for a liquidator to obtain some guidance from the court in conducting a liquidation and so as to give protection against a claim for breach of duty. Applications are so common that it is of little help to catalogue all the situations in which such an application may be made. Instances have been where the liquidator wishes: to know whether testamentary gifts to a charitable company that had gone into liquidation were ineffective (*Alleyne v Attorney-General* [1997] BCC 370); to know how to deal with a claim of a creditor (*Re Polly Peck International plc* [1996] BCC 486); to know whether to admit a particular debt or claim to proof in the winding up; to seek guidance on the sale of a cause of an action (*Craig v Humberclyde Industrial Finance Ltd* [1999] 1 WLR 129, [1998] 2 BCLC 526, CA). The courts have said that in cases of real doubt the correct procedure for a liquidator is to seek directions.
  Courts will not entertain applications for directions where the liquidator is seeking, in effect, to have the court make a commercial decision for him or her: *Re Stetzel Thomson & Co Ltd* (1988) 4 BCC 74; *Shiraz Nominees (in liquidation) v Collinson* (1985) 3 ACLC 706. Also, there is Australian authority to the effect that the section is not to be employed where there is a dispute between two parties over a right to claim company funds. In such a case the liquidator should commence substantive proceedings against the two parties and seek a declaratory order: *Re Everything Australian Pty Ltd* (1993) 11 ACLC 50 at 51; *Re AMN Pty Ltd (in liquidation)* (1997) 15 ACLC 368. While liquidators should not 'run' to the courts at any time that a problem is raised, an application for directions should be initiated if there is any doubt in the liquidator's mind as to what action he or she should take: *Re Windsor Steam Coal Co* [1929] 1 Ch 151 at 159; *Pace v Antlers Pty Ltd (in liquidation)* (1998) 16 ACLC 261.
  Liquidators should inform the court and take directions if a difficulty arises in the course of the liquidation: *Re Windsor Steam Coal Co* [1929] 1 Ch 151 at 159. Directions will be given if a proposed decision of the liquidator is subject to criticism by a creditor or creditors on the basis that it is unreasonable or there is evidence of bad faith: *Re Addstone Pty Ltd (in liquidation)* (1997) 25 ACSR 357 at 363.
  It seems that ex parte hearings of the application for directions are allowed, but every case must be considered on its facts, and where there are conflicting interests to be considered such a procedure may be inappropriate: *Bank of Melbourne Ltd v HPM Pty Ltd* (1998) 16 ACLC 427 at 429.
  It has been known for judges to direct liquidators to apply to the court for directions: *Craig v Humberclyde Industrial Finance Ltd* [1999] 1 WLR 129, sub nom *Re Hinckley Island Hotel Ltd* [1998] 2 BCLC 526, CA.
  The equivalent of s 168(3) for voluntary liquidation is s 112. Even though a liquidator in a voluntary winding up is not an officer of the court (*Re Hill's Waterfall Estate & Gold Mining Co* [1986] 1 Ch 947; *Re John Bateson & Co* [1985] BCLC 259; *In Re Knitwear (Wholesale) Ltd* [1988] 1 Ch 275), much of what has been decided in relation to s 168(5) can be applied to liquidators in voluntary liquidations because s 168(5), which provides, in effect, that courts may supervise liquidators, applies to all liquidators.
  In general s 168(3) and s 112 have been seen as broadly the same. However, the Australian case of *Dean-Willcocks v Soluble Solution Hydroponics Pty Ltd* (1997) 15 ACLC 833 doubted this, as it was noted that the court may, under the equivalent of s 168(3), direct the

liquidator, its officer, to commit a breach of trust or to do something which it is arguable that the liquidator has no power to do, while under s 112(2) the court is only given power to avoid expensive procedures. Also, under s 112 a creditor or contributory, as well as a liquidator, is entitled to apply for directions.

'Person aggrieved'—For the section to operate there must be an application by a person who is 'aggrieved' by an act, omission or decision of the liquidator. The meaning of 'aggrieved' has not yet been settled. It has been said that the person must be someone who has suffered a legal grievance or has been wrongly deprived of something or affected his or her right to something: *Re S ex parte Sidebotham* (1880) 14 Ch D 458 at 465. Yet this might well be regarded as being too narrow, as the expression should not be limited to those with a definite legal grievance. Any attempt at classifying those who may be persons aggrieved has been said to be undesirable: *Re Edennote Ltd* [1996] BCC 718 at 721, [1996] 2 BCLC 389 at 393. Clearly the expression includes creditors, unless the company's liquidation will yield a surplus. So, those who can apply include creditors whose proofs of debt have been rejected by the liquidator (*Re Taylor* [1934] NZLR 117 at 127), creditors wishing to complain about the fact that the liquidator admitted another creditor's claim (*Re Capital Project Homes Pty Ltd* (1992) 10 ACLC 75), creditors where a liquidator has disposed of an asset at a undervalue (*Re Edennote Ltd* [1996] BCC 718 at 721, [1996] 2 BCLC 389 at 393), and those creditors who have been prevented from attending creditors' meetings (*Re Chevron Furnishers Pty Ltd (receiver and manager appointed) (in liquidation)* (1992) 10 ACLC 1537). It also includes contributories in situations where there will be a surplus of assets: *Re Edennote Ltd* [1996] BCC 718 at 721, [1996] 2 BCLC 389 at 393, CA. Additionally, it includes those who are directly affected by the exercise of a liquidator's power and, absent this provision, would be unable to challenge the exercise of power: *Mahomed v Morris* [2000] 2 BCLC 536 at 555, CA. An example is someone prejudiced by a disclaimer of company property: *Re Hans Place Ltd* [1992] BCC 737, [1992] BCLC 768; *Mahomed v Morris* at 555. But outsiders to the liquidation, dissatisfied with some act or decision of the liquidator, will not be able to bring proceedings: *Mahomed v Morris* at 555. Furthermore, courts will not, normally, accede to applications which will lead to interference with matters of day-to-day administration or where the liquidator has exercised discretionary powers in good faith, as this would make it very difficult, if not impossible, to accomplish the winding-up process: *Leon v York-o-Matic Ltd* [1966] 1 WLR 1450; *Re Wyvern Developments Ltd* [1974] 1 WLR 1097; *Mitchell v Buckingham International plc* [1998] 2 BCLC 369 at 390–391, CA.

Review of a decision—The courts are concerned about ensuring that the fiduciary and other duties and powers of liquidators are exercised properly: *Craig v Humberclyde Industrial Finance Ltd* [1999] 1 WLR 129, [1998] 2 BCLC 526, CA. It has been said that the exercise of a liquidator's discretion may be questioned where it can be established that the liquidator, notwithstanding he or she was acting in good faith, considered issues which ought not to have been considered: *Re Edennote Ltd* [1995] 2 BCLC 248 at 257–258. Also, the liquidator's discretion might be queried where it can be demonstrated that the liquidator failed to take into account issues which should have been taken into account: *Re Edennote Ltd* at 257–258.

When assessing an application and deciding what to do about a decision of a liquidator, a court will give significant weight to the commercial decisions of liquidators: *Re Edennote Ltd* [1996] BCC 718 at 720, [1996] 2 BCLC 389 at 394; *Mitchell v Buckingham International plc* [1998] 2 BCLC 369 at 390–391, CA.

Frequently, an application is made to have a liquidator removed because of a decision which he or she has taken. In such cases an application for removal of the liquidator would be more appropriate than to apply pursuant to s 168(5) for a review of the decision.

The court may, after reviewing a liquidator's decision and if the circumstances so demand, reverse a transaction into which a liquidator entered: *Re Edennote Ltd* [1996] BCC 718 at 721, [1996] 2 BCLC 389 at 393.

Proceedings may be taken under s 168(5) by creditors or contributories and they may seek to have the liquidator's decision not to initiate or defend legal proceedings reviewed. The court might see fit to give leave to persons other than the liquidator to take proceedings in the name of the company or that of the liquidator: *Re Imperial Bank of China, Hindustan & Japan* (1866) 1 Ch App 339; *Cape Breton Co v Fenn* (1881) 17 Ch D 198 at 208; *Fargro Ltd v Godfroy* [1986] 1 WLR 1134 at 1136–1138.

'Make such order as it thinks fit'—When hearing applications pursuant to s 168(5) the court will not readily interfere with a decision of the liquidator: *Mitchell v Buckingham*

International plc [1998] 2 BCLC 369 at 391, CA. In fact, it will not do so except where the decision of the liquidator is such that no reasonable liquidator could, properly instructed and advised in the circumstances, come to it: *Re Hans Place Ltd* [1992] BCC 737; *Re Greenhaven Motors Ltd* [1997] BCC 547; *Re Edennote Ltd* [1996] BCC 718, [1996] 2 BCLC 389, CA; *Hamilton v Official Receiver* [1998] BPIR 602. This is particularly the case with commercial decision-making: *Mahomed v Morris* [2000] 2 BCLC 536 at 557, CA. An example of a liquidator acting unreasonably is where the liquidator refused to assign to a former controller of the company in liquidation a claim which the company had against a firm of solicitors: *Hamilton v Official Receiver* [1998] BPIR 602.

See Keay 'The Supervision and Control of Liquidators' [2000] *The Conveyancer and Property Lawyer* 295.

169 Supplementary powers (Scotland)

(1) In the case of a winding up in Scotland, the court may provide by order that the liquidator may, where there is no liquidation committee, exercise any of the following powers, namely—

(a)   to bring or defend any action or other legal proceeding in the name and on behalf of the company, or

(b)   to carry on the business of the company so far as may be necessary for its beneficial winding up,

without the sanction or the intervention of the court.

(2) In a winding up by the court in Scotland, the liquidator has (subject to the rules) the same powers as a trustee on a bankrupt estate.

170 Enforcement of liquidator's duty to make returns etc

(1) If a liquidator who has made any default—

(a)   in filing, delivering or making any return, account or other document, or

(b)   in giving any notice which he is by law required to file, deliver, make or give,

fails to make good the default within 14 days after the service on him of a notice requiring him to do so, the court has the following powers.

(2) On an application made by any creditor or contributory of the company, or by the registrar of companies, the court may make an order directing the liquidator to make good the default within such time as may be specified in the order.

(3) The court's order may provide that all costs of and incidental to the application shall be borne by the liquidator.

(4) Nothing in this section prejudices the operation of any enactment imposing penalties on a liquidator in respect of any such default as is mentioned above.

General note—If a court makes an order under this section and the liquidator fails to comply with it, then he or she is in contempt of court and it can lead to serious consequences for the liquidator: see *Re S & A Conversion Ltd* (1988) 4 BCC 384, CA where a liquidator was ordered to be imprisoned for failing to provide the registrar of companies with the particulars required in what is now s 192, after being ordered to do so by the court;

Re Allan Ellis (Transport and Packing Services) Ltd (1989) 5 BCC 835. The courts in these two cases emphasised the seriousness of not complying with court orders.

Removal; vacation of office

171 Removal etc (voluntary winding up)

(1) This section applies with respect to the removal from office and vacation of office of the liquidator of a company which is being wound up voluntarily.

(2) Subject to the next subsection, the liquidator may be removed from office only by an order of the court or—

   (a)   in the case of a members' voluntary winding up, by a general meeting of the company summoned specially for that purpose, or

   (b)   in the case of a creditors' voluntary winding up, by a general meeting of the company's creditors summoned specially for that purpose in accordance with the rules.

(3) Where the liquidator was appointed by the court under section 108 in Chapter V, a meeting such as is mentioned in subsection (2) above shall be summoned for the purpose of replacing him only if he thinks fit or the court so directs or the meeting is requested, in accordance with the rules—

   (a)   in the case of a members' voluntary winding up, by members representing not less than one-half of the total voting rights of all the members having at the date of the request a right to vote at the meeting, or

   (b)   in the case of a creditors' voluntary winding up, by not less than one-half, in value, of the company's creditors.

(4) A liquidator shall vacate office if he ceases to be a person who is qualified to act as an insolvency practitioner in relation to the company.

(5) A liquidator may, in the prescribed circumstances, resign his office by giving notice of his resignation to the registrar of companies.

(6) Where—

   (a)   in the case of a members' voluntary winding up, a final meeting of the company has been held under section 94 in Chapter III, or

   (b)   in the case of a creditors' voluntary winding up, final meetings of the company and of the creditors have been held under section 106 in Chapter IV,

the liquidator whose report was considered at the meeting or meetings shall vacate office as soon as he has complied with subsection (3) of that section and has given notice to the registrar of companies that the meeting or meetings have been held and of the decisions (if any) of the meeting or meetings.

General note—The provision deals with the removal or resignation of a liquidator in a voluntary liquidation. Compulsory liquidation is covered by s 172.

See r 4.120.

Creditors' meeting—See r 4.224 for the procedure applicable to such meetings.

Vacation of office—A liquidator whose authorisation to act as a liquidator has been suspended may apply for an order of removal and to have another liquidator to replace him or her: *Re AJ Adams (Builders) Ltd* [1991] BCC 62.
See r 4.135.

Resign—The circumstances referred to in s 171(5) are set out in r 4.108(4) (creditors' voluntary) and r 4.142(3) (members' voluntary), although the provisions are identical.

In creditors' voluntary liquidations, liquidators might apply under s 171(5), if a creditors' meeting resolves not to accept the liquidator's resignation, to the court, which may give leave to the liquidator to resign (r 4.111(1)). The Chief Clerk of the Companies Court will determine the application (see r 13.2(2) and *Practice Direction No 3 of 1986* [1987] 1 WLR 53). The court will not exercise its discretion without a good reason: *Re Sankey Furniture Ltd* [1995] 2 BCLC 594.

There is no provision in the Act or Rules dealing with the refusal by the meeting of contributories to accept the resignation of the liquidator. It seems fair to say that the liquidator could apply to the court pursuant to s 112 if one of the grounds for resignation existed.

See the notes accompanying s 108.

Final meeting—Within 1 week of the holding of this meeting the liquidator must send to the registrar of companies a copy of the account laid before the general meeting, and file a return setting out the fact that the meeting was held and on what date (s 94(3)). If there is no quorum at the meeting, as is often the case because creditors might feel that it is not worth attending, the liquidator is, instead of lodging the s 94 return, to make a return that the meeting was held and no quorum was present. Once this is done the liquidator's duties in making a return to the registrar are complete (s 94(5)).

172 Removal etc (winding up by the court)

(1) This section applies with respect to the removal from office and vacation of office of the liquidator of a company which is being wound up by the court, or of a provisional liquidator.

(2) Subject as follows, the liquidator may be removed from office only by an order of the court or by a general meeting of the company's creditors summoned specially for that purpose in accordance with the rules; and a provisional liquidator may be removed from office only by an order of the court.

(3) Where—

    (a)   the official receiver is liquidator otherwise than in succession under section 136(3) to a person who held office as a result of a nomination by a meeting of the company's creditors or contributories, or

    (b)   the liquidator was appointed by the court otherwise than under section 139(4)(a) or 140(1), or was appointed by the Secretary of State,

a general meeting of the company's creditors shall be summoned for the purpose of replacing him only if he thinks fit, or the court so directs, or the meeting is requested, in accordance with the rules, by not less than one-quarter, in value, of the creditors.

(4) If appointed by the Secretary of State, the liquidator may be removed from office by a direction of the Secretary of State.

(5) A liquidator or provisional liquidator, not being the official receiver, shall vacate office if he ceases to be a person who is qualified to act as an insolvency practitioner in relation to the company.

(6) A liquidator may, in the prescribed circumstances, resign his office by giving notice of his resignation to the court.

(7) Where an order is made under section 204 (early dissolution in Scotland) for the dissolution of the company, the liquidator shall vacate office when the dissolution of the company takes effect in accordance with that section.

(8) Where a final meeting has been held under section 146 (liquidator's report on completion of winding up), the liquidator whose report was considered at the meeting shall vacate office as soon as he has given notice to the court and the registrar of companies that the meeting has been held and of the decisions (if any) of the meeting.

General note—This provision accords, as far as it can, with s 171, which deals with voluntary liquidation.

Once a liquidator has vacated office under any of the provisions in this section, he or she is required to deliver up to his or her successor as liquidator all company assets, books, papers and records (r 4.138(1)).

Removed by direction of the Secretary of State—Before the Secretary of State decides to remove the liquidator, (s)he must notify the liquidator and the official receiver of the decision and the basis for it, and indicate a period in which the liquidator may make representations against the decision (r 4.123(1)). If the Secretary of State directs removal, then immediately (s)he is to file notice of the decision in court and send notices of the decision to both the liquidator and the official receiver (r 4.123(2)). Where it is incumbent on the Secretary of State to decide the issue of release, if release is granted it may be revoked on proof that it was obtained by fraud or by suppression or concealment of any material fact: *Re Harris* [1899] 2 QB 97.

Removal under section 172(3)—for an order of removal the applicant had to satisy the court that it was in the best interests of the liquidation to remove the liquidator: *Managa Properties Ltd v Brittain* [2009] EWHC 157 (Ch), [2009] 1 BCLC 689, [2009] BPIR 306.

Resign—A liquidator in compulsory winding up must call a meeting for the purpose of receiving his or her resignation (r 4.108(1)), and the liquidator is only permitted to resign in those circumstances set out in r 4.108(4) and after giving notice to the court (s 172(6)).

In recent times the courts have been willing, on occasions, to by-pass the procedures prescribed for resignation and to make orders removing a practitioner from multiple offices and to appoint some appropriate person in his or her stead: *Re Bullard & Taplin Ltd* [1996] BCC 973; *Re A & C Supplies* [1998] BCC 708; *Re Equity Nominees Ltd* [1999] 2 BCLC 19 at 22. The question that courts have posed is whether the convening of meetings of creditors would serve a useful purpose: *Re Sankey Furniture Ltd* [1995] 2 BCLC 594 at 600 and 601. Where the liquidator is resigning from a firm that is handling the liquidation, because of grounds that are referred to in r 4.108(4), there is no objection to the court ordering the removal of the liquidator and the appointment of another member of his or her former firm, instead of requiring the convening of meetings for every liquidation that is involved, certainly where there is evidence that the cost would be significant: *Re AJ Adams (Builders) Ltd* [1991] BCLC 359; *Re Sankey Furniture Ltd* [1995] 2 BCLC 594. The same goes for the situation where the liquidator is leaving his or her firm and taking up other employment such that he or she would be unable to discharge the duties of a liquidator properly: *Re Equity Nominees Ltd* [1999] 2 BCLC 19.

In a number of cases the courts have been confronted with the situation where a liquidator is resigning from a firm and, so that his or her former firm retains the appointment, an application is made for removal of the liquidator and for him or her to be replaced by one or more members of the original firm. There is some uncertainty as to whether a court would accede to such an application and, if so, on what conditions. In *Re Sankey Furniture Ltd* [1995] 2 BCLC 594 the court was not willing to make the order requested, while in *Re A & C Supplies Ltd* [1998] BCC 708 the court took the opposite view, although *Re Sankey Ltd* was distinguished. In *Re Equity Nominees Ltd* [1999] 2 BCLC 19, [2000] BCC 84 Neuberger J adverted to the apparent conflicting lines taken in *Re Sankey Furniture Ltd* and *Re A & C Supplies Ltd*, and he sought to follow the essential philosophy espoused in the judgments. The order his Lordship ended up making involved a reconciliation between the two approaches. According to the judge, whether the 'short-cut approach' was to be invoked depended on whether or not convening meetings would serve a useful purpose and the use of the approach in cases like *Re A & C Supplies Ltd* was often a practical and sensible approach to take, as it could save costs and, subject to the imposition of conditions and safeguards, should be employed. As part of his order that the liquidator be replaced, Neuberger J ordered that a letter be sent to all creditors within a short time explaining to them the effect of replacing the liquidator and their right to oppose his discharge within a certain time period.

In *Cork v Rolph* (2000) *The Times*, December 13, Neuberger J adopted a similar approach to that taken in *Re Equity Nominees Ltd*, and his Lordship said that every application has to be judged on its own merits, before making the order sought. The judge ordered that the liquidator be replaced by a former colleague and that the creditors should be advised by way of a block advertisement in the London Gazette in relation to each liquidation. A similar order was made in *Saville v Gerrard and Pick* [2004] BPIR 1332, [2005] BCC 433, which appears to manifest an even more liberal approach taken by the courts. In that case there was a reorganisation of the firm in which the liquidator of a group of companies worked, whereby the insolvency work of the firm was to be moved from the Leeds office to other offices around the country. As a result the staff of the firm who had worked on the liquidations were not working in offices that were close to the liquidator. The court permitted two other members of the firm who were experienced office-holders, and who worked out of the Leeds office, to replace the liquidator of the group. The decision was based on the notion of minimising the costs of the liquidations (and other insolvencies).

Where applications are made to remove liquidators in the manner discussed above, the courts are able to appoint extra licensed practitioners to the relevant liquidations if there is any delay in hearing and disposing of the application: *Clements v Udall* [2001] BCC 658, [2002] 2 BCLC 606, [2001] BPIR 454. Additional liquidators can be appointed on the basis of s 108(1), which gives a judge power to appoint a liquidator where there was 'no liquidator acting'.

In *Donaldson v O'Sullivan* [2008] EWCA Civ 879 an appellate court had, first the first time, the opportunity to consider the so-called 'block transfer order'. An order had been made ([2008] EWHC 387 (Ch), [2008] BPIR 288) to remove an insolvency practitioner from many appointments in relation to different kinds of insolvency regime. Included was his removal as the trustee of the appellant's bankrupt estate and his replacement with a new appointee. The bankrupt argued that while the court had power to remove the original trustee, it had no power to order the appointment of the replacement trustee. The Court of Appeal, dealing with the bankruptcy specifically, also considered compulsory liquidations in the same light. The Court did not specifically approve of the process of block transfer, but it did not reject it and in fact said that in the matter before it the order was permissible. The Court said that it was important that bankruptcies and compulory liquidations were dependent on, and controlled by, the court. The Court held that a court was empowered to appoint a replacement trustee pursuant to s 303.

If it is clear that a liquidator should be willing to step aside, but he or she fights a resultant application for removal, indemnity costs should be awarded against the liquidator: *Shepheard v Lamey* [2001] BPIR 939. Similarly, Australian authority holds that if a liquidator resigns after opposing an application to remove him or her, the liquidator will be liable for the costs of the applicant: *Nicou v Ngan* [2005] NSWSC 446, (2005) 53 ACSR 529, NSW Sup Ct.

Release of liquidator

173 Release (voluntary winding up)

(1) This section applies with respect to the release of the liquidator of a company which is being wound up voluntarily.

(2) A person who has ceased to be a liquidator shall have his release with effect from the following time, that is to say—

    (a)   in the case of a person who has been removed from office by a general meeting of the company or by a general meeting of the company's creditors that has not resolved against his release or who has died, the time at which notice is given to the registrar of companies in accordance with the rules that that person has ceased to hold office;

    (b)   in the case of a person who has been removed from office by a general meeting of the company's creditors that has resolved against his release, or by the court, or who has vacated office under section 171(4) above, such time as the Secretary of State may, on the application of that person, determine;

    (c)   in the case of a person who has resigned, such time as may be prescribed;

    (d)   in the case of a person who has vacated office under subsection (6)(a) of section 171, the time at which he vacated office;

    (e)   in the case of a person who has vacated office under subsection (6)(b) of that section–

        (i)   if the final meeting of the creditors referred to in that subsection has resolved against that person's release, such time as the Secretary of State may, on an application by that person, determine, and

        (ii) if that meeting has not resolved against that person's release, the time at which he vacated office.

(3) In the application of subsection (2) to the winding up of a company registered in Scotland, the references to a determination by the Secretary of State as to the time from which a person who has ceased to be liquidator shall have his release are to be read as references to such a determination by the Accountant of Court.

(4) Where a liquidator has his release under subsection (2), he is, with effect from the time specified in that subsection, discharged from all liability both in respect of acts or omissions of his in the winding up and otherwise in relation to his conduct as liquidator.

But nothing in this section prevents the exercise, in relation to a person who has had his release under subsection (2), of the court's powers under section 212 of this Act (summary remedy against delinquent directors, liquidators, etc).

General note—Release is available to liquidators who have resigned or been removed from office, and also to those liquidators who have ceased to be qualified insolvency practitioners, as well as those removed by the direction of the Secretary of State (r 4.122). The usual thing is that the liquidator remains in office until winding up is completed and then obtains a release. This occurs when all the property of the company (or so much as can be realised without needlessly protracting the liquidation) has been realised, the liquidator has distributed a final dividend to the creditors, adjusted the rights of contributories, and made a final return, if any, to the contributories.

If a liquidator has resigned, release is obtained when the resignation is accepted by the creditors' meeting in a creditors' voluntary winding up and the meeting has not resolved to withhold release, and the registrar of companies has been informed of the resignation (r 4.122). In a members' voluntary the release is effective from the time when the registrar of companies is given notice of the resignation (r 4.144(1)).

The compulsory liquidation equivalent provision is s 174.

'Discharged from all liability'—Although release discharges a liquidator from all liability, if a creditor, contributory or the official receiver obtains the leave of the court, an application may be made to the court for it to examine the conduct of a liquidator under s 212 (s 212(4)).

174 Release (winding up by the court)

(1) This section applies with respect to the release of the liquidator of a company which is being wound up by the court, or of a provisional liquidator.

(2) Where the official receiver has ceased to be liquidator and a person becomes liquidator in his stead, the official receiver has his release with effect from the following time, that is to say—

   (a)   in a case where that person was nominated by a general meeting of creditors or contributories, or was appointed by the Secretary of State, the time at which the official receiver gives notice to the court that he has been replaced;

   (b)   in a case where that person is appointed by the court, such time as the court may determine.

(3) If the official receiver while he is a liquidator gives notice to the Secretary of State that the winding up is for practical purposes complete, he has his release with effect from such time as the Secretary of State may determine.

(4) A person other than the official receiver who has ceased to be a liquidator has his release with effect from the following time, that is to say—

   (a)   in the case of a person who has been removed from office by a general meeting of creditors that has not resolved against his release or who has died, the time at which notice is given to the court in accordance with the rules that that person has ceased to hold office;

   (b)   in the case of a person who has been removed from office by a general meeting of creditors that has resolved against his release, or by the court or the Secretary of State, or who has vacated office under section 172(5) or (7), such time as the Secretary of State may, on an application by that person, determine;

   (c)   in the case of a person who has resigned, such time as may be prescribed;

   (d)   in the case of a person who has vacated office under section 172(8) –

         (i)   if the final meeting referred to in that subsection has resolved against that person's release, such time as the Secretary of State may, on an application by that person, determine, and

 (ii) if that meeting has not so resolved, the time at which that person vacated office.

(5) A person who has ceased to hold office as a provisional liquidator has his release with effect from such time as the court may, on an application by him, determine.

(6) Where the official receiver or a liquidator or provisional liquidator has his release under this section, he is, with effect from the time specified in the preceding provisions of this section, discharged from all liability both in respect of acts or omissions of his in the winding up and otherwise in relation to his conduct as liquidator or provisional liquidator.

But nothing in this section prevents the exercise, in relation to a person who has had his release under this section, of the court's powers under section 212 (summary remedy against delinquent directors, liquidators, etc).

(7) In the application of this section to a case where the order for winding up has been made by the court in Scotland, the references to a determination by the Secretary of State as to the time from which a person who has ceased to be liquidator has his release are to such a determination by the Accountant of Court.

General note—This section is, for compulsory liquidations, the corresponding section to s 173.
 See the notes accompanying s 173.

Chapter VIII

Provisions of General Application in Winding Up Preferential Debts

175 Preferential debts (general provision)

(1) In a winding up the company's preferential debts (within the meaning given by section 386 in Part XII) shall be paid in priority to all other debts.

(2) Preferential debts—

 (a) rank equally among themselves after the expenses of the winding up and shall be paid in full, unless the assets are insufficient to meet them, in which case they abate in equal proportions; and

 (b) so far as the assets of the company available for payment of general creditors are insufficient to meet them, have priority over the claims of holders of debentures secured by, or holders of, any floating charge created by the company, and shall be paid accordingly out of any property comprised in or subject to that charge.

General note—While subsection (1) states that the preferential debts are to be paid in priority to all other debts, subsection (2) qualifies that by indicating that the preferential debts do not rank for payment until the winding-up expenses have been satisfied in full.

Preferential debts are defined in s 386 and the kinds of debts that are preferential are enumerated in Sch 6. The types of debts that qualify have gradually been reduced over the years and since the commencement of the provisions in the Enterprise Act 2002 that deal with corporate insolvency, Crown debts no longer rank as preferential debts (Enterprise Act, s 251). Their priority status was abolished from 15 September 2003. The abolition was regarded as an integral part of the objective of government, which is to see more companies rescued. The government wanted to see the funds that would normally be swallowed up by the Crown pass on to the unsecured creditors. However, that will not always be the case because unless a charge was created post 15 September 2003, the floating chargeholder will get the benefit of the abolition of the Crown priority.

Section 754 of the Companies Act 2006 (formerly s 196 of the Companies Act 1985) provides (if the company is not being wound up) that preferential creditors will obtain priority in relation to assets subject to a floating charge where the chargeholder takes possession of the assets. It has been held by the Court of Appeal in *HM Commissioners for Revenue and Customs v Royal Bank of Scotland* [2007] EWCA Civ 1262, [2008] BCC 135 that s 754's precursor provision (s 196) could not apply to all payments made by a company to the credit of its account with the chargeholder, and that it was necessary to distinguish between acts which are, substantially, acts by which the chargeholder realises its security and those acts which are, substantially, no more than the ordinary discharge of a debtor's liability. The substance of each transaction had to be considered.

As regards 'winding-up' expenses, see the notes attaching to r 4.4.218.

Payment—The preferential debts are paid in full, if the company's funds permit, before lower order creditors, such as the unsecured creditors, get paid anything, and if the funds do not permit full payment the preferential debts rank equally and abate in equal proportions. Importantly, the preferential debts are paid out of the funds of the company that are subject to a floating charge, in priority to the chargeholder where the general funds of the company (that are not encumbered by the charge) are not sufficient to pay them in full (s 175(2)(b)).

Floating charge—As a result of the definition in s 251, a floating charge for the purposes of the Act is one that was created as a floating charge. So, any charge that was created as a floating charge and still was at the time of winding-up order is regarded as a floating charge for the purposes of the legislation and, more importantly, so is a floating charge that has crystallised before winding up commences.

A receiver appointed before winding up, and operating under a floating charge is required by s 40 to pay the preferential debts, as they exist at the time of the 'relevant date' in priority to repaying his or her appointor. The relevant date is the date of the appointment of the receiver (s 387(4)(a)). But if winding up occurs subsequent to receivership, s 175 will overtake s 40: *Re Leyland DAF Ltd* [2002] 1 BCLC 571. This leads to the consequence that the receiver has to pay preferential debts that exist at the time of a different 'relevant date'. In the latter circumstance the relevant date is the date of the winding-up order or the date of the resolution to wind up (s 387(3)(b), (c)). But it was held that the assets covered by the charge could not be used by the liquidator to recoup the expenses of winding up, save where they involved the preservation and/or realisation of charged assets: *Buchler v Talbot* [2004] UKHL 9, [2004] 2 AC 298, [2004] 2 WLR 582, [2004] 1 All ER 1289. The effect of the decision was, however, overturned by s 176ZA, which was introduced by Companies Act 2006. See the notes accompanying s 176ZA.

See ss 40, 386 and Sch 6 and the notes accompanying each.

See Keay and Walton 'The Preferential Debts' Regime in Liquidation Law: In the Public Interest?' (1999) 3 *Company Financial and Insolvency Law Review* 84.

176 Preferential charge on goods distrained

(1) This section applies where a company is being wound up by the court in England and Wales, and is without prejudice to section 128 (avoidance of attachments, etc).

(2) Where any person (whether or not a landlord or person entitled to rent) has distrained upon the goods or effects of the company in the period of 3 months ending with the date of the winding-up order, those goods or

effects, or the proceeds of their sale, shall be charged for the benefit of the company with the preferential debts of the company to the extent that the company's property is for the time being insufficient for meeting them.

(3) Where by virtue of a charge under subsection (2) any person surrenders any goods or effects to a company or makes a payment to a company, that person ranks, in respect of the amount of the proceeds of sale of those goods or effects by the liquidator or (as the case may be) the amount of the payment, as a preferential creditor of the company, except as against so much of the company's property as is available for the payment of preferential creditors by virtue of the surrender or payment.

General note—This provision only applies where the action of distress has not been put in force following the commencement of winding up (s 128).

Preferential debts—Where goods are distrained in the three months before the winding-up order, the proceeds from the sale of the goods, or the goods themselves, are charged for the benefit of preferential creditors where the company's funds are not sufficient to pay those creditors in full. So, while distress permits a landlord to get ahead of the general unsecured creditors, he or she falls behind the preferential creditors, in the circumstances mentioned above.

See the notes to accompany s 347.

For further discussion, see Walton 'Landlord's Distress: Past Its Use By Date?' [2000] Conv 508.

Property subject to floating charge

Amendments—Cross-heading inserted by Enterprise Act 2002, s 52.

176ZA Payment of expenses of winding up (England and Wales)

(1) The expenses of winding up in England and Wales, so far as the assets of the company available for payment of general creditors are insufficient to meet them, have priority over any claims to property comprised in or subject to any floating charge created by the company and shall be paid out of any such property accordingly.

(2) In subsection (1)—

    (a)   the reference to assets of the company available for payment of general creditors does not include any amount made available under section 176A(2)(a);

    (b)   the reference to claims to property comprised in or subject to a floating charge is to the claims of—

        (i)   the holders of debentures secured by, or holders of, the floating charge, and

        (ii)   any preferential creditors entitled to be paid out of that property in priority to them.

(3) Provision may be made by rules restricting the application of subsection (1), in such circumstances as may be prescribed, to expenses authorised or approved—

    (a)   by the holders of debentures secured by, or holders of, the floating charge and by any preferential creditors entitled to be paid in priority to them, or

    (b)   by the court.

(4) References in this section to the expenses of the winding up are to all expenses properly incurred in the winding up, including the remuneration of the liquidator.

Amendments—Inserted by the Companies Act 2006, s 1282(1).

General Note—This provision was introduced by the Companies Act 2006 and came into force on 6 April 2008. The provision represents the Government's response to the decision of the House of Lords in *Buchler v Talbot* [2004] UKHL 9, [2004] 2 AC 298, [2004] 2 WLR 582, [2004] 1 All ER 1289, which held that liquidation expenses are not to be paid out of assets subject to a floating charge over company property, because where a company is in both administrative receivership and liquidation, its assets are comprised in two different funds. One fund involved some assets that were subject to a floating charge and the other fund involved assets that were just subject to the liquidation. Generally each fund bears its own costs and, as the chargeholder has no interest in the liquidation, he or she should not have to contribute towards the liquidation expenses (at [30] and [31]). This ruling severely limited liquidators as often a floating charge is granted over most, if not all, of a company's property. Hence, liquidators could not use, without the consent of the chargeholder much (or any) of the company's property to pay for litigation and other expenses. The new provision and accompanying rules acknowledge the fact that floating chargeholders (and in some cases, preferential creditors) have a special interest in the use of assets (covered by a charge) to fund litigation in the liquidation, so they are given a voice in the use of such assets.

    New rules were introduced in light of the introduction of the section (Insolvency (Amendment) Rules 2008 (SI 2008/737), rules 4.218A–4.218E). Liquidators should use Form 4.74 for the request for approval or authorisation.

    Assets that are covered by a floating charge, but which make up the prescribed part under s 176A and are payable to general creditors as a result, cannot be used to pay expenses of the winding up (s 176ZA(2)(a)).

    The payment of expenses out of assets subject to a floating charge is restricted by the need for approval or authorisation to be obtained from those interested in the assets subject to the charge. The procedure for obtaining this approval or authorisation is explained in rather detailed rules, namely rr 4.218A–4.218E. The only kind of expenses that are restricted when it comes to using charged assets for the payment of liquidation expenses are litigation expenses as defined in r 4.218A(1)(d) (see r 4.218A(2)).

    See, A Keay 'Litigation Expenses in Liquidations' (2009) 22 *Insolvency Intelligence* 113.

    See the detailed commentary on rr 4.218A–4.218E.

176A Share of assets for unsecured creditors

(1) This section applies where a floating charge relates to property of a company—

    (a)   which has gone into liquidation,

    (b)   which is in administration,

    (c)   of which there is a provisional liquidator, or

    (d)   of which there is a receiver.

(2) The liquidator, administrator or receiver—

    (a)   shall make a prescribed part of the company's net property available for the satisfaction of unsecured debts, and

(b)   shall not distribute that part to the proprietor of a floating charge except in so far as it exceeds the amount required for the satisfaction of unsecured debts.

(3) Subsection (2) shall not apply to a company if—

(a)   the company's net property is less than the prescribed minimum, and

(b)   the liquidator, administrator or receiver thinks that the cost of making a distribution to unsecured creditors would be disproportionate to the benefits.

(4) Subsection (2) shall also not apply to a company if or in so far as it is disapplied by—

(a)   a voluntary arrangement in respect of the company, or

(b)   a compromise or arrangement agreed under Part 26 of the Companies Act 2006 (arrangements and reconstructions).

(5) Subsection (2) shall also not apply to a company if—

(a)   the liquidator, administrator or receiver applies to the court for an order under this subsection on the ground that the cost of making a distribution to unsecured creditors would be disproportionate to the benefits, and

(b)   the court orders that subsection (2) shall not apply.

(6) In subsections (2) and (3) a company's net property is the amount of its property which would, but for this section, be available for satisfaction of claims of holders of debentures secured by, or holders of, any floating charge created by the company.

(7) An order under subsection (2) prescribing part of a company's net property may, in particular, provide for its calculation—

(a)   as a percentage of the company's net property, or

(b)   as an aggregate of different percentages of different parts of the company's net property.

(8) An order under this section—

(a)   must be made by statutory instrument, and

(b)   shall be subject to annulment pursuant to a resolution of either House of Parliament.

(9) In this section—

'floating charge' means a charge which is a floating charge on its creation and which is created after the first order under subsection (2)(a) comes into force, and

'prescribed' means prescribed by order by the Secretary of State.

(10) An order under this section may include transitional or incidental provision.

Amendments—Inserted by Enterprise Act 2002, s 252. Amended by SI 2008/948.

General note—This provision was introduced by the Enterprise Act 2002. It is part of the package that involved the abolition of the Crown preference. It is to be seen as a counterweight to the benefit that floating chargeholders have received from the elimination of the Crown priority. See the notes to s 175 and Sch 6.

The provision, which applies to four kinds of insolvency administration, provides for what has become known as 'top-slicing'. That is, in relation to floating charges created on or after 15 September 2003, a certain part of the net proceeds (net property) from the realisation of the property covered by floating charges must be set aside for the unsecured creditors.

A secured creditor, who has either a fixed or floating charge over company property, and whose security is not adequate to discharge his or her debt, is not permitted to share in the net property. If the net property is sufficient to pay out all unsecured creditors then the surplus may be paid out to secured creditors: *Re Airbase (UK) Ltd* [2008] EWHC 124 (Ch), [2008] BCC 213, [2008] 1 BCLC 437; *Re Permacell Finesse Ltd (in liq)* [2007] EWHC 3233 (Ch), [2008] BCC 208. But if a floating chargeholder surrendered entirely his or her security under the charge pursuant to, or in accordance with, r.4.88(2),received nothing pursuant to it, and is entitled to prove as if his or her debt were unsecured, the former chargeholder becomes an unsecured creditor and may share in the prescribed part: *Kelly and Sumpton v Inflexion Fund 2 2850 Limited Partnership and Autocruise Co-Investment Limited Partnership* [2010] EWHC (Ch) at [41]). HH Judge Kaye QC (sitting as a High Court judge) who gave judgment in this case made the point that if the chargeholder elects to become an unsecured creditor he or she should be treated as such in relation both to proving under r.4.88(2) and to sharing in the prescribed part (at [48]). In *Re JT Frith Ltd* [2012] EWHC 196 (Ch) it was held that if a secured creditor does not take any action to surrender its security, but lodges a proof of debt for the whole of its debt then it can be assumed that it is surrendering its security and it is entitled to share in the prescribed part, even if the proof of debt does not state that security is surrendered but the creditor states 'None' in answer to the question in the proof 'particulars of any security held' ([29]).

This provision does not apply:

- to charges created before the commencement date (15 September 2003) (s 176A(9)) (hence, benefiting the holders of any pre 15 September 2003 charges substantially as the charges are not placed behind Crown debts and are not subject to top-slicing);
- where the company's net property is less than the prescribed minimum (at present this is £10,000 (Insolvency Act 1986 (Prescribed Part) Order 2003 (SI 2003/2097), art 2)) and the relevant office-holder thinks that the cost of making a distribution to the unsecured creditors would be disproportionate to the benefits received by the unsecured creditors (s 176A(3)(a), (b));
- where it is disapplied by a company voluntary arrangement in respect of the company or a compromise or arrangement under s 895 of the Companies Act 2006 (s 176A(4)(a), (b));
- where the office-holder applies to the court for an order, and one is granted, on the basis that the cost of making a distribution would be disproportionate to the benefits (s 176A(5)(a), (b)) (the right to a dividend was disapplied under this provision in *Re Hydroserve Ltd* [2007] EWHC 3026 (Ch), [2007] All ER (D) 184 (Jun), [2008] BCC 175, but not in either *Re Courts plc* [2008] EWHC 2339 (Ch) or *Re International Sections Ltd (in creditors' voluntary liquidation)* [2009] EWHC 137 (Ch), [2009] BPIR 297.

In the second situation just referred to, both conditions must exist if a payment is to be set aside. So, it is possible that the sum available is less than the minimum, but the office-holder thinks that it might be proportionate to make a distribution. If the minimum is exceeded, then there is no discretion in the office-holder when it comes to distribution.

In the penultimate situation referred to above, the unsecured creditors will have agreed to forego the top-slicing so as to assist the implementation of some arrangement that might benefit them more in the long run. The question is: would dissenting creditors be entitled to challenge the decision, under s 6(1) of the Insolvency Act 1986, on the basis that the arrangement unfairly prejudices his or her interests as a creditor?

The last situation mentioned above might be fulfilled where there are a huge number of creditors and making a distribution would not be worthwhile, given the attendant costs and expenses. But note the approach taken in *Re Courts plc* [2008] EWHC 2339 (Ch) or *Re International Sections Ltd (in creditors' voluntary liquidation)* [2009] EWHC 137 (Ch), [2009] BPIR 297.

As the provision does not have retrospective effect (note s 176A(9)), it might be thought that where there are any subsequent orders to the first order setting the prescribed part, they will only apply to charges created after the commencement of the respective orders (Davies et al *Insolvency and the Enterprise Act 2002* (Jordans, 2003) at 58).

'Shall not apply'—While in *Re Hydroserve Ltd* [2007] EWHC 3026 (Ch), [2007] All ER (D) 184 (Jun), [2008] BCC 175 the court was willing to disapply section 176A(2), in *Re Courts plc* [2008] EWHC 2339 (Ch) Blackburne J took the view that he was not entitled, in his discretion, to order the partial disapplication of the section, as he was asked to do by the applicant (at [15]). In the case the liquidator sought an order under s 176A(5) that s 176A(2) would not apply so as to require a distribution to those unsecured creditors who were owed less than £28,000 on the basis that to make a distribution would be disproportionate to the benefits. His Lordship rejected the application on the basis that if he were to accede to it, it would interfere with a pari passu distribution, as a minority of creditors would be able to take the whole of the prescribed part if the judge made the order sought, and unless Parliament specifically indicated that the pari passu principle should not apply then the learned judge said that it should be applied (at [16]). Furthermore, his Lordship said that if, when averaged out, a liquidator's expenses relating to the processing of each creditor's claim to a share of the prescribed part equals or exceeds the distribution to a particular creditor, that is not a relevant matter to be taken into account in consideration of the operation of this section (at [17]). The judge stated that the cost/benefit balance that is to be considered in relation to s.176A(5) is to be approached on the basis of treating creditors as a body, and one cannot look at individual creditors and see what each would actually receive ([19]). Later, in *Re International Sections Ltd (in creditors' voluntary liquidation)* [2009] EWHC 137 (Ch), [2009] BPIR 297 H H Judge Purle QC also declined to disapply s 176A(2). The learned judge said that in deciding whether to disapply the section a court had to be satisfied that the cost of making a distribution would be disproportionate to the benefits, and that it was right to disapply the section on that ground. It was permissible for a court to adopt the view, even where the cost of making a distribution would be disproportionate, that unsecured creditors should still receive what remained of the prescribed part, after deducting costs. His Lordship said that the court should not be too ready to disapply the section merely because the dividend would be small. His Lordship said that the disapplication of s 176A(2) should be very much the exception, and not the rule (at [9], [15]), a position supported by Lord Glennie in the Scottish case of *Re QMD Hotels Ltd* [2010] CSOH 168 at [4]. Often liquidators and administrators may say that there should be disapplication because of the cost of dealing with the payment out of the prescribed part. Yet in Re QMD Hotels Ltd Lord Glennie said, in relation to the case before him, that the administrators should do no more than was necessary to effect payment of a dividend without carrying out further investigations into the merits of the claims (at [6]).

'Net property'—This term covers the property that would, but for this section, be available to be paid to the floating chargeholder.

'Floating charge'—See the comments relating to s 175.

'Prescribed'—The part that is set aside for unsecured creditors is prescribed by the Secretary of State. The government decided that there should be a minimum amount available to the unsecured creditors and that thereafter payment would be on a sliding scale. At present the prescribed sums are (Insolvency Act 1986 (Prescribed Part) Order 2003 (SI 2003/2097), art 3(1)(a), (b)):

- where the property's value does not exceed £10,000 in value, 50% of that;
- where the company's net property exceeds £10,000 in value, 50% of the first £10,000 in value and 20% of that part that exceeds £10,000 in value.

The above is subject to the fact that the prescribed part is not to exceed £600,000 in satisfying the debts of unsecured creditors (art 3(2)).

Report to creditors—Within 28 days of the creditors' meeting under s 95 or s 98, in a creditors' voluntary liquidation, the liquidator is obliged to send a report to the creditors and contributories and in that report he or she should provide an estimate of the prescribed part, and an estimate of the value of the company's net property (r 4.49(2)(a)).

'Created'—The charges to which the prescribed part apply are ones created after 15 September 2003. Does 'created' here mean the execution of a new document or does it cover the assignment of debenture to a new lender, who lends money on the basis of the debenture? It has been submitted that a charge is created when a debenture is assigned – the parties being the new lender and the company (Simmons 'Some Reflections on Administrations, Crown Preferences and the Ring-Fenced Sums in the Enterprise Act' [2004] JBL 423 at 434).

For further discussion, see A Keay'The Prescribed Part: Sharing Around the Company's Funds' (2011) 24 (6) *Insolvency Intelligence* 81; P Cranston 'The unchartered shallows of the prescribed part' (2010) 5 JIBFL 278.

Special managers

177 Power to appoint special manager

(1) Where a company has gone into liquidation or a provisional liquidator has been appointed, the court may, on an application under this section, appoint any person to be the special manager of the business or property of the company.

(2) The application may be made by the liquidator or provisional liquidator in any case where it appears to him that the nature of the business or property of the company, or the interests of the company's creditors or contributories or members generally, require the appointment of another person to manage the company's business or property.

(3) The special manager has such powers as may be entrusted to him by the court.

(4) The court's power to entrust powers to the special manager includes power to direct that any provision of this Act that has effect in relation to the provisional liquidator or liquidator of a company shall have the like effect in relation to the special manager for the purposes of the carrying out by him of any of the functions of the provisional liquidator or liquidator.

(5) The special manager shall—

   (a)   give such security or, in Scotland, caution as may be prescribed;
   (b)   prepare and keep such accounts as may be prescribed; and
   (c)   produce those accounts in accordance with the rules to the Secretary of State or to such other persons as may be prescribed.

General note—It is normal, where limited circumstances exist, for a court to appoint a special manager, namely if the company's business or affairs are too extensive, too remote or too specialised for the liquidator to be able to exercise personal control over their conduct or administration. For an example of an appointment, see *Re US Ltd* (1983) 1 BCC 98, 985.

The special manager is an officer of the court and under its control: *Re Walter L Jacob & Son Ltd* (1989) 5 BCC 244.

In its order the court is to set the duration of the appointment, which may be for a specific period of time or until the occurrence of a specified event, or alternatively the court may state that the appointment is to be subject to a further order of the court (r 4.206(3)).

See rr 4.206–4.210 for the details of practice and procedure.

Security—The appointment of a special manager does not take effect until the prescribed security has been given to the applicant for the appointment (r 4.207(1)). The security given is not to be less than the value of the assets as estimated by the liquidator in his or her report under r 4.206(1): see r 4.206(3).

Disclaimer (England and Wales only)

178 Power to disclaim onerous property

(1) This and the next two sections apply to a company that is being wound up in England and Wales.

(2) Subject as follows, the liquidator may, by the giving of the prescribed notice, disclaim any onerous property and may do so notwithstanding that he has taken possession of it, endeavoured to sell it, or otherwise exercised rights of ownership in relation to it.

(3) The following is onerous property for the purposes of this section—

(a) any unprofitable contract, and
(b) any other property of the company which is unsaleable or not readily saleable or is such that it may give rise to a liability to pay money or perform any other onerous act.

(4) A disclaimer under this section—

(a) operates so as to determine, as from the date of the disclaimer, the rights, interests and liabilities of the company in or in respect of the property disclaimed; but
(b) does not, except so far as is necessary for the purpose of releasing the company from any liability, affect the rights or liabilities of any other person.

(5) A notice of disclaimer shall not be given under this section in respect of any property if—

(a) a person interested in the property has applied in writing to the liquidator or one of his predecessors as liquidator requiring the liquidator or that predecessor to decide whether he will disclaim or not, and
(b) the period of 28 days beginning with the day on which that application was made, or such longer period as the court may allow, has expired without a notice of disclaimer having been given under this section in respect of that property.

(6) Any person sustaining loss or damage in consequence of the operation of a disclaimer under this section is deemed a creditor of the company to the extent of the loss or damage and accordingly may prove for the loss or damage in the winding up.

General note—This provision, which has caused many problems over the years, permits liquidators to disclaim certain forms of property that can be regarded as onerous. In many ways s 178 closely follows the pattern set by the law of bankruptcy (see s 315) from which it is directly imported. But in bankruptcy, as the bankrupt estate vests in the trustee, the trustee will be personally liable in respect of onerous property if disclaimer does not occur (*Titterton v Cooper* (1882) 9 QBD 473), while liquidators are not liable: *Stead Hazel & Co v Cooper* [1933] 1 KB 480.

The reason for permitting disclaimer is to allow the liquidator to obtain an early closure of the liquidation (*Re Park Air Services plc* [1999] 1 BCLC 155 at 162, HL). Without disclaimer, where a lease exists, for instance, the liquidator would have to retain sufficient sums to pay the rent on the leased premises as they fell due: *Re Park Air Services plc* at 163.

The power to disclaim is available to liquidators in both compulsory and voluntary liquidations. It is a power that exists to allow a liquidator to reduce company liabilities, and thereby boost dividends paid to creditors. The power can be exercised unilaterally by the liquidator now, which differs from the previous law where a liquidator had to secure the leave of the court before he or she was able to disclaim.

Although the power to disclaim is exercised in relation to insolvent companies for the most part, it is exercisable in the case of a solvent company as well (*Re Nottingham General Cemetery Co* [1955] Ch 683; *Re Park Air Services plc* [1999] 1 BCLC 155, HL), where it might hamper the winding up of the company.

The liquidator must disclaim the whole of the property and is not entitled to disclaim just part of it (*Re Fussell* (1882) 20 Ch D 341, CA).

A person who is affected by a proposed disclaimer is able to apply to the court under s 168(5) for a review of the liquidator's decision to disclaim: *Re Hans Place Ltd* [1992] BCC 737, [1992] BCLC 768. See the notes accompanying s 168 to see when a challenge under s 168(5) might be successful.

If a liquidator is unsure about disclaiming some property, he or she might seek directions from the court under s 112, for voluntary liquidations, and s 168(3) for compulsory liquidations.

'Property'—The word is defined widely in s 436 (*Bristol Airport plc v Powdrill* [1990] Ch 744 at 759, CA), but it is not an exhaustive definition. Leases are the kinds of property often the subject of the action of disclaimer.

A licence under the Sea Fish (Conservation) Act 1992 (*Re Rae* [1995] BCC 102) and a waste management licence (*Re Celtic Extraction Ltd; Re Blue Stone Chemicals Ltd* [1999] 2 BCLC 555, CA) have been held to constitute property within s 436 of the Act and constituted onerous property within s 178, as has an interest under a chattel lease: *Re Paramount Airways Ltd* [1990] BCC 130 at 148, and a water use licence under the Water Environment (Controlled Activities) (Scotland) Regulations 2011 (SSI 2011/209): *Joint Liquidators of the Scottish Coal Co Ltd, Petitioners* 2013 SLT 1055.

Where the property consisted of permits provided under legislation whether disclaimer was permitted would depend on the terms of the permits and the statutory provisions: *Joint Liquidators of the Scottish Coal Co Ltd, Petitioners* 2013 SLT 1055.

'Unprofitable contract'—A contract is unprofitable if the cost involved for the company in performing its obligations is greater than the benefit which the company will enjoy under the terms of the contract. A contract is not unprofitable if the amount of profit is small: *Re Bastable* [1901] 2 KB 518, CA, or is merely financially disadvantageous: *Squires v AIG Europe (UK) Ltd* [2006] EWCA Civ 7, [2006] BCC 233. And demonstrating that a better commercial bargain could be made by the liquidator compared with the bargain that was arranged originally (prior to liquidation) does not mean that the original contract was unprofitable: *Re Bastable* [1901] 2 KB 518; *Capital Prime Properties plc v Worthgate Ltd (in liquidation)* [2000] BCC 525; *Squires v AIG Europe (UK) Ltd*. But if a contract that had been entered into before liquidation would take a significant time to complete, then it might be regarded as unprofitable: *Dekala Pty Ltd (in liquidation) v Perth Land & Leisure Ltd* (1989) 17 NSWLR 664 (NSW S Ct) (contract would take eight months to be completed). The Court of Appeal appears to see that this is a critical issue in determining that a contract was unprofitable, as the need to perform future obligations would prejudice the liquidator's responsibility to realise the company's property and pay a dividend to creditors within a reasonable period of time: *Squires v AIG Europe (UK) Ltd*.

Contracts cannot be disclaimed where the effect of disclaimer would be to undo the contract in so far as it had been performed and in so far as interests had been created under it: *Capital Prime Properties plc v Worthgate Ltd (in liquidation)* [2000] BCC 525.

As a liquidator is able to disclaim despite having taken possession of property, attempting to sell it, or exercising an act of ownership in relation to it (s 178(2)), it is probably the case that the right to disclaim unprofitable contracts still exists even if the company or the liquidator has attempted to assign, or has exercised rights in relation to the contract or any property to which the contract relates.

Section 178 does not apply where there is a market contract (a contract defined in s 155(2) of the Companies Act 1989) or a contract effected by the exchange or clearing house for the purpose of realising property provided as margin in relation to market contracts (s 164(1) of the Companies Act 1989), so such contracts cannot be disclaimed as unprofitable.

'Unsaleable'—Given more recent case law, it is probable that a liquidator is not required to show that reasonable efforts were taken to sell the property; rather, he or she can rely on his or her subjective view that the property is not readily saleable, provided that the liquidator's view is not totally unreasonable to the point of being perverse: *Re Hans Place Ltd* [1992] BCC 737. Moreover, property can still be onerous even if one cannot establish unsaleability, such as property that requires expensive repairs before it can be sold (see s 178(3)(b)).

Not affecting the rights or liabilities of other persons—When disclaimer occurs, it is to do as little violence as possible to the rights and liabilities of others (*Capital Prime Properties plc v Worthgate Ltd (in liquidation)* [2000] BCC 525) and only 'to the extent necessary to achieve the primary object: the release of the company from all liability': *Hindcastle Ltd v Barbara Attenborough Associates Ltd* [1996] BCC 636 at 644, HL per Lord Nicholls.

Effect—The disclaimer of a lease (the kind of property often disclaimed) involves an extinguishing of the liability between landlord and tenant, with the consequence that the tenant's liability to pay rent ends, as does the landlord's right to receive it: *Re Park Air Services plc* [1999] 1 BCLC 155, HL. See the notes attached to s 181 for further discussion on the effects of disclaiming leases.

As in many cases, disclaimer releases the company from liability to others, with the persons who are affected by the disclaimer being given a right to prove as creditors of the company for the amount of the loss suffered together with, under s 181(2), a right to apply for a vesting order or order for delivery of the property disclaimed. In assessing damages for a landlord, where the company disclaimed a lease, the landlord should not be regarded as a secured creditor within the meaning of s 248 of the Act, and so the matter should be approached as a claim for damages for breach of contract and the appropriate principles applying in such a claim applied: *Re Park Air Services plc*. Also, the landlord's right of re-entry, which is lost on disclaimer, is not to be taken into account, and allowance should be made in favour of the company for the accelerated receipt of any sums which have not fallen due at the date of disclaimer: *Re Park Air Services plc*. Where a lease is disclaimed, the loss of the lessor will, in general terms, be the rents and other payments which will be payable pursuant to the lease for the balance of the lease period, and subtracted from that amount which the lessor will or is likely to receive by re-letting the premises, and in relation to each amount the court will build in a discount because the lessor has received the amount earlier than he or she would in the normal run of things: *Re Park Air Services plc*.

While the lessee of a lease who subleased the lease to a company that ends up in liquidation and disclaimed the lease, continued to be liable for the rent under the lease until the lease expired or is determined, because the lease continued to exist: *Hill v East & West India Dock Co* (1884) 9 App Cas 448; *Wanford Investments Ltd v Duckworth* [1979] Ch 127, [1978] 2 WLR 741; *WH Smith Ltd v Wyndram Investments Ltd* [1994] 2 BCLC 571, [1994] BCC 699, the enactment of the Landlord and Tenant (Covenants) Act 1995 means that this does not apply to leases entered into after 1 January 1996. But in the scenario just set out, if the original lessee guaranteed rent payments and other covenants by the company, after disclaimer the lessee would be liable under the guarantee for any breaches: *Shaw v Doleman* [2009] EWCA Civ 279, [2009] BCC 730, [2009] 2 BCLC 123, [2009] BPIR 945. According to *Shaw v Doleman* the Landlord and Tenant (Covenants) Act 1995 made no difference as far as the liability of a guarantor was concerned, and the *Hindcastle* ruling applies.So, a disclaimer by a tenant company in liquidation which took an assignment of a lease will free the assignor from liability, but not if the assignor were to have given a guarantee to the landlord concerning compliance with the terms of the covenants.

While the liabilities of a company pursuant to a lease are terminated when a liquidator disclaims an interest in the lease, this does not determine the covenants in the lease for all purposes: *Hindcastle Ltd v Barbara Attenborough Associates Ltd* [1997] AC 70, [1996] BCC 636, HL. So, if a person guaranteed the lease payments which were to be paid by the company whose liquidator has disclaimed the lease, he or she remains liable under the guarantee, because the legal rights of recourse to the guarantor could be determined without releasing the guarantor from his or her liability to the landlord (*Hindcastle Ltd*). The guarantor's liability survived the extinguishment of the guarantor's right of recourse (*Hindcastle Ltd*). The Court of Appeal applied similar reasoning in relation to a charge, which continued to exist after disclaimer of an agreement to sell the land over which the charge was held: *Groveholt Ltd v Hughes* [2005] EWCA Civ 897, [2005] BPIR 1345, [2005] 2 BCLC 421. It follows from the House of Lords' decision in *Hindcastle Ltd* that if the landlord of a disclaimed lease assigns the lease to another, the latter could enforce the obligations of any guarantors of the company's liability under the lease: *Scottish Widows plc v Tripipatkul* [2004] BCC 200. But, if no vesting order is made and the landlord re-takes possession, then the obligations of persons in the position of a guarantor terminate as far as future liability is concerned (*Hindcastle Ltd*). What a guarantor needs to do when a debtor company disclaims a lease is to reduce his or her liability by finding a new tenant for the premises: *Bhogal v Mohinder Singh Cheema* [1999] BPIR 13.

The approach taken in *Hindcastle Ltd v Barbara Attenborough Associates Ltd* has been applied in other areas. For instance, a liquidator who disclaimed a waste management licence was unable to claim any interest in a trust fund that had been established in relation to the licence: *Environment Agency v Hillridge Ltd* [2003] EWHC 3023 (Ch), [2004] BCLC 358. The fund was inextricably linked to the licence, and the company could not keep the interest in the fund and yet be freed from its liabilities under the licence.

The *Hindcastle* approach has been applied in Australia where the one disclaiming the lease is the landlord. Usually the company in liquidation wishes to disclaim a leasehold interest. If it wishes to disclaim a lease that it had granted as landlord, then according to the Australian case of *Re Wilmott Forests Ltd (in liq)* [2012] VCA 202 such disclaimer does extinguish the tenant's interest in the property. Effectively the Victorian Court of Appeal held that the principle in Hindcastle applies equally to the disclaimer of a lease by a landlord, as the disclaimer necessarily extinguishes the tenant's interest.

Unless a court makes a vesting order in relation to the interest of the company which is disclaimed, that interest vests in the Crown automatically as bona vacantia (*Re Mercer & Moore* (1880) 14 Ch D 287), while rights of the company under a contract do not vest in the Crown: they terminate.

If the freehold in land is disclaimed, then the land goes to the Crown on an escheat, unless a vesting order is made in favour of some other person, and the Crown does not have to do anything for this to occur: *Scmlla Properties Ltd v Gesso Properties (BVI) Ltd* [1995] BCC 793. A legal charge and the leases of tenants would survive a disclaimer (*Scmlla Properties Ltd*).

No room exists for any rights or liabilities to be preserved by s 178(4): *Hindcastle Ltd v Barbara Attenborough Associates Ltd* [1997] AC 70 at 90, [1996] BCC 636 at 645, HL.

Loss—It is necessary for the liquidator or (possibly) the court, following a disclaimer, to quantify the loss in money terms in the same way that is done where there is a breach of contract because one party to the contract has repudiated it and the other party has accepted the repudiation as ending the contract: *Re Park Air Services plc* [1999] 1 BCLC 155 at 158, HL. To determine what loss has been sustained the court must compare the pre-disclaimer position with the post-disclaimer position (*Re Park Air Services plc* at 159). The same approach that is adopted for calculating damages for a breach of contract is to be used in calculating compensation where there is a disclaimer, because a lessor is not a secured creditor within the meaning of the Act (*Re Park Air Services plc* at 162, 163–164).

Where a loss is suffered over a period in the future, the calculation has to allow for any advancement that has occurred or else the aggrieved party will be over-compensated (*Re Park Air Services plc* at 158). With disclaimers of leases, the right of the lessor to prove for loss is not a right to prove in relation to any debt due in the future, and r 11.13 does not apply (*Re Park Air Services plc* at 158–159). The lessor's compensation is for the loss of his or her right to future rent and not the rent itself, because he or she has no right to the latter anymore (*Re Park Air Services plc* at 161). The loss of a lessor is the 'aggregate of the differences between the contractual rent and the market rent over a period of the remainder of the lease discounted to allow for advancement' (*Re Park Air Services plc* at 159 per Lord Hobhouse). In calculating the loss of a lessor one has to take into account the sums he or she will be able to obtain from re-letting the premises, so that there should be a discount for early receipt by the lessor (*Re Park Air Services plc* at 161–162). In *Re Park Air Services plc* (at 166) the House of Lords held that the best evidence of the appropriate discount rate to be applied is the yield on gilt-edged securities for an equivalent term.

If a creditor is able to prove for loss as a result of a disclaimer, interest can be claimed from the time of the disclaimer (*Re Park Air Services plc*).

Procedure—See rr 4.187–194 and the notes relating to those rules.

See McCartney 'Disclaimer of leases and its impact: the "pecking order"' (2002) 18 IL & P 79; A Keay *McPherson's Law of Company Liquidation* (3rd edn, Sweet and Maxwell, 2013) at 583–599 for a detailed discussion.

179 Disclaimer of leaseholds

(1) The disclaimer under section 178 of any property of a leasehold nature does not take effect unless a copy of the disclaimer has been served (so far as the liquidator is aware of their addresses) on every person claiming under the company as underlessee or mortgagee and either—

(a) no application under section 181 below is made with respect to that property before the end of the period of 14 days beginning with the day on which the last notice served under this subsection was served; or

(b) where such an application has been made, the court directs that the disclaimer shall take effect.

(2) Where the court gives direction under subsection (1)(b) it may also, instead of or in addition to any order it makes under section 181, make such orders with respect to fixtures, tenant's improvements and other matters arising out of the lease as it thinks fit.

General note—Disclaimer of a lease creates in the lessor of the premises that are subject to lease a right to claim loss or damage which he or she has suffered as a result of the disclaimer, the right to rent having been lost (s 178(6)): *Re Park Air Services plc* [1999] 1 BCLC 155 at 157, 158, HL.

This provision requires liquidators to serve notice on those who might wish to apply for a vesting order pursuant to s 181, namely underlessees and mortgagees.

On disclaimer of a lease, any underlease is destroyed: *Re AE Realisations (1985) Ltd* [1988] 1 WLR 200, (1987) 3 BCC 136. Any underlessees have the right to remain in occupation, paying the rent and discharging the covenants required under the lease for the length of the underlease (*Re AE Realisations (1985) Ltd*).

A landlord is not obliged to mitigate his or her loss on the disclaimer of a lease: *Bhogal v Mohinder Singh Cheema* [1999] BPIR 13.

See the notes relating to s 178. Also, see McCartney 'Disclaimer of leases and its impact: the "pecking order"' (2002) 18 IL & P 79; A Keay *McPherson's Law of Company Liquidation* (3rd edn, Sweet and Maxwell, 2013) at 583–599.

180 Land subject to rentcharge

(1) The following applies where, in consequence of the disclaimer under section 178 of any land subject to a rentcharge, that land vests by operation of law in the Crown or any other person (referred to in the next subsection as 'the proprietor').

(2) The proprietor and the successors in title of the proprietor are not subject to any personal liability in respect of any sums becoming due under the rentcharge except sums becoming due after the proprietor, or some person claiming under or through the proprietor, has taken possession or control of the land or has entered into occupation of it.

General note—This provision serves to keep anyone, including the Crown, in whom land subject to a rentcharge vests by operation of law free from personal liability in respect of any sums becoming due under the rentcharge, except sums becoming due after possession or control of the land or the entering into of occupation following the making of the vesting order.

181 Powers of court (general)

(1) This section and the next apply where the liquidator has disclaimed property under section 178.

(2) An application under this section may be made to the court by—

    (a)   any person who claims an interest in the disclaimed property, or

    (b)   any person who is under any liability in respect of the disclaimed property, not being a liability discharged by the disclaimer.

(3) Subject as follows, the court may on the application make an order, on such terms as it thinks fit, for the vesting of the disclaimed property in, or for its delivery to—

    (a)   a person entitled to it or a trustee for such a person, or

    (b)   a person subject to such a liability as is mentioned in subsection (2)(b) or a trustee for such a person.

(4) The court shall not make an order under subsection (3)(b) except where it appears to the court that it would be just to do so for the purpose of compensating the person subject to the liability in respect of the disclaimer.

(5) The effect of any order under this section shall be taken into account in assessing for the purpose of section 178(6) the extent of any loss or damage sustained by any person in consequence of the disclaimer.

(6) An order under this section vesting property in any person need not be completed by conveyance, assignment or transfer.

General note—This provision empowers a court to order the vesting of property (disclaimed under s 178) in, or delivered to, a person entitled to it or a person subject to a liability because of the disclaimed property. See r 4.194 for the procedure that applies.

Applications—Applications can be made by a person who claims an interest in the disclaimed property, or a person who is under any liability in respect of the disclaimed property (not including a liability discharged by the disclaimer).—This does not include anyone who cannot demonstrate some form of proprietary interest in the disclaimed property and in relation to which a vesting order was sought: *Lloyds Bank SF Nominees v Aladdin Ltd* [1996] 1 BCLC 720 at 721, CA (a person was in occupation of premises and he had agreed to take an assignment provided that the consent of the landlord was secured, and in this case the occupier did not have a proprietary interest); *Re Ballast plc* [2006] EWHC 3189 (Ch), [2007] BCC 620, *sub nom St Paul Travelers Insurance Company Ltd v Dargan and Edwards* [2007] BPIR 117 at [42], [109]. Any right granted to an insurer by way of subrogation did not constitute a proprietary interest in any cause of action which the company (the assured) might have against another party (although it might have an interest in the proceedings of the action) until the action is assigned: *Re Ballast plc* at [41], [100]. For a critical discussion of *Re Ballast plc*, see L Ho, 'Of proprietary restitution, insurers' subrogation and insolvency set-off – the untenable case of *Re Ballast*' (2007) 23 I L & P 103.

A landlord is only able to become entitled to possession of property once all of the interests of all other relevant parties who had, or could obtain, an interest in the property had been cleared away by invoking the mechanism provided in s 182: *Re ITM Corp Ltd (in liquidation)* [1997] 2 BCLC 389, [1997] BCC 554.

It was held in *Re Spirit Motorsport Ltd (in liquidation)* [1996] 1 BCLC 684, [1997] BPIR 288 that the directors of a company that was in liquidation were not able to make an application as persons who were under a liability in respect of disclaimed property of their company, where the property had been disclaimed by the Crown after it had received it as bona vacantia. The directors had guaranteed the debts of the company, but this was not sufficient, as the liability was not in respect of disclaimed property.

The guarantor of the obligations that exist under a lease that has been disclaimed, as well as a lessee who assigned the lease, come within s 181(2)(b) as persons who are under a liability in respect of disclaimed property and who could apply for a vesting order, enabling them to rent out or use the premises that are the subject of the lease.

'Under a liability'—While at common law a lessee who assigns the lease is liable for the payments pursuant to the lease as well as fulfilling the covenants under the lease if the assignee disclaims the sublease (*Hindcastle Ltd v Barbara Attenborough Associates Ltd* [1997] AC 70, [1996] BCC 636, HL), if a lease was entered into after 1 January 1996 and the assignee disclaims, then the original lessee will not be liable for future rent and meeting the covenants of the assignee as he or she is automatically discharged from such liability on assignment of the lease (Landlord and Tenant (Covenants) Act 1995, ss 1(1), (3), 5(1), (2) and 31(1)).

Vesting orders—In making a vesting order under s 181 the court has a wide discretion and it is wide enough to permit a court to order that the surplus proceeds of the sale of a lease, in which no one had an interest, be given back to the liquidator: *Lee v Lee* [1999] BPIR 926, [2000] BCC 500, CA.

The power of a court to make a vesting order is restricted somewhat by s 182(1), and by the fact that it must be just made for the purpose of compensating the person who is liable following the disclaimer (s 181(4)).

182 Powers of court (leaseholds)

(1) The court shall not make an order under section 181 vesting property of a leasehold nature in any person claiming under the company as underlessee or mortgagee except on terms making that person—

    (a) subject to the same liabilities and obligations as the company was subject to under the lease at the commencement of the winding up, or

    (b) if the court thinks fit, subject to the same liabilities and obligations as that person would be subject to if the lease had been assigned to him at the commencement of the winding up.

(2) For the purposes of an order under section 181 relating to only part of any property comprised in a lease, the requirements of subsection (1) apply as if the lease comprised only the property to which the order relates.

(3) Where subsection (1) applies and no person claiming under the company as underlessee or mortgagee is willing to accept an order under section 181 on the terms required by virtue of that subsection, the court may, by order under that section, vest the company's estate or interest in the property in any person who is liable (whether personally or in a representative capacity, and whether alone or jointly with the company) to perform the lessee's covenants in the lease.

The court may vest that estate and interest in such a person freed and discharged from all estates, incumbrances and interests created by the company.

(4) Where subsection (1) applies and a person claiming under the company as underlessee or mortgagee declines to accept an order under section 181, that person is excluded from all interest in the property.

General note—It has been held that s 182(4) does not apply where an application is made by statutory tenants, because the provision is limited to cases where the applicant has a proprietary interest in the land: *Re Vedmay Ltd* [1994] 1 BCLC 676.

Given what Sir William Blackburne said in *Hunt v Conwy CBC* [2013] EWHC 1154 (Ch), [2013] BPIR 790 at [48] in relation to s 320, it might be argued that a vesting of part of the property, if it is possible practically, can be valid.

See the notes accompanying s 181.

Execution, attachment and the Scottish equivalents

183 Effect of execution or attachment (England and Wales)

(1) Where a creditor has issued execution against the goods or land of a company or has attached any debt due to it, and the company is subsequently wound up, he is not entitled to retain the benefit of the execution or attachment against the liquidator unless he has completed the execution or attachment before the commencement of the winding up.

(2) However—

    (a) if a creditor has had notice of a meeting having been called at which a resolution for voluntary winding up is to be proposed, the date on which he had notice is substituted, for the purpose of subsection (1), for the date of commencement of the winding up;

    (b) a person who purchases in good faith under a sale by the enforcement officer or other officer charged with the execution of the writ any goods of a company on which execution has been levied in all cases acquires a good title to them against the liquidator; and

    (c) the rights conferred by subsection (1) on the liquidator may be set aside by the court in favour of the creditor to such extent and subject to such terms as the court thinks fit.

(3) For purposes of this Act—

    (a) an execution against goods is completed by seizure and sale, or by the making of a charging order under section 1 of the Charging Orders Act 1979;

    (b) an attachment of a debt is completed by receipt of the debt; and

    (c) an execution against land is completed by seizure, by the appointment of a receiver, or by the making of a charging order under section 1 of the Act above-mentioned.

(4) In this section, 'goods' includes all chattels personal; and 'enforcement officer' means an individual who is authorised to act as an enforcement officer under the Courts Act 2003.

(5) This section does not apply in the case of a winding up in Scotland.

Amendments—Courts Act 2003, s 109(1), Sch 8, para 295.

General note—The thrust of the provision is that if a creditor has not completed an execution or attachment by the time winding up commences, the creditor is not entitled to retain the benefit of the execution or attachment process. The avoiding effect of the section is enhanced by s 183(2)(a), which provides that if the creditor is to be able to retain the benefit of execution, he or she must have effected completion before the creditor had notice of a meeting called to consider resolving to put the relevant company into liquidation.

The court has no jurisdiction under the section to make an order in relation to a creditor who has engaged in execution in a foreign jurisdiction, as the section has no extra-territorial effect: *Mitchell v Carter* [1997] 1 BCLC 673, [1997] BCC 907.

'Execution' and 'attachment'—The levying of distress is not within the meaning of execution or attachment for the purposes of this section (*Re Herbert Barry Associates Ltd v IRC* [1977] 1 WLR 1437, [1978] 1 All ER 161, HL; *Re Modern Jet Support Centre Ltd* [2005] EWHC 1611 (Ch), [2005] BPIR 1382, [2006] BCC 174), so if the process of distress has commenced before the date of the commencement of winding up it should be allowed to continue unless there are special circumstances, such as fraud or unfair dealing, justifying a stay, the reason being that the distress was not put in force after commencement: *Re G Winterbottom (Leeds) Ltd* [1937] 2 All ER 232; *Re Bellaglade Ltd* [1977] 1 All ER 319 at 321. Liquidation would not constitute 'special circumstances' and justify the distress being halted (*Re Bellaglade Ltd* at 321). See comments relating to s 128.

Ordinarily the word 'execution' was used to describe a process of enforcement of a judgment inter partes. However, the word could take on a broader meaning if the context clearly demanded, such as involving extra-judicial process for the recovery of a debt: *Re Modern Jet Support Centre Ltd* [2005] EWHC 1611 (Ch), [2005] BPIR 1382, [2006] BCC 174 at [17], [21].

Section 183(1)

'Benefit'—It has been said that 'benefit' in this context means the benefit which the charge provides for the creditor as a consequence of the execution and does not mean the money received under the charge: *Re Andrew* [1937] Ch 122, CA.

The benefit of the attachment means 'the right to take the necessary steps to complete the attachment' (*Re Caribbean Products (Yam Importers Ltd)* [1966] Ch 331, CA), and so a creditor who obtained payment of a garnisheed debt after receipt of notice of the meeting called to consider a resolution to wind up was bound to account to the liquidator for the payment received (*Re Caribbean Products (Yam Importers Ltd)*).

'Completed'—In terms of execution there is a completion when there is a sale of the goods seized (*Re Standard Manufacturing Co* [1891] 1 Ch 627) or, if the execution is by the making of a charging order, completion occurs when the order is made absolute (*Clarke v Coutts & Co* [2002] BPIR 916 at 924, CA (reversing [2002] BPIR 762)), and an order will not be made absolute after the debtor company has entered liquidation (*Roberts Petroleum Ltd v Bernard Kelly Ltd* [1983] 2 AC 192 at 208). With attachments, there is completion when the debt is received (s 183(3)(b)): see *Re Walkden Sheet Metal Co Ltd* [1960] Ch 170. The point of completion where land is involved is explained by s 183(3)(c).

Section 183(3)(a)

'Charging order'—A charging order nisi imposes an immediate charge, but it is defeasible until being made absolute, and the intervention of liquidation before the making of the order absolute would mean that the property charged falls into the assets subject to the liquidation: *Roberts Petroleum Ltd v Bernard Kelly Ltd* [1983] 2 AC 192 at 209. In *JGD Construction Ltd v Aaron Mills* [2013] EWHC 572, [2013] BPIR 811 it was said that it would be vey unlikely that an interim charging order would be made final where there was compelling evidence of an imminent insolvency process or of actual insolvency. The case also held that while there was not rule that no charging order could be finalized when there was a formal insolvency regime in existence, the predominant view in the cases was that the finalization of the order would be precluded.

Court discretion—Paragraph (2)(c) gives the court the right to take no account of the liquidator's entitlement under subsection (1) if it thinks fit. The discretion in this respect is wide (*Re Grosvenor Metals Co* [1950] Ch 63 at 64), and allows the court to do what is right and fair according to the circumstances of the case: *Re Suidair International Airways Ltd* [1951] Ch 165. If, because of some deception perpetrated by the company, a creditor is induced not to proceed to execution, the creditor will be permitted by the court to retain the benefit of the execution against the liquidator (*Re Suidair International Airways Ltd*). The rights of a liquidator have been set aside where a creditor's attempts to levy execution were frustrated when the company improperly obtained leave to defend an action on a debt in respect of which it had previously admitted liability (*Re Suidair International Airways Ltd*). The same result has also occurred even where the company has not acted improperly, but persuaded a creditor to delay execution in consequence of requests and representations by the company (*Re Grosvenor Metal Co*). However, where the company has not acted fraudulently, substantial reasons must exist before the court will exercise its discretion and permit a creditor to retain the benefit of an uncompleted execution: *Re Caribbean Products (Yam Importers) Ltd* [1966] Ch 331 at 348, 354. The courts have said that they are careful to ensure that the pari passu principle is not compromised by allowing one or two creditors to benefit through execution when the rest of the creditors receive nothing.

184 Duties of officers charged with execution of writs and other processes (England and Wales)

(1) The following applies where a company's goods are taken in execution and, before their sale or the completion of the execution (by the receipt or recovery of the full amount of the levy), notice is served on the enforcement officer, or other officer, charged with execution of the writ or other process, that a provisional liquidator has been appointed or that a winding-up order has been made, or that a resolution for voluntary winding up has been passed.

(2) The enforcement officer or other officer shall, on being so required, deliver the goods and any money seized or received in part satisfaction of the execution to the liquidator; but the costs of execution are a first charge on the goods or money so delivered, and the liquidator may sell the goods, or a sufficient part of them, for the purpose of satisfying the charge.

(3) If under an execution in respect of a judgment for a sum exceeding £500 a company's goods are sold or money is paid in order to avoid sale, the enforcement officer or other officer shall deduct the costs of the execution from the proceeds of sale or the money paid and retain the balance for 14 days.

(4) If within that time notice is served on the enforcement officer or other officer of a petition for the winding up of the company having been presented, or of a meeting having been called at which there is to be proposed a resolution for voluntary winding up, and an order is made or a resolution passed (as the case may be), the enforcement officer or other officer shall pay the balance to the liquidator, who is entitled to retain it as against the execution creditor.

(5) The rights conferred by this section on the liquidator may be set aside by the court in favour of the creditor to such extent and subject to such terms as the court thinks fit.

(6) In this section, 'goods' includes all chattels personal; and 'enforcement officer' means an individual who is authorised to act as an enforcement officer under the Courts Act 2003.

(7) The money sum for the time being specified in subsection (3) is subject to increase or reduction by order under section 416 in Part XV.

(8) This section does not apply in the case of a winding up in Scotland.

Amendments—SI 1986/1996; Courts Act 2003, s 109(1), Sch 8, para 296.

General note—The section follows along the same lines as some of the matters mentioned in s 183, except that it is focused on the sheriff (defined in s 184(6)) and the work done in the process of execution.

'Completion'—See the notes under 'Completed' in s 183.

'Notice'—Apparently, notice can be served on any interested party. The notice is to be in writing and delivered by hand or sent by recorded delivery (r 12.19(2)). Notice to the sheriff's officer is not, alone, sufficient to invoke the section: *Hellyer v Sheriff of Yorkshire* [1975] Ch 16.

'Execution in respect of judgments exceeding £500'—If the company pays the sheriff a sum, in order to avoid the sale of its assets, the money is not characterised as satisfaction of the execution: *Re Walkden Sheet Metal Co Ltd* [1960] Ch 170 at 177. The sheriff is bound to retain the money, less the costs of execution, for 14 days (the time runs from the time of payment – *Re Walkden Sheet Metal Co Ltd* at 178), but if no notice within s 184(4) is served in the 14 days, then the sheriff is at liberty to pay the money to the execution creditor.

The costs that the sheriff is to deduct from the proceeds of the sale or money paid does not include the creditor's costs of issuing and serving the execution process, but only costs which the sheriff has incurred: *Re Wood (Bristol) Ltd* [1931] 2 Ch 321.

Court discretion—As with s 183, the court has a wide discretion to override the rights of a liquidator. See the comments under 'Court discretion' in the notes accompanying s 183.

185 Effect of diligence (Scotland)

(1) In the winding up of a company registered in Scotland, the following provisions of the Bankruptcy (Scotland) Act 1985—

  (a) subsections (1) to (6) of section 37 (effect of sequestration on diligence); and
  (b) subsections (3), (4), (7) and (8) of section 39 (realisation of estate),

apply, so far as consistent with this Act, in like manner as they apply in the sequestration of a debtor's estate, with the substitutions specified below and with any other necessary modifications.

(2) The substitutions to be made in those sections of the Act of 1985 are as follows—

  (a) for references to the debtor, substitute references to the company;
  (b) for references to the sequestration, substitute references to the winding up;
  (c) for references to the date of sequestration, substitute references to the commencement of the winding up of the company; and
  (d) for references to the trustee, substitute references to the liquidator.

(3) In this section, 'the commencement of the winding up of the company' means, where it is being wound up by the court, the day on which the winding-up order is made.

(4) This section, so far as relating to any estate or effects of the company situated in Scotland, applies in the case of a company registered in England and Wales as in the case of one registered in Scotland.

Amendments—Bankruptcy and Diligence etc (Scotland) Act 2007, s 226(2), Sch 6, Pt 1.

Miscellaneous matters

186 Rescission of contracts by the court

(1) The court may, on the application of a person who is, as against the liquidator, entitled to the benefit or subject to the burden of a contract made with the company, make an order rescinding the contract on such terms as to payment by or to either party of damages for the non-performance of the contract, or otherwise as the court thinks just.

(2) Any damages payable under the order to such a person may be proved by him as a debt in the winding up.

General note—This provision enables an executory contract to be rescinded by court order when liquidation has occurred.

This provision does not apply where there is a market contract (a contract defined in s 155(2) of the Companies Act 1989) or a contract effected by the exchange or clearing house for the purpose of realising property provided as margin in relation to market contracts (s 164(1) of CA 1989).

187 Power to make over assets to employees

(1) On the winding up of a company (whether by the court or voluntarily), the liquidator may, subject to the following provisions of this section, make any payment which the company has, before the commencement of the winding up, decided to make under section 247 of the Companies Act 2006 (power to provide for employees or former employees on cessation or transfer of business).

(2) The liquidator may, after the winding up has commenced, make any such provision as is mentioned in section 247(1) If—

    (a)   the company's liabilities have been fully satisfied and provision has been made for the expenses of the winding up,

    (b)   the exercise of the power has been sanctioned by a resolution of the company, and

    (c)   any requirements of the company's articles as to the exercise of the power conferred by section 247 (1) are complied with.

(3) Any payment which may be made by a company under this section (that is, a payment after the commencement of its winding up) may be made out of the company's assets which are available to the members on the winding up.

(4) On a winding up by the court, the exercise by the liquidator of his powers under this section is subject to the court's control, and any creditor or contributory may apply to the court with respect to any exercise of the power.

(5) Subsections (1) and (2) above have effect notwithstanding anything in any rule of law or in section 107 of this Act (property of company after satisfaction of liabilities to be distributed among members).

Amendments—SI 2007/2194; SI 2009/1941.

General note—The provision refers to s 247 of the Companies Act 2006 expressly empowers a company by resolution to make provision for employees or former employees in relation to the cessation or transfer of the company's business, and this can be done even if it is not in the best interests of the company. Payments may only be made from profits available for dividend pay-outs. Section 247 effectively overruled the decision in *Parke v Daily News Ltd* [1962] Ch 927, which provided that ex gratia payments to employees were ultra vires. Section 187 complements the Companies Act in that the liquidator of a company that, prior to the commencement of winding up, resolved to make payments falling within s 247, is entitled to make those payments. But such payments can only be made from funds that would be available for the members, and this can only occur after the company's liabilities have been satisfied in full and provision has been made for the expenses relating to the winding up. Thus, payments can only be made in relation to solvent companies.

A contributory can apply to the court in relation to the exercise of the power permitted under this section, where the company is being compulsorily wound up. On what basis a contributory might succeed in having the exercise of the power halted or change the way in which the power is used is not easy to ascertain. This is especially so given the fact that s 247(2) provides that the power does not have to be exercised in accordance with s 172 of the Companies Act 2006 (duty to promote the success of the company). Perhaps, though, a claim that the power is not being used for its proper purposes, or the majority in exercising the power was acting oppressively as far as the minority is concerned, might succeed.

188 Notification that company is in liquidation

(1) When a company is being wound up, whether by the court or voluntarily—

(a) every invoice, order for goods or services, business letter or order form (whether in hard copy, electronic or any other form)issued by or on behalf of the company, or a liquidator of the company, or a receiver or manager of the company's property, and

(b) all the company's websites,

must contain a statement that the company is being wound up.

(2) If default is made in complying with this section, the company and any of the following persons who knowingly and wilfully authorises or permits the default, namely, any officer of the company, any liquidator of the company and any receiver or manager, is liable to a fine.

Amendments—SI 2006/3429; SI 2008/1897.

189 Interest on debts

(1) In a winding up interest is payable in accordance with this section on any debt proved in the winding up, including so much of any such debt as represents interest on the remainder.

(2) Any surplus remaining after the payment of the debts proved in a winding up shall, before being applied for any other purpose, be applied in paying interest on those debts in respect of the periods during which they have been outstanding since the company went into liquidation.

(3) All interest under this section ranks equally, whether or not the debts on which it is payable rank equally.

(4) The rate of interest payable under this section in respect of any debt ('the official rate' for the purposes of any provision of this Act in which that expression is used) is whichever is the greater of—

    (a)   the rate specified in section 17 of the Judgments Act 1838 on the day on which the company went into liquidation, and

    (b)   the rate applicable to that debt apart from the winding up.

(5) In the application of this section to Scotland—

    (a)   references to a debt proved in a winding up have effect as references to a claim accepted in a winding up, and

    (b)   the reference to section 17 of the Judgments Act 1838 has effect as a reference to the rules.

General note—Where a debt has accrued interest before the company went into liquidation, it may be proved in winding up, but interest that falls due after the company went into liquidation is not able to be claimed (r 4.93(1)), certainly as far as insolvent companies are generally concerned. But s 189(2) provides that where there is a surplus remaining after the payment of all debts that have been proved, the first call on the surplus is for the payment of interest on those debts in relation to the period following winding up.

As interest payable out of the surplus in a liquidation ranks equally and does not depend on the debts being ranked equally, interest on preferential debts is paid equally with interest on the ordinary unsecured creditors' debts.

Debts known as deferred debts are only provable once all other creditors' claims, together with interest under s 189(2), have been paid (r 12.3(2A)).

See r 4.93.

190 Documents exempt from stamp duty

(1) In the case of a winding up by the court, or of a creditors' voluntary winding up, the following has effect as regards exemption from duties chargeable under the enactments relating to stamp duties.

(2) If the company is registered in England and Wales, the following documents are exempt from stamp duty—

    (a)   every assurance relating solely to freehold or leasehold property, or to any estate, right or interest in, any real or personal property, which forms part of the company's assets and which, after the execution of the assurance, either at law or in equity, is or remains part of those assets, and

    (b)   every writ, order, certificate, or other instrument or writing relating solely to the property of any company which is being wound up as mentioned in subsection (1), or to any proceeding under such a winding up.

'Assurance' here includes deed, conveyance, assignment and surrender.

(3) If the company is registered in Scotland, the following documents are exempt from stamp duty—

    (a)   every conveyance relating solely to property which forms part of the company's assets and which, after the execution of the conveyance, is or remains the company's property for the benefit of its creditors,

(b) any articles of roup or sale, submission and every other instrument and writing whatsoever relating solely to the company's property, and

(c) every deed or writing forming part of the proceedings in the winding up.

'Conveyance' here includes assignation, instrument, discharge, writing and deed.

191 Company's books to be evidence

Where a company is being wound up, all books and papers of the company and of the liquidators are, as between the contributories of the company, prima facie evidence of the truth of all matters purporting to be recorded in them.

192 Information as to pending liquidations

(1) If the winding up of a company is not concluded within one year after its commencement, the liquidator shall, at such intervals as may be prescribed, until the winding up is concluded, send to the registrar of companies a statement in the prescribed form and containing the prescribed particulars with respect to the proceedings in, and position of, the liquidation.

(2) If a liquidator fails to comply with this section, he is liable to a fine and, for continued contravention, to a daily default fine.

General note—If the liquidator fails to comply with the section, an order may be sought from the court by a creditor, contributory or registrar of companies, and under s 170, to force the liquidator to comply. Further failure to comply will constitute a contempt of court and may lead to imprisonment: e g *Re S & A Conversions Ltd* (1988) 4 BCC 384; *Re Allan Ellis (Transport & Packing) Services Ltd* (1989) 5 BCC 835.

'Such intervals'—Rule 4.223, which only applies to creditors' voluntary liquidations, provides that after the end of the first year of the liquidation (from the time of commencement), a statement should be made every 6 months.

193 Unclaimed dividends (Scotland)

(1) The following applies where a company registered in Scotland has been wound up, and is about to be dissolved.

(2) The liquidator shall lodge in an appropriate bank or institution as defined in section 73(1) of the Bankruptcy (Scotland) Act 1985 (not being a bank or institution in or of which the liquidator is acting partner, manager, agent or cashier) in the name of the Accountant of Court the whole unclaimed dividends and unapplied or undistributable balances, and the deposit receipts shall be transmitted to the Accountant of Court.

(3) The provisions of section 58 of the Bankruptcy (Scotland) Act 1985 (so far as consistent with this Act and the Companies Acts) apply with any necessary modifications to sums lodged in a bank or institution under this section as they apply to sums deposited under section 57 of the Act first mentioned.

Amendments—SI 2009/1941.

194 Resolutions passed at adjourned meetings

Where a resolution is passed at an adjourned meeting of a company's creditors or contributories, the resolution is treated for all purposes as having been passed on the date on which it was in fact passed, and not as having been passed on any earlier date.

195 Meetings to ascertain wishes of creditors or contributories

(1) The court may—

(a) as to all matters relating to the winding up of a company, have regard to the wishes of the creditors or contributories (as proved to it by any sufficient evidence), and

(b) if it thinks fit, for the purpose of ascertaining those wishes, direct meetings of the creditors or contributories to be called, held and conducted in such manner as the court directs, and appoint a person to act as chairman of any such meeting and report the result of it to the court.

(2) In the case of creditors, regard shall be had to the value of each creditor's debt.

(3) In the case of contributories, regard shall be had to the number of votes conferred on each contributory.

Amendments—SI 2009/1941.

General note—As the creditors, and possibly the contributories, are the persons primarily interested in a winding up, it seems appropriate that the court has the right to ascertain the wishes of these groups in certain circumstances: see e g *Wilson v PLT Pipetech Pty Ltd* (1989) 7 ACLC 191.

There might well be occasions where convening meetings of creditors and contributories is impracticable: *Re Bank of Credit and Commerce International SA (No 2)* [1992] BCC 715, [1993] BCLC 1490. Where the views are sought, then they should normally be accepted, save in exceptional circumstances (*Re Bank of Credit and Commerce International SA (No 2)*).

Meetings under this section have generally been ordered in the context of whether or not there should be a winding up (*Re Western of Canada Oil Co* (1873) 17 Eq 1; *Re Chapel House Colliery Co* (1883) 24 Ch D 259), whether it is to be compulsory or voluntary and, if voluntary (*Re City & County Bank* (1875) 10 Ch App 470), who is to be the liquidator (*Re Manmac Farmers Ltd* [1968] 1 WLR 572). So that when a winding-up petition is before the court (see *Re Western of Canada Oil Co* and *Re Chapel House Colliery Co*), the views of a meeting of creditors provide the courts with an additional source of discretionary power to refuse a winding-up order (*Re Western of Canada Oil Co* and *Re Chapel House Colliery Co*). See the notes under 'Creditor opposition to the petition' and accompanying s 125.

Where no order of winding up has been made, the court does not have power to order that a meeting be held until the court has been satisfied that a ground for winding up does in fact exist: *Re Joint Stock Coal* (1869) 8 Eq 146; *Re Langham Skating Rink* (1877) 5 Ch D 669.

The court is not bound to accede to the wishes of any meetings that are called: *Re Land Development Association* [1892] WN 23.

'The value of each creditors' debt'—This has been held to refer to the amount of the debt and not what it may ultimately prove to be worth in a liquidation: *Re Manakau Timber Co* (1895) 13 NZLR 319.

196 Judicial notice of court documents

In all proceedings under this Part, all courts, judges and persons judicially acting, and all officers, judicial or ministerial, of any court, or employed in enforcing the process of any court shall take judicial notice—

(a)   of the signature of any officer of the High Court or of a county court in England and Wales, or of the Court of Session or a sheriff court in Scotland, or of the High Court in Northern Ireland, and also

(b)   of the official seal or stamp of the several offices of the High Court in England and Wales or Northern Ireland, or of the Court of Session, appended to or impressed on any document made, issued or signed under the provisions of this Act or the Companies Acts, or any official copy of such a document.

Amendments—SI 2009/1941.

197 Commission for receiving evidence

(1) When a company is wound up in England and Wales or in Scotland, the court may refer the whole or any part of the examination of witnesses—

(a)   to a specified county court in England and Wales, or

(b)   to the sheriff principal for a specified sheriffdom in Scotland, or

(c)   to the High Court in Northern Ireland or a specified Northern Ireland County Court,

('specified' meaning specified in the order of the winding-up court).

(2) Any person exercising jurisdiction as a judge of the court to which the reference is made (or, in Scotland, the sheriff principal to whom it is made) shall then, by virtue of this section, be a commissioner for the purpose of taking the evidence of those witnesses.

(3) The judge or sheriff principal has in the matter referred the same power of summoning and examining witnesses, of requiring the production and delivery of documents, of punishing defaults by witnesses, and of allowing costs and expenses to witnesses, as the court which made the winding-up order.

These powers are in addition to any which the judge or sheriff principal might lawfully exercise apart from this section.

(4) The examination so taken shall be returned or reported to the court which made the order in such manner as that court requests.

(5) This section extends to Northern Ireland.

198 Court order for examination of persons in Scotland

(1) The court may direct the examination in Scotland of any person for the time being in Scotland (whether a contributory of the company or not), in regard to the trade, dealings, affairs or property of any company in course

of being wound up, or of any person being a contributory of the company, so far as the company may be interested by reason of his being a contributory.

(2) The order or commission to take the examination shall be directed to the sheriff principal of the sheriffdom in which the person to be examined is residing or happens to be for the time; and the sheriff principal shall summon the person to appear before him at a time and place to be specified in the summons for examination on oath as a witness or as a haver, and to produce any books or papers called for which are in his possession or power.

(3) The sheriff principal may take the examination either orally or on written interrogatories, and shall report the same in writing in the usual form to the court, and shall transmit with the report the books and papers produced, if the originals are required and specified by the order or commission, or otherwise copies or extracts authenticated by the sheriff.

(4) If a person so summoned fails to appear at the time and place specified, or refuses to be examined or to make the production required, the sheriff principal shall proceed against him as a witness or haver duly cited; and failing to appear or refusing to give evidence or make production may be proceeded against by the law of Scotland.

(5) The sheriff principal is entitled to such fees, and the witness is entitled to such allowances, as sheriffs principal when acting as commissioners under appointment from the Court of Session and as witnesses and havers are entitled to in the like cases according to the law and practice of Scotland.

(6) If any objection is stated to the sheriff principal by the witness, either on the ground of his incompetency as a witness, or as to the production required, or on any other ground, the sheriff principal may, if he thinks fit, report the objection to the court, and suspend the examination of the witness until it has been disposed of by the court.

199 Costs of application for leave to proceed (Scottish companies)

Where a petition or application for leave to proceed with an action or proceeding against a company which is being wound up in Scotland is unopposed and is granted by the court, the costs of the petition or application shall, unless the court otherwise directs, be added to the amount of the petitioner's or applicant's claim against the company.

200 Affidavits etc in United Kingdom and overseas

(1) An affidavit required to be sworn under or for the purposes of this Part may be sworn in the United Kingdom, or elsewhere in Her Majesty's dominions, before any court, judge or person lawfully authorised to take and receive affidavits, or before any of Her Majesty's consuls or vice-consuls in any place outside Her dominions.

(2) All courts, judges, justices, commissioners and persons acting judicially shall take judicial notice of the seal or stamp or signature (as the case may

be) of any such court, judge, person, consul or vice-consul attached, appended or subscribed to any such affidavit, or to any other document to be used for the purposes of this Part.

Chapter IX

Dissolution of Companies After Winding Up

201 Dissolution (voluntary winding up)

(1) This section applies, in the case of a company wound up voluntarily, where the liquidator has sent to the registrar of companies his final account and return under section 94 (members' voluntary) or section 106 (creditors' voluntary).

(2) The registrar on receiving the account and return shall forthwith register them; and on the expiration of 3 months from the registration of the return the company is deemed to be dissolved.

(3) However, the court may, on the application of the liquidator or any other person who appears to the court to be interested, make an order deferring the date at which the dissolution of the company is to take effect for such time as the court thinks fit.

(4) It is the duty of the person on whose application an order of the court under this section is made within 7 days after the making of the order to deliver to the registrar a copy of the order for registration; and if that person fails to do so he is liable to a fine and, for continued contravention, to a daily default fine.

Amendments—SI 2006/3429.

General note—This provision and ss 202–205 address dissolution. Dissolution involves the death of the company, which constitutes the termination of its existence as a legal entity (*Re Working Project Ltd* [1995] BCC 197, [1995] 1 BCLC 226), although in certain circumstances the company's registration might be reinstated (see ss 1024 and 1029 of the Companies Act 2006). The process of dissolution brings winding up to an end (*Re Working Project Ltd*).

Under this section a company, in voluntary liquidation, is dissolved automatically once the conditions provided for here are complied with.

As a company's affairs are able to be regarded as fully wound up in situations where there is property still retained by the liquidator, but where all that can be done has been done, it follows that once the account required by s 106 has been returned to the registrar of companies the company would be dissolved automatically: *Re Wilmott Trading Ltd (in liquidation) (No 1 and 2)*, sub nom *Henry v Environmental Agency (No 2)* [1999] 2 BCLC 541, [1999] BPIR 1021, [2000] BCC 321 (the continued holding of a waste management licence).

Expiration of 3 months—This is designed to provide time for any matters that need resolving to come to light, such as the finding of other assets, and any disagreement between the creditors and the liquidator concerning whether the latter's work is complete: *Re Working Project Ltd* [1995] BCC 197 at 201, [1995] 1 BCLC 226 at 231.

202 Early dissolution (England and Wales)

(1) This section applies where an order for the winding up of a company has been made by the court in England and Wales.

(2) The official receiver, if—

    (a)   he is the liquidator of the company, and

    (b)   it appears to him—

        (i)   that the realisable assets of the company are insufficient to cover the expenses of the winding up, and

        (ii) that the affairs of the company do not require any other investigation,

may at any time apply to the registrar of companies for the early dissolution of the company.

(3) Before making that application, the official receiver shall give not less than 28 days' notice of his intention to do so to the company's creditors and contributories and, if there is an administrative receiver of the company, to that receiver.

(4) With the giving of that notice the official receiver ceases (subject to any directions under the next section) to be required to perform any duties imposed on him in relation to the company, its creditors or contributories by virtue of any provision of this Act, apart from a duty to make an application under subsection (2) of this section.

(5) On the receipt of the official receiver's application under subsection (2) the registrar shall forthwith register it and, at the end of the period of 3 months beginning with the day of the registration of the application, the company shall be dissolved.

However, the Secretary of State may, on the application of the official receiver or any other person who appears to the Secretary of State to be interested, give directions under section 203 at any time before the end of that period.

General note—The provision enables a company that is being wound up compulsorily and is hopelessly insolvent to be dissolved without adding costs where it would be a waste of time and money for a company to go through the formal processes that are involved with a winding up. This procedure would not be invoked where there are suggestions of improper activity, and investigation is needed. The concern for the winding up of companies that have no assets, save expending costs, will be secondary, if there are indications of unlawful conduct in the formation or management of the company.

The section does not provide for the scenario where the official receiver is replaced by a private insolvency practitioner as liquidator and he or she finds that the company does not have the assets it was thought to have. One suspects that the appropriate course of action would be for the practitioner to resign, with the official receiver taking over because of the vacancy (s 136(3)). The official receiver could then invoke the procedure under s 202.

Where the official receiver gives notice of an intention to make an application under the section, any creditor, contributory or administrative receiver may apply to the Secretary of State for directions pursuant to s 203(1) if any of the grounds set out in s 203(2) are cited.

As under s 201, dissolution is automatic when the circumstances in subsection (5) are fulfilled.

203 Consequence of notice under s 202

(1) Where a notice has been given under section 202(3), the official receiver or any creditor or contributory of the company, or the administrative receiver of the company (if there is one) may apply to the Secretary of State for directions under this section.

(2) The grounds on which that application may be made are—

    (a)   that the realisable assets of the company are sufficient to cover the expenses of the winding up;

    (b)   that the affairs of the company do require further investigation; or

    (c)   that for any other reason the early dissolution of the company is inappropriate.

(3) Directions under this section—

    (a)   are directions making such provision as the Secretary of State thinks fit for enabling the winding up of the company to proceed as if no notice had been given under section 202(3), and

    (b)   may, in the case of an application under section 202(5), include a direction deferring the date at which the dissolution of the company is to take effect for such period as the Secretary of State thinks fit.

(4) An appeal to the court lies from any decision of the Secretary of State on an application for directions under this section.

(5) It is the duty of the person on whose application any directions are given under this section, or in whose favour an appeal with respect to an application for such directions is determined, within 7 days after the giving of the directions or the determination of the appeal, to deliver to the registrar of companies for registration such a copy of the directions or determination as is prescribed.

(6) If a person without reasonable excuse fails to deliver a copy as required by subsection (5), he is liable to a fine and, for continued contravention, to a daily default fine.

General note—This section merely provides the mechanism for certain parties to seek directions from the Secretary of State (and possibly from a court if there is an appeal from the decision of the Secretary of State) where a notice pursuant to s 202 has been given by the official receiver.

    See rr 4.224 and 4.225.

204 Early dissolution (Scotland)

(1) This section applies where a winding-up order has been made by the court in Scotland.

(2) If after a meeting or meetings under section 138 (appointment of liquidator in Scotland) it appears to the liquidator that the realisable assets of the company are insufficient to cover the expenses of the winding up, he may apply to the court for an order that the company be dissolved.

(3) Where the liquidator makes that application, if the court is satisfied that the realisable assets of the company are insufficient to cover the expenses of the winding up and it appears to the court appropriate to do so, the court shall make an order that the company be dissolved in accordance with this section.

(4) A copy of the order shall within 14 days from its date be forwarded by the liquidator to the registrar of companies, who shall forthwith register it;

and, at the end of the period of 3 months beginning with the day of the registration of the order, the company shall be dissolved.

(5) The court may, on an application by any person who appears to the court to have an interest, order that the date at which the dissolution of the company is to take effect shall be deferred for such period as the court thinks fit.

(6) It is the duty of the person on whose application an order is made under subsection (5), within 7 days after the making of the order, to deliver to the registrar of companies such a copy of the order as is prescribed.

(7) If the liquidator without reasonable excuse fails to comply with the requirements of subsection (4), he is liable to a fine and, for continued contravention, to a daily default fine.

(8) If a person without reasonable excuse fails to deliver a copy as required by subsection (6), he is liable to a fine and, for continued contravention, to a daily default fine.

205 Dissolution otherwise than under ss 202–204

(1) This section applies where the registrar of companies receives—

    (a)   a notice served for the purposes of section 172(8) (final meeting of creditors and vacation of office by liquidator), or

    (b)   a notice from the official receiver that the winding up of a company by the court is complete.

(2) The registrar shall, on receipt of the notice, forthwith register it; and, subject as follows, at the end of the period of 3 months beginning with the day of the registration of the notice, the company shall be dissolved.

(3) The Secretary of State may, on the application of the official receiver or any other person who appears to the Secretary of State to be interested, give a direction deferring the date at which the dissolution of the company is to take effect for such period as the Secretary of State thinks fit.

(4) An appeal to the court lies from any decision of the Secretary of State on an application for a direction under subsection (3).

(5) Subsection (3) does not apply in a case where the winding-up order was made by the court in Scotland, but in such a case the court may, on an application by any person appearing to the court to have an interest, order that the date at which the dissolution of the company is to take effect shall be deferred for such period as the court thinks fit.

(6) It is the duty of the person—

    (a)   on whose application a direction is given under subsection (3);

    (b)   in whose favour an appeal with respect to an application for such a direction is determined; or

    (c)   on whose application an order is made under subsection (5),

within 7 days after the giving of the direction, the determination of the appeal or the making of the order, to deliver to the registrar for registration such a copy of the direction, determination or order as is prescribed.

(7) If a person without reasonable excuse fails to deliver a copy as required by subsection (6), he is liable to a fine and, for continued contravention, to a daily default fine.

General note—This provision corresponds to s 201 and relates to compulsory liquidations (note references in s 205(1) to s 172(8) and winding up by the court). Under the previous legislation, a compulsory liquidation could only be dissolved by way of court order. But this section allows for automatic dissolution, as in voluntary liquidation, at the end of a three-month period following the registration by the registrar of companies of the receipt of either the return from a private insolvency practitioner who is acting as the liquidator that the final meeting required under s 146 has been summoned and held or, in the case of the official receiver, notice that the winding up is complete.

Although the provision corresponds to s 201, it combines aspects of ss 202 and 203 as well as s 201, particularly in relation to applications to the Secretary of State for directions.

See rr 4.224 and 4.225.

For a detailed discussion of dissolution, including the restoration of dissolved companies, see A Keay *McPherson's Law of Company Liquidation* (3rd edn, Sweet and Maxwell, 2013) at 1072–1090.

Chapter X

Malpractice Before and During Liquidation; Penalisation of Companies and Company Officers; Investigations and Prosecutions

General comment on Chapter X—This Chapter deals with wrongdoing, both before and during a liquidation, and imposes both criminal and civil sanctions.

Sections 206–211 set out specific offences and these sections provide defences to, and impose sanctions for, criminal offences which may be committed prior to or in the course of a liquidation. Notably, certain of the provisions, namely ss 206(4), 207(2)(b), 208(4) and 210(4), reverse the burden of proof from the ordinary position in criminal law whereby the prosecution is required to establish beyond reasonable doubt that a particular offence has been committed by the defendant. These provisions deem the committing of an offence in the circumstances prescribed, subject to a defendant establishing, in contrast to the usual position, that, on a balance of probabilities, any of the defences defined in the provisions are available to him or her: *Morton v Confer* [1963] 2 All ER 765 at 767 (Lord Parker CJ) and 768 (Havers and Edmund Davies JJ agreeing). In considering whether reverse burdens involve a contravention of a defendant's human rights the Court of Appeal has said in *Attorney-General's Reference (No 1 of 2004); R v Edwards* [2004] EWCA Crim 1025, [2004] 1 WLR 2111, [2004] BPIR 1073 that reference should be made only to the House of Lords' decision in *R v Johnstone* [2003] 1 WLR 1736 (and see especially at 1748–1751) and the guidance the Court of Appeal gave in *R v Edwards*. In that case the Court of Appeal was dealing with reverse burden provisions relating to bankruptcy offences, but they are drafted in similar ways to the provisions mentioned above and contained in this Chapter of the Act. The court stated (at 1073) that the common law and the European Convention for the Protection of Human Rights permitted legal reverse burdens in appropriate circumstances. The court also stated (at 1073) that if an evidential reverse burden alone was invoked, and not a legal burden, there was no risk of breach of art 6(2) of the European Convention. The result is that if a defendant is able to adduce evidence supporting a statutory defence, then the burden of proof shifts onto the prosecution, which must establish the constituent parts of the offence beyond reasonable doubt. In *R v Edwards* Lord Woolf stated that insolvency offences have long been regarded as subject to special rules ([80], as the following sections and notes attest. The reason for allowing such burdens is that those involved in companies have the benefit of corporate personality and limited liability ([81]).

The remaining sections of the Chapter address such matters as misfeasance, fraudulent trading, wrongful trading, and the Phoenix Syndrome.

Offences of fraud, deception etc

206 Fraud etc in anticipation of winding up

(1) When a company is ordered to be wound up by the court, or passes a resolution for voluntary winding up, any person, being a past or present officer of the company, is deemed to have committed an offence if, within the 12 months immediately preceding the commencement of the winding up, he has—

    (a)   concealed any part of the company's property to the value of £500 or more, or concealed any debt due to or from the company, or

    (b)   fraudulently removed any part of the company's property to the value of £500 or more, or

    (c)   concealed, destroyed, mutilated or falsified any book or paper affecting or relating to the company's property or affairs, or

    (d)   made any false entry in any book or paper affecting or relating to the company's property or affairs, or

    (e)   fraudulently parted with, altered or made any omission in any document affecting or relating to the company's property or affairs, or

    (f)   pawned, pledged or disposed of any property of the company which has been obtained on credit and has not been paid for (unless the pawning, pledging or disposal was in the ordinary way of the company's business).

(2) Such a person is deemed to have committed an offence if within the period above mentioned he has been privy to the doing by others of any of the things mentioned in paragraphs (c), (d) and (e) of subsection (1); and he commits an offence if, at any time after the commencement of the winding up, he does any of the things mentioned in paragraphs (a) to (f) of that subsection, or is privy to the doing by others of any of the things mentioned in paragraphs (c) to (e) of it.

(3) For purposes of this section, 'officer' includes a shadow director.

(4) It is a defence—

    (a)   for a person charged under paragraph (a) or (f) of subsection (1) (or under subsection (2) in respect of the things mentioned in either of those two paragraphs) to prove that he had no intent to defraud, and

    (b)   for a person charged under paragraph (c) or (d) of subsection (1) (or under subsection (2) in respect of the things mentioned in either of those two paragraphs) to prove that he had no intent to conceal the state of affairs of the company or to defeat the law.

(5) Where a person pawns, pledges or disposes of any property in circumstances which amount to an offence under subsection (1)(f), every person who takes in pawn or pledge, or otherwise receives, the property knowing it to be pawned, pledged or disposed of in such circumstances, is guilty of an offence.

(6) A person guilty of an offence under this section is liable to imprisonment or a fine, or both.

(7) The money sums specified in paragraph (a) and (b) of subsection (1) are subject to increase or reduction by order under section 416 in Part XV.

Amendments—SI 1986/1996.

General note—The provision was formally s 624 of the Companies Act 1985 and it deems a person to be guilty of an offence, and it is for the defendant to extricate himself or herself by establishing his or her innocence on the balance of probabilities. See the note at the commencement of the Chapter and the comments on reverse burden provisions.

Details of any offence under this section should be reported by the liquidator to the Secretary of State for Business Enterprise and Regulatory Reform and should include: details of the date and circumstances of the transaction(s); details of the assets/amount concerned and the director's explanations; and whether there has been a civil recovery under either s 238 or s 239 (Dear IP Millennium Edition, December 2000, chapter 20).

'Officer'—This term is defined in s 1173 of the Companies Act 2006, as incorporated by s 251. The term includes a director. According to s 251 of the Act, 'director' includes anyone occupying that position, no matter what they are called. So, a person who is a 'shadow director' falls within that term, but in any event s 206(3) actually states that a shadow director is included within the term. Section 251(1) of the Companies Act 2006 provides a definition of 'shadow director'. See the notes accompanying that term in s 251 of the Insolvency Act.

The term in s 1173 of the Companies Act 2006 also includes anyone who is a manager of the company. For the meaning of 'manager of the company', see the notes under the heading 'Involved in the management' and following s 217.

'Concealed'—In the Australian case of *Motor Auction Pty Ltd v John Joyce Wholesale Cars Pty Ltd* (1997) 15 ACLC 987 the New South Wales Supreme Court held that the word, in a similar kind of context to which it is found in s 206, included a hiding of property by a person who then deliberately disappeared so as not to be amenable to questioning concerning the property's whereabouts.

'Book or paper affecting or relating to the company's property or affairs' – Computer records are included within this expression as found in s 206(1)(c) (*R v Taylor* [2011] EWCA Civ 728, [2011] 1 WLR 1809).

'Commencement of the winding up'—This phrase is defined in s 129. See the note under this heading and accompanying s 129.

Defence—Note the burden of proof that is placed on the defendant. See the general note at the commencement of the Chapter on this subject. In the circumstances of this offence a legal burden was compatible with the Human Rights Act 1998: *Attorney-General's Reference (No 1 of 2004); R v Edwards* [2004] EWCA Crim 1025, [2004] 1 WLR 2111, [2004] BPIR 1073; *Sheldrake v DPP* [2005] 1 AC 264, HL. According to *R v Richmond Magistrates' Court* [2008] EWHC 84 (Admin), [2008] 1 BCLC 681, [2008] BPIR 468 under this provision the reverse of burden provision is to be regarded as placing a legal as well as an evidential burden on the respondent.

'Penalty'—The penalties for a breach of s 206(1), s 206(2) or s 206(5) are seven years' imprisonment or a fine or both where the prosecution is brought on indictment (s 430 and Sch 10 to the Act). Where the prosecution is a summary one, the punishment is six months' imprisonment or the statutory maximum or both. The statutory maximum fine is £5,000 (Magistrates' Courts Act 1980, s 32 as amended by Criminal Justice Act 1991, s 17).

207 Transactions in fraud of creditors

(1) When a company is ordered to be wound up by the court or passes a resolution for voluntary winding up, a person is deemed to have committed an offence if he, being at the time an officer of the company—

    (a)   has made or caused to be made any gift or transfer of, or charge on, or has caused or connived at the levying of any execution against, the company's property, or

    (b)   has concealed or removed any part of the company's property since, or within 2 months before, the date of any unsatisfied judgment or order for the payment of money obtained against the company.

(2) A person is not guilty of an offence under this section—

    (a)   by reason of conduct constituting an offence under subsection (1)(a) which occurred more than 5 years before the commencement of the winding up, or

    (b)   if he proves that, at the time of the conduct constituting the offence, he had no intent to defraud the company's creditors.

(3) A person guilty of an offence under this section is liable to imprisonment or a fine, or both.

General note—The offences now contained in s 207(1) are broadly based on those which previously appeared in s 625 of the Companies Act 1985, and deem the committing of an offence. See the general note at the commencement of the Chapter on this subject. In *R v Enver* (unreported, 20 January 2000) the defendant was prosecuted under s 207(1)(b) and it was alleged he had stripped the assets of the company in order to pay off a bank and his own company.

    Details of any offence under this section should be reported by the liquidator to the Secretary of State for Business Enterprise and Regulatory Reform. The details that should be included are the same as for offences under s 206. See the General note to s 206.

'Officer'—The term is defined in Companies Act 2006, s 1173 as incorporated by s 251. It is notable, however, that in contrast to s 206(3) and s 208(3) the term 'officer' is not extended here to include a shadow director, such that the offences in this provision must be taken, for no obvious reason, as not extending to shadow directors.

'Commencement of the winding up'—This phrase is defined in s 129. See the note under this heading and accompanying s 129.

    In a compulsory liquidation the 5-year time limit, which is new, is reckoned from the date of presentation of the winding-up petition and not from the date of the winding-up order.

Defence—Note the burden of proof that is placed on the defendant. See the general note at the commencement of the Chapter on this subject.

    This provision infers that a person is taken to have committed the actus reus of the offence with the requisite mens rea of intent to defraud the company's creditors, subject to the statutorily defined defence.

Penalty—The offence is punishable by imprisonment for 2 years or a fine or both, where proceedings have been brought by indictment, and where initiated summarily, the penalty is imprisonment for 6 months or a fine equal to the statutory maximum or both (ss 207(3) and 430, and Sch 10). The statutory maximum fine is £5,000 according to s 32 of the Magistrates' Courts Act 1980 as amended by s 17 of the Criminal Justice Act 1991.

208 Misconduct in course of winding up

(1) When a company is being wound up, whether by the court or voluntarily, any person, being a past or present officer of the company, commits an offence if he—

- (a) does not to the best of his knowledge and belief fully and truly discover to the liquidator all the company's property, and how and to whom and for what consideration and when the company disposed of any part of that property (except such part as has been disposed of in the ordinary way of the company's business), or
- (b) does not deliver up to the liquidator (or as he directs) all such part of the company's property as is in his custody or under his control, and which he is required by law to deliver up, or
- (c) does not deliver up to the liquidator (or as he directs) all books and papers in his custody or under his control belonging to the company and which he is required by law to deliver up, or
- (d) knowing or believing that a false debt has been proved by any person in the winding up, fails to inform the liquidator as soon as practicable, or
- (e) after the commencement of the winding up, prevents the production of any book or paper affecting or relating to the company's property or affairs.

(2) Such a person commits an offence if after the commencement of the winding up he attempts to account for any part of the company's property by fictitious losses or expenses; and he is deemed to have committed that offence if he has so attempted at any meeting of the company's creditors within the 12 months immediately preceding the commencement of the winding up.

(3) For purposes of this section, 'officer' includes a shadow director.

(4) It is a defence—

- (a) for a person charged under paragraph (a), (b) or (c) of subsection (1) to prove that he had no intent to defraud, and
- (b) for a person charged under paragraph (e) of that subsection to prove that he had no intent to conceal the state of affairs of the company or to defeat the law.

(5) A person guilty of an offence under this section is liable to imprisonment or a fine, or both.

General note—Formerly this provision was s 626 of the Companies Act 1985. The provision identifies the nature of seven separate offences, found in s 208(1) and (2) which may arise in the course of a liquidation, save that the second offence in s 208(2), which amounts to a deeming provision, is relevant only to the period preceding the commencement of the winding up. These notes should be read in conjunction with those in relation to the offences in s 206 and the General note to the Chapter.

The actus reus of five separate offences appear here together with, in the case of s 208(1)(d), the mens rea ('knowing or believing that a false debt has been proved by any person in the winding up') of that particular offence. Section 208(4)(a) and (b) infer that a person is taken to have committed the actus reus of the offences prescribed in s 208(1)(a), (b), (c) and (e) with the requisite intent to defraud or intent to conceal the state of affairs of the company etc, subject to the defences in s 208(4)(a) and (b).

The directors are under a continuous duty because of this section to co-operate with the liquidator and to be proactive in disclosing and delivering up company property, and the section is not triggered by the liquidator's inquiry concerning property or request for production: *R v McCredie; R v French* [2000] 2 BCLC 438 at 442, [2000] BCC 617 at 621, CA, Criminal Division.

As would be expected, a cheque is regarded as property for the purposes of the section (*R v McCredie* at 445; 623). The fruits of company property as compiled by a company officer are also part of the property of a company (*R v McCredie* at 445; 623).

In relation to s 208(1)(c) books and records may include computer disks (*McCredie*).

In relation to s 208(1)(d), in contrast to the other subparagraphs in this subsection, the burden of proof rests on the prosecution in establishing beyond reasonable doubt the knowledge or belief as to the proof of a false debt (see s 208(4)).

'Commencement of the winding up'—The term is defined in s 129. See the note accompanying s 129.

'Officer'—See the note to s 206 under the heading of 'officer'.

'Deliver up'—Details of any offence under s 208(1)(c) should be reported by the liquidator to the Secretary of State and should include: details of the attempts to recover records, including a copy of the correspondence with the director; the effect of the failure to deliver up the records; and the director's explanations for failing to deliver up (Dear IP Millennium Edition, December 2000, chapter 20).

Defences—In relation to the burden of proof, see the note at the commencement of this Chapter. Note that no defences are provided to those offences prescribed by s 208(1)(d) or s 208(2). In relation to this offence a legal burden was compatible with the Human Rights Act: *R v Richmond Magistrates' Court* [2008] EWHC 84 (Admin), [2008] 1 BCLC 681, [2008] BPIR 468] at [29]. According to this case under this section the reverse of burden provision Is to be regarded as placing a legal as well as an evidential burden on the respondent.

Penalty—See the note to s 206, under the heading 'penalty'. The severity of the penalty is the same as for s 206. For the imposition of a custodial sentence: see *Re Brevis* [2001] All ER (D) 09. In this case a custodial sentence of 18 months ordered in relation to a director for failure to discover all company property to the liquidator in contravention of s 208(1) was reduced to nine months on appeal on the basis that the offence, whilst involving an element of dishonesty (which was not a technical or administrative offence), was in fact distinguishable from fraudulent trading under Companies Act 2006, s 993.

209 Falsification of company's books

(1) When a company is being wound up, an officer or contributory of the company commits an offence if he destroys, mutilates, alters or falsifies any books, papers or securities, or makes or is privy to the making of any false or fraudulent entry in any register, book of account or document belonging to the company with intent to defraud or deceive any person.

(2) A person guilty of an offence under this section is liable to imprisonment or a fine, or both.

General note—Formerly this provision was s 627 of the Companies Act 1985. The offence identified in this provision is only capable of being committed 'when a company is being wound up'. For a pre-liquidation offence (which extends to concealment, which is not mentioned within the present provision), see s 206(1)(c).

Besides prosecuting officers, contributories can also be prosecuted. For a discussion of who are contributories, see the notes accompanying s 74.

The burden of proof in establishing mens rea ('intent to defraud or deceive any person') rests on the prosecution.

'Officer'—See the note under this heading accompanying s 206.

Penalty—See the note to s 206 dealing with 'Penalty'. The severity of the penalty is the same as for s 206.

210 Material omissions from statement relating to company's affairs

(1) When a company is being wound up, whether by the court or voluntarily, any person, being a past or present officer of the company, commits an offence if he makes any material omission in any statement relating to the company's affairs.

(2) When a company has been ordered to be wound up by the court, or has passed a resolution for voluntary winding up, any such person is deemed to have committed that offence if, prior to the winding up, he has made any material omission in any such statement.

(3) For purposes of this section, 'officer' includes a shadow director.

(4) It is a defence for a person charged under this section to prove that he had no intent to defraud.

(5) A person guilty of an offence under this section is liable to imprisonment or a fine, or both.

General note—This provision creates two separate offences which are limited in scope to the making of any material omission in any statement relating to the company's affairs. Section 210(1) applies to material omissions made by a person 'when a company is being wound up', irrespective of whether the liquidation is compulsory or voluntary. Section 210(2) is a deeming provision which provides for the actus reus of the offence at a time 'prior to the winding up'. This provision should be read in conjunction with the notes to s 206 and the General note to s 211, which addresses false representations – apparently something distinct from omissions – to creditors.

The offence within s 210(2) involves the making of an omission which is material by a person who, at the time of the making of the omission, is or was an officer of the company in 'any statement relating to the company's affairs'. Section 210(4) infers that a person is taken to have committed the actus reus of the offence with the requisite mens rea of intent to defraud, subject to the defence in that subsection.

This offence is plainly not limited to material omissions which appear in the statement of affairs provided for in s 99 (creditors' voluntary winding up) or s 131 (winding up by the court or in provisional liquidation). The provision instead appears to be wide enough to catch omissions in any statement, whether made for the purposes of the legislation or not. Examples might include statements made to a liquidator in the course of the preparation of a statement of affairs under s 95(3) (conversion of members' voluntary winding up to creditors' voluntary winding up) or statements made to creditors or other third parties, such as those made in correspondence or circulars. There would also not appear to be any requirement that the statement from which there is an omission should be in writing, and so the offence may well catch omissions from statements made orally. The offence might also cover omissions from statements made in the course of a public or private examination (on which see s 133 and s 236, respectively), although statements made under oath in the course of such examinations will in any case be covered by s 5 of the Perjury Act 1911.

Positive misstatements relating to the company's affairs are not caught, at least not expressly, by this provision, but will be caught by s 208 and/or s 209.

The offence in s 210(2) mirrors that in s 210(1) and would appear wide enough to catch material omissions from statements made relating to the company's affairs without a requirement that such statements should relate to the winding up itself. Thus, it would follow that the provision would catch material omissions from a statement of officers prepared for the purposes of a company voluntary arrangement (see r 1.5), an administration order (para 47 of Sch B1) or administrative receivership (s 47), together with material omissions in the course of other statements made to creditors or third parties.

'Officer'—See the note under this heading accompanying s 206.

Defences—In relation to the reverse burden of proof, see the General note at the commencement of the Chapter.

Penalty—See the note to s 206 dealing with 'Penalty.' The severity of the penalty is the same as for s 206.

211 False representations to creditors

(1) When a company is being wound up, whether by the court or voluntarily, any person, being a past or present officer of the company—

    (a)   commits an offence if he makes any false representation or commits any other fraud for the purpose of obtaining the consent of the company's creditors or any of them to an agreement with reference to the company's affairs or to the winding up, and

    (b)   is deemed to have committed that offence if, prior to the winding up, he has made any false representation, or committed any other fraud, for that purpose.

(2) For purposes of this section, 'officer' includes a shadow director.

(3) A person guilty of an offence under this section is liable to imprisonment or a fine, or both.

Penalisation of directors and officers

General note—This provision creates two separate offences. Both are limited in scope to the making of any false representation to creditors – but not to any other third party – for the purpose of obtaining consent to an agreement 'with reference to the company's affairs or to the winding up'. Either offence may be committed 'when the company is being wound up' (in the case of s 211(1)(a)) or, by virtue of the deeming provision in s 211(1)(b), prior to the winding up.

The actus reus of each of the offences in s 211(1)(a) and (b) necessarily involves the making of a fraudulent (as opposed to a negligent or innocent) representation, given the subsequent reference to the alternative act of committing 'any other fraud' for the purpose then identified. An offence may be committed under these provisions through the silence of an officer, given that silence may, in certain circumstances, amount to a misrepresentation: see Furmston *Cheshire, Fifoot and Furmston's Law of Contract* (Butterworths, 14th edn, 2001) at pp 297–298; Halson *Contract Law* (Pearson, 2001) at pp 31–34). It appears that silence may also fall susceptible to prosecution under s 210 as a material omission.

The offence does not require the obtaining of consent to an agreement on the part of one or more creditors but, rather, involves only the making of a false representation or the committing of any other fraud for that purpose.

The burden of proof in establishing fraud rests on the prosecution.

'Officer'—See the note under this heading accompanying s 206.

Penalty—See the note to s 206 dealing with 'Penalty'. The severity of the penalty is the same as for s 206.

212 Summary remedy against delinquent directors, liquidators etc

(1) This section applies if in the course of the winding up of a company it appears that a person who—

    (a)   is or has been an officer of the company,

(b)   has acted as liquidator or administrative receiver of the company, or

(c)   not being a person falling within paragraph (a) or (b), is or has been concerned, or has taken part, in the promotion, formation or management of the company,

has misapplied or retained, or become accountable for, any money or other property of the company, or been guilty of any misfeasance or breach of any fiduciary or other duty in relation to the company.

(2) The reference in subsection (1) to any misfeasance or breach of any fiduciary or other duty in relation to the company includes, in the case of a person who has acted as liquidator of the company, any misfeasance or breach of any fiduciary or other duty in connection with the carrying out of his functions as liquidator of the company.

(3) The court may, on the application of the official receiver or the liquidator, or of any creditor or contributory, examine into the conduct of the person falling within subsection (1) and compel him—

(a)   to repay, restore or account for the money or property or any part of it, with interest at such rate as the court thinks just, or

(b)   to contribute such sum to the company's assets by way of compensation in respect of the misfeasance or breach of fiduciary or other duty as the court thinks just.

(4) The power to make an application under subsection (3) in relation to a person who has acted as liquidator of the company is not exercisable, except with the leave of the court, after he has had his release.

(5) The power of a contributory to make an application under subsection (3) is not exercisable except with the leave of the court, but is exercisable notwithstanding that he will not benefit from any order the court may make on the application.

Amendments—Enterprise Act 2002, ss 248(3), 278(2), Sch 17, paras 9, 18, Sch 26.

General note—This provision is often said to cover misfeasance (a term mentioned in s 212(2)), particularly perpetrated by directors of companies, but there is no such distinct wrongful act known to the law as misfeasance. The provision is purely procedural in effect (*Re B Johnson & Co (Builders) Ltd* [1955] Ch 634 at 647–648; *Cohen v Selby* [2001] 1 BCLC 176 at 183); its purpose is to provide a summary mode of enforcing rights which, apart from the section, could have been enforced by the company prior to liquidation. The provision is merely a gateway enabling a claim which was, but for liquidation, able to be brought by the company and so the liquidator can bring it instead: *French v Cipolletta* [2009] EWHC 223 at [9].The section does not affect any right of a liquidator to bring action in the ordinary way, nor does it affect the rights of the liquidator which came into existence by virtue of special statutory provisions: *Re Home & Colonial Insurance Co* [1930] 1 Ch 102 at 132. Liquidators are only able to take proceedings to enforce claims vested in the company, and not actions that vest in other persons, such as creditors: *Re Hill's Waterfall Estate and Gold Mining Co* [1896] 1 Ch 947.

The usual respondent to an action under this provision will be directors, but others as indicated in s 212(1) may be the subject of proceedings. An example of an action against a liquidator is *Centralcrest Engineering Ltd* [2000] BCC 727. It has been held in Australia that before a court will inquire into the conduct of a liquidator the complainant must make out a prima facie case that there is something which requires an inquiry to be conducted: *Vink v Tuckwell* [2008] VSC 100, [2008] 216 FLR 309. A claim against a liquidator can be answered successfully if there is no loss sustained by the company or creditors: *Lomax Leisure Ltd v*

Miller [2007] EWHC 2508 (Ch), [2007] BPIR 1615, [2008] 1 BCLC 262 at [37]. Prior to the commencement of the corporate liquidations provision of Part 10 of the Enterprise Act 2002 on 15 September 2003, administrators could be the subject of proceedings under s 212. Now any proceedings must be brought under para 75 of Sch B1.

It has been held that misfeasance covers the whole spectrum of duties of directors, and the provision is not restricted to cases where the respondent is guilty of moral turpitude: *Re Westlowe Storage and Distribution Ltd* [2000] BCC 851, [2000] 2 BCLC 590.

A liquidator may take action under the provision as well as making application for relief on some other basis, such as wrongful trading under s 214 (*Re DKG Contractors Ltd* [1990] BCC 903; *Re Brian D Pierson (Contractors) Ltd* [1999] BCC 26, [2001] BCLC 275), or at common law (*A & J Fabrications Ltd v Grant Thornton* [1998] 2 BCLC 227).

The difficulty of obtaining summary judgment can be seen in *Phillips v McGregor-Paterson* [2009] EWHC 2385 (Ch), [2010] BPIR 239 at [37]ff. There is going to be a need for a trial very often when the questions involve consideration of whether the defendant was in breach of his or her duties as a director. There may also be the need to consider whether the defendant should be excused under s 1157 of the Companies Act 2006.

In bringing an action under the section proof of loss to the company is a necessary ingredient of a cause of action for breach of fiduciary duty or negligence. There is no basis for saying that the section justifies a laxer approach to pleading than would be called for in an ordinary action. The director is entitled to know what case is being made against him or her and it is necessary that the pleadings allege loss and make clear the types of loss that are alleged to have been caused by the breaches of duty or negligence in question: *French v Cipolletta* [2009] EWHC 223 at [16].

Applicants—The usual applicant will be a liquidator for relief against a director, but the official receiver and creditors are also permitted to apply (for an instance of an application by a creditor, see *Re Loquitur Ltd* [2003] EWHC 999 (Ch), [2003] 2 BCLC 410).

Contributories may apply if they obtain the leave of the court (s 212(5)). Before the 1986 Act, contributories would not be granted leave unless they could demonstrate a real interest in the outcome of the proceedings, but this is no longer the case. It has been said that the provision enables contributories to commence direct proceedings against a director instead of derivative proceedings, which might be unavailable or difficult to institute: *Wightman v Bennett* [2005] BPIR 470 at 473. A contributory is not able to apply under s 212 after a winding-up petition has been presented, but must wait until an order has been made (*Wightman v Bennett*).

A person who made a claim against the company, and the claim had been settled, could not bring an action under s 212 as a creditor: *Re Tertiary Enterprises Ltd* (unreported, 3 August 2006, ChD, Thomas Ivory QC).

Negligence—Negligence is covered by s 212 (*Re D'Jan of London Ltd* [1993] BCC 646, [1994] 1 BCLC 561; *Centralcrest Engineering Ltd* [2000] BCC 727; *Re Simmon Box (Diamonds) Ltd* [2002] BCC 82, CA), because the provision refers not only to misfeasance, but also 'breach of any fiduciary or other duty'. But the liquidator must establish a cause of action whereby the alleged breach of duty of care caused loss or damage: *Re Anglo-Austrian Printing & Publishing Co* [1985] 2 Ch 891.

Contribution—Courts have a broad discretion as to what they order should be paid by the respondent: *Re Home & Colonial Insurance Co* [1930] 1 Ch 102; *Re Westlowe Storage and Distribution Ltd* [2000] BCC 851, [2000] 2 BCLC 590. Courts are able to order compensation as they think fit, and a court can decide to award only part of the compensation sought (*Re Home & Colonial Insurance Co*), as was the case in *Re Loquitur Ltd* [2003] EWHC 999 (Ch), [2003] 2 BCLC 410, where the court felt that it should limit the amount to be paid.

The courts have a discretion as to whether any order should be made: *Re Sunlight Incandescent Gas Lamp Co Ltd* (1900) 16 TLR 535, and there is Australian authority to the effect that in very limited circumstances the court may exonerate a liquidator for breach of duty: *Re ACN 003 671 387 and ACN 008 664 257* [2004] NSWSC 368 (sale to the liquidator's service trust), but in *Re Paycheck Services 3 Ltd* [2008] EWHC 2200 (Ch), [2008] All ER (D) 319 (Jun), Mark Cawson QC doubted whether it had been intended to provide in s 212 a judical ability to relieve from liability, given the existence of s 727 of the Companies Act 1985 (now s 1157 of the Companies Act 2006).

Most frequently a court will order the respondent to pay the amount of the loss suffered because of the misconduct: *Bishopsgate Investment Management Ltd v Maxwell (No 2)*

[1993] BCLC 814, [1993] BCC 120 (affirmed on appeal [1994] 2 All ER 261, [1993] BCLC 1282, CA). Notwithstanding their broad discretion, courts cannot order the rescission of contracts (*Re Centrifugal Butter Co Ltd* [1913] 1 Ch 188) or order the payment of debts owed to the company (*Re Etic Ltd* [1928] Ch 861).

Before any contribution will be ordered, the applicant must demonstrate that the company has suffered loss: *Re Derek Randall Enterprises Ltd* [1990] BCC 749, CA.

Where a claim is made pursuant to both s 212 and s 214 there would be no injustice in ordering payments under both provisions, provided that the liquidator does not recover more than was required to satisfy the liabilities of the company: *Re Purpoint Ltd* [1991] BCC 121.

Any contribution paid by a respondent will, following the deduction of costs of the action, be available to any holders of charges over the present and future property of the company: *Re Anglo-Austrian Printing & Publishing Co* [1985] 2 Ch 891.

Orders—A court is able to order one respondent to indemnify another respondent to the proceedings: *Re Morecombe Bowling Ltd* [1969] 1 WLR 133. But third party procedure cannot be used so as to make a person contribute where he or she is not a respondent (*Re B Johnson & Co (Builders) Ltd*), and this is the case despite the fact that the latter could have been made a respondent: *Re A Singer & Co (Hat Manufacturers) Ltd* [1943] 1 Ch 121, CA.

If an application is brought by a creditor or a contributory, any order can only be made to the benefit of the company, and not to the applicant: *Oldham v Kyrris* [2003] EWCA Civ 1506, [2004] BCC 111.

'Officer'—An auditor has been held to be within this term for the purposes of s 212 (*Re London and General Bank* [1895] 2 Ch 166, CA; *Re Thomas Gerrard & Sons Ltd* [1968] Ch 455), but other professionals who might be involved in providing advice to the company, such as a company's bankers (*Re Imperial Land Co of Marseilles* (1870) LR 10 Eq 298) and solicitors (*Re Great Western Forest of Dean Co* (1886) 31 Ch D 496) are not.

De facto directors are officers for the purposes of this section: *Re Mumtaz Properties Ltd* [2011] EWCA Civ 610, as are shadow directors: *Re Hydrodan (Corby) Ltd* [1994] BCC 161.

Limit on actions—The limitation for taking proceedings would run from the time when the breach upon which the action is brought occurred or was discovered by the company. As s 212 is merely procedural in nature, it does not provide a limitation period that was independent from that applying to the claim underlying the proceedings(*Re Eurocruit Europe Ltd (in liq)* [2007] EWHC 1433 (Ch), [2008] BCC 916, [2007] 2 BCLC 598).

See generally, on breach of duties of directors, A Keay *Directors' Duties* (2nd edn, Jordans, 2009).

213 Fraudulent trading

(1) If in the course of the winding up of a company it appears that any business of the company has been carried on with intent to defraud creditors of the company or creditors of any other person, or for any fraudulent purpose, the following has effect.

(2) The court, on the application of the liquidator may declare that any persons who were knowingly parties to the carrying on of the business in the manner above-mentioned are to be liable to make such contributions (if any) to the company's assets as the court thinks proper.

General note—The law against fraudulent trading dates from 1928. Since then until the Act was enacted, the Companies Acts dealt with fraudulent trading and provided for both civil and criminal liability. Now s 213 deals solely with civil liability. Criminal liability is covered by s 993 of the Companies Act 2006. Sections 213 and 993 are essentially identical, with the primary difference being procedural. The former has the civil standard of proof, namely the balance of probabilities, while the standard for the criminal proceeding under s 993 remains beyond reasonable doubt. Unlike s 993, proceedings can only be brought under s 212 where the company is in liquidation, and can only be initiated by the liquidator.

There are three elements that need to be established by a liquidator. These are: the business of the company in liquidation has been carried on with intent to defraud creditors or for any other fraudulent purpose; the defendant participated in the carrying of business; the defendant did so knowingly: *Re BCCI; Morris v Bank of India* [2004] 2 BCLC 236 at 243.

At one time it was generally thought that this section would not be invoked frequently, certainly given the advent of the action of wrongful trading in s 214, but that is not the case. While s 214 has a lower threshold of proof, and the elements of the section appear prima facie easier to establish, there have been several fraudulent trading actions in recent times with a number being reported (e g *Re Esal (Commodities) Ltd* [1997] 1 BCLC 705, CA; *Morris v Bank of America National Trust and Savings Association* [2000] BPIR 83, [2000] BCC 1076, [2001] 1 BCLC 771, CA; *Re Bank of Credit and Commerce International SA; Morris v State Bank of India* [2004] 2 BCLC 236; *Morphites v Bernasconi* [2003] EWCA Civ 289, [2003] BCC 540, CA; *Morris v Bank of India* [2004] BCC 404 and affirmed on appeal in [2005] EWCA Civ 693); most have revolved around the liquidation of BCCI.

Any court award must be in favour of the liquidator for the whole body of creditors, and not an individual creditor: *Re Esal (Commodities) Ltd* [1997] 1 BCLC 705, CA. The award is to be held by a liquidator for the purpose of making a distribution to the unsecured creditors (*Re Oasis Merchandising Services Ltd* [1995] BCC 911, affirmed on appeal [1997] 1 All ER 1009, [1997] BCC 282, CA) and is, therefore, not available for a chargeholder.

It is probably in order for a liquidator to take proceedings under s 213 where a company is being wound up as an unregistered company: *Re Howard Holdings Inc* [1998] BCC 549 (involving an application under s 214). But a liquidator is unable to assign an action under s 213 because it is an action given to him or her personally in the position of liquidator: *Re Oasis Merchandising Services Ltd*. But proceedings are not available under s 213 in relation to conduct that occurred between the date of the presentation of a winding-up petition and the making of a winding-up order as a company cannot be regarded as carrying on business when any transaction in the course of that business which amounts to a disposition of property is deemed to be void under s 127 of the Insolvency Act 1986 unless the court orders to the contrary (*Carman v Cronos Group SA* [2005] EWHC 2403 (Ch), [2006] BCC 451 at [37]–[38]). But it was held in the same case that people can be held liable under s 213 in relation to actions that occurred when the company had been dissolved at the time, but is later reinstated to the register (at [24]). This is on the basis that ss 1028(1) and 1032(1) (formerly s 653 of the Companies Act 1985) state that a dissolved company, when reinstated, is deemed to have deemed to have continued in existence as if it had not been struck off the register (at [24]).

It appears that it would be in order for a liquidator to bring an action that relied on both ss 213 and 214. There is nothing in s 213 to prevent it, and s 214(8) specifically provides that s 214 is not to prejudice s 213.

Only liquidators can bring proceedings and this does not include a provisional liquidator: *Re Overnight Ltd; Goldfarb v Higgins* [2009] EWHC 601 (Ch), [2010] BCC 787.

Liquidators are required, before taking action, to secure approval from either the liquidation committee or the court (s 165(2)(b) (creditors' voluntary liquidations) or s 167(1)(a) (compulsory liquidations); para 3A of Sch 4).

Respondents—While it is likely that directors will be the usual respondents to any fraudulent trading case, the provision is in fact quite wide, as anyone who was knowingly a party to the carrying on of a business of a company with intent to defraud creditors can be the subject of proceedings, and this can include companies: *Bank of India v Morris* [2005] EWCA Civ 693. The respondent does not have to be someone who performed a managerial or controlling role in the company. In fact, the language of s 213(2) might point towards persons who were not employed by the company, but were in fact outsiders: *Re BCCI; Banque Arabe Internationale D'Investissement SA v Morris* [2002] BCC 407. So, in *Re Gerald Cooper Chemicals Ltd* [1978] 2 WLR 866 a creditor was held liable, and in *Morris v Bank of India* [2004] BCC 404 and affirmed on appeal [2005] EWCA (Civ) 693, CA, a bank was found liable. Similarly, later in *Re BCCI; Banque Arabe Internationale D'Investissement SA v Morris* the court said that a company or other entity that was involved in and assisted and benefited from the action that was fraudulent, and did so knowingly, could be a respondent. Outsider respondents need not know all of the details of any fraudulent action perpetrated by the company or how the fraud was to be carried out before they are held liable, provided that they knew, either from their own observations of what was being done or from what they were told, that the company was intending to carry out a fraud on creditors: *Re BCCI; Morris v State Bank of India* [2004] BCC 404.

Generally, employees of the company that are merely carrying out orders are not able to be made respondents: *Re BCCI; Banque Arabe Internationale D'Investissement SA v Morris* [2002] BCC 407. A company could be held liable even if none of its board members did not have knowledge of the fraudulent trading activity as that would defeat the policy behind the provision (*Bank of India v Morris* [2005] EWCA Civ 693 at [108], [129]). A company employee's knowledge of fraudulent trading may be attributed to his or her employer company (*Bank of India v Morris*). However, there are some circumstances where a person's knowledge of fraudulent trading should not be attributed to the company (*Bank of India v Morris* at [114], [129]).

There is a strong argument that a claim under the section would survive the death of a person allegedly liable under s 213, but who died before the initiation of proceedings, so a liquidator would be able to take proceedings against the personal representative of the deceased's estate: see *Re Sherborne Associates Ltd* [1995] BCC 40 (a s 214 claim).

The provision could be used against respondents who are foreign residents where the company was involved in trade across borders: *Bilta (UK) Ltd v Nazir* [2012] EWHC 2163 (Ch) at [44]. This judgment was confirmed on appeal: [2013] EWCA Civ 968, [2013] 3 WLR 1167.

Extent of liability—The liability of those against whom a liquidator is successful is without limit. Persons who are liable must make such contributions to the company as the court thinks proper. While it has been said that the courts can make an order against respondents that involves requiring them to make payments that exceed the company's indebtedness during the period of fraudulent trading (*Re Cyona Distributors Ltd* [1967] Ch 889 at 902, [1967] 1 All ER 281 at 284, CA), the Court of Appeal has now rejected such a view, stating that the contribution to the assets to be shared amongst the creditors should reflect the loss which has been caused to the creditors by the carrying on of the business in the way that gives rise to the exercise of the power (*Morphites v Bernasconi* [2003] EWCA Civ 289, [2003] BCC 540 at [55]). Again, while in some cases courts have included a punitive element in the order (e g *Re Cyona Distributors Ltd*), in *Morphites v Bernasconi* (at [55]) the Court of Appeal said that there was no power in s 213 permitting the imposition of any punitive element in the amount of any contribution. The court added (at [55]) that the power to punish a guilty party was preserved in s 458 of the Companies Act 1985 (now s 993 of the Companies Act 2006).

'Intent to defraud'—This phrase has never been defined statutorily and there has been inconsistency concerning what test should be applied.

The test for intent to defraud is a subjective test (*Bernasconi v Nicholas Bennett & Co* [2000] BCC 921, [2000] BPIR 8; *Re BCCI; Morris v Bank of India* [2004] 2 BCLC 236), namely the state of mind of the respondent at the time of the alleged fraudulent trading is the decisive factor: the respondent had to evince an intent or a reckless indifference whether creditors were defrauded (*Bernasconi v Nicholas Bennett & Co*).

While the subjective test is applied to respondents, objective considerations are not without some relevance. For instance, the circumstances pertaining to what is being alleged as fraudulent trading must be taken into account and, if a respondent's subjective view is found not to be reasonable, he or she might be found liable. But it has been said that courts must be careful in invoking the concept of the hypothetical decent honest man and what he would have done in the circumstances, as there might be a temptation to treat shortcomings by the respondent as a failure to comply with the necessary objective standard of conduct: *Aktieselskabet Dansk Skibsfinansiering v Brothers* [2001] 2 BCLC 324 at 334 (HKCFA). The Court of Appeal decision in *R v Grantham* [1984] QB 675, seems to suggest that courts can take into account objective considerations when respondents incur debts at a time when they know that their company will clearly not be able to make repayment, or where there is considerable risk that the company will not be able to repay.

The liquidator is required to demonstrate dishonesty on the part of the respondent, and it is this element which caused s 213 to be distinguishable from s 214: *Bernasconi v Nicholas Bennett & Co* [2000] BCC 921 at 925, [2000] BPIR 8 at 13. Whether a person is regarded as being dishonest must depend on an assessment of all of the facts (*Aktieselskabet Dansk Skibsfinansiering v Brothers*). If it was established that the respondent had knowledge of fraud, then it follows that the respondent was dishonest: *Re BCCI; Morris v State Bank of India* [2004] BCC 404.

An intent to defraud in the carrying on of business must be distinguished from misrepresentations and deception in general: *Morphites v Bernasconi* [2003] EWCA Civ 289, [2003] BCC 540, CA at [43].

The payment of preferences, which are within the scope of s 239, will not generally be deemed to be fraud for the purposes of s 213: *Re Sarflax Ltd* [1979] 1 All ER 529 at 535, 545. Inaction cannot constitute fraud, as some positive action must have been taken. So, if an officer of, or adviser to, the company, were to fail to tell the directors that the company is insolvent, that person is not liable: *Re Maidstone Buildings Ltd* [1971] 1 WLR 1085. But a company outsider may be held liable even where he or she does not commit a positive act or is involved in the carrying on of business if the outsider is knowingly a party to a fraudulent act: *Re Augustus Barnett & Sons Ltd* (1986) 2 BCC 98, 904 at 98, 907. Thus, if a creditor were to be paid by the company when the creditor knew that the payment resulted from the carrying on of business with an intent to defraud, he or she might be liable: *Re Gerald Cooper Chemicals Ltd* [1978] Ch 262, [1978] 2 All ER 49.

The actual conduct that constitutes an intent to defraud must be set out clearly in any application (*Morris v Bank of America National Trust* [2001] 1 BCLC 771, [2000] BCC 1076, [2000] BPIR 83, CA – an appeal relating to a strike out application).

See A Keay 'Fraudulent Trading: The Intent to Defraud Element' (2006) 35 *Common Law World Review* 121.

'Knowingly'—In considering whether the respondent was knowingly a party to fraud, if liquidators could demonstrate that respondents had 'blind-eye' knowledge of the intent to defraud, namely deliberately shutting their eyes to the obvious, in that it was obvious to the respondents that fraud was involved, they could succeed: *Re BCCI; Morris v Bank of India* [2004] 2 BCLC 236; *Bank of India v Morris* [2005] EWCA Civ 693. Blind-eye knowledge involves a suspicion that a fraud exists and a deliberate decision to avoid confirming that it exists, and that the suspicion is well-grounded (*Re BCCI; Morris v Bank of India*). To be knowingly parties to the fraud, people do not have to know every detail of the fraud or how it was to be perpetrated: *Re BCCI; Morris v Bank of India* [2004] BCC 404 at 419. To be liable a person must have had the relevant knowledge contemporaneously with giving assistance to effect the fraud: *Re BCCI; Morris v Bank of India* [2004] BCC 404 at 419.

'Fraudulent purpose'—This expression is not designed in any way to restrict the application of s 213. On the contrary, the expression is extremely wide: *R v Kemp* [1988] QB 645 at 654–655. But it should not be construed so as to stultify normal business transactions: *Re BCCI; Banque Arabe Internationale D'Investissement SA v Morris* [2002] BCC 407.

Carrying on business—Carrying on business is interpreted broadly. For fraudulent trading to have been committed, it is not necessary for the liquidator to prove that there has been a course of conduct, as a single transaction or act is able to constitute the basis for action under s 213: *Re Gerald Cooper Chemicals Ltd* [1978] Ch 262, [1978] 2 All ER 49; *Morphites v Bernasconi* [2003] EWCA Civ 289, [2003] BCC 540, CA. Hence, where a company is doing nothing except collecting and distributing its assets, it can be regarded as carrying on business within s 213: *Re Sarflax Ltd* [1979] 1 All ER 529. Fraudulent trading can occur when business is being carried on to defraud just one creditor, but one cannot say that whenever a fraud on a creditor is perpetrated while carrying on business, it is inevitable that a breach of s 213 occurs; critically s 213 only applies where the business has been carried on with intent to defraud (*Morphites v Bernasconi* at [46]–[47]).

Contribution—The liquidator, in order for a contribution to be ordered, has to establish a nexus between the loss caused to creditors because of the fraudulent trading, and the contribution that is being sought from the person allegedly involved in the fraudulent trading (*Morphites v Bernasconi*).

Any order of contribution, while essentially compensatory, could only ever be a reasonable approximation of the damage that the respondent precipitated or to which he or she contributed: *Re BCCI; Morris v State Bank of India* [2004] BCC 404 at 461.

The court is entitled to determine that several persons should be held jointly and severally liable for the loss caused. As the word 'contributions' was used in the section the court is not required to order the contribution is the same for each of the respondents; the court has a wide discretion when it comes to ordering what each respondent should contribute: *Re Overnight Ltd (in liq)* [2010] EWHC 613 (Ch), [2010] 2 BCLC 186. The court held that in relation to the issue of contribution the approach utilized in cases dealing with wrongful trading should apply to s 213 as it would be surprising if different approaches were used in relation to identical wording contained in adjacent provisions of the Act.

Directions—If an order under s 213 is made, a court is, at its discretion, empowered to make further directions to give effect to its declaration. This is covered by s 215. See the comments attaching to that section.

Practice—As a successful claim under s 213 involves an allegation of dishonesty, dishonesty must be pleaded and also put to the respondent in cross-examination: *Dempster v HMRC* [2008] EWHC 63 (Ch), [2008] STC 2079, *Abbey Forwarding Ltd v Hone* [2010] EWHC 2029 (Ch).

Limitation period—It has been held in relation to s 214 that the application can be categorised as a claim in respect of a sum of money within the Limitation Act, and hence, a six-year limitation period applies: *Re Farmizer (Products) Ltd* [1997] 1 BCLC 589 at 598, CA. It appears that the same comments could be applied to s 213. The limitation period would begin from the time of the resolution to wind up in voluntary liquidations, or from the date of the court order in compulsory liquidations, being the time when the cause of action accrued.

See A Keay *Company Directors' Responsibilities to Creditors* (Routledge-Cavendish, 2007), chs 3–6.

214 Wrongful trading

(1) Subject to subsection (3) below, if in the course of the winding up of a company it appears that subsection (2) of this section applies in relation to a person who is or has been a director of the company, the court, on the application of the liquidator, may declare that that person is to be liable to make such contribution (if any) to the company's assets as the court thinks proper.

(2) This subsection applies in relation to a person if—

    (a)   the company has gone into insolvent liquidation,

    (b)   at some time before the commencement of the winding up of the company, that person knew or ought to have concluded that there was no reasonable prospect that the company would avoid going into insolvent liquidation, and

    (c)   that person was a director of the company at that time;

but the court shall not make a declaration under this section in any case where the time mentioned in paragraph (b) above was before 28 April 1986.

(3) The court shall not make a declaration under this section with respect to any person if it is satisfied that after the condition specified in subsection (2)(b) was first satisfied in relation to him that person took every step with a view to minimising the potential loss to the company's creditors as (assuming him to have known that there was no reasonable prospect that the company would avoid going into insolvent liquidation) he ought to have taken.

(4) For the purposes of subsections (2) and (3), the facts which a director of a company ought to know or ascertain, the conclusions which he ought to reach and the steps which he ought to take are those which would be known or ascertained, or reached or taken, by a reasonably diligent person having both—

(a)   the general knowledge, skill and experience that may reasonably be expected of a person carrying out the same functions as are carried out by that director in relation to the company, and

(b)   the general knowledge, skill and experience that that director has.

(5) The reference in subsection (4) to the functions carried out in relation to a company by a director of the company includes any functions which he does not carry out but which have been entrusted to him.

(6) For the purposes of this section a company goes into insolvent liquidation if it goes into liquidation at a time when its assets are insufficient for the payment of its debts and other liabilities and the expenses of the winding up.

(7) In this section 'director' includes a shadow director.

(8) This section is without prejudice to section 213.

General note—The provision fails to specify what action will cause a director to breach it. Claims by liquidators have apparently not been plentiful in recent years and those liquidators taking proceedings have struggled to obtain judgments: see notably *Re Continental Assurance Co of London plc* [2001] BPIR 733; *The Liquidator of Marini Ltd v Dickensen* [2003] EWHC 334 (Ch), [2004] BCC 172. Rarely, it seems, if at all, where directors have made an effort to understand the position of their company, and where they decided to continue doing business, will they be held liable: *Re Sherborne Associates Ltd* [1995] BCC 40; *Re Continental Assurance Co of London plc*. The courts do not appear readily to impose liability on directors, and this is particularly so where the directors have sought and obtained advice from professionals. In most cases where directors have been found liable they have been found to have acted irresponsibly.

This section was introduced to stop directors from continuing to trade while their companies are on a slide into insolvency and to allow a liquidator to recoup the loss to the company caused by the actions of the directors, so as to benefit the creditors as a whole: *Re Purpoint Ltd* [1991] BCLC 491 at 499 per Vinelott J, but it has been made clear that liability is not imposed on the directors necessarily where they knew or ought to have known that the company was insolvent; it is only where the directors knew or ought to have concluded that the company could not avoid entering insolvent liquidation: *Re Hawkes Hill Publishing Co Ltd (in liq)* [2007] BCC 937 at [28].

Claims are able to be made against a director's estate in the event of his or her death: *Re Sherborne Associates Ltd* [1995] BCC 40 at 46. Where there are a number of directors, their liability is several, requiring each director's position to be considered separately and the payment by one director does not automatically discharge the other director(s): *Re Continental Assurance Co of London plc* [2001] BPIR 733 at 846–848. Nevertheless, the court has the discretion of ordering that the liability of any two or more directors is joint and several for the whole or part of the contribution that the court orders to be paid (*Re Continental Assurance Co of London plc* at 847). The courts in *Re Produce Marketing Marketing Consortium Ltd* (1989) 5 BCC 569 at 598 and *Re DKG Contractors Ltd* [1990] BCC 903 at 912 held that the directors were jointly and severally liable.

Claims under s 214 against foreign directors of a foreign company that is being wound up in England or Wales can be commenced (*Re Howard Holdings Inc* [1998] BCC 549 at 552; *Stocznia Gdanska SA v Latreefers Inc (No 2)*, [2001] 2 BCLC 116 at 142, CA) but, in assessing the claims, courts must have regard for the relevant foreign law under which the directors were acting and what obligations a director had to minimise losses to the company's creditors under that law, and it might well be that if the foreign law did not impose obligations akin to s 214, the English court will decide that it is not appropriate to make an order under s 214 (*Re Howard Holdings Inc* at 554).

Liquidators are not permitted to assign actions under s 214 because they are actions given by statute to them personally in the position of liquidator: *Re Oasis Merchandising Services Ltd* [1995] BCC 911, affirmed on appeal [1997] 1 All ER 1009, [1997] BCC 282, CA. This can mean that liquidators have difficulty in funding actions.

de facto directors as well as de jure and shadow directors: *Re Hydrodan (Corby) Ltd* [1994] BCC 161. An insolvency practitioner who advised directors before their company entered liquidation could not be under a common liability with the directors in relation to proceedings brought against the directors (*Re International Championship Management Ltd* [2006] EWHC 768 (Ch)).

'**Every step**'—As part of a defence to an action under s 214, a director has to establish that he or she took every step with a view to minimising creditor losses. The phrase 'every step' is not defined in any shape or form and one cannot really ascertain what is meant by the phrase from the surrounding provisions. It is difficult for a director to know what every step is, and when he or she has completed taking all of the steps necessary. There is the potential for directors to be left uncertain what they should do and whether what they do is adequate. The major step of resigning or even deciding to appoint an administrator might not suffice. The extreme measure of entering liquidation cannot be taken by a single director of a multiple director board (*Re Instrumentation Electrical Services Ltd* (1988) 4 BCC 301), so a concerned director has to convince a majority of directors that liquidation is the appropriate avenue to go down. Steps that directors might take are, amongst many: seeking the advice of insolvency practitioners; appointing an administrator; seeking up-to-date accounts and reports from executive directors; ensuring that adequate inquiries are made of managers. In *Re Continental Assurance*, Park J was impressed with the fact that the directors 'reduced the scale of trading to minimal and cautious levels', and eventually ceased trading when they were advised that their company was insolvent (at 769). In contrast in *Re Idessa (UK) Ltd* [2011] EWHC 804 (Ch), [2011] BPIR 957 the directors failed in their defence as they had not tightened the corporate belt or encouraged cost savings or done anything differently despite the company's state (at [120]).

'Every step' was intended to cover specific steps taken by directors with a view to preserving or realising assets or claims for the benefit of creditors and did not apply to the act of wrongful trading itself, even if that action was undertaken with the intention of attempting to make a profit: *Re Brian D Pierson (Contractors) Ltd* [1999] BCC 26, [2001] BCLC 275.

The directors who are respondents to s 214 claims have the burden of establishing that they took every step, and they must establish their case on the balance of probabilities, but in this regard we must note that courts have cautioned against the use of hindsight (*Re Sherborne Associates Ltd* [1995] BCC 40 at 54; *Re Brian D Pierson (Contractors) Ltd* [1999] BCC 26 at 50, [2001] BCLC 275 at 303), and so a determination whether a director took every step should not be considered in light of later developments that could not be reasonably foreseen by directors.

The test as to whether a director has taken every step depends on courts considering what has been done in light of the criteria contained in s 214(4).

Not carrying out functions—Directors can be held liable for not carrying out functions that were entrusted to them (s 214(5)). So directors are responsible if they omit to do that which they should have done.

Loss—Although not deciding the issue, it has been assumed that it may not be necessary to prove a causal link between the wrongful trading established, and any particular loss: *Re Simmon Box (Diamonds) Ltd* [2000] BCC 275, [2001] 1 BCLC 176, CA. However, subsequently in *Re Continental Assurance Co of London plc* [2001] BPIR 733 at 844 Park J said that it was necessary to establish some connection between the wrongfulness of the directors' conduct with the company's losses which the liquidator seeks to recover. This is in line with the argument that counsel for the liquidator put in *Re Produce Marketing Consortium Ltd*, an argument that appeared to have been accepted by the judge in that case, namely that the test of liability is analogous to the assessment of tortious damages, being dependent on causation. Nevertheless, Park J in *Continental Assurance* said that more had to be established than mere nexus between an incorrect decision to carry on trading and a particular loss sustained by the company (at 844). Park J pointed out that the required nexus will often be obvious, such as where a director turns a blind eye to inherent loss-making (at 844). Not all losses suffered by a company after the directors wrongly decide to continue trading can necessarily be claimed by a liquidator: *Re Continental Assurance* at 844; *The Liquidator of Marini Ltd v Dickensen* [2003] EWHC 334 (Ch) at [68]. The law will limit liability to those consequences which are attributable to the wrongful action(s) (*Re Continental Assurance* at 845).

Liquidators are required to show that there was a net deficiency in company assets when comparing the company's position as at the time when wrongful trading is alleged to have commenced (and trading should have stopped or every step was taken to minimize creditors' loss) and the position when trading actually ceased (perhaps on the commencement of winding up) (*Re Continental Assurance* at 844; *The Liquidator of Marini Ltd v Dickensen* at [68]).

Relief from liability—It has been held that directors cannot be excused for wrongful trading under s 1157 of the Companies Act 2006 (formerly s 727 of the Companies Act 1985), which requires directors to have acted honestly and reasonably, as this defence is incompatible with the objective nature of the test found in s 214 (*Re Produce Marketing Consortium Ltd* [1989] 1 WLR 745, (1989) 5 BCC 399; *Re Brian D Pierson (Contractors) Ltd* [1999] BCC 26, [2001] BCLC 275), the test under s 1157 being essentially a subjective test (*Re Produce Marketing Consortium Ltd; Bairstow v Queens Moat Houses plc* [2000] BCC 1025). Query whether this is correct, as s 214 (as discussed earlier) involves both subjective and objective elements, as does s 1157. Perhaps it can be argued that s 214 and s 1157 are not incompatible after all. It is notable that in *Re D'Jan of London Ltd* [1994] 1 BCLC 561 Hoffmann LJ (as he then was) was prepared to relieve a director from liability for breach of the director's duty of care and skill, and the test for a breach of this duty was, according to his Lordship, the same as that found in s 214. The judge in *Re DKG Contractors Ltd* [1990] BCC 903 did not exclude possible relief for a director liable under s 214. Furthermore, in Australia it has been held that the Australian counterpart of s 1157 (Corporations Act, s 1318) is able to be relied upon by a director if he or she is found guilty of engaging in insolvent trading (broadly equivalent to wrongful trading): *Kenna & Brown Ltd v Kenna* (1999) 32 ACSR 430. But see the argument against the use of s 1157 mounted by Edmunds and Lowry ('The Continuing Value of Relief for Directors' Breach of Duty' (2003) 66 MLR 195 at 211).

Beneficiaries of any award—The award is to be held by a liquidator for the purpose of making a distribution to the unsecured creditors (*Re Oasis Merchandising Services Ltd* [1995] BCC 911, affirmed on appeal [1997] 1 All ER 1009, [1997] BCC 282, CA), and is therefore not available for a chargeholder.

Directions—If an order under s 214 is made, a court is, at its discretion, empowered to make further directions to give effect to its declaration. This is covered by s 215. See the comments attaching to that section.

Limitation period—Claims under the section are regarded as claims for the recovery of sums recoverable under any enactment, so the limitation period is six years (Limitation Act 1989, s 9(1)), and runs from the date when the company entered insolvent liquidation (*Re Farmizer (Products) Ltd* [1997] 1 BCLC 589, [1997] BCC 655, CA), namely either the date of the resolution to wind up or the date of the winding-up order. In any event, unreasonable delay in initiating proceedings by a liquidator could see the proceedings struck out (*Re Farmizer (Products) Ltd*).

See A Keay *Company Directors' Responsibilities to Creditors* (Routledge-Cavendish, 2007), chs 7–10.

215 Proceedings under ss 213–214

(1) On the hearing of an application under section 213, or 214, the liquidator may himself give evidence or call witnesses.

(2) Where under either section the court makes a declaration, it may give such further directions as it thinks proper for giving effect to the declaration; and in particular, the court may—

> (a) provide for the liability of any person under the declaration to be a charge on any debt or obligation due from the company to him, or on any mortgage or charge or any interest in a mortgage or charge on assets of the company held by or vested in him, or

any person on his behalf, or any person claiming as assignee from or through the person liable or any person acting on his behalf, and

(b) from time to time make such further order as may be necessary for enforcing any charge imposed under this subsection.

(3) For the purposes of subsection (2), 'assignee'—

(a) includes a person to whom or in whose favour, by the directions of the person made liable, the debt, obligation, mortgage or charge was created, issued or transferred or the interest created, but

(b) does not include an assignee for valuable consideration (not including consideration by way of marriage or the formation of a civil partnership) given in good faith and without notice of any of the matters on the ground of which the declaration is made.

(4) Where the court makes a declaration under either section in relation to a person who is a creditor of the company, it may direct that the whole or any part of any debt owed by the company to that person and any interest thereon shall rank in priority after all other debts owed by the company and after any interest on those debts.

(5) Sections 213 and 214 have effect notwithstanding that the person concerned may be criminally liable in respect of matters on the ground of which the declaration under the section is to be made.

Amendments—Civil Partnership Act 2004, s 261(1), Sch 27, para 112.

General note—Where a court makes a declaration in relation to either a s 213 or s 214 application, it is, at its discretion, empowered to make further directions to give effect to its declaration. This might even involve directing that any debt owed to the respondent is to rank after the unsecured creditors and the payment of interest (s 215(4)).

216 Restriction on re-use of company names

(1) This section applies to a person where a company ('the liquidating company') has gone into insolvent liquidation on or after the appointed day and he was a director or shadow director of the company at any time in the period of 12 months, ending with the day before it went into liquidation.

(2) For the purposes of this section, a name is a prohibited name in relation to such a person if—

(a) it is a name by which the liquidating company was known at any time in that period of 12 months, or

(b) it is a name which is so similar to a name falling within paragraph (a) as to suggest an association with that company.

(3) Except with leave of the court or in such circumstances as may be prescribed, a person to whom this section applies shall not at any time in the period of 5 years beginning with the day on which the liquidating company went into liquidation—

(a)   be a director of any other company that is known by a prohibited name, or

(b)   in any way, whether directly or indirectly, be concerned or take part in the promotion, formation or management of any such company, or

(c)   in any way, whether directly or indirectly, be concerned or take part in the carrying on of a business carried on (otherwise than by a company) under a prohibited name.

(4) If a person acts in contravention of this section, he is liable to imprisonment or a fine, or both.

(5) In subsection (3) 'the court' means any court having jurisdiction to wind up companies; and on an application for leave under that subsection, the Secretary of State or the official receiver may appear and call the attention of the court to any matters which seem to him to be relevant.

(6) References in this section, in relation to any time, to a name by which a company is known are to the name of the company at that time or to any name under which the company carries on business at that time.

(7) For the purposes of this section a company goes into insolvent liquidation if it goes into liquidation at a time when its assets are insufficient for the payment of its debts and other liabilities and the expenses of the winding up.

(8) In this section 'company' includes a company which may be wound up under Part V of this Act.

General note—This provision is to be read with s 217 and rr 4.227–4.230 (*ESS Production Ltd (in administration) v Sully* [2005] BCC 435 at 438, [2005] EWCA Civ 554 at [2]; s 216(3)) and is designed to prevent the re-use of the name of a company that has entered insolvent liquidation, except where the leave of the court is secured or in certain limited circumstances. This action has been taken to thwart the use of the so-called 'Phoenix syndrome' (*Re Lightning Electrical Contractors Ltd* [1996] BCC 950, [1996] 2 BCLC 302), defined as where a company 'trading under a particular name goes into liquidation or receivership, leaving its creditors behind, and then a new company, with much the same name and all the same assets run by the same people, takes over but shorn of its previous creditors' (*Western Intelligence Ltd v KDO Label Printing Machines Ltd* [1998] BCC 472 at 473 per Jacob J). Chadwick LJ has said, in the Court of Appeal decision of *ESS Production Ltd (in administration) v Sully* [2005] BCC 435 at 454, [2005] EWCA Civ 554 at [91] that there is no breach of the section where an active company had, before the liquidation of the liquidating company, a name that suggested association with the liquidating company.

   The following is the scenario that the provision seeks to prevent. An unscrupulous person who has carried on business by way of a limited liability company that had substantial debts owed to unsecured creditors, and which fails and enters liquidation, carries on the business of the company through another company after, as often occurs, the second company acquires the original company's business as a going concern (as occurred in *ESS Production Ltd (in admin) v Sully*), often at an undervalue, with the new company effectively benefiting from the goodwill of the failed company. It must be emphasised though that while s 216 has Phoenix-type situations as its principal target: *First Independent Factors & Finance v Mountford* [2008] EWHC 835 (Ch), [2008] 2 BCLC 297 at [17], [26], it can apply where the Phoenix situation is not strictly relevant, and that some Phoenix scenarios are not necessarily wrong; it has been held that the section applies to both unscrupulous and honest traders: *First Independent Factors & Finance v Mountford* at [17]. Also there have been suggestions that the section could serve to protect shareholders as well as creditors. In *Re Neath Rugby Ltd; Hawkes v Cuddy* [2007] EWHC 1789 (Ch), [2007] BCC 671, [2008] 1 BCLC 527 at [93], it was said that the provision was quite wide in that it 'creates a free-standing criminal offence. It concerns the management of companies and is designed to protect anyone who is interested in or has dealings with companies from those who act as directors of liquidating companies and then seek to carry on business through another corporate vehicle bearing the same or a similar name. The principal target of section 216 was the phoenix company: but the application of the section is not confined to the phoenix phenomenon.' The court went on to say that a breach of s 216 could form the basis for a successful petition under s 459 of the Companies Act 1985 (now s 994 of the Companies Act 2006) (on appeal the Court of Appeal did not criticise this approach concerning the section: *Cuddy v Hawkes* [2007] EWCA Civ 1072, [2008] BCC 125).

The critical issue is the use of a name that is prohibited and not that a company that is insolvent has transferred assets to another company (*Ricketts v Ad Valorem Factors Ltd* [2004] 1 BCLC 1, CA) or that the goodwill of an insolvent has been exploited: *Thorne v Silverleaf* [1994] BCLC 637 at 642–643, CA. There is no requirement, before holding that s 216 applies, that anyone must be misled by the use of the company name (*Ricketts* at [13], [16]). According to Etherton J in *Re Bowman Power Systems (UK) Ltd* (unreported, ChD, 27 October 2004), the provision was designed to prevent the danger of the insolvent company being acquired at an undervalue and the danger that creditors might be under the misapprehension that there had been no change in the corporate vehicle. In dealing with any cases, it is critical that the purpose behind the section is kept in mind: *ESS Production Ltd (in administration) v Sully* at [91].

Notwithstanding the points made at the end of the last paragraph, one of the judges in the Court of Appeal in *Ricketts* (Simon Brown LJ) was of the view that 'Draconian consequences' of the section meant that courts should 'strive to avoid adopting a construction which penalises someone where the legislator's intention to do so is doubtful' (at [30]).

Details of any offence under this section should be reported by the liquidator to the Secretary of State for Business Enterprise and Regulatory Reform and should include: evidence that the successor business is using the prohibited name in cases where this is not evident from records at Companies House; and any details of any sale of the liquidated company's assets or business by the liquidator in accordance with r 4.228 of the Rules (Dear IP Millennium Edition, December 2000, chapter 20).

'Insolvent liquidation'—See the comments under this heading in relation to s 214.

Section 216(2)

'A prohibited name in relation to such a person'—Section 216 only stops directors and shadow directors of the company in liquidation from using the name of the insolvent company. So a company's name may be re-used, but it must not involve someone who is a prohibited person, ie anyone mentioned in s 216 ('such a person').

Similar name—When determining whether a name of a company is similar to the name of another, the matter is one of fact for the court: *Archer Structures v Christopher Griffiths* [2003] EWHC 957 (Ch), [2003] BPIR 1071 at [15]. Courts will employ an objective test (*Archer Structures* at [18]). The test that is to be used in determining similarity of names is not whether members of the public believed that the company was the same as the one that was in liquidation, but whether the similarity between the two companies is such that it is probable that members of the public, when comparing the names in the appropriate context, would associate the two companies with one another. The impact of the names on a reasonable person in the relevant commercial field, taking into account the manner in which the names were employed, the kind of customers of the companies and the context in which they would do so as well as the sorts of businesses involved, are matters to be considered by courts: *Commissioners for HM Revenue and Customs v Walsh* [2005] EWHC 1304 (Ch), [2005] BPIR 1105, [2005] 2 BCLC 455 (the two companies involved were both building and civil engineering companies); *First Independent Factors & Finance v Mountford* [2008] EWHC 835 (Ch), [2008] 2 BCLC 297 at [18]. It has been held that the addition of words such as 'Contractors' and 'Construction' when used with company names with no other differences does not stop the company names being deemed to be similar (*Archer Structures* at [21]). Hence, where the name of the insolvent company was 'MPJ Construction Ltd', and its assets were transferred to a company with the name of 'MPJ Contractors Ltd', the person prohibited to act because of s 216 had to obtain leave to be involved in the latter company, as the names were similar (*Archer Structures* at [21]). Also see *Re Lightning Electrical Contractors Ltd* [1996] BCC 950, [1996] 2 BCLC 302). It is not possible to circumvent the law in relation to a company in insolvent liquidation. This is confirmed by the recent Court of Appeal decision in *Ricketts v Ad Valorem Factors Ltd* [2004] 1 BCLC 1. In that case the names 'Air Component Co Ltd' and 'Air Equipment Co Ltd' were regarded as being similar for the purposes of the section. The former went into liquidation and, because the latter was a similar name to the former, it was a prohibited name in the context of s 216(2)(b). The court took into account the circumstances in which the names were actually used or likely to be used, namely the types of product in which they carried on business, the location of the businesses, the types of customers, and those who were involved in the operation of the businesses. In this case all of this suggested an association between the two companies, or that they were part of the same group of companies ([22]. Also, see *R v Richmond Magistrates' Court* [2008] EWHC 84 (Admin), [2008] 1 BCLC 681, [2008] BPIR 468) at [9].

If the court finds that two names are similar, then it has no discretion in relation to the personal liability of the director against whom proceedings are brought (*Ricketts* at [22]).

In *Ricketts* Simon Brown LJ said that the 'similarity between the two names must be such as to give rise to a probability that members of the public, comparing the two names in the relevant context, will associate the two companies with each other, whether as successor companies or, as here, as part of the same group' (at [30]).

Leave of the court—If leave of the court is granted, a person who is ordinarily prohibited by the section from using the name, may do so: e g *Re Bonus Breaks Ltd* [1991] BCC 546; *Re Lightning Electrical Contractors Ltd* [1996] BCC 950, [1996] 2 BCLC 302. The court may grant leave subject to conditions. While some principles have been specified by the courts, each case must be taken on its own merits. The courts will, in deciding whether or not to grant leave, examine whether there is any risk to the creditors of the new company: *Penrose v Official Receiver* [1996] 1 WLR 482 at 490. Where there is an application for leave the court should not treat the applicant, without evidence of misconduct, as if the applicant were unfit to be a director, and it would be incorrect for a court to approach the application in the same way that it would with an application for leave under the Company Directors' Disqualification Act 1986: *Re Lightning Electrical Contractors Ltd* [1996] BCC 950, [1996] 2 BCLC 302; *Penrose v Official Receiver* at 489. But if the court heard evidence on a s 216 application that indicated that the applicant was, because of his or her conduct relating to the affairs of the company in liquidation, unfit to be involved in the management of a company, then the court could exercise the discretion that it possesses in accordance with the principles that operate when the court is hearing applications for leave under s 17 of the Company Directors' Disqualification Act 1986 (*Penrose v Official Receiver* at 489).

To aid its deliberations concerning an application for leave, the court may ask the liquidator of the company to provide a report detailing the circumstances of the company's insolvency and the extent (if any) of the applicant's apparent responsibility for the insolvency (r 4.227). It is likely to enable the applicant under s 216 to obtain leave if the receiver or liquidator of the company whose name is being used supports the application: *Re Lightning Electrical Contractors Ltd* [1996] BCC 950, [1996] 2 BCLC 302.

Leave may well be granted to those involved in a company that enters insolvent liquidation to be directors of companies with prohibited names if they were not culpable in the failing of the company: *Re Bonus Breaks Ltd* [1991] BCC 546.

See rr 4.228–4.230 and the relevant notes for three situations where the prohibition in s 216 does not apply. These situations ensure that the disposal of company property in the ordinary course of business is not restricted.

Section 216(3)(b)

'concerned or take part in the ... management'—This is not defined, but from s 217(1)(b) and s 217(4) it would seem that it would mean being involved in the management of a company. See comments under 'Involved in the management' under s 217.

Section 216(3)(c)

'Indirectly'—This is obviously designed to cover the case where a person runs a company by using others who appear, prima facie, to be running the company, but who are effectively puppets, or at least dependent on the prohibited person.

Breach—In a prosecution mens rea in relation to a breach does not have to be proved: *R v Cole* [1998] BCC 87. The offence under this provision is one of strict liability: *R v Doring* [2002] EWCA Crim 1695, [2002] BPIR 1204; *ESS Production Ltd (in administration) v Sully* [2005] BCC 435 at 454, [2005] EWCA Civ 554.

Any breach of s 216 automatically makes the respondent liable under s 217: *Thorne v Silverleaf* [1994] 1 BCLC 637, CA. A breach of s 216 by a director may be taken into account by a court in considering an application for a disqualification order pursuant to the Company Directors' Disqualification Act 1986 on the basis that the director is unfit for office: *Re Migration Services International Ltd* [2000] BCC 1095.

'carrying on of a business carried on (otherwise than by a company)'—this means that the section is not confined to the situation where the defendant has been involved in carrying on a business through a company. It might apply to where he or she was carrying on business as a sole trader or in partnership: *First Independent Factors & Finance v Mountford* [2008] EWHC 835 (Ch), [2008] 2 BCLC 297 at [20].

Penalty—As far as the criminal penalties are concerned, see s 430 and Sch 10 to the Act. The latter provides that the penalty is imprisonment for 2 years or a fine or both where the prosecution is on indictment, and where prosecutions are initiated summarily then the penalty is imprisonment for 6 months or a statutory maximum fine (the statutory maximum is £5,000 according to s 32 of the Magistrates' Courts Act 1980 as amended by s 17 of the Criminal Justice Act 1991).

The penalty for a breach of the section was considered in *R v Enver* (20 January 2000, CA (Crim Div)). The court reduced the fine of £10,000 to £5,000 because of the respondent's previous good character and the severe personal losses that he suffered. In contrast, the defendants in *R v McCredie* [2000] 2 BCLC 438, [2000] BCC 617, CA (Crim Div) were subjected to community service orders of 180 and 100 hours respectively.

If the magistrates hearing a case believe that their own power in sentencing a person under this provision is too limited, they may commit a person to the Crown Court for sentencing: *R v Chelmsford Justices ex parte Lloyd* (2000) *The Times*, December 5.

Where directors trade under a company name which was prohibited, they can be held liable under the Proceeds of Crime Act 2002 s.76(2). What they are liable for is not a proportion of the sum that could be attributed to the name of the company but the full amount that the director actually received in their role as directors: *R v Weintroub* [2011] EWCA Crim 2167.

Section 216(6)

'a name by which a company is known'—This could mean the registered name of the company or any other name that the company carried on business with during the 12 months prior to liquidation, including a change of name during the relevant period: *ESS Production Ltd (in administration) v Sully* [2005] BCC 435 at 454, [2005] EWCA Civ 554 at [68], [70]. The reference to 'any name' indicates that a company could have more than one name in the relevant period before liquidation (*ESS Production Ltd (in administration) v Sully* at [70]).

'carries on business'—This covers the case where a company carries on some of its business, but not necessarily all of it, under a prohibited name (*ESS Production Ltd (in administration) v Sully* at [72]).

'Company'—This can include an unregistered company that is wound up under Part V of the Act. This would include foreign companies.

See the comments relating to s 217 and rr 4.227–4.230.

217 Personal liability for debts, following contravention of s 216

(1) A person is personally responsible for all the relevant debts of a company if at any time—

(a) in contravention of section 216, he is involved in the management of the company, or

(b) as a person who is involved in the management of the company, he acts or is willing to act on instructions given (without the leave of the court) by a person whom he knows at that time to be in contravention in relation to the company of section 216.

(2) Where a person is personally responsible under this section for the relevant debts of a company, he is jointly and severally liable in respect of those debts with the company and any other person who, whether under this section or otherwise, is so liable.

(3) For the purposes of this section the relevant debts of a company are—

(a) in relation to a person who is personally responsible under paragraph (a) of subsection (1), such debts and other liabilities of the company as are incurred at a time when that person was involved in the management of the company, and

(b) in relation to a person who is personally responsible under paragraph (b) of that subsection, such debts and other liabilities of the company as are incurred at a time when that person was acting or was willing to act on instructions given as mentioned in that paragraph.

(4) For the purposes of this section, a person is involved in the management of a company if he is a director of the company or if he is concerned, whether directly or indirectly, or takes part, in the management of the company.

(5) For the purposes of this section a person who, as a person involved in the management of a company, has at any time acted on instructions given (without the leave of the court) by a person whom he knew at that time to be in contravention in relation to the company of section 216 is presumed, unless the contrary is shown, to have been willing at any time thereafter to act on any instructions given by that person.

(6) In this section 'company' includes a company which may be wound up under Part V.

General note— This provision is to be read with s 216 and rr 4.227–4.30: *ESS Production Ltd (in administration) v Sully* [2005] BCC 435, [2005] EWCA Civ 554 at [2]. It appears to have been rarely used until the last few years, when we have seen cases such as *Archer Structures v Christopher Griffiths* [2003] EWHC 957 (Ch), [2003] BPIR 1071; *Inland Revenue Commissioners v Nash* [2003] EWHC 686 (Ch), [2003] BPIR 1138; *ESS Production Ltd v Sully* [2005] EWCA Civ 554; *Revenue and Customs Commissioners v Benton-Diggins* [2006] EWHC 793 (Ch); *Re Neath Rugby Ltd; Hawkes v Cuddy* [2007] EWHC 1789 (Ch), [2007] BCC 671, [2008] 1 BCLC 527, in which creditors have sought orders under it, decided. In the last of these cases the Revenue was seeking an order that a director pay arrears of PAYE income tax and NIC payments relating to former employees of his company.

While the section is primarily invoked by creditors, it has been held that it is not so limited. It simply imposes a personal liability on a director or manager who was formerly a director of a liquidating company: *Re Neath Rugby Ltd; Hawkes v Cuddy* [2007] EWHC 1789 (Ch), [2007] BCC 671, [2008] 1 BCLC 527 at [93].

While only directors and shadow directors can be liable under s 216, the sister provision to s 217, any person involved in the management of a company and acting on the instructions of someone who he or she knows is acting in breach of s 216, may be held liable under s 217.

This provision was included in order to provide a more effective deterrent than would be provided by criminal sanctions: *Thorne v Silverleaf* [1994] BCC 109 at 117.

To assist those proceeding under s 217, there is no need for a director to be found guilty of a breach of s 216 before proceedings can be initiated under s 217. What an applicant under s 217 has to establish is that two companies traded under similar names and that the respondent was a director of one of the companies, that had gone into insolvent liquidation, and was either a director, or involved in the management, of the other company, or acted on the instructions of someone whom he or she knew was liable under s 216: *Inland Revenue Commissioners v Nash* [2003] EWHC 686 (Ch), [2003] BPIR 1138. See notes accompanying s 216.

Even if a person deals with a company that he or she knows has a person who is in breach of s 216 involved in its management, he or she is entitled to recover against the director under s 217: *Thorne v Silverleaf* [1994] 1 BCLC 637.

The section does not specify who can initiate proceedings, and creditors have done so successfully: *Archer Structures v Christopher Griffiths* [2003] EWHC 957 (Ch), [2003] BPIR 1071.

In *City of Glasgow Council v Craig* [2008] CSOH 171, [2010] BCC 235 at [20] (Lord Glennie, Outer House of the Scottish Court of Session) it was said that a director is only liable for liabilities incurred by the company that has used the prohibited name while it is carrying on business using that name, and this does not mean that there is liability for all debts of the company, however incurred.

Where an application is made against a director for a confiscation order under the Proceeds of Crimes Act 2002 in relation to a breach of section 216, the director is liable for the sums that he or she has received in his or her capacity as a director, including salaries and dividends: *R v Weintroub* [2011] EWCA Crim 2167 at [8].

'Involved in the management'—This phrase is defined in s 217(4) and includes taking part in the management of a company. It is likely that it will encompass those acting in relation to the internal workings of the company and its external relations with others: *R v Austen* (1985) 1 BCC 99, 528. Each case will have to be taken on its merits. If a person acts in the capacity of an adviser to the board of a company, this conduct has been regarded as sufficient to constitute taking part in the management of a company: *R v Campbell* (1984) 78 Cr App R 95, CA (Crim Div). The appeal court in *R v Campbell* approved of a distinction drawn by the trial judge between someone involved in the central direction of the company's affairs, which involved taking part in the management of the company, and managing particular aspects of the company's trading affairs, which did not constitute taking part in the management of the company (at 98). Certainly it is not necessary to have control of the company before one can be regarded as being involved in the management of the company: *Re Market Wizard Systems (UK) Ltd* [1998] 2 BCLC 282.

In the Australian case of *Commissioner for Corporate Affairs (Vic) v Bracht* (1988) 14 ACLR 728 (referred to in *Re Market Wizard Systems (UK) Ltd*) a person was charged with breaching the Companies Code of Victoria because he was, allegedly, taking part in the management of a company while an undischarged bankrupt (equivalent to s 11 of the Company Directors' Disqualification Act 1986). Ormiston J of the Victorian Supreme Court, following, inter alia, the English case of *R v Campbell* (above), said that the size of the company should be taken into account in considering what was meant by taking part in the management of a company (at 733–734). His Honour went on to say that the concept of 'taking part in the management of a company' should be construed widely, and would include activities involving some responsibility and participation in the decision-making processes of a company related to its business affairs, but need not involve directly communicating with the board (at 733–734, 735, 736). Taking part in management would neither encompass routine clerical or administrative duties associated with management, nor activities that did not involve any significant discretion or advisory role in decision-making (at 733).

Relevant debts—'Relevant debts' are defined widely in s 217(3) and include liabilities that are not debts in the strict sense of the term. So, a damages award against the company would qualify. As a consequence of the breadth of the expression 'relevant debts' a person liable under s 217 may be liable for claims in damages, and the person is not simply liable for all debts incurred by him or her during the relevant time: he or she can be held liable for all debts incurred. Only debts that are incurred under a prohibited name (and where there is a breach of the section) are to be categorised as relevant for the purposes of the section: *ESS Production Ltd (in administration) v Sully* [2005] BCC 435 at 454, [2005] EWCA Civ 554 at [75].

'A person … has at any time acted on instructions'—Section 217(5) provides that if a person who has been involved in the management of a company and acted at any time on instructions from someone whom he or she knew to be in breach of s 216, then he or she is presumed to have been willing at any time to act on any instructions given by the person in breach of s 216. Consequently, if it is established at one point of time that a person is willing to act on instructions from a person who breached s 216, a continuing presumption prevails that he or she is willing to act on instructions. The presumption can be rebutted.

Relief from liability—Arden LJ in *ESS Production Ltd (in administration) v Sully* [2005] BCC 435, [2005] EWCA Civ 554 at [20] left unresolved whether a director might be able to be relieved from liability under s 1157 of the Companies Act 2006 (formerly s 727 of the Companies Act 1985) where he or she has acted scrupulously. But more recently Lewison J in *First Independent Factors & Finance v Mountford* [2008] EWHC 835 (Ch), [2008] 2 BCLC 297 at [33] has said that where a person is found liable under the section a court cannot give relief under s 1157 for the relieving provision is not available where a stranger is bring proceedings (as against the situation where proceedings are brought by the company itself or someone acting for the company, such as a liquidator)

Generally, see the comments relating to s 217 and rr 4.227–4.230.

See, Werner 'Phoenixing: Avoiding the Ashes' (2009) 22 Ins Intel 105.

Investigation and prosecution of malpractice

218 Prosecution of delinquent officers and members of company

(1) If it appears to the court in the course of a winding up by the court that any past or present officer, or any member, of the company has been guilty of any offence in relation to the company for which he is criminally liable, the court may (either on the application of a person interested in the winding up or of its own motion) direct the liquidator to refer the matter—

    (a)   in the case of a winding up in England and Wales, to the Secretary of State, and

    (b)   in the case of a winding up in Scotland, to the Lord Advocate.

(2) *(Repealed)*

(3) If in the case of a winding up by the court in England and Wales it appears to the liquidator, not being the official receiver, that any past or present officer of the company, or any member of it, has been guilty of an offence in relation to the company for which he is criminally liable, the liquidator shall report the matter to the official receiver.

(4) If it appears to the liquidator in the course of a voluntary winding up that any past or present officer of the company, or any member of it, has been guilty of an offence in relation to the company for which he is criminally liable, he shall forthwith report the matter—

    (a)   in the case of a winding up in England and Wales, to the Secretary of State, and

    (b)   in the case of a winding up in Scotland, to the Lord Advocate,

and shall furnish to the Secretary of State or (as the case may be) the Lord Advocate such information and give to him such access to and facilities for inspecting and taking copies of documents (being information or documents in the possession or under the control of the liquidator and relating to the matter in question) as the Secretary of State or (as the case may be) the Lord Advocate requires.

(5) Where a report is made to the Secretary of State under subsection (4) he may, for the purpose of investigating the matter reported to him and such other matters relating to the affairs of the company as appear to him to require investigation, exercise any of the powers which are exercisable by inspectors appointed under section 431 or 432 of the Companies Act 1985 to investigate a company's affairs.

(6) If it appears to the court in the course of a voluntary winding up that—

(a)   any past or present officer of the company, or any member of it, has been guilty as above-mentioned, and

(b)   no report with respect to the matter has been made by the liquidator under subsection (4),

the court may (on the application of any person interested in the winding up or of its own motion) direct the liquidator to make such a report.

On a report being made accordingly, this section has effect as though the report had been made in pursuance of subsection (4).

Amendments—Insolvency Act 2000, ss 10(1)–(6), 15(1), Sch 5; SI 2009/1941.

General note—The provision is not exhaustive and does not deal with assisting criminal investigators and prosecutors who might seek assistance from liquidators and official receivers: *R v Brady* [2005] BCC 357, [2004] EWCA Crim 1763.

Official receiver—If the official receiver obtains information pursuant to s 218(3), he or she is entitled to pass that on to the relevant prosecuting authority: *Re Arrows Ltd (No 4)* [1995] 2 AC 75, [1994] BCC 641, HL; *R v Brady* [2005] BCC 357, [2004] EWCA Crim 1763. The Court of Appeal has specifically held that the official receiver has the power to disclose any information gleaned under s 235 to the Inland Revenue if it was otherwise lawful and this information could be used to prosecute under this provision (*R v Brady*).

References to the Secretary of State—The powers given to the Secretary of State by s 218(5) to investigate, are wide and not restricted to undertaking inquiries related to criminal activity. Investigations are to be conducted in private, and information disclosed is not to be made public (*Re an Inquiry into Mirror Group Newspapers plc* [2000] BCC 217).

219   Obligations arising under s 218

(1) For the purpose of an investigation by the Secretary of State in consequence of a report made to him under section 218(4), any obligation imposed on a person by any provision of the Companies Act 1985 to produce documents or give information to, or otherwise to assist, inspectors appointed as mentioned in section 218(5) is to be regarded as an obligation similarly to assist the Secretary of State in his investigation.

(2) An answer given by a person to a question put to him in exercise of the powers conferred by section 218(5) may be used in evidence against him.

(2A) However, in criminal proceedings in which that person is charged with an offence to which this subsection applies—

(a)   no evidence relating to the answer may be adduced, and

    (b)   no question relating to it may be asked,

by or on behalf of the prosecution, unless evidence relating to it is adduced, or a question relating to it is asked, in the proceedings by or on behalf of that person.

(2B) Subsection (2A) applies to any offence other than—

    (a)   an offence under section 2 or 5 of the Perjury Act 1911 (false statements made on oath otherwise than in judicial proceedings or made otherwise than on oath), or

    (b)   an offence under section 44(1) or (2) of the Criminal Law (Consolidation) (Scotland) Act 1995 (false statements made on oath or otherwise than on oath).

(3) Where criminal proceedings are instituted by the Director of Public Prosecutions, the Lord Advocate or the Secretary of State following any report or reference under section 218, it is the duty of the liquidator and every officer and agent of the company past and present (other than the defendant or defender) to give to the Director of Public Prosecutions, the Lord Advocate or the Secretary of State (as the case may be) all assistance in connection with the prosecution which he is reasonably able to give.

For this purpose 'agent' includes any banker or solicitor of the company and any person employed by the company as auditor, whether that person is or is not an officer of the company.

(4) If a person fails or neglects to give assistance in the manner required by subsection (3), the court may, on the application of the Director of Public Prosecutions, the Lord Advocate or the Secretary of State (as the case may be) direct the person to comply with that subsection; and if the application is made with respect to a liquidator, the court may (unless it appears that the failure or neglect to comply was due to the liquidator not having in his hands sufficient assets of the company to enable him to do so) direct that the costs shall be borne by the liquidator personally.

Amendments—Insolvency Act 2000, ss 10(1), (7), 11; SI 2009/1941.

Use of evidence—Answers given by those who are the subject of Secretary of State inquiries, may be used in subsequent civil proceedings, but not in criminal proceedings save in limited circumstances set out in s 219(2A). The bar to the use of answers in criminal proceedings would conform to the European Convention on Human Rights, which gives the right of a fair trial to people, and to ensure that this occurs they are not to be forced to give evidence that will incriminate themselves.

PART V
WINDING UP OF UNREGISTERED COMPANIES

General comment on Part V—This Part deals solely with the winding up of unregistered companies. While the term 'unregistered company' in relation to the power to wind up was originally aimed at dealing with the situation which existed in the mid-nineteenth century with some companies which had not registered pursuant to relevant companies legislation, the primary type of company to which the provisions have been applied are oversea companies, namely those that are not registered in this jurisdiction, but which have been carrying on business in Great Britain or have some other relevant connection with Great Britain: *Re Real Estate Development Co Ltd* [1991] BCLC 210. Other types that will be covered are unincorporated registered friendly societies and unincorporated building societies, as well as certain insolvent partnerships (see s 420 and arts 7 and 9 of the Insolvent Partnerships Order 1994 (SI 1994/2421).

Leaving aside oversea companies, the companies that have been wound up in the past under the precursor of this Part, are companies incorporated by special Acts of Parliament (*Re South London Fish Market* (1888) 39 Ch D 324; *Re Barton-upon-Humber Water Co* (1889) 42 Ch D 585) and companies incorporated by Royal Charter (*Re Oriental Bank Corporation* (1884) 28 Ch D 634; *Re Bank of South Australia* [1895] 1 Ch 578).

Oversea companies are treated as unregistered companies for the purposes of British company law (see *Banco Nacional de Cuba v Cosmos Trading Corp* [2000] 1 BCLC 813 at 816–817, CA) and may be wound up by the courts of England and Wales, or Scotland. In winding up such companies, all of the provisions of the Act and the Companies Acts 1985 and 2006 relating to winding up apply to an unregistered company with the exceptions and additions mentioned in s 221.

In *Re International Tin Council* [1989] Ch 309, (1988) 4 BCC 653 the Court of Appeal held that English courts should not wind up a corporate body established by international treaty, as Parliament, in enacting the forerunner of s 221 (Companies Act 1985, s 665) could not have intended to subject the body to the winding-up jurisdiction of English courts.

220 Meaning of 'unregistered company'

For the purposes of this Part 'unregistered company' includes any association and any company, with the exception of a company registered under the Companies Act 2006 in any part of the United Kingdom.

Amendments—Insolvency Act 1986, s 220(2); Transport and Works Act 1992, ss 65(1)(f), 68(1), Sch 4, Pt I; SI 2009/1941.

General note—The provision defines the bodies that may be regarded as unregistered companies and wound up as such in England and Wales or Scotland.

The provision only applies to truly unregistered companies falling within the Companies (Unregistered Companies) Regulations 1985 (SI 1985/680): *Re National Union of Flint Glassworkers* [2006] BCC 828 at [12].

'Association'—In this context 'any' is not to be given its literal meaning, and so it is not without limit: *Re St James's Club* (1852) 2 De GM & G 383, 42 ER 920. Association is a word that has been held, in relation to earlier and different legislation, to refer only to associations which are conducted for profit or gain: see *Re St James's Club* and *Re International Tin Council* [1989] Ch 309, (1988) 4 BCC 653 (affirming [1987] 1 BCLC 272, (1987) 3 BCC 103). In *Re Witney Town Football and Social Club* [1993] BCC 874 it was held that a club established solely for professional football was not an association and could not be wound up as an unregistered company within s 220.

'Company'—This covers any company except for a company registered in any part of the United Kingdom under the Joint Stock Companies Act or under the legislation (past or present) relating to companies in Great Britain.

221 Winding up of unregistered companies

(1) Subject to the provisions of this Part, any unregistered company may be wound up under this Act; and all the provisions of this Act about winding up apply to an unregistered company with the exceptions and additions mentioned in the following subsections.

(2) If an unregistered company has a principal place of business situated in Northern Ireland, it shall not be wound up under this Part unless it has a principal place of business situated in England and Wales or Scotland, or in both England and Wales and Scotland.

(3) For the purpose of determining a court's winding-up jurisdiction, an unregistered company is deemed—

(a) to be registered in England and Wales or Scotland, according as its principal place of business is situated in England and Wales or Scotland, or

(b) if it has a principal place of business situated in both countries, to be registered in both countries;

and the principal place of business situated in that part of Great Britain in which proceedings are being instituted is, for all purposes of the winding up, deemed to be the registered office of the company.

(4) No unregistered company shall be wound up under this Act voluntarily, except in accordance with the EC Regulation.

(5) The circumstances in which an unregistered company may be wound up are as follows—

(a) if the company is dissolved, or has ceased to carry on business, or is carrying on business only for the purpose of winding up its affairs;

(b) if the company is unable to pay its debts;

(c) if the court is of opinion that it is just and equitable that the company should be wound up.

(6) (*Repealed*)

(7) In Scotland, an unregistered company which the Court of Session has jurisdiction to wind up may be wound up by the court if there is subsisting a floating charge over property comprised in the company's property and undertaking, and the court is satisfied that the security of the creditor entitled to the benefit of the floating charge is in jeopardy.

For this purpose a creditor's security is deemed to be in jeopardy if the court is satisfied that events have occurred or are about to occur which render it unreasonable in the creditor's interests that the company should retain power to dispose of the property which is subject to the floating charge.

Amendments—Trustee Savings Banks Act 1985, ss 4(3), 7(3), Sch 4; SI 2002/1240; SI 2009/1941.

General note—So as to ascertain the jurisdiction in which a company is to be wound up, an unregistered company is deemed to be registered in England and Wales or Scotland if its principal place of business is situated in those countries, or if it has a principal place of business in both jurisdictions (ie overseas and in Great Britain) and the principal place of business situated in that part of Great Britain in which proceedings are being instituted is, for all purposes of the winding up, deemed to be the registered office of the company (s 221(3)).

This section cannot be considered without taking into account the possible application of either the EC Regulation on Insolvency Proceedings or the Cross-Border Regulations 2006. Both of these pieces of legislation are set out later in the book with commentary, hence the commentary to this section does not discuss these legislative instruments in any great detail. Many of the comments provided have to be read subject to the aforementioned internationally focused legislation.

Much of the winding-up law that applies to registered companies applies equally to unregistered companies.

Principal place of business in Northern Ireland—While a company that is an unregistered company in Northern Ireland cannot be wound up in England and Wales, a company registered in Northern Ireland and with a principal place of business in England or Wales may be wound up as an unregistered company: *Re Normandy Marketing Ltd* [1994] Ch 198, [1993] BCC 879.

Oversea companies—As indicated in the introduction to this Part, s 221 is primarily used to wind up oversea companies. No definitive principles have been formulated as to when such companies will be wound up; it falls completely within the discretion of the courts. Where oversea companies can be wound up satisfactorily in their jurisdiction of incorporation, they will not usually be wound up in England and Wales: *Re Standard Contract and Debenture Corporation* (1892) 8 TLR 485; *Re Jarvis Conklin Mortgage Co* (1895) 11 TLR 373. Initially, the courts have to be satisfied that there is a sufficient connection between the company and the jurisdiction of England and Wales or Scotland before winding-up procedures can be set in train, as the company is essentially beyond the limits of its territory: *Re Real Estate Development Co Ltd* [1991] BCLC 210 at 217; *Stocznia Gdanska SA v Latreefers Inc (No 2)* [2001] 2 BCLC 116 at 140, CA. The connections with Great Britain that have been said to suffice are: a place of business (see *South India Shipping Corporation Ltd v The Export-Import Bank of Korea* [1985] 1 WLR 585); a branch office; assets within the jurisdiction (see *Banque des Marchands de Moscou (Koupetchesky) v Kindersley* [1951] Ch 112, [1950] 2 All ER 549; *Re Titan International Inc* [1998] 1 BCLC 102); the fact that if the company is wound up in England the employees of the foreign company would be entitled to receive statutory benefits on termination of their employment (*Re Eloc Electro-Optieck and Communicatie BV* [1982] Ch 43, [1981] 2 All ER 1111); and winding up in England would benefit creditors of the company: *Re a Company No 00359 of 1987* [1988] Ch 210, (1987) 3 BCC 160, sub nom *International Westminster Bank plc v Okeanos Maritime Corporation* [1987] 3 All ER 137 (the liquidator had claims under s 213 or s 214); *Re Paramount Airways Ltd* [1993] Ch 223 at 240, [1992] BCLC 710 at 722. In some cases, such as *Atlantic & General Investment Trust Ltd v Richbell Information Services Inc* [2000] BCC 111, the court will base its right to jurisdiction on a number of factors. In this case they were: the directors were resident in England; the company was part of a group consisting of English companies; the transaction that led to the bringing of the petition was arranged in England; the company conducted correspondence from a London address; there were assets in the UK. But just because a connection has been established, it does not necessarily mean that the English courts will accede to a petition for winding up: *Re Compania Merabello San Nicholas SA* [1973] Ch 75 at 86; *Stocznia Gdanska SA v Latreefers Inc (No 2)* [2001] 2 BCLC 116 at 140, CA. Any consideration now might well involve the court deciding where the company's centre of main interests is to be found, as required under both the EC Regulation on Insolvency Proceedings (where the company operates in the EU (excepting Denmark)) or the Cross-Border Regulations 2006.

While the presence of an asset in the jurisdiction might be a sufficient connection, in the recent case of *Re OJSC ANK Yugraneft* [2008] EWHC 2614 (Ch) it was said that the fact that there was an asset within the jurisdiction to which the company laid claim was not automatically a reason for the court to exercise the winding-up jurisdiction. The asset might be so small or of such a character that the link with the jurisdiction said to be constituted by it was too tenuous to justify invoking the winding-up jurisdiction (at [58]). The asset must be one of substance and a valuable chose in action would qualify (at [41]).

If the connection with the jurisdiction is that there are assets within Great Britain, then the court must, before deciding whether to order winding up, consider whether there is any likelihood of the assets being administered by the courts of another jurisdiction: *Re Compania Merabello San Nicholas SA* [1973] Ch 75 at 86–87. This occurred in *New Hampshire Insurance Co v Rush & Tompkins Group plc* [1998] 2 BCLC 471, where the Court of Appeal refused to wind up two Dutch companies that were part of a group of companies which included English companies, all of which were being wound up compulsorily.

There is nothing that requires the oversea company that is the subject of a winding-up petition ever to have had a place of business, or carried on business in England or Wales, nor to have had assets within the jurisdiction (*Re Real Estate Development Co Ltd* [1991] BCLC 210; *Re a Company No 00359 of 1987* [1988] Ch 210, (1987) 3 BCC 160, sub nom *International Westminster Bank plc v Okeanos Maritime Corporation* [1987] 3 All ER 137; *Stocznia Gdanska SA v Latreefers Inc (No 2)* [2001] 2 BCLC 116 at 140, CA), before a court will agree to order winding up: *Re Compania Merabello San Nicholas SA*. But besides requiring a sufficient connection with the jurisdiction, a court must be satisfied that making a winding-up order would benefit the petitioner (*Re Compania Merabello San Nicholas SA* [1973] Ch 75; *Re Latreefers Inc* [1999] 1 BCLC 271; *Banco Nacional de Cuba v Cosmos Trading Corp* [2000] 1 BCLC 813 at 817, CA), and that it is able to exercise jurisdiction over at least one person who has the right to share in the distribution of the company's assets: *Re Real Estate Development Co Ltd* [1991] BCLC 210.

In the situation where a foreign company has been dissolved in its home jurisdiction, it could be wound up in the UK: *Re Eurodis Electron Ltd plc* [2011] EWHC 1025 (Ch) at [22]. Where a company had been dissolved in its home jurisdiction the English courts will not make it a prerequisite for jurisdiction to wind up that the company had a branch or place of business in Great Britain before its dissolution. In such a case it suffices if there are assets within the jurisdiction and there are creditors claiming debts owed by the company: *Banque des Marchands de Moscou (Koupetchesky) v Kindersley*.

In *Re Real Estate Development Co Ltd* Knox J laid down a three-fold test (affirmed by the Court of Appeal in *Banco Nacional de Cuba v Cosmos Trading Corp* [2000] 1 BCLC 813 at 817–818 and recently approved of in *Re OJSC ANK Yugraneft* [2008] EWHC 2614 (Ch) at [20] also Re *HSBC Bank plc* 2010 SLT 281) (and summarising what has been mentioned above) that must be satisfied for jurisdiction to exist. They are:

- a sufficient connection with England and Wales (which may include, though it is not necessary, the presence of assets within the jurisdiction);
- a reasonable possibility of benefiting those petitioning;
- one or more of the persons who would be recipients in a distribution of the company's assets had to be persons over whom the court had jurisdiction.

While it is not a requirement that assets must exist in the jurisdiction before English courts will make a winding-up order, it was said in the Court of Appeal in *Banco Nacional de Cuba v Cosmos Trading Corp* [2000] 1 BCLC 813 that the courts should hesitate before they subject foreign companies with no assets in the UK to being wound up here (at 819), and in fact caution should be shown where a company continues to trade in its place of incorporation and in other places in the world (at 819). It was said that making a winding-up order in such a situation would be 'thoroughly undesirable' (at 819).

Overall the courts, while having a broad discretion concerning whether to make a winding-up order or not, have proceeded cautiously, and on many occasions they have decided that it was more appropriate that the company be wound up in another jurisdiction: *Re a Company No 00359 of 1987* [1988] Ch 210, (1987) 3 BCC 160, sub nom *International Westminster Bank plc v Okeanos Maritime Corporation* [1987] 3 All ER 137; *Re a Company (No 003102 of 1991) ex parte Nyckeln Finance Co Ltd* [1991] BCLC 539; *Re Wallace Smith & Co Ltd* [1992] BCLC 970. With the advent of the EC Regulation on Insolvency Proceedings and the Cross-Border Regulations 2006, it is likely that this conclusion might be reached more often, at least certainly after considering where the centre of main interests of the company is.

A court has the power, where it decides to order winding up, to place conditions on the order, and this might include a provision that the winding up is to be conducted as ancillary to a main liquidation being conducted in another country: In *Re Commercial Bank of South Australia* (1886) 33 Ch D 174 at 178; *Re Hibernian Merchants Ltd* [1958] Ch 76 at 80. But, of course, conditions might be inappropriate (*Re Hibernian Merchants Ltd*).

There is authority for the proposition that where the winding up of an oversea company is pending or proceeding in the place of its incorporation and base, it may be wound up in England and Wales: *Re Matheson Brothers* (1884) 27 Ch D 225; *Re Commercial Bank of South Australia* (1886) 33 Ch D 174; *Re Federal Bank of Australia* [1893] WN 77. However, now one must take into account the EC Regulation on Insolvency Proceedings 2000 (1346/2000) in this regard, and in regard to all issues surrounding the winding up of companies that operate in Member States of the EU. The Regulation provides, in effect, that UK courts could make winding-up orders in relation to companies that have the centre of their main interests in the UK (art 3(1)). An example, although addressing administration, is *Re Daisytek-Isa Ltd* [2004] BPIR 30, [2003] BCC 562, where the English courts were held to have jurisdiction because the company had its main centre of interests in Bradford. The decision was challenged in a French court, and while the French court held that Bradford was not the company's centre of main interests, on appeal a French appellate court reversed the earlier French decision and affirmed the decision of the English court: *Klempka v ISA* [2003] BCC 984 (CA of Versailles). It is likely that companies that have the centre of their main interests in the UK will have assets here. UK courts could not make winding-up orders in relation to companies that have the centre of their main interests in another Member State of the EU, even if they operate in the UK and have some connection with the jurisdiction, unless these companies possess establishments within the UK, and the UK proceedings may only affect the assets of the companies situated in the UK (art 3(2)), whereby such proceedings the UK would be secondary proceedings. Proceedings initiated pursuant to art 3(2) in the UK will only be permitted in the event that proceedings cannot be opened in the Member State where the centre of the company's main interests is situated or where the opening of proceedings is requested by a creditor who has his domicile, habitual residence or registered office (if a company) in the UK where the debtor company has an establishment, or whose claim arises as a result of the operation of the establishment, such as incurring debts (art 3(4)). It is emphasised that the Regulation only affects companies that have the centre of a company's main interests in the EU, but of course that could include companies that are incorporated outside of the Member States of the EU but conduct the substantial part of their business in one or more of the States of the EU. Nevertheless, the Regulation has the capacity to limit the number of occasions on which UK courts will assume jurisdiction and order the winding up of foreign companies. For further discussion of the Regulation and its impact, see the comments to the Regulation.

One must also take into account the Cross-Border Insolvency Regulations 2006 when considering the winding up of a foreign company that is registered in a non-EU Member State or in Denmark. If foreign insolvency proceedings have been opened then it would seem, because of art 28 of the Regulations, liquidation proceedings will not be permitted under s 221. But if no foreign insolvency proceedings have been instigated s 221 could be relied on.

Voluntary winding up—While the section provides in subsection (4) that unregistered companies cannot be wound up in voluntary liquidation, this has to be qualified, because they can be where the EC Regulation on Insolvency Proceedings 2000 applies. So companies that were, for instance, incorporated in a Member State of the EU and which have the centre of their main interests in the UK will be able to wind up in voluntary liquidation here: *Re TXU Europe German Finance BV* [2005] BCC 90, [2005] BPIR 209. This decision also suggests that companies from outside of the EU may be wound up pursuant to the creditors' voluntary liquidation process in the UK, provided that the centre of their main interests is in the UK. This follows from the case of *Re BRAC Rent-a-car International Inc* [2003] BCC 248, where a foreign non-EU company was made the subject of an administration order in England.

See s 97.

Circumstance for winding up—While including some of the grounds that permit the winding up of registered domestic companies, the number of grounds mentioned in subsection (5) is fewer. As for registered companies, the main ground will be that the company cannot pay its debts, ie insolvent.

See Dawson 'The Doctrine of Forum Non Conveniens and the Winding Up of Insolvent Foreign Companies' [2005] JBL 28.

222 Inability to pay debts: unpaid creditor for £750 or more

(1) An unregistered company is deemed (for the purposes of section 221) unable to pay its debts if there is a creditor, by assignment or otherwise, to whom the company is indebted in a sum exceeding £750 then due and—

   (a) the creditor has served on the company, by leaving at its principal place of business, or by delivering to the secretary or some director, manager or principal officer of the company, or by otherwise serving in such manner as the court may approve or direct, a written demand in the prescribed form requiring the company to pay the sum due, and

   (b)   the company has for 3 weeks after the service of the demand neglected to pay the sum or to secure or compound for it to the creditor's satisfaction.

(2) The money sum for the time being specified in subsection (1) is subject to increase or reduction by regulations under section 417 in Part XV; but no increase in the sum so specified affects any case in which the winding-up petition was presented before the coming into force of the increase.

General note—This provision, with some changes, replicates s 123(1)(a). Like s 123(1)(a) it allows for a company to be deemed to be unable to pay its debts. The provision, when it comes to service of the demand, provides for greater flexibility. For a discussion of the demand and the matters affecting service, see the comments applying to s 123.

223 Inability to pay debts: debt remaining unsatisfied after action brought

An unregistered company is deemed (for the purposes of section 221) unable to pay its debts if an action or other proceeding has been instituted against any member for any debt or demand due, or claimed to be due, from the company, or from him in his character of member, and—

   (a)   notice in writing of the institution of the action or proceeding has been served on the company by leaving it at the company's principal place of business (or by delivering it to the secretary, or some director, manager or principal officer of the company, or by otherwise serving it in such manner as the court may approve or direct), and

   (b)   the company has not within 3 weeks after service of the notice paid, secured or compounded for the debt or demand, or procured the action or proceeding to be stayed or sisted, or indemnified the defendant or defender to his reasonable satisfaction against the action or proceeding, and against all costs, damages and expenses to be incurred by him because of it.

General note—This provision does not follow a corresponding provision applying to registered companies. It provides creditors of unregistered companies with greater flexibility in establishing the insolvency of a company.

224 Inability to pay debts: other cases

(1) An unregistered company is deemed (for purposes of section 221) unable to pay its debts—

   (a)   if in England and Wales execution or other process issued on a judgment, decree or order obtained in any court in favour of a creditor against the company, or any member of it as such, or any person authorised to be sued as nominal defendant on behalf of the company, is returned unsatisfied;

   (b)   if in Scotland the induciae of a charge for payment on an extract decree, or an extract registered bond, or an extract registered protest, have expired without payment being made;

(c)   if in Northern Ireland a certificate of unenforceability has been granted in respect of any judgment, decree or order obtained as mentioned in paragraph (a);

(d)   if it is otherwise proved to the satisfaction of the court that the company is unable to pay its debts as they fall due.

(2) An unregistered company is also deemed unable to pay its debts if it is proved to the satisfaction of the court that the value of the company's assets is less than the amount of its liabilities, taking into account its contingent and prospective liabilities.

General note—This section brings into play the remaining bases in s 123 for deeming a company to be insolvent. See the comments accompanying that section.

Subsection (1) is broader than the corresponding provision in s 123 in that it permits execution against a person who represents the company to be considered.

225 Company incorporated outside Great Britain

(1) Where a company incorporated outside Great Britain which has been carrying on business in Great Britain ceases to carry on business in Great Britain, it may be wound up as an unregistered company under this Act, notwithstanding that it has been dissolved or otherwise ceased to exist as a company under or by virtue of the laws of the country under which it was incorporated.

(2) This section is subject to the EC Regulation.

Amendments—SI 2002/1240; SI 2009/1941.

General note—This is an additional provision to s 221, which enables the court to exercise jurisdiction to wind up an oversea company. That provision permits the winding up of a company, while incorporated outside of Great Britain, that has carried on business in Great Britain and has now ceased carrying on business, even though the company has been dissolved or otherwise ceased to exist as a company under the laws of the country where it was incorporated.

The power in this provision is more restricted compared with that found in s 221, and it is not as frequently invoked.

As with s 221, the provision is subject to the EC Regulation on Insolvency Proceedings 2000 (1346/2000). See the comments under 'Overseas companies' in relation to s 221 for further discussion of the function and operation of the Regulation.

226 Contributories in winding up of unregistered company

(1) In the event of an unregistered company being wound up, every person is deemed a contributory who is liable to pay or contribute to the payment of any debt or liability of the company, or to pay or contribute to the payment of any sum for the adjustment of the rights of members among themselves, or to pay or contribute to the payment of the expenses of winding up the company.

(2) Every contributory is liable to contribute to the company's assets all sums due from him in respect of any such liability as is mentioned above.

(3) In the case of an unregistered company engaged in or formed for working mines within the stannaries, a past member is not liable to

contribute to the assets if he has ceased to be a member for 2 years or more either before the mine ceased to be worked or before the date of the winding-up order.

(4) (*Repealed*)

Amendments—SI 2009/1941.

General note—This provision inserts provisions that correspond to those sections found elsewhere in the Act as far as registered companies are concerned. It confirms the requirement of contributories to contribute to company funds in relation to what is outstanding on their shares, for instance.

227 Power of court to stay, sist or restrain proceedings

The provisions of this Part with respect to staying, sisting or restraining actions and proceedings against a company at any time after the presentation of a petition for winding up and before the making of a winding-up order extend, in the case of an unregistered company, where the application to stay, sist or restrain is presented by a creditor, to actions and proceedings against any contributory of the company.

General note—This provision causes provisions such as s 126 to apply to unregistered companies. See the notes accompanying that section.

228 Actions stayed on winding-up order

Where an order has been made for winding up an unregistered company, no action or proceeding shall be proceeded with or commenced against any contributory of the company in respect of any debt of the company, except by leave of the court, and subject to such terms as the court may impose.

General note—This provision corresponds to s 130(2) for registered companies. See the comments relating to that latter provision.

229 Provisions of this Part to be cumulative

(1) The provisions of this Part with respect to unregistered companies are in addition to and not in restriction of any provisions in Part IV with respect to winding up companies by the court; and the court or liquidator may exercise any powers or do any act in the case of unregistered companies which might be exercised or done by it or him in winding up companies registered under the Companies Act 2006 in England and Wales or Scotland.

(2) (*Repealed*)

Amendments—SI 2009/1941.

PART VI
MISCELLANEOUS PROVISIONS APPLYING TO COMPANIES WHICH ARE INSOLVENT OR IN LIQUIDATION

Amendments—SI 2009/1941.

General comment on Part VI—This Part deals with miscellaneous provisions that are relevant to a company that is being administered pursuant to some formal insolvency regime or liquidation (if the company is not insolvent). While the provisions can be described as miscellaneous, there is very much of an emphasis on the function of office-holders. The majority of the Part focuses on provisions that can support the investigative work of office-holders as well as those that can assist in the recovery of money or property, namely the adjustment provisions (ss 238–246).

Office-holders

230 Holders of office to be qualified insolvency practitioners

(1) (*Repealed*)

(2) Where an administrative receiver of a company is appointed, he must be a person who is so qualified.

(3) Where a company goes into liquidation, the liquidator must be a person who is so qualified.

(4) Where a provisional liquidator is appointed, he must be a person who is so qualified.

(5) Subsections (3) and (4) are without prejudice to any enactment under which the official receiver is to be, or may be, liquidator or provisional liquidator.

Amendments—Enterprise Act 2002, ss 248(3), 278(2), Sch 17, paras 9, 19, Sch 26.

General note—This provision clearly states that those who act as different types of office-holders in relation to companies must be qualified to act as an insolvency practitioner. If anyone does act as one of the office-holders mentioned in the section, and he or she is not qualified as an insolvency practitioner, that person is guilty of an offence pursuant to s 389. See the comments accompanying s 389.

It is notable that the nominee or supervisor of a company voluntary arrangement is omitted from the section, yet the person occupying this position must be qualified as an insolvency practitioner (ss 1(2), 7(5)).

'Act as an insolvency practitioner'—This is defined in s 388 and covers the types of office-holder mentioned in s 230 as well as supervisors of company voluntary arrangements and office-holders in relation to individual insolvent estates.

'Qualified'—This is explained in s 390. See the comments applying to that section.

Official receiver—Official receivers occupy statutory offices and in carrying out the functions of their office they are to act under the directions of the Secretary of State, and are officers of the court when exercising those functions (s 400(2)). Official receivers are not regulated by the scheme that governs insolvency practitioners.

231 Appointment to office of two or more persons

(1) This section applies if an appointment or nomination of any person to the office of administrative receiver, liquidator or provisional liquidator—

    (a)   relates to more than one person, or

    (b)   has the effect that the office is to be held by more than one person.

(2) The appointment or nomination shall declare whether any act required or authorised under any enactment to be done by the administrative receiver, liquidator or provisional liquidator is to be done by all or any one or more of the persons for the time being holding the office in question.

Amendments—Enterprise Act 2002, ss 248(3), 278(2), Sch 17, paras 9, 20, Sch 26.

232 Validity of office-holder's acts

The acts of an individual as administrative receiver, liquidator or provisional liquidator of a company are valid notwithstanding any defect in his appointment, nomination or qualifications.

Amendments—Enterprise Act 2002, ss 248(3), 278(2), Sch 17, paras 9, 21, Sch 26.

General note—Notwithstanding the apparent breadth of the section – which may be regarded as a fair approach as a person acting as a purported agent may affect the legal position of the purported principal – there is Australian authority that indicates that it can only apply where there has been at least a purported appointment, in the form of a genuine attempt to appoint, say a liquidator (*Mercantile Bank of Australia Ltd v Dinwoodie* (1902) 28 VLR 491 at 501), and the acts of liquidators are validated only in so far as any defects in qualification or appointment are discovered after the acts in question have been done: *Re Bridport Old Brewery Co* (1867) 2 Ch App 191. This suggests that upon the discovery of any such defects, the liquidator cannot validly perform further acts in purported reliance upon this validating provision (*Re Bridport Old Brewery Co*).

In *OBG v Allan* [2005] BPIR 928 the Court of Appeal (Peter Gibson and Carnwath LJJ, Manie LJ dissenting) held that the tort of unlawful interference with contractual relations could not be extended to an improperly appointed receiver who takes over the management of the contractual commitments of a company. Neither does English law recognise the tort of conversion of a chose in action.

Management by administrators, liquidators etc

233 Supplies of gas, water, electricity etc

(1) This section applies in the case of a company where—

    (a)   the company enters administration, or

    (b)   an administrative receiver is appointed, or

    (ba)   a moratorium under section 1A is in force, or

    (c)   a voluntary arrangement approved under Part I, has taken effect, or

    (d)   the company goes into liquidation, or

    (e)   a provisional liquidator is appointed;

and 'the office-holder' means the administrator, the administrative receiver, the nominee, the supervisor of the voluntary arrangement, the liquidator or the provisional liquidator, as the case may be.

(2) If a request is made by or with the concurrence of the office-holder for the giving, after the effective date, of any of the supplies mentioned in the next subsection, the supplier—

    (a)   may make it a condition of the giving of the supply that the office-holder personally guarantees the payment of any charges in respect of the supply, but

(b)   shall not make it a condition of the giving of the supply, or do anything which has the effect of making it a condition of the giving of the supply, that any outstanding charges in respect of a supply given to the company before the effective date are paid.

(3) The supplies referred to in subsection (2) are—

(a)   a supply of gas by a gas supplier within the meaning of Part I of the Gas Act 1986,

(b)   a supply of electricity by an electricity supplier within the meaning of Part I of the Electricity Act 1989

(c)   a supply of water by a water undertaker or, in Scotland, Scottish Water,

(d)   a supply of communications services by a provider of a public electronic communications service.

(4) 'The effective date' for the purposes of this section is whichever is applicable of the following dates—

(a)   the date on which the company entered administration,

(b)   the date on which the administrative receiver was appointed (or, if he was appointed in succession to another administrative receiver, the date on which the first of his predecessors was appointed),

(ba)   the date on which the moratorium came into force

(c)   the date on which the voluntary arrangement took effect,

(d)   the date on which the company went into liquidation,

(e)   the date on which the provisional liquidator was appointed.

(5) The following applies to expressions used in subsection (3)—

(a)   (*repealed*)

(b)   (*repealed*)

(c)   (*repealed*)

(d)   'communications services' do not include electronic communications services to the extent that they are used to broadcast or otherwise transmit programme services (within the meaning of the Communications Act 2003).

Amendments—Water Act 1989, s 190(1), Sch 25, para 78(1); Gas Act 1995 ss 16(1), 17(5), Sch 4, para 14, Sch 6; Insolvency Act 2000, s 1, Sch 1, paras 1, 8; Utilities Act 2000, s 108, Sch 6, para 47, Sch 8; Enterprise Act 2002, s 248(3), Sch 17, paras 9, 22; Communications Act 2003, s 406(1), Sch 17, para 82; SI 2004/1822.

General note—This provision was introduced to stop suppliers of critical utilities refusing to continue to supply office-holders when the latter were appointed to companies, unless any charges outstanding were paid or security given in relation to them. Where the office-holder was administering a company, the supply of some or all of the utilities mentioned in the section could be critical, and the utilities had the office-holder 'over a barrel' in that the office-holder could not carry on, or even wind up, the company's business without supplies, something that the utility suppliers realised to their advantage.

234 Getting in the company's property

(1) This section applies in the case of a company where—

(a)   the company enters administration, or

(b)   an administrative receiver is appointed, or

(c)   the company goes into liquidation, or

(d)   a provisional liquidator is appointed;

and 'the office-holder' means the administrator, the administrative receiver, the liquidator or the provisional liquidator, as the case may be.

(2) Where any person has in his possession or control any property, books, papers or records to which the company appears to be entitled, the court may require that person forthwith (or within such period as the court may direct) to pay, deliver, convey, surrender or transfer the property, books, papers or records to the office-holder.

(3) Where the office-holder—

(a)   seizes or disposes of any property which is not property of the company, and

(b)   at the time of seizure or disposal believes, and has reasonable grounds for believing, that he is entitled (whether in pursuance of an order of the court or otherwise) to seize or dispose of that property,

the next subsection has effect.

(4) In that case the office-holder—

(a)   is not liable to any person in respect of any loss or damage resulting from the seizure or disposal except in so far as that loss or damage is caused by the office-holder's own negligence, and

(b)   has a lien on the property, or the proceeds of its sale, for such expenses as were incurred in connection with the seizure or disposal.

Amendments—Enterprise Act 2002, s 248(3), Sch 17, paras 9, 23.

General note—This provision creates a summary procedure for office-holders in obtaining payment, delivery, or transfer of property, books, papers or records from any person: *Re Oakwell Collieries Co* [1879] WN 65. The purpose of this form of procedure is simply to facilitate the administrative side of an insolvency regime.

The section replaced s 551 of the Companies Act 1985, and as s 234 states that the liquidator is able to get property from 'any person', this means that it is easier for the liquidator (and now other office-holders) than under the former provision, as there is no need, as there was under s 551, to have to assert, and to establish, that the holder of the property falls into any specified categories.

The section does not give an office-holder a better right to property than that held by the company: *Re Leyland DAF Ltd* [1994] BCC 166, CA.

The application must be commenced in the office-holder's own name, and not that of the company: *Re Cosslett (Contractors) Ltd* [2001] BCC 740. Applications ex parte should only be sought in exceptional circumstances: *Re First Express Ltd* [1991] BCC 782 at 785.

The provision protects the office-holder from liability if, in taking the property and disposing of it, he or she had reasonable grounds for believing that the company was entitled to it: *Euromex Ventures Ltd v BNP Paribas Real Estate Advisory and Property Management UK Ltd* [2013] EWHC 3007 (Ch).

Court's powers—While s 234(2) refers to the court requiring a person to deliver etc, r 4.185 makes it clear that a liquidator may invoke the power of the court. The rule applies only to a compulsory winding up, wher which is measured in money or money's worth; is significantly less than the value eas in voluntary windings up, applications under s 112 must be made to the court for it to exercise these powers.

The courts will deal with any disputes over the ownership of property covered by a s 234 demand (*Re London Iron & Steel Co Ltd* [1990] BCC 159 (motor cars); *Euro Commercial Leasing Ltd v Cartwright & Lewis* [1995] BCC 830 (company money held by its solicitors); *Re Cosslett (Contractors) Ltd* [2001] BCC 740, HL (heavy plant)), but are not entitled to do so where the issue of ownership of property is subject to the jurisdiction of the courts of a foreign country: *Re Leyland DAF Ltd* [1994] BCC 166, CA.

Whilst the provision is broad, it might not be broad enough to permit office-holders to use the procedure to take proceedings that should be commenced in another manner. For instance, in *Byers v Yacht Bull Corp* [2010] EWHC 133 (Ch), [2010] 2 BCLC 169, [2010] BCC 368 at [11] the office-holder added ss 238 and 239 to the s 234 application as grounds for taking action.

Section 234(2)

'Books, papers and records'—Books, papers and records has been held by the Supreme Court of Appeal of South Africa in *Le Roux v Viana* 2008 (2) SA 173 in that jurisdiction's equivalent provision, to include any information relating to the company in liquidation where it is located on a computer's hard drive and where the computer is owned by a third party.

Section 234(3)

'Property'—This does not embrace the improper seizure of choses in action, as it only covers tangible property: *Welsh Development Agency Ltd v Export Finance Co* [1992] BCC 270 (by receivers interfering in a contract in this case).

For a discussion of whether s 234 may be used to recover debts, see A Keay 'The Office-Holder's Delivery Up Power and the Recovery of Debts' [2011] 4 *Corporate Rescue and Insolvency* 3.

235 Duty to co-operate with office-holder

(1) This section applies as does section 234; and it also applies, in the case of a company in respect of which a winding-up order has been made by the court in England and Wales, as if references to the office-holder included the official receiver, whether or not he is the liquidator.

(2) Each of the persons mentioned in the next subsection shall—

    (a) give to the office-holder such information concerning the company and its promotion, formation, business, dealings, affairs or property as the office-holder may at any time after the effective date reasonably require, and

    (b) attend on the office-holder at such times as the latter may reasonably require.

(3) The persons referred to above are—

    (a) those who are or have at any time been officers of the company,

    (b) those who have taken part in the formation of the company at any time within one year before the effective date,

    (c) those who are in the employment of the company, or have been in its employment (including employment under a contract for services) within that year, and are in the office-holder's opinion capable of giving information which he requires,

    (d) those who are, or have within that year been, officers of, or in the employment (including employment under a contract for services) of, another company which is, or within that year was, an officer of the company in question, and

(e) in the case of a company being wound up by the court, any person who has acted as administrator, administrative receiver or liquidator of the company.

(4) For the purposes of subsections (2) and (3), 'the effective date' is whichever is applicable of the following dates—

(a) the date on which the company entered administration,
(b) the date on which the administrative receiver was appointed or, if he was appointed in succession to another administrative receiver, the date on which the first of his predecessors was appointed,
(c) the date on which the provisional liquidator was appointed, and
(d) the date on which the company went into liquidation.

(5) If a person without reasonable excuse fails to comply with any obligation imposed by this section, he is liable to a fine and, for continued contravention, to a daily default fine.

Amendments—Enterprise Act 2002, s 248(3), Sch 17, paras 9, 24.

General note—This section is an investigative power providing for an informal procedure to allow office-holders to obtain information: *Re Arrows Ltd (No 4)* [1994] BCC 641 at 643, HL. The provision was part of statutory investigative powers that had as their purpose the identification of potential criminal or other misconduct and the initiation of the relevant steps to prosecute or apply for a director's disqualification: *R v Brady* [2004] EWCA Crim 1763, [2005] BCC 357.

Office-holders who are permitted to obtain formal examinations under s 236 should first, ordinarily, seek to avail themselves of s 235 in order to gain information.

Any information or documents obtained pursuant to s 235 may be disclosed by the official receiver or liquidator to the Secretary of State for Business, Innovation and Skills so that a decision can be made as to whether proceedings for the disqualification of a director should be commenced: *Re Polly Peck International plc* [1994] BCC 15. It makes no difference if an undertaking was given that the information or documents would only be used for the purposes of winding up as disclosure would fall within the purposes of the administration (*Polly Peck*).

Information obtained under this provision is confidential and should only be used for the purpose for which it had been obtained (*R v Brady* [2004] EWCA Crim 1763, [2005] BCC 357), but the Court of Appeal has held that confidentiality was not absolute and might be outweighed by the public interest. So, the Court held information could be passed to the appropriate prosecuting authority, as a matter of public interest. In that case it was said that the official receiver has the power to disclose any information gleaned under s 235 to the Inland Revenue if it was otherwise lawful (*R v Brady* at [18]). An office-holder could apply to obtain an order of the court to permit the office-holder to disclose material to another office-holder, but a court would not give a blanket order as it would wish to know what material was being disclosed: *Re Bernard L Madoff Investment Securities LLC* [2009] EWHC 442 (Ch), [2009] 2 BCLC 78, [2010] BCC 328 at [13].

Details of any breach of this section should be reported by the liquidator to the Secretary of State for Business, Innovation and Skills and should include: details of efforts of the liquidator to enforce co-operation by the director, officer or other person; details of any action taken by the liquidator to enforce compliance; and the consequences of non-co-operation on the part of the director, officer or other person (Dear IP, Millennium Edition, December 2000, chapter 20).

There was nothing in s 235 which limited the ability of the office-holder to have whoever he or she pleased at interview when he or she required it to be conducted under s 235: *Re Bernard L Madoff Investment Securities LLC* [2009] EWHC 442 (Ch), [2009] 2 BCLC 78, [2010] BCC 328 at [15].

An interviewee at an interview convened under this section could only be required to answer questions about the company to which the office-holder was appointed: *Re Bernard L Madoff Investment Securities LLC* [2009] EWHC 442 (Ch), [2009] 2 BCLC 78, [2010] BCC 328 at [15].

If a person fails to co-operate with the office-holder, then the latter may apply to the court under r 7.20(1)(c) for an order against the person in order to enforce compliance. In such a case the person against whom an order is made might be made liable for costs (r 7.20(3)).

236 Inquiry into company's dealings etc

(1) This section applies as does section 234; and it also applies in the case of a company in respect of which a winding-up order has been made by the court in England and Wales as if references to the office-holder included the official receiver, whether or not he is the liquidator.

(2) The court may, on the application of the office-holder, summon to appear before it—

(a)   any officer of the company,

(b)   any person known or suspected to have in his possession any property of the company or supposed to be indebted to the company, or

(c)   any person whom the court thinks capable of giving information concerning the promotion, formation, business, dealings, affairs or property of the company.

(3) The court may require any such person as is mentioned in subsection (2)(a) to (c) to submit to the court an account of his dealings with the company or to produce any books, papers or other records in his possession or under his control relating to the company or the matters mentioned in paragraph (c) of the subsection.

(3A) An account submitted to the court under subsection (3) must be contained in—

(a)   a witness statement verified by a statement of truth (in England and Wales), and

(b)   an affidavit (in Scotland).

(4) The following applies in a case where—

(a)   a person without reasonable excuse fails to appear before the court when he is summoned to do so under this section, or

(b)   there are reasonable grounds for believing that a person has absconded, or is about to abscond, with a view to avoiding his appearance before the court under this section.

(5) The court may, for the purpose of bringing that person and anything in his possession before the court, cause a warrant to be issued to a constable or prescribed officer of the court—

(a)   for the arrest of that person, and

(b)   for the seizure of any books, papers, records, money or goods in that person's possession.

(6) The court may authorise a person arrested under such a warrant to be kept in custody, and anything seized under such a warrant to be held, in

accordance with the rules, until that person is brought before the court under the warrant or until such other time as the court may order.

Amendments—SI 2010/18.

General note—This provision is to be read together with ss 235 (*Shierson v Rastogi*, sub nom *Re RGB Resources plc* [2002] EWCA Civ 1624, [2003] 1 WLR 586, [2003] BPIR 148, [2002] BCC 1005) and 237. Sections 235 and 236 differ in that s 235 includes a mandatory requirement that officers give information that is reasonably required and s 236 gives a court a discretion as to whether there should in fact be an examination (*Shierson v Rastogi*). Section 236 provides a composite code to enable office-holders to obtain information from books, papers and records relating to the company and information from witnesses who may have relevant information to give concerning the company: *Re Trading Partners Ltd* [2002] BPIR 606, [2002] 1 BCLC 655.

The provision involves an examination in private: *Bishopsgate Investment Management Ltd (in provisional liquidation) v Maxwell* [1992] Ch 1, [1992] 2 All ER 856, [1992] BCLC 475, [1992] BCC 222, CA.

While the power might be exercised by any office-holder, it is liquidators who have employed it most frequently.

The power to examine privately is very broad and extraordinary: *Re British & Commonwealth Holdings plc (No 2)* [1992] Ch 342, CA (affirmed on appeal by the House of Lords [1993] AC 476). And as the power is broad the courts are concerned about possible abuse, and so they have said that the power must be exercised carefully in order to ensure that the examinee is not unfairly disadvantaged: *Re North Australian Territory Company* (1890) 45 Ch D 87 at 93; *Ex parte Willey* (1883) 23 Ch D 118 at 128; *Re Rolls Razor Ltd (No 2)* [1970] Ch 576 at 591, [1969] 3 All ER 1386 at 1396. The courts are careful to ensure that the rights of a person to privacy and confidentiality are not unfairly interfered with: *Hamilton v Oades* (1989) 166 CLR 486 (Australian High Court). The courts have to engage in a balancing exercise between the requirements of the liquidator, to ascertain all of the relevant information about the company, and the possible oppression of the examinee: *Cloverbay Ltd (Joint Administrators) v Bank of Credit and Commerce International SA* [1991] BCLC 135 at 138, CA; *Re British and Commonwealth Holdings plc* [1992] BCC 977 at 984 per Lord Slynn.

The provision binds the Crown, so an office-holder might require inspectors appointed by the Department of Business Enterprise and Regulatory Reform to disclose transcripts of evidence given to them in relation to the company in winding up. In such a case, those giving evidence are to be given a right to be heard on whether disclosure should be permitted: *Soden v Burns* [1996] 1 WLR 1512, [1996] 3 All ER 967, [1996] 2 BCLC 636, [1997] BCC 308.

If the prospective examinee is the subject of criminal proceedings, an examination may still be held. The usual balancing exercise, to weigh up the importance to the office-holder of the information sought as against the extent of oppression likely to be suffered by the examinee, will be undertaken: *Re Arrows Ltd (No 2)* [1992] BCC 446; *Re British and Commonwealth Holdings plc* [1992] BCC 977, HL.

It has been held that it is not appropriate to use an examination to test the proof of debt that a liquidator has rejected: *Re BCCI (No7)* [1994] BCLC 455.

Purpose—The purpose of private examinations is to assist a liquidator to ascertain the truth concerning the affairs of the company and obtain information concerning the company's trading and dealings. This is to be done with the object of allowing the liquidator, as effectively and as inexpensively as possible to fulfil the functions that liquidators have; to put the affairs of the company in order; and to carry out all aspects of the liquidation, including the getting in of any assets of the company: *Re Rolls Razor Ltd* [1968] 3 All ER 698 at 700 per Buckley J (approved in *Re British and Commonwealth Holdings plc (No 2)* [1992] BCC 977 at 983, HL). In *Shierson v Rastogi*, sub nom *Re RGB Resources plc* [2002] EWCA Civ 1624, [2003] 1 WLR 586, [2003] BPIR 148, [2002] BCC 1005 Peter Gibson LJ stated that: 'The primary duty of the liquidator being wound up by the court is to collect its assets with a view to discharging its liabilities to the extent the assets permit. To perform that function the liquidator needs information, and the companies legislation has for very many years given the liquidator power to obtain it from those who can be expected to have relevant information' (at [23]).

In referring to examinations, some emphasis has been given to the idea that it can be a vital aspect in relation to the ascertaining and collection of the assets to which the company is entitled (*Shierson v Rastogi*). But the purpose of examinations is not limited to one purpose: *Re Pantmaenog Timber Co Ltd (in liquidation); Official Receiver v Wadge Rapps & Hunt* [2003] UKHL 49, [2003] 2 BCLC 257. In *Official Receiver v Wadge Rapps & Hunt*, the House of Lords held that it is permissible for the official receiver to use the examination process only for the purpose of obtaining evidence to be employed in disqualification proceedings against a director of a company in liquidation (reversing *Re Pantmaenog Timber Co Ltd (in liquidation)* [2001] 2 BCLC 555, [2002] BCC 11, CA).

Examinations are often used to enable the liquidator to ascertain whether any substantive claims can be mounted against third parties or whether there are defences against proceedings brought against the company: *Re Gold Company* (1897) 12 Ch D 77; *Re Castle New Homes Ltd* [1979] 2 All ER 775 at 788. Also, the objective of examinations is to permit liquidators to investigate the conduct of directors and others, where necessary (*Re Arrows Ltd (No 4)* [1994] BCC 641; *Re Pantmaenog Timber Co Ltd (in liquidation); Official Receiver v Wadge Rapps & Hunt* [2003] UKHL 49, [2003] 2 BCLC 257) and to investigate the causes of the failure of a company (*Re Pantmaenog Timber Co Ltd (in liquidation); Official Receiver v Wadge Rapps & Hunt*).

The power to examine may not, however, be used to conduct a fishing expedition: *Re Castle New Homes Ltd* [1979] 2 All ER 775 at 790; *Re James McHale Automobiles Ltd* [1997] 1 BCLC 273, [1997] BCC 202. Having said that, recently Newey J stated in *Re Chesterfield United Inc* [2012] EWHC 244 (Ch) at [16] that within limits, s 236 can properly be used for what might be termed 'fishing,' but his Lordship did not indicate what the limits in fact were.

Where a company is in members' voluntary liquidation, an examination will not be permitted, as the examination process is designed to protect the interests of creditors and not to provide a windfall for the shareholders of the solvent company: *Re Galileo Group Ltd* [1998] 2 WLR 364, [1998] 1 BCLC 318, [1998] BCC 228.

Court discretion—The court has a discretion as to whether it will make the order sought (s 236(2)). However, there are some principles that must be considered by a court in arriving at its decision. Justice and fairness must demand that an order be made: *Re BCCI (No 7)* [1994] 1 BCLC 458. The discretion is to be exercised judicially and following a careful balancing of the interests and factors involved, including taking into account the purpose of the examination power and whether the making of an order would be unreasonable, unnecessary or oppressive: *Re British & Commonwealth Holdings plc (No 2)* [1993] AC 426, [1992] BCC 977, HL. Of the principles that must be taken into account, the overarching ones are that any examination must be necessary in the interests of the insolvency administration involved (*Re Embassy Art Products* (1987) 3 BCC 292), and that the liquidator has a reasonable need for the information sought (*Re Galileo Group Ltd* [1998] 2 WLR 364, [1998] 1 BCLC 318), as well as the fact that the examination should not be unreasonably oppressive as far as the examinee is concerned (*British & Commonwealth Holdings plc (No 2)*). Some of the factors that a court may well consider in making their decision are: the purpose of an examination; the reasonable requirements of the liquidator to wind up the company; the oppression of the prospective examinee; and the width of the order sought (*Re British & Commonwealth Holdings plc (No 2)*). An example of oppression occurred in *Re PFTZM Ltd (in liquidation)* [1995] 2 BCLC 354, [1995] BCC 280, where the liquidator was seeking to discover whether third parties were shadow directors of the company.

In striking the balance between permitting the promotion of the public interest of allowing examinations so as to ensure the efficient administration of an insolvency regime, on the one hand, and protecting the private interests of individual examinees, on the other, the court has to weigh up the need to uncover wrongdoing with the possible oppression of an innocent party: *Morris v European Islamic Ltd* [1999] CLY 3283, Neuberger J. The cases indicate that applications to examine insiders, namely directors and officers of the company, are treated more liberally compared with applications to examine third parties, but having said that, applications in respect of insiders can be set aside on the basis of oppression, such as where they are accused of serious wrongdoing and an examination would constitute an occasion for the office-holder to prove the case against them (*Shierson v Rastogi*, sub nom *Re RGB Resources plc* [2002] EWCA Civ 1624, [2003] 1 WLR 586, [2003] BPIR 148, [2002] BCC 1005, CA); the fact is that the degree of possible oppression with third parties is greater than with insiders (*Shierson v Rastogi*). In *Shierson* Peter Gibson LJ indicated that requiring something that is effectively oppressive can in fact be outweighed by the legitimate requirements of the liquidator (at [39]).

The principles that govern the exercise of the court's discretion were set out in two Court of Appeal decisions, *Cloverbay Ltd (Joint Administrators) v Bank of Credit and Commerce International SA* [1991] 1 BCLC 135, and *Re British & Commonwealth Holdings plc (No 2)* [1992] Ch 342 (affirmed on appeal by the House of Lords at [1993] AC 476), which considered examinations in liquidations. In *Cloverbay* it was said that courts, in engaging in balancing the requirements of the liquidator as against the possible oppression of the examinee, should consider the importance to the office-holder of obtaining the information sought and the degree of oppression to the examinee (at 141). Browne-Wilkinson V-C stated that a court should consider, in exercising its discretion, the following points (in relation to a liquidation), but the points can, for the most part, apply to other office-holders:

- the liquidator arrives on the scene with no previous knowledge and often important documents cannot be found; but the examination process is not to put the liquidator in a better position than would have been enjoyed if liquidation had not occurred;
- the test is not whether the liquidator has an absolute need for the information, but whether obtaining the information is a reasonable requirement;
- generally, liquidators have a stronger argument for the examination of officers or former officers of the company compared with the examination of third parties;
- any order for oral examination of a person is more likely to be oppressive than an order for the production of documents.

Later, in *Re British & Commonwealth Holdings plc (No 2)* [1992] Ch 342, Ralph Gibson LJ in a judgment that was ultimately approved of by the House of Lords ([1993] AC 426), formulated the principles which should guide a court when considering the power to examine. They were (at 370–372): the court has an unfettered discretion whether or not to permit an examination; the exercise of the discretion involves balancing the liquidator's requirements as against possible oppression to the prospective examinee; the power is to enable the court to help the liquidator discharge his or her function as effectively and as speedily as possible.

It may be oppressive for a court to permit certain questions where the amount of work required to answer them is not justified by the benefit to the inquiry of the answers to be given: *Re Richbell Strategic Holdings Ltd (in liquidation) (No 2)* [2000] 2 BCLC 794. It is probably oppressive to seek an examination where the prospective examinee has already given a detailed witness statement, unless the office-holder can demonstrate that it is necessary for the examinee to come to court to be questioned: *Re Westmead Consultants Ltd (in liquidation)* [2002] 1 BCLC 384.

Liquidators of a foreign company who make an application under Art 21(1)(d) of the UNCITRAL Model Law on Cross-Border Insolvency as incorporated by the Cross-Border Insolvency Regulations 2006 can clearly obtain an order from an English court for examination of persons under s 236 (*Re Chesterfield United Inc* [2012] EWHC 244 (Ch) at [10].

The application—The person who applies for an examination must provide reasonable grounds for the belief that the respondent is able to provide information which may assist the applicant in carrying out his or her duties, but it is unlikely that a court will dismiss an application unless it is oppressive as far as the respondent is concerned or an abuse of process: *Re Metropolitan Bank* (1880) 15 Ch D 139, CA; *Re Embassy Art Products* (1987) 3 BCC 292; *Re Adlards Motor Group Holdings Ltd* [1990] BCLC 68. Office-holders have the onus of establishing the need for the examination (*Re BCCI v Bank of America National Trust & Savings Association* [1997] BCC 561; *Joint Liquidators of Sasea Finance Ltd v KPMG* [1998] BCC 216), but a good deal of weight is given to the views of administrators and liquidators (*Cloverbay Ltd (Joint Administrators) v Bank of Credit and Commerce International SA* [1991] BCLC 135 at 146, CA; *Joint Liquidators of Sasea Finance Ltd v KPMG* [1998] BCC 216 at 220), and there is a general tendency for more latitude to be extended to office-holders in recent days because of the greater concern over the perpetration of fraud, particularly by company officers: *Re Arrows Ltd (No 4)* [1994] BCC 641 at 650, HL, per Lord Browne-Wilkinson. Consequently, office-holders do not have to demonstrate an absolute need for the information sought: *Cloverbay Ltd (Joint Administrators) v Bank of Credit and Commerce International SA* [1991] BCLC 135, CA.

Creditors are not given the right to apply for an examination and it has been held that s 112, cannot be used in voluntary liquidations as an alternative basis for a creditor instigating the examination process: *Re James McHale Automobiles Ltd* [1997] 1 BCLC 273, [1997] BCC 202.

314

Where office-holders wish to ascertain information from a company, they are not able to ask in the application for an order to be issued against the company. The order must be directed to the proper officer, who will give evidence on behalf of the company: *Re JN Taylor Pty Ltd* [1999] BCC 197 at 203, [1998] BPIR 347 at 353.

The application is made to a registrar of the Companies Court, who may refer it to a judge, or a district judge where the application is made in the county court. An application will be governed by art 6 of the European Convention on Human Rights, namely the right to a fair hearing.

The Rules do permit an application to be made ex parte (r 9.2(4)), but it seems that now the general rule in practice is that applications must be made inter partes (*Re PFTZM Ltd (in liquidation)* [1995] 2 BCLC 354, [1995] BCC 280; *Re Murjani* [1996] 1 BCLC 272, [1996] BCC 278, [1996] BPIR 325 (a bankruptcy case)), unless there are compelling reasons for having an ex parte application. Such reasons might include: urgency or concern over the likelihood of documents disappearing: *Re Maxwell Communications Corporation plc* [1994] BCC 741 at 747; *Re PFTZM Ltd (in liquidation)*. The preference for an inter partes application is consistent with the general principle that a person is entitled to be heard before a court delivers an order that has significant impact on the person (see *Re Maxwell Communications Corporation plc* and *Re PFTZM Ltd (in liquidation)*). Such an approach seems to be in accord with art 6 of the European Convention on Human Rights, which provides persons with the right to a fair hearing.

Contemporaneous or contemplated proceedings—A significant amount of litigation has resulted from office-holders seeking to examine a person who is likely to be a party to (or a witness at the hearing of) legal proceedings which the office-holder is either contemplating or has already commenced. The potential examinee's worry is that the office-holder may be able to gain significant forensic advantages in the conduct of contemplated or pending litigation.

As with any application for an examination, the courts need to engage in balancing the need of the liquidator to gain information and the possible oppression of the respondent (*Re British and Commonwealth Holdings plc* [1992] BCC 977 at 984, per Lord Slynn; *Re Atlantic Computers plc* [1998] BCC 200 at 209–210; *Joint Liquidators of Sasea Finance Ltd v KPMG* [1998] BCC 216 at 220), and this is necessary even if the persons to be examined are insiders, because they can be the subject of oppression: *Shierson v Rastogi*, sub nom *Re RGB Resources plc* [2002] EWCA Civ 1624, [2003] 1 WLR 586, [2003] BPIR 148, [2002] BCC 1005, CA.

Simply because a liquidator has decided to proceed, or has initiated proceedings, against the examinee or someone related to the examinee, does not necessarily preclude the holding of an examination (*Re Castle New Homes Ltd* [1979] 2 All ER 775 at 782; *Re British and Commonwealth Holdings plc* [1992] BCC 97) because the presiding officer at the examination can disallow questions if they are oppressive (*Shierson v Rastogi*), and an examination of insiders is particularly likely to be permitted where there are reasonable grounds for suspecting that the insiders have pocketed company funds (*Shierson v Rastogi*). Having said that, if litigation has been commenced and the examination is sought in order to improve the position of a liquidator as a litigant, this will not be permitted: *Re Spiraflite Ltd* [1979] 2 All ER 766 at 769; *Re Castle New Homes Ltd* [1979] 2 All ER 775 at 789. The purpose of the office-holder in seeking the examination might well be considered (*Re Spiraflite Ltd*). The purpose of the power to examine is to enable an office-holder to discharge his or her functions and not to improve the prospects of any litigation, so the liquidator's purpose must be the former and not the latter (*Re Spiraflite Ltd*). Recent cases have moved away from the purpose of the office-holder and focused almost totally on the balancing exercise, referred to above, but they have said that in undertaking the balancing, the court should consider the importance to the office-holder of obtaining the information sought as well as the degree of oppression to the examinee: *Cloverbay Ltd (Joint Administrators) v Bank of Credit and Commerce International SA* [1991] 1 BCLC 135 at 141.

An examination will not be prevented merely because the office-holder has completed litigation against the examinee (*Re JT Rhodes Ltd* (1986) 2 BCC 99, 284 – but cf the view of Evans-Lombe J in *Re JN Taylor Pty Ltd* [1999] BCC 197 at 209, [1998] BPIR 347 at 361, where he regarded the former case as 'a case arising from unusual facts'). However, an office-holder will not be permitted to have an examination if litigation is discontinued in order to make an application for an examination: *Re Bletchley Boat Co Ltd* [1974] 1 WLR 630, [1974] 1 All ER 1225.

Where an examination is sought and the information to be given may be of assistance to the office-holder in legal proceedings already commenced, the court might permit the examination to be held if it is the case that gaining the information relevant to the proceedings is merely an incidental consequence of inquiries that are necessary to enable the office-holder to discharge his or her duties: *Re Brook Martin & Co (Nominees) Ltd* [1993] BCLC 328. This might be difficult for a court to determine.

'Affairs or property of the company'—It has been held in Australia that the affairs or property of a company includes the company's choses in action: *Grosvenor Hill (Qld) Pty Ltd v Barber* (1994) 120 ALR 262; *Gerah Imports Pty Ltd v The Duke Group Ltd (in liquidation)* (1994) 12 ACLC 116, (1994) 12 ACSR 513; *Re Interchase Corporation Ltd* (1996) 21 ACSR 375. It has been held that office-holders are entitled to documents relating to a trading relationship between one of the company's subsidiaries and a third party where those documents are kept by the third party, on the basis that such documents involved the affairs of the company: *Re PNC Telecom Plc* [2003] EWHC 2220 (Ch).

Section 236(3)

Books, papers or other records—This subsection covers information that is contained in books, papers and records that are the property of the company, whether or not still in its possession: *Re Trading Partners Ltd* [2002] BPIR 606, [2002] 1 BCLC 655. The office-holder is not limited to papers that came into existence before the advent of an insolvency administration. For example, if the company became insolvent and came under the control of administrative receivers, a subsequent liquidator is entitled to have access to papers that relate to the company's affairs even if they came into existence after the receivers took office and the papers were produced at the expense of the chargeholder who appointed the receivers: *Re Trading Partners Ltd* [2002] BPIR 606, [2002] 1 BCLC 655. In *Re Trading Partners Ltd* the court ordered the production of working and litigation papers held by the receivers. Books, papers and records has been held by the Supreme Court of Appeal of South Africa in *Le Roux v Viana* 2008 (2) SA 173 to include any information relating to the company in liquidation where it is located on a computer's hard drive and where the computer is owned by a third party.

In seeking documents, it is not sufficient for a liquidator to state merely that the documents are needed in the winding-up process, for the liquidator must state why the documents are necessary: *Re XL Communications Group plc* [2005] EWHC 2413 (Ch).

Liquidators of a foreign company who make an application under Art 21(1)(g) of the UNCITRAL Model Law on Cross-Border Insolvency as incorporated by the Cross-Border Insolvency Regulations 2006 may obtain an order from an English court for disclosure of documents relating to the company under s 236: *Re Chesterfield United Inc* [2012] EWHC 244 (Ch).

It has been held that a court could exercise its discretion under s 236 to order HM Revenue and Customs to disclose information to a liquidator which had been obtained from a foreign authority under a letter of request (*XYZ v Revenue and Customs Commissioners* [2010] EWHC 1645 (Ch), [2010] BPIR 1297).

In *Re Delberry Ltd* [2008] EWHC 925, [2008] BPIR 1277 it was said that the court could consider, inter alia, the following factors when hearing an application under s 236(3): '(i) should be necessary for the liquidator to obtain the documents in the interests of the winding up; (ii) that production should not be oppressive or unfair to the respondent; (iii) the onus of establishing the need for the documents is on the office-holder (albeit a great deal of weight is to be given to the office-holder's views that production is required) and the status of the person to whom the order is addressed; (iv) if the person is a stranger to the company the court may be slower to make an order but where the person owed fiduciary duties to the company, and was an ex-officer of the company, the court may be more ready to make the order; (v) s 236 is not intended to give the office-holder special advantages in ordinary litigation and in general the court is disinclined to make an order where the office holder has commenced litigation against the respondent to the s 236 application. However, there is no hard and fast rule in relation to that issue and (vi) the volume of documentation requested and the effort required to produce it; (vii) s 236 is not limited to documents belonging to the company in liquidation'. (at [25])

The order—In making an order, the courts have the power to limit the ambit of the examination, if they feel that it is too wide as sought in the application: In *Re Richbell Strategic Holdings Ltd (in liquidation) (No 2)* [2000] 2 BCLC 794. Alternatively, the court may restrict the material that is sought to be produced: *Re Galileo Group Ltd* [1998] 2 WLR 364, [1998] 1 BCLC 318, [1998] BCC 228; *Re Atlantic Computers plc* [1998] BCC 200.

If an order is made that the respondent must produce documents, then the liquidator is not able to demand that he or she be given copies. The respondent's duty is to produce and let the liquidator inspect, and it is then for the liquidator to make copies at his or her expense: *Re Maxwell Communications Corporation plc (No 3)* [1994] BCC 741, [1995] 1 BCLC 521.

If exceptional circumstances exist, a court is able to make an order, pursuant to its powers under the Supreme Court Act 1981, preventing an examinee from absconding abroad prior to the examination and restraining the examinee from leaving the jurisdiction: *Re Oriental Credit Ltd* [1988] 2 WLR 172. A court may order, although this would be done rarely, that the examinee surrender his or her passport or order that the examinee not leave the jurisdiction pending the examination: *Daltel Europe Ltd (in liquidation) v Makki* [2005] 1 BCLC 594. If a court takes any of the foregoing actions, a person who wishes to leave the jurisdiction may obtain court permission to go, on condition that security be given, so as to ensure that the examinee will adhere to the order: *Re a Company (No 003318 of 1987)* (1987) 3 BCC 564; *Re BCCI (No 7)* [1994] 1 BCLC 455.

In *Re BCCI (No 7)* [1994] 1 BCLC 455 an order against a person domiciled overseas, but resident in the UK, was supported by a requirement that he should give security in the amount of £500,000 before being permitted to leave the country: *Re a Company (No 003318 of 1987)* (1987) 3 BCC 564.

If the office-holder who applied for and obtained an order subsequently vacates office, the order ceases to have any force: *Re Kingscroft Insurance Co Ltd* [1994] BCC 343.

Rescission of order—Where an order for examination is made, the examinee may apply, under r 7.47, to have the order set aside, perhaps because the examination would be unreasonable or oppressive. In hearing an application the court is required to carry out a balancing of interests, just as it did when the application for the examination was determined.

If the respondent does apply to a judge against a registrar's order for examination, the judge may exercise a discretion, not being fettered by the registrar's exercise of discretion, and the judge's discretion supplants that of the registrar: *Re Rolls Razor Ltd (No 2)* [1970] Ch 576 at 594.

Where an application for a rescission of an order is opposed, the costs will usually be awarded against the party who loses. If that is the examinee then, unless special circumstances exist, he or she will be ordered to pay the costs of the liquidator: *Re Cloverbay Ltd* [1989] 1 BCLC 724 at 733; *Re BCCI (No 12)* [1997] BCC 561 at 579.

See r 7.47 and the comments accompanying it.

Examinees—While it is not usual, it appears that a creditor may be examined in certain circumstances (*Massey v Allen* (1878) 9 Ch D 164; *Re Tyne Chemical Co* (1874) 43 LJ Ch 354), for example in relation to a proof of debt (*Bellmex International v British American Tobacco* [2001] BCC 253). But such orders should only be made when office-holders demonstrate a clear necessity for them (*Bellmex International*).

Persons who are residing in England and Wales and whose examination is sought in a letter of request from a foreign court to a court in England and Wales, under s 426, may be ordered to be examined (*Re Southern Equities Corp* [2000] BCC 123, CA (a letter of request from the South Australian Supreme Court to High Court in England and Wales)), and will be summoned to appear by the court in England and Wales to be examined, provided that the examination is justified under the law of the foreign jurisdiction and notwithstanding that an order would not be granted if the request came from an office-holder administering an insolvent administration in England and Wales (*Re Southern Equities Corp*).

As far as costs and expenses of examinees go, see r 9.6 and the notes accompanying it.

Section 236(2)

'Officer'—There are a number of definitions of 'officer' in the Act (e g ss 206(3), 208(3), 210(3) and 211(2)), as well as a definition in the Companies Act 2006 (s 1173). The latter section includes directors, managers and secretaries. 'Director' is explained in s 250 as including any person occupying the position of director by whatever name called. For the purposes of s 236, auditors of the company are also officers: *Joint Liquidators of Sasea Finance Ltd v KPMG* [1998] BCC 216 at 222.

Section 236(2)

'Person'—This has been interpreted so as to include corporate bodies, so they can be examined through their appropriate officer: *Re Highgrade Traders Ltd* [1984] BCLC 151, CA.

Examinees residing outside of the jurisdiction—It has been held that a court may order, pursuant to r 12.12, the service of an order of public examination on a person who is outside the jurisdiction, whether or not that person is a British subject: *Re Seagull Manufacturing Co Ltd (in liquidation)* [1993] Ch 345, [1993] BCC 241. However, at first instance in that case, it was said that this was not the position with private examinations, and in *Re Tucker* [1990] Ch 148, [1988] 1 All ER 603 the Court of Appeal said that it would not order, under a bankruptcy equivalent of s 236, the examination in Belgium of a person if it could not compel that person to attend. But that is inconsistent with the law relating to public examinations (*Re Casterbridge Properties Ltd (in liquidation)* [2002] BCC 453, [2002] BPIR 428), and in the Scottish case of *McIsaac, Petitioners; Joint Liquidators of First Tokyo Index Trust Ltd* [1994] BCC 410, the Court of Session held that there was no reason why an order under s 236 could not be made in relation to a person resident in New York. The court indicated that whether or not it was proper to make an order for a person residing overseas depended, not on a consideration of s 236, but rather on whether the court could effectively invoke s 426 in obtaining assistance from the courts of the place of the person's residence. In *Re Casterbridge Properties Ltd (in liq)* Burton J. doubted the correctness of the reason given in *McIsaac*. His Lordship did not have to decide whether s 236 could be used extra-territorially, although he was willing to say that s 236 had partial extra-judicial effect (at [43]). He was of the view that a summons for an examination could be served overseas and be effective if the examination was to take place where the examinee was residing (at [48]).

The Court of Appeal in *Re Mid-East Trading Ltd* [1998] 1 BCLC 240 said that an order under s 236 could be made in relation to documents that are held overseas. An order would only be made in circumstances where the office-holder required to see the documents in order to discharge the duties and functions of office and production of the documents did not unnecessarily or unreasonably burden the person required to produce.

The examination—A person may be examined orally or by interrogatories (see s 237(4)).

The registrar or judge who presides at the examination has a complete discretion in determining how the examination ought to be conducted and what questions may be put to the examinee: In *Re North Australian Territory Company* (1890) 45 Ch D 87 at 93; *Re Maville Hose Ltd* [1938] 1 Ch D 32 at 40; *Rottmann v Brittain* [2009] EWCA Civ 473, [2010] 1 WLR 67, [2009] BPIR 1148 at [16]). However, only relevant questions should be permitted: In *Re Pennington ex parte Pennington* (1888) 5 Mor 268 at 269.

The content of without prejudice negotiations involving the applicant for the examination and the examinee will not be able to be admitted at the examination, although a court may be advised that without prejudice negotiations have occurred: *Re Anglo-American Insurance Co Ltd* [2003] BPIR 793.

Those examined are required to provide the best answers they are able, possibly supplemented by documents where necessary: *Re Richbell Strategic Holdings Ltd (in liquidation) (No 2)* [2000] 2 BCLC 794. If the examinee refuses to answer a question then the practice is for the registrar to adjourn the hearing to a judge of the Companies Court, before whom the question is repeated and, if not answered, the judge may make necessary punitive orders: *Re JN Taylor Pty Ltd* [1999] BCC 197 at 199, [1998] BPIR 347 at 349.

See r 9.4 and the notes accompanying that rule.

Privilege against self-incrimination—It has been held that an officer of an insolvent company is unable to refuse to answer questions at an examination on the basis that those answers might incriminate him or her: *Bishopsgate Investment Management Ltd (in provisional liquidation) v Maxwell* [1992] Ch 1, [1992] 2 All ER 856, [1992] BCLC 475, [1992] BCC 222, CA. This is because the purpose of s 236 necessitates the abrogation of the privilege, or else an officer who is examined could frustrate the purpose of the section: *Re Jeffery S Levitt Ltd* [1992] BCC 137, [1992] BCLC 250; *Bishopsgate Investment Management Ltd (in provisional liquidation) v Maxwell*. If the examinee refuses to answer, on the basis of self-incrimination, the examinee is in contempt of court: *Bishopsgate Investment*

Management Ltd (in provisional liquidation) v Maxwell. Even if the prospective examinee is being investigated by the Serious Fraud Office, no right to claim the privilege exists: *Re AE Farr Ltd* [1992] BCC 150.

Any statement made that incriminates the examinee can be used in subsequent civil proceedings if the trial judge permits, but it cannot be used in any criminal proceedings, save those mentioned in s 433(3): see *R v Faryabb* [1999] BPIR 569, CA. For further details, see the notes accompanying s 433. In a civil action, if a trial judge acts in a proportionate way, that is considering the strength of the case for interference with the rights of the former examinee against the seriousness of the interference, it would appear that there would not be a breach of the rights under the European Convention on Human Rights if statements given at a s 236 hearing were admitted: Simmons and Smith 'The Human Rights Act 1998: the practical impact on insolvency' (2000) 16 IL & P 167 at 171–172.

The Court of Appeal has stated, in the context of an examination, that the privilege against self-incrimination did not apply where the criminal offence arose under the law of another country: *Rottmann v Brittain* [2009] EWCA Civ 473, [2010] 1 WLR 67, [2009] BPIR 1148.

Legal professional privilege—This privilege cannot be asserted by the solicitors of the company which is in liquidation in relation to documents which belonged to the company: *Re Brook Martin & Co (Nominees) Ltd* [1993] BCLC 328 at 336. Also, the company's solicitors could not assert the privilege in answer to a question relating to the company's affairs. It is not clear whether the privilege may be asserted in relation to clients other than the company. But in Australia, it has been held that a liquidator is able to claim or waive privilege on behalf of the company if it were in the interests of the company or its creditors: *Re Dallhold Investments Pty Ltd* (1994) 53 FCR 339 at 348.

If solicitors for a company officer, or other person examined under s 236, are examined and asked a question, privilege is not able to be claimed if their client would be lawfully required to answer the question and divulge the information which is the subject of the question: *Re Murjani* [1996] 1 BCLC 272, [1996] BCC 278, [1996] BPIR 325.

Requiring documents to be kept confidential—There is Scottish authority to the effect that where a liquidator seeks production of documents under s 236, the person delivering the documents is not entitled to obtain from the liquidator an undertaking of confidentiality with respect to the documents: *McIsaac, Petitioners; Joint Liquidators of First Tokyo Index Trust Ltd* [1994] BCC 410. English courts have not gone this far, stating that the obligation of an office-holder to keep information obtained under s 236 confidential may be waived by court order if the court was satisfied that either such action enabled the purposes of the office-holder's position to be fulfilled, or it was otherwise justified by the balance of considerations of how justice was to be secured: *Re Esal (Commodities) Ltd (No 2)* [1990] BCC 708 at 723; *Re a Company (No 005374 of 1993)* [1993] BCC 734.

Information secured pursuant to an order under s 236 by a liquidator of a holding company can be disclosed to the directors and liquidators of subsidiary companies (*Re Esal (Commodities) Ltd* [1989] BCLC 59 at 65, CA), on the basis that disclosure may assist the officers of the subsidiaries getting in assets or defending actions for the ultimate benefit of the holding company.

While the application for an examination is governed by Art 6 of the European Convention on Human Rights, the examination itself is not, as it does not determine the respondent's substantive rights (see Trower 'Bringing Human Rights Home to the Insolvency Practitioner' (Part 1) (2000) 13 *Insolvency Intelligence* 41 at 43). But, as a result of the decision of the European Court of Human Rights in *Saunders v United Kingdom* [1997] EHRR 313, [1997] BCC 872, [1998] 1 BCLC 362, evidence given by the examinee will not be able to be used in subsequent criminal proceedings because the evidence is given under compulsion, and permitting the use of such evidence would constitute a contravention of Art 6(1) of the European Convention on Human Rights. Notwithstanding this, the court did say that testimony obtained under compulsion which appeared to be of a non-incriminating nature could later be used in criminal proceedings to contradict or cast doubt on the other statements of the person or otherwise to undermine his or her credibility.

Enforcement—Provision for enforcing an order against an examinee who fails to appear at the examination or absconds is provided for in s 236(4), (5) and (6). Also, see s 237 and r 7.23 and the comments that accompany these provisions.

For a more detailed discussion of private examinations, see A Keay *McPherson's Law of Company Liquidation* (3rd edn, Sweet and Maxwell, 2013) at 964–1002.
Also, see the comments accompanying rr 9.1–9.6.

237 Court's enforcement powers under s 236

(1) If it appears to the court, on consideration of any evidence obtained under section 236 or this section, that any person has in his possession any property of the company, the court may, on the application of the office-holder, order that person to deliver the whole or any part of the property to the office-holder at such time, in such manner and on such terms as the court thinks fit.

(2) If it appears to the court, on consideration of any evidence so obtained, that any person is indebted to the company, the court may, on the application of the office-holder, order that person to pay to the office-holder, at such time and in such manner as the court may direct, the whole or any part of the amount due, whether in full discharge of the debt or otherwise, as the court thinks fit.

(3) The court may, if it thinks fit, order that any person who if within the jurisdiction of the court would be liable to be summoned to appear before it under section 236 or this section shall be examined in any part of the United Kingdom where he may for the time being be, or in a place outside the United Kingdom.

(4) Any person who appears or is brought before the court under section 236 or this section may be examined on oath, either orally or (except in Scotland) by interrogatories, concerning the company or the matters mentioned in section 236(2)(c).

Flexibility on place and mode of examination—In an attempt to be flexible and to ensure that the powers of examination are not easily thwarted, the court is provided with a discretion to order that any person who, if within England and Wales, would be liable to be summoned to appear before it, be examined in any part of the UK where he or she may for the time being be, or in a place outside of the UK. Furthermore, the person may be examined in person or through interrogatories.

Costs—If a court makes orders, under either s 237(1) or s 237(2), it may order the costs to be paid by the examinee under s 236 (r 9.6(2)).

Adjustment of prior transactions (administration and liquidation)

238 Transactions at an undervalue (England and Wales)

(1) This section applies in the case of a company where—

    (a)   the company enters administration, or
    (b)   the company goes into liquidation;

and 'the office-holder' means the administrator or the liquidator, as the case may be.

(2) Where the company has at a relevant time (defined in section 240) entered into a transaction with any person at an undervalue, the office-holder may apply to the court for an order under this section.

(3) Subject as follows, the court shall, on such an application, make such order as it thinks fit for restoring the position to what it would have been if the company had not entered into that transaction.

(4) For the purposes of this section and section 241, a company enters into a transaction with a person at an undervalue if—

(a)   the company makes a gift to that person or otherwise enters into a transaction with that person on terms that provide for the company to receive no consideration, or

(b)   the company enters into a transaction with that person for a consideration the value of which, in money or money's worth, is significantly less than the value, in money or money's worth, of the consideration provided by the company.

(5) The court shall not make an order under this section in respect of a transaction at an undervalue if it is satisfied—

(a)   that the company which entered into the transaction did so in good faith and for the purpose of carrying on its business, and

(b)   that at the time it did so there were reasonable grounds for believing that the transaction would benefit the company.

Amendments—Enterprise Act 2002, s 248(3), Sch 17, paras 9, 25.

General note—The section is, in many ways, to be viewed as a successor to s 42 of the Bankruptcy Act 1914, which provided for the avoidance of voluntary settlements and was, until the advent of the Insolvency Act, incorporated by reference by the Companies Act. Section 42 was seen as being outmoded, not sufficiently broad and difficult to apply in relation to companies. Section 238 has its roots in the law which first provided for the avoidance of fraudulent conveyances, the Statute of Elizabeth in 1571, although there is now no need to establish fraud. Section 423 tends to be closer to the fraudulent conveyance language, although it is also related to s 238 in that both deal with transactions at an undervalue. Hence, there is some overlap between the provisions, and office-holders have, on occasions, brought proceedings under both sections. See the comments attached to s 423. Section 238 aims to prevent insolvent companies disposing of property at an undervalued amount just before winding up (as a means of asset-stripping), thereby reducing the pool of property which would be available to the liquidator to distribute to creditors.

Administrators and liquidators are able to invoke the section. The section corresponds to s 339, which relates to bankruptcy and is able to be employed by a trustee in bankruptcy.

The section only applies to a transaction entered into by the company that is in administration or liquidation, and does not cover transactions that are entered into by a party other than the company, such as the company's mortgagee: *Re Brabon* [2000] BCC 1171.

The burden of establishing that a transaction was entered into at an undervalue lies squarely on the shoulders of the applicant: *Stone & Rolls Ltd v Micro Communications Inc* [2005] EWHC 1052 (Ch) at [93]). However the circumstances might be such that an evidential burden is placed on the respondent: *Phillips v Brewin Dolphin Bell Lawrie Ltd* [2001] 1 WLR 143 at [26] (HL).

There is no obligation on the applicant to prove that the insolvent company intended to sell at an undervalue or pay over the market value for an asset, but if that can be established then it may have an effect on the remedy that is ordered: *Stanley and Wood v TMK Finance Ltd* [2010] EWHC 3349 (Ch), [2011] BPIR 876 at [7].

In *Re MC Bacon Ltd* [1990] BCLC 324 at 335, a case involving an application under both s 238 and s 239, Millett J protested, in relation to arguments concerning the application of s 239, at counsel citing cases which dealt with previous preference provisions. In dealing with a transaction at an undervalue case, *Hill v Haines* [2007] EWCA Civ 1284, [2007] BPIR 1280, [2008] 2 All ER 901, the Court of Appeal did not take the same view as far as such transactions were concerned (at [18]).

Liquidators are required, before taking action, to secure approval from either the liquidation committee or the court (s 165(2)(b) (creditors' voluntary liquidations) or s 167(1)(a) (compulsory liquidations); para 3A of Sch 4).

'**Relevant time**'—This is defined in s 240, and involves two aspects. First, the transaction must have occurred in a particular time zone, namely the two years preceding the onset of insolvency. 'Onset of insolvency' is defined in s 240(3). Second, besides falling within this time zone, the transaction must have been entered into at a time when the company was unable to pay its debts within the meaning of s 123 or the entering into of the transaction resulted in the company being unable to pay its debts. The latter requirement is not relevant where the transaction was entered into with a person connected with the company (s 240(2)), although in such a case, the two-year time period still applies. See the comments under 'Relevant time' and 'Unable to pay debts' in relation to s 240 and 'Connected person' in relation to s 249.

Section 238(2)

'**Any person**'—While the section does not indicate that it operates extraterritorially, it has been said that the use of 'any person' should bear its literal and natural meaning: anyone, wherever he or she is situated. So s 238 could have effect outside of the country in which the court making the order is situated, and an order could be made against a foreign resident who has no place of business in the UK and who does not carry on business in the jurisdiction, provided that the court is satisfied, in exercising its discretion, that the respondent has a sufficient connection with England for it to be just and proper to make an order against the person: *Re Paramount Airways Ltd (No 2)* [1993] Ch 223, [1992] BCC 416. But where a case involves a foreign element, the court will have to be persuaded that the defendant was sufficiently connected with England for it to be just and proper to make an order: *Re Paramount Airways Ltd (No 2)* at 239–240, 425.

'**Transaction at an undervalue**'—The most critical element of a s 238 action is to prove that the company entered into a transaction that involved an undervalue. The office-holder must establish that the transaction involved a gift given by the company or one where the company agrees to accept from a person consideration the value of which, in money or money's worth, is significantly less than the value, in money or money's worth, of the consideration provided by the company.

In *Re MC Bacon Ltd* [1990] BCLC 324 at 340 Millett J said that there were six elements to be established, namely: 'a transaction entered into by the company; for a consideration; the value of which is measured in money or money's worth; is significantly less than the value; also measured in money or money's worth; of the consideration provided by the company.' This assessment was approved of by the House of Lords in *Phillips v Brewin Dolphin Bell Lawrie Ltd* [2001] 1 WLR 143 at [21].

'**Entered into a transaction**'—The Court of Appeal in *Ovenden Colbert Printers Ltd (in liq) (sub nom Hunt v Hosking)* [2013] EWCA Civ 1408 stated that this expression connoted the taking of some step or act of participation by the company.

Transaction—'Transaction' is defined in s 436 as including 'a gift, agreement or arrangement' and it is indicated that the references to 'entering into a transaction' in the Act are to be construed accordingly. 'Transaction' is defined broadly and embraces a potentially wide range of possibilities (*Re Taylor Sinclair (Capital) Ltd* [2001] 2 BCLC 176 at 184, *Re HHO Licensing Ltd* [2007 EWHC 2953 (Ch), [2007] BPIR 1363, [2008] 1 BCLC 223 at [31]) and the courts have said that they should not strain to limit the width of the definition: *Phillips v Brewin Dolphin Bell Lawrie Ltd* [1999] BCC 557 at 565, CA (the House of Lords ([2001] 1 WLR 143) dismissed the appeal). For there to be a transaction under s 238 the existence of a contract is not required: *Re HHO Licensing Ltd* [2007 EWHC 2953 (Ch), [2007] BPIR 1363, [2008] 1 BCLC 223 at [31]. It is probable that something like a guarantee would constitute a transaction. The giving of security by a company to a creditor constitutes a transaction, but, the generally-held view since *Re MC Bacon Ltd* [1990] BCLC 324 is that it is not one that falls within s 238, as all that the company loses is the ability to apply the proceeds of the realisation of the security otherwise than in satisfaction of the secured debt: *Re Mistral Finance Ltd (in liquidation)* [2001] BCC 27. That is not something capable of valuation in monetary terms and is not customarily disposed of for value (*Re MC Bacon Ltd* at 340). But, in light of the comments of Arden LJ (with whom the other judges agreed on all points save the issue of the limitation period – see later) in the Court of Appeal in *Hill v Spread Trustee Company Ltd* [2006] EWCA Civ 542, [2006] BPIR 789, [2007] 1 All ER 1106, [2006] BCC 646, [2007] 1 BCLC 450, [2007] 1 WLR 2404, it does not follow from this that a transaction involving the grant of security can never amount to a transaction for no consideration, as such a grant is no different from any other transaction in that respect (at [93]).

The House of Lords in *Phillips v Brewin Dolphin Bell Lawrie Ltd* [2001] 1 WLR 143 indicated that it was not necessary to search for one transaction, as inter-connected transactions could be considered in assessing whether there was a transaction at an undervalue. Their Lordships actually said that the focus should not be on finding the transaction, but on finding the consideration (if any) that is given and received (at [20]). Lord Scott gave the following example to explain the view: 'if a company agrees to sell an asset to A on terms that B agrees to enter into some collateral agreement with the company, the consideration for the asset will, in my opinion, be the combination of the consideration, if any, expressed in the agreement with A and the value of the agreement with B.' (at [20]). Unfortunately, the decision does not indicate how far one can go in including transactions that were not entered into between the company and the respondent.

To claim successfully under s 238, the office-holder must be able to prove that there was some form of dealing between the company and the respondent (*Re Taylor Sinclair (Capital) Ltd* [2001] 2 BCLC 176 at 185), but indications are that it is sometimes difficult to isolate the transaction that can be challenged.

See Mokal and Ho 'Consideration, Characterisation and evaluation: Transactions at an Undervalue after Phillips v Brewin Dolphin' (2001) 1 JCLS 359.

Undervalue—Besides actually establishing a transaction, an undervalue element must be proved, and that can be difficult in some cases. The House of Lords in *Phillips v Brewin Dolphin Bell Lawrie Ltd* [2001] 1 WLR 143 at [27] said that if the value of the consideration for which a company enters into a transaction is speculative, then the party who relies on the consideration is required to establish the value. Lord Scott in that case said that: 'The value of an asset that is being offered for sale is, prima facie, not less than the amount which a reasonably well-informed purchaser is prepared, in arm's length negotiations, to pay for it.' (at [30]). His Lordship went on to consider the situation where a unique asset is involved in the transaction. Unique assets can cause valuation problems. His Lordship said that the price for such an asset can be presumed to be market value, and, therefore, not transferred at something than an undervalue within the section, if it was sold after arm's length negotiations and after proper marketing and both parties acted 'knowledeably, prudently and without compulsion.' (at [30]).

Any transfer that is expressed to be simply for natural love and affection will constitute a transfer at an undervalue unless there is some other explanation of it (*Simms v Oakes* [2002] EWCA Civ 8, [2002] BPIR 1244 at [5].

If a joint tenant of property that is subject to a mortgage transfers his or her interest to the other joint tenant for no consideration except that the transferee tenant assumes sole liability under the mortgage, the transfer would be a transaction at an undervalue: *Re Kumar* [1993] 1 WLR 224.

Clearly, office-holders must establish a significant undervalue by proving the respective values of the consideration given by the parties to the transaction, and this must be done in money terms: *Re Brabon* [2000] BPIR 537 at 562.

The issue of valuation can play a significant part in establishing whether or not the required transaction was entered into. It is incumbent on the office-holder, as just indicated, to establish the respective values in money or money terms of the consideration given and received by the company and, also, to demonstrate that what it received was significantly less than what it provided: *Re MC Bacon Ltd* [1990] BCLC 324 at 340–341. So, if consideration is not able to be valued in money terms, it is not able to be considered as part of any consideration passing between the parties. In relation to a s 423 action, it has been said that when determining whether consideration received by the defendant was significantly less than the consideration passed to the debtor, the court is obliged to form the view as to the price which could be obtained in the open market in relation to the property representing the consideration given by the defendant and that given by the debtor: *National Westminster Bank plc v Jones* [2000] BPIR 1092 at 1115. It will be necessary for the court to compare the value of property in relation to the consideration given for it, and then consider 'in percentage terms, how much less the consideration is than the value' (*National Westminster Bank plc v Jones* at 1115).

It would appear that in determining whether there is an inequality of benefit, a court must be aware of all aspects of the transaction, including the totality of the benefits received in practice: see *Agricultural Mortgage Corporation v Woodward* [1994] BCC 688.

There is nothing in the section which requires the court to ascribe a precise figure either to the outgoing value or to the incoming value relating to the relevant transaction. The provision will apply whenever the court is satisfied that, whatever the precise values may be, the incoming value is on any view 'significantly less' than the outgoing value: *Ramlort Ltd v Reid* [2004] EWCA Civ 800, [2004] BPIR 985 at [103] per Jonathan Parker LJ. The judge did accept that it was preferable if a judge could find precise figures (at [105]). His Lordship said that he could 'see no reason why the court, if it considers it appropriate to do so, should not address the issue of undervalue by taking from a range of possible values those which are most favourable to the party seeking to uphold the transaction' (at [104]). For a recent discussion, see *Ailyan and Fry v Smith* [2010] EWHC 24 (Ch), [2010] BPIR 289 at [48]-[49].

If property was purchased by the company from a person at arm's length, and after it had been offered for sale publicly, this will suggest the price paid by the company was market value: *Re Brabon* [2000] BPIR 537.

The same valuation principles should be employed for valuing both the consideration received by the company and the consideration disposed of by the company (*Re Thoars* [2003] 1 BCLC 499). While the consideration should be valued as at the date of the transfer, in appropriate circumstances the occurrence or non-occurrence of events subsequent to the transfer that is impugned, and before the assessment of the consideration, may be considered in assessing the value of consideration in money or money's worth (*Re Thoars* at [8], [17]), an approach that the House of Lords in *Phillips v Brewin Dolphin Bell Lawrie Ltd* [2001] UKHL 2, [2001] 1 WLR 143, [2001] BPIR 119 appeared to endorse. An example of this might be where a property, when sold, was expected to receive planning permission that would boost its value and those in the market for a property with such permission might be willing to pay more for it, and the property did in fact attract the necessary permission post sale. The value of an asset that is being offered for sale is, prima facie as not less than the amount that a reasonably well informed purchaser is prepared, in arms' length negotiations, to pay for it.': *Phillips v Brewin Dolphin Bell Lawrie Ltd* [2001] UKHL 2, [2001] 1 WLR 143, [2001] BPIR 119 at [30] per Lord Scott.

In determining value the court could take into account a subsequent sale of the property as the basis for establishing the value of the property at the relevant time, however this depended on the fact that there had been no significant change in market conditions and the circumstances surrounding the sale could be regarded as proving a reliable base for inferring market value at the relevant time, namely the sale from the company to the defendant: *Stanley and Wood v TMK Finance Ltd* [2010] EWHC 3349 (Ch), [2011] BPIR 876.

As far as valuation goes it has been said that the question in every case would be whether there was a 'significant' disparity in the consideration moving from and to the debtor: *Ramlort v Reid* [2004] BPIR 985 at [102]-[105]).

It has been accepted that a preferential payment which is susceptible to challenge cannot amount to consideration for the purposes of this provision (or s 339): *Re Peppard* [2009] BPIR 331 at [28].

A court might say that there is an undervalue, not because the purchase price given or received is an undervalue, but because of the terms of the agreement relating to the transfer. For instance, if A Ltd was to sell a property to B for what is regarded as market value, a court might hold that the transfer is an undervalue if the purchase price was not due to be paid for 12 months and no interest component was factored in.

The compromise or release of, or forebearance to press, a valid claim, or even a doubtful or invalid claim, as long as it is not known to be invalid but is advanced in good faith, can provide good consideration in this context: *Hill v Haines* [2007] EWCA Civ 1284, [2007] BPIR 1280, [2008] 2 All ER 901 at [79].

See G Peters 'Undervalues and the Value of Creditor and Debtor Covenants: A Comparative Analysis' (2008) 21 *Insolvency Intelligence* 81.

Defence—Provided that the office-holder is able to establish that there was a transaction at an undervalue, that it was entered into during the two years before the onset of insolvency and either the company was insolvent at the time of the transaction or was made insolvent as a consequence of entering into the transaction, to resist the claim the defendant must establish a two-limbed defence. This requires proving that:

*   the company entered into the transaction in good faith for the purpose of carrying on its business; *and*
*   when entering the transaction there were reasonable grounds for believing that the transaction would benefit the company.

It is the company that must act in good faith, and so the mind of the respondent is not at issue: *Re Baron Manufacturing Co Ltd* [1998] BCC 827, [1999] 1 BCLC 740 (a case where the defence failed, even though the respondent acted in innocence). The defence is rarely successful, but was in *Levy McCallum Ltd v Allen* [2007] NICh 3, [2007] NIJB 366 (and noted in Capper (2008) 21 *Insolvency Intelligence* 59). In that case Treacy J found that a guarantee given by a company that ended up in liquidation was given in good faith for the purpose of carrying on the business of the company and with reasonable grounds for believing that it would benefit the company. The company had guaranteed the debt of a another company (in the same corporate group) that owed it money.

The second limb introduces an objective factor. If no consideration was given to the company, the defendant has a much harder task in fulfilling this limb of the defence.

Whether or not reasonable grounds existed must be determined at the time of the transaction.

Court order—If a court believes that the office-holder has succeeded in proving a case under s 238, it will make a declaration to that effect. Then the court must consider what orders, if any, will be made to restore the position to what it would have been if the company had not entered the transaction (s 238(3)). Section 238(3) is a restitutionary, rather than a compensatory provision. Examples of the kinds of orders that a court might make are set out in s 241. Importantly, courts are not restricted to those orders contained in s 241, but generally one or more of them will be incorporated into the orders of courts. Where there is a transaction at an undervalue, involving the company having purchased an asset at an inflated price, often courts will order, in the terms of s 241(1)(a), that the property that is the subject of the transaction at undervalue be re-transferred to the company: e g *Re Schuppan* [1997] BPIR 271 (shares). Where the liquidator does not seek the return of the property which was transferred under the transaction challenged under s 238, or the court does not think it appropriate to order the re-transfer of the property, it is likely that the hearing of an application under s 238 will end up involving a battle of valuations by experts: *Walker v WA Personnel Ltd* [2002] BPIR 621 at 635.

See s 241 and the comments accompanying that section.

The idea that the courts can only make an order by way of monetary compensation has been expressly rejected, and it has been said that a court can order restitution of assets even where the nature and substance of the assets had changed significantly since the transfer that is under attack: *Walker v WA Personnel Ltd* [2002] BPIR 621 at 634. Courts will be slow to allow a transferee of property that is later subject to a successful claim pursuant to s 238 to retain the property and pay the difference between the purchase price and a fair value, where the transferee had notice that the transaction might be challenged by a liquidator: *Walker v WA Personnel Ltd* at 634–635. The Court of Appeal in *Ramlort Ltd v Reid* [2004] EWCA Civ 800, [2004] BPIR 985 has approved of that general approach. It has stated that the court is not to start with a presumption that favours monetary compensation as against a setting aside of the relevant transaction. Courts must fashion the most appropriate remedy, as far as practicable, in order to restore the position pre-transaction: *Ramlort Ltd v Reid.*

Notwithstanding the use of 'shall' in s 238(3), usually indicating something that is mandatory, there is authority that provides that a court is not obliged to make an order, if it thinks fit: *Re Paramount Airways Ltd (No 2)* [1993] Ch 223 at 229, [1992] BCC 416 at 425. This is perhaps illustrated in *Re MDA Investment Management Ltd* [2004] 1 BCLC 217 where Park J declined to make an order even though he found the elements of s 238 to be established. His Lordship said that if he were to order the position to be restored to what it was before the relevant transaction, the company in liquidation would have been in a worse position.

It has been said that it is impossible to say that delay by the office-holder can never be a factor in the exercise of discretion under this section. However, delay by itself cannot be a relevant reason for not exercising the discretion to grant relief which would otherwise seem to be appropriate: *Stonham v Ramrattan* [2010] EWHC 1033 (Ch) (Mann J) at [34].

Interest could be claimed by a successful office-holder. From what date the interest may be calculated is somewhat of a moot point. In *Re Barton Manufacturing Ltd* [1999] BCLC 740 at 747–748 the court adopted the date of the liquidation. See the comments dealing with interest under the heading 'Orders' in relation to s 239.

A third party (someone other than the defendant who was a party to the transaction) who benefited from the transaction at an undervalue might be able to secure some protection where the transaction is declared to be at an undervalue within s 238. See the comments under 'Safeguarding third parties' relating to s 241.

Benefits of orders—As far as the destination of the benefits of orders, see the comments under 'Benefits of orders' relating to s 239.

Market contracts are exempted—This provision is specifically disapplied in relation to market contracts if a recognised investment exchange or clearing-house is a party to those contracts, and does not affect a disposition of property in pursuance of a market contract (Companies Act 1989, ss 155, 165(1)(a), 165(3)). Similar exemptions applicable to financial and security settlements and associated security arrangements are provided for in the Financial Markets and Insolvency (Settlement Finality) Regulations 1999 (SI 1999/2979).

Limitation period—Actions under this section are generally to be regarded as actions on a specialty, covered by ss 8 and 9 of the Limitation Act 1980, and as a consequence there is a 12-year time period in which office-holders can commence proceedings, *provided* that the substance of the application is to set aside a transaction, and not to recover a sum that is recoverable: *Re Priory Garages (Walthamstow) Ltd* [2001] BPIR 144 at 149, 160; *Re Yates* [2005] BPIR 476. Also, see *Hill v Spread Trustee Company Ltd* [2006] EWCA Civ 542, [2006] BPIR 789, [2007] 1 All ER 1106, [2006] BCC 646, [2007] 1 BCLC 450, [2007] 1 WLR 2404 (discussed in the notes to s 423). If a claim for a sum is ancillary to a primary head of relief that involves the setting aside of transactions, then the time limit is 12 years (*Re Priory Garages* at 160).

For further discussion, see Parry *Transaction Avoidance in Insolvencies* (OUP, 2nd edn, 2011); Armour 'Transactions at an Undervalue' in Armour and Bennett (eds) *Vulnerable Transactions in Corporate Insolvency* (Hart Publishing, 2003) at 95–122; A Keay *McPherson's Law of Company Liquidation* (3rd edn, Sweet and Maxwell, 2013) at 664–685. For a discussion of a possible challenge pursuant to the Human Rights Act 1998, see Ulph and Allen 'Transactions at an Undervalue, Purchasers and the Impact of the Human Rights Act 1998' [2004] JBL 1.

239 Preferences (England and Wales)

(1) This section applies as does section 238.

(2) Where the company has at a relevant time (defined in the next section) given a preference to any person, the office-holder may apply to the court for an order under this section.

(3) Subject as follows, the court shall, on such an application, make such order as it thinks fit for restoring the position to what it would have been if the company had not given that preference.

(4) For the purpose of this section and section 241, a company gives a preference to a person if—

    (a)   that person is one of the company's creditors or a surety or guarantor for any of the company's debts or other liabilities, and

    (b)   the company does anything or suffers anything to be done which (in either case) has the effect of putting that person into a position which, in the event of the company going into insolvent liquidation, will be better than the position he would have been in if that thing had not been done.

(5) The court shall not make an order under this section in respect of a preference given to any person unless the company which gave the preference was influenced in deciding to give it by a desire to produce in relation to that person the effect mentioned in subsection (4)(b).

(6) A company which has given a preference to a person connected with the company (otherwise than by reason only of being its employee) at the time the preference was given is presumed, unless the contrary is shown, to have been influenced in deciding to give it by such a desire as is mentioned in subsection (5).

(7) The fact that something has been done in pursuance of the order of a court does not, without more, prevent the doing or suffering of that thing from constituting the giving of a preference.

General note—This section permits courts to adjust transactions that constitute preferences. These are transactions that involve a creditor getting paid more (the debt being paid in full or in part) than would be paid to other creditors in a winding up. If such a transaction could not be adjusted, then creditors would grab what they could as quickly as possible when there was an inkling that a company was insolvent or heading towards, insolvency, and this would affect the statutorily regulated system laid down for the payment of creditors (and, some would say, derogates from the pari passu principle). A preference is where a transaction confers a priority or advantage on a creditor in relation to past indebtedness of the insolvent company and the advantage is given at the expense of other creditors who are owed debts at the time of transaction, thus preventing a distribution of the insolvent's property amongst the creditors according to the statutory scheme.

The Insolvency Law Review Committee's *Insolvency Law and Practice* ('the Cork Report') (Cmnd 858) provided the following as examples of preferences: paying the whole or part of a debt, providing security or further security for an existing debt, and returning goods that have been delivered but not paid for (at para 1208).

Where the preference involves the creation of a security interest, orders can be made under s 239 setting aside the security interest even though another secured creditor (ranking behind the secured creditor whose security is declared to be a preference) would benefit from the action of the liquidator: *Mills v Edict Ltd* [1999] BPIR 391 at 394.

When assessing whether a transaction is a preference, the court is to have regard for the transaction as a whole, in much the same way that the House of Lords in *Phillips v Brewin Dolphin Bell Lawrie Ltd* [2001 1 WLR 143 approached s 238: *Damon v Widney plc* [2002] BPIR 465 at 469–470. See the comments under 'Transaction at an undervalue' in relation to s 238.

Actions under this section are generally to be regarded as actions on a specialty, covered by ss 8 and 9 of the Limitation Act 1980, and as a consequence there is a 12-year time period in which office-holders can commence proceedings, *provided* that the substance of the application is to set aside a transaction, and not to recover a sum that is recoverable: *Re Priory Garages (Walthamstow) Ltd* [2001] BPIR 144 at 149, 160. If a claim for a sum is ancillary to a primary head of relief that involves the setting aside of transactions, then the time limit is 12 years (*Re Priory Garages* at 160).

Liquidators are required, before taking action, to secure approval from either the liquidation committee or the court (s 165(2)(b) (creditors' voluntary liquidations) or s 167(1)(a) (compulsory liquidations); para 3A of Sch 4).

'Relevant time'—This is defined in s 240, and involves two aspects. First, the transaction must have occurred in a particular time zone, namely either the six months preceding the onset of insolvency, or, where the defendant is a person connected with the company, two years before the onset of insolvency. 'Onset of insolvency' is defined in s 240(3). Second, besides falling within this time zone, the transaction must have been entered into at a time when the company was unable to pay its debts within the meaning of s 123 or the entering into of the transaction resulted in the company being unable to pay its debts. See the comments under 'Relevant time' and 'Unable to pay debts' in relation to s 240 and 'Connected person' in relation to s 249.

Creditors—The word 'creditor' is not defined. But taking into account rr 12.3 and 13.12, it must be someone who can prove for a debt in the winding up.

The reference to 'creditor' sought to identify the creditor in the legal sense of the word: *Re Thirty-Eight Building Ltd* [1999] BCC 260.

Where a supplier delivers goods on the basis of cash-on-delivery, any payment made at the time of delivery is not able to be regarded as being a preference (*Ferrier & Knight v Civil Aviation Authority* (1994) 48 FCR 163 at 169), because the supplier was not at any time a creditor for any of the company's debts, ie there was no creditor-debtor relationship.

See the comments under 'Creditor' relating to s 124.

Amelioration of a creditor's position—This is required by para 4(b) of the section and it means establishing that the defendant received more from the company before winding up than would be received if no payment were received and the defendant proved for the debt in a winding up and was given a dividend, pari passu with all of the other creditors. This assessment could be based on either what the creditor would have received if liquidation occurred at the time of the alleged preference, or what the creditor would receive in the actual winding up. The legislation does not specify the time. But it seems that the former position is correct given the wording of s 239(4)(b) and some comments in the case law: *Re FP & CH Matthews Ltd* [1982] 1 Ch 257, [1982] 2 WLR 495, CA; *Re Ledingham-Smith* [1993] BCLC 635; *Re Hawkes Hill Publishing Co Ltd (in liq); Ward v Perks* [2007] BCC 937, [2007] BPIR 1305 at [31].

Any payments made to secured creditors who have valid security does not improve the position of the secured creditor and it does not affect the position vis-à-vis the other creditors in winding up: *National Australia Bank Ltd v KDS Construction Services Pty Ltd* (1987) 163 CLR 668 (Aust HC). It is generally acknowledged that a payment in discharge of a valid security is not a preference (*National Australia Bank Ltd v KDS Construction Services Pty* at 679), but the giving of security to cover existing indebtedness would be preferential: *Re Transworld Trading Ltd* ([1999] BPIR 628. If there was to be a change in the form of security held by the creditor, there is still no preference, for example in *Sharyn Development Co Pty Ltd (in liquidation) v Official Receiver in Bankruptcy as Trustee of the Estate of Bridgland* (1980) 5 ACLR 1 (where a registered mortgage replaced a vendor's lien for unpaid purchase money). In the case where security is created over company property in order to secure both past indebtedness and new advances, the security is able to be challenged as a preference as far as the giving of the security related to the debtor's existing indebtedness is concerned: *Burns v Stapleton* (1959) 102 CLR 97 (Aust HC); *Re Mistral Finance Ltd* [2001] BCC 27.

The Australian High Court had stated in obiter comments that payments to creditors out of assets not usually available to unsecured creditors, such as those belonging to secured creditors, can constitute preferences: *G & M Aldridge Pty Ltd v Walsh* [2002] BPIR 482, (2001) 179 ALR 416.

Influenced by a desire to provide a preference—Section 239(5) demands that office-holders prove, on a subjective basis (see *Re MC Bacon Ltd* [1990] BCLC 324), that the company, when deciding to give the alleged preference, desired to produce the effect of a preference, although this is not required where the defendant is a person connected to the company (s 239(6)). In this latter situation there is a presumption that the desire was present (eg *Mills v Edict Ltd* [1999] BPIR 391, sub nom *Re Shapland Inc* [2000] BCC 106) unless the defendant can show the contrary.

In establishing the desire of the company, the office-holder need not necessarily prove that the controllers of the company knew that their company was insolvent (*Katz v McNally* [1999] BCC 291 at 296, CA), or that the controllers knew that the company would enter insolvent liquidation: *Wills v Corfe Joinery Ltd* [1997] BCC 511 at 514; *Katz v McNally* at 296. But it has been suggested that knowledge of impending liquidation may assist the office-holder in establishing desire: *Re Living Images Ltd* [1996] BCC 112 at 127, and *Re Agriplant Services Ltd* [1997] BCC 842 at 851.

It has been held that it is not always necessary to adduce direct evidence of the requisite desire as a court might infer desire from the facts: *Re MC Bacon Ltd* [1990] BCLC 324 at

335–336; *Rooney v Das* [1999] BPIR 404 at 406. Critically, the desire must have influenced the decision of the company to enter into the transaction that is the subject of the action (*Re MC Bacon Ltd* at 335–336). There must be a nexus between the desire and the making of the transaction, but it is not necessary to prove that the requisite desire is the only or decisive factor that caused the company to give the preference, for the desire might only be one of the factors that led to the payment or transfer (*Re MC Bacon Ltd* at 336). Also, it is not necessary for the liquidator to prove that if the requisite desire had not been present then the company would not have entered into the transaction impugned (*Re MC Bacon Ltd* at 336). The point at which to assess whether the necessary desire existed is when the decision to enter the transaction was made and not when the transaction was effected (*Re MC Bacon Ltd* at 336, *Re Stealth Construction Ltd* [2011] EWHC 1305 (Ch), [2011] BPIR 1173). The question of when the decision to enter the transaction is made is a matter to be decided the facts of each case: *Re Stealth Construction Ltd* at [62]. It is clear from this decision, and others, that it is the state of mind of the directors that is critical and not the creditor who is paid or any other person.

Liquidators are not required to prove that the sole or dominant desire of the company was to effect an improvement in the position of the creditor who benefited from the preference, and it is probably sufficient if some desire to provide an improvement is established: *Re Fairway Magazines Ltd* [1992] BCC 924.

In ascertaining the desire of a corporate entity, it has been said that it is 'necessary to explore the mind of the company which gave the preference' (*Re Transworld Trading Ltd* [1999] BPIR 628 at 629). As it is an abstraction, a company has no mind of its own, for it acts through human agents (*Tesco Supermarkets Ltd v Nattrass* [1972] AC 153 at 170; *El Ajou v Dollar Land Holdings plc* [1994] BCC 143 at 150), and so it is necessary to ascertain the human agents whose desire needs to be considered. Usually the board of directors is given, by the articles of association, the power to manage the affairs of the company (eg art 70 of Table A of the Companies (Tables A to F) Regulations 1985), and so the desire of the board may need to be taken into account. But it is not going to be easy, in many cases, for the liquidator to know whose desire needs to be established, and, even when that can be ascertained, how that desire is to be in fact established. In *Re Agriplant Services Ltd* [1997] BCC 842, Jonathan Parker J equated the state of mind of the director who essentially ran the company with the state of mind of the company (at 851). It is going to be easier for a liquidator to establish desire in 'one-man companies' as the desire of the controller will be attributable to the company.

Even where the director who makes the payment that is being challenged has no personal desire to improve the position of the creditor to whom the payment was made, if the controllers of the company with whom the creditor was connected were behind the payment then there would be necessary desire within s 239: *Katz v McNally* [1999] BCC 291 at 297, CA.

It is probably notable, and indicative of the difficulty of establishing a desire, that there are few reported cases in which a court has found there to be a preference in favour of a person other than a connected person: *Re Living Images Ltd* [1996] BCC 112; *Re Agriplant Services Ltd* [1997] BCC 842; *Re Mistral Finance Ltd* [2001] BCC 27.

If it can be demonstrated that in making a payment to a creditor, the company is motivated solely by commercial considerations, such as ensuring the provision of future supplies or credit, and has no desire to improve the creditor's position, there is no preference, because the company is not positively wishing that the creditor be given a preference: *Re MC Bacon Ltd* at 335, 336; *Re DKG Contractors Ltd* [1990] BCC 903, 910; *Re Fairway Magazines Ltd* [1992] BCC 924, 930; *Wills v Corfe Joinery Ltd (in liquidation)* [1997] BCC 511 at 512. Probably the most common commercial consideration is the pressure brought to bear by a major creditor. So, if a payment is made to a creditor who threatens that if he is not paid then he will not supply the company with any raw materials that it needs to carry on its business, it is likely that a court would not rule that the payment constituted a preference, as the desire of the company, in making the payment, was not to prefer the creditor but to ensure that its business could continue.

It has been suggested that events subsequent to the giving of the alleged preference can be considered in determining whether there was a desire to prefer and whether that desire influenced the company to enter into the transaction: *Re Transworld Trading Ltd* [1999] BPIR 628 at 634. Such events will not be as relevant as events occurring before the transaction was entered into, and while inferences may be drawn from these subsequent events, courts must do so with care (*Re Transworld Trading Ltd*).

For further discussion of this element of preference law, see Keay 'Preferences in Liquidation Law: A Time for a Change' (1998) 2 *Company Financial and Insolvency Law Review* 198.

Presumption—Where connected persons are involved in a transaction, the presumption in s 239(6) comes into play. It is only in such circumstances that liquidators have experienced any real success (see, for example, *Re DKG Contractors Ltd* [1990] BCC 903; *Weisgard v Pilkington* [1995] BCC 1108; *Wills v Corfe Joinery Ltd (in liquidation)* [1997] BCC 511; *Re Transworld Trading Ltd* [1999] BPIR 628; *Katz v McNally* [1999] BCC 291, CA; *Conquest v Fox* [2003] All ER (D) 360; *Re Conegrade Ltd* [2003] BPIR 358), although in two cases, admittedly some time ago, the presumption has been rebutted: *Re Fairway Magazines Ltd* [1992] BCC 924; *Re Beacon Leisure Ltd* [1992] BCLC 565. The rationale for this presumption is that those connected with the company are more likely to know about the financial position of the company and will seek to benefit at the expense of the general body of creditors. But the presumption does not apply to a creditor who receives a benefit only because he or she is a company employee. Most frequently, preferences have been alleged where companies have paid directors, and in such cases the liquidator is able to avail himself or herself of the benefit of the presumption: e g *Re DKG Contractors Ltd* [1990] BCC 903; *Weisgard v Pilkington* [1995] BCC 1108; *Wills v Corfe Joinery Ltd (in liquidation)* [1997] BCC 511; *Re Brian D Pierson (Contractors) Ltd* [1999] BCC 26.

It has been held in *Re Exchange Travel Holdings Ltd*, sub nom *Katz v McNally* [1999] BCC 291 at 295, CA that persons connected with the company are not able to rebut the presumption that the company desired to give a preference to the defendant, merely by establishing that they did not know the company was insolvent at the time of the preference being made and, therefore, could not have had the requisite desire. Also, defendants have failed to rebut the presumption where they believed that there was reason to be optimistic concerning the prospects of the company: *Re Conegrade Ltd* [2003] BPIR 358. See the comments under 'Connected person' in relation to s 249.

Orders—If a court believes that the office-holder has succeeded in proving a case under s 239, it will make a declaration to that effect. Then the court must consider what orders, if any, will be made to restore the position to what it would have been if the company had not entered the transaction (s 239(3)). Section 239(3) is a restitutionary, rather than a compensatory, provision. Examples of the kinds of orders that a court might make are set out in s 241. And although courts are not restricted to those orders contained in s 241, additional orders are usually in terms of one of the paragraphs in s 241(1). For instance para (c) indicates that a court could order the release or discharge of any security given by the company as part of a preference: *Mills v Edict Ltd* [1999] BPIR 391 at 394. It is likely that most often courts will make orders pursuant to s 241(1)(d): e g *Re Conegrade Ltd* [2003] BPIR 358.

A court can, either pursuant to the Insolvency Act, or (more likely) pursuant to the Supreme Court Act 1981, award interest. Section 35A of the Supreme Court Act provides, inter alia, that in proceedings for the recovery of a debt there may be included in any sum for which judgment is given simple interest from the date on which the cause of action arose and the date of judgment, and the recovery of an amount as a preference would be regarded as the recovery of a debt: *Re FP & CH Matthews Ltd* [1982] 1 All ER 338, CA. While there is some doubt as to the date from which interest will be calculated, existing authority seems to suggest that it will be from the time of the commencement of winding up, as that is the date when the liquidator's cause of action arose (*Re FP & CH Matthews Ltd*). However, it is submitted that the time should run from the date on which the liquidator first demands repayment of the sum paid to the creditor. This view is based on the fact that, arguably, it would be unfair to make a creditor liable for interest before any demand, as the creditor cannot be sure that he or she will be pursued until that time, and until a demand is made a preferred creditor may not actually be aware that he or she is liable to disgorge benefits: see *Star v O'Brien* (1997) 15 ACLC 144. For further discussion on this point, see Keay 'The Recovery of Voidable Preferences: Aspects of Restoration' [2000] *Company Financial and Insolvency Law Review* 1 and reproduced in Francis Rose (ed) *Restitution and Insolvency* (Mansfield Press, 2000) at 237 ff.

Benefits of orders—Traditionally, it has been held that any benefits flowing from orders made are held on statutory trust for the benefit of the general body of creditors, not the chargeholders, as they did not exist as part of the company's property at the time of the commencement of the winding up: *Re Yagerphone* [1935] Ch 392; *Re Oasis Merchandising Services Ltd* [1995] BCC 911; affirmed on appeal [1998] Ch 170, [1997] 1 All ER 1009, [1997] BCC 282, CA (dealing with a claim under s 214); *Lewis v Commissioners of Inland Revenue* [2001] 3 All ER 499). It is only when the liquidator or administrator was appointed that the action under s 239 came into being, and the action is personal to the liquidator or administrator (*Re Oasis Merchandising Services Ltd*). But see the comments of Neuberger J (as he then was) in *Ciro Citterio Menswear plc v Thakrar* (unreported) 10 July 2002 (discussed in P Fleming 'Sharing the Spoils of a Preference Action: Save a Slice for the Secured Creditors' (2003) 16(5) *Insolvency Intelligence* 33). For further discussion, see Parry 'The Destination of Proceeds of Insolvency Liquidation' (2002) 23 *Company Lawyer* 49; Armour and Walters, ''The Proceeds of Office-holder Actions under the Insolvency Act: Charged Assets of Free Estate?' [2006] LMCLQ 27.

See the comments under 'Court orders' in relation to s 238. Also, see the comments relating to ss 240 and 241.

Market contracts are exempted—This provision is specifically disapplied in relation to market contracts if a recognised investment exchange or clearing-house is a party to those contracts, and does not affect a disposition of property in pursuance of a market contract (Companies Act 1989, ss 155, 165(1)(b), 165(3)). Similar exemptions applicable to financial and security settlements and associated security arrangements are provided for in the Financial Markets and Insolvency (Settlement Finality) Regulations 1999 (SI 1999/2979).

For further discussion on preferences, see Parry et al *Transaction Avoidance in Insolvencies* (OUP, 2nd edn, 2011); Walters 'Preferences' in J Armour and H Bennett (eds) *Vulnerable Transactions in Corporate Insolvency* (Hart Publishing, 2003) at 123–181; A Keay *McPherson's Law of Company Liquidation* (3rd edn, Sweet and Maxwell, 2013) at 685–718. Also, see Wilkes 'Setting aside vulnerable transactions – an update (2011) 4 *Corporate Rescue and Insolvency* 189; J Morgan 'Preference – when is the decision made?' (2011) 5 *Corporate Rescue and Insolvency* 75.

240 'Relevant time' under ss 238, 239

(1) Subject to the next subsection, the time at which a company enters into a transaction at an undervalue or gives a preference is a relevant time if the transaction is entered into, or the preference given—

    (a)   in the case of a transaction at an undervalue or of a preference which is given to a person who is connected with the company (otherwise than by reason only of being its employee), at a time in the period of 2 years ending with the onset of insolvency (which expression is defined below),

    (b)   in the case of a preference which is not such a transaction and is not so given, at a time in the period of 6 months ending with the onset of insolvency,

    (c)   in either case, at a time between the making of an administration application in respect of the company and the making of an administration order on that application, and

    (d)   in either case, at a time between the filing with the court of a copy of notice of intention to appoint an administrator under paragraph 14 or 22 of Schedule B1 and the making of an appointment under that paragraph.

(2) Where a company enters into a transaction at an undervalue or gives a preference at a time mentioned in subsection (1)(a) or (b), that time is not a relevant time for the purposes of section 238 or 239 unless the company—

    (a)   is at that time unable to pay its debts within the meaning of section 123 in Chapter VI of Part IV, or

> (b)   becomes unable to pay its debts within the meaning of that section in consequence of the transaction or preference;

but the requirements of this subsection are presumed to be satisfied, unless the contrary is shown, in relation to any transaction at an undervalue which is entered into by a company with a person who is connected with the company.

(3) For the purposes of subsection (1), the onset of insolvency is—

> (a)   in a case where section 238 or 239 applies by reason of an administrator of a company being appointed by administration order, the date on which the administration application is made,
>
> (b)   in a case where section 238 or 239 applies by reason of an administrator of a company being appointed under paragraph 14 or 22 of Schedule B1 following filing with the court of a copy of a notice of intention to appoint under that paragraph, the date on which the copy of the notice is filed,
>
> (c)   in a case where section 238 or 239 applies by reason of an administrator of a company being appointed otherwise than as mentioned in paragraph (a) or (b), the date on which the appointment takes effect,
>
> (d)   in a case where section 238 or 239 applies by reason of a company going into liquidation either following conversion of administration into winding up by virtue of Article 37 of the EC Regulation or at the time when the appointment of an administrator ceases to have effect, the date on which the company entered administration (or, if relevant, the date on which the application for the administration order was made or a copy of the notice of intention to appoint was filed), and
>
> (e)   in a case where section 238 or 239 applies by reason of a company going into liquidation at any other time, the date of the commencement of the winding up.

Amendments—Enterprise Act 2002, ss 248(3), 278(2), Sch 17, paras 9, 26, Sch 26.

General note—This section limits the actions that can be brought under either s 238 or s 239. Not all transactions at an undervalue and preference can be challenged. Only those transactions that occurred in the relevant time can be attacked. The provision sets out two factors that will limit the transactions that a liquidator can impugn. First, the transaction must have been effected within a certain time zone prior to liquidation or administration. Second, there is a financial restriction on the bringing of actions, for in order to succeed, a company must have been unable to pay its debts at the time of the transaction or, as a result of the transaction, the company is unable to pay its debts.

Relevant time—The actual time zone applicable will depend on several circumstances, including what type of transaction is alleged to have been made, but what is uniform with all transactions is that the time zone is calculated in relation to a specific date: the onset of insolvency (s 240(3)) (see below).

Transaction at an undervalue—For a successful action under s 238 the transaction must have taken place during the two years preceding the onset of insolvency (discussed below), or, where administration occurred, in the interim period between either the presentation of a petition for an administration order and the making of such an order or the filing with the court of a copy of a notice of intention to appoint an administrator pursuant to para 14 or 22 of Sch B1 and the making of the appointment.

Preference—For a successful action under s 238 the transaction must have taken place during the six months preceding the onset of insolvency, unless the recipient of the alleged preference is a connected party, and then the period is extended to two years, or, where administration occurred, either during the interim period between the presentation of a petition for an administration order and the making of such an order or the filing with the court of a copy of a notice of intention to appoint an administrator pursuant to para 14 or 22 of Sch B1 and the making of the appointment.

The date of payment is the critical point of time: *Wills v Corfe Joinery Ltd (in liquidation)* [1997] BCC 511.

Unable to pay debts—While the transaction that a liquidator wants to attack occurs during the necessary time zone, s 240(2) provides that he or she will not succeed unless the debtor company was unable to pay its debts at the time of the transaction or, as a result of the transaction, the company was unable to pay its debts. 'Unable to pay its debts' means the same as the manner in which the phrase is defined in s 123. See the comments relating to s 123, and especially those under the headings: 'Unable to pay debts as they fall due'; 'Value of assets less than liabilities'.

An important proviso is that if the respondent to a s 238 action is a person connected with the company, then the company is presumed to have been unable to pay its debts at the time or unable to pay its debts as a consequence of entering into the transaction. This exception accommodates the fact that for provisions like s 238, which are designed to prevent asset-stripping in favour of persons connected with companies, insolvency should not be a required factor, unlike with preferences where the concern is to ensure that there is a division of the assets of the company amongst creditors according to the statutory scheme. With a preference the recipient is actually entitled to be paid (even if he or she is a connected person, provided that the debt was incurred bona fide) as a debt is owed to him or her, but with a transaction at an undervalue, entered into in favour of a connected person, the recipient is not entitled to the benefit. In the majority of cases the respondent is likely to be a connected person.

The ability of a company to pay its debts must be determined given the circumstances that existed at the relevant time with no use of hindsight: *Lewis v Doran* [2005] NSWCA 243, (2005) 219 ALR 555.

See the comments under this heading and accompanying s 123.

'Onset of insolvency'—This is an expression which is used as a matter of convenience to establish the end point for the time zone in which transactions must occur if they are to be able to be challenged. The use of the expression is somewhat confusing at first blush because it does not identify the beginning of insolvency, but identifies steps in the advent of formal insolvency proceedings. Section 240(3) explains what this phrase means, where action is taken in an administration or in a liquidation. To ensure that the time zone for transactions is not unreasonably reduced when a liquidation follows an administration, the provision will not take effect at the time at which liquidation commences, but when the administration commenced. If this were not done then the onset of insolvency would not occur until the commencement of winding up (the presentation of a petition to wind up), and this might permit transactions that would have just been in the relevant time when the administration was occurring to 'escape'.

If the company's liquidation occurred in any circumstances, other than following administration, then the date of the commencement of the winding up is the onset of insolvency. The commencement of winding up is not really the beginning of the liquidation; it is a deemed commencement of winding up. In voluntary winding up the deemed date of commencement is at the time of the passing of the resolution for voluntary winding up (s 86). In compulsory liquidation, winding up is deemed to have commenced at the time of the presentation of the petition (s 129(2)). If a voluntary liquidation was commenced prior to the presentation of a petition on which a winding up order is subsequently made, then the commencement of winding up is deemed to be the date of the resolution to wind up (s 129(1)). If a petition is presented and then there is a substitution order made, leading to an amended petition, with a different petitioner, the date of the commencement of the winding up is deemed to be the date of the presentation of the first petition: *Re Western Welsh International System Buildings Ltd* (1985) 1 BCC 99, 296. If action is brought in a liquidation, that followed the conversion of an administration into a liquidation through the agency of Art 37 of the EC Regulation on Insolvency Proceedings, the date of the presentation of the administration petition is the date of the onset of insolvency. Article 37 provides that a liquidator in main proceedings may request that proceedings covered by the Regulation (for the UK this means compulsory and creditors' voluntary liquidations, provisional liquidations, administrations, company and individual voluntary arrangements and bankruptcy) previously commenced in another State of the EU (secondary proceedings) be converted into winding-up proceedings if this is for the benefit of the creditors. The court may order conversion into compulsory or creditors' voluntary liquidation or bankruptcy.

241 Orders under ss 238, 239

(1) Without prejudice to the generality of sections 238(3) and 239(3), an order under either of those sections with respect to a transaction or preference entered into or given by a company may (subject to the next subsection)—

(a) require any property transferred as part of the transaction, or in connection with the giving of the preference, to be vested in the company,

(b) require any property to be so vested if it represents in any person's hands the application either of the proceeds of sale of property so transferred or of money so transferred,

(c) release or discharge (in whole or in part) any security given by the company,

(d) require any person to pay, in respect of benefits received by him from the company, such sums to the office-holder as the court may direct,

(e) provide for any surety or guarantor whose obligations to any person were released or discharged (in whole or in part) under the transaction, or by the giving of the preference, to be under such new or revived obligations to that person as the court thinks appropriate.

(f) provide for security to be provided for the discharge of any obligation imposed by or arising under the order, for such an obligation to be charged on any property and for the security or charge to have the same priority as a security or charge released or discharged (in whole or in part) under the transaction or by the giving of the preference, and

(g) provide to the extent to which any person whose property is vested by the order in the company, or on whom obligations are imposed by the order, is to be able to prove in the winding up of the company for debts or other liabilities which arose from, or were released or discharged (in whole or in part) under or by, the transaction or the giving of the preference.

(2) An order under section 238 or 239 may affect the property of, or impose any obligation on, any person whether or not he is the person with whom the company in question entered into the transaction or (as the case may be) the person to whom the preference was given; but such an order—

(a) shall not prejudice any interest in property which was acquired from a person other than the company and was acquired in good faith and for value, or prejudice any interest deriving from such an interest, and

(b) shall not require a person who received a benefit from the transaction or preference in good faith and for value to pay a sum to the office-holder, except where that person was a party to the transaction or the payment is to be in respect of a preference given to that person at a time when he was a creditor of the company.

(2A) Where a person has acquired an interest in property from a person other than the company in question, or has received a benefit from the transaction or preference, and at the time of that acquisition or receipt—

(a) he had notice of the relevant surrounding circumstances and of the relevant proceedings, or

(b) he was connected with, or was an associate of, either the company in question or the person with whom that company entered into the transaction or to whom that company gave the preference,

then, unless the contrary is shown, it shall be presumed for the purposes of paragraph (a) or (as the case may be) paragraph (b) of subsection (2) that the interest was acquired or the benefit was received otherwise than in good faith.

(3) For the purposes of subsection (2A)(a), the relevant surrounding circumstances are (as the case may require)—

(a) the fact that the company in question entered into the transaction at an undervalue; or

(b) the circumstances which amounted to the giving of the preference by the company in question;

and subsections (3A) to (3C) have effect to determine whether, for those purposes, a person has notice of the relevant proceedings.

(3A) Where section 238 or 239 applies by reason of a company's entering administration, a person has notice of the relevant proceedings if he has notice that—

(a) an administration application has been made,

(b) an administration order has been made,

(c) a copy of a notice of intention to appoint an administrator under paragraph 14 or 22 of Schedule B1 has been filed, or

(d) notice of the appointment of an administrator has been filed under paragraph 18 or 29 of that Schedule.

(3B) Where section 238 or 239 applies by reason of a company's going into liquidation at the time when the appointment of an administrator of the company ceases to have effect, a person has notice of the relevant proceedings if he has notice that—

(a) an administration application has been made,

(b) an administration order has been made,

(c) a copy of a notice of intention to appoint an administrator under paragraph 14 or 22 of Schedule B1 has been filed,

(d) notice of the appointment of an administrator has been filed under paragraph 18 or 29 of that Schedule, or

(e) the company has gone into liquidation.

(3C) In a case where section 238 or 239 applies by reason of the company in question going into liquidation at any other time, a person has notice of the relevant proceedings if he has notice—

(a) where the company goes into liquidation on the making of a winding-up order, of the fact that the petition on which the winding-up order is made has been presented or of the fact that the company has gone into liquidation;

(b) in any other case, of the fact that the company has gone into liquidation.

(4) The provisions of sections 238 to 241 apply without prejudice to the availability of any other remedy, even in relation to a transaction or preference which the company had no power to enter into or give.

Amendments—Insolvency (No 2) Act 1994, s 1; Enterprise Act 2002, s 248(3), Sch 17, paras 9, 27.

General note—This provision addresses the issue of orders made in relation to ss 238 and 239 claims. Where claims under either of these sections have been made out, the requirement for a court is to restore the position to what it would have been had the transaction at an undervalue or a preference not taken place (ss 238(3) and 239(3)). In order to do this the court might make any order that it sees fit. If an order cannot be made that fully restores the parties to the pre-transaction position, then the court is able to make such order that restores the parties' positions as far as possible: *Chohan v Saggar* [1994] 1 BCLC 706 at 713; *Walker v WA Personnel Ltd* [2002] BPIR 621. Full restoration might not be possible because property in the hands of the party to the preference or transaction at an undervalue has passed to an innocent third party (see below under 'Safeguarding third parties'). Whilst all of this gives the courts a wide discretion, s 241(1) provides a number of examples of orders that a court might make. The language of s 241(1) ('without prejudice to the generality of sections 238(3) and 239(3) ...') makes it clear that the kinds of orders set out there are not meant to be seen as exhaustive. The orders set out in s 241 merely indicate the wide range that court orders may take. Courts are able to make any of the kinds of orders set out in s 241(1) where they find that a transaction at an undervalue was entered into or a preference granted, but clearly some provisions in s 241 will be more suited to transactions at an undervalue and others more suited to preferences.

The provision goes on to restrict courts in making orders where a third party might be prejudiced by the court's order.

The orders—It has been said in relation to a transaction at an undervalue case (under s 339, the bankruptcy equivalent of s 238) that the court is not to start with a presumption that favours monetary compensation as against a setting aside of the relevant transaction. Courts must fashion the most appropriate remedy, as far as practicable, in order to restore the position pre-transaction: *Ramlort Ltd v Reid* [2004] EWCA Civ 800, [2004] BPIR 985. The court in *Ramlort* went on to say that when a court exercises its discretion in relation to what is the most appropriate remedy, the events subsequent to the impugned transaction will be considered.

Section 241(1)(a)

Scope of provision—This provision is most likely to be invoked with transactions at an undervalue, where the company has either purchased an asset at an inflated price or sold one of its assets for a significantly smaller sum than market value would dictate: see *Walker v WA Personnel Ltd* [2002] BPIR 621. The paragraph involves an order whereby the court requires the vesting of any property transferred in connection with the transaction at an undervalue in the company. The order could be invoked where the company, which is now in liquidation or administration, transferred property prior to its liquidation or administration to a creditor to discharge its indebtedness, with such a transfer being regarded as preferential. If the order involves the respondent having to re-transfer property to the liquidator or administrator and the property has been enhanced in value by the respondent, one would think that the court would include in the order some requirement that the respondent be paid, or allowed a sum to cover his or her expenses in enhancing the property.

Section 241(1)(b)

Scope of provision—This provides that property is to be vested in the company where the property represents in anyone's hands the application of either the proceeds of property, or money, transferred by the company as part of the preference transaction. The order allows for tracing, and might be useful where the company made a payment or transferred property to a person who is, when proceedings are ready to be commenced, insolvent. If the money or property had been transferred to a third person, the liquidator or administrator might investigate the possibility of proceeding against that other person. Whether such action is able to succeed will depend, partly, on whether the third person can make use of the protections for third parties contained elsewhere in the section.

Section 241(1)(c)

Scope of provision—Effectively, the order in *Mills v Edict Ltd* [1999] BPIR 391 at 394 fell within this broad category. It could be applied where a company granted a mortgage to a creditor over some property which it owns, either in exchange for some property it transferred (where a transaction at an undervalue is concerned) or in payment of a debt owed (in the case of a preference). A release or discharge would enable the company to regain the property and return it to the position it enjoyed prior to the transaction.

Section 241(1)(d)

Scope of provision—Commonly this will apply in preference cases and involve the creditor, who was paid by the company in relation to a debt owed by the company, being ordered to repay that sum to the liquidator or administrator. This order could also be made in a transaction at an undervalue case, where property has been transferred at an undervalue, and instead of the court ordering a re-transfer of the property, perhaps in circumstances where re-transfer is impossible, the court might order the transferee to repay the company the difference between what the respondent paid and a fair price: see *Phillips v Brewin Dolphin Bell Lawrie Ltd* [2001 1 WLR 143.

Section 241(1)(e)

Scope of provision—The order envisaged by this paragraph will visit new or revived obligations on a guarantor who was released or discharged from obligations under a transaction or as a result of the giving of a preference. This kind of order could well be coupled with a s 241(1)(d) type order. The restoration of the obligations of a guarantor may not only benefit the company. Take a situation where a director of the company in liquidation or administration guaranteed the company's debts to a creditor and ensures that the creditor is paid off before liquidation or administration ensues. This extinguishes the guarantor's obligations. The liquidator or administrator will take preference proceedings against the creditor (assuming the payment falls in the relevant time) and if he or she succeeds the creditor will be ordered to repay the payment to the liquidator. To ensure that the creditor is restored to his or her pre-preference position, an order might be made under this paragraph to provide that the director's guarantee obligations be revived and the creditor could, once again, rely on the guarantee.

Section 241(1)(f)

Scope of provision—This paragraph covers the case where a court makes an order which requires the provision of security for the discharge of any obligation imposed by the court's order, for the obligation to be charged on any property and for the security to have the same priority as a security released or discharged by the giving of the preference or a transaction at an undervalue.

Section 241(1)(g)

Scope of provision—This paragraph allows courts to limit the amount that could be proved in the winding up by a party. It is the type of order that has to be used carefully, remembering that the purpose of orders is to restore the position to what it was before the impugned transaction was entered into. The order will probably see a preferred creditor being given the right to prove in the liquidation of the insolvent company for the debt owed to him or her, and which he or she has been ordered to repay to the company.

The safeguarding of third parties—Section 241(2) acknowledges that court orders may affect the property of, or impose an obligation on, persons (third parties) other than the company now in liquidation or administration, and the other party to the transaction at an undervalue or the preference. In such a case the court is obliged in making its order not to prejudice the interest in property which a third party acquired from anyone other than the company and where the third party was not a party to the transaction at an undervalue or a preference. If a third party acquired property in good faith and for value, then his or her successor in title will also be safeguarded from the attack of an office-holder. All of this accords with the position at common law, where traditionally the effect of the avoidance of transactions in relation to preferences and transactions at an undervalue has been limited to immediate parties and their privies: see *Stevenson v Newnham* (1853) CB 286 at 302, (1853) 138 ER 1208 at 1215.

A third party who relies on the ground of good faith has the onus of establishing good faith. There are indications from *Re Sonatacus Ltd* [2007] EWCA Civ 31, [2007] 1 BCLC 627, [2007] BCC 186 at [29], that establishing good faith may not be easy. *Re Sonatacus Ltd* represents a case where the court used s 241(2) to order the repayment of a preference.

Presumption against third parties—But a third party, if he or she at the time of receiving a benefit from anyone other than the company had notice of both the surrounding circumstances and relevant proceedings, or he or she is a person connected with, or was an associate of, the company or the person who entered into the transaction (under challenge) with the company, a presumption exists that the third party had not acted in good faith (s 240(2A)). The presumption is rebuttable. Where the situation is not covered by any of the factors in this paragraph the onus is on the office-holder to demonstrate that the third party did not act in good faith.

'Surrounding circumstances'—This is defined in s 241(3) and means the fact that the company had entered into a transaction that amounted to a transaction at an undervalue or a preference. The meaning of 'relevant proceedings' is determined whether the company has entered administration, liquidation following administration or straight liquidation, and is defined in subsections (3A), (3B), and (3C) respectively.

See Keay 'The Recovery of Voidable Preferences: Aspects of Restoration' [2000] *Company Financial and Insolvency Law Review* 1 and reproduced in Francis Rose (ed) *Restitution and Insolvency*, (Mansfield Press, 2000) at 237 ff.

For a discussion of a possible challenge by third parties, who are affected by orders made as a result of a successful claim under either s 238 or s 239, pursuant to the Human Rights Act 1998, see Ulph and Allen 'Transactions at an Undervalue, Purchasers and the Impact of the Human Rights Act 1998' [2004] JBL 1.

242 Gratuitous alienations (Scotland)

(1) Where this subsection applies and—

    (a)   the winding up of a company has commenced, an alienation by the company is challengeable by –

        (i)   any creditor who is a creditor by virtue of a debt incurred on or before the date of such commencement, or

        (ii)   the liquidator;

    (b)   a company enters administration, an alienation by the company is challengeable by the administrator.

(2) Subsection (1) applies where—

(a) by the alienation, whether before or after 1 April 1986 (the coming into force of section 75 of the Bankruptcy (Scotland) Act 1985), any part of the company's property is transferred or any claim or right of the company is discharged or renounced, and

(b) the alienation takes place on a relevant day.

(3) For the purposes of subsection (2)(b), the day on which an alienation takes place is the day on which it becomes completely effectual; and in that subsection 'relevant day' means, if the alienation has the effect of favouring—

(a) a person who is an associate (within the meaning of the Bankruptcy (Scotland) Act 1985) of the company, a day not earlier than 5 years before the date on which –
(i) the winding up of the company commences, or
(ii) as the case may be, the company enters administration; or

(b) any other person, a day not earlier than 2 years before that date.

(4) On a challenge being brought under subsection (1), the court shall grant decree of reduction or for such restoration of property to the company's assets or other redress as may be appropriate; but the court shall not grant such a decree if that person seeking to uphold the alienation establishes—

(a) that immediately, or at any other time, after the alienation the company's assets were greater than its liabilities, or
(b) that the alienation was made for adequate consideration, or
(c) that the alienation—
(i) was a birthday, Christmas or other conventional gift, or
(ii) was a gift made, for a charitable purpose, to a person who is not an associate of the company,

which, having regard to all the circumstances, it was reasonable for the company to make:

Provided that this subsection is without prejudice to any right or interest acquired in good faith and for value from or through the transferee in the alienation.

(5) In subsection (4) above, 'charitable purpose' means any charitable, benevolent or philanthropic purpose, whether or not it is charitable within the meaning of any rule of law.

(6) For the purposes of the foregoing provisions of this section, an alienation in implementation of a prior obligation is deemed to be one for which there was no consideration or no adequate consideration to the extent that the prior obligation was undertaken for no consideration or no adequate consideration.

(7) A liquidator and an administrator have the same right as a creditor has under any rule of law to challenge an alienation of a company made for no consideration or no adequate consideration.

(8) This section applies to Scotland only.

Amendments—Enterprise Act 2002, s 248(3), Sch 17, paras 9, 28.

243 Unfair preferences (Scotland)

(1) Subject to subsection (2) below, subsection (4) below applies to a transaction entered into by a company, whether before or after 1 April 1986, which has the effect of creating a preference in favour of a creditor to the prejudice of the general body of creditors, being a preference created not earlier than 6 months before the commencement of the winding up of the company or the company enters administration.

(2) Subsection (4) below does not apply to any of the following transactions—

   (a)   a transaction in the ordinary course of trade or business;

   (b)   a payment in cash for a debt which when it was paid had become payable, unless the transaction was collusive with the purpose of prejudicing the general body of creditors;

   (c)   a transaction whereby the parties to it undertake reciprocal obligations (whether the performance by the parties of their respective obligations occurs at the same time or at different times) unless the transaction was collusive as aforesaid;

   (d)   the granting of a mandate by a company authorising an arrestee to pay over the arrested funds or part thereof to the arrester where –

      (i)   there has been a decree for payment or a warrant for summary diligence, and

      (ii)   the decree or warrant has been preceded by an arrestment on the dependence of the action or followed by an arrestment in execution.

(3) For the purposes of subsection (1) above, the day on which a preference was created is the day on which the preference became completely effectual.

(4) A transaction to which this subsection applies is challengeable by—

   (a)   in the case of a winding up—

      (i)   any creditor who is a creditor by virtue of a debt incurred on or before the date of commencement of the winding up, or

      (ii)   the liquidator; and

   (b)   where the company has entered administration, the administrator.

(5) On a challenge being brought under subsection (4) above, the court, if satisfied that the transaction challenged is a transaction to which this section applies, shall grant decree of reduction or for such restoration of property to the company's assets or other redress as may be appropriate:

Provided that this subsection is without prejudice to any right or interest acquired in good faith and for value from or through the creditor in whose favour the preference was created.

(6) A liquidator and an administrator have the same right as a creditor has under any rule of law to challenge a preference created by a debtor.

(7) This section applies to Scotland only.

Amendments—Enterprise Act 2002, s 248(3), Sch 17, paras 9, 29.

244 Extortionate credit transactions

(1) This section applies as does section 238, and where the company is, or has been, a party to a transaction for, or involving, the provision of credit to the company.

(2) The court may, on the application of the office-holder, make an order with respect to the transaction if the transaction is or was extortionate and was entered into in the period of 3 years ending with the day on which the company entered administration or went into liquidation.

(3) For the purposes of this section a transaction is extortionate if, having regard to the risk accepted by the person providing the credit—

    (a)   the terms of it are or were such as to require grossly exorbitant payments to be made (whether unconditionally or in certain contingencies) in respect of the provision of the credit, or

    (b)   it otherwise grossly contravened ordinary principles of fair dealing;

and it shall be presumed, unless the contrary is proved, that a transaction with respect to which an application is made under this section is or, as the case may be, was extortionate.

(4) An order under this section with respect to any transaction may contain such one or more of the following as the court thinks fit, that is to say—

    (a)   provision setting aside the whole or part of any obligation created by the transaction,

    (b)   provision otherwise varying the terms of the transaction or varying the terms on which any security for the purposes of the transaction is held,

    (c)   provision requiring any person who is or was a party to the transaction to pay to the office-holder any sums paid to that person, by virtue of the transaction, by the company,

    (d)   provision requiring any person to surrender to the office-holder any property held by him as security for the purposes of the transaction,

    (e)   provision directing accounts to be taken between any persons.

(5) The powers conferred by this section are exercisable in relation to any transaction concurrently with any powers exercisable in relation to that transaction as a transaction at an undervalue or under section 242 (gratuitous alienations in Scotland).

Amendments—Enterprise Act 2002, s 248(3), Sch 17, paras 9, 30.

General note—Effectively, the provision will allow for the re-opening of a transaction that can be deemed to be extortionate and which occurred within the stated time zone. The provision was modelled on ss 137–140 of the Consumer Credit Act 1974.

    The provision's object is to ensure that the assets of a company that has gone into liquidation or administration are not reduced by reason of the company having entered into a loan arrangement for which the consideration paid by the company is excessive. The aim is not to attack loans which ultimately end up being bad bargains, but to allow for the impugning of those loans which are grossly unfair, i e loans which no reasonable company in normal circumstances would enter into except where the true intention was to confer an undue benefit on the lender.

The section does not appear as yet to have been the subject of any reported decision, suggesting that it has not been invoked frequently, or at all, by liquidators and administrators.

The powers conferred by s 244 are exercisable in relation to any transaction concurrently with any powers exercisable under s 238 (transaction at an undervalue) (s 244(5)).

In dealing with a case under the Consumer Credit Act the Court of Appeal in *Paragon Finance plc v Nash* [2001] EWCA Civ 1466, [2002] 1 WLR 685 said that the nature of the test for what is an extortionate transaction is stringent, and this was adopted in relation to a consideration of s 244 in *White v Davenham Trust Ltd* (2010) [2010] EWHC 2784 (Ch).

Time zone—The transaction, to be impugned, must have been entered into in the period of three years before the date of the administration order or the date when the company went into liquidation. Unusually, the point of time that rules this type of transaction, where liquidation has occurred, is not the commencement of winding up (as it is for transactions at an undervalue and preferences), but the going into of liquidation. Going into liquidation is defined in s 247 to mean the date of the resolution to wind up, for voluntary liquidations, and the date of the winding-up order, in compulsory liquidations, and so it is submitted that these dates will be the ones from which the liquidator will calculate the three year time zone.

'Credit'—This is not defined, but in the Consumer Credit Act, s 9 the word is defined broadly to include 'a cash loan, and any other form of financial accommodation', and it is likely that this is the same meaning that Parliament intended to apply here as the provision is based on aspects of the Consumer Credit Act.

'Extortionate'—This word is, obviously, the critical part of the provision. Section 244(3) states what is meant by the term. 'Extortionate' does not mean unwise: *Broadwick Financial Services Ltd v Spencer* [2002] EWCA Civ 35 at [79]. It has been said, in relation to the Consumer Credit Act, that any transaction must not only be unfair but also oppressive, reflecting an imbalance in bargaining power of which the other party took improper advantage (*Wills v Wood* (1984) CCLR 7, (1984) 128 SJ 222; *Broadwick Financial Services Ltd* at [79]), while another view is that only unfairness is required (*Davies v Direct Loans Ltd* [1986] 1 WLR 823 at 831). In *Batooneh v Asombang* [2004] BPIR 1 (a case involving an allegation that a loan was extortionate under the Consumer Credit Act 1974) it was said that to be within the idea of extortionate, the loan had to be grossly exorbitant or in some other way it had to grossly contravene the principles of fair dealing.

Courts might well consider, when interpreting this provision, s 138 of the Consumer Credit Act. The latter provision states that in determining whether a bargain is extortionate, regard must be had to a number of specified matters.

Presumption—The office-holder is assisted by the fact that a transaction to which an application under s 244 relates is presumed, unless the contrary is proved, to be extortionate. It is unclear how much an office-holder has to establish before the presumption operates. The legislation suggests that the office-holder would merely have to prove that the company entered into a credit transaction within the three years of going into administration or liquidation.

Orders—Unlike where there are transactions at an undervalue or preferences, there is no general provision that requires the position of the parties to be restored to what they were prior to the entering into of the transaction. Rather, if a liquidator can establish that a transaction was an extortionate credit transaction, then the court may make any order it sees fit and this might contain one of the orders set out in subsection (4). These orders are designed to liberate the company from the burdens associated with the transaction. As with ss 238 and 239 actions, it is assumed that the court could decline to make an order if it chooses.

These orders are somewhat similar to the powers given to courts under s 139(2) of the Consumer Credit Act.

245 Avoidance of certain floating charges

(1) This section applies as does section 238, but applies to Scotland as well as to England and Wales.

(2) Subject as follows, a floating charge on the company's undertaking or property created at a relevant time is invalid except to the extent of the aggregate of—

    (a)   the value of so much of the consideration for the creation of the charge as consists of money paid, or goods or services supplied, to the company at the same time as, or after, the creation of the charge,

    (b)   the value of so much of that consideration as consists of the discharge or reduction, at the same time as, or after, the creation of the charge, of any debt of the company, and

    (c)   the amount of such interest (if any) as is payable on the amount falling within paragraph (a) or (b) in pursuance of any agreement under which the money was so paid, the goods or services were so supplied or the debt was so discharged or reduced.

(3) Subject to the next subsection, the time at which a floating charge is created by a company is a relevant time for the purposes of this section if the charge is created—

    (a)   in the case of a charge which is created in favour of a person who is connected with the company, at a time in the period of 2 years ending with the onset of insolvency,

    (b)   in the case of a charge which is created in favour of any other person, at a time in the period of 12 months ending with the onset of insolvency,

    (c)   in either case, at a time between the making of an administration application in respect of the company and the making of an administration order on that application, or

    (d)   in either case, at a time between the filing with the court of a copy of notice of intention to appoint an administrator under paragraph 14 or 22 of Schedule B1 and the making of an appointment under that paragraph.

(4) Where a company creates a floating charge at a time mentioned in subsection (3)(b) and the person in favour of whom the charge is created is not connected with the company, that time is not a relevant time for the purposes of this section unless the company—

    (a)   is at that time unable to pay its debts within the meaning of section 123 in Chapter VI of Part IV, or

    (b)   becomes unable to pay its debts within the meaning of that section in consequence of the transaction under which the charge is created.

(5) For the purposes of subsection (3), the onset of insolvency is—

    (a)   in a case where this section applies by reason of an administrator of a company being appointed by administration order, the date on which the administration application is made,

(b) in a case where this section applies by reason of an administrator of a company being appointed under paragraph 14 or 22 of Schedule B1 following filing with the court of a copy of notice of intention to appoint under that paragraph, the date on which the copy of the notice is filed,

(c) in a case where this section applies by reason of an administrator of a company being appointed otherwise than as mentioned in paragraph (a) or (b), the date on which the appointment takes effect, and

(d) in a case where this section applies by reason of a company going into liquidation, the date of the commencement of the winding up.

(6) For the purposes of subsection (2)(a) the value of any goods or services supplied by way of consideration for a floating charge is the amount in money which at the time they were supplied could reasonably have been expected to be obtained for supplying the goods or services in the ordinary course of business and on the same terms (apart from the consideration) as those on which they were supplied to the company.

Amendments—Enterprise Act 2002, ss 248(3), 278(2), Sch 17, paras 9, 31, Sch 26.

General note—The provision permits office-holders to take proceedings to have certain floating charges avoided. If this can be done, the chargeholders become unsecured creditors and, therefore, more funds should be available to the general body of creditors. Primarily, the section aims to prevent companies on their last legs from creating floating charges in favour of certain creditors in order to secure past debts (see *Re Orleans Motor Co* [1911] 2 Ch 41 at 45), so the purpose and effect of the provision is similar to that of s 239. The section proscribes the granting of a charge unless the chargeholder has advanced fresh value, in the form of funds, goods or services to the company. Where a charge has been given to secure past indebtedness, an office-holder could take action under s 239, but action under s 245 might be more effective. In particular, the time zone in which charges can be set aside is longer under s 245 when compared with s 239 where a non-connected party is involved, and with s 245 there is not a requirement that the company had to have been influenced by a desire to give a preference, as there is with s 239.

See R Parry *Transaction Avoidance in Insolvencies* (OUP, 2002) at 357–379.

Floating charge—The floating charges that are avoided are those that were created in the relevant time (see below), but if the charge was created in favour of a non-connected person, then the company had to be insolvent at the time of the creation of the charge or became so as a result of the entering into of the charge. 'Floating charge' is defined in s 251 and provides that the phrase includes a charge that was created as a floating charge, so s 245 would apply where a floating charge covered by the section is converted into a fixed charge by crystallisation before the onset of insolvency. If a floating charge that is covered by s 245 crystallises before the onset of insolvency and an administrative receiver appointed by the chargeholder makes payments to the chargeholder under the charge, such payments would have to be challenged, if at all, as preferences: *Mace Builders (Glasgow) Ltd v Lunn* [1987] Ch 191, CA.

Relevant time—As with ss 238 and 239, the provision limits the transactions that can be adjusted to those occurring within a specified time before administration or liquidation.

The time zone is defined in s 245(3). The critical thing is the time of creation of the charge. There are two time zones in which a charge may be created for it to be subject to invalidation. First, any floating charge created within the 12 months preceding the onset of insolvency may be invalid. 'Onset of insolvency' is defined in subsection (5). Also, see the comments under that heading in relation to s 240. The second zone is in relation to charges created in favour of a connected person, and they may be invalidated where they were created within the period of two years prior to the onset of insolvency. This is designed to stop a connected person, such as a director, from taking a charge and enjoying security when the company may be on the verge of insolvency (but still technically solvent). For 'connected person', see under that heading in relation to s 249.

Where a charge is created in the 12 months prior to the onset of insolvency, and in favour of a person who is not a connected person, the charge is not created within the relevant time unless, according to s 245(4), the company is either unable to pay its debts within the meaning of s 123 or became unable to pay its debts within s 123 as a result of the entering into of the transaction under which the charge is created.

Also, the time zone covers the period between the presenting of a petition for an administration order and the making of an order on the petition.

Exceptions—Section 245(2) enumerates certain cases where the charges will not be avoided. These exceptions are applicable whether the chargeholder is a connected person or not.

Paragraph (a) purports to make an exception where funds are lent in order to revitalise a failing company. The legislature wants to encourage persons who lend in such circumstances, and they should be entitled to their security. Whether there has, in fact, been money advanced by the chargeholder within para (a) is going to depend upon the circumstances, and in considering the circumstances, the courts will probably examine substance and not form: *Re Matthew Ellis Ltd* [1933] Ch 458. There have been attempts to use this exception to hide a charge that would ordinarily be avoided. These have included cases in which there appears to be a payment of money to the company, but this was really no more than a transparent subterfuge designed to secure a creditor in respect of an existing debt, such as where a loan to the company in cash is immediately repaid to the lender (*Revere Trust Ltd v Wellington Handkerchief Works Ltd* [1931] NI 55), or where directors who had guaranteed the company's bank overdraft take a floating charge over its assets in return for a payment to the company of money which was to be applied in reducing its overdraft: *Re Orleans Motor Co* [1911] 2 Ch 41.

For para (a) to operate, it is important that any cash is paid or provided to the company, becoming part of the assets of the company and available to the company to be used as it likes (*Re Fairway Magazines Ltd* [1992] BCC 924), and not paid to a third person (*Re Orleans Motor Co*). Unless this occurs, a chargeholder might have to attempt to rely on para (b) on the basis that it discharges or reduces the liability of a debt of the company.

The meaning of 'at the same time as' in para (a) has never been interpreted in such a way as to require strict contemporaneity as far as the creation of the charge and the payment of the money is concerned; provided that the advance follows the creation of the charge there seems to be no problem. The problem is where the advance is made before the creation, for unless the advance is regarded as being made at the time of the charge's creation, the charge is not an exception within para (a): *Re Shoe Lace Ltd*, sub nom *Power v Sharp Investments Ltd* [1993] BCC 609, [1994] 1 BCLC 111. In recent times a fairly strict approach appears to have been applied (*Re Shoe Lace Ltd*). In *Re Shoe Lace* it was said in the Court of Appeal ([1993] BCC 609 at 620, per Sir Christopher Slade) that 'no moneys paid before the execution of the debenture will qualify for exemption ... unless the interval between payment and execution is so short that it can be regarded as minimal and payment and execution can be regarded as contemporaneous'. So, it would appear that any delay would have to be very short.

Paragraph (a) also requires that exception is to be given in relation to 'the value of so much of the consideration for the creation of the charge', and, therefore, if the chargeholder is to benefit from this exception in relation to any advance subsequent to creation of the charge, it must be established that it was in consideration of the charge. 'Consideration' here does not mean what might be regarded as good consideration in contract law, and so past consideration will suffice: *Re Yeovil Glove Co* [1965] Ch 148 at 184–185, CA.

The effect—If a charge falls foul of this section, any debt owed to the chargeholder will continue to be able to be claimed, but the claim will only be that of an unsecured creditor. The chargeholder will lose its right to priority when it comes to payment.

For further discussion, see A Keay *McPherson's Law of Company Liquidation* (3rd edn, Sweet and Maxwell, 2013) at 721–729.

246 Unenforceability of liens on books etc

(1) This section applies in the case of a company where—

> (a) the company enters administration, or
> (b) the company goes into liquidation, or
> (c) a provisional liquidator is appointed;

and 'the office-holder' means the administrator, the liquidator or the provisional liquidator, as the case may be.

(2) Subject as follows, a lien or other right to retain possession of any of the books, papers or other records of the company is unenforceable to the extent that its enforcement would deny possession of any books, papers or other records to the office-holder.

(3) This does not apply to a lien on documents which give a title to property and are held as such.

Amendments—Enterprise Act 2002, s 248(3), Sch 17, paras 9, 32.

General note—The provision aims to stop persons, especially accountants and solicitors, from withholding documents on the basis that they have a lien over them, e g for the payment of fees, and thereby placing themselves in a formidable position as far as getting paid.

There is an equivalent provision in personal insolvency. See s 349.

'Enforcement'—The exercise of a right to retain property under a lien constitutes the enforcement of the security: *Bristol Airport plc v Powdrill* [1990] Ch 744 at 762, CA.

'Documents which give a title to property and are held as such'—This clearly permits a bank or other lender that has a fixed charge over assets of the company to retain the indicia of title, such as the title deeds to real property.

The section would cover documents like share certificates, charges over land, debentures and any other document that was evidence of possession of, or right to, land or personal property or anything covered by the definition of 'property' in s 436, but would not encompass a motor vehicle registration certificate: *Joblin v Watkins & Rosaveare (Motors) Ltd* [1949] 1 All ER 47.

The wording of s 246 as a whole is inconsistent with any requirement that for the document to be held 'as such' it had to be held so as to confer a proprietary title on the holder of the document: *Re SEIL Trade Finance Ltd* [1992] BCC 538, sub nom *Brereton v Nicholls* [1993] BCLC 593. It has been said that the words, 'as such' referred to the circumstances, manner or capacity in which the documents gave rise to the lien, in order to distinguish that situation from those where the documents were held by someone who would sometimes be entitled to assert a lien, but in the situation when a lien did not arise (*Re SEIL Trade Finance Ltd*). This means that, provided that the documents fall within subsection (3), such as debentures and share certificates, it does not matter that the only reason that the documents are being held is to obtain payment, so solicitors and accountants could retain such documents so as to obtain their fees.

246A Remote attendance at meetings

(1) Subject to subsection (2), this section applies to—

> (a) any meeting of the creditors of a company summoned under this Act or the rules, or
> (b) any meeting of the members or contributories of a company summoned by the office-holder under this Act or the rules, other than a meeting of the members of a company in a members' voluntary winding up.

(2) This section does not apply where—

> (a) a company is being wound up in Scotland, or
>
> (b) a receiver is appointed under section 51 in Chapter 2 of Part 3.

(3) Where the person summoning a meeting ('the convener') considers it appropriate, the meeting may be conducted and held in such a way that persons who are not present together at the same place may attend it.

(4) Where a meeting is conducted and held in the manner referred to in subsection (3), a person attends the meeting if that person is able to exercise any rights which that person may have to speak and vote at the meeting.

(5) For the purposes of this section—

> (a) a person is able to exercise the right to speak at a meeting when that person is in a position to communicate to all those attending the meeting, during the meeting, any information or opinions which that person has on the business of the meeting; and
>
> (b) a person is able to exercise the right to vote at a meeting when—
>
> > (i) that person is able to vote, during the meeting, on resolutions put to the vote at the meeting, and
> >
> > (ii) that person's vote can be taken into account in determining whether or not such resolutions are passed at the same time as the votes of all the other persons attending the meeting.

(6) The convener of a meeting which is to be conducted and held in the manner referred to in subsection (3) shall make whatever arrangements the convener considers appropriate to—

> (a) enable those attending the meeting to exercise their rights to speak or vote, and
>
> (b) ensure the identification of those attending the meeting and the security of any electronic means used to enable attendance.

(7) Where in the reasonable opinion of the convener—

> (a) a meeting will be attended by persons who will not be present together at the same place, and
>
> (b) it is unnecessary or inexpedient to specify a place for the meeting,

any requirement under this Act or the rules to specify a place for the meeting may be satisfied by specifying the arrangements the convener proposes to enable persons to exercise their rights to speak or vote.

(8) In making the arrangements referred to in subsection (6) and in forming the opinion referred to in subsection (7)(b), the convener must have regard to the legitimate interests of the creditors, members or contributories and others attending the meeting in the efficient despatch of the business of the meeting.

(9) If—

> (a) the notice of a meeting does not specify a place for the meeting,
>
> (b) the convener is requested in accordance with the rules to specify a place for the meeting, and

347

(c)   that request is made—
     (i)   in the case of a meeting of creditors or contributories, by not less than ten percent in value of the creditors or contributories, or
    (ii)   in the case of a meeting of members, by members representing not less than ten percent of the total voting rights of all the members having at the date of the request a right to vote at the meeting,

it shall be the duty of the convener to specify a place for the meeting.

(10) In this section, 'the office-holder', in relation to a company, means—

(a)   its liquidator, provisional liquidator, administrator, or administrative receiver, or
(b)   where a voluntary arrangement in relation to the company is proposed or has taken effect under Part 1, the nominee or the supervisor of the voluntary arrangement.

Amendments—Inserted by SI 2010/18.

246B Use of websites

(1) Subject to subsection (2), where any provision of this Act or the rules requires the office-holder to give, deliver, furnish or send a notice or other document or information to any person, that requirement is satisfied by making the notice, document or information available on a website—

(a)   in accordance with the rules, and
(b)   in such circumstances as may be prescribed.

(2) This section does not apply where—

(a)   a company is being wound up in Scotland, or
(b)   a receiver is appointed under section 51 in Chapter 2 of Part 3.

(3) In this section, 'the office-holder' means—

(a)   the liquidator, provisional liquidator, administrator, or administrative receiver of a company, or
(b)   where a voluntary arrangement in relation to a company is proposed or has taken effect under Part 1, the nominee or the supervisor of the voluntary arrangement.

Amendments—Inserted by SI 2010/18.

PART VII
INTERPRETATION FOR FIRST GROUP OF PARTS

247 'Insolvency' and 'go into liquidation'

(1) In this Group of Parts, except in so far as the context otherwise requires, 'insolvency', in relation to a company, includes the approval of a voluntary arrangement under Part I, or the appointment of an administrator or administrative receiver.

(2) For the purposes of any provision in this Group of Parts, a company goes into liquidation if it passes a resolution for voluntary winding up or an order for its winding up is made by the court at a time when it has not already gone into liquidation by passing such a resolution.

(3) The reference to a resolution for voluntary winding up in subsection (2) includes a reference to a resolution which is deemed to occur by virtue of—

    (a)   paragraph 83(6)(b) of Schedule B1, or

    (b)   an order made following conversion of administration or a voluntary arrangement into winding up by virtue of Article 37 of the EC Regulation.

Amendments—SI 2002/1240; Enterprise Act 2002, s 248(3), Sch 17, paras 9, 33.

General note—The provision is a little vague in referring to 'this Group of Parts'. Undoubtedly the reference is to Parts I–VI of the Act (the Parts preceding the Part now under review), dealing with company voluntary arrangements, administration, administrative receivership and winding up, as well as some provisions that apply generally to corporate insolvency proceedings.

'Insolvency'—In this context it does not have the meaning suggested in s 123, but means entering one of the forms of insolvency regime set out in Parts I–III.

'Goes into liquidation'—This phrase signifies when a company practically enters liquidation, and is to be contrasted with 'the commencement of liquidation', although as far as voluntary liquidation is concerned the point of time when a company commences liquidation is the same as when it goes into liquidation, namely the passing of the resolution to wind up.

Conversion under Art 37—The meaning of s 247(3) is not clear. Let us begin with Art 37. It covers the case where main proceedings are initiated in a Member State, the place of the debtor's centre of main interests, when proceedings have already been commenced in another Member State. The liquidator (as the person administering the insolvent estate is generally known, no matter what kind of regime is involved (Art 2(b)) may apply to have the latter proceedings (secondary proceedings) converted into winding-up proceedings. The scenario envisaged by s 247(3) is where proceedings, such as the entering into of either a company voluntary arrangement or administration, have commenced as secondary proceedings, and liquidation has subsequently been initiated in the UK (where the company's centre of main interests exist), and the liquidator applies to have the voluntary arrangement or administration converted to winding-up proceedings. If a conversion order is made, then the company is deemed to have passed a resolution to wind up on the date of the order. It is from this date that the company goes into liquidation for the purposes of the Act, and not when the original proceedings (company voluntary arrangement or administration) were commenced.

'Paragraph 83(6)(b)'—Paragraph 83 deals with the conversion of administration into a creditors' voluntary liquidation. The company is to be wound up as if a resolution to wind up had been passed on the day when the administrator's notice that para 83 applies directed to the registrar of companies is registered.

248 'Secured creditor' etc

In this Group of Parts, except in so far as the context otherwise requires—

    (a)   'secured creditor', in relation to a company, means a creditor of the company who holds in respect of his debt a security over property of the company, and 'unsecured creditor' is to be read accordingly; and

(b)　'security' means—
(i)　in relation to England and Wales, any mortgage, charge, lien or other security, and
(ii)　in relation to Scotland, any security (whether heritable or moveable), any floating charge and any right of lien or preference and any right of retention (other than a right of compensation or set off).

General note—This provision deals with the meaning of security, an important concept in Parts I–VI.

'Secured creditor'—The definition provides little assistance. Consideration of the case law is necessary to ascertain the scope of the expression.

A landlord is not a secured creditor within s 248, as he or she does not hold a security interest over company property: *Re Park Air Services plc* [1999] 1 BCLC 155 at 163, HL.

Security—Again, the definition is of little assistance, only specifying mortgages, charges and liens as securities. One would expect these interests to have given the holders security interests. The provision, by the use of the words 'other security', obviously leaves open the fact that other kinds of security interests may well qualify. While some interests, such as retention of title rights under contracts, do not qualify as security interests, they might provide the holder with similar rights.

249 'Connected' with a company

For the purposes of any provision in this Group of Parts, a person is connected with a company if—

(a)　he is a director or shadow director of the company or an associate of such a director or shadow director, or
(b)　he is an associate of the company;

and 'associate' has the meaning given by section 435 in Part XVIII of this Act.

General note—The provision deals with a term that is important, particularly for the provisions that cover the adjustment of pre-administration or pre-liquidation transactions, such as preferences (s 239). The use of the term in the context of the adjustment provisions is designed to prevent persons and companies associated with the company that has subsequently entered administration or liquidation, or directors of that company, from benefiting from transactions that occurred not long before the advent of administration or liquidation, but outside of the normal time zone for the setting aside of such transactions. The Insolvency Law Review Committee, in its *Insolvency Law and Practice* report ('the Cork Report') said (at para 1033):

'If the law of insolvency is to reflect the social and economic conditions of modern society, and is to be accepted as fair and just by the general public, then it cannot treat husband and wife, or persons living together as man and wife, or other closely connected persons, as if they were unrelated parties accustomed to deal with each other at arms' length. Nor can it treat companies which are members of the same group, or other closely associated companies, as if they were wholly unrelated. Special relationships call for special provisions to be made.'

The expression 'connected' is not defined simply. To appreciate the full impact of the term, one has to have reference to s 251 of the Act, as explained below. The expression has two main limbs to it. First, it covers directors and shadow directors of the company and their associates. Second, it encompasses associates of the company.

See the comments under 'Director' and 'Shadow director' in relation to s 251.

Associate—The expression 'associate' is defined far more fully than the other elements of s 249, but in s 435. 'Associate' includes a broad range of persons and relationships.

The expression was considered in *Mills v Edict Ltd* [1999] BPIR 391, where a Liberian company entered liquidation and its liquidator sought to attack, under s 239, security given to Edict Ltd, the only shareholder of the former company. The Liberian company had borrowed money from Edict, and when it was insolvent it had created a charge in favour of Edict. It was held that Edict was connected to the Liberian company on the basis that the former was an associate of the latter, Edict having control of the Liberian company.

See the comments under s 435.

250 'Member' of a company

For the purposes of any provision in this Group of Parts, a person who is not a member of a company but to whom shares in the company have been transferred, or transmitted by operation of law, is to be regarded as a member of the company, and references to a member or members are to be read accordingly.

General note—The word 'member' is defined by s 122 of the Companies Act 2006 and covers those who were the subscribers to the memorandum of association (the first members) and those who have been registered as members. This provision encompasses others, who are the owners or holders of the shares, but who are not registered as such. Prime amongst these are the personal representatives of deceased shareholders and the trustee in bankruptcy of bankrupt members.

The definition means that persons who were not registered as members may be held liable to pay contributions pursuant to s 74.

251 Expressions used generally

In this Group of Parts, except in so far as the context otherwise requires—

'administrative receiver' means—
> (a) an administrative receiver as defined by section 29(2) in Chapter I of Part III, or
> (b) a receiver appointed under section 51 in Chapter II of that Part in a case where the whole (or substantially the whole) of the company's property is attached by the floating charge;

'agent' does not include a person's counsel acting as such;

'books and papers" and 'books or papers' includes accounts, deeds, writing and documents;

'business day' means any day other than a Saturday, a Sunday, Christmas Day, Good Friday or a day which is a bank holiday in any part of Great Britain;

'chattel leasing agreement' means an agreement for the bailment or, in Scotland, the hiring of goods which is capable of subsisting for more than 3 months;

'contributory' has the meaning given by section 79;

'the court', in relation to a company, means a court having jurisdiction to wind up the company;

'director' includes any person occupying the position of director, by whatever name called;

'document' includes summons, notice, order and other legal process, and registers;

'floating charge' means a charge which, as created, was a floating charge and includes a floating charge within section 462 of the Companies Act (Scottish floating charges);

'the Gazette' means—

(a) as respects companies registered in England and Wales, the London Gazette;

(b) as respects companies registered in Scotland, the Edinburgh Gazette;

'officer', in relation to a body corporate, includes a director, manager or secretary;

'the official rate', in relation to interest, means the rate payable under section 189(4);

'prescribed' means prescribed by the rules;

'receiver', in the expression 'receiver or manager', does not include a receiver appointed under section 51 in Chapter II of Part III;

'retention of title agreement' means an agreement for the sale of goods to a company, being an agreement—

(a) which does not constitute a charge on the goods, but

(b) under which, if the seller is not paid and the company is wound up, the seller will have priority over all other creditors of the company as respects the goods or any property representing the goods;

'the rules' means rules under section 411 in Part XV; and

'shadow director', in relation to a company, means a person in accordance with whose directions or instructions the directors of the company are accustomed to act (but so that a person is not deemed a shadow director by reason only that the directors act on advice given by him in a professional capacity);

(*repealed*)

Amendments—SI 2007/2194; SI 2009/1941.

General note—The provision defines some important terms for Parts I–VI.

'Director'—The definition incorporates the definition in s 250 of the Companies Act 2006. The definition means that not only de jure directors, but also de facto directors are encompassed.

There is no legislative provision that defines the term 'de facto director', but it has been used for a long time (*Re Kaytech International plc* [1999] 2 BCLC 351, CA), and covers a person who is held out as a director by the company and claims to be one and acts as a director while never being appointed according to law. A de facto director is a person who assumes the functions and status of a director (*Re Kaytech International*). A person will only be held to be a de facto director if it can be established that he or she carried out director-like functions, and they are functions that could only be discharged by a director: see *Secretary of State for Trade and Industry v Becker* [2003] 1 BCLC 555. There is not one decisive test that establishes that a person was or was not a de facto director. Courts have to take into account all relevant factors including:

- whether there was a holding out of the person as a director;
- whether the person used the title;
- whether the person had proper information on which to base decisions;
- whether the person had to make major decisions: *Secretary of State for Trade and Industry v Tjolle* [1998] 1 BCLC 333, CA.

But none of these factors are necessarily decisive on their own (eg *Secretary of State for Trade and Industry v Tjolle*), and even where a person uses the title of 'director' a court might not hold that the person is a de facto director (*Secretary of State for Trade and Industry v Tjolle*).

A person does not have to believe that he or she is a director before being regarded as a de facto director (*Re Kaytech International*).

'Shadow director'—The definition incorporates that contained in s 251 of the Companies Act 2006: see *Re Hydrodam (Corby) Ltd* [1994] BCLC 180, [1994] BCC 161.

While professional advisers are not considered to be shadow directors, they might act in such a way that they cross the line and move from advising to instructing.

In determining whether a person is a shadow director, courts will look at the communications between the alleged shadow and the board, and ascertain, from an objective perspective, whether those communications might be able to be regarded as directions or instructions. In this regard the outcome of the communication is the important element on which to focus: *Secretary of State for Trade and Industry v Deverell* [2001] Ch 340, [2000] 2 WLR 907, [2000] 2 BCLC 133, CA. If the board is able to be characterised as subservient, that indicates shadow directorship, but it is not necessary to establish subservience before one can establish that someone is a shadow director (*Secretary of State for Trade and Industry v Deverell*). While a bank will not usually be regarded as a connected person, it might be if the liquidator can establish that it is a shadow director. The possibility of this being proven has been raised (*Re a Company (No 005009 of 1987)* (1988) 4 BCC 424), but banks will not be categorised as shadow directors when they merely lay down terms for continuing to provide credit for the business of a company, as these cannot be taken as instructions, for the company can take or leave the terms (*Re PFTZM Ltd* [1995] BCC 280 at 292).

It is important that one distinguishes between a shadow and a de facto director (*Re Hydrodam (Corby) Ltd*). A de facto director claims to act for the company as a director and is held out as such by the company even though he or she has never been appointed properly. In contrast, a shadow does not make such a claim; on the contrary he or she says that he or she is not a director. Shadows tend to act behind the scene (although this is not necessary) while the activity of de facto directors may well be more obvious.

PART VIIA
DEBT RELIEF ORDERS

Amendments—Inserted by Tribunals, Courts and Enforcement Act 2007, s 108(1), Sch 17.

251A Debt relief orders

(1) An individual who is unable to pay his debts may apply for an order under this Part ('a debt relief order') to be made in respect of his qualifying debts.

(2) In this Part 'qualifying debt' means (subject to subsection (3)) a debt which—

(a) is for a liquidated sum payable either immediately or at some certain future time; and

(b) is not an excluded debt.

(3) A debt is not a qualifying debt to the extent that it is secured.

(4) In this Part 'excluded debt' means a debt of any description prescribed for the purposes of this subsection.

Amendments—Inserted by Tribunals, Courts and Enforcement Act 2007, s 108(1), Sch 17.

251B Making of application

(1) An application for a debt relief order must be made to the official receiver through an approved intermediary.

(2) The application must include—

    (a)   a list of the debts to which the debtor is subject at the date of the application, specifying the amount of each debt (including any interest, penalty or other sum that has become payable in relation to that debt on or before that date) and the creditor to whom it is owed;

    (b)   details of any security held in respect of any of those debts; and

    (c)   such other information about the debtor's affairs (including his creditors, debts and liabilities and his income and assets) as may be prescribed.

(3) The rules may make further provision as to—

    (a)   the form of an application for a debt relief order;

    (b)   the manner in which an application is to be made; and

    (c)   information and documents to be supplied in support of an application.

(4) For the purposes of this Part an application is not to be regarded as having been made until—

    (a)   the application has been submitted to the official receiver; and

    (b)   any fee required in connection with the application by an order under section 415 has been paid to such person as the order may specify.

Amendments—Inserted by Tribunals, Courts and Enforcement Act 2007, s 108(1), Sch 17.

251C Duty of official receiver to consider and determine application

(1) This section applies where an application for a debt relief order is made.

(2) The official receiver may stay consideration of the application until he has received answers to any queries raised with the debtor in relation to anything connected with the application.

(3) The official receiver must determine the application by—

    (a)   deciding whether to refuse the application;

    (b)   if he does not refuse it, by making a debt relief order in relation to the specified debts he is satisfied were qualifying debts of the debtor at the application date;

but he may only refuse the application if he is authorised or required to do so by any of the following provisions of this section.

(4) The official receiver may refuse the application if he considers that—

    (a)   the application does not meet all the requirements imposed by or under section 251B;

(b)   any queries raised with the debtor have not been answered to the satisfaction of the official receiver within such time as he may specify when they are raised;

(c)   the debtor has made any false representation or omission in making the application or on supplying any information or documents in support of it.

(5) The official receiver must refuse the application if he is not satisfied that—

(a)   the debtor is an individual who is unable to pay his debts;

(b)   at least one of the specified debts was a qualifying debt of the debtor at the application date;

(c)   each of the conditions set out in Part 1 of Schedule 4ZA is met.

(6) The official receiver may refuse the application if he is not satisfied that each condition specified in Part 2 of Schedule 4ZA is met.

(7) If the official receiver refuses an application he must give reasons for his refusal to the debtor in the prescribed manner.

(8) In this section 'specified debt' means a debt specified in the application.

Amendments—Inserted by Tribunals, Courts and Enforcement Act 2007, s 108(1), Sch 17.

251D Presumptions applicable to the determination of an application

(1) The following presumptions are to apply to the determination of an application for a debt relief order.

(2) The official receiver must presume that the debtor is an individual who is unable to pay his debts at the determination date if—

(a)   that appears to the official receiver to be the case at the application date from the information supplied in the application and he has no reason to believe that the information supplied is incomplete or inaccurate; and

(b)   he has no reason to believe that, by virtue of a change in the debtor's financial circumstances since the application date, the debtor may be able to pay his debts.

(3) The official receiver must presume that a specified debt (of the amount specified in the application and owed to the creditor so specified) is a qualifying debt at the application date if—

(a)   that appears to him to be the case from the information supplied in the application; and

(b)   he has no reason to believe that the information supplied is incomplete or inaccurate.

(4) The official receiver must presume that the condition specified in paragraph 1 of Schedule 4ZA is met if—

(a)   that appears to him to be the case from the information supplied in the application;

(b)   any prescribed verification checks relating to the condition have been made; and

  (c) he has no reason to believe that the information supplied is incomplete or inaccurate.

(5) The official receiver must presume that any other condition specified in Part 1 or 2 of Schedule 4ZA is met if—

  (a) that appears to him to have been the case as at the application date from the information supplied in the application and he has no reason to believe that the information supplied is incomplete or inaccurate;

  (b) any prescribed verification checks relating to the condition have been made; and

  (c) he has no reason to believe that, by virtue of a change in circumstances since the application date, the condition may no longer be met.

(6) References in this section to information supplied in the application include information supplied to the official receiver in support of the application.

(7) In this section 'specified debt' means a debt specified in the application.

Amendments—Inserted by Tribunals, Courts and Enforcement Act 2007, s 108(1), Sch 17.

251E Making of debt relief orders

(1) This section applies where the official receiver makes a debt relief order on determining an application under section 251C.

(2) The order must be made in the prescribed form.

(3) The order must include a list of the debts which the official receiver is satisfied were qualifying debts of the debtor at the application date, specifying the amount of the debt at that time and the creditor to whom it was then owed.

(4) The official receiver must—

  (a) give a copy of the order to the debtor; and

  (b) make an entry for the order in the register containing the prescribed information about the order or the debtor.

(5) The rules may make provision as to other steps to be taken by the official receiver or the debtor on the making of the order.

(6) Those steps may include in particular notifying each creditor to whom a qualifying debt specified in the order is owed of—

  (a) the making of the order and its effect,

  (b) the grounds on which a creditor may object under section 251K, and

  (c) any other prescribed information.

(7) In this Part the date on which an entry relating to the making of a debt relief order is first made in the register is referred to as 'the effective date'.

Amendments—Inserted by Tribunals, Courts and Enforcement Act 2007, s 108(1), Sch 17.

251F Effect of debt relief order on other debt management arrangements

(1) This section applies if—

  (a)   a debt relief order is made, and
  (b)   immediately before the order is made, other debt management arrangements are in force in respect of the debtor.

(2) The other debt management arrangements cease to be in force when the debt relief order is made.

(3) In this section 'other debt management arrangements' means—

  (a)   an administration order under Part 6 of the County Courts Act 1984;
  (b)   an enforcement restriction order under Part 6A of that Act;
  (c)   a debt repayment plan arranged in accordance with a debt management scheme that is approved under Chapter 4 of Part 5 of the Tribunals, Courts and Enforcement Act 2007.

Amendments—Inserted by Tribunals, Courts and Enforcement Act 2007, s 108(1), Sch 17.

251G Moratorium from qualifying debts

(1) A moratorium commences on the effective date for a debt relief order in relation to each qualifying debt specified in the order ('a specified qualifying debt').

(2) During the moratorium, the creditor to whom a specified qualifying debt is owed—

  (a)   has no remedy in respect of the debt, and
  (b)   may not—
        (i)   commence a creditor's petition in respect of the debt, or
        (ii)   otherwise commence any action or other legal proceedings against the debtor for the debt,

except with the permission of the court and on such terms as the court may impose.

(3) If on the effective date a creditor to whom a specified qualifying debt is owed has any such petition, action or other proceeding as mentioned in subsection (2)(b) pending in any court, the court may—

  (a)   stay the proceedings on the petition, action or other proceedings (as the case may be), or
  (b)   allow them to continue on such terms as the court thinks fit.

(4) In subsection (2)(a) and (b) references to the debt include a reference to any interest, penalty or other sum that becomes payable in relation to that debt after the application date.

(5) Nothing in this section affects the right of a secured creditor of the debtor to enforce his security.

Amendments—Inserted by Tribunals, Courts and Enforcement Act 2007, s 108(1), Sch 17.

251H The moratorium period

(1) The moratorium relating to the qualifying debts specified in a debt relief order continues for the period of one year beginning with the effective date for the order, unless—

    (a)   the moratorium terminates early; or

    (b)   the moratorium period is extended by the official receiver under this section or by the court under section 251M.

(2) The official receiver may only extend the moratorium period for the purpose of—

    (a)   carrying out or completing an investigation under section 251K;

    (b)   taking any action he considers necessary (whether as a result of an investigation or otherwise) in relation to the order; or

    (c)   in a case where he has decided to revoke the order, providing the debtor with the opportunity to make arrangements for making payments towards his debts.

(3) The official receiver may not extend the moratorium period for the purpose mentioned in subsection (2)(a) without the permission of the court.

(4) The official receiver may not extend the moratorium period beyond the end of the period of three months beginning after the end of the initial period of one year mentioned in subsection (1).

(5) The moratorium period may be extended more than once, but any extension (whether by the official receiver or by the court) must be made before the moratorium would otherwise end.

(6) References in this Part to a moratorium terminating early are to its terminating before the end of what would otherwise be the moratorium period, whether on the revocation of the order or by virtue of any other enactment.

Amendments—Inserted by Tribunals, Courts and Enforcement Act 2007, s 108(1), Sch 17.

251I Discharge from qualifying debts

(1) Subject as follows, at the end of the moratorium applicable to a debt relief order the debtor is discharged from all the qualifying debts specified in the order (including all interest, penalties and other sums which may have become payable in relation to those debts since the application date).

(2) Subsection (1) does not apply if the moratorium terminates early.

(3) Subsection (1) does not apply in relation to any qualifying debt which the debtor incurred in respect of any fraud or fraudulent breach of trust to which the debtor was a party.

(4) The discharge of the debtor under subsection (1) does not release any other person from—

    (a)   any liability (whether as partner or co-trustee of the debtor or otherwise) from which the debtor is released by the discharge; or

(b)   any liability as surety for the debtor or as a person in the nature of such a surety.

(5) If the order is revoked by the court under section 251M after the end of the moratorium period, the qualifying debts specified in the order shall (so far as practicable) be treated as though subsection (1) had never applied to them.

Amendments—Inserted by Tribunals, Courts and Enforcement Act 2007, s 108(1), Sch 17.

251J Providing assistance to official receiver etc

(1) The duties in this section apply to a debtor at any time after the making of an application by him for a debt relief order.

(2) The debtor must—

(a)   give to the official receiver such information as to his affairs,
(b)   attend on the official receiver at such times, and
(c)   do all such other things,

as the official receiver may reasonably require for the purpose of carrying out his functions in relation to the application or, as the case may be, the debt relief order made as a result of the application.

(3) The debtor must notify the official receiver as soon as reasonably practicable if he becomes aware of—

(a)   any error in, or omission from, the information supplied to the official receiver in, or in support of, the application;
(b)   any change in his circumstances between the application date and the determination date that would affect (or would have affected) the determination of the application.

(4) The duties under subsections (2) and (3) apply after (as well as before) the determination of the application, for as long as the official receiver is able to exercise functions of the kind mentioned in subsection (2).

(5) If a debt relief order is made as a result of the application, the debtor must notify the official receiver as soon as reasonably practicable if—

(a)   there is an increase in his income during the moratorium period applicable to the order;
(b)   he acquires any property or any property is devolved upon him during that period;
(c)   he becomes aware of any error in or omission from any information supplied by him to the official receiver after the determination date.

(6) A notification under subsection (3) or (5) must give the prescribed particulars (if any) of the matter being notified.

Amendments—Inserted by Tribunals, Courts and Enforcement Act 2007, s 108(1), Sch 17.

251K Objections and investigations

(1) Any person specified in a debt relief order as a creditor to whom a specified qualifying debt is owed may object to—

(a) the making of the order;
(b) the inclusion of the debt in the list of the debtor's qualifying debts; or
(c) the details of the debt specified in the order.

(2) An objection under subsection (1) must be—

(a) made during the moratorium period relating to the order and within the prescribed period for objections;
(b) made to the official receiver in the prescribed manner;
(c) based on a prescribed ground;
(d) supported by any information and documents as may be prescribed;

and the prescribed period mentioned in paragraph (a) must not be less than 28 days after the creditor in question has been notified of the making of the order.

(3) The official receiver must consider every objection made to him under this section.

(4) The official receiver may—

(a) as part of his consideration of an objection, or
(b) on his own initiative,

carry out an investigation of any matter that appears to the official receiver to be relevant to the making of any decision mentioned in subsection (5) in relation to a debt relief order or the debtor.

(5) The decisions to which an investigation may be directed are—

(a) whether the order should be revoked or amended under section 251L;
(b) whether an application should be made to the court under section 251M; or
(c) whether any other steps should be taken in relation to the debtor.

(6) The power to carry out an investigation under this section is exercisable after (as well as during) the moratorium relating to the order.

(7) The official receiver may require any person to give him such information and assistance as he may reasonably require in connection with an investigation under this section.

(8) Subject to anything prescribed in the rules as to the procedure to be followed in carrying out an investigation under this section, an investigation may be carried out by the official receiver in such manner as he thinks fit.

Amendments—Inserted by Tribunals, Courts and Enforcement Act 2007, s 108(1), Sch 17.

251L Power of official receiver to revoke or amend a debt relief order

(1) The official receiver may revoke or amend a debt relief order during the applicable moratorium period in the circumstances provided for by this section.

(2) The official receiver may revoke the order on the ground that—

    (a) any information supplied to him by the debtor—
        (i) in, or in support of, the application, or
        (ii) after the determination date,

was incomplete, incorrect or otherwise misleading;

    (b) the debtor has failed to comply with a duty under section 251J;
    (c) a bankruptcy order has been made in relation to the debtor; or
    (d) the debtor has made a proposal under Part 8 (or has notified the official receiver of his intention to do so).

(3) The official receiver may revoke the order on the ground that he should not have been satisfied—

    (a) that the debts specified in the order were qualifying debts of the debtor as at the application date;
    (b) that the conditions specified in Part 1 of Schedule 4ZA were met;
    (c) that the conditions specified in Part 2 of that Schedule were met or that any failure to meet such a condition did not prevent his making the order.

(4) The official receiver may revoke the order on the ground that either or both of the conditions in paragraphs 7 and 8 of Schedule 4ZA (monthly surplus income and property) are not met at any time after the order was made.

For this purpose those paragraphs are to be read as if references to the determination date were references to the time in question.

(5) Where the official receiver decides to revoke the order, he may revoke it either—

    (a) with immediate effect, or
    (b) with effect from such date (not more than three months after the date of the decision) as he may specify.

(6) In considering when the revocation should take effect the official receiver must consider (in the light of the grounds on which the decision to revoke was made and all the other circumstances of the case) whether the debtor ought to be given the opportunity to make arrangements for making payments towards his debts.

(7) If the order has been revoked with effect from a specified date the official receiver may, if he thinks it appropriate to do so at any time before that date, revoke the order with immediate effect.

(8) The official receiver may amend a debt relief order for the purpose of correcting an error in or omission from anything specified in the order.

(9) But subsection (8) does not permit the official receiver to add any debts that were not specified in the application for the debt relief order to the list of qualifying debts.

(10) The rules may make further provision as to the procedure to be followed by the official receiver in the exercise of his powers under this section.

Amendments—Inserted by Tribunals, Courts and Enforcement Act 2007, s 108(1), Sch 17.

251M Powers of court in relation to debt relief orders

(1) Any person may make an application to the court if he is dissatisfied by any act, omission or decision of the official receiver in connection with a debt relief order or an application for such an order.

(2) The official receiver may make an application to the court for directions or an order in relation to any matter arising in connection with a debt relief order or an application for such an order.

(3) The matters referred to in subsection (2) include, among other things, matters relating to the debtor's compliance with any duty arising under section 251J.

(4) An application under this section may, subject to anything in the rules, be made at any time.

(5) The court may extend the moratorium period applicable to a debt relief order for the purposes of determining an application under this section.

(6) On an application under this section the court may dismiss the application or do one or more of the following—

    (a) quash the whole or part of any act or decision of the official receiver;

    (b) give the official receiver directions (including a direction that he reconsider any matter in relation to which his act or decision has been quashed under paragraph (a));

    (c) make an order for the enforcement of any obligation on the debtor arising by virtue of a duty under section 251J;

    (d) extend the moratorium period applicable to the debt relief order;

    (e) make an order revoking or amending the debt relief order;

    (f) make an order under section 251N; or

    (g) make such other order as the court thinks fit.

(7) An order under subsection (6)(e) for the revocation of a debt relief order—

    (a) may be made during the moratorium period applicable to the debt relief order or at any time after that period has ended;

    (b) may be made on the court's own motion if the court has made a bankruptcy order in relation to the debtor during that period;

    (c) may provide for the revocation of the order to take effect on such terms and at such a time as the court may specify.

(8) An order under subsection (6)(e) for the amendment of a debt relief order may not add any debts that were not specified in the application for the debt relief order to the list of qualifying debts.

Amendments—Inserted by Tribunals, Courts and Enforcement Act 2007, s 108(1), Sch 17.

251N Inquiry into debtor's dealings and property

(1) An order under this section may be made by the court on the application of the official receiver.

(2) An order under this section is an order summoning any of the following persons to appear before the court—

    (a)   the debtor;

    (b)   the debtor's spouse or former spouse or the debtor's civil partner or former civil partner;

    (c)   any person appearing to the court to be able to give information or assistance concerning the debtor or his dealings, affairs and property.

(3) The court may require a person falling within subsection (2)(c)—

    (a)   to provide a written account of his dealings with the debtor; or

    (b)   to produce any documents in his possession or under his control relating to the debtor or to the debtor's dealings, affairs or property.

(4) Subsection (5) applies where a person fails without reasonable excuse to appear before the court when he is summoned to do so by an order under this section.

(5) The court may cause a warrant to be issued to a constable or prescribed officer of the court—

    (a)   for the arrest of that person, and

    (b)   for the seizure of any records or other documents in that person's possession.

(6) The court may authorise a person arrested under such a warrant to be kept in custody, and anything seized under such a warrant to be held, in accordance with the rules, until that person is brought before the court under the warrant or until such other time as the court may order.

Amendments—Inserted by Tribunals, Courts and Enforcement Act 2007, s 108(1), Sch 17.

251O False representations and omissions

(1) A person who makes an application for a debt relief order is guilty of an offence if he knowingly or recklessly makes any false representation or omission in making the application or providing any information or documents to the official receiver in support of the application.

(2) A person who makes an application for a debt relief order is guilty of an offence if—

(a) he intentionally fails to comply with a duty under section 251J(3) in connection with the application; or

(b) he knowingly or recklessly makes any false representation or omission in providing any information to the official receiver in connection with such a duty or otherwise in connection with the application.

(3) It is immaterial for the purposes of an offence under subsection (1) or (2) whether or not a debt relief order is made as a result of the application.

(4) A person in respect of whom a debt relief order is made is guilty of an offence if—

(a) he intentionally fails to comply with a duty under section 251J(5) in connection with the order; or

(b) he knowingly or recklessly makes any false representation or omission in providing information to the official receiver in connection with such a duty or otherwise in connection with the performance by the official receiver of functions in relation to the order.

(5) It is immaterial for the purposes of an offence under subsection (4)—

(a) whether the offence is committed during or after the moratorium period; and

(b) whether or not the order is revoked after the conduct constituting the offence takes place.

Amendments—Inserted by Tribunals, Courts and Enforcement Act 2007, s 108(1), Sch 17.

251P Concealment or falsification of documents

(1) A person in respect of whom a debt relief order is made is guilty of an offence if, during the moratorium period in relation to that order—

(a) he does not provide, at the request of the official receiver, all his books, papers and other records of which he has possession or control and which relate to his affairs;

(b) he prevents the production to the official receiver of any books, papers or other records relating to his affairs;

(c) he conceals, destroys, mutilates or falsifies, or causes or permits the concealment, destruction, mutilation or falsification of, any books, papers or other records relating his affairs;

(d) he makes, or causes or permits the making of, any false entries in any book, document or record relating to his affairs; or

(e) he disposes of, or alters or makes any omission in, or causes or permits the disposal, altering or making of any omission in, any book, document or record relating to his affairs.

(2) A person in respect of whom a debt relief order is made is guilty of an offence if—

(a) he did anything falling within paragraphs (c) to (e) of subsection (1) during the period of 12 months ending with the application date; or

(b) he did anything falling within paragraphs (b) to (e) of subsection (1) after that date but before the effective date.

(3) A person is not guilty of an offence under this section if he proves that, in respect of the conduct constituting the offence, he had no intent to defraud or to conceal the state of his affairs.

(4) In its application to a trading record subsection (2)(a) has effect as if the reference to 12 months were a reference to two years.

(5) In subsection (4) 'trading record' means a book, document or record which shows or explains the transactions or financial position of a person's business, including—

(a) a periodic record of cash paid and received,
(b) a statement of periodic stock-taking, and
(c) except in the case of goods sold by way of retail trade, a record of goods sold and purchased which identifies the buyer and seller or enables them to be identified.

(6) It is immaterial for the purposes of an offence under this section whether or not the debt relief order in question is revoked after the conduct constituting the offence takes place (but no offence is committed under this section by virtue of conduct occurring after the order is revoked).

Amendments—Inserted by Tribunals, Courts and Enforcement Act 2007, s 108(1), Sch 17.

251Q Fraudulent disposal of property

(1) A person in respect of whom a debt relief order is made is guilty of an offence if he made or caused to be made any gift or transfer of his property during the period between—

(a) the start of the period of two years ending with the application date; and
(b) the end of the moratorium period.

(2) The reference in subsection (1) to making a transfer of any property includes causing or conniving at the levying of any execution against that property.

(3) A person is not guilty of an offence under this section if he proves that, in respect of the conduct constituting the offence, he had no intent to defraud or to conceal the state of his affairs.

(4) For the purposes of subsection (3) a person is to be taken to have proved that he had no such intent if—

(a) sufficient evidence is adduced to raise an issue as to whether he had such intent; and
(b) the contrary is not proved beyond reasonable doubt.

(5) It is immaterial for the purposes of this section whether or not the debt relief order in question is revoked after the conduct constituting an offence takes place (but no offence is committed by virtue of conduct occurring after the order is revoked).

Amendments—Inserted by Tribunals, Courts and Enforcement Act 2007, s 108(1), Sch 17.

251R Fraudulent dealing with property obtained on credit

(1) A person in respect of whom a debt relief order is made is guilty of an offence if during the relevant period he disposed of any property which he had obtained on credit and, at the time he disposed of it, had not paid for it.

(2) Any other person is guilty of an offence if during the relevant period he acquired or received property from a person in respect of whom a debt relief order was made (the 'debtor') knowing or believing—

    (a)   that the debtor owed money in respect of the property, and

    (b)   that the debtor did not intend, or was unlikely to be able, to pay the money he so owed.

(3) In subsections (1) and (2) 'relevant period' means the period between—

    (a)   the start of the period of two years ending with the application date; and

    (b)   the determination date.

(4) A person is not guilty of an offence under subsection (1) or (2) if the disposal, acquisition or receipt of the property was in the ordinary course of a business carried on by the debtor at the time of the disposal, acquisition or receipt.

(5) In determining for the purposes of subsection (4) whether any property is disposed of, acquired or received in the ordinary course of a business carried on by the debtor, regard may be had, in particular, to the price paid for the property.

(6) A person is not guilty of an offence under subsection (1) if he proves that, in respect of the conduct constituting the offence, he had no intent to defraud or to conceal the state of his affairs.

(7) In this section references to disposing of property include pawning or pledging it; and references to acquiring or receiving property shall be read accordingly.

(8) It is immaterial for the purposes of this section whether or not the debt relief order in question is revoked after the conduct constituting an offence takes place (but no offence is committed by virtue of conduct occurring after the order is revoked).

Amendments—Inserted by Tribunals, Courts and Enforcement Act 2007, s 108(1), Sch 17.

251S Obtaining credit or engaging in business

(1) A person in respect of whom a debt relief order is made is guilty of an offence if, during the relevant period—

    (a)   he obtains credit (either alone or jointly with any other person) without giving the person from whom he obtains the credit the relevant information about his status; or

(b)   he engages directly or indirectly in any business under a name other than that in which the order was made without disclosing to all persons with whom he enters into any business transaction the name in which the order was made.

(2) For the purposes of subsection (1)(a) the relevant information about a person's status is the information that—

(a)   a moratorium is in force in relation to the debt relief order,

(b)   a debt relief restrictions order is in force in respect of him, or

(c)   both a moratorium and a debt relief restrictions order is in force,

as the case may be.

(3) In subsection (1) 'relevant period' means—

(a)   the moratorium period relating to the debt relief order, or

(b)   the period for which a debt relief restrictions order is in force in respect of the person in respect of whom the debt relief order is made,

as the case may be.

(4) Subsection (1)(a) does not apply if the amount of the credit is less than the prescribed amount (if any).

(5) The reference in subsection (1)(a) to a person obtaining credit includes the following cases—

(a)   where goods are bailed to him under a hire-purchase agreement, or agreed to be sold to him under a conditional sale agreement;

(b)   where he is paid in advance (in money or otherwise) for the supply of goods or services.

Amendments—Inserted by Tribunals, Courts and Enforcement Act 2007, s 108(1), Sch 17.

251T Offences: supplementary

(1) Proceedings for an offence under this Part may only be instituted by the Secretary of State or by or with the consent of the Director of Public Prosecutions.

(2) It is not a defence in proceedings for an offence under this Part that anything relied on, in whole or in part, as constituting the offence was done outside England and Wales.

(3) A person guilty of an offence under this Part is liable to imprisonment or a fine, or both (but see section 430).

Amendments—Inserted by Tribunals, Courts and Enforcement Act 2007, s 108(1), Sch 17.

251U Approved intermediaries

(1) In this Part 'approved intermediary' means an individual for the time being approved by a competent authority to act as an intermediary between a person wishing to make an application for a debt relief order and the official receiver.

(2) In this section 'competent authority' means a person or body for the time being designated by the Secretary of State for the purposes of granting approvals under this section.

(3) Designation as a competent authority may be limited so as to permit the authority only to approve persons of a particular description.

(4) The Secretary of State may by regulations make provision as to—

    (a)   the procedure for designating persons or bodies as competent authorities;

    (b)   descriptions of individuals who are ineligible to be approved under this section;

    (c)   the procedure for granting approvals under this section;

    (d)   the withdrawal of designations or approvals under this section;

and provision made under paragraph (a) or (c) may include provision requiring the payment of fees.

(5) The rules may make provision about the activities to be carried out by an approved intermediary in connection with an application for a debt relief order, which may in particular include—

    (a)   assisting the debtor in making the application;

    (b)   checking that the application has been properly completed;

    (c)   sending the application to the official receiver.

(6) The rules may also make provision about other activities to be carried out by approved intermediaries.

(7) An approved intermediary may not charge a debtor any fee in connection with an application for a debt relief order.

(8) An approved intermediary is not liable to any person in damages for anything done or omitted to be done when acting (or purporting to act) as an approved intermediary in connection with a particular application by a debtor for a debt relief order.

(9) Subsection (8) does not apply if the act or omission was in bad faith.

(10) Regulations under subsection (4) shall be made by statutory instrument subject to annulment in pursuance of a resolution of either House of Parliament.

Amendments—Inserted by Tribunals, Courts and Enforcement Act 2007, s 108(1), Sch 17.

251V Debt relief restrictions orders and undertakings

Schedule 4ZB (which makes provision about debt relief restrictions orders and debt relief restrictions undertakings) has effect.

Amendments—Inserted by Tribunals, Courts and Enforcement Act 2007, s 108(1), Sch 17.

251W Register of debt relief orders etc

The Secretary of State must maintain a register of matters relating to—

    (a)   debt relief orders;

(b)   debt relief restrictions orders; and

(c)   debt relief restrictions undertakings.

Amendments—Inserted by Tribunals, Courts and Enforcement Act 2007, s 108(1), Sch 17.

251X Interpretation

(1) In this Part—

'the application date', in relation to a debt relief order or an application for a debt relief order, means the date on which the application for the order is made to the official receiver;

'approved intermediary' has the meaning given in section 251U(1);

'debt relief order' means an order made by the official receiver under this Part;

'debtor' means—

    (a)   in relation to an application for a debt relief order, the applicant; and

    (b)   in relation to a debt relief order, the person in relation to whom the order is made;

'debt relief restrictions order' and 'debt relief restrictions undertaking' means an order made, or an undertaking accepted, under Schedule 4ZB;

'the determination date', in relation to a debt relief order or an application for a debt relief order, means the date on which the application for the order is determined by the official receiver;

'the effective date' has the meaning given in section 251E(7);

'excluded debt' is to be construed in accordance with section 251A;

'moratorium' and 'moratorium period' are to be construed in accordance with sections 251G and 251H;

'qualifying debt', in relation to a debtor, has the meaning given in section 251A(2);

'the register' means the register maintained under section 251W;

'specified qualifying debt' has the meaning given in section 251G(1).

(2) In this Part references to a creditor specified in a debt relief order as the person to whom a qualifying debt is owed by the debtor include a reference to any person to whom the right to claim the whole or any part of the debt has passed, by assignment or operation of law, after the date of the application for the order.

Amendments—Inserted by Tribunals, Courts and Enforcement Act 2007, s 108(1), Sch 17.

PART VIII
INDIVIDUAL VOLUNTARY ARRANGEMENTS

Introductory note to Part VIII—The individual voluntary arrangement ('IVA') was a creation of the 1986 Act and followed recommendations made by the Cork Committee which had observed that, in effect, an individual debtor in financial difficulties had no practical option between bankruptcy and an arrangement requiring registration under the Deeds of Arrangement Act 1914, a procedure which was cumbersome, if not unworkable, in a large number of cases. In *Re Bradley-Hole (a Bankrupt)* [1995] 1 WLR 1097 at 1108–1109 Rimer J identified that 'the essence of a voluntary arrangement is that under it each creditor compromises or releases his right against the debtor in respect of his pre-existing debts and receives in exchange and full satisfaction whatever terms are being offered by the debtor.'

IVAs have become common in everyday insolvency practice and have doubtless provided a workable rescue mechanism, as an alternative to bankruptcy, in a large number of cases. One challenge in the immediate future lies in the professional bodies remaining alive to and taking steps as necessary in relation to those non-authorised undertakings which peddle the procedure as an apparently quick-fix solution to individuals suffering the consequences of the massive and largely unchecked increase in consumer credit since the 1990s in circumstances where those individuals are simply passed on to a licensed practitioner for a fee, invariably payable up front, where, in reality, little, if any, thought has been given to the appropriateness of the procedure. This is not to say that the new-style 'fast-track' IVA does not have its place. That procedure, which allows a debtor to go forward without the protection of an interim order, is no doubt more streamlined and likely to be less costly than the original model. Again, however, the IVA procedure is reliant on the skill and judgment of a professional individual fulfilling the roles of nominee and, usually thereafter, supervisor. It is that individual who must initially form a view as to whether the procedure is appropriate and, even if it may be, whether bankruptcy under the new 'one-year (or sooner) undischarged' period might not be an alternative which better serves the interests of the debtor, if not his creditors.

The IVA procedure has been described variously in the authorities as a form of quasi-contract or a form of statutory binding. Whilst contractually based, the real essence of the procedure lies in what American practitioners would term a cramming down by way of the ability of a debtor and a requisite majority of his creditors to reach agreement in compromising the debtor's liability whilst, at the same time, binding into the same arrangement any dissentient creditors. An aggrieved party may make application under s 262 to challenge the arrangement on the grounds of a material irregularity in relation to the creditors' meeting at which the proposal is approved or on the grounds that the operation of the arrangement is unfairly prejudicial to, at least, the applicant. These matters are discussed further in the notes to s 262.

252 Interim order of court

(1) In the circumstances specified below, the court may in the case of a debtor (being an individual) make an interim order under this section.

(2) An interim order has the effect that, during the period for which it is in force—

    (a)   no bankruptcy petition relating to the debtor may be presented or proceeded with,

    (aa) no landlord or other person to whom rent is payable may exercise any right of forfeiture by peaceable re-entry in relation to premises let to the debtor in respect of a failure by the debtor to comply with any term or condition of his tenancy of such premises, except with the leave of the court and

    (b)   no other proceedings, and no execution or other legal process, may be commenced or continued and no distress may be levied against the debtor or his property except with the leave of the court.

Amendments—Insolvency Act 2000, s 3, Sch 3, paras 1, 2(a), 2(b).

General note—Prior to the introduction of s 256A, effective from 1 January 2003, the obtaining of an interim order had been held to be a prerequisite to the approval of an IVA by creditors without which any purported approved arrangement was void and incapable of being saved by an application for an interim order with retrospective effect: *Fletcher v Vooght* [2000] BPIR 435 (Lloyd J, as he then was, approval of IVA proposal by creditors in ignorance of fact that no interim order obtained). Section 256A, it is submitted, undermines the previous observation in *Fletcher v Vooght* that an interim order is an integral part of the procedure under Part VIII.

The moratorium provided by way of an interim order operates to confer wide-ranging protection on a debtor and his property so as to allow a debtor to formulate an IVA proposal, albeit within relatively tight time constraints. Following an application for an interim order under s 253 the protection in s 254(1) and (2) is brought into force, following which the interim order has the effect prescribed in s 252(2) upon it being made. Subject to extension by the court under s 256(5), an interim order will cease to have effect at the end of the period of 14 days beginning with the day after the making of the order, by virtue of s 255(6). The tight initial 14-day period, coupled with the court's power to extend the effect of an interim order under s 256(5), has led to the common practice of the court making so-called 'concertina' orders, on which see the note under that heading below.

For an interesting suggested use of the interim order procedure, see the decision of the Court of Appeal in *Bramston v Haut* [2012] EWCA Civ 1637 [2013] BPIR 25 in which Kitchin LJ considered that it was open to an undischarged bankruptcy to make an application for an interim order which would also invite the Court to stay his discharge from bankruptcy. The Court of Appeal's decision contains a useful review of the interim order procedure.

Section 252(1)

'in the circumstances specified below'—The eligible applicants for an interim order are as prescribed in s 253(3). An application may not be made in the circumstances identified in s 253(5). The conditions for the making of an interim order by the court are stipulated in s 255(1).

Insolvent partnerships—The words 'a debtor (being an individual)' refer to an individual but not a partnership, company or any other undertaking. An IVA is not available to an insolvent partnership. Although art 11 of the Insolvent Partnerships Order 1986 (SI 1986/2142), made pursuant to s 420, extended Part VIII to individual partners of insolvent partnerships where a winding-up order was made against the partnership and bankruptcy orders made against individual members, the Insolvent Partnerships Order 1994 (SI 1994/2421), which revoked the 1986 Order, only applies the CVA procedure, appropriately modified, to insolvent partnerships, on which see art 4 and Sch 1 thereto.

Interim orders and the 'concertina' order—Either of two forms of order are commonly made on an application for an order. First, the court may make a 14-day interim order with the application adjourned for a 14-day period to allow for consideration of the nominee's report. Alternatively, the court may make a standard order, on consideration of the nominee's report, extending the interim order to a date seven weeks after the date of the proposed meeting, directing the creditors' meeting to be summoned and adjourning the hearing to a date on or around three weeks after the creditors' meeting. As a further alternative, particularly in straightforward cases, the court may make a 'concertina' order which combines both of those orders just mentioned. In suitable cases, where the papers are in order and where there is no bankruptcy order in existence and, so far as is known, there is no pending bankruptcy petition, the court may consider making any such order without the attendance of the parties, on which see para 16 of the *Practice Direction: Insolvency Proceedings*.

Note also s 260(4), which provides for the automatic lapse of an interim order 28 days after the filing of the chairman's report with the court, subject to contrary order.

Section 252(2)

Effect of the interim order—The scope of the moratorium in s 252(2)(aa) and (b) was bolstered by s 3 of and Sch 3 to the Insolvency Act 2000 by expressly extending the protection to forfeiture by peaceable re-entry by a landlord and the levying of distress so as to reverse the effect of previous contrary authority: see *Re A Debtor (No 13AIO and 14AIO of 1994)* [1995] 1 WLR 1127 and *McMullen & Sons v Cerrone* [1994] BCC 25.

The prohibition against the presentation of or proceeding with a bankruptcy petition is absolute; in contrast to s 252(2)(aa) and (b), the court has no jurisdiction to give leave for a bankruptcy petition to proceed. The protection against a bankruptcy petition will operate irrespective of the circumstances giving rise to its presentation, including failure to comply with a statutory demand.

Section 252(2)(aa)

'no landlord or other person to whom rent is payable ...'—Subject to the leave of the court, this provision protects against the exercise of any right of forfeiture by peaceable re-entry. The protection is restricted to premises which are let to the debtor, but not necessarily occupied by the debtor. The reference to a failure by the *debtor* 'to comply with any term or condition of his tenancy' makes clear that the protection of the sub-provision extends to forfeiture by peaceable re-entry whether arising on breach of a covenant for rent or any other covenant which, but for the moratorium, would give rise to such relief. Furthermore, the draftsman's use of the words 'tenancy of such premises' provides a debtor with no protection where the substance of his interest amounts only to a licence: see *Street v Mountford* [1985] AC 809.

Section 252(2)(b)

'no other proceedings, and no execution or other legal process may be commenced or continued ... except with the leave of the court'—The term 'proceedings' is a more compendious expression than the word 'action' used previously and most recently in s 9 of the Bankruptcy Act 1914. The former term is apt to denote any legal or quasi-legal proceedings and has been held to extend to arbitration proceedings (*Bristol Airport plc v Powdrill* [1990] Ch 744 (Browne-Wilkinson V-C)), proceedings before an industrial tribunal (*Carr v British International Helicopters Ltd (in administration)* [1994] 2 BCLC 474 (EAT)), a statutory adjudication process under s 108 of the Housing Grants, Construction and Regeneration Act 1996 and under cl 41A of the standard-form JCT 80 contract (*A Straume (UK) Ltd v Bradlor Developments Ltd* [2000] BCC 333 (His Honour Judge Behrens)), criminal prosecution under the Environmental Protection Act 1990 (*Environment Agency v Clark* [2000] BCC 653 (Robert Walker and Henry LJJ and Scott-Baker J) and, but not without some degree of doubt given the diametrically opposed views of Sir Anthony Morritt V-C and Lord Woolf (with whom Waller and Robert Walker LJJ had agreed), an application by a special freight train operator for a replacement access contract under s 17 of the Railways Act 1993 (*Winsor v Special Railway Administrators of Railtrack plc* [2002] 2 BCLC 308). The conclusion of the Scottish Court of Session in *Air Ecosse Ltd v Civil Aviation Authority* [1987] 3 BCC 492, to the effect that the words 'other proceedings ... against the company' in the form of s 11(3)(d) were confined to the activities of creditors and did not extend to courses of action which might be open to persons who were not creditors, such as competitors, under different statutes, is now extremely doubtful and should not be followed, given the later authorities which construe the term far more broadly.

In *Re Olympia & York Canary Wharf Ltd* [1993] BCLC 453 at 457A Millett J, as he then was, identified that the words 'legal process' refer to a process which requires the assistance of the court and which would not, therefore, extend, for example, to the service of a contractual notice, whether or not the service of such a notice was a pre-condition to the bringing of legal proceedings. If the view is taken that a particular process does not require the assistance of the court, then careful consideration should be given to the question of whether that process falls within the scope of 'proceedings' above. It is doubtful, however, that the service of a counter-notice under Part II of the Landlord and Tenant Act 1954 for a fresh tenancy constitutes 'proceedings': *Bristol Airport plc v Powdrill* [1990] Ch 744 at 766 (Browne-Wilkinson V-C).

When will leave be granted by the court?—Although interim order cases requiring the leave of the court are necessarily decided on a case by case basis, useful guidance, it is submitted, may be gleaned from the guidance given in the Court of Appeal in *Re Atlantic Computer Systems plc* [1992] Ch 505, which is set out in full, together with further commentary, in the note to para 43 of Sch B1 (on administrations). That guidance is relevant here to the extent that the court's approach will be rooted in establishing the purpose for which the interim order has been obtained and the extent to which, if leave was granted, the assertion of third party rights would operate to undermine that purpose. In *Hall and Shivers v Van Der Heiden* [2010] EWHC 537 (TCC), [2010] BPIR 585, the Technology and Construction Court

(Coulson J) was faced with a situation where a defendant debtor, on the last business day before a trial, obtained an interim order from the Swindon County Court. The claimants in the proceedings, on the first day of the trial, applied for leave to continue the proceedings. The judge held both that he had jurisdiction to make the order, and that it was appropriate to make the order.

Criminal proceedings which are not protected against by an interim order—Certain criminal statutes allow for the making of orders against the assets of a defendant by way of charging orders, confiscation orders and the like. The effect of the making of a restraint order under s 8 of the Drug Trafficking Offences Act 1986, for example, takes effect so as to take such property out of the scope of the defendant's estate. Provisions to like effect appear in Part V of the Criminal Justice Act 1988 and the Proceeds of Crime Act 2002. In *Re M (Restraint Order)* [1992] QB 377 Otton J held that an interim order did not prevent the making of an application by the prosecuting authorities and the making of an order appointing a receiver over such property which would remain outside of the scope of the defendant's estate pending the discharge of the restraint order. Neither will the interim order protect against the enforcement of an order imposed by a magistrates court for the payment of compensation following the defendant's conviction for VAT offences, since the purpose of an IVA is to provide an alternative to bankruptcy in which a claim under a criminal compensation order is not provable: *R v Barnet Magistrates' Court ex parte Philippou* [1997] BPIR 134.

Creditor and third party remedies not protected against by an interim order—Like the protection of the moratorium in administration under paras 40–43 of Sch B1 – which, in substance, resembles the protection previously afforded by ss 10 and 11 – nothing within the interim order provisions suggests that the statutory protection afforded to a debtor is intended to deprive a creditor or third party from utilising any self-help remedies against the debtor, even where the effect of such remedies is harmful to the financial interests or standing of the debtor. These self-help remedies would include determination by repudiation of a contract, service of a contractual notice (such as one making time of the essence, as in *Re Olympia & York Canary Wharf Ltd* [1993] BCLC 453 (Millett J)) or forfeiture (though not by peaceable re-entry) of a lease. Neither would the protection of the moratorium appear to catch the combination of accounts, most obviously by a bank or trading customer, or an application for an extension of time for the registration of a charge over the company's property, as in *Re Barrow Borough Transport Ltd* [1990] Ch 227. Since the exercise of a right of set-off cannot sensibly be characterised as proceedings, execution or other legal process, such a right – whether legal, equitable or contractual – should also remain available to a third party, in support of which proposition see *Electromagnetic (S) Ltd v Development Bank of Singapore* [1994] SLR 734, a decision of the High Court of Singapore, in which jurisdiction the administration regime had been modelled on the former English scheme. It is suggested that the service of a demand, say for the return of goods, constitutes no more than self-help and will not fall within the scope of s 252(2)(b) (on which see *Barclays Mercantile Business Finance Ltd v Sibec Developments Ltd* [1992] 1 WLR 1253), although it is arguable that the position is different where the service of such a demand or other notice is a contractual pre-condition for the taking of any step within s 252(2)(b), on which see *Re Olympia & York Canary Wharf Ltd* [1993] BCLC 453 at 454G–454H (Millett J).

Secured creditors—In contrast with the position under para 43 of Sch B1 in relation to company administration, the interim order in an IVA offers no protection against the enforcement of the rights of a secured creditor. Neither is an IVA capable of modifying the rights of a secured creditor, save with that creditor's consent: see s 258(4).

253 Application for interim order

(1) Application to the court for an interim order may be made where the debtor intends to make a proposal under this Part, that is, a proposal to his creditors for a composition in satisfaction of his debts or a scheme of arrangement of his affairs (from here on referred to, in either case, as a 'voluntary arrangement').

(2) The proposal must provide for some person ('the nominee') to act in relation to the voluntary arrangement either as trustee or otherwise for the purpose of supervising its implementation and the nominee must be a person who is qualified to act as an insolvency practitioner, or authorised to act as nominee, in relation to the voluntary arrangement.

(3) Subject as follows, the application may be made—

    (a)   if the debtor is an undischarged bankrupt, by the debtor, the trustee of his estate, or the official receiver, and

    (b)   in any other case, by the debtor.

(4) An application shall not be made under subsection (3)(a) unless the debtor has given notice of the proposal to the official receiver and, if there is one, the trustee of his estate.

(5) An application shall not be made while a bankruptcy petition presented by the debtor is pending, if the court has, under section 273 below, appointed an insolvency practitioner to inquire into the debtor's affairs and report.

Amendments—Insolvency Act 2000, s 3, Sch 3, paras 1, 3(a)–(c).

General note—An IVA backed by a moratorium is open to a debtor who has not made an application for an interim order within the 12 months ending with the day of the application (on which see s 255(1)(c)) or an undischarged bankrupt. An application may not be made in the circumstances prescribed in s 253(5). A debtor may not propose an IVA proposal to a meeting of creditors where he has received his automatic discharge from bankruptcy after the date of an interim order but before the date of the creditors' meeting: *Re Ravichandran* [2004] BPIR 814 (Registrar Nicholls). Neither is the IVA procedure available to a discharged bankrupt in respect of the bankruptcy debts since those debts will have been released on discharge by operation of s 281: *Wright v Official Receiver* [2001] BPIR 196 (District Judge Caddick, Medway County Court). An IVA would, however, be available to a discharged bankrupt in respect of non-bankruptcy debts which are not released by s 281(1); in those circumstances the debtor will fall within s 253(3)(b). Equally, a discharged bankrupt would have standing to propose an IVA in respect of post-bankruptcy debts.

Unliquidated debts—Rule 5.21(3) provides that a creditor voting in respect of an unliquidated amount or any debt whose value is not ascertained 'shall', not may, for voting purposes only, have his debt valued at £1 unless the chairman agrees to put a higher value on it. For further illustrations on the treatment of such creditor claims see *Beverley Group plc v McClue* [1995] BCC 751 (Knox J); *Re Sweatfield Ltd* [1997] BCC 744 (His Honour Judge Weeks QC); *Re Wisepark Ltd* [1994] BCC 221 (untaxed (ie unassessed) litigation costs not a debt for voluntary arrangement purposes) and *County Bookshops Ltd v Grove* [2002] BPIR 772 (Neuberger J, as he then was, contractual instalment payments which had not fallen due as at date of CVA admitted to arrangement as contingent debts), *Sofaer v Anglo Irish Asset Finance plc* [2011] EWHC 1480 (Ch), [2011] BPIR 1736 (Lewison J, as he then was), is a case in which one of the debtor's arguments was that his liability to the relevant creditor was under a guarantee and so was unliquidated. That argument was rejected by Lewison J, who held in any event, following *Re Newlands (Seaford) Educational Trust (In Administration); Chittenden and Others v Pepper and Others* [2006] EWHC 1511 (Ch), [2006] BPIR 1230 that r 5.21(3) was not engaged where the chairman agreed to put a higher valuer on the debt.

Disputed debts—In the case of disputed debts the proper course under r 5.22(4) is for the chairman to mark the claims objected to and allow the creditor to vote for the full amount, on which see *Re A Debtor (No 222 of 1990) ex parte Bank of Ireland* [1992] BCLC 137 at 144F–144H (Harman J) and the commentary to rule 5.22.

Court control over the admission of creditor's proof—The court has jurisdiction to direct that a creditor be admitted to proof in an arrangement: *Re FMS Financial Management*

Services Ltd (1989) 5 BCC 191 (Hoffmann J, as he then was, nominees proposing arrangement directed to admit to proof shareholders with prima facie good claim against the company for misrepresentation).

Section 253(1)

The scope of the terms 'voluntary arrangement', 'composition' and 'scheme of arrangement'—The distinction between the terms 'composition' and 'scheme of arrangement' was considered by the Court of Appeal in *Commissioners of Inland Revenue v Adams* [2001] 1 BCLC 222 at 230G–231F (Mummery LJ), affirming the decision of Nicholas Warren QC, sitting as he then was as a deputy High Court judge, at [1999] 2 BCLC 730. A composition is an arrangement to pay a sum in lieu of a larger debt or other obligation, or forbearance to sue for the full amount being exchanged for a money payment or other consideration. A scheme of arrangement, on the other hand, involves something less than the release or discharge of creditor debts (as on a composition) and might include nothing more than a moratorium on the enforcement of creditor claims so as to suspend the date for repayment of such debts, with or without the payment of a dividend in the interim: see *March Estates plc v Gunmark* [1996] 2 BCLC 1 at 5A–5G (Lightman J). Accordingly, the approved proposal in *Adams*, which imposed a moratorium on the prosecution of creditor claims for a 3-year period with no prospect of a dividend to preferential or unsecured creditors, constituted a scheme of arrangement so as to amount to a voluntary arrangement within s 253(1). A scheme of arrangement which amounts to nothing more than a moratorium on creditor claims, even if capable of being brought within the definition of a voluntary arrangement, will not usually be of great attraction to a debtor for the simple reason that arrangement creditors will be free to pursue their claims against the debtor on the cessation of the moratorium. In practice, therefore, a debtor might seek to obtain the fuller advantage of a composition by offering a dividend, even a very small dividend, to creditors in consideration for the discharge in full of creditor claims.

Proposals which do not amount to a composition or a scheme of arrangement—If a proposal is put to creditors which amounts to neither a composition nor a moratorium, then the original proposal remains a nullity such that the proposal is not capable of being saved by modifications introduced at the first statutory meeting of creditors, even where the creditors support such modifications: *Commissioners of Inland Revenue v Bland* [2003] BPIR 1274 (Lloyd J, as he then was, original IVA proposal which offered nothing to creditors successfully challenged by Inland Revenue under s 262 notwithstanding modifications introduced to provide for dividend). The same considerations as apply to IVAs apply to CVAs: *Bland* at [39].

The effect of an arrangement on third parties—Although a CVA is capable either expressly or by necessary implication of varying the relationship between a creditor of the company and a third party (eg so as to release a co-debtor or security which is not itself a party to the arrangement), an arrangement will ordinarily be construed as reserving the rights of creditors against third parties: see *March Estates plc v Gunmark* [1996] 2 BCLC 1 at 5H–6G (Lightman J) and the cases cited therein. Construction of an arrangement term purporting to modify third party rights is not a matter of general principle and depends on the surrounding circumstances and account being taken not only of the express words employed in the arrangement but also any terms which may be properly implied: *Johnson v Davies* [1998] 2 BCLC 252 at 259B–259D (Chadwick LJ). On the release of a surety on the IVA of a principal debtor see *Greene King plc v Stanley* [2002] BPIR 491 at [58]–[86] (Jonathan Parker LJ).

For the appropriate procedure where one of two co-debtors has entered into an IVA where the creditor wishes to pursue the debt and the non-IVA co-debtor wishes to pursue an indemnity and contribution claim against the IVA co-debtor see *Lloyds Bank plc v Ellicott* [2003] BPIR 632 at [54] (Chadwick LJ).

For further general guidance on the construction of voluntary arrangements see the notes under that heading to s 260(2)(b) below.

Section 253(2)

Scope of provision—A valid proposal is implemented on it being approved under s 258(1) at a creditors' meeting summoned under s 257 by the requisite majority of creditors as provided for in r 5.23(1). Thereafter, the nominee – or any person appointed in his stead under s 256(3) or s 258(3) – is known as the supervisor of the voluntary arrangement: see s 263(2) and the notes thereto.

Qualifications of the nominee—In addition to the observations as to the nature of a voluntary arrangement in the notes to s 253(1) above, the legislation imposes a requirement that, so as to constitute a proposal, a proposed IVA must provide for a person who is qualified to act as an insolvency practitioner 'in relation to the voluntary arrangement either as trustee or otherwise for the purpose of supervising its implementation'.

The term 'act as an insolvency practitioner' is defined in s 388; and see also s 419. By virtue of s 4 of the Insolvency Act 2000 certain persons who are not licensed insolvency practitioners (commonly termed turnaround specialists) may also be authorised under s 389A to act as nominees and supervisors in relation to IVAs.

Identity of the nominee—In practice, the nominee is invariably the same individual who takes office subsequently as supervisor, although s 258(3) provides that a modification to the proposal replacing the nominee with another individual (who will then take office as supervisor) may be approved by creditors at the meeting summoned to consider the proposal. The nominee may also be replaced by the court under s 256(3) on prescribed grounds.

'to act ... either as trustee or otherwise for the purpose of supervising its implementation'—In *Re Leisure Study Group Ltd* [1994] 2 BCLC 65 at 68A Harman J suggested that a nominee acting in relation to a voluntary arrangement would so act as a trustee. In *Re Bradley-Hole (a Bankrupt)* [1995] 4 All ER 865 Rimer J adopted the same reasoning in relation to the status of the supervisor of an approved arrangement to whom assets had been transferred by the debtor. Given this approach, it would not appear to matter whether the proposal provides expressly that a nominee is to hold arrangement assets as trustee. The words 'or otherwise' would appear to catch any action by a nominee other than in his capacity as a trustee of the proposed arrangement's assets.

Role of the nominee—The legislation confers no powers on a nominee in relation to a debtor or his assets so far as the proposed IVA is concerned. In practice, the nominee will usually play a significant role in assisting a debtor in the drafting of the proposal, although the proposal itself remains that of the debtor. The nominee is not the agent of the debtor: *Re A Debtor (No 222 of 1990) ex parte Bank of Ireland (No 2)* [1993] BCLC 233 at 235D (Harman J).

The involvement of the nominee in the proposal process must be tempered with the fundamental requirement for the nominee to retain objectivity in the discharge of his function and in the preparation of his report to the court under s 256(1).

SIP 3 identifies best practice in relation to voluntary arrangements; para 2.2 provides that 'In dealing with a VA the member should bear in mind his overriding duty to ensure a fair balance between the interests of the company/debtor, the creditors and any other parties involved. In considering whether to accept appointment as either nominee or supervisor, the member should have regard to the ethical guidelines of his authorising body.' The DTI's Dear IP Letter of March 1995 suggests that practitioners pose the following questions in relation to a proposed arrangement: (1) Is it feasible? (2) Is it fair to the creditors? (3) Is it an acceptable alternative to formal insolvency? (4) Is it fit to be considered by the creditors? (5) Is it fair to the debtor? The loss of professional objectivity plainly carries with it the risk of professional criticism and sanction. In addition, where a nominee falls significantly below the standards required of a licensed insolvency practitioner, the court may, on an application under s 262, require the nominee to pay all or part of the costs of any proceedings arising out of the inadequate discharge of his duties, including his conduct as chairman of the creditors' meeting: *Re A Debtor (No 222 of 1990) ex parte Bank of Ireland (No 2)* [1993] BCLC 233 (Harman J). This is the case even where the application could have been pursued by way of an appeal under r 5.22(3), in relation to which r 5.22(7) provides that a chairman of a creditors' meeting may not be personally liable for the costs of such an appeal. It is vitally important, therefore, that a nominee (or supervisor) maintains his objectivity throughout, remaining, in effect, between the debtor and his creditors, and is not seen to take up the debtor's cause where a creditor raises a legitimate complaint. See, in this respect, *Tradition (UK) Limited v Ahmed & Others* [2008] EWHC 3448 (Ch) [2009] BPIR 626 in which, as from para 20, Mr Andrew Simmonds QC, sitting as a deputy High Court judge considered whether to make the nominee liable for the applicant's costs of successfully challenging an individual voluntary arrangement. Although he had previously found that the nominee's conduct had been manifestly inappropriate, the judge was not satisfied that there was a causal connection between that conduct and the incurring of legal costs by the applicant, and so he declined to order the nominee to pay the costs.

Duties of the nominee—For commentary see the notes to s 256(2) below.

The status of arrangement assets in a winding-up or bankruptcy—In *Re NT Gallagher & Son Ltd, Shierson v Tomlinson* [2002] 2 BCLC 133, [2002] EWCA Civ 404 Peter Gibson LJ, giving the judgment of the court (also comprising Ward and Dyson LJJ), considered the issue of whether arrangement assets held on a trust for CVA creditors survived liquidation and whether the arrangement creditors were entitled to prove in an ensuing liquidation. The guidance provided in the *Gallagher* judgment was much needed, given the eleven hardly reconcilable first instance decisions considered in the judgment. The following conclusions were identified (at [54]):

'(1) Where a CVA or IVA provide for money or other assets to be paid to or transferred or held for the benefit of CVA or IVA creditors, this will create a trust of those moneys or assets for those creditors. (2) The effect of the liquidation of the company or the bankruptcy of the debtor on a trust created by the CVA or IVA will depend on the provision of the CVA or IVA relating thereto. (3) If the CVA or IVA provides what is to happen on liquidation or bankruptcy (or a failure of the CVA or IVA), effect must be given thereto. (4) If the CVA or IVA does not so provide, the trust will continue notwithstanding the liquidation, bankruptcy or failure and must take effect according to its terms. (5) The CVA or IVA creditors can prove in the liquidation or bankruptcy for so much of their debt as remains after payment of what has been or will be recovered under the trust.'

For the purposes of conclusion (1) it should be noted that the Court of Appeal approved of the concession by counsel for the CVA supervisors, by reference to the decision of Harman J in *Re Leisure Study Group Ltd* [1994] 2 BCLC 65, to the effect that the supervisors were trustees of the assets in their hands notwithstanding the absence of an express trust having been created by the CVA. The combined effects of conclusions (3) and (4) is that arrangement assets will remain ring-fenced for arrangement creditors on a liquidation or bankruptcy or failure of the arrangement unless the arrangement itself specifically provides that the arrangement assets are to be treated differently, most obviously by way of falling into the liquidation or bankruptcy for the benefit of liquidation or bankruptcy creditors. The justification for what might be termed the default rule on ring-fencing in conclusions (3) and (4) appears in the judgment at [50] and provided, following an observation that the general law leaves trusts of assets not held for a company unaffected by the debtor's liquidation or bankruptcy:

'Further, as a matter of policy, in the absence of any provision in the CVA as to what should happen to trust assets on liquidation of the company, the court should prefer a default rule which furthers rather than hinders what might be taken to be the statutory purpose of Part I of the Act. Parliament plainly intended to encourage companies and creditors to enter into CVAs so as to provide creditors with a means of recovering what they are owed without recourse to the more expensive means provided by winding-up or administration, thereby giving many companies the opportunity to continue to trade.'

Precisely the same rationale justifies the operation of the default rule on ring-fencing in IVAs under Part VIII, which were introduced as a means of avoiding the consequences of bankruptcy, subject to approval by the statutory requisite majority of creditors.

The court has no jurisdiction to authorise the supervisor of a CVA to breach the trust of the CVA assets for the benefit of the CVA creditors: *Re Beloit Walmsley Ltd* [2008] EWHC 1888 (Ch), [2008] BPIR 1445 (HHJ Pelling QC, sitting as a judge of the High Court), a decision which includes a very useful review of the authorities dealing with the court's jurisdiction to interfere with the terms of a voluntary arrangement, *Re FMS Financial Management Services Ltd* (1989) 5 BCC 191, in particular, being identified as doubtful, or at least 'seriously circumscribed'.

Section 253(4)

Scope of provision—Two clear days' notice must be given to the official receiver or trustee: r 5.7(4)(a).

Section 253(5)

Scope of provision—Note that the bankruptcy court may make an interim order under s 252 under s 274(3)(a), without the need for an application.

254 Effect of application

(1) At any time when an application under section 253 for an interim order is pending,

    (a)   no landlord or other person to whom rent is payable may exercise any right of forfeiture by peaceable re-entry in relation to premises let to the debtor in respect of a failure by the debtor to comply with any term or condition of his tenancy of such premises, except with the leave of the court, and

    (b)   the court may forbid the levying of any distress on the debtor's property or its subsequent sale, or both, and stay any action, execution or other legal process against the property or person of the debtor.

(2) Any court in which proceedings are pending against an individual may, on proof that an application under that section has been made in respect of that individual, either stay the proceedings or allow them to continue on such terms as it thinks fit.

Amendments—Insolvency Act 2000, s 3, Sch 3, paras 1, 4(a), (b).

General note—Section 254 takes effect for the period starting with the filing of an application for an interim order under s 253 and ending with either the making of an interim order or the dismissal of the application.

Subparagraphs (1)(a) and (b) provide protection very similar to that provided under an interim order in s 252(2)(aa) and (b). The protection in s 254(1)(a) arises automatically on the filing of an interim order application and may only be circumvented with leave of the court. The protection in s 254(1)(b), on the other hand, requires the intervention of either the debtor or the nominee by way of an application to court.

Section 254(1)(a)

Scope of provision—Subject to the leave of the court, this provision protects against the exercise of any right of forfeiture by peaceable re-entry. The protection is restricted to premises which are let to the debtor, but not necessarily occupied by the debtor. The reference to a failure by the *debtor* 'to comply with any term or condition of his tenancy' makes clear that the protection of the provision extends to forfeiture by peaceable re-entry whether arising on breach of a covenant for rent or any other covenant which, but for the moratorium, would give rise to such relief. Furthermore, the draftsman's use of the words 'tenancy of such premises' provides a debtor with no protection where the substance of his interest amounts only to a licence: see *Street v Mountford* [1985] AC 809. The extension of the provision to protection against the exercise of rights of forfeiture was effected by s 3 of the Insolvency Act 2000 and Sch 3 thereto.

Section 254(1)(b)

Scope of provision—This provision allows the court to prevent not only the levying of distress against the debtor's property – following amendment introduced by s 3 and Sch 3 of the Insolvency Act 2000 – but also the continuation of any distress by way of the sale of any of the debtor's property.

The reference to the court staying 'any action' in s 254(1)(b) differs from the reference in s 252(2)(b), which refers to 'proceedings'; if anything, the latter term is broader than the former, although it is doubtful that any meaningful distinction could have been intended. In any case, the reference to 'action' would allow for the stay of an extant bankruptcy petition in the absence of any specific reference to a petition as appears in s 252(2)(a). The subsection would not appear, however, to prevent the presentation of a bankruptcy petition prior to or during the period in which an application for an interim order under s 252 is pending.

For the scope of the terms 'execution or other legal process against the property or person of the debtor' see the notes under that heading to s 252.

Section 254(2)

The appropriate court on an application for continuance or stay—Where proceedings are pending against an individual (i e under s 254(1)(b)) it is the court in which those proceedings have been commenced which has jurisdiction to stay the proceedings or allow them to continue, subject to any stipulated terms on being satisfied that an application has been made under s 253, very possibly in another court. The court to which the s 253 application is made does not appear capable of exercising such jurisdiction based on the wording in s 254(2). The position is different where leave of the court is sought as against the automatic bars imposed by s 254(1)(a), since the reference to 'the court' in that provision must be read as being the court to which the interim order application under s 253 is made by virtue of the definition in s 385(1).

When will the court grant leave or allow proceedings to continue?—The considerations here will be the same as those identified under this heading in the notes to s 252.

255 Cases in which interim order can be made

(1) The court shall not make an interim order on an application under section 253 unless it is satisfied—

    (a)   that the debtor intends to make a proposal under this Part;

    (b)   that on the day of the making of the application the debtor was an undischarged bankrupt or was able to petition for his own bankruptcy;

    (c)   that no previous application has been made by the debtor for an interim order in the period of 12 months ending with that day; and

    (d)   that the nominee under the debtor's proposal is willing to act in relation to the proposal.

(2) The court may make an order if it thinks that it would be appropriate to do so for the purpose of facilitating the consideration and implementation of the debtor's proposal.

(3) Where the debtor is an undischarged bankrupt, the interim order may contain provision as to the conduct of the bankruptcy, and the administration of the bankrupt's estate, during the period for which the order is in force.

(4) Subject as follows, the provision contained in an interim order by virtue of subsection (3) may include provision staying proceedings in the

bankruptcy or modifying any provision in this Group of Parts, and any provision of the rules in their application to the debtor's bankruptcy.

(5) An interim order shall not, in relation to a bankrupt, make provision relaxing or removing any of the requirements of provisions in this Group of Parts, or of the rules, unless the court is satisfied that that provision is unlikely to result in any significant diminution in, or in the value of, the debtor's estate for the purposes of the bankruptcy.

(6) Subject to the following provisions of this Part, an interim order made on an application under section 253 ceases to have effect at the end of the period of 14 days beginning with the day after the making of the order.

Amendments—Insolvency Act 2000, ss 3, 15(1), Sch 3, paras 1, 5(a), (b), Sch 5.

General note—There are two features to this provision. First, the first two subsections stipulate preconditions for the making of an interim order and direct the circumstances in which an order may be made respectively. Secondly, subsections (3)–(5) specifically allow, where the debtor is an undischarged bankrupt, for the interim order to include provisions providing for the future conduct of the bankruptcy, the administration of the bankrupt's estate and the staying of proceedings and the modification of any statutory rules within this Group of Parts provided, in the last case, that the provision is unlikely to result in any significant reduction in the debtor's estate or the value thereof.

Section 255(1)(a)

Scope of provision—This precondition will be satisfied by the court having sight of what appears to it to be a genuine proposal.

Section 255(1)(b)

Scope of provision—This condition would not appear to be met if, on the day of the application, the debtor was not an undischarged bankrupt but was unable to petition for his own bankruptcy, for example by virtue of there being an extant bankruptcy petition against the debtor.

Section 255(1)(c)

Scope of provision—This provision requires only that an application has been made, rather than an interim order obtained, within the preceding 12-month period. In *Hurst v Bennett (No 2)* [2002] BPIR 102 the Court of Appeal (Mummery and Jonathan Parker LJJ), in refusing permission to appeal, upheld the decision of Ferris J on an appeal from the Registrar to the effect that it is an improper use of the review procedure under s 375(1) to challenge the dismissal of an interim order application within the preceding 12 months whilst, at the same time, seeking to advance a fresh application, albeit in relation to a reformulated proposal with the support of a new nominee.

Section 255(1)(d)

Scope of provision—The court need only be satisfied that the nominee is willing to act in relation to the proposal. It will be necessary in any case for the nominee to be authorised to act as such: see s 389A.

Section 255(2)

Scope of provision—In effect, this provision amounts to an additional precondition to the four subsections above, in that an interim order may only be made if the court 'thinks' (on the meaning of which see the commentary in the notes to para 36 in Sch B1) that the making of the order would be appropriate for facilitating 'the consideration and implementation of the debtor's proposal', being a reference to the views and decision of the creditors' meeting and the viability thereafter of the proposal. Although the provision provides that the court 'may make' – as opposed to 'may only make' – an order, it is implausible that Parliament might have intended that the court should even consider making an interim order in any circumstances other than where it would be appropriate to do so for the specific purpose identified above.

It is well established that, in determining the appropriateness of making an interim order, the court will consider whether the proposal is 'serious or viable' on which test see the notes to s 256(1)(aa) below. The wording of s 255(2) is apt to confer on the court a discretion as to whether to make an interim order.

Section 255(3)–(5)

Scope of provision—The discretion of the court and the scope of any additional provisions which may be provided for by the court is unfettered and broad.

Section 255(6)

Scope of provision—Although an interim order would ordinarily expire 14 days from the date on which it was made, see the note headed 'Interim orders' and the 'Concertina order' to s 252.

256 Nominee's report on debtor's proposal

(1) Where an interim order has been made on an application under section 253, the nominee shall, before the order ceases to have effect, submit a report to the court stating—

    (a)   whether, in his opinion, the voluntary arrangement which the debtor is proposing has a reasonable prospect of being approved and implemented,

    (aa) whether, in his opinion, a meeting of the debtor's creditors should be summoned to consider the debtor's proposal, and

    (b)   if in his opinion such a meeting should be summoned, the date on which, and time and place at which, he proposes the meeting should be held.

(2) For the purpose of enabling the nominee to prepare his report the debtor shall submit to the nominee—

    (a)   a document setting out the terms of the voluntary arrangement which the debtor is proposing, and

    (b)   a statement of his affairs containing—

        (i)   such particulars of his creditors and of his debts and other liabilities and of his assets as may be prescribed, and

        (ii)   such other information as may be prescribed.

(3) The court may—

    (a)   on an application made by the debtor in a case where the nominee has failed to submit the report required by this section or has died, or

    (b)   on an application made by the debtor or the nominee in a case where it is impracticable or inappropriate for the nominee to continue to act as such, direct that the nominee shall be replaced as such by another person qualified to act as an insolvency practitioner, or authorised to act as nominee, in relation to the voluntary arrangement.

(3A) The court may, on an application made by the debtor in a case where the nominee has failed to submit the report required by this section, direct that the interim order shall continue, or (if it has ceased to have effect) be renewed, for such further period as the court may specify in the direction.

(4) The court may, on the application of the nominee, extend the period for which the interim order has effect so as to enable the nominee to have more time to prepare his report.

(5) If the court is satisfied on receiving the nominee's report that a meeting of the debtor's creditors should be summoned to consider the debtor's proposal, the court shall direct that the period for which the interim order has effect shall be extended, for such further period as it may specify in the direction, for the purpose of enabling the debtor's proposal to be considered by his creditors in accordance with the following provisions of this Part.

(6) The court may discharge the interim order if it is satisfied, on the application of the nominee—

(a) that the debtor has failed to comply with his obligations under subsection (2), or

(b) that for any other reason it would be inappropriate for a meeting of the debtor's creditors to be summoned to consider the debtor's proposal.

Amendments—Insolvency Act 2000, s 3, Sch 3, paras 1, 6(a), (b), 7.

General note—The counterpoint to s 256 appears in s 256A, which applies to cases where no interim order is sought, whether or not the debtor is an undischarged bankrupt. The detailed procedural rules governing the preparation and contents of an IVA proposal together with the preparation of the proposal and the nominee's report to the court are set out in rr 5.2–5.14B.

Section 256(1)

Scope of provision—Section 256 applies where an interim order has been made and requires action before the interim order ceases to have effect.

The viability of the proposal and the duties of the nominee in reporting to the court—In *Re A Debtor (No 222 of 1990) ex parte Bank of Ireland and Others (No 2)* [1993] BCLC 233 at 234E–234G Harman J, in the course of a judgment heavily critical of a nominee, expressed the following view:

'In my judgment, the nominee both in making his report and in acting as chairman of the meeting is to be taken as having a duty (arising from the requirement in the statute that he shall report his own opinion to the court) to exercise a professional independent judgment. The fact that judgment is required to be that of a licensed insolvency practitioner emphasises the fact that the court is to receive a report from a qualified person skilled and experienced in these matters, who is exercising his own professional functions in judging whether the matter is, in his opinion, fit to go forward.'

The substance of the judgment in *Bank of Ireland* is reflected in the guidance in SIP 3 and was referred to in the Dear IP Letter of March 1995 noted under the heading 'Role of the nominee' to s 253(2) above.

In *Greystoke v Hamilton-Smith* [1997] BPIR 24 at 28B–28F Lindsay J made reference to the Dear IP Letter of March 1995 as representing 'a fair view in general terms of responsibilities which the legislation casts upon a nominee.' The judge, however, went on to express the view that a nominee cannot be expected in every case to have verified personally every figure and to have tested every part of the proposal where, for example, financial resources preclude such enquiries. Lindsay J did, nonetheless, consider that a nominee has an obligation to satisfy himself of three specific matters, 'at least in those cases where the fullness or candour of the debtor's information has properly come into question', namely (1) that the debtor's true position as to assets and liabilities does not appear to him in any material respect to differ substantially from that as it is to be represented to creditors, (2) that the debtor's proposal to creditors has a real prospect of being implemented in the way it is to be represented that it will be (bearing in mind that a measure of modification to proposals is possible under s 258), and (3) that the information provides a basis for the view that no already-manifest yet unavoidable prospective unfairness in relation to the nominee's functions of admitting or rejecting claims to vote and agreeing values for voting purposes is present. In each particular case, therefore, it is submitted that the question of further enquiry or investigation by the nominee remains a judgment call for the nominee, which decision must be capable of being justified, objectively speaking, in those circumstances which are known or ought to be known to him. His Lordship also considered but rejected the proposition that the arrangement must appear to offer a reasonable prospect of a better recovery than bankruptcy.

Having identified the above three minimum steps, Lindsay J went on in *Greystoke* (at 28H 29A) to qualify his view with the proviso that the steps which it is reasonable for a nominee to take in satisfying himself of the matters identified will, amongst a host of variables particular to any case, include the availability of funds to meet the expense entailed in such further enquiries. That view is consistent with the approach adopted subsequently by His Honour Judge Cooke, sitting as a judge of the High Court in *Pitt v Mond* [2001] BPIR 624 at 640F–641B, to the effect that, whilst a nominee is entitled to rely on information provided to him by a debtor, he is under a duty to investigate further any fact or matter which appears to him to be doubtful, but only by the taking of such steps as are reasonable on the facts of the case. This scope for limited enquiry is reflected in the best practice guidance in SIP 3, para 5(d). Any limitation imposed by a lack of funds, however, should not obviate the court being made aware by the nominee of any concerns on his part in relation to the three basic minimum points identified by Lindsay J in *Greystoke* (above). SIP 3, para 6.2 specifically provides that 'If the nominee cannot satisfy himself of the above three conditions [in *Greystoke*] are met but still recommends that a meeting should be held, he should explain in his comments the basis on which he is making that recommendation and qualify his comments so that the fact that the conditions are not met is conspicuously brought to the attention of the court.' As such, a nominee would be obliged, at least as a matter of best practice, and almost certainly as a matter of law, to bring to the court's attention the nature of his concerns and the reasons (e g lack of funding) for his being unable to assuage those concerns.

For further cases involving claims against nominees see *Heritage Joinery (a firm) v Krasner* [1999] BPIR 683; *Harmony Carpets v Chaffin-Laird* [2000] BPIR 61 (Rattee J); and *Prosser v Castle Sanderson (a firm)* [2002] BPIR 1163 (Mummery, Clarke and Hale LJJ, insolvency practitioner did not owe duty of care to debtor as nominee or chairman of creditors' meeting, but did owe such a duty in his capacity as the debtor's adviser during the short adjournment of the creditors' meeting).

Section 256(1)(a)

'Whether ... the proposed voluntary arrangement has a reasonable prospect of being approved and implemented'—This requirement in s 256(1)(a) differs from that in s 256(1)(aa) in that the latter requires consideration of whether a creditors' meeting should be summoned (which brings into play the 'serious and viable' test considered under the next heading) whereas the former provision requires the nominee to express a view not only as to whether the proposal has a reasonable prospect of being approved by creditors but also, it is submitted, whether the approved arrangement is capable of being implemented as envisaged by the proposal.

The formation of an opinion on the prospects of approval must, it is submitted, involve a consideration of the likely attitude of the debtor's unsecured creditors to the proposal. SIP 3, para 6.3(f) indicates that, as a matter of best practice, the nominee's report will normally include 'information on the attitude of any major unsecured creditor which may affect the approval of the arrangement by creditors'. It is submitted that s 256(1)(a) does not of itself impose an obligation on the nominee to make contact with creditors for the purpose of taking soundings, although a nominee may well regard such a step as prudent in a particular case. Equally, the nominee may, in the absence of suspicion, rely upon representations made to him by the directors as to the likely attitude of any particular creditor. In many cases, however, neither the debtor nor the nominee will be in a position to express an opinion as to the likely position of creditors, other than where the proposal is plainly derisory in terms of any proposed dividend.

The question of implementation involves the nominee making an informed assessment as to the viability of the proposal on its terms. It is submitted that any mechanism within the proposal for the post-approval modification of the arrangement will usually constitute a factor affecting implementation.

There is no authority on the meaning of the term 'reasonable prospect' in the present context. It is suggested that this threshold test is relatively low and, by definition, will not be met only where there is no reasonable prospect of the proposal being both approved and – just as importantly and perhaps rather more stringently – implemented.

Section 256(1)(aa)

'Whether ... meetings of the company and its creditors should be summoned to consider the proposal': the 'serious and viable' test—In *Cooper v Fearnley* [1997] BPIR 20 at 21B–21C Aldous J (as he then was) considered, in the context of an appeal against the decision of a deputy district judge to refuse the making of an interim order in relation to a proposed individual voluntary arrangement, that a proposal must be 'serious and viable'. That yardstick was adopted by Sir Richard Scott V-C in *Hook v Jewson Ltd* [1997] BPIR 100 at 105D, and is now well established.

The 'serious and viable' threshold requires not merely that a proposal is seriously made or is made bona fide; rather, the proposal must have both substance and be one which should seriously be considered by the creditors or, alternatively, be capable of serious consideration by creditors, even if there were serious and well-founded doubts and questions over the proposal itself: *Shah v Cooper* [2003] BPIR 1018 (Deputy Registrar Schekerdemian). The fact that a proposal offers only a modest projected dividend to creditors is a relevant factor, but need not of itself mean that the proposal is not serious and viable, since the matter can be left for approval or rejection by creditors: *Knowles v Coutts* [1998] BPIR 96 at 99E–100F (proposal of 1.4 pence in the pound) and *National Westminster Bank plc v Scher* [1998] BPIR 224 (proposed dividend of 0.06 pence in the pound). For a case in which Blackburne J regarded the proposal as 'an essay in make-believe' see *Davidson v Stanley* [2004] EWHC 2595 (Ch) [2005] BPIR 279.

For best practice guidance see SIP 3, para 6.

Section 256(2)

'a document setting out the terms of the proposed voluntary arrangement'—The proposal, as distinct from the statement of the company's affairs, provides the basis for the conduct of the voluntary arrangement. The detailed information which must appear in the debtor's proposal is prescribed in r 5.3. Best practice guidance appears in SIP 3, paras 2 and 5.

A proposal does not extend to an agreement or other understanding between a third party and creditors where the distribution to those creditors is to be made from funds advanced by the third party: *IRC v Wimbledon Football Club Ltd* [2004] EWCA Civ 44, [2005] 1 BCLC 66 at [59] (Neuberger LJ).

In practice, it will frequently be necessary to supplement that information prescribed by r 5.3 with further details, so as to enable the nominee to report to the court and for the purpose of enabling creditors to make an informed assessment of what is proposed. For example, in the case of a 'trading' arrangement – something more common in CVAs than IVAs – the debtor will usually wish to provide something akin to a business plan which extends beyond the very general and which identifies the company's strategy and objectives through ongoing trading. A proposal will also usually identify clearly those assets of the debtor which are included within an arrangement and those which are not. In *Supperstone v Hurst* [2005] BPIR 1231 it was held that statements in an IVA proposal as to the nature and extent of a debtor's interest in a property could not constitute declarations of trust and could not form the basis of inferring a shared common intention of beneficial ownership.

A proposal will also commonly include certain procedural and administrative provisions which allow for the operation of the arrangement itself. Such provisions commonly include an express statement of the supervisor's powers, together with an indication of whether the supervisor is deemed to act as agent for the debtor in the exercise of those powers, given the absence of any statutory provision providing for such agency.

It is also common for arrangements to provide for the treatment of disputed, contingent and/or prospective debts, the status of claims asserted against the debtor which are not known to exist at the time of the proposal together with a facility for the subsequent modification of the arrangement by, typically, 75% of creditors voting on any modification, given that an arrangement may only be modified with the unanimous approval of all creditors in the absence of such a provision: *Raja v Rubin* [1999] 3 WLR 606, CA and see *Re Alpa Lighting Ltd, Mills v Samuels* [1997] BPIR 341, CA (court has no jurisdiction to direct modifications to approved proposal).

The debtor's proposal may be amended at any time prior to the delivery of the nominee's report to the court under s 256 or s 256A: r 5.3(3).

The Appendix to SIP 3 suggests that a proposal should include sections covering six key areas and also identifies other matters which should be considered in order to facilitate the practical implementation of a proposal.

Notice of the debtor's proposal, together with a copy of the proposal itself, must be delivered to the nominee, or some person authorised by him, for which a receipt must be given and returned to the debtor: see r 5.4.

'a statement of [the debtor's] affairs'—The statement of the debtor's affairs must be delivered to the nominee at the same time as the delivery of the debtor's proposal: r 5.5(1). In practice, in any event, both documents are almost always delivered together.

The statement of affairs must include those particulars prescribed by r 5.5(3) and must supplement or amplify those particulars already given in the debtor's proposal 'so far as is necessary for clarifying the state of the debtor's affairs'.

Best practice guidance on the preparation of the statement of affairs and the obtaining of additional information by the nominee appears in SIP 3, para 4.

A mis-statement of the amount of the assets and liabilities of the debtor may be actionable by an aggrieved creditor as a material irregularity within the meaning of s 262(1)(b) with the potential for revocation of approval of the arrangement.

False representations etc—For the criminal consequences of a debtor falsely or fraudulently obtaining approval of the creditors of an IVA proposal see s 262A.

Section 256(3)

Scope of provision—Section 256(3)(a) allows for the replacement (and not merely the removal) of the nominee by the court, where the nominee has died or failed to submit his report to the court. Applications to replace a nominee in default of his reporting obligations will be rare since, in cases where the nominee is unwilling to vacate office voluntarily, the debtor is properly entitled to abort the process and to proceed with an alternative nominee. In those circumstances it is submitted that the original nominee would not, on being given notice of the debtor's position, fall within the definition of 'nominee' in s 253(2) and would therefore have no obligation to report to the court under s 256(1).

'in a case where it is impracticable or inappropriate for the nominee to continue to act as such'—The observations above in relation to s 256(3)(a) apply equally to s 256(3)(b). Alternatively, the person intending to make the proposal or the nominee may make application if, say, the nominee is subject to geographical relocation or is professionally embarrassed.

If an application is made to replace a nominee on professional grounds, then the proposed replacement nominee should, as a matter of good practice, confirm to the court that his appointment does not conflict with any statement of professional ethics or professional guidelines which apply to him.

Section 256(5)

It has been stated judicially that the court is not a rubber-stamp and must consider the contents of and reasons for a nominee's report and whether or not a meeting of creditors ought to be summoned: *Re a Debtor (No 140-IO-1995)* [1996] 2 BCLC 429 at 436 (Lindsay J).

If the court has not directed that a meeting of creditors ought to be summoned then any meeting of creditors convened to consider a proposal is not a statutory meeting within s 257 such that the court will be unable to entertain any complaint under s 262 in relation to it: *Vleiland-Boddy v Dexter* [2004] BPIR 235 (Roger Kaye QC, sitting as a deputy High Court judge).

256A Debtor's proposal and nominee's report

(1) This section applies where a debtor (being an individual)—

> (a) intends to make a proposal under this Part (but an interim order has not been made in relation to the proposal and no application for such an order is pending), and
>
> (b) if he is an undischarged bankrupt, has given notice of the proposal to the official receiver and, if there is one, the trustee of his estate,

unless a bankruptcy petition presented by the debtor is pending and the court has, under section 273, appointed an insolvency practitioner to inquire into the debtor's affairs and report.

(2) For the purpose of enabling the nominee to prepare a report under subsection (3), the debtor shall submit to the nominee—

> (a) a document setting out the terms of the voluntary arrangement which the debtor is proposing, and
>
> (b) a statement of his affairs containing—
>
>> (i) such particulars of his creditors and of his debts and other liabilities and of his assets as may be prescribed, and
>>
>> (ii) such other information as may be prescribed.

(3) If the nominee is of the opinion that the debtor is an undischarged bankrupt, or is able to petition for his own bankruptcy, the nominee shall, within 14 days (or such longer period as the court may allow) after receiving the document and statement mentioned in subsection (2), submit a report to the debtor's creditors stating—

> (a) whether, in his opinion, the voluntary arrangement which the debtor is proposing has a reasonable prospect of being approved and implemented,
>
> (b) whether, in his opinion, a meeting of the debtor's creditors should be summoned to consider the debtor's proposal, and
>
> (c) if in his opinion such a meeting should be summoned, the date on which, and time and place at which, he proposes the meeting should be held.

(4) The court may—

> (a) on an application made by the debtor in a case where the nominee has failed to submit the report required by this section or has died, or

(b)   on an application made by the debtor or the nominee in a case where it is impracticable or inappropriate for the nominee to continue to act as such,

direct that the nominee shall be replaced as such by another person qualified to act as an insolvency practitioner, or authorised to act as nominee, in relation to the voluntary arrangement.

(5) The court may, on an application made by the nominee, extend the period within which the nominee is to submit his report.

Amendments—Inserted by the Insolvency Act 2000, s 3, Sch 3, paras 1, 7. Amended by SI 2010/18.

General note—Section 256A was introduced by s 3 of and Sch 3 to the Insolvency Act 2000 and took effect from 1 January 2003. Section 256A closely resembles s 256. The significance of the new provisions, however, lies in their facilitating the implementation of an individual debtor's IVA proposal without any requirement for an application for an interim order. Prior to the introduction of s 256A an interim order had been held to be an integral part of the IVA procedure under Part VIII and a pre-requisite for the approval of a valid IVA which could not be cured retrospectively: *Fletcher v Vooght* [2000] BPIR 435 (Lloyd J, as he then was). Neither, in the absence of a provision equivalent to s 256(5), is the court under any duty to consider the report of the nominee submitted under s 256A(3) with a view to satisfying itself that a meeting of the debtor's creditors should be summoned to consider the debtor's proposal. The court will be under a duty to consider the report, however, if any application is made in relation to the debtor's proposal: see r 5.14B.

Where the s 256A procedure is used, the summoning of a creditors' meeting by the nominee is pursuant to s 257(1) and is dependent solely on the submission to the creditors of a positive report by the nominee under s 256A(3). The court remains open to applications under ss 256A(4) and (5), 262 and 263, on which see r 5.16.

Cases in which s 256A will be of use—IVAs implemented under the s 256A procedure will be obtainable more quickly and cheaply than under the interim order route. The real question for the debtor, and those advising him, is whether the debtor requires the protection of an interim order immediately or is likely to need such protection upon creditors becoming aware of his IVA proposal. In a borderline case where no interim order is sought in the belief that no creditor will resort to pre-emptive action, there is no reason why a debtor should not resort to the interim order procedure for protection where that belief turns out to be mistaken, subject to the restrictions imposed by s 253(3) and (5) and the conditions in s 255(1).

Procedure—See rr 5.14A and 5.14B.

Section 256A(2)

Scope of provision—This provision is almost identical to s 256(2), on which see the notes thereto.

Section 256A(3)

Scope of provision—The s 256A procedure is not available if the nominee is of the opinion that the debtor is a discharged bankrupt seeking to make a proposal in respect of debts released in the bankruptcy, on which see *Wright v Official Receiver* [2001] BPIR 196 and the General note to s 253. Neither may an individual propose an IVA under s 256A if a bankruptcy petition presented by the individual himself under s 264(1)(b) is outstanding, since in those circumstances the debtor would not be able to petition for his own bankruptcy. Subject to the nominee's opinion – the absence of a reference to the nominee being 'satisfied' suggests that the nominee may take the documents submitted to him under s 256A(2) at face value without the need for further investigation, in the absence of any suspicion – that the debtor is an undischarged bankrupt or is able to petition for his own bankruptcy these provisions are otherwise identical to those in s 256(1), on which see the notes thereto.

Section 256A(4)

Scope of provision—This provision is identical to s 256(3), on which see the notes thereto.

Section 256A(5)

Scope of provision—The nominee's report must be submitted to the debtor's creditors of whose address the nominee is aware, if the debtor is an undischarged bankrupt to the official receiver and the trustee, and any person who has presented a bankruptcy petition against the debtor within 14 days after receiving those documents prescribed in s 256A(2): r 5.14A. The court should not extend the period for the submission of the nominee's report without a proper explanation for the reasons giving rise to the need for extra time.

257 Summoning of creditors' meeting

(1) Where it has been reported to the court under section 256 or to the debtor's creditors under section 256A that a meeting of debtor's creditors should be summoned, the nominee (or the nominee's replacement under section 256(3) or 256A(4)) shall summon that meeting for the time, date and place proposed in the nominee's report unless, in the case of a report to which section 256 applies, the court otherwise directs.

(2) The persons to be summoned to the meeting are every creditor of the debtor of whose claim and address the person summoning the meeting is aware.

(3) For this purpose the creditors of a debtor who is an undischarged bankrupt include—

    (a)   every person who is a creditor of the bankrupt in respect of a bankruptcy debt, and

    (b)   every person who would be such a creditor if the bankruptcy had commenced on the day on which notice of the meeting is given.

Amendments—Insolvency Act 2000, s 3, Sch 3, paras 1, 8(a), (b); SI 2010/18.

General note—For the detailed procedural rules governing the summoning of meetings see rr 5.17–5.24. A meeting is not valid if not summoned in accordance with s 256(5): *Vlieland-Boddy v Dexter* [2004] BPIR 235.

Failure to give notice of a creditors' meeting to a person entitled to receive it is capable of having serious practical consequences, since a person not properly summoned may challenge the arrangement on the 'material irregularity' grounds in s 262(1)(b).

For best practice on the summoning of meetings see SIP 3, para 7.1.

Section 257(1)

Scope of provision—If the nominee (or his replacement) files a positive report for the purposes of s 256(1)(aa) or s 256A(3)(b), then he is under an obligation to summon a meeting of the debtor's creditors, subject to contrary order of the court, in accordance with the time, date and venue proposed in his report. In practice, a positive report will not usually elicit any response from the court such that the nominee will normally proceed to summon the meetings as a matter of course. The subsection appears to anticipate that a contrary order of the court may be made of the court's own volition or following an application by any party with a genuine interest in the business of the proposed meeting of creditors.

In *Re N (a Debtor)* [2002] BPIR 1024 at [6] Registrar Baister emphasised that s 257(1) is mandatory and that a meeting should be convened in strict compliance with it. If, as in that case, the nominee fails to hold the meeting at the time and date stipulated then the meeting, and any arrangement there approved, is a nullity and the nominee is at risk of costs personally on any subsequent proceedings in relation thereto.

Timing of the meeting of creditors—Where an interim order has not been obtained, r 5.17(1) provides that the meeting of creditors must be held not more than 28 days from the date on which the nominee receives the document and statement referred to in s 256A(2) Where an interim order is in force, the meeting of creditors must be held not less than 14 days from the date on which the nominee's report is filed in court nor more than 28 days from the date on which it is considered by the court.

The reference to 14 days' notice is to 14 days' clear notice being given to a creditor; there is no scope for arguing for 'substantial compliance' with the provision where less than 14 days' clear notice has been given: *Mytre Investments Ltd v Reynolds (No 2)* [1996] BPIR 464 at 468H–470H. This point is relevant to the question of whether a creditor can be said to have had notice of a creditors' meeting 'in accordance with the rules' under s 262(3)(b).

Section 257(2)

Scope of provision—The most obvious source of information regarding the identity of the creditors of a debtor is the statement of affairs submitted to the nominee by the debtor under s 256(2) or s 256A(2). Plainly the nominee should not rely blindly on the list of creditors particularised in the statement of affairs if he has reason to believe that other creditors may exist, given that the subsection is based on the nominee's state of knowledge.

The scope of the term 'creditor'—The scope of the term 'creditor' and related terms is provided for in ss 382, 383 and 385, a point relevant to a proposal by an undischarged bankrupt, on which see s 257(3) and the notes thereto. In *Re A Debtor, JP v A Debtor* [1999] BPIR 206 Sir John Vinelott held that, whilst r 12.3(2) provides that a matrimonial debt is not provable in bankruptcy, a petitioning former wife was a creditor within the scope of s 383(1)(a) and was therefore bound by the arrangement proposed by her former husband.

The term extends not only to unliquidated debts (given the above provisions and the specific language to that effect in r 5.21(3)) but also to future or contingently payable debts: *Re Cancol Ltd* [1996] 1 All ER 37 (Knox J, future payments of rents to fall due under an existing lease) applying to CVAs the reasoning applied by the Court of Appeal in *Doorbar v Alltime Securities Ltd (No 2)* [1995] BCC 1149, which affirmed Knox J at first instance [1994] BCC 728, in relation to individual voluntary arrangements.

The Court of Appeal has expressed the view informally that an IVA may extend to joint debts: *Re Cupit (Note)* [1996] BPIR 560 at 563E–564E (Sir Thomas Bingham MR).

There is no conceptual difficulty in the terms of an arrangement being construed so as to extend to post-arrangement debts, subject to the particular terms and circumstances of each case: *Re Goldspan Ltd* [2003] BPIR 93 (Leslie Kosmin QC sitting as a deputy High Court judge).

Unliquidated debts—Rule 5.21(3) provides that a creditor voting in respect of an unliquidated amount or any debt whose value is not ascertained shall, for voting purposes only, have his debt valued at £1 unless the chairman agrees to put a higher value on it. For further illustrations on the treatment of such creditor claims see *Beverley Group plc v McClue* [1995] BCC 751 (Knox J); *Re Sweatfield Ltd* [1997] BCC 744 (His Honour Judge Weeks QC); *Re Wisepark Ltd* [1994] BCC 221 (untaxed – ie unassessed – litigation costs not a debt for voluntary arrangement purposes) and *County Bookshops Ltd v Grove* [2002] BPIR 772 (Neuberger J, as he then was, contractual instalment payments which had not fallen due as at date of CVA admitted to arrangement as contingent debts). See also the commentary to s 253 above.

Disputed debts—In the case of disputed debts the proper course under r 5.22(4) is for the chairman to mark the claims objected to and allow the creditor to vote for the full amount, on which see *Re A Debtor (No 222 of 1990) ex parte Bank of Ireland* [1992] BCLC 137 at 144F–144H (Harman J).

Court control over the admission of creditor's proof—The court has jurisdiction to direct that a creditor be admitted to proof in an arrangement: *Re FMS Financial Management*

Services Ltd (1989) 5 BCC 191 (Hoffmann J, nominees proposing arrangement directed to admit to proof shareholders with prima facie good claim against the company for misrepresentation).

For the binding effect of an IVA on persons entitled to notice of the creditors' meeting in accordance with the rules, see s 262(2) and the notes thereto.

The importance of complying with s 257(2) was emphasised in *(1) Namulas Pension Trustees Ltd (2) Boyd v (1) Mouzakis (2) Mouzakis (3) Hogg (4) Grant* [2011] BPIR 1724.

Section 257(3)

Scope of provision—This subsection applies only to any proposal made by an undischarged bankrupt. Its effect is to extend the scope of creditors entitled to be summoned to a creditors' meeting under s 257(2) beyond the creditors in the bankruptcy so as to include post-bankruptcy creditors. The rationale behind s 257(3)(b) is self-evident. Without the subsection a debtor could not succeed in binding a post-bankruptcy creditor in any approved arrangement, with the consequence that any such creditor would remain entitled to pursue his debt, ultimately to a second bankruptcy.

'bankruptcy debt'—The scope of bankruptcy debts in delineating the creditors of a debtor under s 257(3) is as provided for in ss 382, 383 and 385.

258 Decisions of creditors' meeting

(1) A creditors' meeting summoned under section 257 shall decide whether to approve the proposed voluntary arrangement.

(2) The meeting may approve the proposed voluntary arrangement with modifications, but shall not do so unless the debtor consents to each modification.

(3) The modifications subject to which the proposed voluntary arrangement may be approved may include one conferring the functions proposed to be conferred on the nominee on another person qualified to act as an insolvency practitioner or authorised to act as nominee, in relation to the voluntary arrangement.

But they shall not include any modification by virtue of which the proposal ceases to be a proposal under this Part.

(4) The meeting shall not approve any proposal or modification which affects the right of a secured creditor of the debtor to enforce his security, except with the concurrence of the creditor concerned.

(5) Subject as follows, the meeting shall not approve any proposal or modification under which—

   (a)   any preferential debt of the debtor is to be paid otherwise than in priority to such of his debts as are not preferential debts, or

   (b)   a preferential creditor of the debtor is to be paid an amount in respect of a preferential debt that bears to that debt a smaller proportion than is borne to another preferential debt by the amount that is to be paid in respect of that other debt.

However, the meeting may approve such a proposal or modification with the concurrence of the preferential creditor concerned.

(6) Subject as above, the meeting shall be conducted in accordance with the rules.

(7) In this section 'preferential debt' has the meaning given by section 386 in Part XII; and 'preferential creditor' is to be construed accordingly.

Amendments—Insolvency Act 2000, s 3, Sch 3, paras 1, 9.

General note—For the procedural rules governing the meeting of creditors see rr 5.17–5.24.

A proposal does not extend to an agreement or other understanding between a third party and creditors where the money from which a distribution is to be made from the third party's 'free money', being money which is not advanced at the cost of the debtor company: *IRC v Wimbledon Football Club Ltd* [2004] EWCA Civ 55, [2005] 1 BCLC 66 at [59] (Neuberger LJ).

Section 258(1)

Scope of provision—Although this subsection places approval of a proposed voluntary arrangement in the hands of 'a creditors' meeting summoned under s 257' alone, the provision cannot be read as requiring a decision to be made at the first such meeting. Indeed, a chairman may adjourn a creditors' meeting under r 5.24(1) without putting the IVA proposal to a vote, on which see the notes to r 5.24.

'with or without modifications'—In practice, proposed modifications, particularly those introduced at the last moment, can create difficulties and may prompt the chairman to consider adjourning the creditors' meeting, even for a short time, under r 5.24(1), where creditors require time to consider their respective positions.

Where modifications are introduced, it is prudent to include a provision of a kind frequently required as a condition of support for a proposal by Crown creditors to the effect that any modification is deemed to override any term in the original proposal where an inconsistency arises between the two.

Section 258(2)

Scope of provision—This subsection should be read in conjunction with s 258(3), which limits the scope of modifications.

'unless the debtor consents to each modification'—In contrast to the position in CVAs, where the debtor company's consent to modifications proposed by creditors is not required, in respet of an IVA, the debtor's consent is a pre-condition of any modification. If a debtor does not consent to a modification, then the arrangement is void in its entirety: *Reid v Hamblin* [2001] BPIR 929 (District Judge Tetlow, Milton Keynes County Court). Furthermore, the debtor's consent is a condition precedent for the approval of a proposal which is itself subject to any proposed modifications since s 258 provides that it is only the creditors' meeting which can give approval, and 'it shall not do so unless the debtor consents': *Re Plummer* [2004] BPIR 767 at [21]–[24] (Registrar Baister).

Section 258(3)

Scope of provision—Any modification altering the identity of the nominee squares with s 253(2) in that the amendment will not deprive the IVA proposal of its status as such.

'... any modification by virtue of which the proposal ceases to be a proposal ...'—Section 258(2) imposes no limitation on the extent of the modifications which may be proposed, subject to the debtor's consent. In practice, such modifications are common enough and may be insisted upon by a significant creditor or creditors as the price for their support of the proposal, subject to the standing of an eligible applicant making application to the court complaining of unfair prejudice or material irregularity under s 262(1). In theory, therefore, there is no good reason why the proposal should not be modified extensively at the meetings stage, provided that the modifications do not fall within the scope of challenge under s 262(1).

The specific limitation imposed by s 258(3) prevents the proposal being modified so as to deprive it of its status as a composition or a scheme of arrangement such that, if approved, the proposal would not constitute a voluntary arrangement as defined in s 253(1).

Section 258(4)

Scope of provision—A proposal or modified proposal is incapable of affecting the rights of the secured creditor 'to enforce his security' other than with the 'concurrence' of the secured creditor. For the definition of 'secured creditor' and of 'security' see s 383.

'**... to enforce his security ...**'—The prohibition in s 258(4) does not safeguard the rights of a non-concurring secured creditor generally, but only the rights of such a creditor 'to enforce his security'. In *Razzaq v Pala* [1998] BCC 66 Lightman J confirmed (in the context of the former s 11(3)(c)) that the term 'security' does not include a landlord's right of re-entry, as Lightman J had previously held to be the case, albeit without full argument on the point, in *March Estates plc v Gunmark Ltd* [1996] BPIR 439. The adoption of Lightman J's approach in *Razzaq* by the House of Lords in *Re Park Air Services plc* [1999] 2 WLR 396 confirms that a landlord's right of re-entry does not constitute security for the performance of lease covenants, including, most obviously, a covenant for the payment of rent reserved. It follows that an IVA may affect the right of a landlord to exercise his right of re-entry under a lease without the concurrence of the landlord, subject to the standing of the landlord to challenge such a decision as unfairly prejudicial under s 262(1)(a). A voluntary arrangement is capable of modifying a landlord's right as a creditor in relation to reserved rent, including arrears and/or future rent: *Re Cancol Ltd* [1996] 1 All ER 37. In *Re Naeem (a Bankrupt)* [1990] 1 WLR 48 at 50 Hoffmann J (as he then was) rejected a landlord's complaint of unfair prejudice and held that, in keeping with the modification of the claims of other creditors, the right of the landlord to forfeit under a lease should operate for the recovery of rent as modified by the arrangement and not the landlord's original claim. The decision in *Re Naeem*, it is submitted, is consistent with that in *Razzaq*.

It is suggested that there are at least two obvious reasons why the reasoning of Hoffmann J in *Re Naeem*, as it applies to the modification of a landlord's claim for rent, would not apply to a debt due to a creditor secured by a mortgage or charge. First, a mortgagee or chargee obtains an immediate proprietary interest by way of security in the debtor's property, which encumbrance the debtor is only able to discharge through payment in full of the underlying indebtedness. A landlord, on the other hand, obtains no such proprietary interest in the debtor's property but enjoys instead proprietary *remedies* (forfeiture, re-entry etc) which are exercisable in relation to the leased property. Secondly, it is extremely unlikely that Parliament could have intended to allow for the modification of the security rights of a non-concurring mortgage or charge holder under the terms of a voluntary arrangement where, as is the case, the same rights would be unaffected by the process of liquidation or administration.

'**... except with the concurrence of the creditor concerned ...**'—The word 'concurrence', it is suggested, would allow for the passive acquiescence of a secured creditor as something distinct from the pro-active approval on the part of the same creditor which would otherwise have been required if the word 'consent' had been employed in the provision. As such, it would appear that a secured creditor will be bound by any modification to his security rights, in terms of the enforcement of such rights, merely by virtue of that creditor being entitled to vote at the creditors' meeting within the meaning of s 260(2)(b) and doing nothing, but not, it would appear, if the secured creditor did not have actual notice of the meeting, since in those circumstances he could not be said to have concurred with the modification approved.

A secured creditor is not automatically deemed to have waived its security rights through the acceptance of a dividend under a voluntary arrangement: *Whitehead v Household Mortgage Corporation* [2002] EWCA Civ 1657; compare *Khan v Permayer* [2001] BPIR 95.

Section 258(5)

Scope of provision—This subsection prohibits the variation of the priority status afforded to preferential debts and the treatment of any preferential debt vis-à-vis other preferential debts other than with the concurrence of the preferential creditor concerned.

A decision under s 258(1) cannot take away the priority afforded to preferential debts by statute. Neither is a voluntary arrangement capable of modifying the claim of a single preferential creditor such that the reduction in that preferential creditor's claim would be greater than the reduction suffered by any other preferential creditor.

For the meaning of 'preferential debts' and 'preferential creditors' see s 258(7). On the term 'concurrence' see the note to s 258(4) above.

Section 258(6)

Scope of provision—For the relevant rules see rr 5.17–5.24. Note also rr 5.25–5.34 which relate to implementation of the arrangement.

Subject to s 258(2)–(5), a meeting which is not conducted in accordance with rr 5.17–5.24 will not, by virtue of s 258(6), constitute a creditors' meeting for the purposes of s 258(1), even if summoned in compliance with s 257.

Section 258(7)

Scope of provision—Where the debtor is not an undischarged bankrupt, the 'relevant date' for the assessment of preferential debts is the date of any interim order made under s 252 or, where no interim order is made, the date on which the arrangement takes effect: s 387(5). Where the debtor is an undischarged bankrupt, the 'relevant date' is the date of the bankruptcy order or the date of the appointment of an interim receiver where such an appointment was made after presentation of the bankruptcy petition but prior to the bankruptcy order: s 387(6).

259 Report of decisions to court

(1) After the conclusion in accordance with the rules of the meeting summoned under section 257, the chairman of the meeting shall—

    (a)   give notice of the result of the meeting to such persons as may be prescribed, and

    (b)   where the meeting was summoned under section 257 pursuant to a report to the court under section 256(1)(aa), report the result of it to the court.(2) If the report is that the meeting has declined (with or without modifications) to approve the voluntary arrangement proposed under section 256, the court may discharge any interim order which is in force in relation to the debtor.

Amendments—SI 2010/18.

General note—The filing of the chairman's report with the court amounts to a reporting obligation only and has no substantive consequence. The IVA comes into being as a consequence of approval under s 258 alone; the court is not involved in the ongoing conduct of the arrangement in the absence of an application to it.

Rule 5.27(1) provides that a report of the creditors' meeting is to be prepared by the chairman. Just as there is only one creditors' meeting – which may be adjourned – so there is only a single chairman's report; the legislation does not provide for or envisage any sort of interim report: *Re Symes* [1995] 2 BCLC 651 at 666E–666F (James Munby QC, sitting as a deputy High Court judge). Rule 5.27(2) prescribes the contents of the report, which must be filed with the court under r 5.27(3) within four business days of the meeting being held. The chairman must also send a notice of the result of the meeting – but not necessarily a copy of the chairman's report – to all those persons who were sent notice of each of the meetings summoned under s 257 and any other creditor of whom the chairman is aware, as well as the official receiver and the trustee-in-bankruptcy (if any) where the debtor is an undischarged bankrupt.

Section 259(2)

Scope of provision—Although the court has an unlimited discretion under this provision, the only power conferred on the court is a power to discharge the interim order or to decline to discharge the interim order; the court has no power to extend the period for which the interim order has effect or to authorise the calling of a further creditors' meeting: *Re Symes* [1995] 2 BCLC 651 at 669H–670A. The practical utility in the court declining to discharge the interim order is in affording a debtor some final breathing space in appropriate circumstances or in affording protection to the debtor where the court is satisfied that the making of an application under s 262 challenging the arrangement will follow.

260 Effect of approval

(1) This section has effect where the meeting summoned under section 257 approves the proposed voluntary arrangement (with or without modifications).

(2) The approved arrangement—

    (a)   takes effect as if made by the debtor at the meeting, and

    (b)   binds every person who in accordance with the rules—

        (i)   was entitled to vote at the meeting (whether or not he was present or represented at it), or

        (ii)   would have been so entitled if he had had notice of it,

as if he were a party to the arrangement.

(2A) If—

    (a)   when the arrangement ceases to have effect any amount payable under the arrangement to a person bound by virtue of subsection (2)(b)(ii) has not been paid, and

    (b)   the arrangement did not come to an end prematurely,

the debtor shall at that time become liable to pay to that person the amount payable under the arrangement.

(3) The Deeds of Arrangement Act 1914 does not apply to the approved voluntary arrangement.

(4) Any interim order in force in relation to the debtor immediately before the end of the period of 28 days beginning with the day on which the report with respect to the creditors' meeting was made to the court under section 259 ceases to have effect at the end of that period.

This subsection applies except to such extent as the court may direct for the purposes of any application under section 262 below.

(5) Where proceedings on a bankruptcy petition have been stayed by an interim order which ceases to have effect under subsection (4), the petition is deemed, unless the court otherwise orders, to have been dismissed.

Amendments—Insolvency Act 2000, s 3, Sch 3, paras 1, 10.

General note—Only the meeting of creditors summoned under s 257 is capable of bringing an IVA into effect. An approved arrangement remains in force until either revoked by way of a modification validly approved by creditors or until the making of any order setting aside the arrangement under s 262.

Section 260(2)

Scope of provision—This is a deeming provision which provides for the binding nature of the IVA. The effect of the arrangement taking effect as if made by the debtor operates so as to bind the debtor to the arrangement.

Section 260(2)(a)

Scope of provision—The word 'made' replaced the word 'approved' by amendment under Sch 5 of the Insolvency Act 2000.

Section 260(2)(b)

The meaning of 'notice'—This new provision was inserted by s 3 of the Insolvency Act 2000 and Sch 3 thereto and represents a significant change from the previous position. Formerly, it had been held that a creditor must have actual notice of the creditors' meeting so as to be bound by the arrangement; in particular, the court had rejected the operation of a doctrine of deemed notice: see *Re a Debtor (No 64 of 1992)* [1994] BCC 55, and *Skipton Building Society v Collins* [1998] BPIR 267 (Jonathan Parker J). The court had, however, been prepared to find that proper notice had been given where it had been obtained from a third party, as in *Beverley Group plc v McClue* [1995] 2 BCLC 407 (Knox J). The new provision does away with the requirement for actual notice. Instead, s 260(2)(b) binds two classes of person (see below) as party to the IVA on the assumption that any such person would have been entitled to vote at the creditors' meeting. In this regard, r 5.21(1) (entitlement to vote) must be read in light of s 260(2)(b) to the extent that the former provision refers to 'every creditor who has notice of the creditors' meeting'; s 260(2)(b) suggests that those words must be interpreted as meaning every creditor who has notice or would have been entitled to have had notice of the creditors' meeting.

The two classes of person within s 260(2)(b)—The two classes of person bound by s 260(2)(b) are (i) every person entitled to vote at the creditors' meeting (ie who had notice of the meeting, irrespective of whether or not he was present or represented), or (ii) any person who would have been entitled to have had such notice (ie irrespective of whether such notice was received or otherwise communicated). Class (i) will not extend to a person who is not entitled to vote at the creditors' meeting: *RA Securities Ltd v Mercantile Credit Co Ltd* [1994] BCC 598 at 600H (Jacob J, as he then was); and see also *Burford Midland Properties Ltd v Marley Extrusions Ltd* [1994] BCC 604 (His Honour Judge Roger Cooke sitting as a High Court judge). Class (ii) will catch both creditors who are not known to the nominee summoning the creditors' meeting and also creditors who are known but to whom notice is not given through, say, an administrative oversight or even a deliberate omission.

Failure to give notice as ground for alleging unfair prejudice/material irregularity under s 262—The fact of a creditor being bound by an arrangement under s 260(2)(b) in circumstances where that creditor can establish, as a matter of fact, that it had not been given notice of the creditors' meeting is capable of founding an application alleging material irregularity and/or, possibly, unfair prejudice under s 262(1), but only where that creditor would have been capable of affecting or influencing the outcome of the creditors' meeting.

Unliquidated, future or contingent debts, co-debtors and third parties—For the treatment of unliquidated, future or contingent debts in an IVA and the position of co-debtors and third parties, see the notes to s 253 above.

The effect of an arrangement on assignees—Subject to an effective contrary term within an arrangement, the assignee of a contractual right which is modified by an arrangement prior to assignment acquires only the benefit of that right as modified by the arrangement. In the context of leases it is well established that an assignee may reach agreement with his landlord to alter the terms on which the assignee holds the estate so as to bind an original tenant: *Baynton v Morgan* (1888) 22 QBD 74; and see *Centrovincial Estates plc v Bulk Storage Ltd* (1983) 46 PCR 393. Whether or not future rent under a lease falls within the scope of the arrangement as a prospective debt will depend on the particular terms and construction of the arrangement. Note that, pursuant to the decision of the Court of Appeal in *Kapoor v (1) National Westminster Bank plc (2) Tan* [2011] EWCA Civ 1083 [2011] BPIR 1680 an assignee of a creditor is able to vote at a meeting of creditors called to consider an IVA proposal.

Single creditor with a claim within and a claim outside of the arrangement—One problem which may arise in relation to s 260(2)(b) concerns the position where a creditor maintains two separate claims against the debtor where one of the claims does not fall plainly within the scope of the arrangement. The decision of Knox J in *Doorbar v Alltime Securities Ltd* [1994] BCC 994 involved claims by a landlord in respect of arrears and interest for a liquidated sum together with a further claim for the aggregate of rent prospectively payable until the end of the contractual term of the lease, disregarding possible upward rent reviews. At 1000E of his judgment Knox J opined that a creditor entitled to vote in respect of one debt was not bound by an approved arrangement in respect of a different debt if (as was the case on the facts of *Doorbar*) the creditor was not entitled to vote in respect of that different debt. That position appears to have been assumed in the judgment of the Court of Appeal given by Peter Gibson LJ: see [1995] BCC 1149 at 1155C. That view, as expressed, however, runs contrary to the decision of Rimer J in *Re Bradley-Hole (a Bankrupt)* [1995] BCC 418 at 434B–434C which held that a creditor is bound by an arrangement in respect of both debts where one carried an entitlement to vote and the other did not. This problem is probably now more apparent than real following the Court of Appeal's decision in *Doorbar* and the finding (at 1157E) that a chairman is entitled to place an estimated minimum value on an unliquidated debt for voting purposes, on which see now the express wording in r 5.21(3) and the notes to that provision. Where a creditor disagrees with that minimum value it can hardly be said that the creditor has no entitlement to vote for the purposes of s 260(2)(b). In *Peterkin v London Borough of Merton and Another* [2011] EWHC 376 (Ch), [2012] BPIR 388, Vos J held that a moratorium imposed by an IVA could not preclude a participating creditor from seeking to enforce a debt which arose after the IVA and which were outside the scope of the IVA. *Cornelius v Casson* [2008] BPIR 504 is another example of a case in which the court (Thomas Ivory QC, sitting as a deputy High Court Judge) considered which debts of a participating creditor fell within an IVA.

Where the chairman declines to admit a claim for unliquidated damages and attributes to it only a nominal value, in circumstances where the same creditor is admitted to the arrangement for a liquidated sum relating to a separate debt so as to be bound by it in respect of the liquidated debt, any entitlement to pursue the unliquidated claim outside of the terms of the arrangement will depend on a construction of the terms of the IVA. In *Sea Voyager Maritime Inc v Bielecki (t/a Hughes Hooker & Co)* [1999] 1 BCLC 133 at 150–151, Richard McCombe QC, sitting as he then was as a deputy High Court judge, held that it was implicit in the terms of that particular arrangement that those bound by it were prevented from commencing or pursuing proceedings outside of the arrangement. No such bar was held to have been implied in the less elaborately drawn arrangement considered by Rimer J in *Alman v Approach Housing Ltd* [2001] BPIR 203. Ultimately, the implication of a term into an IVA turns on whether the term is necessary to give efficacy to the arrangement; although such terms will not be implied lightly: see *Johnson v Davies* [1999] Ch 117 at 128G–128H (Chadwick LJ).

Single creditor pursuing only part of single debt in arrangement—What of the position where a single creditor seeks to be bound only in respect of part of that debt? It is submitted that that possibility now seems doubtful, given the revised wording in s 260(2)(b)(i).

In *Re CJ Hoare* [1997] BPIR 683 Edward Nugee QC, sitting as a deputy High Court judge, held (at 695D), following the decision of the Court of Appeal in *Doorbar v Alltime Securities Ltd* and adopting the approach of Knox J in *Re Cancol Ltd* [1996] 1 All ER 37, that it is not open to a creditor to put an estimated figure on his debt which is stated as being subject to verification and possible amendment only to claim later that he is owed some other debt which was not included in the original figure and in respect of which he is not bound by the arrangement. Whilst the deputy judge accepted the possibility of a distinction being drawn between two separate debts arising out of the same claim (at 694G), it now seems unlikely, given the amended form of s 260(2), that a single debt might be divided so as to allow part of it to be pursued outside of the arrangement other than where the terms of the arrangement expressly provide for such an outcome.

The court's approach to the construction of voluntary arrangements—The judgment of Blackburne J in *Welsby v Brelec Installations Ltd* [2000] 2 BCLC 576 concerned in part the construction of certain express terms employed in a CVA for the purpose of determining if and when there had been 'failure' for the purposes of that arrangement. The following passage (at 585I–586B), it is submitted, will be of general assistance in construing the express terms of a voluntary arrangement:

'An arrangement is usually put together with some haste. Modifications to it are frequently made at the statutory meeting of creditors with little time to reflect on how they relate to the other terms of the debtor's proposal. Quite often, as this case demonstrates, the resulting terms are clumsily worded. The arrangement ought therefore to be construed in a practical fashion. Otherwise there is a risk that careless drafting coupled with a too-literal approach to its construction will serve to frustrate rather than achieve the purpose of the arrangement. The underlying purpose in most arrangements – and certainly this one – is to provide the arrangement creditors with a means of debt recovery which avoids the need to have recourse to the formal and more expensive mechanisms of winding-up or administration (or bankruptcy in the case of an individual) and, if the arrangement is successful, to give the debtor the chance to continue trading in the longer term.'

Although necessarily based on the specific terms employed in each particular case, examples of the court's broad approach to construction of the terms of an arrangement can be found in *Re Energy Holdings (No 3) Ltd (in liquidation)* [2008] BPIR 1473 (Morritt C) and *Simpson v Bowker* [2008] BPIR 1114, CA. In construing the terms of an IVA, and by analogy with CVAs, it must be borne in mind that the IVA must be read as a whole, and further that specific terms must not be analysed so closely as to overlook the overall commercial context or the practical consequences: see *Tucker and Spratt (Joint Supervisors of Energy Holdings (No 3) (In Liquidation) v Gold Fields Mining LLC* [2009] EWCA Civ 173 [2009] BPIR 704.

The implication of terms into an arrangement—As regards terms implied into a voluntary arrangement, given that an arrangement is ordinarily a lengthy and complex document and has the effect by statutory force under s 260(2) of binding all creditors entitled to notice of it, it is perhaps not surprising that the court will be very slow to imply a term unless it is absolutely necessary to give efficacy to an arrangement. In the words of Chadwick LJ in *Johnson v Davies* [1998] 2 BCLC 252 at 270A–270B, in the context of a case which considered whether an arrangement was capable of releasing a co-debtor from liability:

'Under Part VIII of the 1986 Act, the discharge of the debtor depends entirely on the terms of the arrangement. One must look at the arrangement, and nothing else, in order to find the terms (if any) under which the debtor is discharged. This is emphasised by the words in s 260(2) of the 1986 Act ...'

Section 260(2A)

Scope of provision—This provision was inserted by Insolvency Act 2000, s 3 and Sch 3. Its effect is such that, where an arrangement does not end prematurely, a creditor who is bound by an arrangement but has not had notice of it by virtue of s 260(2)(b)(ii) is entitled to any sum due to him under the arrangement to the extent that that creditor has not already been paid.

For the meaning of the term 'comes to an end prematurely' see s 262C.

Section 260(3)

Deeds of Arrangement Act 1914—The express disapplication of the 1914 Act avoids any suggestion that an IVA might otherwise be deemed void for non-registration and stamping in accordance with those earlier provisions which have little relevance in modern practice.

Section 260(4) and (5)

Lapse of certain interim orders and effect on extant bankruptcy petition—In the absence of contrary order, an interim order will cease to have effect at the end of the 28-day period beginning with the day on which the chairman's report of the creditors' meeting under s 259 is filed with the court.

On the cessation of an interim order under s 260(4), any bankruptcy petition stayed by virtue of s 252(2)(a) is deemed dismissed by virtue of s 260(5), subject to contrary order of the court.

261 Additional effect on undischarged bankrupt

(1) This section applies where—

  (a)   the creditors' meeting summoned under section 257 approves the proposed voluntary arrangement (with or without modifications), and

  (b)   the debtor is an undischarged bankrupt.

(2) Where this section applies the court shall annul the bankruptcy order on an application made—

  (a)   by the bankrupt, or

  (b)   where the bankrupt has not made an application within the prescribed period, by the official receiver.

(3) An application under subsection (2) may not be made—

  (a)   during the period specified in section 262(3)(a) during which the decision of the creditors' meeting can be challenged by application under section 262,

  (b)   while an application under that section is pending, or

  (c)   while an appeal in respect of an application under that section is pending or may be brought.

(4) Where this section applies the court may give such directions about the conduct of the bankruptcy and the administration of the bankrupt's estate as it thinks appropriate for facilitating the implementation of the approved voluntary arrangement.

Amendments—Enterprise Act 2002, s 264(1), Sch 22, para 1.

General note—This provision provides for the annulment of the bankruptcy order where a creditors' meeting summoned under s 257 approves an IVA proposed by an undischarged bankrupt. The annulment is not automatic and requires an application by either the bankrupt within the prescribed period (ie 28 days) or by the official receiver, but only where the bankrupt has not made an application within the prescribed period: see s 261(2). Such an application may not be made, however, in any of the three circumstances in s 261(3) which each relate to an application or an appeal from an order under s 262.

The strategic advantage to a debtor of annulment under s 261—Annulment of a bankruptcy order is usually, though not always, the motive behind an undischarged bankrupt seeking approval of an IVA. Assuming the bankruptcy order to be beyond procedural challenge under s 282(1)(a), the only other alternative route to annulment for an undischarged bankrupt is in seeking to satisfy the court under s 282(1)(b) that the bankruptcy debts and expenses of the bankruptcy have been paid or secured for. Since there is no requirement that an annulment under s 261 is dependent on unsecured creditors being paid in full in the IVA – the debtor's proposal as to dividends or returns to creditors in the IVA is a matter for the requisite majority of the unsecured creditors alone – a debtor may find an annulment via this provision less expensive than under s 282(1)(b).

There is an additional potential for the saving of expense where a bankrupt, whose bankruptcy estate comprises assets not yet realised, is able to procure third party funds for the purpose of providing returns to creditors in an IVA since, in those circumstances, the sums arising from the realisation of the bankruptcy estate will not fall subject to the DTI levy which would arise on payments being made into the Insolvency Services Account by a trustee-in-bankruptcy.

Procedure—Rules 6.206–6.212 formerly applied to a s 261 annulment application as they did to an application under s 282(1)(a) by virtue of r 6.212A until that provision was revoked with effect from 1 April 2004 by the Insolvency (Amendment) Rules 2003 (SI 2003/1730). The contents of the court's order and the requirements regarding advertisement remain as in r 6.213.

An application for annulment will proceed by way of an ordinary application in the bankruptcy proceedings and will usually be issued with a witness statement or affidavit in support: see the notes to r 7.3. Although the legislation makes no such stipulation, it is suggested that the respondents to the application should normally include the creditor upon whose petition the bankruptcy order was made and the trustee-in-bankruptcy. There are also good reasons why the official receiver should at least be given notice of the application and be permitted to report to or appear before the court if the official receiver considers such action appropriate.

262 Challenge of meeting's decision

(1) Subject to this section, an application to the court may be made, by any of the persons specified below, on one or both of the following grounds, namely—

    (a)   that a voluntary arrangement approved by a creditors' meeting summoned under section 257 unfairly prejudices the interests of a creditor of the debtor;

    (b)   that there has been some material irregularity at or in relation to such a meeting.

(2) The persons who may apply under this section are—

    (a)   the debtor;

    (b)   a person who—

        (i)   was entitled, in accordance with the rules, to vote at the creditors' meeting, or

        (ii)   would have been so entitled if he had had notice of it;

    (c)   the nominee (or his replacement under section 256(3), 256A(4) or 258(3)); and

    (d)   if the debtor is an undischarged bankrupt, the trustee of his estate or the official receiver.

(3) An application under this section shall not be made—

    (a)   after the end of the period of 28 days beginning with the day on which the report of the creditors' meeting was made to the court under section 259, or

    (b)   in the case of a person who was not given notice of the creditors' meeting, after the end of the period of 28 days beginning with the day on which he became aware that the meeting had taken place,

but (subject to that) an application made by a person within subsection (2)(b)(ii) on the ground that the arrangement prejudices his interests may be made after the arrangement has ceased to have effect, unless it has come to an end prematurely.

(4) Where on an application under this section the court is satisfied as to either of the grounds mentioned in subsection (1), it may do one or both of the following, namely—

    (a)   revoke or suspend any approval given by the meeting;

(b)   give a direction to any person for the summoning of a further meeting of the debtor's creditors to consider any revised proposal he may make or, in a case falling within subsection (1)(b), to reconsider his original proposal.

(5) Where at any time after giving a direction under subsection (4)(b) for the summoning of a meeting to consider a revised proposal the court is satisfied that the debtor does not intend to submit such a proposal, the court shall revoke the direction and revoke or suspend any approval given at the previous meeting.

(6) Where the court gives a direction under subsection (4)(b), it may also give a direction continuing or, as the case may require, renewing, for such period as may be specified in the direction, the effect in relation to the debtor of any interim order.

(7) In any case where the court, on an application made under this section with respect to a creditors' meeting, gives a direction under subsection (4)(b) or revokes or suspends an approval under subsection (4)(a) or (5), the court may give such supplemental directions as it thinks fit and, in particular, directions with respect to—

(a)   things done since the meeting under any voluntary arrangement approved by the meeting, and

(b)   such things done since the meeting as could not have been done if an interim order had been in force in relation to the debtor when they were done.

(8) Except in pursuance of the preceding provisions of this section, an approval given at a creditors' meeting summoned under section 257 is not invalidated by any irregularity at or in relation to the meeting.

Amendments—Insolvency Act 2000, s 3, Sch 3, paras 1, 11(1)(a), (b), (2)(a), (b).

General note—This section allows for an application to court by any of the applicants within s 262(2) on either or both of the grounds identified in s 262(1), either of which may extend to breach of a substantive statutory prohibition: *IRC v Wimbeldon Football Club Ltd* [2004] EWCA Civ 655, [2005] 1 BCLC 66 at [37] (Neuberger LJ). The use of the words 'an application to the court may be made' in s 262(1) together with the reference to 'a voluntary arrangement approved by a creditors' meeting' in s 262(1)(a) (to which s 262(1)(b) implicitly makes reference) strongly suggests that an application may only be made once an arrangement has actually been approved by creditors such that no grounds are available for an application in respect of prospective or anticipated unfair prejudice or material irregularity prior to approval of the arrangement.

The court has wide powers under s 262(4)–(6) to tailor its order to the circumstances of the case, including the revocation of the approval of the voluntary arrangement or directions for the summoning of further meetings to consider either the original proposal or any revised proposal with which the debtor seeks to proceed. Many of the reported first instance decisions on applications under s 262 (and its equivalent in s 6 in relation to company voluntary arrangements) are of very limited assistance in terms of general application, given that the grounds in s 262(1), and any order or direction made by the court, in any particular case, necessarily depend on the particular facts of each such case.

Save for s 262, an application to court may also be available under s 263(3): see the notes to that subsection. A creditor or member of the company may also appeal the chairman's decision on the admission of any creditor claim for voting purposes under r 5.22(3). The 28-day time limit imposed by s 262, which is not extendable by the court, is of considerable practical significance, since it is doubtful that the court retains any inherent jurisdiction to revoke or otherwise stay a voluntary arrangement, given the specific terms in which s 262 is drafted.

Section 262(1)(a)

Scope of provision—The language of the subsection requires that the unfair prejudice complained of must be caused by the voluntary arrangement, and not merely the voluntary arrangement itself taking effect through statutory force under s 258(1) and s 260(2).

In *Re A Debtor (No 222 of 1990) ex parte Bank of Ireland* [1992] BCLC 137 at 145C–145G Harman J considered that s 262(1)(a) 'plainly looks at the arrangement itself and requires consideration of whether it prejudices the creditor, presumably because of some differential treatment, some restriction upon the creditors or some advantage to another creditor so that there is an unfair prejudice by reason of the voluntary arrangement itself'; see also *Re A Debtor (No 87 of 1993) (No 2)* [1996] 1 BCLC 63 at 86 (Rimer J) in which, having cited and relied upon the above passage, counsel for the claimant was forced to abandon an argument to the effect that the court may embark upon consideration of the overall merits of the arrangement on an unfair prejudice complaint and to accept that there is no relevant prejudice to any creditor if each creditor under the scheme is put in the same position as the other creditors and suffers no discriminatory treatment as a consequence. Section 262(1)(b), on the other hand, 'seems plainly to divide the matter into events occurring at the meeting which are wrong, which are irregularities, and matters in relation to the voluntary arrangement which could be unfairly prejudicial.' Accordingly, a wrong decision at a meeting to exclude or prohibit a vote gives rise to a complaint of material irregularity and not unfair prejudice.

To similar effect, in *Peck v Craighead* [1995] 1 BCLC 337 Martin Mann QC, sitting as a deputy High Court judge, observed at 343E that 'Irregularity involving unlawfulness at a meeting of creditors is conceptually different from unfair prejudice which predicates unfairness inherent in a proposal or modification which otherwise lawfully affects a creditor's interest.'

'... unfairly prejudices the interests of the creditor, member or contributory of the company'—The term 'unfairly prejudicial' is also employed in s 994 of the Companies Act 2006, ss 459 and 460 of the Companies Act 1985 which, together with their predecessors in the Companies Acts of 1948 and 1980, have given rise to a plethora of reported case law. The term 'unfairly prejudicial' is, however, employed in a very different context in s 994 of the 2006 Act in that it relates to the conduct of the management of a company. As a consequence, authorities on s 994 and its predecessors are unlikely to be of any assistance in the present context, on which see the comments in *Doorbar v Alltime Securities Ltd* [1995] BCC 1149 at 1159A (Peter Gibson LJ).

The meaning and scope of unfair prejudice—In the context of voluntary arrangements, the term 'unfairly prejudices' has not been the subject of very detailed analysis in any of the authorities. At least two key principles, however, are clear enough. First, the unfair prejudice must result from the arrangement itself: *Re A Debtor (No 222 of 1990) ex parte Bank of Ireland* [1992] BCLC 137. Secondly, whether the interests of an applicant are unfairly prejudiced requires the court to consider all the circumstances of the case: *Re A Debtor (No 101 of 1999)* [2001] 1 BCLC 54 at 63D (Ferris J). It is not sufficient that an applicant establishes mere prejudice resulting from the arrangement; rather, the prejudice must be unfair.

In *Doorbar v Alltime Securities Ltd* [1995] BCC 1149 the Court of Appeal upheld a finding of Knox J at first instance to the effect that a landlord, who was precluded from petitioning for bankruptcy of the debtor on the arrangement taking effect, with the consequence that the landlord could not rely on a clause in the lease which required that the debtor and his wife would take a new lease on the debtor's bankruptcy, was prejudiced by the arrangement, but not unfairly prejudiced. The taking into account of all relevant circumstances required the court to balance the prejudice to the landlord in having its rights against the debtor's wife restricted on the one hand, and the prejudice to the general body of creditors in being prevented from having the benefits of any voluntary arrangement (which included future payments of rent) under the lease on the other. Accordingly, the court would not exercise its discretion in interfering with the arrangement.

Differential treatment of creditors which is not assented to by a creditor who considers that he has been less favourably treated than other creditors may give cause for an inquiry but does not of itself necessarily establish unfair prejudice in that there may well be an explanation justifying such differential treatment. In *Re A Debtor (No 101 of 1999)* [2001]

1 BCLC 54 Ferris J overturned the decision of the judge below who had failed to consider all of the circumstances of the case in this regard. At a meeting of creditors, various friends of the debtor, with a collective claim of £440,000, approved an arrangement whereby a sum of £20,000 would be introduced by a third party, which sum, subject to costs and expenses of £5,000, would leave some £15,000 in discharge of the Crown's debt of £77,000 whilst doing nothing to modify the total indebtedness due to the debtor's friends. The use of the friends' voting power to achieve a differential treatment for the Crown, whilst at the same time preserving their rights and remedies in full, was held to constitute unfair prejudice. The court was, however, prepared to allow the debtor a direction under s 262(4)(b) for the summoning of a further meeting of creditors to consider a revised proposal.

Cases on unfair prejudice—For further cases on unfair prejudice see *Cadbury Schweppes plc v Somji* [2001] 1 WLR 615, CA (secret deal with two creditors inducing their support of a voluntary arrangement not unfairly prejudicial but a fraud on creditors); *National Westminster Bank plc v Scher* [1998] BPIR 224 (John Martin QC, sitting as a deputy High Court judge, no unfair prejudice to two bank creditors prevented from enforcing rights against debtor's wife under terms of arrangement where wife had no separate assets or income); *Sea Voyager Maritime Inc v Bielecki (t/a Hughes Hooker & Co)* [1999] 1 BCLC 133 (Richard McCombe QC (as he then was) creditor unfairly prejudiced by arrangement which prevented creditor from proceeding to judgment against debtor with consequence that creditor unable to make recovery from debtor's insurers under the Third Parties (Rights Against Insurers) Act 1930); *Re Naeem (a Bankrupt) (No 18 of 1988)* [1990] 1 WLR 48 (Hoffmann J (as he then was), arrangement reducing debtor's liability for rent for which landlord retained usual enforcement remedies prejudicial but not unfairly prejudicial to landlord); and *Re Cancol Ltd* [1995] BCC 1133 (Knox J, no unfair prejudice to landlord under terms of arrangement providing for landlord to be paid either rent in full whilst debtor occupied premises or a dividend on premises being vacated where landlord not deprived of right of forfeiture on rent ceasing to be paid in full). A creditor may also apply to court alleging unfair prejudice where an arrangement has the effect of releasing a co-debtor against whom that creditor would otherwise have a right of action: *Johnson v Davies* [1998] 3 WLR 1299 at 1317B (Chadwick LJ). *Child Maintenance and Enforcement Commission v Beesley and Whyman* [2010] EWCA Civ 1344 (Ch), [2011] BPIR 608 was a case in which CMEC brought a challenge in the context of an individual voluntary arrangement and in which the Court of Appeal considered CMEC's alternative contention that the voluntary arrangement was unfairly prejudicial. Both at first instance in that case, and on appeal, the Court concluded that the voluntary arrangement was unfairly prejudicial to CMEC.

Unfair prejudice based on lower projected dividend than in bankruptcy—It is submitted that an allegation that the interests of a creditor are unfairly prejudiced on the sole ground that the approved arrangement will produce a lower return to a class of creditors than that projected on bankruptcy (or liquidation) will be bound to fail, since an arrangement cannot unfairly prejudice the interests of a creditor where the modification of a creditor's entitlement comes about through the operation of an arrangement with statutory force consequent upon the approval of the prescribed requisite majority of creditors.

Section 262(1)(b)

The meaning and scope of material irregularity—Section 262(8) expressly provides that, in the absence of an application under s 262, the mere fact of an irregularity at or in relation to either the company meeting or the meeting of creditors does not of itself invalidate any decision in relation to the arrangement. To obtain a remedy under s 262 an applicant must establish not only an irregularity but also the fact of its materiality: *Re Sweatfield Ltd* [1997] BCC 744 at 750E (His Honour Judge Weeks QC, sitting as a High Court judge).

In *Cadbury Schweppes plc v Somji* [2001] 1 WLR 615 at 626 Robert Walker LJ, as he then was, identified that the test for materiality is whether objectively assessed an error or omission 'would be likely to have made a material difference to the way in which creditors would have considered and assessed the terms of the proposed IVA'. That test is not the same as asking whether votes cast at a further creditors' meeting would produce any different result: *Monecar (London) Ltd v Ahmed* [2008] BPIR 458 at [17] (Paul Chaisty QC, sitting as a deputy High Court judge).

Perhaps the most obvious form of material irregularity in relation to meetings concerns the assertion and treatment of voting rights. In *Doorbar v Alltime Securities Ltd* [1995] BCC 1149 at 1158D–1158H the Court of Appeal, upholding the decision of Knox J below, rejected an allegation of material irregularity by a landlord in circumstances where the chairman of the creditors' meeting had placed a minimum value of one year's rent on the landlord's claim in making allowance for the possibility that the landlord would exercise its power of re-entry and, in so doing, had rejected the landlord's claim for the aggregate of the whole of the future rent under the lease. Given that the chairman's approach was entirely reasonable, and that the landlord would only have had 25% or more of the voting power of the meeting if the estimated value of its claim was increased threefold, there could be no material irregularity

In *Commissioners of Inland Revenue v Duce* [1999] BPIR 189 Hazel Williamson QC, sitting as a deputy High Court judge, considered an allegation of material irregularity by the Inland Revenue where a debtor had failed to disclose the fact that a significant creditor supporting approval of the arrangement had taken assignment of the debt from a company in which the debtor had a substantial interest and where the debtor had failed to identify accurately the creditor which was to purchase the debtor's property for full market value less £90,000 so as to produce funds in full and final settlement of all creditor claims. The deputy judge took the view that the judge below had erred in principle in failing to undertake a balancing exercise which took full account of the circumstances of the case, namely the seriousness and heinousness of the irregularity on the one hand, and the likely attitude of the other creditors on the other. On the basis that creditors ought to be given the opportunity to reconsider an arrangement with knowledge of the proper facts, the deputy judge directed the re-convening of the creditors' meeting and overturned the decision of the judge below which had revoked approval of the arrangement and directed that no further meeting of creditors should be convened.

Material irregularity may also arise by virtue of a meeting failing to acknowledge the security rights of a creditor whose consent would otherwise be required for the modification of such rights. For example, in *Peck v Craighead* [1995] 1 BCLC 337 Martin Mann QC, sitting as a deputy High Court judge, found material irregularity under s 262(1)(b) where the meeting of creditors had approved an arrangement which envisaged the sale of chattels which had been used by the debtors but over which the complainant creditor had obtained a writ of fieri facias and walking possession pursuant to a consent judgment. Given that the complainant creditor had not consented to the modification of what amounted to its rights as a secured creditor, the deputy judge held that the approval constituted a material irregularity, as a consequence of which the complainant creditor's execution could proceed notwithstanding the approval of the arrangement.

It is plainly arguable that an application may be made under s 262(1)(b) by a creditor who is bound by an arrangement through the operation of s 260(2)(b) where the creditor would have been entitled at the creditors' meeting but did not have notice of it in circumstances where that creditor could have affected or influenced the outcome of the meeting: see, for example, *Tager v Westpac Banking Corp* [1997] 1 BCLC 313 at 325F–325G (His Honour Judge Weeks QC, sitting as a High Court judge).

In *Coutts & Co v Passey* [2007] BPIR 323 Registrar Nicholls allowed an appeal against the decision of the chairman of a creditors' meeting on the basis that the chairman should have allowed the creditor to vote in full for legal costs incurred by it, but not assessed by the court, where the creditor had a contractual entitlement to such costs incurred from the debtor. The chairman's decision constituted a material irregularity justifying the setting aside of the IVA and discharge of the interim order given that the appellant was thus capable of voting down the debtor's proposal. Where a liability to pay costs arises out of a pre-IVA agreement, but is not imposed until after approval of the IVA, the costs claim, subject to the terms of the IVA, will not be caught by the IVA: *Cornelius v Casson* [2008] BPIR 504 (Thomas Ivory QC, sitting as a deputy High Court judge).

For a finding of material irregularity resulting in the revocation of the approval of an individual voluntary arrangement see *Re Cardona* [1997] BCC 697, where the chairman of the creditors' meeting wrongly refused to allow the Inland Revenue, being the debtor's largest creditor, to withdraw a proxy form lodged for the purposes of a creditors' meeting, which was adjourned, and to lodge a second proxy for the purposes of the re-convened meeting.

For an unsuccessful allegation of material irregularity which was based on fundamental misunderstandings on the part of the secured creditor as to the effect of the CVA and unsubstantiated allegations of irregularities at the creditors' meeting and the counting of votes see *Swindon Town Properties Ltd v Swindon Town Football Co Ltd* [2003] BPIR 253 (Hart J).

The Court of Appeal in *Kapoor v (1) National Westminster Bank plc (2) Tan* [2011] EWCA Civ 1083, [2011] BPIR 1680 considered that it was a material irregularity for a connected creditor to have assigned his debt to an unconnected creditor (notwithstanding that the assignment was effective) for the purposes of circumventing rule 5.23.A challenge based on a material irregularity succeeded in *National Westminster Bank Plc v Yadgaroff* [2011] EWHC 1130 (Ch).

Commissioners for Her Majesty's Revenue and Customs v (1) Earley (2) Heron (3) Fisher [2011] EWHC 1783 (Ch), [2011] BPIR 1590 is a decision of Sir Andrew Morritt, the then Chancellor of the High Court, in which he found that there was a material irregularity in relation to an IVA (a without notice injunction had been obtained against HMRC preventing HMRC from voting at the meeting in the full amount of its debt in circumstances where, pursuant to s 21 of the Crown Proceedings Act 1947, the Court could not make an injunction against the Crown).

Re Linfoot (A Debtor); Linfoot v (1) Adamson (2) Bank of Scotland plc (3) National Westminster Bank plc [2012] BPIR 1033 was a case in which an individual had made an application challenging a decision taken at a creditors meeting called by the supervisor of the IVA some time after the IVA had been approved. HHJ Behrens held that s.262 was not engaged on such an application, whereas s 263 was.

Section 262(1)(b) is sufficiently broad to extend to a material irregularity in a debtor's proposal or statement of affairs: *Re A Debtor (No 87 of 1993) (No 2)* [1996] BCC 80 at 107C–108E (Rimer J). That case, which resulted in the court revoking the arrangement, involved an application by four creditors of the debtor alleging that the debtor's proposal was dishonest and misleading in that it falsely disclosed a non-existent asset, it failed to disclose all of the debtor's assets and made false representation with regard to those assets and liabilities which had been disclosed by the debtor.

It is submitted that a finding of material irregularity involves a finding of fact alone and is no way dependent on any finding of fault.

Paragraph 4.1 of SIP 3 advises that a mis-statement of the amount of the assets and liabilities in the debtor's statement of affairs is capable of constituting a material irregularity.

Section 262(2)

Scope of provision—For the standing of the FSA to apply and be heard on applications under s 262 see ss 356 and 357 of the Financial Services and Markets Act 2000.

Eligible applicants—Categories (a) and (b) are clear enough by reference to the two grounds in s 262(1).

For the purposes of categories (c) and (d) it appears that either the nominee (or his replacement) or a trustee-in-bankruptcy or the official receiver (where the debtor is an undischarged bankrupt) has standing to make application under s 262(1)(a), although such an application may only proceed on the basis of alleged unfair prejudice to the interests of a creditor; as such, and in the absence of an application by either such party, such applications are unlikely. More obviously plausible are applications under s 262(1)(b), since these are not restricted to prejudice to the interests of a creditor.

Procedure on a s 262(2) application—Care must be taken in naming the respondents to an application under s 262(1). In *Re Naeem (a Bankrupt) (No 18 of 1988)* [1990] 1 WLR 48, a case involving an unsuccessful allegation of unfairly prejudicial conduct, Hoffmann J (as he then was) indicated that the applicant had been wrong to join the nominee and two creditors as respondents to the application. His Lordship also held that a nominee should not be ordered to pay the costs of a successful application in the absence of actual misconduct on the nominee's part. Hoffmann J did comment, however, that convenience may dictate giving the nominee notice of the application in such a case (at 51): 'If there had been some personal conduct on the part of the nominee which would justify an order for costs against him, that could be done.'

It is suggested that it will usually be appropriate to join the nominee, and possibly one or more creditors, to an application alleging material irregularity at or in relation to a meeting at which the nominee and/or such creditors have played a part.

For further discussion on costs in the context of a s 262(1) application, see *Re A Debtor (No 222 of 1990) ex parte Bank of Ireland* [1992] BCLC 137 and *(No 2)* [1993] BCLC 233 (Harman J); and *Harmony Carpets v Chaffin-Laird* [2000] BPIR 61 (Rattee J, no order for costs against nominee notwithstanding criticisms of nominee in reporting to court on the basis that it was not clear, had proper reports been made, that the court would have declined to allow meetings of creditors to take place such that the complainant would still have incurred the costs of challenging the decision of the meeting). See also the decision of Andrew Simmonds QC in *Tradition (UK) Ltd v Ahmed and Others* [2008] EWHC 3448 (Ch), [2009] BPIR 626 for an unsuccessful attempt at making the nominee liable for all of the costs of an application to challenge a voluntary arrangement – the decision of Andrew Simmonds QC contains a useful analysis of the principles to be applied when determining whether a proposed nominee should be liable for costs.

For further general guidance on procedure see the notes to rr 7.1, 7.2 and 7.10(2).

Section 262(3)

'... **shall not be made ... after the end of the period of 28 days ...**'—These words are not a common formulation for the computation of time under statute. The 28-day period begins with and includes the dates specified in subsections (a) and (b). Furthermore, the 28-day period in s 262(3) is capable of extension under s 376 (time-limits): *Tager v Westpac Banking Corp* [1997] 1 BCLC 313 (His Honour Judge Weeks QC). The position is different in CVA cases where the 28-day period in the analogous s 6(3) cannot be extended by the court in the absence of any equivalent to s 376 in Part I of the Act: *Re Bournemouth & Boscombe Athletic Football Club Co Ltd* [1998] BPIR 183 (Lloyd J, as he then was). In the context of IVAs His Honour Judge Weeks QC held in *Tager* (at 325D) that the factors relevant to the exercise of discretion and extending time are the length of delay, the reasons for the delay, the apparent merits of the underlying application and the prejudice to each side, other than the inevitable prejudice inherent in re-opening the question of approval of the arrangement. The decision in *Tager* extending time was approved of by Carnwath J in *Plant v Plant* [1998] 1 BCLC 38. In *Warley Continental Services Ltd (in liquidation) v Johal* (2002) *The Times*, October 28 His Honour Judge Norris QC, sitting as a High Court judge, also identified the conduct of the parties as being of potential significance in a wide range of cases; an extension of time in that case was refused given the unjustifiable and significant delay in making the application, notwithstanding the obvious merits of the case. Plainly the 28-day period will not be extended as a matter of course without proper explanation in evidence being tendered to the court.

If a proposal has been approved, but can nonetheless be shown to have been invalid then, at least where the proposal is advanced bona fide and approved and implemented accordingly, and in particular where the invalidity is overlooked by all concerned up to the time of approval and expiration of the 28-day period, the arrangement should be treated as valid notwithstanding the infringement giving rise to the apparent invalidity: *IRC v Wimbledon Football Club Ltd* [2004] EWCA Civ 655, [2005] 1 BCLC 66 at [38] (Neuberger LJ). Equally, even where a proposal is made a debtor with the assistance of a professional adviser can be shown to be defective in terms of a number of minor procedural irregularities, the court will not entertain an application under s 262 to revoke, especially following a significant passage of time: *Tanner v Everitt* [2004] BPIR 1026 (Mann J).

For the meaning of the words 'has come to an end prematurely' see s 262C.

Section 262(4)

Remedies and relief on a s 262(2) application—Whilst the discretion of the court in making an order under this subsection appears unfettered through the use of the word 'may', the court has a positive duty to act in setting aside an arrangement where the arrangement is in clear conflict with a statutory provision (see below). In other cases the court would be perfectly entitled in the exercise of its discretion to refuse to make any order if the practical effect of, most obviously, setting aside an arrangement would be to harm the interests of the creditors of the debtor generally, say where the purpose of the arrangement was all but complete, even where the court was satisfied as to the fact of unfair prejudice and/or material irregularity.

The scope of any order made is defined in fairly restrictive terms by s 262(4)(a) and (b), which do not read as being mutually exclusive in that the court may make an order suspending the decision under (a) whilst at the same time providing directions under (b). In particular, the court has no power to direct the modification of a proposal or that any particular modification should be considered by any further meeting, since the formulation of the proposal remains at all times entirely a matter for the party making the proposal. *Davis v Price* [2013] EWHC 323 (Ch), [2013] BPIR 200 is a case in which David Richards J considered the relief which a Court can grant on an application under s 262 and in particular the effect of a suspension of an IVA.

The court's discretion in granting relief—The exercise of the court's powers under s 262(4) – upon which the powers in s 262(25) and s 262(6) are dependent – is discretionary. However, where an approved arrangement conflicts with a clear statutory prohibition, which goes to the substance of the proposal and has resulted in clear prejudice, the court must revoke the arrangement save, possibly, in the most exceptional circumstances: *IRC v Wimbledon Football Club Ltd* [2004] EWCA Civ 655, [2005] 1 BCLC 66 at [39] (Neuberger LJ). *IRC v Wimbledon* involved an unsuccessful challenge to an arrangement by the Inland Revenue which complained of a breach of s 4(4)(a) (being the statutory equivalent of s 258(5)(a) in CVAs) on the grounds that so-called football creditors would receive 100 pence in the pound, whereas the Revenue would receive only 30. The application and appeal by the Revenue failed, since the football creditors were to be discharged by third party monies such that there was no infringement of s 4(4)(a). Another example of interference with statutory provisions might include an arrangement which purported to vary and undermine the statutory trust created in favour of the Law Society under Sch 6 of the Solicitors Act 1974 following a Law Society intervention into a solicitors' practice.

Section 262(4)(a)

Scope of provision—If an arrangement is revoked or suspended then, in the absence of some contrary supplemental direction under s 6(6), there is nothing to prevent a fresh proposal being formulated and advanced, even, it would appear, by way of a proposal in identical terms to that revoked or suspended.

Section 262(4)(b)

Scope of provision—The provision for the giving of a direction 'to any person' for the summoning of further meetings is probably designed to allow for summoning by a person other than the incumbent nominee where the court forms the view that future conduct by that individual is inappropriate, although in those circumstances further steps would be required to replace the nominee for the purposes of s 253(2).

The court will not ordinarily be inclined to direct the summoning of further meetings to consider any revised proposal if it is satisfied on evidence before it that a sufficient number of creditors in value will vote against, so as to defeat, approval of the proposal.

Section 262(5)

Scope of provision—The court may revoke an arrangement under s 262(5) if satisfied that the party making the original proposal does not intend to proceed with a revised proposal and squarely accepts the merit of the application under s 262(1).

For action following the revocation or suspension of an arrangement see r 5.30.

Section 262(6)

Scope of provision—This provision provides specifically for control of any interim order where a further creditors' meeting is ordered under s 262(4)(b). The usual course will be for the interim order to continue in effect pending the decision of the further meeting.

Section 262(7)

Scope of provision—Although the court may tailor any supplemental directions to complement any order under s 262(4) or (5), this provision addresses in particular the interim period between the approval of an arrangement and the making of any such order, given that an arrangement remains valid pending the making of such an order.

Section 262(8)

Scope of provision—See the notes to s 262(1)(b) and s 262(3).

262A False representations etc

(1) If for the purpose of obtaining the approval of his creditors to a proposal for a voluntary arrangement, the debtor—

    (a)   makes any false representation, or

    (b)   fraudulently does, or omits to do, anything,

he commits an offence.

(2) Subsection (1) applies even if the proposal is not approved.

(3) A person guilty of an offence under this section is liable to imprisonment or a fine, or both.

Amendments—Inserted by Insolvency Act 2000, s 3, Sch 3, paras 1, 12.

General note—These provisions, carrying criminal liability, were effective from 1 January 2003 on implementation under s 3 of the Insolvency Act 2000 and Sch 3 thereto. In practice, a proposal will typically include a declaration that a debtor has been made aware of s 262A. Some proposals also include a statement of truth of the kind employed in witness statements and statements of case under the Civil Procedure Rules 1998 which verifies the deponent's belief as to the matters of fact represented in the proposal.

Section 262A(1)

Scope of provision—The actus reus of the offence includes the making of a false representation or, alternatively, the fraudulent commission, or omission, of anything for the purpose of obtaining the approval of the members or creditors of a company to a proposal.

    For a criminal prosecution for fraudulent representation in the context of an IVA proposal see *R v Dawson* (unreported) 29 June 2001. The wording of the sub-section, it is suggested, does not extend to the obtaining of approval for a modification to the terms of a subsisting arrangement.

Section 262A(2)

Scope of provision—The fact that a proposal is not approved has no bearing on the committing of an offence under s 6A(1), which requires only proof of the acts or omissions within its scope 'for the purpose' of obtaining approval of the arrangement.

Section 262A(3)

Scope of provision—On penalties see s 430 and Sch 10.

262B Prosecution of delinquent debtors

(1) This section applies where a voluntary arrangement approved by a creditors' meeting summoned under section 257 has taken effect.

(2) If it appears to the nominee or supervisor that the debtor has been guilty of any offence in connection with the arrangement for which he is criminally liable, he shall forthwith—

    (a)   report the matter to the Secretary of State, and

    (b)   provide the Secretary of State with such information and give the Secretary of State such access to and facilities for inspecting and taking copies of documents (being information or documents in his possession or under his control and relating to the matter in question) as the Secretary of State requires.

(3) Where a prosecuting authority institutes criminal proceedings following any report under subsection (2), the nominee or, as the case may be, supervisor shall give the authority all assistance in connection with the prosecution which he is reasonably able to give.

For this purpose, 'prosecuting authority' means the Director of Public Prosecutions or the Secretary of State.

(4) The court may, on the application of the prosecuting authority, direct a nominee or supervisor to comply with subsection (3) if he has failed to do so.

Amendments—Inserted by Insolvency Act 2000, s 3, Sch 3, paras 1, 12.

General note—The heart of this provision lies in s 262B(2) in the obligation to report to the Secretary of State, which triggers the possibility of a criminal prosecution and the consequences in s 262B(3). That obligation is triggered on it appearing to the nominee or supervisor that the debtor has been guilty of an offence. The term 'appears' does not envisage steps having to be taken by the nominee or supervisor by way of investigating matters, although the office-holder may well consider such steps to be appropriate where a suspicion is aroused as to the possible commission of an offence.

Section 262B(2)(b) is unlimited in affording the Secretary of State access to and facilities for the inspection and copying of such documents as he requires. In the absence of any provision providing for the costs of such an exercise it is submitted, given the unconditional wording in s 262B(2)(b), that such costs must fall on the office-holder, who might in turn seek to recover such sums by way of an enhanced nominee's fee or as an expense or disbursement in the arrangement.

262C Arrangements coming to an end prematurely

For the purposes of this Part, a voluntary arrangement approved by a creditors' meeting summoned under section 257 comes to an end prematurely if, when it ceases to have effect, it has not been fully implemented in respect of all persons bound by the arrangement by virtue of section 260(2)(b)(i).

Amendments—Inserted by Insolvency Act 2000, s 3, Sch 3, paras 1, 12.

General note—For the relevance of this definition, introduced by s 3 and Sch 3 of the Insolvency Act 2000 with effect from 1 January 2003, see ss 260(2A) and 262(3).

263 Implementation and supervision of approved voluntary arrangement

(1) This section applies where a voluntary arrangement approved by a creditors' meeting summoned under section 257 has taken effect.

(2) The person who is for the time being carrying out, in relation to the voluntary arrangement, the functions conferred by virtue of the approval on the nominee (or his replacement under section 256(3), 256A(4) or 258(3)) shall be known as the supervisor of the voluntary arrangement.

(3) If the debtor, any of his creditors or any other person is dissatisfied by any act, omission or decision of the supervisor, he may apply to the court; and on such an application the court may—

    (a)   confirm, reverse or modify any act or decision of the supervisor,

    (b)   give him directions, or

    (c)   make such other order as it thinks fit.

(4) The supervisor may apply to the court for directions in relation to any particular matter arising under the voluntary arrangement.

(5) The court may, whenever—

    (a)   it is expedient to appoint a person to carry out the functions of the supervisor, and

    (b)   it is inexpedient, difficult or impracticable for an appointment to be made without the assistance of the court,

make an order appointing a person who is qualified to act as an insolvency practitioner or authorised to act as supervisor, in relation to the voluntary arrangement, either in substitution for the existing supervisor or to fill a vacancy.

This is without prejudice to section 41(2) of the Trustee Act 1925 (power of court to appoint trustees of deeds of arrangement).

(6) The power conferred by subsection (5) is exercisable so as to increase the number of persons exercising the functions of the supervisor or, where there is more than one person exercising those functions, so as to replace one or more of those persons.

Amendments—Insolvency Act 2000, s 3, Sch 3, paras 1, 13(a), (b).

General note—These provisions provide for the automatic appointment of the supervisor following approval of the voluntary arrangement (under s 263(2)) and for the making of applications to court in the event of dissatisfaction with the conduct of the supervisor (under s 263(3)) or where the supervisor requires the assistance of the court by way of directions (under s 263(4)).

Best practice guidance on the implementation of a voluntary arrangement following the meeting of creditors and the conclusion/termination of the arrangement appears in paras 8 and 9 of SIP 3. The supervisor is expected to keep creditors abreast of developments in the conduct of the arrangement. In particular para 8.1 of SIP 3 provides:

'If actual events suggest a deviation from the terms of the arrangement, the supervisor should take appropriate action. Such action should correspond to further detailed provisions of the proposal. If he is authorised to exercise discretion in any area, and that discretion is exercised, the supervisor should explain the circumstances to creditors (and members in a CVA) at the next available opportunity.'

Despite the heading to s 263 its provisions provide no specific guidance on the implementation of the proposal itself. Detailed procedural rules do, however, appear in rr 5.25–5.34. In addition, the terms of the arrangement itself will dictate the method of implementation on a case by case basis.

On the declaration of payment of dividends see rr 11.1–11.13.

In practice, it is common to find that the terms of an IVA import the provisions in rr 6.96–6.114, which provide a procedure for proof and quantification of claims for dividend purposes in bankruptcy.

Section 263(1)

Scope of provision—For guidance see the notes to s 257(1), ss 258(1) and 260(2)(b).

Section 263(2)

Scope of provision—The nominee, or his replacement, becomes known as the supervisor of the voluntary arrangement automatically by force of this provision on the arrangement coming into effect under ss 257(1) and 258(1).

The circumstances in which the nominee does not become supervisor are specified in ss 256(3), 256A(4) and 258(2). The first arises where the court has appointed a replacement nominee because the original nominee failed to submit his report to the court in accordance with ss 256(1) and 256A(3). The second situation arises where the proposal has been modified so as to confer the functions of the nominee on another appropriately qualified person.

The consequence of the supervisor's appointment is that the person so appointed becomes entitled, indeed obliged, to discharge his functions and exercise his powers under and in accordance with the arrangement.

Section 263(3)

Scope of provision—This subsection is concerned only with complaints directed against a supervisor; it has no bearing on whether a creditor is able to sustain a claim against a debtor notwithstanding the approval of the voluntary arrangement, on which see the notes to s 260(2)(b).

'... any other person ...'—This term will, it is submitted, extend to any person capable of establishing to the court that he has a sufficient interest in the voluntary arrangement. This might include a person with a beneficial interest in the arrangement assets: see *Port v Auger* [1994] 1 WLR 862 at 873–874 (Harman J, considering similar wording in s 303). The provision might also catch a third party who claims not to be bound by an arrangement but is treated as such by the supervisor in circumstances where the supervisor refuses to seek clarification of the issue by way of an application under s 262 at the behest of the third party: *Re Timothy* [2006] BPIR 329 at [49] (Warren J). HHJ Langan QC, in *Stericker v Horner* [2012] BPIR 645 gave some limited consideration to the scope of the phrase 'any other person' (see paras 37 and 38 of his judgment).

'... is dissatisfied ...'—This phrase also appears in s 303(1) in relation to complaints made against a trustee-in-bankruptcy. The term is to be contrasted with 'is aggrieved by', which applies to complaints made against a liquidator under s 168(5) in a compulsory liquidation and which also appeared in the former s 80 of the Bankruptcy Act 1914 in relation to trustees-in-bankruptcy. In *Re Dennis Michael Cooke* [1999] BPIR 881 Stanley Burnton QC, sitting as he then was as a deputy High Court judge, considered (at 883F–883G), in the context of an application under s 303, that the word 'dissatisfied' is no narrower than the term 'aggrieved' employed in s 80 of the Bankruptcy Act 1914, and is arguably wider. Accordingly, the term should not be given a restricted interpretation and will include a person who has a genuine grievance against the actions of the office-holder, but not a mere busybody interfering in things which do not concern him. That interpretation, it is submitted, would apply equally in the context of the present provision.

'... by any act, omission or decision of the supervisor ...'—The subsection distinguishes a 'decision' from an 'act' or 'omission'. If those three terms are mutually exclusive, then it would follow that an omission extends to a failure to do something, say through an oversight or through ignorance, but not a failure to do something as a consequence of a decision to that effect. The scope of the conduct capable of falling within the cumulative scope of the three terms is plainly broad, but will only include relevant conduct on the part of the supervisor acting as such, including such conduct undertaken on his behalf, say by a member of the supervisor's staff.

For further commentary see the notes to s 303(1).

Does s 263(3) preclude the existence of a private right of action outside of the provision in favour of a creditor?—In *King v Anthony* [1999] BPIR 73 the Court of Appeal (Nourse, Schiemann and Brooke LJJ) held (in the judgment of Brooke LJ at 78H–79B) that a creditor had no private right of action allowing for complaint to be made against a supervisor, since s 263(3) provided an effective means of enforcing the duties of a supervisor. Furthermore,

Part VIII of the 1986 Act constitutes a self-contained statutory scheme which in s 263(3) provides expressly for the court to give appropriate directions to a supervisor, thereby allowing the court to maintain control over the performance of its officer. This issue had arisen in that case in the context of a claim by a supervisor against two debtors who had served a defence and counterclaim which alleged a private law remedy against the supervisor which sounded in damages and which constituted a set-off against the supervisor's claim. Based on its construction of s 263 the Court of Appeal upheld the decision of the judge below in striking out the defence and counterclaim.

Is a private law remedy available against a nominee?—Section 263(3) applies only to a supervisor. *King v Anthony*, therefore, cannot operate so as to limit any private law remedy available against a nominee, as opposed to a supervisor. It would appear to follow from the reasoning in *King v Anthony* that misconduct by a nominee which constitutes unfair prejudice and/or material irregularity within the meaning of s 262(1)(a) and/or (b) is actionable only under those provisions and will not be open to a private law remedy. However, to the extent that any breach of the nominee's duties falls outside s 262(1) that conduct would appear actionable by way of a private law remedy, say in a claim for breach of duty and/or negligence.

Section 263(4)

'... directions in relation to any particular matter arising under the voluntary arrangement ...'—There is no authority which deals with the scope of s 263(4)(a), most likely because the court will usually be willing to respond to a genuine request for assistance by a supervisor in connection with any specific (or 'particular') matter which arises under – seemingly, in connection with or caused by – the IVA. The objective of the provision, it is submitted, is to afford a supervisor easy access to court for the resolution of such genuine difficulties. Whilst plainly drafted more broadly in scope than s 263(3), the s 263(4)(a) facility should not be employed for the purpose of seeking the court's approval or 'rubber stamp' – which will most likely be refused in any case – where the substance of the particular matter raised amounts to a commercial decision for the office-holder personally. Neither, it is submitted, is an application for directions appropriate where the application constitutes an obvious attempt on the part of the supervisor to avoid alternative and plainly more appropriate proceedings.

The court has no jurisdiction to give directions modifying the terms of an approved arrangement: *Re Alpa Lighting Ltd* [1997] BPIR 341.

Supervisor's petition for bankruptcy order—In practice, the provisions of an IVA will commonly require a supervisor either to petition or to consider petitioning for bankruptcy in the event of one or more specified defaults. The standing of a supervisor to petition is expressly provided for in s 264(1)(c). The supervisor of an IVA does not necessarily lose standing to petition by virtue of the fact that an arrangement is no longer functioning as originally envisaged. In *Re Arthur Rathbone Kitchens Ltd* [1997] 2 BCLC 280 Roger Kaye QC, sitting as deputy High Court judge, rejected submissions in a CVA case to the effect that a supervisor could not petition for winding up under s 7(4)(b) – which, in contrast to the present provisions, expressly provides a CVA supervisor with standing to petition for a winding-up order – if the CVA was not still on foot so as to deprive the supervisor of locus standi as 'supervisor' within the meaning of s 7(2). The deputy judge identified that, on the particular terms of the CVA, the arrangement had not terminated, although the company was in default, at the time of the presentation of the supervisor's petition. Neither does a supervisor lose standing to petition on the expiration of a fixed-term arrangement, provided that, at the time of presentation of the petition, the supervisor was still 'carrying out in relation to the voluntary arrangement the functions' conferred on the supervisor by virtue of s 263(2): *Harris v Gross* [2001] BPIR 586 (His Honour Judge Maddocks sitting as a High Court judge; bankruptcy orders made on petitions presented by IVA supervisor one month after expiration of 4-year fixed term interlocking IVAs in respect of ongoing defaults committed during the fixed arrangement terms).

263A Availability

Section 263B applies where an individual debtor intends to make a proposal to his creditors for a voluntary arrangement and—

(a) the debtor is an undischarged bankrupt,
(b) the official receiver is specified in the proposal as the nominee in relation to the voluntary arrangement, and
(c) no interim order is applied for under section 253.

Amendments—Inserted by Enterprise Act 2002, s 264(1), Sch 22, para 2.

263B Decision

(1) The debtor may submit to the official receiver—

(a) a document setting out the terms of the voluntary arrangement which the debtor is proposing, and
(b) a statement of his affairs containing such particulars as may be prescribed of his creditors, debts, other liabilities and assets and such other information as may be prescribed.

(2) If the official receiver thinks that the voluntary arrangement proposed has a reasonable prospect of being approved and implemented, he may make arrangements for inviting creditors to decide whether to approve it.

(3) For the purposes of subsection (2) a person is a 'creditor' only if—

(a) he is a creditor of the debtor in respect of a bankruptcy debt, and
(b) the official receiver is aware of his claim and his address.

(4) Arrangements made under subsection (2)—

(a) must include the provision to each creditor of a copy of the proposed voluntary arrangement,
(b) must include the provision to each creditor of information about the criteria by reference to which the official receiver will determine whether the creditors approve or reject the proposed voluntary arrangement, and
(c) may not include an opportunity for modifications to the proposed voluntary arrangement to be suggested or made.

(5) Where a debtor submits documents to the official receiver under subsection (1) no application under section 253 for an interim order may be made in respect of the debtor until the official receiver has—

(a) made arrangements as described in subsection (2), or
(b) informed the debtor that he does not intend to make arrangements (whether because he does not think the voluntary arrangement has a reasonable prospect of being approved and implemented or because he declines to act).

Amendments—Inserted by Enterprise Act 2002, s 264(1), Sch 22, para 2.

263C Result

As soon as is reasonably practicable after the implementation of arrangements under section 263B(2) the official receiver shall notify the Secretary of State whether the proposed voluntary arrangement has been approved or rejected.

Amendments—Inserted by Enterprise Act 2002, s 264(1), Sch 22, para 2. Amended by SI 2010/18.

263D Approval of voluntary arrangement

(1) This section applies where the official receiver notifies the Secretary of State under section 263C that a proposed voluntary arrangement has been approved.

(2) The voluntary arrangement—

- (a) takes effect,
- (b) binds the debtor, and
- (c) binds every person who was entitled to participate in the arrangements made under section 263B(2).

(3) The court shall annul the bankruptcy order in respect of the debtor on an application made by the official receiver.

(4) An application under subsection (3) may not be made—

- (a) during the period specified in section 263F(3) during which the voluntary arrangement can be challenged by application under section 263F(2),
- (b) while an application under that section is pending, or
- (c) while an appeal in respect of an application under that section is pending or may be brought.

(5) The court may give such directions about the conduct of the bankruptcy and the administration of the bankrupt's estate as it thinks appropriate for facilitating the implementation of the approved voluntary arrangement.

(6) The Deeds of Arrangement Act 1914 (c 47) does not apply to the voluntary arrangement.

(7) A reference in this Act or another enactment to a voluntary arrangement approved under this Part includes a reference to a voluntary arrangement which has effect by virtue of this section.

Amendments—Inserted by Enterprise Act 2002, s 264(1), Sch 22, para 2. Amended by SI 2010/18.

263E Implementation

Section 263 shall apply to a voluntary arrangement which has effect by virtue of section 263D(2) as it applies to a voluntary arrangement approved by a creditors' meeting.

Amendments—Inserted by Enterprise Act 2002, s 264(1), Sch 22, para 2.

263F Revocation

(1) The court may make an order revoking a voluntary arrangement which has effect by virtue of section 263D(2) on the ground—

> (a) that it unfairly prejudices the interests of a creditor of the debtor, or
>
> (b) that a material irregularity occurred in relation to the arrangements made under section 263B(2).

(2) An order under subsection (1) may be made only on the application of—

> (a) the debtor,
>
> (b) a person who was entitled to participate in the arrangements made under section 263B(2),
>
> (c) the trustee of the bankrupt's estate, or
>
> (d) the official receiver.

(3) An application under subsection (2) may not be made after the end of the period of 28 days beginning with the date on which the official receiver notifies the Secretary of State under section 263C.

(4) But a creditor who was not made aware of the arrangements under section 263B(2) at the time when they were made may make an application under subsection (2) during the period of 28 days beginning with the date on which he becomes aware of the voluntary arrangement.

Amendments—Inserted by Enterprise Act 2002, s 264(1), Sch 22, para 2. Amended by SI 2010/18.

263G Offences

(1) Section 262A shall have effect in relation to obtaining approval to a proposal for a voluntary arrangement under section 263D.

(2) Section 262B shall have effect in relation to a voluntary arrangement which has effect by virtue of section 263D(2) (for which purposes the words 'by a creditors' meeting summoned under section 257' shall be disregarded).

Amendments—Inserted by Enterprise Act 2002, s 264(1), Sch 22, para 2.

****

Chapter I

Bankruptcy Petitions; Bankruptcy Orders

Preliminary

264 Who may present a bankruptcy petition

(1) A petition for a bankruptcy order to be made against an individual may be presented to the court in accordance with the following provisions of this Part—

> (a) by one of the individual's creditors or jointly by more than one of them,
>
> (b) by the individual himself,

(ba) by a temporary administrator (within the meaning of Article 38 of the EC Regulation),

(bb) by a liquidator (within the meaning of Article 2(b) of the EC Regulation) appointed in proceedings by virtue of Article 3(1) of the EC Regulation,

(c) by the supervisor of, or any person (other than the individual) who is for the time being bound by, a voluntary arrangement proposed by the individual and approved under Part VIII, or

(d) where a criminal bankruptcy order has been made against the individual, by the Official Petitioner or by any person specified in the order in pursuance of section 39(3)(b) of the Powers of Criminal Courts Act 1973.

(2) Subject to those provisions, the court may make a bankruptcy order on any such petition.

Amendments—SI 2002/1240.

General note—The court can only make a bankruptcy order on a petition presented by any of the class of persons in s 264(1), subject to the conditions relating to a debtor in s 265(1) in the case of a creditor's or debtor's petition. The conditions in s 265 do not apply to a default petition under s 264(1)(c): *Loy v O'Sullivan* [2010] EWHC 3583 (Ch), [2011] BPIR 181.

Section 264(1)(a)

Scope of provision—The term 'creditor' is defined in s 383(1)(a) and (b), on which see also r 6.6 and the general power to dismiss or stay in s 266(3). It is permissible for separate debts owed to different creditors to be joined in a single petition, provided that the combined level of such petition debts exceeds the bankruptcy level of £750 in s 267(4): *Re Allen, Re a Debtor (No 367 of 1992)* [1998] BPIR 319 at 320F–320G (Ferris J).

In *Levy v Legal Services Commission* [2000] BPIR 1065 at 1075A–1075F (Jonathan Parker LJ, Peter Gibson LJ and Waller J agreeing) the Court of Appeal held that, given that no distinction is made between provable and non-provable debts in ss 264 and 383(1), the court had jurisdiction to make a bankruptcy order upon a petition based on a non-provable debt although it would only do so in very exceptional circumstances, which, indeed, the court was unable to envisage save where a supporting creditor with a provable debt obtained a change of carriage order pursuant to r 6.31.

Once s 115 of the Tribunals, Courts and Enforcement Act 2007 is commenced, an unsecured creditor with a qualifying debt will require the Court's permission to present a bankruptcy petition against a debtor who has entered into a debt repayment plan in accordance with an approved scheme under that Act.

Section 264(1)(b)

Scope of provision—For the grounds of a debtor's petition see s 272.

Section 264(1)(c)

Scope of provision—Where a bankruptcy petition is presented by the supervisor of an IVA or a creditor bound by an IVA under this provision, the court may not make a bankruptcy order unless it is satisfied as to the fulfilment of any one of the three conditions in s 276(1) on which see also the notes thereto.

In *Harris v Gross* [2001] BPIR 586 at 589D–589H His Honour Judge Maddocks, sitting as a High Court judge, held that a supervisor may present a default petition even after the expiration of any fixed term for which the arrangement subsists, although such petition must be presented within a reasonable period following expiration.

For the consequences of an order made on a supervisor's petition following the decision of the Court of Appeal in *Re NT Gallagher & Son Ltd* [2002] EWCA Civ 404, [2002] 1 WLR 2380 see the notes to s 2(2).

Where a voluntary arrangement fails on the making of a bankruptcy order the proper destination of funds paid into the arrangement will depend on the terms of the arrangement and the possibility of any Quistelose trust: see, for example, *Cooper v Official Receiver* [2003] BPIR 55.

The court may appoint a supervisor as trustee on a s 264(1)(c) petition under s 297(5). Although such appointments are common, any such appointment may be challenged if not judiciously exercised: *Landsman v De Concilio* [2005] EWHC 267 (Ch), [2005] BPIR 829. The court is unlikely, however, to consider objections by a debtor alone when the substance of those objections amounts to little more than a sense of irritation or grievance, however misguided, on the part of the debtor.

Section 264(1)(d)

Scope of provision—This obsolete provision is to be repealed from a date to be appointed pursuant to s 170(2) of and Sch 16 to the Criminal Justice Act 1988, on which see further the general note to ss 277 and 280.

The Financial Services Authority may present its own petition or be heard on any other person's petition, on which see ss 372 and 374(2) of the Financial Services and Markets Act 2000 respectively.

Petition deposits and court fees—Under the Insolvency Proceedings (Fees) Order 2004 (SI 2004/593) as amended by the Insolvency Proceedings (Fees) (Amendment) Order 2011 (SI 2011/1167) with effect from 1 June 2011 the deposit payable under s 264(1)(a),(ba), (bb), (c) and (d) is £700, whereas the deposit on a debtor's petition under s 264(1)(b) is £525. The Court fee for issuing a bankruptcy petition is £175 if it is issued by the debtor or their personal representative and £220 issued by the creditor or other person: Civil Proceedings Fees (Amendment) Order 2011 (SI 2011/586).

Section 264(2)

The court's discretion—On the exercise of the court's discretion on a creditor's petition see the notes to s 271, which incorporate reference to r 6.25 (decision on the hearing) and r 6.26 (non-appearance of creditor).

On the exercise of the court's discretion on the supervisor's petition see the notes to s 276.

Procedure—A bankruptcy petition should be in Form 6.7, 6.8, 6.9, 6.10, or 6.27 (debtor's own petition) as appropriate.

The procedure applicable to a creditor's bankruptcy petition appears in rr 6.6–6.35, that for a debtor's is in rr 6.37–6.47.

265 Conditions to be satisfied in respect of debtor

(1) A bankruptcy petition shall not be presented to the court under section 264(1)(a) or (b) unless the debtor—

- (a)   is domiciled in England and Wales,
- (b)   is personally present in England and Wales on the day on which the petition is presented, or
- (c)   at any time in the period of 3 years ending with that day—
    - (i)   has been ordinarily resident, or has had a place of residence, in England and Wales, or
    - (ii)   has carried on business in England and Wales.

(2) The reference in subsection (1)(c) to an individual carrying on business includes—

- (a)   the carrying on of business by a firm or partnership of which the individual is a member, and

(b) the carrying on of business by an agent or manager for the individual or for such a firm or partnership.

(3) This section is subject to Article 3 of the EC Regulation.

Amendments—SI 2002/1240.

General note—In the case of a creditor's or debtor's petition (but not that of an IVA supervisor: *Loy v O'Sullivan* [2010] EWHC 3583 (Ch), [2011] BPIR 181) there is a requirement that the petitioner can satisfy the court as to the debtor's geographical connection with the jurisdiction by the fulfilment of any one of what amount to the three requirements in s 265(1) and (2). Save for s 265(1)(c)(i), there is no requirement that the debtor need be resident in England and Wales. Neither do the provisions make any reference to the debtor's nationality or the state of his citizenship.

Section 265(1)

Conditions for presentation of a bankruptcy petition—Each of the conditions amounts to a question of fact.

The leading authorities on the issue of domicile in s 265(1)(a) are the Court of Appeal's decisions in *Re Bird* [1962] 1 WLR 686 and *Re Brauch (a Debtor)* [1978] Ch 316, and the decision on tax legislation in *Plummer v IRC* [1988] 1 WLR 292. Where a person abandons his domicile of choice, his domicile of origin is revived as a matter of law: *Barlow Clowes International Ltd v Henwood* [2008] EWCA Civ 577, [2008] BPIR 778 (Waller, Arden and Moore-Bick LJJ), the judgment of Arden LJ containing a useful survey of the authorities

Section 265(1)(b) requires only that the debtor is personally present in the jurisdiction, even in passing through for a very short period: see *Re Thulin* [1995] 1 WLR 165 (Jules Sher QC, sitting as a deputy High Court judge).

On 'ordinarily resident' under s 265(1)(c)(i) see the authorities mentioned above in relation to s 265(1)(a). The fact that an individual has not appealed tax assessments made against him by the Inland Revenue does not estop a debtor from disputing his alleged residence within the jurisdiction based on the fact of those assessments alone: *Wilkinson v IRC* [1998] BPIR 418 (His Honour Judge Collyer QC, sitting as a deputy High Court judge).

Section 265(2)

Scope of provision—The question of whether an individual has 'carried on business' within the preceding 3-year period under s 265(1)(c)(ii) 'includes', but is not therefore limited to, those two circumstances in s 265(2). If an individual has carried on business within the jurisdiction and has left debts of the business unpaid then, notwithstanding the cessation of the business operation, the individual is deemed to continue to carry on business so as to be susceptible to a petition: *Theophile v Solicitor General* [1950] AC 186, which was followed by Hoffmann J, as he then was, in *Re a Debtor (No 784 of 1991)* [1992] Ch 554.

Section 265(3)

EC Regulation—This provision, effective from 31 May 2002, was inserted by reg 14 of the Insolvency Act 1986 (Amendment) (No 2) Regulations 2002 (SI 2002/1240). Article 3 of the Regulation allows for the opening of main proceedings in relation to a debtor where the debtor's centre of main interests is in another Member State subject to the Regulation. In those circumstances any bankruptcy proceedings within England and Wales are only capable of amounting to secondary or territorial proceedings. Section 265 will still provide the basis for the making of a bankruptcy order where the EC Regulation has no application on account of the debtor having no centre of main interests within a Member State: *Geveran Trading Co v Skjevesland* [2002] EWHC 2898 (Ch), [2003] BCC 391.

Centre of main interests ('COMI')—A debtor's centre of main interests is to be determined at the time when the court is first required to decide whether to open insolvency proceedings and should correspond not by reference to the place where his debts were incurred but, rather, by reference to the place where the debtor conducted the administration of his interests so as to be ascertainable by an objective third party: *Shierson v Vlieland-Boddy*

[2005] BPIR 1170 and 1190 (Chadwick LJ, Longmore LJ and Sir Martin Nourse). For an example of the Court refusing jurisdiction on a creditor's petition because the link between the debtor and the English jurisdiction was too tenuous, see Anglo Irish Bank Corporation v Flannery [2012] EWHC 4090 (Ch). See also the notes to s 272 for further cases relating to COMI in the context of debtor's petitions.

266 Other preliminary conditions

(1) Where a bankruptcy petition relating to an individual is presented by a person who is entitled to present a petition under two or more paragraphs of section 264(1), the petition is to be treated for the purposes of this Part as a petition under such one of those paragraphs as may be specified in the petition.

(2) A bankruptcy petition shall not be withdrawn without the leave of the court.

(3) The court has a general power, if it appears to it appropriate to do so on the grounds that there has been a contravention of the rules or for any other reason, to dismiss a bankruptcy petition or to stay proceedings on such a petition; and, where it stays proceedings on a petition, it may do so on such terms and conditions as it thinks fit.

(4) Without prejudice to subsection (3), where a petition under section 264(1)(a), (b) or (c) in respect of an individual is pending at a time when a criminal bankruptcy order is made against him, or is presented after such an order has been so made, the court may on the application of the Official Petitioner dismiss the petition if it appears to it appropriate to do so.

General note—The two procedural conditions in s 266(1) and (2) are conveniently located with the general power in subsection (3) within this provision: see also IR 1986, r 6.25 and the notes thereto. Section 266(4) is to be repealed from a day to be appointed pursuant to s 170(2) and Sch 16 of the Criminal Justice Act 1988 with the effect of finally rendering obsolete the criminal bankruptcy regime.

Section 266(1)

Scope of provision—The requirement that a petition must specify the ground under which the petitioner proceeds where the petitioner has standing to proceed under more than one ground serves to prevent a debtor having to deal, in effect, with more than one ground for the making of a bankruptcy order at any one time. The scheme of the legislation prevents more than one bankruptcy petition proceeding against a debtor simultaneously. In practice, however, the court may well be prepared to allow an amendment to cure any such defect, particularly where it can be shown that the debtor has placed no reliance on an omission or suffers no prejudice as a consequence of it or is plainly well aware of the ground upon which the petition has proceeded.

Section 266(2)

Withdrawal of a petition—This provision applies to *all* bankruptcy petitions. Its effect is not only to prevent abuse of the bankruptcy procedure through the presentation of groundless petitions (which will come under the scrutiny of the court on being withdrawn) but also to allow other creditors to substitute or effect a change of carriage of the petition under rr 6.30 and 6.31, as appropriate. The procedure on dismissal or leave to withdraw a petition, including evidence which must support such an application, appears in r 6.32.

Section 266(3)

The court's general power to dismiss or stay a petition—The court's general power to dismiss or stay arises only where 'there has been a contravention of rules or for any other reason.' In *Re Micklethwaite* [2003] BPIR 101 at [11] Peter Smith J observed in relation to s 266(3) that 'Earlier cases as to when petitions have been adjourned or dismissed under such a discretionary power are of no assistance, except in drawing to my attention the fact that I have a discretionary power. It is the facts of each case which indicate how, if at all, the discretion should be exercised.' In that case his Lordship made bankruptcy orders on three petitions where the petition debts were undisputed, unpaid and longstanding and refused to grant open-ended adjournments so as to allow the debtors, who were Lloyd's names, to pursue cross-claims which faced significant procedural hurdles, even if the claims could be said to exist at all. In *TSB Bank plc v Platts* [1997] BPIR 151 His Honour Judge Weekes QC, sitting as a High Court judge, held that s 266(3) does confer a discretion on the court to strike out a petition on the grounds of delay. Although in that case there had been delay following which the bankruptcy petition was re-listed of the court's own motion, the judge did not dismiss the petition, having taken account of the possibility of the bankruptcy proceedings starting again and the waste of costs that would entail together with the fact that the bankruptcy petition was, by that time, ready for trial.

There is no closed class of circumstances in which the court will dismiss a bankruptcy petition. The court's power, being a general one, has been held to justify dismissal where the petitioner could be shown to have been guilty of extortion or where the purpose of the proceedings is to gain some collateral advantage for himself: see *Re Majory* [1955] Ch 600 at 623, CA and compare, on its facts, *Re Malcolm Robert Ross (a Bankrupt) (No 2)* [2000] BPIR 636 at 643A–645E (Nourse LJ, Mantell LJ agreeing). The court may also dismiss a petition based on a non-provable debt, on which see the notes to s 264, or an unliquidated debt, on which see the notes to s 267 and the other examples therein. As regards going behind a judgment debt upon which a petition is based, Etherton J, following a review of the authorities, held in *Dawodu v American Express* [2001] BPIR 983 at 990D–990E that: '... what is required before the court is prepared to investigate a judgment debt, in the absence of an outstanding appeal or an application to set it aside, is some fraud, collusion, or miscarriage of justice. The latter phrase is of course capable of wide application according to the particular circumstances of the case. What in my judgment is required is that the court be shown something from which it can conclude that had there been a properly conducted judicial process then it would have been found, or very likely would have been found, that nothing was in fact due to the claimant.' These propositions were applied by Henderson J in *Dias v Havering LBC* [2011] EWHC 172 (Ch), [2011] BPIR 395 where he declined to investigate liability orders in respect of unpaid business rates. In *HMRC v Crossman* [2007] BPIR 1068 Rimer J held that HMRC was entitled to a bankruptcy order on a petition based on the difference between unpaid duty of £343,450 and the sum of £55,965.46 paid by the debtor pursuant to a confiscation order made under s 71 of the Criminal Justice Act 1988 notwithstanding the failure of HMRC to notify the criminal court at the time of the confiscation order proceedings of the possibility of it seeking to make a civil recovery for the balance. In *Dunbar Assets Plc v Fowler* [2013] BPIR 46 (at para 37) Chief Registrar Baister indicated the section could be used to 'deal with any serious abuse that did result in prejudice to a debtor by dismissing a petition presented in circumstances that did give rise to unfairness to the debtor'.

The court should not dismiss a bankruptcy petition merely on the ground that the debtor has no assets, since bankruptcy is a class action which is justifiable on grounds other than the realisation and distribution of assets by way of an investigation by a trustee of the affairs of the debtor: *Shepherd v Legal Services Commission* [2003] BPIR 140 at 146F–146H (Gabriel Moss QC, sitting as a deputy High Court judge) applying *Re Field (a Debtor)* [1978] Ch 371 (Sir Robert Megarry V-C) which is authority (at 375) for the proposition that the court may dismiss a petition subject to a heavy burden resting on the debtor to show that he has no assets and has no prospect of assets by reference to evidence of a source other than himself. The 'no assets' point also finds authority in the decision of Jules Sher QC, sitting as a deputy High Court judge, in *Re Thulin* [1995] 1 WLR 165 at 169 and in the decision of Rimer J in *HMRC v Crossman* [2007] BPIR 1068 at [42]. In the unusual case of *Amihyia v Official Receiver* [2005] BPIR 264 Evans-Lombe J allowed annulment of a bankruptcy order under s 375 where the order had been made through no fault of the bankrupt's where there were no assets to realise in the bankruptcy.

Neither should the court engage in the task of ascertaining whether a bankruptcy order is a disproportionate remedy in the circumstances of the case since the question of proportionality is not appropriate to a bankruptcy petition in the absence of an unreasonable refusal by the petitioning creditor, any serious procedural defect or abuse of process: *John Lewis plc v Pearson Burton* [2004] BPIR 70 (Pumfrey J). The relevance or otherwise of the concept of proportionality is discussed in greater detail in the notes to r 6.25.

There have been a number of cases in which the Local Government Ombudsman has criticised local authorities for bankrupting residents over small arrears of council tax and considered this to be maladministration causing injustice (see *Ford v Wolverhampton CC (Local Government's Ombudsman's Report)* [2008] BPIR 1304; *Report of an investigation into Complaint 07/A/12661 Against Camden LBC* [2008] BPIR 1572; Report of an Investigation in No 08002300 against Exeter City Council [2009] BPIR 598 and other LGO reports to similar effect noted in [2010] BPIR at 464, 476,1407, 1420 and [2011] BPIR at 1098). In *Hunt v Fylde* BC [2008] BPIR 1368 (an annulment case) the district judge referred (at para 19) to the possibility of human rights issues arising 'as we contemplate an individual losing his home for a small tax liability when the more proportionate remedy of a charging order subject to court control is available'. The question was put off for submissions at the future hearing of the bankruptcy petition. However, the Court of Appeal in *Lonergan v Gedling Borough Council* [2009] EWCA Civ 1569, [2010] BPIR 911 considered that a local authority is entitled to present a petition in respect of a liability order and rejected arguments that the practice violated the debtor's human rights (see paras 30–32 of the judgment).

Creditor's petition

267 Grounds of creditor's petition

(1) A creditor's petition must be in respect of one or more debts owed by the debtor, and the petitioning creditor or each of the petitioning creditors must be a person to whom the debt or (as the case may be) at least one of the debts is owed.

(2) Subject to the next three sections, a creditor's petition may be presented to the court in respect of a debt or debts only if, at the time the petition is presented—

    (a)   the amount of the debt, or the aggregate amount of the debts, is equal to or exceeds the bankruptcy level,

    (b)   the debt, or each of the debts, is for a liquidated sum payable to the petitioning creditor, or one or more of the petitioning creditors, either immediately or at some certain, future time, and is unsecured,

    (c)   the debt, or each of the debts, is a debt which the debtor appears either to be unable to pay or to have no reasonable prospect of being able to pay, and

    (d)   there is no outstanding application to set aside a statutory demand served (under section 268 below) in respect of the debt or any of the debts.

(3) A debt is not to be regarded for the purposes of subsection (2) as a debt for a liquidated sum by reason only that the amount of the debt is specified in a criminal bankruptcy order.

(4) 'The bankruptcy level' is £750; but the Secretary of State may by order in a statutory instrument substitute any amount specified in the order for that amount or (as the case may be) for the amount which by virtue of such an order is for the time being the amount of the bankruptcy level.

(5) An order shall not be made under subsection (4) unless a draft of it has been laid before, and approved by a resolution of, each House of Parliament.

General note—The substance of this provision is in identifying the nature of the debt upon which a creditors' petition under s 264(1)(a) may be based. Section 267(3) refers to the now obsolete criminal bankruptcy regime and is to be repealed from a day to be appointed under s 171(1) of the Criminal Justice Act 1988. The bankruptcy level of £750 in s 267(4) was originally fixed at that level by the Insolvency Proceedings (Increase of Monetary Limits) Regulations 1984 (SI 1984/1199), having previously been fixed at £200, but has not been increased since.

The four conditions in s 267(2) are cumulative. If a petition debt does not fall within each of those criteria, then the court has power to dismiss the petition under s 266(3).

The words 'subject to the next three sections' in s 267(2) means that s 267 must be read as subject to ss 268–270. Accordingly, the procedure for an expedited petition under s 270 may be engaged despite the fact of an outstanding application to set aside a statutory demand as mentioned in s 267(2)(d): *Re a Debtor (No 22 of 1993)* [1994] 1 WLR 46 (Mummery J, as he then was). Further, where a statutory demand seeks payment of an unsecured debt and a secured debt and the debtor discharges the unsecured debt the petitioner is precluded from amending the petition to revalue its security where the security has become unrealisable such that the debtor is entitled to have the petition dismissed because the unsecured element of the petition debt has been discharged. The reference in s 267(2)(c) is to the unsecured debt alone given that s 269(2) stipulates that the securerd and unsecured debts are separate debts: *Dubai Aluminium Company Ltd v Salaam* [2007] BPIR 690 (Registrar Simmonds).

Malicious petitions—A cause of action in tort lies in respect of injury caused by the malicious and unreasonable commencement of bankruptcy proceedings against an individual: *Gregory v Portsmouth City Council* [2000] 1 AC 419 at 427. The five elements of such an action are: (a) the presentation of a bankruptcy petition, (b) the termination of that petition in favour of the party against whom it was presented, (c) the absence of reasonable and probable cause for presentation of the petition, (d) the malicious presentation of the petition, and (e) the identification of damage caused by the malicious presentation of that petition. The authorities were considered by HHJ Peter Coulson QC, sitting as a judge of the High Court, in *Jacob v Vockrodt* [2007] BPIR 1568. The Privy Council has since confirmed in the corporate insolvency context in *Ebbvale Ltd v Hosking* [2013] UKPC 1, [2013] BPIR 219 that provided a winding up order is objectively likely to be of substantial advantage to the petitioner as a creditor, it is irrelevant that the petitioner's principle purpose behind presenting the petition was illegitimate.

Unliquidated debts—A creditor's petition may only be based on a debt for a 'liquidated sum', with the consequence that a petition based on a claim for damages or a claim for an account and payment is liable to be dismissed: *Hope v Premierpace (Europe) Ltd* [1999] BPIR 695 (Rimer J). The sum must be a 'liquidated sum' at the time the statutory demand is presented. If it is not, the statutory demand is irredeemably defective and cannot be saved by the fact the debt may become liquidated by the date the petition is presented (e g by agreement with the debtor): *Orrick, Herrington and Sutcliffe (Europe) LLP v Frohlich* [2012] BPIR 169.

Where a guarantor can be regarded as the principle debtor his liability under the guarantee can be regarded as a liquidated sum: *McGuiness v Norwich & Peterborough Building Society* [2011] EWCA Civ 1286, [2012] BPIR 145 which contains a detailed discussion of the classification of different types of guarantee liability as damages (unliquidated, even if the quantum is readily ascertainable) or a debt (a liquidated sum). See also *Sofaer v Anglo Irish Asset Finance plc* [2011] EWHC 1480 (Ch), [2011] BPIR 1736, *Dunbar Assets plc v Fowler* [2013] BPIR 46 and *Francis v Solomon Taylor & Shaw* [2013] EWHC 9 (Ch), [2013] BPIR 314 (in each of which the debtor's guarantee liability was held to be a liquidated sum).

Where, despite some irregularity its signing, the court was able to order specifc performance of a tenancy agreement, the rent due thereunder is a contingent debt in a liquidated sum: *Hurley v The Darjan Estate Company Plc* [2012] EWHC 189 (Ch), [2012] BPIR 1021.

Disputed debts—The court will not make a bankruptcy order where the petition debt is disputed, although an order is properly made if the undisputed element of the petition debt exceeds the bankruptcy level of £750: *TSB Bank plc v Platts (No 2)* [1998] BPIR 284 at 293A–293E (Peter Gibson and Otton LJJ and Sir John Balcombe). Where the debtor claims to have a counterclaim, set-off or cross-demand or otherwise disputes the debt, the question before the bankruptcy court is whether, on the evidence, there is a genuine triable issue. This follows from the test applied by para 13.4.4 of the *Practice Direction: Insolvency Proceedings* by which a rule of practice is established such that the court will normally set aside a statutory demand in those circumstances. If a statutory demand stands to be set aside on those grounds, then it follows that a bankruptcy petition must also be dismissed. The question of whether a debtor is entitled to raise such grounds on the hearing of a bankruptcy petition where the same grounds were raised on an application to set aside a statutory demand is considered in the notes to r 6.5(4).

Statute-barred debts—A statutory demand may not be based on a statute-barred debt, with the consequence that a petition based on such a debt must be dismissed: *Jelly v All Type Roofing* [1997] BCC 465 (HHJ Paul Baker QC). A petition based on a judgment debt, however, is not subject to the 6-year limitation period within s 24(1) of the Limitation Act 1980 since a petition is neither an action upon a judgment nor a process of execution of the judgment: *Ridgeway Motors (Isleworth) Ltd v ALTS Ltd* [2005] 2 All ER 304 (Brooke, Mummery and Scott Baker LJJ).

Petition based on costs—A sum awarded in respect of costs is capable of founding a bankruptcy petition, but only at the point at which the costs are assessed or the client is otherwise prevented from disputing them on the basis of a binding agreement or an estoppel. A solicitor's bill which has not been assessed is not a liquidated debt within s 267(2) such that it is incapable of founding a bankruptcy petition or a statutory demand: *Klamer v Kyrkiakides and Braier (a firm)* [2005] BPIR 1142 (Registrar Simmonds). In *Truex v Toll* [2009] EWHC 396 (Ch), [2009] BPIR 692 Proudman J held that a simple admission by the client of his costs bill, unsupported by consideration, was not sufficient to convert an unliquidated debt into a liquidated one. The client had to be bound by an agreement or an estopppel. The fact that the solicitor had incurred the cost of presenting the statutory demand and petition in reliance on the admission was insufficient detriment to found an estoppel. An example of a case where an estoppel argument succeeded is *Moseley v Else Solicitors LLP* [2010] BPIR 1192 where the petitioning solicitors had continued to work for the debtor in reliance upon his representation that a disputed invoice would be paid. An estoppel argument failed on the facts in *Wallace LLP v Yates* [2010] BPIR 1041. An interim order in respect of costs for a liquidated sum would also be capable of founding a petition. For the position on sums due in publicly funded cases see *Galloppa v Galloppa* [1999] BPIR 352 (Jonathan Parker J). A petition may also be based on an unpaid bill raised by a solicitor for a liquidated sum for non-contentious work, even where the reasonableness of those fees is challenged by way of the debtor client seeking a Law Society taxation: *Re a Debtor (No 88 of 1991)* [1993] Ch 286 at 292 (Sir Donald Nicholls V-C).

A costs liability incurred post-IVA, arising out of an agreement entered into pre-IVA, is, subject to the terms of the IVA, capable of founding a bankruptcy petition as a debt not caught by the IVA: *Cornelius v Casson* [2008] BPIR 504 (Thomas Ivory QC, sitting as a deputy High Court judge): see also *Coutts & Co v Passey* [2007] BPIR 323.

Bankruptcy debts—A debt owed jointly by a partner is capable of founding a bankruptcy petition against that partner: *Schooler v Commissioners of Customs & Excise* [1996] BPIR 207 (Nourse LJ, Roch and Hobhouse LJJ agreeing).

Gambling debts—As a matter of public policy English law regards gambling debts as unenforceable. However, a gambling debt which is enforceable in a foreign jurisdiction may found a bankruptcy petition, even where the foreign gambling debt has been compromised under a deed which states expressly that the deed is subject to English law: *Rio Properties Inc v Al-Midani* [2003] BPIR 128 (His Honour Judge Maddocks, sitting as a High Court judge; compromised $1.8 million Nevada gaming debt justified bankruptcy order).

Payment of petition debt by date of hearing—In *Lilley v American Express Europe Ltd* [2000] BPIR 70 John Jarvis QC, sitting as a deputy High Court judge, held that the court retained jurisdiction to make a bankruptcy order even where the debtor had reduced the outstanding petition debt to beneath the bankruptcy level by the time of the hearing of the petition. However, having made reference to r 6.25 and s 271, the deputy judge observed that this was a course which the court should approach cautiously. He went on (at 74H–75B):

'It seems to me clear that the court cannot make a bankruptcy order if the whole of the debt has been paid by the time it comes for hearing, but the Act says nothing to prevent a court from making an order if only part of the debt has been paid. In my judgment a court must retain a discretion as to whether or not it is proper to make an order in these circumstances. One can imagine a case where a debtor has played a cat and mouse game with the petitioning creditor and has paid off just under the bankruptcy level on a number of petitions, and one can imagine in those circumstances that a court will be reluctant to permit a bankrupt to behave in that way. It seems to me that the court would retain a discretion then to make an order in those circumstances. If, on the other hand, the case is one where there were genuine difficulties for the debtor and the debtor has made efforts to pay money in and it was not a cat and mouse game, then the court would consider carefully whether or not it should exercise its discretion to make a bankruptcy order.'

It is submitted that where the court was satisfied as to the genuine efforts of the debtor then, subject to the facts of the case, the court would be justified in adjourning the petition, albeit for a relatively short period. Notably, the deputy judge also went on (at 76D–77G) to hold that it is wrong in principle to add to a petition debt the costs of the petition to date so as to bring the petition debt above the bankruptcy level.

Tax assessments—The bankruptcy court has no standing to interfere with assessments made by the General Commissioner on evidence supplied by the Inland Revenue where a bankruptcy order has been made on such assessments and where the bankrupt seeks to challenge the evidence supplied by the Revenue: *Cullinane v Commissioners of Inland Revenue* [2000] BPIR 996 (Hart J) and see *Flett v HMRC* [2010] EWHC 2662 (Ch), [2010] BPIR 1075. The position is no different when the court is invited to look behind the Revenue's assessments on the ground that the taxpayer complains that assessments are unfair since such complaints should be channelled through the tax appeals system: *Worby v Inland Revenue* [2005] BPIR 1249 (Sir Donald Rattee). This is not to say, however, that the fact of a tax assessment and its notification to the taxpayer must automatically result in a bankruptcy order being made. In *HM Customs & Excise v D & D Marketing (UK) Ltd* [2002] EWHC 660, [2003] BPIR 539 (a winding-up case) Evans-Lombe J found that a manually assessed liability for VAT was due and payable but was mindful of an extant appeal instituted by the taxpayer under the tax legislation. Whilst making a winding-up order based on evidence which showed that the appeal could not succeed his Lordship identified that '[The making of an order] is a matter for my discretion. It does not follow that, because the debt is still deemed to be due, it would be appropriate to make a winding-up order if I were satisfied that the company on its appeal to the VAT Tribunal stood a reasonable chance of succeeding with that appeal.' To like effect, in *HMRC v Potter* [2008] BPIR 1033 Deputy Registrar Nicholas Briggs dismissed a bankruptcy petition based on manual VAT assessments totaling £2,220,351.57 on the basis that, first, at [73], the court is not ousted entirely from jurisdiction in matters between taxpayer and Crown and, secondly, at [78], and given the dispute raised by the debtor following the judgment of Blackburne J in *Lam v Inland Revenue* [2006] EWHC 592 (Ch), [2006] STC 893 at [13] and [30] to the effect that the bankruptcy court may look behind an assessment in an exceptional case, the making of an order in light of the basis of the debtor's objections could be unjust, disproportionate and might result in a miscarriage of justice. Further, HMRC must have regard to its obligations under the Disability Discrimination Act 1995 in conducting its affairs: in *Re Haworth* [2011] EWHC 36 (Ch), [2011] BPIR 428 HHJ Pelling QC annulled a bankruptcy order made on a petition by HMRC where the debtor had lacked capacity to deal with the bankruptcy proceedings. Moreover it was held that as HMRC knew of the debtor's mental impairment it was in breach of its obligations under the Disability Discrimination Act 1995 in acting as it did. HMRC was ordered in principle to pay the fees and expenses of the bankruptcy, once they were determined.

Council Tax—A council tax liability order is a 'debt' for the purpose of s 267 (*Smolen v Tower Hamlets LBC* [2007] BPIR 448). The Court of Appeal have confirmed that unpaid council tax arrears still constitue a debt even if no liability order has been made (*Bolsover*

DC v Ashfield Nominees Ltd [2010] EWCA Civ 1129, [2011] BPIR 7. For some discussion on proportionality and bankruptcy petitions based on council tax arrears see the notes to s 266.

Section 267(2)(c)

Scope of provision—See s 268 and the notes thereto.

Section 267(2)(d)

Scope of provision—An application to set aside the statutory demand must be in the prescribed form and made in time and is subject to the prescribed fee being paid: *Ariyo v Sovereign Leasing plc* [1998] BPIR 177 (Nourse, Roch and Phillips LJJ).

There is 'no outstanding application to set aside a statutory demand' if such an application has been dismissed but is subject to an appeal at the time a petition is presented: *Ahmad v IR Commissioners* [2005] BPIR 541 at [7] and [8] (Evans-Lombe J).

In the unusual case of *Regis Direct Ltd v Hakeem* (unreported, 3 October 2012) Norris J refused to set aside a bankruptcy order, even though there was an extant application to set aside the statutory demand when the petition was presented. He considered there was no point in doing so, because the set aside application had been dismissed three days after the bankruptcy order had been made and there was no injustice to the debtor.

Setting aside a statutory demand—See r 6.5(4) and the notes thereto.

268 Definition of 'inability to pay', etc; the statutory demand

(1) For the purposes of section 267(2)(c), the debtor appears to be unable to pay a debt if, but only if, the debt is payable immediately and either—

    (a)   the petitioning creditor to whom the debt is owed has served on the debtor a demand (known as 'the statutory demand') in the prescribed form requiring him to pay the debt or to secure or compound for it to the satisfaction of the creditor, at least 3 weeks have elapsed since the demand was served and the demand has been neither complied with nor set aside in accordance with the rules, or

    (b)   execution or other process issued in respect of the debt on a judgment or order of any court in favour of the petitioning creditor, or one or more of the petitioning creditors to whom the debt is owed, has been returned unsatisfied in whole or in part.

(2) For the purposes of section 267(2)(c) the debtor appears to have no reasonable prospect of being able to pay a debt if, but only if, the debt is not immediately payable and—

    (a)   the petitioning creditor to whom it is owed has served on the debtor a demand (also known as 'the statutory demand') in the prescribed form requiring him to establish to the satisfaction of the creditor that there is a reasonable prospect that the debtor will be able to pay the debt when it falls due,

    (b)   at least 3 weeks have elapsed since the demand was served, and

    (c)   the demand has been neither complied with nor set aside in accordance with the rules.

General note—This provision provides the definition relevant to s 267(2)(c) by reference to a statutory demand or an unsatisfied execution. It is not concerned with the grounds for the setting aside of a statutory demand, which are considered in r 6.5(4) and the notes thereto.

Form and procedure on a statutory demand—Although no forms are specifically prescribed by the Rules, Form 6.1, 6.2 or 6.3 are invariably employed, as appropriate. The procedure is provided for in rr 6.1–6.3.

The use of a statutory demand by a creditor constitutes a form of self-help. The statutory demand procedure does not, however, involve the court (other than where there is an application to set aside the demand) and, as such the demand does not constitute 'insolvency proceedings' which are capable of cure under r 7.55 in the event of irregularity: *Re a Debtor (No 340 of 1992)* [1996] 2 All ER 211, CA. Neither does pursuit of a statutory demand constitute 'legal proceedings' for the purposes of s 9 of the Arbitration Act 1996: *Shalson v D F Keane Ltd* [2003] BPIR 1045 at [13] (Blackburne J).

Future debts—Section 268 and Form 6.3 provide no guidance as to what a creditor must allege in respect of a future debt other than the grounds upon which it is alleged that the debtor has no reasonable prospect of paying the debt. A creditor will frequently be at risk in pursuing this ground, since the creditor will have to satisfy the court as to the basis upon which the court can be satisfied that the debtor will be unable to pay the debt as and when it falls due if it is has not fallen due by the date of the bankruptcy hearing. In practice this is most likely to arise in a case where the debtor is hopelessly insolvent and/or has given an indication that he will be unable to pay in future.

If the requirements of this section are satisfied, the debtor cannot avoid a bankruptcy order being made by demonstrating that he is solvent – if the debt which is the subject of the statutory demand is due and owing it must be paid: *Johnson v Tandridge DC* [2008] BPIR 405.

Section 268(1)(b)

'… **execution or other process … returned unsatisfied in whole or in part'**—Although, strictly speaking, only an execution, as opposed to any 'other process', is capable of involving anything being 'returned unsatisfied', in *Skarzynski v Chalford Property Co Ltd* [2001] BPIR 673 at [13] Jacob J, as he then was, held that the words 'returned unsatisfied' meant 'proof that the execution or other process failed to satisfy the debt – the upshot of the execution or other process.' As such, it is open to a creditor to go down the 'execution or other process' route and, where that route produces no money or insufficient money, to petition for bankruptcy. In that case the fact that the sheriff had failed to endorse a statement on the writ of execution had not been fatal to the writ's validity as an unsatisfied return. That decision should be read with that of the Court of Appeal in *Re a Debtor (No 340 of 1992)* [1996] 2 All ER 211, and the judgment of Millett J to which Jacob J referred. *Re a Debtor*, however, as Jacob J pointed out, was a case which involved no valid execution such that there could be no return, as opposed to the position in *Skarzynski* where there had been a valid execution but a failure by the sheriff to endorse the writ subsequently.

269 Creditor with security

(1) A debt which is the debt, or one of the debts, in respect of which a creditor's petition is presented need not be unsecured if either—

    (a)   the petition contains a statement by the person having the right to enforce the security that he is willing, in the event of a bankruptcy order being made, to give up his security for the benefit of all the bankrupt's creditors, or

    (b)   the petition is expressed not to be made in respect of the secured part of the debt and contains a statement by that person of the estimated value at the date of the petition of the security for the secured part of the debt.

(2) In a case falling within subsection (1)(b) the secured and unsecured parts of the debt are to be treated for the purposes of sections 267 and 270 as separate debts.

General note—The fact that a creditor holds security does not preclude the creditor from proceeding on a bankruptcy petition subject to compliance with either s 269(1)(a) or (b). The position of a secured creditor who petitions for a debtor's bankruptcy is provided for in s 383(3). Section 383(2) provides that a creditor is secured if he 'holds any security for the debt (whether a mortgage, charge or lien or other security) over any property of the [debtor].' On the interplay between s 269 and and r 6.5(4)(c) (which states in effect that the court may set aside a statutory demand if the debt is fully secured) see 1st Credit (Finance) Ltd v Bartram [2010] EWHC 2910 (Ch), [2011] BPIR 1.

Section 269 is available to a petitioning creditor even if the debtor has no other creditors and the petitioning creditor would otherwise be entitled to rely on its security rights: *Zandfarid v Bank of Credit & Commerce International (SA) (in liquidation)* [1996] BPIR 501 at 509G–509H (Jonathan Parker J, as he then was).

In *Barclays Bank plc v Mogg* [2004] BPIR 259 David Richards J held that, whilst a failure to comply with s 269 constituted a serious flaw, the proper course was to allow an amendment to a petition, rather than dismissing it, where the omission was not deliberate and where the debtor had not been misled and had suffered no prejudice as a consequence of the omission.

Rules 6.115–6.119 deal with the valuation etc of a creditor's security.

270 Expedited petition

In the case of a creditor's petition presented wholly or partly in respect of a debt which is the subject of a statutory demand under section 268, the petition may be presented before the end of the 3-week period there mentioned if there is a serious possibility that the debtor's property or the value of any of his property will be significantly diminished during that period and the petition contains a statement to that effect.

General note—This provision allows for the presentation of a petition without the need for the elapse of the 3-week period mentioned in s 268(1)(a) following service of a statutory demand, but only 'if there is a serious possibility that the debtor's property or the value of any of his property will be significantly diminished during that period ...'. The court will, therefore, require evidence of the jeopardy alleged; in keeping with the threshold applied to interim, and in particular freezing, injunctions, the court will require something over and above mere suspicion or fear.

Section 270 applies only to cases where a statutory demand has been served: *Wehmeyer v Wehmeyer* [2001] BPIR 548 (Mr Registrar James). The fact that there is an outstanding application to set aside a statutory demand within s 267(2)(d) does not prevent the expedition of a petition: *Re a Debtor (No 22 of 1993)* [1994] 1 WLR 46 (Mummery J). Rule 6.18(2) provides that an expedited petition may be heard within the 14-day period which must ordinarily elapse following service of a bankruptcy petition. In theory at least, it would follow that, in the most extreme case, the statutory demand might be served contemporaneously with the bankruptcy petition and the matter listed immediately for hearing although in practice a creditor would usually be better proceeding directly down the petition route and seeking an expedited hearing under r 6.18(2), although a hearing would remain subject to s 271(2).

271 Proceedings on creditor's petition

(1) The court shall not make a bankruptcy order on a creditor's petition unless it is satisfied that the debt, or one of the debts, in respect of which the petition was presented is either—

    (a)   a debt which, having been payable at the date of the petition or having since become payable, has been neither paid nor secured or compounded for, or

    (b)   a debt which the debtor has no reasonable prospect of being able to pay when it falls due.

(2) In a case in which the petition contains such a statement as is required by section 270, the court shall not make a bankruptcy order until at least 3 weeks have elapsed since the service of any statutory demand under section 268.

(3) The court may dismiss the petition if it is satisfied that the debtor is able to pay all his debts or is satisfied—

(a) that the debtor has made an offer to secure or compound for a debt in respect of which the petition is presented,

(b) that the acceptance of that offer would have required the dismissal of the petition, and

(c) that the offer has been unreasonably refused;

and, in determining for the purposes of this subsection whether the debtor is able to pay all his debts, the court shall take into account his contingent and prospective liabilities.

(4) In determining for the purposes of this section what constitutes a reasonable prospect that a debtor will be able to pay a debt when it falls due, it is to be assumed that the prospect given by the facts and other matters known to the creditor at the time he entered into the transaction resulting in the debt was a reasonable prospect.

(5) Nothing in sections 267 to 271 prejudices the power of the court, in accordance with the rules, to authorise a creditor's petition to be amended by the omission of any creditor or debt and to be proceeded with as if things done for the purposes of those sections had been done only by or in relation to the remaining creditors or debts.

General note—The key provisions here are in s 271(1) and (3) which, respectively, impose two alternative conditions which arise for consideration on the hearing of the bankruptcy petition together with a single ground, made up of three cumulative criteria, which, if fulfilled, afford the court a discretion to dismiss the petition.

Section 271(1) should also be read in conjunction with r 6.25 which, in addition to corresponding with the former provision, adds a further fetter to the court's jurisdiction in the case of an over-stated debt in a statutory demand, as considered below. Section 271(2) should be read in conjunction with the notes to s 270.

On procedure generally on a bankruptcy petition see paras 14–16 of the *Practice Direction: Insolvency Proceedings* [2012] BPIR 409. As to circumstances which might justify the imposition of a stay pending the hearing of an appeal see *Emap Active Ltd v Hill* [2007] EWHC 1592 (Ch), [2007] BPIR 1228 (Morgan J, stay granted on undertakings where real harm would be done if the order under appeal remained in force and effect in the event that the appeal was successful). Where a bankruptcy order is successfully appealed after a trustee has been installed it is important that the appeal court be invited to address the trustee's remuneration and expenses incurred in the interim, and the court has an inherent jurisdiction to do so: *Appleyard v Wewelwala* [2012] EWHC 3302 (Ch).

Section 271(1)

'the court … is satisfied'—In the absence of authority it is submitted that the word 'satisfied' equates to the court being satisfied on a balance of probabilities.

A debtor is not precluded from disputing that a debt is due at the petition stage if he has not challenged a statutory demand leading to the petition: *Royal Bank of Scotland v Farley* [1996] BPIR 638 at 640. In *Barnes v Whitehead* [2004] BPIR 693 at 697 HHJ Maddocks, sitting as a judge of the High Court, said this:

'Furthermore the terms of r 6.25 of the 1986 Rules expressly require the court to be satisfied that the statements in the petition are true. One of those statements is that the debt is due. If the debt is the subject of a genuine dispute on substantial grounds, then the court cannot be so satisfied. The principle is well settled, and frequently applied in relation to company winding-up petitions, that the insolvency procedure is not the appropriate procedure for resolving disputed debts. The proper course is to issue a claim and obtain a judgment. The court does in any case have a discretion and once it appears that there is a dispute on substantial grounds it would be wrong to make a bankruptcy order. On principle therefore it would seem to me that the court would be bound to hear the case that the debt was disputed, notwithstanding the failure of the debtor to raise it by a preliminary application to set aside the demand. I would finally note that r 6.25(3) seems to contemplate a situation in which a debt, disputed as to part, would be resolved on the hearing of the petition.'

Section 271(1)(a)

'a debt which … has been neither paid nor secured nor compounded for'—The word 'paid' is not controversial. Either the debt has been paid or it has not, and, if paid in part, the court must be satisfied that the amount outstanding exceeds £750 although, even if it does not, the court retains a discretion in making an order: *Lilley v American Express Europe Ltd* [2000] BPIR 70 (John Jarvis QC sitting as a deputy High Court judge).

For debts capable of founding a bankruptcy petition see the notes to s 267.

The term 'secured' is best understood by reference to s 383(2) which provides that 'a debt is secured … to the extent that the person to whom the debt is owed holds any security for the debt (whether a mortgage, charge, lien or other security) over any property of the person by whom the debt is owed.'

In *Smith v Ian Simpson & Co* [2000] BPIR 667 (Laws LJ and Jonathan Parker J, Evans LJ dissenting on result but not reasoning) it was held that the reference to payment in s 271(1)(a) is to unconditional payment such that a payment from the debtor's funds which is liable to be avoided under s 284(1) on a bankruptcy order being made cannot constitute payment. In such circumstances the court retains the power to make a bankruptcy order, which will be relevant where a supporting creditor seeks carriage of the petition under r 6.31. If there are no such supporting creditors, then the court is entitled to dismiss the bankruptcy petition notwithstanding the fact that the petition debt has been discharged out of the debtor's own estate: *Re Marr (a Bankrupt)* [1990] Ch 773, CA.

For further commentary see the notes to s 123 under the heading 'Secure or compound to the reasonable satisfaction of the creditor'.

In *Marquis de Louville de Toucy v Bonhams 1793 Ltd* [2011] EWHC 3809 (Ch), [2012] BPIR 793 Vos J allowed an appeal against a bankruptcy order made against a debtor who lacked capacity to deal with his financial affairs. In the circumstances, given the incomplete nature of the information before the Court, the Registrar could not have been sure that the debt could not in fact have been discharged from the debtor's assets and could not have been sure whether or not s 271(1) was satisfied without investigation and hearing submissions from somebody who could represent the debtor, and the petition should have been adjourned to allow such a representative to be appointed.

Section 271(1)(b)

'… no reasonable prospect of being able to pay …'—This provision requires the court to reach a finding of fact as to whether, on the balance of probabilities, a debtor has no reasonable prospect of being able to pay a future debt when it falls due. Thus, the court must not make a bankruptcy order if satisfied that there is a 'reasonable prospect' that the debtor will be able to pay the future debt at a due date. This assessment may amount to a very difficult exercise for the court which may dictate that further evidence is required other than in extreme cases, as do arise in practice, such as where the debtor is hopelessly insolvent, where promises of future funding are unevidenced and plainly speculative or where the debtor himself has admitted that he will be unable to make payment in the future. It should also be noted that, in reaching a finding on the evidence, by virtue of s 271(4), the facts and other matters known to the creditor at the time the future debt came into being was a reasonable prospect such that the burden rests on the creditor to establish some new fact or matter which has come to his knowledge since the debt came into being which detracts from that statutorily presumed reasonable prospect.

Section 271(3)

Scope of provision—The court retains a discretion to dismiss a petition in the circumstances listed within subsection (3). The fact of a debtor asserting his solvency is no answer to a petition based on a debt which remains unpaid: *Johnson v Tandridge District Council* [2008] BPIR 405 at [37] (HHJ Kaye QC sitting as judge of the High Court).

The final part of the provision requires that, in reaching its conclusion, the court must take into account both the debtor's contingent liabilities (ie those which will crystallise subject to a condition which may or may not occur) and the debtor's prospective liabilities (ie those liabilities which will crystallise at some future time. The relevant principles, which draw on the judgments of Timothy Lloyd QC, sitting as he then was as a deputy High Court judge in *Re a Debtor (No 32 of 1993)* [1994] 1 WLR 899, and of Robert Walker J, as he then as, in *Commissioners of Inland Revenue v the Debtor, Re a Debtor (No 6349 of 1994)* [1996] BPIR 271, are summarised conveniently in the judgment of Lightman J in *HM Customs & Excise v Dougall* [2001] BPIR 269 at 272F–272H thus:

'First, the test of unreasonableness is whether an unreasonable creditor in the position of the petitioning creditor and in the light of the actual history as disclosed to the court could have reached the conclusion that the petitioning creditor reached. There may be a range of reasonable positions on the part of the hypothetical reasonable creditors and a rejection of an offer by the petitioner is only to be categorised as unreasonable if no reasonable creditor would have refused the offer and accordingly the refusal is beyond the range of reasonable responses to it. Secondly, the test is objective, namely the response of the hypothetical reasonable creditor. The court is not limited to considering the considerations that were taken into account by the petitioning creditor himself when he refused to agree to the offer. The court must look at all the relevant factors and decide what are the relevant and what impact those relevant factors would have on the hypothetical reasonable creditor. The third proposition is that the debtor must be full, frank and open and provide all the necessary information to enable an informed decision to be made by the creditor.'

The identification of the relevant principles as above is important because, whilst any reported authority on s 271(3) may illustrate the court's approach to any particular set of facts, each case may only be determined by a comparison of the response of any particular creditor to the range of reasonable positions open to a hypothetical reasonable creditor on the particular facts before the court.

The test has been elaborated upon in the detailed judgment of Chief Registrar Baister in *HMRC v Garwood* [2012] BPIR 575, particularly at para 23 where he gives a comprehensive summariy of the principle propositions that emerge from the authorities. (Unusually) in that case it was held that HMRC had unreasonably refused an offer of security where, if it had applied thought and not acted mechanistically, it would have been clear that the offer had increased the possibility of recovering the tax due. This position can be contrasted with the prior decision *Ross v HMRC* [2010] BPIR 652, where the contrary result was reached on the facts (although the court did caution HMRC against adopting a blanket policy of refusing security in every case).

For recent examples of cases where a debtor has unsuccessfully argued a creditor had not acted reasonably in rejecting his offer see: *Nottingham County Council v Pennant* [2010] BPIR 430 (HHJ Purle QC held that a local authority had been entitled to reject an offer of repayment over 2 years where the debtor had defaulted on payment arrangments in the past, and the district judge had erred in treating the situation as analogous to an application in a mortgagee repossession case under s 36 of the Administration of Justice Act 1970, since in bankruptcy cases an undisputed creditor was prima facie entitled to the bankruptcy order which was petitioned for); *Shrimpton v Darby's Solicitors LLP* [2011] EWHC 3796 (Ch), [2012] BPIR 631 (where the offer to pay was based upon a future income stream which was too speculative). In *Dunbar Assets plc v Fowler* [2013] BPIR 46 Chief Registrar Baister was faced with the seemingly novel submission that offers made by third parties were not offers made by the debtor and did not engage s 271(3)(a). He said (at para 21) 'I venture to express the tentative view that it could be possible for an offer from the debtor to include an offer that contemplates fulfilment of some or all of what is on offer by a third party as, for example, agent of the debtor. However, it is unnecessary for me to reach a definitive view in the circumstances of this case' (since the offers were not unreasonbly refused).

Section 271(5)

Amendment to creditor's petition—The only provision in the Insolvency Rules 1986 allowing for amendment of a bankruptcy petition appears in r 6.22 which, subject to the leave of the court, allows a petition to be amended 'at any time after presentation by the omission of any creditor or any debt'. The general power in the present provision allows for the omission of a creditor or a debt mentioned therein so as to allow for the continuance of the petition with the remaining creditors or debts and is not limited in scope by the narrower r 6.22: *Aspinall's Club Ltd v Halabi* [1998] BPIR 322 (John Martin QC, sitting as a deputy High Court judge).

The standing of the debtor to raise arguments raised previously on an application to set aside a statutory demand—See the notes to r 6.5(4).

Debtor's petition

272 Grounds of debtor's petition

(1) A debtor's petition may be presented to the court only on the grounds that the debtor is unable to pay his debts.

(2) The petition shall be accompanied by a statement of the debtor's affairs containing—

    (a)   such particulars of the debtor's creditors and of his debts and other liabilities and of his assets as may be prescribed, and

    (b)   such other information as may be prescribed.

General note—A debtor may petition for his own bankruptcy, but only on the ground of inability to pay debts. No minimum level of debt or debts is prescribed, although the court may not be prepared to consider making an order on a petition where the level of the debts is very low and where the debtor does not fall within all of the four conditions in s 273(1) which preclude the court from making a bankruptcy order where those criteria are met.

A debtor's right to petition for his own bankruptcy does not amount to a fundamental constitutional right; as such, the deposit fee payable under the Insolvency Fees Order 1986 to cover the costs of the official receiver in addition to the petition fee is not unlawful and does not contravene Arts 6 and 14 of the European Convention on Human Rights, since a bankruptcy petition does not involve the determination of disputed civil rights: *Lightfoot v Lord Chancellor* [2000] BPIR 120 (Simon Browne and Chadwick LJJ and Rattee J).

Bankruptcy Tourism—The courts are becoming more alive to the emerging issue of forum shopping or 'bankruptcy tourism', and should be careful to consider when considering a petition presented by a foreign debtor whether there has been a genuine transfer of the debtor's centre of main interests ('COMI') into the English jurisdiction for the purpose of EC Regulation 1346/2000. All too often this is not considered on the hearing of the petition (often only attended by the debtor him or herself who is then unchallenged), leading to the necessity for later applications for an annulment by the OR or creditors on the ground that the bankruptcy order should not have been made: see for instance *OR v Mitterfellner* [2009] BPIR 1075; *OR v Keelan* [2012] BPIR 613; *Re Eichler (No 2)* [2011] BPIR 1293 (which contains a review of the authorities and some very helpful guidance as to what the court's practice should be when faced with a debtor's petition where there are doubts as to jurisdiction by Chief Registrar Baister) and *Die Sparkeasse Bremen AG v Armutcu* [2012] EWHC 4026 (Ch), [2013] BPIR 210 (where Proudman J emphasised the importance of full disclosure where a debtor's petition was presented on an ex parte basis). The practice has developed in some courts of requiring a debtor presenting his own petition to serve the petition on his creditors before the bankruptcy order will be made. This has much to recommend it since it gives the opportunity for the creditors to object beforethe event, rather than having to do so by way of an application for an annulment.

On a debtor's petition the burden of proof is on the debtor as petitioner to establish COMI and not on the objecting creditor to disprove it: *Eck v Zapf* [2012] BPIR 499. Detailed consideration was given to the caselaw on COMI and the principles to be applied when assessing oral evidence in *O'Mahoney v National Irish Bank* [2012] BPIR 1174, where the Court found that the debtor had in fact extablished COMI in the jurisdiction and the challenge to the bankruptcy order failed.

In *Re Hagemeister* [2010] BPIR 1093 it was emphasised that once a court, rightly or wrongly, opens main proceedings, they remain as main proceedings until they are annulled, rescinded or otherwise set aside and cannot be simply re-characterised as secondary proceedings if it is discovered that 'main-proceedings' in another state pre-dated them.

Section 272(1)

'... **the debtor is unable to pay his debts**'—In *Re Coney (a Bankrupt)* [1998] BPIR 333 at 335G–335H David Oliver QC, sitting as a deputy High Court judge, held that these words in the present provision referred to an inability to pay debts at the time that such debts are due. The court is therefore not concerned with what might be an excess of assets over liabilities but, rather, the debtor's liquidity. The question is whether at the time of his petition the debtor has some tangible and immediate prospect of being able to meet his liabilities in due course: see *F v F (S Intervening) (Financial Provison: Bankruptcy Reviewable Disposition)* [2002] EWHC 2814 (Fam), [2003] 1 FLR 911 at 928 (Coleridge J; bankruptcy order annulled, applying *Coney*, on the basis that husband not insolvent on facts of case). *Coney* was approved by the Court of Appeal in *Paulin v Paulin* [2009] EWCA Civ 221, [2009] BPIR 572. In *Gittins v Serco Home Affairs* [2012] EWHC 651 (Ch), [2012] BPIR 560 HHJ Behrens held (relying on *BNY Corporate Trustee Services Ltd v Eurosail-UK 2007-3BL plc and Others* [2011] EWCA Civ 227, [2011] 1 WLR 2524 at paras 45-47) that 'the primary test for an inability to pay debts as they fall due for an individual under s 272 of the 1986 Act is the cash flow test in respect of assets and immediate liabilities. However there is a limited role in respect of future liabilities which comes into play when it can be said that the individual's use of cash or other assets for current purposes can be said to be a fraud on the future creditors' (para 33). It was unnecessary to show any actual demand for payment had been made which could not be satisfied. This is consistent with r 6.39(1) which requires that the debtor's petition should include a statement that the petitioner is unable to pay his debts.

Statement of debtor's affairs—The statement of affairs must be in Form 6.28 and must be verified by an affidavit: r 6.41(1).

The term 'debt' is defined in s 385(1) as being construed in accordance with s 382(3) which imports very wide meaning to any reference to the term 'debt' or 'liability' such that 'It is immaterial whether the debt or liability is present or future, whether it is certain or contingent or whether its amount is fixed or liquidated, or is capable of being ascertained by fixed rules or as a matter of opinion.' Notwithstanding the breadth of those words, it is submitted that the term 'debts' in s 272(1) will not extend to the legal or unenforceable debts, such as gaming debts incurred in England and Wales, although the term would appear to catch a gaming debt incurred and enforceable in another jurisdiction: *Rio Properties Inc v Al-Midani* [2003] BPIR 128 (His Honour Judge Maddocks sitting as a High Court judge, $1.8 million gaming debt enforceable in Nevada capable of founding a creditor's petition).

Court in which petition to be filed—See r 6.40, which also deals with the position where a voluntary arrangement is in force.

Procedure generally—See rr 6.37–6.50.

273 Appointment of insolvency practitioner by the court

(1) Subject to the next section, on the hearing of a debtor's petition the court shall not make a bankruptcy order if it appears to the court—

    (a)   that if a bankruptcy order were made the aggregate amount of the bankruptcy debts, so far as unsecured, would be less than the small bankruptcies level,

(b)   that if a bankruptcy order were made, the value of the bankrupt's estate would be equal to or more than the minimum amount,

(c)   that within the period of 5 years ending with the presentation of the petition the debtor has neither been adjudged bankrupt nor made a composition with his creditors in satisfaction of his debts or a scheme of arrangement of his affairs, and

(d)   that it would be appropriate to appoint a person to prepare a report under section 274.

'The minimum amount' and 'the small bankruptcies level' mean such amounts as may for the time being be prescribed for the purposes of this section.

(2) Where on the hearing of the petition, it appears to the court as mentioned in subsection (1), the court shall appoint a person who is qualified to act as an insolvency practitioner in relation to the debtor—

(a)   to prepare a report under the next section, and

(b)   subject to section 258(3) in Part VIII, to act in relation to any voluntary arrangement to which the report relates either as trustee or otherwise for the purpose of supervising its implementation.

General note—This provision finds no counterpart in the case of a creditor's petition and is designed to avoid the making of a bankruptcy order in certain cases where a voluntary arrangement might produce what might be termed a more satisfactory outcome for both debtor and creditors. The mechanism for the proposal of such a voluntary arrangement is provided for in s 274, but is conditional on the fulfilment of the four conditions in s 273(1) and the willingness of the debtor to make a proposal for a voluntary arrangement.

Just as there is no mechanism on a debtor's petition for creditors to give notice of intention to appear on the petition – compared to rr 6.18(3), 6.23 and 6.24 in the case of a creditor's petition – there is no mechanism for the giving of notice to creditors of any voluntary arrangement proposal under s 274 prior to their being summoned to the meeting of creditors under s 274(5).

Insolvent partnerships—Sections 273–277 have no application to insolvent partnerships: see the Insolvent Partnerships Order 1994 (SI 1994/2421).

Section 273(1)

Scope of provision—Conditions (a)–(c) of s 273(1) involve objective issues of fact. Notably, condition (c) requires the fact of a bankruptcy, or a composition or scheme of arrangement within the definition of a voluntary arrangement under s 253(1) and not the fact of circumstances which might conceivably have led to either. Condition (d) involves an exercise of discretion dependent on the court's perception of the appropriateness in the circumstances of the preparation of a report under s 274. In assessing the appropriateness of ordering a report the court apparently has an unfettered discretion which may, it is submitted, be affected by the overall picture conveyed by the debtor's statement of affairs (which will include any other liabilities, as well as debts), the court's impression as to whether the financial circumstances disclosed are reasonably capable of producing a voluntary arrangement proposal which is 'serious and viable' (on which see the notes to s 2(2)) and the views expressed to the court by the debtor on the hearing of the petition.

'The minimum amount' and 'the small bankruptcies level'—With effect from 1 April 2004 the level and amount were £40,000 and £4,000 respectively under the Insolvency Proceedings (Monetary Limit) Order 2004 (SI 2004/547), which replaced the 1986 Order (SI 1986/1996) which provides figures of £20,000 and £2,000.

Section 273(2)

Procedure—See r 6.44. The court's order is in Form 6.29.

Where the court has appointed a person under s 273(2), the debtor may not make an application for an interim order in relation to a voluntary arrangement proposal by virtue of s 253(5).

274 Action on report of insolvency practitioner

(1) A person appointed under section 273 shall inquire into the debtor's affairs and, within such period as the court may direct, shall submit a report to the court stating whether the debtor is willing, for the purposes of Part VIII, to make a proposal for a voluntary arrangement.

(2) A report which states that the debtor is willing as above mentioned shall also state—

    (a)   whether, in the opinion of the person making the report, a meeting of the debtor's creditors should be summoned to consider the proposal, and

    (b)   if in that person's opinion such a meeting should be summoned, the date on which, and time and place at which, he proposes the meeting should be held.

(3) On considering a report under this section the court may—

    (a)   without any application, make an interim order under section 252, if it thinks that it is appropriate to do so for the purpose of facilitating the consideration and implementation of the debtor's proposal, or

    (b)   if it thinks it would be inappropriate to make such an order, make a bankruptcy order.

(4) An interim order made by virtue of this section ceases to have effect at the end of such period as the court may specify for the purpose of enabling the debtor's proposal to be considered by his creditors in accordance with the applicable provisions of Part VIII.

(5) Where it has been reported to the court under this section that a meeting of the debtor's creditors should be summoned, the person making the report shall, unless the court otherwise directs, summon that meeting for the time, date and place proposed in his report.

The meeting is then deemed to have been summoned under section 257 in Part VIII, and subsections (2) and (3) of that section, and sections 258 to 263 apply accordingly.

General note—This provision only comes into operation on the making of an appointment under s 273(2). The relevant procedure is provided for in r 6.44. There is no prescribed form for the insolvency practitioner's report. On submission of the report the insolvency practitioner is entitled to a fee of £450, inclusive of VAT: Insolvency Proceedings (Fees) Order 2004 (SI 2004/593) as amended by the Insolvency Proceedings (Fees) (Amendment) Order 2010 (SI 2010/732).

Cessation of the interim order and summoning of the creditors' meeting—In keeping with a concertina-type order, the interim order under s 274(4) should be continued for a sufficient period to allow for the summoning of a creditors' meeting within the timescales prescribed by r 5.17. It is difficult to conceive of circumstances where the summoning of a meeting following a positive report would be subject to a contrary court order, other perhaps than where the debtor is actively opposed to a voluntary arrangement.

274A Debtor who meets conditions for a debt relief order

(1) This section applies where, on the hearing of a debtor's petition—

    (a)   it appears to the court that a debt relief order would be made in relation to the debtor if, instead of presenting the petition, he had made an application under Part 7A; and

    (b)   the court does not appoint an insolvency practitioner under section 273.

(2) If the court thinks it would be in the debtor's interests to apply for a debt relief order instead of proceeding on the petition, the court may refer the debtor to an approved intermediary (within the meaning of Part 7A) for the purposes of making an application for a debt relief order.

(3) Where a reference is made under subsection (2) the court shall stay proceedings on the petition on such terms and conditions as it thinks fit; but if following the reference a debt relief order is made in relation to the debtor the court shall dismiss the petition.

Amendments—Inserted by Tribunals, Courts and Enforcement Act 2007, s 108(1), Sch 20, Pt 1, paras 1, 3.

275 (*Repealed*)

General note—Summary administration in bankruptcy was repealed with effect from 1 April 2004 by virtue of s 269 of and Sch 23 to the Enterprise Act 2002.

Other cases for special consideration

276 Default in connection with voluntary arrangement

(1) The court shall not make a bankruptcy order on a petition under section 264(1)(c) (supervisor of, or person bound by, voluntary arrangement proposed and approved) unless it is satisfied—

    (a)   that the debtor has failed to comply with his obligations under the voluntary arrangement, or

    (b)   that information which was false or misleading in any material particular or which contained material omissions—

        (i)   was contained in any statement of affairs or other document supplied by the debtor under Part VIII to any person, or

        (ii)   was otherwise made available by the debtor to his creditors at or in connection with a meeting summoned under that Part, or

    (c)   that the debtor has failed to do all such things as may for the purposes of the voluntary arrangement have been reasonably required of him by the supervisor of the arrangement.

(2) Where a bankruptcy order is made on a petition under section 264(1)(c), any expenses properly incurred as expenses of the administration of the voluntary arrangement in question shall be a first charge on the bankrupt's estate.

General note—The three alternative conditions in s 276(1)(a)–(c) apply where the court is asked to make a bankruptcy order on a petition presented under s 264(1)(c). These conditions will not, it is submitted, apply where a person who is bound by a voluntary arrangement proceeds by way of a creditor's petition under s 264(1)(a) in respect of a debt which is not caught by the voluntary arrangement, such as, for example, fresh indebtedness arising after approval of the arrangement. Even where any of these conditions are fulfilled the court retains a discretion in making a bankruptcy order under s 264(2) and r 6.25(1).

Time for presentation of a supervisor's default petition—The basis for the presentation of a bankruptcy petition by a supervisor will depend on the particular terms of the voluntary arrangement. Although the arrangement will often require presentation of a petition in the event of default, often following the issue of a so-called certificate of non-compliance or default, the arrangement may confer a discretion on the supervisor as to whether or not to present. In either case a petition should be presented timeously once the requirement or the decision to present is made, particularly where the debtor may otherwise continue to make contributions to the supervisor which are capable of being ring-fenced from any ensuing bankruptcy following the decision of the Court of Appeal in *Re NT Gallagher & Son Ltd* [2002] 1 WLR 2380 (on which see the note to s 2(2)).

In *Harris v Gross* [2001] 586 at 589G His Honour Judge Maddocks, sitting as a High Court judge, held that the standing of a supervisor to petition under s 264(1)(c) does not determine on the termination of the period of a fixed-term arrangement. Judge Maddocks did point out (at 589G), however, that the fact of any delay in presenting a petition would be a factor which would influence the court in the exercise of its discretion in making a bankruptcy order.

The absence of a requirement for a deliberate or culpable act by the debtor for s 276(1)(a) and (b) purposes—In *Re Keenan* [1998] BPIR 205 Jacob J, as he then was, rejected submissions to the effect that s 276(1)(a) only applies where there is a culpable failure by a debtor to comply with an obligation; the test, therefore, in approaching that provision is objective. It was common ground that it did not matter whether the debtor had supplied false or misleading information intentionally or not for the purposes of s 276(1)(b), to which the approach is also objective.

In *Re Keenan* [1998] BPIR 205 at 210F Jacob J employed the example of a case where a debtor had agreed to pay £1,000 per month and for some reason did not make one payment but was in a position to make and did make twice the payment the month after. In considering a bankruptcy petition his Lordship suggested that: 'that would be a failure to comply with an obligation of the agreement, but the court would not regard it as blameworthy or sufficiently important to justify the bankruptcy, save perhaps where the failure to make the first payment involved a degree of culpability ...'.

Section 276(1)(a)

'**... the debtor has failed to comply with his obligations ...**'—This condition requires a finding of fact as to (a) the obligations of the debtor under the voluntary arrangement, and (b) whether there has been a failure to comply with such obligations. In terms of construing the terms of any particular voluntary arrangement, some assistance may be gleaned from the extract of the judgment of Blackburne J in *Wellsby v Brelec Installations Ltd* [2000] 2 BCLC 576 as appears in the note to s 5(2).

One practical difficulty which can arise in relation to this provision comes about where the debtor is guilty of a minor or de minimis breach of his obligations under an arrangement which, dependent on the terms of the arrangement, may trigger the presentation of a bankruptcy petition. Alternatively, the debtor may have committed a fundamental breach of his obligations through, say, a failure to make monthly contributions to the supervisor, which have been fully remedied following presentation of the petition. Unless the supervisor is empowered by the arrangement, either by an express or implied term or by a variation validly approved by creditors, to withdraw the petition, the court may find itself faced with either a petition which is resisted by the debtor or a petition which the supervisor has no real enthusiasm for prosecuting, given the remedied breach and the likelihood, as will usually have been the case at the time of approval, that the continuance of the arrangement will provide a better return for creditors. Although the decision of Neuberger J, as he then was, in *Carter-Knight v Peat* [2000] BPIR 968 at 971H–973D is authority for the proposition that it is not necessary on a default petition presented by a supervisor that the alleged breach of the terms of an arrangement should continue at the date of the hearing of the petition, his Lordship did identify (at 973D) that the court retains a discretion under r 6.25(1) – as also arises under s 264(2) – as to whether or not to make a bankruptcy order. It is submitted that the fact that a petition is presented by the supervisor of a voluntary arrangement should not, of itself, incline the court towards the making of an order where the court might otherwise be inclined to adjourn or even dismiss the petition. The fact that a petition is presented by a supervisor amounts to no more than the supervisor acting in accordance with the terms of an arrangement; the creditors approving the arrangement, however, can do no more than require the supervisor to seek an order, which remains entirely in the discretion of the court, through the presentation of a petition. On the other hand, the court will plainly give weight to the seriousness of any breach and any other relevant surrounding circumstances such as a failure or repeated failure to honour any previous promise by a debtor to remedy a breach. In *Kaye v Bourne* [2005] BPIR 590 Patten J held that, where a petition is presented by a supervisor based on defaults under an arrangement, but where the debtor is able to show that the defaults have been remedied at the date of the hearing of the petition, the court retains a discretion under s 276 to refuse a bankruptcy order and to allow the arrangement to continue if satisfied that such a course would secure a better return for creditors. Each case will be decided upon its own facts and careful consideration of the terms of the IVA. In *Clarke v Birkin* [2006] EWHC 340 (Ch), [2006] BPIR 632 a bankruptcy order was made upon a petition brought by IVA participating creditors, despite the fact that the debtor's defaults had been partially remedied by the bankrupt who had made significant payments under the IVA. The bankrupt's appeal on the basis that his default in making payments was not a material default was dismissed by Evans-Lombe J. The IVA had contained a term making it clear that failure to pay installments on time could not be remedied by later payment, and although the Registrar had a discretion whether or not to make a bankruptcy order where a breach of the terms of the voluntary arrangement had been established (see *Re Keenan* [1998] BPIR 205), there were no grounds for interfering with the Registrar's exercise of his discretion in this case.

Section 276(1)(b)

'... **information which was false or misleading in any material particular or which contained material omissions** ...'—Initially, what should be noted here is the scope of the documents in s 276(1)(b)(i) and the fact that s 276(1)(b)(ii) apparently extends beyond the scope of documents and might conceivably catch oral representations made at a creditors' meeting or in connection with it, say prior to it in response to an enquiry by a creditor.

In *Re Tack* [2000] BPIR 164 at 204C–204D Rimer J held that information in a proposal or statement of affairs will be false or misleading in a material way for the purposes of s 276(1)(b) if, had the truth been told, it would be likely to have made a material difference to the way in which creditors would have considered and assessed the particular arrangement to which they were being invited to agree. In *Somji v Cadbury Schweppes plc* [2001] BPIR 172 at [25] Robert Walker LJ, in a court also comprising Judge LJ and Sir Christopher Staughton, approved of Rimer J's formulation, subject to two provisos. First, the test must be answered objectively. Secondly, it is necessary to bear in mind that any number of creditors might themselves be unrepresented, having given proxies in favour of the nominee as chairman of the meeting; as such, the court should bear in mind that it would ordinarily be the chairman's duty as chairman to adjourn the meeting and to report to creditors on learning of the true position, even if such a course would mean having to obtain an extension of time under s 376. In *Somji* the Court of Appeal confirmed a bankruptcy order made in the court below by Anthony Boswood QC on the basis that a secret agreement under which two creditors were to be paid sums by a third party in return for voting in support of the proposal constituted a material omission, as did non-disclosure of the fact that two previously dissentient creditors were at an advanced stage in negotiations for improved returns over any return under the arrangement in which they would not participate.

Where there is an air of suspicion as to the veracity of information or an omission, it may be appropriate to order cross-examination to confirm or dispel the suspicion: *Re A Debtor (No 574 of 1995)* [1998] 2 BCLC 124 at 130H (John Martin QC sitting as a deputy High Court judge).

Section 276(1)(c)

'... **the debtor has failed to do all such things as may ... have been reasonably required of him by the supervisor ...**'—There is no specific statutory term requiring a debtor to do things required of him by a supervisor. Such an obligation would, however, appear implicit, given the present provision. Whether in any particular case a thing required by a supervisor of a debtor can be said to have been reasonably required will turn on the facts of the arrangement under consideration and the circumstances of the case in which the supervisor has come to require a particular thing to be done by the debtor.

In *Vadher v Weisgard* [1998] BPIR 295 at 298F–298G Chadwick J, as he then was, identified that the provisions in Part VIII 'require a degree of co-operation between the debtor and the supervisor. In particular, they are provisions which require that the debtor does honour faithfully the proposals to which his creditors have agreed.' So far as non-co-operation on the part of the debtor went, so as to give rise to increased time costs due to the supervisor, his Lordship went on to identify that, 'Those [Part VIII] provisions are not working in a situation where the cost of supervising the voluntary arrangement represented by the insolvency practitioner's time and correspondence costs absorbing whatever contributions are being made by the debtor ... If the debtor is failing to co-operate to such an extent that the contributions are being absorbed in the supervisor's proper expenses, then the arrangements are not working and should be brought to an end.'

277 Petition based on criminal bankruptcy order

(1) Subject to section 266(3), the court shall make a bankruptcy order on a petition under section 264(1)(d) on production of a copy of the criminal bankruptcy order on which the petition is based.

This does not apply if it appears to the court that the criminal bankruptcy order has been rescinded on appeal.

(2) Subject to the provisions of this Part, the fact that an appeal is pending against any conviction by virtue of which a criminal bankruptcy order was made does not affect any proceedings on a petition under section 264(1)(d) based on that order.

(3) For the purposes of this section, an appeal against a conviction is pending—

    (a)   in any case, until the expiration of the period of 28 days beginning with the date of conviction;

    (b)   if notice of appeal to the Court of Appeal is given during that period and during that period the appellant notifies the official receiver of it, until the determination of the appeal and thereafter for so long as an appeal to the Supreme Court is pending within the meaning of subsection (4).

(4) For the purposes of subsection (3)(b) an appeal to the Supreme Court shall be treated as pending until any application for leave to appeal is disposed of and, if leave to appeal is granted, until the appeal is disposed of; and for the purposes of this subsection an application for leave to appeal shall be treated as disposed of at the expiration of the time within which it may be made, if it is not made within that time.

Amendments—Constitutional Reform Act 2005, s 40(4), Sch 9, Pt 1, para 44.

General note—Criminal bankruptcy orders were previously provided for under the Powers of the Criminal Courts Act 1973. The power to make such orders, which were rare in any case in practice, was abolished with effect from 3 April 1989 by s 101 of the Criminal Justice Act 1988. The standing of the Official Petitioner or any other person within s 264(1)(d) to present a bankruptcy petition where a criminal bankruptcy order has been made against an individual is therefore redundant, at least for practical purposes.

Section 277 was repealed prospectively by s 170(2) of and Sch 16 to the Criminal Justice Act 1988 from a date to be appointed under s 171(1) of the Criminal Justice Act 1988.

Commencement and duration of bankruptcy; discharge

278 Commencement and continuance

The bankruptcy of an individual against whom a bankruptcy order has been made—

    (a)   commences with the day on which the order is made, and

    (b)   continues until the individual is discharged under the following provisions of this Chapter.

General note—In contrast to a compulsory winding up under s 129(2), bankruptcy commences not with the presentation of the bankruptcy petition but with the day on which the order is made.

Although the bankruptcy itself ends with the discharge of the bankrupt – on which see ss 279 and 280 and the notes thereto – the effect of discharge itself is as provided for in s 281, which allows for the continuation of the functions of the trustee, the right of any creditor to prove in the bankruptcy for any debt from which the bankrupt is released, the right of any secured creditor to enforce his security for the payment of a debt from which the bankrupt has been released and the continuance in effect of certain bankruptcy debts incurred through fraud, together with those particular species of debt identified in s 281(4)–(8).

Third Parties (Rights Against Insurers) Act 1930—It is well established that the statutory transfer to a third party of an insured's right against his insurer under s 1 of the 1930 Act takes place at the moment of the insured's bankruptcy: see *Law Society v Official Receiver* [2007] BPIR 1595 at [27] and the cases cited therein.

Procedures and Forms on the making of a bankruptcy order—See r 6.33 (settlement and content of bankruptcy order made on creditor's petition in Form 6.25), r 6.34 (action by the court and the official receiver to follow making of bankruptcy order on creditor's petition), r 6.45 (settlement and content of bankruptcy order made on debtor's petition in Form 6.30) and r 6.46 (action by the court and the official receiver to follow making of bankruptcy order on debtor's petition).

279 Duration

(1) A bankrupt is discharged from bankruptcy at the end of the period of one year beginning with the date on which the bankruptcy commences.

(2) If before the end of that period the official receiver files with the court a notice stating that investigation of the conduct and affairs of the bankrupt under section 289 is unnecessary or concluded, the bankrupt is discharged when the notice is filed.

(3) On the application of the official receiver or the trustee of a bankrupt's estate, the court may order that the period specified in subsection (1) shall cease to run until—

(a)   the end of a specified period, or

(b)   the fulfilment of a specified condition.

(4) The court may make an order under subsection (3) only if satisfied that the bankrupt has failed or is failing to comply with an obligation under this Part.

(5) In subsection (3)(b) 'condition' includes a condition requiring that the court be satisfied of something.

(6) In the case of an individual who is adjudged bankrupt on a petition under section 264(1)(d)—

(a)   subsections (1) to (5) shall not apply, and

(b)   the bankrupt is discharged from bankruptcy by an order of the court under section 280.

(7) This section is without prejudice to any power of the court to annul a bankruptcy order.

Amendments—Enterprise Act 2002, s 256(1). Subsection (2) omitted in relation to a bankruptcy order made on or after 1 October 2013, Enterprise and Regulatory Reform Act 2013, s 73, Sch 21, Pt 3, para 5.

General note—This new version of s 279 was introduced by s 256 of and Sch 19 to the Enterprise Act 2002 with effect from 1 April 2004. These provisions apply to all individuals against whom a bankruptcy order is made on or after that date.

The principal amendment made by the new provision is that the bankrupt is automatically discharged, in the absence of a contrary order under s 279(3), after a one-year period beginning with the date of the bankruptcy order, or sooner under s 279(2), on the official receiver filing a s 289 notice – on which see r 6.214A on procedure. There can be no doubt that, particularly at a time of record levels of consumer debt, the reduction of the former three-year period before automatic discharge will reduce both the disincentive and any degree of stigma formerly associated with bankruptcy, irrespective of the continued availability of the newly streamlined IVA procedure.

The effect of discharge is provided for in s 281.

In *Shierson v Rastogi* [2007] BPIR 891 at [65], and whilst resiling from expressing a concluded view on this issue, Morritt C opined that the purpose of s 279 in allowing for the postponement of discharge from bankruptcy lies in the continuance of the disabilities arising from an individual being an undischarged bankrupt, as opposed to the providing of an incentive to full compliance by the bankrupt with his statutory obligations, since otherwise Parliament might have been expected to provide that discharge was conditional upon full compliance. The Court of Appeal had cause to consider the purpose and grounds for suspension of discharge in the rather unusual case of *Bramston v Haut* [2012] EWHC 1279 (Ch), [2012] BPIR 672. There it was the bankrupt himself who wanted his discharge suspended so that he might put forward an IVA proposal to his creditors, the trustee being opposed to this course of action. On the bankrupt's own application Arnold J granted a period of suspension, concluding that the trustee had acted 'Wednesbury' unreasonably and that the court should have ordered the trustee to make the application to suspend under s 303 if necessary. The Court of Appeal overturned this decision on the trustee's appeal since the bankrupt was acting for an impermissible purpose outside the scope of s 279(3). The suspension was not linked to the failure by the bankrupt to comply with his obligations, nor was it made to ensure that he continued to suffer from the disabilities of being an undischarged bankrupt until he had fully complied with those obligations, nor for any other purpose that might be within s 279(3) of the 1986 Act. The trustee could not therefore have acted perversely in refusing to authorise the bankrupt to make the application on his behalf. This case also contains a useful discussion of the circumstances in which the court will interfere with the day to day administration by the trustee of a bankruptcy estate at [68]-[74].

Application and order that discharge period ceases to run—An application under s 279(3) may be made either by the official receiver or, in contrast to the former s 279, by the trustee of a bankrupt's estate. The procedure on such an application is as provided for in r 6.215. The procedure on the lifting of a suspension of discharge appears in r 6.216. The lifting of a suspension of discharge is not retrospective and can only permit the period of bankruptcy to continue to run from the point at which the period was previously suspended.

In *Hardy v Focus Insurance Co Ltd* [1997] BPIR 77 at 82F–82G Robert Walker J, as he then was, held that the court has no jurisdiction, whether under s 303 or otherwise, to give directions to the official receiver to make an application for a suspension of discharge in the course of what amounts to his public law functions. That decision, of course, was made under the former s 279 under which the official receiver was the only eligible applicant. The new s 279 allows for an application to be made by a trustee. While it might be thought that the jurisdiction of the Court should be no different from that identified by Robert Walker J, in that an application by a trustee is hardly distinguishable from an application by the official receveir in terms of its public law function, it was taken for granted by Arnold J in *Bramston v Haut* [2012] EWHC 1279 (Ch), [2012] BPIR 672 that, in a suitable case, the court had power to direct the trustee to make an application under s 279, and the Court of Appeal did not disagree (although it overturned his decision on other grounds).

Notwithstanding the requirement in r 6.215(5) that evidence in support of an application to suspend must reach the bankrupt at least 21 days before the date fixed for the suspension hearing, it is doubtful that it is impossible to make an application under s 279(3) within the last 21 days before the expiration of the automatic discharge period: *Hardy v Focus Insurance Co Ltd* [1997] BPIR 77 at 81F–81G. Given the practical consequence that no action can be taken to reverse an automatic discharge from bankruptcy, the Court of Appeal has confirmed that the court has power to make an interim order on an urgent and without notice basis under r 7.4(6) suspending the bankrupt's automatic discharge until the substantive hearing of an application to suspend under s 279(3): *Bagnall v Official Receiver* [2004] 2 All ER 294 (Arden LJ, Latham LJ agreeing). In *Jacobs v Official Receiver* [1998] 3 All ER 250, which was considered by Arden LJ in *Bagnall*, Michael Burton QC, sitting as a deputy High Court judge, held at 255B–255C that the making of an interim order is appropriate where an on-notice hearing has to be adjourned, as in that case where insufficient time was available for the hearing, if, ignoring any dispute raised by the bankrupt, the court can be satisfied that there would be sufficient evidence for making a final order if that evidence were unchallenged and undisputed. However, it was emphasized in *Hellard v Kapoor* [2013] EWHC 2204, [2013] BPIR 745 (at para [10]) by Penelope Reed QC (sitting as a judge of the High Court) that the trustee should not wait to the last minute to seek suspension of discharge or (s)he runs the risk of the Court refusing to exercise its discretion to suspend.

The practice under the former s 279, as it is understood, was that the official receivers were generally unwilling to make an application to suspend discharge where representations were made by a trustee only in the final six-month period of the bankruptcy. Whilst that may well have been the case, two points warrant mention. First, given that automatic discharge is generally obtained now after only one year, it may well be that an official receiver who acts as a trustee will have to consider an application at a late stage of the bankruptcy, particularly where the bankrupt has prevaricated or apparently taken steps to mislead the official receiver. Secondly, the very sensible move of bringing the trustee within the scope of a s 279(3) application leaves the suspension process to an office-holder who in most cases will invariably be much closer than the official receiver to the conduct of the bankruptcy and who will usually be prepared to take steps, even at a very late stage, to suspend discharge if proper grounds can be made out.

Grounds for the making of a suspension order under s 279(3)—Although the court has a wide discretion in making an order under s 279(3), the breadth of that discretion gives no clue as to the way in which it should be exercised. Bankruptcy is of a very serious nature both to a debtor and to the public interest. Nevertheless, whilst an order should not be made lightly, it is respectfully submitted that the test espoused by His Honour Judge Rich QC, sitting as a High Court judge in *Official Receiver v Milburn* (1999) *The Independent*, July 26, to the effect that the court must be satisfied on the evidence as to a bankrupt's non-compliance with his obligations such that reasonable suspicion of non-compliance will not suffice, goes too far and overlooks the level of subtlety involved in some cases. In practice, a trustee or the official receiver will very frequently be prompted into making an application for suspension in cases where the bankrupt's non-compliance with his obligations is not abject. Difficult cases very commonly involve bankrupts who provide partial disclosure of relevant facts and

(b)   arises under any order made in family proceedings or under a maintenance assessment made under the Child Support Act 1991.

(6) Discharge does not release the bankrupt from such other bankruptcy debts, not being debts provable in his bankruptcy, as are prescribed.

(7) Discharge does not release any person other than the bankrupt from any liability (whether as partner or co-trustee of the bankrupt or otherwise) from which the bankrupt is released by the discharge, or from any liability as surety for the bankrupt or as a person in the nature of such a surety.

(8) In this section—

'family proceedings' means—
>   (a)   family proceedings within the meaning of the Magistrates' Courts Act 1980 and any proceedings which would be such proceedings but for section 65(1)(ii) of that Act (proceedings for variation of order for periodical payments); and
>   (b)   family proceedings within the meaning of Part V of the Matrimonial and Family Proceedings Act 1984.

'fine' means the same as in the Magistrates' Courts Act 1980; and
'personal injuries' includes death and any disease or other impairment of a person's physical or mental condition.

Amendments— Consumer Protection Act 1987, Children Act 1989, ss 92(11), 108(7) Sch 11, Pt II, para 11(1), (2), Sch 15; s 48, Sch 4, para 12; Child Support Act 1991, s 58(13), Sch 5, para 7; Proceeds of Crime Act 2002, s 456, Sch 11, paras 1, 16(1), (2).

General note—The most significant consequence of discharge from bankruptcy is the release of the bankrupt from his bankruptcy debts, subject to the exceptions identified in this section. Discharge does not, however, operate so as to re-vest any part of the bankruptcy estate in the discharged individual, a point which can come as a surprise to some bankrupts.

The process of discharge itself has no bearing either on the conduct of the bankruptcy by the trustee, whose general functions remain as provided for under s 305, or on the procedure for the proving of debt under rr 6.96–6.114.

Discharge takes effect immediately to remove the disqualifications imposed by s 427 (membership of either House of Parliament), s 63A of the Justices of the Peace Act 1979 (Justice of the Peace) and s 11 of the Company Directors Disqualification Act 1986 (company director).

'Discharge and the running of time for limitation period purposes'—In *Anglo Manx Group Ltd v Aitken* [2002] BPIR 215 at [69] John Jarvis QC, sitting as a deputy High Court judge, held, following the Court of Appeal's decision in *Re Benzon, Bower v Chetwynd* [1914] 2 Ch 68, that the 1986 Act contains nothing which should detract from the earlier established principle that time does not cease to run for limitation purposes during the period of bankruptcy. This point is of particular relevance to those debts, considered under the next two sub-headings below, which are not released on discharge.

Section 281(1)

'… the discharge releases him from all the bankruptcy debts …'—The term 'bankruptcy debt' is defined in s 382(1) and should be read in conjunction with s 382(2)–(4), which give the term an extremely broad scope. It includes a liability to repay overpaid benefits, so that upon discharge, this liability is released and deductions cannot be made against future benefit payments: *Secretary of State for Work and Pensions v Balding* [2007] EWCA Civ 1327, [2007] BPIR 1669; approved by the Supreme Court in *Secretary of State for Work and Pensions v*

Payne [2011] UKSC 60, [2012] BPIR 224 (which held that such deductions were a 'remedy' caught by the moratorium imposed by s 251G(2)(a) of the Insolvency Act 1986 when a Debt Relief Order was in place). A solicitor's liability to pay compensation imposed by the Legal Complaints Service is not a 'bankruptcy debt' where the matter complained of arose prior to the bankruptcy but the award was not made until afterwards, since the obligation to pay compensation could not properly be characterised as a contingent liability prior to the bankruptcy: *Casson and Wales v The Law Society* [2009] EWHC 1943 (Admin), [2010] BPIR 49.

The exceptions in s 281(3)–(7) to the general release under s 281(1) are justifiable in each case on public policy grounds and serve to avoid the abuse of the bankruptcy procedure as a means of escaping such liabilities. It remains, however, that bankruptcy is a procedure ordinarily lasting only one year – or even less, given s 279(2) – which carries a much reduced social stigma in comparison even with relatively recent times and which amounts to a lawful mechanism by which an individual might effectively divest himself of an unlimited level of personal indebtedness within the scope of s 382(1).

The proviso in the final part of s 261(1) operates to preserve the underlying cause of action giving rise to a creditor's claim so as to allow for its proof in the bankruptcy after discharge: *Law Society v Official Receiver* [2007] BPIR 1595 at [34]–[37] (Floyd J).

The effect of discharge on debts from which a bankrupt is not released—Discharge has a different effect on debts which are not released under s 281(1), depending on whether any such debt is provable or not provable in the bankruptcy.

Rule 12.3(1) provides a general rule that all claims by creditors are provable, subject to specific exceptions in r 12.3(2)(a) and (b) and r 12.3(2A)(a), which provisions extend to obligations arising under an order made in family proceedings (as defined therein) or under a maintenance assessment made under the Child Support Act 1991, a confiscation order under Parts 2, 3 or 4 of the Proceeds of Crime Act 2002 and any claim arising under s 382(1)(a) of the Financial Services and Markets Act 2000, not being a claim under s 382(1)(b) of the 2000 Act. If a debt which is not released is provable in the bankruptcy then, prior to discharge, a creditor may not commence any action or legal proceedings in respect of the debt other than with leave of the court, by virtue of s 285(3), subject to ss 346 (enforcement procedures) and 347 (limited right to distress). On the other hand, a creditor whose debt is not released, and which is not provable, is not caught by the limitations imposed by the bankruptcy procedure or by s 285(3), with the consequence that the creditor may pursue the bankrupt prior to or following discharge. Thus, in *Re X (a Bankrupt)* [1996] BPIR 494 Singer J, sitting in the Family Division of the High Court, held that a bankrupt father was not protected by his bankruptcy or by s 285(3) from a lump sum order made in favour of the mother of the bankrupt's child under para 5 of Sch 1 to the Children Act 1989, since that debt was neither provable nor released on discharge.

The effect of discharge on after-acquired property claims under s 307 and income payments orders under s 310—A trustee may not claim after-acquired property for the benefit of the estate after discharge: s 307(2)(c). Neither may an income payments order be made after discharge, although the period for which such an order is made may extend beyond discharge: s 310(1A)(b) and (6)(a).

Section 281(3)

'Any bankruptcy debt ... incurred in respect of, or forbearance in respect of which was secured by means of, any fraud or fraudulent breach of trust ...'—In *Mander v Evans* [2001] BPIR 902 at [25] Ferris J held that the word 'fraud' in this provision means actual fraud in the sense explained by the House of Lords in *Derry v Peek* (1889) 14 App Cas 337. In rejecting an argument for a wider definition of the term his Lordship went on to say that he found it 'much less comprehensible that [the bankrupt] should remain liable for constructive fraud, which covers a wide range of conduct regarded by equity as unconscionable but not necessarily involving actual dishonesty.' In *Woodland-Ferrari v UCL Group Retirement Benefit Schemes* [2002] BPIR 1270 Ferris J went on to identify at [37]–[50] that the term 'fraudulent breach of trust' has no wider meaning than the term 'fraud' in s 281(3) and therefore requires proof of dishonesty as an essential ingredient.

The burden of proof in establishing fraud within the meaning of *Mander v Evans* will rest on a creditor. That burden will not be discharged, however, merely by production of a foreign default judgment based purely on a single cause of action alleging fraud: *Masters v Leaver* [2000] BPIR 284 (Morritt and Thorpe LJJ and Sir Oliver Popplewell, appeal against summary judgment upheld where deputy judge below granted judgment based on a Texan default judgment which, notably, was itself based on actual fraud against bankrupt). For another example of a case where an allegation that certain of the bankrupt's debts fell within 281(3) failed on the facts see *Soutzos v Asombang* [2010] BPIR 960, where it was empahasised the burden of proof was on the creditor, and the creditors' claims against the bankrupt in deceit and the tort of conspiracy to injure by unlawful means were not made out.

The reference to 'forbearance' is a reference to a forbearance relating to a bankruptcy debt which will not be released on discharge where the creditor's forbearance was secured by the requisite *Mander v Evans* fraud or fraudulent breach of trust. Although the provision makes no reference to the time at which the forbearance must have been secured, it is submitted that a fraudulently secured forbearance is only capable of avoiding discharge if it can be shown – the burden, again, resting on the creditor – that there was a real likelihood that the underlying debt would have been paid in full but for the forbearance, since there is no good reason why liability for an ordinary debt should not be so discharged, irrespective of the debtor's fraud, where there was in any case no such prospect of the debt being discharged in full.

Section 281(4)

Fines and other penalties—A fine imposed for an offence is not provable by virtue of r 12.3(2)(a). Section 281(8) provides that the term 'fine' is as defined in s 150(1) of the Magistrates Courts Act 1980 as extended by s 281(4A) below. The term 'recognisance' may be more readily understood by English lawyers as equating to the American bail bond.

Section 281(4A)

Scope of provision—This provision was inserted by s 456 of, and para 16 of Sch 11 to the Proceeds of Crime Act 2002.

Section 281(5)

The Court's discretion to order release—The discretion afforded to the court under this section to order the debtor's release from the bankruptcy debts described in s 281(5)(a) and (b) was subject to detailed examination by HHJ Pelling QC in *Hayes v Hayes* [2012] EWHC 1240 (Ch), [2012] BPIR 739 and Hildyard J in *McRoberts v McRoberts* [2012] EWHC 2966 (Ch), [2013] BPIR 77. These cases indicate that the discretion is unfettered, and has to be exercised by reference to all the relevant circumstances as they existed at the date when the application was determined, including: (a) any lapse of time between the date when the discharge occurred and the date of any application for release, and the reasons for any delay; (b) the future earning capacity of the applicant, the possibility of some future income or capital receipt or windfall, the prospect accordingly of the obligation being fulfilled in whole or in part if not released, and in the round whether there was any good reason for maintaining the obligation; (c) the risk of the respondent to the application using the fact of the obligation (if not released) to harass the applicant, for example by seeking to diminish the applicant in the eyes of the community, or his future prospects, by reference to the stigma still relating to bankruptcy, or by bringing new and abusive bankruptcy proceedings calculated to restrict the applicant in building a new life; and (d) the duration of time that had elapsed since the relevant obligation arose. The default position is that the obligation should remain in place and the burden is on the applicant to show the balance of prejudice favours its release.

Section 281(6)

Other bankruptcy debts as prescribed—This provision extends to non-provable debts on which see r 6.223. Neither is liability for a student loan discharged by virtue of s 42 of the Higher Education Act 2004 and reg 5 of the Education (Student Support) (No 2) Regulations 2002 (Amendment) Regulations 2004 (SI 2004/2041).

Section 281(7)

Liability as surety etc—Discharge only releases the bankrupt from liability and has no bearing on a partner, co-trustee, co-indemnifier or surety who is personally liable for the same debt. In the case of sureties, this provision overrides earlier authorities (as did s 28(4) of the Bankruptcy Act 1914), such as *Re Moss* [1905] 2 KB 307, in which a surety was held to have no liability for interest on a debt for which the debtor would have been liable had he not been made bankrupt.

281A Post-discharge restrictions

Schedule 4A to this Act (bankruptcy restrictions order and bankruptcy restrictions undertaking) shall have effect.

Amendments—Inserted by Enterprise Act 2002, s 257(1).

General note—With effect from 1 April 2004, s 257 of and Schs 20 and 21 to the Enterprise Act 2002 introduced the new concepts of bankruptcy restriction orders ('BROs') and bankruptcy restriction undertakings ('BRUs') to which this provision gives effect. No transitional provisions govern the new provisions. However, art 7 of the Enterprise Act 2002 (Commencement No 4 and Transitional Provisions and Savings) Order 2003 (SI 2003/2093) provides that, in considering whether or not to make a BRO, the court shall not take into account any conduct of the bankrupt before 1 April 2004.

The substance of the provisions governing BROs and BRUs appears in Sch 4A, although those provisions do not prescribe the effect of a BRO, which is to be found in the amendments in Sch 21 to the Enterprise Act 2001.

In short, para 1 of Sch 4A allows for a BRO to be made on application to the Secretary of State or the official receiver acting on a direction of the Secretary of State. Paragraph 3 requires an application to be made within one year of the bankruptcy order (even, apparently, if the bankrupt is discharged within the one-year period) or later with the permission of the court. The ordinary one-year period ceases to run whilst discharge is suspended under s 279(3). In considering the making of an order para 2(1) provides that the court 'shall' grant an application for a BRO 'if it thinks it appropriate having regard to the conduct of the bankrupt (whether before or after the making of the bankruptcy order).' Paragraph 2(2) requires that the court 'shall, in particular, take into account' any of 13 specific factors, whilst para 2(3) also requires the court to consider whether the bankrupt was an undischarged bankrupt at some time during the period of six years ending with the date of the bankruptcy to which the application relates. Paragraph 4 allows the court to make a BRO for a period of between two years and 15 years in addition to provision being made in para 5 for the making of an interim BRO pending determination of a substantive application. Paragraphs 7 and 9 provide for the entering into of BRUs. Paragraphs 10 and 11 provide for the differing effects of annulment on a BRO or BRU, depending on the provision under which the annulment is granted.

The principal restrictions imposed on a person subject to a BRO are (i) a prohibition on the obtaining of credit of more than £500 without disclosure that the individual is subject to a BRO, (ii) a prohibition against an individual acting in the promotion, formation or management of a company without permission of the court, (iii) a prohibition against trading under any name other than that in which the individual was made bankrupt without disclosure of that name, (iv) a prohibition against acting as an LPA receiver of the property of a company other than in the very unlikely circumstances of a court appointment, and (v) a prohibition against acting as an insolvency practitioner. The additional disqualifications identified in the notes to s 281 also apply, in addition to which the Secretary of State may provide for additional restrictions under s 268 of the Enterprise Act 2002.

Exercise of the court's jurisdiction—In *Randhawa v Official Receiver* [2006 EWHC 2946 (Ch), [2007] BPIR 87, Mr Launcelot Henderson QC, sitting as he then was as a deputy High Court judge, considered the BRO jurisdiction in some detail. The following four principles appear from the judgment. First, the purpose of a BRO is one of public protection comprising three distinct elements: (a) keeping bankrupts whose conduct warrants a BRO 'off the road'; (b) deterring such bankrupts from repeating such conduct (individual deterrence); and (c) deterring others (general deterrence): see [69] and [72]-[75]. Secondly, the jurisdiction is not one of general discretion but one entirely analogous to the regime under s 6 of the Company Directors' Disqualification Act 1986. Accordingly, the court is required to determine whether any of the conduct alleged has been established and, if so, to determine whether that conduct, viewed individually and cumulatively, and taking account of any extenuating circumstances, is such as to establish that the defendant has so seriously failed to meet the proper standards of probity and competence as fixed by courts, being the standards required of individuals in conducting their financial affairs, as to warrant the making of a BRO; if it does then the court has no discretion and is required to make an order: see [64], [65], [68] and [71]-[75]. Thirdly, although the court will consider conduct within para 2(2) of Sch 4A, and any prior bankruptcy under para 2(3), the fact of such conduct does not of itself warrant the making of a BRO. Further, conduct not falling within para 2(2) may be sufficiently serious to justify a BRO: [66]. Fourthly, the period of a BRO is in the discretion of the judge but should be fixed by reference to the principles in *Re Sevenoaks Stationers (Retail) Ltd* [1991] Ch 164 at 174E-174G: [88].

In *Official Receiver v Doganci* [2007] BPIR 87 Chief Registrar Baister, considering *Randhawa*, dismissed an application for a BRO where the sole ground relied on by the Official Receiver was an allegation that the debtor, made bankrupt on his own petition, had rented a piano worth over £9,000 and had failed to account satisfactorily for its disposal. Though not entirely satisfactory, the bankrupt's evidence was not unbelievable.

In *Official Receiver v Southay* [2009] BPIR 89 the Court refused to make a BRO because it was not satisfied that the bankrupt had incurred a debt which he had no reasonable expectation of being able to repay – there had been a reasonable chance of repayment (albeit not a likelihood). The bankrupt had incurred debt previously which he had always managed to repay and had simply misjudged his ability to make repayment on this occasion. This conduct fell short of the relatively high threshold required for a BRO.

Period of the BRO—In *Jenkins v The Official Receiver* [2007] EWHC 1402 (Ch), [2007] BPIR 740 Rimer J dismissed an appeal against a BRO of 4 years imposed upon an individual who could be shown to have acted in wilful defiance of a bankruptcy restrictions undertaking entered into by the debtor who had continued to act as a company director irresponsibly and without sanction contrary to terms which had been stressed to him at the outset. It did not matter that the individual might have obtained leave to act as a director or that the order annulling the bankruptcy had been obtained.

In *Official Receiver v Pyman* [2007] EWHC 2002 (Ch), [2007] BPIR 1150 Stuart Isaacs QC, sitting as a deputy judge of the High Court, allowed an appeal by the Official Receiver against an order of a deputy district judge imposing a BRO for 4 years, extending the period to 7 years. Although necessarily fact specific, the deputy judge emphasised at [24] that, whilst the main object of making a BRO must undoubtedly be the protection of the public, the jurisdiction also had a deterrent effect which has two distinct aspects by way of, first, the deterrence of the bankrupt himself repeating the misconduct complained of and, secondly, the deterrence of others.

In *Official Receiver v Bathurst* [2008] EWHC 1724 (Ch), [2008] BPIR 1548 Morritt C allowed an appeal from a district judge and imposed a BRO for 9 years in place of the 3-year order below. In particular, the district judge had failed to take proper account of the bankrupt's failure to co-operate with the Official Receiver and the level of the bankrupt's personal expenditure.

Where a district judge had formed the view that a bankrupt's conduct was culpable, so as to constitute that justifying the making of a BRO, she had no discretion to refuse to make a BRO and was obliged to impose such an order for at least 2 years: *Official Receiver v May* [2008] EWHC 1778 (Ch), [2008] BPIR 1562 (Christopher Nugee QC sitting as a deputy High Court judge; BRO of 2 years and 6 months imposed on Official Receiver's appeal).

An 8 year BRO was successfully appealed in *Official Receiver v Going* [2011] EWHC 786 (Ch), [2011] BPIR 1069 on the basis that the conclusions reached by the district judge at first instance could not be supported on the evidence. HHJ Pelling QC rejected the OR's argument that the BRO should nevertheless be maintained (albeit for a reduced period) on the basis of additional allegations which, although set out in the allegations in the OR's report, had not been the subject of submissions and about which not findings had been made by the district judge: it was not open to an appeal court to make essentially an entirely new order by reference to issues which had not been argued before the court below.

Time period for making an application—An application for a BRO must be made within a year from the date of the bankruptcy or the Court's permission is required. The Court considered the factors to be considered in deciding whether to grant permission for a late application in *Official Recevier v Baars* [2009] BPIR 524. The main factors to be taken into account were the length of the delay, the reason for the delay and the strength of the case against the bankrupt. A failure to comply with disclosure obligations so that an asset was not discovered until after the expiry of the one-year period was an obvious circumstance when, depending on the facts, such an application should be allowed to proceed

The Impact of the Human Rights Act 1998—The bankrupt's challenge the interim BRO procedure on the ground that it infringed his human rights under Art 6 of the ECHR (right to a fair trial) failed in *Michael v Official Receiver* [2010] EWHC 2246 (Ch).

282 Court's power to annul bankruptcy order

(1) The court may annul a bankruptcy order if it at any time appears to the court—

    (a)   that, on the grounds existing at the time the order was made, the order ought not to have been made, or

    (b)   that, to the extent required by the rules, the bankruptcy debts and the expenses of the bankruptcy have all, since the making of the order, been either paid or secured for to the satisfaction of the court.

(2) The court may annul a bankruptcy order made against an individual on a petition under paragraph (a), (b) or (c) of section 264(1) if it at any time appears to the court, on an application by the Official Petitioner—

    (a)   that the petition was pending at a time when a criminal bankruptcy order was made against the individual or was presented after such an order was so made, and

    (b)   no appeal is pending (within the meaning of section 277) against the individual's conviction of any offence by virtue of which the criminal bankruptcy order was made;

and the court shall annul a bankruptcy order made on a petition under section 264(1)(d) if it at any time appears to the court that the criminal bankruptcy order on which the petition was based has been rescinded in consequence of an appeal.

(3) The court may annul a bankruptcy order whether or not the bankrupt has been discharged from the bankruptcy.

(4) Where the court annuls a bankruptcy order (whether under this section or under section 261 or 263D in Part VIII)—

    (a)   any sale or other disposition of property, payment made or other thing duly done, under any provision in this Group of Parts, by or under the authority of the official receiver or a trustee of the bankrupt's estate or by the court is valid, but

    (b)   if any of the bankrupt's estate is then vested, under any such provision, in such a trustee, it shall vest in such person as the court may appoint or, in default of any such appointment, revert to the bankrupt on such terms (if any) as the court may direct;

and the court may include in its order such supplemental provisions as may be authorised by the rules.

(5) (*Repealed*)

Amendments—Enterprise Act 2002, ss 269, 278(2), Sch 23, paras 1, 4(a), (b), Sch 26.

General note—The two grounds in s 282(1) replace those in s 29 of the Bankruptcy Act 1914. An annulment may also be obtained under s 261(2) on the approval of an IVA proposed by an undischarged bankrupt. Alternatively, the same *effect* may be obtained through the rescission of a bankruptcy order under s 375(1). Where the court makes a bankruptcy order upon being satisfied as to service of a bankruptcy petition, the proper course in challenging the order is for the bankrupt to apply for rescission under s 282(1)(a), as opposed to appealing the bankruptcy order: *Johnson v Tandridge District Council* [2008] BPIR 405 at [29]–[32] (HHJ Kaye QC sitting as a judge of the High Court).

Annulment and bankruptcy restrictions orders—Where an annulment order was made under s 282(1)(b) the court retained jurisdiction to make a bankruptcy restrictions order on the same day provided the application for the BRO had been made prior to the annulment and before the one year period commencing with the date of the bankruptcy order: *Jenkins v The Official Receiver* [2007] BPIR 740 at [12] (Rimer J).

The court's jurisdiction to annul—Prior to the Bankruptcy Act 1914 it had been held in *Ex parte Ashworth* (1874) LR 18 Eq 705 that, in the absence of statutory enactment, there was an inherent jurisdiction in the court to annul what was previously termed a receiving order where good reason could be established. In *Re A Debtor (No 68 of 1992), Royal Bank of Scotland v The Debtor* [1996] BPIR 478 at 479A–479D, Harman J (in the course of overturning an annulment granted by a deputy district judge) held that there is no longer a general discretion or inherent jurisdiction in the court and that the only basis for annulling a bankruptcy order – apart from the alternative methods identified in the general note above, which were not relevant – is as provided for in s 282(1)(a) and (b). Those observations were not the subject of the appeal from that decision, reported as *Royal Bank of Scotland v Farley* [1996] BPIR 638, in which appeal Hoffmann LJ identified at 640A–640D that it is appropriate for a bankruptcy court on an annulment application to go behind a default judgment: see, for example, *Hunter v Lex Vehicles Ltd* [2005] BPIR 586 (David Richards J).

Since there is a single High Court, in which judges are assigned to any particular Division, each Division applies precisely the same principles on an application to annul: *Whig v Whig* [2007] EWHC 1856 (Fam), [2007] BPIR 1418 at [55]–[60] (Munby J).

Eligible applicants—In contrast to s 29 of the Bankruptcy Act 1914, which allowed for an application for an annulment only by 'any person interested', the present provision makes no mention of persons who might apply for an annulment. Indeed, s 282 itself makes no reference to the making of an order on an application, which might suggest that the court has jurisdiction to make an order, at least under s 282(1)(a), of its own volition. Rule 6.206(6) indicates that, in the case of application being made, the application need not be made by the bankrupt. In *F v F (divorce: insolvency: annulment of bankruptcy order)* [1994] 1 FLR 359, for example, the court ordered an annulment under s 282(1)(a) on the application of a bankrupt's wife who satisfied the court that the bankrupt's bankruptcy petition misrepresented his true financial circumstances. Further in *Die Sparkasse Bremen AG v Armutcu* [2012] EWHC 4026 (Ch), [2013] BPIR 210 Proudman J considered that even a secured creditor could apply for an annulment where it could show a legitimate interest in the matter, as for instance where there was likely to be be a significant shortfall when the security was realised. The court will, however, approach with some caution an application by a person with no immediately obvious interest in the annulment.

The question of motive on the part of a debtor in obtaining a bankruptcy order in the context of an application to annul by a person interested—Where an applicant seeks an order under s 282(1)(a) the burden of proof rests on the applicant on the balance of probabilities. It had been held that, where an annulment is sought on the basis that the debtor has presented a false picture of his financial position in obtaining a bankruptcy order, a high standard of proof is required to reflect the gravity of the stain on the debtor's integrity: *Whig v Whig*

[2007] EWHC 1856 (Fam), [2007] BPIR 1418 at [51] (Munby J) but the Court of Appeal have confirmed in *Paulin v Paulin* [2009] BPIR 572 that this reference to a higher standard should be regarded as wrong. While the onus is on the applicant to show the bankruptcy order should never have been made, the burden of proof is the ordinary burden in civil cases. Furthermore, the Court of Appeal considered that where the applicant establishes the debtor was not insolvent on a balance sheet basis, the debtor falls under an evidential burden to establish commercial insolvency (ie that nevertheless he was unable to pay his debts). Adverse inferences could be drawn against a debtor who prevaricated and failed to give a condid account of his affairs. In *Arif v Zar* [2012] EWCA Civ 986, [2012] BPIR 948 the Court of Appeal emphasized the fact that the Courts should be alive to the real possibility of debtors attempting to use the protection of a bankruptcy order as a shield against ancilliary relief proceedings and, where there is credible evidence of this, judges and registrars should not be afraid to use their powers of ordering full disclosure and cross examination and for this purpose it may be more cost effective to transfer the matter to be dealt with alongside the ancilliary relief proceedings.

However, if satisfied that the debtor was, in fact, insolvent within the meaning of s 272(1) – on which see the notes thereto – the court cannot annul the bankruptcy order under s 282(1)(a), even if the debtor's purpose was corrupt or self-serving: see *Whig* at [54] and the survey of the cases at [55]–[66].]. See also *Paulin v Paulin* [2009] BPIR 572 at where the Court of Appeal considered that it is safe to assume that if a debtor is insolvent on the date of his petition its presentation is not an abuse of process (at [48]) but if, on the other hand, the debtor was solvent and the court must then go on to exercise its discretion as to whether to anull the bankruptcy, the debtor's motive in procuring his bankruptcy will be a relevant factor (at [53]). For an example of a failed annulment application by a wife in respect of her estranged husband's bankruptcy see *Re Ruiz* [2011] EWHC 913 (Ch), [2011] BPIR 1139 (permission to appeal refused at a hearing before the Court of Appeal – see [2012] BPIR 446).

The court's two stage approach to a s 282(1)(a) application—In *Society of Lloyds v Waters* [2001] BPIR 698 at 704G–705C Park J identified that s 282(1)(a) requires the court to proceed in two stages:

'First, it must ask whether, at the time that the bankruptcy order was made … any grounds existed on the basis of which the order ought not to have been made. If it does not appear to the court that any such grounds existed, the bankruptcy order stays in place and the second stage is not reached. If, however, it does appear to the court that such grounds existed, the second stage is reached. At that stage the court has a discretion whether or not to annul the bankruptcy. It is only a discretion, not a duty; the word is "may", not "shall".'

Park J went on in *Waters* to make the following observations as to the first of the two stages. In looking back to the time of the bankruptcy order, it does not matter that the debtor did not put before the court those grounds which existed at that time and on which the bankruptcy order ought not to have been made. In other words, it is sufficient for the debtor to put those grounds before the court on the hearing of the annulment application, provided that they can be shown to have existed at the time of the hearing of the bankruptcy petition. However, the burden of proof in establishing the existence of those grounds at the earlier time rests on the applicant; it is not good enough for the bankrupt to say that such grounds *may* have existed at that time. Furthermore, a debtor is not entitled to an annulment and must still make out his grounds in the event of a petitioning creditor's non-attendance: *Leicester v Plumtree Farms Ltd* [2004] BPIR 296 (Lloyd J, as he then was). An application may in any case be open to challenge by a creditor who argues that grounds raised by the bankrupt on the annulment application were available to him at the bankruptcy hearing and, as such, constitute abuse of process. Such an argument is plainly consistent with the decision of the House of Lords in *Johnson v Gore Wood & Co (a firm)* [2001] 1 All ER 481, although it should be noted that in *Johnson* their Lordships resisted the establishment of a hard and fast rule where a claim or defence could have been raised in earlier proceedings and preferred a broad, merits-based approach which takes account of the public and private interests involved and the facts of the case and, in particular, whether, in all the circumstances, a party was misusing or abusing the process of the court by seeking to raise before it an issue which could have been raised before. A very similar approach in the context of grounds raised in opposition to a bankruptcy petition which had been raised previously on an application to set aside a statutory demand appears in the judgment of the Court of Appeal in *Royal Bank of Scotland v Turner* [2000] BPIR 683.

In *Cramner v West Bromwich Building Society* [2012] EWCA Civ 517, [2012] BPIR 963 the Court of Appeal confirmed that the Court can take into account in the exercise of its discretion any matters which which had not already been adjudicated upon, even if they could have been raised earlier, but if the creditor had acted reasonably in seeking the bankruptcy order and the debtor had failed to raise defences open to him at an earlier stage the court was not bound to grant the annulment. By contrast, it would be only in exceptional circumstances that the Court would allow points already raised and rejected at the statutory demand/ hearing of the petition to be re-litigated on an annulment application.

Where an application proceeds under s 282(1)(a) on the basis of the bankrupt disputing the petition debt, it has been held by Neuberger J that the appropriate test should equate to that under CPR r 24.2 as to whether there is a real issue to be tried: *Guinan III v Caldwell Associates Ltd* [2004] BPIR 531 at [32]–[33]. However, in *Flett v HMRC* [2010] BPIR 1075 Anthony Ellray QC (sitting as a deputy High Court judge) drew a distinction between a debtor challenging the making of a bankruptcy order (where the question for the court is whether the debtor's evidence establishes a real prospect of making out the alleged defence) and a debtor making an application under s 282(1)(a), where the bankrupt is trying to establish that the bankruptcy order ought not to have been made on grounds existing at the time the order was made: 'In context it appears to me that the court hearing the application of the debtor for annulment must be satisfied as to those grounds on the balance of probability. It may not be enough in my view for a debtor to say at the time of an application for annulment: 'I had an arguable defence to a given case'. He should be saying: "I did not in fact owe the money for this or that reason," and it is for that reason that he now seeks the annulment of the order.'[46]. (*Flett* also contains an interesting discussion of the relationship between s 282 and the s 375 review jurisdiction, on which see also: *HMRC v Cassells* [2009] BPIR 284.)

As regards the second stage of the process identified in *Waters*, the court retains a very wide discretion in the exercise of which some general guidance may be gleaned from some of the reported authorities. In *Askew v Peter Dominic Ltd* [1997] BPIR 163 Millett LJ (with whom Sir John Balcombe agreed) refused leave to appeal from a decision of His Honour Judge Cooke who, on an appeal from a district judge, had refused to exercise his discretion in annulling a bankruptcy order notwithstanding the fact that Judge Cooke had described the statutory demand and the bankruptcy petition leading to the order as 'sheer nonsense', given technical defects which mis-described the source of the appellant's indebtedness but which, notably, could not possibly have misled the appellant. More importantly, however, Millett LJ identified (at 164F–164H) that, despite those observations, Judge Cooke had relied heavily upon the fact that the appellant was plainly indebted to the petitioning creditor, that the appellant did not dispute the debt and that, if sued, the appellant would have no defence to the petitioning creditor's claim. Accordingly, the only effect of annulling the bankruptcy order would have been to compel the petitioning creditor to serve a fresh statutory demand which the appellant could neither satisfy nor have set aside. *Askew* was accepted as authoritiy for the proposition that the court may refuse to annul a bankruptcy order even if prima facie grounds to annul are made out by Chief Registrar Baister in *Omokwe v HFC Bank Ltd* [2007] BPIR 1157 at [37] and [38]. Further, in exercising its discretion the court should always have regard to the ability of a debtor to meet his liabilities: see, for example, *Owo-Samson v Barclays Bank* [2003] EWCA Civ 714, [2003] BPIR 1373.

In *Housiaux v HM Customs & Excise* [2003] BPIR 858 at [25] and [26] Chadwick LJ (with whom Morland J and Thorpe LJ agreed) identified bankruptcy as a class remedy which necessitated that, when asked to make an order under s 282(1)(a), a court ought to satisfy itself, by such investigation of the facts as it thinks necessary, that the bankruptcy order ought not to have been made. Accordingly, the court should not annul a bankruptcy order by consent and without investigation. Even where a petitioning creditor does not oppose an annulment of a bankruptcy order, the petitioning creditor should make it clear that he does not challenge the factual basis, or identified parts of the factual basis, upon which the application for annulment is made.

In *Hope v Premierpace (Europe) Ltd* [1999] BPIR 695 Rimer J held at 698E–698H, again in the course of an appeal, that a district judge had been wrong to refuse an annulment where a bankruptcy petition had been made in the debtor's absence, where the debtor's solicitor could show that he had not attended at the hearing because he had not only been told by an unidentified individual at the court that the bankruptcy hearing would not be effective but also he had subsequently confirmed to the chief clerk in writing what he had been told. That decision is also authority for the proposition that an annulment should be ordered under s 282(1)(a) where, contrary to s 267(2)(b), the petition is based on an unliquidated debt.

In *Henwood v Customs & Excise* [1998] BPIR 339 Evans and Rose LJJ gave leave to appeal (ie without deciding the issue) against an order of Millett J (as he then was) which had dismissed the applicant's appeal against a refusal to annul a bankruptcy order where the applicant's solicitors had failed to appear at the bankruptcy hearing through a mix-up in relation to the solicitors and in circumstances where the bulk of the petition debt – sufficient to bring the petition debt below the statutory minimum – could be shown to be disputed on substantial grounds.

In the exercise of its discretion the court will also wish to consider any prima facie evidence requiring investigation that the bankrupt has concealed assets and the existence of other debts which make it likely that the bankrupt might be made bankrupt again: *Society of Lloyds v Reuters* [2001] BPIR 698 at 707B–707C; and see *Re a Bankrupt (No 622 of 1995), Artman v Artman* [1996] BPIR 511 at 517A–517D (Robert Walker J).

For an annulment, which was not opposed by the official receiver, in very unusual circumstances where justice required such a course see *Amihyia v Official Receiver* [2005] BPIR 264 (Evans-Lombe J). See also *Parveen v Manchester City Council* [2010] BPIR 152 (bankruptcy order should not have been made as it represented a disproportionate response to council tax arrears and caused injustice to the debtor). For another case made in good faith but too late in the day, where many creditors could not be contacted because bankruptcy records had been destroyed, see *Gill v Quinn* [2004] EWHC 883 (Ch), [2005] BPIR 129 (Mann J).

For discussion of a spate of recent cases where the Court have annulled a bankruptcy order made on the debtor's own petition on the s 282 (1)(b) ground on the basis that the debtor did not in fact have a genuine centre of main interest in the jurisdiction, see the notes to s 272.

Section 282(1)(b)

'... to the extent required by the rules, the bankruptcy debts and the expenses of the bankruptcy have all, since the making of the order, been either paid or secured for ...'—The reference here to 'the rules' was identified by Warner J in *Re Robertson (a Bankrupt)* [1989] 1 WLR 1139 as being a reference to rr 6.209 and 6.211. Following *Robertson*, it is not open to a bankrupt to argue that the term 'the bankruptcy debts' extends only to such of the bankruptcy debts in respect of which a proof has been lodged. Rather, it is a pre-condition of annulment under s 282(1)(b) that all creditors must be given an opportunity to prove following an application for annulment on that ground. Rule 6.209 provides a mechanism for such steps to be taken and for the adjournment of the application in the interim. The fact that a particular creditor may choose not to prove in the bankruptcy following notice of the application need not be fatal, although the court may, dependent on circumstances, require clarification of the position of a significant creditor. This, at least, is the theory. In practice, steps are not always taken to clarify the position with creditors who, for whatever reason, have not proved, with the consequence that the court is at risk of granting what might be an invalid annulment.

The term 'bankruptcy debts' is as defined in the broadest terms in s 382(1) and (2). The latter subsection begs the question as to how it might be that an unliquidated debt can be 'paid', although it is easy to see how such a debt might be secured. In practice, this 'paid' difficulty is most obviously overcome by the creditor placing an agreed figure on its claim.

The term 'paid or secured for' was considered by Mr John Jarvis QC, sitting as a deputy High Court judge, in *Halabi v London Borough of Camden* [2008] BPIR 370. The primary significance of the judgment lies in paras [13]–[15] where the wording in s 282(1)(b) was construed, by reference to the wording in r 6.211(2) and (3), as meaning that 'paid' means just that – 'A debt is either paid or not paid' – and that the words 'to the satisfaction of the court' refer to and qualify only the words 'secured for', and not the word 'paid'. As such, paid could not mean secured by an undertaking. The question of undertakings was relevant given the practice that had evolved in the county courts by which, commonly, a mortgage advance would be paid over to the bankrupt's solicitors on an undertaking that the solicitor would hold the funds in client account and would not release the funds until the making of the annulment order. At [13] the deputy judge held that the making of an order under s 282(1)(b) on the basis that debts could be said to have been paid on the strength of such undertakings was beyond the jurisdiction of the court. This did not, however, preclude the court from accepting, in an appropriate case, that payment could be made to a trustee-in-bankruptcy to be held as security provided – and this, it is submitted – amounts to the potential practical difficulty on this point – the trustee has instructions from *all* creditors to act as their agent, and nothing less than all creditors will do for this purpose. Equally, the court could make a conditional order to take effect at such date as the court might specify under CPR r 40.7(1). Such an order could be tailored to trigger on the satisfaction of certain conditions, the usual conditions being that the Official Receiver had notified the court that the debts in the sums specified in the order had been paid together with costs and that security had been provided in respect of any unproven claims in the bankruptcy. This inconvenient ruling has been reversed by the Insolvency Amendment Rules 2010 (SI 2010/686) which, by the insertion of r 6.211(6), makes clear that security includes an undertaking given by a solicitor and accepted by the court.

Statutory interest—An application under s 282(1)(b) does not require the court to be satisfied that interest which would accrue on bankruptcy debts after the date of the bankruptcy order has either been paid or secured, since the term 'bankruptcy debt' does not, by reason of the reference to s 322(2) and s 382(1)(d), extend to interest payable in any period *after* the making of the bankruptcy order. Certainly the Court of Appeal had held in *Re A Debtor (No 37 of 1976) ex parte Taylor v the Debtor* [1980] Ch 565 that the court was entitled to grant an annulment without any provision being made for statutory interest. In *Harper v Buchler* [2004] BPIR 724 Deputy Registrar Barnett, considering *Taylor*, held that statutory interest is not a bankruptcy debt within s 382, and identified the following general principles (at 727G–728B):

'(1) The grant of an annulment is a privilege. The court has a completely unfettered discretion in deciding whether or not to grant it. (2) In considering the exercise of its discretion the court may have regard to all of the circumstances of the matter before it. I do not think that the court is limited to an analysis of the applicant's conduct. (3) The length of time between the date of the bankruptcy order and the date of the application for the annulment of the order is one such factor that the court may take into consideration. If an application for annulment is made very promptly it may well be that the court would disregard the issue of statutory interest. Equally, if the application was not made until some years later the court may very well have regard to that. (4) The court would also have regard to the source of the funds being made available to discharge creditors and will doubtless have regard to the question of whether the bankruptcy estate, if realised, is sufficient to discharge both the principal debts and any statutory interest that would ordinarily accrue in the bankruptcy.'

It is now clear from the new r 6.211(5) (inserted by SI 2010/686) that payment of post commencement interest on the bankruptcy debts which have been proved is a relevant factor to the court's discretion and the court may take such payment into account if it thinks just.

Third party funds—Adopting the above principles in *Harper v Buchler (No 2)* [2005] BPIR 577 Registrar Derrett identified at [12] that statutory interest should be paid in circumstances where there are more than sufficient assets in the bankruptcy estate. However, where third party funds are being made available, and those funds are insufficient to meet the claims of creditors for interest in full, the burden lies on the bankrupt to show that the third party funds are in no way linked (eg by re-mortgaging) to assets within the bankruptcy estate: *Wilcock v Duckworth* [2005] BPIR 682 at [8]–[9] (Deputy Registrar Shaffer).

One practical difficulty which can arise in the course of an annulment application is that a third party or lender – usually a secured lender – will not complete on an advance unless an order for annulment is obtained. The potential difficulties for debtors have been mitigated by the new rule 6.211(5) which endorses the practice of annulments based on solicitor's undertakings to pay the creditors (reversing the decision in *Halabi v London Borough of Camden* [2008] BPIR 370, noted above. The term 'secured for' is more flexible than the term 'paid' such that the court may make an order if satisfied that the debts and expenses cannot exceed a particular amount and that amount is fully secured: *Engel v Peri* [2002] BPIR 961 at [42]. The court may grant an annulment conditionally on payment of such sums: see, for example, *Hirani v Rendle* [2004] BPIR 274 (Lawrence Collins J) (annulment conditional on debtor securing Inland Revenue debt and any unpaid costs and expenses of the trustee), and see *Thornhill v Atherton* [2004] EWCA Civ 1858, [2005] BPIR 437 (Waller and Jonathan Parker LJJ, Lloyd J) (appeal upholding annulment order under s 282(1)(a) on terms that order not to be perfected until order that the debtor paid the trustee-in-bankruptcy's costs and expenses in full).

Annulment funding agreements have been the subject of judicial consideration in *Annulment Funding Co Ltd v Cowey* [2010] EWCA Civ 711, [2010] BPIR 1304; *Consolidated Finance Limited v Hunter* [2010] BPIR 1322; *Cook v Consolidated Finance Limited* [2010] EWCA Civ 369, [2010] BPIR 1331; *Consolidated Finance Limited v (1) Collins (2) Collins* [2013] EWCA Civ 475, [2013] BPIR 543 (loan and charge unenforceable as they did not comply with the terms of the Consumer Credit Act 1974).

If an annulment order under s 282(1)(b) is made on the basis of an undertaking to pay monies and that undertaking is not honoured then the appropriate course is to apply to set aside the annulment order, and not to present a fresh bankruptcy petition: *Inland Revenue Commissioners v Khan* [2005] BPIR 409 (Registrar Rawson).

The effect of r 6.211(2)—Rule 6.211(2) provides that 'All bankruptcy debts which have been proved must have been paid in full' as one of the matters to be proved in a s 282(1)(b) application. The court, therefore, has no jurisdiction to annul an order where payment is to be made in less than full even where some or all of the creditors in the bankruptcy have expressly agreed to accept less than their full claim for the purposes of obtaining the annulment. However sympathetic the court may be to a debtor in these circumstances it remains that the term 'bankruptcy debt' is as defined in s 382(1) by reference to debt or liability and to which the debtor 'is subject' at the commencement of the bankruptcy or to which he 'may become subject' after commencement in the case of a pre-commencement obligation, together with interest. Section 282(1)(b) does not contemplate annulment on the debtor discharging anything less than the full extent of the bankruptcy debts as so defined, and the court has no jurisdiction to facilitate such a course, although payment of less than his full bankruptcy debts remains achievable by way of an IVA by a debtor.

The effect of annulment—The effect of an annulment is to treat the bankruptcy order as if it had never been made. Upon annulment taking effect those assets then vested in the trustee-in-bankruptcy will re-vest in the former bankrupt: see *Bell v Brown* [2007] EWHC 2788 (QB), [2008] BPIR 829 at [60] (Tugendhat J), albeit the point did not require final resolution in that case.

'The distinction between an appeal and an annulment'—The distinction between an appeal and an annulment was identified by Peter Smith J in *Hore v Commissioners of Inland Revenue* [2002] BPIR 986 at [10] and [11] as, in the latter case, allowing the court to look at the facts from the point of view of circumstances that existed at the time of the making of the bankruptcy order.

Costs—Whilst the making of an order for costs necessarily remains subject to the court's discretion on the facts of any particular case, the starting point in respect of liability for the trustee-in-bankruptcy's costs is with the petitioning creditor in a s 282(1)(a) case, whereas the starting point is with the debtor in a s 282(1)(b) case: *Butterworth v Soutter* [2000] BPIR 582 (Neuberger J, as he then was). For a case in which that presumption was rebutted in a s 282(1)(a) case because of delay on the part of a debtor see *Tetteh v London Borough of Lambeth* [2008] BPIR 241 (Registrar Nicholls). See also the detailed discussion in *Redbridge LBC v Mustafa* [2010] EWHC 1105 (Ch), [2010] BPIR 893 and the difficult case of *Re Haworth* [2011] EWHC 36 (Ch), [2011] BPIR 428.

Credit Reference Agencies—For an interesting case where a bankrupt successfully established a cause of action in negligence and breach of statutory duty against a credit reference agency for their failure to update their records to show a bankruptcy had been stayed and then rescinded see *Smeaton v Equifax* [2013] EWCA Civ 108 (principles equally applicable to an annulment).

Procedure—See rr 6.206–6.214. Although it may be possible to effect equivalent compliance with r 6.209 by way of making efforts to contact creditors in the bankruptcy, the court is very unlikely to grant an annulment where there is a significant passage of time and where records have been destroyed making such contact difficult: *Gill v Quinn* [2005] BPIR 129 (Mann J). In *Howard v Savage* [2007] BPIR 1097 at [8] Lewison J identified that the Rules are silent on the position where there may be unknown creditors in the absence of a report under r 6.207 that there are known creditors who have not proved. In upholding the decision of a district judge not to direct advertisement under r 6.211(4) his Lordship held at [10] and [14] that the decision as to whether or not advertisement is appropriate forms part of the discretion under s 282(1)(b) and amounts to a fact-sensitive exercise which depends on the particular circumstances of any case. *Howard* involved an annulment application made some 12 or 13 years after the making of the bankruptcy order and the district judge was, in those circumstances, entitled to form the view that advertisement would be pointless in terms of bringing forward unknown claims.

Rule 6.215 neither excludes the operation of r 7.4(6) (urgent applications) in an appropriate case, nor does it necessarily require a hearing of an application within the three year period in which the application itself must be made: *Bagnall v Official Receiver* [2004] BPIR 445 (Latham and Arden LJJ). Rule 6.214(1) allows a bankrupt to challenge a trustee's costs, even following annulment: *Hirani v Rendle* [2004] BPIR 274 at [65].

On the question of the introduction of fresh evidence see *Oraki v Dean and Dean (A Firm)* [2012] EWHC 2885 (Ch), [2013] BPIR 88.

Chapter II

Protection of Bankrupt's Estate and Investigation of His Affairs

283 Definition of bankrupt's estate

(1) Subject as follows, a bankrupt's estate for the purposes of any of this Group of Parts comprises—

(a) all property belonging to or vested in the bankrupt at the commencement of the bankruptcy, and

(b) any property which by virtue of any of the following provisions of this Part is comprised in that estate or is treated as falling within the preceding paragraph.

(2) Subsection (1) does not apply to—

(a) such tools, books, vehicles and other items of equipment as are necessary to the bankrupt for use personally by him in his employment, business or vocation;

(b) such clothing, bedding, furniture, household equipment and provisions as are necessary for satisfying the basic domestic needs of the bankrupt and his family.

This subsection is subject to section 308 in Chapter IV (certain excluded property reclaimable by trustee).

(3) Subsection (1) does not apply to—

(a) property held by the bankrupt on trust for any other person, or

(b) the right of nomination to a vacant ecclesiastical benefice.

(3A) Subject to section 308A in Chapter IV, subsection (1) does not apply to—

(a) a tenancy which is an assured tenancy or an assured agricultural occupancy, within the meaning of Part I of the Housing Act 1988, and the terms of which inhibit an assignment as mentioned in section 127(5) of the Rent Act 1977, or

(b)   a protected tenancy, within the meaning of the Rent Act 1977, in respect of which, by virtue of any provision of Part IX of that Act, no premium can lawfully be required as a condition of assignment, or

(c)   a tenancy of a dwelling-house by virtue of which the bankrupt is, within the meaning of the Rent (Agriculture) Act 1976, a protected occupier of the dwelling-house, and the terms of which inhibit an assignment as mentioned in section 127(5) of the Rent Act 1977, or

(d)   a secure tenancy, within the meaning of Part IV of the Housing Act 1985, which is not capable of being assigned, except in the cases mentioned in section 91(3) of that Act.

(4) References in any of this Group of Parts to property, in relation to a bankrupt, include references to any power exercisable by him over or in respect of property except in so far as the power is exercisable over or in respect of property not for the time being comprised in the bankrupt's estate and—

(a)   is so exercisable at a time after either the official receiver has had his release in respect of that estate under section 299(2) in Chapter III or a meeting summoned by the trustee of that estate under section 331 in Chapter IV has been held, or

(b)   cannot be so exercised for the benefit of the bankrupt;

and a power exercisable over or in respect of property is deemed for the purposes of any of this Group of Parts to vest in the person entitled to exercise it at the time of the transaction or event by virtue of which it is exercisable by that person (whether or not it becomes so exercisable at that time).

(5) For the purposes of any such provision in this Group of Parts, property comprised in a bankrupt's estate is so comprised subject to the rights of any person other than the bankrupt (whether as a secured creditor of the bankrupt or otherwise) in relation thereto, but disregarding—

(a)   any rights in relation to which a statement such as is required by section 269(1)(a) was made in the petition on which the bankrupt was adjudged bankrupt, and

(b)   any rights which have been otherwise given up in accordance with the rules.

(6) This section has effect subject to the provisions of any enactment not contained in this Act under which any property is to be excluded from a bankrupt's estate.

Amendments—Housing Act 1988, s 117(1).

General note—The definition of the bankrupt's estate identifies the scope of that property which vests automatically in a trustee or the official receiver under s 306(1). In brief terms, the bankrupt's estate includes all property to which the bankrupt is entitled legally or beneficially, save for those domestic or business assets in s 283(2), property held on trust for another and those 'personal' claims which are identified under that heading below and which, for reasons of public policy, remain vested in a debtor despite the making of a bankruptcy order against him. The bankruptcy estate is also subject to the rights, including the security rights, of third parties, save to the extent that such rights are abandoned under s 283(5). Section 283(6) expressly provides that legislation may expressly or impliedly override s 283 so as to exclude particular property from the scope of the bankrupt's estate. This point is also considered below.

Section 283 should be read in conjunction with ss 306–310, especially s 307 (after-acquired property) and s 310 (income payments orders), which are specifically concerned with property which does not fall within the definition of the bankrupt's estate under s 283 but which becomes claimable by a trustee in the course of the bankruptcy.

Joint property—The making of a bankruptcy order gives rise to the severance of an equitable joint tenancy to which the bankrupt is party by operation of law: *Re Dennis (a bankrupt)* [1993] 1 Ch 72, [1993] 1 FLR 313.

Section 283(1) and (4)

'**... property ...**'—Although it is commonly said that s 436 contains a definition of the term 'property', what appears in that provision is in fact a non-exhaustive list of certain forms of property which are included within the term. Given the breadth of the wording employed in s 436, it is difficult indeed to conceive of a form of tangible or intangible property which would not fall within its scope.

However, the bankrupt's estate will include any power exercisable by the bankrupt over property. A power which is not exercisable by the bankrupt, therefore, falls outside of the estate; equally, a power will be excluded if exercised by the bankrupt in trust for a third party: *Clarkson v Clarkson* [1994] BCC 921 at 931D (Hoffmann LJ, Stuart-Smith and Saville LJJ agreeing).

If property vests in a trustee then, unless the trustee disclaims that property under s 315, the bankrupt has no standing to apply to the court for an order re-vesting such property in him: *Khan-Ghauri v Dunbar Bank plc* [2001] BPIR 618 at 622B–622G (Pumfrey J).

Benefits arising from the use of the bankrupt's estate by third parties—In *Trustee of FC Jones & Sons v Jones* [1996] BPIR 644 the Court of Appeal (Nourse, Beldam and Millett LJJ) held that a wife who had used monies to which a trustee-in-bankruptcy was entitled, and who had made substantial profits from engaging in speculation with those monies, was liable to account to the trustee on the basis of common law tracing for both the original monies and interest thereon together with the profits derived from its use. Although *Jones* was decided under the Bankruptcy Act 1914, the same principles will continue to apply under the 1986 Act. It should be noted, however, that the wife in *Jones* had conceded that she had no claim to the original monies to which her husband had been entitled, in contrast with a case where, say, the wife had obtained the monies under a voidable contract which was subsequently set aside by a trustee as a transaction-at-undervalue or a preference. In the case of a voidable contract it is doubtful that the making of an order to restore the position to what it would have been but for the transaction challenged – on which see ss 339(2) and 340(2) – would provide for the payment over of such a windfall, although interest would be claimable by the trustee.

Trust assets—In bankruptcy, perhaps the most common example of property held on trust involves the matrimonial home. If a debtor is the sole legal owner of a property which is held on trust for himself and his wife in bankruptcy, then the consequence of a bankruptcy order is that the trustee will acquire the legal estate and hold the beneficial interest in equity for himself and the bankrupt's wife. Where, however, the legal estate is owned by the debtor and his wife on trust for themselves, then the consequence of the bankruptcy is that the legal estate will be held by the bankrupt and his wife with the trustee and the bankrupt's wife being entitled to the beneficial interest in the property. The making of a bankruptcy order operates to sever a joint tenancy.

Property which is subject to an individual voluntary arrangement constitutes trust property, even where the arrangement contains no express trust clause. That proposition and the consequences of bankruptcy on an individual voluntary arrangement are explained in the notes to s 2(2).

For a novel case in which a bankrupt was held to hold lottery winnings on a resulting trust for an individual on whose behalf the bankrupt had purchased the lottery ticket, see *Abrahams v Trustee of Property of Abrahams* [1999] BPIR 637.

Where a trustee in bankruptcy realises an asset for the benefit of a secured creditor with the agreement of that creditor, the trustee is entitled to look to that creditor for the costs of realisation: *Re Sobey (a Bankrupt)* [1999] BPIR 1009 (Mr Registrar Baister).

For a complex proprietary claim including discussion of the possibility of tracing by the Official Receveir see *KK v MA* [2012] EWHC 788 (Fam), [2012] BPIR 1137.

Pension interests—In any case where a bankruptcy petition is presented on or after 31 May 2000, ss 11 and 12 of the Welfare Reform and Pensions Act 1999 operate so as to exclude from the scope of the bankrupt's estate any interest in a pension scheme as defined very broadly in the 1999 Act. Certain unapproved schemes and other specialist arrangements are not subject to that exclusion.

The Occupational and Personal Pension Schemes (Bankruptcy) Regulations 2002 (SI 2002/427) allow for agreement between a trustee and a bankrupt as to the exclusion of pension rights from the bankrupt's estate where such rights would otherwise vest in the estate.

Section 283(5)

Secured and other third party rights—Section 283(5) is sufficiently broad so as to protect the rights of secured creditors and any party entitled to an equitable interest in property otherwise comprised in the bankrupt's estate other than to the extent that such rights or interests are waived or abandoned.

In *Mountney v Treharne* [2003] Ch 135, [2002] EWCA Civ 1174 the Court of Appeal held that an order in ancillary relief proceedings created a specifically enforceable contract and immediate equitable interest in a property which would be sufficient to take that interest out of the estate for present purposes: to similar effect see *Roberts v Nunn and Tiffany* [2004] BPIR 623 (Nicholas Strauss QC sitting as a Deputy High Court judge), and see also the notes on 'disposition' to s 284.

A trustee-in-bankruptcy assumes the rights of a bankrupt under an ancillary relief consent order for the purposes of the Trusts of Land and Appointment of Trustees Act 1996 unless the order can be shown to have some special force going beyond the agreement of the parties to it: *Avis v Turner* [2007] EWCA Civ 748, [2007] BPIR 663 (Ward, Chadwick and May LJJ).

'Personal' claims which are not comprised in the bankruptcy estate—In *Heath v Tang* [1993] 1 WLR 1421 at 1423A–1423B Hoffmann LJ, as he then was, identified that the courts have long recognised that certain causes of action can be said to be personal to the bankrupt such that they do not vest in his trustee. Almost a century and a half earlier, Earle J indicated in *Beckham v Drake* (1849) 2 HL Cas 579 at 604 that these cases include those where 'damages are to be estimated by immediate reference to pain felt by the bankrupt in respect of his body, mind, or character, without immediate reference to his rights of property.' In recent years the courts have been busy in this area and have reached findings which extend beyond what Lord Atkinson had, in *Hollinshead v Hazelton* [1916] 1 AC 428 at 436, termed 'compassionate allowances' for the maintenance of the bankrupt. The authorities do not, however, suggest that there is any sort of trend or inclination in finding that any particular species of claim should fall inside or outside of the bankrupt's estate, since each particular cause of action must be assessed according to its own characteristics.

See *Young v Hamilton* [2010] BPIR 1468 and *Young v OR* [2010] BPIR 1477 for a recent discussion of the rule that bankruptcy deprives the bankrupt from the right to commence or continue proceedings in his/ her own name. Neither the English and Irish courts considered that this infringed the Bankrupt's human rights under the European Convention. In *Thames Chambers Solicitors v Miah* [2013] EWHC 1245 (QC) Tugendhat J upheld a wasted costs order made against solicitors who conducted proceedings on behalf of a bankrupt without the consent of the OR or trustee, despite being aware of the bankruptcy.

Those causes of action which have been held to be 'personal' to the bankrupt and therefore outside of the scope of the bankrupt's estate include:

- A claim for damages for slander: *Re Wilson ex parte Vine* (1878) 8 Ch D 364.
- A claim for damages for loss of reputation: *Wilson v United Counties Bank Ltd* [1920] AC 102.
- The hope or expectation of a payment by the Criminal Injuries Compensation Board which remains subject to the Board's discretion such that the hope or expectation did

not exist as a right to which some future or contingent entitlement could relate: *Re Campbell (a Bankrupt)* [1996] 2 All ER 537.

- An aviation licence awarded to an individual as a fit and proper person: *Griffiths v Civil Aviation Authority* [1997] BPIR 50 (Federal Court of Australia).
- Social security benefits of an income nature: *Mulvey v Secretary of State for Social Security* [1997] BPIR 696, considered in *Secretary of State for Work and Pensions v Payne* [2011] UKSC 60, [2012] BPIR 224.
- A claim for medical negligence giving rise to personality change: *Davis v Trustee in Bankruptcy of the Estate of Davis* [1998] BPIR 572.
- A claim for damages for professional negligence in respect of conduct which gave rise to the bankruptcy of the bankrupt: *Mulkerrins v PricewaterhouseCoopers* [2003] UKHL 41, [2003] 1 WLR 1937.
- Claim for unfair dismissal under the Employment Rights Act 1996: *Grady v Prison Service* [2003] EWCA Civ 527, [2003] 3 All ER 745.

The following causes of action have been held to be within the scope of the bankrupt's estate:

- Damages for breaking, entering and damaging the property of the bankrupt: *Rogers v Spence* (1846) 12 Cl & Fin 700.
- A claim for damages for breach of a contract of employment (but not, according to a majority of the Exchequer Chamber, a claim in respect of mental suffering): *Beckham v Drake* (1849) 2 HL Cas 579.
- Damages equating to 6 months' salary in lieu of proper notice of dismissal: *Walding v Oliphant* (1875) 1 QBD 145.
- Entitlement to a licence allowing for use of registered fishing vessels: *Re Rae* [1995] BCC 102. At 113C–113D Warner J observed that, 'I am not persuaded that one can, merely from a consideration of the purposes of the Insolvency Act and the non-exhaustive nature of the definition of 'property' in s 436, reach the conclusion that any asset of the bankrupt which can be realised or turned to account is "property" within the meaning of the act.'
- Right to appeal pre-bankruptcy summary judgment: *Wordsworth v Dixon* [1997] BPIR 337. See also *Cowey v Insol Funding Ltd* [2012] EWHC 2421 (Ch), [2012] BPIR 958 for confirmation that a bankrupt has no right to appeal in his own name from a judgment against him which is enforceable only against the estate vested in his trustee.
- A claim for a grant of a new tenancy under Part II of the Landlord & Tenant Act 1954: *Saini v Petroform Ltd* [1997] BPIR 515.
- A claim under a contingency fee agreement entered into by a solicitor prior to his bankruptcy: *Royal Bank of Canada v Chetty* [1997] BPIR 137.
- Right to receive royalties from the Performing Rights Society: *Performing Rights Society v Rowland* [1998] BPIR 128.
- An award of damages to compensate the bankrupt for loss of earning capacity: *Re Bell (a Bankrupt)* [1998] BPIR 26 (British Columbia Supreme Court).
- A claim for damages for breach of joint venture agreement: *Morris v Morgan* [1998] BPIR 764.
- A claim on the critical illness element of a life assurance policy which produced a fixed sum in the event of a varying range of disabilities: *Cork v Rawlins* [2001] EWCA Civ 197, [2001] Ch 792. The judgment of Peter Gibson LJ in *Rawlins* is of note, since it draws attention to the fact that there is no authority supporting the proposition that a contractual claim is capable of remaining vested in a bankrupt.
- The entitlement to one half of the policy proceeds of a joint life policy payable upon the bankrupt's wife being diagnosed terminally ill where the joint tenancy in equity representing entitlement to the policy proceeds had been severed upon the husband's earlier bankruptcy: *Re Pritchard (a bankrupt), Williams v Pritchard* [2007] BPIR 1385 (Registrar Derrett).
- The right to challenge a tax assessment (at least where the assessment was raised prior to the bankruptcy): *R (Singh) v HMRC* [2010] BPIR 933. See also *McNulty v HMRC* [2012] STC 2110 (the right to appeal in tax cases vests in the trustee pursuant to s 306, and the bankrupt tax payer therefore has no locus stnadi to pursue an appeal). In *Re GP Aviation Group International Ltd* [2013] EWHC 1447 (Ch), [2013] BPIR 576 the court accepted that only the trustee was entitled to appeal a tax assessment but considered that, for the purposes of assignment, the right to appeal was not property within the meaning of s 436 and was not capable of being sold by the liquidator.

- A payment protection insurance refund (either because it was an 'interest incidental to property' ie the policy itself, or because it was the fruit of a cause of action which was in itself property encompassed within the estate: see the definition of property in s 436): *Ward v Official Receiver* [2012] BPIR 1073.
- An equitable interest arising under a proprietary estoppel: *Walden v Atkins (Executor of the Estate of Dennis Walden)* [2013] EWHC 1387 (Ch), [2013] BPIR 943.

The fact that any particular item of property is of no value when in the hands of the bankrupt is not determinative of whether the item constitutes property: *Rothschild v Bell* [1999] 2 All ER 722 at 734.

'Hybrid' claims—It is possible that a single cause of action will comprise two or more heads of damage in respect of loss which is respectively personal and non-personal. In *Ord v Upton* [2001] 1 All ER 193 the Court of Appeal considered a claim for medical negligence which comprised separate heads of claim for loss of earnings and pain and suffering. Aldous LJ, with whom Mantell and Kennedy LJJ agreed, held at 207J–208B that the single cause of action vested in the trustee, but that the trustee held the proceeds of the pain and suffering element of the claim on a constructive trust for the bankrupt, with the consequence that the trustee would have to account to the bankrupt for any such damages recovered. It would also, of course, be open to the trustee to consider assigning the cause of action to the bankrupt, subject to the bankrupt accounting to the trustee for the proceeds of the loss of income element of the claim.

The position between bankruptcy order and appointment of a trustee-in-bankruptcy—The vesting of a property in a trustee-in-bankruptcy only occurs under s 306 upon the appointment of the trustee. As regards the interim period during which the Official Receiver is receiver of the bankruptcy estate under s 287, and as regards pursuit of any claim relating to a claim *against* the bankrupt for a debt or damages, the bankrupt has no standing to pursue such a claim because s 285(3) renders the claim for debt or damages unenforceable against the bankrupt personally such that the bankrupt no longer has any interest in the claim: *Heath v Tang* [1993] 1 WLR 1423 at 1427. The court does, however, retain a discretion in allowing the bankrupt to act in exceptional circumstances where, for example, the time limit for an appeal is about to expire: *Dadourian Group International Inc v Simms* [2008] EWHC 723 (Ch), [2008] BPIR 508 at [13] (Warren J). The Court of Appeal has held that such a discretion exists even where a trustee has been appointed: *Boyd & Hutchinson (a firm) v Foenander* [2003] EWCA Civ 1516, [2004] BPIR 20.

Property excluded from the bankruptcy estate by other statutes—The exclusion of pensions from the scope of the bankrupt's estate is considered above.

By s 417 of the Proceeds of Crime Act 2002, property which is subject to an order under that legislation is automatically excluded from the bankrupt's estate.

Under reg 80(2)(a) of the Education (Student Loans) (Repayment) Regulations 2009 (SI 2009/470) any part of a student loan received by a bankrupt after the bankruptcy is excluded from his estate.

Section 308(1)(b) allows the trustee to claim property excluded by s 283(2) (tools of trade, household effects etc) if 'it appears to the trustee that the realisable value of the whole or any part of the property exceeds the cost of a reasonable replacement for that property'.

283A Bankrupt's home ceasing to form part of estate

(1) This section applies where property comprised in the bankrupt's estate consists of an interest in a dwelling-house which at the date of the bankruptcy was the sole or principal residence of—

    (a)   the bankrupt,

    (b)   the bankrupt's spouse or civil partner, or

    (c)   a former spouse or former civil partner of the bankrupt.

(2) At the end of the period of three years beginning with the date of the bankruptcy the interest mentioned in subsection (1) shall—

    (a)   cease to be comprised in the bankrupt's estate, and

    (b)   vest in the bankrupt (without conveyance, assignment or transfer).

(3) Subsection (2) shall not apply if during the period mentioned in that subsection—

    (a)   the trustee realises the interest mentioned in subsection (1),

    (b)   the trustee applies for an order for sale in respect of the dwelling-house,

    (c)   the trustee applies for an order for possession of the dwelling-house,

    (d)   the trustee applies for an order under section 313 in Chapter IV in respect of that interest, or

    (e)   the trustee and the bankrupt agree that the bankrupt shall incur a specified liability to his estate (with or without the addition of interest from the date of the agreement) in consideration of which the interest mentioned in subsection (1) shall cease to form part of the estate.

(4) Where an application of a kind described in subsection (3)(b) to (d) is made during the period mentioned in subsection (2) and is dismissed, unless the court orders otherwise the interest to which the application relates shall on the dismissal of the application—

    (a)   cease to be comprised in the bankrupt's estate, and

    (b)   vest in the bankrupt (without conveyance, assignment or transfer).

(5) If the bankrupt does not inform the trustee or the official receiver of his interest in a property before the end of the period of three months beginning with the date of the bankruptcy, the period of three years mentioned in subsection (2)—

    (a)   shall not begin with the date of the bankruptcy, but

    (b)   shall begin with the date on which the trustee or official receiver becomes aware of the bankrupt's interest.

(6) The court may substitute for the period of three years mentioned in subsection (2) a longer period—

    (a)   in prescribed circumstances, and

    (b)   in such other circumstances as the court thinks appropriate.

(7) The rules may make provision for this section to have effect with the substitution of a shorter period for the period of three years mentioned in subsection (2) in specified circumstances (which may be described by reference to action to be taken by a trustee in bankruptcy).

(8) The rules may also, in particular, make provision—

    (a)   requiring or enabling the trustee of a bankrupt's estate to give notice that this section applies or does not apply;

    (b)   about the effect of a notice under paragraph (a);

    (c)   requiring the trustee of a bankrupt's estate to make an application to the Chief Land Registrar.

(9) Rules under subsection (8)(b) may, in particular—

    (a)   disapply this section;

    (b)   enable a court to disapply this section;

    (c)   make provision in consequence of a disapplication of this section;

    (d)   enable a court to make provision in consequence of a disapplication of this section;

    (e)   make provision (which may include provision conferring jurisdiction on a court or tribunal) about compensation.

Amendments—Inserted by Enterprise Act 2002, s 261(1). Amended by Civil Partnership Act 2004, s 261(1), Sch 27, para 113.

General note—Section 283A – together, with s 313A, the so-called 'use it or lose it' provisions – was introduced with effect from 1 April 2004 by s 261 of the Enterprise Act 2002. These provisions should be read in conjunction with s 313 (charge on bankrupt's home) and s 313A (application for sale, possession or charge of low value home) and engender Parliament's attempt at addressing the highly unsatisfactory practice by which a trustee could previously take no action in relation to a bankrupt's home and later, often years later, and usually to the surprise of the by now discharged bankrupt, take steps to realise not only the property but also its enhanced value over time. The new provisions require action of the trustee, irrespective of the state of the property market. This obligation, however, is subject to s 313, which permits a trustee to apply for a charge on a bankrupt's interest in a dwelling-house where 'the trustee is, for any reason, unable for the time being to realise that property.' Such a charge will secure the value of the bankrupt's interest, as assessed by the court, together with interest, and is enforceable notwithstanding the subsequent discharge of the bankrupt or the release of the trustee. On the other hand, s 313A imposes restrictions on actions by a trustee where the bankrupt's interest in a dwelling-house is of no value, as defined in that provision.

    The policy underlying s 283A was discussed by Lawrence Collins J, as he then was, in *Re Byford (Deceased)* [2003] EWHC 1267 (Ch), [2003] BPIR 1089 in the context of the relevance of that policy to cases involving equitable accounting.

    The mechanism employed in s 283A is to exclude any interest of the bankrupt in a dwelling-house – as defined in s 385(1) – from the scope of the bankrupt's estate, as defined in s 283, at the end of the three-year period identified in s 283A(2), subject to extension under s 283A(5) and (6).

    Section 283A has no application to a bankruptcy commenced prior to 29 December 1986 (ie under the Bankruptcy Act 1914): *Pannell v The Official Receiver* [2008] EWHC 736 (Ch), [2008] BPIR 629 (HHJ Havelock-Allan QC, sitting as a judge of the High Court).

    For discussion of the transitional provisions applying to s 283A see *Stonham v Ramrattan* [2011] EWCA Civ 119, [2011] BPIR 518.

Property to which s 283A applies—Section 283A(1) defines the property or properties to which the provision applies. The provision catches any dwelling-house at the date of the bankruptcy order in which the bankrupt had a legal or beneficial interest where any such property was 'the sole or principal residence' of the bankrupt, the bankrupt's spouse, or a former spouse (without limitation in number) of the bankrupt. Although, by definition, a person may have only one sole or principal residence, s 283A(1) plainly envisages more than one property falling within its scope. Any property which is not the sole or principal residence of any of those persons mentioned in s 283A(1), such as an investment property or holiday home, will not fall within the protection of s 283A or, indeed, s 313A. Section 283A does not apply to property vested in a third party at the date of the bankruptcy but later recovered by the trustee by virtue of s 342 (orders made in respect of transactions at an undervalue/ preferences): *Stonham v Ramrattan* [2011] EWCA Civ 119, [2011] BPIR 518.

    For the position where a trustee's interest was bought out by the bankrupt and his wife and the bankrupt was then made bankrupt for a second time, see *Garwood v Ambrose* [2012] EWHC 1494 (Ch), [2012] BPIR 996, where the trustee's argument that the bankrupt's interest re-vested in him pursuant to s 283A was successful on the facts (since the evidence did not establish any agreement that the wife would solely own the property). See also *Miller v Gallo* (unreported, 13 June 2013, Mann J) for a case where the opposite conclusion was reached on the evidence.

The combined effect of s 283A(2)–(4)—The starting point here lies in the automatic re-vesting of the bankrupt's interest in the bankrupt at the end of the three-year period beginning with the date of the bankruptcy order. That period has no application, however, where the trustee realises the bankrupt's interest, by virtue of s 283A(3)(a), or reaches agreement with the bankrupt for s 283A(3)(e) purposes within the three-year period (note the Court of Appeal's decision in *Lewis v Metropolitan Property Realisations Ltd* [2009] EWCA Civ 448, [2009] BPIR 820 that effecting a sale for future cash consideration does not amount to 'realization' until the cash is actually received, differing from the view of Proudman J in the Court below (reported at [2009] BPIR 79)). The trustee will also avoid the automatic re-vesting in the bankrupt of the bankrupt's interest if he 'applies' – that is, issues an application – for any of the orders listed in s 283A(3)(b)–(d) within the three-year period. On the other hand, if any such application is issued and dismissed – and only dismissed – within the three-year period then, by virtue of s 283A(4), the interest re-vests in the bankrupt (although note *Hunt and Another v Conwy County Borough Council* [2013] EWHC 1154 (Ch), [2013] BPIR 790, where Sir William Blackburne (sitting as a High Court judge) confirmed that where a trustee had disclaimed the property as onerous by the time his application for possession and sale was dismissed, the property did not re-vest in the bankrupt under s 283A. He did not think there was anything improper in allowing the Trustee to extend the 3-year time period by making an application within such a period to enable him to disclaim an asset). The onus, therefore, is squarely on the trustee to ensure that he has undertaken appropriate investigations into any interest to which the bankrupt's estate is entitled within the applicable time-limit, and that the application is properly prepared and technically sound. Where the trustee has obtained an order for sale, but has not enforced it, the three year time limit does not apply to prevent a later application to affirm the previous order: *Re Ellis Carr (in Bankruptcy); Levy v Ellis- Carr* [2012] EWHC 63 (Ch), [2012] BPIR 347.

Section 283A (5)

The period of 3 years runs from the date of the bankruptcy order only if the bankrupt notifies the trustee or Official Receiver of his interest in the property within 3 months of that date. Otherwise, the period runs from the date on which the trustee or Official Receiver becomes aware of the bankrupt's interest. For detailed discussion on s 283A(5) see *Stonham v Ramrattan* [2011] EWCA Civ 119, [2011] BPIR 518.

Section 283A(6)

Substitution of period exceeding three years—Rule 6.237C allows the court to substitute, for the purposes of s 283A(2), 'such longer period as the court thinks just and reasonable in all the circumstances of the case'.

Section 283A(7)

Substitution of shorter period than three years—Rule 6.237CA allows for automatic re-vesting in the bankrupt one month from the date of a notice – for which there is no prescribed form – sent by the trustee to the bankrupt to the effect that the trustee considers that the continued vesting of the property in the bankrupt's estate is of no benefit to creditors or, alternatively, that the re-vesting in the bankrupt will facilitate a more efficient administration of the bankrupt's estate.

Procedure—For the notification of a property falling within s 283A see rr 6.237, 6.237A, 6.237B and 6.237E for which Forms 6.83 and 6.84 are prescribed.

284 Restrictions on dispositions of property

(1) Where a person is adjudged bankrupt, any disposition of property made by that person in the period to which this section applies is void

except to the extent that it is or was made with the consent of the court, or is or was subsequently ratified by the court.

(2) Subsection (1) applies to a payment (whether in cash or otherwise) as it applies to a disposition of property and, accordingly, where any payment is void by virtue of that subsection, the person paid shall hold the sum paid for the bankrupt as part of his estate.

(3) This section applies to the period beginning with the day of the presentation of the petition for the bankruptcy order and ending with the vesting, under Chapter IV of this Part, of the bankrupt's estate in a trustee.

(4) The preceding provisions of this section do not give a remedy against any person—

(a)   in respect of any property or payment which he received before the commencement of the bankruptcy in good faith, for value and without notice that the petition had been presented, or

(b)   in respect of any interest in property which derives from an interest in respect of which there is, by virtue of this subsection, no remedy.

(5) Where after the commencement of his bankruptcy the bankrupt has incurred a debt to a banker or other person by reason of the making of a payment which is void under this section, that debt is deemed for the purposes of any of this Group of Parts to have been incurred before the commencement of the bankruptcy unless—

(a)   that banker or person had notice of the bankruptcy before the debt was incurred, or

(b)   it is not reasonably practicable for the amount of the payment to be recovered from the person to whom it was made.

(6) A disposition of property is void under this section notwithstanding that the property is not or, as the case may be, would not be comprised in the bankrupt's estate; but nothing in this section affects any disposition made by a person of property held by him on trust for any other person.

General note—This provision renders void any disposition of property that is made between the time when a bankruptcy petition is presented and the time when a debtor's property vests in the trustee, unless court approval is obtained. Section 284 is the bankruptcy equivalent of s 127, which applies in the liquidation of companies, and basically many of the same principles will apply, or at least provide legitimate guidelines (*Re Flint* [1993] Ch 319 at 328). But s 284 is in different terms to s 127 and so one cannot approach this section with the assumption that it is designed to achieve the same outcome as s 127, and one cannot necessarily apply a case decided under one section to the other section: *Pettit v Novakovic* [2007] BPIR 1643, [2007] BCC 462. The aim of the provision is to ensure that the bankrupt's estate is not dissipated, between the dates mentioned above, and so prevent a rateable distribution of the bankrupt's estate amongst his or her creditors.

HHJ David Cooke considered the application of s 284 to the insolvent estate of a deceased person (see s 421) in *Williams v Lawrence* [2011] EWHC 2001 (Ch), [2011] BPIR 1761.

The provision is expressly disapplied in the case of certain financial market transactions prescribed in Companies Act 1989, ss 164(3), 173(3)–(5). Similar exemptions applicable to financial and security settlements and associated security arrangements are provided for in the Financial Markets and Insolvency (Settlement Finality) Regulations 1999 (SI 1999/2979). These provisions seek to protect certain transactions from the normal effects of a company's insolvency.

'**Disposition**'—See the notes under the same heading in relation to s 127. Disposition is to be interpreted broadly in this context. It includes, as s 284(2) indicates, cash, and this would, consequently, cover things such as direct debits, cheques and the use of debit cards. For the application of s 284 to a power of attorney see *Sanders v Donovan* [2012] BPIR 219.

Whether the disposition of a debtor in the relevant time and pursuant to an order under s 24 of the Matrimonial Causes Act 1973 is a disposition within s 284 has been the subject of divergent views over the years. It was held in *Re Flint* [1993] Ch 319 that a transfer of a husband's interest in the matrimonial home, within the time-zone mentioned in s 284, to his wife pursuant to an order (whether or not by consent) under s 24 of the Matrimonial Causes Act 1973 constitutes a disposition for the purposes of s 284. This decision was made even though the debtor had not actually effected a transfer before bankruptcy ensued, although the order of the court was made during the s 284 period. The position taken by the judge was that the court order was effectively a disposition by the debtor. This diverged from the view in *Burton v Burton* [1986] 2 FLR 419 that a transfer order is not a disposition of property, as there is not a transfer until the completion of the relevant documentation effecting it. In Australia it has been held that a disposition made under an order pursuant to the Australian Family Law Act 1975 is protected from the impact of the Australian equivalent (although Australia retains the relation back doctrine that formerly applied in England and Wales) (*Corke v Corke and Official Trustee in Bankruptcy* (1994) 121 ALR 320). *Re Flint* was not followed in *Beer v Higham* [1997] BPIR 349, where Jonathan Parker J sided with the view expressed in *Burton*. However, in *Mountney v Treharne* [2003] Ch 135, [2002] EWCA Civ 1174 at [77], a case distinguishable from *Flint*, his Lordship, who was by now Jonathan Parker LJ, accepted that his decision in *Beer* was wrong and that the view expressed in *Flint* was correct. In the decision of *Treharne and Sand v Forrester* [2004] BPIR 338, [2003] EWHC 2784 (Ch), Lindsay J followed the approach taken in *Re Flint*. As a consequence we now appear to have some certainty and can say that any disposition of a debtor's property in the time covered by s 284 will, even if it is pursuant to a court in family law proceedings, be void. A matrimonial settlement which had not been finalised by the date of the bankruptcy petition was struck down as a void disposition by HHJ Cooke in *Warwick v Trustee of Bankruptcy of Yarwood* [2010] EWHC 2272 (Ch), [2010] BPIR 1443.

'**Void**'—A disposition is not void at the point of the transaction taking place. It only becomes void once the bankruptcy order is made, because unless an order is made, the disposition cannot be impugned. See the comments under the same heading for s 127.

'**Payment**' – a payment within s 284(2) could, but was not necessarily, a disposition of property within s 284(1): *Pettit v Novakovic* [2007] BPIR 1643, [2007] BCC 462.

'**Consent of the court**'—This can be obtained at the time of any disposition or subsequently.

Validation—Payments to solicitors and barristers by the debtor, in order to obtain advice and representation in relation to the bankruptcy petition that has been presented against him or her, may be validated by the court, even where the payments will prejudice creditors (*Re Sinclair ex parte Payne* (1885) 15 QBD 616; *Rio Properties Inc v Al-Midani* [2003] BPIR 128). But under s 284, and in order to validate payments, the court would require evidence as to the financial position of the debtor and of the grounds for validation (*Rio Properties Inc v Al-Midani* at 139). However, funds used to pay for costs related to attempts to finalise arrangements with creditors, and so avoid bankruptcy, will not be validated (*Re Spackman ex parte Foley* (1890) 24 QBD 728, distinguishing *Re Sinclair*).

The most recent set of guidelines for such applications are in *Practice Direction: Insolvency Proceedings* [2012] BPIR 409.

See the notes under 'Validating Orders' in relation to s 127, as the validation process under s 127 has been regarded as not unlike the process under s 284 (*Treharne and Sand v Forrester* [2004] BPIR 338, [2003] EWHC 2784 (Ch) at [57]).

Time—With debtors' petitions, namely where the debtor presents his or her own petition, the practice is that presentation is taken to be on the same day as the bankruptcy order is made (*Treharne and Sand v Forrester* [2004] BPIR 338, [2003] EWHC 2784 (Ch) at [23]), thereby reducing the period in which s 284 can operate. This is to be compared with the situation where a compulsory bankruptcy order is made on a creditor's petition.

Tomlinson v Bridging Finance Ltd [2010] BPIR 759 clarified that, although s 284 only applies to a disposition made between presentation of the bankruptcy petition and the vesting of the estate in the trustee, dispositions made the bankrupt of property within the bankruptcy estate after it had vested in the trustee are also void (see in particular para [10]).

Third party protection—Section 284(4) protects a third party who receives property or money before the date of the bankruptcy order, provided that he or she was a bona fide purchaser without notice.

Good faith—This element involves the state of mind of the beneficiary of the disposition. It connotes the fact that some duty is owed, and that is to the general body of creditors. Good faith goes beyond mere personal honesty, requiring more than absence of dishonesty, and more than absence of a conscious attempt to defraud (*Re Dalton* [1963] Ch 336 at 355, dealing with the old relation back doctrine under Bankruptcy Act 1914). If a person is aware that the debtor (soon to become a bankrupt) had failed to comply with a statutory demand, then it might be that good faith would not exist for the purposes of this section. The same would occur if the person who received the disposition did not know, but shut his or her eyes to some suspicion, that the debtor was the subject of bankruptcy proceedings. For an example of an unsuccessful attempt to rely on the good faith exception, see sands and *Treharne v Wright* [2010] BPIR 1437, where the test in Dalton was applied.

There is Australian authority to the effect that a person would be acting in good faith if he or she believed that the disposition was regularly and properly done (*PT Garuda Indonesia v Grellman* (1992) 107 ALR 199).

Value—Obviously this would rule out any disposition by way of gift. See the notes under 'Value' related to s 238.

Section 284(5)

Commencement of bankruptcy—This is the date on which the bankruptcy order is made. See s 278. See the notes accompanying s 127.

285 Restriction on proceedings and remedies

(1) At any time when proceedings on a bankruptcy petition are pending or an individual has been adjudged bankrupt the court may stay any action, execution or other legal process against the property or person of the debtor or, as the case may be, of the bankrupt.

(2) Any court in which proceedings are pending against any individual may, on proof that a bankruptcy petition has been presented in respect of that individual or that he is an undischarged bankrupt, either stay the proceedings or allow them to continue on such terms as it thinks fit.

(3) After the making of a bankruptcy order no person who is a creditor of the bankrupt in respect of a debt provable in the bankruptcy shall—

    (a)   have any remedy against the property or person of the bankrupt in respect of that debt, or

    (b)   before the discharge of the bankrupt, commence any action or other legal proceedings against the bankrupt except with the leave of the court and on such terms as the court may impose.

This is subject to sections 346 (enforcement procedures) and 347 (limited right to distress).

(4) Subject as follows, subsection (3) does not affect the right of a secured creditor of the bankrupt to enforce his security.

(5) Where any goods of an undischarged bankrupt are held by any person by way of pledge, pawn or other security, the official receiver may, after giving notice in writing of his intention to do so, inspect the goods.

Where such a notice has been given to any person, that person is not entitled, without leave of the court, to realise his security unless he has given the trustee of the bankrupt's estate a reasonable opportunity of inspecting the goods and of exercising the bankrupt's right of redemption.

(6) References in this section to the property or goods of the bankrupt are to any of his property or goods, whether or not comprised in his estate.

General note—Although grouped together, these provisions address distinct issues which, in the case of s 285(3), should be read in conjunction with ss 346 and 347, together with the analogous provisions in s 130 and the commentary thereto.

Section 285 is effectively disapplied in relation to action by an exchange or clearing house in the context of default proceedings by s 161(4) of the Companies Act 1989.

Scope of provision—Section 285(1) allows the court with bankruptcy jurisdiction over an individual to stay any action, execution or other legal process against the property or the debtor at any time when a bankruptcy petition is pending against the debtor or following the making of a bankruptcy order against him, to stay the proceedings or allow them to continue subject to such terms as the court thinks fit. The purpose of the provision lies in protecting the bankrupt's estate for the whole body of creditors and preventing unsecured creditors from taking steps to obtain advantages over other creditors following the presentation of a bankruptcy petition: *Re Smith ex parte Braintree District Council* [1990] 2 AC 215, HL. Subsection (2), on the other hand, allows *any* court in which 'proceedings' are pending against the respondent to a bankruptcy petition or an undischarged bankrupt to stay those proceedings or to allow them to continue on such terms as the court considers appropriate. The purpose behind s 285(2) is the same as that underlying s 285(1); the differences between the two lies in s 285(1) being limited to the staying of a variety of proceedings and the greater elaboration in s 285(2) on the scope of proceedings subject to that provision.

Section 285(1) and (2)

'... other legal process ...'—In *Braintree District Council* (above) the House of Lords held that a warrant of committal for non-payment of rates fell within the term 'other legal process' which the court therefore had standing to stay, consistent with the purpose of s 285(1), as identified above, notwithstanding the punitive element of the warrant.

In the important case of *Sharples v Place for People Homes Ltd* [2011] EWCA Civ 813, [2011] BPIR 1488, the Court of Appeal held that where a bankruptcy order was made against the tenant of property, the automatic stay in s 285(3) did not apply to a landlord's application for possession on the grounds of rent arrears, although it does apply to any claim for the arrears themselves (the same analysis applies in the context of debt relief orders and s 251G: *Godfrey v A2 Dominion Homes Ltd*, reported together with *Sharples*).

By which principles, if any, should the court be guided in exercising its discretion under s 285(1) or (2)?—Although there is no reported authority in which the exercise of the court's jurisdiction is considered by reference to any reasoned general principles, it is submitted that, certainly as regards the stay or continuance of proceedings prior to bankruptcy, the principles identified in the judgment of Lord Brandon in the Court of Appeal in *Roberts Petroleum Ltd v Bernard Kenny Ltd* [1982] 1 All ER 685 at 690F–690J in relation to the making of a charging order or garnishee order absolute will be of some assistance. Although reversed on appeal, those principles were not called into question in any of the opinions of the House of Lords in *Roberts Petroleum Ltd v Bernard Kenny Ltd* [1983] AC 192.

Consistent with the purpose of s 285(1) and (2) (see above) and, it is submitted, the principles established by Lord Brandon in *Roberts Petroleum*, the court might be expected to allow for the continuance of proceedings which advance a liability from which the bankrupt would not be released on discharge, the most obvious example being a claim for fraudulent breach of trust: see *Re Blake ex parte Coker* (1875) 10 Ch App 652. Equally, the court may be prepared to permit a claim which seeks a remedy which, in substance, will not reduce the level of assets comprised within the bankrupt's estate, such as a monetary claim which will give rise to a debt which is not provable under r 12.3(2) (see, for example, *Albert v Albert* [1996] BPIR 232, CA) or a claim for specific performance or an injunction, on which see *Re Coregrange Ltd* [1984] BCLC 453 (on the former but analogous liquidation provisions). For the same reasons the court will usually be inclined to allow proceedings which are brought to obtain a judgment so as to allow the claimant to pursue the bankrupt's insurer under the Third Parties (Rights against Insurers) Act 1999, which proceedings have no effect on the bankrupt's estate itself: see *Post Office v Norwich Union* [1967] 2 QB 363 at 377–378.

The scope of s 285(3) and the principles governing permission to proceed—Section 285(3) only applies where a bankruptcy order is made and a creditor with a provable debt seeks to *commence* any action or other legal proceedings – which will have the broadest scope – against the bankrupt. In *Bristol & West Building Society v Trustee of the Property of John Julius Bach (a Bankrupt) and Stuart Samuel Melinek (a Bankrupt)* [1997] BPIR 358 at 361G–362F David Young QC, sitting as a deputy High Court judge, drew on the following principles set out in the judgment of Master Lee QC in *Ex parte Walker* (1982) 6 ACLR 423 at 426 as guiding the court in the exercise of its discretion, albeit not exhaustively:

(1) If, on the face of the matter, there is no arguable claim, leave should be refused.
(2) There must be no prejudice to the creditors or to the orderly administration of the bankruptcy if the action is to proceed.
(3) The claim must be of a type that should proceed by action rather than through the proofing procedure of bankruptcy.
(4) Leave is more likely to be granted where the defendant is insured – s 285(3) is not designed to protect an insurer.
(5) A condition is often imposed that a claimant cannot enforce any judgment against the defendant without the leave of the bankruptcy court.
(6) Mere delay in applying for leave will not prevent leave being granted.
(7) Leave may be granted after the expiry of the relevant period of limitation to continue an action commenced within the limitation period without the leave of the court.

The use of the mandatory leave requirement in s 285(3) does not infringe art 6 of the European Convention for the Protection of Human Rights for if an applicant for leave had an arguable case leave would be granted: *Seal v Chief Constable of South Wales Police* [2007] UKHL 31, [2007] BPIR 1396.

Section 285(4) specifically provides that the rights of a secured creditor are not affected by s 285(3).

The judgment of Lindsay J in *Bristol & West Building Society v Saunders* [1996] 3 WLR 473 is authority for the proposition that the court has jurisdiction under s 285(3) to grant leave retrospectively although *Saunders* was not followed by HHJ Kershaw, sitting as a judge of the High Court, in *Re Taylor (a bankrupt)* [2007] BPIR 175. *Saunders* was preferred by Chief Registrar Baister in *Bank of Scotland plc v Breytenbach* [2012] BPIR 1 and by David Richards J in *Bank of Ireland v Colliers International*.

The meaning of s 285(6)—Sections 283 and 283A define the scope of a bankrupt's estate. Subsection (6) makes clear that s 285 applies to proceedings against *any* property or goods of the bankrupt, irrespective of whether such property or goods is comprised in the bankrupt's estate, such that a creditor is susceptible to the court's control where he attacks property excluded from the scope of the bankrupt's estate, on which see s 283 and the notes thereto.

286 Power to appoint interim receiver

(1) The court may, if it is shown to be necessary for the protection of the debtor's property, at any time after the presentation of a bankruptcy petition and before making a bankruptcy order, appoint the official receiver to be interim receiver of the debtor's property.

(2) Where the court has, on a debtor's petition, appointed an insolvency practitioner under section 273 and it is shown to the court as mentioned in

subsection (1) of this section, the court may, without making a bankruptcy order, appoint that practitioner, instead of the official receiver, to be interim receiver of the debtor's property.

(3) The court may by an order appointing any person to be an interim receiver direct that his powers shall be limited or restricted in any respect; but, save as so directed, an interim receiver has, in relation to the debtor's property, all the rights, powers, duties and immunities of a receiver and manager under the next section.

(4) An order of the court appointing any person to be an interim receiver shall require that person to take immediate possession of the debtor's property or, as the case may be, the part of it to which his powers as interim receiver are limited.

(5) Where an interim receiver has been appointed, the debtor shall give him such inventory of his property and such other information, and shall attend on the interim receiver at such times, as the latter may for the purpose of carrying out his functions under this section reasonably require.

(6) Where an interim receiver is appointed, section 285(3) applies for the period between the appointment and the making of a bankruptcy order on the petition, or the dismissal of the petition, as if the appointment were the making of such an order.

(7) A person ceases to be interim receiver of a debtor's property if the bankruptcy petition relating to the debtor is dismissed, if a bankruptcy order is made on the petition or if the court by order otherwise terminates the appointment.

(8) References in this section to the debtor's property are to all his property, whether or not it would be comprised in his estate if he were adjudged bankrupt.

General note—The appointment of an interim receiver in the period between the presentation of a bankruptcy petition and the making of a bankruptcy order is a draconian measure which is designed to safeguard against the depletion of the bankruptcy estate and which finds a broad equivalent in the appointment of a provisional liquidator under s 135 in winding up. By s 286(6) the appointment of an interim receiver triggers the limitation on creditors' actions under s 285(3), which would otherwise only apply on the making of a bankruptcy order.

The circumstances in which an interim receiver will be appointed—The requirement that an applicant must show that the appointment of an interim receiver is 'necessary for the protection of the debtor's property' has not been the subject of reported judicial analysis. It is suggested that the test must necessarily reflect the scope for the divergence of circumstances in which such an application might be made and, as such, should equate to the requirements for the appointment of a provisional liquidator under s 135 in winding up, on which see the notes thereto.

Identity of the interim receiver—Although an interim receiver will ordinarily be the official receiver, as provided for in s 286(1), the Court of Appeal has held that a person other than the official receiver may be appointed in an appropriate case: *Gibson Dunn & Crutcher v Rio Properties Inc* [2004] BPIR 1203. The court also retains a discretion to appoint as interim receiver an insolvency practitioner already appointed under s 273.

Appointment of a special manager—Given that the function of the interim receiver is essentially protective, it may be appropriate for the official receiver to consider an application under s 370(2) for the appointment of another person as special manager where the particular nature of the estate, property or business comprised in the debtor's estate or the interests of creditors generally require such an appointment to be made.

Rights and powers of the interim receiver—In the absence of contrary order under s 286(3), the rights and powers of the interim receiver are those set out in s 287(2) and (3). In an appropriate case, however, the court may be receptive to a submission that the provision of express powers is appropriate, as in *Re Baars* [2003] BPIR 523 at 530D–530E, where Lloyd J, as he then was, was prepared to declare 'that the interim receiver's powers shall extend to the powers that he would have under ss 366 and 367 [which he would have in any case] and 426 of the Insolvency Act 1986 just in case there is otherwise room for arguing that he does not have those powers.'

Immunities of the interim receiver—Section 268(3) invokes the two-stage process in s 287(4).

The combined effect of s 286(4) and (8) is that the interim receiver is not bridled with the risk of seizing property which he reasonably believes to be the property of the debtor, or which is subject to contrary representations as to ownership by the debtor or an interested third party, or property which cannot easily be removed or separated from other property for the purpose of taking immediate possession.

Contents of court order—Form 6.32 elaborates on the basic requirement on the making of an order in s 286(4). Apart from the question of powers, the circumstances of the case may require further express provision, although the legislation makes no stipulation as to such terms. For example, an order may identify specific property which is not subject to immediate possession by the interim receiver. Further provisions might include sums to be made available to a debtor for the obtaining of legal advice, sums to be available in respect of living expenses, the sale or charge of property subject to the consent of the official receiver and, possibly, the requirement for co-operation with the interim receiver in any particular respect. It is usually the case that any appointment of a special manager is incorporated within a single order, together with any further consequential provisions such as those just mentioned. It may also be appropriate that undertakings are provided by the debtor; for example, in *Re Baars* (above) the debtor gave an undertaking that he would not gamble pending the determination of the bankruptcy petition.

The inclusion in an order allowing a debtor to expend monies on, most commonly, legal advice and living expenses mirrors a similar provision commonly found within a freezing order made under CPR, Pt 25. Where a dispute arises as to what constitutes the very common 'reasonable' provision made for such items in the context of a freezing order, the resolution of that issue is a matter for the parties to the litigation. On the other hand, in the case of an interim receiver's appointment the issue will concern the petitioner only indirectly and, ultimately, the dispute is one between the interim receiver himself and the debtor. Given the inherent difficulty that the interim receiver may not be in a position to assess what is reasonable and what is not, in the circumstances of any particular case, one solution, as employed by Lloyd J in the *Re Baars* case, is for an order to impose a cap on the amount that may be spent on legal advice etc and living expenses, the interim receiver thereby being in a position to object to and refuse plainly extravagant requests for monies.

Appointment to estate of deceased person—The court may appoint an interim receiver in the administration of a deceased person's insolvent estate if the court considers it necessary to protect the estate's property: art 3 and Sch 1, Pt II, para 13 of the Administration of Insolvent Estates of Deceased Persons Order 1986.

Position of interim receiver where order in effect under Proceeds of Crime Act 2002—An interim receiver takes subject to any order made under the 2002 Act, in that the interim receiver's powers are not exercisable over property which is subject to such an order by virtue of s 417(4) of the 2002 Act.

Procedure—The procedure governing the appointment of an interim receiver and the giving of security appears in rr 6.51–6.57. Most significantly, eligible applicants – being a closed class of five persons, including a creditor or debtor – together with the mandatory contents of the affidavit or witness statement in support of an application appear in r 6.51. An order appointing an interim receiver should be in Form 6.32. Section 268(7) identifies the three circumstances in which the appointment of an interim receiver may terminate; r 6.57(2) allows the court to give appropriate directions on termination.

Paragraph 9 of Sch 9 allows for the making of rules under s 412 as to the manner in which an interim receiver is to carry out his functions. No such rules have yet been introduced.

287 Receivership pending appointment of trustee

(1) Between the making of a bankruptcy order and the time at which the bankrupt's estate vests in a trustee under Chapter IV of this Part, the official receiver is the receiver and (subject to section 370 (special manager)) the manager of the bankrupt's estate and is under a duty to act as such.

(2) The function of the official receiver while acting as receiver or manager of the bankrupt's estate under this section is to protect the estate; and for this purpose—

(a) he has the same powers as if he were a receiver or manager appointed by the High Court, and

(b) he is entitled to sell or otherwise dispose of any perishable goods comprised in the estate and any other goods so comprised the value of which is likely to diminish if they are not disposed of.

(3) The official receiver while acting as receiver or manager of the estate under this section—

(a) shall take all such steps as he thinks fit for protecting any property which may be claimed for the estate by the trustee of that estate,

(b) is not, except in pursuance of directions given by the Secretary of State, required to do anything that involves his incurring expenditure,

(c) may, if he thinks fit (and shall, if so directed by the court) at any time summon a general meeting of the bankrupt's creditors.

(4) Where—

(a) the official receiver acting as receiver or manager of the estate under this section seizes or disposes of any property which is not comprised in the estate, and

(b) at the time of the seizure or disposal the official receiver believes, and has reasonable grounds for believing, that he is entitled (whether in pursuance of an order of the court or otherwise) to seize or dispose of that property,

the official receiver is not to be liable to any person in respect of any loss or damage resulting from the seizure or disposal except in so far as that loss or damage is caused by his negligence; and he has a lien on the property, or the proceeds of its sale, for such of the expenses of the bankruptcy as were incurred in connection with the seizure or disposal.

(5) This section does not apply where by virtue of section 297 (appointment of trustee; special cases) the bankrupt's estate vests in a trustee immediately on the making of the bankruptcy order.

General note—The general rule, as provided for by s 287(1) and (5), is that the official receiver is the receiver and manager of the bankrupt's estate, and is under a duty to act as such, between the making of a bankruptcy order and the time at which the bankrupt's estate vests in a trustee under s 306 on his appointment. There are three exceptions to that general rule, namely, where a special manager has been appointed under s 370, where a person is appointed as trustee under s 297(4) following a negative report for the purposes of s 274(1), and where the supervisor of an IVA is appointed trustee under s 297(5) on the making of a bankruptcy order.

Rules 10.1–10.4 govern the status of the official receiver.

Section 287(2)

Functions and powers of the official receiver—The powers of a receiver and manager appointed by the High Court are at the court's discretion and will depend on the facts of any particular case.

Section 287(2)(b) applies only to either 'perishable goods' or any other goods comprised within the estate 'the value of which is likely to diminish if they are not disposed of.' This latter reference is narrower than the scope of onerous property under s 315(2) and, in contrast to s 315(2)(b), requires the likelihood of diminishment in value as opposed to the risk that the property may give rise to a liability to pay money or perform any other onerous act which amounts to a very different requirement.

The role of the official receiver in exercising his powers must be read in conjunction with s 287(3).

Section 287(3)

Steps towards protecting property—The three provisions of s 287(3) are independent of each other. Section 287(3)(a) allows the official receiver a good deal of leeway in exercising his discretion in taking steps to protect any property comprised within the scope of the bankruptcy estate without, under s 287(3)(b), being required to do anything involving the incurring of expenditure other than on the direction of the Secretary of State. It should be noted, however, that 287(3)(b) does not require the direction of the Secretary of State where the official receiver is prepared to involve himself in the incurring of expenditure voluntarily.

Although 287(3)(c) allows for the summoning of a general meeting of creditors, such meetings are rare in practice. The provision would allow for an application to court by the official receiver if he is uncertain as to whether or not a meeting of creditors should be summoned, or an application by a creditor where the official receiver refuses to summon a meeting voluntarily and where the court can be satisfied that the summoning of a meeting is appropriate in the circumstances.

Section 287(4)

Limitation on liability of the official receiver—Other than in a case of negligence, the official receiver is protected from any claim for loss or damage following the seizure or disposal of property which is not comprised in the debtor's estate, subject to the official receiver discharging the burden of proof upon him in establishing both that he believed (ie subjectively) and had reasonable grounds for believing (ie objectively) that he was entitled to seize or dispose of that property. The substance of that protection is now mirrored in s 432(2) of the Proceeds of Crime Act 2002. Provided the official receiver is able to establish both grounds, he is equally entitled to the statutory lien created by s 287(4) in respect of expenses incurred in connection with the seizure or disposal.

Appointment to estate of deceased person—The court may appoint an interim receiver in the administration of a deceased person's insolvent estate if the court considers it necessary to protect the estate's property: art 3 and Sch 1, Pt II, para 13 of the Administration of Insolvent Estates of Deceased Persons Order 1986.

288 Statement of affairs

(1) Where a bankruptcy order has been made otherwise than on a debtor's petition, the bankrupt shall submit a statement of his affairs to the official receiver before the end of the period of 21 days beginning with the commencement of the bankruptcy.

(2) The statement of affairs shall contain—

(a) such particulars of the bankrupt's creditors and of his debts and other liabilities and of his assets as may be prescribed, and

(b) such other information as may be prescribed.

(3) The official receiver may, if he thinks fit—

(a) release the bankrupt from his duty under subsection (1), or

(b) extend the period specified in that subsection;

and where the official receiver has refused to exercise a power conferred by this section, the court, if it thinks fit, may exercise it.

(4) A bankrupt who—

(a) without reasonable excuse fails to comply with the obligation imposed by this section, or

(b) without reasonable excuse submits a statement of affairs that does not comply with the prescribed requirements,

is guilty of a contempt of court and liable to be punished accordingly (in addition to any other punishment to which he may be subject).

General note—This provision applies in all cases other than on a debtor's petition, for which see s 272 and rr 6.67–6.72. The statement of affairs itself is of fundamental importance in enabling the official receiver and creditors to reach an informed assessment of the assets and liabilities in the bankruptcy. Section 433 also allows for the use of the statement in evidence against any person making or concurring with its contents.

The obligation in s 288(1) and the power of dispensation under s 288(3)—The bankrupt's statement of affairs must be in Form 6.33 and must contain all the particulars required by that form: r 6.59. The bankrupt may request an extension of the 21-day period for submission of the statement of affairs and may apply to the court for an extension if the request is refused by the official receiver: r 6.62(2).

The release from the obligation to submit a statement of affairs may apparently only be granted if requested by the bankrupt, who may again seek a release from the court if refused by the official receiver: see rr 6.62(1) and (2).

Contents of the statement of affairs—See rr 6.59 and 6.64–6.66.

Rules relating to the statement of affairs generally—See rr 6.58–6.66.

Deceased insolvents' estates—These provisions apply to such estates: para 15 of the Administration of Insolvent Estates of Deceased Persons Order 1986 (SI 1986/1999).

289 Investigatory duties of official receiver

(1) The official receiver shall—

(a) investigate the conduct and affairs of each bankrupt (including his conduct and affairs before the making of the bankruptcy order), and

> (b) make such report (if any) to the court as the official receiver
> thinks fit.

(2) Subsection (1) shall not apply to a case in which the official receiver
thinks an investigation under that subsection unnecessary.

(3) Where a bankrupt makes an application for discharge under
section 280 —

> (a) the official receiver shall make a report to the court about such
> matters as may be prescribed, and
> (b) the court shall consider the report before determining the
> application.

(4) A report by the official receiver under this section shall in any
proceedings be prima facie evidence of the facts stated in it.

Amendments—Enterprise Act 2002, s 248.

General note—Section 289 was amended by s 248 of the Enterprise Act 2002 with effect
from 1 April 2004 and applies to all bankruptcies commencing after that date. The new
provision represents a relaxation of the obligation under the former s 289(1) which imposed
a duty on the official receiver to investigate the conduct and affairs of *every* bankrupt other
than in the case of summary administration under s 275 (which has itself now been
repealed). Despite this amendment, the significance of the investigatory duties imposed on
the official receiver by s 289 remains as identified by the Court of Appeal in *R v Kearns*
[2002] 1 WLR 2815.

**The grounds for and consequences of the official receiver thinking an investigation to be
unnecessary**—The word 'shall' in s 289(1) raises a presumption that the obligations within
that provision will apply to any particular bankruptcy. The presumption, however, is capable
of being rebutted if the official receiver 'thinks' an investigation is unnecessary. The word
'thinks' is new: see the commentary on possible interpretation in the notes to para 3(3) of
Sch B1. In the absence of any guidance – there is certainly no good reason why the grounds
for the making of a bankruptcy restrictions order in Sch 4A should be of any particular
relevance here – it is suggested that an investigation might only be considered unnecessary if
the official receiver thinks, based on proper consideration of the information available to
him, and in the absence of suspicion as to the accuracy of that information, that the time
and cost likely to be involved in an investigation outweighs any practical benefit of an
investigation, bearing in mind in particular the public interest element of an investigation.
  Where the official receiver intends to file a notice that an investigation is unnecessary, he is
obliged under r 6.214A(1) to give notice to that effect to all creditors and any trustee, any of
whom may object within 28 days under r 6.214A(2). That procedure is relevant because, in
the absence of any objections, the filing of a notice by the official receiver with the court, as
a general rule, has the irreversible effect of discharging the bankrupt under s 279(2) within
the one-year period after which discharge is ordinarily obtained under s 279(1).

Statements made in the report under s 289(4)—The official receiver enjoys absolute privilege
for the purpose of a claim for libel by any person named within his report: *Bottomley v
Brougham* [1908] 1 KB 584; and see also *Burr v Smith* [1909] 2 KB 306.

Deceased insolvents' estates—These provisions apply to such estates: para 16 of the
Administration of Insolvent Estates of Deceased Persons Order 1986 (SI 1986/1999); the
official receiver is not under a duty to investigate the conduct of a deceased debtor but may
do so if he thinks fit.

290 Public examination of bankrupt

(1) Where a bankruptcy order has been made, the official receiver may at any time before the discharge of the bankrupt apply to the court for the public examination of the bankrupt.

(2) Unless the court otherwise orders, the official receiver shall make an application under subsection (1) if notice requiring him to do so is given to him, in accordance with the rules, by one of the bankrupt's creditors with the concurrence of not less than one-half, in value, of those creditors (including the creditor giving notice).

(3) On an application under subsection (1), the court shall direct that a public examination of the bankrupt shall be held on a day appointed by the court; and the bankrupt shall attend on that day and be publicly examined as to his affairs, dealings and property.

(4) The following may take part in the public examination of the bankrupt and may question him concerning his affairs, dealings and property and the causes of his failure, namely—

    (a)   the official receiver and, in the case of an individual adjudged bankrupt on a petition under section 264(1)(d), the Official Petitioner,

    (b)   the trustee of the bankrupt's estate, if his appointment has taken effect,

    (c)   any person who has been appointed as special manager of the bankrupt's estate or business,

    (d)   any creditor of the bankrupt who has tendered a proof in the bankruptcy.

(5) If a bankrupt without reasonable excuse fails at any time to attend his public examination under this section he is guilty of a contempt of court and liable to be punished accordingly (in addition to any other punishment to which he may be subject).

General note—The examination of bankrupts has a long lineage, going back to the Act of 1604 (1 Jac 1 c 15). Under s 15 the Bankruptcy Act 1914 a public examination of a bankrupt was obligatory in all cases save for where the bankrupt was afflicted with a physical or mental disability. The time and expense, if nothing else, was hardly justifiable in the majority of cases. There is now no obligation in any case for a public examination, other than where the court makes an order under s 290(2) on the application of the official receiver – and only the official receiver – under s 290(1). Although the official receiver must make application to the court for an examination if required to do so by at least one-half in value of the creditors, it remains open to the official receiver to seek an examination of his own volition, irrespective of the position of creditors.

    Those persons in s 290(4) and, again, only those persons, may question the bankrupt in the course of the public examination as to the bankrupt's 'affairs, dealings and property and the causes of his failure.' The court will not allow an examination to stray beyond the scope of those matters.

    Much of the discussion under s 133 will also apply here, although under s 290 only the bankrupt may be summoned to an examination. This contrasts with s 366 under which others may be summoned to appear for a private examination as to the bankrupt or his dealings, affairs or property.

Persons resident outside the jurisdiction—The power of the court to order a person resident outside the jurisdiction to attend for a public examination under s 133, as confirmed by the

Court of Appeal in *Re Seagull Manufacturing Co Ltd* [1993] BCC 241 in the context of winding up, must, it is submitted, extend to bankruptcy.

Fails to attend—If a bankrupt fails to attend he or she can be held to be in contempt and imprisoned. For an instance of this, see *R v Scriven* [2004] EWCA Civ 683, [2004] BPIR 972.

Self-incrimination—The decision of the Court of Appeal in *Bishopgate Investments Ltd v Maxwell* [1993] Ch 1 confirmed that a bankrupt is not entitled to refuse to answer any question on the ground of privilege against self-incrimination in the course of a public examination. This was also the position previously under the Bankruptcy Act 1914, on which see *Re Paget ex parte Official Receiver* [1947] 2 Ch 85. Refusal to answer any question within the scope of a public examination will constitute a contempt on the part of the bankrupt. Under s 433 a bankrupt's answers at his/her public examination would not generally be admissible against him in criminal proceedings. If the Court is concerned about the use to which the transcript might be put in proceedings outside the English jurisdiction, it can adjourn and order proceedings to continue in private: see *Rottman v Official Receiver* [2009] BPIR 617 (affirmed on appeal).

Deceased person's estate—See the Administration of Insolvent Estates of Deceased Persons Order 1986 (SI 1986/1999) and *Re Jawett* [1929] 1 Ch 108.

Procedure—See rr 6.173–6.177 and the prescribed forms mentioned in the notes thereto. Rule 6.176 specifically allows the court to adjourn a public examination either to a fixed date or generally. By r 6.177(2) the costs and expenses of a public examination cannot fall on the official receiver personally in any case.

291 Duties of bankrupt in relation to official receiver

(1) Where a bankruptcy order has been made, the bankrupt is under a duty—

    (a)   to deliver possession of his estate to the official receiver, and

    (b)   to deliver up to the official receiver all books, papers and other records of which he has possession or control and which relate to his estate and affairs (including any which would be privileged from disclosure in any proceedings).

(2) In the case of any part of the bankrupt's estate which consists of things possession of which cannot be delivered to the official receiver, and in the case of any property that may be claimed for the bankrupt's estate by the trustee, it is the bankrupt's duty to do all such things as may reasonably be required by the official receiver for the protection of those things or that property.

(3) Subsections (1) and (2) do not apply where by virtue of section 297 below the bankrupt's estate vests in a trustee immediately on the making of the bankruptcy order.

(4) The bankrupt shall give the official receiver such inventory of his estate and such other information, and shall attend on the official receiver at such times, as the official receiver may reasonably require—

    (a)   for a purpose of this Chapter, or

    (b)   in connection with the making of a bankruptcy restrictions order.

(5) Subsection (4) applies to a bankrupt after his discharge.

(6) If the bankrupt without reasonable excuse fails to comply with any obligation imposed by this section, he is guilty of a contempt of court and liable to be punished accordingly (in addition to any other punishment to which he may be subject).

Amendments—Enterprise Act 2002, s 269, Sch 23.

General note—In some ways parts of this section are the counterpart of s 235, which applies to company officers and others, although one must remember that in bankruptcy, unlike with company insolvency administrations, the property of the bankrupt vests in the trustee immediately on the making of a bankruptcy order. Besides this provision, s 363(2) also obliges bankrupts (discharged and undischarged) to do all such things as they may be directed to do by their trustees for the purposes of the bankruptcy or the administration of the estate. Failure to assist involves a contempt of court (s 363(4)). The obligations imposed by s 291(1), (2) and (4) apply to the interim period between the making of a bankruptcy order and the appointment of a trustee, during which, by virtue of s 287(1), the official receiver is the receiver and manager of the bankrupt's estate. Section 291(3) provides that these provisions have no application, however, where a trustee is appointed immediately on the making of a bankruptcy order under s 297(4) (no certificate for summary administration) and s 297(5) (supervisor of voluntary arrangement appointed as trustee). Even if applicable, the provisions will cease to apply on the appointment of a trustee by a meeting of creditors summoned under s 293 or s 294, an appointment by the Secretary of State under s 296(2), or upon the official receiver assuming the office of trustee under s 293(3).

The nature of the obligations in s 291(1), (2) and (4)—The substance of the obligations imposed on the bankrupt by these provisions is virtually identical to those imposed vis-à-vis a trustee by ss 312(1) and 333(1). Reference should be made to the notes to those provisions. See *DBIS v Compton* [2012] BPIR 1108 for an example of the Magistrate's practical (although perhaps surprisingly lenient) approach to the obligations of a bankrupct under s 291 in the context of criminal charges under s 356 and s 357.

The purpose of the provisions is in assisting the official receiver in the discharge of his function as receiver and manager and facilitating the mandatory investigation required by s 289(1). In its revised form, s 291(4) (see below) also anticipates that the official receiver may have an ongoing requirement for the provision of information, including information in connection with what is specifically termed 'the making' of a bankruptcy restrictions order under s 281A.

Section 291(4)

Scope of provision—This provision was revised with effect from 1 April 2004 by s 269 of and Sch 23 to the Enterprise Act 2002 so as to provide for the reference to bankruptcy restrictions orders in s 291(4)(b), on which see the notes to s 281A. Whilst the reference to 'the making' of a bankruptcy restrictions order might be read restrictively so as to limit the scope of the obligation imposed on the bankrupt, it is doubtful, if not absurd, that the bankrupt should only be obliged to provide information in connection with the making of a bankruptcy restrictions order, as opposed to having to provide information within the scope of the subsection where, most obviously, the official receiver is looking into the *possibility* of making application for such an order. Like s 333(1), the obligation to provide information survives discharge.

In practice, the official receiver attached to the court in which a bankruptcy order is made will, for the purpose of his investigatory duties under s 289(1), require the bankrupt to attend on him for an initial interview at which a sworn statement detailing the bankrupt's assets, liabilities and pre-bankruptcy dealings is produced, usually in a Preliminary Bankruptcy Questionnaire, Form B40.01.

Chapter III

Trustees in Bankruptcy

Tenure of office as trustee

292 Power to make appointments

(1) The power to appoint a person as trustee of a bankrupt's estate (whether the first such trustee or a trustee appointed to fill any vacancy) is exercisable—

    (a)   by a general meeting of the bankrupt's creditors;

    (b)   under section 295(2), 296(2) or 300(6) below in this Chapter, by the Secretary of State; or

    (c)   under section 297, by the court.

(2) No person may be appointed as trustee of a bankrupt's estate unless he is, at the time of the appointment, qualified to act as an insolvency practitioner in relation to the bankrupt.

(3) Any power to appoint a person as trustee of a bankrupt's estate includes power to appoint two or more persons as joint trustees; but such an appointment must make provision as to the circumstances in which the trustees must act together and the circumstances in which one or more of them may act for the others.

(4) The appointment of any person as trustee takes effect only if that person accepts the appointment in accordance with the rules. Subject to this, the appointment of any person as trustee takes effect at the time specified in his certificate of appointment.

(5) This section is without prejudice to the provisions of this Chapter under which the official receiver is, in certain circumstances, to be trustee of the estate.

Amendments—Enterprise Act 2002, ss 269, 278(2), Sch 23, paras 1, 6, Sch 26.

General note—This provision applies to both the first appointment of a trustee and the making of an appointment following death, resignation etc. The power to appoint extends to two or more joint appointees under s 292(3), subject to the requirements of the second part of that provision.

    Although an appointment may be made by the bankrupt's creditors, the Secretary of State or by the court in the circumstances described in s 292(1), the appointment will usually, but need not be, made by the creditors. Section 292 is not exhaustive of the circumstances in which a trustee can be appointed, for example the general powers of the court under the Insolvency Act 1986 ss 303(2) (to give directions) and 363 (to exercise control of bankruptcy proceedings) could be used to confer jurisdiction on the court to appoint trustees under a block transfer arrangement: *Donaldson v O'Sullivan* [2008] EWHC 387 (Ch), [2008] BPIR 288 (confirmed on appeal: [2008] EWCA Civ 879, [2008] BPIR 1288).

    For the purposes of s 292(5) the three circumstances in which the official receiver may be appointed trustee are identified in the general note to s 306.

Procedure—See rr 6.120–6.125.

293 Summoning of meeting to appoint first trustee

(1) Where a bankruptcy order has been made it is the duty of the official receiver, as soon as practicable in the period of 12 weeks beginning with the day on which the order was made, to decide whether to summon a general meeting of the bankrupt's creditors for the purpose of appointing a trustee of the bankrupt's estate.

This section does not apply where the bankruptcy order was made on a petition under section 264(1)(d) (criminal bankruptcy); and it is subject to the provision made in sections 294(3) and 297(6) below.

(2) Subject to the next section, if the official receiver decides not to summon such a meeting, he shall, before the end of the period of 12 weeks above mentioned, give notice of his decision to the court and to every creditor of the bankrupt who is known to the official receiver or is identified in the bankrupt's statement of affairs.

(3) As from the giving to the court of a notice under subsection (2), the official receiver is the trustee of the bankrupt's estate.

Amendments—Enterprise Act 2002, ss 269, 278(2), Sch 23, paras 1, 7, Sch 26.

General note—Section 293(1) imposes a duty 'to decide whether to summon a general meeting of the bankrupt's creditors' for the sole purpose of appointing a trustee of the bankrupt's estate. That duty is not triggered, however, in the case of the now obsolete criminal bankruptcy petition and is subject to (ie overridden by) the circumstances in ss 294(3) and 297(6), which are self-explanatory.

Section 293(2) and (3) are only triggered if, in discharge of his duty under s 293(1), the official receiver decides not to summon a general meeting of the bankrupt's creditors.

Procedure—The procedure governing creditors' meetings appears in rr 6.79–6.95.

294 Power of creditors to requisition meeting

(1) Where in the case of any bankruptcy—

  (a) the official receiver has not yet summoned, or has decided not to summon, a general meeting of the bankrupt's creditors for the purpose of appointing the trustee,

  (b) (*repealed*)

any creditor of the bankrupt may request the official receiver to summon such a meeting for that purpose.

(2) If such a request appears to the official receiver to be made with the concurrence of not less than one-quarter, in value, of the bankrupt's creditors (including the creditor making the request), it is the duty of the official receiver to summon the requested meeting.

(3) Accordingly, where the duty imposed by subsection (2) has arisen, the official receiver is required neither to reach a decision for the purposes of section 293(1) nor (if he has reached one) to serve any notice under section 293(2).

Amendments—Enterprise Act 2002, ss 269, 278(2), Sch 23, paras 1, 8, Sch 26.

General note—Section 294(1) and (2) allow a minimum of one-quarter in value of the bankrupt's creditors to request the official receiver to summon a general meeting for the purpose of appointing a trustee of the bankrupt's estate. The making of that request imposes a 'duty' to summon such a meeting. The standing of the requisite level of creditors to make a request of the official receiver continues beyond the twelve-week period in s 293(1) without limit where, under the duty imposed on him by that provision, the official receiver has decided not to summon a meeting of creditors. Equally, where the official receiver's duty is triggered under s 249(2) by the making of a request, the obligations in s 293(1) and/or (2) are disapplied by s 249(3).

In practice, requests of the official receiver are not common, since the official receiver will usually be made aware of the broad wishes of creditors following the making of a bankruptcy order and is unlikely to resist representations to the effect that the requisite level of creditors would wish to see a trustee appointed.

Procedure—See r 6.83.

295 Failure of meeting to appoint trustee

(1) If a meeting summoned under section 293 or 294 is held but no appointment of a person as trustee is made, it is the duty of the official receiver to decide whether to refer the need for an appointment to the Secretary of State.

(2) On a reference made in pursuance of that decision, the Secretary of State shall either make an appointment or decline to make one.

(3) If—

    (a)   the official receiver decides not to refer the need for an appointment to the Secretary of State, or

    (b)   on such a reference the Secretary of State declines to make an appointment,

the official receiver shall give notice of his decision or, as the case may be, of the Secretary of State's decision to the court.

(4) As from the giving of notice under subsection (3) in a case in which no notice has been given under section 293(2), the official receiver shall be trustee of the bankrupt's estate.

General note—The fact that a creditors' meeting is convened under either s 293 or s 294 does not dictate that the meeting will resolve to appoint a person as trustee. If no appointment is made, then the duty imposed on the official receiver in s 295(1) is triggered. It should be noted that the official receiver's duty is not to refer the matter to the Secretary of State but, rather, to decide whether to refer the need for an appointment to the Secretary of State. If the official receiver's decision is to refer the matter to the Secretary of State, then s 295(2), (3)(a) and (4) are triggered.

Where a reference is made under s 295(2), then the Secretary of State will usually make an appointment, although both the reasons for no appointment having been made by any meeting summoned under s 294(2) and the level of assets and/or liabilities in the bankrupt's estate will usually feature in the making of that decision.

Procedure—See rr 6.122–6.124.

296 Appointment of trustee by Secretary of State

(1) At any time when the official receiver is the trustee of a bankrupt's estate by virtue of any provision of this Chapter (other than section 297(1)

below) he may apply to the Secretary of State for the appointment of a person as trustee instead of the official receiver.

(2) On an application under subsection (1) the Secretary of State shall either make an appointment or decline to make one.

(3) Such an application may be made notwithstanding that the Secretary of State has declined to make an appointment either on a previous application under subsection (1) or on a reference under section 295 or under section 300(4) below.

(4) Where the trustee of a bankrupt's estate has been appointed by the Secretary of State (whether under this section or otherwise), the trustee shall give notice to the bankrupt's creditors of his appointment or, if the court so allows, shall advertise his appointment in accordance with the court's directions.

(5) In that notice or advertisement the trustee shall—

(a)   state whether he proposes to summon a general meeting of the bankrupt's creditors for the purposes of establishing a creditor's committee under section 301, and

(b)   if he does not propose to summon such a meeting, set out the power of the creditors under this Part to require him to summon one.

General note—The circumstances in which the official receiver may be trustee of the bankrupt's estate are identified in the General note to s 306. At any time at which the official receiver is trustee, without limitation, he may apply to the Secretary of State for the appointment of a person as trustee in his stead. The official receiver's standing in this regard is unaffected by the fact of any previous application of the kind mentioned in s 296(3). This is not surprising, since an application under s 296(1) is most likely to be made where the official receiver becomes aware of information which has a significant bearing on his perception of the nature of the bankruptcy and, for example, the need for further investigation, proceedings etc where no such action was previously considered necessary or appropriate.

Although s 296(2) allows the Secretary of State to decline to make an appointment following an application under s 296(1), the grounds giving rise to the application will usually give rise to an appointment being made.

Procedure—Section 296(4) and (5) are only triggered on an appointment being made by the Secretary of State under s 296(2). See rr 6.122–6.124.

297 Special cases

(1) Where a bankruptcy order is made on a petition under section 264(1)(d) (criminal bankruptcy), the official receiver shall be trustee of the bankrupt's estate.

(2) (*Repealed*)

(3) (*Repealed*)

(4) Where a bankruptcy order is made in a case in which an insolvency practitioner's report has been submitted to the court under section 274, the court, if it thinks fit, may on making the order appoint the person who made the report as trustee.

(5) Where a bankruptcy order is made (whether or not on a petition under section 264(1)(c)) at a time when there is a supervisor of a voluntary arrangement approved in relation to the bankrupt under Part VIII, the court, if it thinks fit, may on making the order appoint the supervisor of the arrangement as trustee.

(6) Where an appointment is made under subsection (4) or (5) of this section, the official receiver is not under the duty imposed by section 293(1) (to decide whether or not to summon a meeting of creditors).

(7) Where the trustee of a bankrupt's estate has been appointed by the court, the trustee shall give notice to the bankrupt's creditors of his appointment or, if the court so allows, shall advertise his appointment in accordance with the directions of the court.

(8) In that notice or advertisement he shall—

  (a)   state whether he proposes to summon a general meeting of the bankrupt's creditors for the purpose of establishing a creditor's committee under section 301 below, and

  (b)   if he does not propose to summon such a meeting, set out the power of the creditors under this Part to require him to summon one.

Amendments—Enterprise Act 2002, ss 269, 278(2), Sch 23, paras 1, 9(a), (b), Sch 26.

Scope of provision—On s 297(5) see the notes to s 264(1)(c).

298 Removal of trustee; vacation of office

(1) Subject as follows, the trustee of a bankrupt's estate may be removed from office only by an order of the court or by a general meeting of the bankrupt's creditors summoned specially for that purpose in accordance with the rules.

(2) Where the official receiver is trustee by virtue of section 297(1), he shall not be removed from office under this section.

(3) (*Repealed*)

(4) Where the official receiver is trustee by virtue of section 293(3) or 295(4) or a trustee is appointed by the Secretary of State or (otherwise than under section 297(5)) by the court, a general meeting of the bankrupt's creditors shall be summoned for the purpose of replacing the trustee only if—

  (a)   the trustee thinks fit, or

  (b)   the court so directs, or

  (c)   the meeting is requested by one of the bankrupt's creditors with the concurrence of not less than one-quarter, in value, of the creditors (including the creditor making the request).

(5) If the trustee was appointed by the Secretary of State, he may be removed by a direction of the Secretary of State.

(6) The trustee (not being the official receiver) shall vacate office if he ceases to be a person who is for the time being qualified to act as an insolvency practitioner in relation to the bankrupt.

(7) The trustee may, in the prescribed circumstances, resign his office by giving notice of his resignation to the court.

(8) The trustee shall vacate office on giving notice to the court that a final meeting has been held under section 331 in Chapter IV and of the decision (if any) of that meeting.

(9) The trustee shall vacate office if the bankruptcy order is annulled.

Amendments—Enterprise Act 2002, ss 269, 278(2), Sch 23, paras 1, 10, Sch 26.

General note—The principles applying to removal of a trustee by order of the court under s 298(1) are the same as those considered in the notes to the analogous provision in liquidation in s 108, and in s 171. Although it was identified by Registrar Nicholls in *Smedley v Brittain* [2008] BPIR 219 at [16] that a bankruptcy case may not be analogous to a liquidation case to the extent that an application may be brought by a debtor in bankruptcy, whereas the authorities in liquidation are, for the most part, concerned with applications to remove by creditors, it is respectfully submitted that such a distinction is only of any practical relevance to the extent that a debtor's application in bankruptcy can be shown to serve the debtor himself, as opposed to the interests of creditors, that is, to the extent that those two sets of interest cannot be shown to coincide. *Smedley* also provides guidance at [24]–[26] upon the removal of, specifically, a trustee by the court. In particular:

'... if the trustee has gone about his or her actions effectively, honestly, reasonably, without misconduct or maladministration, the court must think carefully and long and hard before deciding to remove him or her and that is especially the case if an application is made by a debtor. It should not be seen as easy to remove a trustee because, say, one or two actions are subject to criticism and especially if that comes with hindsight ... the test to be achieved by the debtor is a particularly high one, if he is to be successful in removing from office the trustee, and he must shown a very real and substantial cause.'

See also *Doffman and Isaacs v Wood and Hellard* [2011] EWHC 4008 (Ch), [2012] BPIR 972 for an example of an unsuccessful application for removal where a conflict of interest was alleged. Proudman J considered that (1) the interests of creditors were paramount and they had no objection to the appointment which would save costs and (2) the potential conflict could be managed on the basis of undertakings.

Procedure—On procedure on removal or vacation see rr 6.126–6.135 and 6.144.

299 Release of trustee

(1) Where the official receiver has ceased to be the trustee of a bankrupt's estate and a person is appointed in his stead, the official receiver shall have his release with effect from the following time, that is to say—

    (a)   where that person is appointed by a general meeting of the bankrupt's creditors or by the Secretary of State, the time at which the official receiver gives notice to the court that he has been replaced, and

    (b)   where that person is appointed by the court, such time as the court may determine.

(2) If the official receiver while he is the trustee gives notice to the Secretary of State that the administration of the bankrupt's estate in accordance with Chapter IV of this Part is for practical purposes complete, he shall have his release with effect from such time as the Secretary of State may determine.

(3) A person other than the official receiver who has ceased to be the trustee shall have his release with effect from the following time, that is to say—

(a) in the case of a person who has been removed from office by a general meeting of the bankrupt's creditors that has not resolved against his release or who has died, the time at which notice is given to the court in accordance with the rules that that person has ceased to hold office;

(b) in the case of a person who has been removed from office by a general meeting of the bankrupt's creditors that has resolved against his release, or by the court, or by the Secretary of State, or who has vacated office under section 298(6), such time as the Secretary of State may, on an application by that person, determine;

(c) in the case of a person who has resigned, such time as may be prescribed;

(d) in the case of a person who has vacated office under section 298(8)—

(i) if the final meeting referred to in that subsection has resolved against that person's release, such time as the Secretary of State may, on an application by that person, determine; and

(ii) if that meeting has not so resolved, the time at which the person vacated office.

(4) Where a bankruptcy order is annulled, the trustee at the time of the annulment has his release with effect from such time as the court may determine.

(5) Where the official receiver or the trustee has his release under this section, he shall, with effect from the time specified in the preceding provisions of this section, be discharged from all liability both in respect of acts or omissions of his in the administration of the estate and otherwise in relation to his conduct as trustee.

But nothing in this section prevents the exercise, in relation to a person who has had his release under this section, of the court's powers under section 304.

General note—This provision deals with the timing and effect of a trustee's release. The timing of release varies depending on the circumstances in s 299(1)–(4).

The effect of release is provided for in s 299(5) and effectively exonerates a trustee from all liability save for any liability imposed by the court under s 304, which is entirely unaffected.

Procedure—See rr 6.136–6.137A.

300 Vacancy in office of trustee

(1) This section applies where the appointment of any person as trustee of a bankrupt's estate fails to take effect or, such an appointment having taken effect, there is otherwise a vacancy in the office of trustee.

(2) The official receiver shall be trustee until the vacancy is filled.

(3) The official receiver may summon a general meeting of the bankrupt's creditors for the purpose of filling the vacancy and shall summon such a meeting if required to do so in pursuance of section 314(7) (creditors' requisition).

(4) If at the end of the period of 28 days beginning with the day on which the vacancy first came to the official receiver's attention he has not summoned, and is not proposing to summon, a general meeting of creditors for the purpose of filling the vacancy, he shall refer the need for an appointment to the Secretary of State.

(5) (*Repealed*)

(6) On a reference to the Secretary of State under subsection (4) the Secretary of State shall either make an appointment or decline to make one.

(7) If on a reference under subsection (4) no appointment is made, the official receiver shall continue to be trustee of the bankrupt's estate, but without prejudice to his power to make a further reference.

(8) References in this section to a vacancy include a case where it is necessary, in relation to any property which is or may be comprised in a bankrupt's estate, to revive the trusteeship of that estate after the holding of a final meeting summoned under section 331 or the giving by the official receiver of notice under section 299(2).

Amendments—Enterprise Act 2002, ss 269, 278(2), Sch 23, paras 1, 11(a), (b), Sch 26.

General note—This provision applies to a vacancy in the office of trustee as defined in s 300(1) and (8). By s 300(2) the official receiver is trustee in all cases until a vacancy is filled.

The reference to it being necessary to 'revive the trusteeship' in s 300(8) caters for the need for a trustee to be appointed following the release of the official receiver as trustee under s 299(2), or the release of a trustee following the release determined by a meeting of the bankrupt's creditors under s 331(2)(b). Such a need might arise where property enures for the benefit of the bankruptcy estate following release or, for example, where any charge on the bankrupt's home under s 313(2) becomes enforceable following release.

Control of trustee

301 Creditors' committee

(1) Subject as follows, a general meeting of a bankrupt's creditors (whether summoned under the preceding provisions of this Chapter or otherwise) may, in accordance with the rules, establish a committee (known as 'the creditors' committee') to exercise the functions conferred on it by or under this Act.

(2) A general meeting of the bankrupt's creditors shall not establish such a committee, or confer any functions on such a committee, at any time when the official receiver is the trustee of the bankrupt's estate, except in connection with an appointment made by that meeting of a person to be trustee instead of the official receiver.

General note—A creditors' committee may be established by a meeting of creditors in any bankruptcy. Where at any time there is no creditors' committee, s 302 vests the functions of such a committee in the Secretary of State. The provisions governing the formation and function of a creditors' committee appear in rr 6.150–6.166. The functions of a creditors' committee are essentially in monitoring the trustee and holding him to account on matters of genuine concern with respect to the bankruptcy: see rr 6.152 and 6.153. In addition, a creditors' committee has specific powers under certain provisions, namely s 314(3) (permission to trustee to appoint bankrupt to superintend management of estate or carry on business for benefit of creditors), s 326(2) (permission to distribute bankrupt's property in specie), and ss 314(4) and 326(3) (retrospective permission for acts undertaken without committee's permission in certain circumstances). However, where the official receiver is trustee, the role of the committee is limited by s 301(2), other than in connection with an appointment by the meeting of creditors of a person to be trustee in the place of the official receiver.

Rule 6.162 specifically provides for resolutions of the committee to be effected by post, subject to the standing of any committee member to require the trustee to summon a committee meeting.

The decision of the Court of Appeal in *Re Bulmer ex parte Greaves* [1937] Ch 499 is authority for the proposition that a member of a Committee of Inspection, as a committee was known under the Bankruptcy Act 1914, is a fiduciary in relation to the bankrupt's estate so far as a committee member deals in property comprised in the estate. Although that authority almost certainly remains good, its practical relevance is now very much limited by the fact that, in contrast with the position under the earlier legislation, the committee has no standing to direct the trustee in the conduct of the bankruptcy. Furthermore, detailed and restrictive provisions governing dealings by committee members and others in the bankrupt's estate are now imposed by r 6.165.

Rule 12A.51 authorises a trustee to refuse inspection of a document comprising part of the records of the bankruptcy from any member of the creditors' committee if the document should be treated as confidential or its disclosure would be prejudicial to the conduct of the proceedings or might reasonably be expected to lead to violence against any person.

For the position of the Financial Services Authority, see s 374(4) of the Financial Services and Markets Act 2000.

302 Exercise by Secretary of State of functions of creditors' committee

(1) The creditors' committee is not to be able or required to carry out its functions at any time when the official receiver is trustee of the bankrupt's estate; but at any such time the functions of the committee under this Act shall be vested in the Secretary of State, except to the extent that the rules otherwise provide.

(2) Where in the case of any bankruptcy there is for the time being no creditors' committee and the trustee of the bankrupt's estate is a person other than the official receiver, the functions of such a committee shall be vested in the Secretary of State, except to the extent that the rules otherwise provide.

General note—See the notes to s 301. On procedure see r 6.166.

303 General control of trustee by the court

(1) If a bankrupt or any of his creditors or any other person is dissatisfied by any act, omission or decision of a trustee of the bankrupt's estate, he may apply to the court; and on such an application the court may confirm, reverse or modify any act or decision of the trustee, may give him directions or may make such other order as it thinks fit.

(2) The trustee of a bankrupt's estate may apply to the court for directions in relation to any particular matter arising under the bankruptcy.

(2A) Where at any time after a bankruptcy petition has been presented to the court against any person, whether under the provisions of the Insolvent Partnerships Order 1994 or not, the attention of the court is drawn to the fact that the person in question is a member of an insolvent partnership, the court may make an order as to the future conduct of the insolvency proceedings and any such order may apply any provisions of that Order with any necessary modifications.

(2B) Where a bankruptcy petition has been presented against more than one individual in the circumstances mentioned in subsection (2A) above, the court may give such directions for consolidating the proceedings, or any of them, as it thinks just.

(2C) Any order or directions under subsection (2A) or (2B) may be made or given on the application of the official receiver, any responsible insolvency practitioner, the trustee of the partnership or any other interested person and may include provisions as to the administration of the joint estate of the partnership, and in particular how it and the separate estate of any member are to be administered.

Amendments—SI 1994/2421.

General note—These two provisions allow matters within the scope of either to be resolved by way of the procedure provided for in Part 7 of the Insolvency Rules 1986. An application will usually proceed by way of an ordinary application in the existing bankruptcy proceedings.

Although broad in scope, this section should be read in conjunction with s 363. In particular, an application by a trustee or the official receiver that an undischarged or discharged bankrupt should do as directed by the court falls within s 363(2) and not s 303(2). Reference should also be made to s 298 (removal of trustee) and the notes thereto.

It is extremely doubtful that s 303 is appropriate for the fixing of a trustee's remuneration, although the court does have such power under s 363(1) or its own inherent jurisdiction: *Engel v Peri* [2002] BPIR 961 at [33]–[35] (Ferris J). His Lordship went on to identify that s 303 does confer the necessary jurisdiction for the court to fix a trustee's legal fees 'although the challenge to the legal fees actually incurred may well be a difficult one to make successfully'. See also *Freeburn v Hunt* [2010] BPIR 325. Further commentary on a trustee's remuneration appears in the notes to s 363.

Section 303(1)

'... **or any other person is dissatisfied** ...'—In *Port v Auger* [1994] 1 WLR 862 at 874A Harman J considered that 'a person can only be "dissatisfied" if he can show that he has some substantial interest which has been adversely affected by whatever is complained of.' A person dissatisfied may therefore include a discharged bankrupt (on which see *Osborn v Cole* [1999] BPIR 251 at 254C–254F (Registrar Baister)) or a person in respect of whom a bankruptcy order has been annulled (on which see *Engel v Peri* [2002] BPIR 961 (Ferris J)). In *Re Dennis Michael Cook* [1999] BPIR 881 at 883G Stanley Burnton QC, sitting as he then was as a deputy High Court judge, adopted a wider interpretation than that of Harman J in expressing the view at 883F–883G that the term 'dissatisfied' is no narrower than the term 'aggrieved', as employed in the former s 80 of the Bankruptcy Act 1914, and was arguably wider. Accordingly, the term should not be given a restricted interpretation and will extend to a person who has a genuine grievance whose interests are prejudicially affected by any act, omission or decision of a trustee, but will not include a mere busybody who is interfering with things which do not concern him. Following consideration of these authorities in *Woodbridge v Smith* [2004] BPIR 247 Registrar Baister held that the wife of a bankrupt with an interest in the matrimonial home who wished to challenge a trustee's claim to remuneration, apparently approved at a meeting of which proper notice had not been given, fell within the scope of s 303(1) as a person 'dissatisfied'.

'... **by any act, omission or decision of a trustee** ...'—Unless some unnecessary overlap was intended, the terms 'decision', 'act' and 'omission' are mutually exclusive. It would follow that an omission extends to a failure to do something, say through an oversight or through ignorance, but not a failure to do something as a consequence of a conscious decision as to such inaction.

Circumstances in which the court's jurisdiction under s 303(1) should be invoked—Practicality and justice, including the need to protect the interests of creditors, are not always served by allowing the time and expense necessarily involved in an application challenging a trustee's conduct, however genuine the sense of grievance on the part of the applicant. It was for this reason that Harman J expressed the view in *Port v Auger* [1994] 1 WLR 862 at 873–874 that s 303(1) should not be invoked lightly, and only where the applicant can be shown to have some substantial interest (see above) which has been adversely affected by whatever conduct is under complaint. In *Engel v Peri* [2002] BPIR 961 at [18] Ferris J held that it is the establishing of this 'substantial interest' which is determinative of whether an applicant has standing to proceed under s 303 (1). The judge considered, but rejected, a submission to the effect that it was also necessary for an applicant to show that there would be a surplus after all the bankruptcy debts and the expenses of the bankruptcy had been paid in full. That proposition had been based on the judgment of Charles Harman J in *Re A Debtor ex parte the Debtor v Dodwell (the Trustee)* [1949] Ch 236 at 240. Ferris J considered (at [18]) that 'While this decision will obviously be applicable to the great majority of cases where a bankrupt seeks to interfere with the day to day administration of his estate in the course of the bankruptcy, I do not think it can be shown as laying down a universal requirement that a bankrupt must show that there will or may be a surplus before he has standing to apply under s 303.'

It is submitted that a creditor will usually be able to establish the 'substantial interest' requirement if the decision, act or omission complained of can be shown to have a potential and real effect on the creditor's financial interest in the bankruptcy. Perhaps the most obvious form of such conduct involves the trustee in refusing to pursue a cause of action vested in the bankruptcy estate, as suggested by Hoffmann J, as he then was, in *Heath v Tang* [1993] 1 WLR 1421, or the taking of steps by a trustee which are indefensible on any objective scrutiny. The court will not, however, interfere with a decision of a trustee in the course of his discharging his function under s 305(2), other than where, as Registrar Baister put the matter in *Osborn v Cole* [1999] BPIR 251 at 255G–255H, following a review of the authorities, 'it can be shown that [the trustee] has acted in bad faith or so perversely that no trustee properly advised or properly instructing himself could so have acted, alternatively if he had acted fraudulently or in a manner so unreasonable and absurd that no reasonable person would have acted in that way': see to the same effect *Hamilton v The Official Receiver* [1998] BPIR 602 at 605C–606A (Laddie J, as he then was) and *Re Don Basil Williams* [2003] BPIR 545 at 546A–546D (Jacob J, as he then was). *Osborne v Cole* was approved in *Supperstone v Hurst (No 3)* [2006] EWHC 2147 (Ch), [2006] BPIR 1263 and in *Bank of Baroda v Patel* [2009] BPIR 255. Arnold J proposed a slightly more interventionist approach at first instance in *Bramston v Haut* [2012] EWHC 1279 (Ch), [2012] BPIR 672, but the Court of Appeal confirmed that the court should only intervene if the trustee's decision was 'perverse' ([2012] EWCA Civ 1637, [2013] BPIR 25). It follows that an applicant is plainly at risk on costs unless he can show that he has arguable grounds for challenging a decision of a trustee, given that onerous test.

In *Shepherd v The Official Receiver* [2007] BPIR 101 Gabriel Moss QC, sitting as a deputy High Court judge, dismissed an application by a bankrupt under s 303 challenging the Official Receiver's decision not to investigate what the bankrupt had maintained tenaciously, but unreasonably, was a claim in the bankruptcy estate against the Legal Services Commission.

The court may direct a trustee to assign a cause of action against a third party although it may refuse to do so on the ground that the cause of action is doubtful or that the assignee's financial position is so weak as to pose a real risk as to a costs order being made against the trustee in any ensuing litigation: *Re Shettar* [2003] BPIR 1055 (Park J). See also *Hunt v Harb* [2011] EWCA Civ 1239, [2012] BPIR 117.

Neither s 303(1) nor s 303(2) confers on the court jurisdiction or power to give directions to the official receiver as to the performance of his public law functions: *Hardy v Focus Insurance Co Ltd* [1997] BPIR 77 at 82F (Robert Walker J, as he then was).

Applicants under s 303(2)—Although s 303(2) only makes reference to the trustee in making an application, the judgment of Blackburne J in *Re A & C Supplies Ltd* [1998] 1 BCLC 603 at 608G – a case on block-transfer orders – is authority for the proposition that an application may be made by any person with a sufficient interest to invoke the court's jurisdiction. That decision was followed by Park J in *Supperstone v Auger* [1999] BPIR 152 at 154B–154C, another block-transfer case. In *Craig v Humberclyde Industrial Finance Group Ltd* [1999] 1 WLR 129 the Court of Appeal confirmed the approach of Chadwick J, as he then was, at first instance in treating an application by the official receiver under the analogous s 168(3) (in a compulsory winding-up) for directions as to whether a claim by the company in liquidation ought to be compromised or assigned to the company's directors as akin to a *Beddoe* application.

In *Re Michael* [2010] BPIR 418 Sales J held that the test according to which the court would intervene to overturn decisions of a trustee in the administration of a bankrupt's estate was the same whether an application was made by a person under s 303(1) of the Insolvency Act 1986 (the Act) or by the trustee in bankruptcy himself under s 303(2) of the Act. He considered trhat the usual test was that, fraud and bad faith apart, the court would only interfere with the act of a trustee in bankruptcy if he had done something so utterly unreasonable and absurd that no reasonable person would have done it, and the basic approach was that the court should be very slow to second-guess commercial decisions made by a trustee in bankruptcy in the exercise of the statutory discretion conferred on him by s 305(2) of the Act.

Section 303(2A)–(2C)—The court has jurisdiction to give directions in relation to a partnership dissolution where the partnership is not being wound up as an unregistered company but where its two partners are subject to bankruptcy orders: *Official Receiver v Hollens* [2007] BPIR 830 (Blackburne J).

Costs of a s 303 application—There is no hard and fast rule as to where the costs of a s 303 application will fall. In addition to the exercise of its discretion in ordering costs against a particular party, the court may have to consider whether or not any costs should rank as an expense in the bankruptcy. In the context of a contentious application the court is perfectly entitled to take the view, in the exercise of its discretion under CPR, rr 44.3 and 44.5, as invoked by r 7.51A, that the costs of an unsuccessful party should not fall as an expense of the bankruptcy, so as to be borne, in effect, by creditors in the bankruptcy, and that an unsuccessful party should meet the cost of other litigants whose conduct in the proceedings is either proper and justifiable or of assistance to the court.

304 Liability of trustee

(1) Where on an application under this section the court is satisfied—

> (a)   that the trustee of a bankrupt's estate has misapplied or retained, or become accountable for, any money or other property comprised in the bankrupt's estate, or
>
> (b)   that a bankrupt's estate has suffered any loss in consequence of any misfeasance or breach of fiduciary or other duty by a trustee of the estate in the carrying out of his functions,

the court may order the trustee, for the benefit of the estate, to repay, restore or account for money or other property (together with interest at such rate as the court thinks just) or, as the case may require, to pay such sum by way of compensation in respect of the misfeasance or breach of fiduciary or other duty as the court thinks just.

This is without prejudice to any liability arising apart from this section.

(2) An application under this section may be made by the official receiver, the Secretary of State, a creditor of the bankrupt or (whether or not there is, or is likely to be, a surplus for the purposes of section 330(5) (final distribution)) the bankrupt himself.

But the leave of the court is required for the making of an application if it is to be made by the bankrupt or if it is to be made after the trustee has had his release under section 299.

(3) Where—

(a)   the trustee seizes or disposes of any property which is not comprised in the bankrupt's estate, and

(b)   at the time of the seizure or disposal the trustee believes, and has reasonable grounds for believing, that he is entitled (whether in pursuance of an order of the court or otherwise) to seize or dispose of that property,

the trustee is not liable to any person (whether under this section or otherwise) in respect of any loss or damage resulting from the seizure or disposal except in so far as that loss or damage is caused by the negligence of the trustee; and he has a lien on the property, or the proceeds of its sale, for such of the expenses of the bankruptcy as were incurred in connection with the seizure or disposal.

General note—The effect of s 304(1)(a) and (b) is to create two distinct statutory causes of action which may be advanced by those applicants listed in s 304(2), subject to the limitations therein. Although s 304(1) closely resembles s 212(3) (misfeasance proceedings) the latter provision does not create any cause of action but is procedural in facilitating the advancing of already existing causes of action. It is for this reason that the words 'This is without prejudice to any liability arising apart from this section' appear in s 304(1) but are absent from s 212, since s 304(1) cannot prejudice any other cause of action – for breach of trust, breach of duty etc – which may also be available to a person eligible to proceed under s 304. However, even if other causes of action co-exist with s 304, the effect of a trustee's release under s 299 exonerates a trustee from all liability, save for liability imposed by court order under s 304(1).

For examples of claims under s 304 see *Green v Satsangi* [1998] BPIR 55 (Rimer J); *A & J Fabrications Ltd v Grant Thornton* [1998] 2 BCLC 227 (a liquidation case under s 212) (Jacob J, as he then was); *Brown v Beat* [2002] BPIR 421 (Hart J); see also *Chapper v Jackson* [2012] EWHC 3897 (Ch), [2012] BPIR 257 and McAteer v Lismore [2012] NICh 7, [2012] BPIR 812 (dealing with the comparable provision in art 277 of the Northern Ireland Insolvency Order 1989) – cases on each side of the line as to whether a trustee had breached his duties in relation to property. In the former the trustee had not fallen short of the standard of a reasonably skilled and careful IP where he had refused to intervene in a court ordered sale at a price alleged to be an undervalue. A relevant but not determinative factor was the fact that the trustee had taken and followed legal advice. In the latter the trustee was found to have breached his duty of care by failing to properly advertise a property and selling at a price deemed to be an undervalue.

Who benefits from an order under s 304(1)—Despite the varying class of applicants in s 304(2), the words 'for the benefit of the estate' in s 304(1) must be taken, it is submitted, as meaning that the court may only make an order which results in an award being made in favour of the bankruptcy estate, and not in favour of any individual applicant or creditor. That analysis is consistent with the class nature of bankruptcy and the concept of pari passu.

Leave under s 304(2)—A bankrupt requires the leave of the court to proceed with a s 304 claim in all cases. Any other person within s 304(2) requires leave of the court once the trustee has had his release under s 299. In *Brown v Beat* [2002] BPIR 421 at 424D Hart J identified that the requirement that a bankrupt requires leave under s 304(2) reflects Parliament's recognition 'that applications by bankrupts against their trustees may well have a tendency to be vexatious'.

In any case requiring leave, the court will wish to be satisfied that the claim advanced has at least a real prospect of succeeding.

Section 304(3)

'... **property** ...'—In *Welsh Development Agency v Export Finance Co Ltd* [1992] BCC 270 the Court of Appeal held, in the context of s 234, that the word 'seizes' is only capable of extending to tangible property.

Chapter IV

Administration by Trustee

Preliminary

305 General functions of trustee

(1) This Chapter applies in relation to any bankruptcy where either—

    (a)   the appointment of a person as trustee of a bankrupt's estate takes effect, or

    (b)   the official receiver becomes trustee of a bankrupt's estate.

(2) The function of the trustee is to get in, realise and distribute the bankrupt's estate in accordance with the following provisions of this Chapter; and in the carrying out of that function and in the management of the bankrupt's estate the trustee is entitled, subject to those provisions, to use his own discretion.

(3) It is the duty of the trustee, if he is not the official receiver—

    (a)   to furnish the official receiver with such information,

    (b)   to produce to the official receiver, and permit inspection by the official receiver of, such books, papers and other records, and

    (c)   to give the official receiver such other assistance,

as the official receiver may reasonably require for the purpose of enabling him to carry out his functions in relation to the bankruptcy.

(4) The official name of the trustee shall be 'the trustee of the estate of, a bankrupt' (inserting the name of the bankrupt); be he may be referred to as 'the trustee in bankruptcy' of the particular bankrupt.

General note—The key provision in defining the general functions of a trustee appears in s 305(2). The powers of a trustee should, of necessity, be exercised directly or indirectly in pursuit of those general functions. Furthermore, the trustee is subject not only to the rule in *Ex parte James*, which is discussed in more detail in the notes to para 5 of Sch B1, but is also obliged to maintain his independence. In the words of Lightman J in *Re Ng (a Bankrupt)* [1997] BPIR 267 at 269H–270A – words which were approved of subsequently by the Court of Appeal in *Trustee in Bankruptcy of Bukhari v Bukhari* [1999] BPIR 157 – 'A trustee in bankruptcy is not vested with the powers and privileges of his office so as to enable himself to accept engagement as a hired gun. His duty is to exercise his powers and privileges for the benefit of the creditors for whom he is appointed a trustee.'

The generality of the words in s 305(2), and the reliance of the procedure of bankruptcy on the professional judgment of a trustee-in-bankruptcy, afford the trustee a considerable breadth of discretion in discharging his functions. The court, therefore, is only likely to interfere with the trustee's conduct, perhaps in the course of an application under s 303(1), where the conduct complained of is so manifestly beyond the scope of that in which a competent and reasonable trustee might engage as to justify the court's interference. Absent such conduct, the court will not entertain complaints which amount, in substance, to a difference of opinion as between the complainant and the trustee, or complaints which are plainly frivolous or vexatious. Conversely, a trustee should not approach any given situation blindly and thereafter seek to argue that any steps taken by him were only undertaken pursuant to his functions under s 305(2); so, for example, and commonly enough, a trustee must weigh up all relevant circumstances, including litigation risk, when making what amounts to a commercial decision as to whether proceedings should be instituted in connection with the bankruptcy.

As a general principle it is not unreasonable for a trustee-in-bankruptcy to retain the solicitors which acted for the petitioning creditor: *Re Schuppan (a Bankrupt) (No.1)* [1996] 2 All ER 664 (Robert Walker J, as he then was), as considered with further cases in the notes to s 314 under the heading 'Employment of solicitors'.

For the position of the Financial Services Authority see s 373 of the Financial Services and Markets Act 2000.

Acquisition, control and realisation of bankrupt's estate

306 Vesting of bankrupt's estate in trustee

(1) The bankrupt's estate shall vest in the trustee immediately on his appointment taking effect or, in the case of the official receiver, on his becoming trustee.

(2) Where any property which is, or is to be, comprised in the bankrupt's estate vests in the trustee (whether under this section or under any other provision of this Part), it shall so vest without any conveyance, assignment or transfer.

General note—The vesting of property in a trustee-in-bankruptcy on his appointment – in contrast to the position in liquidation where property remains vested in the company – is fundamental to the discharge of the trustee's functions under s 305(2). At a practical level, a trustee will also wish to ensure that adequate insurance arrangements are in place.

The fact that a third party is unaware of the trustee's entitlement to property does not excuse that third party from dealings in respect of the property. The third party will not be able to give a good receipt for property to which the trustee is entitled: *Rooney v Cardona* [1991] 1 WLR 1388, CA (bankrupt husband could not give good receipt for proceeds of life policy written by wife on her life for his benefit where wife deceased prior to bankruptcy order, following which husband claimed and obtained policy proceeds from life assurance company which was ignorant of bankruptcy order).

In contrast to the automatic vesting of a bankrupt's estate on the making of an adjudication order under ss 18(1) and 53(1) of the Bankruptcy Act 1914, the bankrupt's estate, as defined in s 283, remains vested in the bankrupt on the making of a bankruptcy order pending appointment of a trustee-in-bankruptcy. The official receiver is, however, by virtue of s 287(1), the receiver and manager of the bankrupt's estate in the period between the making of the bankruptcy order and the appointment of a trustee and is under a duty to act as such.

The appointment of a trustee—The official receiver may be appointed trustee-in-bankruptcy of the estate in four situations. First, under s 279(1), where a bankruptcy order is made on a criminal bankruptcy petition presented under s 264(1)(d), although such petitions are obsolete in practice. Secondly, under s 293(3), as from the giving to the court of a notice under s 293(2) of the official receiver's decision not to summon a meeting of creditors. Thirdly, under s 295(4), on the giving of a notice under s 295(3) to the effect that the official receiver has decided not to refer a need for an appointment of a trustee to the Secretary of State or on the Secretary of State declining to make an appointment following such a reference. Fourthly, under s 300(2), where the official receiver becomes trustee to fill a vacancy in that office until the vacancy is otherwise fulfilled.

For the appointment of a trustee-in-bankruptcy see ss 292–296 and rr 6.120–6.124.

Location of property comprised in the bankrupt's estate—The definition of property in the Bankruptcy Act 1869 made no reference to the location of such property, although the definition in s 167 of the Bankruptcy Act 1914 referred to property 'whether situated in England or elsewhere'. The absence of any qualification in s 306 means that all property to which the bankrupt is legally or beneficially entitled, wherever situated in the world, will, save for those exceptions identified in the notes to s 283, vest in the trustee: see *Pollard v Ashurst* [2001] BPIR 131.

Ascertaining the extent of the bankrupt's estate—Specific provisions envisage the trustee taking steps to identify the property comprised in the bankrupt's estate as soon as practicable. First, there is an express obligation under s 311(1) to take possession of all books, papers and other records which relate to the bankrupt's estate or affairs. Second, and more generally, the functions of the trustee, as defined in s 305(2), envisage the trustee exercising those powers conferred on him by s 315 and Sch 5 '... to get in, realise and distribute the bankrupt's estate' as soon as is reasonably practicable in the circumstances. The trustee also has statutory powers of inquiry into the bankrupt's dealings and property in addition to his standing to enforce those duties owed to him by the bankrupt under s 333.

Steps securing property—Notwithstanding the automatic vesting of property in a trustee without the requirement for any further formality, a trustee may consider it prudent to take steps to secure his position by reason of noting his title on any register maintained in respect of such property so as to give notice of his title or interest to third parties. Furthermore, whilst a trustee is not entitled to property previously transferred out of the bankruptcy estate under a transaction which is susceptible to challenge as a transaction-at-undervalue or a preference it is usually prudent to register a caution against dealings in favour of the trustee where that property comprises registered land or an equivalent entry where title is determined by reference to a register of interests. Failure to take such steps which results in loss to the bankruptcy estate may give rise to a claim against the trustee under s 304(1).

Shares—Where a bankrupt owns shares and the company is regulated by Table A, reg 30 thereof allows a trustee to elect, on producing such evidence as the directors may require, to be registered as holder of the shares or to nominate some other person to be so registered. A bankrupt who remains a registered holder of shares is allowed to vote at general meetings, although a trustee may direct a bankrupt under s 333(1) as to how he should vote: *Wise v Landsell* [1921] 1 Ch 420.

Registered land—Previously a trustee obtained title to registered land automatically without the need for his entry on the title register: under s 61(5) of the Land Registration Act 1925. For the registration of a bankruptcy petition as a pending action under the Land Charges Act 1972 and the registration of a trustee as proprietor, see now s 86 of the Land Registration Act 2002. For the interaction betwees s 303 and the LRA 2002 see *Pick v Chief Land Registrar* [2011] EWHC 206 (Ch) (cf *Tomlinson v Bridging Finance Ltd* [2010] BPIR 759).

Contractual prohibition against assignment—A contractual prohibition preventing assignment of a thing in action does not affect the deemed assignment of such property to a trustee under s 306 and s 311(4), since vesting by reference to the latter provision is deemed to take effect without assignment: *Re Landau* [1998] Ch 223 (Ferris J).

Claims which are 'personal' to the bankrupt—Certain causes of action which are regarded as being 'personal' to a bankrupt do not, by virtue of decisions of the court, vest in the trustee despite the fact that they would otherwise fall within the scope of the bankrupt's estate. These are considered in the notes to s 283.

Pension rights—The recent case law on this area is of diminishing importance, given the exclusion of the vast majority of pension interests from the scope of the bankrupt's estate by virtue of ss 11 and 12 of the Welfare Reform and Pensions Act 1999. For pre-existing and ongoing cases the case law remains that in *Re Landau* [1998] Ch 223; *Krasner v Dennison* [2001] Ch 76; *Patel v Jones* [2001] BPIR 919; *Rowe v Sanders* [2002] BPIR 847; *Re the Trusts of the Scientific Investment Pension Plan* [1998] BPIR 410; and *Malcolm v Benedict Mackenzie* [2004] EWCA Civ 1748, [2005] BPIR 176.

306A Property subject to restraint order

(1) This section applies where—

    (a) property is excluded from the bankrupt's estate by virtue of section 417(2)(a) of the Proceeds of Crime Act 2002 (property subject to a restraint order),

    (b) an order under section 50, 128, or 198 of that Act has not been made in respect of the property, and

    (c) the restraint order is discharged.

(2) On the discharge of the restraint order the property vests in the trustee as part of the bankrupt's estate.

(3) But subsection (2) does not apply to the proceeds of property realised by a management receiver under section 49(2)(d) or 197(2)(d) of that Act (realisation of property to meet receiver's remuneration and expenses).

Amendments—Inserted by Proceeds of Crime Act 2002, s 456, Sch 11, paras 1, 16(1), (3). Amended by Serious Crime Act 2007, ss 74(2)(g), 92, Sch 8, Pt 7, para 151, Sch 14.

General note—Sections 306A to 306C were introduced by s 456 and paras 1 and 16 of Sch 11 to the Proceeds of Crime Act 2002 and took effect from 24 March 2003. The provisions are necessary to cater expressly for the vesting in a trustee of property which becomes available as a result of the three specific and differing circumstances identified in each of the new sections. Sections 306A(3) and 306C(3) afford protection to a management receiver appointed under the 2002 Act in respect of remuneration and expenses which may be drawn from the proceeds of property realised which would otherwise vest automatically in the trustee under ss 306A(2) or 306C(2).

Property subject to a restrain order, a receivership, or administration or confiscation order does not comprise part of the bankruptcy estate in a subsequent bankruptcy, although those enforcement sanctions are not exercisable where the debtor has previously been made bankrupt. A fuller discussion of the scope of the 2002 Act is beyond the scope of this text; further reference should be made initially to ss 50, 52, 128, 198, 200, 417, 418 and 419 of the 2002 Act.

306B Property in respect of which receivership or administration order made

(1) This section applies where—

    (a) property is excluded from the bankrupt's estate by virtue of section 417(2)(b), (c) or (d) of the Proceeds of Crime Act 2002 (property in respect of which an order for the appointment of a receiver or administrator under certain provisions of that Act is in force),

    (b) a confiscation order is made under section 6, 92 or 156 of that Act,

    (c) the amount payable under the confiscation order is fully paid, and

    (d) any of the property remains in the hands of the receiver or administrator (as the case may be).

(2) The property vests in the trustee as part of the bankrupt's estate.

Amendments—Inserted by Proceeds of Crime Act 2002, s 456, Sch 11, paras 1, 16(1), (3).

General note—See the general note to s 306A.

306C Property subject to certain orders where confiscation order discharged or quashed

(1) This section applies where—

    (a) property is excluded from the bankrupt's estate by virtue of section 417(2)(a), (b), (c) or (d) of the Proceeds of Crime Act 2002 (property in respect of which a restraint order or an order for the appointment of a receiver or administrator under that Act is in force),

    (b) a confiscation order is made under section 6, 92 or 156 of that Act, and

    (c) the confiscation order is discharged under section 30, 114 or 180 of that Act (as the case may be) or quashed under that Act or in pursuance of any enactment relating to appeals against conviction or sentence.

(2) Any such property in the hands of a receiver appointed under Part 2 or 4 of that Act or an administrator appointed under Part 3 of that Act vests in the trustee as part of the bankrupt's estate.

(3) But subsection (2) does not apply to the proceeds of property realised by a management receiver under section 49(2)(d) or 197(2)(d) of that Act (realisation of property to meet receiver's remuneration and expenses).

Amendments—Inserted by Proceeds of Crime Act 2002, s 456, Sch 11, paras 1, 16(1), (3).

General note—See the general note to s 306A.

307 After-acquired property

(1) Subject to this section and section 309, the trustee may by notice in writing claim for the bankrupt's estate any property which has been acquired by, or has devolved upon, the bankrupt since the commencement of the bankruptcy.

(2) A notice under this section shall not served in respect of—

    (a) any property falling within subsection (2) or (3) of section 283 in Chapter II,

    (aa) any property vesting in the bankrupt by virtue of section 283A in Chapter II,

    (b) any property which by virtue of any other enactment is excluded from the bankrupt's estate, or

    (c) without prejudice to section 280(2)(c) (order of court on application for discharge), any property which is acquired by or, devolves upon, the bankrupt after his discharge.

(3) Subject to the next subsection, upon the service on the bankrupt of a notice under this section the property to which the notice relates shall vest in the trustee as part of the bankrupt's estate; and the trustee's title to that property has relation back to the time at which the property was acquired by, or devolved upon, the bankrupt.

(4) Where, whether before or after service of a notice under this section—

(a) a person acquires property in good faith, for value and without notice of the bankruptcy, or

(b) a banker enters into a transaction in good faith and without such notice,

the trustee is not in respect of that property or transaction entitled by virtue of this section to any remedy against that person or banker, or any person whose title to any property derives from that person or banker.

(5) References in this section to property do not include any property which, as part of the bankrupt's income, may be the subject of an income payments order under section 310.

Amendments—Enterprise Act 2002, s 261(4).

General note—Only that property comprised in the bankrupt's estate as at the date of the trustee's appointment vests in the trustee automatically under s 306. Any property which is subsequently acquired by or devolves upon the bankrupt after the commencement of the bankruptcy – as defined in s 278(a) as the date of the bankruptcy order – is property to which the bankrupt is entitled in the absence of either the trustee utilising s 307 or the court making an income payments order under s 310, or an income payments agreement being entered into under s 310A. The notes to s 310 include commentary as to the distinction between property subject to s 307 and the mutually exclusive s 310. In particular, income within the meaning of s 310(7) is incapable of being claimed as after-acquired property: see s 307(5). A single one-off payment for services rendered is capable of constituting 'income' for s 307(7) purposes: *Supperstone v Lloyd's Names Association Working Party* [1999] BPIR 832 (Evans-Lombe J).

The operation of s 307 presupposes compliance by the bankrupt with his duty under s 333(2) to give notice to the trustee within 21 days of property devolving upon him. More specifically, r 6.200 imposes a specific duty on a bankrupt to give notice to his trustee of after-acquired property. The safeguard for the trustee in the event of non-compliance by the bankrupt with his duties lies in s 309(1)(a), under which the 42-day period in which the trustee must serve a notice only commences upon the trustee obtaining knowledge of the property in question.

Property to which s 307 applies—Apart from the observations above as to income, s 307 applies to 'property' – as defined very broadly in non-exhaustive terms in s 436 – but does not catch any property which falls within the scope of the bankrupt's estate under ss 283 or 283A.

Although the general rule is that property subject to an order under the Proceeds of Crime Act 2002 will not be available in bankruptcy, s 418(3) of the 2002 Act precludes the exercise of the court's power under that statute in relation to property in respect of which a trustee may serve a notice under ss 307, 308 or 308A, but only where the notice may be served without leave of the court.

Service of the s 307(1) notice—In *Pike v Cork Gully* [1997] BPIR 723 the Court of Appeal (Millett and Schiemann LJJ) considered the position where a trustee had seized money in a bank account following which he served the requisite notice. At 724C–724D Millett LJ, with whom Schiemann LJ agreed, concurred with the reasoning of the judge below to the effect that, once the notice had been given, it was effective and related back to the date on which the bankrupt acquired the money such that, whilst the seizure was not proper at that time, the later service of the notice and the operation of the relation-back cured the technical defect. That reasoning no doubt served the justice of the case in *Pike*. Nevertheless, and with respect, it is rather difficult to square that conclusion with the wording in s 307(3), which specifically provides that property which is subject to a notice shall only vest in the trustee upon service of the notice on the bankrupt. On the other hand, even if a trustee does seize money without service of a notice, Millett LJ's observation that no conversion and no recoverable loss could be complained of by the bankrupt, at least on the facts of *Pike*, is unassailable.

Extension of the 42-day period for service of the s 307(1) notice—Section 309(1)(a) allows for the extension of the 42-day period after its expiration. In *Solomons v Williams* [2001] BPIR 1123 at 1136F–1136H Pumfrey J identified that 'good cause' must be established to justify extension of the period. His Lordship considered that each case must be determined on its own facts, but that relevant factors would include the period of delay both in serving the notice under s 307 and seeking the extension, the merits of the application having regard to the overall position of the bankrupt, any prejudice caused to the bankrupt by the lateness of the application and the reasons for the delay. An order should not be made, however, if it causes prejudice to the bankrupt which is disproportionate to the likely benefit conferred on the creditors. An extension was refused in *Solomans v Williams* [2001] BPIR 1123 where there was a four month delay in serving the s 307 notice but where the application was only made two years later: for a refusal on even longer delay see *Franses v Oomerjee* [2005] BPIR 1320 (Registrar Derrett). Neither is it sufficient simply for an application to be made by a trustee since the court must have evidence upon which any permissive discretion can be based: *Vickers v Mitchell* [2004] All ER (D) 414 (Sir Donald Rattee) and see also *Warley Continental Services Ltd v Johal* [2004] BPIR 353 at [30]–[33] (HHJ Norris QC).

Procedure—There is no prescribed form for a s 307(1) notice. The relevant procedure appears in rr 6.200–6.202A.

308 Vesting in trustee of certain items of excess value

(1) Subject to section 309, where—

    (a)   property is excluded by virtue of section 283(2) (tools of trade, household effects, etc) from the bankrupt's estate, and

    (b)   it appears to the trustee that the realisable value of the whole or any part of that property exceeds the cost of a reasonable replacement for that property or that part of it,

the trustee may by notice in writing claim that property or, as the case may be, that part of it for the bankrupt's estate.

(2) Upon the service on the bankrupt of a notice under this section, the property to which the notice relates vests in the trustee as part of the bankrupt's estate; and, except against a purchaser in good faith, for value and without notice of the bankruptcy, the trustee's title to that property has relation back to the commencement of the bankruptcy.

(3) The trustee shall apply funds comprised in the estate to the purchase by or on behalf of the bankrupt of a reasonable replacement for any property vested in the trustee under this section; and the duty imposed by this subsection has priority over the obligation of the trustee to distribute the estate.

(4) For the purposes of this section property is a reasonable replacement for other property if it is reasonably adequate for meeting the needs met by the other property.

Amendments—Housing Act 1988, s 140(1), Sch 17, para 73.

General note—The purpose of this provision lies in permitting the trustee to claim property for the benefit of the bankrupt's estate where that property is excluded by s 283(2) but where it appears that the realisable value of any part of that excluded property exceeds the cost of a reasonable replacement. The trustee is, however, necessarily constrained by s 308(3), which imposes an overriding duty to apply funds in purchasing a reasonable replacement for any property claimed under this provision. Thus, s 308 will require the trustee to be satisfied that he is both able to sell a particular item of property and to replace it – within the meaning of s 308(4) – so as to produce a net benefit for the bankruptcy estate which justifies the time and cost of that exercise.

In practice, applications under s 308 are not common. Moreover, it is submitted that there is some scope for a bankrupt challenging a claim by a trustee on the basis that the term 'reasonable replacement' in s 308(1)(b) and (4) should not be construed by reference to some objective minimum standard applicable to all individuals but is capable of reflecting the particular circumstances of an individual bankrupt. In other words, what is a reasonable replacement in one case will not necessarily be a reasonable replacement in another. This approach would certainly be consistent with that adopted by the courts to the concept of reasonable domestic needs in the context of income payments order applications under s 310, on which see the notes thereto.

Procedure—See rr 6.187 and 6.188.

308A Vesting in trustee of certain tenancies

Upon the service on the bankrupt by the trustee of a notice in writing under this section, any tenancy—

> (a)   which is excluded by virtue of section 283(3A) from the bankrupt's estate, and
> (b)   to which the notice relates,

vests in the trustee as part of the bankrupt's estate; and, except against a purchaser in good faith, for value and without notice of the bankruptcy, the trustee's title to that tenancy has relation back to the commencement of the bankruptcy.

Amendments—Inserted by Housing Act 1988, s 117(2).

309 Time-limit for notice under s 307 or 308

(1) Except with the leave of the court, a notice shall not be served—

> (a)   under section 307, after the end of the period of 42 days beginning with the day on which it first came to the knowledge of the trustee that the property in question had been acquired by, or had devolved upon, the bankrupt;
> (b)   under section 308 or section 308A, after the end of the period of 42 days beginning with the day on which the property or tenancy in question first came to the knowledge of the trustee.

(2) For the purposes of this section—

> (a)   anything which comes to the knowledge of the trustee is deemed in relation to any successor of his as trustee to have come to the knowledge of the successor at the same time; and
> (b)   anything which comes (otherwise than under paragraph (a)) to the knowledge of a person before he is the trustee is deemed to come to his knowledge on his appointment taking effect or, in the case of the official receiver, on his becoming trustee.

Amendments—Housing Act 1988, s 117(3).

General note—See the notes to ss 307 and 308.

310 Income payments orders

(1) The court may make an order ('an income payments order') claiming for the bankrupt's estate so much of the income of the bankrupt during the period for which the order is in force as may be specified in the order.

(1A) An income payments order may be made only on an application instituted—

    (a)   by the trustee, and
    (b)   before the discharge of the bankrupt.

(2) The court shall not make an income payments order the effect of which would be to reduce the income of the bankrupt when taken together with any payments to which subsection (8) applies below what appears to the court to be necessary for meeting the reasonable domestic needs of the bankrupt and his family.

(3) An income payments order shall, in respect of any payment of income to which it is to apply, either—

    (a)   require the bankrupt to pay the trustee an amount equal to so much of that payment as is claimed by the order, or
    (b)   require the person making the payment to pay so much of it as is so claimed to the trustee, instead of to the bankrupt.

(4) Where the court makes an income payments order it may, if it thinks fit, discharge or vary any attachment of earnings order that is for the time being in force to secure payments by the bankrupt.

(5) Sums received by the trustee under an income payments order form part of the bankrupt's estate.

(6) An income payments order must specify the period during which it is to have effect; and that period—

    (a)   may end after the discharge of the bankrupt, but
    (b)   may not end after the period of three years beginning with the date on which the order is made.

(6A) An income payments order may (subject to subsection (6)(b)) be varied on the application of the trustee or the bankrupt (whether before or after discharge).

(7) For the purposes of this section the income of the bankrupt comprises every payment in the nature of income which is from time to time made to him or to which he from time to time becomes entitled, including any payment in respect of the carrying on of any business or in respect of any office or employment and (despite anything in section 11 or 12 of the Welfare Reform and Pensions Act 1999) any payment under a pension scheme but excluding any payment to which subsection (8) applies.

(8) This subsection applies to—

    (a)   payments by way of guaranteed minimum pension; and
    (b)   . . .

(9) In this section, "guaranteed minimum pension" has the same meaning as in the Pension Schemes Act 1993.

Amendments—Pensions Act 1995, s 122, Sch 3, para 15(a), (b); Welfare Reform and Pensions Act 1999, s 18, Sch 2, para 2; Enterprise Act 2002, ss 259(1)–(4), 278(2), Sch 26, SI 2011/1730 (as amended by SI 2012/709).

General note—Under the former legislation – on which see *Tennant's Application* [1956] 1 WLR 876, CA and *Re Cohen* [1961] Ch 246 – s 51(2) of the Bankruptcy Act 1914 provided that 'salary and income' received or receivable by a bankrupt vested in the trustee, subject to an order of the court to the contrary and s 38(1) of the 1914 Act, which dealt with after-acquired property and provided that all such property devolved automatically on the trustee before discharge.

The income payments order is an invention of the 1986 Act. Section 310 represents a marked shift from the old law, in that income now remains vested in the bankrupt subject to the making of an income payments order which itself requires the court to safeguard the bankrupt's reasonable domestic needs. This change in the law followed recommendations in paras 591–598 of the Cork Committee Report (1982, Cmnd 8558) to the effect that, consistent with the wider principle of seeking, so far as possible, to the rehabilitation of the debtor, as espoused in paras 192 and 193 of the Cork Report, whilst income should remain available for payment of creditors, the legislation should facilitate a more realistic and humane attitude being taken than previously in relation to the debtor and his family. In particular, there was no intention that earning capacity should automatically be made available for payment of debts such that 'the debtor must in no circumstances become the slave of his creditors', a point now also found in Art 3 of the European Convention on Human Rights. Nevertheless, whilst the policy of the Act appears to be to allow a bankrupt to enhance his post-bankruptcy estate by retention of his income and receipts, whether earned or not, it seems equally clear from the breadth of the definition of 'income' in s 310(7) that a trustee may lay claim to all such income and receipts, unless protected by statute, in the absence of an unconditional statutory exclusion of such income and receipts from the bankrupt's estate and the plain intention of Parliament that income should be available for distribution to creditors subject to the protection of the reasonable domestic needs of the bankrupt and his family.

Is a trustee-in-bankruptcy obliged to make an application for an income payments order?—A trustee has a discretion, not a duty, to make an application under s 310 in the discharge of his functions under s 305. Where no application is made in a very obvious case of surplus income over reasonable domestic needs, an aggrieved creditor might consider an application under s 303(1).

The trustee should not approach an application blindly and should give consideration to the likely benefit to creditors as against the overall cost of an application and any consequent hardship to the bankrupt and his family. The reported judgment of a district judge in *Boyden v Watson* [2004] BPIR 1131 is instructive in terms of the blistering criticism levelled at a trustee, his solicitors and counsel in relation to the apparent motives behind and conduct of what was ultimately an unsuccessful application in which the trustee's costs of the application itself amounted to one-half of the relatively modest total sum sought over a three-year period which, costs and the bankrupt's evidence that he had no surplus income available apart, would only have produced approximately three pence in the pound, if that, for creditors over that period.

However, Newey J confirmed in *Official Receiver v Negus* [2011] EWHC 3719 (Ch), [2012] BPIR 382 that the Court can still grant an IPO where the creditors will receive no direct benefit because the entirety of the sum generated will go to discharge bankruptcy expenses.

Timing- An application for an IPO must be made before the bankrupt is discharged. An application to suspend a bankrupt's discharge where the underlying motivation of the trustee appeared to be to try and facilitate an income payments arrangement attracted criticism (and was roundly rejected) in circumstances where action to obtain an IPO could and should have been taken much earlier in *Chadwick v Nash* [2012] BPIR 70.

Income payments agreements under s 310A—So as to avoid the cost associated with an income payments order, even one made by consent, particularly given the relatively modest amounts often involved, with effect from 1 April 2004, by virtue of s 310A as introduced by s 260 of the Enterprise Act 2002, a bankrupt may reach agreement for payments of contributions by himself or a third party to his trustee (or the official receiver, as appropriate), which agreement is enforceable as an order under s 310A(2).

The procedure governing such agreements appears in rr 6.193A–6.193C.

The inter-relationship between s 307 and s 310—The most useful analysis of the interplay of ss 307 and 310 appears in the judgment of Chadwick LJ in *Dennison v Krasner* [2000] BPIR 410 at 421B–421C. After-acquired property does not automatically form part of the bankrupt's estate, as defined in s 283(1)(a), other than where a notice is served by the trustee under s 307(1). However, after-acquired property which, as part of the bankrupt's income, could be the subject of an income payments order under s 310 cannot be the subject of a notice under s 307(1), by virtue of s 307(5). In other words, ss 307 and 310 are mutually exclusive. Section 310 itself provides a separate regime in relation to after-acquired property which is in the nature of income. Such property does not, however, form part of the bankrupt's estate unless it is received by the trustee under an income payments order. Section 310 does not control and qualify the vesting provisions in ss 306 or 307 but instead supplements those provisions in that s 310 applies to property which would not otherwise fall within those provisions. Accordingly, there is no need, indeed no justification, for construing s 310 as having any application to property which has vested in the trustee on his appointment under s 306(1), on which see the finding of Ferris J in *Re Landau* [1997] BPIR 229 at 233C–234D, approved of by Chadwick LJ in *Dennison* at 421E, to the effect that contractual rights to either income or capital under a retirement annuity contract vested automatically in a trustee-in-bankruptcy under s 306 on his appointment on the basis that the future entitlement constituted an existing chose in action within the meaning of property in s 436 irrespective of whether benefits were actually in payment at the commencement of the bankruptcy.

The approach to distinguishing between income and after-acquired property—Nothing analogous to s 310(7) appears in s 307. Accordingly, given the observation by Chadwick LJ in *Dennison* to the effect that s 310 provides what amounts, in effect, to an exception to the after-acquired property regime under s 307 – which itself amounts to an exception to the automatic vesting rule under s 306 – it is submitted that the proper approach is to consider in the first place whether a particular payment is capable of falling within s 310 as income before falling back on the s 307 provisions.

Section 310(2)

'the reasonable domestic needs of the bankrupt and his family'—The reference in s 310(2) to 'the reasonable domestic needs of the bankrupt and his family' is not to be construed as meaning that which 'is necessary to enable the bankrupt to live' (as had been the position under the Bankruptcy Act 1914 and at common law following *Re Roberts* [1903] 1 QB 122): *Re Rayatt (a Bankrupt)* [1998] BPIR 495 at 499G–500E (Michael Hart QC, sitting as he then was as a deputy High Court judge). *Rayatt* (which concerned an unsuccessful attempt by a trustee to claim monies expended by the bankrupt on private education fees) established (at 500G–500H) a two-stage test which, it is submitted, should be adopted in relation to any particular item of expenditure challenged by the trustee as involving monies which are claimed as falling subject to an income payments order. First, can expenditure by the bankrupt on a particular item be said to constitute the meeting of a *domestic need* of the bankrupt and his family? The court should note here that the deputy judge identified (at 502F–502G) the 'implicit notion' in para 591 of the Cork Committee Report that, given that income does not form part of the bankruptcy estate in the absence of an order under s 310, and that the bankrupt is under no legal obligation to work, 'within reasonable limits the debtor should retain some freedom of choice as to the lifestyle he adopts for himself and his family on the basis of the earnings which he is able to achieve by the deployment of his professional or other skills'. The second stage of the test involves the court establishing how much expenditure of that particular kind can be described as meeting a *reasonable* domestic need, given the particular facts of the case. This is a question of fact which, consistent with para 591 of the Cork Committee Report, necessitates the court considering the particular circumstances of the particular bankrupt and ascertaining to what the bankrupt intends applying his income and *not* what others might do with such monies (*Kilvert v Flackett* [1998] BPIR 721, Peter Scott QC, sitting as a deputy High Court judge). *Rayatt* (at 502H) is further authority for the proposition that, to the extent that an order imposes real hardship, there must be some reasonable proportionality between the hardship imposed and the benefit which will be recouped by creditors. The same point was also made subsequently in *Kilvert* (at 723H).

The term 'reasonable domestic needs' finds no elucidation in the cases. The starting point, it is submitted, lies in the non-exhaustive list of items identified in s 283(2) and other items capable of falling within those terms. Ultimately, however, it is impossible to state further items which might fall within 'reasonable domestic needs' in all cases, since each case can only be determined on its own facts. In *Rayatt*, for example, the deputy judge was satisfied that private school fees were capable of amounting to a reasonable domestic need, given medical evidence demonstrating the possible effect of removing a child from her private schooling. In *Scott v Davis* [2003] BPIR 1009 at [13] Anthony Mann QC, sitting as he then was as a deputy High Court judge, identified that there is no presumption one way or the other in relation to school fees – or, it is submitted, any particular item of expenditure – and that 'it all depends on the facts of the individual case.' In *Malcolm v Official Receiver* [1999] BPIR 97 at 100C–100E Rattee J held that it was unreasonable for a bankrupt to pay £820 on mortgage payments out of £1,100 net monthly income where the property was also occupied by the bankrupt's wife and where unsecured liabilities in the bankruptcy amounted to £144,000-odd, although the judge took the view that the bankrupt should be afforded some time to revise his domestic arrangements. See also the comments of HHJ Jarman QC in *Official Receiver v Wilson* [2013] BPIR 907 (the OR's appeal against the decision at first instance to refuse an application for an IPO was successful and the matter remitted for reconsideration where the bankrupt's joint mortgage was £1,750 per month and there was evidence that an equivalent property could be rented for £700pcm, albeit there was some uncertainty as to how difficult or otherwise iot might be for the undischarged bankrupt to obtain a tenancy).

Accordingly, if it can be shown that no real benefit will enure for creditors on particular expenditure being appropriated to the bankruptcy estate, it is submitted that it will in an appropriate case be at least well arguable that monies expended on tobacco, alcohol, satellite television subscription or, say, gym membership – other than in cases of plain excess – are capable of amounting to reasonable domestic needs, not because a bankrupt can be said to be entitled to what might be called such luxury items as of right, but on the basis that the bankrupt may be able to show that his day-to-day life, which might well mean his day-to-day working life, involves and should involve any such item as a reasonable method of relaxation or spending leisure time. The court should not consider any sort of penal element in imposing an income payments order, since the provision does not feature and is not based on any punitive element or policy.

Section 310(7)

'... **income** ...'—The wording of s 310(7) expressly extends the provision beyond merely 'income' to 'every payment in the nature of income', without the limitations of the term 'salary' as appeared in s 51(2) of the Bankruptcy Act 1914 and previously in s 53(2) of the Bankruptcy Act 1883. In *Dennison v Krasner* [2000] BPIR 410 at 420E Chadwick LJ expressed the view that s 310(7) extends to income other than earnings, 'say, an allowance from a parent or other relative, or income under a discretionary trust.' It is respectfully submitted that the scope of 'payment in the nature of income' probably extends far beyond the examples given by Chadwick LJ in *Dennison* – which examples were provided in passing as illustrations on a point for which numerous other examples might have been given – to any cash or cash equivalent receipt by a bankrupt save where the payment actually forms part of the bankruptcy estate. Obvious examples would include wages, salary, commission, bonus or gratuity payments, whether or not paid regularly, or a gratuity or a payment made as compensation for loss of office, including a statutory redundancy payment, or a payment in lieu of notice.

Even though pension interests are ordinarily excluded from the scope of the bankruptcy estate where the bankruptcy commenced after 1 May 2001 by virtue of the provisions recited in s 310(7), pension income is capable of being claimed under an income payments order, subject to the exclusions in s 310(8) and (9). In *Kilvert Flackett* [1998] BPIR 721, Peter Scott QC, sitting as a deputy High Court judge, held, on the facts of that case, that a lump sum payment under an occupational pension scheme constituted income which was susceptible to an income payments order. The report in *Kilvert*, however, makes clear that the point was not fully argued and was based on a concession by counsel.In *C Brooks III v Rajapakse* [2008] BPIR 283 at [17] Registrar Nicholls reached the same conclusion but observed that the finding in *Kilvert* had been reached notwithstanding the court retaining a discretion on the point which had to be exercised with reference to the general purpose of the legislation which provided that surplus income received between bankruptcy and discharge should be available for the benefit of creditors unless there were reasons to the contrary. In *Raithatha v Williamson* [2012] EWHC 909 (Ch), [2012] 1 WLR 3559, [2012] BPIR 621 Bernard Livesey QC (sitting in the High Court) confirmed that the one off payment of a lump sum under a pension scheme could qualify as income for the purpose of s 310. Further (asnd more controversially) he held that, even where the bankrupt had not made an election prior to his bankruptcy to take up his rights under a pension scheme, the payments he was entitled to receive under that scheme could be taken into account as income under s 310.

The exercise of the court's discretion in making an order—The court need not grant the specific relief sought and might even dismiss an application. In particular, the court will wish to consider the age, health and likely future earning capacity of the debtor as well as the broader issues of income and expenditure.

'… from time to time …'—The words 'from time to time' in s 310(7) equate to 'at any time' and do not envisage or necessitate periodical payments such that the provision may catch a one-off payment: *Supperstone v Lloyds Names Associations' Working Party* [1999] BPIR 832 at 840G–841G (Evans-Lombe J, one-off payment for services rendered susceptible to income payments order); and see *Kilvert v Flackettt* [1998] BPIR 721 at 722C–724D (single lump sum payment under NHS occupational pension within s 310) and *Raithatha v Williamson* [2012] EWHC 909 (Ch), [2012] 1 WLR 3559, [2012] BPIR 621 at [30].

Varying an existing income payments order—Variation of an existing order is provided for in s 310(6A).

The power to increase an income payments order under r 6.193 should only be exercised in the case of a material change of circumstances which can be shown by an applicant to justify such an increase (*Jones v Patel* [1999] BPIR 509 at 515D–515E). A reduction on an application by the bankrupt under the same provision will also, it is submitted, require a material change of circumstances.

Procedure—The procedure on s 310 orders, including variations, appears in rr 6.189–6.193. Rules 6.189(3) and 6.194(3) and (4), it is submitted, do not envisage an original or variation application being anything other than a relatively short, summary assessment by the court other, possibly, than in an exceptionally complex or controversial case.

310A Income payments agreement

(1) In this section 'income payments agreement' means a written agreement between a bankrupt and his trustee or between a bankrupt and the official receiver which provides—

(a) that the bankrupt is to pay to the trustee or the official receiver an amount equal to a specified part or proportion of the bankrupt's income for a specified period, or

(b) that a third person is to pay to the trustee or the official receiver a specified proportion of money due to the bankrupt by way of income for a specified period.

(2) A provision of an income payments agreement of a kind specified in subsection (1)(a) or (b) may be enforced as if it were a provision of an income payments order.

(3) While an income payments agreement is in force the court may, on the application of the bankrupt, his trustee or the official receiver, discharge or vary an attachment of earnings order that is for the time being in force to secure payments by the bankrupt.

(4) The following provisions of section 310 shall apply to an income payments agreement as they apply to an income payments order—

    (a)   subsection (5) (receipts to form part of estate), and

    (b)   subsections (7) to (9) (meaning of income).

(5) An income payments agreement must specify the period during which it is to have effect; and that period—

    (a)   may end after the discharge of the bankrupt, but

    (b)   may not end after the period of three years beginning with the date on which the agreement is made.

(6) An income payments agreement may (subject to subsection (5)(b)) be varied—

    (a)   by written agreement between the parties, or

    (b)   by the court on an application made by the bankrupt, the trustee or the official receiver.

(7) The court—

    (a)   may not vary an income payments agreement so as to include provision of a kind which could not be included in an income payments order, and

    (b)   shall grant an application to vary an income payments agreement if and to the extent that the court thinks variation necessary to avoid the effect mentioned in section 310(2).

Amendments—Inserted by Enterprise Act 2002, s 260.

General note—See the notes under the heading referring to this section in the notes to s 310 above.

    In *Re Hargreaves (Booth v Mond)* [2010] BPIR 1111, the court considered that arrears due under an income payments agreement could rank as debts in the subsequent IVA of the former bankrupt. Since under s 310A the terms of the IPA could be varied, the trustee in bankrupty could compromise the sums due under the IPA under an IVA.

311 Acquisition by trustee of control

(1) The trustee shall take possession of all books, papers and other records which relate to the bankrupt's estate or affairs and which belong to him or are in his possession or under his control (including any which would be privileged from disclosure in any proceedings).

(2) In relation to, and for the purpose of acquiring or retaining possession of, the bankrupt's estate, the trustee is in the same position as if he were a receiver of property appointed by the High Court; and the court may, on his application, enforce such acquisition or retention accordingly.

(3) Where any part of the bankrupt's estate consists of stock or shares in a company, shares in a ship or any other property transferable in the books of a company, office or person, the trustee may exercise the right to transfer the property to the same extent as the bankrupt might have exercised it if he had not become bankrupt.

(4) Where any part of the estate consists of things in action, they are deemed to have been assigned to the trustee; but notice of the deemed

assignment need not be given except in so far as it is necessary, in a case where the deemed assignment is from the bankrupt himself, for protecting the priority of the trustee.

(5) Where any goods comprised in the estate are held by any person by way of pledge, pawn or other security and no notice has been served in respect of those goods by the official receiver under subsection (5) of section 285 (restriction on realising security), the trustee may serve such a notice in respect of the goods; and whether or not a notice has been served under this subsection or that subsection, the trustee may, if he thinks fit, exercise the bankrupt's right of redemption in respect of any such goods.

(6) A notice served by the trustee under subsection (5) has the same effect as a notice served by the official receiver under section 285(5).

General note—The obligation imposed by s 311(1) should be read in conjunction with the corresponding obligation imposed on the bankrupt by s 312. The trustee's obligation is unqualified and ongoing to the extent that the collective term 'books, papers and other records' within the meaning of s 311(1) is capable of relating to property which does not form part of the bankruptcy estate at the commencement of the bankruptcy, whether or not such property is capable of being claimed by the trustee for the estate as after-acquired property under s 307. It is submitted that the trustee's obligation under s 311(1) will continue following discharge of the bankrupt as regards property forming part of the bankruptcy estate. The obligation under s 311(1) would not, however, continue beyond discharge in respect of property acquired by or devolved upon the bankrupt after discharge, since such property cannot be claimed as after-acquired property, by virtue of s 307(2)(c).

Section 311(1)

'**... books, papers and other records ...**'—The term 'records' is defined non-exhaustively in s 436 as including 'computer records and other non-documentary records'. The term would, therefore, extend to e-mail communications and web-based records.

'**... which relate to the bankrupt's estate or affairs ...**'—These words, taken together with 'books, papers and other records', appear to impose a limitation on the scope of the records to which the trustee's obligation relates by way of excluding records which do not relate to the bankrupt's estate or affairs.
There is no requirement that the records to which s 311(1) relates should form part of the bankruptcy estate. Indeed, in *Haig v Jonathan Aitken* [2000] BPIR 462 at 470E–470F Rattee J expressed the view that s 311(1) contemplated and made express provision for records outside of the scope of the estate.
Personal correspondence, even correspondence between a famous bankrupt and parliamentary colleagues or distinguished statesmen which may be worth a considerable sum to the media, does not form part of the bankruptcy estate and cannot therefore be subject to acquisition by a trustee under s 311: see *Haig v Jonathan Aitken* [2000] BPIR 462 at 470A–470D, in which Rattee J also expressed the view that it was 'at least strongly arguable' that a contrary construction of the provision might give rise to a breach of the right of privacy under Art 8 of the European Convention on Human Rights.

'**... which belong to him or are in his possession or under his control ...**'—As identified under the immediately preceding heading, the present provision extends to property which does not form part of the bankruptcy estate. Although the provision would not on its face appear to extend to records which are neither within the bankrupt's possession nor under his control, the court is unlikely to take anything but a dim view of any arrangement under which the bankrupt has sought to divest himself of such 'control'.

Privileged records—Legal professional privilege may be of significant practical relevance to an individual and is also of fundamental importance in the administration of justice: see *R v Derby Magistrates* [1995] 4 All ER 526.

In *Re Konisberg (a Bankrupt)* [1989] 3 All ER 289 at 297A–297J, Peter Gibson J, as he then was, held that a trustee, as the individual in whom a bankrupt's estate vests, constitutes a successor in title to the bankrupt's property and is therefore entitled to assert the privilege of the bankrupt as his predecessor in title: see *Crescent Farm (Sidcup) Sports Ltd v Sterling Officers Ltd* [1971] 3 All ER 1192. As such, the trustee in *Konisberg* was entitled to require communications relating to a transaction – to which the bankrupt had been party prior to the bankruptcy order – to be disclosed to him where such communications would otherwise have been protected by legal professional privilege in relation to an 'ordinary' third party. See also the discussion in *Doffman and Isaacs v Wood v Hellard* [2011] EWHC 4008 (Ch), [2012] BPIR 972 at [30]–[38].

The general rule is that, whilst a bankrupt is not entitled to assert legal professional privilege against a trustee, s 366 does not operate so as to override privilege, with the consequence that a trustee is not entitled to an order for the disclosure of privileged documents against an individual other than the bankrupt: *Re Ouvaroff (a Bankrupt)* [1997] BPIR 712 at 720C (Stanley Burnton QC, sitting as he then was as a deputy High Court judge) and see also *Re Murjani (a Bankrupt)* [1996] 1 BCLC 272 (Lightmann J, a bankrupt's solicitor may not claim privilege on behalf of a bankrupt where such privilege would not have been available to the bankrupt himself). Note also the decision of the Supreme Court in *R (on the application of Prudential plc) v Special Commissioner of Income Tax* [2013] UKSC 1 on limitations to the scope of legal advice privilege (it does not apply to person other than a member of the legal profession and therefore does not cover legal advice given by accountants in relation to a tax avoidance scheme).

A trustee is entitled to waive privilege relating to matters which concern the estate and affairs of the bankrupt: *Re Dennis Michael Cooke* [1999] BPIR 881 (Stanley Burnton QC). In *Re Omar (a Bankrupt)* [1999] BPIR 1001 Jacob J, as he then was, considered an application for directions by a trustee as to whether he should disclose documents obtained by him under s 311(1) to the administrators of the estate of the bankrupt's deceased husband who were to take part in a proposed examination of the bankrupt by the trustee and who intended to use the documents in an action against the bankrupt in which there was strong evidence that the bankrupt fraudulently concealed monies to which the bankruptcy estate would be entitled. In authorising disclosure, subject to undertakings by administrators to use the documents only for the purposes just mentioned, Jacob J relied in particular (at 1007H) on the fact in that case of fraud on the part of the bankrupt in earlier litigation and the use by the bankrupt of her previous lawyers for the advancement of what amounted to a fraudulent defence. Given that legal professional privilege is capable of being overridden by other factors, in particular fraud, consideration should be given to an application for directions where, as in *Re Omar*, the bankrupt objects to the disclosure on the grounds of privilege.

Section 311(2)

Trustee like receiver—The most obvious significance of the trustee being treated as if he were a receiver of property appointed by the High Court is that the trustee acquires the protection of the law of contempt. Any proceedings for enforcement brought under s 311(2), therefore, may be accompanied with an application against the respondent for contempt of court.

'... and the court may, on his application, enforce such acquisition or retention accordingly'—Only the trustee may make an application for enforcement under this provision. An order for enforcement under s 311(2) should be distinguished from an order for enforcement under s 367 for s 366 purposes in that the present provision relates to the trustee taking possession 'of all books, papers and other records which relate to the bankrupt's estate or affairs' (which need not form part of the bankruptcy estate), whereas s 367 provides inter alia for the making of an order for delivery up of property comprised in the bankrupt's estate.

Section 311(3)

Exercise by the trustee of rights of transfer of transferable property—Although a trustee obtains ownership of all property comprised in the bankruptcy estate automatically under s 306(1), including intangible property incapable of physical delivery, the present provision operates so as to override any external procedural mechanism which might otherwise operate to preclude the trustee from transferring property to a third party. The trustee's standing to transfer, however, which would be enforceable most obviously by way of an application for directions under s 303(2), can be no better than the position in which the bankrupt would otherwise have been. Thus, a trustee would be entitled to transfer shares in a limited company, but only subject to the articles of association.

Although a company may refuse to register a trustee as a member under the terms of its articles, the decision in *Morgan v Gray* [1953] Ch 83 is authority for the proposition that, whilst a bankrupt may exercise voting rights attached to the shares and give proxies, he may be required by the trustee to exercise the voting rights as directed. Although it was held in *Re HL Belton Engineering Co* [1956] Ch 577 that a trustee who is not registered as a member may not petition for relief under what is now s 994 of the Companies Act 2006, there is nothing which prevents the bankrupt presenting a petition on behalf of the trustee: *Re K/9 Meter Supplies (Guildford) Ltd* [1966] 1 WLR 112.

Section 311(4)

Things in action—The first part of this provision repeats in substance the effect of s 306(2). A statutory deemed assignment does not contravene any contractual provision prohibiting assignment, such as a term commonly being included within private pension policies as a condition of tax approval: *Re Landau (a Bankrupt)* [1998] Ch 223 (Ferris J).

The balance of the provision provides a general rule dispensing with the need for notice of the deemed assignment. Consequently, a life insurer which is ignorant of the bankruptcy of the beneficiary of a life policy, and which makes payment of the policy proceeds to the bankrupt, remains liable to the bankrupt's trustee for an equivalent sum in the absence of the bankrupt being in a position to give a good receipt for the proceeds: *Rooney v Cardona* [1999] 1 WLR 1388, CA.

The exception to the general rule on deemed assignment arises where notice is necessary for protecting the priority of the trustee, but only where the deemed assignment is from the bankrupt to the trustee; for examples of circumstances warranting protection of a trustee see *Weddell v JEA Pearce & Major* [1988] Ch 26 at 31–32 on the substantively identical provision under s 48(5) of the Bankruptcy Act 1914.

Section 311(5) and (6)

Goods held by pledge etc—Prior to bankruptcy an individual in worsening financial circumstances may have chosen to pawn, pledge or use his goods as security for his debts. The present provision operates for the benefit of the bankruptcy estate to the extent that the true value of the goods is significantly in excess of the amount for which those goods were pawned etc, as is often the case in practice. Subject to the service of a notice – for which there is no prescribed form – the trustee may exercise the bankrupt's right of redemption, although it would follow that the trustee can obtain no better right than that to which the bankrupt would otherwise have been entitled.

Where a notice has been given to any person under s 285(5), that person is not entitled, without the leave of the court, to realise his security unless he has given the trustee of the bankrupt's estate a reasonable opportunity of inspecting the goods and of exercising the bankrupt's right of redemption.

312 Obligation to surrender control to trustee

(1) The bankrupt shall deliver up to the trustee possession of any property, books, papers or other records of which he has possession or control and of which the trustee is required to take possession.

This is without prejudice to the general duties of the bankrupt under section 333 in this Chapter.

(2) If any of the following is in possession of any property, books, papers or other records of which the trustee is required to take possession, namely—

(a)   the official receiver,

(b)   a person who has ceased to be trustee of the bankrupt's estate, or

(c)   a person who has been the supervisor of a voluntary arrangement approved in relation to the bankrupt under Part VIII,

the official receiver or, as the case may be, that person shall deliver up possession of the property, books, papers or records to the trustee.

(3) Any banker or agent of the bankrupt or any other person who holds any property to the account of, or for, the bankrupt shall pay or deliver to the trustee all property in his possession or under his control which forms part of the bankrupt's estate and which he is not by law entitled to retain as against the bankrupt or trustee.

(4) If any person without reasonable excuse fails to comply with any obligation imposed by this section, he is guilty of a contempt of court and liable to be punished accordingly (in addition to any other punishment to which he may be subject).

General note—This provision should be read alongside s 333 and corresponds with but exceeds the scope of s 311, in that the present provision refers to the trustee taking possession of 'any property' in addition to books, papers and other records. The obligation in s 312(1) mirrors the duty of a bankrupt in relation to the official receiver in s 291(1). The burden on the debtor to deliver up is a heavy one: *Smedley v Brittain* [2008] BPIR 219 at [45] (Registrar Nicholls).

Related provisions—See also r 6.125 (handover of estate by official receiver to trustee) and r 6.146 (trustee's duties on vacating office).

313 Charge on bankrupt's home

(1) Where any property consisting of an interest in a dwelling house which is occupied by the bankrupt or by his spouse or former spouse or by his civil partner or former civil partner is comprised in the bankrupt's estate and the trustee is, for any reason, unable for the time being to realise that property, the trustee may apply to the court for an order imposing a charge on the property for the benefit of the bankrupt's estate.

(2) If on an application under this section the court imposes a charge on any property, the benefit of that charge shall be comprised in the bankrupt's estate and is enforceable, up to the charged value from time to time, for the payment of any amount which is payable otherwise than to the bankrupt out of the estate and of interest on that amount at the prescribed rate.

(2A) In subsection (2) the charged value means—

(a)   the amount specified in the charging order as the value of the bankrupt's interest in the property at the date of the order, plus

(b)   interest on that amount from the date of the charging order at the prescribed rate.

(2B) In determining the value of an interest for the purposes of this section the court shall disregard any matter which it is required to disregard by the rules.

(3) An order under this section made in respect of property vested in the trustee shall provide, in accordance with the rules, for the property to cease to be comprised in the bankrupt's estate and, subject to the charge (and any prior charge), to vest in the bankrupt.

(4) Subsection (1), (2), (4), (5) and (6) of section 3 of the Charging Orders Act 1979 (supplemental provisions with respect to charging orders) have effect in relation to orders under this section as in relation to charging orders under that Act.

(5) But an order under section 3(5) of that Act may not vary a charged value.

Amendments— Enterprise Act 2002, s 261(2)(a)–(c); Civil Partnership Act 2004, s 261(1), Sch 27, para 114; Tribunals, Courts and Enforcement Act 2007, s 93(5).

General note—The circumstances in which a trustee may make an application under this provision are precisely the same as those to which s 283A applies, on which see the commentary thereto. Section 313 will be of heightened relevance to a trustee, given the introduction of s 283A which requires action on the part of the trustee within a variable three year period, failing which the bankrupt's interest in a dwelling-house reverts to the bankrupt. The provision is not concerned with the extent of the bankrupt's interest in a dwelling-house but, rather, the realisation of that interest. Specifically, s 313(2) allows for the imposition by the court of a charge – a charging order by virtue of s 313(4) – securing the interest to which the bankrupt's estate is entitled. This will be of assistance to the trustee where, as can commonly arise in practice, there are no assets in the estate to fund litigation where the possession and sale of the property is disputed or, alternatively, where an order for possession and sale is likely to be postponed on the establishment of exceptional circumstances under either s 335A(3) or s 336(5).

The 'charged value' in s 313(2A), (2B) and (5)—These subsections were inserted with effect from 1 April 2004 by s 260 of the Enterprise Act 2002 and represent a marked shift from the previous position in favour of the bankrupt and his family. If the court grants a charge under s 313(2), then it is obliged to value the bankrupt's interest at that date under s 313(2B), which thereafter constitutes the charged value when taken together with interest on that amount from that date. Interest, for those purposes, will be the applicable rate under s 17 of the Judgments Act 1838, which at present is 8% per annum. The charged value is incapable of variation under s 3(5) of the Charging Orders Act 1979. Section 313(3) is necessary to reflect the vesting of the charged interest in the bankrupt, without which the charge would secure nothing, since the relevant interest would remain vested in the bankrupt's estate. The 'charged value', therefore, is capped as at the date of the charging order and can increase only at the applicable level of interest. In a rising property market this will be advantageous to the bankrupt and his family, although in a falling market a trustee will retain the value of his security as fixed by the court together with ongoing interest.

Limitation—Section 20(1) of the Limitation Act 1980 does not apply to the enforcement of a charge under s 313(2) with the consequence that enforcement will not be statute-barred 12 years after the making of such an order: *Doodes v Gotham* [2006] EWCA Civ 1080, [2006] BPIR 1178 reversing Lindsay J at [2006] BPIR 36 below. The right to receive the amounts provided for in s 313 does not accrue for the purposes of the 1980 Act until the making of an order for sale of the property by the court.

Procedure—See rr 6.237D and 6.237E.

313A Low value home: application for sale, possession or charge

(1) This section applies where—

    (a)   property comprised in the bankrupt's estate consists of an interest in a dwelling-house which at the date of the bankruptcy was the sole or principal residence of—

(i)   the bankrupt,

(ii)   the bankrupt's spouse or civil partner, or

(iii)   a former spouse or former civil partner of the bankrupt, and

(b)   the trustee applies for an order for the sale of the property, for an order for possession of the property or for an order under section 313 in respect of the property.

(2) The court shall dismiss the application if the value of the interest is below the amount prescribed for the purposes of this subsection.

(3) In determining the value of an interest for the purposes of this section the court shall disregard any matter which it is required to disregard by the order which prescribes the amount for the purposes of subsection (2).

Amendments—Inserted by the Enterprise Act 2002, s 261(3); Civil Partnership Act 2004, s 261(1), Sch 27, para 115.

General note—This provision can only apply on any one of the applications in s 313A(1)(b) (applications for possession and sale usually being combined) where the bankrupt's estate consists of an interest in a dwelling-house, as defined in s 385(1), within s 313A(1)(a). The concept of 'sole or principal residence' in relation to a dwelling-house is discussed in the notes to s 283A.

The purpose of the provision is in avoiding the hardship associated with the sale of a dwelling-house, even one which is not the sole or principal residence of the bankrupt himself, where the value of net realisations is modest and therefore unlikely to make any real difference to the position of unsecured creditors.

Section 313A(2)

Scope of provision—The court has no discretion and must dismiss an application brought by a trustee if the value of the interest to which the application relates is below £1,000, as currently prescribed by art 2 of the Insolvency Proceedings (Monetary Limits) (Amendment) Order 2004 (SI 2004/547). In determining the value of an interest, art 3 of the 2004 Order directs, for the purposes of s 313A(3), that the court must disregard the value of the property equal to the value of any loan secured by mortgage or other charge against the property, the value of any third party interest and the value of reasonable costs of sale.

Consequences of dismissal of trustee's application—An application within s 313A(1)(b) will fall within s 283A(3)(b)–(d), with the consequence that, if dismissed, the interest will cease to be comprised in the bankrupt's estate and will vest automatically in the bankrupt, subject to contrary order of the court, by virtue of s 283A(4).

Practical considerations—Section 313A does nothing to prevent a negotiated sale of any interest vested in the bankrupt's estate. Such a course may be satisfactory to all parties where there is a genuine dispute as to valuation of the interest or where the bankrupt's estate includes two or more properties potentially within the scope of the provision.

314 Powers of trustee

(1) The trustee may—

(a)   with the permission of the creditors' committee or the court, exercise any of the powers specified in Part I of Schedule 5 to this Act, and

(b)   without that permission, exercise any of the general powers specified in Part II of that Schedule.

(2) With the permission of the creditors' committee or the court, the trustee may appoint the bankrupt—

(a)   to superintend the management of his estate or any part of it,

(b)   to carry on his business (if any) for the benefit of his creditors, or

(c)   in any other respect to assist in administering the estate in such manner and on such terms as the trustee may direct.

(3) A permission given for the purposes of subsection (1)(a) or (2) shall not be a general permission but shall relate to a particular proposed exercise of the power in question; and a person dealing with the trustee in good faith and for value is not to be concerned to enquire whether any permission required in either case has been given.

(4) Where the trustee has done anything without the permission required by subsection (1)(a) or (2), the court or the creditors' committee may, for the purpose of enabling him to meet his expenses out of the bankrupt's estate, ratify what the trustee has done.

But the committee shall not do so unless it is satisfied that the trustee has acted in a case of urgency and has sought its ratification without undue delay.

(5) Part III of Schedule 5 to this Act has effect with respect to the things which the trustee is able to do for the purposes of, or in connection with, the exercise of any of his powers under any of this Group of Parts.

(6) Where the trustee (not being the official receiver) in exercise of the powers conferred on him by any provision in this Group of Parts—

(a)   disposes of any property comprised in the bankrupt's estate to an associate of the bankrupt, or

(b)   employs a solicitor,

he shall, if there is for the time being a creditors' committee, give notice to the committee of that exercise of his powers.

(7) Without prejudice to the generality of subsection (5) and Part III of Schedule 5, the trustee may, if he thinks fit, at any time summon a general meeting of the bankrupt's creditors.

Subject to the preceding provisions in this Group of Parts, he shall summon such a meeting if he is requested to do so by a creditor of the bankrupt and the request is made with the concurrence of not less than one-tenth, in value, of the bankrupt's creditors (including the creditor making the request).

(8) Nothing in this Act is to be construed as restricting the capacity of the trustee to exercise any of his powers outside England and Wales.

General note—The powers of a trustee are set out in Sch 5. Only those powers listed in Part II of the Schedule are exercisable without sanction: s 314(1)(b). By s 314(1)(a) a power within Part I may only be exercised with the permission of the creditors' committee or, if no committee exists or permission is refused by it, the court. Although the powers in Part III of the Schedule do not require sanction, those ancillary powers may only be exercised for the purposes of, or in connection with, the exercise of any of the powers of the trustee under Parts VIII to XI: s 314(5) and Sch 5, para 14.

The specific powers in s 314(6) and (7) may be exercised without sanction, although s 314(6) requires notice to be given to any creditors' committee. On the other hand, the exercise of the specific powers in s 314(2) do require the permission of any creditors' committee or the court.

The nature of permission—Any permission given for the purposes of s 314(1)(a) or (2) must be specific and, by s 314(3), cannot be given in general terms. Section 314(4) allows permission to be given retrospectively by a creditors' committee, but only where the committee is satisfied that the trustee has acted in a case of urgency and has sought sanction without undue delay. The obtaining of permission, where required, is of practical significance, because without permission the trustee has no authority to act and, equally, is not properly entitled to meet the cost of his unauthorised acts as an expense of the bankruptcy estate. A third party acting in good faith and for value, but only such a third party, is protected in dealing with a trustee as to the authority of the trustee so to act by the latter part of s 314(3): *Weddell v JA Pearce & Major* [1988] Ch 26 (bankrupt acting in good faith and without notice entitled to sue on cause of action after taking assignment of cause of action from trustee acting without permission), following *Re Branson* [1914] 2 KB 701.

Employment of solicitors—Section 56(3) of the Bankruptcy Act 1914 required the obtaining of permission by a trustee before employing a solicitor (or other agent), although Scott J held in *Re a Debtor (26A of 1975)* [1985] 1 WLR 6 that the court had jurisdiction to give permission retrospectively. Section 314(6)(b) specifically sanctions the employment of solicitors without any requirement for permission, but subject to the giving of notice to any creditors' committee.

Although it is understood to be the official receiver's practice not to employ the same solicitors as a petitioning creditor, in *Re Schuppan (a Bankrupt) (No 1)* [1996] 2 All ER 664 at 668 Robert Walker J, as he then was, expressed the view that that practice was a 'counsel of perfection which need not necessarily be followed by all insolvency practitioners in all circumstances.' Indeed, as his Lordship went on, 'In a case where the real difficulties that are foreseen are in connection with the identification, tracing and recovery of assets for the bankrupt's estate, the retainer of solicitors who already have a good grasp of these difficulties can be of great advantage to all creditors, not just the petitioning creditor.' In particular, if the petitioning creditor is the largest creditor, and no difficulties are foreseen in quantifying the provable debts of the petitioning creditor or other creditors, the risk of a conflict of interest would appear to be, in the words of Hoffmann J, as he then was, in *Re Maxwell Communication Corp plc* [1992] BCLC 465 at 468, 'a mere distant possibility.' In *Re Baron Investments (Holdings) Ltd* [2000] 1 BCLC 272 (a liquidation case) Pumfrey J expressed the view that, whilst all cases must turn on their own facts, the retention of a petitioning creditors' solicitors by an office-holder contemporaneous with the employment of other solicitors in relation to particular matters in which a conflict was perceived was only justifiable where there is a reasonable apprehension of potential conflict and not a mere theoretical possibility. In dealing with potential conflicts it is necessary to adopt a pragmatic approach, although an actual conflict cannot be ignored and must be addressed with appropriate steps.

The judgment of Lord Millett in *Prince Jefri Bolkiah v KPMG (a firm)* [1999] 2 AC 222 at 234 includes a useful summary of the duties of solicitors and other fiduciaries.

Exercise of trustee's powers outside of the jurisdiction—Section 314(8) clearly allows for the exercise of any of the trustee's powers outside England and Wales. The court must, however, consider whether, on the facts of any particular case, any application before it is concerned with English bankruptcy law or whether, in reality, the action is in substance a matter of foreign law. That issue is one determined by reference to the Civil Jurisdiction and Judgments Act 1982, which gives effect to the Convention on Jurisdiction and the Enforcement of Judgments in Civil and Commercial Matters 1968, commonly known as the Brussels Convention.

In *Re Hayward (Deceased)* [1997] Ch 45 Rattee J struck out a trustee's application, which had sought declaratory and consequential relief, including the rectification of a property register located in the foreign jurisdiction, in relation to the bankrupt's alleged beneficial half-share in a Spanish property. In distinguishing the decision of the European Court of Justice in *Webb v Webb* [1994] QB 696, his Lordship held that Art 16 of the Brussels Convention required the proceedings to proceed in the Spanish courts, since the trustee was seeking to enforce a right in rem in the land and to rectify the Spanish property register. A contrary decision on different facts was reached in *Ashurst v Pollard* [2001] BPIR 131, which followed the European court's decision in *Webb* and which required a bankrupt and his wife to transfer title in a Portuguese property to the trustee so as to allow for a sale with vacant possession, notwithstanding the fact that art 16 of the Brussels Convention dictated that the English courts had no jurisdiction to authorise a sale by the trustee.

Disclaimer of onerous property

315 Disclaimer (general power)

(1) Subject as follows, the trustee may, by the giving of the prescribed notice, disclaim any onerous property and may do so notwithstanding that he has taken possession of it, endeavoured to sell it or otherwise exercised rights of ownership in relation to it.

(2) The following is onerous property for the purposes of this section, that is to say—

    (a)   any unprofitable contract, and

    (b)   any other property comprised in the bankrupt's estate which is unsaleable or not readily saleable, or is such that it may give rise to a liability to pay money or perform any other onerous act.

(3) A disclaimer under this section—

    (a)   operates so as to determine, as from the date of the disclaimer, the rights, interests and liabilities of the bankrupt and his estate in or in respect of the property disclaimed, and

    (b)   discharges the trustee from all personal liability in respect of that property as from the commencement of his trusteeship,

but does not, except so far as is necessary for the purpose of releasing the bankrupt, the bankrupt's estate and the trustee from any liability, affect the rights or liabilities of any other person.

(4) A notice of disclaimer shall not be given under this section in respect of any property that has been claimed for the estate under section 307 (after-acquired property) or 308 (personal property of bankrupt exceeding reasonable replacement value) or 308A, except with the leave of the court.

(5) Any person sustaining loss or damage in consequence of the operation of a disclaimer under this section is deemed to be a creditor of the bankrupt to the extent of the loss or damage and accordingly may prove for the loss or damage as a bankruptcy debt.

Amendments—Housing Act 1988, s 117(4).

General note—The power of disclaimer can be of great practical assistance to a trustee who, unlike any ordinary person, has the ability under these provisions to disown property with the characteristics prescribed by s 315(2). The utility of the power of disclaimer lies in the trustee's ability to jettison property which might otherwise pose an unavoidable financial drain on the bankrupt's estate or which might otherwise unduly protract the administration of the bankruptcy, ultimately at the expense of creditors.

The power to disclaim is unaffected by the trustee having dealt with the relevant property: s 315(1). Further, no time limit applies to the power of disclaimer, save where the trustee is put to a decision on service of a notice under s 316.

Corresponding provisions on disclaimer in winding up appear in ss 178–182. Reference may also be made to the commentary on those provisions.

Section 315(2)

Onerous property—The term 'property' is defined in non-exhaustive terms in s 436.

In *Re Celtic Extraction Ltd (in liquidation)* [2001] Ch 475 the Court of Appeal (Morritt and Roch LJJ and Rattee J) upheld the decision of Neuberger J, as he then was, albeit on different grounds, to the effect that a waste management licence issued under the terms of the Environmental Protection Act 1990 constituted 'property', with the consequence that a liquidator was entitled to exercise his power of disclaimer in relation to it.

The question of whether property is 'onerous' is a question of fact and one for the trustee in the discharge of his functions under s 305(2). A trustee's decision to disclaim particular property might be challenged by way of a claim under s 304(1). An eligible applicant might also consider injunctive relief so as to prevent the exercise of the power of disclaimer, which would be coupled, most obviously, with a claim under s 303(1), in an appropriate case. The court will not, however, interfere with an office-holder's decision to disclaim unless there is a challenge to the bona fides of the office-holder or a suggestion that his decision to disclaim can be categorised as perverse: *Re Hans Place Ltd* [1992] BCC 737 at 749D (Edward Evans-Lombe QC, sitting as he then was as a deputy High Court judge).

Subject to particular circumstances, examples of onerous property might include a cause of action (on which see *Khan-Ghauri v Dunbar Bank plc* [2001] BPIR 618, *Young v Hamilton* [2010] BPIR 1468 and *Young v Official Receiver* [2010] BPIR 1477), a property giving rise to ongoing environmental or other liabilities, property for which there is no market or in respect of which the costs of marketing and sale are disproportionate to the likely proceeds of sale or an unduly onerous contract.

Section 315(3)

Effect of disclaimer—Section 315(3) provides for the determination of the rights, interests and liabilities of the bankrupt and his estate in relation to the property disclosed and, secondly, the discharge of the trustee's personal liability in respect of that property. The determination of rights etc is 'as from the date of the disclaimer' and cannot, therefore, be retrospective, although a trustee is discharged from all personal liability in respect of that property as from the date of the bankruptcy order. Furthermore, the decision of Neuberger J, as he then was, in *Capital Prime Properties plc v Worthgate Ltd (in liquidation)* [2000] 1 BCLC 647 is authority for the proposition that the exercise of the power of disclaimer cannot operate so as to undo contractual rights and benefits which had vested prior to that date. The following extract from the judgment, at 655B–655C, provides a useful analysis:

'In the context of a commercial contract, eg where A agrees to sell 1,000 tonnes of aluminium a month to B for two years, it seems to me that, if A went into liquidation after a year, the liquidator would be able to disclaim the contract if A did not have the aluminium and would have had to have purchased it in the market at a price considerably in excess of £1,000 a tonne. But it cannot be sensibly suggested that the effect of the disclaimer would be to undo the rights which had been acquired by B in relation to the aluminium which had already been supplied to B.'

It is not possible for a trustee to disclaim onerous liabilities for rent under a lease whilst at the same time retaining the property itself: *MEPC Ltd v Scottish Amicable* [1996] BPIR 447 at 450E–450G (Dillon LJ, Leggatt LJ agreeing).

Property disclaimed by a trustee devolves on the Crown Estate.

The effect of disclaimer on third parties—Disclaimer affects third parties insofar as the rights, interests and liabilities of the bankrupt and his estate are determined under s 315(3) in relation to the property disclaimed, but no further. The operation of that rule is illustrated by the House of Lords' decision in *Hindcastle Ltd v Barbara Attenborough Associates* [1997] AC 70, which held that a disclaimer does not operate so as to release a guarantor or surety for future rent and obligations under a lease from such liability where the guarantor's remedy on disclaimer is to prove in the bankruptcy in respect of the indemnity to which the guarantor is entitled by operation of law.

Section 315(4)

Leave to disclaim under—The court will require a clear explanation as to the circumstances giving rise to the trustee's decision to disclaim property caught by s 315(4) where he has previously taken steps to claim that property for the benefit of the bankrupt's estate. Even if satisfied that disclaimer is appropriate, it is open to the court to take the view that the costs incurred by the trustee either in claiming and/or disclaiming the property should not rank as an expense of the bankruptcy if a trustee can be shown to have acted unreasonably in discharging his function.

Financial markets etc—Section 315 has no application to market contracts and the like: see s 164(1) of the Companies Act 1989.

Section 315(5)

Assessment of loss or damage—This provision should be read in conjunction with s 320(5).

Procedure—See rr 6.178–6.186.

316 Notice requiring trustee's decision

(1) Notice of disclaimer shall not be given under section 315 in respect of any property if—

    (a)   a person interested in the property has applied in writing to the trustee or one of his predecessors as trustee requiring the trustee or that predecessor to decide whether he will disclaim or not, and

    (b)   the period of 28 days beginning with the day on which that application was made has expired without a notice of disclaimer having been given under section 315 in respect of that property.

(2) The trustee is deemed to have adopted any contract which by virtue of this section he is not entitled to disclaim.

General note—Although the trustee's power to disclaim under s 315 is not subject to any time limit, 'a person interested in' any particular property may impose a 28-day period in which the trustee must elect whether or not to disclaim that property. The 28-day period in s 316(1)(b) begins with the day on which the trustee receives that person's notice in writing, which must be in Form 6.62 and follow the procedure in r 6.183(1) and (2). The 28-day period is extendable by an application to the court by the trustee under r 6.183(3) where the trustee requires leave to disclaim (on which see ss 315(4) and ss 317–321). The 28-day period is not otherwise extendable, with the consequence that the trustee will be fixed with being unable to disclaim if he does not act by disclaiming within that period following service of a notice on him.

A trustee may use r 6.184, for which Form 6.63 is prescribed, to require a person to declare within 14 days whether he claims any interest in property which the trustee has the right to disclaim.

Procedure—See the notes to s 315 and see rr 6.178–6.186.

317 Disclaimer of leaseholds

(1) The disclaimer of any property of a leasehold nature does not take effect unless a copy of the disclaimer has been served (so far as the trustee is aware of their addresses) on every person claiming under the bankrupt as underlessee or mortgagee and either—

    (a)   no application under section 320 below is made with respect to the property before the end of the period of 14 days beginning with the day on which the last notice served under this subsection was served, or

    (b)   where such an application has been made, the court directs that the disclaimer is to take effect.

(2) Where the court gives a direction under subsection (1)(b) it may also, instead of or in addition to any order it makes under section 320, make such orders with respect to fixtures, tenant's improvements and other matters arising out of the lease as it thinks fit.

General note—This provision applies only to leasehold property which is onerous within the meaning of s 315(2) and is only triggered where the disclaimer is communicated to persons interested in compliance with r 6.179(1), (2) and (4) and either s 317(1)(a) or (b) applies. Curiously, there is no requirement for a copy of the disclaimer to be served on the lessor or the landlord, despite the fact that either person would have standing to apply for a vesting order under s 320.

For further commentary see the notes to the analogous s 179 applicable in winding up.

Procedure—See the notes to s 315 and see rr 6.178–6.186.

318 Disclaimer of dwelling house

Without prejudice to section 317, the disclaimer of any property in a dwelling house does not take effect unless a copy of the disclaimer has been served (so far as the trustee is aware of their addresses) on every person in occupation of or claiming a right to occupy the dwelling house and either—

    (a)   no application under section 320 is made with respect to the property before the end of the period of 14 days beginning with the day on which the last notice served under this section was served, or

    (b)   where such an application has been made, the court directs that the disclaimer is to take effect.

General note—This provision applies where a dwelling-house constitutes onerous property within the meaning of s 315(2), and is very similar in substance to s 317. The term 'dwelling-house' is defined in s 385. Notably, it is a specific requirement of s 318 that a copy of the disclaimer is served not only on every person in occupation of a dwelling-house but also on every person *claiming* a right to occupy.

Procedure—See the notes to s 315 and see rr 6.178–6.186.

319 Disclaimer of land subject to rentcharge

(1) The following applies where, in consequence of the disclaimer under section 315 of any land subject to a rentcharge, that land vests by operation of law in the Crown or any other person (referred to in the next subsection as 'the proprietor').

(2) The proprietor, and the successors in title of the proprietor, are not subject to any personal liability in respect of any sums becoming due under the rentcharge, except sums becoming due after the proprietor, or some person claiming under or through the proprietor, has taken possession or control of the land or has entered into occupation of it.

General note—This provision will most commonly be relevant on the disclaimer of freehold land where, as a consequence, the freehold vests in the Crown or some other person who, but for s 319(2), would be personally liable to pay any rent charge on the land. The term 'rent charge' is defined in s 205(1)(xxiii) of the Law of Property Act 1925. The leading case under the old law is the House of Lords' decision in *Attorney-General v Parsons* [1956] AC 421.

Procedure—See the notes to s 315 and see rr 6.178–6.186, and in particular r 6.180.

320 Court order vesting disclaimed property

(1) This section and the next apply where the trustee has disclaimed property under section 315.

(2) An application may be made to the court under this section by—

(a) any person who claims an interest in the disclaimed property,

(b) any person who is under any liability in respect of the disclaimed property, not being a liability discharged by the disclaimer, or

(c) where the disclaimed property is property in a dwelling-house, any person who at the time when the bankruptcy petition was presented was in occupation of or entitled to occupy the dwelling house.

(3) Subject as follows in this section and the next, the court may, on an application under this section, make an order on such terms as it thinks fit for the vesting of the disclaimed property in, or for its delivery to—

(a) a person entitled to it or a trustee for such a person,

(b) a person subject to such a liability as is mentioned in subsection (2)(b) or a trustee for such a person, or

(c) where the disclaimed property is property in a dwelling-house, any person who at the time when the bankruptcy petition was presented was in occupation of or entitled to occupy the dwelling house.

(4) The court shall not make an order by virtue of subsection (3)(b) except where it appears to the court that it would be just to do so for the purpose of compensating the person subject to the liability in respect of the disclaimer.

(5) The effect of any order under this section shall be taken into account in assessing for the purposes of section 315(5) the extent of any loss or damage sustained by any person in consequence of the disclaimer.

(6) An order under this section vesting property in any person need not be completed by any conveyance, assignment or transfer.

General note—Following disclaimer under s 315, any of those persons listed in s 320(2) may apply for what is commonly termed a 'vesting order' under s 320(3). Section 320(3)(b) must be read in the light of s 320(4).

Section 320(2)(a)

'Any person who claims an interest ...'—A person with a statutory charge over disclaimed property constitutes a person 'who claims an interest' in the disclaimed property: *London Borough of Hackney v Crown Estates Commissioners* [1996] BPIR 428 (Knox J). See also *Fenland DC v Shappard* [2011] EWHC 2829 (Ch), [2012] BPIR 289 (a vesting order in favour of a mortgagee will not operate to merge the freehold interest with the interest under the charge where that result was not intended). By s 320(2)(c) a person has standing to make application for a vesting order on the sole ground of being in occupation or entitled to occupy a dwelling-house at the time of the bankruptcy petition. This provision is important, since the mere fact of occupation, in the context of a person who had agreed to take an assignment subject to the consent of the landlord, does not give rise to a proprietary interest within s 181(2)(a), the liquidation equivalent of s 320(2)(a): *Lloyds Bank SF Nominees v Aladdin Ltd* [1996] 1 BCLC 720 (Leggatt and Peter Gibson LJJ).

In *Hunt and Another v Conwy County Borough Council* [2013] EWHC 1154 (Ch), [2013] BPIR 790 Sir William Blackburne (sitting in the High Court) confirmed that it was open to the court to make a vesting order in respect of part only of the disclaimed property. He also confirmed that, to qualify under s 320(2)(c), it was not necessary that the whole of the disclaimed property had to comprise a dwellinghouse. He considered that the discretion to make a vesting order was at large in the sense that there was no statutory guidance but in the absence of some competing applicant and in the absence of some good reason to the contrary the court ought ordinarily to exercise its discretion in favour of a qualifying applicant at least in relation to a freehold

'Disclaimed property'—According to Sir William Blackburne in *Hunt v Conwy CBC* [2013] EWHC 1154 (Ch), [2013] BPIR 790 at [48] a vesting of part of the property can be valid. The judge also said that in relation to s 320(2)(c) he did not consider that to qualify under that provision the whole of the disclaimed property must comprise a dwelling-house (at [48]).

Procedure—See the notes to s 315 and rr 6.178–6.186, in particular r 6.186 which, in r 6.186(2), imposes a 3-month time limit for the making of an application for a vesting order.

321 Order under s 320 in respect of leaseholds

(1) The court shall not make an order under section 320 vesting property of a leasehold nature in any person, except on terms making that person—

    (a)   subject to the same liabilities and obligations as the bankrupt was subject to under the lease on the day the bankruptcy petition was presented, or

    (b)   if the court thinks fit, subject to the same liabilities and obligations as that person would be subject to if the lease had been assigned to him on that day.

(2) For the purposes of an order under section 320 relating to only part of any property comprised in a lease, the requirements of subsection (1) apply as if the lease comprised only the property to which the order relates.

(3) Where subsection (1) applies and no person is willing to accept an order under section 320 on the terms required by that subsection, the court may (by order under section 320) vest the estate or interest of the bankrupt in the property in any person who is liable (whether personally or in a representative capacity and whether alone or jointly with the bankrupt) to perform the lessee's covenants in the lease.

The court may by virtue of this subsection vest that estate and interest in such a person freed and discharged from all estates, incumbrances and interests created by the bankrupt.

(4) Where subsection (1) applies and a person declines to accept any order under section 320, that person shall be excluded from all interest in the property.

General note—See the notes to s 320. Where the trustee of an under-lessor disclaims the head-lease, the under-lease continues to exist and remains subject to the rights of the lessor to distrain for rent or to re-enter for breach of covenant: *Re Town Investment Ltd's Under-lease* [1954] Ch 301.

Distribution of bankrupt's estate

322 Proof of debts

(1) Subject to this section and the next, the proof of any bankruptcy debt by a secured or unsecured creditor of the bankrupt and the admission or rejection of any proof shall take place in accordance with the rules.

(2) Where a bankruptcy debt bears interest, that interest is provable as part of the debt except in so far as it is payable in respect of any period after the commencement of the bankruptcy.

(3) The trustee shall estimate the value of any bankruptcy debt which, by reason of its being subject to any contingency or contingencies or for any other reason, does not bear a certain value.

(4) Where the value of a bankruptcy debt is estimated by the trustee under subsection (3) or, by virtue of section 303 in Chapter III, by the court, the amount provable in the bankruptcy in respect of the debt is the amount of the estimate.

General note—A creditor 'proves' for his debt by asserting his claim by way of a document known as a 'proof'. The forms and procedure for proving appear in rr 6.96–6.114.

A creditor bears the costs of proving its own debt: r 6.100(1).

Other than non-provable and postponed debts (see below), r 12.3(1) provides that all claims by creditors are provable as debts against a bankrupt, whether they are present or future, certain or contingent, ascertained or sounding only in damages.

Section 322(1)

'... **bankruptcy debt** ...'—This term is defined very broadly in s 382.

Non-provable debts—Debts which are not provable, and postponed debts which are only provable after all other creditors have been paid in full, appear in rr 12.3(2) and (2A).

Secured creditors—The term 'secured creditor' and the position of a secured creditor who petitions for a debtor's bankruptcy are provided for in s 383.

A secured creditor is entitled to rely on his security without submission of a proof. Any proof must, however, provide particulars of any security held, the date it was given and the value which the creditor puts upon it: r 6.98(1)(e). A secured creditor is entitled to alter the value which is put upon his security in his proof of debt with the agreement of the trustee or with the leave of the court, although the leave of the court must be obtained if the secured creditor has put a value on his security in the bankruptcy petition or has voted in respect of the unsecured balance of his debt: r 6.115(1) and (2).

Interest—The calculation of interest is provided for in r 6.113; and see also s 328(5).

Under s 322(2) interest is provable as part of a debt but not in respect of any period after the date of the bankruptcy order. A contractual provision for the capitalisation of interest cannot be relied upon in relation to any post-bankruptcy order period: *Re Amalgamated Investment & Property Co Ltd* [1984] BCLC 341.

Section 322(3) and (4)

Scope of provision—The quantification of claims is a matter for the trustee. The particular rules governing negotiable instruments etc, secured creditors, discounts, debt in a foreign currency, periodical payments, interest and debts payable at a future time appear in rr 6.108–6.114 and r 11.13. A creditor has a right of appeal against the trustee's decision on a proof under r 6.105. Such an appeal is not a true appeal and is determined by the court on the facts before it at the date of the hearing: *Cadwell v Jackson* [2001] BPIR 966 at 967E–967F (Neuberger J, as he then was).

323 Mutual credit and set-off

(1) This section applies where before the commencement of the bankruptcy there have been mutual credits, mutual debts or other mutual dealings between the bankrupt and any creditor of the bankrupt proving or claiming to prove for a bankruptcy debt.

(2) An account shall be taken of what is due from each party to the other in respect of the mutual dealings and the sums due from one party shall be set off against the sums due from the other.

(3) Sums due from the bankrupt to another party shall not be included in the account taken under subsection (2) if that other party had notice at the time they became due that a bankruptcy petition relating to the bankrupt was pending.

(4) Only the balance (if any) of the account taken under subsection (2) is provable as a bankruptcy debt or, as the case may be, to be paid to the trustee as part of the bankrupt's estate.

General note—The provision specifically allows set-off, which is an exception to the pari passu rule, for reasons of policy and justice.

The provision mirrors r 4.90, which applies to liquidations. There appears no good reason for the fact that set-off for liquidation is covered by the Rules and set-off for bankruptcy is dealt with by the Act.

A debt arising from a market contract cannot be set-off until the completion of default proceedings (Companies Act 1989, ss 159(4), 163(1), (2)). These are proceedings brought pursuant to the relevant investment exchange or clearing house rules, where default occurs.

Time—The set-off takes place, in relation to the respective parties' rights, as at the date of the bankruptcy order.

Application of set-off—Set-off is a statutory directive and therefore applies automatically without any action having to be taken by the bankrupt's trustee or the other party (*Stein v Blake* [1996] AC 243, [1995] BCC 543).

'What is due from each party to the other… and the sums due from one party shall be set off against the sums due from the other'—This means that the sums that are owed are treated as having been owing as at the date of bankruptcy with the benefit and estimation laid down by the bankruptcy law: *Stein v Blake* at 256 (AC).

A contingent liability that is owed to X by Y is sufficient to allow X to claim set-off if there is liability of Y to X: *Bateman v Williams* [2009] EWHC 1760 (Ch), [2009] BPIR 973 at [10].

The effect—Once set-off has occurred, the original choses in action of the parties cease to exist, and the party with the greater claim then has a right to the net balance (*Stein v Blake*). The right to the net balance may be assigned (*Stein v Blake*).

See the notes accompanying r 4.90, which deal with set-off in some depth.

324 Distribution by means of dividend

(1) Whenever the trustee has sufficient funds in hand for the purpose he shall, subject to the retention of such sums as may be necessary for the expenses of the bankruptcy, declare and distribute dividends among the creditors in respect of the bankruptcy debts which they have respectively proved.

(2) The trustee shall give notice of his intention to declare and distribute a dividend.

(3) Where the trustee has declared a dividend, he shall give notice of the dividend and of how it is proposed to distribute it; and a notice given under this subsection shall contain the prescribed particulars of the bankrupt's estate.

(4) In the calculation and distribution of a dividend the trustee shall make provision—

    (a)   for any bankruptcy debts which appear to him to be due to persons who, by reason of the distance of their place of residence, may not have had sufficient time to tender and establish their proofs,

    (b)   for any bankruptcy debts which are the subject of claims which have not yet been determined, and

    (c)   for disputed proofs and claims.

General note—Section 324(1) imposes an unqualified duty on a trustee to declare and distribute dividends among creditors which have proved in respect of bankruptcy debts 'whenever' the trustee has sufficient funds in hand, subject to the retention of sums necessary for the expenses of the bankruptcy. It is unhelpful that the unqualified nature of the duty takes no account of the fact that in some cases the cost of distributing the dividend may be disproportionate to the level of the dividend itself.

The purpose of the giving of the notice of intention to declare and distribute a dividend under s 324(2) is to afford an opportunity to any creditor which has not proved to do so, on which see rr 11.2 and 11.3. There is no form prescribed for the giving of a notice of intention to pay dividends, although the notice must be in writing unless the court permits notice to be given in some other way: r 12A.7. Even where a trustee is unable to declare any dividend, or any further dividend where an interim dividend has been paid, he must give notice of the fact to creditors: see r 11.7. The trustee is obliged to state that payment of a dividend will be made within a period of four months from the last date for proving: see r 11.2(2) and (3). A dividend may be distributed simultaneously with the notice declaring it: r 11.6(3).

Undistributed and unclaimed dividends—See regs 23 and 31 of the Insolvency Regulations 1994.

Procedure—See the detailed provisions in rr 11.1–11.13.

325 Claims by unsatisfied creditors

(1) A creditor who has not proved his debt before the declaration of any dividend is not entitled to disturb, by reason that he has not participated in it, the distribution of that dividend or any other dividend declared before his debt was proved, but—

    (a)   when he has proved that debt he is entitled to be paid, out of any money for the time being available for the payment of any further dividend, any dividend or dividends which he has failed to receive; and

    (b)   any dividend or dividends payable under paragraph (a) shall be paid before that money is applied to the payment of any such further dividend.

(2) No action lies against the trustee for a dividend, but if the trustee refuses to pay a dividend the court may, if it thinks fit, order him to pay it and also to pay, out of his own money—

    (a)   interest on the dividend, at the rate for the time being specified in section 17 of the Judgments Act 1838, from the time it was withheld, and

    (b)   the costs of the proceedings in which the order to pay is made.

General note—The two subsections in this provision deal with very different situations.

Section 325(1)

Scope of provision—This subsection is only triggered where a creditor who has not proved his debt before the declaration of any dividend but subsequently proves. In those circumstances, whilst the late creditor is not entitled to disturb any dividend previously made, he obtains a right to be paid his original dividend, effectively as if he had proved on time, from any monies available for the payment of any future dividend.

Section 325(2)

Scope of provision—This subsection insulates a trustee from personal liability for any claim in relation to a dividend, although the court may, if it thinks fit, order the trustee to pay any dividend which he *refuses* to pay; that is, from the fund available to the trustee for the payment of dividends. In those circumstances, however, the trustee may be made personally liable for interest on any such dividend and the costs of any proceedings in which the order to pay is made.

326 Distribution of property in specie

(1) Without prejudice to sections 315 to 319 (disclaimer), the trustee may, with the permission of the creditors' committee, divide in its existing form amongst the bankrupt's creditors, according to its estimated value, any property which from its peculiar nature or other special circumstances cannot be readily or advantageously sold.

(2) A permission given for the purposes of subsection (1) shall not be a general permission but shall relate to a particular proposed exercise of the power in question; and a person dealing with the trustee in good faith and for value is not to be concerned to enquire whether any permission required by subsection (1) has been given.

(3) Where the trustee has done anything without the permission required by subsection (1), the court or the creditors' committee may, for the purpose of enabling him to meet his expenses out of the bankrupt's estate, ratify what the trustee has done.

But the committee shall not do so unless it is satisfied that the trustee acted in a case of urgency and has sought its ratification without undue delay.

General note—A distribution of property in specie is only permitted where the property to be distributed cannot be readily or advantageously sold on account of its 'peculiar nature', such as perishable goods or goods for which the market is so specialised that the costs of realisation are disproportionate to the likely proceeds of sale, or 'other special circumstances' which are not defined. Such special circumstances might include the absence of any ready market for the property in question.

Permission of and ratification by the creditors' committee—The distribution of property in specie is subject to the permission of the creditors' committee. That permission may only be given in relation to particular proposed exercise of the power to distribute in specie and must not be general. Section 326(3) permits the creditors' committee to ratify the act of a trustee in distributing in specie without permission – without which permission the trustee would not be entitled to recover the expense of the distribution exercise as an expense of the bankrupt's estate – but only if the committee is satisfied that the trustee acted in a case of urgency and that ratification was sought without undue delay.

327 Distribution in criminal bankruptcy

Where the bankruptcy order was made on a petition under section 264(1)(d) (criminal bankruptcy), no distribution shall be made under sections 324 to 326 so long as an appeal is pending (within the meaning of section 277) against the bankrupt's conviction of any offence by virtue of which the criminal bankruptcy order on which the petition was based was made.

General note—This provision is now obsolete and is to be repealed from a date to be appointed by virtue of s 170(2) of Sch 16 to the Criminal Justice Act 1988.

328 Priority of debts

(1) In the distribution of the bankrupt's estate, his preferential debts (within the meaning given by section 386 in Part XII) shall be paid in priority to other debts.

(2) Preferential debts rank equally between themselves after the expenses of the bankruptcy and shall be paid in full unless the bankrupt's estate is insufficient for meeting them, in which case they abate in equal proportions between themselves.

(3) Debts which are neither preferential debts nor debts to which the next section applies also rank equally between themselves and, after the preferential debts, shall be paid in full unless the bankrupt's estate is insufficient for meeting them, in which case they abate in equal proportions between themselves.

(4) Any surplus remaining after the payment of the debts that are preferential or rank equally under subsection (3) shall be applied in paying interest on those debts in respect of the periods during which they have been

outstanding since the commencement of the bankruptcy; and interest on preferential debts ranks equally with interest on debts other than preferential debts.

(5) The rate of interest payable under subsection (4) in respect of any debt is whichever is the greater of the following—

    (a)   the rate specified in section 17 of the Judgments Act 1838 at the commencement of the bankruptcy, and

    (b)   the rate applicable to that debt apart from the bankruptcy.

(6) This section and the next are without prejudice to any provision of this Act or any other Act under which the payment of any debt or the making of any other payment is, in the event of bankruptcy, to have a particular priority or to be postponed.

General note—The priority of debts in bankruptcy is as follows:

- Expenses of the bankruptcy (on which see r 6.224).
- Preferential claims (which abate in equal proportions between themselves, and on which see the commentary to Sch 6).
- Unsecured claims (which abate in equal proportions between themselves).
- Interest on preferential and unsecured claims from the date of the bankruptcy order (such claims for interest being treated as a single class). On 328(5), see *KK v MA* [2012] EWHC 788 (Ch) at [79].

Section 328(6) allows for other legislation varying the above priority regime. Examples include postponed debts under ss 2 and 3 of the Partnership Act 1890 and fees paid to a bankrupt by an apprentice or clerk under s 348.

329 Debts to spouse or civil partner

(1) This section applies to bankruptcy debts owed in respect of credit provided by a person who (whether or not the bankrupt's spouse or civil partner at the time the credit was provided) was the bankrupt's spouse or civil partner at the commencement of the bankruptcy.

(2) Such debts—

    (a)   rank in priority after the debts and interest required to be paid in pursuance of section 328(3) and (4), and

    (b)   are payable with interest at the rate specified in section 328(5) in respect of the period during which they have been outstanding since the commencement of the bankruptcy;

and the interest payable under paragraph (b) has the same priority as the debts on which it is payable.

Amendments—Civil Partnership Act 2004, s 261(1), Sch 27, para 116.

General note—These provisions are limited to the priority of a debt owed by the bankrupt to an individual who was the bankrupt's spouse at the commencement of the bankruptcy, as defined at the date of the bankruptcy order by s 278(a), irrespective of whether that creditor was the bankrupt's spouse at the time that the credit was provided or, indeed, whether or not that individual was the bankrupt's spouse at the date at which the priority of debts comes to be assessed.

The effect of s 329(2) is to subordinate a debt to which the provision applies, together with interest thereon, to debts and any surplus ranking within s 328(3) and (4).

330 Final distribution

(1) When the trustee has realised all the bankrupt's estate or so much of it as can, in the trustee's opinion, be realised without needlessly protracting the trusteeship, he shall give notice in the prescribed manner either—

    (a)   of his intention to declare a final dividend, or

    (b)   that no dividend, or further dividend, will be declared.

(2) The notice under subsection (1) shall contain the prescribed particulars and shall require claims against the bankrupt's estate to be established by a date ('the final date') specified in the notice.

(3) The court may, on the application of any person, postpone the final date.

(4) After the final date, the trustee shall—

    (a)   defray any outstanding expenses of the bankruptcy out of the bankrupt's estate, and

    (b)   if he intends to declare a final dividend, declare and distribute that dividend without regard to the claim of any person in respect of a debt not already proved in the bankruptcy.

(5) If a surplus remains after payment in full and with interest of all the bankrupt's creditors and the payment of the expenses of the bankruptcy, the bankrupt is entitled to the surplus.

(6) Subsection (5) is subject to Article 35 of the EC Regulation (surplus in secondary proceedings to be transferred to main proceedings).

Amendments—SI 2002/1240.

General note—These provisions govern the closure of the bankruptcy and should be read in conjunction with s 331 (final meeting) below. Although s 305(2) provides that the function of a trustee includes the realisation and distribution of the bankrupt's estate, the trustee is permitted by s 330(1) to give notice of his intention to declare a final dividend etc where he is of the opinion that any remaining part of the bankrupt's estate is incapable of being realised without needlessly protracting the trusteeship. This squares with s 331(1) which is triggered where it appears to the trustee that the administration of a bankrupt's estate 'is for practical purposes complete'.

The 'final date' identified in s 330(2) is of significance since its passing allows the trustee to take those steps in s 330(4) without regard to the claim of any person who has not already proved in the bankruptcy.

For the purpose of any surplus payable under s 330(5) – which very rarely arises in practice – the term 'expenses' is as defined in r 12.2.

Unclaimed dividends are subject to regs 23 and 31 of the Insolvency Regulations 1994.

Procedure—No form has been prescribed for either s 330(1) or (2).

Although the class of persons eligible to apply to postpone the final date of the bankruptcy under s 330(3) is not defined, it is unlikely that the court would entertain an application by any person other than one with a financial interest in the outcome of the bankruptcy.

331 Final meeting

(1) Subject as follows in this section and the next, this section applies where—

(a) it appears to the trustee that the administration of the bankrupt's estate in accordance with this Chapter is for practical purposes complete, and

(b) the trustee is not the official receiver.

(2) The trustee shall summon a final general meeting of the bankrupt's creditors which—

(a) shall receive the trustee's report of his administration of the bankrupt's estate, and

(b) shall determine whether the trustee should have his release under section 299 in Chapter III.

(3) The trustee may, if he thinks fit, give the notice summoning the final general meeting at the same time as giving notice under section 330(1); but, if summoned for an earlier date, that meeting shall be adjourned (and, if necessary, further adjourned) until a date on which the trustee is able to report to the meeting that the administration of the bankrupt's estate is for practical purposes complete.

(4) In the administration of the estate it is the trustee's duty to retain sufficient sums from the estate to cover the expenses of summoning and holding the meeting required by this section.

General note—Section 331(1) comes into operation where the trustee is not the official receiver and it appears to the trustee that the administration of the estate 'is for practical purposes complete'. As identified in the general note to s 330, the trustee does not therefore have to be satisfied that the entirety of the assets comprised in the bankrupt's estate have been realised but, rather, that there is nothing further which is capable of practical completion. The calling of a meeting under s 331 is subject to s 332.

The practical significance of the final meeting of creditors lies in the general meeting receiving the trustee's report of his administration of the estate and the determination by the meeting of whether the trustee should have his release under s 299. The time of the trustee's release is determined by s 299(3)(d). Furthermore, s 298(8) provides that the trustee shall vacate office on giving notice to the court that a final meeting has been held under s 331, although, it should be noted, that notice will not affect the release of the trustee under s 299(3)(d).

332 Saving for bankrupt's home

(1) This section applies where—

(a) there is comprised in the bankrupt's estate property consisting of an interest in a dwelling house which is occupied by the bankrupt or by his spouse or former spouse or by his civil partner or former civil partner, and

(b) the trustee has been unable for any reason to realise that property.

(2) The trustee shall not summon a meeting under section 331 unless either—

(a) the court has made an order under section 313 imposing a charge on that property for the benefit of the bankrupt's estate, or

(b) the court has declined, on an application under that section, to make such an order, or

(c)   the Secretary of State has issued a certificate to the trustee stating that it would be inappropriate or inexpedient for such an application to be made in the case in question.

Amendments—Civil Partnership Act 2004, s 261(1), Sch 27, para 117.

General note—The effect of this provision is to preclude the convening of a final meeting under s 331 in the circumstances set out in s 332(1), subject to the exceptions in s 332(2).

Further assistance may be found in the commentary to ss 313, 336 and 337. The term 'dwelling-house' is defined in s 385 and extends under s 322(1)(a) not only to a dwelling-house occupied by the bankrupt or an interest therein, but also to any dwelling-house occupied by the bankrupt's spouse or one occupied by the bankrupt's former spouse.

Supplemental

333 Duties of bankrupt in relation to trustee

(1) The bankrupt shall—

(a)   give to the trustee such information as to his affairs,
(b)   attend on the trustee at such times, and
(c)   do all such other things,

as the trustee may for the purposes of carrying out his functions under any of this Group of Parts reasonably require.

(2) Where at any time after the commencement of the bankruptcy any property is acquired by, or devolves upon, the bankrupt or there is an increase of the bankrupt's income, the bankrupt shall, within the prescribed period, give the trustee notice of the property or, as the case may be, of the increase.

(3) Subsection (1) applies to a bankrupt after his discharge.

(4) If the bankrupt without reasonable excuse fails to comply with any obligation imposed by this section, he is guilty of a contempt of court and liable to be punished accordingly (in addition to any other punishment to which he may be subject).

General note—Section 333(1) sets out the duties owed by a bankrupt to his trustee. These duties apply to a bankrupt both before and after discharge (emphasised by Mr Registrar Nicholls in Chadwick v Nash [2012] BPIR 70 at [13]. Broadly, these duties correspond with the duties of a bankrupt in relation to the official receiver under s 291. The duties owed to both previously appeared in rather more elaborate terms in s 22 of the Bankruptcy Act 1914. In *Morris v Murjani* [1996] BPIR 458 at 462H–463A Peter Gibson LJ (with whom Buxton J and Hirst LJ agreed) observed that there is no corporate insolvency equivalent to s 333, with the consequence that decisions on corporate cases, including decisions made under s 561 of the Companies Act 1985, should not be treated as binding in a s 333 case.

Section 333 should also be read in conjunction with s 312 (which gives rise to an independent obligation to surrender control of property, books etc to the trustee), and s 307 (standing of trustee to claim after-acquired property) with which s 333(2) corresponds.

The scope of the trustee's duties under s 333(1)—In *Murjani* Peter Gibson LJ identified the nature of s 333(1) as follows (at 462B–462D):

'... it is not in dispute that s 333(1) has imposed a type of public duty on the bankrupt, though not one, in my view, such as would be enforceable only at the suit of the Attorney-General. The duties are owed, as [counsel for the bankrupt] accepts, to the trustee who is the person designated as being able to require the performance and determine the content of that duty and who can enforce it. A trustee has the right, and in appropriate circumstances it may be said that he also has the duty, to enforce the statutory duty owed by the bankrupt. The bankrupt's estate has become vested in the trustee as a result of the adjudication [bankruptcy] order made by the court. The trustee must therefore collect the assets of the estate as speedily as possible, which may require the obtaining of information in order to trace the relevant assets. His ultimate object is to make a distribution in accordance with the statutory scheme. The duties imposed on the bankrupt are all plainly designed to assist the trustee in the performance by him of his statutory functions.'

The final two sentences of the above extract, it is submitted, provide the benchmark against which any application by a trustee to enforce the bankrupt's duties should be tested. Relief should be granted only if what is required of the bankrupt is necessary to assist a trustee in the performance by him of his statutory functions, as identified in s 305(2). The question of enforcement of the s 333(1) duties is dealt with below.

The requirement that a bankrupt shall '(c) do all such other things' as his trustee may reasonably require extends to a duty to execute any document necessary for the discharge of the trustee's functions. Where a bankrupt is in default of that obligation, as can arise where a bankrupt refuses to execute a transfer or conveyance of property which the bankrupt holds as co-trustee or co-owner in law, a registrar or district judge has power under s 39(1) of the Supreme Court Act 1981 to execute the document in the name of the bankrupt: *Savage v Norton* [1908] 1 Ch 290. By parity of reasoning it would follow that the court would have jurisdiction to execute any document, such as a power of attorney or other written authority, reasonably required by the trustee to discharge his functions in the face of the bankrupt's refusal to do so.

The position of the bankrupt—A bankrupt should be extremely cautious in refusing to comply with the reasonable requirements of a trustee under s 333(1), given the public nature of the bankrupt's duties as identified in *Murjani* (above) and the risk of the bankrupt's liability for contempt of court under s 333(4) (see below). As noted above, the court has the ability in any case to execute documents in the name of the bankrupt under s 39(1) of the Senior Courts Act 1981.

In a judgment handed down on 19 July 1984 in relation to the former but analogous s 22(3) of the Bankruptcy Act 1914 the Court of Appeal (Oliver LJ and Balcombe J) held in *Fryer and Thompson v Brooke* [1998] BPIR 687 that the nature of the bankrupt's duties precludes him from raising against the trustee some personal right of occupation in property so as to impede and inhibit the sale of the property at its best value where the bankrupt's estate was also entitled to an interest in the property which was capable of being realised for the purpose of paying off creditors. In *Christofi v Barclays Bank plc* [2000] 1 WLR 937 the Court of Appeal (Stuart-Smith and Chadwick LJJ) affirmed the decision of Lawrence Collins QC, sitting as he then was as a deputy High Court judge, to the effect that an instruction by a bankrupt to his bank to have no contact with and provide no information to his trustee (who, in that case, was investigating pre-bankruptcy transactions) would constitute a breach of the bankrupt's duties. Further, the bank would be justified, notwithstanding the bankrupt's instructions, to respond to the trustee's legitimate enquiries in connection with an account in which the bankrupt had an interest and of which the bank had every reason to suppose the trustee was already aware: see *Tournier v National Provincial & Union Bank of England* [1924] 1 KB 461.

A transaction entered into for the illegal purpose of enabling a bankrupt to escape his disclosure obligations under s 333(2) cannot be used to assert a proprietary claim and is liable to be struck out: *Barrett v Barrett* [2008] EWHC 1061 (Ch), [2008] BPIR 817 (David Richards J).

Enforcement of the s 333(1) duties—A trustee may enforce the bankrupt's duties by seeking an order under s 366 or, it is submitted, by an application under s 363(2). Further, or in the alternative, a trustee might institute contempt proceedings under s 333(4). In an appropriate case the court may also grant an injunction ordering the bankrupt not to leave the jurisdiction and to deliver up his passport, as in *Murjani*. As Peter Gibson LJ observed in that case (at 462F), 'It would be extraordinary if the trustee could obtain an order for the arrest of the bankrupt but could not obtain a less severe remedy restraining the bankrupt from leaving the jurisdiction.' Failure to comply with s 333 duties will also often form the basis for an application for suspension of the bankrupt's discharge under s 279 eg *Hellard v Kapoor* [2013 EWHC 2204 (Ch), [2013] BPIR 745 (see also the cases in the notes to s 279).

In *Re M (a minor) (contact order: committal)* (1998) *The Times*, December 31 the Court of Appeal gave guidance, albeit in the context of a claim under the Children Act 1989, on the exercise of the power of committal for non-compliance with a court order; in particular, it is inadvisable that the judge initiating the committal procedure should also rule on the decision to commit.

In finding that a bankrupt was in contempt it lies within the court's inherent jurisdiction to regulate or stay any proceedings pursued by the bankrupt until further order or until the contempt is purged.

Procedure—On s 333(2) see the 21-day period in r 6.200(1).

334 Stay of distribution in case of second bankruptcy

(1) This section and the next apply where a bankruptcy order is made against an undischarged bankrupt; and in both sections—

- (a) 'the later bankruptcy' means the bankruptcy arising from that order,
- (b) 'the earlier bankruptcy' means the bankruptcy (or, as the case may be, most recent bankruptcy) from which the bankrupt has not been discharged at the commencement of the later bankruptcy, and
- (c) 'the existing trustee' means the trustee (if any) of the bankrupt's estate for the purposes of the earlier bankruptcy.

(2) Where the existing trustee has been given the prescribed notice of the presentation of the petition for the later bankruptcy, any distribution or other disposition by him of anything to which the next subsection applies, if made after the giving of the notice, is void except to the extent that it was made with the consent of the court or is or was subsequently ratified by the court.

This is without prejudice to section 284 (restrictions on dispositions of property following bankruptcy order).

(3) This subsection applies to—

- (a) any property which is vested in the existing trustee under section 307(3) (after-acquired property);
- (b) any money paid to the existing trustee in pursuance of an income payments order under section 310; and
- (c) any property or money which is, or in the hands of the existing trustee represents, the proceeds of sale or application of property or money falling within paragraph (a) or (b) of this subsection.

General note—These provisions must be read in conjunction with s 335 and are only triggered where a bankruptcy order is made against an undischarged bankrupt.

The purpose of the provisions is in protecting the assets in what is termed 'the earlier bankruptcy' so as to allow for the adjustment between the earlier bankruptcy and the later bankruptcy under s 335.

Section 334(2)

'Where the existing trustee has been given a prescribed notice ...'—Form 6.78 is prescribed for the giving of notice. It is not clear whether the notice is to be given by the petitioning creditor or the existing trustee. In either case, however, it is the giving of the prescribed notice which brings s 334(2) into operation. A disposition will not be rendered void by s 334(2) until such notice is given.

Property subject to s 334(2)—Although the wording in the opening of s 334(3) might suggest that only the property listed within that provision is subject to s 334(2), this is not the case. Section 334(2) applies not only to the property listed in s 334(3) but also to all of the property comprised in the bankrupt's estate in the earlier bankruptcy. Subsection (3) appears to have been included in the provisions for the avoidance of any doubt which might otherwise have arisen.

The effect of a void disposition—Any property which is lost to the bankruptcy estate under a disposition rendered void by s 334(2) may be recovered by the trustee in the earlier bankruptcy or, it is submitted, the trustee in the later bankruptcy. The principles applicable to such a void disposition are the same as those which apply to any void disposition under s 127 or s 284.

The effect of s 284—It is not clear how s 284 might apply in a case to which s 344 applies, not least because s 284(1) specifically makes reference to any disposition of property made by a person who is adjudged bankrupt. It is also doubtful that what was intended by the draftsman was that s 284 should apply to dispositions by 'the existing trustee' as if the existing trustee were the bankrupt, since the first part of s 334(2) would in those circumstances be entirely superfluous.

Procedure—See rr 6.225–6.228 which provide, in r 6.226, for the general duty of the existing trustee in the event of a second bankruptcy.

335 Adjustment between earlier and later bankruptcy estates

(1) With effect from the commencement of the later bankruptcy anything to which section 334(3) applies which, immediately before the commencement of that bankruptcy, is comprised in the bankrupt's estate for the purposes of the earlier bankruptcy is to be treated as comprised in the bankrupt's estate for the purposes of the later bankruptcy and, until there is a trustee of that estate, is to be dealt with by the existing trustee in accordance with the rules.

(2) Any sums which in pursuance of an income payments order under section 310 are payable after the commencement of the later bankruptcy to the existing trustee shall form part of the bankrupt's estate for the purposes of the later bankruptcy; and the court may give such consequential directions for the modification of the order as it thinks fit.

(3) Anything comprised in a bankrupt's estate by virtue of subsection (1) or (2) is so comprised subject to a first charge in favour of the existing trustee for any bankruptcy expenses incurred by him in relation thereto.

(4) Except as provided above and in section 334, property which is, or by virtue of section 308 (personal property of bankrupt exceeding reasonable replacement value) or section 308A (vesting in trustee of certain tenancies) is capable of being, comprised in the bankrupt's estate for the purposes of the earlier bankruptcy, or of any bankruptcy prior to it, shall not be comprised in his estate for the purposes of the later bankruptcy.

(5) The creditors of the bankrupt in the earlier bankruptcy and the creditors of the bankrupt in any bankruptcy prior to the earlier one, are not

to be creditors of his in the later bankruptcy in respect of the same debts; but the existing trustee may prove in the later bankruptcy for—

  (a) the unsatisfied balance of the debts (including any debt under this subsection) provable against the bankrupt's estate in the earlier bankruptcy;

  (b) any interest payable on that balance; and

  (c) any unpaid expenses of the earlier bankruptcy.

(6) Any amount provable under subsection (5) ranks in priority after all the other debts provable in the later bankruptcy and after interest on those debts and, accordingly, shall not be paid unless those debts and that interest have first been paid in full.

Amendments—Housing Act 1988, s 140, Sch 17, Part I, para 74.

General note—These provisions must be read in conjunction with s 334. Their effect is to denude an earlier bankruptcy of property comprised in that bankruptcy estate, together with any income payments order, save to the extent of property within ss 308 or 308A, in favour of the later bankruptcy. In addition, s 335(6) confers priority on creditors in the later bankruptcy over creditors in the earlier bankruptcy whose claims may only be advanced under s 335(5) by the existing trustee for the unsatisfied balance in the earlier bankruptcy and interest thereon together with any unpaid expenses of the earlier bankruptcy. Notably, s 335(3) confers the benefit of a statutory first charge in favour of the existing trustee for any bankruptcy expenses incurred by him in relation to the earlier bankruptcy estate.

Procedure—See rr 6.225–6.228 which provide, in r 6.226, for the general duty of the existing trustee in the event of the second bankruptcy.

Chapter V

Effect of Bankruptcy on Certain Rights, Transactions, Etc

Rights under trusts of land

335A Rights under trusts of land

(1) Any application by a trustee of a bankrupt's estate under section 14 of the Trusts of Land and Appointment of Trustees Act 1996 (powers of court in relation to trusts of land) for an order under that section for the sale of land shall be made to the court having jurisdiction in relation to the bankruptcy.

(2) On such an application the court shall make such order as it thinks just and reasonable having regard to—

  (a) the interests of the bankrupt's creditors;

  (b) where the application is made in respect of land which includes a dwelling house which is or has been the home of the bankrupt or the bankrupt's spouse or civil partner or former spouse or former civil partner—

    (i) the conduct of the spouse, civil partner, former spouse or former civil partner, so far as contributing to the bankruptcy,

    (ii) the needs and financial resources of the spouse, civil partner, former spouse or former civil partner, and

> (iii) the needs of any children; and
>
> (c) all the circumstances of the case other than the needs of the bankrupt.

(3) Where such an application is made after the end of the period of one year beginning with the first vesting under Chapter IV of this Part of the bankrupt's estate in a trustee, the court shall assume, unless the circumstances of the case are exceptional, that the interests of the bankrupt's creditors outweigh all other considerations.

(4) The powers conferred on the court by this section are exercisable on an application whether it is made before or after the commencement of this section.

Amendments—Inserted by the Trusts of Land and Appointment of Trustees Act 1996, s 25(1), Sch 3, para 23; Civil Partnership Act 2004, s 261(1), Sch 27, para 118.

General note—Section 335A was inserted by s 25(1) of and Sch 3 to the Trusts of Land and Appointment of Trustees Act 1996 and took effect from 1 January 1997. The new provision replaced s 336(3) and disapplied s 336(4) to cases involving trusts of land.

Sections 14 and 15 of the 1996 Act replaced s 30 of the Law of Property Act 1925. Section 15 of the 1996 Act, however, is disapplied by s 15(4) thereof if s 335A is applicable. Section 335A(1) expressly provides that an application for the sale of land is made to the court having jurisdiction in relation to the bankruptcy. The issue of court jurisdiction is dealt with in ss 373 and 374 and the notes thereto.

Application of s 335A—Despite the reference to the bankrupt's 'spouse' or 'former spouse' in s 335A(2), it is clear from s 335A(1) that the section applies in any case where a trustee applies for an order under s 14 of the 1996 Act. The provision will, therefore, apply to *any* trust of land under which the bankrupt has an interest, irrespective of whether the beneficial co-owner is a spouse, a former spouse, an unmarried co-habitee or any other person.

Other statutory considerations—Regard should be had initially to s 283A (bankrupt's home ceasing to form part of bankrupt's estate in certain circumstances) and s 313A (low value home) and, in particular, s 313A(2) which requires the court to dismiss an application for possession and sale etc if the value of the trustee's interest in the dwelling-house is below the £1,000 figure presently prescribed under that provision.

The court's approach to a s 335A case—Section 335A does not, of course, create a new cause of action but, rather, provides for the position where an application is made for an order for sale by a trustee under s 14 of the 1996 Act. In *Mortgage Corporation plc v Shaire* [2000] BPIR 483 Neuberger J, as he then was, concluded (at 497H–500A) that s 15, and the factors to be taken into account under the provision, represented a change in the law from the previous s 30 of the Law of Property Act 1925 as exemplified by the Court of Appeal's decision in *Re Citro* [1991] Ch 142. Notwithstanding the considerable body of authoritative case law under the previous legislation, his Lordship went on to express the view that 'It would be wrong to throw over all the earlier cases without paying them any regard. However, they have to be treated with caution, in light of the change in the law, and in many cases they are unlikely to be of great, let alone decisive, assistance.' Subsequently, in *Bank of Ireland Home Mortgages v Bell* [2001] BPIR 429 at [31] Peter Gibson LJ made reference to the decision in *Shaire* without detracting in any way from Neuberger J's expressed view. Following *Shaire*, not only should the authorities under s 30 be treated with the need for caution expressed by Neuberger J, but also, in particular, for the purpose of what would amount to all the circumstances of the case other than the needs of the bankrupt under s 335A(2)(c), a powerful consideration is and ought to be whether a creditor is receiving proper recompense for being kept out of his money where repayment of that money is overdue.

Once an order for possession has been made the court will not direct the trustee to delay implementation of the order, although it is within the trustee's powers to consider doing so if there is a reasonable prospect of the bankruptcy debts and expenses being paid: *Awoyemi v Bowell* [2006] BPIR 1 (Evans-Lombe J).

A custodial 6-month prison sentence for contempt of court by way of willful breach of a possession order (in addition to breach of obligations under ss 313, 333 and 363) was not manifestly excessive: *Boyden v Canty (No 2)* [2007] BPIR 299 (Chadwick and Lloyd LJJ).

In *French v Barcham* [2008] BPIR 857 Blackburne J held that ss 12–15 of the 1996 Act do not provide an exhaustive a regime for compensation for exclusion of a beneficiary from occupation of property held subject to a trust of land. In particular, where a trustee-in-bankrutpcy has no statutory right of occupation under s 12 there is no scope for the operation of s 13 (exclusion and restriction of right to occupy). However, whilst the trustee had no statutory right to occupy, it was wrong (as the district judge below had held) that the bankrupt's co-owning spouse was not liable to be charged an occupation rent (or equitable compensation) for her occupation from the time the bankrupt's interest in the property vested in his trustee because it was not reasonable to expect the trustee to exercise the right of occupation attaching to his interest in the property. This conclusion was entirely consistent with the line of authorities on equitable accounting culminating in *Re Byford (Deceased)* [2003] BPIR 1089 which remained good law notwithstanding the explanation of ss 12–15 of the 1996 Act by the House of Lords in *Stack v Dowden* [2007] AC 423. See also the notes under the heading 'Equitable accounting' below.

Factors considered under s 335A(2)—The court must make such order as it thinks just and reasonable having regard to those factors within s 335A(2), together with 'all the circumstances of the case' in s 335A(2)(c) which will extend to all *relevant* circumstances before the court. Neither those circumstances, however, nor any other factor within s 335A(2) extends to the needs of the bankrupt. Accordingly, the court may not have regard for the need of the bankrupt, say, to use the property in issue for earning his livelihood, or evidence that the bankrupt may suffer some adverse mental or physical consequence as a result of the property being sold. Section 335A(2)(b)(i) is broad enough to include excessive or irresponsible spending on the part of a spouse or former spouse or, it is submitted, a refusal by a spouse or former spouse to assist the bankrupt in avoiding bankruptcy from assets available to that individual.

Neither the term 'spouse' nor 'former spouse' is defined in the 1986 Act. It is submitted that the term should be attributed a meaning in line with s 30 of the Family Law Act 1996 which extends to husband and wife, including parties to a polygamous marriage.

Section 335A(3)

'... unless the circumstances of the case are exceptional ...'—Following the expiration of one year from the vesting of the bankrupt's estate in a trustee s 335A(3) raises a rebuttable presumption that the interests of the bankrupt's creditors outweigh all other considerations such that an order for sale should be made. In seeking to rebut that presumption two points should be borne in mind. First, as appears from the authorities (see below) the court will not be receptive to arguments which, in substance, are based on nothing more than inconvenience and the like. Secondly, each case must be determined on its own facts such that the *facts* of any other reported decision will be of very limited use, since each case necessarily involves a weighing-up exercise on a case-by-case basis. For a case in which exceptional circumstances were not established see *Barca v Mears* [2005] BPIR 15 (Nicholas Strauss QC sitting as a deputy High Court judge, applying *Re Citro* [1991] Ch 142). In *Barca*, at [33]–[43], the deputy judge considered, but left open, the question of whether the narrow approach to exceptional circumstances in *Re Citro* (on which see sub-para (d) below) is consistent with Art 8 of the European Convention for the Protection of Human Rights (right to respect for private family life and home). The point was, however, engaged by His Honour judge Norris QC, sitting as a judge of the High Court, in *Foyle v Turner* [2007] BPIR 43. *Foyle* is authority for the proposition (at [16]–[19]) that, in light of the decision of the House of Lords in *Kay v London Borough of Lambeth* [2006] UKHL 10, s 335A is compliant with Convention rights in that Art 8 of the Convention added nothing to the substance of the protection already provided by domestic law on the provision: see also to the same effect the decision of Paul Morgan QC, sitting as he then was as a deputy High Court judge in *Nicholls v Lan* [2006] BPIR 1243 at [43] and *Turner v Avis* [2008] BPIR 1143 in which His Honour Judge Pelling QC adopted the analysis of Judge Norris QC in *Foyle*. In *Ford v Alexander* [2012] EWHC 266 (Ch), [2012] BPIR 528, Peter Smith J came to the view that the s 335A procedure was compliant with Art 8. In the Northern Irish case of Official Receiver for Northern Ireland v O'Brien [2012] NICh 12, [2012] BPIR 826, however, Deeny J was willing to accept an argument based on Art 6 and Art 8 from a co-owner. Weir J similarly accepted human rights arguments under Art 6 and Art 8 in *Official Receiver for Northern Ireland v Rooney and Paulson* [2008] NICh 22, [2009] BPIR 536. Both of these cases were ones in which there had been very considerable delay.

The judgment of Lawrence Collins QC, sitting as he then was as a deputy High Court judge, in *Harrington v Bennett* [2000] BPIR 630 at 633G–634C provides the following convenient summary of the principles discernible from the authorities upon which provides an entirely accurate summary of the relevant law:

'(a) The presence of exceptional circumstances is a necessary condition to displace the assumption that the interests of the creditors outweigh all other considerations, but the presence of the exceptional circumstances does not debar the court from making an order for sale: *Re DR Raval* [1998] BPIR 389.

(b) Typically the exceptional circumstances in the modern cases relate to the personal circumstances of one of the joint owners, such as medical or mental condition: see *Judd v Brown, Re Bankrupts (Nos 9587 and 9588 of 1994)* [1997] BPIR 470; *Re DR Raval* [1998] BPIR 389; *Claughton v Charalamabous* [1998] BPIR 558.

(c) But the categories of exceptional circumstances are not to be categorised or defined. The court makes a value judgment after looking at all the circumstances: *Claughton v Charalamabous* [1998] BPIR 558.

(d) But the circumstances must be "exceptional", and this expression was intended to apply the same test as the pre-Insolvency Act 1986 decisions on bankruptcy: *Re Citro* [1991] Ch 142, pp 159, 160 referring to the identical wording in s 336(5), i e exceptional or special circumstances which are outside the usual "melancholy consequences of debt and improvidence" at p 157, per Nourse LJ; or "compelling reasons, not found in the ordinary run of cases", at p 161, per Bingham LJ.

(e) For the purposes of weighing the interests of the creditors, the creditors have an interest in the order for sale being made even if the whole of the net proceeds will go towards the expenses of the bankruptcy; and the fact that they will be swallowed up in paying those expenses is not an exceptional circumstance justifying the displacement of the assumption that the interests of the creditors outweigh all other considerations: *Trustee of the Estate of Eric Bowe (a Bankrupt) v Bowe* [1997] BPIR 747.'

In *Dean v Stout* [2005] BPIR 1113 Lawrence Collins J, as he then was, repeated the above principles but also pointed out, at [6], that, whilst the presence of exceptional circumstances is a necessary condition for displacing the presumption that the interests of creditors outweigh all other considerations after the statutory one year period, 'the presence of exceptional circumstances does not debar the court from making an order for sale'. Despite the use of the words 'assume' and 'unless' in s 335A(3), the court therefore appears to have jurisdiction to make an order for sale notwithstanding it having concluded by way of a value judgment on the facts that the case before it does involve exceptional circumstances of the *Citro* variety. In *Hosking v Michaelides* [2006] BPIR 1192 Paul Morgan QC, sitting as he then was as a deputy High Court judge, adopted the definition given by the Court of Appeal of the term 'exceptional' in *R v Kelly (Edward)* [2000] 1 QB 198 as meaning '… a circumstance … which is out of the ordinary course, or unusual, or special or uncommon. To be exceptional, a circumstance need not be unique, unprecedented or very rare, but it cannot be one that is regularly or routinely encountered.'

The fact that it may well be possible for a debtor to make full repayment, including statutory interest, over a period of time does not of itself constitute exceptional circumstances: *Donohoe v Ingram* [2006] BPIR 417 (Stuart Isaacs QC sitting as a deputy High Court judge). Neither is the court concerned with the degree of interest displayed by the bankrupt's creditors in pursuing their debts in bankruptcy; rather, the interest of the bankrupt's creditors is a reference to the creditors' legal rights to be paid the debts due to them: *Foyle v Turner* [2007] BPIR 43 (HHJ Norris QC sitting as a judge of the High Court; order for sale sought (and obtained) 13 years after bankruptcy orders).

As to the importance of the court approaching an appropriate case with a view to the protection of creditors, see *Pick v Sumpter* [2010] EWHC 685 (Ch), [2010] BPIR 638.

In *Martin-Sklan v White* [2007] BPIR 76 Evans-Lombe J upheld on appeal a decision of a district judge that, for the purposes of the equivalent provision in s 337(6), the bankrupt's partner's alcoholism and the support network available through neighbours and a relative living locally for two children aged 10 and 14 together with the poor state of the property (valued at £120,000 and subject to a mortgage of £41,000) constituted exceptional circumstances justifying postponement of an order for sale for a period of some six years and ten months. Exceptional circumstances were not established in *Turner v Avis* [2008] BPIR 1143 (HHJ Pelling QC sitting as a judge of the High Court) based on a wife's reliance on the terms of an ancillary relief order and an allegation of delay in bringing the possession proceedings. Exceptional circumstances did arise in respect of the requirements of a very severely disabled child in *Re Haghighat* [2009] EWHC 90 (Ch), [2009] BPIR 268 (although this was, in fact, a case decided with reference to ss 336 and 337). This case was unsuccessfully appealed as *Brittain v Haghighat* [2010] EWCA Civ 1521, [2011] BPIR 328. In *Everitt v Budhram* [2009] EWHC 1219 (Ch), [2010] Ch 170, in finding exceptional circumstances on the facts, Henderson J noted that the term 'needs' was to be more widely defined than merely encompassing financial needs.

Equitable accounting—The decision of the Court of Appeal (Auld and Jonathan Parker LJJ) in *Wilcox v Tait* [2006] EWCA Civ 1867, [2007] BPIR 262 provides valuable guidance on the approach to equitable accounting in cases under the 1996 Act. Equitable accounting is not to be confused with an enquiry as to beneficial interests and can only be undertaken once such interests have been determined. Although fact-sensitive, the Court of Appeal approved of the general proposition identified by His Honour Judge Behrens, sitting as a judge of the High Court in *Clarke v Marlowe* [2006] BPIR 636 at [39] that in the ordinary case equitable accounting commences at the date of separation since it is open to the court to infer a common intention that neither partner should have to account to the other during the period of co-habitation although, again, the drawing of such necessarily depends on the facts of any particular case.

It should be understood, as identified by the Court of Appeal in *Murphy v Gooch* [2007] EWCA Civ 603, [2007] BPIR 1123 at [11] (Lightman J, Sedley and Mummery LJJ agreeing), that the resolution of the subsidiary issue before the House of Lords in *Stack v Dowden* [2007] UKHL 17, [2007] 2 WLR 831 holds that the court's power to order payment to a co-owner of an occupation rent is no longer governed by the doctrine of equitable accounting as developed by the courts but, rather, by the statutory provisions now laid down in ss 12–15 of the 1996 Act (on which see, in particular, the opinion of Baroness Hale in *Stack v Dowden* at [12]). Cases, therefore, such as *Re Pavlou* [1993] 1 WLR 1046 (Millett J, as he then was), *Re Byford (Deceased)* [2003] BPIR 1089 (Lawrence Collins J, as he then was) and *Brassford v Patel* [2007] BPIR 1049 (Richard Sheldon QC sitting as a deputy High Court judge) no longer govern the position. However, whilst the difference between the two approaches lies in the equitable doctrine developed in the case law concerning itself with the achievement of a just result between the parties, as compared with the statutory provisions by which s 15 stipulates matters to which the court must give its consideration, it was observed by Lord Neuberger in *Stack v Dowden* at [150] that it would be a rare case in which the application of the equitable and statutory principles would produce a different result. See also the view of Blackburne J in *French v Barcham* [2008] BPIR 857.

As to the reasoning in *Stack v Dowden* generally as regards the beneficial interests of co-owners, now see also *Jones v Kernott* [2011] UKSC 53, [2012] 1 AC 776.

Rights of occupation

336 Rights of occupation etc of bankrupt's spouse or civil partner

(1) Nothing occurring in the initial period of the bankruptcy (that is to say, the period beginning with the day of the presentation of the petition for the bankruptcy order and ending with the vesting of the bankrupt's estate in a trustee) is to be taken as having given rise to any home rights under Part IV of the Family Law Act 1996 in relation to a dwelling house comprised in the bankrupt's estate.

(2) Where a spouse's or civil partner's home rights under the Act of 1996 are a charge on the estate or interest of the other spouse or civil partner, or of trustees for the other spouse or civil partner, and the other spouse or civil partner is adjudged bankrupt—

(a) the charge continues to subsist notwithstanding the bankruptcy and, subject to the provisions of that Act, binds the trustee of the bankrupt's estate and persons deriving title under that trustee, and

(b) any application for an order under section 33 of that Act shall be made to the court having jurisdiction in relation to the bankruptcy.

(3) (*Repealed*)

(4) On such an application as is mentioned in subsection (2) the court shall make such order under section 33 of the Act of 1996 as it thinks just and reasonable having regard to—

(a) the interests of the bankrupt's creditors,

(b) the conduct of the spouse or former spouse or civil partner or former civil partner, so far as contributing to the bankruptcy,

(c) the needs and financial resources of the spouse or former spouse or civil partner or former civil partner,

(d) the needs of any children, and

(e) all the circumstances of the case other than the needs of the bankrupt.

(5) Where such an application is made after the end of the period of one year beginning with the first vesting under Chapter IV of this Part of the bankrupt's estate in a trustee, the court shall assume, unless the circumstances of the case are exceptional, that the interests of the bankrupt's creditors outweigh all other considerations.

Amendments—Family Law Act 1996, s 66(1), Sch 8, para 57(2), (3)(a), (b), (4); Trusts of Land and Appointment of Trustees Act 1996, s 25(2), Sch 4; Civil Partnership Act 2004, s 82, Sch 9.

General note—This provision applies where a bankrupt's spouse asserts matrimonial home rights under the Family Law Act 1996, as opposed to rights under a trust of land in which case s 335A will apply. The present provisions specifically provide for the relevant court and the factors to be considered by the court on an application being made under s 33 of the 1996 Act for what is commonly termed an 'occupation order'. Such an application may be made by the trustee (ie so as to require the bankrupt's non-owning spouse to vacate the dwelling-house) or by a non-owning spouse seeking to assert her matrimonial home rights under the 1996 Act which amount to a charge on the state or interest of the bankrupt, or of trustees for the bankrupt: see s 336(2).

Other statutory considerations—Regard should be had initially to s 283A (bankrupt's home ceasing to form part of bankrupt's estate in certain circumstances) and s 313A (low value home) and, in particular, s 313A(2) which requires the court to dismiss an application for possession and sale etc if the value of the trustee's interest in the dwelling-house is below the £1,000 figure currently prescribed under that provision.

Definitions—The terms 'family' and 'dwelling-house' are defined in s 385. The term 'spouse' is not defined in the 1986 Act. A definition does appear, however, in the 1996 Act so as to catch a husband or wife, including any such party to a polygamous marriage. The term 'former spouse' should be construed accordingly.

The spouse's rights of occupation as a charge on the bankrupt's estate—Section 336(1) precludes anything giving rise to any matrimonial home rights under the 1996 Act in favour of the bankrupt's non-owning spouse in the period between the presentation of the petition and the vesting of the bankrupt's estate in the trustee under s 306, although s 336(1) does nothing to inhibit matrimonial home rights which came into existence prior to the presentation of the petition. Such rights continue to bind the bankrupt's estate by virtue of s 336(2)(a), but do not take the home permanently beyond the reach of creditors, as made clear in Mekarska v Ruiz [2011] EWHC 913 (Fam), [2011] 2 FCR 608. Permission to appeal was not granted ([2011] EWCA Civ 1646, [2012] BPIR 446).

The appropriate court for an application under s 33 of the 1996 Act—Irrespective of the provisions of the 1996 Act, the application is made to the court having jurisdiction in relation to the bankruptcy: s 336(2)(b). Sections 373 and 374 and the notes thereto deal with the bankruptcy court having jurisdiction.

Section 336(4)

Scope of provision—Section 336(4) requires the court to make an order 'as it thinks just and reasonable' having regard to the four specific factors in s 336(4)(a)–(d) and the particular circumstances of the case in (e) which, notably, do not include the needs of the bankrupt. Accordingly, the court should not take account of any particular need of the bankrupt in relation to the dwelling-house other than to the extent that such needs might have a bearing on those factors in (c) or (d). For the purposes of (b) the court will be justified in taking into account any conduct on the part of a spouse or former spouse which might properly be said to have contributed to the bankruptcy such as an excessive level of personal expenditure or, arguably, a refusal to assist the bankrupt in his financial difficulties from assets available to the spouse or former spouse.

Section 336(5)

'... unless the circumstances of the case are exceptional ...'—See the notes on exceptional circumstances to s 335A.

337 Rights of occupation of bankrupt

(1) This section applies where—

> (a) a person who is entitled to occupy a dwelling house by virtue of a beneficial estate or interest is adjudged bankrupt, and
>
> (b) any persons under the age of 18 with whom that person had at some time occupied that dwelling house had their home with that person at the time when the bankruptcy petition was presented and at the commencement of the bankruptcy.

(2) Whether or not the bankrupt's spouse or civil partner (if any) has home rights under Part IV of the Family Law Act 1996—

> (a) the bankrupt has the following rights as against the trustee of his estate—
>
> > (i) if in occupation, a right not to be evicted or excluded from the dwelling house or any part of it, except with the leave of the court,
> >
> > (ii) if not in occupation, a right with the leave of the court to enter into and occupy the dwelling house, and
>
> (b) the bankrupt's rights are a charge, having the like priority as an

equitable interest created immediately before the commencement of the bankruptcy, on so much of his estate or interest in the dwelling house as vests in the trustee.

(3) The Act of 1996 has effect, with the necessary modifications, as if—

    (a)   the rights conferred by paragraph (a) of subsection (2) were home rights under that Act,

    (b)   any application for such leave as is mentioned in that paragraph were an application for an order under section 33 of that Act, and

    (c)   any charge under paragraph (b) of that subsection on the estate or interest of the trustee were a charge under that Act on the estate or interest of a spouse or civil partner.

(4) Any application for leave such as is mentioned in subsection (2)(a) or otherwise by virtue of this section for an order under section 33 of the Act of 1996 shall be made to the court having jurisdiction in relation to the bankruptcy.

(5) On such an application the court shall make such order under section 33 of the Act of 1996 as it thinks just and reasonable having regard to the interests of the creditors, to the bankrupt's financial resources, to the needs of the children and to all the circumstances of the case other than the needs of the bankrupt.

(6) Where such an application is made after the end of the period of one year beginning with the vesting (under Chapter IV of this Part) of the bankrupt's estate in a trustee, the court shall assume, unless the circumstances of the case are exceptional, that the interests of the bankrupt's creditors outweigh all other considerations.

Amendments—Family Law Act 1996, s 66(1), Sch 8, para 58(2)–(4); Civil Partnership Act 2004, s 82, Sch 9.

General note—This provision applies where, on the making of a bankruptcy order, a bankrupt is entitled to occupy a dwelling-house (as defined in s 385) by virtue of a beneficial estate or interest where, at the time of the presentation of the bankruptcy petition *and* on the making of the bankruptcy order, a minor had his home with the bankrupt at that dwelling-house. Section 337(1) makes no mention of, and is therefore not concerned with, the presence of a spouse, former spouse or co-habitee, or any rights of occupation in favour of such an individual, although s 337(2) makes clear that nothing within s 337 should be understood as detracting from any such rights of occupation. The provision therefore most obviously addresses the position of a single, separated or divorced bankrupt who occupies a dwelling-house with one or more minors at the relevant times.

Section 337(1), (2) and (3)

Scope of provision—Where the conditions in s 337(1) are met, the bankrupt acquires those rights identified in s 337(2)(a), dependent on whether or not the bankrupt is in occupation of the dwelling-house, which take effect under s 337(2)(b) as a statutory charge enforceable against the trustee with the priority of an equitable interest created immediately prior to the making of the bankruptcy order. Section 337(3) then takes effect by treating the rights in s 337(2)(a) as matrimonial home rights under the Family Law Act 1996, enforceable by way of an occupation order under s 33 of that Act, and the statutory charge encapsulating those rights under s 337(2)(b) as a charge on the estate or interest of a spouse for the purposes of the 1996 Act.

Notably, s 337 creates no specific rights in favour of a minor (or, indeed, any other person).

As with applications under s 335A or s 336, an application for an occupation order under s 33 of the 1996 Act is made to the court having bankruptcy jurisdiction. Bankruptcy court jurisdiction is dealt with in ss 273 and 374 and the notes thereto.

Section 337(5)

Factors to be considered by the court—The court must make such occupation order as it thinks just and reasonable having regard to those factors in s 337(5). Those factors mirror those in s 335A(2) and s 336(4). Given s 337(1)(b), it may be that, in weighing the various factors and the particular circumstances of the case, the court is prepared to give greater weight than would otherwise be the case to the needs of those children whose home was the dwelling-house referred to in s 337(1).

Section 337(6)

'... unless the circumstances of the case are exceptional ...'—See the note on exceptional circumstances to s 335A.

338 Payments in respect of premises occupied by bankrupt

Where any premises comprised in a bankrupt's estate are occupied by him (whether by virtue of the preceding section or otherwise) on condition that he makes payments towards satisfying any liability arising under a mortgage of the premises or otherwise towards the outgoings of the premises, the bankrupt does not, by virtue of those payments, acquire any interest in the premises.

General note—If, by virtue of the making of an occupation order under s 33 of the Family Law Act 1996 or otherwise, premises forming part of the bankrupt's estate are occupied by the bankrupt on condition that the bankrupt makes payment towards any liability arising under a mortgage of those premises or otherwise on the outgoings of the premises, then the bankrupt acquires no interest in the premises by the fact of making such payments.

It would follow from the prohibition on the bankrupt acquiring any interest in premises, that any benefit which might accrue as a consequence of such payments, say on the reduction of capital liability under a mortgage, must accrue for the benefit of the bankrupt's estate. Certainly it would not seem possible for any such interest to be claimed by the trustee as after-acquired property since s 338 specifically precludes the possibility of such property being acquired by or devolving upon the bankrupt, as a consequence of which such property cannot fall within the scope of s 307(1).

339 Transactions at an undervalue

(1) Subject as follows in this section and sections 341 and 342, where an individual is adjudged bankrupt and he has at a relevant time (defined in section 341) entered into a transaction with any person at an undervalue, the trustee of the bankrupt's estate may apply to the court for an order under this section.

(2) The court shall, on such an application, make such order as it thinks fit for restoring the position to what it would have been if that individual had not entered into that transaction.

(3) For the purposes of this section and sections 341 and 342, an individual enters into a transaction with a person at an undervalue if—

(a)   he makes a gift to that person or he otherwise enters into a transaction with that person on terms that provide for him to receive no consideration,

(b)   he enters into a transaction with that person in consideration of marriage or the formation of a civil partnership, or

(c)   he enters into a transaction with that person for a consideration the value of which, in money or money's worth, is significantly less than the value, in money or money's worth, of the consideration provided by the individual.

Amendments—Civil Partnership Act 2004, s 261(1), Sch 27, para 119.

General note—This is equivalent to s 238, which deals with companies. The provision is almost identical save for the fact that, in addition to the transaction covered by s 238, transactions in consideration of marriage (s 339(3)(b)) may be caught by the section. The inclusion of this category is probably to address the fact that in equity marriage constitutes valid consideration (*Attorney-General v Jacobs Smith* [1895] 2 QB 341) and also under the previous legislation (Bankruptcy Act 1914, s 42) marriage could render an otherwise voidable transaction valid.

Trustees in bankruptcy need to secure approval from either the creditors' committee or the court before initiating proceedings under s 339 (s 314(1)(a); para 2A of Sch 5).

There is no equivalent to the defence that is potentially available in cases involving corporate insolvency under s 238(5). Also, the 'relevant time' that is explained in s 341 is different in some cases from that applying to s 238. See the comments accompanying s 341.

In something of a controversial decision, the Court of Appeal, in reversing the decision at first instance ([2007] EWHC 1012 (Ch)), held in *Hill v Haines* [2007] EWCA Civ 1284, [2007] BPIR 1280, [2008] 2 All ER 901, that a transfer made pursuant to an ancillary order for relief granted by the court under the Matrimonial Causes Act 1973, in relation to a divorce, was not a transaction at an undervalue. The Court held that the order did constitute consideration for the purposes of s 339. Inter alia, the property adjustment order made by the court involved the husband transferring his property to his wife. After the order the husband became bankrupt. The Court of Appeal held that s 339(3)(a) was inapplicable as the wife was deemed to have given consideration, namely that her claim had been turned into financial provision by the husband, and consequently the husband received consideration. Effectively, the order of the court quantifies the value of the wife's statutory right by reference to the value of the money or property thereby ordered to be paid or transferred by the husband to the wife (at [35] also, see [79]). Additionally, s 339(3)(c) was not applicable as the consideration provided by the wife constituted money's worth and its value was not less than the value of the consideration provided by the husband whether significantly or at all. This was the case whether an order was made with or without consent, absent fraud, mistake, misrepresentation or other vitiating factor (at [35], [47]). If a transfer occurs as a result of the couple colluding, dishonestly, it could be regarded as a transaction at an undervalue (at [46]). In *Re French* [2008] BPIR 1051, Chief Registrar Baister rejected the notion that any agreement between spouses that placed one of them ahead of creditors was collusive and dishonest ([64]). The Chief Registrar said that what was needed to establish collusion and dishonesty was evidence that the spouses had sought to put assets out of the reach of a trustee in bankruptcy (at [64]). The Court of Appeal in *Hill v Haines* could not accept that it was Parliament's intention that one of the most common orders made in matrimonial matters could be nullified by the action of a trustee in bankruptcy (at [36]). Leave to appeal to the House of Lords was denied.

See J Briggs 'Haines v Hill: Where Does This Leave a Trustee in Bankruptcy?' (2008) 21 *Insolvency Intelligence* 90.

See *Hargreaves v Salt* [2010] EWHC 3549 (Fam), [2011] BPIR 656 for a case where the court dealt with a s 339 application alongside an application under s 37 of the Matrimonial Causes Act 1973, both arising as a result of the same transaction.

In the Northern Irish case of *Official Receiver for Northern Ireland v Stranaghan* [2010] NICh 8, [2010] BPIR 928, the grant of a mortgage security for an existing loan was held to be void as a transaction at an undervalue where it was entered into only for the past consideration represented by the existing loan. See also *Re Peppard* [2009] BPIR 331, where various claimed elements of consideration were rejected by the court in the context of a transfer between family members. In particular the argument that good consideration could be given by a transferee by waiving repayment of a debt, repayment of which could have been challenged as a preference, was rejected.

The requirements for a transaction at an undervalue have also been reviewed by the court in the context of investments in an alleged pyramid scheme, and were found to be met on the facts: *Ailyan v Smith* [2010] EWHC 24 (Ch), [2010] BPIR 289.

A court has the discretion to make no remedial order even if a transaction falls foul of s 339, where justice requires: *Singla v Brown* [2007] EWHC 405 (Ch), [2007] BPIR 424 at [52]; *Trustee in Bankruptcy of Claridge v Claridge* [2011] EWHC 2047 (Ch), [2011] BPIR 1529 at [41]). Such action is likely to be something that is very much out of the ordinary (at [59]; *Hill v Haines* [2007] EWCA Civ 1284, [2007] BPIR 1280, [2008] 2 All ER 901 at [5]), and it would only be in exceptional circumstances would a court be justified in withholding relief to which the trustee in bankruptcy otherwise would seem to be entitled: *Stonham v Ramrattan* [2010] EWHC 1033 (Ch), [2010] BPIR 1210 at [40] (appeal to the Court of Appeal was dismissed ([2011] EWCA Civ 119, [2011] 1 WLR 1617), *Trustee in Bankruptcy of Claridge v Claridge* [2011] EWHC 2047 (Ch), [2011] BPIR 1529.

In *Re French* [2008] BPIR 1051, Chief Registrar Baister said that a court will take into account, where a claim originates from an order relating to a dissolution of marriage, the personal effect of a restitutionary order (at [68]). In that case the Chief Registrar would have taken into account, if the section applied, the fact that an order in favour of the trustee would have made homeless a man in serious ill health and who had a child living with him. He also would have taken into account the fact that he was not satisfied that the creditors would receive a real, tangible benefit (at [68]). As far as delay in taking action is concerned, it alone cannot be a relevant reason for not exercising the discretion to grant relief which would otherwise seem to be appropriate: *Stonham v Ramrattan* [2010] EWHC 1033 (Ch), [2010] BPIR 1210 (Mann J) at [34].

Limitation period – As with actions under s 238 in relation to companies, actions under this section are generally to be regarded as actions on a specialty, covered by ss 8 and 9 of the Limitation Act 1980, and as a consequence there is a 12-year time period in which office-holders can commence proceedings, *provided* that the substance of the application is to set aside a transaction: *Segal v Pasram* [2007] EWHC 3448 (Ch), [2007] BPIR 881.

See the notes relating to s 238.

340 Preferences

(1) Subject as follows in this and the next two sections, where an individual is adjudged bankrupt and he has at a relevant time (defined in section 341) given a preference to any person, the trustee of the bankrupt's estate may apply to the court for an order under this section.

(2) The court shall, on such an application, make such order as it thinks fit for restoring the position to what it would have been if that individual had not given that preference.

(3) For the purposes of this and the next two sections, an individual gives a preference to a person if—

    (a)   that person is one of the individual's creditors or a surety or guarantor for any of his debts or other liabilities, and

    (b)   the individual does anything or suffers anything to be done which (in either case) has the effect of putting that person into a position which, in the event of the individual's bankruptcy, will be better than the position he would have been in if that thing had not been done.

(4) The court shall not make an order under this section in respect of a preference given to any person unless the individual who gave the preference

was influenced in deciding to give it by a desire to produce in relation to that person the effect mentioned in subsection (3)(b) above.

(5) An individual who has given a preference to a person who, at the time the preference was given, was an associate of his (otherwise than by reason only of being his employee) is presumed, unless the contrary is shown, to have been influenced in deciding to give it by such a desire as is mentioned in subsection (4).

(6) The fact that something has been done in pursuance of the order of a court does not, without more, prevent the doing or suffering of that thing from constituting the giving of a preference.

General note—This is equivalent to s 239, which deals with companies, and is generally identical.

See the comments attaching to s 239.

Matrimonial Proceedings—In *Re French* [2008] BPIR 1051, Chief Registrar Baister rejected the argument that the spouse who benefitted under an ancilliary relief order could be regarded, for the purposes of the Insolvency Act, as a creditor of the spouse who had to make good on the relief, and who subsequently became a bankrupt. Hence a claim for a preference failed.

Influenced by a desire to provide a preference—This requirement is the same as in s 239, but it might be a little easier for a trustee to establish the desire of the bankrupt than a liquidator to try to establish the desire of a corporate body. However, after saying that, as with liquidators claiming preferences in relation to the corporate equivalent (s 239), trustees in bankruptcy have had little success in impugning transactions as preferences where the recipient of the alleged preference is not connected with the bankrupt (eg *Rooney v Das* [1999] BPIR 404; *Re Ledingham-Smith* [1993] BCLC 635).

See the comments under the same heading in relation to s 239.

Initiating proceedings—Trustees in bankruptcy need to secure approval from either the creditors' committee or the court before initiating proceedings under s 339 (s 314(1)(a); para 2A of Sch 5).

341 'Relevant time' under ss 339, 340

(1) Subject as follows, the time at which an individual enters into a transaction at an undervalue or gives a preference is a relevant time if the transaction is entered into or the preference given—

> (a) in the case of a transaction at an undervalue, at a time in the period of 5 years ending with the day of the presentation of the bankruptcy petition on which the individual is adjudged bankrupt,
>
> (b) in the case of a preference which is not a transaction at an undervalue and is given to a person who is an associate of the individual (otherwise than by reason only of being his employee), at a time in the period of 2 years ending with that day, and
>
> (c) in any other case of a preference which is not a transaction at an undervalue, at a time in the period of 6 months ending with that day.

(2) Where an individual enters into a transaction at an undervalue or gives a preference at a time mentioned in paragraph (a), (b) or (c) of subsection

(1) (not being, in the case of a transaction at an undervalue, a time less than 2 years before the end of the period mentioned in paragraph (a)), that time is not a relevant time for the purposes of sections 339 and 340 unless the individual—

    (a)   is insolvent at that time, or

    (b)   becomes insolvent in consequence of the transaction or preference;

but the requirements of this subsection are presumed to be satisfied, unless the contrary is shown, in relation to any transaction at an undervalue which is entered into by an individual with a person who is an associate of his (otherwise than by reason only of being his employee).

(3) For the purposes of subsection (2), an individual is insolvent if—

    (a)   he is unable to pay his debts as they fall due, or

    (b)   the value of his assets is less than the amount of his liabilities, taking into account his contingent and prospective liabilities.

(4) A transaction entered into or preference given by a person who is subsequently adjudged bankrupt on a petition under section 264(1)(d) (criminal bankruptcy) is to be treated as having been entered into or given at a relevant time for the purposes of sections 339 and 340 if it was entered into or given at any time on or after the date specified for the purposes of this subsection in the criminal bankruptcy order on which the petition was based.

(5) No order shall be made under section 339 or 340 by virtue of subsection (4) of this section where an appeal is pending (within the meaning of section 277) against the individual's conviction of any offence by virtue of which the criminal bankruptcy order was made.

General note—This is equivalent to s 240, which applies to companies. One major difference is that while s 240 only provides for a two-year time zone prior to the onset of insolvency for transactions at an undervalue, s 341 provides for an extended period of 5 years prior to the date of the presentation of the petition which led to the debtor's bankruptcy. Another difference is that if it can be established in a bankruptcy that the transaction at an undervalue was effected in the 2 years before the presentation of the bankruptcy petition, then there is no requirement to prove that the debtor was insolvent at the time of the transaction or became insolvent as a consequence of the entering into of the transaction.

Insolvent—Apart from where a transaction at an undervalue within the 2-year period preceding the bankruptcy is alleged, the trustee must establish either that the bankrupt was insolvent at the time of the transaction or that he or she became insolvent as a result of the transaction. Insolvency here means either cash flow or balance sheet insolvency, as set out in s 123(1)(e) and s 123(2), whereas, where a company is involved, insolvency can be in terms of any of the provisions in s 123. For a discussion of insolvency, see the comments under the heading 'Unable to pay debts' relating to s 123. As to the presumption of insolvency under s 341(2) in relation to an associate, see *Re Calder; Salter v Wetton* [2011] EWHC 3192 (Ch), [2012] BPIR 63 regarding what is required to overcome this presumption where the trustee advances a specific case as to the basis of insolvency.

    See the comments under s 240.

342 Orders under ss 339, 340

(1) Without prejudice to the generality of section 339(2) or 340(2), an order under either of those sections with respect to a transaction or preference entered into or given by an individual who is subsequently adjudged bankrupt may (subject as follows)—

(a)   require any property transferred as part of the transaction, or in connection with the giving of the preference, to be vested in the trustee of the bankrupt's estate as part of that estate;

(b)   require any property to be so vested if it represents in any person's hands the application either of the proceeds of sale of property so transferred or of money so transferred;

(c)   release or discharge (in whole or in part) any security given by the individual;

(d)   require any person to pay, in respect of benefits received by him from the individual, such sums to the trustee of his estate as the court may direct;

(e)   provide for any surety or guarantor whose obligations to any person were released or discharged (in whole or in part) under the transaction or by the giving of the preference to be under such new or revived obligations to that person as the court thinks appropriate;

(f)   provide for security to be provided for the discharge of any obligation imposed by or arising under the order, for such an obligation to be charged on any property and for the security or charge to have the same priority as a security or charge released or discharged (in whole or in part) under the transaction or by the giving of the preference; and

(g)   provide for the extent to which any person whose property is vested by the order in the trustee of the bankrupt's estate, or on whom obligations are imposed by the order, is to be able to prove in the bankruptcy for debts or other liabilities which arose from, or were released or discharged (in whole or in part) under or by, the transaction or the giving of the preference.

(2) An order under section 339 or 340 may affect the property of, or impose any obligation on, any person whether or not he is the person with whom the individual in question entered into the transaction or, as the case may be, the person to whom the preference was given; but such an order—

(a)   shall not prejudice any interest in property which was acquired from a person other than that individual and was acquired in good faith and for value, or prejudice any interest deriving from such an interest, and

(b)   shall not require a person who received a benefit from the transaction or preference in good faith and for value to pay a sum to the trustee of the bankrupt's estate, except where he was a party to the transaction or the payment is to be in respect of a preference given to that person at a time when he was a creditor of that individual.

(2A) Where a person has acquired an interest in property from a person other than the individual in question, or has received a benefit from the transaction or preference, and at the time of that acquisition or receipt—

(a)   he had notice of the relevant surrounding circumstances and of the relevant proceedings, or

(b)   he was an associate of, or was connected with, either the individual in question or the person with whom that individual entered into the transaction or to whom that individual gave the preference,

then, unless the contrary is shown, it shall be presumed for the purposes of paragraph (a) or (as the case may be) paragraph (b) of subsection (2) that the interest was acquired or the benefit was received otherwise than in good faith.

(3) Any sums required to be paid to the trustee in accordance with an order under section 339 or 340 shall be comprised in the bankrupt's estate.

(4) For the purposes of subsection (2A)(a), the relevant surrounding circumstances are (as the case may require)—

    (a)   the fact that the individual in question entered into the transaction at an undervalue; or

    (b)   the circumstances which amounted to the giving of the preference by the individual in question.

(5) For the purposes of subsection (2A)(a), a person has notice of the relevant proceedings if he has notice—

    (a)   of the fact that the petition on which the individual in question is adjudged bankrupt has been presented; or

    (b)   of the fact that the individual in question has been adjudged bankrupt.

(6) Section 249 in Part VII of this Act shall apply for the purposes of subsection (2A)(b) as it applies for the purposes of the first Group of Parts.

Amendments—Insolvency (No 2) Act 1994, s 2(1)–(3).

General note—This is equivalent to s 241, which deals with companies. Just like ss 238(3) and 239(3), with successful proceedings under either s 339 or s 340 the court is required to restore the position to what it was before the transaction that is adjusted (ss 339(2), 340(2)), but s 342 sets out some examples of orders that the court can make. As with s 241, courts are not limited to what is enumerated in s 342. The primary differences between s 342 and s 241 turn on the fact that the latter is dealing with companies.

Vesting—Several of the orders refer to property vesting in the trustee in bankruptcy. This is because the bankrupt's estate vests in the trustee in bankruptcy at the date of the appointment of the trustee (s 306), so orders involving the re-transfer of a bankrupt's property will involve providing that the property will vest in the trustee. In liquidation, by contrast, the property is transferred to the company, as usually the company property is not vested in the liquidator. As to the interaction between s 283A, s 339 and s 342, see *Stonham v Ramrattan* [2011] EWCA Civ 119, [2011] 1 WLR 1617, referred to above in relation to s 339.

    See the comments under s 241.

342A Recovery of excessive pension contributions

(1) Where an individual who is adjudged bankrupt—

    (a)   has rights under an approved pension arrangement, or

    (b)   has excluded rights under an unapproved pension arrangement,

the trustee of the bankrupt's estate may apply to the court for an order under this section.

(2) If the court is satisfied—

(a)   that the rights under the arrangement are to any extent, and whether directly or indirectly, the fruits of relevant contributions, and

(b)   that the making of any of the relevant contributions ('the excessive contributions') has unfairly prejudiced the individual's creditors,

the court may make such order as it thinks fit for restoring the position to what it would have been had the excessive contributions not been made.

(3) Subsection (4) applies where the court is satisfied that the value of the rights under the arrangement is, as a result of rights of the individual under the arrangement or any other pension arrangement having at any time become subject to a debit under section 29(1)(a) of the Welfare Reform and Pensions Act 1999 (debits giving effect to pension-sharing), less than it would otherwise have been.

(4) Where this subsection applies—

(a)   any relevant contributions which were represented by the rights which became subject to the debit shall, for the purposes of subsection (2), be taken to be contributions of which the rights under the arrangement are the fruits, and

(b)   where the relevant contributions represented by the rights under the arrangement (including those so represented by virtue of paragraph (a)) are not all excessive contributions, relevant contributions which are represented by the rights under the arrangement otherwise than by virtue of paragraph (a) shall be treated as excessive contributions before any which are so represented by virtue of that paragraph.

(5) In subsections (2) to (4) 'relevant contributions' means contributions to the arrangement or any other pension arrangement—

(a)   which the individual has at any time made on his own behalf, or

(b)   which have at any time been made on his behalf.

(6) The court shall, in determining whether it is satisfied under subsection (2)(b), consider in particular—

(a)   whether any of the contributions were made for the purpose of putting assets beyond the reach of the individual's creditors or any of them, and

(b)   whether the total amount of any contributions—

(i)   made by or on behalf of the individual to pension arrangements, and

(ii)   represented (whether directly or indirectly) by rights under approved pension arrangements or excluded rights under unapproved pension arrangements,

is an amount which is excessive in view of the individual's circumstances when those contributions were made.

(7) For the purposes of this section and sections 342B and 342C ('the recovery provisions'), rights of an individual under an unapproved pension

arrangement are excluded rights if they are rights which are excluded from his estate by virtue of regulations under section 12 of the Welfare Reform and Pensions Act 1999.

(8) In the recovery provisions—

'approved pension arrangement' has the same meaning as in section 11 of the Welfare Reform and Pensions Act 1999;

'unapproved pension arrangement' has the same meaning as in section 12 of that Act.

Amendments—Welfare Reform and Pensions Act 1999, s 15.

General note—Sections 342A to 342F came into force on 29 May 2000 and were introduced by Sch 12 to the Welfare Reform and Pensions Act 1999 and the Welfare Reform and Pensions Act 1999 (Commencement No 7) Order 2000 (SI 2000/1382).

These new provisions are necessary, given ss 11 and 12 of the 1999 Act which, in effect, exclude pension rights from the scope of the bankrupt's estate, subject to certain but uncommon exceptions. The consequence of those provisions is that a pension arrangement, as defined, represents a vehicle to which an individual in financial difficulties facing bankruptcy might be tempted to transfer assets with a view to those assets escaping the scope of the bankruptcy. These provisions, framed, as they are, in necessarily technical language, provide the basis by which a trustee might seek to challenge such conduct on the part of a bankrupt.

342B Orders under section 342A

(1) Without prejudice to the generality of section 342A(2), an order under section 342A may include provision—

(a) requiring the person responsible for the arrangement to pay an amount to the individual's trustee in bankruptcy,

(b) adjusting the liabilities of the arrangement in respect of the individual,

(c) adjusting any liabilities of the arrangement in respect of any other person that derive, directly or indirectly, from rights of the individual under the arrangement,

(d) for the recovery by the person responsible for the arrangement (whether by deduction from any amount which that person is ordered to pay or otherwise) of costs incurred by that person in complying in the bankrupt's case with any requirement under section 342C(1) or in giving effect to the order.

(2) In subsection (1), references to adjusting the liabilities of the arrangement in respect of a person include (in particular) reducing the amount of any benefit or future benefit to which that person is entitled under the arrangement.

(3) In subsection (1)(c), the reference to liabilities of the arrangement does not include liabilities in respect of a person which result from giving effect to an order or provision falling within section 28(1) of the Welfare Reform and Pensions Act 1999 (pension sharing orders and agreements).

(4) The maximum amount which the person responsible for an arrangement may be required to pay by an order under section 342A is the lesser of—

(a) the amount of the excessive contributions, and

(b) the value of the individual's rights under the arrangement (if the arrangement is an approved pension arrangement) or of his excluded rights under the arrangement (if the arrangement is an unapproved pension arrangement).

(5) An order under section 342A which requires the person responsible for an arrangement to pay an amount ('the restoration amount') to the individual's trustee in bankruptcy must provide for the liabilities of the arrangement to be correspondingly reduced.

(6) For the purposes of subsection (5), liabilities are correspondingly reduced if the difference between—

(a) the amount of the liabilities immediately before the reduction, and

(b) the amount of the liabilities immediately after the reduction,

is equal to the restoration amount.

(7) An order under section 342A in respect of an arrangement—

(a) shall be binding on the person responsible for the arrangement, and

(b) overrides provisions of the arrangement to the extent that they conflict with the provisions of the order.

Amendments—Welfare Reform and Pensions Act 1999, s 15.

342C Orders under section 342A: supplementary

(1) The person responsible for—

(a) an approved pension arrangement under which a bankrupt has rights,

(b) an unapproved pension arrangement under which a bankrupt has excluded rights, or

(c) a pension arrangement under which a bankrupt has at any time had rights,

shall, on the bankrupt's trustee in bankruptcy making a written request, provide the trustee with such information about the arrangement and rights as the trustee may reasonably require for, or in connection with, the making of applications under section 342A.

(2) Nothing in—

(a) any provision of section 159 of the Pension Schemes Act 1993 or section 91 of the Pensions Act 1995 (which prevent assignment and the making of orders that restrain a person from receiving anything which he is prevented from assigning),

(b) any provision of any enactment (whether passed or made before or after the passing of the Welfare Reform and Pensions Act 1999) corresponding to any of the provisions mentioned in paragraph (a), or

    (c)   any provision of the arrangement in question corresponding to any of those provisions,

applies to a court exercising its powers under section 342A.

(3) Where any sum is required by an order under section 342A to be paid to the trustee in bankruptcy, that sum shall be comprised in the bankrupt's estate.

(4) Regulations may, for the purposes of the recovery provisions, make provision about the calculation and verification of—

    (a)   any such value as is mentioned in section 342B(4)(b);

    (b)   any such amounts as are mentioned in section 342B(6)(a) and (b).

(5) The power conferred by subsection (4) includes power to provide for calculation or verification—

    (a)   in such manner as may, in the particular case, be approved by a prescribed person; or

    (b)   in accordance with guidance from time to time prepared by a prescribed person.

(6) References in the recovery provisions to the person responsible for a pension arrangement are to—

    (a)   the trustees, managers or provider of the arrangement, or

    (b)   the person having functions in relation to the arrangement corresponding to those of a trustee, manager or provider.

(7) In this section and sections 342A and 342B—

'prescribed' means prescribed by regulations;
'the recovery provisions' means this section and sections 342A and 342B;
'regulations' means regulations made by the Secretary of State.

(8) Regulations under the recovery provisions may—

    (a)   make different provision for different cases;

    (b)   contain such incidental, supplemental and transitional provisions as appear to the Secretary of State necessary or expedient.

(9) Regulations under the recovery provisions shall be made by statutory instrument subject to annulment in pursuance of a resolution of either House of Parliament.

Amendments—Welfare Reform and Pensions Act 1999, s 15; Pensions Act 2007, s 17, Sch 5, para 3.

General note—See the general note to s 342A.

342D Recovery of excessive contributions in pension-sharing cases

(1) For the purposes of sections 339, 341 and 342, a pension-sharing transaction shall be taken—

    (a)   to be a transaction, entered into by the transferor with the transferee, by which the appropriate amount is transferred by the transferor to the transferee; and

(b) to be capable of being a transaction entered into at an undervalue only so far as it is a transfer of so much of the appropriate amount as is recoverable.

(2) For the purposes of sections 340 to 342, a pension-sharing transaction shall be taken—

(a) to be something (namely a transfer of the appropriate amount to the transferee) done by the transferor; and

(b) to be capable of being a preference given to the transferee only so far as it is a transfer of so much of the appropriate amount as is recoverable.

(3) If on an application under section 339 or 340 any question arises as to whether, or the extent to which, the appropriate amount in the case of a pension-sharing transaction is recoverable, the question shall be determined in accordance with subsections (4) to (8).

(4) The court shall first determine the extent (if any) to which the transferor's rights under the shared arrangement at the time of the transaction appear to have been (whether directly or indirectly) the fruits of contributions ('personal contributions')—

(a) which the transferor has at any time made on his own behalf, or

(b) which have at any time been made on the transferor's behalf,

to the shared arrangement or any other pension arrangement.

(5) Where it appears that those rights were to any extent the fruits of personal contributions, the court shall then determine the extent (if any) to which those rights appear to have been the fruits of personal contributions whose making has unfairly prejudiced the transferor's creditors ('the unfair contributions').

(6) If it appears to the court that the extent to which those rights were the fruits of the unfair contributions is such that the transfer of the appropriate amount could have been made out of rights under the shared arrangement which were not the fruits of the unfair contributions, then the appropriate amount is not recoverable.

(7) If it appears to the court that the transfer could not have been wholly so made, then the appropriate amount is recoverable to the extent to which it appears to the court that the transfer could not have been so made.

(8) In making the determination mentioned in subsection (5) the court shall consider in particular—

(a) whether any of the personal contributions were made for the purpose of putting assets beyond the reach of the transferor's creditors or any of them, and

(b) whether the total amount of any personal contributions represented, at the time the pension-sharing transaction was made, by rights under pension arrangements is an amount which is excessive in view of the transferor's circumstances when those contributions were made.

(9) In this section and sections 342E and 342F—

'appropriate amount', in relation to a pension-sharing transaction, means the appropriate amount in relation to that transaction for the purposes of section 29(1) of the Welfare Reform and Pensions Act 1999 (creation of pension credits and debits);

'pension-sharing transaction' means an order or provision falling within section 28(1) of the Welfare Reform and Pensions Act 1999 (orders and agreements which activate pension-sharing);

'shared arrangement', in relation to a pension-sharing transaction, means the pension arrangement to which the transaction relates;

'transferee', in relation to a pension-sharing transaction, means the person for whose benefit the transaction is made;

'transferor', in relation to a pension-sharing transaction, means the person to whose rights the transaction relates

Amendments—Welfare Reform and Pensions Act 1999, s 84(1), Sch 12, Pt II, paras 70, 71.

General note—See the general note to s 342A.

342E Orders under section 339 or 340 in respect of pension-sharing transactions

(1) This section and section 342F apply if the court is making an order under section 339 or 340 in a case where—

(a) the transaction or preference is, or is any part of, a pension-sharing transaction, and

(b) the transferee has rights under a pension arrangement ('the destination arrangement', which may be the shared arrangement or any other pension arrangement) that are derived, directly or indirectly, from the pension-sharing transaction.

(2) Without prejudice to the generality of section 339(2) or 340(2), or of section 342, the order may include provision—

(a) requiring the person responsible for the destination arrangement to pay an amount to the transferor's trustee in bankruptcy,

(b) adjusting the liabilities of the destination arrangement in respect of the transferee,

(c) adjusting any liabilities of the destination arrangement in respect of any other person that derive, directly or indirectly, from rights of the transferee under the destination arrangement,

(d) for the recovery by the person responsible for the destination arrangement (whether by deduction from any amount which that person is ordered to pay or otherwise) of costs incurred by that person in complying in the transferor's case with any requirement under section 342F(1) or in giving effect to the order,

(e) for the recovery, from the transferor's trustee in bankruptcy, by the person responsible for a pension arrangement, of costs incurred by that person in complying in the transferor's case with any requirement under section 342F(2) or (3).

(3) In subsection (2), references to adjusting the liabilities of the destination arrangement in respect of a person include (in particular) reducing the amount of any benefit or future benefit to which that person is entitled under the arrangement.

(4) The maximum amount which the person responsible for the destination arrangement may be required to pay by the order is the smallest of—

    (a)   so much of the appropriate amount as, in accordance with section 342D, is recoverable,

    (b)   so much (if any) of the amount of the unfair contributions (within the meaning given by section 342D(5)) as is not recoverable by way of an order under section 342A containing provision such as is mentioned in section 342B(1)(a), and

    (c)   the value of the transferee's rights under the destination arrangement so far as they are derived, directly or indirectly, from the pension-sharing transaction.

(5) If the order requires the person responsible for the destination arrangement to pay an amount ('the restoration amount') to the transferor's trustee in bankruptcy it must provide for the liabilities of the arrangement to be correspondingly reduced.

(6) For the purposes of subsection (5), liabilities are correspondingly reduced if the difference between—

    (a)   the amount of the liabilities immediately before the reduction, and

    (b)   the amount of the liabilities immediately after the reduction,

is equal to the restoration amount.

(7) The order—

    (a)   shall be binding on the person responsible for the destination arrangement, and

    (b)   overrides provisions of the destination arrangement to the extent that they conflict with the provisions of the order.

Amendments—Welfare Reform and Pensions Act 1999, s 84(1), Sch 12, Pt II, paras 70, 71.

General note—See the general note to s 342A.

342F Orders under section 339 or 340 in pension-sharing cases: supplementary

(1) On the transferor's trustee in bankruptcy making a written request to the person responsible for the destination arrangement, that person shall provide the trustee with such information about—

    (a)   the arrangement,

    (b)   the transferee's rights under it, and

    (c)   where the destination arrangement is the shared arrangement, the transferor's rights under it,

as the trustee may reasonably require for, or in connection with, the making of applications under sections 339 and 340.

(2) Where the shared arrangement is not the destination arrangement, the person responsible for the shared arrangement shall, on the transferor's trustee in bankruptcy making a written request to that person, provide the trustee with such information about—

    (a)   the arrangement, and
    (b)   the transferor's rights under it,

as the trustee may reasonably require for, or in connection with, the making of applications under sections 339 and 340.

(3) On the transferor's trustee in bankruptcy making a written request to the person responsible for any intermediate arrangement, that person shall provide the trustee with such information about—

    (a)   the arrangement, and
    (b)   the transferee's rights under it,

as the trustee may reasonably require for, or in connection with, the making of applications under sections 339 and 340.

(4) In subsection (3) 'intermediate arrangement' means a pension arrangement, other than the shared arrangement or the destination arrangement, in relation to which the following conditions are fulfilled—

    (a)   there was a time when the transferee had rights under the arrangement that were derived (directly or indirectly) from the pension-sharing transaction, and
    (b)   the transferee's rights under the destination arrangement (so far as derived from the pension-sharing transaction) are to any extent derived (directly or indirectly) from the rights mentioned in paragraph (a).

(5) Nothing in—

    (a)   any provision of section 159 of the Pension Schemes Act 1993 or section 91 of the Pensions Act 1995 (which prevent assignment and the making of orders which restrain a person from receiving anything which he is prevented from assigning),
    (b)   any provision of any enactment (whether passed or made before or after the passing of the Welfare Reform and Pensions Act 1999) corresponding to any of the provisions mentioned in paragraph (a), or
    (c)   any provision of the destination arrangement corresponding to any of those provisions,

applies to a court exercising its powers under section 339 or 340.

(6) Regulations may, for the purposes of sections 339 to 342, sections 342D and 342E and this section, make provision about the calculation and verification of—

    (a)   any such value as is mentioned in section 342E(4)(c);
    (b)   any such amounts as are mentioned in section 342E(6)(a) and (b).

(7) The power conferred by subsection (6) includes power to provide for calculation or verification—

  (a) in such manner as may, in the particular case, be approved by a prescribed person; or

  (b) in accordance with guidance from time to time prepared by a prescribed person.

(8) In section 342E and this section, references to the person responsible for a pension arrangement are to—

  (a) the trustees, managers or provider of the arrangement, or

  (b) the person having functions in relation to the arrangement corresponding to those of a trustee, manager or provider.

(9) In this section—

  'prescribed' means prescribed by regulations;
  'regulations' means regulations made by the Secretary of State.

(10) Regulations under this section may—

  (a) make different provision for different cases;

  (b) contain such incidental, supplemental and transitional provisions as appear to the Secretary of State necessary or expedient.

(11) Regulations under this section shall be made by statutory instrument subject to annulment in pursuance of a resolution of either House of Parliament.

Amendments—Welfare Reform and Pensions Act 1999, s 84(1), Sch 12, Pt II, paras 70, 71; Pensions Act 2007, s 17, Sch 5, para 4.

General note—See the general note to s 342A.

343 Extortionate credit transactions

(1) This section applies where a person is adjudged bankrupt who is or has been a party to a transaction for, or involving, the provision to him of credit.

(2) The court may, on the application of the trustee of the bankrupt's estate, make an order with respect to the transaction if the transaction is or was extortionate and was not entered into more than 3 years before the commencement of the bankruptcy.

(3) For the purposes of this section a transaction is extortionate if, having regard to the risk accepted by the person providing the credit—

  (a) the terms of it are or were such as to require grossly exorbitant payments to be made (whether unconditionally or in certain contingencies) in respect of the provision of the credit, or

  (b) it otherwise grossly contravened ordinary principles of fair dealing;

and it shall be presumed, unless the contrary is proved, that a transaction with respect to which an application is made under this section is or, as the case may be, was extortionate.

(4) An order under this section with respect to any transaction may contain such one or more of the following as the court thinks fit, that is to say—

- (a) provision setting aside the whole or part of any obligation created by the transaction;
- (b) provision otherwise varying the terms of the transaction or varying the terms on which any security for the purposes of the transaction is held;
- (c) provision requiring any person who is or was party to the transaction to pay to the trustee any sums paid to that person, by virtue of the transaction, by the bankrupt;
- (d) provision requiring any person to surrender to the trustee any property held by him as security for the purposes of the transaction;
- (e) provision directing accounts to be taken between any persons.

(5) Any sums or property required to be paid or surrendered to the trustee in accordance with an order under this section shall be comprised in the bankrupt's estate.

(6) .The powers conferred by this section are exercisable in relation to any transaction concurrently with any powers exercisable under this Act in relation to that transaction as a transaction at an undervalue.

Amendments—Consumer Credit Act 2006, s 70, Sch 4.

General note—These provisions allow a trustee to make application to the court for relief under s 343(2) and (4) in relation to any credit transaction entered into by the bankrupt in the three years prior to the making of the bankruptcy order on the grounds that the transaction is or was extortionate. As such, these provisions bear a close resemblance to s 139(1)(a) of the Consumer Credit Act 1974 which allow a debtor to apply to the court to re-open a credit agreement on the grounds that what is termed therein a 'credit bargain' is extortionate.

It appears from *Davies v Directloans Ltd* [1986] 1 WLR 823 (a case decided under the Consumer Credit Act 1974) that the court is limited to having regard to those factors in s 343(3) alone in assessing whether a transaction is extortionate. In reversing the usual position the subsection places the burden of proof on the other party to the transaction in establishing that the transaction was not extortionate.

The second sentence in s 343(6) confirms that, notwithstanding s 343, a trustee retains standing to challenge a credit transaction as a transaction-at-undervalue under s 339, but not, apparently, as a preference under s 340.

The commentary on the analogous provision in s 244, applicable in liquidations, should also be considered here.

344 Avoidance of general assignment of book debts

(1) The following applies where a person engaged in any business makes a general assignment to another person of his existing or future book debts, or any class of them, and is subsequently adjudged bankrupt.

(2) The assignment is void against the trustee of the bankrupt's estate as regards book debts which were not paid before the presentation of the bankruptcy petition, unless the assignment has been registered under the Bills of Sale Act 1878.

(3) For the purposes of subsections (1) and (2)—

- (a) 'assignment' includes an assignment by way of security or charge on book debts, and
- (b) 'general assignment' does not include—

(i)   an assignment of book debts due at the date of the assignment from specified debtors or of debts becoming due under specified contracts, or

(ii)   an assignment of book debts included either in a transfer of a business made in good faith and for value or in an assignment of assets for the benefit of creditors generally.

(4) For the purposes of registration under the Act of 1878 an assignment of book debts is to be treated as if it were a bill of sale given otherwise than by way of security for the payment of a sum of money; and the provisions of that Act with respect to the registration of bills of sale apply accordingly with such necessary modifications as may be made by rules under that Act.

General note—This provision renders void a general assignment of book debts, a term which includes an assignment by way of security or charge of book debts, to the extent that such book debts were not paid before the presentation of a bankruptcy petition other than where the assignment was registered under the Bills of Sale Act 1878. A specific assignment of particular debts falls outside of the provision, as does an assignment effected in the transfer of a business made in good faith or an assignment for the benefit of creditors generally, as might arise in the context of an IVA: s 344(3).

If, prior to bankruptcy, an individual enters into a general assignment of book debts and subsequently enters into a specific assignment of particular book debts, then s 344 will render the general assignment void but will not affect the specific assignment: *Hill v Alex Lawrie Factors* [2000] BPIR 1038 (Jacob J, as he then was).

345 Contracts to which bankrupt is a party

(1) The following applies where a contract has been made with a person who is subsequently adjudged bankrupt.

(2) The court may, on the application of any other party to the contract, make an order discharging obligations under the contract on such terms as to payment by the applicant or the bankrupt of damages for non-performance or otherwise as appear to the court to be equitable.

(3) Any damages payable by the bankrupt by virtue of an order of the court under this section are provable as a bankruptcy debt.

(4) Where an undischarged bankrupt is a contractor in respect of any contract jointly with any person, that person may sue or be sued in respect of the contract without the joinder of the bankrupt.

General note—It is a long-established rule at common law that a contract is not determined by the bankruptcy of one of the parties to the agreement: *Ex parte Chalmers* (1873) LR 8 Ch App 289, CA. Whilst a trustee might disclaim a contract as onerous property under s 315(2), the present provision allows the other party to the contract to make an application to court for an order discharging obligations under the contract on terms envisaged by s 345(2). Subsection (3) then permits that party to prove for any damages payable by virtue of the court's order as a bankruptcy debt.

In practice, s 345 will often have no application, particularly where the parties contract on the basis of detailed standard form terms, since commercial contracts frequently provide for automatic termination, together with the agreed consequences thereof, on bankruptcy or even the presentation of a bankruptcy petition or, equally commonly, stipulated events in connection with an IVA proposal.

346 Enforcement procedures

(1) Subject to section 285 in Chapter II (restrictions on proceedings and remedies) and to the following provisions of this section, where the creditor of any person who is adjudged bankrupt has, before the commencement of the bankruptcy—

  (a) issued execution against the goods or land of that person, or
  (b) attached a debt due to that person from another person,

that creditor is not entitled, as against the official receiver or trustee of the bankrupt's estate, to retain the benefit of the execution or attachment, or any sums paid to avoid it, unless the execution or attachment was completed, or the sums were paid, before the commencement of the bankruptcy.

(2) Subject as follows, where any goods of a person have been taken in execution, then, if before the completion of the execution notice is given to the enforcement officer or other officer charged with the execution that that person has been adjudged bankrupt—

  (a) the enforcement officer or other officer shall on request deliver to the official receiver or trustee of the bankrupt's estate the goods and any money seized or recovered in part satisfaction of the execution, but
  (b) the costs of the execution are a first charge on the goods or money so delivered and the official receiver or trustee may sell the goods or a sufficient part of them for the purpose of satisfying the charge.

(3) Subject to subsection (6) below, where—

  (a) under an execution in respect of a judgment for a sum exceeding such sum as may be prescribed for the purposes of this subsection, the goods of any person are sold or money is paid in order to avoid a sale, and
  (b) before the end of the period of 14 days beginning with the day of the sale or payment the enforcement officer or other officer charged with the execution is given notice that a bankruptcy petition has been presented in relation to that person, and
  (c) a bankruptcy order is or has been made on that petition,

the balance of the proceeds of sale or money paid, after deducting the costs of execution, shall (in priority to the claim of the execution creditor) be comprised in the bankrupt's estate.

(4) Accordingly, in the case of an execution in respect of a judgment for a sum exceeding the sum prescribed for the purposes of subsection (3), the enforcement officer or other officer charged with the execution—

  (a) shall not dispose of the balance mentioned in subsection (3) at any time within the period of 14 days so mentioned or while there is pending a bankruptcy petition of which he has been given notice under that subsection, and
  (b) shall pay that balance, where by virtue of that subsection it is

557

comprised in the bankrupt's estate, to the official receiver or (if there is one) to the trustee of that estate.

(5) For the purposes of this section—

    (a)   an execution against goods is completed by seizure and sale or by the making of a charging order under section 1 of the Charging Orders Act 1979;

    (b)   an execution against land is completed by seizure, by the appointment of a receiver or by the making of a charging order under that section;

    (c)   an attachment of a debt is completed by the receipt of the debt.

(6) The rights conferred by subsections (1) to (3) on the official receiver or the trustee may, to such extent and on such terms as it thinks fit, be set aside by the court in favour of the creditor who has issued the execution or attached the debt.

(7) Nothing in this section entitles the trustee of a bankrupt's estate to claim goods from a person who has acquired them in good faith under a sale by an enforcement officer or other officer charged with an execution.

(8) Neither subsection (2) nor subsection (3) applies in relation to any execution against property which has been acquired by or has devolved upon the bankrupt since the commencement of the bankruptcy, unless, at the time the execution is issued or before it is completed—

    (a)   the property has been or is claimed for the bankrupt's estate under section 307 (after-acquired property), and

    (b)   a copy of the notice given under that section has been or is served on the enforcement officer or other officer charged with the execution.

(9) In this section 'enforcement officer' means an individual who is authorised to act as an enforcement officer under the Courts Act 2003.

Amendments—Courts Act 2003, s 109(1), Sch 8, para 297(1)–(4).

General note—These provisions provide, in fairly elaborate terms, for the circumstances in which a creditor is entitled to retain the benefit of an execution or attachment where the execution was issued or debt due attached prior to the commencement of the bankruptcy (ie the date of the bankruptcy order: s 278(a)). The court may also stay an execution under s 285(1) or (2). Section 285(3)(a) expressly provides that a creditor has no remedy against the property or person of a bankrupt after the making of a bankruptcy order, a provision which, in contrast to s 285(3)(b), is not subject to contrary leave of the court.

    The commentary on the analogous provisions in liquidation in ss 183 and 184 will also be of assistance here.

The sum prescribed for the purposes of s 346(3) and (4)—With effect from 1 April 2004 the sum prescribed is £1,000 by virtue of the Insolvency Proceedings (Monetary Limits) (Amendment) Order 2004 (SI 2004/547).

Challenge to execution or attachment completed before the commencement of the bankruptcy—Despite the terms of s 346(1), a trustee may challenge a charging order absolute or a garnishee order absolute, particularly where any such order was obtained only a short period prior to the making of the bankruptcy order, as can arise in practice where a bankruptcy petition is not presented in the same court as that in which the order absolute is obtained. The trustee's standing to challenge an order absolute arises under CPR, r 40.9: *Industrial Diseases Compensation Ltd v Marrons* [2001] BPIR 600 at 606C–606F (His

Honour Judge Behrens sitting as a High Court judge). The court's discretion in setting aside an order absolute will be based on the seven principles summarised by Lord Brandon in the Court of Appeal in *Roberts Petroleum v Bernard Kenny Ltd* [1982] 1 All ER 685 at 690E–690J, as elaborated upon in the opinion of Lord Brightman in the House of Lords [1983] AC 192 at 207E–208C. The reasoning in *Marrons* was approved and the House of Lords' judgment, and its effect on the principles espoused by Lord Brandon in the Court of Appeal in that case, was analysed in the decision of David Hodge QC, sitting as a deputy High Court judge, in *Morris Dean (a firm) v Bryan Hilton Slater* (Chancery Division, Manchester District Registry, 23 June 2005). See also *Wright v Nationwide Building Society* [2009] EWCA Civ 811, [2010] Ch 318, where it was held that legislative policy was not to be taken as requiring that a creditor having completed execution ought to be deprived of the benefit of it on an application by the trustee under s 3(5) of the Charging Orders Act 1979 merely on the basis of a subsequent bankruptcy order.

Application by creditor to set aside rights conferred on official receiver or trustee under s 346(6)—See *Tagore Investments SA v Official Receiver* [2008] EWHC 3495 (Ch), [2009] BPIR 392 for a consideration of the circumstances in which an application by a creditor having issued execution or attached a debt may be entertained.

Procedure—For the procedure as to notice in a case under ss 346(2) or 346(3)(b) see r 12.19. The assessment of a sheriff's bill for the purposes of s 346(2) or (3) is governed by r 7.36.

347 Distress, etc

(1) The right of any landlord or other person to whom rent is payable to distrain upon the goods and effects of an undischarged bankrupt for rent due to him from the bankrupt is available (subject to sections 252(2)(b) and 254(1) above and subsection (5) below) against goods and effects comprised in the bankrupt's estate, but only for 6 months' rent accrued due before the commencement of the bankruptcy.

(2) Where a landlord or other person to whom rent is payable has distrained for rent upon the goods and effects of an individual to whom a bankruptcy petition relates and a bankruptcy order is subsequently made on that petition, any amount recovered by way of that distress which—

(a) is in excess of the amount which by virtue of subsection (1) would have been recoverable after the commencement of the bankruptcy, or

(b) is in respect of rent for a period or part of a period after the distress was levied,

shall be held for the bankrupt as part of his estate.

(3) Where any person (whether or not a landlord or person entitled to rent) has distrained upon the goods or effects of an individual who is adjudged bankrupt before the end of the period of 3 months beginning with the distraint, so much of those goods or effects, or of the proceeds of their sale, as is not held for the bankrupt under subsection (2) shall be charged for the benefit of the bankrupt's estate with the preferential debts of the bankrupt to the extent that the bankrupt's estate is for the time being insufficient for meeting those debts.

(4) Where by virtue of any charge under subsection (3) any person surrenders any goods or effects to the trustee of a bankrupt's estate or makes a payment to such a trustee, that person ranks, in respect of the amount of the proceeds of the sale of those goods or effects by the trustee

or, as the case may be, the amount of the payment, as a preferential creditor of the bankrupt, except as against so much of the bankrupt's estate as is available for the payment of preferential creditors by virtue of the surrender or payment.

(5) A landlord or other person to whom rent is payable is not at any time after the discharge of a bankrupt entitled to distrain upon any goods or effects comprised in the bankrupt's estate.

(6) Where in the case of any execution—

    (a)   a landlord is (apart from this section) entitled under section 1 of the Landlord and Tenant Act 1709 or section 102 of the County Courts Act 1984 (claims for rent where goods seized in execution) to claim for an amount not exceeding one year's rent, and

    (b)   the person against whom the execution is levied is adjudged bankrupt before the notice of claim is served on the enforcement officer, or other officer charged with the execution,

the right of the landlord to claim under that section is restricted to a right to claim for an amount not exceeding 6 months' rent and does not extend to any rent payable in respect of a period after the notice of claim is so served.

(7) Nothing in subsection (6) imposes any liability on an enforcement officer or other officer charged with an execution to account to the official receiver or the trustee of a bankrupt's estate for any sums paid by him to a landlord at any time before the enforcement officer or other officer was served with notice of the bankruptcy order in question.

But this subsection is without prejudice to the liability of the landlord.

(8) Subject to sections 252(2)(b) and 254(1) above nothing in this Group of Parts affects any right to distrain otherwise than for rent; and any such right is at any time exercisable without restriction against property comprised in a bankrupt's estate, even if that right is expressed by any enactment to be exercisable in like manner as a right to distrain for rent.

(9) Any right to distrain against property comprised in a bankrupt's estate is exercisable notwithstanding that the property has vested in the trustee.

(10) The provisions of this section are without prejudice to a landlord's right in a bankruptcy to prove for any bankruptcy debt in respect of rent.

(11) In this section 'enforcement officer' means an individual who is authorised to act as an enforcement officer under the Courts Act 2003.

Amendments—Insolvency Act 2000, s 3, Sch 3, paras 1, 14(a), (b); Courts Act 2003, s 109(1), (4), Sch 8, para 298(1)–(3).

General note—These intricate provisions provide, essentially, in s 347(1), that bankruptcy has no effect on the right of a landlord or other person to whom rent is payable to distrain upon the goods and effects of an undischarged bankrupt, save that the distraint is limited to six months' rent accrued due before the bankruptcy order. The fact that the bankrupt's estate will have vested in the trustee under s 306, or conceivably under ss 307 or 310, is immaterial: s 347(9). Sections 347(2)–(10) follow from the basic rule in s 347(1). Three particular points warrant mention. First, the combined effect of s 347(3) and (4) is to create a statutory charge to secure preferential debts over the goods or effects distrained upon, or the proceeds of sale thereof, consequential upon which the landlord or person entitled to rent is subrogated to the position of the preferential creditors so secured for an equivalent sum. Secondly, the discharge of a bankrupt terminates the right of a landlord or other person to distrain upon any goods or effects comprised in the bankrupt's estate: s 347(5). Thirdly, s 347(10) makes clear that a landlord retains standing to prove for outstanding rent as a bankruptcy debt. However, whilst a landlord is not precluded from distraining by virtue of submitting a proof in respect of rent, the landlord is put to election as between a dividend and distraint at the time the dividend becomes payable: *Holmes v Watt* [1935] 2 KB 300, CA.

348 Apprenticeships, etc

(1) This section applies where—

    (a)   a bankruptcy order is made in respect of an individual to whom another individual was an apprentice or articled clerk at the time when the petition on which the order was made was presented, and

    (b)   the bankrupt or the apprentice or clerk gives notice to the trustee terminating the apprenticeship or articles.

(2) Subject to subsection (6) below, the indenture of apprenticeship or, as the case may be, the articles of agreement shall be discharged with effect from the commencement of the bankruptcy.

(3) If any money has been paid by or on behalf of the apprentice or clerk to the bankrupt as a fee, the trustee may, on an application made by or on behalf of the apprentice or clerk, pay such sum to the apprentice or clerk as the trustee thinks reasonable, having regard to—

    (a)   the amount of the fee,

    (b)   the proportion of the period in respect of which the fee was paid that has been served by the apprentice or clerk before the commencement of the bankruptcy, and

    (c)   the other circumstances of the case.

(4) The power of the trustee to make a payment under subsection (3) has priority over his obligation to distribute the bankrupt's estate.

(5) Instead of making a payment under subsection (3), the trustee may, if it appears to him expedient to do so on an application made by or on behalf of the apprentice or clerk, transfer the indenture or articles to a person other than the bankrupt.

(6) Where a transfer is made under subsection (5), subsection (2) has effect only as between the apprentice or clerk and the bankrupt.

General note—These provisions are more or less self-explanatory and are rarely applicable in practice. For the payment to an apprentice or articled clerk from the National Insurance Fund see ss 182 and 184 of the Employment Rights Act 1996.

349 Unenforceability of liens on books, etc

(1) Subject as follows, a lien or other right to retain possession of any of the books, papers or other records of a bankrupt is unenforceable to the extent that its enforcement would deny possession of any books, papers or other records to the official receiver or the trustee of the bankrupt's estate.

(2) Subsection (1) does not apply to a lien on documents which give a title to property and are held as such.

General note—Reference should be made here to the commentary on s 246, which is identical in substance to s 349.

349A Arbitration agreements to which bankrupt is party

(1) This section applies where a bankrupt had become party to a contract containing an arbitration agreement before the commencement of his bankruptcy.

(2) If the trustee in bankruptcy adopts the contract, the arbitration agreement is enforceable by or against the trustee in relation to matters arising from or connected with the contract.

(3) If the trustee in bankruptcy does not adopt the contract and a matter to which the arbitration agreement applies requires to be determined in connection with or for the purposes of the bankruptcy proceedings—

    (a)   the trustee with the consent of the creditors' committee, or
    (b)   any other party to the agreement,

may apply to the court which may, if it thinks fit in all the circumstances of the case, order that the matter be referred to arbitration in accordance with the arbitration agreement.

(4) In this section—

    'arbitration agreement' has the same meaning as in Part I of the Arbitration Act 1996; and
    'the court' means the court which has jurisdiction in the bankruptcy proceedings.

Amendments—Inserted by Arbitration Act 1996, s 107(1), Sch 3, para 46.

Chapter VI

Bankruptcy Offences

Reference should be had to the introduction to Chapter X of Part IV of the Act.

Preliminary

350 Scheme of this Chapter

(1) Subject to section 360(3) below, this Chapter applies where the court has made a bankruptcy order on a bankruptcy petition.

(2) This Chapter applies whether or not the bankruptcy order is annulled, but proceedings for an offence under this Chapter shall not be instituted after the annulment.

(3) Without prejudice to his liability in respect of a subsequent bankruptcy, the bankrupt is not guilty of an offence under this Chapter in respect of anything done after his discharge; but nothing in this Group of

Parts prevents the institution of proceedings against a discharged bankrupt for an offence committed before his discharge.

(3A) Subsection (3) is without prejudice to any provision of this Chapter which applies to a person in respect of whom a bankruptcy restrictions order is in force.

(4) It is not a defence in proceedings for an offence under this Chapter that anything relied on, in whole or in part, as constituting that offence was done outside England and Wales.

(5) Proceedings for an offence under this Chapter or under the rules shall not be instituted except by the Secretary of State or by or with the consent of the Director of Public Prosecutions.

(6) A person guilty of an offence under this Chapter is liable to imprisonment or a fine, or both.

Amendments—Enterprise Act 2002, s 257(3), Sch 21, para 2.

General note—This provision, together with the definitions in s 351, relates to those offences in ss 353–360.

Under s 350(2) proceedings for an offence are not affected by an annulment provided that the proceedings are instituted prior to the annulment. On the other hand, by virtue of s 350(3), proceedings may be instituted irrespective of discharge, but only in respect of an offence committed prior to discharge.

Human rights—On the question of whether the Human Rights Act 1998 can operate in a retrospective way to render unsafe convictions which were unimpeachable at the date of trial see the survey of the law expressed in the opinions of the House of Lords in *R v Kansal* [2001] UKHL 62, [2002] BPIR 370.

Documentary evidence relied upon by the Crown—In *Re Attorney General's Reference (No 7 of 2000)* (2001) *The Times*, April 12 the Criminal Division of the Court of Appeal held that a bankrupt's right to a fair trial under Art 6 of the European Convention on Human Rights was not breached where the Crown relied upon documents which had been delivered to the official receiver under s 291(1)(b) (duties of bankrupt in relation to official receiver) where the delivery up had been made under compulsion but where the documents did not contain any statement made by the bankrupt under compulsion.

Other offences—Schedule 5 details five further offences which may be committed under the rules; in the context of bankruptcy only r 12.18 (false representation of status for purpose of inspection documents) is relevant.

Penalties—See s 430 and Sch 10. Schedule 5 deals with the punishment of offences under the rules and should be read in conjunction with r 12.21.

351 Definitions

In the following provisions of this Chapter—

    (a)   references to property comprised in the bankrupt's estate or to property possession of which is required to be delivered up to the official receiver or the trustee of the bankrupt's estate include any property which would be such property if a notice in respect of it were given under section 307 (after-acquired property), section 308 (personal property and effects of bankrupt having more than replacement value) or section 308A (vesting in trustee of certain tenancies);

(b) 'the initial period' means the period between the presentation of the bankruptcy petition and the commencement of the bankruptcy; and

(c) a reference to a number of months or years before petition is to that period ending with the presentation of the bankruptcy petition.

Amendments—Housing Act 1988, s 140, Sch 17, Part I.

General note—The offences in ss 353–359 should be read with references to these definitions. The definition in s 351(a) extends the basic definition of the bankruptcy estate in s 283(1).

352 Defence of innocent intention

Where in the case of an offence under any provision of this Chapter it is stated that this section applies, a person is not guilty of the offence if he proves that, at the time of the conduct constituting the offence, he had no intent to defraud or to conceal the state of his affairs.

General note—The effect of this provision is to bring the availability of the defence of innocent intention into play in the case of any of the offences in ss 353–359 in which reference to s 352 is made. The defence will not, therefore, be available to defendants in proceedings instituted under ss 354(3), 356(2), 359(2) and 360(1).

The burden of proof—In *R v Daniel* [2002] EWCA Crim 959, [2002] BPIR 1193 the Court of Appeal (Auld LJ, Newman and Roderick-Evans JJ) held at [31] and [36] that, in the context of an appeal against conviction under s 354(1)(b), the burden of proof in establishing concealment rests with the prosecution but, once discharged, and for the purpose of the defence of innocent intention, the burden of proof then switches to the defendant, who must establish on the balance of probabilities that he did not intend to conceal the property. The burden of proof on the defendant is persuasive and legal, and not merely evidential: *Attorney-General's Reference (No 1 of 2004); R v Edwards* [2004] EWCA Crim 1025, [2004] 1 WLR 2111, [2004] BPIR 1073. In this case the Court was concerned with the interaction of s 352 with the offences in ss 353 and 357, and concluded that (1) where s 352 is read with s 353, the legal burden created does not infringe Art 6 of the European Convention on Human Rights but (2) the same cannot be said as regards s 357. However, s 352 could be interpreted when read in conjunction with s 357 such that it imposes a merely evidential burden upon the defendant, which would not breach Art 6. See also *DBIS v Compton* [2012] BPIR 1108 for further discussion of the burden of proof as regards the interaction between s 352 and 357.

Wrongdoing by the bankrupt before and after bankruptcy

353 Non-disclosure

(1) The bankrupt is guilty of an offence if—

(a) he does not to the best of his knowledge and belief disclose all the property comprised in his estate to the official receiver or the trustee, or

(b) he does not inform the official receiver or the trustee of any disposal of any property which but for the disposal would be so comprised, stating how, when, to whom and for what consideration the property was disposed of.

(2) Subsection (1)(b) does not apply to any disposal in the ordinary course of a business carried on by the bankrupt or to any payment of the ordinary expenses of the bankrupt or his family.

(3) Section 352 applies to this offence.

General note—Perhaps given the very obvious evidential difficulties, there is no reported authority on a conviction under this provision under the 1986 Act, which reproduces the provision in s 154(1) of the Bankruptcy Act 1914. Note *Williams v Mohammed* [2011] BPIR 1787 where HHJ Hodge QC upheld an order that the bankrupt deliver up an attendance note of a meeting between himself and his solicitor on the basis that the usual privilege attaching to the document had been abrogated by the iniquity exception: the bankrupts underlying purpose in seeking advice at the meeting was to attempt to conceal from the trustee assets comprised in his estate (contrary to s 353 and s 354).

The judgment in *Re Bolus* (1870) 23 LT 339 considers the phrase 'in the ordinary course of business' in the context of the now repealed s 11 of the Debtors Act 1969, although the antiquity of that authority and the new legislative code in the 1986 Act, as amended, really call for a more contemporary judicial view on the point.

Defence of innocent intention—See the notes to s 352.

354 Concealment of property

(1) The bankrupt is guilty of an offence if—

(a) he does not deliver up possession to the official receiver or trustee, or as the official receiver or trustee may direct, of such part of the property comprised in his estate as is in his possession or under his control and possession of which he is required by law so to deliver up,

(b) he conceals any debt due to or from him or conceals any property the value of which is not less than the prescribed amount and possession of which he is required to deliver up to the official receiver or trustee, or

(c) in the 12 months before petition, or in the initial period, he did anything which would have been an offence under paragraph (b) above if the bankruptcy order had been made immediately before he did it.

Section 352 applies to this offence.

(2) The bankrupt is guilty of an offence if he removes, or in the initial period removed, any property the value of which was not less than the prescribed amount and possession of which he has or would have been required to deliver up to the official receiver or the trustee.

Section 352 applies to this offence.

(3) The bankrupt is guilty of an offence if he without reasonable excuse fails, on being required to do so by the official receiver, the trustee or the court—

(a) to account for the loss of any substantial part of his property incurred in the 12 months before petition or in the initial period, or

(b) to give a satisfactory explanation of the manner in which such a loss was incurred

Amendments—Enterprise Act 2002, s 269, Sch 23, paras 1, 12.

General note—The offences within this provision are closely related to those in s 353 and references should be made to the notes thereto. See also the notes accompanying s 206. For the purposes of the Human Rights Act 1998 s 354 is indistinguishable from s 206: *R v Daniel* [2002] EWCA Crim 959).

'conceals'—See the note to s 206.

The direction of the jury in a s 354(2) case—It is irrelevant for the purposes of this offence that a debt settled by the bankrupt out of property which ought to have been delivered up was not a provable debt: *Woodley v Woodley (No 2)* [1994] 1 WLR 1167.

Section 354(2)

'... the prescribed amount ...'—With effect from 1 April 2004 the prescribed amount was increased from £500 to £1,000 under the Insolvency Proceedings (Monetary Limits) (Amendment) Order 2004 (SI 2004/547).

Section 354(3)

Failure to account for loss—In the words of Sachs LJ in *R v Salter* [1968] 2 QB 793 at 809, in commenting on the similarly worded predecessor to s 354(2), this provision:

> 'intends to and does, in the interests of the business community as a whole, put in peril the man who goes bankrupt without having so conducted his affairs as to be able satisfactorily to explain why some substantial loss has been incurred. It is as well to make it plain, as the offence is absolute, it follows that, once a prosecution has been initiated, no issue arises before verdict as to the reason why the failure has occurred or as to any motive which led to that failure.'

> A jury should be directed that an offence has been committed if they are satisfied, as regards the total sum of money constituting the loss of any substantial part of his estate, that the bankrupt had not at the time of the alleged failure given, with such reasonable details as was appropriate in the circumstances, an explanation which is both reasonably clear and true of how such sum was made up (as the loss may be composed of more than one component), of how it came to be lost, and where the money has gone. The degree of particularity required of the bankrupt will depend on the facts of the case and may vary greatly between cases.

Human rights—Given the public interest served by the investigation and realisation of assets caught by the bankruptcy estate, the Court of Appeal held in *R v Kearns* [2002] EWCA Crim 748, [2002] 1 WLR 2815 that s 354(3) is proportionate to the extent that a bankrupt is deprived of his right to silence or a right against self-incrimination, with the consequence that a prosecution under that provision does not violate an individual's right to a fair trial under Art 6 of the European Convention on Human Rights.

Defence of innocent intention in s 354(1) and (2)—See the notes to s 352.

355 Concealment of books and papers; falsification

(1) The bankrupt is guilty of an offence if he does not deliver up possession to the official receiver or the trustee, or as the official receiver or trustee may direct, of all books, papers and other records of which he has possession or control and which relate to his estate or his affairs.

Section 352 applies to this offence.

(2) The bankrupt is guilty of an offence if—

(a) he prevents, or in the initial period prevented, the production of any books, papers or records relating to his estate or affairs;

(b) he conceals, destroys, mutilates or falsifies, or causes or permits the concealment, destruction, mutilation or falsification of, any books, papers or other records relating to his estate or affairs;

(c) he makes, or causes or permits the making of, any false entries in any book, document or record relating to his estate or affairs; or

(d) in the 12 months before petition, or in the initial period, he did anything which would have been an offence under paragraph (b) or (c) above if the bankruptcy order had been made before he did it.

Section 352 applies to this offence.

(3) The bankrupt is guilty of an offence if—

(a) he disposes of, or alters or makes any omission in, or causes or permits the disposal, altering or making of any omission in, any book, document or record relating to his estate or affairs, or

(b) in the 12 months before petition, or in the initial period, he did anything which would have been an offence under paragraph (a) if the bankruptcy order had been made before he did it.

Section 352 applies to this offence.

(4) In their application to a trading record subsections (2)(d) and (3)(b) shall have effect as if the reference to 12 months were a reference to two years.

(5) In subsection (4) 'trading record' means a book, document or record which shows or explains the transactions or financial position of a person's business, including—

(a) a periodic record of cash paid and received,

(b) a statement of periodic stock-taking, and

(c) except in the case of goods sold by way of retail trade, a record of goods sold and purchased which identifies the buyer and seller or enables them to be identified.

Amendments—Enterprise Act 2002, s 269, Sch 23, paras 1, 13.

General note—Section 355(4) and (5) took effect from 1 April 2004 and were introduced by s 269 of and Sch 23 to the Enterprise Act 2002.

'conceals'—See the note to s 206.

Defence of innocent intention in s 356(1)—See the notes to s 352.

356 False statements

(1) The bankrupt is guilty of an offence if he makes or has made any material omission in any statement made under any provision in this Group of Parts and relating to his affairs.

Section 352 applies to this offence.

(2) The bankrupt is guilty of an offence if—

    (a)   knowing or believing that a false debt has been proved by any person under the bankruptcy, he fails to inform the trustee as soon as practicable; or

    (b)   he attempts to account for any part of his property by fictitious losses or expenses; or

    (c)   at any meeting of his creditors in the 12 months before petition or (whether or not at such a meeting) at any time in the initial period, he did anything which would have been an offence under paragraph (b) if the bankruptcy order had been made before he did it; or

    (d)   he is, or at any time has been, guilty of any false representation or other fraud for the purpose of obtaining the consent of his creditors, or any of them, to an agreement with reference to his affairs or to his bankruptcy.

General note—The defence of innocent intention under s 352 is not available in relation to any of the four offences provided for in s 356(2).

The offence in s 356(1) extends beyond bankruptcy to 'any statement made under any provision in this group of Parts' which relates to the bankrupt's affairs. It follows that a prosecution under s 356(1) may be instituted in relation to any material omission in any statement made in connection with the proposal for or approval of an individual voluntary arrangement under Part VIII.

Omissions from the statement of affairs required by s 288(1) are not actionable under s 5 of the Perjury Act 1911, which relates only to the making of a 'false statement'. Such omissions may, however, be actioned under s 356(1).

In *Re Johnson* (unreported, 12 April 2013, Bristol Crown Court) the bankrupt was sentenced to four months imprisonment, suspended for 18 months for a breach of s 356(2)(b).

See *DBIS v Compton* [2012] BPIR 1108 (Davison DJ sitting in the Magistrate's Court) for an example of how charges under this provision (and s 357) are dealt with by the criminal courts and discussion of the burden of proof.

357 Fraudulent disposal of property

(1) The bankrupt is guilty of an offence if he makes or causes to be made, or has in the period of 5 years ending with the commencement of the bankruptcy made or caused to be made, any gift or transfer of, or any charge on, his property.

Section 352 applies to this offence.

(2) The reference to making a transfer of or charge on any property includes causing or conniving at the levying of any execution against that property.

(3) The bankrupt is guilty of an offence if he conceals or removes, or has at any time before the commencement of the bankruptcy concealed or removed, any part of his property after, or within 2 months before, the date on which a judgment or order for the payment of money has been obtained against him, being a judgment or order which was not satisfied before the commencement of the bankruptcy.

Section 352 applies to this offence.

General note—Two separate offences are provided for in s 357(1) and (3). Section 357(2) refers to s 357(1).

At a practical level it is difficult to imagine proceedings being instituted under s 357(1) in the absence of civil proceedings alleging a transaction-at-undervalue and/or a preference under s 339 and/or s 340 or a transaction defrauding creditors under s 423, although any such civil claim is plainly not a prerequisite to criminal proceedings.

The burden that was placed on the bankrupt was evidential and not legal: *Attorney-General's Reference (No 1 of 2004); R v Edwards* [2004] EWCA Crim 1025, [2004] 1 WLR 2111, [2004] BPIR 1073. See also *DBIS v Compton* [2012] BPIR 1108 and the note to s 352.

Penalties—These are as provided for in ss 350 and 430 and Sch 10. In *R v Mungroo* [1998] BPIR 784 the Criminal Division of the Court of Appeal (McCowan LJ, Ognall and Sedley JJ) had no difficulty in upholding a short custodial sentence of two months imposed by a recorder in the Crown Court against a 44-year-old man of previously excellent character with a 20-year exemplary army career who had received a gratuity of £31,000 on leaving the service and who had used those monies to pay off debts, including gambling debts, debts due to family members and a debt incurred in putting an extension onto the family home, and who thereafter failed to provide information concerning the gratuity to the official receiver following a bankruptcy order based on a judgment debt which pre-dated the payment out of the gratuity. Giving the judgment of the court Ognall J pointed out at 78D–78E that, notwithstanding evidence of good character, in all normal circumstances conduct in contravention of s 357 crosses the custody threshold.

358 Absconding

The bankrupt is guilty of an offence if—

    (a)   he leaves, or attempts or makes preparations to leave, England and Wales with any property the value of which is not less than the prescribed amount and possession of which he is required to deliver up to the official receiver or the trustee, or

    (b)   in the 6 months before petition, or in the initial period, he did anything which would have been an offence under paragraph (a) if the bankruptcy order had been made immediately before he did it.

Section 352 applies to this offence.

General note—Despite its heading, it is sufficient for the commission of this offence that the bankrupt merely 'attempts or makes preparations' to leave the jurisdiction with property of the prescribed value. Under s 358(b) the offence may be committed in the 6-month period preceding presentation of the bankruptcy petition.

'... prescribed amount ...'—The figure is modest. With effect from 1 April 2004 the amount was increased from £500 to £1,000 by the Insolvency Proceedings (Monetary Limits) (Amendment) Order 2004 (SI 2004/547).

Defence of innocent intention—See the notes to s 352.

359 Fraudulent dealing with property obtained on credit

(1) The bankrupt is guilty of an offence if, in the 12 months before petition, or in the initial period, he disposed of any property which he had obtained on credit and, at the time he disposed of it, had not paid for it.

Section 352 applies to this offence.

(2) A person is guilty of an offence if, in the 12 months before petition or in the initial period, he acquired or received property from the bankrupt knowing or believing—

    (a)   that the bankrupt owed money in respect of the property, and

    (b)   that the bankrupt did not intend, or was unlikely to be able, to pay the money he so owed.

(3) A person is not guilty of an offence under subsection (1) or (2) if the disposal, acquisition or receipt of the property was in the ordinary course of a business carried on by the bankrupt at the time of the disposal, acquisition or receipt.

(4) In determining for the purposes of this section whether any property is disposed of, acquired or received in the ordinary course of a business carried on by the bankrupt, regard may be had, in particular, to the price paid for the property.

(5) In this section references to disposing of property include pawning or pledging it; and references to acquiring or receiving property shall be read accordingly.

General note—The purpose of the offences created by and sanctions imposed under this provision is in seeking to prevent an individual in financial difficulties, other than a person acting in the ordinary course of business, from obtaining property on credit and then disposing of that property – within the broad scope of s 359(5) – without paying for it. Those acquiring or receiving property from a bankrupt, subject to proof of the relevant state of mind in subsection (2), are also caught by the provisions.

    Section 359(1) provides for an offence which may be committed by the bankrupt in the period commencing 12 months prior to presentation of the petition and ending with the bankruptcy order. Section 359(2) provides for a separate offence which comprises the actus reus of acquiring or receiving property from a bankrupt together with the mens rea of knowledge or belief as to those two matters in s 359(2)(a) and (b). No offence may be committed if the bankrupt acts in the ordinary course of business, as defined in s 359(3) and qualified in s 359(4).

Defence of innocent intention in s 359(1)—See the notes to s 352.

360 Obtaining credit; engaging in business

(1) The bankrupt is guilty of an offence if—

    (a)   either alone or jointly with any other person, he obtains credit to the extent of the prescribed amount or more without giving the person from whom he obtains it the relevant information about his status; or

    (b)   he engages (whether directly or indirectly) in any business under a name other than that in which he was adjudged bankrupt without disclosing to all persons with whom he enters into any business transaction the name in which he was so adjudged.

(2) The reference to the bankrupt obtaining credit includes the following cases—

    (a)   where goods are bailed to him under a hire-purchase agreement, or agreed to be sold to him under a conditional sale agreement, and

(b)   where he is paid in advance (whether in money or otherwise) for
the supply of goods or services.

(3) A person whose estate has been sequestrated in Scotland, or who has
been adjudged bankrupt in Northern Ireland, is guilty of an offence if,
before his discharge, he does anything in England and Wales which would
be an offence under subsection (1) if he were an undischarged bankrupt and
the sequestration of his estate or the adjudication in Northern Ireland were
an adjudication under this Part.

(4) For the purposes of subsection (1)(a), the relevant information about
the status of the person in question is the information that he is an
undischarged bankrupt or, as the case may be, that his estate has been
sequestrated in Scotland and that he has not been discharged.

(5) This section applies to the bankrupt after discharge while a bankruptcy
restrictions order is in force in respect of him.

(6) For the purposes of subsection (1)(a) as it applies by virtue of
subsection (5), the relevant information about the status of the person in
question is the information that a bankruptcy restrictions order is in force in
respect of him.

Amendments—Enterprise Act 2002, s 257(3), Sch 21, para 3.

General note—There are two distinct offences in s 360(1)(a) and (b). The purpose of the
provision in the former case is in affording protection to any third party advancing credit
meeting the prescribed amount (see below) to whom a bankrupt must disclose his status. The
latter provision also provides protection to third parties, in that a bankrupt is prohibited
from engaging in business under any name other than that in which he was adjudged
bankrupt without disclosing that name 'to all persons with whom he enters into any business
transaction'. Strictly speaking, s 360(1)(b) does not preclude a bankrupt from engaging in
business under a name other than his bankruptcy name, in that the disclosure obligation is
only triggered on the entry into a business transaction.
No equivalent offences apply to a debtor subject to an individual voluntary arrangement.

Section 360(1)

'... **the prescribed amount** ...'—With effect from 1 April 2004 the amount is £500 by virtue of
the Insolvency Proceedings (Monetary Limits) (Amendment) Order 2004 (SI 2004/547).

Section 360(1)(a)

'... **the relevant information about his status** ...'—The relevant information is that prescribed
in s 360(4) and, perhaps surprisingly, given the form of words employed here, requires no
more than the disclosure of the fact that the bankrupt is an undischarged bankrupt, or its
Scottish equivalent.

Section 360(1)(b)

'... **any business transaction** ...'—This term is not specifically defined in the legislation,
although the term 'transaction' is defined in very broad, non-exhaustive terms in s 436 as
including a gift, agreement or arrangement.

Strict liability—The predecessor to s 360(1), in the substantially similar s 155 of the
Bankruptcy Act 1914, provided offences of strict liability: see *R v Duke of Leinster* [1924]
1 KB 311. In *R v Scott* [1998] BPIR 471 the Supreme Court of South Australia, the Court of
Criminal Appeal (Doyle CJ, Cox and Matheson JJ) held that an offence under s 369(1)(a) or
(b) of the Australian Bankruptcy Act 1966, which creates offences very similar to those in

s 360(1), were offences of strict liability. Consequently, all that was required was that the appellant had failed to disclose her status as an undischarged bankrupt to the provider of credit in that case. It was immaterial that the lender knew that she was an undischarged bankrupt, just as it was no defence for the appellant to say that she believed that the credit provider was aware that she was an undischarged bankrupt.

Section 360(2)

'... **obtaining credit** ...'—Section 360(2) does no more than identify two forms of agreement and one form of arrangement, albeit in very general terms, which fall within the scope of the term 'obtaining credit'. Given the purpose of the provision, identified in the general note above, it is submitted that, subject to the prescribed amount, s 360(1)(a) will extend to the obtaining of any credit whatsoever. The absence of any express exclusion from the scope of the provision militates against any argument that any particular form of credit, say credit obtained in the course of the conduct of a bank account in overdraft, will fall outside the provision.

Section 360(5) and (6)—These provisions were introduced with effect from 1 April 2004 by s 257 of and Sch 21 to the Enterprise Act 2002; for commentary on BROs see the notes to s 281A.

361   (*Repealed*)

General note—This provision provided for offences in relation to a failure to maintain accounting records and was repealed with effect from 1 April 2004 by s 263 of the Enterprise Act 2002. The court may, however, take into account such conduct under para 2(2)(a) of Sch 4A in considering the making of a bankruptcy restrictions order under para 1 thereof, as discussed in the notes to s 281A, where such conduct is perpetrated on or after 1 April 2004.

362   (*Repealed*)

General note—This provision provided for offences in relation to gambling and to rash and hazardous speculations and was repealed with effect from 1 April 2004 by s 263 of the Enterprise Act 2002. The court may, however, take into account such conduct under para 2(2)(j) of Sch 4A in considering the making of a bankruptcy restrictions order under para 1 thereof, as discussed in the notes to s 281A, where such conduct is perpetrated on or after 1 April 2004.

Chapter VII

Bankruptcy Offences

Power of court in bankruptcy

363 General control of court

(1) Every bankruptcy is under the general control of the court and, subject to the provisions in this Group of Parts, the court has full power to decide all questions of priorities and all other questions, whether of law or fact, arising in any bankruptcy.

(2) Without prejudice to any other provision in this Group of Parts, an undischarged bankrupt or a discharged bankrupt whose estate is still being administered under Chapter IV of this Part shall do all such things as he

may be directed to do by the court for the purposes of his bankruptcy or, as the case may be, the administration of that estate.

(3) The official receiver or the trustee of a bankrupt's estate may at any time apply to the court for a direction under subsection (2).

(4) If any person without reasonable excuse fails to comply with any obligation imposed on him by subsection (2), he is guilty of a contempt of court and liable to be punished accordingly (in addition to any other punishment to which he may be subject).

General note—These provisions subject all bankruptcies to the power of 'the court', as defined in s 385(1), and on which see ss 373 and 374 and the notes thereto. Section 363 allows for an application to court only by the official receiver or a trustee for the determination of issues within the very broadly cast s 363(1) or so as to require action of an undischarged or discharged bankrupt under s 363(2). The class of eligible applicants has nevertheless been held to be wider in scope: *Hardy v Buchler* [1997] BPIR 643. Subsection (1) should be read in conjunction with s 303(2). The former provision alone anticipates determination of any question of priorities of law or fact. Nothing equivalent to s 363(2) appears in s 303. Furthermore, only s 303(1) provides for an application by a dissatisfied bankrupt or any of his creditors.

As with s 303, the court's jurisdiction under s 363 is exercisable irrespective of whether a bankrupt is undischarged or discharged, or whether the bankruptcy has been annulled: *Engel v Peri* [2002] EWHC 799 (Ch), [2002] BPIR 961 (Ferris J). The provision gives power to a court to set the remuneration of a trustee in bankruptcy: *Engel v Peri*.

Examples of matters within s 363(1)—The court has jurisdiction under s 363(1), and under its inherent jurisdiction, to fix a trustee's remuneration although it is doubtful that s 303(2) extends to such an application: *Engel v Peri* [2002] BPIR 961 at [33] (Ferris J). The provision also extends to the appointment of an additional trustee: *Clements v Udal* [2001] BPIR 454. For guidance on the proper approach to the fixing of remuneration (in an administration case) see *Re Cabletel Installation Ltd* [2005] BPIR 28 (Chief Registrar Baister) and the review of the English authorities in the judgment of Weatherup J in the decision of the Northern Ireland High Court in *Re Cooper (a bankrupt), Houston v Finnegan* [2007] BPIR 1206 at [9] and [10]. In the wake of *Cabletel* the *Practice Statement: The Fixing and Approval of the Remuneration of Appointees* (which appears as an appendix to this text) was brought into force in relation to the vast majority of applications (see para 2) to fix remuneration brought after 1 October 2004. The Practice Statement prescribes information which should be provided by an office-holder for the purposes of fixing remuneration (see paras 5.2 and 5.3) together with guiding principles in relation to the Practice Statement's main objective of ensuring that remuneration fixed by the court 'is fair, reasonable and commensurate with the nature and extent of the work properly undertaken by the appointee in any given case and is fixed and approved by reference to a process which is consistent and predictable' (see para 3). The Court of Appeal reviewed the Practice Statement in *Brook v Reid* [2011] EWCA Civ 331 which contains an excellent summary and analysis of the case law relating to office holders remuneration. The 2004 Practice Statement has now been replaced by Practice *Direction: Insolvency Proceedings* [2012] BCC 265 with effect from 23 February 2012. See also IR 6.138-6.142 on remuneration.

Cabletel is authority for the proposition that the court should only interfere with a trustee's decision as to the taking of and paying for legal advice if the trustee acts unreasonably and outside the generous scope of his discretion: *Barker v Bajjon* [2008] BPIR 771 at [17] (Chief Registrar Baister).

Far more commonly, s 363 provides a mechanism for the determination by the court of common issues as to, say, the ranking or validity of security, the extent of any particular interest in property comprised in the bankrupt's estate or issues of disputed fact relevant to the administration of the bankruptcy.

The section has a very wide ambit: for instance in *Holtham v Kelmanson* [2006] BPIR 1422 the Court indicated that, where a bankrupt is the absolute owner of land (and therefore there is no trust of land), he could be ordered to deliver it up to the trustee under this provision, with no need for an application under s 335A or s 14 of the Trusts of Land and Appointment of Trustees Act 1996. Further, in *Re Gonsalves* [2011] BPIR 419 the Court held that under s 363, every bankruptcy was under the general control of the court and the court had full power to decide all questions of priorities and all other questions, whether of law or fact, arising in any bankruptcy including the right to suspend an order for sale made under s 363.

In *Dunbar Assets Plc v Fowler* [2013] BPIR 46 (at para 37) Chief Registrar Baister indicated the section might perhaps be used to dismiss a bankruptcy petition presented in circumstances that gave rise to unfairness to the debtor.

Section 363(4)

Contempt—In *Re M (a minor) (contact order: committal)* (1998) *The Times*, December 31 the Court of Appeal gave guidance, albeit in the context of a claim under the Children Act 1989, on the exercise of the power of committal for non-compliance with a court order; in particular, it is inadvisable that the judge initiating the committal procedure should also rule on the decision to commit. In finding that a bankrupt is in contempt it lies within the court's inherent jurisdiction to regulate or stay any proceedings pursued by the bankrupt until further order or until the contempt is purged.

One bankrupt was, on the application of the official receiver, imprisoned for 20 months for a number of defalcations in assisting his trustee and failing to adhere to orders and undertakings, including consistently refusing to answer questions put to him properly by the official receiver in and out of court, not complying with court orders, lying on oath in court in the course of applications relating to the administration of the bankrupt estate, and falsely excusing himself from attending court on the basis of false grounds of ill health (*Official Receiver v Cummings-John* [2000] BPIR 320).

In finding that a bankrupt is in contempt it lies within the court's inherent jurisdiction to regulate or stay any proceedings pursued by the bankrupt until further order or until the contempt is purged.

Procedure—Form 7.15 is prescribed for contempt proceedings.

364 Power of arrest

(1) In the cases specified in the next subsection the court may cause a warrant to be issued to a constable or prescribed officer of the court—

    (a)   for the arrest of a debtor to whom a bankruptcy petition relates or of an undischarged bankrupt, or of a discharged bankrupt whose estate is still being administered under Chapter IV of this Part, and

    (b)   for the seizure of any books, papers, records, money or goods in the possession of a person arrested under the warrant,

and may authorise a person arrested under such a warrant to be kept in custody, and anything seized under such a warrant to be held, in accordance with the rules, until such time as the court may order.

(2) The powers conferred by subsection (1) are exercisable in relation to a debtor or undischarged or discharged bankrupt if, at any time after the presentation of the bankruptcy petition relating to him or the making of the bankruptcy order against him, it appears to the court—

    (a)   that there are reasonable grounds for believing that he has absconded, or is about to abscond, with a view to avoiding or delaying the payment of any of his debts or his appearance to a bankruptcy petition or to avoiding, delaying or disrupting any proceedings in bankruptcy against him or any examination of his affairs, or

    (b)   that he is about to remove his goods with a view to preventing or delaying possession being taken of them by the official receiver or the trustee of his estate, or

(c) that there are reasonable grounds for believing that he has concealed or destroyed, or is about to conceal or destroy, any of his goods or any books, papers or records which might be of use to his creditors in the course of his bankruptcy or in connection with the administration of his estate, or

(d) that he has, without the leave of the official receiver or the trustee of his estate, removed any goods in his possession which exceed in value such sum as may be prescribed for the purposes of this paragraph, or

(e) that he has failed, without reasonable excuse, to attend any examination ordered by the court.

General note—These provisions should be read along with s 366(3) and (4) and the potential liability of a bankrupt for contempt under ss 291(6) and 333(4).

This provision is triggered if, following presentation of a bankruptcy petition against a debtor or the making of a bankruptcy order against an undischarged bankrupt, and without any requirement for the petition to be served on the debtor or the bankrupt to be made aware of the order, 'it appears to the court' that any of the five circumstances listed in s 364(2) have arisen, with the consequence that the court 'may cause a warrant' to be issued for the arrest of a debtor 'and' the seizure of any books, papers, records etc 'in the possession of a person arrested under the warrant', together with the discretion to authorise those further steps identified in the latter part of s 364(1).

The powers exercisable under s 364(1) expressly extend to a discharged bankrupt whose estate continues to be administered under Chapter IV (ie ss 305–335): see *Oakes v Simms* [1997] BPIR 499. The section can apply to a discharged bankrupt: *Oakes v Simms*. There needs to be a distinction drawn, when it comes to the issue of arrest warrants, where the bankrupt absents himself or herself because the bankrupt believes the bankruptcy proceedings to be at an end (where he or she has been discharged), on the one hand, and, on the other, where a bankrupt absconds so as to delay the examination of his or her affairs (*Oakes v Simms* [1997] BPIR 499 at 503).

Section 364(2)(b)

Scope of provision—The word 'goods' is used here, and not the broader term 'property'. The word 'his' goods cannot be taken as applying to 'goods' which form part of the bankrupt's estate under s 283 vesting in a trustee under s 306 following the making of a bankruptcy order, although the term would catch goods subsequently acquired by or devolved upon a bankrupt which have yet to be claimed as after-acquired property under s 307. It also appears doubtful that the words 'his goods' can apply to items of excess value which do not form part of the bankrupt's estate under s 308, but which are claimable by a trustee.

Section 364(2)(c)

Scope of provision—For the term 'records' see the definition of s 436.

Section 364(2)(d)

Scope of provision—Compare the requirement here for an individual to have 'removed any goods in his possession' with the requirement under s 364(2)(b), 'he is about to remove his goods', with a view to the consequences identified therein.

The sum prescribed for the purposes of s 364(2)(d) is £1,000 with effect from 1 April 2004 by virtue of the Insolvency Proceedings (Monetary Limits) (Amendment) Order 2004 (SI 2004/547).

Procedure—See rr 7.21, 7.22 and 7.24.

Although Art 5 of the European Convention on Human Rights does not require notice of an application to commit under s 364, the evidence in support of such an application must make clear why a without notice application is said to be justified as an exception to the normal rule: *Hickling v Baker* [2007] EWCA Civ 287, [2007] BPIR 346.

365 Seizure of bankrupt's property

(1) At any time after a bankruptcy order has been made, the court may, on the application of the official receiver or the trustee of the bankrupt's estate, issue a warrant authorising the person to whom it is directed to seize any property comprised in the bankrupt's estate which is, or any books, papers or records relating to the bankrupt's estate or affairs which are, in the possession or under the control of the bankrupt or any other person who is required to deliver the property, books, papers or records to the official receiver or trustee.

(2) Any person executing a warrant under this section may, for the purpose of seizing any property comprised in the bankrupt's estate or any books, papers or records relating to the bankrupt's estate or affairs, break open any premises where the bankrupt or anything that may be seized under the warrant is or is believed to be and any receptacle of the bankrupt which contains or is believed to contain anything that may be so seized.

(3) If, after a bankruptcy order has been made, the court is satisfied that any property comprised in the bankrupt's estate is, or any books, papers or records relating to the bankrupt's estate or affairs are, concealed in any premises not belonging to him, it may issue a warrant authorising any constable or prescribed officer of the court to search those premises for the property, books, papers or records.

(4) A warrant under subsection (3) shall not be executed except in the prescribed manner and in accordance with its terms.

General note—These provisions, which are capable of being triggered only after a bankruptcy order has been made, are draconian in nature and allow not only for the issue of a warrant authorising the seizure of any property comprised in a bankrupt's estate or any books, papers or records relating to the bankrupt's estate or affairs from either the bankrupt or a third party, but also the breaking open of any premises and any receptacle which contains 'or is believed to contain' (ie believed subjectively but reasonably by the trustee or his agent) anything capable of seizure. The power to authorise a search under s 365(3) is independent of s 365(1) and (2).

For discussion of the test to be applied to an application under this section, see *Williams v Mohammed* (No 2) [2012] BPIR 238. HHJ Hodge QC (sitting as a judge of the the High Court) considered the relevant questions are threefold: (i) Is there a real risk that the respondent's possessions might be dissipated, destroyed or otherwise disposed of unless the warrant was issued? (ii) Does the value of the property liable to be seized justify the grant of such a draconian remedy? (iii) Can the rights of third parties be respected as far as possible? The task of the court was to find a balance between such rights and the need to advance the bankruptcy in the interests of the creditors.

It is submitted that the nature of the powers in s 365(1)–(3) is so serious that the court will not engage such extreme measures lightly, and certainly not without a very detailed consideration of the evidence and the grounds upon which it is alleged that such steps should be taken. For example, the court is very unlikely to exercise its power under s 365(3) without clear evidence, which extends beyond mere suspicion, as to the specific property or books, papers etc which are alleged to be subject to concealment. Furthermore, the court will not exercise any of its powers in a vacuum and will wish to be satisfied that the likely benefit to creditors consequent, directly or indirectly, upon the exercise of its discretion is proportionate to the very extreme remedy or remedies which the court is being asked to grant.

An order under s 365 was made by Chief Registrar Baister in favour of a German Insolvency Admininstrator in *Re A Bankrupt* [2012] BPIR 238.

Procedure—See rr 7.21, 7.24 and 7.25. Rule 7.25 corresponds with s 365(4).

366 Inquiry into bankrupt's dealings and property

(1) At any time after a bankruptcy order has been made the court may, on the application of the official receiver or the trustee of the bankrupt's estate, summon to appear before it—

(a) the bankrupt or the bankrupt's spouse or former spouse or civil partner or former civil partner,

(b) any person known or believed to have any property comprised in the bankrupt's estate in his possession or to be indebted to the bankrupt,

(c) any person appearing to the court to be able to give information concerning the bankrupt or the bankrupt's dealings, affairs or property.

The court may require any such person as is mentioned in paragraph (b) or (c) to submit a witness statement verified by a statement of truth to the court containing an account of his dealings with the bankrupt or to produce any documents in his possession or under his control relating to the bankrupt or the bankrupt's dealings, affairs or property.

(2) Without prejudice to section 364, the following applies in a case where—

(a) a person without reasonable excuse fails to appear before the court when he is summoned to do so under this section, or

(b) there are reasonable grounds for believing that a person has absconded, or is about to abscond, with a view to avoiding his appearance before the court under this section.

(3) The court may, for the purpose of bringing that person and anything in his possession before the court, cause a warrant to be issued to a constable or prescribed officer of the court—

(a) for the arrest of that person, and

(b) for the seizure of any books, papers, records, money or goods in that person's possession.

(4) The court may authorise a person arrested under such a warrant to be kept in custody, and anything seized under such a warrant to be held, in accordance with the rules, until that person is brought before the court under the warrant or until such other time as the court may order.

Amendments—Civil Partnership Act 2004, s 261(1), Sch 27, para 120; SI 2010/18.

General note—This is the bankruptcy equivalent of s 236 and much of what is included in the comments relating to s 236 can be applied to this section.

The court has a discretion whether or not to order an examination and this will depend on the circumstances.

A bankrupt can be required to be examined even after he or she has obtained a discharge (*Oakes v Simms* [1997] BPIR 499 at 501–502, CA (trustee seeking to ascertain whether the bankrupt had concealed assets)).

Any such person—if an application were made in relation to anyone who is abroad the court would take into account the need for that person to comply with obligations under local laws: *Buchler v Al-Midani* [2005] EWHC 3183 (Ch), [2006] BPIR 867. For an example of the enforcement of an order made under s366 by an English Court abroad see *Handelsveem BV v Hill* [2011] BPIR 1024 (enforcement by the Dutch Supreme Court).

Affidavit containing an account of his dealings with the bankrupt—If an order is made that a person covered by s 336 is to provide an affidavit of his dealings with the bankrupt, he or she is expected to take reasonable steps to ascertain the true facts. If he fails to do so and does not provide an accurate explanation, he or she is in contempt of court (*Bird v Hadkinson* [1999] BPIR 653). If the person does take reasonable steps and provides information honestly, then if it is inaccurate he will not be in contempt of court (*Bird v Hadkinson*).

Legal professional privilege—If solicitors of a bankrupt, or other persons who can be examined under s 366 are examined, they are not able to rely on the privilege in circumstances where it would be incumbent on their client to reveal the information which is the subject of the question (*Re Murjani* [1996] 1 BCLC 272, [1996] BCC 278, [1996] BPIR 325). See also the discussion on the interaction between s 366 and legal professional privilege in *Hooper v Duncan Lewis (Solicitors) Ltd* [2010] BPIR 591.

See the notes relating to s 236 and rr 9.1 ff.

367 Court's enforcement powers under s 366

(1) If it appears to the court, on consideration of any evidence obtained under section 366 or this section, that any person has in his possession any property comprised in the bankrupt's estate, the court may, on the application of the official receiver or the trustee of the bankrupt's estate, order that person to deliver the whole or any part of the property to the official receiver or the trustee at such time, in such manner and on such terms as the court thinks fit.

(2) If it appears to the court, on consideration of any evidence obtained under section 366 or this section, that any person is indebted to the bankrupt, the court may, on the application of the official receiver or the trustee of the bankrupt's estate, order that person to pay to the official receiver or trustee, at such time and in such manner as the court may direct, the whole or part of the amount due, whether in full discharge of the debt or otherwise as the court thinks fit.

(3) The court may, if it thinks fit, order that any person who if within the jurisdiction of the court would be liable to be summoned to appear before it under section 366 shall be examined in any part of the United Kingdom where he may be for the time being, or in any place outside the United Kingdom.

(4) Any person who appears or is brought before the court under section 366 or this section may be examined on oath, either orally or by interrogatories, concerning the bankrupt or the bankrupt's dealings, affairs and property.

General note—This is the bankruptcy counterpart to s 237. See the comments relating to s 237.

368 Provision corresponding to s 366, where interim receiver appointed

Sections 366 and 367 apply where an interim receiver has been appointed under section 286 as they apply where a bankruptcy order has been made, as if—

- (a) references to the official receiver or the trustee were to the interim receiver, and
- (b) references to the bankrupt and to his estate were (respectively) to the debtor and his property.

General note—This provides for private examinations to be conducted where a bankruptcy order has not been made against a person, but an interim receiver has been appointed (under s 286) over his or her estate before the hearing of a bankruptcy petition, but after the presentation of the petition. This is usually done to protect the estate for the benefit of creditors. See the comments accompanying s 286.

369 Order for production of documents by inland revenue

(1) For the purposes of an examination under section 290 (public examination of bankrupt) or proceedings under sections 366 to 368, the court may, on the application of the official receiver or the trustee of the bankrupt's estate, order an inland revenue official to produce to the court—

- (a) any return, account or accounts submitted (whether before or after the commencement of the bankruptcy) by the bankrupt to any inland revenue official,
- (b) any assessment or determination made (whether before or after the commencement of the bankruptcy) in relation to the bankrupt by any inland revenue official, or
- (c) any correspondence (whether before or after the commencement of the bankruptcy) between the bankrupt and any inland revenue official.

(2) Where the court has made an order under subsection (1) for the purposes of any examination or proceedings, the court may, at any time after the document to which the order relates is produced to it, by order authorise the disclosure of the document, or of any part of its contents, to the official receiver, the trustee of the bankrupt's estate or the bankrupt's creditors.

(3) The court shall not address an order under subsection (1) to an inland revenue official unless it is satisfied that that official is dealing, or has dealt, with the affairs of the bankrupt.

(4) Where any document to which an order under subsection (1) relates is not in the possession of the official to whom the order is addressed, it is the duty of that official to take all reasonable steps to secure possession of it and, if he fails to do so, to report the reasons for his failure to the court.

(5) Where any document to which an order under subsection (1) relates is in the possession of an inland revenue official other than the one to whom the order is addressed, it is the duty of the official in possession of the document, at the request of the official to whom the order is addressed, to deliver it to the official making the request.

(6) In this section 'inland revenue official' means any inspector or collector of taxes appointed by the Commissioners of Inland Revenue or any person appointed by the Commissioners to serve in any other capacity.

(7) This section does not apply for the purposes of an examination under sections 366 and 367 which takes place by virtue of section 368 (interim receiver).

General note—The power of the court to make and direct an order under s 369(1) to a particular Inland Revenue official or officials is rather more restricted than might at first appear, for two reasons. First, the court's power is not independent and free-standing and may only be exercised in the course of a public examination under s 290 or inquiries under ss 366 and 367, but not such inquiries undertaken by an interim receiver where no bankruptcy order will have been made. Secondly, the court's power extends, at least in the first instance, only to the production of documents to the court. As a second stage to the exercise of this power s 369(2) then empowers the court to authorise the disclosure of any such document to the official receiver or the trustee or the bankrupt's creditors, who are apparently not caught by an order for disclosure in favour of the trustee under this provision.

The Commissioners of the Inland Revenue are required either to consent or to object to the making of an order under s 369: see r 6.194(3)–(6).

Procedure—See rr 6.194–6.196.

370 Power to appoint special manager

(1) The court may, on an application under this section, appoint any person to be the special manager—

    (a)   of a bankrupt's estate, or
    (b)   of the business of an undischarged bankrupt, or
    (c)   of the property or business of a debtor in whose case the official receiver has been appointed interim receiver under section 286.

(2) An application under this section may be made by the official receiver or the trustee of the bankrupt's estate in any case where it appears to the official receiver or trustee that the nature of the estate, property or business, or the interests of the creditors generally, require the appointment of another person to manage the estate, property or business.

(3) A special manager appointed under this section has such powers as may be entrusted to him by the court.

(4) The power of the court under subsection (3) to entrust powers to a special manager includes power to direct that any provision in this Group of Parts that has effect in relation to the official receiver, interim receiver or trustee shall have the like effect in relation to the special manager for the purposes of the carrying out by the special manager of any of the functions of the official receiver, interim receiver or trustee.

(5) A special manager appointed under this section shall—

    (a)   give such security as may be prescribed,
    (b)   prepare and keep such accounts as may be prescribed, and
    (c)   produce those accounts in accordance with the rules to the Secretary of State or to such other persons as may be prescribed.

General note—For the purposes of s 370(1) the power of the court to appoint a special manager arises under s 286(1) or (2), s 287(1), or on an application by a trustee.

Although the court retains a discretion to make an appointment under s 370(1), the court is very likely to weigh heavily the fact that, for the purposes of s 370(2), it 'appears' to the official receiver or trustee that the circumstances of the case require the appointment of another person as special manager. In practice, the requirement for a special manager most commonly arises where the nature of any business or assets comprised in the bankrupt's estate is particularly specialist or idiosyncratic and where it is inappropriate to involve the bankrupt in the management of such business or assets. Inevitably, the court will, in the exercise of its discretion, be concerned that the benefit to creditors consequent upon the appointing of a special manager is proportionate to the likely costs of such an appointment.

Section 370(3)

Powers of a special manger—As in the case of a court appointed receiver, the court's order should expressly provide for the powers of a special manager. The court will not confer powers which exceed those reasonably required by a special manager, dependent on the facts of any particular case, although the court will be equally alive to the risk of unduly restricting its appointee and the time and expense involved in an application to extend such powers. The powers listed in Sch 5, free of the restrictions imposed as to sanction, may provide a useful starting point for the selection of appropriate powers.

Procedure—See rr 6.167–6.171.

For the cost of the security of the special manager where a bankruptcy order is made see r 6.224(1)(e). The remuneration of a special manager is governed by para 20 of Sch 9.

371 Re-direction of bankrupt's letters, etc

(1) Where a bankruptcy order has been made, the court may from time to time, on the application of the official receiver or the trustee of the bankrupt's estate, order a postal operator (within the meaning of Part 3 of the Postal Services Act 2011) to re-direct and send or deliver to the official receiver or trustee or otherwise any postal packet (within the meaning of that Act) which would otherwise be sent or delivered by the operator concerned to the bankrupt at such place or places as may be specified in the order.

(2) An order under this section has effect for such period, not exceeding 3 months, as may be specified in the order.

Amendments—Postal Services Act 2000, s 127(4), Sch 8, para 20(a)–(c); Postal Services Act 2011, s 91(1), (2), Sch 12, Pt 3, paras 124, 125.

General note—The exercise of the court's power under this provision constitutes a serious intrusion into a bankrupt's privacy. In *Foxley v United Kingdom* [2000] BPIR 1009 the European Court of Human Rights held that, whilst the interception of mail clearly interfered with the right of privacy under Art 8 of the European Convention on Human Rights, interference sanctioned by court order was 'in accordance with the law' of the United Kingdom jurisdiction and fell within the margin of appreciation afforded to a Member State in determining the level of interference permissible. However, the continued interception of mail after a three-month period stipulated in the court's order was not in accordance with the law. Neither was the opening and copying of mail from the bankrupt's legal advisers justified at any time as a proportionate response or 'necessary in a democratic society' within the terms of Art 8.2 of the Convention. For an opposite finding in relation to the law of Finalnd see *Narinen v Finland* [2004] BPIR 914. In *Smedley v Brittain* [2008] BPIR 219 at [67] and [68] Registrar Nicholls identified, in the context of Art 8 of the Convention, that the reasonableness of a trustee-in-bankruptcy seeking and obtaining an order for re-direction would necessarily be determined by reference to the conduct of and approach adopted by the debtor. On the evidence in that case there had been no breach of Art 8 in the trustee obtaining a re-direction order in accordance with the legislation.

Section 371 has no application to mail of any sort emanating from a bankrupt.

Duration of order—Although s 371(2) envisages an order not exceeding three months in duration, the words 'from time to time' would allow the court to make a fresh order for up to three months following the expiration of a previous order.

Procedure—Whilst the procedure governing redirection of a bankrupt's mail may be made without notice and need only be supported by a letter setting out the grounds upon which the order is sought, in *Singh v Official Receiver* [1997] BPIR 530 Sir Richard Scott V-C expressed concern at those requirements and commented (at 532A–532C):

'... in any event in my view all applications to the court ought to be supported by something more substantial than merely a letter informing the courts that the order was being sought on the grounds of non-co-operation or whatever. The material ought to give chapter and verse of the non-co-operation relied on. In the case of applications under s 279 rules have been prescribed which provide for the official receiver to lodge with the court a report, a copy of which is then to be supplied to the respondent bankrupt, in which the details of the non-co-operation relied on for the purposes of the application are set out. In my view a similar procedure ought to be introduced for the purposes of applications under s 371. I think it is unreasonable for an application to be made in circumstances where the substantive allegations on which the application are based are not set out in some written form available to be provided to the bankrupt respondent.'

A new r 6.235A inserted by the Insolvency (Amendment) Rules 2005 (SI 2005/527) allows the court to give broad effect to the above observations.

Chief Registrar Baister made an order under s 371 in favour of a German insolvency administrator (pursuant to the co-operation mechanisms in Art 25 of the EC Regulation on Insolvency Proceedings (1346/2000) in *Re A Bankrupt* [2012] BPIR 469.

PART X
INDIVIDUAL INSOLVENCY: GENERAL PROVISIONS

372 Supplies of gas, water, electricity, etc

(1) This section applies where on any day ('the relevant day')—

(a) a bankruptcy order is made against an individual or an interim receiver of an individual's property is appointed, or

(b) a voluntary arrangement proposed by an individual is approved under Part VIII, or

(c) a deed of arrangement is made for the benefit of an individual's creditors;

and in this section 'the office-holder' means the official receiver, the trustee in bankruptcy, the interim receiver, the supervisor of the voluntary arrangement or the trustee under the deed of arrangement, as the case may be.

(2) If a request falling within the next subsection is made for the giving after the relevant day of any of the supplies mentioned in subsection (4), the supplier—

(a) may make it a condition of the giving of the supply that the office-holder personally guarantees the payment of any charges in respect of the supply, but

(b) shall not make it a condition of the giving of the supply, or do anything which has the effect of making it a condition of the giving of the supply, that any outstanding charges in respect of a supply given to the individual before the relevant day are paid.

(3) A request falls within this subsection if it is made—

(a) by or with the concurrence of the office-holder, and

(b) for the purposes of any business which is or has been carried on by the individual, by a firm or partnership of which the individual is or was a member, or by an agent or manager for the individual or for such a firm or partnership.

(4) The supplies referred to in subsection (2) are—

(a) a supply of gas by a gas supplier within the meaning of Part I of the Gas Act 1986;

(b) a supply of electricity by an electricity supplier within the meaning of Part I of the Electricity Act 1989;

(c) a supply of water by a water undertaker,

(d) a supply of communications services by a provider of a public electronic communications service.

(5) The following applies to expressions used in subsection (4)—

(a) (*repealed*)

(b) (*repealed*)

(c) 'communications services' do not include electronic communications services to the extent that they are used to broadcast or otherwise transmit programme services (within the meaning of the Communications Act 2003).

Amendments—Water Act 1989, s 190(1), Sch 25, para 78(1); Gas Act 1995, ss 16(1), 17(5), Sch 4, para 14(3), (4), Sch 6; Utilities Act 2000, s 108, Sch 6, Pt III, para 47(1), (3)(a), (b), Sch 8; Communications Act 2003, s 406(1), Sch 17, para 82(1), (3)(a), (b).

General note—These provisions apply in any of the three circumstances set out in s 372(1) and, in effect, prohibit any supplier of utilities within the meaning of s 372(4) from imposing conditions in relation to outstanding utility charges for the continued supply of utilities or extracting any personal guarantee relating to the payment of outstanding or future charges. Amendments were made to s 372(4)(d) and (5)(c) by the Broadcasting Act 2003.

Further commentary appears in the notes to s 233 which applies in corporate insolvencies and which provision corresponds in substance with s 372.

373 Jurisdiction in relation to insolvent individuals

(1) The High Court and the county courts have jurisdiction throughout England and Wales for the purposes of the Parts in this Group.

(2) For the purposes of those Parts, a county court has, in addition to its ordinary jurisdiction, all the powers and jurisdiction of the High Court; and the orders of the court may be enforced accordingly in the prescribed manner.

(3) Jurisdiction for the purposes of those Parts is exercised—

(a) by the High Court or the Central London County Court in relation to the proceedings which, in accordance with the rules, are allocated to the London insolvency district, and

(b)   by each county court in relation to the proceedings which are so allocated to the insolvency district of that court.

(4) Subsection (3) is without prejudice to the transfer of proceedings from one court to another in the manner prescribed by the rules; and nothing in that subsection invalidates any proceedings on the grounds that they were initiated or continued in the wrong court.

Amendments—SI 2011/761.

General note—Section 373(1) confers co-existing bankruptcy jurisdiction on the High Court and the county courts of England and Wales. Section 373(2) is necessary to bring the powers and jurisdiction of a county court into line with those of the High Court. Notwithstanding the co-existing jurisdiction of the High Court and the county courts, s 373(3) allocates jurisdiction in bankruptcy cases between the High Court, which exercises jurisdiction in relation to the London bankruptcy district as defined in s 374(4)(a), and the county court exercising jurisdiction in relation to that court's insolvency district as defined in s 374(4)(b) and (c). Other than where a bankruptcy petition must be presented in the High Court (as provided for in r 6.40(1)), r 6.40(2)–(3A) provides for the county court in which a bankruptcy petition may be presented. The county courts exercising bankruptcy jurisdiction, together with the nearest full-time court in relation to those which do not, appear in Sch 2 to the Insolvency Rules 1986. It does not appear from these provisions that any District Registry of the High Court has standing to exercise bankruptcy jurisdiction, although in practice the district registries frequently entertain and hear bankruptcy matters. See in this regard the decision of Morritt C in *HMRC v Earley* [2011] EWHC 1783 (Ch) on the jusrisdiction of the High Court.

Transfer of proceedings—Rules 7.11–7.15 deal with the transfer of proceedings between courts; see the commentary to those provisions.

374 Insolvency districts

(1) The Lord Chancellor may, with the concurrence of the Lord Chief Justice, by order designate the areas which are for the time being to be comprised, for the purposes of the Parts in this Group, in the London Insolvency district and the insolvency district of each county court; and an order under this section may—

(a)   exclude any county court from having jurisdiction for the purposes of those Parts, or

(b)   confer jurisdiction for those purposes on any county court which has not previously had that jurisdiction.

(2) An order under this section may contain such incidental, supplemental and transitional provisions as may appear to the Lord Chancellor and the Lord Chief Justice necessary or expedient.

(3) An order under this section shall be made by statutory instrument and, after being made, shall be laid before each House of Parliament.

(4) Subject to any order under this section—

(a)   the district which, immediately before the appointed day, is the London bankruptcy district becomes, on that day, the London insolvency district;

(b)   any district which immediately before that day is the bankruptcy district of a county court becomes, on that day, the insolvency district of that court, and

(c)   any county court which immediately before that day is excluded from having jurisdiction in bankruptcy is excluded, on and after that day, from having jurisdiction for the purposes of the Parts in this Group.

(5) The Lord Chief Justice may nominate a judicial office holder (as defined in section 109(4) of the Constitutional Reform Act 2005) to exercise his functions under this section.

Amendments—Constitutional Reform Act 2005, s 15(1), Sch 4.

General note—See the commentary to s 373 and r 6.40 and Sch 2 to the Insolvency Rules 1986.

375   Appeals etc from courts exercising insolvency jurisdiction

(1) Every court having jurisdiction for the purposes of the Parts in this Group may review, rescind or vary any order made by it in the exercise of that jurisdiction.

(2) An appeal from a decision made in the exercise of jurisdiction for the purposes of those Parts by a county court or by a registrar in bankruptcy of the High Court lies to a single judge of the High Court; and an appeal from a decision of that judge on such an appeal lies to the Court of Appeal.

(3) A county court is not, in the exercise of its jurisdiction for the purposes of those Parts, to be subject to be restrained by the order of any other court, and no appeal lies from its decision in the exercise of that jurisdiction except as provided by this section.

Amendments—Access to Justice Act 1999, s 106, Sch 15, Pt III.

General note—Section 375 corresponds in substance with r 7.47(1)–(3) which applies in winding up. (Rule 7.47(4) finds no counterpart in s 375.) The commentary to r 7.47, which includes reference to the authorities decided under s 375, may also be read as a commentary to the present provision.

Procedure—See rr 7.48–7.50 and Part 4 of the *Practice Direction: Insolvency Proceedings* [2012] BPIR 409.

376   Time-limits

Where by any provision in this Group of Parts or by the rules the time for doing anything is limited, the court may extend the time, either before or after it has expired, on such terms, if any, as it thinks fit.

General note—Section 376 has its origins in s 105(4) of the Bankruptcy Act 1883 and applies to any time-limit for the doing of anything imposed by 'any provision in this Group of Parts' (ie the Second Group of Parts, being ss 252–385) or 'by the rules' (ie seemingly the entirety of the Insolvency Rules 1986, without limitation). The power of the court lies in its discretion to extend time either prospectively or retrospectively, and subject to any terms the court considers appropriate.

Extension of time in relation to the provisions of the First Group of Parts is dealt with by r 4.3. Despite the apparent restriction on the power in r 4.3 to winding up, in *Tager v Westpac Banking Corporation* [1998] BCC 73 at 78D–78E His Honour Judge Weeks QC, sitting as a High Court judge, held that the substance of r 4.3 and s 376 was the same. As such, the judge did not consider that he would be justified 'into torturing the clear wording of s 376 so as to exclude appeals relating to individual voluntary arrangements.' See also *Legal and Equitable Securities plc v Linton* [2010] EWHC 2046 (Ch).

The discretion of the court in extending time is one to be determined on the facts of any particular case. In *Tager*, for example, the judge was prepared to exercise his jurisdiction in extending time retrospectively, given that the delay in that case (of two months) was not too long, that the reasons for the delay were understandable, that the party seeking to rely on the extension was able to demonstrate an arguable case and that there was no significant prejudice to any other party.

Formerly s 376 corresponded in substance with r 12.9(2) which applied to the extension or shortening of time for anything to be done under the rules. Rule 12.9(2) was replaced by r 12A.55(2) (introduced by the Insolvency (Amendment) Rules 2010 (SI 2010/686)) which provides the provisions of CPR r 3.1(2)(a) (the Court's general powers of management) apply so as to enable the Court to extend or shorten the time limit for ampliance with anything required or authorized to be done by the rules.

Procedure—The court manager of the bankruptcy court (on which see r 13.2(2)) is authorised under para 15.1(1) of the *Practice Direction: Insolvency Proceedings* [2012] BPIR 409 to extend time for the hearing of a petition on an application by a petitioning creditor.

377 Formal defects

The acts of a person as the trustee of a bankrupt's estate or as a special manager, and the acts of the creditors' committee established for any bankruptcy, are valid notwithstanding any defect in the appointment, election or qualifications of the trustee or manager or, as the case may be, of any member of the committee.

General note—The substance of this provision in relation to the acts of a trustee, special manager or a creditors' committee in bankruptcy is precisely the same as s 232, which operates in relation to the office-holders identified therein, and para 104 of Sch B1 in relation to administrators. Reference should be made to the commentary to s 232.

Section 377, like, s 232 and para 104 of Sch B1, is concerned with the acts of an office-holder, as well as the acts of a creditors' committee. Unlike its predecessor in s 147(1) of the Bankruptcy Act 1914, no cure is provided for formal defects or irregularities in insolvency proceedings. Such a provision, however, does appear in r 7.55, on which see the commentary thereto. Rule 12.5 (evidence of proceedings at meetings) and r 12.6 (presumption relating to documents issuing from the Secretary of State) may also be of assistance in relation to formal defects or procedural irregularities in relation to such matters.

378 Exemption from stamp duty

Stamp duty shall not be charged on—

(a) any document, being a deed, conveyance, assignment, surrender, admission or other assurance relating solely to property which is comprised in a bankrupt's estate and which, after the execution of that document, is or remains at law or in equity the property of the bankrupt or of the trustee of that estate,

(b) any writ, order, certificate or other instrument relating solely to the property of a bankrupt or to any bankruptcy proceedings.

General note—Documents relating to bankruptcy matters are exempt from stamp duty. Section 378 is a simplified version of the former provision in s 148 of the Bankruptcy Act 1914.

379 Annual report

As soon as practicable after the end of 1986 and each subsequent calendar year, the Secretary of State shall prepare and lay before each House of Parliament a report about the operation during that year of so much of this Act as is comprised in this Group of Parts, and about proceedings in the course of that year under the Deeds of Arrangement Act 1914.

General note—This provision provides for the laying before Parliament of an annual report by the Secretary of State which extends to proceedings under the Deeds of Arrangement Act 1914. Some of the raw material upon which the annual report is based emanates from the court under r 7.29(1).

379A Remote attendance at meetings

(1) Where—

  (a) a bankruptcy order is made against an individual or an interim receiver of an individual''s property is appointed, or
  (b) a voluntary arrangement in relation to an individual is proposed or is approved under Part 8,

this section applies to any meeting of the individual's creditors summoned under this Act or the rules.

(2) Where the person summoning a meeting ('the convener') considers it appropriate, the meeting may be conducted and held in such a way that persons who are not present together at the same place may attend it.

(3) Where a meeting is conducted and held in the manner referred to in subsection (2), a person attends the meeting if that person is able to exercise any rights which that person may have to speak and vote at the meeting.

(4) For the purposes of this section—

  (a) a person exercises the right to speak at a meeting when that person is in a position to communicate to all those attending the meeting, during the meeting, any information or opinions which that person has on the business of the meeting; and
  (b) a person exercises the right to vote at a meeting when—
    (i)   that person is able to vote, during the meeting, on resolutions put to the vote at the meeting, and
    (ii) that person's vote can be taken into account in determining whether or not such resolutions are passed at the same time as the votes of all the other persons attending the meeting.

(5) The convener of a meeting which is to be conducted and held in the manner referred to in subsection (2) may make whatever arrangements the convener considers appropriate to—

  (a) enable those attending the meeting to exercise their rights to speak or vote, and
  (b) ensure the identification of those attending the meeting and the security of any electronic means used to enable attendance.

(6) Where in the reasonable opinion of the convener—

(a)   a meeting will be attended by persons who will not be present together at the same place, and

(b)   it is unnecessary or inexpedient to specify a place for the meeting,

any requirement under this Act or the rules to specify a place for the meeting may be satisfied by specifying the arrangements the convener proposes to enable persons to exercise their rights to speak or vote.

(7) In making the arrangements referred to in subsection (5) and in forming the opinion referred to in subsection (6)(b), the convener must have regard to the legitimate interests of the creditors and others attending the meeting in the efficient despatch of the business of the meeting.

(8) If—

(a)   the notice of a meeting does not specify a place for the meeting,

(b)   the convener is requested in accordance with the rules to specify a place for the meeting, and

(c)   that request is made by not less than ten percent in value of the creditors,

it shall be the duty of the convener to specify a place for the meeting.

Amendments—Inserted by SI 2010/18.

This self explanatory provision mirrors s 246A. See also IR 12A.22 and 12A.23.

379B   Use of websites

(1) This section applies where—

(a)   a bankruptcy order is made against an individual or an interim receiver of an individual's property is appointed, or

(b)   a voluntary arrangement in relation to an individual is proposed or is approved under Part 8,

and 'the office-holder' means the official receiver, the trustee in bankruptcy, the interim receiver, the nominee or the supervisor of the voluntary arrangement, as the case may be.

(2) Where any provision of this Act or the rules requires the office-holder to give, deliver, furnish or send a notice or other document or information to any person, that requirement is satisfied by making the notice, document or information available on a website—

(a)   in accordance with the rules, and

(b)   in such circumstances as may be prescribed.

Amendments—Inserted by SI 2010/18.

This self explanatory provisions mirrors s 246B. See also IR 12A.12

PART XI
INTERPRETATION FOR SECOND GROUP OF PARTS

Introduction to Part XI—This Part includes just five sections and these provisions define words and expressions used in what is called 'the Second Group of Parts'. The provisions covered in the Second Group of Parts are ss 254–379, being provisions that deal with individual insolvency, including bankruptcy.

380 Introductory

The next five sections have effect for the interpretation of the provisions of this Act which are comprised in this Group of Parts; and where a definition is provided for a particular expression, it applies except so far as the context otherwise requires.

General note—In addition to ss 381–385 a number of useful definitions relating to bankruptcy appear in Part XIII of the Insolvency Rules 1986.

381 'Bankrupt' and associated terminology

(1) 'Bankrupt' means an individual who has been adjudged bankrupt and, in relation to a bankruptcy order, it means the individual adjudged bankrupt by that order.

(2) 'Bankruptcy order' means an order adjudging an individual bankrupt.

(3) 'Bankruptcy petition' means a petition to the court for a bankruptcy order.

382 'Bankruptcy debt', 'liability'

(1) 'Bankruptcy debt', in relation to a bankrupt, means (subject to the next subsection) any of the following—

(a) any debt or liability to which he is subject at the commencement of the bankruptcy,

(b) any debt or liability to which he may become subject after the commencement of the bankruptcy (including after his discharge from bankruptcy) by reason of any obligation incurred before the commencement of the bankruptcy,

(c) any amount specified in pursuance of section 39(3)(c) of the Powers of Criminal Courts Act 1973 in any criminal bankruptcy order made against him before the commencement of the bankruptcy, and

(d) any interest provable as mentioned in section 322(2) in Chapter IV of Part IX.

(2) In determining for the purposes of any provision in this Group of Parts whether any liability in tort is a bankruptcy debt, the bankrupt is deemed to become subject to that liability by reason of an obligation incurred at the time when the cause of action accrued.

(3) For the purposes of references in this Group of Parts to a debt or liability, it is immaterial whether the debt or liability is present or future, whether it is certain or contingent or whether its amount is fixed or

liquidated, or is capable of being ascertained by fixed rules or as a matter of opinion; and references in this Group of Parts to owing a debt are to be read accordingly.

(4) In this Group of Parts, except in so far as the context otherwise requires, 'liability' means (subject to subsection (3) above) a liability to pay money or money's worth, including any liability under an enactment, any liability for breach of trust, any liability in contract, tort or bailment and any liability arising out of an obligation to make restitution.

(5) Liability under the Child Support Act 1991 to pay child support maintenance to any person is not a debt or liability for the purposes of Part 8.

Amendments—Welfare Reform Act 2012, s 142(1), (2).

General note—The provision explains what constitutes a bankruptcy debt, namely a debt that permits a creditor to petition for bankruptcy, although a bankruptcy debt is not necessarily provable. In theory, a creditor can base a petition on a non-provable debt: *Levy v Legal Services Commission* [2001] 1 All ER 895, [2000] BPIR 1065. See r 12.3 and the comments applying to it for consideration of the debts which are provable.

The definition of 'bankruptcy debt' has most obvious significance to s 281(1), by which the effect of discharge is to release a bankrupt from all such debts.

A liability to repay benefit overpayments (in respect of income support) arising on a decision by the Secretary of State to recover such an overpayment made prior to the recipient's bankruptcy, and in the absence of fraud, constitutes a bankruptcy debt from which the recipient is released on discharge: *Secretary of State for Work and Pensions v Balding* [2007] BPIR 1669 (Mummery, Thomas and Lloyd LJJ). *Balding* was approved by the Supreme Court in *Secretary of State for Work and Pensions v Payne* [2011] UKSC 60. The liability will not constitute a bankruptcy debt and will not therefore be released on discharge if the decision to recover the overpayment is made after the commencement of the bankruptcy: *Steele v Birmingham City Council* [2006] 1 WLR 2380.

Section 382(1)(c), which is obsolete in any case, is to be repealed from a date to be appointed by virtue of s 170(2) and Sch 16 to the Criminal Justice Act 1988.

The scope of the term 'bankruptcy debt', which extends not only to debts but also to 'liability', on which see s 382(3) and (4), is extremely broad and extends to all manner of unliquidated claims.

For the purposes of s 382(3) a liability is contingent if it arises out of an existing legal commitment or state of affairs but which is dependent on the happening or non-happening of a stipulated event: *Re Sutherland* [1963] AC 253, HL.

In *Glenister v Rowe* [2000] Ch 76, [1999] BPIR 674 the Court of Appeal held that liability for an opposing party's costs in proceedings commenced prior to the making of a bankruptcy order does not constitute a contingent liability, since an order for costs remains a matter for the court's discretion and, until that discretion is exercised, there cannot be said to be a contingency in the *Sutherland* sense. Neither can a costs order, under which costs are to be assessed, constitute a future liability, since there is no certainty that the court will exercise its discretion in assessing costs. See also *Casson v The Law Society* [2009] EWHC 1943 (Admin), [2010] BPIR 49. *Glenister* was distinguished in *Coutts & Co v Passey* [2007] BPIR 323 (Registrar Nicholls) in which the applicant (who successfully appealed against the refusal of the chairman of the creditors' meeting to allow it to vote in full for legal costs incurred but not assessed by the court) had a specific contractual right to full payment by the debtor of its costs incurred. Lord Neuberger, in giving the leading judgment in *Re Nortel GmbH* [2013] UKSC 52, [2013] 3 WLR 504 (at [91]) said by way of obiter, in the course of considering r 13.12(1)(b) and contingent liabilities, that he felt that *Glenister v Rowe and Steele v Birmingham City Council* [2006] 1 WLR 2380 were wrongly decided, although he could see how they might justified on the basis of the rules of precedent. Lord Sumption also cast some doubts on the judgments (at [136]).

'Contingent'—See under the heading 'Contingent or prospective creditors' in relation to s 124.

383 'Creditor', 'security', etc

(1) 'Creditor'—

    (a)   in relation to a bankrupt, means a person to whom any of the bankruptcy debts is owed (being, in the case of an amount falling within paragraph (c) of the definition in section 382(1) of 'bankruptcy debt', the person in respect of whom that amount is specified in the criminal bankruptcy order in question), and

    (b)   in relation to an individual to whom a bankruptcy petition relates, means a person who would be a creditor in the bankruptcy if a bankruptcy order were made on that petition.

(2) Subject to the next two subsections and any provision of the rules requiring a creditor to give up his security for the purposes of proving a debt, a debt is secured for the purposes of this Group of Parts to the extent that the person to whom the debt is owed holds any security for the debt (whether a mortgage, charge, lien or other security) over any property of the person by whom the debt is owed.

(3) Where a statement such as is mentioned in section 269(1)(a) in Chapter I of Part IX has been made by a secured creditor for the purposes of any bankruptcy petition and a bankruptcy order is subsequently made on that petition, the creditor is deemed for the purposes of the Parts in this Group to have given up the security specified in the statement.

(4) In subsection (2) the reference to a security does not include a lien on books, papers or other records, except to the extent that they consist of documents which give a title to property and are held as such.

General note—Apart from the definition of the term 'creditor' in s 383(1), s 383(2) and (3) are most obviously relevant to s 269, which deals with a petitioning creditor with security. In addition to the more common mortgage or charge, a debt may be secured by 'lien or other security' such as a trust arrangement as arises in favour of the Law Society under the Solicitors Act 1974 following an intervention, but not including a landlord's right of re-entry: *Razzaq v Pala* [1998] BCC 66. For commentary on the two lines of authority as to whether money in court is capable of constituting security see the Court of Appeal's judgment in *Flightline Ltd v Edwards* [2003] 1 WLR 1200 at [23].

Secured creditor—As one would expect, a creditor is only a secured creditor if he or she holds security over the property of a debtor who becomes bankrupt, and not if security is held over the property of a third party (*Re A Debtor (No 310 of 1988)* [1989] 1 WLR 452, [1989] 2 All ER 42): see also *Fagg v Rushton* [2007] BPIR 1059 (Evans-Lombe J) and *Sofaer v Anglo Irish Finance Plc* [2011] EWHC 1480 (Ch), [2011] BPIR 1736.

    A landlord who has a right to distrain is not a secured creditor: *Re Coal Consumers' Association* (1876–1877) 4 Ch D 625; *Re Bridgewater Engineering Co* (1879) 12 Ch D 181 at 186.

Security and surrender—Section 383(3) relates to s 269(1)(a) which provides that if a petitioning creditor bases a bankruptcy petition on a secured debt, he or she must be ready to surrender security for the benefit of all creditors of the debtor, if a bankruptcy order is made. See also the note to s 269(1)(a).

384 'Prescribed' and 'the rules'

(1) Subject to the next subsection and sections 342C(7) and 342F(9) in Chapter V of Part IX, 'prescribed' means prescribed by the rules; and 'the rules' means rules made under section 412 in Part XV.

(2) References in this Group of Parts to the amount prescribed for the purposes of any of the following provisions—

    section 251S(4);
    section 273;
    section 313A;
    section 346(3);
    section 354(1) and (2);
    section 358;
    section 360(1);
    section 361(2);
    section 364(2)(d),
    paragraphs 6 to 8 of Schedule 4ZA,

and references in those provisions to the prescribed amount are to be read in accordance with section 418 in Part XV and orders made under that section.

Amendments—Welfare Reform and Pensions Act 1999, s 84(1), Sch 12, Pt II, paras 70, 72; Enterprise Act 2002, s 261(5); Tribunals, Courts and Enforcement Act 2007, s 108(3), Sch 20, Pt 1, paras 1, 4.

'Debt'—This will include (because of the reference to s 382(3)) future and contingent claims.

385 Miscellaneous definitions

(1) The following definitions have effect—

    'the court', in relation to any matter, means the court to which, in accordance with section 373 in Part X and the rules, proceedings with respect to that matter are allocated or transferred;
    'creditor's petition' means a bankruptcy petition under section 264(1)(a);
    'criminal bankruptcy order' means an order under section 39(1) of the Powers of Criminal Courts Act 1973;
    'debt' is to be construed in accordance with section 382(3);
    'the debtor'—

      (za) in relation to a debt relief order or an application for such an order, has the same meaning as in Part 7A,
      (a) in relation to a proposal for the purposes of Part VIII, means the individual making or intending to make that proposal, and
      (b) in relation to a bankruptcy petition, means the individual to whom the petition relates;

    'debtor's petition' means a bankruptcy petition presented by the debtor himself under section 264(1)(b);
    'debt relief order' means an order made by the official receiver under Part 7A
    'dwelling house' includes any building or part of a building which is occupied as a dwelling and any yard, garden, garage or outhouse belonging to the dwelling house and occupied with it;
    'estate', in relation to a bankrupt is to be construed in accordance with section 283 in Chapter II of Part IX;

'family', in relation to a bankrupt, means the persons (if any) who are living with him and are dependent on him;

'insolvency administration order' means an order for the administration in bankruptcy of the insolvent estate of a deceased debtor (being an individual at the date of his death);

'insolvency administration petition' means a petition for an insolvency administration order;

'the Rules' means the Insolvency Rules 1986.

'secured' and related expressions are to be construed in accordance with section 383; and

'the trustee', in relation to a bankruptcy and the bankrupt, means the trustee of the bankrupt's estate.

(2) References in this Group of Parts to a person's affairs include his business, if any.

Amendments—SI 1986/1999; Tribunals, Courts and Enforcement Act 2007, s 108(3), Sch 20, Pt 1, paras 1, 5.

On the meaning of the 'Court' and questions of jurisdiction see *Hall and Shivers v Van Der Heiden* [2010] BPIR 585.

THIRD GROUP OF PARTS
MISCELLANEOUS MATTERS BEARING ON BOTH COMPANY AND INDIVIDUAL INSOLVENCY; GENERAL INTERPRETATION; FINAL PROVISIONS

PART XII
PREFERENTIAL DEBTS IN COMPANY AND INDIVIDUAL INSOLVENCY

General comment on Part XII—This Part only consists of two sections and simply deals with one topic, namely preferential debts that can be claimed in both corporate and personal insolvency. The provisions also apply to limited liability partnerships through reg 5(1)(b) of the Limited Liability Partnerships Regulations 2001 (SI 2001/1090) (operative from 6 April 2001) and insolvent partnerships due to arts 10 and 11 and Sch 7 (paras 1 and 23) of the Insolvent Partnerships Order 1994 (SI 1994/2421).

The scheme provided by this Part (and Sch 6) allows certain unsecured creditors to get a right to payment in priority to other unsecured creditors, and, in relation to companies that have given floating charges, priority over a secured creditor. See the notes accompanying s 107 in relation to the position where a company is subject to a floating charge.

At one time there were two main preferential creditors, namely employees of the debtor and the Crown. The Crown's right to recover unremitted taxes and duties was gradually eroded in the latter part of the twentieth century, until s 251 of the Enterprise Act 2002 abolished Crown priority totally (in accord with the actions of a number of countries, such as Austria, Australia and Germany). Now the Crown is treated effectively like all unsecured creditors. A large number of countries around the world still retain priority for debts owed to government. Spain, France, Italy and South Africa are examples.

See the notes accompanying Sch 6 and s 175.

See A Keay *McPherson's Law of Company Liquidation* (3rd edn, Sweet and Maxwell, 2013), ch 13 for a detailed discussion of the preferential debts scheme.

386 Categories of preferential debts

(1) A reference in this Act to the preferential debts of a company or an individual is to the debts listed in Schedule 6 to this Act (contributions to occupational pension schemes; remuneration, &c of employees; levies on coal and steel production); and references to preferential creditors are to be read accordingly.

(2) In that Schedule 'the debtor' means the company or the individual concerned.

(3) Schedule 6 is to be read with Schedule 4 to the Pension Schemes Act 1993 (occupational pension scheme contributions).

Amendments—Pension Schemes Act 1993, s 190, Sch 8, para 18; Enterprise Act 2002, s 251(3).

General note—See Sch 6 for the debts that are preferential. Also, see the notes accompanying that Schedule for more details.

387 'The relevant date'

(1) This section explains references in Schedule 6 to the relevant date (being the date which determines the existence and amount of a preferential debt).

(2) For the purposes of section 4 in Part I (meetings to consider company voluntary arrangement), the relevant date in relation to a company which is not being wound up is—

    (a)   if the company is in administration, the date on which it entered administration, and

    (b)   if the company is not in administration, the date on which the voluntary arrangement takes effect.

(2A) For the purposes of paragraph 31 of Schedule A1 (meetings to consider company voluntary arrangement where a moratorium under section 1A is in force), the relevant date in relation to a company is the date of filing.

(3) In relation to a company which is being wound up, the following applies—

    (a)   if the winding up is by the court, and the winding-up order was made immediately upon the discharge of an administration order, the relevant date is the date on which the company entered administration;

    (aa)   if the winding up is by the court and the winding-up order was made following conversion of administration into winding up by virtue of Article 37 of the EC Regulation, the relevant date is the date on which the company entered administration;

    (ab)   if the company is deemed to have passed a resolution for voluntary winding up by virtue of an order following conversion of administration into winding up under Article 37 of the EC Regulation, the relevant date is the date on which the company entered administration;

(b) if the case does not fall within paragraph (a), (aa) or (ab) and the company—
    (i) is being wound up by the court, and
    (ii) had not commenced to be wound up voluntarily before the date of the making of the winding-up order,

the relevant date is the date of the appointment (or first appointment) of a provisional liquidator or, if no such appointment has been made, the date of the winding-up order;

(ba) if the case does not fall within paragraph (a), (aa), (ab) or (b) and the company is being wound up following administration pursuant to paragraph 83 of Schedule B1, the relevant date is the date on which the company entered administration;

(c) if the case does not fall within paragraph (a), (aa), (ab), (b) or (ba), the relevant date is the date of the passing of the resolution for the winding up of the company.

(3A) In relation to a company which is in administration (and to which no other provision of this section applies) the relevant date is the date on which the company enters administration.

(4) In relation to a company in receivership (where section 40 or, as the case may be, section 59 applies), the relevant date is—

(a) in England and Wales, the date of the appointment of the receiver by debenture-holders, and

(b) in Scotland, the date of the appointment of the receiver under section 53(6) or (as the case may be) 54(5).

(5) For the purposes of section 258 in Part VIII (individual voluntary arrangements), the relevant date is, in relation to a debtor who is not an undischarged bankrupt—

(a) where an interim order has been made under section 252 with respect to his proposal, the date of that order, and

(b) in any other case, the date on which the voluntary arrangement takes effect.

(6) In relation to a bankrupt, the following applies—

(a) where at the time the bankruptcy order was made there was an interim receiver appointed under section 286, the relevant date is the date on which the interim receiver was first appointed after the presentation of the bankruptcy petition;

(b) otherwise, the relevant date is the date of the making of the bankruptcy order.

Amendments—Insolvency Act 2000, s 1, Sch 1, paras 1, 9; Enterprise Act 2002, s 248(3), Sch 17, paras 9, 34; SI 2002/1240.

General note—The section explains what 'relevant date' means for the various insolvency regimes. The expression is used frequently in Sch 6 and is the point used for determining and quantifying a preferential debt.
    Paragraph 23 of Sch 7 of the Insolvent Partnerships Order 1994 (SI 1994/2421) modifies s 387 as far as it applies to insolvent partnerships.

PART XIII
INSOLVENCY PRACTITIONERS AND THEIR QUALIFICATION

General comment on Part XIII—The Insolvency Law Review Committee's Report, entitled *Insolvency Law and Practice* (and known as 'the Cork Report') (Cmnd 8558, 1982), acknowledged that the success of an insolvency regime was heavily dependent on those who administer it, namely the insolvency practitioners in private practice who did the work of liquidators, receivers, trustees and so on (at para 732). At the time of the Cork Committee's review of insolvency law and practice, insolvency practitioners were not required to have any particular qualifications, and this was identified by many as a major shortcoming in the system (at para 735). There was general recognition in the commercial world that there were some persons who were acting as insolvency practitioners, who might be termed 'cowboys', and who were not really qualified to act, and who engaged in questionable activities in administering the affairs of the insolvent. The Cork Committee agreed with the need for regulation and standards for qualification as an insolvency practitioner. This Part seeks to fulfil many of the Cork Committee's recommendations, with the heart of the Part being the requirement that practitioners should be members of professional bodies that could regulate and discipline their members. The aim of the Part is to ensure that there is a qualified, independent and competent insolvency profession that is marked by integrity.

People unhappy with the actions of insolvency practitioners who are members of recognised bodies should initially complain to those bodies. If no satisfaction is obtained, the person should then go to the Department of Trade and Industry. The latter action is the appropriate course for anyone who is aggrieved about the conduct of insolvency practitioners not members of recognised bodies, but who were granted authorisation to act as practitioners by the Secretary of State or other competent authority. The professional bodies as well as the Association for Business Recovery Professionals (formerly the Society for Practitioners of Insolvency) provide guidance to practitioners on ethics and professional conduct in material that they publish.

Besides being members of recognised professional bodies, many practitioners have become members of the Association for Business Recovery Professionals, known as 'R3' (standing for Rescue, Recovery and Renewal). This Association is involved in training practitioners and also determining ethical issues.

The Insolvency Practitioners Regulations 2005 (SI 2005/524) set out the requirements for a person to be authorised as an insolvency practitioner. The Regulations prescribe rules in relation to education, practical training and experience. The Insolvency Practitioners Regulations 1990 (SI 1990/439) (and amended by SI 1993/221) apply to applications for authorisation under s 393 to act as an insolvency practitioner made before 1 April 2005 (Insolvency Practitioners Regulations 2005, reg 4(2)), as well as cases in which an insolvency practitioner was appointed before that date (reg 4(3)).

To assist practitioners the Insolvency Service issues what are known as 'Dear IP' letters.

In the following commentary, unless it is indicated to the contrary, the term 'insolvency practitioner' refers to licensed insolvency practitioners carrying out any of the following roles: liquidator, provisional liquidator, administrator, administrative receiver, a supervisor of a company voluntary arrangement, trustee in bankruptcy, interim receiver and a supervisor of an individual voluntary arrangement.

Restrictions on unqualified persons acting as liquidator, trustee in bankruptcy, etc

388 Meaning of 'act as insolvency practitioner'

(1) A person acts as an insolvency practitioner in relation to a company by acting—

    (a)   as its liquidator, provisional liquidator, administrator or administrative receiver, or

    (b)   where a voluntary arrangement in relation to the company is proposed or approved under Part I, as nominee or supervisor.

(2) A person acts as an insolvency practitioner in relation to an individual by acting—

    (a)   as his trustee in bankruptcy or interim receiver of his property or as permanent or interim trustee in the sequestration of his estate; or

    (b)   as trustee under a deed which is a deed of arrangement made for the benefit of his creditors or, in Scotland, a trust deed for his creditors; or

    (c)   where a voluntary arrangement in relation to the individual is proposed or approved under Part VIII, as nominee or supervisor; or

    (d)   in the case of a deceased individual to the administration of whose estate this section applies by virtue of an order under section 421 (application of provisions of this Act to insolvent estates of deceased persons), as administrator of that estate.

(2A) A person acts as an insolvency practitioner in relation to an insolvent partnership by acting—

    (a)   as its liquidator, provisional liquidator or administrator, or

    (b)   as trustee of the partnership under article 11 of the Insolvent Partnerships Order 1994, or

    (c)   where a voluntary arrangement in relation to the insolvent partnership is proposed or approved under Part I of the Act, as nominee or supervisor.

(2B) In relation to a voluntary arrangement proposed under Part I or VIII, a person acts as nominee if he performs any of the functions conferred on nominees under the Part in question.

(3) References in this section to an individual include, except in so far as the context otherwise requires, references to any debtor within the meaning of the Bankruptcy (Scotland) Act 1985.

(4) In this section—

'administrative receiver' has the meaning given by section 251 in Part VII;
'company' means—

    (a)   a company registered under the Companies Act 2006 in England and Wales or Scotland, or

    (b)   a company that may be wound up under Part 5 of this Act (unregistered companies); 'interim trustee' and 'permanent trustee' mean the same as in the Bankruptcy (Scotland) Act 1985.

(5) Nothing in this section applies to anything done by—

    (a)   the official receiver; or

    (b)   the Accountant in Bankruptcy (within the meaning of the Bankruptcy (Scotland) Act 1985).

(6) Nothing in this section applies to anything done (whether in the United Kingdom or elsewhere) in relation to insolvency proceedings under the EC Regulation in a member State other than the United Kingdom.

Amendments—Bankruptcy (Scotland) Act 1993, s 11(1); SI 1994/2421; Insolvency Act 2000, s 4(1), (2); SI 2002/1240; SI 2002/2708; SI 2009/1941.

General note—The provision explains what acting as an insolvency practitioner entails. This is done by setting out the fact that acting in certain roles means one is acting as an insolvency practitioner. This is important, as it is acting as an insolvency practitioner that is regarded as an offence (see s 389). Official receivers are not required to be qualified insolvency practitioners (s 388(5)(a)). Their work is, of course, monitored in different ways within the civil service and by the courts.

Section 388(2A)(c) was amended by the Insolvent Partnerships (Amendment) (No 2) Order 2002 (SI 2002/2708).

389 Acting without qualification an offence

(1) A person who acts as an insolvency practitioner in relation to a company or an individual at a time when he is not qualified to do so is liable to imprisonment or a fine, or to both.

(1A) This section is subject to section 389A.

(2) This section does not apply to the official receiver or the Accountant in Bankruptcy (within the meaning of the Bankruptcy (Scotland) Act 1985).

Amendments—Bankruptcy (Scotland) Act 1993, s 11(2); Insolvency Act 2000, s 4(1), (3).

General note—This provision gives the bite to the whole regime for insolvency practitioners, making it a criminal offence to act as an insolvency practitioner when not authorised to do so. Schedule 10 to the Act sets out the penalty for breaching this provision. It can be severe with, in a trial on indictment, a prison sentence of up to 2 years and/or a fine. The provision is subject to certain exceptions contained in s 389A.

389A Authorisation of nominees and supervisors

(1) Section 389 does not apply to a person acting, in relation to a voluntary arrangement proposed or approved under Part I or Part VIII, as nominee or supervisor if he is authorised so to act.

(2) For the purposes of subsection (1) and those Parts, an individual to whom subsection (3) does not apply is authorised to act as nominee or supervisor in relation to such an arrangement if—

(a) he is a member of a body recognised for the purpose by the Secretary of State or of a body recognised for the purpose of Article 348A(2)(a) of the Insolvency (Northern Ireland) Order 1989 by the Department of Enterprise, Trade and Investment for Northern Ireland, and

(b) there is in force security (in Scotland, caution) for the proper performance of his functions and that security or caution meets the prescribed requirements with respect to his so acting in relation to the arrangement.

(3) This subsection applies to a person if—

(a) he has been adjudged bankrupt or sequestration of his estate has been awarded and (in either case) he has not been discharged, (aa) a moratorium period under a debt relief order applies in relation to him (under Part 7A of this Act),

(b) he is subject to a disqualification order made or a disqualification undertaking accepted under the Company Directors Disqualification Act 1986 or the Company Directors Disqualification (Northern Ireland) Order 2002,

(c) he is a patient within the meaning of section 329(1) of the Mental Health (Care and Treatment) (Scotland) Act 2003, or

(d) he lacks capacity (withing the meaning of the Mental Health Capacity Act 2005) to act as nominee of supervisor.

(4) The Secretary of State may by order declare a body which appears to him to fall within subsection (5) to be a recognised body for the purposes of subsection (2)(a).

(5) A body may be recognised if it maintains and enforces rules for securing that its members—

(a) are fit and proper persons to act as nominees or supervisors, and

(b) meet acceptable requirements as to education and practical training and experience.

(6) For the purposes of this section, a person is a member of a body only if he is subject to its rules when acting as nominee or supervisor (whether or not he is in fact a member of the body).

(7) An order made under subsection (4) in relation to a body may be revoked by a further order if it appears to the Secretary of State that the body no longer falls within subsection (5).

(8) An order of the Secretary of State under this section has effect from such date as is specified in the order; and any such order revoking a previous order may make provision for members of the body in question to continue to be treated as members of a recognised body for a specified period after the revocation takes effect.

Amendments—Inserted by Insolvency Act 2000, s 4(1), (4). Amended by SI 2004/1941; SI 2005/2078; Mental Capacity Act 2005, s 67(1), (2), Sch 6; SI 2009/1941; SI 2009/3081; SI 2012/2404.

389B Official receiver as nominee or supervisor

(1) The official receiver is authorised to act as nominee or supervisor in relation to a voluntary arrangement approved under Part VIII provided that the debtor is an undischarged bankrupt when the arrangement is proposed.

(2) The Secretary of State may by order repeal the proviso in subsection (1).

(3) An order under subsection (2)—

(a) must be made by statutory instrument, and

(b) shall be subject to annulment in pursuance of a resolution of either House of Parliament.

Amendments—Inserted by Enterprise Act 2002, s 264(1), Sch 22, para 3.

General note—Originally official receivers could not act in relation to IVAs, but this provision, part of the Enterprise Act 2002 reforms, permits official receivers to act in relation to so-called 'fast track' IVAs under s 263A. See that section and the notes accompanying it.

The requisite qualification, and the means of obtaining it

390 Persons not qualified to act as insolvency practitioners

(1) A person who is not an individual is not qualified to act as an insolvency practitioner.

(2) A person is not qualified to act as an insolvency practitioner at any time unless at that time—

    (a)   he is authorised so to act by virtue of membership of a professional body recognised under section 391 below, being permitted so to act by or under the rules of that body, or

    (b)   he holds an authorisation granted by a competent authority under section 393; or

    (c)   he holds an authorisation granted by the Department of Enterprise, Trade and Investment for Northern Ireland under Article 352 of the Insolvency (Northern Ireland) Order 1989.

(3) A person is not qualified to act as an insolvency practitioner in relation to another person at any time unless—

    (a)   there is in force at that time security or, in Scotland, caution for the proper performance of his functions, and

    (b)   that security or caution meets the prescribed requirements with respect to his so acting in relation to that other person.

(4) A person is not qualified to act as an insolvency practitioner at any time if at that time—

    (aa)   a moratorium period under a debt relief order applies in relation of him,

    (a)   he has been adjudged bankrupt or sequestration of his estate has been awarded and (in either case) he has not been discharged,

    (b)   he is subject to a disqualification order made or a disqualification undertaking accepted under the Company Directors Disqualification Act 1986 or the Company Directors Disqualification (Northern Ireland) Order 2002,

    (c)   he is a patient within the meaning of section 329(1) of the Mental Health (Care and Treatment) (Scotland) Act 2003 or has had a guardian appointed to him under the Adults with Incapacity (Scotland) Act 2000 (asp 4), or

    (d)   he lacks capacity (within the meaning of the Mental Capacity Act 2005) to act as an insolvency practioner.

(5) A person is not qualified to act as an insolvency practitioner while a bankruptcy restrictions order or a debt relief restrictions order is in force in respect of him.

Amendments—Insolvency Act 2000, s 8, Sch 4, paras 1, 16; Adults with Incapacity (Scotland) Act 2000, s 88(2), Sch 5, para 18; Enterprise Act 2002, s 257(3), Sch 21, para 4; SI 2004/1941; SI 2005/2078; Mental Capacity Act 2005, s 67(1), (2), Sch 6, para 31(1), (3), Sch 7; Tribunals, Courts and Enforcement Act 2007, s 108(3), Sch 20, Pt 1, paras 1, 6; SI 2009/1941; SI 2009/3081.

General note—The provision explains who is not qualified to act as an insolvency practitioner, and implicitly indicates what must be done to act legitimately.

Authorisation—Persons will only be authorised to act as insolvency practitioners if they are members of recognised professional bodies or they secure the right to be able to act as insolvency practitioners by successfully applying to the Secretary of State or a competent authority (see s 392) for an authorisation to act (under s 393). Applicants may be authorised to act as insolvency practitioners if they are fit and proper persons (Insolvency Practitioners Regulations 2005 (SI 2005/524), reg 6). The Insolvency Practitioners Regulations 2005 (SI 2005/524) set out matters that might be considered in determining whether a person is a fit and proper person to act as an insolvency practitioner. Examples are whether: the applicant has been convicted of any offences involving fraud, dishonesty or violence; the applicant's practice has adequate systems of control and adequate records; such systems and records have been maintained.

Security—The requirement in s 390(3) is designed to safeguard the positions of creditors where an insolvency practitioner has acted in such as way as to cause loss to creditors. See Insolvency Practitioners Regulations 2005 (SI 2005/524), Sch 2, paras 2–8 for the details of any security bond. The Regulations provide that the surety under the bond that is given undertakes to be jointly and severally liable with the insolvency practitioner for the proper performance by the practitioner of the duties and obligations imposed upon the practitioner.

391 Recognised professional bodies

(1) The Secretary of State may by order declare a body which appears to him to fall within subsection (2) below to be a recognised professional body for the purposes of this section.

(2) A body may be recognised if it regulates the practice of a profession and maintains and enforces rules for securing that such of its members as are permitted by or under the rules to act as insolvency practitioners—

    (a)   are fit and proper persons so to act, and

    (b)   meet acceptable requirements as to education and practical training and experience.

(3) References to members of a recognised professional body are to persons who, whether members of that body or not, are subject to its rules in the practice of the profession in question.

The reference in section 390(2) above to membership of a professional body recognised under this section is to be read accordingly.

(4) An order made under subsection (1) in relation to a professional body may be revoked by a further order if it appears to the Secretary of State that the body no longer falls within subsection (2).

(5) An order of the Secretary of State under this section has effect from such date as is specified in the order; and any such order revoking a previous order may make provision whereby members of the body in question continue to be treated as authorised to act as insolvency practitioners for a specified period after the revocation takes effect.

General note—The Secretary of State is granted the power under this provision to declare bodies to be recognised professional bodies, to which a person who wishes to act as an insolvency practitioner must belong.

Recognised professional bodies—Bodies that have been recognised for the purposes of s 391 as being ones that were professional and able to discipline and regulate members are set out in the Insolvency Practitioners (Recognised Professional Bodies) Order (SI 1986/1764). They are, save for one, bodies that regulate accountants and solicitors. The bodies number seven and are (art 2): the Chartered Association of Certified Accountants, the Institute of Chartered Accountants in England and Wales, the Institute of Chartered Accountants of Scotland, the Institute of Chartered Accountants in Ireland, the Insolvency Practitioners' Association, the Law Society and the Law Society of Scotland. While the professional bodies that are recognised exercise control over their own qualified members, there is governmental monitoring, as the Insolvency Service supervises the regulatory process, conducts regular visits to all of the professional bodies and endeavours to ensure that necessary standards are maintained. Besides being a member of a professional body that is recognised, a person must also satisfy other requirements in order to be able to practise as an insolvency practitioner. These requirements include passing examinations and practical experience. Hence, the mere fact that one is a member of one of the professional bodies does not mean that one is qualified to practise as an insolvency practitioner.

The professional bodies must determine whether a member is a fit and proper person to act as an insolvency practitioner. The bodies operate various processes to control and correct those acting improperly, with revocation of a practitioner's licence to operate as an insolvency practitioner as one critical measure that can be taken. Obviously, if this were done, the practitioner would no longer be qualified to act as an insolvency practitioner. Bodies may withdraw a licence with immediate effect and before the exhausting of the appeal process, if it is deemed necessary in order to protect the public (*R v Institute of Chartered Accountants* [2001] BPIR 363, 2000 WL 1918639 at [33], a case concerning an application for judicial review in relation to the withdrawal of an insolvency practitioner's licence to act).

392 Authorisation by competent authority

(1) Application may be made to a competent authority for authorisation to act as an insolvency practitioner.

(2) The competent authorities for this purpose are—

    (a)   in relation to a case of any description specified in directions given by the Secretary of State, the body or person so specified in relation to cases of that description, and

    (b)   in relation to a case not falling within paragraph (a), the Secretary of State.

(3) The application—

    (a)   shall be made in such manner as the competent authority may direct,

    (b)   shall contain or be accompanied by such information as that authority may reasonably require for the purpose of determining the application, and

    (c)   shall be accompanied by the prescribed fee;

and the authority may direct that notice of the making of the application shall be published in such manner as may be specified in the direction.

(4) At any time after receiving the application and before determining it the authority may require the applicant to furnish additional information.

(5) Directions and requirements given or imposed under subsection (3) or (4) may differ as between different applications.

(6) Any information to be furnished to the competent authority under this section shall, if it so requires, be in such form or verified in such manner as it may specify.

(7) An application may be withdrawn before it is granted or refused.

(8) Any sums received under this section by a competent authority other than the Secretary of State may be retained by the authority; and any sums so received by the Secretary of State shall be paid into the Consolidated Fund.

(9) Subsection (3)(c) shall not have effect in respect of an application made to the Secretary of State (but this subsection is without prejudice to section 415A).

Amendments—Enterprise Act 2002, s 270(3).

393 Grant, refusal and withdrawal of authorisation

(1) The competent authority may, on an application duly made in accordance with section 392 and after being furnished with all such information as it may require under that section, grant or refuse the application.

(2) The authority shall grant the application if it appears to it from the information furnished by the applicant and having regard to such other information, if any, as it may have—

    (a)   that the applicant is a fit and proper person to act as an insolvency practitioner, and

    (b)   that the applicant meets the prescribed requirements with respect to education and practical training and experience.

(3) An authorisation granted under this section, if not previously withdrawn, continues in force for one year.

(3A) But where an authorisation is granted under this section the competent authority must, before its expiry (and without a further application made in accordance with section 392) grant a further authorisation under this section taking effect immediately after the expiry of the previous authorisation, unless it appears to the authority that the subject of the authorisation no longer complies with subsection (2)(a) and (b).

(4) An authorisation granted under this section may be withdrawn by the competent authority if it appears to it—

    (a)   that the holder of the authorisation is no longer a fit and proper person to act as an insolvency practitioner, or

    (b)   without prejudice to paragraph (a), that the holder—

        (i)   has failed to comply with any provision of this Part, or of any regulations made under this Part or Part XV, or

      (ii)   in purported compliance with any such provision, has furnished the competent authority with false, inaccurate or misleading information.

(5) An authorisation granted under this section may be withdrawn by the competent authority at the request or with the consent of the holder of the authorisation.

(6) Where an authorisation granted under this section is withdrawn—

      (a)   subsection (3A) does not require a further authorisation to be granted, or

      (b)   if a further authorisation has already been granted at the time of the withdrawal, the further authorisation is also withdrawn.

Amendments—SI 2009/3081

General note—An alternative way of qualifying to act as an insolvency practitioner, besides being a member of a recognised professional body, is to secure the right to be able to act by applying to the Secretary of State or a competent authority for an authorisation. Applicants may be authorised to act as insolvency practitioners if they are fit and proper persons (Insolvency Practitioners Regulations 2005 (SI 2005/524), reg 6). Educational requirements and practical training and experience demands are set out in regs 7 and 8 of the Regulations. Besides holding qualifications, a person must have passed the Joint Insolvency Examination set by the Joint Insolvency Examination Board or have acquired, or been awarded, in a country or territory outside the United Kingdom professional or vocational qualifications which indicate that the applicant has the knowledge and competence that is attested by a pass in that examination (reg 7).

If a person is refused an authorisation to act (or has his or her authorisation withdrawn), the person may make representations to the Secretary of State or competent authority (s 395). If this does not bring success, the person may require the matter to be referred to the Insolvency Practitioners' Tribunal (s 396).

Any authorisation that is granted is for a maximum of 3 years (Insolvency Practitioners Regulations 1990, reg 10).

The Insolvency Practitioners Regulations 1990 (SI 1990/439) (and amended by SI 1993/221) apply to applications for authorisation under s 393 to act as an insolvency practitioner made before 1 April 2005.

394 Notices

(1) Where a competent authority grants an authorisation under section 393, it shall give written notice of that fact to the applicant, specifying the date on which the authorisation takes effect.

(2) Where the authority proposes to refuse an application, or to withdraw an authorisation under section 393(4), it shall give the applicant or holder of the authorisation written notice of its intention to do so, setting out particulars of the grounds on which it proposes to act.

(3) In the case of a proposed withdrawal the notice shall state the date on which it is proposed that the withdrawal should take effect.

(4) A notice under subsection (2) shall give particulars of the rights exercisable under the next two sections by a person on whom the notice is served.

395 Right to make representations

(1) A person on whom a notice is served under section 394(2) may within 14 days after the date of service make written representations to the competent authority.

(2) The competent authority shall have regard to any representations so made in determining whether to refuse the application or withdraw the authorisation, as the case may be.

396 Reference to Tribunal

(1) The Insolvency Practitioners Tribunal ('the Tribunal') continues in being; and the provisions of Schedule 7 apply to it.

(2) Where a person is served with a notice under section 394(2), he may—

    (a)   at any time within 28 days after the date of service of the notice, or

    (b)   at any time after the making by him of representations under section 395 and before the end of the period of 28 days after the date of the service on him of a notice by the competent authority that the authority does not propose to alter its decision in consequence of the representations,

give written notice to the authority requiring the case to be referred to the Tribunal.

(3) Where a requirement is made under subsection (2), then, unless the competent authority—

    (a)   has decided or decides to grant the application or, as the case may be, not to withdraw the authorisation, and

    (b)   within 7 days after the date of the making of the requirement, gives written notice of that decision to the person by whom the requirement was made,

it shall refer the case to the Tribunal.

General note—A person who has been refused an authorisation to act as an insolvency practitioner or whose authorisation has been withdrawn under s 393 may either require the Secretary of State or competent authority to refer the matter to the Insolvency Practitioners' Tribunal, or he or she can do so if, after first making representations to the Secretary of State or competent authority, he or she fails to persuade the Secretary of State or the competent authority that there should not be refusal of an application for an authorisation (or that there should not be a withdrawal of an authorisation).

The procedure for the referral of a matter to the Tribunal is covered in the Insolvency Practitioners' Tribunal (Conduct of Investigations) Rules 1986 (SI 1986/952).

See Sch 7 for consideration of the constitution and processes of the Tribunal.

397 Action of Tribunal on reference

(1) On a reference under section 396 the Tribunal shall—

    (a)   investigate the case, and

(b)   make a report to the competent authority stating what would in their opinion be the appropriate decision in the matter and the reasons for that opinion,

and it is the duty of the competent authority to decide the matter accordingly.

(2) The Tribunal shall send a copy of the report to the applicant or, as the case may be, the holder of the authorisation; and the competent authority shall serve him with a written notice of the decision made by it in accordance with the report.

(3) The competent authority may, if he thinks fit, publish the report of the Tribunal.

General note—The Tribunal investigates any matter referred to it pursuant to the Insolvency Practitioners' Tribunal (Conduct of Investigations) Rules 1986 (SI 1986/952).

The Tribunal does not make the final decision concerning a person's authorisation. The Tribunal advises the Secretary of State or competent authority of its opinion and the Secretary of State or competent authority makes a decision. However, the terms of the section indicate that the decision is to reflect the opinion of the Tribunal. An unsuccessful applicant could seek judicial review of the decision.

398 Refusal or withdrawal without reference to Tribunal

Where in the case of any proposed refusal or withdrawal of an authorisation either—

(a)   the period mentioned in section 396(2)(a) has expired without the making of any requirement under that subsection or of any representations under section 395, or

(b)   the competent authority has given a notice such as is mentioned in section 396(2)(b) and the period so mentioned has expired without the making of any such requirement,

the competent authority may give written notice of the refusal or withdrawal to the person concerned in accordance with the proposal in the notice given under section 394(2).

Adjudicators

398A Appointment etc of adjudicators and assistants

(1) The Secretary of State may appoint persons to the office of adjudicator.

(2) A person appointed under subsection (1)—

(a)   is to be paid out of money provided by Parliament such salary as the Secretary of State may direct,

(b)   holds office on such other terms and conditions as the Secretary of State may direct, and

(c)   may be removed from office by a direction of the Secretary of State.

(3) A person who is authorised to act as an official receiver may not be appointed under subsection (1).

(4) The Secretary of State may appoint officers of the Secretary of State's department to assist adjudicators in the carrying out of their functions.

Amendments—Inserted by Enterprise and Regulatory Reform Act 2013, s 71(1), with effect from 25 April 2013 for the purpose of enabling the exercise, on or after that date, of any power to make provision by regulations, rules or order made by statutory instrument.

PART XIV
PUBLIC ADMINISTRATION (ENGLAND AND WALES)

General comment on Part XIV—This Part deals with the public administration of insolvency law and practice. Its primary focus is on the office of official receiver and the financing and accounting arrangements in the Insolvency Service for monies held in insolvent estates.

Official receivers

399 Appointment etc of official receivers

(1) For the purposes of this Act the official receiver, in relation to any bankruptcy, winding up, individual voluntary arrangement, debt relief order or application for such an order, is any person who by virtue of the following provisions of this section or section 401 below is authorised to act as the official receiver in relation to that bankruptcy, winding up, individual voluntary arrangement, debt relief order or application for such an order.

(2) The Secretary of State may (subject to the approval of the Treasury as to numbers) appoint persons to the office of official receiver, and a person appointed to that office (whether under this section or section 70 of the Bankruptcy Act 1914)—

    (a)   shall be paid out of money provided by Parliament such salary as the Secretary of State may with the concurrence of the Treasury direct,

    (b)   shall hold office on such other terms and conditions as the Secretary of State may with the concurrence of the Treasury direct, and

    (c)   may be removed from office by a direction of the Secretary of State.

(3) Where a person holds the office of official receiver, the Secretary of State shall from time to time attach him either to the High Court or to a county court having jurisdiction for the purposes of the second Group of Parts of this Act.

(4) Subject to any directions under subsection (6) below, an official receiver attached to a particular court is the person authorised to act as the official receiver in relation to every bankruptcy, winding up, individual voluntary arrangement, debt relief order or application for such an order falling within the jurisdiction of that court.

(5) The Secretary of State shall ensure that there is, at all times, at least one official receiver attached to the High Court and at least one attached to

each county court having jurisdiction for the purposes of the second Group of Parts; but he may attach the same official receiver to two or more different courts.

(6) The Secretary of State may give directions with respect to the disposal of the business of official receivers, and such directions may, in particular—

    (a)   authorise an official receiver attached to one court to act as the official receiver in relation to any case or description of cases falling within the jurisdiction of another court;

    (b)   provide, where there is more than one official receiver authorised to act as the official receiver in relation to cases falling within the jurisdiction of any court, for the distribution of their business between or among themselves.

(7) A person who at the coming into force of section 222 of the Insolvency Act 1985 (replaced by this section) is an official receiver attached to a court shall continue in office after the coming into force of that section as an official receiver attached to that court under this section.

Amendments—Enterprise Act 2002, s 269, Sch 23, paras 1, 14; Tribunals, Courts and Enforcement Act 2007, s 108(3), Sch 20, Pt 1, paras 1, 7.

General note—Official receivers carry out an important role in relation to many aspects of insolvency law, including acting as the first liquidator in compulsory windings up (s 136(2)) and investigating the causes of failure of insolvents (ss 132 and 295). Before being appointed as official receivers, such persons have usually occupied positions as civil servants within the Department of Business Enterprise and Regulatory Reform, but when appointed as official receivers they cease 'to be civil servants in the proper sense of servants of the Crown employed in the business of government within (in this case) a department of state' (*Re Minotaur Data Systems Ltd* [1999] 2 BCLC 766 at 772, per Aldous LJ). Because Beldam LJ in *Mond v Hyde* [1999] 2 WLR 499 at 516, [1998] 2 BCLC 340 at 357 was of the view that the relationship between the Department of Business Enterprise and Regulatory Reform and official receivers was not that of master and servant, each official receiver is entitled to initiate legal proceedings in his or her own name, and is able to have a right of audience before the court to which he or she is attached.

See *Re Minotaur Data Systems Ltd* [1999] 2 BCLC 766; sub nom *Official Receiver v Brunt* [1999] BPIR 560 (CA) for a judicial discussion of the nature of the office of official receiver.

400 Functions and status of official receivers

(1) In addition to any functions conferred on him by this Act, a person holding the office of official receiver shall carry out such other functions as may from time to time be conferred on him by the Secretary of State.

(2) In the exercise of the functions of his office a person holding the office of official receiver shall act under the general directions of the Secretary of State and shall also be an officer of the court in relation to which he exercises those functions.

(3) Any property vested in his official capacity in a person holding the office of official receiver shall, on his dying, ceasing to hold office or being otherwise succeeded in relation to the bankruptcy or winding up in question by another official receiver, vest in his successor without any conveyance, assignment or transfer.

Officers of the court—Because official receivers have the status of officers of the court in carrying out their functions, if there is any interference with their work, it could constitute a contempt of court.

401 Deputy official receivers and staff

(1) The Secretary of State may, if he thinks it expedient to do so in order to facilitate the disposal of the business of the official receiver attached to any court, appoint an officer of his department to act as deputy to that official receiver.

(2) Subject to any directions given by the Secretary of State under section 399 or 400, a person appointed to act as deputy to an official receiver has, on such conditions and for such period as may be specified in the terms of his appointment, the same status and functions as the official receiver to whom he is appointed deputy.

Accordingly, references in this Act (except section 399(1) to (5)) to an official receiver include a person appointed to act as his deputy.

(3) An appointment made under subsection (1) may be terminated at any time by the Secretary of State.

(4) The Secretary of State may, subject to the approval of the Treasury as to numbers and remuneration and as to the other terms and conditions of the appointments, appoint officers of his department to assist official receivers in the carrying out of their functions.

402 Official Petitioner

(1) There continues to be an officer known as the Official Petitioner for the purpose of discharging, in relation to cases in which a criminal bankruptcy order is made, the functions assigned to him by or under this Act; and the Director of Public Prosecutions continues, by virtue of his office, to be the Official Petitioner.

(2) The functions of the Official Petitioner include the following—

- (a) to consider whether, in a case in which a criminal bankruptcy order is made, it is in the public interest that he should himself present a petition under section 264(1)(d) of this Act;
- (b) to present such a petition in any case where he determines that it is in the public interest for him to do so;
- (c) to make payments, in such cases as he may determine, towards expenses incurred by other persons in connection with proceedings in pursuance of such a petition; and
- (d) to exercise, so far as he considers it in the public interest to do so, any of the powers conferred on him by or under this Act.

(3) Any functions of the Official Petitioner may be discharged on his behalf by any person acting with his authority.

(4) Neither the Official Petitioner nor any person acting with his authority is liable to any action or proceeding in respect of anything done or omitted to be done in the discharge, or purported discharge, of the functions of the

Official Petitioner.(5) In this section 'criminal bankruptcy order' means an order under section 39(1) of the Powers of Criminal Courts Act 1973.

Insolvency Service finance, accounting and investment

403 Insolvency Services Account

(1) All money received by the Secretary of State in respect of proceedings under this Act as it applies to England and Wales shall be paid into the Insolvency Services Account kept by the Secretary of State with the Bank of England; and all payments out of money standing to the credit of the Secretary of State in that account shall be made by the Bank of England in such manner as he may direct.

(2) Whenever the cash balance standing to the credit of the Insolvency Services Account is in excess of the amount which in the opinion of the Secretary of State is required for the time being to answer demands in respect of bankrupts' estates or companies' estates, the Secretary of State shall—

(a) notify the excess to the National Debt Commissioners, and
(b) pay into the Insolvency Services Investment Account ('the Investment Account') kept by the Commissioners with the Bank of England the whole or any part of the excess as the Commissioners may require for investment in accordance with the following provisions of this Part.

(3) Whenever any part of the money so invested is, in the opinion of the Secretary of State, required to answer any demand in respect of bankrupt's estates or companies' estates, he shall notify to the National Debt Commissioners the amount so required and the Commissioners—

(a) shall thereupon repay to the Secretary of State such sum as may be required to the credit of the Insolvency Services Account, and
(b) for that purpose may direct the sale of such part of the securities in which the money has been invested as may be necessary.

404 Investment Account

Any money standing to the credit of the Investment Account (including any money received by the National Debt Commissioners by way of interest on or proceeds of any investment under this section) may be invested by the Commissioners, in accordance with such directions as may be given by the Treasury, in any manner for the time being specified in Part II of Schedule 1 to the Trustee Investments Act 1961.

405 (*Repealed*)

406 Interest on money received by liquidators or trustees in bankruptcy and invested

Where under rules made by virtue of paragraph 16 of Schedule 8 to this Act (investment of money received by company liquidators) or paragraph 21 of Schedule 9 to this Act (investment of money received by trustee in bankruptcy) a company or a bankrupt's estate has become entitled to any sum by way of interest, the Secretary of State shall certify that sum and the amount of tax payable on it to the National Debt Commissioners; and the Commissioners shall pay, out of the Investment Account—

    (a)   into the Insolvency Services Account, the sum so certified less the amount of tax so certified, and

    (b)   to the Commissioners of Inland Revenue, the amount of tax so certified.

Amendments—Insolvency Act 2000, s 13(2).

407 Unclaimed dividends and undistributed balances

(1) The Secretary of State shall from time to time pay into the Consolidated Fund out of the Insolvency Services Account so much of the sums standing to the credit of that Account as represents—

    (a)   dividends which were declared before such date as the Treasury may from time to time determine and have not been claimed, and

    (b)   balances ascertained before that date which are too small to be divided among the persons entitled to them.

(2) For the purposes of this section the sums standing to the credit of the Insolvency Services Account are deemed to include any sums paid out of that Account and represented by any sums or securities standing to the credit of the Investment Account.

(3) The Secretary of State may require the National Debt Commissioners to pay out of the Investment Account into the Insolvency Services Account the whole or part of any sum which he is required to pay out of that account under subsection (1); and the Commissioners may direct the sale of such securities standing to the credit of the Investment Account as may be necessary for that purpose.

408 Adjustment of balances

(1) The Treasury may direct the payment out of the Consolidated Fund of sums into—

    (a)   the Insolvency Services Account;

    (b)   the Investment Account.

(2) The Treasury shall certify to the House of Commons the reason for any payment under subsection (1).

(3) The Secretary of State may pay sums out of the Insolvency Services Account into the Consolidated Fund.

(4) The National Debt Commissioners may pay sums out of the Investment Account into the Consolidated Fund.

Amendments—Substituted by Enterprise Act 2002, s 272(2).

General note—This provision was amended by the Enterprise Act 2002, s 272(2) and became operative from 1 April 2004.

409 Annual financial statement and audit

(1) The National Debt Commissioners shall for each year ending on 31 March prepare a statement of the sums credited and debited to the Investment Account in such form and manner as the Treasury may direct and shall transmit it to the Comptroller and Auditor General before the end of November next following the year.

(2) The Secretary of State shall for each year ending 31st March prepare a statement of the sums received or paid by him under section 403 above in such form and manner as the Treasury may direct and shall transmit each statement to the Comptroller and Auditor General before the end of November next following the year.

(3) Every such statement shall include such additional information as the Treasury may direct.

(4) The Comptroller and Auditor General shall examine, certify and report on every such statement and shall lay copies of it, and of his report, before Parliament.

Supplementary

410 Extent of this Part

This Part of this Act extends to England and Wales only.

PART XV
SUBORDINATE LEGISLATION

General comment on Part XV—This Part deals with subordinate legislation that can be enacted to make the insolvency process work, and includes: the power to make rules and orders; provision for fees; and the power to make regulations for insolvency practice.

General insolvency rules

411 Company insolvency rules

(1) Rules may be made—

    (a)   in relation to England and Wales, by the Lord Chancellor with the concurrence of the Secretary of State and, in the case of rules that affect court procedure, with the concurrence of the Lord Chief Justice, or

    (b)   in relation to Scotland, by the Secretary of State,

for the purpose of giving effect to Parts I to VII of this Act or the EC Regulation.

(1A) Rules may also be made for the purpose of giving effect to Part 2 of the Banking Act 2009 (bank insolvency orders); and rules for that purpose shall be made—

(a) in relation to England and Wales, by the Lord Chancellor with the concurrence of—
    (i) the Treasury, and
    (ii) in the case of rules that affect court procedure, the Lord Chief Justice, or

(b) in relation to Scotland, by the Treasury.

(1B) Rules may also be made for the purpose of giving effect to Part 3 of the Banking Act 2009 (bank administration); and rules for that purpose shall be made—

(a) in relation to England and Wales, by the Lord Chancellor with the concurrence of—
    (i) the Treasury, and
    (ii) in the case of rules that affect court procedure, the Lord Chief Justice, or

(b) in relation to Scotland, by the Treasury.

(2) Without prejudice to the generality of subsection (1), (1A) or (1B) or to any provision of those Parts by virtue of which rules under this section may be made with respect to any matter, rules under this section may contain—

(a) any such provision as is specified in Schedule 8 to this Act or corresponds to provision contained immediately before the coming into force of section 106 of the Insolvency Act 1985 in rules made, or having effect as if made, under section 663(1) or (2) of the Companies Act 1985 (old winding-up rules), and

(b) such incidental, supplemental and transitional provisions as may appear to the Lord Chancellor or, as the case may be, the Secretary of State or the Treasury necessary or expedient.

(2A) For the purposes of subsection (2), a reference in Schedule 8 to this Act to doing anything under or for the purposes of a provision of this Act includes a reference to doing anything under or for the purposes of the EC Regulation (in so far as the provision of this Act relates to a matter to which the EC Regulation applies).

(2B) Rules under this section for the purpose of giving effect to the EC Regulation may not create an offence of a kind referred to in paragraph 1(1)(d) of Schedule 2 to the European Communities Act 1972.

[(2C) For the purposes of subsection (2), a reference in Schedule 8 to this Act to doing anything under or for the purposes of a provision of this Act includes a reference to doing anything under or for the purposes of Part 2 of the Banking Act 2009.

[(2D) For the purposes of subsection (2), a reference in Schedule 8 to this Act to doing anything under or for the purposes of a provision of this Act includes a reference to doing anything under or for the purposes of Part 3 of the Banking Act 2009.

(3) In Schedule 8 to this Act 'liquidator' includes a provisional liquidator or bank liquidator or administrator; and references above in this section to Parts I to VII of this Act or Part 2 or 3 of the Banking Act 2009 are to be read as including the Companies Acts so far as relating to, and to matters connected with or arising out of, the insolvency or winding up of companies.

(3A) In this section references to Part 2 or 3 of the Banking Act 2009 include references to those Parts as applied to building societies (see section 90C of the Building Societies Act 1986).

(4) Rules under this section shall be made by statutory instrument subject to annulment in pursuance of a resolution of either House of Parliament.

(5) Regulations made by the Secretary of State or the Treasury under a power conferred by rules under this section shall be made by statutory instrument and, after being made, shall be laid before each House of Parliament.

(6) Nothing in this section prejudices any power to make rules of court.

(7) The Lord Chief Justice may nominate a judicial office holder (as defined in section 109(4) of the Constitutional Reform Act 2005) to exercise his functions under this section.

Amendments—SI 2002/1037; Constitutional Reform Act 2005, s 15(1), Sch 4; SI 2007/2194; Banking Act 2009, ss 125, 160; SI 2009/805; SI 2009/1941.

General note—This provision only deals with corporate insolvency (Parts I–VII of the Act) and the EC Regulation on Insolvency Proceedings.

Section 411(2A) and (2B) were introduced by reg 3 of the Insolvency Act 1986 (Amendment) Regulations 2002 (SI 2002/1037) to accommodate the advent of the EC Regulation on Insolvency Proceedings.

412 Individual insolvency rules (England and Wales)

(1) The Lord Chancellor may, with the concurrence of the Secretary of State and, in the case of rules that affect court procedure, with the concurrence of the Lord Chief Justice, make rules for the purpose of giving effect to Parts 7A to 11 of this Act or the EC Regulation.

(2) Without prejudice to the generality of subsection (1), or to any provision of those Parts by virtue of which rules under this section may be made with respect to any matter, rules under this section may contain—

(a) any such provision as is specified in Schedule 9 to this Act or corresponds to provision contained immediately before the appointed day in rules made under section 132 of the Bankruptcy Act 1914; and

(b) such incidental, supplemental and transitional provisions as may appear to the Lord Chancellor necessary or expedient.

(2A) For the purposes of subsection (2), a reference in Schedule 9 to this Act to doing anything under or for the purposes of a provision of this Act includes a reference to doing anything under or for the purposes of the EC Regulation (in so far as the provision of this Act relates to a matter to which the EC Regulation applies).

(2B) Rules under this section for the purpose of giving effect to the EC Regulation may not create an offence of a kind referred to in paragraph 1(1)(d) of Schedule 2 to the European Communities Act 1972.

(3) Rules under this section shall be made by statutory instrument subject to annulment in pursuance of a resolution of either House of Parliament.

(4) Regulations made by the Secretary of State under a power conferred by rules under this section shall be made by statutory instrument and, after being made, shall be laid before each House of Parliament.

(5) Nothing in this section prejudices any power to make rules of court.

(6) The Lord Chief Justice may nominate a judicial office holder (as defined in section 109(4) of the Constitutional Reform Act 2005) to exercise his functions under this section.

Amendments—SI 2002/1037; Constitutional Reform Act 2005, s 15(1), Sch 4; Tribunals, Courts and Enforcement Act 2007, s 108(3), Sch 20, Pt 1, paras 1, 8.

General note—This provision is the personal insolvency equivalent of s 411.
Section 412(2A) and (2B) were introduced by reg 3 of the Insolvency Act 1986 (Amendment) Regulations 2002 (SI 2002/1037) to accommodate the advent of the EC Regulation on Insolvency Proceedings.

413 Insolvency Rules Committee

(1) The committee established under section 10 of the Insolvency Act 1976 (advisory committee on bankruptcy and winding-up rules) continues to exist for the purpose of being consulted under this section.

(2) The Lord Chancellor shall consult the committee before making any rules under section 411 or 412 other than rules which contain a statement that the only provision made by the rules is provision applying rules made under section 411, with or without modifications, for the purposes of provision made by any of sections 23 to 26 of the Water Industry Act 1991 or Schedule 3 to that Act or by any of sections 59 to 65 of, or Schedule 6 or 7 to, the Railways Act 1993.

(3) Subject to the next subsection, the committee shall consist of—

    (a)   a judge of the High Court attached to the Chancery Division;
    (b)   a circuit judge;
    (c)   a registrar in bankruptcy of the High Court:
    (d)   the registrar of a county court;
    (e)   a practising barrister;
    (f)   a practising solicitor; and
    (g)   a practising accountant;

and the appointment of any person as a member of the committee shall be made in accordance with subsection (3A) or (3B).

(3A) The Lord Chief Justice must appoint the persons referred to in paragraphs (a) to (d) of subsection (3), after consulting the Lord Chancellor.

(3B) The Lord Chancellor must appoint the persons referred to in paragraphs (e) to (g) of subsection (3), after consulting the Lord Chief Justice.

(4) The Lord Chancellor may appoint as additional members of the committee any persons appearing to him to have qualifications or experience that would be of value to the committee in considering any matter with which it is concerned.

(5) The Lord Chief Justice may nominate a judicial office holder (as defined in section 109(4) of the Constitutional Reform Act 2005) to exercise his functions under this section.

Amendments—Water Act 1989, s 190(1), Sch 25, para 78(2); Water Consolidation (Consequential Provisions) Act 1991, s 2(1), Sch 1, para 46; Railways Act 1993, s 152(1), Sch 12, para 25; Constitutional Reform Act 2005, s 15(1), Sch 4.

Fees orders

414 Fees orders (company insolvency proceedings)

(1) There shall be paid in respect of—

    (a)   proceedings under any Parts I to VII of this Act, and,

    (b)   the performance by the official receiver or the Secretary of State of functions under those Parts,

such fees as the competent authority may with the sanction of the Treasury by order direct.

(2) That authority is—

    (a)   in relation to England and Wales, the Lord Chancellor, and

    (b)   in relation to Scotland, the Secretary of State.

(3) The Treasury may by order direct by whom and in what manner the fees are to be collected and accounted for.

(4) The Lord Chancellor may, with the sanction of the Treasury, by order provide for sums to be deposited, by such persons, in such manner and in such circumstances as may be specified in the order, by way of security for fees payable by virtue of this section.

(5) An order under this section may contain such incidental, supplemental and transitional provisions as may appear to the Lord Chancellor, the Secretary of State or (as the case may be) the Treasury necessary or expedient.

(6) An order under this section shall be made by statutory instrument and, after being made, shall be laid before each House of Parliament.

(7) Fees payable by virtue of this section shall be paid into the Consolidated Fund.

(8) References in subsection (1) to Parts I to VII of this Act are to be read as including the Companies Acts so far as relating to, and to matters connected with or arising out of, the insolvency or winding up of companies.

(8A) This section applies in relation to Part 2 of the Banking Act 2009 (bank insolvency) as in relation to Parts I to VII of this Act.

(8B) This section applies in relation to Part 3 of the Banking Act 2009 (bank administration) as in relation to Parts I to VII of this Act.

(8C) In subsections (8A) and (8B) the reference to Parts 2 and 3 of the Banking Act 2009 include references to those Parts as applied to building societies (see section 90C of the Building Societies Act 1986)

(9) Nothing in this section prejudices any power to make rules of court; and the application of this section to Scotland is without prejudice to section 2 of the Courts of Law Fees (Scotland) Act 1895.

Amendments—SI 2007/2194; Banking Act 2009, ss 126, 161; SI 2009/805.

415 Fees orders (individual insolvency proceedings in England and Wales)

(1) There shall be paid in respect of—

    (za)   the costs of persons acting as approved intermediaries under Part 7A,

    (a)   proceedings under Parts 7A to 11 of this Act,

    (b)   the performance by the official receiver or the Secretary of State of functions under those Parts, and

    (c)   the performance by an adjudicator of functions under Part 9 of this Act,

such fees as the Lord Chancellor may with the sanction of the Treasury by order direct.

(1A) An order under subsection (1) may make different provision for different purposes, including by reference to the manner or form in which proceedings are commenced.

(2) The Treasury may by order direct by whom and in what manner the fees are to be collected and accounted for.

(3) The Lord Chancellor may, with the sanction of the Treasury, by order provide for sums to be deposited, by such persons, in such manner and in such circumstances as may be specified in the order, by way of security for—

    (a)   fees payable by virtue of this section, and

    (b)   fees payable to any person who has prepared an insolvency practitioner's report under section 274 in Chapter I of Part IX.

(4) An order under this section may contain such incidental, supplemental and transitional provisions as may appear to the Lord Chancellor or, as the case may be, the Treasury, necessary or expedient.

(5) An order under this section shall be made by statutory instrument and, after being made, shall be laid before each House of Parliament.

(6) Fees payable by virtue of this section shall be paid into the Consolidated Fund.

(7) Nothing in this section prejudices any power to make rules of court.

Amendments—Tribunals, Courts and Enforcement Act 2007, s 108(3), Sch 20, Pt 1, paras 1, 9. Enterprise and Regulatory Reform Act 2013, s 71(3), Sch 19, paras 1, 59.

415A Fees orders (general)

(A1) The Secretary of State—

  (a)   may by order require a person or body to pay a fee in connection with the grant or maintenance of a designation of that person or body as a competent authority under section 251U, and

  (b)   may refuse to grant, or may withdraw, any such designation where a fee is not paid.

(1) The Secretary of State—

  (a)   may by order require a body to pay a fee in connection with the grant or maintenance of recognition of the body under section 391, and

  (b)   may refuse recognition, or revoke an order of recognition under section 391(1) by a further order, where a fee is not paid.

(2) The Secretary of State—

  (a)   may by order require a person to pay a fee in connection with the grant or maintenance of authorisation of the person under section 393, and

  (b)   may disregard an application or withdraw an authorisation where a fee is not paid.

(3) The Secretary of State may by order require the payment of fees in respect of—

  (a)   the operation of the Insolvency Services Account;

  (b)   payments into and out of that Account.

(4) The following provisions of section 414 apply to fees under this section as they apply to fees under that section –

  (a)   subsection (3) (manner of payment),

  (b)   subsection (5) (additional provision),

  (c)   subsection (6) (statutory instrument),

  (d)   subsection (7) (payment into Consolidated Fund), and

  (e)   subsection (9) (saving for rules of court).

Amendments—Inserted by Enterprise Act 2002, s 270(1). Amended by Tribunals, Courts and Enforcement Act 2007, s 108(3), Sch 20, Pt 1, paras 1, 10.

General note—The provision allows for the making of orders that provide for the payment of fees. It was introduced by Enterprise Act 2002, s 270. The Insolvency Practitioners and

Insolvency Services Account (Fees) Order 2003 (SI 2003/3363) was made pursuant to the provision. This Order, since amended by Insolvency Practitioners and Insolvency Services Account (Fees) Order 2004 (SI 2004/476, art 1) and the Insolvency Practitioners and Insolvency Services Account (Fees) Order 2005 (SI 2005/523, art 2) (commenced 1 April 2005), includes providing for the payment of fees by applicants seeking authorisation to act as insolvency practitioners (art 3).

Specification, increase and reduction of money sums relevant in the operation of this Act

416 Monetary limits (companies winding up)

(1) The Secretary of State may by order in a statutory instrument increase or reduce any of the money sums for the time being specified in the following provisions in the first Group of Parts—

> section 117(2) (amount of company's share capital determining whether county court has jurisdiction to wind it up);
> section 120(3) (the equivalent as respects sheriff court jurisdiction in Scotland);
> section 123(1)(a) (minimum debt for service of demand on company by unpaid creditor);
> section 184(3) (minimum value of judgment, affecting sheriff's duties on levying execution);
> section 206(1)(a) and (b) (minimum value of company property concealed or fraudulently removed, affecting criminal liability of company's officer).

(2) An order under this section may contain such transitional provisions as may appear to the Secretary of State necessary or expedient.

(3) No order under this section increasing or reducing any of the money sums for the time being specified in section 117(2), 120(3) or 123(1)(a) shall be made unless a draft of the order has been laid before and approved by a resolution of each House of Parliament.

(4) A statutory instrument containing an order under this section, other than an order to which subsection (3) applies, is subject to annulment in pursuance of a resolution of either House of Parliament.

417 Money sum in s 222

The Secretary of State may by regulations in a statutory instrument increase or reduce the money sum for the time being specified in section 222(1) (minimum debt for service of demand on unregistered company by unpaid creditor); but such regulations shall not be made unless a draft of the statutory instrument containing them has been approved by resolution of each House of Parliament.

417A Money sums (company moratorium)

(1) The Secretary of State may by order increase or reduce any of the money sums for the time being specified in the following provisions of Schedule A1 to this Act—

paragraph 17(1) (maximum amount of credit which company may obtain without disclosure of moratorium);

paragraph 41(4) (minimum value of company property concealed or fraudulently removed, affecting criminal liability of company's officer).

(2) An order under this section may contain such transitional provisions as may appear to the Secretary of State necessary or expedient.

(3) An order under this section shall be made by statutory instrument subject to annulment in pursuance of a resolution of either House of Parliament.

Amendments—Inserted by Insolvency Act 2000, s 1, Sch 1, paras 1, 10.

418 Monetary limits (bankruptcy)

(1) The Secretary of State may by order prescribe amounts for the purposes of the following provisions in the second Group of Parts—

section 251S(4) (maximum amount of credit which a person in respect of whom a debt relief order is made may obtain without disclosure of his status);

section 273 (minimum value of debtor's estate determining whether immediate bankruptcy order should be made; small bankruptcies level);

section 313A (value of property below which application for sale, possession or charge to be dismissed);

section 346(3) (minimum amount of judgment, determining whether amount recovered on sale of debtor's goods is to be treated as part of his estate in bankruptcy);

section 354(1) and (2) (minimum amount of concealed debt, or value of property concealed or removed, determining criminal liability under the section);

section 358 (minimum value of property taken by a bankrupt out of England and Wales, determining his criminal liability);

section 360(1) (maximum amount of credit which bankrupt may obtain without disclosure of his status);

section 361(2) (exemption of bankrupt from criminal liability for failure to keep proper accounts, if unsecured debts not more than the prescribed minimum);

section 364(2)(d) (minimum value of goods removed by the bankrupt, determining his liability to arrest);

paragraphs 6 to 8 of Schedule 4ZA (maximum amount of a person's debts monthly surplus income and property for purposes of obtaining a debt relief order);

and references in the second Group of Parts to the amount prescribed for the purposes of any of those provisions, and references in those provisions to the prescribed amount, are to be construed accordingly.

(2) An order under this section may contain such transitional provisions as may appear to the Secretary of State necessary or expedient.

(3) An order under this section shall be made by statutory instrument subject to annulment in pursuance of a resolution of either House of Parliament.

Amendments—Enterprise Act 2002, s 261(6); Tribunals, Courts and Enforcement Act 2007, s 108(3), Sch 20, Pt 1, paras 1, 11.

Insolvency practice

419 Regulations for purposes of Part XIII

(1) The Secretary of State may make regulations for the purpose of giving effect to Part XIII of this Act; and 'prescribed' in that Part means prescribed by regulations made by the Secretary of State.

(2) Without prejudice to the generality of subsection (1) or to any provision of that Part by virtue of which regulations may be made with respect to any matter, regulations under this section may contain—

    (a)   provision as to the matters to be taken into account in determining whether a person is a fit and proper person to act as an insolvency practitioner;

    (b)   provision prohibiting a person from so acting in prescribed cases, being cases in which a conflict of interest will or may arise;

    (c)   provision imposing requirements with respect to—

        (i)   the preparation and keeping by a person who acts as an insolvency practitioner of prescribed books, accounts and other records, and

        (ii)   the production of those books, accounts and records to prescribed persons;

    (d)   provision conferring power on prescribed persons –

        (i)   to require any person who acts or has acted as an insolvency practitioner to answer any inquiry in relation to a case in which he is so acting or has so acted, and

        (ii)   to apply to a court to examine such a person or any other person on oath concerning such a case;

    (e)   provision making non-compliance with any of the regulations a criminal offence; and

    (f)   such incidental, supplemental and transitional provisions as may appear to the Secretary of State necessary or expedient.

(3) Any power conferred by Part XIII or this Part to make regulations, rules or orders is exercisable by statutory instrument subject to annulment by resolution of either House of Parliament.

(4) Any rule or regulation under Part XIII or this Part may make different provision with respect to different cases or descriptions of cases, including different provision for different areas.

General note—The provision enables the Secretary of State to make regulations to effect the objectives of the section that deal with the qualification of insolvency practitioners. The prime example of this is the Insolvency Practitioners Regulations 1990 (SI 1990/439). A more recent instance is the Insolvency Practitioners (Amendment) Regulations 1990 (SI 2004/473). These last Regulations revoke reg 9 of the Insolvency Practitioners Regulations 1990 which makes provision for the charging of a fee on the making of an application to the Secretary of State for the granting of an authorisation to act as an insolvency practitioner. This is because the relevant provisions regarding the Secretary of State's powers in relation to fees are now contained within s 415A.

Other order-making powers

420 Insolvent partnerships

(1) The Lord Chancellor may, by order made with the concurrence of the Secretary of State and the Lord Chief Justice, provide that such provisions of this Act as may be specified in the order shall apply in relation to insolvent partnerships with such modifications as may be so specified.

(1A) An order under this section may make provision in relation to the EC Regulation.

(1B) But provision made by virtue of this section in relation to the EC Regulation may not create an offence of a kind referred to in paragraph 1(1)(d) of Schedule 2 to the European Communities Act 1972.

(2) An order under this section may make different provision for different cases and may contain such incidental, supplemental and transitional provisions as may appear to the Lord Chancellor and the Lord Chief Justice necessary or expedient.

(3) An order under this section shall be made by statutory instrument subject to annulment in pursuance of a resolution of either House of Parliament.

(4) The Lord Chief Justice may nominate a judicial office holder (as defined in section 109(4) of the Constitutional Reform Act 2005) to exercise his functions under this section.

Amendments—SI 2002/1037; Constitutional Reform Act 2005, s 15(1), Sch 4.

General note—The Insolvent Partnerships Orders are instances of the use of this power. The Insolvent Partnerships Order 1994 (SI 1994/2421) governs insolvent partnerships at present (replacing Insolvent Partnerships Order 1986 (SI 1986/2142)). There have been subsequent amendments to the Order. In 1996 (SI 1996/1308), there was a minor change that involved simply amending art 7 to broaden the list of possible petitioners for winding up.
  The Insolvent Partnerships (Amendment) Order 2001 (SI 2001/767) effected a modification of Sch 8 of the 1994 Order to reflect the changes to the Company Directors Disqualification Act 1986 brought about by the Insolvency Act 2000. The Insolvent Partnerships (Amendment) Order 2002 (SI 2002/1308) amended the Insolvent Partnerships Order 1994 in light of the EC Regulation on Insolvency Proceedings. It amended arts 7 and 8 and Schs 3–6 and9 of the 1994 Order. Subsequently, the Insolvent Partnerships (Amendment) (No 2) Order 2002 (SI 2002/2708) effected other amendments to the 1994 Order. It amended arts 4 and 19 and Schs 1–4, and reflected the amendments to voluntary arrangements contained in the Insolvency Act 2000.
  Section 420(1A) and (1B) were introduced by reg 3 of the Insolvency Act 1986 (Amendment) Regulations 2002 (SI 2002/1037) to accommodate the commencement of the EC Regulation on Insolvency Proceedings.

421 Insolvent estates of deceased persons

(1) The Lord Chancellor may, by order made with the concurrence of the Secretary of State and the Lord Chief Justice, provide that such provisions of this Act as may be specified in the order shall apply in relation to the administration of the insolvent estates of deceased persons with such modifications as may be so specified.

(1A) An order under this section may make provision in relation to the EC Regulation.

(1B) But provision made by virtue of this section in relation to the EC Regulation may not create an offence of a kind referred to in paragraph 1(1)(d) of Schedule 2 to the European Communities Act 1972.

(2) An order under this section may make different provision for different cases and may contain such incidental, supplemental and transitional provisions as may appear to the Lord Chancellor and the Lord Chief Justice necessary or expedient.

(3) An order under this section shall be made by statutory instrument subject to annulment in pursuance of a resolution of either House of Parliament.

(4) For the purposes of this section the estate of a deceased person is insolvent if, when realised, it will be insufficient to meet in full all the debts and other liabilities to which it is subject.

(5) The Lord Chief Justice may nominate a judicial office holder (as defined in section 109(4) of the Constitutional Reform Act 2005) to exercise his functions under this section.

Amendments—Insolvency Act 2000, s 12(2); SI 2002/1037; Constitutional Reform Act 2005, s 15(1), Sch 4.

General note—The Administration of Insolvent Estates of Deceased Persons Order 1986 (SI 1986/1999), an example of the power to make orders under this section, deals with many of the issues relating to insolvent estates of deceased debtors. This Order, which applies to England and Wales, specifies the provisions of the Insolvency Act 1986 which apply to the administration in bankruptcy of the insolvent estates of deceased persons and the modifications to those provisions. It applies to the estates of persons who die before the presentation of a bankruptcy petition. If a person dies after the presentation of a petition, the petition stands and proceedings continue just as if the person remained alive (Administration of Insolvent Estates of Deceased Persons Order 1986, art 5(1)).

If there is any inconsistency between the Order and the Act, the former is paramount (art 3(2)). The 1986 Order has been amended by the Administration of Insolvent Estates of Deceased Persons (Amendment) Order 2002 (SI 2002/1309) to provide for the operation of the EC Regulation on Insolvency Proceedings.

Section 421(1A) and (1B) were introduced by reg 3 of the Insolvency Act 1986 (Amendment) Regulations 2002 (SI 2002/1037) to accommodate the commencement of the EC Regulation on Insolvency Proceedings.

421A Insolvent estates: joint tenancies

(1) This section applies where—

    (a)   an insolvency administration order has been made in respect of the insolvent estate of a deceased person,

    (b)   the petition for the order was presented after the commencement of this section and within the period of five years beginning with the day on which he died, and

    (c)   immediately before his death he was beneficially entitled to an interest in any property as joint tenant.

(2) For the purpose of securing that debts and other liabilities to which the estate is subject are met, the court may, on an application by the trustee appointed pursuant to the insolvency administration order, make an order under this section requiring the survivor to pay to the trustee an amount not exceeding the value lost to the estate.

(3) In determining whether to make an order under this section, and the terms of such an order, the court must have regard to all the circumstances of the case, including the interests of the deceased's creditors and of the survivor; but, unless the circumstances are exceptional, the court must assume that the interests of the deceased's creditors outweigh all other considerations.

(4) The order may be made on such terms and conditions as the court thinks fit.

(5) Any sums required to be paid to the trustee in accordance with an order under this section shall be comprised in the estate.

(6) The modifications of this Act which may be made by an order under section 421 include any modifications which are necessary or expedient in consequence of this section.

(7) In this section, 'survivor' means the person who, immediately before the death, was beneficially entitled as joint tenant with the deceased or, if the person who was so entitled dies after the making of the insolvency administration order, his personal representatives.

(8) If there is more than one survivor—

    (a)   an order under this section may be made against all or any of them, but

    (b)   no survivor shall be required to pay more than so much of the value lost to the estate as is properly attributable to him.

(9) In this section—

'insolvency administration order' has the same meaning as in any order under section 421 having effect for the time being,

'value lost to the estate' means the amount which, if paid to the trustee, would in the court's opinion restore the position to what it would have been if the deceased had been adjudged bankrupt immediately before his death.

Amendments—Inserted by the Insolvency Act 2000, s 12(1).

General note—This provision overcomes the common law to the effect that where a person dies insolvent his or her interest in a joint tenancy passed automatically to the other joint tenant and could not be regarded as part of the insolvent's estate. Under this provision the surviving joint tenant can be ordered by a court, on the application of the trustee in bankruptcy, to pay to the bankrupt estate an amount up to the value that the estate has lost. The value is defined in s 421A(9).

422 Formerly authorised banks

(1) The Secretary of State may by order made with the concurrence of the Treasury and after consultation with the Financial Conduct Authority and the Prudential Regulation Authority provide that specified provisions in the first Group of Parts shall apply with specified modifications in relation to any person who—

    (a)   has a liability in respect of a deposit which he accepted in accordance with the Banking Act 1979 (c. 37) or 1987 (c. 22), but

    (b)   does not have permission under Part 4A of the Financial Services and Markets Act 2000 (c. 8) (regulated activities) to accept deposits.

(1A) Subsection (1)(b) shall be construed in accordance with—

    (a)   section 22 of the Financial Services and Markets Act 2000 (classes of regulated activity and categories of investment),

    (b)   any relevant order under that section, and

    (c)   Schedule 2 to that Act (regulated activities).

(2) An order under this section may make different provision for different cases and may contain such incidental, supplemental and transitional provisions as may appear to the Secretary of State necessary or expedient.

(3) An order under this section shall be made by statutory instrument subject to annulment in pursuance of a resolution of either House of Parliament.

Amendments—Enterprise Act 2002, s 248(3), Sch 17, paras 9, 35; SI 2002/1555; Financial Services Act 2012, s 114(1), Sch 18, Pt 2, paras 51, 53.

PART XVI

PROVISIONS AGAINST DEBT AVOIDANCE (ENGLAND AND WALES ONLY)

423 Transactions defrauding creditors

(1) This section relates to transactions entered into at an undervalue; and a person enters into such a transaction with another person if—

    (a)   he makes a gift to the other person or he otherwise enters into a transaction with the other on terms that provide for him to receive no consideration;

    (b)   he enters into a transaction with the other in consideration of marriage or the formation of a civil partnership; or

    (c)   he enters into a transaction with the other for a consideration the value of which, in money or money's worth, is significantly less than the value, in money or money's worth, of the consideration provided by himself.

(2) Where a person has entered into such a transaction, the court may, if satisfied under the next subsection, make such order as it thinks fit for—

(a)   restoring the position to what it would have been if the transaction had not been entered into, and

(b)   protecting the interests of persons who are victims of the transaction.

(3) In the case of a person entering into such a transaction, an order shall only be made if the court is satisfied that it was entered into by him for the purpose—

(a)   of putting assets beyond the reach of a person who is making, or may at some time make, a claim against him, or

(b)   of otherwise prejudicing the interests of such a person in relation to the claim which he is making or may make.

(4) In this section 'the court' means the High Court or—

(a)   if the person entering into the transaction is an individual, any other court which would have jurisdiction in relation to a bankruptcy petition relating to him;

(b)   if that person is a body capable of being wound up under Part IV or V of this Act, any other court having jurisdiction to wind it up.

(5) In relation to a transaction at an undervalue, references here and below to a victim of the transaction are to a person who is, or is capable of being, prejudiced by it; and in the following two sections the person entering into the transaction is referred to as 'the debtor'.

Amendments—Civil Partnership Act 2004, s 261(1), Sch 27, para 121.

General note—Whilst an action to avoid transactions entered into in fraud of creditors was first introduced by statute in the so-called Statute of Elizabeth 1571 (which rendered transactions 'clearly and utterly void, frustrated and of no effect' and which remained in force until replaced by the Law of Property Act 1925, s 172), the common law had also previously recognised a similar action, analogous to the actio Pauliana available to creditors under Roman law: see *Cadogen v Kennett* (1776) 2 Cowp 432 at 434. Section 172 of the 1925 Act provided a remedy in respect of so-called 'fraudulent conveyance' in that '... every conveyance of property, made whether before or after commencement of this Act, with intent to defraud creditors, shall be voidable at the instance of any person thereby prejudiced.'

Section 423 of the 1986 Act makes four significant amendments to the law. First, even if the requisite element in s 423(3) can be satisfied, a transaction is only capable of being avoided if it meets the definition of a transaction-at-undervalue in s 423(1). Secondly, s 423(3) provides that the transaction under challenge must have been entered into by the transferor 'for the purpose' of putting assets beyond the reach of actual or potential claimants or otherwise prejudicing the interests of any such person. Thirdly, unlike the fraudulent conveyance, transactions under s 423 are subject to the remedial powers of the court pursuant to s 423(2), and not void. Fourthly, the new provision attributes no relevance to the state of mind of the counterparty, an approach adopted by Mervyn Davies J in *Moon v Franklin* [1996] BPIR 196 at 202E–202F in ignoring a wife's evidence to the effect that she did not attribute any value to benefits transferred to her by her husband. It remains, however, that it is open to the court to draw inferences from the evidence of the counterparty or, indeed, the evidence of any other party, in construing as a matter of fact the mind of the transferor at the relevant time.

Whilst s 423 allows not only office-holders under the legislation but also 'victims' of transactions (on which see the note to s 423(3) below) to challenge transactions without any time-limit of the sort imposed in the case of transactions-at-undervalue and preferences, the applicant carries the evidential burden in establishing the transferor's purpose. No presumption operates in favour of an applicant, even when a transaction is effected in favour of a connected party. Whilst each case must turn on its own facts, the court will not entertain speculative claims, particularly where the allegations reach back many years: see, for example, the Court of Appeal's dismissal of a claim under CPR, Pt 24 (reversing Hart J below) in *Law Society v Southall* [2002] BPIR 336, in which Peter Gibson LJ identified that the allegation of an attempt to defeat creditors over 30 years previously was 'mere speculation' and that it was 'wishful thinking on the [applicant's] part that the pre-trial procedures, or cross-examination, would yield valuable support for its case' (at [52]).

A critical thing with the provision is that there must be an entering into of a transaction. According to *Defra v Feakins* [2004] EWHC 2735 (Ch), [2005] BPIR 292, this includes participating in an arrangement. This was upheld on appeal ([2005] EWCA Civ 1513, [2007] BCC 54) and the court said that the word 'arrangement' was to be given its natural meaning, and included an agreement or understanding, whether formal or informal, oral or in writing. Hence the term, 'transaction' is broad: *Griffin v Awoderu* [2008] EWHC 349 (Ch) at [25].

Any application brought under this provision is brought on behalf of all victims of the impugned transaction: *Hill v Spread Trustee Company Ltd* [2006] EWCA Civ 542, [2006] BPIR 789, [2007] 1 All ER 1106, [2006] BCC 646, [2007] 1 BCLC 450, [2007] 1 WLR 2404 at [104].

It is not necessary for the claimant to establish that when the transaction impugned was effected the debtor was engaging, or about to engage, in risky or hazardous business: *Midland Bank v Wyatt* [1997] 1 BCLC 242; *Sands v Clitheroe* [2006] BPIR 1000. Engaging in such activity was merely a factor which might well justify the court making an inference that the debtor's intention was to put assets beyond the reach of creditors.

Section 423(1)

Scope of provision—This subsection reproduces the definition of a transaction-at-undervalue as it appears in s 339(3) (bankruptcy) and, in substantially similar terms, in s 238(4) (winding up): see further the notes to those sections.

'Value' – see the notes accompanying s.238. In considering a transaction under s.423 the court is to look at the value received from the point of view of the debtor *re (Re MC Bacon Limited* [1991] Ch 127 and affirmed in *Delaney v Chen* [2010] EWCA Civ 1455, [2011] BPIR 39 at [15].

Section 423(2)

Scope of provision—Although s 423(2)(a) mirrors ss 238(3) and 339(2) (transaction-at-undervalue) in identifying the end to which the powers of the court under s 423 should be directed, s 423(2)(b) adds an additional purpose which should also feature in the mind of the court for the purposes of the discretion exercised by it in granting relief. These two paragraphs must be read conjunctively so that '... Any order made under [s 423(2)] must seek, so far as practicable, both to restore the position to what it would have been if the transaction had not been entered into and to protect the victims of it': *Chohan v Saggar* [1994] 1 BCLC 706 at 714D–714E (Nourse LJ, Balcombe and Waite LJJ agreeing in varying the trial judge's order on the basis that it had given insufficient protection to victims of the transaction so as to restore the full net value lost to it by way of impugned transaction). In other words, the restorative purpose in s 423(2)(a) is not pursued by way of an order under s 423 in isolation; rather, the court should restore the position so far as is necessary to protect the interests of creditors. In *Moon v Franklin* [1996] BPIR 196, for example, the respondent had sold his accountancy practice for £65,000 and gifted the bulk of the proceeds to his wife at a time when the respondent was facing a possible professional negligence claim. The husband subsequently transferred the beneficial interest in the couple's joint property to his wife. Whilst the professional negligence proceedings were pending Mervyn Davies J (whilst, unhelpfully, construing paragraphs (a) and (b) disjunctively, at 205D) declared the gift of the practice proceeds and the transfer of the matrimonial home interest to be in contravention of s 423, whilst requiring the wife to repay only the £5,000 of the proceeds remaining in her hands and ordering that there be no further dealings in the matrimonial property. For an order in a case where improper transfers from one trading company L, to another, F, were impugned see *Arbuthnot Leasing International Ltd v Havelet Leasing (No 2)* [1990] BCC 636 at 645G (Scott J) where it was said:

'The mechanics of the reversal must take into account that since the date of the transfer F has been carrying on business on its own account and will have creditors who are not creditors of L and who have become its creditors since the date of the transfers. Those creditors are entitled prima facie to look at the assets standing in the name of F for payment of the debts due to them. Accordingly, it seems to me that I ought to order that the business and assets of F, including the sums held on its behalf by H, are held by F, upon trust for L but without prejudice to the claims of creditors of F who have become creditors since the date of the transfers.'

Section 423(2) differs from ss 238(3) and 339(2) in its use of the word 'may' as opposed to 'shall'. This would appear to allow the court some scope for making an order which seeks to protect the interests, even where it is not possible to restore by order the pre-transaction position.

Relief granted under s 423(2) by way of an order and s 425 does not invalidate the transaction attacked in the applicant's claim, although it may do so. Rather, an order pursuant to s 423(2) requires the counterparty to the transaction challenged to confer on the transferor's estate the benefit received by it unjustly on a restitutionary basis, subject to the protection afforded to bona fide third parties by s 425(2).

Section 423(3)

Scope of provision—As a pre-condition of the granting of any relief by order, this provision imposes a requirement that the court makes a finding of fact as to either of those matters set out in s 423(3)(a) or (b). Despite the heading to the section, there is no requirement in the provision for a finding of fraud or dishonesty.

Reliance on legal advice will not necessarily provide a transferor with a defence to a s 423 claim, although it is a point which the court may consider on the facts: *Arbuthnot Leasing International Ltd v Havelet Leasing Ltd (No 2)* [1990] BCC 636 at 644B–644D.

In *Barclays Bank v Eustice* [1995] 2 BCLC 630 the Court of Appeal upheld the decision of the judge below in granting specific discovery of documents which would otherwise be protected by legal professional privilege on the basis that privilege did not protect communications between client and legal advisers where there was strong evidence of a s 423 transaction. The scope of those persons referred to in s 423(3)(a) and (b) are considered in the notes to s 423(6) below.

'Purpose'—As a matter of law the term 'purpose' has been the subject of some judicial consideration. The point is not an issue where the transferor can be shown to have acted only for either of the purposes in s 423(3)(a) or (b) where the transferor is unable to offer some legitimate and credible explanation for his actions, as in *Barclays Bank v Eustice* [1995] 2 BCLC 630 (assignment of agricultural tenancy and equipment at nominal rate without disclosure to a bank one week following Inland Revenue distraint and one week before the bank appointed receivers upheld by Court of Appeal as disclosing strong prima facie case); *Midland Bank v Wyatt* [1997] 1 BCLC 242 (protection of assets where transferor executed voluntary settlement of his interest in matrimonial property in favour of daughters at a time when the transferor was contemplating setting up his own business); or *Hashmi v Inland Revenue* [2002] EWCA Civ 981, [2002] BPIR 974, [2002] 2 BCLC 489 (Court of Appeal upheld inference drawn by Hart J at first instance to the effect that a deceased shopkeeper who defrauded Revenue and who transferred interest in commercial property to his son did so to put assets beyond the reach of creditors, given likelihood of substantial tax claims against him): see also *Aiglon Ltd v Gau Shan Co Ltd* [1993] BCLC 1321 (Hirst J) and *Agricultural Mortgage Corporation v Woodward* [1994] BCC 688, CA. The Court of Appeal in *Williams v Taylor* [2012] EWCA Civ 1443, [2013] BPIR 133 at [30] provided that the required intention to defraud might be based on objective factors that are in evidence. Neither is s 423 intended to catch only transactions where either of the statutory purposes in s 423(3) is capable of being shown to be the sole purpose of the transferor: *Royscott Spa Leasing Ltd v Lovett* [1995] BCC 502 at 507D (Sir Christopher Slade). Indeed, it is the question of mixed purposes which poses the real difficulty in construing s 423(3). In *Chohan v Saggar*, at first instance, Edward Evans-Lombe QC, then sitting as a deputy High Court judge, held that s 423(3) required the applicant to show a dominant purpose on the part of a transferor in achieving either of the s 423(3) objects, without excluding the possibility that some other purpose might exist for the transferor. This in fact followed the formulation of a 'predominant test' by Mervyn Davies J in *Moon v Franklin* [1996] BPIR 196 at 204, a case actually decided in 1990. Subsequently in *Pinewood Joinery v Starelm Properties Ltd* [1994] 2 BCLC 412, His Honour Judge Moseley QC, sitting as a High Court judge, doubted that it was necessary to find a dominant purpose. Later, in the Court of Appeal, Sir Christopher Slade, in no more than touching on the point in *Spa Leasing Ltd v Lovett* [1995] BCC 502 at 507G, and after referring to the judgment in *Chohan v Saggar*, assumed for the purpose of the appeal that 'the relevant purpose which has to be established is ... substantial purpose, rather than the stricter test of dominant purpose.' In *Re Brabon* [2000] BPIR 537, Jonathan Parker J also preferred the less demanding 'substantial purpose' to the 'dominant purpose' test, although he commented that the applicant could not meet the dominant test in any event on the facts of that case if he was unable to meet the substantial test. Some much-needed clarification appeared in the Court of Appeal's judgment in *Hashmi v Inland Revenue* [2002] EWCA Civ 981, [2002] BPIR 974, [2002] 2 BCLC 489 where Arden LJ, after considering the authorities, opined that s 423 does not require proof of a dominant purpose, only 'a real substantial purpose' (at [23]–[25]): 'It is sufficient if the statutory purpose can properly be described as a purpose, and not merely as a consequence ... Moreover, I agree with the observation of [Hart J below] that it will often be the case that the motive to defeat creditors and the motive to secure family protection will co-exist in such a way that even the transferor himself may be unable to say what was uppermost in his mind'; and see to like effect the comments of Laws LJ at [32]–[33].

The following caveat of Simon Brown LJ (who agreed that the arguments supporting a test involving substantial purpose rather than a test of dominant purpose were compelling) must not be ignored. If a judge '[W]ere to find in any given case that the transaction is one which the debtor might well have entered into in any event, he should not then too readily infer that the debtor also had the substantial purpose of escaping his liabilities.' (at [40]).

A person can be said to have the necessary purpose even if he or she is mistaken as to whether the entering into the transaction challenged can have the effect of being detrimental to the interests of a victim: *Hill v Spread Trustee Company Ltd* [2006] EWCA Civ 542, [2006] BPIR 789, [2007] 1 WLR 2404, [2007] 1 All ER 1106, [2006] BCC 646, [2007] 1 BCLC 450 at [102]. Also, if a person knows that the entering into of a transaction alone will not cause prejudice, but some other event must also occur for that to happen, that will not save the transaction from successful attack, provided that the person had the necessary purpose; this is because it is the entering into of the transaction that is critical for a s 423 action: *Hill v Spread Trustee Company Ltd* at [102].

For the application of the above principles on specific facts see also *Menzies v National Bank of Kuwait* [1994] BCC 119, CA; *Re Schuppan* [1997] BPIR 271; *Ashe v Mumford* [2001] BPIR 1, CA; *Re Taylor Sinclair (Capital) Ltd* [2002] BPIR 203; *Trowbridge v Trowbridge* [2002] EWHC 3114 (Ch), [2003] 2 FLR 231; *Pena v Coyne (No 2)* [2004] EWHC 2685 (Ch), [2004] 2 BCLC 730; *Beckenham MC Ltd v Centralex Ltd* [2004] EWHC 1287 (Ch), [2004] 2 BCLC 764; *Gil v Baygreen* [2005] BPIR 95; and *Hocking v Canyon Holdings Ltd* [2005] BPIR 160.

See A Keay 'Transactions Defrauding Creditors: The Problem of Purpose Under Section 423 of the Insolvency Act' [2003] *The Conveyancer and Property Lawyer* 272

Section 423(4)

Scope of provision—This provision is determinative of the courts having jurisdiction to deal with a s 423 claim. For further guidance, see the notes on 'Forms and procedure' below.

Section 423(5)

'Victim'—The term 'victim' is employed here as shorthand for the purposes of the three categories of persons eligible to bring a claim under s 423 by s 424(1). The term is used to characterise those persons who are capable of being prejudiced by the transaction-at-undervalue defined in s 423(1) and who fall within either s 423(3)(a) or (b).

The definition of 'victim' by its indirect reference to the persons within the scope of s 423(3) is broad and extends to existing and future creditors, including putative – further unascertained – creditors. Thus, whilst the term 'victim' will catch unsecured creditors (*Re Ayala Holdings Ltd* [1993] BCLC 256 (Chadwick J)), members as creditors (*Soden v British and Commonwealth Holdings plc* [1997] BCC 952), a mortgagee (*Agricultural Mortgage Corporation plc v Woodward* [1994] BCC 688) or a claimant or prospective claimant in litigation (as in *Moon v Franklin* [1996] BPIR 196), an individual with no creditors at the time of a transaction may face a claim in future on the basis that the debtor may be construed as having entered into the transaction at issue for the purpose of defeating future claims, even if he was solvent at that time. In *Sands v Clitheroe* [2006] BPIR 1000 it was indicated that a person could be regarded as a victim provided that he or she could prove to have been prejudiced by the transaction; victims were not limited to those who became creditors as a consequence of the activity that the debtor had in mind when entering into the transaction (at [18]–[20]). It was made clear in *Clydesdale Financial Services Ltd v Smailes* [2009] EWHC 3190 (Ch) that 'victim' is a term that is wider than creditors; the critical thing is that the applicant can demonstrate that he or she was capable of being prejudiced by the transaction.

Whilst the recommendation of the Cork Committee in para 1215(b) of its Report to the effect that a debtor may be taken to have acted for the purpose of prejudicing victims where that consequence was a reasonably foreseeable (ie natural and probable) consequence, given the debtor's knowledge of his financial circumstances at the time of the transaction, was not enacted in express terms, it is suggested that, in fact, the authorities do actually bear out such an approach to s 423(3). Consistent with this analysis, there is first instance authority in which the court has accepted the pre-1986 Act proposition, established in *Mackay v Douglas* (1872) 14 Eq 106, and *Re Butterworth ex parte Russell* (1882) 19 Ch D 588, to the effect that, in circumstances in which a transferor has no creditors at the time of a disposition but is contemplating a new business venture, the court will more readily infer the requisite intention (or purpose), the more hazardous the business contemplated: *Midland Bank v Wyatt* [1997] 1 BCLC 242 at 255C (David Young QC sitting as a deputy High Court judge). Specifically the Court of Appeal has recently stated that a victim might be someone who may not have been the person within the purpose of the person entering into the impugned transaction; in fact the person entering into the transaction may not have been aware of the victim's existence: *Hill v Spread Trustee Company Ltd* [2006] EWCA Civ 542, [2006] BPIR 789, [2007] 1 All ER 1106, [2006] BCC 646, [2007] 1 BCLC 450, [2007] 1 WLR 2404 at [101]. In *Fortress Value Recovery Fund I LLC v Blue Skye Special Opportunites Fund LP* [2013] EWHC 14 (Comm) at [110] Flaux J said that the scope of persons falling within s 423(3), namely those who are making or may at some time make a claim, is to be given a broad interpretation and is not necessarily limited to 'victims' under s 423(5).

It has been held that s 423(3) does not require that the transaction sought to be impugned was entered into in order to prejudice the particular person now bringing the claim. It is enough that the transferor acted with the purpose of defrauding any person who had made or might make a claim against him: *4 Eng v Harper* [2009] EWHC 2633 (Ch), [2010] BPIR 1, [2010] 1 BCLC 176 at [22], *Fortress Value Recovery Fund I LLC v Blue Skye Special Opportunites Fund LP* [2013] EWHC 14 (Comm) at [111].

Forms and procedure—A claim under s 423 does not constitute 'insolvency proceedings' within the meaning of r 13.7: *J Syke Bank Ltd v Spieldnaes* [1999] 2 BCLC 101 at 124A (Evans-Lombe J, referring to an unreported interim application on 5 October 1998); *Re Baillies Ltd* [2012] EWHC 285 (Ch), [2012] BPIR 665, [2012] BCC 554). Section 423 claims are now subject to r 12A(20) of the Insolvency Rules 1986 (service outside the jurisdiction) (also, see r 12A.16) and as under previous rules claims will fall within CPR, r 6.19(2) and require leave for service out of the jurisdiction in light of the comments of Dillon LJ in *Re Harrods (Buenos Aires) Ltd (No 2)* [1991] 4 All ER 334 at 359J: *Banca Carige v Banco Nacional* [2001] 2 BCLC 407 at [19] (Lightman J).

Insofar as actions do not seek the recovery of a sum recoverable by virtue of an enactment within s 9 of the Limitation Act 1980, they are actions for a specialty: *Hill v Spread Trustee Company Ltd* [2006] EWCA Civ 542, [2006] BPIR 789, [2007] 1 All ER 1106, [2006] BCC 646, [2007] 1 BCLC 450, [2007] 1 WLR 2404 at [116].

A claim under s 423 may be commenced in any Division of the High Court. The Insolvency Rules 1986 do not apply to a s 423 claim other than where the claim is brought in existing proceedings in the Companies Court or in the Bankruptcy Court: *TSB Bank v Katz* [1997] 147 at 149E–150C (Arden J, as she then was). Where a claim under s 423 is issued in the wrong form as an originating or ordinary application under the Insolvency Rules 1986 where there are no existing proceedings in the Companies Court or the Bankruptcy Court, the court has power to cure the defect and to treat the application as a claim form: *Banca Carige v Banco Nacional* [2001] 2 BCLC 407 at [16].

For procedure on a s 423 claim see the note under that heading to r 7.2.

A claimant under s 423 may also consider seeking declaratory and consequential relief alleging that a transaction constitutes a sham, as identified by Diplock LJ in *Snook v London and West Riding Investments Ltd* [1967] 2 QB 786 at 802, on which see further the comments of David Young QC, sitting as a deputy High Court judge, in *Midland Bank v Wyatt* [1997] 1 BCLC 242 at 245A–245J as to the need for any common intention between the parties to the sham transaction.

Limitation period—It was generally accepted that pre-1986 Act claims alleging a fraudulent conveyance were not subject to a limitation period on the basis that such conveyances were rendered void. Notwithstanding the apparent presumption in earlier cases that no statutory limitation period applied to actions under s 423 (for example, *Law Society v Southall* [2001] EWCA Civ 2001, [2002] BPIR 336), the Court of Appeal has now ruled that there is: *Hill v Spread Trustee Company Ltd* [2006] EWCA Civ 542, [2006] BPIR 789, [2007] 1 All ER 1106, [2006] BCC 646, [2007] 1 BCLC 450, [2007] 1 WLR 2404 at [117]–[118], [143]. The period is 12 years if s 9 of the Limitation Act 1980 applied (actions upon a specialty), and six years if s 8 of that Act applies (a claim for monetary relief): *Hill v Spread* at [116]. It was accepted in *Hill v Spread* that there could be separate limitation periods for different applicants (at [149]). For instance, where the applicant was a bankruptcy trustee the period would not start to run until the making of a bankruptcy order (applied in *Rubin v Dweck* [2012] BPIR 854), for it was not until then that the applicant could bring proceedings; the appointment of the trustee is an ingredient in the cause of action (see [150], Arden LJ dissenting on this point at [120]–[122]). It was held that it was of no consequence that at the time of the bringing of an action by a trustee in bankruptcy there might be creditors whose action under s 423 was statute-barred and who would benefit from the trustee's action ([150]).

The Court of Appeal allowed the extension of the limitation period in the case of *Giles v Rhind* [2008] EWCA Civ 118, [2008] BPIR 342, [2008] 2 BCLC 1. Arden LJ (with whom the other judges agreed) held that a claim under s 423 could be within the expression, 'breach of duty,' in s 32(2) of the Limitation Act 1980, as 'breach of duty' bears a wide meaning. Section 32(2) provides that the deliberate commission of a breach of duty in circumstances in which it is unlikely to be discovered for some time amounts to a deliberate concealment of the facts and the deliberate concealing of facts permits, according to s 32(1) of the Limitation Act 1980, a court to extend time (at [38]–[39]. The time runs from the time the plaintiff discovers that the improper action occurred. Her Ladyship noted that a transaction covered by s 423 is the kind of transaction of which there was likely to be concealment and 'thus there would be a heightened policy reason for the application of s 32(2) to claims under that section.' (at [54]).

Generally, see R Stubbs 'Section 423 of the Insolvency Act in Practice' (2008) 21 *Insolvency Intelligence* 17.

424 Those who may apply for an order under s 423

(1) An application for an order under section 423 shall not be made in relation to a transaction except—

  (a) in a case where the debtor has been adjudged bankrupt or is a body corporate which is being wound up or is in administration, by the official receiver, by the trustee of the bankrupt's estate or the liquidator or administrator of the body corporate or (with the leave of the court) by a victim of the transaction;

  (b) in a case where a victim of the transaction is bound by a voluntary arrangement approved under Part I or Part VIII of this Act, by the supervisor of the voluntary arrangement or by any person who (whether or not so bound) is such a victim; or

  (c) in any other case, by a victim of the transaction.

(2) An application made under any of the paragraphs of subsection (1) is to be treated as made on behalf of every victim of the transaction.

Amendments—Enterprise Act 2002, s 248(3), Sch 17, paras 9, 36.

General note—This provision provides distinct categories of claimant who are deemed by s 424(2) to proceed on behalf of every victim of the particular transaction challenged. For the standing of the FSA to make application in an appropriate case, see s 375 of the Financial Services and Markets Act 2000.

Section 424(1)(a)

Scope of provision—Where any of the insolvency procedures specified in this provision are in place the cause of action under s 423 falls to the office-holder such that a victim of the transaction requires leave of the court to enable him or her to bring proceedings. Leave should ordinarily be given by the court where the claim is plainly arguable on its face and where the incumbent office-holder consents. Such consent might be forthcoming where there are no assets in the estate to fund the proceedings, as in *Re Ayala Holdings* [1993] BCLC 256 at 266–267. Where the debtor has been adjudged bankrupt or entered a formal corporate insolvency regime after proceedings have been instituted under s 423, the claimant does not need to obtain leave of the court: *Godfrey v Torpy* [2007] EWHC 919 (Ch), [2007] BPIR 1538, *The Times* May 16 2007 at [39]. In any event, if leave is required in such a situation it can be granted retrospectively by the court: *Godfrey v Torpy* at [43].

Where a claimant does require leave and the office-holder has declined to bring proceedings under s 423 then the claimant must demonstrate that he or she has a realistic prospect of establishing: the transaction is covered by s 423; the claimant was a victim of the transaction within s 423; and there is a good reason why he or she should bring proceedings when the liquidator had not: *Re Simon Carves Ltd* [2013] EWHC 685 (Ch) at [27].

The nature of the court's relief—The court's remedial power is, it is submitted, restitutionary and not compensatory in nature. The proceeds of a s 423 action will in any case enure for the benefit of the insolvent estate, irrespective of the identity of the claimant, since, whilst in contrast to s 238(3), which concerns the court with the making of an order for the purpose of restoring the pre-transaction position, s 423(2) admits of the court also seeking to protect the interests of the victims of a challenged transaction. Accordingly, the position should only be returned to what it would have been by way of the court asking what is necessary to restore what has been lost to the debtor, albeit by allowing for the restoration of assets to the debtor so as to make those assets available for execution by victims: see *Chohan v Saggar* [1994] BCLC 706 at 714 (Nourse LJ, with whom Balcombe and Waite LJJ agreed).

Section 424(1)(b)

Scope of provision—Where a voluntary arrangement is in place, the claim may be pursued by the supervisor, an arrangement creditor, or a non-arrangement creditor – provided either is a victim as defined in s 423(5) – without any requirement for the leave of the court.

Section 424(1)(c)

Scope of provision—A victim may proceed with a claim without a requirement for leave if none of the preceding circumstances apply. Such a claim will be available where a debtor company is in receivership (of any form) or subject to a company voluntary arrangement, although a CVA backed by a moratorium will ordinarily prevent such proceedings.

425 Provision which may be made by order under s 423

(1) Without prejudice to the generality of section 423, an order made under that section with respect to a transaction may (subject as follows)—

    (a) require any property transferred as part of the transaction to be vested in any person, either absolutely or for the benefit of all the persons on whose behalf the application for the order is treated as made;

    (b) require any property to be so vested if it represents, in any person's hands, the application either of the proceeds of sale of property so transferred or of money so transferred;

(c) release or discharge (in whole or in part) any security given by the debtor;

(d) require any person to pay to any other person in respect of benefits received from the debtor such sums as the court may direct;

(e) provide for any surety or guarantor whose obligations to any person were released or discharged (in whole or in part) under the transaction to be under such new or revived obligations as the court thinks appropriate;

(f) provide for security to be provided for the discharge of any obligation imposed by or arising under the order, for such an obligation to be charged on any property and for such security or charge to have the same priority as a security or charge released or discharged (in whole or in part) under the transaction.

(2) An order under section 423 may affect the property of, or impose any obligation on, any person whether or not he is the person with whom the debtor entered into the transaction; but such an order—

(a) shall not prejudice any interest in property which was acquired from a person other than the debtor and was acquired in good faith, for value and without notice of the relevant circumstances, or prejudice any interest deriving from such an interest, and

(b) shall not require a person who received a benefit from the transaction in good faith, for value and without notice of the relevant circumstances to pay any sum unless he was a party to the transaction.

(3) For the purposes of this section the relevant circumstances in relation to a transaction are the circumstances by virtue of which an order under section 423 may be made in respect of the transaction.

(4) In this section 'security' means any mortgage, charge, lien or other security.

General note—For the purpose of orders under s 425(1) see s 423(2) and the notes thereto.

It has been held that the nature and the extent of relief should take into account the mental state of either the transferee of the property that is the subject of the impugned transaction or any other person against whom an order is sought, as well as their involvement in the scheme of the debtor to put assets out of the reach of creditors: *4Eng Ltd v Harper* [2009] EWHC 2633 (Ch), [2010] BPIR 1, [2010] 1 BCLC 176 at [11], [13]. Sales J in this case said that where a person receives property in good faith and he or she has changed his or her position as a result, then it would not be appropriate to require the transferee to return the property ([14]). The decision is analysed and criticised in Morgan, '*4Eng Ltd v Harper* – an unjustified change?' (2010) 3(1) CRI 5. The decision has been the subject of reasonably wide criticism(e g Goode *Principles of Corporate Insolvency Law* (Sweet and Maxwell, 4th edn 2011) at 633-634).

Section 425(1)

Scope of provision—Judges are granted wide discretion when it comes to ordering relief: *Griffin v Awoderu* [2008] EWHC 349 (Ch) at [40].The range of orders in s 425(1)(a)–(f) closely resemble those in ss 241(1) and 342(1), save that those sections feature an additional sub-para (g) which allows the court to control proofs in a winding up or bankruptcy. This range of orders is, however, no more than illustrative of the types of orders, singly or in any combination, which the court may choose to make in its discretion under s 423(2) in meeting the two purposes in that subsection. Neither does the range of orders set out here limit the scope of the court's power given the words 'without prejudice to the generality of Section 423 ...'

What relief is ordered is heavily dependent on the facts. The provision allows for flexibility in tailoring orders to permit justice to be done. Hard and fast rules cannot be laid down: *4Eng Ltd v Harper* [2009] EWHC 2633 (Ch), [2010] BPIR 1, [2010] 1 BCLC 176 at [16].

Where property has been transferred to a person who had no knowledge of the transferor's internation to put assets out of the reach of creditors and the transferee had simply held the property then the appropriate order should normally be one that transfers the property either to the creditors or the transferor: *4Eng Ltd v Harper* [2009] EWHC 2633 (Ch), [2010] BPIR 1, [2010] 1 BCLC 176 at [14]. The court in this case said that there was no obligation on the court to inquire, when providing for relief, into the need to maintain the standard of living of the transferee.

Section 425(2) and (3)

Scope of provision—Whilst it is open to the court to upset third party rights, s 425(2) provides mandatory protection for two categories of bona fide purchasers for value without notice of the relevant circumstances defined in s 425(3). (Compare here the more complex third party protection provisions in ss 241(2)–(3) and 341(2)–(3).)

For an example of protection of third party rights, see the order of Scott J in *Arbuthnot Leasing International Ltd v Havelet Leasing Ltd (No 2)* [1990] BCC 636, noted above, to s 423(2).

PART XVII
MISCELLANEOUS AND GENERAL

General comment on Part XVII—This Part covers a number of diverse matters including provisions for: co-operation with overseas courts exercising insolvency jurisdiction; dealing with Members of Parliaments and Assemblies who are subject to bankruptcy restriction orders or undertakings; penalties for breach of the Insolvency Act; and the admissibility of certain statements in evidence.

426 Co-operation between courts exercising jurisdiction in relation to insolvency

(1) An order made by a court in any part of the United Kingdom in the exercise of jurisdiction in relation to insolvency law shall be enforced in any other part of the United Kingdom as if it were made by a court exercising the corresponding jurisdiction in that other part.

(2) However, without prejudice to the following provisions of this section, nothing in subsection (1) requires a court in any part of the United Kingdom to enforce, in relation to property situated in that part, any order made by a court in any other part of the United Kingdom.

(3) The Secretary of State, with the concurrence in relation to property situated in England and Wales of the Lord Chancellor, may by order make provision for securing that a trustee or assignee under the insolvency law of any part of the United Kingdom has, with such modifications as may be specified in the order, the same rights in relation to any property situated in

another part of the United Kingdom as he would have in the corresponding circumstances if he were a trustee or assignee under the insolvency law of that other part.

(4) The courts having jurisdiction in relation to insolvency law in any part of the United Kingdom shall assist the courts having the corresponding jurisdiction in any other part of the United Kingdom or any relevant country or territory.

(5) For the purposes of subsection (4) a request made to a court in any part of the United Kingdom by a court in any other part of the United Kingdom or in a relevant country or territory is authority for the court to which the request is made to apply, in relation to any matters specified in the request, the insolvency law which is applicable by either court in relation to comparable matters falling within its jurisdiction.

In exercising its discretion under this subsection, a court shall have regard in particular to the rules of private international law.

(6) Where a person who is a trustee or assignee under the insolvency law of any part of the United Kingdom claims property situated in any other part of the United Kingdom (whether by virtue of an order under subsection (3) or otherwise), the submission of that claim to the court exercising jurisdiction in relation to insolvency law in that other part shall be treated in the same manner as a request made by a court for the purpose of subsection (4).

(7) Section 38 of the Criminal Law Act 1977 (execution of warrant of arrest throughout the United Kingdom) applies to a warrant which, in exercise of any jurisdiction in relation to insolvency law, is issued in any part of the United Kingdom for the arrest of a person as it applies to a warrant issued in that part of the United Kingdom for the arrest of a person charged with an offence.

(8) Without prejudice to any power to make rules of court, any power to make provision by subordinate legislation for the purpose of giving effect in relation to companies or individuals to the insolvency law of any part of the United Kingdom includes power to make provision for the purpose of giving effect in that part to any provision made by or under the preceding provisions of this section.

(9) An order under subsection (3) shall be made by statutory instrument subject to annulment in pursuance of a resolution of either House of Parliament.

(10) In this section 'insolvency law' means—

    (a)   in relation to England and Wales, provision extending to England and Wales and made by or under this Act or sections 1A, 6 to 10, 12 to 15, 19(c) and 20 (with Schedule 1), of the Company Directors Disqualification Act 1986, Part XVIII of the Companies Act and sections 1 to 17 of that Act as they apply for the purposes of those provisions of that Act;

    (b)   in relation to Scotland, provision extending to Scotland and made by or under this Act, sections 1A, 6 to 10, 12 to 15, 19(c) and 20 (with Schedule 1) of the Company Directors

Disqualification Act 1986 and sections 1 to 17 of that Act as they apply for the purposes of those provisions of that Act, Part XVIII of the Companies Act or the Bankruptcy (Scotland) Act 1985;

(c)   (*not reproduced*)

(d)   in relation to any relevant country or territory, so much of the law of that country or territory as corresponds to provisions falling within any of the foregoing paragraphs;

and references in this subsection to any enactment include, in relation to any time before the coming into force of that enactment the corresponding enactment in force at that time.

(11) In this section 'relevant country or territory' means—

(a)   any of the Channel Islands or the Isle of Man, or

(b)   any country or territory designated for the purposes of this section by the Secretary of State by order made by statutory instrument.

(12) In the application of this section to Northern Ireland—

(a)   for any reference to the Secretary of State there is substituted a reference to the Department of Economic Development in Northern Ireland;

(b)   in subsection (3) for the words 'another part of the United Kingdom' and the words 'that other part' there are substituted the words 'Northern Ireland';

(c)   for subsection (9) there is substituted the following subsection—

'(9) An order made under subsection (3) by the Department of Economic Development in Northern Ireland shall be a statutory rule for the purposes of the Statutory Rules (Northern Ireland) Order 1979 and shall be subject to negative resolution within the meaning of section 41(6) of the Interpretation Act (Northern Ireland) 1954.'.

(13) Section 129 of the Banking Act 2009 provides for provisions of that Act about bank insolvency to be 'insolvency law' for the purposes of this section.

(14) Section 165 of the Banking Act 2009 provides for provisions of that Act about bank administration to be 'insolvency law' for the purposes of this section.

Amendments—SI 1989/2405; Insolvency Act 2000, s 8, Sch 4, paras 1, 16; Banking Act 2009, ss 129, 165.

General note—This provision is designed to promote co-operation between the UK courts and the courts of certain other designated countries and territories. It permits the UK courts to give assistance to a foreign court in an insolvency matter. Only countries or territories that are designated for the purposes of s 426 may apply and they are known as 'relevant countries or territories': s 426(11). At the present time they are: Anguilla, Australia, the Bahamas, Bermuda, Botswana, Canada, Cayman Islands, Falkland Islands, Gibraltar, Hong Kong, the Republic of Ireland, Montserrat, New Zealand, St Helena, Turks and Caicos Islands, Tuvalu and the Virgin Islands. These were designated by the Co-operation of Insolvency Courts (Designation of Relevant Countries and Territories) Order 1986 (SI 1986/2123). Subsections

(4), (5), (10) and (11) of s 426 now apply to the Bailiwick of Guernsey by Insolvency Act 1986 (Guernsey) Order 1989 (SI 1989/2409). Malaysia and the Republic of South Africa were added to the list by SI 1996/253, and Brunei was the last country to be designated by SI 1998/2766. This means that, although the purpose of s 426 is to encourage co-operation, only a very limited number of countries can ask for assistance, thereby limiting the utility of the provision. Nevertheless, now that the EC Regulation on Insolvency Proceedings 1346/2000 has come into force, there would be little need to add any other EU countries to the list (the Republic of Ireland is the only EU country on the list at the present time) since the Regulation sets out a framework for co-operation between, and co-ordination of, insolvency proceedings in the EU.

The UNCITRAL Model Law, which has been brought into effect in Great Britain by s 14 of the Insolvency Act 2000 through the Cross-Border Insolvency Regulations 2006 (SI 2006/1030) is relevant to the application of s 426. The aim of the Model Law is to foster the efficient administration of cross-border insolvency proceedings where there is an international element. One great benefit of the Model Law is that, its effects are not limited to specific countries, as is the case with s 426 and the EC Regulation. However this also means that there is the potential for conflict between s 426 and the Model Law. Where an insolvency proceeding is connected to a country that is designated under s 426(11), an application may still be made under the Model Law. Under Article 7 of schedule 1 of the Cross-Border Insolvency Regulations 2006 it is stated that any additional assistance that may be forthcoming under the laws of Great Britain may be given in conjunction with assistance under the Model Law.

See also the introduction to the Cross-Border Insolvency Regulations 2006.

Section 426(1) and (2)

Reciprocal enforcement of orders within the UK—Sections 426(1) and (2) state that any court order made in relation to insolvency law in any part of the UK is enforceable throughout the UK, except with regard to orders relating to property.

Section 426(3) and (9)

Rights to property—Sections 426(3) and (9) permit the Secretary of State to make an order by statutory instrument which gives a trustee or liquidator the same rights with regard to property situated in another part of the UK, as a trustee or assignee would have in that other part. By virtue of s 426(6) a trustee or liquidator is able to claim property situated in any other part of the UK by asking for assistance from the UK court with jurisdiction over the property. The request is to be treated in the same way as a request under s 426(4).

Section 426(4)

The jurisdiction of the UK courts – the discretion to grant a request—It is fair to say that, although cross-border insolvency has become increasingly important in recent times, there has not been a deluge of cases under these provisions. This may be because of the countries and territories that have been designated as there are significant omissions, such as the USA and Japan. However, there have been a number of cases that have clarified the court's approach to its jurisdiction under s 426.

It is possible to put into administration, or apply the CVA procedure to, a foreign company. See *Re Dallhold Estates (UK) Ltd* [1992] 1 BCLC 621, where an Australian company was put into administration, and *Re Television Trade Rentals Ltd* [2002] BPIR 859, where the CVA procedure was applied to companies incorporated in the Isle of Man.

Section 426(4) states that the UK courts 'shall assist' any other UK court or any 'relevant country or territory' (defined in s 426(11)) with regard to insolvency law. These apparently mandatory words have not been interpreted as meaning that the UK courts have to assist in every case. Instead, in *Hughes v Hannover* [1997] BCLC 497, the Court of Appeal stated that the court has a discretion to refuse to give assistance where it is appropriate. The case involved an insurance company being wound up in Bermuda. The defendants were re-insurers of the company and sought arbitration under the re-insurance contracts. A letter of request from the Bermudan court sought a worldwide injunction restraining any actions or proceedings being commenced against the company. The court did refuse assistance in this case because the circumstances, the basis of which the application under s 426(4) were made, had changed by the time the court came to make its decision.

In setting down guidelines for deciding whether assistance should be given, Morritt LJ referred with approval to early cases involving s 426, eg *Re Dallhold Estates (UK) Ltd* [1992] 1 BCLC 621 and *Re Focus Insurance Co Ltd* [1997] 1 BCLC 219, in which the judges concerned acknowledged that assistance was not to be granted automatically: rather the courts had a discretion to determine whether to accede to a letter of request. Assistance should be given if, in accordance with the law to be applied, the relief sought may be properly granted. Public policy might be a reason for refusing to give assistance, but it is not the only one. He stressed that the fact that a request has been made is a weighty factor to be taken into account in deciding whether to grant the assistance sought; nevertheless it is not in itself conclusive that assistance should be given. Furthermore, Jonathan Parker LJ in *England v Smith (Re Southern Equities Corp)* [2001] Ch 419 (see below) stated that since countries and territories are specifically designated for the purpose of s 426, this indicated that public policy favours the giving of assistance. He then went on to say that the court would not make an order if it considered that such action would be oppressive.

The case of *Hughes v Hannover* also makes clear that in deciding whether to give assistance the courts may apply their own inherent jurisdiction, English insolvency law, or the insolvency law of the foreign jurisdiction applying for assistance. In that case the court could have granted a worldwide injunction only under its general jurisdiction, as both of the relevant insolvency provisions of England and Bermuda were limited territorially in their scope.

In *Re Focus Insurance Co Ltd* [1996] BCC 659 Scott VC declined to make an order for the assistance of foreign liquidators in the recovery of English assets in an English bankruptcy where the liquidators were the petitioning creditors in the bankruptcy and the relief sought could be obtained in the bankruptcy proceedings by the trustee in bankruptcy. The same judge also held in *Re BCCI (No 11)* [1997] 1 BCLC 80 that s 426 assistance could not be given where its effect would be to disapply the mandatory English set off rules prescribed by the Insolvency Rules.

Section 426(5)

Application of foreign law—In a Court of Appeal case, *England v Smith (Re Southern Equities Corp)* [2001] Ch 419, Morritt LJ, giving the leading judgment, stated that an examination under Australian law would be permitted pursuant to a request under s 426. (Under s 426(5) the UK court is permitted to apply the law of the foreign court making the request.) The English provision, IA 1986, s 236 identified s 596B as a provision of the Australian Corporations Law. But once the decision to apply provisions of the foreign law has been made, any corresponding English provisions cease to have any relevance.

So, despite the fact the Australian law pertaining to examinations was different to English law and under the latter provisions the examination could not have gone ahead, that was no reason to refuse to grant assistance. The object of s 426 was to provide reciprocal assistance in insolvencies; it would be inconsistent with the need for comity if the English courts stigmatised the law of the requesting court as oppressive because it did not correspond to English law. Both the Australian and English provisions were interpreted to avoid oppression, but this was achieved in different ways. By acknowledging that a provision of the insolvency law of the foreign court should not be divorced from the principles and practice by which the provision is applied in that jurisdiction, s 426 could be given full effect. In the alternative, if the English court applied a foreign provision only when it corresponded to English law, there would have been little point in the legislature giving the court the power to apply foreign law. In so deciding, the Court of Appeal disapproved of *Re JN Taylor Finance Pty Ltd* [1999] 2 BCLC 256, where a similar request to that in *England v Smith* was made for an examination under Australian law. The request was refused because the examination could not go ahead under English law.

In insolvency matters where choice of law is concerned, there has been a traditional emphasis placed on the law of the place of the forum (the lex fori) and the power to apply foreign law is at variance with this traditional emphasis. In deciding what law to apply, s 426(5) provides that an English court 'shall have regard, in particular' to the rules of private international law. It is not entirely clear what this statement is intended to imply. In

Re Television Trade Rentals Ltd[1] [2002] BPIR 859 Lawrence Collins J while suggesting that the provision was 'obscure and ill thought out' also expressed the view that the requested court should take the foreign elements into account in deciding what law to apply. Where these elements point to the application of the foreign law, this may influence the court in deciding to apply that law, although courts would seem still to have a discretion to disregard the English conflicts rule in an appropriate case. This view appears to correspond to the view articulated by some that, in applying s 426, an English court should not regard common law rules of jurisdiction and recognition as inhibiting its statutory power to give assistance if, in the circumstances, it is felt otherwise appropriate to offer the assistance requested.[2] Others have suggested however, that s 426(5) should be accorded a more decisive meaning.[3] In other words, and as a matter of principle, when a court is confronted with a choice between the provisions of two different systems of law from which to derive the basis for its decision, it should select the rule contained within that system which, according to the rules of private international law, is properly applicable to the issue which forms the subject matter of the request to which the court is responding.[4]

Handing over assets to a foreign liquidator—An English ancillary liquidation is conducted in accordance with English insolvency rules in deciding, for example, what proofs can be admitted and what counts as a preferential debt but once secured and preferential debts have been paid off it is common to remit the remaining assets to the jurisdiction where the principal liquidation is taking place. In *Re HIH Casualty and General Insurance Ltd* [2008] 1 WLR 852 the question arose whether this power to remit assets should be exercised where the foreign law of distribution does not coincide with English law. The case concerned the liquidation of an Australian insurance company where the assets of the company would be distributed on a different basis from that in an English liquidation to the disadvantage of certain creditors.[5] At first instance, David Richards J held that ([2006] 2 All ER 671 at para 8): 'in an English liquidation of a foreign company, the court has no power to direct the liquidator to transfer funds for distribution in the principal liquidation, if the scheme for pari passu distribution in that liquidation is not substantially the same as under English law.'

The decision was confirmed by the Court of Appeal, which, nevertheless, did introduce some qualifications to this general statement of principle. Morritt VC said ([2007] 1 All ER 177 at para 41):

'There may be circumstances in which it is for the benefit of the creditors that a transfer should be made, notwithstanding that their interests in the liquidation in England, when viewed in isolation would be adversely affected. For example, the savings in cost by avoiding duplication may offset any reduction in prospective dividend. Similarly a loss of priority may be sufficiently offset by an increase in the pool available for distribution to those whose priority was changed. The admission of further creditors may be offset by an increase in the pool available for distribution to that class of creditor. In such cases it may be that an order sanctioning the transfer may properly be made.'

The Court of Appeal pointed to *Daewoo Motor Co Ltd* [2006] BPIR 415 as an example of the operation of this qualification in practice. In that case Lewison J authorised the transfer

[1] See also Lord Neuberger in *RE HIH Casualty and General Insurance Ltd* [2008] 1 WLR 852 at para 81 talking about the reference as 'slightly mystifying'.

[2] See CGJ Morse 'Principles and Pragmatism in English Cross-Border Insolvency Law' in Harry Rajak (ed) *Insolvency Law: Theory and Practice* (Sweet & Maxwell, 1993) 201 at 223.

[3] For a slightly different view see Carnwath LJ in *Re HIH Casualty and General Insurance Ltd* [2007] 1 All ER 177 at para 71 who suggested that it was for those seeking to justify a departure from English principles, to show that there is some rule of Private International Law which so requires.

[4] See the discussion in I Fletcher *Insolvency in Private International Law* 2nd edn (Oxford, 2005) at pp 236–237.

[5] Under Australian law insurance creditors were treated better and non-insurance creditors worse than under English law. As Lord Hoffmann pointed out at para 32 English law has now adopted a regime for the winding-up of insurance companies which gives preference to insurance creditors – reg 21(2) of the Insurers (Reorganisation and Winding Up) Regulations 2004, SI 2004/353 giving effect to Directive 2001/17/EC on the reorganisation and winding up of insurance companies.

of the assets collected by provisional liquidators to a receiver appointed by a Korean court. The transfer was ordered because it was being done with the consent of the three creditors whose interests might be prejudiced and to the overall advantage of all the others.

In *Re HIH Casualty and General Insurance Ltd* the request to transfer assets came from an Australian court pursuant to s 426 of the Insolvency Act 1986 and the House of Lords overturned the Court of Appeal holding that it failed to take sufficient heed of the section. Lord Hoffmann said that the section should not be deprived of its intended potential to enable a single universal scheme for insolvency distribution to be achieved. Australia was a designated country for s 426 purposes and there was nothing unacceptably discriminatory or otherwise contrary to public policy in the Australian insolvency provisions. Lord Neuberger said a fundamental principle of English insolvency law would not be offended or unfairness perpetrated by the application of the Australian insolvency regime.

Lord Hoffmann was prepared to go further placing greater emphasis on the principle of universalism and suggesting that a remission of assets to Australia could be ordered at common law. The differences between English and foreign systems of distribution were relevant only to discretion and in this case the application of Australian law to the distribution of all the assets was more likely to give effect to the expectations of creditors as a whole than the distribution of some of the assets according to English law.

Section 426(10)

Meaning of insolvency law—Insolvency law is defined under this provision and in *Hughes v Hannover* [1997] BCLC 49, where the court asserted that s 426(10) states what insolvency law means, not what it includes.

There may be difficulties with the application of the 'correspondence' test to foreign schemes of arrangement as these may or may not be equivalent to company voluntary arrangements under Part 1 Insolvency Act 1986. The point however was glossed over in *Re Business City Express Ltd* [1997] BCC 826 where a scheme of arrangement entered into pursuant to the Irish examinership procedures was made binding on English creditors.

Section 426(11)

Countries and territories to which s 426 applies—Any of the Channel Islands, the Isle of Man and any place designated by statutory instrument can be a relevant country or territory for the purposes of making a request to the UK courts: see s 426(11). Section 426 applies to Northern Ireland by virtue of s 426(12). It should be noted that although s 426 applies in Northern Ireland, the Cross-Border Insolvency Regulations 2006 (SI 2006/1030) apply within Great Britain.

See the general note for a list of those countries or territories that are currently designated.

426A Disqualification from Parliament (England and Wales and Northern Ireland)

(1) A person in respect of whom a bankruptcy restrictions order or a debt relief restrictions order has effect shall be disqualified—

  (a) from membership of the House of Commons,
  (b) from sitting or voting in the House of Lords, and
  (c) from sitting or voting in a committee of the House of Lords or a joint committee of both Houses.

(2) If a member of the House of Commons becomes disqualified under this section, his seat shall be vacated.

(3) If a person who is disqualified under this section is returned as a member of the House of Commons, his return shall be void.

(4) No writ of summons shall be issued to a member of the House of Lords who is disqualified under this section.

(5) If a court makes a bankruptcy restrictions order or interim order, or a debt relief restrictions order or an interim debt relief restrictions order, in respect of a member of the House of Commons or the House of Lords the court shall notify the Speaker of that House.

(6) If the Secretary of State accepts a bankruptcy restrictions undertaking or a debt relief restrictions undertaking made by a member of the House of Commons or the House of Lords, the Secretary of State shall notify the Speaker of that House.

(7) If the Department of Enterprise, Trade and Investment for Northern Ireland accepts a bankruptcy restrictions undertaking made by a member of the House of Commons or the House of Lords under Schedule 2A to the Insolvency (Northern Ireland) Order 1989, the Department shall notify the Speaker of that House.

(8) In this section a reference to a bankruptcy restrictions order or an interim order includes a reference to a bankruptcy restrictions order or an interim order made under Schedule 2A to the Insolvency (Northern Ireland) Order 1989.

Amendments—Inserted by Enterprise Act 2002, s 266(1); Tribunals, Courts and Enforcement Act 2007, s 108(3), Sch 20, Pt 1, paras 1, 12; SI 2012/1544.

426B Devolution

(1) If a court in England and Wales makes a bankruptcy restrictions order or interim order in respect of a member of the Scottish Parliament, the Northern Ireland Assembly or the National Assembly for Wales, or makes a debt relief restrictions order or interim debt relief restrictions order in respect of such a member, the court shall notify the presiding officer of that body.

(1A) If the High Court in Northern Ireland makes a bankruptcy restrictions order or interim order under Schedule 2A to the Insolvency (Northern Ireland) Order 1989 in respect of a member of the Scottish Parliament or the National Assembly for Wales, the Court shall notify the presiding officer of that body.

(2) If the Secretary of State accepts a bankruptcy restrictions undertaking or a debt relief restrictions undertaking made by a member of the Scottish Parliament, the Northern Ireland Assembly or the National Assembly for Wales, the Secretary of State shall notify the presiding officer of that body.

(3) If the Department of Enterprise, Trade and Investment for Northern Ireland accepts a bankruptcy restrictions undertaking made by a member of the Scottish Parliament or the National Assembly for Wales under Schedule 2A to the Insolvency (Northern Ireland) Order 1989, the Department shall notify the presiding officer of that body.

Amendments—Inserted by Enterprise Act 2002, s 266(1); Tribunals, Courts and Enforcement Act 2007, s 108(3), Sch 20, Pt 1, paras 1, 13; SI 2012/1544.

426C Irrelevance of privilege

(1) An enactment about insolvency applies in relation to a member of the House of Commons or the House of Lords irrespective of any Parliamentary privilege.

(2) In this section 'enactment' includes a provision made by or under—

    (a)   an Act of the Scottish Parliament, or
    (b)   Northern Ireland legislation.

Amendments—Inserted by Enterprise Act 2002, s 266(1).

427 Disqualification from Parliament (Scotland)

(1) Where a court in Scotland awards sequestration of an individual's estate, the individual is disqualified—

    (a)   for sitting or voting in the House of Lords,
    (b)   for being elected to, or sitting or voting in, the House of Commons, and
    (c)   for sitting or voting in a committee of either House.

(2) Where an individual is disqualified under this section, the disqualification ceases—

    (a)   except where the award is recalled or reduced without the individual having been first discharged, on the discharge of the individual, and
    (b)   in the excepted case, on the recall or reduction, as the case may be.

(3) No writ of summons shall be issued to any lord of Parliament who is for the time being disqualified under this section for sitting and voting in the House of Lords.

(4) Where a member of the House of Commons who is disqualified under this section continues to be so disqualified until the end of the period of 6 months beginning with the day of the award, his seat shall be vacated at the end of that period.

(5) A court which makes an award such as is mentioned in subsection (1) in relation to any lord of Parliament or member of the House of Commons shall forthwith certify the award to the Speaker of the House of Lords or, as the case may be, to the Speaker of the House of Commons.

(6) Where a court has certified an award to the Speaker of the House of Commons under subsection (5), then immediately after it becomes apparent which of the following certificates is applicable, the court shall certify to the Speaker of the House of Commons—

    (a)   that the period of 6 months beginning with the day of the award has expired without the award having been recalled or reduced, or
    (b)   that the award has been recalled or reduced before the end of that period.

(6A) Subsections (4) to (6) have effect in relation to a member of the Scottish Parliament but as if—

(a) references to the House of Commons were to the Parliament and references to the Speaker were to the Presiding Officer, and

(b) in subsection (4), for 'under this section' there were substituted 'under section 15(1)(b) of the Scotland Act 1998 by virtue of this section'.

(6B) Subsections (4) to (6) have effect in relation to a member of the National Assembly for Wales but as if—

(a) references to the House of Commons were to the Assembly and references to the Speaker were to the presiding officer, and

(b) in subsection (4), for 'under this section' there was substituted 'under section 16 (2) of the Government of Wales Act 2006 by virtue of this section'.

(6C) –Subsections (4) to (6) have effect in relation to a member of the Northern Ireland Assembly but as if—

(a) references to the House of Commons were to the Assembly and references to the Speaker were to the Presiding Officer; and

(b) in subsection (4), for 'under this section' there were substituted 'under section 36(4) of the Northern Ireland Act 1998 by virtue of this section'.

(7) (*Repealed*)

Amendments—Government of Wales Act 2006, s160 (1); Enterprise Act 2002, ss 266(1)–(2)(b), 278(2), Sch 26; Scotland Act 1998, s 125, Sch 8, para 23(6); Government of Wales Act 1998, s 125, Sch 12, para 24; Northern Ireland Act 1998, s 99, Sch 13, para 6; SI 2012/1544.

General note—While a Member of the UK Parliament was disqualified from his or her position if he or she became bankrupt, now, as a result of changes brought about by the Enterprise Act 2002, that does not apply in relation to Members who have been adjudged bankrupt in England and Wales.

428 Exemptions from Restrictive Trade Practices Act

(1) (*Repealed*)

(2) (*Repealed*)

(3) In this section 'insolvency services' means the services of persons acting as insolvency practitioners or carrying out under the law of Northern Ireland functions corresponding to those mentioned in section 388(1) or (2) in Part XIII, in their capacity as such.

Amendments—SI 2000/311.

429 Disabilities on revocation of administration order against an individual

(1) The following applies where a person fails to make any payment which he is required to make by virtue of an administration order under Part VI of the County Courts Act 1984.

(2) The court which is administering that person's estate under the order may, if it thinks fit—

(a) revoke the administration order, and

(b) make an order directing that this section and section 12 of the Company Directors Disqualification Act 1986 shall apply to the person for such period, not exceeding one year, as may be specified in the order.

(3) A person to whom this section so applies shall not—

(a) either alone or jointly with another person, obtain credit to the extent of the amount prescribed for the purposes of section 360(1)(a) or more, or

(b) enter into any transaction in the course of or for the purposes of any business in which he is directly or indirectly engaged,

without disclosing to the person from whom he obtains the credit, or (as the case may be) with whom the transaction is entered into, the fact that this section applies to him.

(4) The reference in subsection (3) to a person obtaining credit includes—

(a) a case where goods are bailed or hired to him under a hire-purchase agreement or agreed to be sold to him under a conditional sale agreement, and

(b) a case where he is paid in advance (whether in money or otherwise) for the supply of goods or services.

(5) A person who contravenes this section is guilty of an offence and liable to imprisonment or a fine, or both.

Amendments—Enterprise Act 2002, s 269, Sch 23, paras 1, 15.

General note—This provision covers the situation where a person has neglected to adhere to the terms of an administration order that has been given pursuant to the County Courts Act 1984. The administration order may be revoked and the debtor will be subject to some of the restrictions that are imposed on a bankrupt.

The penalty for contravention of any restrictions placed on a debtor is set out in Sch 10 to the Insolvency Act 1986.

430 Provision introducing Schedule of punishments

(1) Schedule 10 to this Act has effect with respect to the way in which offences under this Act are punishable on conviction.

(2) In relation to an offence under a provision of this Act specified in the first column of the Schedule (the general nature of the offence being described in the second column), the third column shows whether the offence is punishable on conviction on indictment, or on summary conviction, or either in the one way or the other.

(3) The fourth column of the Schedule shows, in relation to an offence, the maximum punishment by way of fine or imprisonment under this Act which may be imposed on a person convicted of the offence in the way

specified in relation to it in the third column (that is to say, on indictment or summarily) a reference to a period of years or months being to a term of imprisonment of that duration.

(4) The fifth column shows (in relation to an offence for which there is an entry in that column) that a person convicted of the offence after continued contravention is liable to a daily default fine; that is to say, he is liable on a second or subsequent conviction of the offence to the fine specified in that column for each day on which the contravention is continued (instead of the penalty specified for the offence in the fourth column of the Schedule).

(5) For the purpose of any enactment in this Act whereby an officer of a company who is in default is liable to a fine or penalty, the expression 'officer who is in default' means any officer of the company who knowingly and wilfully authorises or permits the default, refusal or contravention mentioned in the enactment.

General note—The section indicates that Sch 10 to the Act sets out the penalties for offences against sections of the Act. Schedule 5 to the Insolvency Rules sets out the penalties for breaching the Rules.

'Officer who is in default'—This expression is identical to that used in the equivalent provision in the Companies Act 2006 (s 1121(1)).

431 Summary proceedings

(1) Summary proceedings for any offence under any of Parts I to VII of this Act may (without prejudice to any jurisdiction exercisable apart from this subsection) be taken against a body corporate at any place at which the body has a place of business, and against any other person at any place at which he is for the time being.

(2) Notwithstanding anything in section 127(1) of the Magistrates' Courts Act 1980, an information relating to such an offence which is triable by a magistrates' court in England and Wales may be so tried if it is laid at any time within 3 years after the commission of the offence and within 12 months after the date on which evidence sufficient in the opinion of the Director of Public Prosecutions or the Secretary of State (as the case may be) to justify the proceedings comes to his knowledge.

(3) Summary proceedings in Scotland for such an offence shall not be commenced after the expiration of 3 years from the commission of the offence.

Subject to this (and notwithstanding anything in section 136 of the Criminal Procedure (Scotland) Act 1995), such proceedings may (in Scotland) be commenced at any time within 12 months after the date on which evidence sufficient in the Lord Advocate's opinion to justify the proceedings came to his knowledge or, where such evidence was reported to him by the Secretary of State, within 12 months after the date on which it came to the knowledge of the latter; and subsection (3) of that section applies for the purpose of this subsection as it applies for the purpose of that section.

(4) For purposes of this section, a certificate of the Director of Public Prosecutions, the Lord Advocate or the Secretary of State (as the case may be) as to the date on which such evidence as is referred to above came to his knowledge is conclusive evidence.

Amendments—Criminal Procedure (Consequential Provisions) (Scotland) Act 1995, s 5, Sch 4, para 61.

432 Offences by bodies corporate

(1) This section applies to offences under this Act other than those excepted by subsection (4).

(2) Where a body corporate is guilty of an offence to which this section applies and the offence is proved to have been committed with the consent or connivance of, or to be attributable to any neglect on the part of, any director, manager, secretary or other similar officer of the body corporate or any person who was purporting to act in any such capacity he, as well as the body corporate, is guilty of the offence and liable to be proceeded against and punished accordingly.

(3) Where the affairs of a body corporate are managed by its members, subsection (2) applies in relation to the acts and defaults of a member in connection with his functions of management as if he were a director of the body corporate.

(4) The offences excepted from this section are those under sections 30, 39, 51, 53, 54, 62, 64, 66, 85, 89, 164, 188, 201, 206, 207, 208, 209, 210 and 211 and those under paragraphs 16(2), 17(3)(a), 18(3)(a), 19(3)(a), 22(1) and 23(1)(a) of Schedule A1.

Amendments—Insolvency Act 2000, s 1, Sch 1, paras 1, 11.

General note—This mirrors former s 733 of the Companies Act 1985.

433 Admissibility in evidence of statements of affairs etc

(1) In any proceedings (whether or not under this Act)—

    (a)   a statement of affairs prepared for the purposes of any provision of this Act which is derived from the Insolvency Act 1985,

    (aa)   a statement made in pursuance of a requirement imposed by or under Part 2 of the Banking Act 2009 (bank insolvency),

    (ab)   a statement made in pursuance of a requirement imposed by or under Part 3 of that Act (bank administration), and

    (b)   any other statement made in pursuance of a requirement imposed by or under any such provision or by or under rules made under this Act,

may be used in evidence against any person making or concurring in making the statement.

(2) However, in criminal proceedings in which any such person is charged with an offence to which this subsection applies—

(a) no evidence relating to the statement may be adduced, and

(b) no question relating to it may be asked,

by or on behalf of the prosecution, unless evidence relating to it is adduced, or a question relating to it is asked, in the proceedings by or on behalf of that person.

(3) Subsection (2) applies to any offence other than—

(a) an offence under section 22(6), 47(6), 48(8), 66(6), 67(8), 95(8), 98(6), 99(3)(a), 131(7), 192(2), 208(1)(a) or (d) or (2), 210, 235(5), 353(1), 354(1)(b) or (3) or 356(1) or (2)(a) or (b) or paragraph 4(3)(a) of Schedule 7;

(b) an offence which is—
   (i)   created by rules made under this Act, and
   (ii)   designated for the purposes of this subsection by such rules or by regulations made by the Secretary of State;

(c) an offence which is—
   (i)   created by regulations made under any such rules, and
   (ii)   designated for the purposes of this subsection by such regulations;

(d) an offence under section 1, 2 or 5 of the Perjury Act 1911 (false statements made on oath or made otherwise than on oath); or

(e) an offence under section 44(1) or (2) of the Criminal Law (Consolidation) (Scotland) Act 1995 (false statements made on oath or otherwise than on oath).

(4) Regulations under subsection (3)(b)(ii) shall be made by statutory instrument and, after being made, shall be laid before each House of Parliament.

Amendments—Youth Justice and Criminal Evidence Act 1999, s 59, Sch 3, para 7; Banking Act 2009, ss 128, 162.

General note—The provision was added to, but the effect of it was circumscribed, as a result of the enactment of the Youth Justice and Criminal Evidence Act 1999. Section 59 and Sch 3, para 7(1) of that Act introduced sub-ss (2)–(4) of s 433. The section now drafted means that statements obtained by compulsion cannot be used in most criminal proceedings, i e those not mentioned in s 433(3). The changes made to s 433 resulted from the decision of the European Court of Human Rights in *Saunders v United Kingdom* (1997) 23 EHRR 313, [1998] 1 BCLC 362, [1997] BCC 872, where it was held that the use of evidence that was obtained by company inspectors from persons who were compelled to answer was a contravention of the right to a fair trial under art 6(1) of the European Convention on Human Rights.

434 Crown application

For the avoidance of doubt it is hereby declared that provisions of this Act which derive from the Insolvency Act 1985 bind the Crown so far as affecting or relating to the following matters, namely—

(a) remedies against, or against the property of, companies or individuals;

(b) priorities of debts;

(c) transactions at an undervalue or preferences;

(d)　voluntary arrangements approved under Part I or Part VIII, and

(e)　discharge from bankruptcy.

PART XVIIA
SUPPLEMENTARY PROVISIONS

434A Introductory

The provisions of this Part have effect for the purposes of—

(a)　the First Group of Parts, and

(b)　sections 411, 413, 414, 416 and 417 in Part 15.

Amendments—Inserted by SI 2008/948.

434B Representation of corporations at meetings

(1) If a corporation is a creditor or debenture-holder, it may by resolution of its directors or other governing body authorise a person or persons to act as its representative or representatives—

(a)　at any meeting of the creditors of a company held in pursuance of this Act or of rules made under it, or

(b)　at any meeting of a company held in pursuance of the provisions contained in a debenture or trust deed.

(2) Where the corporation authorises only one person, that person is entitled to exercise the same powers on behalf of the corporation as the corporation could exercise if it were an individual creditor or debenture-holder.

(3) Where the corporation authorises more than one person, any one of them is entitled to exercise the same powers on behalf of the corporation as the corporation could exercise if it were an individual creditor or debenture-holder.

(4) Where the corporation authorises more than one person and more than one of them purport to exercise a power under subsection (3)—

(a)　if they purport to exercise the power in the same way, the power is treated as exercised in that way;

(b)　if they do not purport to exercise the power in the same way, the power is treated as not exercised.

Amendments—Inserted by SI 2008/948.

434C Legal professional privilege

In proceedings against a person for an offence under this Act nothing in this Act is to be taken to require any person to disclose any information that he is entitled to refuse to disclose on grounds of legal professional privilege (in Scotland, confidentiality of communications).

Amendments—Inserted by SI 2008/948.

434D Enforcement of company's filing obligations

(1) This section applies where a company has made default in complying with any obligation under this Act—

(a)   to deliver a document to the registrar, or
(b)   to give notice to the registrar of any matter.

(2) The registrar, or any member or creditor of the company, may give notice to the company requiring it to comply with the obligation.

(3) If the company fails to make good the default within 14 days after service of the notice, the registrar, or any member or creditor of the company, may apply to the court for an order directing the company, and any specified officer of it, to make good the default within a specified time.

(4) The court's order may provide that all costs (in Scotland, expenses) of or incidental to the application are to be borne by the company or by any officers of it responsible for the default.

(5) This section does not affect the operation of any enactment imposing penalties on a company or its officers in respect of any such default.

Amendments—Inserted by SI 2009/1941.

434E Application of filing obligations to overseas companies

The provisions of this Act requiring documents to be forwarded or delivered to, or filed with, the registrar of companies apply in relation to an overseas company that is required to register particulars under section 1046 of the Companies Act 2006 as they apply in relation to a company registered under that Act in England and Wales or Scotland.

Amendments—Inserted by SI 2009/1941.

PART XVIII
INTERPRETATION

General comment on Part XVIII—This Part explains the meaning of certain expressions.

435 Meaning of 'associate'

(1) For the purposes of this Act any question whether a person is an associate of another person is to be determined in accordance with the following provisions of this section (any provision that a person is an associate of another person being taken to mean that they are associates of each other).

(2) A person is an associate of an individual if that person is—

(a)   the individual's husband or wife or civil partner,
(b)   a relative of—
    (i)   the individual, or

(ii) the individual's husband or wife or civil partner, or

(c) the husband or wife or civil partner of a relative of—
  (i) the individual, or
  (ii) the individual's husband or wife or civil partner.

(3) A person is an associate of any person with whom he is in partnership, and of the husband or wife or civil partner or a relative of any individual with whom he is in partnership; and a Scottish firm is an associate of any person who is a member of the firm.

(4) A person is an associate of any person whom he employs or by whom he is employed.

(5) A person in his capacity as trustee of a trust other than—

(a) a trust arising under any of the second Group of Parts or the Bankruptcy (Scotland) Act 1985, or

(b) a pension scheme or an employees' share scheme,

is an associate of another person if the beneficiaries of the trust include, or the terms of the trust confer a power that may be exercised for the benefit of, that other person or an associate of that other person.

(6) A company is an associate of another company—

(a) if the same person has control of both, or a person has control of one and persons who are his associates, or he and persons who are his associates, have control of the other, or

(b) if a group of two or more persons has control of each company, and the groups either consist of the same persons or could be regarded as consisting of the same persons by treating (in one or more cases) a member of either group as replaced by a person of whom he is an associate.

(7) A company is an associate of another person if that person has control of it or if that person and persons who are his associates together have control of it.

(8) For the purposes of this section a person is a relative of an individual if he is that individual's brother, sister, uncle, aunt, nephew, niece, lineal ancestor or lineal descendant, treating—

(a) any relationship of the half blood as a relationship of the whole blood and the stepchild or adopted child of any person as his child, and

(b) an illegitimate child as the legitimate child of his mother and reputed father;

and references in this section to a husband or wife include a former husband or wife and a reputed husband or wife and references to a civil partner include a former civil partner and a reputed civil partner.

(9) For the purposes of this section any director or other officer of a company is to be treated as employed by that company.

(10) For the purposes of this section a person is to be taken as having control of a company if—

(a) the directors of the company or of another company which has control of it (or any of them) are accustomed to act in accordance with his directions or instructions, or

(b) he is entitled to exercise, or control the exercise of, one third or more of the voting power at any general meeting of the company or of another company which has control of it;

and where two or more persons together satisfy either of the above conditions, they are to be taken as having control of the company.

(11) In this section 'company' includes any body corporate (whether incorporated in Great Britain or elsewhere); and references to directors and other officers of a company and to voting power at any general meeting of a company have effect with any necessary modifications.

Amendments—Civil Partnership Act 2004, s 261(1), Sch 27, para 122; SI 2005/3129; SI 2009/1941.

General note—The provision deals, in great detail, with the meaning of 'associate', and covers relatives, companies, employment and trusts. The term is of particular importance in relation to claims to adjust preferential transfers under s 239 or s 340. It is integral to the meaning of 'connected person' in s 249. 'Connected person' is used in relation to the adjustment provisions in Part IV of the Act, but also in several other places in the First Group of Parts of the Act.

It is clear that if A is associated with B, and B is associated with C, it does not follow that A is also associated with C:

See the comments accompanying s 249 and specifically under the heading 'associate'.

436 Expressions used generally

(1) In this Act, except in so far as the context otherwise requires (and subject to Parts VII and XI)—

'the appointed day' means the day on which this Act comes into force under section 443;

'associate' has the meaning given by section 435;

'body corporate' includes a body incorporated outside Great Britain, but does not include—

(a) a corporation sole, or

(b) a partnership that, whether or not a legal person, is not regarded as a body corporate under the law by which it is governed;

'business' includes a trade or profession;

' the Companies Act' means the Companies Act (as defined in section 2 of the Companies Act 2006) as they have effect in Great Britain;

'conditional sale agreement' and 'hire-purchase agreement' have the same meanings as in the Consumer Credit Act 1974;

'the EC Regulation' means Council Regulation (EC) No 1346/2000;

'EEA State' means a state that is a Contracting Party to the Agreement on the European Economic Area signed at Oporto on 2nd May 1992 as adjusted by the Protocol signed at Brussels on 17th March 1993;

'employees' share scheme' means a scheme for encouraging or facilitating the holding of shares in or debentures of a company by or for the benefit of—

> (a)   the bona fide employees or former employees of—
> > (i)   the company,
> > (ii)   any subsidiary of the company, or
> > (iii)   the company's holding company or any subsidiary of the company's holding company, or
> (b)   the spouses, civil partners, surviving spouses, surviving civil partners, or minor children or step-children of such employees or former employees;

'modifications' includes additions, alterations and omissions and cognate expressions shall be construed accordingly;

'property' includes money, goods, things in action, land and every description of property wherever situated and also obligations and every description of interest, whether present or future or vested or contingent, arising out of, or incidental to, property;

'records' includes computer records and other non-documentary records;

'subordinate legislation' has the same meaning as in the Interpretation Act 1978; and

'transaction' includes a gift, agreement or arrangement, and references to entering into a transaction shall be construed accordingly.

(2) The following expressions have the same meaning in this Act as in the Companies Acts—

'articles', in relation to a company (see section 18 of the Companies Act 2006);

'debenture' (see section 738 of that Act);

'holding company' (see sections 1159 and 1160 of, and Schedule 6 to, that Act);

'the Joint Stock Companies Acts' (see section 1171 of that Act);

'overseas company' (see section 1044 of that Act);

'paid up' (see section 583 of that Act);

'private company' and 'public company' (see section 4 of that Act);

'registrar of companies' (see section 1060 of that Act);

'share' (see section 540 of that Act);

'subsidiary' (see sections 1159 and 1160 of, and Schedule 6 to, that Act).

Amendments—SI 2002/1037; SI 2005/879; SI 2007/2194; SI 2009/1941.

'Property'—The provision defines 'property' very broadly. In *Bristol Airport plc v Powdrill* [1990] Ch 744 at 759, Sir Nicholas Browne-Wilkinson said, in relation to the definition, that: 'It is hard to think of a wider definition of property.'

A licence under the Sea Fish (Conservation) Act 1992 (*Re Rae* [1995] BCC 102) and a waste management licence (*Re Celtic Extraction Ltd; Re Blue Stone Chemicals Ltd* [1999] 2 BCLC 555, CA) have been held to constitute property within s 436.

In *Re The Estate of Bertha Hemming* [2008] EWHC 2731 (Ch) it was held that a residuary legatee's entitlement to receive assets that comprise the residue in the future of a deceased estate, and the right to compel due administration of the estate, constituted a chose in action which was transmissible to the legatee's trustee in bankruptcy and so was property for the purposes of this section.

But, a right of appeal against a tax assessment has been held not to be property and could not be assigned by a liquidator: *Re GP Aviation Group International (in liq)* [2013] EWHC 1447 (Ch), [2013] BPIR 576.

'Transaction'—This also is a very widely defined term (see *Phillips v Brewin Dolphin Lawrie Bell Ltd* [1999] BCC 557 at 565, CA).

436A Proceedings under EC Regulation: modified definition of property

In the application of this Act to proceedings by virtue of Article 3 of the EC Regulation, a reference to property is a reference to property which may be dealt with in the proceedings.

Amendments—Inserted by SI 2002/1240.

436B References to things in writing

(1) A reference in this Act to a thing in writing includes that thing in electronic form.

(2) Subsection (1) does not apply to the following provisions—

    (a)   section 53 (mode of appointment by holder of charge),

    (b)   section 67(2) (report by receiver),

    (c)   section 70(4) (reference to instrument creating a charge),

    (d)   section 111(2) (dissent from arrangement under s 110),

    (e)   in the case of a winding up of a company registered in Scotland, section 111(4),

    (f)   section 123(1) (definition of inability to pay debts),

    (g)   section 198(3) (duties of sheriff principal as regards examination),

    (h)   section 222(1) (inability to pay debts: unpaid creditor for £750 or more), and

    (i)   section 223 (inability to pay debts: debt remaining unsatisfied after action brought).

Amendments—Inserted by SI 2010/18.

PART XIX
FINAL PROVISIONS

437 Transitional provisions, and savings

The transitional provisions and savings set out in Schedule 11 to this Act shall have effect, the Schedule comprising the following Parts—

Part I: company insolvency and winding up (matters arising before appointed day, and continuance of proceedings in certain cases as before that day);

Part II: individual insolvency (matters so arising, and continuance of bankruptcy proceedings in certain cases as before that day);

Part III: transactions entered into before the appointed day and capable of being affected by orders of the court under Part XVI of this Act;

Part IV: insolvency practitioners acting as such before the appointed day; and

Part V: general transitional provisions and savings required consequentially on, and in connection with, the repeal and replacement by this Act and the Company Directors Disqualification Act 1986 of provisions of the Companies Act 1985, the greater part of the Insolvency Act 1985 and other enactments.

438 Repeals

The enactments specified in the second column of Schedule 12 to this Act are repealed to the extent specified in the third column of that Schedule.

Amendments—SI 2009/1941.

General note—Schedule 12, to which the section makes reference, provides primarily for the repeal of a number of sections in the Companies Act 1985 (those dealing with insolvency and insolvency-related matters that are now covered in the Act) and most of the Insolvency Act 1985. For a brief explanation of the reason for these repeals and how they relate to the advent of the 1986 Act, see the Introduction to the Insolvency Legislation at the beginning of the book.

439 Amendment of enactments

(1) The Companies Act is amended as shown in Parts I and II of Schedule 13 to this Act, being amendments consequential on this Act and the Company Directors Disqualification Act 1986.

(2) The enactments specified in the first column of Schedule 14 to this Act (being enactments which refer, or otherwise relate, to those which are repealed and replaced by this Act or the Company Directors Disqualification Act 1986) are amended as shown in the second column of that Schedule.

(3) The Lord Chancellor may by order make such consequential modifications of any provision contained in any subordinate legislation made before the appointed day and such transitional provisions in connection with those modifications as appear to him necessary or expedient in respect of—

(a) any reference in that subordinate legislation to the Bankruptcy Act 1914;

(b) any reference in that subordinate legislation to any enactment repealed by Part III or IV of Schedule 10 to the Insolvency Act 1985; or

(c) any reference in that subordinate legislation to any matter provided for under the Act of 1914 or under any enactment so repealed.

(4) An order under this section shall be made by statutory instrument subject to annulment in pursuance of a resolution of either House of Parliament.

440 Extent (Scotland)

(1) Subject to the next subsection, provisions of this Act contained in the first Group of Parts extend to Scotland except where otherwise stated.

(2) The following provisions of this Act do not extend to Scotland—

(a)   in the first Group of Parts—
      section 43;
      section 238 to 241;
      section 246;

(b)   the second Group of Parts;
(c)   in the third Group of Parts—
      sections 399 to 402,
      sections 412, 413, 415, 415A(3), 418, 420 and 421,
      sections 423 to 425, and
      section 429(1) and (2); and

(d)   in the Schedules—
      Parts II and III of Schedule 11; and
      Schedules 12 and 14 so far as they repeal or amend enactments
      which extend to England and Wales only.

Amendments—Enterprise Act 2002, s 270(4).

441 Extent (Northern Ireland)

(1) The following provisions of this Act extend to Northern Ireland—

(a)   sections 197, 426, 425A, 426B, 427 and 428; and
(b)   so much of section 439 and Schedule 14 as relates to enactments
      which extend to Northern Ireland.

(2) Subject as above, and to any provision expressly relating to companies
incorporated elsewhere than in Great Britain, nothing in this Act extends to
Northern Ireland or applies to or in relation to companies registered or
incorporated in Northern Ireland.

Amendments—SI 2012/1544.

442 Extent (other territories)

Her Majesty may, by Order in Council, direct that such of the provisions of
this Act as are specified in the Order, being provisions formerly contained in
the Insolvency Act 1985, shall extend to any of the Channel Islands or any
colony with such modifications as may be so specified.

443 Commencement

This Act comes into force on the day appointed under section 236(2) of the
Insolvency Act 1985 for the coming into force of Part III of that Act
(individual insolvency and bankruptcy), immediately after that Part of that
Act comes into force for England and Wales.

444 Citation

This Act may be cited as the Insolvency Act 1986.

SCHEDULES

SCHEDULE A1
MORATORIUM WHERE DIRECTORS PROPOSE VOLUNTARY ARRANGEMENT

Introductory note on moratorium-backed company voluntary arrangements—The provisions in Sch A1 were enacted by s 1 and Sch 1 of the Insolvency Act 2000 and brought into effect on 1 January 2003 by the Insolvency Act 2000 (Commencement No 3 and Transitional Provisions) Order (SI 2002/2711). These new provisions introduce an optional procedure whereby an eligible company may obtain a moratorium where the directors intend to propose a company voluntary arrangement ('CVA'). Schedule A1 operates in addition to the provisions in Part I which govern 'non-moratorium' CVAs and which some of the new provisions closely resemble. Where a moratorium is or has been in force in relation to a CVA, the procedure applicable to the arrangement is as provided for in Sch A1, as opposed to ss 2–7 which remain applicable to non-moratorium arrangements. Reference should also be made to the notes to those earlier provisions.

Whatever the theory of the new moratorium regime under Sch A1, the fact remains that the procedure is fundamentally commercially unsound; perhaps most obviously, and by specific reference to para 16, how likely is it that a supplier or other third party will be willing to deal on even vaguely commercial terms with a company which is patently insolvent but which remains under the control of its directors?

Purpose of the moratorium provisions—Prior to the introduction of Sch A1, one practical difficulty commonly associated with CVAs was the absence of any protective provisions akin to the interim order in an individual voluntary arrangement or the moratorium formerly provided for in ss 10 and 11 and now contained in paras 40–43 of Sch B1 in relation to administrations. The need for such protection from creditor action in the course of a CVA being proposed and implemented dictated previously that, notwithstanding the additional expense involved, a proposal would commonly be made under the protection of an administration order obtained for the specific purpose provided for in the formerly operative s 8(3)(b) with the approved arrangement providing the exit route from administration, which would in some cases, depending on the circumstances, remain in force for protection purposes.

The use of the moratorium model in practice—Despite widespread expectation as to the popular usage of the new moratorium procedure by eligible companies in place of the 'stand-alone' CVA, the use in practice of the moratorium model as a rescue mechanism is relatively rare. There are at least four possible reasons for this. First, the promotion of the new regime was not assisted by the delay in bringing the voluntary arrangement provisions in the Insolvency Act 2000 into force, primarily on account of the need for the drafting of the detailed underlying rules and prescribed forms. Secondly, and despite some publicity on the introduction of the new provisions, it appears that many insolvency practitioners are more comfortable with the use of the more popular and familiar liquidation procedure and, it seems, the new administration procedure in relation to which a 'stand-alone' CVA will often provide an exit route. Thirdly, and allied to what appears to be a widespread lack of enthusiasm for these new provisions amongst practitioners, is the fact that the moratorium procedure is more complex than (most obviously) the procedure for the placing of a company into administration. Fourthly, it may be that practitioners view the new reporting and monitoring obligations in paras 6 and 24 as unduly onerous, although, for the reasons identified in the notes to those provisions, such concerns, it is submitted, are not well founded.

Some shortcomings in the new moratorium provisions—Paragraph 3(2) provides that the moratorium provisions apply only to 'small' companies as defined in s 382(3) of the Companies Act 2006. Although, under para 5, the Secretary of State may modify the qualifications for eligibility for a moratorium, no such regulations are presently envisaged, with the consequence that larger companies, which might well benefit from the moratorium-backed process, are kept out of the procedure. It is difficult to see why such a widespread exclusion should apply to a rescue mechanism which is essentially creditor-based and which might well, at the option and risk of a requisite majority of creditors, result in a cost-effective and improved return in comparison with what might otherwise be obtained in a more costly liquidation, administration or receivership. It is equally difficult to reconcile the exclusion of larger companies from the moratorium procedure, given Parliament's intention in the Enterprise Act 2002 in restricting the scope for the appointment of administrative receivers over companies; the moratorium procedure precludes the enforcement of security by a debenture-holder unless the appointment of an administrative receiver has already been effected (see para 4(1)(c)).

PART I
INTRODUCTORY

1 Interpretation

In this Schedule—

'the beginning of the moratorium' has the meaning given by paragraph 8(1),

'the date of filing' means the date on which the documents for the time being referred to in paragraph 7(1) are filed or lodged with the court,

'hire-purchase agreement' includes a conditional sale agreement, a chattel leasing agreement and a retention of title agreement,

'market contract' and 'market charge' have the meanings given by Part VII of the Companies Act 1989,

'moratorium' means a moratorium under section 1A,

'the nominee' includes any person for the time being carrying out the functions of a nominee under this Schedule,

'the settlement finality regulations' means the Financial Markets and Insolvency (Settlement Finality) Regulations 1999,

'system-charge' has the meaning given by the Financial Markets and Insolvency Regulations 1996.

2 Eligible companies

(1) A company is eligible for a moratorium if it meets the requirements of paragraph 3, unless—

(a) it is excluded from being eligible by virtue of paragraph 4, or
(b) it falls within sub-paragraph (2).

(2) A company falls within this sub-paragraph if—

(a) it effects or carries out contracts of insurance, but is not exempt from the general prohibition, within the meaning of section 19 of the Financial Services and Markets Act 2000, in relation to that activity,
(b) it has permission under Part IV of that Act to accept deposits,
(bb) it has a liability in respect of a deposit which it accepted in accordance with the Banking Act 1979 (c 37) or 1987 (c 22),
(c) it is a party to a market contract, or any of its property is subject to a market charge, or a system-charge, or
(d) it is a participant (within the meaning of the settlement finality regulations) or any of its property is subject to a collateral security charge (within the meaning of those regulations).

(3) Paragraphs (a), (b) and (bb) of sub-paragraph (2) must be read with—

    (a)   section 22 of the Financial Services and Markets Act 2000;

    (b)   any relevant order under that section; and

    (c)   Schedule 2 to that Act.

'eligible company'—See the note under this heading to para 3 below and note the exclusions in para 4.

'regulated company' under the Financial Services and Markets Act 2000—For the function of the Financial Services Authority in relation to a regulated company see para 44.

3

(1) A company meets the requirements of this paragraph if the qualifying conditions are met—

    (a)   in the year ending with the date of filing, or

    (b)   in the financial year of the company which ended last before that date.

(2) For the purposes of sub-paragraph (1)—

    (a)   the qualifying conditions are met by a company in a period if, in that period, it satisfies two or more of the requirements for being a small company specified for the time being in section 382(3) of the Companies Act 2006, and

    (b)   a company's financial year is to be determined in accordance with that Act.

(3) Section 382(4), (5) and (6) of that Act apply for the purposes of this paragraph as they apply for the purposes of that section.

(4) A company does not meet the requirements of this paragraph if it is a parent company of a group of companies which does not qualify as a small group or a medium-sized group in relation to the financial year of the company which ended last before the date of filing.

(5) For the purposes of sub-paragraph (4)—

    (a)   'group' has the same meaning as in Part 15 of the Companies Act 2006 (see section 474(1) of that Act); and

    (b)   a group qualifies as small in relation to a financial year if it so qualifies under section 383(2) to (7) of that Act, and qualifies as medium-sized in relation to a financial year if it so qualifies under section 466(2) to (7) of that Act.

(6) Expressions used in this paragraph that are defined expressions in Part 15 of the Companies Act 2006 (accounts and reports) have the same meaning in this paragraph as in that Part.

Amendments—SI 2008/948; SI 2009/1941.

'eligible company'—Subject to para 2(1), a company is a 'small' company if it meets two or more of the requirements specified in s 382(3) of the Companies Act 2006 namely (a) the company has an annual turnover of not more than £6.5 million; and/or (b) the company has a 'balance sheet total' which is less than £3.26 million; and/or (c) the company has less than 50 employees.

For the purposes of para 3(2)(b) Companies Act 2006, s 390 provides that a company's financial year is determined by reference to its accounting reference period. Section 382(4),(5) and (6), which are expressly invoked by para 3(3), provide that a proportionate adjustment should be made to the value of turnover and/or a company's balance sheet for the purpose of ascertaining whether or not the company qualifies as a 'small' company where the company's accounting reference period is less than one year.

A small company is not an eligible company if it falls within paras 2(2) or 4(1). A small company is also excluded from being an eligible company if it falls within the scope of paras 4A to 4J which apply to companies which are parties to an agreement which is or forms part of a capital market arrangement, public-private partnership project companies, a company which has a liability under an agreement for £10 million or more or any partnership or other unincorporated group of persons falling within those categories.

Holding companies under para 3(4) and (5)—In addition to the exclusions in paras 2(2) and 4(1) a company is not an eligible company if it is a holding company of a group which does not qualify as a small group or a medium-sized group as defined. These provisions do not, however, exclude from eligibility a small company, for the purposes of para 3(2), which is the member of a group, subject to the exclusions identified under the previous heading.

4

(1) A company is excluded from being eligible for a moratorium if, on the date of filing—

   (a)   the company is in administration,

   (b)   the company is being wound up,

   (c)   there is an administrative receiver of the company,

   (d)   a voluntary arrangement has effect in relation to the company,

   (e)   there is a provisional liquidator of the company,

   (f)   a moratorium has been in force for the company at any time during the period of 12 months ending with the date of filing and—

      (i)   no voluntary arrangement had effect at the time at which the moratorium came to an end, or

      (ii)   a voluntary arrangement which had effect at any time in that period has come to an end prematurely,

   (fa)   an administrator appointed under paragraph 22 of Schedule B1 has held office in the period of 12 months ending with the date of filing, or

   (g)   a voluntary arrangement in relation to the company which had effect in pursuance of a proposal under section 1(3) has come to an end prematurely and, during the period of 12 months ending with the date of filing, an order under section 5(3)(a) has been made.

(2) Sub-paragraph (1)(b) does not apply to a company which, by reason of a winding-up order made after the date of filing, is treated as being wound up on that date.

General note—See paras 2 and 3 and the notes thereto.

4A Capital market arrangement

A company is also excluded from being eligible for a moratorium if, on the date of filing, it is a party to an agreement which is or forms part of a capital market arrangement under which—

    (i)   a party has incurred, or when the agreement was entered into was expected to incur, a debt of at least £10 million under the arrangement, and

    (ii)   the arrangement involves the issue of a capital market investment.

General note—Paragraph 4A should be read in conjunction with para 1 (which incorporates technical definitions found in Part VII of the Companies Act 1989, the Financial Markets and Insolvency (Money Market) Regulations 1995, the Financial Markets and Insolvency (Settlement Finality) Regulations 1999, and the Financial Markets and Insolvency Regulations 1996), and paras 4D and 4E (which provide further definitions). These provisions were introduced by the Insolvency Act 1986 (Amendment) (No 3) Regulations 2002 (SI 2002/1990).

    The exclusion of companies operating within the capital markets from mainstream insolvency procedures is not unusual and, in common with banks and insurance companies (on which see para 2(2)), is explained by reference to the specialist insolvency procedures provided for in regulations which cater for the idiosyncratic nature of such companies and their business and which, broadly speaking, seek to protect the interests of participants therein.

4B Public private partnership

A company is also excluded from being eligible for a moratorium if, on the date of filing, it is a project company of a project which—

    (i)   is a public-private partnership project, and
    (ii)   includes step-in rights.

4C Liability under an arrangement

(1) A company is also excluded from being eligible for a moratorium if, on the date of filing, it has incurred a liability under an agreement of £10 million or more.

(2) Where the liability in sub-paragraph (1) is a contingent liability under or by virtue of a guarantee or an indemnity or security provided on behalf of another person, the amount of that liability is the full amount of the liability in relation to which the guarantee, indemnity or security is provided.

(3) In this paragraph—

    (a)   the reference to 'liability' includes a present or future liability whether, in either case, it is certain or contingent,
    (b)   the reference to 'liability' includes a reference to a liability to be paid wholly or partly in foreign currency (in which case the sterling equivalent shall be calculated as at the time when the liability is incurred).

4D Interpretation of capital market arrangement

(1) For the purposes of paragraph 4A an arrangement is a capital market arrangement if—

(a) it involves a grant of security to a person holding it as trustee for a person who holds a capital market investment issued by a party to the arrangement, or

(b) at least one party guarantees the performance of obligations of another party, or

(c) at least one party provides security in respect of the performance of obligations of another party, or

(d) the arrangement involves an investment of a kind described in articles 83 to 85 of the Financial Services and Markets Act 2000 (Regulated Activities) Order 2001 (SI 2001/544) (options, futures and contracts for differences).

(2) For the purposes of sub-paragraph (1)—

(a) a reference to holding as trustee includes a reference to holding as nominee or agent,

(b) a reference to holding for a person who holds a capital market investment includes a reference to holding for a number of persons at least one of whom holds a capital market investment, and

(c) a person holds a capital market investment if he has a legal or beneficial interest in it.

(3) In paragraph 4A, 4C, 4J and this paragraph—

'agreement' includes an agreement or undertaking effected by—

(a) contract,

(b) deed, or

(c) any other instrument intended to have effect in accordance with the law of England and Wales, Scotland or another jurisdiction, and

'party' to an arrangement includes a party to an agreement which—

(a) forms part of the arrangement,

(b) provides for the raising of finance as part of the arrangement, or

(c) is necessary for the purposes of implementing the arrangement.

4E Capital market investment

(1) For the purposes of paragraphs 4A and 4D, an investment is a capital market investment if—

(a) it is within article 77 or 77A of the Financial Services and Markets Act 2000 (Regulated Activities) Order 2001 (SI 2001/544) (debt instruments) and

(b) it is rated, listed or traded or designed to be rated, listed or traded.

(2) In sub-paragraph (1)—

'listed' means admitted to the official list within the meaning given by section 103(1) of the Financial Services and Markets Act 2000 (interpretation), 'rated' means rated for the purposes of investment by an internationally recognised rating agency,

'traded' means admitted to trading on a market established under the rules of a recognised investment exchange or on a foreign market.

(3) In sub-paragraph (2)—

'foreign market' has the same meaning as 'relevant market' in article 67(2) of the Financial Services and Markets Act 2000 (Financial Promotion) Order 2001 (SI 2001/1335) (foreign markets),

'recognised investment exchange' has the meaning given by section 285 of the Financial Services and Markets Act 2000 (recognised investment exchange).

Amendments—SI 2010/86.

4F

(1) For the purposes of paragraphs 4A and 4D an investment is also a capital market investment if it consists of a bond or commercial paper issued to one or more of the following—

(a)   an investment professional within the meaning of article 19(5) of the Financial Services and Markets Act 2000 (Financial Promotion) Order 2001,

(b)   a person who is, when the agreement mentioned in paragraph 4A is entered into, a certified high net worth individual in relation to a communication within the meaning of article 48(2) of that order,

(c)   a person to whom article 49(2) of that order applies (high net worth company, etc),

(d)   a person who is, when the agreement mentioned in paragraph 4A is entered into, a certified sophisticated investor in relation to a communication within the meaning of article 50(1) of that order, and

(e)   a person in a State other than the United Kingdom who under the law of that State is not prohibited from investing in bonds or commercial paper.

(2) For the purposes of sub-paragraph (1)—

(a)   in applying article 19(5) of the Financial Services and Markets Act 2000 (Financial Promotion) Order 2001 for the purposes of sub-paragraph (1)(a)—
(i)   in article 19(5)(b), ignore the words after 'exempt person',
(ii)   in article 19(5)(c)(i), for the words from 'the controlled activity' to the end substitute 'a controlled activity', and
(iii)   in article 19(5)(e) ignore the words from 'where the communication' to the end, and

(b)   in applying article 49(2) of that order for the purposes of sub-paragraph (1)(c), ignore article 49(2)(e).

(3) In sub-paragraph (1)—

'bond' shall be construed in accordance with article 77 of the Financial Services and Markets Act 2000 (Regulated Activities) Order 2001 (SI 2001/544), and includes any instrument falling within article 77A of that Order, and

'commercial paper' has the meaning given by article 9(3) of that order.

Amendments—SI 2010/86.

4G Debt

The debt of at least £10 million referred to in paragraph 4A—

(a) may be incurred at any time during the life of the capital market arrangement, and

(b) may be expressed wholly or partly in a foreign currency (in which case the sterling equivalent shall be calculated as at the time when the arrangement is entered into).

4H Interpretation of project company

(1) For the purposes of paragraph 4B a company is a 'project company' of a project if—

(a) it holds property for the purpose of the project,

(b) it has sole or principal responsibility under an agreement for carrying out all or part of the project,

(c) it is one of a number of companies which together carry out the project,

(d) it has the purpose of supplying finance to enable the project to be carried out, or

(e) it is the holding company of a company within any of paragraphs (a) to (d).

(2) But a company is not a 'project company' of a project if—

(a) it performs a function within sub-paragraph (1)(a) to (d) or is within sub-paragraph (1)(e), but

(b) it also performs a function which is not—

(i) within sub-paragraph (1)(a) to (d),

(ii) related to a function within sub-paragraph (1)(a) to (d), or

(iii) related to the project.

(3) For the purposes of this paragraph a company carries out all or part of a project whether or not it acts wholly or partly through agents.

4I Public-private partnership project

(1) In paragraph 4B 'public-private partnership project' means a project—

(a) the resources for which are provided partly by one or more public bodies and partly by one or more private persons, or

(b) which is designed wholly or mainly for the purpose of assisting a public body to discharge a function.

(2) In sub-paragraph (1) 'resources' includes—

    (a)   funds (including payment for the provision of services or facilities),

    (b)   assets,

    (c)   professional skill,

    (d)   the grant of a concession or franchise, and

    (e)   any other commercial resource.

(3) In sub-paragraph (1) 'public body' means—

    (a)   a body which exercises public functions,

    (b)   a body specified for the purposes of this paragraph by the Secretary of State, and

    (c)   a body within a class specified for the purposes of this paragraph by the Secretary of State.

(4) A specification under sub-paragraph (3) may be—

    (a)   general, or

    (b)   for the purpose of the application of paragraph 4B to a specified case.

4J Step-in rights

(1) For the purposes of paragraph 4B a project has 'step-in rights' if a person who provides finance in connection with the project has a conditional entitlement under an agreement to—

    (i)   assume sole or principal responsibility under an agreement for carrying out all or part of the project, or

    (ii)   make arrangements for carrying out all or part of the project.

(2) In sub-paragraph (1) a reference to the provision of finance includes a reference to the provision of an indemnity.

4K 'Person'

For the purposes of paragraphs 4A to 4J, a reference to a person includes a reference to a partnership or another unincorporated group of persons.

5

The Secretary of State may by regulations modify the qualifications for eligibility of a company for a moratorium.

Amendments—Inserted by Insolvency Act 2000, s 1, Sch 1, paras 1, 4. Amended by Enterprise Act 2002, s 248(3), Sch 17, paras 9, 37(1), (2); SI 2002/1555; SI 2002/1990.

General note—See the introductory notes to Sch A1.

PART II
OBTAINING A MORATORIUM

6 Nominee's statement

(1) Where the directors of a company wish to obtain a moratorium, they shall submit to the nominee—

  (a)   a document setting out the terms of the proposed voluntary arrangement,

  (b)   a statement of the company's affairs containing—

    (i)   such particulars of its creditors and of its debts and other liabilities and of its assets as may be prescribed, and

    (ii)   such other information as may be prescribed, and

  (c)   any other information necessary to enable the nominee to comply with sub-paragraph (2) which he requests from them.

(2) The nominee shall submit to the directors a statement in the prescribed form indicating whether or not, in his opinion—

  (a)   the proposed voluntary arrangement has a reasonable prospect of being approved and implemented,

  (b)   the company is likely to have sufficient funds available to it during the proposed moratorium to enable it to carry on its business, and

  (c)   meetings of the company and its creditors should be summoned to consider the proposed voluntary arrangement.

(3) In forming his opinion on the matters mentioned in sub-paragraph (2), the nominee is entitled to rely on the information submitted to him under sub-paragraph (1) unless he has reason to doubt its accuracy.

(4) The reference in sub-paragraph (2)(b) to the company's business is to that business as the company proposes to carry it on during the moratorium.

General note—The requirement for the submission of documents by the directors to the nominee and the response by the nominee of a statement in the prescribed form, which is submitted to the directors and subsequently filed with the court in obtaining a CVA moratorium, is new and has no equivalent provision in the non-moratorium CVA procedure.

The expression of opinion by and the obligations of the nominee—The requirement for a nominee's statement under para 6(2) is intended as a means of avoiding abuse of the moratorium procedure in that the nominee is required not only to express a view as to whether the proposed voluntary arrangement has a real prospect of being approved and implemented (ie the proposal is serious and viable), as applies also to the nominee's report to court in a non-moratorium case under s 2(2), but also to consider whether the company is likely to have sufficient funds during the proposed moratorium to enable it to carry on its business. The additional reporting requirement imposed on the nominee by s 6(2) is not unduly burdensome or disproportionate, given the practical consequences of the moratorium for third parties; furthermore, the expression of opinion as to whether the arrangement is serious and viable, for the purposes of para 6(2)(a), will in any case have required some regard to have been had by the nominee to the question of funding, since the expression of opinion under para 6(2) is concerned not only with approval of the arrangement but also its implementation.

Note should also be made here of the new provision in para 24 which should be read in conjunction with para 6 and which imposes a more onerous burden on the nominee to the extent that the nominee is required to monitor the company's affairs on an ongoing basis for the specific purposes identified in para 24(1)(a) and (b).

Paragraph 6(1)(b)

Scope of provision—For certification of the statement see r 1.37(4).

Paragraph 6(1)(c)

Scope of provision—This provision equates to r 1.6 in a non-moratorium case.

Paragraph 6(2)

Scope of provision—In substance, this provision equates to the nominee's reporting obligations to the court in a non-moratorium case under s 2(2)(a) and (aa). For guidance see the notes to those provisions.

In the formation of his opinion for the purposes of para 6(2) the nominee will wish to consider the particular facts of any case, but in particular, and perhaps most obviously, the risk of excessively optimistic trading forecasts or reliance on unsubstantiated funding proposals on the part of directors anxious to secure a voluntary arrangement under the protection of a moratorium.

In addition to the expression of opinion under para 6(2)(a), the requirement for the nominee's expression of opinion under para 6(2)(b) is, in context, not unduly onerous. In some cases the expression of opinion will involve the nominee making further enquiries of the directors as to funding arrangements before expressing his opinion. Paragraph 6(1)(c) provides a mechanism by which the nominee may request such information. In practice it is suggested that the nominee should consider couching any such request in terms which explain to the directors the reasons for his making further enquiries of them and the potential consequences of his expressing a negative view as to the approval or implementation of the proposal, or the funding of the arrangement, or his having doubts as to the accuracy of any information provided to him further to his request (on which see the notes to para 6(3) below).

The nominee is under an ongoing obligation to monitor the company's activities as regards the seriousness and viability of a proposed arrangement and the sufficiency of funding, just as the directors are under an ongoing obligation to provide the nominee with any information necessary to form a view on such matters: see para 24(1) and (2). If the nominee subsequently forms a negative opinion as to either of these matters, then he is obliged to withdraw his consent to act, consequent upon which the moratorium comes to an end: see para 25(2)(a) and 25(4).

The consequences of the nominee expressing a negative opinion—If the nominee's statement is negative as to any of the matters in para 6(2)(a)–(c), then the directors will be unable to obtain a moratorium by filing those documents mentioned in para 7(1).

Amendment of the proposal—Rule 1.35 provides that the directors may amend the proposal, apparently without limitation, at any time prior to the nominee issuing his statement under para 6(2).

Paragraph 6(3)

Scope of provision—The entitlement of the nominee under para 6(3) to rely on information submitted to him by the directors under para 6(1), other than where he has reasonable grounds to doubt the accuracy of that information, amounts, it is submitted, to a statutory rule which equates to the position of the nominee in non-moratorium cases as expressed by Lindsay J in *Greystoke v Hamilton-Smith* [1997] BPIR 24 at 28B–29A, on which see the notes to s 2(2).

The nominee's entitlement to act on the basis of information supplied to him by the directors is ongoing for the purposes of monitoring the company's activities and the formation of an opinion on an ongoing basis as to the seriousness and viability of the proposal and the sufficiency of funding under para 24(1): see para 24(3).

Paragraph 6(4)

Scope of provision—The nominee is only required to consider the sufficiency of funding available during the proposed moratorium to enable the company to carry on that business which the company proposes to carry on during the moratorium, and not any other business.

7 Documents to be submitted to court

(1) To obtain a moratorium the directors of a company must file (in Scotland, lodge) with the court—

(a)   a document setting out the terms of the proposed voluntary arrangement,

(b)   a statement of the company's affairs containing—

     (i)   such particulars of its creditors and of its debts and other liabilities and of its assets as may be prescribed, and

     (ii)   such other information as may be prescribed,

(c)   a statement that the company is eligible for a moratorium,

(d)   a statement from the nominee that he has given his consent to act, and

(e)   a statement from the nominee that, in his opinion—

     (i)   the proposed voluntary arrangement has a reasonable prospect of being approved and implemented,

     (ii)   the company is likely to have sufficient funds available to it during the proposed moratorium to enable it to carry on its business, and

     (iii)   meetings of the company and its creditors should be summoned to consider the proposed voluntary arrangement.

(2) Each of the statements mentioned in sub-paragraph (1)(b) to (e), except so far as it contains the particulars referred to in paragraph (b)(i), must be in the prescribed form.

(3) The reference in sub-paragraph (1)(e)(ii) to the company's business is to that business as the company proposes to carry it on during the moratorium.

(4) The Secretary of State may by regulations modify the requirements of this paragraph as to the documents required to be filed (in Scotland, lodged) with the court in order to obtain a moratorium.

General note—Paragraph 7(2) requires the document submitted to the court to be in the prescribed form. No regulations have been implemented modifying the requirements as to those documents.

On the statement from the nominee under para 7(1)(e) see para 6(2) and the notes to para 6 above.

8 Duration of moratorium

(1) A moratorium comes into force when the documents for the time being referred to in paragraph 7(1) are filed or lodged with the court and references in this Schedule to 'the beginning of the moratorium' shall be construed accordingly.

(2) A moratorium ends at the end of the day on which the meetings summoned under paragraph 29(1) are first held (or, if the meetings are held on different days, the later of those days), unless it is extended under paragraph 32.

(3) If either of those meetings has not first met before the end of the period of 28 days beginning with the day on which the moratorium comes into force, the moratorium ends at the end of the day on which those meetings were to be held (or, if those meetings were summoned to be held on different days, the later of those days), unless it is extended under paragraph 32.

(4) If the nominee fails to summon either meeting within the period required by paragraph 29(1), the moratorium ends at the end of the last day of that period.

(5) If the moratorium is extended (or further extended) under paragraph 32, it ends at the end of the day to which it is extended (or further extended).

(6) Sub-paragraphs (2) to (5) do not apply if the moratorium comes to an end before the time concerned by virtue of—

(a) paragraph 25(4) (effect of withdrawal by nominee of consent to act),
(b) an order under paragraph 26(3), 27(3) or 40 (challenge of actions of nominee or directors), or
(c) a decision of one or both of the meetings summoned under paragraph 29.

(7) If the moratorium has not previously come to an end in accordance with sub-paragraphs (2) to (6), it ends at the end of the day on which a decision under paragraph 31 to approve a voluntary arrangement takes effect under paragraph 36.

(8) The Secretary of State may by order increase or reduce the period for the time being specified in sub-paragraph (3).

General note—For the effect of the moratorium see paras 12–19 and the notes thereto.

9 Notification of beginning of moratorium

(1) When a moratorium comes into force, the directors shall notify the nominee of that fact forthwith.

(2) If the directors without reasonable excuse fail to comply with sub-paragraph (1), each of them is liable to imprisonment or a fine, or both.

General note—Paragraphs 9 and 10 should be read together. Paragraph 9(1) expressly requires the directors to notify the nominee of the fact that the moratorium has come into force, being the time at which the documents prescribed by para 7(1) are lodged with the court: see para 8(1). Although para 9(2) carries with it criminal sanctions on the directors failing without reasonable excuse to comply with para 9(1), the obligation on the nominee to advertise and give notice of the moratorium coming into force under para 10(1) is triggered not by notice being given to him by the directors but, it seems, the fact of the moratorium itself coming into force. In practice, a nominee will almost always be aware of the moratorium coming into force, not least because the nominee, his firm or his solicitors will commonly take responsibility for the filing of the prescribed documents with the court.

10

(1) When a moratorium comes into force, the nominee shall, in accordance with the rules—

(a) advertise that fact forthwith, and
(b) notify the registrar of companies, the company and any petitioning creditor of the company of whose claim he is aware of that fact.

(2) In sub-paragraph (1)(b), 'petitioning creditor' means a creditor by whom a winding-up petition has been presented before the beginning of the moratorium, as long as the petition has not been dismissed or withdrawn.

(3) If the nominee without reasonable excuse fails to comply with sub-paragraph (1)(a) or (b), he is liable to a fine.

General note—See the general note to para 9 above. Failure to comply without reasonable excuse again carries criminal sanctions restricted, for no obvious reason when compared to para 9(2), to a fine.

'petitioning creditor' in para 10(2)—Literally construed, the definition of the term 'petitioning creditor' would not catch a substituted creditor by whom a winding-up petition had not been presented but who retained carriage of the petition at the time for notification by the nominee under para 10(1). Practically speaking, this is unhelpful since the original petitioning creditor for whom substitution has been made will very rarely have any real interest in the continuing conduct of the petition. It is suggested that the best course for a nominee, notwithstanding the restricted definition of 'petitioning creditor', is to give notice not only to the original petitioning creditor but also to any substituted petitioner and any supporting creditors of whom the nominee is aware.

The above suggestion can be reconciled with the purpose of giving notice of the moratorium to third parties. Since the general effect of the moratorium is to prevent action being commenced or continued against a company or its property, the purpose of the notice provision in para 10(1)(b) must be to ensure that third parties (most obviously a creditor petitioning for winding up) are made aware of the fact of the moratorium so as to avoid any inadvertent breach of the statutory protection thereby provided. In those circumstances it is difficult to see why notice should be restricted to a petitioning creditor (as defined), just as it is difficult to see why notice should not also be given to any sheriff or other officer charged with an execution or other legal process against the company or its property, or any person who has distrained against the company or its property – as required under r 2.7 in administration cases – so as to avoid an inadvertent breach of the moratorium.

11 Notification of end of moratorium

(1) When a moratorium comes to an end, the nominee shall, in accordance with the rules—

(a) advertise that fact forthwith, and
(b) notify the court, the registrar of companies, the company and any creditor of the company of whose claim he is aware of that fact.

(2) If the nominee without reasonable excuse fails to comply with sub-paragraph (1)(a) or (b), he is liable to a fine.

Amendments—Inserted by the Insolvency Act 2000, s 1, Sch 1, paras 1, 4.

General note—See the general note to para 9 above. Failure to comply without reasonable excuse again carries criminal sanctions restricted to a fine.

A moratorium may come to an end in the circumstances envisaged in para 8(2) and (5) on the withdrawal by a nominee of his consent to act under para 25(4), on the making of an order by the court on the challenge of the actions of the nominee or the directors under paras 26(3), 27(3) and 40, or on a decision to that effect by either one or both meetings of the company and its creditors to consider the proposal under para 29.

PART III
EFFECTS OF MORATORIUM

12 Effect on creditors, etc

(1) During the period for which a moratorium is in force for a company—

(a) no petition may be presented for the winding up of the company,

(b) no meeting of the company may be called or requisitioned except with the consent of the nominee or the leave of the court and subject (where the court gives leave) to such terms as the court may impose,

(c) no resolution may be passed or order made for the winding up of the company,

(d) no administration application may be made in respect of the company,

(da) no administrator of the company may be appointed under paragraph 14 or 22 of Schedule B1,

(e) no administrative receiver of the company may be appointed,

(f) no landlord or other person to whom rent is payable may exercise any right of forfeiture by peaceable re-entry in relation to premises let to the company in respect of a failure by the company to comply with any term or condition of its tenancy of such premises, except with the leave of the court and subject to such terms as the court may impose,

(g) no other steps may be taken to enforce any security over the company's property, or to repossess goods in the company's possession under any hire-purchase agreement, except with the leave of the court and subject to such terms as the court may impose, and

(h) no other proceedings and no execution or other legal process may be commenced or continued, and no distress may be levied, against the company or its property except with the leave of the court and subject to such terms as the court may impose.

(2) Where a petition, other than an excepted petition, for the winding up of the company has been presented before the beginning of the moratorium, section 127 shall not apply in relation to any disposition of property, transfer of shares or alteration in status made during the moratorium or at a time mentioned in paragraph 37(5)(a).

(3) In the application of sub-paragraph (1)(h) to Scotland, the reference to execution being commenced or continued includes a reference to diligence being carried out or continued, and the reference to distress being levied is omitted.

(4) Paragraph (a) of sub-paragraph (1) does not apply to an excepted petition and, where such a petition has been presented before the beginning of the moratorium or is presented during the moratorium, paragraphs (b) and (c) of that sub-paragraph do not apply in relation to proceedings on the petition.

(5) For the purposes of this paragraph, 'excepted petition' means a petition under—

(a) section 124A or 124B of this Act,
(b) section 72 of the Financial Services Act 1986 on the ground mentioned in subsection (1)(b) of that section, or
(c) section 92 of the Banking Act 1987 on the ground mentioned in subsection (1)(b) of that section.
(d) section 367 of the Financial Services and Markets Act 2000 on the ground mentioned in subsection (3)(b) of that section.

General note—These provisions provide stout protection against action by third parties against the company or its property. In addition to the commentary in paras 40–43 of Sch B1, which provides guidance on the analogous moratorium provisions in administration, the following matters are of particular note.

Paragraph 12(1)(a)

Winding-up petitions—Under para 12(1)(a) no winding-up petition may be presented against the company whilst the moratorium is in force, in default of which any such petition will amount to an abuse of process and should be dismissed as such with an appropriate order for costs; the moratorium does not, however, stand as a bar to certain public interest winding-up petitions – each defined as an 'excepted' petition, as provided for in para 12(5).

The bar against the presentation of a winding-up petition overcomes the practical difficulty illustrated by the decision of His Honour Judge Collyer QC, sitting as a High Court judge, in *Re Piccadilly Property Management Ltd* [1999] 2 BCLC 145 where, in refusing an appeal and an application for a review from the decision of the registrar below, the judge upheld the making of a winding-up order based on a petition presented by the Inland Revenue, notwithstanding the company's application for an adjournment and the support of at least three sympathetic and significant creditors who wished the company to be afforded a further opportunity to put in place proposals for a CVA.

The effect of the moratorium is to stay a winding-up petition extant at the beginning of the moratorium. The petitioner will, however, be bound by the arrangement under para 37(2) to the extent that the petitioner is entitled to notice of the meeting of creditors in respect of the petition debt under para 37(2). Section 127 is expressly disapplied in respect of dispositions during the moratorium or the 28-day period beginning with the day on which the reports of meetings of the company and members required by para 30(3) has been made to the court – on which see para 37(5)(a).

The approval of the CVA requires the dismissal of a winding-up petition presented before the beginning of the moratorium by virtue of para 37(4), save that the court 'shall not dismiss a petition' at any time before the expiration of the 28-day period beginning with the first day on which each of the reports required by para 30(3) has been made to the court, or at any time within which an application alleging unfair prejudice or material irregularity under para 38(1) may be brought or is pending.

Paragraph 12(1)(b)

Management of the company—Paragraph 12(1)(b) should be read in conjunction with paras 16–22, which restrict the management of the company during the moratorium.

Paragraph 12(1)(d), (da) and (e)

The enforcement of floating charges—Paragraph 12(1)(d), (da) and (e) prevents either the making of an administration application to the court or the appointment of an administrator by the holder of a floating charge, a company or its directors.

Appointment of an administrative receiver—An administrative receiver, as formerly defined in s 29(2) and as now defined in para 14 of Sch B1, may only be appointed under a floating charge extending to the whole or substantially the whole of a company's property which was created prior to 15 September 2003: see s 72A(1) and (3). The moratorium imposes a complete bar against such appointments; there is no saving provision which allows for the veto of a moratorium-backed CVA by the holder of a floating charge akin to the formerly operative s 9(3)(a), which allowed such a chargeholder to veto the making of an administration order, and s 10(2)(b), which allowed for the appointment of an administrative receiver notwithstanding a petition having been presented for an administration order.

Crystallisation of floating charges—See paras 13 and 43 and the notes thereto.

Paragraph 12(1)(f)

'No landlord or other person to whom rent is payable may exercise any right of forfeiture by peaceable re-entry ...'—Paragraph 12(1)(f) is in identical form to the formerly operative s 10(1)(aa) and s 11(3)(ba) in relation to the moratorium in administration, which now appears in a more basic form in para 43(4) of Sch B1. Those former provisions were introduced by way of a statutory reversal of the decision of Neuberger J (as he then was) in *Re Lomax Leisure Ltd* [1999] 3 WLR 652, which held, in following the decision of Lightman J in *Rozzaq v Pala* [1997] 1 WLR 1336, and in rejecting the view of Harman J in *Exchange Travel Agency v Triton* [1991] BCLC 396, that the prohibition on the enforcement of 'any security over the company's property' did not prevent a landlord's right of re-entry for non-payment of rent or other breach of a lease covenant. Notably, the nominee is not empowered to consent to peaceable re-entry, which may only be permitted with the permission of the court and subject to any terms imposed by it.

Paragraph 12(1)(g)

'No other steps may be taken to enforce any security over the company's property, or to any possessed goods in the company's possession under any hire-purchase agreement ...'—The wording in this provision very closely resembles that in para 43(2) and (3) of Sch B1 in relation to administrations. Guidance may be gleaned from the judicial analysis of the formerly operative ss 10 and 11, which were in virtually identical form, and which is incorporated into the commentary on para 43(2) and (3) of Sch B1.

Paragraph 13(5) specifically prohibits an application for leave with a view to obtaining the crystallisation of a floating charge or the imposition of any restriction conferred in the security instrument against the disposal of any property of the company. That bar is designed to prevent avoidance of the restrictions imposed by para 13(2)–(4).

Paragraph 12(1)(h)

'No other proceedings and no execution or other legal process may be commenced or continued, and no distress may be levied, against the company or its property ...'—Like para 12(1)(g) above, the wording of para 12(1)(h) closely resembles that in para 43(6) of Sch B1 in relation to administrations – on which see the notes thereto.

Paragraph 12(2)

The disapplication of s 127—See the note on winding-up petitions above.

'excepted petition'—The moratorium does not prevent the presentation of an 'excepted petition'. Neither does para 12(2) disapply the operation of s 127 on the presentation of such a petition. The term 'excepted petition' extends to winding-up petitions presented in the public interest under s 124A and s 367 of the Insolvency Act 2000 and petitions presented by way of assistance to an overseas regulatory authority or a banking or financial services regulator.

For the rules governing disposals and payments of company money during the moratorium see paras 18 and 19.

The granting of leave by the court under para 12(1)(b), (f), (g) and (h)—It is submitted that the guidelines identified by Nicholls LJ in *Re Atlantic Computer Systems plc* [1992] Ch 505 at 542–544 on the court's approach to the granting of leave in the context of the statutory moratorium under the formerly operative administration regime under Part II will apply equally to the present provisions. Those guidelines are set out in the notes to para 43 in Sch B1.

The continued availability of self-help remedies during the moratorium—As discussed in the introductory notes to administration under Sch B1, the moratorium in administration – and, by parity of reasoning, in the case of a moratorium-backed CVA under Sch A1 – does not prevent the exercise of self-help remedies. It follows that the moratorium will not prevent the automatic termination of a contract (provided that the contract accurately identifies the CVA as having such effect), any contractual or legal right to terminate or rescind a contract or to give notice under a contractual term, or the exercise of a right of set-off (ie contractual, legal or equitable) – but note the new automatic set-off provisions in administration under r 2.85 – or combination of accounts.

The operation of one specific type of 'self-terminating' contractual provision as a self-remedy is specifically curtailed by para 43, which renders void any provision in an instrument creating a floating charge which stipulates that the obtaining of a moratorium or anything done with a view to obtaining a moratorium (including any preliminary decision or investigation) is an event causing the floating charge to crystallise or, alternatively, is an event causing restrictions which would not otherwise apply to be imposed on the disposal of property by the company or, alternatively, is a ground for the appointment of a receiver within the meaning of para 43(2).

Supplies of gas, water, electricity etc—By virtue of s 233(2) a public utility supplier, as defined in s 233(3) – but not a private supplier – may not make the continued supply of a utility subject to a condition that any outstanding charges are paid, although the office-holder may be required to provide a personal guarantee in respect of future charges. Amendments introduced by s 1 and Sch 1 of the Insolvency Act 2000 brought into effect s 233(1)(ba) so as to bring the nominee or supervisor of a moratorium-backed CVA within the scope of s 233.

13

(1) This paragraph applies where there is an uncrystallised floating charge on the property of a company for which a moratorium is in force.

(2) If the conditions for the holder of the charge to give a notice having the effect mentioned in sub-paragraph (4) are met at any time, the notice may not be given at that time but may instead be given as soon as practicable after the moratorium has come to an end.

(3) If any other event occurs at any time which (apart from this sub-paragraph) would have the effect mentioned in sub-paragraph (4), then—

    (a)   the event shall not have the effect in question at that time, but

    (b)   if notice of the event is given to the company by the holder of the charge as soon as is practicable after the moratorium has come to an end, the event is to be treated as if it had occurred when the notice was given.

(4) The effect referred to in sub-paragraphs (2) and (3) is—

    (a)   causing the crystallisation of the floating charge, or

    (b)   causing the imposition, by virtue of provision in the instrument creating the charge, of any restriction on the disposal of any property of the company.

(5) Application may not be made for leave under paragraph 12(1)(g) or (h) with a view to obtaining—

    (a)   the crystallisation of the floating charge, or

    (b)   the imposition, by virtue of provision in the instrument creating the charge, of any restriction on the disposal of any property of the company.

General note—These provisions substantially intrude on what would otherwise be the rights of the holder of an uncrystallised floating charge.

The anti-crystallisation provisions in para 13(1)–(4)—These provisions provide what amounts to an extension to para 43, which renders void any provision in an instrument creating a floating charge which provides, first, that the obtaining of a moratorium, or anything done with a view to obtaining a moratorium, causes the automatic crystallisation of the floating charge or, secondly, brings about restrictions on the disposal of the company's property or, thirdly, provides a ground for the appointment of a receiver.

The provisions cater for two specific scenarios. First, para 13(2) prevents the holder of a floating charge from giving notice to the company so as to crystallise the charge where the conditions for the giving of such notice – which can only be a reference to conditions stipulated in the security instrument – 'are met at any time'. The effect of this provision is to suspend the time for the giving of such notice to a time 'as practicable after the moratorium has come to an end'. Secondly, para 13(3) addresses events of automatic crystallisation. The provision does not distinguish between automatic events provided for expressly in the security instrument and those events which, as is well settled on the authorities, will cause a floating charge to crystallise in any event, namely, as applicable here, either (a) a debenture holder taking possession of charged assets, or (b) the appointment of a receiver, or (c) the cessation of the company's business: see *Re Woodroffes (Musical Instruments) Ltd* [1986] Ch 366 (Nourse J, as he then was). Paragraph 13(3)(a) suspends the effect of any such crystallising event subject to para 13(3)(b) which introduces a requirement, exercisable at the option of the floating charge holder, that notice of the crystallising event may be given to the company as soon as practicable after the moratorium has come to an end, consequent upon which the crystallising event is treated as if it had occurred when the notice was given.

14

Security granted by a company at a time when a moratorium is in force in relation to the company may only be enforced if, at that time, there were reasonable grounds for believing that it would benefit the company.

General note—Nothing within the moratorium regime under para 12 prevents a company from granting security whilst a moratorium is in force. In practice, the creation of security over a company's assets in favour of a lender may be the only means by which the directors are able to obtain fresh or even continued funding for the purposes of the CVA. Such circumstances would almost certainly have to feature within the nominee's statement – specifically given para 6(2)(b) – unless, perhaps, where the source of funding originally relied upon was lost through unavoidable and unforeseeable circumstances.

Given that the granting of security is not prohibited by the moratorium, this provision can only operate as an added disincentive to lenders who in the ordinary course would usually require some persuading to lend to a company in financial difficulties evident from the existence of a CVA but who, under this provision, must also establish that there were reasonable grounds for believing that the creation of the security would benefit the company.

'security ... may only be enforced ...'—It appears from the wording employed here that the reference to the enforcement of security is not restricted to the period of the moratorium – for which the leave of the court would be required in any case under para 12(1)(g) – but extends beyond the end of the moratorium.

'... there were reasonable grounds for believing that it would benefit the company'—There is an ambiguity here as to whether the relevant belief is on the part of the company, acting by its directors, or on the part of the lender. It would seem unduly harsh on a lender prepared to advance monies on the strength of security to rely upon the belief of the company's directors as to the benefit conferred on the company. Far preferable, and far more workable, it is submitted, is the burden of proof resting on the lender itself. In those circumstances any lender taking security during a moratorium should ensure that the grounds for its belief as to the benefit served to the company on the creation of the security are clearly documented.

15 Effect on company

(1) Paragraphs 16 to 23 apply in relation to a company for which a moratorium is in force.

(2) The fact that a company enters into a transaction in contravention of any of paragraphs 16 to 22 does not—

    (a)   make the transaction void, or

    (b)   make it to any extent unenforceable against the company.

General note—These provisions impose criminal sanctions on the breach of provisions designed variously to protect third parties dealing with the company and the assets of the company during the moratorium. The imposition of such liability on the company and the directors reflects the fact that the directors remain in office during the course of the moratorium subject to the monitoring obligation imposed on the nominee by para 24.

The most obvious protection for third parties lies in the saving provision in para 15(2).

16 Company invoices, etc

(1) Every invoice, order for goods or services, business letter (whether in hard copy, electronic or any other form) issued by or on behalf of the company, and all the company's websites, must also contain the nominee's name and a statement that the moratorium is in force for the company.

(2) If default is made in complying with sub-paragraph (1), the company and (subject to sub-paragraph (3)) any officer of the company is liable to a fine.

(3) An officer of the company is only liable under sub-paragraph (2) if, without reasonable excuse, he authorises or permits the default.

Amendments—SI 2008/1897.

General note—The purpose of this provision is in providing parties with notice of the fact of the nominee's appointment and the fact of the moratorium being in force. Accordingly, the reference to 'business letter' should be construed very broadly and, it is submitted, will extend to every document bearing the company's name, so far as is reasonably practicable.

17 Obtaining credit during moratorium

(1) The company may not obtain credit to the extent of £250 or more from a person who has not been informed that a moratorium is in force in relation to the company.

(2) The reference to the company obtaining credit includes the following cases—

    (a) where goods are bailed (in Scotland, hired) to the company under a hire-purchase agreement, or agreed to be sold to the company under a conditional sale agreement, and

    (b) where the company is paid in advance (whether in money or otherwise) for the supply of goods or services.

(3) Where the company obtains credit in contravention of sub-paragraph (1)—

    (a) the company is liable to a fine, and

    (b) if any officer of the company knowingly and wilfully authorised or permitted the contravention, he is liable to imprisonment or a fine, or both.

(4) The money sum specified in sub-paragraph (1) is subject to increase or reduction by order under section 417A in Part XV.

General note—Two observations call to be made where a company proceeds to obtain credit. First, the figure here is minimal and will not apply to the majority of trade creditors. Secondly, if a person from whom credit is obtained is given notice of the fact that a moratorium is in force, the company is at liberty to obtain such unlimited credit as may be made available to it, subject to para 14 on the creation of any security. If a person has not been informed that a moratorium is in force, the company may not obtain credit to the extent of £250 or more.

18 Disposals and payments

(1) Subject to sub-paragraph (2), the company may only dispose of any of its property if—

    (a) there are reasonable grounds for believing that the disposal will benefit the company, and

    (b) the disposal is approved by the committee established under paragraph 35(1) or, where there is no such committee, by the nominee.

(2) Sub-paragraph (1) does not apply to a disposal made in the ordinary way of the company's business.

(3) If the company makes a disposal in contravention of sub-paragraph (1) otherwise than in pursuance of an order of the court—

    (a) the company is liable to a fine, and

    (b) if any officer of the company authorised or permitted the contravention, without reasonable excuse, he is liable to imprisonment or a fine, or both.

General note—In para 18 the term 'disposal' is used in contrast to the term 'payment' in para 19 which addresses only payments in respect of any debt or other liability of the company which is in existence before the beginning of the moratorium. The term 'disposal' in para 18, therefore, must be taken as referring to both disposals and payments by the company after the beginning of the moratorium.

Further restrictions on the entering of a company into market contracts and the like are imposed by para 23.

Disposals under para 18(1)—Paragraph 18(1) only addresses disposals which are not made in the ordinary way of the company's business. The reasonable grounds for the belief that the disposal will benefit the company, it is suggested, should equate to the standard of a director's duty of care, skill and diligence imposed by s 214(4), so as to set the threshold as that of a reasonably diligent person having the general knowledge, skill and experience that may reasonably be expected of any particular director carrying out his functions, together with any subjective knowledge, skill and experience possessed by any particular director: see *Re d'Jan of London Ltd* [1993] BCC 646 (Hoffmann LJ, as he then was, sitting as an additional judge of the Chancery Division). In practice, neither a creditors' committee nor the nominee should approve any disposal if the directors are unable to provide and substantiate an explanation as to the benefit to the company on the disposal being made.

Breach of s 18(1)—In contrast to the analogous scheme under s 127, any disposal in contravention of s 18(1) gives rise only to the sanctions in s 18(3). Paragraph 15(2) makes clear that any such disposal is neither void nor unenforceable against the company.

Disposals under para 18(2)—Paragraph 18(2) makes clear that nothing prevents a disposal made in the ordinary way of the company's business. Any payment, sale, transfer of assets etc in the ordinary course of business will not require any approval, although the nominee will wish to monitor the company's activities generally in discharging his obligation under para 24.

19

(1) Subject to sub-paragraph (2), the company may only make any payment in respect of any debt or other liability of the company in existence before the beginning of the moratorium if—

    (a)   there are reasonable grounds for believing that the payment will benefit the company, and

    (b)   the payment is approved by the committee established under paragraph 35(1) or, where there is no such committee, by the nominee.

(2) Sub-paragraph (1) does not apply to a payment required by paragraph 20(6).

(3) If the company makes a payment in contravention of sub-paragraph (1) otherwise than in pursuance of an order of the court—

    (a)   the company is liable to a fine, and

    (b)   if any officer of the company authorised or permitted the contravention, without reasonable excuse, he is liable to imprisonment or a fine, or both.

General note—These provisions in relation to the payment of any pre-moratorium debt or other liability closely resemble those in para 18, on which see the notes thereto.

Despite the protection of the moratorium, one obvious example of payments for the benefit of the company can arise where a supplier requires discharge of a pre-moratorium trading debt as a pre-condition of continued supply in circumstances where it is not reasonably practicable for the company to obtain such goods or services from an alternative supplier without the imposition of such a condition.

Further restrictions on the entering of a company into market contracts and the like are imposed by para 23.

20 Disposal of charged property, etc

(1) This paragraph applies where—

    (a)   any property of the company is subject to a security, or

    (b)   any goods are in the possession of the company under a hire-purchase agreement.

(2) If the holder of the security consents, or the court gives leave, the company may dispose of the property as if it were not subject to the security.

(3) If the owner of the goods consents, or the court gives leave, the company may dispose of the goods as if all rights of the owner under the hire-purchase agreement were vested in the company.

(4) Where property subject to a security which, as created, was a floating charge is disposed of under sub-paragraph (2), the holder of the security has the same priority in respect of any property of the company directly or indirectly representing the property disposed of as he would have had in respect of the property subject to the security.

(5) Sub-paragraph (6) applies to the disposal under sub-paragraph (2) or (as the case may be) sub-paragraph (3) of—

    (a)   any property subject to a security other than a security which, as created, was a floating charge, or

    (b)   any goods in the possession of the company under a hire-purchase agreement.

(6) It shall be a condition of any consent or leave under sub-paragraph (2) or (as the case may be) sub-paragraph (3) that—

    (a)   the net proceeds of the disposal, and

    (b)   where those proceeds are less than such amount as may be agreed, or determined by the court, to be the net amount which would be realised on a sale of the property or goods in the open market by a willing vendor, such sums as may be required to make good the deficiency,

shall be applied towards discharging the sums secured by the security or payable under the hire-purchase agreement.

(7) Where a condition imposed in pursuance of sub-paragraph (6) relates to two or more securities, that condition requires—

    (a)   the net proceeds of the disposal, and

    (b)   where paragraph (b) of sub-paragraph (6) applies, the sums mentioned in that paragraph,

to be applied towards discharging the sums secured by those securities in the order of their priorities.

(8) Where the court gives leave for a disposal under sub-paragraph (2) or (3), the directors shall, within 14 days after leave is given, send a copy of the order giving leave to the registrar of companies.

(9) If the directors without reasonable excuse fail to comply with sub-paragraph (8), they are liable to a fine.

Amendments—SI 2009/1941.

General note—These provisions allow the company to seek the leave of the court in disposing of property as if it were not subject to any fixed charge security or subject to the interest of the lessor under a hire-purchase agreement in the absence of the consent of a holder of security. Leave is unlikely to be granted as a matter of course. Instead, the court will need to be satisfied that any perceived prejudice to a holder of security will be outweighed by the benefit to the company of a sale, specifically in terms of furthering what is identified as the underlying purpose of the CVA for the benefit of creditors.

In terms of drafting, para 20 reads at first sight as similar to s 43, which allows an administrative receiver to make application to the court for leave to dispose of relevant property which is subject to prior ranking security, subject to the approval of the court. In substance, however, the two provisions are very different in that para 20 applies only to fixed charges and has no application to any charge which, as created, was a floating charge (including, therefore, a crystallised floating charge). Paragraph 20 is also very similar to para 71 of Sch B1, which allows an administrator to make application to court for leave to dispose of non-floating security assets. In contrast to the present provision, however, an administrator is specifically empowered by para 70(1) of Sch B1 to dispose of any floating charge asset as if it were not subject to that charge, without any requirement for an application to court. There is little justification, it is submitted, for effectively limiting the scope of a CVA by leaving out floating charge assets from the scope of an application to court under para 20.

Paragraph 13 prevents the improvement of the position of the holder of an uncrystallised floating charge which extends to the property of the company whilst a CVA moratorium is in force. The consequence of that position, somewhat ironically, is that the floating charge-holder will be protected from a para 20 application through the protection of para 13, without which a crystallised floating charge would constitute a fixed equitable charge and therefore be susceptible to a leave application in respect of the assets to which the security attached.

Paragraph 20 has no application to charges arising out of market contracts and the like: see para 23(5).

For the consequences of contravention of para 20, see para 22.

The court's approach to para 20(6)—See the notes to s 43 on the identical s 43(3).

Procedure—See r 1.43.

21

(1) Where property is disposed of under paragraph 20 in its application to Scotland, the company shall grant to the disponee an appropriate document of transfer or conveyance of the property, and—

    (a)   that document, or

    (b)   where any recording, intimation or registration of the document is a legal requirement for completion of title to the property, that recording, intimation or registration,

has the effect of disencumbering the property of, or (as the case may be) freeing the property from, the security.

(2) Where goods in the possession of the company under a hire-purchase agreement are disposed of under paragraph 20 in its application to Scotland, the disposal has the effect of extinguishing, as against the disponee, all rights of the owner of the goods under the agreement.

22

(1) If the company—

    (a)   without any consent or leave under paragraph 20, disposes of any of its property which is subject to a security otherwise than in accordance with the terms of the security,

    (b)   without any consent or leave under paragraph 20, disposes of any goods in the possession of the company under a hire-purchase agreement otherwise than in accordance with the terms of the agreement, or

    (c)   fails to comply with any requirement imposed by paragraph 20 or 21,

it is liable to a fine.

(2) If any officer of the company, without reasonable excuse, authorises or permits any such disposal or failure to comply, he is liable to imprisonment or a fine, or both.

23 Market contracts, etc

(1) If the company enters into any transaction to which this paragraph applies—

    (a)   the company is liable to a fine, and

    (b)   if any officer of the company, without reasonable excuse, authorised or permitted the company to enter into the transaction, he is liable to imprisonment or a fine, or both.

(2) A company enters into a transaction to which this paragraph applies if it—

    (a)   enters into a market contract,

    (b)   gives a transfer order,

    (c)   grants a market charge or a system-charge, or

    (d)   provides any collateral security.

(3) The fact that a company enters into a transaction in contravention of this paragraph does not—

    (a)   make the transaction void, or

    (b)   make it to any extent unenforceable by or against the company.

(4) Where during the moratorium a company enters into a transaction to which this paragraph applies, nothing done by or in pursuance of the transaction is to be treated as done in contravention of paragraphs 12(1)(g), 14 or 16 to 22.

(5) Paragraph 20 does not apply in relation to any property which is subject to a market charge, a system-charge or a collateral security charge.

(6) In this paragraph, 'transfer order', 'collateral security' and 'collateral security charge' have the same meanings as in the settlement finality regulations.

Amendments—Inserted by Insolvency Act 2000, s 1, Sch 1, paras 1, 4. Amended by Enterprise Act 2002, s 248(3), Sch 17, paras 9, 37(1), (3); SI 2002/1555; SI 2004/2326.

General note—Where a moratorium is in effect, the entry by the company into a market contract etc renders the company and its officers liable to those criminal sanctions in para 23(1). Any such contract, however, is not treated as being in contravention of the moratorium provisions by virtue of para 23(4).

PART IV
NOMINEES

24 Monitoring of company's activities

(1) During a moratorium, the nominee shall monitor the company's affairs for the purpose of forming an opinion as to whether—

(a)   the proposed voluntary arrangement or, if he has received notice of proposed modifications under paragraph 31(7), the proposed arrangement with those modifications has a reasonable prospect of being approved and implemented, and

(b)   the company is likely to have sufficient funds available to it during the remainder of the moratorium to enable it to continue to carry on its business.

(2) The directors shall submit to the nominee any information necessary to enable him to comply with sub-paragraph (1) which he requests from them.

(3) In forming his opinion on the matters mentioned in sub-paragraph (1), the nominee is entitled to rely on the information submitted to him under sub-paragraph (2) unless he has reason to doubt its accuracy.

(4) The reference in sub-paragraph (1)(b) to the company's business is to that business as the company proposes to carry it on during the remainder of the moratorium.

General note—Paragraph 24 should be read in conjunction with para 6. Paragraph 24, however, imposes a new obligation on the nominee as to the monitoring of the company's affairs which finds no analogy elsewhere in the voluntary arrangement provisions. The purpose underlying the provision demands that the grounds upon which the nominee's statement is made for the purposes of para 6 are maintained throughout the course of the moratorium, given the risk to creditors (in particular those who advance further credit to the company during the CVA) of the moratorium remaining in place where the voluntary arrangement has no real prospect of being implemented or is incapable of being sufficiently funded so as to enable the company to carry on its business.

Procedure—For guidance see the notes to para 6(2)–(4).

Paragraph 24(1)

Scope of provision—The consequence of the nominee forming a negative opinion as to either matter within this para 24(1) is the mandatory withdrawal of his consent to act under para 25(2), with the consequence that the moratorium comes to an end under para 25(4).

'... **the nominee shall monitor the company's affairs ...**'—Paragraph 24(1) places an obligation on the nominee to monitor the company's affairs for the purpose stated. The discharge of the nominee's function is facilitated by the specific power in para 24(2).

'... **for the purpose of forming an opinion as to whether ...**'—The nominee is not under an obligation to monitor the company's affairs generally. Rather, he is required to monitor the company's affairs so far as is necessary for the purpose of forming opinions as to para 24(1)(a) and (b).

'... **a reasonable prospect of being approved and implemented ...**'—The test applicable here is whether or not the approval and implementation of the proposal is serious and viable: see the notes to s 2(2).

Paragraph 24(2)

Scope of provision—A failure on the part of the directors to comply with their obligation under para 24(2) results in the mandatory withdrawal of the nominee's consent to act: see para 25(2)(c).

'**The directors shall submit to the nominee any information ... which he requests from them**'—The obligation to supply information to the nominee is dependent upon a request being made for such information, and can operate only so far as such information is necessary to enable the nominee to comply with para 24(1) (see below). Paragraph 24(2), therefore, imposes a burden squarely on the nominee in the obtaining of information.

It is suggested that, subject to the need to raise more specific enquiries of the directors as circumstances and the information already disclosed dictate, there is no good reason in practice why a nominee should not discharge his obligation under this para 24(2) by the raising of a request for the disclosure of specific information on a periodic basis, say weekly or monthly, subject to the particular requirements of any case and the need for the nominee to act on that information. In practice, the nominee will also wish to ensure that the directors are fully aware of the purpose for which such information is requested by him, particularly given para 24(3).

'... **any information necessary to enable him to comply with sub-paragraph (1) ...**'—In practice, the information sought by a nominee is likely to include management accounts, trading reports and the like, together with the directors' comments on the same. Given para 24(3), and the fact of the obligation to request information resting on the nominee, the nominee should be concerned to ensure that he is provided with, and understands, the basis or source of the information supplied to him.

Paragraph 24(3)

Scope of provision—See the note to the identical para 6(3).

Paragraph 24(4)

Scope of provision—See the note to the virtually identical para 6(4).

25 Withdrawal of consent to act

(1) The nominee may only withdraw his consent to act in the circumstances mentioned in this paragraph.

(2) The nominee must withdraw his consent to act if, at any time during a moratorium—

> (a)　he forms the opinion that—
>> (i)　the proposed voluntary arrangement or, if he has received notice of proposed modifications under paragraph 31(7),

the proposed arrangement with those modifications no longer has a reasonable prospect of being approved or implemented, or
  (ii) the company will not have sufficient funds available to it during the remainder of the moratorium to enable it to continue to carry on its business,

  (b) he becomes aware that, on the date of filing, the company was not eligible for a moratorium, or

  (c) the directors fail to comply with their duty under paragraph 24(2).

(3) The reference in sub-paragraph (2)(a)(ii) to the company's business is to that business as the company proposes to carry it on during the remainder of the moratorium.

(4) If the nominee withdraws his consent to act, the moratorium comes to an end.

(5) If the nominee withdraws his consent to act he must, in accordance with the rules, notify the court, the registrar of companies, the company and any creditor of the company of whose claim he is aware of his withdrawal and the reason for it.

(6) If the nominee without reasonable excuse fails to comply with sub-paragraph (5), he is liable to a fine.

Paragraph 25(1)

Scope of provision—The only circumstances in which the nominee may withdraw his consent to act are those set out in para 25(2). The nominee may also be replaced by order of the court, on the application of the directors or the nominee, under para 28(1).

Paragraph 25(2)

Scope of provision—See the notes to para 24(1) and (2).
For the eligibility of a company for a moratorium see paras 2 and 3.
In respect of para 25(2)(b) see paras 4, 5 and 45.

Paragraph 25(3)

Scope of provision—See the notes to the virtually identical para 6(4).

Paragraph 25(4)

Scope of provision—The nominee must be careful that the withdrawal of his consent to act is given timeously. If the nominee makes a decision not to withdraw his consent, but anticipates opposition to his decision by one or more creditors, then he should be careful to document the reasons for his decision.
It is conceivable that a nominee may face action under paras 26 and/or 27 if he acts improperly in withdrawing his consent to act prematurely or, alternatively, if he fails to withdraw his consent in circumstances where such conduct is unreasonable.

Paragraph 25(5)

Procedure—The reference here to 'the rules' is to r 1.44.

Paragraph 25(6)

Scope of provision—The criminal sanction imposed here is for non-compliance with the procedural requirements under para 25(5), and not for a failure to withdraw consent to act.

26 Challenge of nominee's actions, etc

(1) If any creditor, director or member of the company, or any other person affected by a moratorium, is dissatisfied by any act, omission or decision of the nominee during the moratorium, he may apply to the court.

(2) An application under sub-paragraph (1) may be made during the moratorium or after it has ended.

(3) On an application under sub-paragraph (1) the court may—

  (a)   confirm, reverse or modify any act or decision of the nominee,
  (b)   give him directions, or
  (c)   make such other order as it thinks fit.

(4) An order under sub-paragraph (3) may (among other things) bring the moratorium to an end and make such consequential provision as the court thinks fit.

Procedure—See the notes to r 1.47.

27

(1) Where there are reasonable grounds for believing that—

  (a)   as a result of any act, omission or decision of the nominee during the moratorium, the company has suffered loss, but
  (b)   the company does not intend to pursue any claim it may have against the nominee,

any creditor of the company may apply to the court.

(2) An application under sub-paragraph (1) may be made during the moratorium or after it has ended.

(3) On an application under sub-paragraph (1) the court may—

  (a)   order the company to pursue any claim against the nominee,
  (b)   authorise any creditor to pursue such a claim in the name of the company, or
  (c)   make such other order with respect to such a claim as it thinks fit,

unless the court is satisfied that the act, omission or decision of the nominee was in all the circumstances reasonable.

(4) An order under sub-paragraph (3) may (among other things)—

  (a)   impose conditions on any authority given to pursue a claim,
  (b)   direct the company to assist in the pursuit of a claim,
  (c)   make directions with respect to the distribution of anything received as a result of the pursuit of a claim,

(d)   bring the moratorium to an end and make such consequential provision as the court thinks fit.

(5) On an application under sub-paragraph (1) the court shall have regard to the interests of the members and creditors of the company generally.

Procedure—See the notes to r 1.47.

28 Replacement of nominee by court

(1) The court may—

(a)   on an application made by the directors in a case where the nominee has failed to comply with any duty imposed on him under this Schedule or has died, or

(b)   on an application made by the directors or the nominee in a case where it is impracticable or inappropriate for the nominee to continue to act as such,

direct that the nominee be replaced as such by another person qualified to act as an insolvency practitioner, or authorised to act as nominee, in relation to the voluntary arrangement.

(2) A person may only be appointed as a replacement nominee under this paragraph if he submits to the court a statement indicating his consent to act.

Amendments—Inserted by the Insolvency Act 2000, s 1, Sch 1, paras 1, 4.

General note—These provisions very much follow the form of s 2(4) with variations which are self-explanatory. The reference to 'any duty imposed on him under this Schedule' in para 28(1)(a) is most obviously a reference to those obligations under paras 6(2) and 24(1). For further guidance see the notes to s 2(4).

PART V
CONSIDERATION AND IMPLEMENTATION OF VOLUNTARY ARRANGEMENT

29 Summoning of meetings

(1) Where a moratorium is in force, the nominee shall summon meetings of the company and its creditors for such a time, date (within the period for the time being specified in paragraph 8(3)) and place as he thinks fit.

(2) The persons to be summoned to a creditors' meeting under this paragraph are every creditor of the company of whose claim the nominee is aware.

General note—For the summoning of meetings see r 1.48.
  The summoning of meetings is relevant to the duration of the moratorium, which ends at the end of the day on which the meetings summoned under para 29(1) are first held (or the later of those days if held on different days), subject to the moratorium being extended for a maximum period of two months as provided for in para 32(2).

30 Conduct of meetings

(1) Subject to the provisions of paragraphs 31 to 35, the meetings summoned under paragraph 29 shall be conducted in accordance with the rules.

(2) A meeting so summoned may resolve that it be adjourned (or further adjourned).

(3) After the conclusion of either meeting in accordance with the rules, the chairman of the meeting shall report the result of the meeting to the court, and, immediately after reporting to the court, shall give notice of the result of the meeting to such persons as may be prescribed.

General note—For the conduct of meetings, the admission of creditors' claims for voting purposes, voting rights and requisite majorities see rr 1.49–1.53.

31 Approval of voluntary arrangement

(1) The meetings summoned under paragraph 29 shall decide whether to approve the proposed voluntary arrangement (with or without modifications).

(2) The modifications may include one conferring the functions proposed to be conferred on the nominee on another person qualified to act as an insolvency practitioner, or authorised to act as nominee, in relation to the voluntary arrangement.

(3) The modifications shall not include one by virtue of which the proposal ceases to be a proposal such as is mentioned in section 1.

(4) A meeting summoned under paragraph 29 shall not approve any proposal or modification which affects the right of a secured creditor of the company to enforce his security, except with the concurrence of the creditor concerned.

(5) Subject to sub-paragraph (6), a meeting so summoned shall not approve any proposal or modification under which—

    (a)   any preferential debt of the company is to be paid otherwise than in priority to such of its debts as are not preferential debts, or

    (b)   a preferential creditor of the company is to be paid an amount in respect of a preferential debt that bears to that debt a smaller proportion than is borne to another preferential debt by the amount that is to be paid in respect of that other debt.

(6) The meeting may approve such a proposal or modification with the concurrence of the preferential creditor concerned.

(7) The directors of the company may, before the beginning of the period of seven days which ends with the meetings (or either of them) summoned under paragraph 29 being held, give notice to the nominee of any modifications of the proposal for which the directors intend to seek the approval of those meetings.

(8) References in this paragraph to preferential debts and preferential creditors are to be read in accordance with section 386 in Part XII of this Act.

General note—These provisions very much follow the form of s 4. For guidance see the notes to those provisions.

For the meaning of 'meetings' and 'meeting' in these provisions see para 36 and the notes thereto.

32 Extension of moratorium

(1) Subject to sub-paragraph (2), a meeting summoned under paragraph 29 which resolves that it be adjourned (or further adjourned) may resolve that the moratorium be extended (or further extended), with or without conditions.

(2) The moratorium may not be extended (or further extended) to a day later than the end of the period of two months which begins—

    (a)   where both meetings summoned under paragraph 29 are first held on the same day, with that day,

    (b)   in any other case, with the day on which the later of those meetings is first held.

(3) At any meeting where it is proposed to extend (or further extend) the moratorium, before a decision is taken with respect to that proposal, the nominee shall inform the meeting—

    (a)   of what he has done in order to comply with his duty under paragraph 24 and the cost of his actions for the company, and

    (b)   of what he intends to do to continue to comply with that duty if the moratorium is extended (or further extended) and the expected cost of his actions for the company.

(4) Where, in accordance with sub-paragraph (3)(b), the nominee informs a meeting of the expected cost of his intended actions, the meeting shall resolve whether or not to approve that expected cost.

(5) If a decision not to approve the expected cost of the nominee's intended actions has effect under paragraph 36, the moratorium comes to an end.

(6) A meeting may resolve that a moratorium which has been extended (or further extended) be brought to an end before the end of the period of the extension (or further extension).

(7) The Secretary of State may by order increase or reduce the period for the time being specified in sub-paragraph (2).

General note—Although in practice the moratorium will usually last for 28 days following its commencement by operation of para 8(1), these provisions allow for the extension, or further extension, of the moratorium for a maximum period of two months, with or without conditions, but only on a meeting of the company or of creditors summoned under para 29 resolving that the original or adjourned meeting be adjourned, or further adjourned. In the case of any meeting proposing to extend, or further extend, the moratorium, para 32(3) imposes an express obligation on the nominee to report on the discharge of his obligation under para 24 and his intentions for continued compliance with that obligation. Sub-paragraphs (4) and (5) dictate that the nominee's reporting obligation extends to his giving an indication of the expected cost of his intended actions; if the meeting resolves not to approve that expected cost, then the moratorium is brought to an end.

For the meaning of 'meetings' and 'meeting' in these provisions see para 36 and the notes thereto.

33

(1) The conditions which may be imposed when a moratorium is extended (or further extended) include a requirement that the nominee be replaced as such by another person qualified to act as an insolvency practitioner, or authorised to act as nominee, in relation to the voluntary arrangement.

(2) A person may only be appointed as a replacement nominee by virtue of sub-paragraph (1) if he submits to the court a statement indicating his consent to act.

(3) At any meeting where it is proposed to appoint a replacement nominee as a condition of extending (or further extending) the moratorium—

    (a)   the duty imposed by paragraph 32(3)(b) on the nominee shall instead be imposed on the person proposed as the replacement nominee, and

    (b)   paragraphs 32(4) and (5) and 36(1)(e) apply as if the references to the nominee were to that person.

General note—The conditions envisaged by para 32(1) on the resolution by a meeting to extend, or further extend, the moratorium may include a requirement that the nominee is replaced by another appropriately qualified individual, subject to the replacement nominee submitting a written consent to act to the court.

34

(1) If a decision to extend, or further extend, the moratorium takes effect under paragraph 36, the nominee shall, in accordance with the rules, notify the registrar of companies and the court.

(2) If the moratorium is extended, or further extended, by virtue of an order under paragraph 36(5), the nominee shall, in accordance with the rules, send a copy of the order to the registrar of companies.

(3) If the nominee without reasonable excuse fails to comply with this paragraph, he is liable to a fine.

Amendments—SI 2009/1941.

General note—The extension, or further extension, of a moratorium must be notified to the Registrar of Companies, and to the court if the decision to extend was made under para 36(1). Where the court makes an order under para 36(5) to the effect that the decision of the company meeting is to have effect instead of the decision of the creditors' meeting (ie following an application by a member of the company), the nominee must send a copy of the order to the Registrar of Companies.

35 Moratorium committee

(1) A meeting summoned under paragraph 29 which resolves that the moratorium be extended (or further extended) may, with the consent of the nominee, resolve that a committee be established to exercise the functions conferred on it by the meeting.

(2) The meeting may not so resolve unless it has approved an estimate of the expenses to be incurred by the committee in the exercise of the proposed functions.

(3) Any expenses, not exceeding the amount of the estimate, incurred by the committee in the exercise of its functions shall be reimbursed by the nominee.

(4) The committee shall cease to exist when the moratorium comes to an end.

General note—What is termed the 'moratorium committee', a term which does not feature elsewhere in the legislation, would appear to equate to a creditors' committee despite the fact that the legislation makes no provision for the formation of a creditors' committee in a non-moratorium CVA. In practice, though not so provided for, creditors' committees are commonly enough formed in non-moratorium CVAs.

SIP 15 provides a useful commentary which, it is suggested, may be adapted for the purposes of a CVA in a moratorium committee or a creditors' committee in a non-moratorium case. The main areas to be addressed, which correspond with those matters identified in rr 4.151–4.172A on liquidations, are: the number of members of a committee (which in liquidation is to be not more than five and not less than three and subject to a member being admitted to proof in respect of an unsecured debt); conformation by a member of his agreement to act; the duty of the office-holder to report to the committee; the holding of committee meetings (on at least 7 days' notice in liquidation); the appointment of the office-holder or his nominee as chairman of committee meetings; the number of members required to form a valid quorum (two in liquidation); the standing of a committee member to be represented by a duly authorised person; the standing of a member to resign, together with rules for the removal and replacement of a member; the voting rights of members and the passing of committee resolutions (on a simple majority in liquidation); the passing of resolutions by post; the claiming by committee members of expenses; and a bar against any member of the committee taking any remuneration or other benefit.

Reimbursement of a member's expenses—Paragraph 35(3) provides that any committee member has a right to be reimbursed in respect of expenses approved under para 35(2) by the nominee, who in turn will have an entitlement to recoup such expenses from arrangement assets under r 1.28.

Meetings—For the meaning of the terms 'meetings' and 'meeting' see para 36 and the notes thereto.

36 Effectiveness of decisions

(1) Sub-paragraph (2) applies to references to one of the following decisions having effect, that is, a decision, under paragraph 31, 32 or 35, with respect to—

    (a)   the approval of a proposed voluntary arrangement,
    (b)   the extension (or further extension) of a moratorium,
    (c)   the bringing of a moratorium to an end,
    (d)   the establishment of a committee, or

(e)   the approval of the expected cost of a nominee's intended actions.

(2) The decision has effect if, in accordance with the rules—

(a)   it has been taken by both meetings summoned under paragraph 29, or

(b)   (subject to any order made under sub-paragraph (5)) it has been taken by the creditors' meeting summoned under that paragraph.

(3) If a decision taken by the creditors' meeting under any of paragraphs 31, 32 or 35 with respect to any of the matters mentioned in sub-paragraph (1) differs from one so taken by the company meeting with respect to that matter, a member of the company may apply to the court.

(4) An application under sub-paragraph (3) shall not be made after the end of the period of 28 days beginning with—

(a)   the day on which the decision was taken by the creditors' meeting, or

(b)   where the decision of the company meeting was taken on a later day, that day.

(5) On an application under sub-paragraph (3), the court may—

(a)   order the decision of the company meeting to have effect instead of the decision of the creditors' meeting, or

(b)   make such other order as it thinks fit.

General note—Those decisions referred to in para 36(1) have effect by virtue of para 36(2) if, in accordance with the rules, (a) the decision has been taken by both meetings summoned under para 29, or (b) subject to any contrary order made under para 36(5) on an application by a member raising objection, the decision has been taken by the creditors' meeting summoned under para 29. In the absence of an aggrieved member making application to court within the 28-day period provided for in para 36(4), therefore, the decision of the creditors' meeting will prevail over any conflicting resolution of the company meeting.

It may be appropriate to combine an application by an aggrieved member objecting to a decision to approve a proposed voluntary arrangement under para 36(3) with an application under para 38(1)(b) alleging that there has been some material irregularity at or in relation to either the company meeting and/or the creditors' meeting.

37 Effect of approval of voluntary arrangement

(1) This paragraph applies where a decision approving a voluntary arrangement has effect under paragraph 36.

(2) The approved voluntary arrangement—

(a)   takes effect as if made by the company at the creditors' meeting, and

(b)   binds every person who in accordance with the rules—

(i)   was entitled to vote at that meeting (whether or not he was present or represented at it), or

(ii)   would have been so entitled if he had had notice of it,

as if he were a party to the voluntary arrangement.

(3) If—

(9) Except in pursuance of the preceding provisions of this paragraph, a decision taken at a meeting summoned under paragraph 29 is not invalidated by any irregularity at or in relation to the meeting.

General note—These provisions virtually replicate s 6. For guidance see the notes to those provisions.

39 Implementation of voluntary arrangement

(1) This paragraph applies where a voluntary arrangement approved by one or both of the meetings summoned under paragraph 29 has taken effect.

(2) The person who is for the time being carrying out in relation to the voluntary arrangement the functions conferred—

    (a)   by virtue of the approval of the arrangement, on the nominee, or

    (b)   by virtue of paragraph 31(2), on a person other than the nominee,

shall be known as the supervisor of the voluntary arrangement.

(3) If any of the company's creditors or any other person is dissatisfied by any act, omission or decision of the supervisor, he may apply to the court.

(4) On an application under sub-paragraph (3) the court may—

    (a)   confirm, reverse or modify any act or decision of the supervisor,

    (b)   give him directions, or

    (c)   make such other order as it thinks fit.

(5) The supervisor—

    (a)   may apply to the court for directions in relation to any particular matter arising under the voluntary arrangement, and

    (b)   is included among the persons who may apply to the court for the winding up of the company or for an administration order to be made in relation to it.

(6) The court may, whenever—

    (a)   it is expedient to appoint a person to carry out the functions of the supervisor, and

    (b)   it is inexpedient, difficult or impracticable for an appointment to be made without the assistance of the court,

make an order appointing a person who is qualified to act as an insolvency practitioner, or authorised to act as supervisor, in relation to the voluntary arrangement, either in substitution for the existing supervisor or to fill a vacancy.

(7) The power conferred by sub-paragraph (6) is exercisable so as to increase the number of persons exercising the functions of supervisor or, where there is more than one person exercising those functions, so as to replace one or more of those persons.

Amendments—Inserted by the Insolvency Act 2000, s 1, Sch 1, paras 1, 4.

General note—These provisions virtually replicate those in s 7. For guidance see the notes to those provisions.

PART VI
MISCELLANEOUS

40 Challenge of directors' actions

(1) This paragraph applies in relation to acts or omissions of the directors of a company during a moratorium.

(2) A creditor or member of the company may apply to the court for an order under this paragraph on the ground—

    (a)   that the company's affairs, business and property are being or have been managed by the directors in a manner which is unfairly prejudicial to the interests of its creditors or members generally, or of some part of its creditors or members (including at least the petitioner), or

    (b)   that any actual or proposed act or omission of the directors is or would be so prejudicial.

(3) An application for an order under this paragraph may be made during or after the moratorium.

(4) On an application for an order under this paragraph the court may—

    (a)   make such order as it thinks fit for giving relief in respect of the matters complained of,

    (b)   adjourn the hearing conditionally or unconditionally, or

    (c)   make an interim order or any other order that it thinks fit.

(5) An order under this paragraph may in particular—

    (a)   regulate the management by the directors of the company's affairs, business and property during the remainder of the moratorium,

    (b)   require the directors to refrain from doing or continuing an act complained of by the petitioner, or to do an act which the petitioner has complained they have omitted to do,

    (c)   require the summoning of a meeting of creditors or members for the purpose of considering such matters as the court may direct,

    (d)   bring the moratorium to an end and make such consequential provision as the court thinks fit.

(6) In making an order under this paragraph the court shall have regard to the need to safeguard the interests of persons who have dealt with the company in good faith and for value.

(7) Sub-paragraph (8) applies where—

    (a)   the appointment of an administrator has effect in relation to the company and that appointment was in pursuance of—

        (i)   an administration application made, or

        (ii) a notice of intention to appoint filed,

before the moratorium came into force, or

(b) the company is being wound up in pursuance of a petition presented before the moratorium came into force.

(8) No application for an order under this paragraph may be made by a creditor or member of the company; but such an application may be made instead by the administrator or (as the case may be) the liquidator.

General note—Paragraph 40(1)–(6) is not dissimilar to the formerly operative s 27 in relation to administrations, but more closely resembles s 994 of the Companies Act 2006. The former provision allowed for an application to court by a creditor'or member on the grounds of actual or proposed unfair prejudice in the management of the company's affairs; business and property by an administrator, on the approach to which see the judgment of Millett J (as he then was) in *Re Charnley Davies Ltd (No 2)* [1990] BCLC 760 at 783–784. Paragraph 40(2), however, in common with s 994 of the 2006 Act, allows for such a claim to be brought complaining of management by the directors of the company. Although the words 'unfairly prejudicial' appear in s 6(1)(a), the term is employed in that provision in a very different context to that in para 40(2) and s 994 of the 2006 Act: see *Doorbar v Alltime Securities Ltd* [1995] BCC 1149 at 1159A (Peter Gibson LJ).

On the scope of s 994 of the Companies Act 2006 see the seminal judgment of Lord Hoffmann in *O'Neill v Phillips* [1999] 2 BCLC 2, and see also the judgments of Hoffmann LJ and Neill LJ in *Re Saul D Harrison & Sons plc* [1995] 1 BCLC 14 at 19–20 and 31–32 respectively. For an analysis of the scope of the remedies available to the court under provisions broadly equivalent to para 40(4) in s 459 cases see *Gore-Browne on Companies* (50th edn), ch 19, paras 22–39. Although the court may make such order as it thinks fit under para 40(4)(a), in addition to the alternative forms of relief identified, a complainant should indicate the general nature of the relief sought in his application: see *Re Antigen Laboratories* [1951] 1 All ER 110. The court is obliged under para 40(6) to have regard to the need to safeguard the interests of persons who have dealt with the company in good faith and for value, with or without, it would appear, notice of those matters complained of by a creditor or member under para 40(2).

Paragraph 40(7) and (8)

Claims by an administrator or liquidator—A claim alleging those matters in para 40(2) may be brought by an administrator appointed prior to the moratorium coming into effect or a liquidator appointed in a compulsory liquidation where the winding-up petition is presented prior to the moratorium coming into effect.

41 Offences

(1) This paragraph applies where a moratorium has been obtained for a company.

(2) If, within the period of 12 months ending with the day on which the moratorium came into force, a person who was at the time an officer of the company—

(a) did any of the things mentioned in paragraphs (a) to (f) of sub-paragraph (4), or

(b) was privy to the doing by others of any of the things mentioned in paragraphs (c), (d) and (e) of that sub-paragraph,

he is to be treated as having committed an offence at that time.

(3) If, at any time during the moratorium, a person who is an officer of the company—

(a)   does any of the things mentioned in paragraphs (a) to (f) of sub-paragraph (4), or

(b)   is privy to the doing by others of any of the things mentioned in paragraphs (c), (d) and (e) of that sub-paragraph,

he commits an offence.

(4) Those things are—

(a)   concealing any part of the company's property to the value of £500 or more, or concealing any debt due to or from the company, or

(b)   fraudulently removing any part of the company's property to the value of £500 or more, or

(c)   concealing, destroying, mutilating or falsifying any book or paper affecting or relating to the company's property or affairs, or

(d)   making any false entry in any book or paper affecting or relating to the company's property or affairs, or

(e)   fraudulently parting with, altering or making any omission in any document affecting or relating to the company's property or affairs, or

(f)   pawning, pledging or disposing of any property of the company which has been obtained on credit and has not been paid for (unless the pawning, pledging or disposal was in the ordinary way of the company's business).

(5) For the purposes of this paragraph, 'officer' includes a shadow director.

(6) It is a defence—

(a)   for a person charged under sub-paragraph (2) or (3) in respect of the things mentioned in paragraph (a) or (f) of sub-paragraph (4) to prove that he had no intent to defraud, and

(b)   for a person charged under sub-paragraph (2) or (3) in respect of the things mentioned in paragraph (c) or (d) of sub-paragraph (4) to prove that he had no intent to conceal the state of affairs of the company or to defeat the law.

(7) Where a person pawns, pledges or disposes of any property of a company in circumstances which amount to an offence under sub-paragraph (2) or (3), every person who takes in pawn or pledge, or otherwise receives, the property knowing it to be pawned, pledged or disposed of in circumstances which—

(a)   would, if a moratorium were obtained for the company within the period of 12 months beginning with the day on which the pawning, pledging or disposal took place, amount to an offence under sub-paragraph (2), or

(b)   amount to an offence under sub-paragraph (3),

commits an offence.

(8) A person guilty of an offence under this paragraph is liable to imprisonment or a fine, or both.

(9) The money sums specified in paragraphs (a) and (b) of sub-paragraph (4) are subject to increase or reduction by order under section 417A in Part XV.

42

(1) If, for the purpose of obtaining a moratorium, or an extension of a moratorium, for a company, a person who is an officer of the company—

    (a)   makes any false representation, or

    (b)   fraudulently does, or omits to do, anything,

he commits an offence.

(2) Sub-paragraph (1) applies even if no moratorium or extension is obtained.

(3) For the purposes of this paragraph, 'officer' includes a shadow director.

(4) A person guilty of an offence under this paragraph is liable to imprisonment or a fine, or both.

43 Void provisions in floating charge documents

(1) A provision in an instrument creating a floating charge is void if it provides for—

    (a)   obtaining a moratorium, or

    (b)   anything done with a view to obtaining a moratorium (including any preliminary decision or investigation),

to be an event causing the floating charge to crystallise or causing restrictions which would not otherwise apply to be imposed on the disposal of property by the company or a ground for the appointment of a receiver.

(2) In sub-paragraph (1), 'receiver' includes a manager and a person who is appointed both receiver and manager.

General note—These provisions complement the anti-crystallisation provisions in para 13(1)–(4), on which see the notes thereto.

'a provision in an instrument creating a floating charge ...'—The wording in para 43(1) is curious in that, at least taken literally, it would not appear to catch a provision which offends against para 43(1)(a) and (b) but which is not contained in an instrument creating a floating charge, such as a facility letter or a side letter between a lender and a debtor company. It seems inconceivable that such avoidance of the provision could have been intended by Parliament. Taking a purposive approach to para 43 as a whole, therefore, it is suggested that the words 'a provision in an instrument creating a floating charge is void' should be read as 'any provision is void', with the reference to 'the floating charge' immediately below para 43(1)(b) being read as 'a floating charge'.

44 Functions of the Financial Services Authority

(1) This Schedule has effect in relation to a moratorium for a regulated company with the modifications in sub-paragraphs (2) to (16) below.

(2) Any notice or other document required by virtue of this Schedule to be sent to a creditor of a regulated company must also be sent to the Authority.

(3) The Authority is entitled to be heard on any application to the court for leave under paragraph 20(2) or 20(3) (disposal of charged property, etc).

(4) Where paragraph 26(1) (challenge of nominee's actions, etc.) applies, the persons who may apply to the court include the Authority.

(5) If a person other than the Authority applies to the court under that paragraph, the Authority is entitled to be heard on the application.

(6) Where paragraph 27(1) (challenge of nominee's actions, etc.) applies, the persons who may apply to the court include the Authority.

(7) If a person other than the Authority applies to the court under that paragraph, the Authority is entitled to be heard on the application.

(8) The persons to be summoned to a creditors' meeting under paragraph 29 include the Authority.

(9) A person appointed for the purpose by the Authority is entitled to attend and participate in (but not to vote at)—

    (a)   any creditors' meeting summoned under that paragraph,

    (b)   any meeting of a committee established under paragraph 35 (moratorium committee).

(10) The Authority is entitled to be heard on any application under paragraph 36(3) (effectiveness of decisions).

(11) Where paragraph 38(1) (challenge of decisions) applies, the persons who may apply to the court include the Authority.

(12) If a person other than the Authority applies to the court under that paragraph, the Authority is entitled to be heard on the application.

(13) Where paragraph 39(3) (implementation of voluntary arrangement) applies, the persons who may apply to the court include the Authority.

(14) If a person other than the Authority applies to the court under that paragraph, the Authority is entitled to be heard on the application.

(15) Where paragraph 40(2) (challenge of directors' actions) applies, the persons who may apply to the court include the Authority.

(16) If a person other than the Authority applies to the court under that paragraph, the Authority is entitled to be heard on the application.

(17) This paragraph does not prejudice any right the Authority has (apart from this paragraph) as a creditor of a regulated company.

(18) In this paragraph—

    'the Authority' means the Financial Services Authority, and
    'regulated company' means a company which—

        (a)   is, or has been, an authorised person within the meaning given by section 31 of the Financial Services and Markets Act 2000,

(b)   is, or has been, an appointed representative within the meaning given by section 39 of that Act, or

(c)   is carrying on, or has carried on, a regulated activity, within the meaning given by section 22 of that Act, in contravention of the general prohibition within the meaning given by section 19 of that Act.

General note—These provisions apply only to a 'regulated company' (as defined in para 44(18)) and require – by virtue of the word 'must' – notice of and supporting documents in relation to a proposal under Sch A1 to be sent to the FSA as if the FSA were a creditor by virtue of para 44(2). The FSA must, therefore, be entitled not only to attend but also to be heard at the creditors' meeting, where any views expressed by it may well have an impact on the consideration by creditors of a proposal. The provisions do not, however, confer any rights on the FSA to vote at the creditors' meeting, although the FSA will be entitled to vote to the extent that it is, in fact, a creditor by virtue of para 44(17). The remainder of the provisions operate where the FSA is not a creditor and confer specific rights on the FSA to attend, to make application and to be heard at those meetings and applications listed in which participation would otherwise require creditor status as a pre-condition.

45 Subordinate legislation

(1) Regulations or an order made by the Secretary of State under this Schedule may make different provision for different cases.

(2) Regulations so made may make such consequential, incidental, supplemental and transitional provision as may appear to the Secretary of State necessary or expedient.

(3) Any power of the Secretary of State to make regulations under this Schedule may be exercised by amending or repealing any enactment contained in this Act (including one contained in this Schedule) or contained in the Company Directors Disqualification Act 1986.

(4) Regulations (except regulations under paragraph 5) or an order made by the Secretary of State under this Schedule shall be made by statutory instrument subject to annulment in pursuance of a resolution of either House of Parliament.

(5) Regulations under paragraph 5 of this Schedule are to be made by statutory instrument and shall only be made if a draft containing the regulations has been laid before and approved by resolution of each House of Parliament.

Amendments—Inserted by Insolvency Act 2000, s 1, Sch 1, paras 1, 4. Amended by Enterprise Act 2002, s 248(3), Sch 17, paras 9, 37(1), (4); SI 2004/2312.

SCHEDULE B1
ADMINISTRATION

ARRANGEMENT OF SCHEDULE

Introductory notes to administration—Administration was a regime introduced by Part II of the 1986 Act. Whilst that regime provided a workable mechanism for rescue or, at least, asset maximisation, it was not without its difficulties. First, the procedure was expensive and was not therefore readily available to small or even medium sized concerns, which would have no option but to go into liquidation or seek to pursue an unprotected CVA. Secondly, the original administration procedure was more unwieldy than was strictly necessary for achieving the end objective envisaged by the Cork Committee whose recommendations had led to the new provisions.

The new regime in Sch B1 seeks to address these difficulties and introduces a reformulated procedure which incorporates the enforcement of floating charges which would otherwise have allowed for the appointment of an administrative receiver if created prior to 15 September 2003: see s 72A. Judicial analysis and development of Sch B1 has continued apace since its inception. The annotations and commentary which follow seek to provide some detailed elaboration in particular on the new statutory purpose (para 3), the new extendable time constraints (paras 4 and 76), the alternative methods of appointment (paras 10, 13, 14 and 22) and the wide procedure governing the conduct of administration, together with the various remedies available to creditors and third parties, including the new provisions in para 74 which allow the creditor or member to challenge the administrator's conduct of the administration.

With the implementation of Sch B1 the DTI issued Explanatory Notes to the new provisions which, whilst not having statutory force, are of some practical assistance and are referred to in the text which follows.

Pre-pack sales—So-called pre-packaged or pre-pack sales, by which the whole or part of a company's business is sold on by an administrator, usually immediately upon the appointment being made or shortly thereafter, commonly arise in practice. This technique of preserving or rescuing a business is both a matter of controversy in some quarters and carries the potential for abuse where, in reality, the real purpose of the sale out of administration is the thwarting of creditor claims. SIP 16, effective from 1 January 2009, which appears in the appendices to this work, provides guidance specifically on pre-pack sales out of administration.

In *Re Kayley Vending Limited* [2009] BCC 578, HHJ Cooke QC held that in exercising its discretion in pre-pack cases, the court must be alert to see, so far as it could, that the procedure was at least not being obviously abused to the disadvantage of creditors. If it was, or may be, the court may conclude that it was inappropriate to give the pre-pack the apparent blessing conferred by making the administration order. Accordingly, in most cases the information required by SIP 16 should be included in the administration application.

In *DKLL Solicitors v HM Revenue and Customs* [2007] EWHC 2067 (Ch), [2007] BCC 908, two equity partners in an insolvent firm of solicitors which was a limited liability partnership applied for an administration order in relation to the partnership where the proposal was to effect a pre-pack sale of the partnership's business immediately upon the appointment of the administrators without the necessity of the approval by a creditors' meeting. The proposal was opposed by HMRC, the partnership's majority creditor, which had presented a winding up petition. Nevertheless, Andrew Simmonds QC (sitting as a deputy judge of the High Court) granted an administration order.

In 2012, there were there were 728 pre-pack deals, accounting for 29% of all administrations.

On 15 July 2013, an independent review of of pre-packs was announced by the Government.

Pre-appointment costs—IR 1986, r 2.67(1)(c) provides that where an administration order is made, the costs of the applicant are payable as an administration expenses.

In *Re Kayley Vending*, the court held it was not appropriate to hold that an administrator's pre-appointment costs were in all cases part of the costs of the applicant that must be allowed under IR 1986 r.2.67(1)(c)). Rather, it was appropriate to use the general power under para 13(1)(f) to order on a discretionary basis that the pre-appointment costs of the proposed administrator be treated as an expense of the administration where the court was satisfied that the balance of benefit arising from the incurring of pre-appointment costs was in favour of the creditors rather than the management as potential purchasers of the business.

In contrast, in *Re Johnson Machine and Tool Co Ltd* [2010] EWHC 582 (Ch), [2010] BCC 382, the directors of a company applied for an administration order. It was proposed that following the administrator's appointment there would be an immediate pre-pack sale of the company's business and assets to a connected company. Following the making of an administration order, HHJ Purle QC declined to allow the administrator's pre-appointment costs to be treated as an administration expense. Although he was satisfied that the pre-pack sale would result in a better return for creditors if the company were placed into liquidation, he noted that where the directors (or a company which they control or have a substantial connection with) are the purchasers, it is rarely possible to establish clearly that the balance of advantage is in the creditors' favour.

TUPE Regulations 2006—The Transfer of Undertakings (Protection of Employment) Regulations 2006 (SI 2006/246) give statutory protection to employees by providing that where a company transfers a business situated immediately before the transfer in the United Kingdom to another person where there is a transfer of an economic entity which retains its identity, the contract of employment of any person employed by the company in relation to that business will have effect after the transfer as if originally made between the employee and the transferee. However, reg 8(7) provides that these regulations do not apply if at the time of a relevant transfer the transferor is subject to 'bankruptcy proceedings or any analogous insolvency proceedings which have been instituted with a view to the liquidation of the assets of the transferor and are under the supervision of an insolvency practitioner'.

In *Oakland v Wellswood (Yorkshire) Limited* [2009] EWCA Civ 1094, [2010] BCC 263, the Court of Appeal held that whether or not an administration falls within the terms of reg 8(7) will depend upon the purpose of the administration.

However, in *OTG Limited v Barke* [2011] BCC 608, the Employment Appeals Tribunal rejected this approach and held that reg 8(7) applies to all administrations. This was affirmed by the Court of Appeal in *Key2Law (Surrey) LLP v De'Antiquis* [2011] EWCA Civ 1567, [2012] BCC 375.

In consequence, where the administrators transfer the company's business as a going concern, its employees will be entitled to the statutory protection of TUPE.

Partnerships—A partnership may be placed into administration under the Insolvent Partnerships (Amendment) Order 2005 (SI 2005/1516) which came into force on 1 July 2005.

Insurance companies—See the Insurers (Reorganisation and Winding-Up) Regulations 2003 (SI 2003/1102) and the Insurers (Reorganisation and Winding-Up) Regulations 2004 (SI 2004/353), effective 20 April 2003 and 18 February 2004 respectively.

Generally, see A Keay 'A Comparative Analysis of the Administration Regimes in Australia and the United Kingdom' in P Omar (ed) *International Insolvency Law: Themes and Perspectives* (Aldershot, Ashgate, 2008), at 105ff.

NATURE OF ADMINISTRATION

1 Administration

(1) For the purposes of this Act 'administrator' of a company means a person appointed under this Schedule to manage the company's affairs, business and property.

(2) For the purposes of this Act—

    (a)   a company is 'in administration' while the appointment of an administrator of the company has effect,

    (b)   a company 'enters administration' when the appointment of an administrator takes effect,

    (c)   a company ceases to be in administration when the appointment of an administrator of the company ceases to have effect in accordance with this Schedule, and

    (d)   a company does not cease to be in administration merely because an administrator vacates office (by reason of resignation, death or otherwise) or is removed from office.

General note—The practical significance of these provisions is in the change of language adopted by the draftsman over that employed in the former administration provisions in Part II.

'administrator'—This term refers to an appropriately qualified individual (on which see para 6) who is appointed administrator by one of the three alternative methods identified in para 2.

'enters administration'—A company cannot be 'in administration' (see below) until such time as it 'enters administration'. The term 'enters administration' is defined by reference to the appointment of an administrator taking effect, as opposed to the time of any administration application or the taking of preparatory steps to effect an out-of-court appointment. A company may enter administration in one of three ways: first, on the making of an administration order under paras 10 and 13(1)(a), secondly, on the satisfaction of the requirements of para 18 on an out-of-court appointment by a floating charge holder under para 14 (see para 19) or, thirdly, on the satisfaction of the requirements of para 29 in an out-of-court appointment by a company or its directors under para 22 (see para 31).

'in administration'—Once a company 'enters administration' (as defined in para 1(2)(b)) the company remains 'in administration' until such time as the appointment of the administrator ceases to have effect. The new terminology should be contrasted with that employed under the former Part II under which a company was deemed to be in administration on the making of an administration order under s 8(2) until such time as the court made an order discharging the administration order under s 18(3).

'a company'—In *Re Eurodis Electron Plc (in Administration)* [2011] EWHC 1025 (Ch), [2011] BPIR 1372 an administration order was made in respect of a company incorporated in Belgium which had its centre of main interests in England. Subsequently, the company was subsequently wound up and dissolved in Belgium. Mann J held that once the company had been dissolved it was not possible for the administration to continue.

When does the appointment of an administrator cease to have effect for the purposes of para 1(2)(c)?—The starting point here is para 1(2)(d) which provides that a company does not cease to be in administration by reason of an administrator vacating or being removed from office. Thus, despite para 1(2), a company will remain 'in administration' during the period in which no administrator remains in office following the vacation or removal of an administrator pending the appointment of a replacement. The appointment of an administrator 'ceases to have effect' for the purposes of para 1(2)(c) in any one of seven circumstances, namely:

(a) under para 76(1) at the end of the period of one year beginning with the date of the appointment of the administrator, subject to extension of the one-year period under para 76(2);
(b) by order of the court on the application of an administrator under para 79(1);
(c) under para 80(3) on the filing of the prescribed forms where the administrator thinks that the purpose of an administration has been sufficiently achieved;
(d) by order of the court on the application of a creditor under para 81(1);
(e) under para 82(3)(a) by order of the court following the presentation of a public interest winding-up petition;
(f) under para 83(6)(a) following the registration of the requisite notice by an administrator prior to the company moving into creditors' voluntary liquidation;
(g) under para 84(4) on the registration of the requisite notice by the administrator prior to a company moving to dissolution.

Consequences of a court order providing for the appointment of an administrator to cease to have effect where the administrator was appointed by an administration order—In these circumstances the court is obliged to discharge the administration order under para 85(2).

2

A person may be appointed as administrator of a company—

    (a)   by administration order of the court under paragraph 10,

    (b)   by the holder of a floating charge under paragraph 14, or

    (c)   by the company or its directors under paragraph 22.

General note—This provision identifies the three possible methods by which an administrator of a company may be appointed. Note, however, that despite such a purported appointment, in or out of court, the appointment may be invalidated by any of those general restrictions in paras 6–9.

3 Purpose of administration

(1) The administrator of a company must perform his functions with the objective of—

    (a)   rescuing the company as a going concern, or

    (b)   achieving a better result for the company's creditors as a whole than would be likely if the company were wound up (without first being in administration), or

    (c)   realising property in order to make a distribution to one or more secured or preferential creditors.

(2) Subject to sub-paragraph (4), the administrator of a company must perform his functions in the interests of the company's creditors as a whole.

(3) The administrator must perform his functions with the objective specified in sub-paragraph (1)(a) unless he thinks either—

    (a)   that it is not reasonably practicable to achieve that objective, or

    (b)   that the objective specified in sub-paragraph (1)(b) would achieve a better result for the company's creditors as a whole.

(4) The administrator may perform his functions with the objective specified in sub-paragraph (1)(c) only if—

(a) he thinks that it is not reasonably practicable to achieve either of the objectives specified in sub-paragraph (1)(a) and (b), and

(b) he does not unnecessarily harm the interests of the creditors of the company as a whole.

General note—This key provision identifies, in para 3(1), the purpose – or, rather, a hierarchy of three specific purposes – in all administrations, whether instigated by an out of court appointment or by a court order. This approach represents a marked shift from that in the formerly operative s 8(3) under which the court could make an order providing for any one or more of the four purposes specified therein.

Paragraph 3(1)

Scope of provision—The new provisions place greater emphasis than previously on company rescue. The use of the term 'purpose', in both the heading to the provision and in para 3(1), is not altogether helpful since para 3(1), albeit under what might be termed a single overarching purpose, encapsulates three separate and fundamentally different purposes or, rather, 'sub-purposes', which, as provided for in para 3(3) and (4), and subject to the provisos therein, an administrator *must* pursue in turn unless the administrator forms the view that the achievement of any particular sub-purpose is not reasonably practicable.

'The administrator of a company must perform his functions with the objective of ...'—These words suggest that the exercise of any power under Sch 1 or those powers identified in the notes to para 60 must be exercised, and only exercised, in pursuit of such purposes or purposes as the administrator considers to be reasonably practicably capable of achievement.

Paragraph 3(1)(a)

'Rescuing the company as a going concern ...'—An administrator must pursue the primary objective of rescuing the company as a going concern unless, according to para 3(3), either it is not reasonably practicable to achieve that purpose or the achievement of the purpose in para 3(1)(b) would bring about a better result for the company's creditors as a whole.

The term 'rescuing the company as a going concern' contrasts with that in the former s 8(3)(a) which referred to 'the survival of the company, and the whole or any part of its undertaking, as a going concern'. In *Re Rowbotham Baxter Ltd* [1990] BCC 113 at 115E–115F Harman J held, in construing the wording in s 8(3)(a), that the subsection required the survival of the company itself together with all or part of its undertaking as a going concern, an outcome which was incapable of being achieved through what is commonly termed the hiving down of the company's business into a new company. Hiving down might, however, have led to the achievement of the purpose in the former s 8(3)(d), which corresponds in substance with the sub-purpose now found in para 3(1)(b).

The wording now employed in para 3(1)(a), it is submitted, should be construed as having the same meaning as that under the former s 8(3)(a) as interpreted in *Rowbotham Baxter* (above). That approach finds support in para 647 of the DTI's Explanatory Notes which indicates that the objective of rescuing the company as a going concern 'is intended to mean the company and as much of its business as possible'. The survival of a company intact, but with no subsisting going concern undertaking, would not fall within the scope of para 3(1)(a) since, in line with para 649 of the DTI's Explanatory Notes, a proposal resulting in nothing more than a 'shell' company does not constitute a rescue. Such an outcome might, however, fall within para 3(1)(b).

In considering the prospects of achievement of the sub-purpose in para 3(1)(a), as with sub-paras (1)(b) and (c), the court is concerned with the weighing up of evidence, and not mere assertions. For example, in *Doltable Ltd v Lexi Holdings plc* [2005] EWHC 1804 (Ch), [2006] 1 BCLC 384 Mann J refused to make an administration order in the absence of evidence that, in a liquidation, creditors would be no worse off, nor indeed any better off, than in an administration.

DTI's examples of para 3(1)(a) rescue—By way of illustration, the DTI's Explanatory Notes suggest that a hypothetical example of a reasonably practicable rescue for para 3(1)(a) purposes would include the following. Company A is operating at a profit and has excellent

704

products, a loyal customer base and a healthy order book. However, major investment in a new IT system, which is late and over budget, has knocked the company off its business plan, its cash flow has suffered and it is unable to pay its debts. The company has been placed in administration and the administrator has had an offer for its business that would provide sufficient funds to pay the secured creditors and give 35p in the pound for unsecured creditors. However, the administrator determines that the problems are short-term and they can be resolved and will not have any ongoing effect. The company's bankers have given their support to the administrator's plans to continue trading, the company's business is profitable and the administrator is confident that the company can be rescued by trading its way out of its current financial difficulties and provide 65p in the pound return for unsecured creditors within twelve months. Whilst no exit route is suggested in this hypothetical example, para 649 of the DTI's Explanatory Notes suggests that company rescue is most likely to involve creditors agreeing to a CVA or a scheme of arrangement under Part 26 of the Companies Act 2006.

The DTI's Explanatory Notes go on to provide the following as a hypothetical example of a case where a rescue would not be reasonably practicable. A company is in financial difficulties and it is clear that the only viable options depend on the continuing support of the company's bankers. The administrator knows that this support will not be forthcoming and that there is no alternative means of financing the company.

In the above circumstances it would follow that the administrator would be required to consider the purpose in para 3(1)(b) upon forming the view that the rescue purpose in para 3(1)(a) is not reasonably practicably capable of achievement. If that purpose, or that in para 3(1)(c) is not, in the opinion of the administrator, reasonably practicably capable of achievement, then the administrator would necessarily have to consider terminating the administration under para 79(2).

Paragraph 3(1)(b)

'Achieving a better result for the company's creditors as a whole than would be likely if the company were wound up (without first being in administration)'—This objective only comes into play where either of the two conditions in para 3(3) is satisfied.

Paragraph 3(1)(b) is substantially equivalent to the purpose in the former s 8(3)(d). What is envisaged here is the sale of a company's business or businesses as a going concern or concerns to one or more buyers, including a so-called 'pre-pack' sale, or a sale other than on a going concern basis as might arise where, for example, an administrator has been unable to sustain a going concern business through lack of funding or in the absence of a ready and willing purchaser.

In *Logitech UK Ltd* [2004] EWHC 2899 (Ch), [2005] 1 BCLC 326 Lindsay J was prepared to make an administration order where a non-trading, insolvent company had no assets save for a number of potential causes of action for transaction-at-undervalue and breach of directors' duties where the applicant, a substantial creditor, was prepared to fund those claims to the tune of £50,000 in administration, but not in liquidation, so as to produce a better projected outcome in administration.

DTI example of para 3(1)(b) case—Paragraph 650 of the DTI's Explanatory Notes provides the following hypothetical example of the para 3(1)(b) objective being achieved. Company B has good products and a sound customer base. The company is making losses, its plant and machinery are outdated, and its overheads and debts have been rising for some time. The company has been placed in administration and the administrator has determined that there are no funds available to maintain its entire trading operation or invest in new machinery and it is therefore not reasonably practicable to rescue the company. The administrator has reviewed the company and determined that a sale of its business on a going concern basis would provide a better return than a break-up sale of its assets. The administrator markets the businesses and the best offer he or she receives would provide sufficient funds to pay the secured creditors and give 40p in the pound for unsecured creditors. The administrator reports to the creditors at a meeting and explains why it was not reasonably practicable to rescue the company.

Paragraph 3(1)(c)

'Realising property in order to make a distribution to one or more secured or preferential creditors'—This objective only comes into play on the two conditions in para 3(4) being satisfied: further commentary appears in the notes to that provision below.

The wording in this provision envisages no distribution being made to unsecured creditors. Although in practice this objective will usually involve a company which is not viable with no business that can be sold as a going concern, there is no reason why the sale of a company's assets and/or business as a going concern should not be effected pursuant to the achievement of this objective. Where the achievement of the objectives in paras 3(1)(a) and (b) is not reasonably practicable the viability of this sub-purpose will necessarily depend on the level of unsecured, secured and preferential claims relative to the projected level of property realisations.

DTI example of a para 3(1)(c) case—Paragraph 651 of the DTI's Explanatory Notes provides the following hypothetical example of the achievement of this objective. Company C is a service company whose business and reputation were built around its excellent standards of customer service. But a number of key personnel have recently left, the quality of the company's service and its reputation have suffered badly, customers have become dissatisfied and the company is no longer able to attract and retain business. It has been making losses for a number of months and is unable to pay its debts. The company is then placed in administration. The administrator reviews the company and concludes that its business is not viable and a sale is not possible. The administrator markets the company's assets and realises funds that are sufficient to make a part-payment to the secured creditors, and there are no funds available to pay unsecured creditors, except for those resulting from the operation of the ring-fence (ie under s 176A). The administrator reports to the creditors and explains why it was not reasonably practicable to achieve either a company rescue or a better return for unsecured creditors.

Paragraph 3(2)

The requirement that an administrator performs his functions in the interests of the company's creditors as a whole—This provision encapsulates the distinction between the office of administrator and that of the virtually abolished administrative receiver. A receiver managing mortgaged property primarily owes duties to the appointing charge holder and anyone else with an interest in the equity of redemption, the primary duty of the receiver being to try to bring about a situation in which interest on the secured debt can be paid and the debt itself repaid: *Medforth v Blake* [1999] 2 BCLC 221 at 237A–237D (Sir Richard Scott V-C, Swinton Thomas and Tuckey LJJ agreeing). Neither is a receiver under any general duty to carry on a business on the mortgaged premises as previously carried on by the mortgagor: (*Medforth v Blake*). The effect of para 3(2) is that an administrator – even one appointed under para 14 by the holder of a qualifying floating charge – must perform his functions in the interests of the company's creditors (ie unsecured, secured and preferential creditors) as a whole. An administrator must not merely have regard to or consider the interests of creditors, or purport to do so, but, rather, is required to perform his functions with the interests of unsecured creditors weighing equally with those of preferential and secured creditors. This is a significant step and one by which the new legislation has substantially altered the position as it was (and remains) under the general law governing receivership. The most obvious practical consequence of the new provision is that an administrator will be obliged to *consider* objectives (a) and (b) in all cases, even where the level of secured indebtedness exceeds the value of secured assets. Paragraph 3(4)(b) expressly provides that even where the achievement of the objectives in para 3(1)(a) and (b) is not reasonably practicable – such that consideration will necessarily have to be given to the enforcement of any security for the purpose of making a distribution to any secured creditor – the administrator may only pursue the objective in para 3(1)(c) provided 'he does not unnecessarily harm the interests of the creditors of the company as a whole'.

Given the conflict between the interests of a secured creditor and unsecured creditors generally where a company is or is likely to become unable to pay its debts (on which see para 11(a)) it remains to be seen whether the concept of 'the interests of the company's creditors as a whole', in the context of administration, is sufficient in itself in providing a workable basis for disgruntled unsecured creditors to mount a challenge, most obviously under para 74, to the actions or proposed conduct of an administrator, and in particular one appointed by a floating charge holder whose appointee appears disinclined to pursue either of the objectives in para 3(1)(a) and (b) without justification. The administrator is in any case required to nail his colours firmly to the mast at an early stage, in that IR 1986, r 2.33(2)(m) requires that the administrator's statement of proposals under para 49(1) must contain a statement of how it is envisaged the purpose of the administration will be achieved whilst, more specifically, para 49(2)(b) requires an explanation to be included within the statement as to why the administrator thinks that the objective in para 3(1)(a) or (b) cannot be achieved. It should also be noted that each of the examples drawn from paras 650 and 651 of the DTI's Explanatory Notes, above, envisages the administrator reporting to creditors and explaining why the achievement of any particular objective was not reasonably practicable.

Paragraph 3(3)

'... **unless he thinks** ...'—The use of the verb 'thinks' on the part of the administrator – a term which also appears in paras 49, 52, 79, 80, 83 and 84 – is interesting in that the draftsman has not employed the more common 'considers', 'is satisfied' or 'in his opinion'. Whilst it is possible that the use of the word 'thinks' is nothing more than the use of simple, modern language, it is submitted that the term actually conveys something less exacting than the three alternative terms just mentioned. The verb 'thinks', it is suggested, is more akin to 'believes' without, apparently, the requirement for an exhaustive analysis or very detailed consideration of the position on the part of the thinker. On the other hand, it must be the case that an administrator will have had to undertake at the very least some initial steps in order to 'think' that the achievement of any particular objective in para 3(1) is reasonably practicable, since the term 'thinks' would otherwise have no useful purpose. It is further suggested that the word 'thinks' cannot have been intended as imposing a purely subjective test which is not qualified by a requirement for rationality – but one imposed by a fixed standard of objective reasoanbleness – on the part of the administrator. Such an outcome would lead to unworkable and, very possibly, unacceptable results. It is submitted that, by use of the word 'thinks', Parliament must be taken as imposing a subjective requirement on an insolvency practitioner which must be rational in terms of being gauged against the objective test of the range of conclusions which might be reached by a hypothetical reasonable and reputable insolvency practitioner acting in the particular circumstances of the case. Indeed the Government's suggestion was that it was not seeking to apply any other test than expecting the court to assess whether the administrator has been 'rational' – which suggests, it is submitted, a subjective test incorporating a requirement for some rational objective reasonableness – see *Hansard*, 21 October 2002, col 1105.

The above observations, it is submitted, are in keeping with the new streamlined administration procedure and the need in some cases for an administrator to act with haste without, at the same time, running the risk of liability for breach of some onerous investigation requirement. Neither, it is submitted, are they inconsistent with the approach taken by Lewison J in *Unidare plc v Cohen and Power* [2005] EWHC 1410 (Ch), [2005] BPIR 1472, a case in part concerning the word 'thinks' as it appears in para 83(1), in which, at [71], his Lordship expressed the view that 'I accept that the process of thinking involves a rational thought process; but I do not accept that what the administrator thinks is subject to any form of test by reference to an objective *standard*' (emphasis added). In practice, an administrator should not derogate from the obtaining of such information as can reasonably be obtained in the circumstances of any particular case for the purpose of enabling the administrator to consider and act on such information appropriately in the discharge of his functions.

Paragraph 3(3)(a)

'... **that it is not reasonably practicable to achieve that objective** ...'—It is submitted that the achievement of an objective, or sub-purpose, is not reasonably practicable either if it is incapable of achievement or if it is capable of achievement, but not reasonably so, by reference to the net effect on creditors of the time and/or cost reasonably anticipated as being necessary for the achievement of that objective.

Paragraph 3(3)(b)

Scope of provision—See the note to para 3(1)(b) above.

Paragraph 3(3) and (5)

Is an administrator obliged to take steps in seeking to achieve each of the sub-purposes in para 3(1) in turn?—There is nothing in para 3 which requires the administrator to take steps in all cases to seek to achieve, in turn, the three sub-purposes within para 3(1). In some cases it will be obvious from the outset that sub-purpose (a) or sub-purposes (a) and (b) cannot be achieved within the reasonably practicable test identified in the note to para 3(3)(a) above. In those circumstances the administrator is required to pursue either sub-purpose (b) or (c) as appropriate, subject to the requirement under para 3(4)(b) in the latter case that the administrator must not unnecessarily harm the interests of creditors of the company as a whole. What is of utmost importance, however, at a practical level, is that the administrator is able to produce appropriate details, objectively speaking, of the method of his reasoning in reaching that conclusion and the facts and opinions upon which his decision is based.

Paragraph 3(4)(a)

Scope of provision—See the notes to paras 3(3)(a) and (b) above.

Paragraph 3(4)(b)

'**... he does not unnecessarily harm the interests of the creditors of the company as a whole'**—This provision is closely related to para 3(2). Its purpose is to provide protection to unsecured, preferential and any secured creditor which is junior to any one or more secured creditors to whom an administrator proposes making a distribution following the realisation of property on the pursuit of the objective in para 3(1)(c). Although these separate classes of 'protected' creditor are grouped together, it is difficult to envisage how an unsecured creditor might have grounds to complain of an administrator's performance given that, by definition, the objective in para 3(1)(c) does not envisage any distribution being made to unsecured creditors. On the other hand, a junior ranking secured creditor with an interest in the equity of redemption in secured assets might conceivably allege that the administrator has placed the value of that equity in jeopardy through his conduct of the administration. Notably, such a claim would be available to a junior ranking secured creditor against a receiver who owes duties in managing mortgaged property not only to the mortgagor but also to anyone else with an interest in the equity of redemption: *Medforth v Blake* [1999] 2 BCLC 221 at 237A (Sir Richard Scott V-C). Given that there is more than a passing resemblance between an administrator pursuing the sub-purpose in para 3(1)(c) and an administrative receiver, there are good grounds for supposing that an administrator in those circumstances is also capable of being fixed with such a duty.

Although para 3(4)(b), like para 3(2), makes reference to the interests of the creditors of the company 'as a whole', any claim by a creditor alleging a breach of para 3(4)(b) will, under para 74(1), require that the administrator is, has or proposes to act so as to unfairly harm the interests of the applicant, whether alone or in common with some or all other members or creditors.

'**... harm ...'**—The term 'harm' appears both in this provision and, in the same context, in para 74(1). Although there is an obvious and neat question as to whether the term 'harm' means the same as the more commonly employed 'prejudice', as appeared in s 27 in Part II coupled with the word 'unfair', recourse to the Parliamentary debates on the terms of the Enterprise Act 2002 reveal that no such distinction was intended. On 21 October 2002, in resisting an amendment from 'harm' to 'prejudice', Lord McIntosh of Haringey stated (HL Deb, col 1120), 'For the purposes of *Pepper v Hart*, I am advised that there is no distinction between "harm" and "prejudice" – but "harm" is a common word and more understandable to lawyers.' At the third reading of the Bill in the House of Lords Lord McIntosh went on to say that '"harm" is a word more likely to be understood not only by the courts and practitioners but also by professional advisers and above all by the public' (HL Deb, col 84 (28 October 2002)).

4

The administrator of a company must perform his functions as quickly and efficiently as is reasonably practicable.

General note—This provision corresponds with the new time-constricting provisions in paras 76 and 77, which provide for the automatic ending of administration after one year, subject to extension of that period by the court or creditors subject to the limitations prescribed therein. What is now expressly stipulated, however, would almost certainly have been implicit in any case, since it could hardly have been the case that an administrator might not have been obliged to perform his functions as quickly and efficiently as is reasonably practicable in the circumstances of any particular case. In remains, however, that in practice not all administrations under the former Part II were conducted with as much expedition as might in fact have been reasonably achievable.

It is suggested that it is extremely doubtful that para 4 creates any fresh duty in favour of an individual creditor on account of the specific cause of action provided for in para 74(2) which allows a creditor or member to apply to the court claiming that an administrator is not performing his functions in accordance with this provision. The relief available on such an application, as provided for in para 74(4), does not appear sufficiently broad to allow the court to make an order for damages or other financial recompense arising as a consequence of a breach of para 4. It is further suggested, however, that a claim may be made in respect of loss so arising on behalf of the company in administration by an applicant eligible to bring a misfeasance claim under para 75(3)(c) on the basis that para 4 amounts to an 'other duty', if not a fiduciary duty, in relation to the company.

5 Status of administrator

An administrator is an officer of the court (whether or not he is appointed by the court).

General note—Under the former administration regime under Part II an administrator was an officer of the court: *Re Atlantic Computer Systems plc* [1992] Ch 505. Paragraph 5 confirms that position, even where an administrator is appointed out-of-court. Whilst the new provision will avoid any suggestion that an out-of-court appointee is not an officer of the court, particularly in light of the decision of the Court of Appeal in *Re TH Knitwear (Wholesale) Ltd* [1988] Ch 275, which is authority for the proposition that a liquidator in a voluntary liquidation is not an officer of the court, its real significance lies in ensuring that an out-of-court appointee is treated as a court appointee for the purposes of the EC Regulation on Insolvency Proceedings (1346/2000) (of which see Article 1 thereof and Annex A thereto).

The consequences of the administrator's status as an officer of the court—There are three obvious consequences which follow from the administrator's status as an officer of the court.

First, an administrator is subject to the rule in *Re Condon ex parte James* (1874) 9 Ch App 609. The elusive and difficult principle enshrined in that rule was identified in *Re Tyler* [1907] 1 KB 865 at 871 as being based on morality and requires that an officer of the court should behave in a high-minded and honourable way. More recently, the matter was identified by His Honour Judge Weeks QC, sitting as a High Court judge, in the following terms in *Re South West Car Sales Ltd (in liquidation)* (1998) BCC 163 at 170, 'The principle underlying the rule in *Ex parte James* is that officers of the court should behave decently and honourably and not retain money which a decent and honourable man would think it dishonest to keep.' In *Re Condon* a trustee-in-bankruptcy was ordered to restore monies paid to him under a mistake of law and which would otherwise have been irrecoverable from him. However, following the decision in *Re Tyler* [1907] 1 KB 865, the courts have extended the application of the rule beyond the recovery of payments made pursuant to a mistake of law to cases which turn on the enrichment of the bankruptcy estate, irrespective of how the enrichment came about: see, for example, *Green v Satangi* [1998] BPIR 55. Indeed, in *Re Clarke* [1975] 1 WLR 559 at 563 Walton J identified the requirement for some form of enrichment of the insolvent estate as being the universal characteristic of all of the cases in which the rule had been applied, in addition to establishing the further conditions required for the rule to operate. Subsequent authorities, however, militate against an inflexible approach to the scope of the rule: see, for example, *Re T H Knitwear (Wholesale) Ltd* [1988] Ch 275 at 289 per Slade LJ, 'The entire basis of the principle, as I discern it from the cases, is that the court will not allow its own officer to behave in a dishonourable manner. There is no doubt much to be said in favour of the principle.' It is suggested that there is much to be said for the subsuming of the rule in *Ex parte James* into the law of restitution, since the courts could then be seen to be applying the rule on a legal basis, as opposed to the less predictable basis of morality, given that the enforcement of the rule relies on the court reaching a finding of unfairness or inequity. This matter is developed further in Dawson 'The Administrator, Morality and the Court' [1996] JBL 437 at 454. For the application and further elaboration on the development of the rule see *Scranton's Trustee v Pearce* [1922] 2 Ch 87 (trustee not permitted to recover unenforceable gambling debts); *Re Wyvern Developments Ltd* [1974] 1 WLR 1097; *Re Multi-Guarantee Co Ltd* [1987] BCLC 257, CA; *Re Thellusson* [1999] 2 KB 735 (trustee required to repay monies loaned to bankrupt in ignorance of receiving order having been made); *Re Japan Leasing (Europe) plc* [1999] BPIR 911; *Re Spring Valley Properties Ltd* [2001] BCC 793. For the restrictive approach to the scope of the rule in Australia see the commentary in A Keay *McPherson's Law of Company Liquidation* (3rd edn Sweet and Maxwell, 2013) at 581–583. It will be apparent from the above analysis that the rule in *Ex parte James* can only operate subject to relatively exacting requirements and does not amount to some generally applicable ground upon which all manner of complaints against an office-holder might be advanced, as can arise in practice.

The second consequence of an administrator being an officer of the court is that an officer of the court has access to the court for the provision of directions. In administration such a facility is in any case expressly provided for in paras 63 and 68(2), on which see the notes thereto. An officer of the court is also subject to the direction of the court by way of the court's inherent jurisdiction: *Re Sabre International Products Ltd* [1991] BCC 694.

Finally, an officer of the court enjoys the very useful protection of the law of contempt from interference with the performance of his duties: see *Bristol Airport plc v Powdrill* [1990] Ch 744 and *Re Sabre International Products Ltd* [1991] BCC 694.

6 General restrictions

A person may be appointed as administrator of a company only if he is qualified to act as an insolvency practitioner in relation to the company.

General note—An administrator must be both 'qualified to act as an insolvency practitioner' (on which see ss 388(1)(a) and 390) and eligible to act as such in relation to any particular company.

7

A person may not be appointed as administrator of a company which is in administration (subject to the provisions of paragraphs 90 to 97 and 100 to 103 about replacement and additional administrators).

General note—This provision expressly precludes the contemporaneous appointment of two or more administrators, in or out of court, save for the appointment of joint, replacement and additional administrators.

Save for the overriding rights of a qualifying charge holder – on which see para 12(2) – the race for appointment will go to the quicker or quickest appointor.

8

(1) A person may not be appointed as administrator of a company which is in liquidation by virtue of—

(a)   a resolution for voluntary winding up, or

(b)   a winding-up order.

(2) Sub-paragraph (1)(a) is subject to paragraph 38.

(3) Sub-paragraph (1)(b) is subject to paragraphs 37 and 38.

General note—Subject to one very limited exception, a person may not be appointed as administrator of a company which is in liquidation. Contemporaneous liquidation and administration may come about in a single and, in practice, relatively rare case, namely where a winding-up order is made on a public interest petition presented under s 124A or on a petition presented by the Financial Services Authority under s 367 of the Financial Services and Markets Act 2000 – neither of which is precluded by the moratorium in administration, as to which see para 40(2) – where the court makes an order that the appointment of the administrator shall continue to have effect under para 82(3)(b).

Paragraph 37 allows the court to discharge a winding-up order, together with the giving of appropriate directions on the making of an administration application by a qualifying floating charge holder. Paragraph 38 also enables the court to make such an order on the making of an administration application by a liquidator.

9

(1) A person may not be appointed as administrator of a company which—

(a) has a liability in respect of a deposit which it accepted in accordance with the Banking Act 1979 or 1987, but

(b) is not an authorised deposit taker.

(2) A person may not be appointed as administrator of a company which effects or carries out contracts of insurance.

(3) But sub-paragraph (2) does not apply to a company which—

(a) is exempt from the general prohibition in relation to effecting or carrying out contracts of insurance, or

(b) is an authorised deposit taker effecting or carrying out contracts of insurance in the course of a banking business.

(4) In this paragraph—

'authorised deposit taker' means a person with permission under Part IV of the Financial Services and Markets Act 2000 to accept deposits, and

'the general prohibition' has the meaning given by section 19 of that Act.

(5) This paragraph shall be construed in accordance with—

(a) section 22 of the Financial Services and Markets Act 2000 (classes of regulated activity and categories of investment), oversight

(b) any relevant order under that section, and

(c) Schedule 2 to that Act (regulated activities).

General note—These provisions re-enact the general bar excluding banks and insurance companies from the previous Part II of the 1986 Act, and the concessions thereto.

For the continued relevance of Part II of the 1986 Act in relation to certain undertakings see the note to para 10 below.

APPOINTMENT OF ADMINISTRATOR BY COURT

10 Administration order

An administration order is an order appointing a person as the administrator of a company.

General note—An administration order may only be made by the court under para 13(1)(a) on the making of an administration application by any one or more of those applicants identified in para 12(1)(a)–(d).

Administration applications by parties eligible to appoint out of court—There is nothing to prevent the holder of a qualifying floating charge, the company or its directors making an application for an administration order notwithstanding the right of any such party to effect an out-of-court appointment under paras 14 or 22. Such an application may be considered appropriate by an applicant who perceives a wide degree of interest on the part of third parties, as well as creditors, in a company's affairs and/or who wishes to avoid the potentially adverse impression conveyed by an out-of-court appointment with the attendant lack of publicity. Administration orders made in respect of Football League clubs post 15 September 2003 provide good examples of such court appointments.

Moreover, giving the present uncertainty surrounding the effect of formal defects on the validity of out-of-court appointments (see notes to para 26), an application for an administration order may be perceived to be a 'safer' route.

It is submitted that an applicant for an administration order who is entitled to appoint out-of-court will nevertheless remain subject to the burden of proof under para 11(b) in satisfying the court that an administration order is reasonably likely to achieve the purpose of administration. In other words, a court application is not merely an exercise in the court 'rubber stamping' the application, even though the application will necessarily be supported by a statement by the proposed administrator in Form 2.2B, as required by IR 1986, r 2.3(5)(c), confirming his opinion that it is reasonably likely that that purpose will be achieved. Paragraph 11 places the requirement for satisfaction as to the fulfilment of the conditions therein squarely on the court, although the court will no doubt have regard to the opinion expressed by the proposed administrator in conjunction with the evidence in support, as required by r 2.4(1) and (2). Such an opinion, however, is not always conclusive. For example, in *Re Rowbotham Baxter Ltd* [1990] BCC 113 Harman J dismissed a petition for an administration order despite giving 'considerable weight' to the proposed administrator's opinion that the making of an administration order carried with it the real prospect of the approval of a company voluntary arrangement. Neither will, or should, the court necessarily accept the view of a proposed administrator, or his appreciation of the administration procedure. For example, the judgment of Jacob J, as he then was, in *Re Colt Telecom Group plc* [2003] BPIR 324, a case under the former Part II, includes serious criticism of both the contents of a r 2.2 report produced by a proposed administrator and that individual's apparent lack of understanding of the former administration regime.

Undertakings to which the former Part II of the 1986 Act continues to apply—There are three categories of undertaking to which the original Part II provisions continue to apply. First, any company in respect of which an administration order was made prior to 15 September 2003 will remain subject to the former regime pending discharge of the order. There is, it should be noted, no scope for the two regimes applying contemporaneously to a single undertaking. Secondly, Part II continues to apply to those special cases identified in s 249(1) of the Enterprise Act 2002 (ie appointed water and sewerage undertakers, a protected railway company, a licensed air traffic services company, certain public-private partnership companies and building societies within the meaning of s 119 of the Building Societies Act 1986), by virtue of s 249(2) of the 2002 Act). Thirdly, by virtue of reg 5(2)–(4) of the Insolvency (Amendment) Regulations 2003 (SI 2003/1730), certain applications remain subject to Part II, namely those made under the Insolvent Partnerships Order 1994, the Limited Liability Partnerships Regulations 2001 and the Financial Services and Markets Act 2002 (Administration Orders Relating to Insurers) Order 2002 (SI 2002/1242, as amended by SI 2003/2134 and reg 52 of SI 2004/353, effective from 18 February 2004).

Procedure—For the parties entitled to appear on an administration application, the form of order (in Form 2.4B), the costs of the application and the giving of notice of an order, see IR 1986, rr 2.12–2.14.

11 Conditions for making order

The court may make an administration order in relation to a company only if satisfied—

(a)   that the company is or is likely to become unable to pay its debts, and

(b)   that the administration order is reasonably likely to achieve the purpose of administration.

General note—These two conditions for the making of an administration order mirror those which appeared in s 8(1)(a) and (b).

Where the holder of a qualifying floating charge makes an application to court for the appointment of an administrator, in circumstances where the charge holder could appoint an administrator out of court under para 14, para 35(2)(a) effectively disapplies the requirement in para 11(a) that the company is or is likely to become unable to pay its debts.

'The court may make an administration order'—The use of the word 'may' indicates that the court is not required to make an administration order, even if satisfied of the two pre-conditions in para 11. In some cases the court may prefer, exceptionally, to adjourn the hearing of the application, conditionally or unconditionally, most obviously to allow for the filing of further evidence under para 13(1)(c), where the court harbours concerns as to the material presented to it. The nature of the administration regime, however, with its emphasis on the relevance of time, dictates that such an adjournment would ordinarily be for only a short period, typically a period of days.

In *Re Information Governance Limited; Hall v Popham* [2013] EWHC 2611 (Ch), the sole director of a company applied for an administration order. Prior to the hearing of the application, the respondents exercised their rights under a shareholder agreement to appoint themselves as directors and opposed the application. Although the conditions in para 11 were satisfied, David Richards J held it was not appropriate for the court to exercise its discretion to make an administration order.

Paragraph 11(a)

Threshold test—The wording here is identical to that in the form of s 8(1)(a). The analysis of that former provision provided by Jacob J, as he then was, in *Re Colt Telecom Group plc* [2003] BPIR 324 will continue to be of relevance here. In *Colt* Jacob J drew a distinction between the evidential test applicable to the two pre-conditions in s 8(1). The two were not the same. In the case of establishing that a company is or is likely to become unable to pay its debts the burden rests on the applicant in satisfying the court on a balance of probabilities that the requirement is met. This differs from the less onerous 'real prospect' test applicable to the second purpose pre-condition, on which see the note to para 11(b) below.

'... is or is likely to become unable to pay its debts'—The term 'unable to pay its debts' has the meaning given by s 123: para 111(1). Section 123 provides either a 'cash-flow' or a 'balance sheet' test of insolvency.

In *BNY Corporate Trustee Services Limited v Eurosail-UK 2007-3BL PLC* [2013] UKSC 28, the Supreme Court confirmed that the cash-flow test is concerned both with presently-due debts and with debts falling due from time to time in the 'reasonably near' future (which will depend on all the circumstances, but especially on the nature of the company's business). Beyond the reasonably near future any attempt to apply a cash-flow test is completely speculative, and a comparison of present assets with present and future liabilities (discounted for contingencies and deferment) becomes the only sensible test, although it is far from an exact science.

Although the vast majority of cases involve companies which are insolvent, an administration application may be made in respect of a company which is solvent but which is likely to become unable to pay its debts.

Paragraph 11(b)

'that the administration order is reasonably likely to achieve the purpose of administration'—An analysis of para 11(b) warrants consideration of the threshold test established under the former administration provisions under Part II, which continues to be of relevance. In *Re Harris Simons Construction Ltd* [1989] 5 BCC 11 Hoffmann J, as he then was, held (at 13H–14A) that the requirements of the former s 8(1)(b) were satisfied if the court considered there to be a 'real prospect' that one or more of the former purposes might

713

be achieved. This relatively low threshold, it should be noted, was lower than that adopted by Peter Gibson J, as he then was, in *Re Consumer & Industrial Press Ltd* (1988) 4 BCC 68 at 70, which had pitched the requirement as being above 50%. Although Hoffmann J accepted in *Harris Simons* that terms such as 'real prospect' might be said to lack precision, he likened such phrases to tempo markings in music; thus, 'although there is inevitably a degree of subjectivity in the way they are interpreted, they are nonetheless meaningful and useful.' In *Re Lomax Leisure Ltd* [2000] BCC 352 Neuberger J, as he then was, confirmed (at 363H) that the 'real prospect' test expounded in *Harris Simons* 'is now well established'.

The wording in para 11(b) is not identical to the equivalent provision in the form of s 8(1)(b). Whereas the former provision required that the court 'considers' that the making of an administration order would be 'likely' to achieve one or more of the former statutory purposes, the new provision requires the court to be 'satisfied' that the administration order is 'reasonably likely' to achieve the purpose of administration. Those differences, however, raise no practical distinction. In keeping with the standard estasblished under the former legislation, the decision of Lewison J in *Re A A Mutual International Insurance Co Ltd* [2005] 2 BCLC 8, a Sch B1 case, is authority for the propositions that 'reasonably likely' requires the court to be satisfied that there is a real prospect that a particular objective will be achieved and that real prospect does not equate to more than a 50% probability: to like effect see also *Re C:4net* [2005] BCC 277. For further discussion see the notes to para 13(1)(a) below.

In *Auto Management Services Ltd v Oracle Fleet UK Ltd* [2007] EWHC 392 (Ch), [2008] BCC 761, Warren J suggested that if an administration can be shown in all but the most unlikely circumstances to produce a result no worse than a liquidation and there are reasonably likely circumstances where the result will be better, that will be significant in influencing the court towards making an order.

It is not necessary to identify in advance with certainty which of the statutory objectives is intended to be attained: *Hammonds (a firm) v Pro-fit USA Ltd* [2007] EWHC 1998 (Ch), [2008] 2 BCLC 159.

12 Administration application

(1) An application to the court for an administration order in respect of a company (an 'administration application') may be made only by—

    (a)   the company,

    (b)   the directors of the company,

    (c)   one or more creditors of the company,

    (d)   the justices' chief executive for a magistrates' court in the exercise of the power conferred by section 87A of the Magistrates' Courts Act 1980 (fine imposed on company), or

    (e)   a combination of persons listed in paragraphs (a) to (d).

(2) As soon as is reasonably practicable after the making of an administration application the applicant shall notify—

    (a)   any person who has appointed an administrative receiver of the company,

    (b)   any person who is or may be entitled to appoint an administrative receiver of the company,

    (c)   any person who is or may be entitled to appoint an administrator of the company under paragraph 14, and

    (d)   such other persons as may be prescribed.

(3) An administration application may not be withdrawn without the permission of the court.

(4) In sub-paragraph (1) 'creditor' includes a contingent creditor and a prospective creditor.

(5) Sub-paragraph (1) is without prejudice to section 7(4)(b).

General note—Although certain of the eligible applicants for an administration order appear in para 12(1)(a)–(d), it should be noted that there are three further eligible applicants, namely (a) a liquidator under para 38(1)(b) a supervisor of a company voluntary arrangement under s 7(4)(b) (and see also para 12(5)), and (c) the Financial Services Authority under s 359 of the Financial Services and Markets Act 2000, as amended by para 55 of Sch 17 of the Enterprise Act 2002.

Paragraph 12(1)(a)

'the company'—In *Re Frontsouth (Witham) Ltd (In Administration)* [2011] EWHC 1668 (Ch), [2011] BPIR 1382 Henderson J held (obiter) that where the company's articles included reg 70 of Table A, which provides that 'the business of the company shall be managed by the directors who may exercise all the powers of the company', as a matter of general company law the decision whether or not to place the company into administration is one to be taken by the directors. The decision cannot be taken by an ordinary resolution of the shareholders, although by a special resolution they may direct the board to take such a step. This may significantly reduce the utility of para 12(1)(a).

Paragraph 12(1)(b)

'the directors of the company'—Paragraph 105 specifically provides that 'something done by the directors of a company' includes 'the same thing done by a majority of the directors of a company'. Accordingly, the directors may act by a simple majority. However, in *Minmar (929) Ltd v Khalastchi* [2011] EWHC 1159 (Ch), [2011] BCC 485, Sir Andrew Morritt C held that an out-of-court appointment purportedly made with the informal consent of a majority of directors was invalid; a board resolution was required. It is suggested that the same approach applies to an application under para 12.

Paragraph 12(1)(c)

'one or more creditors of the company'—This class will include a secured creditor, including the holder of a qualifying floating charge which is specifically identified in the standard form of administration application in Form 2.1B as an eligible applicant. In *Bank of Scotland Plc v Targetfollow Properties Holdings Limited* [2010] EWHC 3606 (Ch), a qualifying charge holder chose to apply for an administration order where another secured creditor claimed that under the terms of an inter-creditor deed it had a contractual right to consultation as a pre-condition to the out-of-court appointment of administrators.

The term 'creditor' includes a contingent or prospective creditor: see para 12(4).

Paragraph 12(2)

Notification of application to floating charge holders and others—Paragraph 12(2)(a) and (b) require notification of an application to be given to any person who was appointed an administrative receiver (ie where the administrative receiver remains in office) or any person who is or may be entitled to effect such an appointment. For the definition of an administrative receiver see s 29(2) and the notes thereto. There is a requirement for notification to the holder of requisite security for the appointment of an administrative receiver, since Sch B1 does nothing to prevent the appointment of an administrative receiver in the case of security granted prior to 15 September 2003 or in any of those excepted cases in ss 72B–72GA. Paragraph 39 provides that the court must dismiss an administration application where an administrative receiver is appointed prior to or following the making of an administration application other than in specified circumstances.

Paragraph 12(2)(c) operates so as to give notice of the holder of a qualifying floating charge who may take any of three steps on receipt of an application. First, the floating charge holder may effect an out-of-court appointment under para 14. Secondly, the charge holder may join in the application for the purpose of seeking the appointment of an administrator other than the person proposed by the administration applicant. The third option involves the charge holder simply acquiescing in the administration application.

For the persons prescribed for the purpose of para 12(2)(d) see IR 1986, rr 2.6(3) and 2.7. Notably, service of the application must be effected on persons within the former provision, whereas the latter requires only the giving of notice, as opposed to service of the application itself, to persons identified therein. The reason for this is that the purpose of giving notice under r 2.7 is primarily to avoid an inadvertent contempt by way of the levying of any execution, legal process of distraint against the company or its property in ignorance of the moratorium provisions having been triggered on the presentation of an administration application.

Paragraph 12(3)

Withdrawal of application only with permission of the court—The purpose of this provision is in guarding against unmeritorious administration applications of the kind which might be made for the sole purpose of obtaining the temporary protection of the statutory moratorium and which, as such, would constitute an abuse of process. The making of an administration application is a significant step and the court will require an explanation as to why an application has to be aborted.

Paragraph 12(5)

A supervisor's application—An application by a supervisor is treated as if it were an application by the company: r 2.2(4).

Practice where dispute as to standing of applicant as creditor of the company— There is no established practice in relation to administration applications which equates to the practice on a disputed winding-up petition. In an administration case the court will have to be satisfied, save in an exceptional case, that the applicant is in fact a creditor, as it would have to determine the status of any alleged cross-claim: *Hammonds (a firm) v Pro-Fit USA Ltd* [2008] 2 BCLC 159 at [49]–[57] (Warren J); compare the comments on Carnwath J in *Re MGI Trading Systems Ltd (in administration)* [1998] 2 BCLC 246 (under the former Part II regime) to the effect that the 1986 Act calls for a realistic interpretation and that, particularly where there is a need for an administration order to be made urgently, it would frustrate the purpose of the provisions if any dispute as to locus or jurisdiction had to be decided before an order could be made.

Procedure—For the procedure applicable to the appointment of an administrator by the court see rr 2.2–2.14 and the notes and form references therein.

13 Powers of court

(1) On hearing an administration application the court may—

    (a)   make the administration order sought;

    (b)   dismiss the application;

    (c)   adjourn the hearing conditionally or unconditionally;

    (d)   make an interim order;

    (e)   treat the application as a winding-up petition and make any order which the court could make under section 125;

    (f)   make any other order which the court thinks appropriate.

(2) An appointment of an administrator by administration order takes effect—

    (a)   at a time appointed by the order, or

    (b)   where no time is appointed by the order, when the order is made.

(3) An interim order under sub-paragraph (1)(d) may, in particular—

    (a)   restrict the exercise of a power of the directors or the company;

(b)   make provision conferring a discretion on the court or on a person qualified to act as an insolvency practitioner in relation to the company.

(4) This paragraph is subject to paragraph 39.

General note—The court has the widest jurisdiction in making an order on the hearing or at an adjourned hearing of an administration application. The practical relevance of para 13(2) lies in para 1(2)(a) which provides that a company is 'in administration' while the appointment of an administrator of the company has effect: see further the notes to para 13(2) below.

Eligible applicants—In addition to the classes of person identified in para 12(1) an application for an administration order may also be made by the holder of a qualifying floating charge where the company is in compulsory liquidation – but not, for any obviously good reason, where the company is in voluntary liquidation – under para 37(2) or by a liquidator under para 38(1). An application may also be made by the supervisor of a CVA under s 7(4)(b) (on which see para 12(5)) or the Financial Services Authority under s 359 of the Financial Services and Markets Act 2000.

Paragraph 13(1)(a)

'... make the administration order sought ...'—In considering the making of an administration order the court will wish to consider not only the interests of all of the company's creditors as a whole, as well as the particular interests of secured, preferential and unsecured creditors, but also the attitude of creditors generally to the administration. The interests of any secured creditor will weigh less heavily where that creditor is fully secured: *Re Consumer & Industrial Press Ltd* [1988] BCLC 177 at 181A (Peter Gibson J, as he then was) and *Re Imperial Motors (UK) Ltd* [1990] BCLC 29. The court is unlikely to make an administration order if satisfied that a majority of creditors are either opposed to the order or are unlikely to support the administrator's proposals: *Re Arrows Ltd (No 3)* [1992] BCLC 555; and see *Re Stalton Distribution Ltd* [2002] BCC 486, and *Re West Park Golf & Country Club* [1997] 1 BCLC 20, but compare *Re Structures and Computers Ltd* [1998] 1 BCLC 292 and see the notes to para 55 and the cases cited therein. An order was made in *Re DKLL Solicitors* [2008] 1 BCLC 112 (Andrew Simmonds QC, sitting as a deputy High Court judge) where, notwithstanding the opposition of the Revenue as a creditor for some £1.7m of total debts of approximately £2.4m, the order would allow for a pre-pack sale of a firm of solicitors' business which would operate to save more than 50 employees' jobs, minimise disruption to clients' affairs and avoid a Law Society intervention. The fact that an administration order is sought by directors prompted by an ulterior motive did not preclude the making of an order by Blackburne J in *Re Dianoor Jewels Ltd* [2001] 1 BCLC 450 where a former wife alleged that a petition had been instituted by her managing director husband in an attempt to scupper ancillary relief proceedings. Opposition to an application on the grounds that incumbent management or owners of a company claim to be able to achieve an outcome equivalent to any of the statutory purposes at a reduced cost should ordinarily, it is submitted, be attributed only modest weight, if any.

The decision of Warren J in *El Ajou v Dollar Land (Manhattan) Ltd* [2007] BCC 953 involved the question of whether the court should make an administration order on the application of the company (which was no longer trading) or a winding-up order on a petition presented by a creditor based on a judgment debt which was subject to an outstanding appeal by the company. Adopting the view that the outstanding appeal did not affect the judgment creditor's status as a creditor, and whilst ultimately a matter of discretion on the facts of the case, his Lordship, in making a winding-up order, took particular notice of the fact that there was no ongoing business on which a winding-up order could have any serious effect, that the Official Receiver would take office as liquidator subject to any replacement being subject to the control of creditors generally and that the only advantage of administration appeared to be a saving of some £2,000 in costs which, in the circumstances, was trivial.

Identity of the administrator—There may be a conflict as to the choice of administrator. In *Re World Class Homes Ltd* [2005] 2 BCLC 1 a petitioning creditor had presented a winding-up petition following which the debtor company made an application for an administration order. The petitioning creditor argued that its nominee should be appointed administrator because the majority of creditors favoured his appointment and had lost confidence in the company's nominees on account of their refusal to provide relevant information to the petitioning creditor and because of doubts as to their ability to obtain the best possible price for the company's assets. In upholding the company's choice of administrators (and refusing the petitioning creditor's nominees' costs of attendance) Lindsay J held that there was no substance to the petitioning creditor's objections and that the unwillingness to disclose information was explicable on the ground that the company's nominees had not yet been appointed with the consequence that there were no grounds for a lack of confidence and concern as to the independence of professional individuals who already had some acquaintance with the company's affairs.

In *The Oracle (North West) Ltd v Pinnacle Services (UK) Ltd* [2008] EWHC 1930 the directors of the company applied for an administration order in response to which a winding-up petitioner, which was also the largest unsecured creditor, made its own cross-application. Whilst it was not in issue that the making of an administration order was appropriate, each party sought the appointment of different office-holders and made allegations as to the motives of the other as to their proposed appointees. In considering that a joint appointment as between the two sets of proposed administrators was inappropriate (in the absence of evidence as to an agreed strategy), and taking account of the facts that the secured creditor remained neutral and that the winding-up petitioner applicant (who was supported by the next most significant creditor) would effectively control a creditors' meeting, Patten J held that where significant creditors have a clear preference for one administrator over another, and the secured and other creditors remain neutral, the court should ordinarily give effect to the wishes of those creditors given that administration is intended to operate for the benefit of creditors.

In *Healthcare Management Services Ltd v Caremark Properties Ltd* [2012] EWHC 1693 (Ch) the conflict as to the choice of administrator arose between the applicant creditor and another creditor. Morgan J held thatin the ordinary case where the conflict was between the views of one group of creditors and the views of a rival group of creditors, the majority in terms of value would prevail as between the creditors, although the majority view did not bind a court which has the final say.

Paragraph 13(1)(c)

There is no limit to the scope of the conditions upon which the court may adjourn an administration application. Conceivably, especially where the adjournment is granted on the application of the applicant and with any degree of reluctance on the part of the court, such conditions might require that the application is withdrawn, dismissed or moved at the adjourned hearing.

The court is unlikely to granted a lengthy adjournment or repeated adjournments given the exceptional nature of the interim moratorium and its effect upon the legitimate rights of third parties."

Paragraph 13(1)(d)

'... make an interim order ...'—No indication appears in Sch B1 as to the scope of an interim order, which was also available to the court previously under s 9(4). Such an order may only be made on the hearing of an administration application – and therefore cannot be sought in the period between presentation of the application and its hearing unless the court is prepared to abridge time for the hearing of the application – and, by its nature, will take effect where the hearing of the application is adjourned under para 13(1)(c). However, in *Re Switch Services Ltd (in administration), SB Corporate Solutions Ltd v Prescott* [2012] Bus LR D91, HHJ McCahill QC (sitting as a High Court judge) held that that the court had the power to grant interim relief prior to a formal application being issued and without written evidence.

The purpose of an interim order will usually be something analogous to an interim injunction so as to hold the proverbial ring pending the determination of the administration application. This is envisaged in the terms of para 13(3) which reflects orders made in the earlier case law. For example, in *Re a Company (No 00175 of 1987)* (1987) 3 BCC 124 Vinelott J made an interim order appointing an insolvency practitioner to take control of a company's property and manage its affairs pending the adjourned hearing and identified that appointment as something akin to a receiver appointed over disputed property which was in jeopardy. In addition to such an appointment, or as an alternative to it, as in *Re Gallidoro Trawlers Ltd* [1991] BCC 691, the court may make an order which restricts the powers of a company's directors so far as deemed necessary pending the hearing of the application. There is also no good reason why the court should not make an interim order which restricts the enforcement of security over the company's property and undertaking where the validity or enforceability of that security can be called into question on genuinely arguable grounds, for the purposes of para 39(1) or otherwise, and where such enforcement might otherwise have a prejudicial effect on the administration application.

Part II did not provide expressly for the appointment of an interim administrator. Neither does any such provision appear in Sch B1. As such, it is almost certainly the case that the court has no power to appoint an interim administrator: see *Re a Company (No 00175 of 1987)* [1987] 3 BCC 124 (Vinelott J). Certainly an interim order under Part II was held not to constitute an administration order for the purposes of s 6(2)(b) of the Company Directors Disqualification Act 1986: *Secretary of State for Trade and Industry v Palmer* [1994] BCC 990.

Paragraph 13(1)(e)

'... **treat the application as a winding-up petition ...**'—This provision is new and allows the court to make any order available to it under s 125, most obviously a winding-up order notwithstanding the absence of a winding-up petition (other than where such a petition is extant but stayed by para 42(3)). This is a useful facility which effectively allows for the avoidance of the time and expense of instituting the winding-up procedure where the court is satisfied that there is no real prospect of an administration application succeeding and where the court takes the view that it is appropriate on the facts for a formal insolvency procedure to be put in place. This approach was adopted by the court in *Re UK Steelfixers Limited* [2012] EWHC 2409 (Ch); *Re Bowen Travel* [2012] EWHC 3405 (Ch), [2013] BCC 182 and *Re Integral Limited* [2013] EWHC 164 (Ch).

Alternatively, the court might be prepared to resile from the making of a winding-up order, so as to avoid the DTI levy in a compulsory liquidation, on being given suitable undertakings for the placing of the company into voluntary liquidation.

Although the usual practice in the Companies Court on the making of a winding-up order is for the petitioner's costs to be paid by the company, the usual order on the making of a winding-up order under para 13(1)(e) should, it is submitted, provide that the costs of an administration application be treated as costs in the winding up where a winding-up order is made under para 13(1)(e): see *Re Gosscott (Groundworks) Ltd* [1988] BCLC 363.

Paragraph 13(1)(f)

'... **any other order which the court thinks appropriate**'—An order under this provision will be one falling outside of the scope of para 13(1)(a)–(e). Such an order would include one appointing an administrator other than the appointee proposed by an applicant where other creditors, who will in the ordinary course face an uphill struggle, are able to convince the court that an alternative appointee is more appropriate. Paragraph 13(1)(f) would also extend to the provision of directions under para 68(2). The utility of the former provision lies in the court having the widest discretion to tailor its order to meet the particular facts of a case.

Paragraph 13(2)

Scope of the provision—Note (j) to the prescribed form of administration order in Form 2.4B allows for the inclusion of the time at which the order was made. Paragraph 13(2)(b) implies the time of the order in the event that no time is so stipulated. It appears, however, that the court has power under para 13(2)(a) to provide that an order takes effect at a time other than when the order is made. It is not at all clear why the court should wish an appointment to take effect after the making of an administration order, although it is conceivable that such an order might be desirable in a case where other administration-type applications are pursued in other jurisdictions in respect of other group or associated companies and where there can be shown to be good commercial reasons for the synchronizing of the effect of such orders. Nevertheless, it is even less clear upon what basis the court might order, as appears possible from the wording employed, that the appointment is to take effect at a time *before* the order is made. Until an appointment takes effect the administrator has no standing to exercise any of his statutory powers, as identified in the note to para 60, such that the court should give consideration in such circumstances to the making of an interim order under para 13(1)(d) for the intervening period.

In *Re G-Tech Construction Ltd* [2007] BPIR 1275, Hart J held that the wording of para 13 was wide enough to give the court jurisdiction to make an administration order with retrospective effect. However, the court may only make a retrospective order if the conditions in para 11 are satisfied at the time when the order is made: *Re Care Matters Partnership Limited* [2011] EWHC 2543 (Ch), [2011] BCC 957. This jurisdiction has been used extensively in recent times in cases where a purported out-of-court appointment has subsequently been discovered to be invalid as a result of a technical defect (e g *Re Derfshaw Limited* [2011] EWHC 1565 (Ch)).

Paragraph 13(4)

The effect of para 39—The court must dismiss an administration application under para 39(1) where an administrative receiver has been appointed before or after the making of an administration application unless any of the four exceptions in that provision apply. Where any of the four circumstances in para 39(1) are alleged, it is submitted that the court should not undertake a detailed and rigorous examination of the challenge to the security, but should adopt an approach of the sort suggested in the notes to para 38. On the other hand, the court may take the view that it is possible to resolve the issue finally in the course of a short hearing after a relatively brief adjournment allowing for the filing of any evidence without undermining the essential element of speed and economy at the heart of the administration regime.

Procedure—See r 2.12 which lists those persons who may appear or be represented on the hearing of an administration application, identifies the form of an administration order as Form 2.4B and provides for the costs of an application, and r 2.14 which provides for the giving of notice of an administration order.

In practice, the court will ordinarily allow for the appearance or representation of a creditor under r 2.12(1)(k), although the court will be unlikely to entertain numerous appearances where the interests of each party are essentially the same. The court may also give permission under r 2.12(1)(k) to contributories, although it will be justified in refusing to do so where there is no prospect of financial participation amongst that class in the administration: *Re Chelmsford City Football Club (1980) Ltd* [1991] BCC 133. The court may also consider it appropriate to warn any party appearing as to the risk on costs (as to which see the note to para 13(1)(a) above).

If the court makes an interim order under para 13(1)(d), then r 2.14(3) requires that the court give directions as to the persons to whom, and how, notice of that order is to be given. The interim order need not follow any prescribed form.

The Financial Services Authority also has standing to be heard on an application under s 362(2)(a) of the Financial Services and Markets Act 2000.

APPOINTMENT OF ADMINISTRATOR BY HOLDER OF FLOATING CHARGE

14 Power to appoint

(1) The holder of a qualifying floating charge in respect of a company's property may appoint an administrator of the company.

(2) For the purposes of sub-paragraph (1) a floating charge qualifies if created by an instrument which—

(a)   states that this paragraph applies to the floating charge,

(b)   purports to empower the holder of the floating charge to appoint an administrator of the company,

(c)   purports to empower the holder of the floating charge to make an appointment which would be the appointment of an administrative receiver within the meaning given by section 29(2), or

(d)   purports to empower the holder of a floating charge in Scotland to appoint a receiver who on appointment would be an administrative receiver.

(3) For the purposes of sub-paragraph (1) a person is the holder of a qualifying floating charge in respect of a company's property if he holds one or more debentures of the company secured—

(a)   by a qualifying floating charge which relates to the whole or substantially the whole of the company's property,

(b)   by a number of qualifying floating charges which together relate to the whole or substantially the whole of the company's property, or

(c)   by charges and other forms of security which together relate to the whole or substantially the whole of the company's property and at least one of which is a qualifying floating charge.

General note—The basis of the power of the holder of a qualifying floating charge to appoint an administrator lies in para 14(1) which is provisoed by paras 14(2), 14(3) and 16. Paragraph 16 provides that 'an administrator may not be appointed under para 14 while a floating charge on which the appointment relies is not enforceable'. A proper understanding of the two provisions requires a distinction to be drawn between a purported power to appoint an administrator (under para 14(2)), the property comprised in the charge holder's security (under para 14(3)) and the enforceability of the floating charge pursuant to which the appointment of the administrator is to be made (see para 16).

Paragraph 14(2) is concerned with the existence of a purported power to appoint. *Prima facie* it is the existence of such a purported power by which a floating charge 'qualifies' as a qualifying floating charge for the purpose of para 14(1) although, for the reasons identified below in relation to para 14(3), the floating charge must also meet one of the conditions in that provision so as to qualify as a floating charge, in addition to the charge being enforceable for the purposes of para 16. If the floating charge pursuant to which the appointment is made comprises a purported power to appoint which, it is argued, has not been triggered then, it is submitted, para 16 would come into operation given that the *purported* power to appoint requirement in para 14(2) could be shown to have been met.

The wording in the opening part of para 14(3) is less clear than it might have been since the impression is conveyed that the holder of the security defined within the provision 'is the holder of a qualifying floating charge' whereas para 14(2) stipulates that the floating charge comprising such security only 'qualifies' subject to its terms. The position might have been made clearer by omitting the word 'qualifying' from the opening part of para 14(3) or, alternatively, by reading para 14(1) as being expressly subject to para 14(2) and omitting the mechanism by which 'a floating charge qualifies' from that latter provision.

The following commentary should be read in conjunction with the notes to para 16.

Security enforcement as alternatives to administration—The holder of security meeting the requirements of s 29(2)(a) remains entitled to appoint an administrative receiver within the meaning of s 29(2) where the requisite floating charge element of that security was created prior to 15 September 2003: see s 72A(4)(a). Irrespective of the date of its creation, the holder of a fixed charge, or a floating charge which does not meet any of the para 14(3) requirements, may appoint a non-administrative or LPA receiver pursuant to that security. There are also certain exceptional cases provided for in s 72B–72GA which allow for the appointment of an administrative receiver, irrespective of the date of the creation of the requisite security. An administrative receiver must, however, vacate office on the appointment of an administrator (para 41(1)), as must a non-administrative/LPA receiver, but only if the administrator requires him to do so (para 41(2)).

No insolvency requirement on appointment of administrator by holder of floating charge out-of-court—In the case of an out-of-court appointment by a floating charge holder there is no requirement that the company is or is likely to become unable to pay its debts as there is where the court makes an administration order (see para 11(a)) or where an out-of-court appointment is effected by a company or its directors (see para 27(2)). Neither is there such a requirement where a floating charge holder seeks an administration order under para 35, subject to the conditions therein.

The triggering of the statutory moratorium—The moratorium provided for in paras 40–43 will only trigger in a para 14 appointment case when the requirements of para 18 are satisfied. In practice, whilst the para 18 formalities go rather beyond the more basic steps necessary to effect the appointment of an administrative receiver, compliance with the statutory requirements should be capable of being met within a very short period of time in most cases, at least where speed is a factor; furthermore, provision is made for a para 14 appointment taking place out of court business hours by faxing the notice of appointment in Form 2.7B to the court under IR 1986, r 2.19, on which see the notes thereto.

Where there exists a prior floating charge holder entitled to notice of intention to appoint under para 15(1)(a), an interim moratorium – equivalent in substance to paras 42 and 43, but operating so as to dismiss any winding-up petition under para 40 – is triggered on the filing of a copy of the prescribed Form 2.5B notice of intention to appoint. The interim moratorium is effective until the appointment of the administrator takes effect or upon the expiration of five days beginning with the date of filing: para 44(2)–(5).

Paragraph 14(1)

'The holder of a qualifying floating charge ... may appoint an administrator of the company'—As noted in the introductions to Sch B1 and Part III on receiverships, the holder of a floating charge compliant with s 29(2)(a) but created on or after 15 September 2003 may no longer appoint an administrative receiver other than in those excepted cases identified in ss 72B to 72GA. Such a charge holder is specifically entitled by virtue of this provision to appoint an administrator. The position of the charge-holder may, however, be said to be significantly weaker than previously, since the out-of-court appointee is obliged, in common with any other administrator, to perform his functions with the objectives identified in para 3(1). From a practical perspective, an administrator appointed out-of-court by a qualifying floating charge holder will be obliged at least to consider whether it is reasonably practicable to achieve the objectives in para 3(1)(a) or (b), even when, in reality, the real wish on the part of the charge holder is to realise its security. Further commentary on this issue appears in the notes to para 3.

It remains to be seen whether in practice the new administration regime can be shown to have produced any marked improvement in terms of rehabilitation and recovery, by whatever criteria that term might be measured, in cases where it might otherwise reasonably be supposed that the company would have been placed into administrative receivership.

Paragraph 14(2)

'... floating charge qualifies if created by an instrument which ...'—There are four separate grounds upon which a floating charge 'qualifies' for the purpose of para 14(1). Although only para 14(2)(b)–(d) make express reference to the instrument purporting to empower the floating charge holder to make an appointment, para 14(2)(a) is to the same effect (given the heading 'power to appoint' to para 14). Whilst in practice it would not strictly be necessary, for the purposes of para 14(2)(a), for an instrument to expressly make reference to a power to appoint (it being apparently sufficient for the instrument merely to make reference to para 14 alone, without more), a well-drawn, standard-form debenture or other instrument will invariably, if only for the avoidance of doubt and clarity, make specific reference to a power to appoint.

In the cases of para 14(2)(b)–(d) the purported power to appoint must relate to the specific type of office-holder identified in each provision.

Paragraph 14(2)(c) relates to a floating charge created prior to 15 September 2003 which is compliant with para 14(3).

Paragraph 14(3)

'... is the holder of a qualifying floating charge in respect of a company's property if he holds one or more debentures of the company secured ...'—There are three alternative scenarios by any of which a charge holder may qualify as the holder of a floating charge within this provision. The language used and the substance of the three subparagraphs, it should be noted, very closely resemble, but are not identical to, the language employed in the definition of an administrative receiver in s 29(2)(a) ('a receiver or manager of the whole (or substantially the whole) of a company's property appointed by or on behalf of the holders of any debentures of the company secured by a charge which, as created, was a floating charge, or by such a charge and one or more other securities').

There are two requirements common to each of the four constituent elements in para 14(3), namely (i) the requirement that the security is constituted by a floating charge (ie as defined in para 111(1)) or charges, and (ii) the requirement that the requisite security (ie a single floating charge or number of floating charges which, whether or not in combination, extend to the whole or substantially the whole of the company's property). The words 'one or more debentures' means that there is no requirement that the requisite security is created by a single instrument or provided for in a single security document.

Paragraph 14(3)(b) differs from the substance of s 29(2) in that the former provision now allows the charge holder to meet the requisite security requirements if two or more floating charges, taken together, constitute security over the whole or substantially the whole of the company's property. Although it was held in *Re Croffbell Ltd* [1990] BCLC 844 by Vinelott J that a floating charge remains a valid basis for the appointment of an administrative receiver for the purposes of s 29(2), notwithstanding the fact that the security actually catches on no assets (so as to constitute a so-called 'lightweight floating charge'), such a position is highly unlikely in practice since a floating charge is usually framed in terms so as to catch any assets not subject to any fixed charge such that the floating charge would catch nothing on crystallisation only if the debtor company had no assets whatsoever or if the entirety of the company's assets were subject to a valid fixed charge.

Paragraph 14(3)(c) addresses the position where the charge holder holds two or more 'charges and other forms of security' of which at least one constitutes a qualifying floating charge. However, in such a case the presence of the qualifying floating charge itself would appear to entitle the charge holder to qualify as a floating charge holder under para 14(3)(a), such that the existence of charges and other forms of security which do not constitute a qualifying floating charge would appear irrelevant. In *Meadrealm Ltd* (unreported, Chancery Division, 29 November 1991, the decision never being reduced to an approved judgment) Vinelott J held that a receiver could not amount to an administrative receiver where appointed pursuant to a fixed charge only when the appointor was the holder of a floating charge and a fixed charge which cumulatively extended to the whole or substantially the whole of the company's assets. The substance of the decision, it is respectfully submitted, is doubtful. Nothing in s 29(2) requires an appointment of an administrative receiver to be effected pursuant to any particular security. Rather, the provision is concerned with the substance of the security held by a debenture holder. Paragraph 14(3) adopts precisely the same approach. In both cases, it is submitted, the common requirement is for a floating charge (or two or more such charges in the case of para 14(3)) which extends to the whole or substantially the whole of the assets of the company. Although para 14(2) does make reference to the existence of a purported power to appoint, there is no requirement that the appointment of an administrator should actually be effected pursuant to that power provided that, by way of substance over form, the requirements in both para 14(2) and (3), contrary to the form over substance approach in *Meadrealm*, are met.

The inter-relationship between para 14(1), (2) and (3)—The appointment of an administrator under para 14(1) requires an intended appointor and the security held by the intended appointor to come within both para 14(3) and (2) respectively.

The language used in the three subparagraphs is not as straightforward or as clear as it might have been. The starting point lies in para 14(3) which, though determinative of the appointor's status as the 'holder' of a qualifying floating charge, is actually concerned with the substance of the appointor's security, as discussed under the immediately preceding heading. Paragraph 14(2), on the other hand, determines whether a floating charge constitutes a qualifying floating charge not by reference to the substance of the security itself (which, of course, is addressed by para 14(2)), but by reference (and no more) to either, in the case of para 14(1), the label (and no more) attached to the instrument by which the floating charge is created or, in the case of each of the subparas (b)–(d), the existence of a purported power to appoint.

An appointment under para 14(1) will not be possible where the intended appointor's security does not meet the requirements in para 14(3), even though either of the requirements in para 14(2) can be met, since, in those circumstances, the intended appointor would not be the 'holder' of a qualifying floating charge, and only such a 'holder ... may appoint an administrator ...' under para 14(1).

15 Restrictions on power to appoint

(1) A person may not appoint an administrator under paragraph 14 unless—

> (a) he has given at least two business days' written notice to the holder of any prior floating charge which satisfies paragraph 14(2), or
>
> (b) the holder of any prior floating charge which satisfies paragraph 14(2) has consented in writing to the making of the appointment.

(2) One floating charge is prior to another for the purposes of this paragraph if—

> (a) it was created first, or
>
> (b) it is to be treated as having priority in accordance with an agreement to which the holder of each floating charge was party.

(3) Sub-paragraph (2) shall have effect in relation to Scotland as if the following were substituted for paragraph (a)—

> '(a) it has priority of ranking in accordance with section 464(4)(b) of the Companies Act 1985,'.

General note—This provision operates as a further pre-condition to a valid appointment under para 14, although it only arises where the security of the intending appointor under para 14(3) ranks subject to any prior floating charge – of which there may be more than one – which meets the appointment criteria in para 14(2).

The intending appointor must give at least two business days' written notice of the intention to appoint to the senior charge holder(s) under para 15(1)(a). Where the senior charge holder is content with the identity of the proposed appointee, the senior charge holder may consent in writing to the making of the appointment under para 15(1)(b). In the first of these two cases the senior charge holder(s) has no standing to prevent the proposed appointment proceeding other than where a challenge is made to the enforceability of the intending appointor's security, say on grounds of illegality in the creation of the charge. Instead, the giving of the relatively short period of notice of intention to appoint is designed to provide a senior qualifying floating charge holder the opportunity to effect the appointment of his own administrator, whether by court order or out-of-court, thereby guaranteeing an appointee of his choice and precluding the appointment by the junior charge holder on the basis that only one administrator, or joint appointees, may hold office at any one time.

In *Re Eco Link Resources Ltd (in CVL)* [2012] BCC 731, HHJ David Cooke (sitting as a High Court judge) held that failure to comply with para 15 is a defect which renders an appointment by a second charge holder invalid from the beginning and is not capable of being cured retrospectively.

In contrast, in *Re Care People Limited* [2013] EWHC 1734 (Ch), HHJ Purle QC (sitting as a High Court judge) held that an appointment which was made before a floating charge had become enforceable (i.e. in breach of para 16) was not a nullity; the defect was capable of cure under IR 1986, r 7.55.

Paragraph 15(1)(a)

'**... written notice ...**'—Strictly speaking, there is no requirement that written notice is given in the prescribed Form 2.5B since, although any document accompanying the notice of appointment for the purpose of filing with the court under para 18(1) 'must be in the prescribed form' by virtue of para 18(5), IR 1986, r 2.16(2) does not impose a requirement for the filing of the actual notice of intention to appoint. The use of Form 2.5B, however, has two distinct advantages. First, on being filed with the court in the prescribed form, the act of filing triggers the protection of the interim moratorium by virtue of para 44(2)–(5). Secondly, Form 2.5B includes a section on which a prior ranking qualifying floating charge holder may indicate his consent to the intended appointment the absence of which his written consent must include those particular details listed in r 2.16(5)(a)–(g).

'**... the holder of any prior floating charge which satisfies para 14(2)**'—In identifying the party or parties entitled to written notice a junior intending appointor is apparently only concerned with the senior charge holder's ability to appoint under para 14(2) without any consideration as to the extent of the senior security for the purposes of para 14(3). The giving of notice is required without regard to the question of whether the standing to appoint has arisen or, it seems, any other question as to the enforceability of the senior ranking security. (This analysis was approved of by HHJ Hodge QC, sitting as a judge of the High Court, in *Re OMP Leisure Ltd* [2008] BCC 67 at [6]). In practice it is very unlikely that the ability of the senior charge holder to effect an appointment will be apparent from a search of Companies House since such information does not fall within the scope of the prescribed particulars necessary on the registration of a debenture although, in theory, such additional information may be included within the statutory form by which registration of a charge is effected. In the interests of certainty a junior charge holder should consider giving notice to all senior ranking charge holders, including fixed charge holders, whose security, particularly over intangibles, receivables and movables, might well, on closer analysis, not in fact have been created as such so as to constitute a floating charge within the para 111(1) definition: see now in particular the decision of the House of Lords in *National Westminster Bank plc v Spectrum Plus Ltd* [2005] UKHL 41 in relation to charges over book debts.

In practice, where an apparently senior charge holder can be shown to have been discharged the court may be prepared to make the order sought subject to granting the senior charge holder liberty to apply.

Priority of floating charges for the purposes of para 15(2)—This provision gives statutory effect to floating charges ranking chronologically in time, save that effect is given to any agreement varying that priority, such as a subrogation or subordination agreement, to which the intending appointor must have been party. Paragraph 15(1)(a) and (b) each make reference to 'the holder of any prior floating charge which satisfied para 14(2)'. In the absence of express provision it is submitted that there can be no requirement read into the provisions that the holder of a qualifying floating charge ranking equally with the intending appointor should be afforded notice of intention to appoint. As such, the appointment will go to the quicker of any two equal ranking and eligible appointors.

16

An administrator may not be appointed under paragraph 14 while a floating charge on which the appointment relies is not enforceable.

General note—Like para 15, this provision operates as a further pre-condition to a valid appointment under para 14. The language employed precludes an appointment where the underlying floating charge 'is not enforceable', as a consequence of which the appointment itself would be 'invalid', to use the language employed in para 21(1) (invalid appointment: indemnity).

Quite apart from the possibility of a floating charge being 'not enforceable' – say, through a failure of consideration (on which see s 245) – this provision raises the specific question of whether a floating charge on which an appointment relies is 'not enforceable' by virtue of the power to appoint an administrator, as identified in para 14(2), having yet to arise. Whilst in most cases that power will almost always have arisen, at least under the terms of a well-drawn standard form debenture, the point warrants confirmation since the term 'enforceable' in para 16 should, it is submitted, be read as meaning that the floating charge holder must be entitled to enforce its security of which a power to appoint within the meaning of para 14(2) is plainly a constituent part.

In *Lovett v Carson Country Homes Limited* [2009] EWHC 1143 (Ch), [2011] BCC 789, the administrators of a company applied to the court to determine if they were properly appointed after it was discovered that the signature of one of the company's directors on a debenture in favour of a bank under which the bank appointed the administrators had been forged. Davis J held that the bank was entitled to assume that the debenture had been validly executed by virtue of s 44 of the Companies Act 2006.

In *Re Care People Limited* [2013] EWHC 1734 (Ch), HHJ Purle QC (sitting as a High Court judge) held that para 16 is not of such fundamental importance that an appointment made shortly before the charge had become enforceable was rendered a nullity. In that case a floating charge became enforceable if a written demand was not met in full. The chargeholder served a demand upon the company and purported to appoint an administrator without having given the company an opportunity to comply with the demand. The appointment was therefore premature. However, there was no evidence to suggest that the company could comply with the demand. It was held that the premature appointment was properly characterised as a defective exercise of an undoubted power of appointment, which was procedural in nature but not fundamental to the existence of the power. In the circumstances, the defect could be waived under IR 1986, r 7.55.

In keeping with the former position under Part II, the appointment of an administrator under Sch B1 is not rendered invalid because of the existence of a bona fide dispute as to the enforceability of the security pursuant to which an administrator is appointed: *BCPMS (Europe) Ltd v GMAC Commercial Finance* [2006] All ER (D) 285 (Lewison J).

17

An administrator of a company may not be appointed under paragraph 14 if—

    (a)   a provisional liquidator of the company has been appointed under section 135, or

    (b)   an administrative receiver of the company is in office.

General note—Paragraph 17(a) and (b) constitute the only circumstances preventing an out-of-court appointment of an administrator by the holder of a qualifying floating charge. In contrast to an out-of-court appointment by a company or its directors under para 22 the existence of an outstanding winding-up petition or administration application presents no bar to an appointment: see para 25 and the notes thereto. A provisional liquidator may only be removed from office by an order of the court under IR 1986, r 4.31, the holder of a floating charge having standing to make such an application under r 4.25(1)(b). In those circumstances, however, the court would be concerned at maintaining the preservation and custody of the company's assets if those factors were relevant, as will invariably be the case, on the appointment of the provisional liquidator. An administrative receiver may only vacate office on removal by order of the court or on resigning in compliance with s 45(1) or on the making of an administration order under para 13(1): see para 41(1). The holder of a qualifying floating charge has standing to seek an administration order by virtue of para 12(1)(c).

In contrast to the position on the making of an administration order, which has the effect of dismissing a winding-up petition, an appointment under para 14 only suspends a winding-up petition for the period of the administration other than in the case of a public interest or Financial Services Authority petition which is unaffected by such an appointment: see paras 40(1)(b) and 40(2) and the notes thereto.

18 Notice of appointment

(1) A person who appoints an administrator of a company under paragraph 14 shall file with the court—

    (a)   a notice of appointment, and

    (b)   such other documents as may be prescribed.

(2) The notice of appointment must include a statutory declaration by or on behalf of the person who makes the appointment—

    (a)   that the person is the holder of a qualifying floating charge in respect of the company's property,

    (b)   that each floating charge relied on in making the appointment is (or was) enforceable on the date of the appointment, and

    (c)   that the appointment is in accordance with this Schedule.

(3) The notice of appointment must identify the administrator and must be accompanied by a statement by the administrator—

    (a)   that he consents to the appointment,

    (b)   that in his opinion the purpose of administration is reasonably likely to be achieved, and

    (c)   giving such other information and opinions as may be prescribed.

(4) For the purpose of a statement under sub-paragraph (3) an administrator may rely on information supplied by directors of the company (unless he has reason to doubt its accuracy).

(5) The notice of appointment and any document accompanying it must be in the prescribed form.

(6) A statutory declaration under sub-paragraph (2) must be made during the prescribed period.

(7) A person commits an offence if in a statutory declaration under sub-paragraph (2) he makes a statement—

    (a)   which is false, and

    (b)   which he does not reasonably believe to be true.

General note—These provisions prescribe the formalities necessary to give effect to the appointment of an administrator, on which see para 19 and the notes thereto.

Paragraph 18(1)

Documents for filing with the court—The notice of appointment is in Form 2.6B. That form incorporates a statutory declaration (required under para 18(2)) which must be made not more than five business days before the form is filed with the court: IR 1986, r 2.16(3). The reference in para 18(1)(b) to 'other documents as may be prescribed' is to those identified in r 2.16(2), being (a) the administrator's written statement in Form 2.2B (stating those matters set out in r 2.3(5)); (b) evidence (there being no prescribed form) of the giving of any notice required by para 15(1)(a) or copies of the written consent of those required to give consent under para 15(1)(b); and (c) a statement of those matters provided for in para 100(2) (joint and concurrent administrators) for which there is, again, no prescribed form.

If an appointment takes place out of court business hours, then the notice of appointment shall be in Form 2.7B: r 2.19(1). Form 2.7B must also have attached to it a statement under r 2.19 setting out reasons for the out-of-hours filing.

If previously filed in the prescribed Form 2.5B, a notice of intention to appoint will have the effect of triggering the interim moratorium provided for in para 44(2)–(5): r 2.15(1).

Paragraph 18(5) stipulates that the notice of appointment and any document appointing it must be in the prescribed form, in default of which the requirements of para 18 cannot be said to be satisfied for the purpose of para 19. Although there is no requirement that the notice of intention to appoint is in Form 2.5B, the advantages of using the prescribed form are noted under para 15(1)(a) ('written notice') above.

Paragraph 18(7)

Criminal liabilities—The penalties provided for in s 430 and Sch 10 are also provided for in s 5 of the Perjury Act 1911.

The obtaining of advice on the validity of the administrator's appointment—The statutory declaration made by or on behalf of the appointing charge holder carries with it potential criminal liability where any statement therein is false and is not reasonably believed to be true by the maker: see para 18(7). Despite the statutory indemnity to which an invalidly appointed appointee might have recourse under para 21, an administrator will also wish to be confident as to the validity of his appointment. Previously, on or shortly following the appointment of an administrative receiver an office-holder would very commonly seek legal advice as to the validity of his appointment. Not least, given the requirements as to the enforceability of the floating charge pursuant to which the appointment is effected and the requirement for compliance with para 18 by virtue of paras 16 and 19 respectively – matters in or of which an appointee in a para 14 case may not be involved or have knowledge – there are, it is suggested, very good practical reasons why an administrator appointed by the holder of a qualifying floating charge might wish to seek legal advice on the validity of his appointment.

Appointment of administrator taking place out of court business hours—See r 2.19 and the notes thereto.

Procedure—See IR 1986, rr 2.15–2.19.

19 Commencement of appointment

The appointment of an administrator under paragraph 14 takes effect when the requirements of paragraph 18 are satisfied.

General note—This provision predicates the effectiveness of a para 14 appointment on satisfaction of the requirements in para 18. This is an event of some moment, since it is at this point, and no sooner, that the administrator becomes entitled to exercise those statutory powers identified in the note to para 60.

The reference in para 19 is to 'paragraph 18', and not merely para 18(1); consequently, an appointment is not effective unless there is strict compliance with paras 18(2), (3), (5) and (6): *Fliptex Ltd v Hogg* [2004] EWHC 1280 (Ch), [2004] BCC 870 (Peter Smith J). Despite any defects in his appointment in relation to those provisions, however, para 104 would operate to render valid any act on the part of the administrator, although that provision does not operate to validate the defective appointment itself, which might be remedied either through the taking of the administrative step necessary to secure compliance with para 18 or, in an appropriate case, through an application to court for an appropriate direction under para 63. It is also arguable that a defective appointment might be capable of being cured under IR 1986, r 7.55, since out-of-court appointments seem likely to constitute 'insolvency proceedings' for the purpose of that provision, given that such appointments are attributed a case number, title and court file and, by virtue of para 5, out-of-court appointees are officers of the court. A challenge to the validity of an administrator's appointment may also be subject to estoppel arguments: see the comments of Peter Smith J in *Fliptex* (above).

The effectiveness of a para 14 appointment is unaffected by any non-compliance with para 20(a).

20

A person who appoints an administrator under paragraph 14—

(a) shall notify the administrator and such other persons as may be prescribed as soon as is reasonably practicable after the requirements of paragraph 18 are satisfied, and

(b) commits an offence if he fails without reasonable excuse to comply with paragraph (a).

General note—This provision imposes notice obligation on the appointing holder of a qualifying floating charge. Notice obligations are also imposed by para 46(2) on the administrator following appointment.

Rule 2.17(2) requires that the administrator's appointor must send a copy of the sealed order to the administrator as soon as reasonably practicable. No 'other persons' have been prescribed for the purposes of para 20(a).

Non-compliance with para 20(a) will not affect the validity of the appointment of an administrator or his standing to act as such, the sanction for default lying in the criminal penalties under para 20(b), on which see s 430, Sch 10 and the daily default fine imposed by para 106(2)(a).

Procedure—See rr 2.17(2) and 2.18 (which applies where a para 14 appointment is made after the holder of a qualifying floating charge receives notice that an administration application has been made) and para 2.19 on an out-of-court business hours appointment.

21 Invalid appointment: indemnity

(1) This paragraph applies where—

(a) a person purports to appoint an administrator under paragraph 14, and

(b) the appointment is discovered to be invalid.

(2) The court may order the person who purported to make the appointment to indemnify the person appointed against liability which arises solely by reason of the appointment's invalidity.

General note—This provision bears a very close resemblance, and, it is suggested, is identical in substance, to that in s 34 which provides for an indemnity by court order where the appointment of a receiver and manager appointed out-of-court is discovered to be invalid. The authorities considered below arise in relation to s 34 but, by analogy, will apply equally to para 21.

Paragraph 21(1)(a) and (b)

Scope of the provision—The power of the court to make an order under para 21(2) only arises where both para 21(a) and (b) are met and, as a separate matter, can only extend to liability which arises solely by reason of the invalidity of the appointment. There is nothing in the language employed in the provision to suggest that the invalidity of the appointment, for the purposes of para 21(b), should arise solely by virtue of any lack of standing to appoint under para 14.

Invalid and defective appointments distinguished—A distinction is drawn between invalidity in appointment under this provision, say where there is no power to appoint or no substantive appointment (on which see *Morris v Kanssen* [1946] AC 459 in relation to a receivership appointment), and mere defects in the formalities or procedure by which appointment is effected, which defects may be cured by para 104.

Paragraph 21(2)

'... **liability which arises solely by reason of the appointment's invalidity** ...'—These words appear wide enough to cover liabilities flowing solely from the invalidity of the appointment which are incurred by the appointee either to the company itself, say for wrongful interference with goods or conversion, or to a third party with whom the appointee has had dealings as receiver. However, it is doubtful that any such liability will arise 'solely' from any invalidity in appointment where the liability is incurred by the appointee contracting with personal liability on the basis of an indemnity from the company's assets (which indemnity would be lost by virtue of the invalidity of the appointment).

The exercise of the court's discretion under this provision – which arises through the use of the word 'may' in para 21(2) – will depend on the extent to which the appointor and appointee can each be shown to have been aware of the invalidity of the appointment or capable of establishing such invalidity on reasonable investigation.

Invalidly appointed administrator agent of appointor?—In the case of an invalidly appointed administrator, quite apart from para 21, the appointor will be vicariously liable for the acts of his agent, the purported administrator, where the purported administrator acts on the instructions or directions of his appointor: *Standard Chartered Bank v Walker* [1982] 1 WLR 1410 at 1416A, CA (a receivership case). Paragraph 21, it is suggested, does not preclude the existence of such an agency relationship; compare the reasoning of Walton J in *Bank of Baroda v Panessar* [1986] 3 All ER 564 to the opposite effect. However, neither does the mere fact of appointment automatically trigger an agency relationship between appointor and appointee in the usual absence of a provision to such effect in the debenture pursuant to which an administrator may be appointed: *National Bank of Greece v Pinios* [1990] 1 AC 637 at 648–649 (Lloyd LJ).

Indemnities beyond para 21—The statutory indemnity provided for in para 21 is also discrete from any indemnity which may be claimed by an administrator who incurs liability to the chargor company or any third party in the course of acting on the instructions of his appointor: *Re B Johnson & Co (Builders) Ltd* [1955] Ch 634 at 647–648 (Evershed MR, a receivership case).

Where there are concerns over the validity of an appointment, a prospective appointee may seek a contractual indemnity, usually in the form of a deed, from his appointor to cover consequential liabilities as a condition of his appointment. The provision of indemnities very much varies in practice. An indemnity will ordinarily only protect an administrator from liability arising from invalidity in the debenture or in the form of appointment.

There is no good reason why the court's discretion should not be invoked under para 21 notwithstanding the existence of a contractual indemnity between an appointor and appointee.

APPOINTMENT OF ADMINISTRATOR BY COMPANY OR DIRECTORS

22 Power to appoint

(1) A company may appoint an administrator.

(2) The directors of a company may appoint an administrator.

General note—Subject to the conditions identified below, either a company or its directors may appoint an administrator out-of-court, though such standing does not affect the entitlement of either party to make an application for an administration order under para 12(1). Neither a company nor its directors has standing to appoint an administrator out of court business hours, as in the case of the holder of a qualifying floating charge under IR 1986, r 2.19, which provision effectively serves to preserve the contractual right to enforce a floating charge as previously on the appointment of an administrative receiver.

The decision of the directors—The reference in r 2.22 to 'the resolution of the company to appoint an administrator' requires that a resolution of shareholders is necessary where appointment is to be effected by the company, as opposed to the directors. The requirement will generally be met by either an ordinary resolution or a unanimous informal agreement which is equivalent to such a resolution, either at common law or under ss 288-289 of the Companies Act 2006. However, in *Re Frontsouth (Witham) Ltd (In Administration)* [2011] EWHC 1668 (Ch), [2011] BPIR 1382 Henderson J held that where the company's articles included reg 70 of Table A, which provides that 'the business of the company shall be managed by the directors who may exercise all the powers of the company', as a matter of general company law the decision whether or not to place the company into administration is one to be taken by the directors. The decision cannot be taken by an ordinary resolution of the shareholders, although by a special resolution they may direct the board to take such a step.

Rule 2.22 refers not to a 'resolution' (as in the case of a company) but 'a record of the decision of the directors' to appoint. Para 105 (which provides that a decision of the directors may be made by a majority of the board under para 105), does not apply to para 22: *Minmar (929) Ltd v Khalastchi* [2011] EWHC 1159 (Ch), [2011] BCC 485.

Conditions for out-of-court appointment by company or directors—An out-of-court appointment may only be made by the company or its directors if all of the following five conditions are satisfied:

(a)   the company has not been in administration following an out-of-court appointment effected by the company or its directors – the fact of any administration application or order on any such application being irrelevant – nor subject to a moratorium in respect of a failed CVA under Sch A1 in the previous twelve months: see paras 23(2) and 24(1) and (3) and the differing dates therein on which the twelve-month period is to commence;

(b)   the company is or is likely to become unable to pay its debts: see para 27(2)(a) and the definition in para 111(1) by reference to s 23;

(c)   there is no outstanding winding-up petition or application for an administration order in respect of the company: see para 25(a) and (b);

(d)   the company is not in liquidation: see para 8(1)(a) and (b); and

(e)   there is no administrator or administrative receiver in office: see paras 7 and 25(c).

23   Restrictions on power to appoint

(1) This paragraph applies where an administrator of a company is appointed—

  (a)   under paragraph 22, or
  (b)   on an administration application made by the company or its directors.

(2) An administrator of the company may not be appointed under paragraph 22 during the period of 12 months beginning with the date on which the appointment referred to in sub-paragraph (1) ceases to have effect.

General note—See here para 22 and the notes thereto.

These restrictions apply only to an out-of-court appointment under para 22; they do not restrict the company or its directors in making an application for an administration order.

24

(1) If a moratorium for a company under Schedule A1 ends on a date when no voluntary arrangement is in force in respect of the company, this paragraph applies for the period of 12 months beginning with that date.

(2) This paragraph also applies for the period of 12 months beginning with the date on which a voluntary arrangement in respect of a company ends if—

(a) the arrangement was made during a moratorium for the company under Schedule A1, and

(b) the arrangement ends prematurely (within the meaning of section 7B).

(3) While this paragraph applies, an administrator of the company may not be appointed under paragraph 22.

General note—See para 4(1)(f) of Sch A1 and the notes to that provision.

These restrictions apply only to an out-of-court appointment under para 22; they do not restrict the company or its directors in making an application for an administration order.

25

An administrator of a company may not be appointed under paragraph 22 if—

(a) a petition for the winding up of the company has been presented and is not yet disposed of,

(b) an administration application has been made and is not yet disposed of, or

(c) an administrative receiver of the company is in office.

General note—See here paras 22 and 23 and the notes thereto.

Given the language in r 4.7 and r 13.13 a winding-up petition is presented for the purposes of para 25(a) upon its presentation to the court, and not upon its issue by the court: *Re Blights Builders Ltd* [2008] 1 BCLC 245 (HHJ Norris QC, sitting as a High Court judge; para 22 appointment held invalid where made on 24 July 2006 in ignorance of creditor's winding-up petition presented on 5 July 2006 but only issued by the court on 25 July 2006).The restrictions in para 25 apply only to an out-of-court appointment under para 22. They do not prevent the company or its directors from making an application for an administration order, although, where there is an administrative receiver in office, whether appointed before or after the making of the administration application, the court must dismiss the application unless any of the four conditions in para 39(1) are satisfied.

These restrictions on a para 22 appointment are more extensive than those imposed by para 17 in relation to a para 14 appointment. The major practical difference between paras 17 and 25 is that the former does not prevent the holder of a qualifying floating charge from making an out-of-court appointment following the presentation of a winding-up petition or an administration application. Such an appointment would also have the effect of suspending a winding-up petition under para 40(1)(b), subject to those exceptional cases in para 40(2), as well as preventing the appointment of an administrator on the hearing of an administration application. Subject to the general restriction in para 39, on the other hand, para 25 does nothing to prevent a company and/or its directors from making an administration application under para 12(1)(a) and/or (b) where a winding-up petition or an administration application presented by a third party is on foot.

If a winding up petition is presented after a Notice of Intention to Appoint has been filed, although the petition was not a nullity, it was prohibited by the interim mortatorium. In the circumstances, para 25(a) did not prevent the appointment of an administrator: *Re Ramora UK Ltd* [2011] EWHC 3959 (Ch), [2012] BCC 672.

26 Notice of intention to appoint

(1) A person who proposes to make an appointment under paragraph 22 shall give at least five business days' written notice to—

(a) any person who is or may be entitled to appoint an administrative receiver of the company, and

(b) any person who is or may be entitled to appoint an administrator of the company under paragraph 14.

(2) A person who proposes to make an appointment under paragraph 22 shall also give such notice as may be prescribed to such other persons as may be prescribed.

(3) A notice under this paragraph must—

(a) identify the proposed administrator, and

(b) be in the prescribed form.

General note—Paragraph 28 prohibits an out-of-court appointment by a company and/or its directors under para 22 where there has been a failure to comply with any requirement in paras 26 and 27.

The purpose behind para 26(1) differs from that behind para 26(2). The former provision affords any person who is or may be entitled to appoint an administrative receiver or an administrator to a minimum of 5 business days' written notice of the intention to appoint. Any such person is thereby afforded the opportunity to effect its own appointment within that 5-day period, failing which the company and/or its directors are able to effect an appointment of which notice must be given in the period commencing with the expiry of the 5 business days' written notice and ending with the 10 business days period prescribed in para 28(2). The purpose behind para 26(2), on the other hand, is in affording those four classes of person identified in IR 1986, r 2.20(2) notice of the intended appointment so as to avoid an inadvertent contempt through an innocent breach of the interim moratorium triggered under para 44(4) on a copy of the notice of intention to appoint being filed with the court under para 27(1).

The contrast between the purpose of these two provisions was recognised by HHJ McCahill QC (sitting as a High Court judge) in *Hill v Stokes plc* [2010] EWHC 3726, [2011] BCC 473 (at [51]).

However, the submission that the purpose behind para 26(2) was to prevent inadvertent breach of the interim moratorium was rejected by Warren J in *Westminster Bank plc v Msaada Group* [2011] EWHC 3423 (Ch), [2012] BCC 226 (at [32]), although the judge did not identify what other purpose is served by this rule.

The repeated service of a notice of intention to appoint, without an appointment being made, but nevertheless invoking the protection of the interim moratorium, constitutes an abuse which should be capable of control by the court. In *Re Cornercare Ltd* [2010] EWHC 893 (Ch), [2010] BCC 592, HHJ Purle QC suggested that this could be achieved either by restraining the lodgement of further notices of intention to appoint unless followed by an actual appointment or even, in an extreme case, vacating and removing from the file under its inherent jurisdiction any abusive notice of intention to appoint, coupled with a blanket order for permission under para 43 during the unexpired period of the illicit moratorium.

Paragraph 26(1)

'**... is or may be entitled to appoint ...**'—The use of the words 'or may be' requires notice to be given to a person whose security is not presently enforceable or whose security is challenged as void or voidable where that challenge is disputed on genuinely arguable grounds. It follows that the holder of a floating charge within the meaning of s 29(2) or the holder of a qualifying floating charge is entitled to notice, even where the charge presently secures no presently outstanding indebtedness. This is an important point, because in practice the view is sometimes taken that it is unnecessary to serve such a charge-holder. The notes to para 15(1) provide further commentary relevant here.

In *Adjei v Law for All* [2011] EWHC 2672 (Ch), [2011] BCC 963, it was accepted that the failure by the directors to give notice of intention to appoint to the holder of a qualifying floating charge rendered the subsequent appointment of administrators invalid notwithstanding that the debt had been discharged in full and the continued registration of the debenture had merely been overlooked.

Paragraph 26(2)

The position where no person is entitled to notice under para 26(1)—The requirement to serve notice of intention to appoint on those persons specified in IR 1986, r 2.20(2) prior to appointment where there is no person entitled to notice under para 26(1) has recently been the subject of detailed consideration. Unhelpfully, there is a clear divergence of judicial opinion.

In *Hill v Stokes plc* [2010] EWHC 3726, [2011] BCC 473, the directors failed to give notice of intention to appoint to landlords who, to their knowledge, had distrained against the company's property (as required by IR 1986, r 2.20(2)(b)). HHJ McCahill QC (sitting as a High Court judge) held that the reference in para 28(1) to compliance with 'any requirement of paragraphs 26 and 27' should be read as 'any requirement of paragraphs 26(1) and 27. Alternatively, the requirements of paragraph 26(2) should be construed as 'non-fundamental', such that non-compliance was not necessarily fatal to the validity of appointment.

In contrast, in *Minmar (929) Ltd v Khalastchi* [2011] EWHC 1159 (Ch), [2011] BCC 485, the Chancellor held that the failure by directors to give notice of intention to appoint to the company (as required by IR 1986, r 2.20(2)(d)) caused the appointment to be invalid. The requirement in para 26(2) that notice 'also' be given to such persons as may be prescribed made it plain that it was an additional obligation.

Although *Hill v Stokes plc* was decided before *Minmar*, it was not reported until afterwards. It was not therefore referred to by the Chancellor in his judgment.

Subsequently, there have been a number of decisions in which the court has adopted differing approaches. The lack of resulting lack of clarity is starkly illustrated by the fact that on 21 December 2011 two directly conflicting judgments were handed down by the High Court. In *Westminster Bank plc v Msaada Group* [2011] EWHC 3423 (Ch), [2012] BCC 226, Warren J followed the reasoning in *Minmar*, holding that the failure to give notice of intention to appoint to the company invalidated the subsequent appointment. In contrast, in *Re Virtualpurple Professional Services Ltd* [2011] EWHC 3487 (Ch), Norris J followed *Hill v Stokes plc* in reaching the opposite conclusion.

In *Re BXL Services* [2012] EWHC 1877 (Ch), [2012] BCC 657, HHJ Purle QC held that in light of the fact that Arnold J had followed Virtualpurple in Re Ceart Risk Services Limited [2012] EWHC 1178 (Ch), [2012] BCC 541, 'the law must now be taken as settled at first instance' that the failure to comply with para 26(2) was not fatal.

Procedure—The notice of intention to appoint must be in Form 2.8B, of which an amended version appears in the Schedule to the Insolvency (Amendment) Rules 2004 (SI 2004/584). Rule 2.20(2) makes reference only to the giving of a copy of the notice of intention to appoint to the classes of person identified therein without reference to the statutory declaration referred to in para 27(2).

Rule 2.22 requires that the notice of intention to appoint must be accompanied by either a copy of the resolution of the company to appoint an administrator or a record of the decision of the directors to appoint, as appropriate.

Paragraph 28(1) specifically prohibits an appointment under para 22 before the expiry of the five clear days' notice period where a notice of intention to appoint is given to any person entitled to such notice, unless that person consents in writing.

27

(1) A person who gives notice of intention to appoint under paragraph 26 shall file with the court as soon as is reasonably practicable a copy of—

    (a)   the notice, and
    (b)   any document accompanying it.

(2) The copy filed under sub-paragraph (1) must be accompanied by a statutory declaration made by or on behalf of the person who proposes to make the appointment—

(a) that the company is or is likely to become unable to pay its debts,

(b) that the company is not in liquidation, and

(c) that, so far as the person making the statement is able to ascertain, the appointment is not prevented by paragraphs 23 to 25, and

(d) to such additional effect, and giving such information, as may be prescribed.

(3) A statutory declaration under sub-paragraph (2) must—

(a) be in the prescribed form, and

(b) be made during the prescribed period.

(4) A person commits an offence if in a statutory declaration under sub-paragraph (2) he makes a statement—

(a) which is false, and

(b) which he does not reasonably believe to be true.

General note—Paragraph 28 prohibits an out-of-court appointment by a company and/or its directors under para 22 where there has been a failure to comply with any requirement in paras 26 and 27.

The filing of the notice of intention to appoint with the court under para 27(1), but not apparently any other document required under IR 1986, r 2.22, triggers the interim moratorium in para 44(4).

During the currency of the interim moratorium, it will not be possible for the directors of the company to resolve to put the company into creditors' voluntary liquidation. Any such purported resolution is invalid and incapable of retrospective validation: *Re Business Dream Limited* [2011] EWHC 2860 (Ch), [2012] BCC 115.

Paragraph 27(2)

Statutory declaration—Form 2.8B actually includes a statutory declaration despite the reference in para 27(2) to the copy of the notice of intention to appoint filed with the court being 'accompanied by a statutory declaration'.

Paragraph 27(3)(b)

'**... the prescribed period...** '—Rule 2.21 provides that the statutory declaration must not be made more than five business days before the notice of intention to appoint is filed with the court.

Paragraph 27(4)

Criminal liabilities under para 27(4)—The penalties prescribed by s 430 and Sch 10 are also provided for in s 5 of the Perjury Act 1911.

28

(1) An appointment may not be made under paragraph 22 unless the person who makes the appointment has complied with any requirement of paragraphs 26 and 27 and—

(a) the period of notice specified in paragraph 26(1) has expired, or

(b) each person to whom notice has been given under paragraph 26(1) has consented in writing to the making of the appointment.

(2) An appointment may not be made under paragraph 22 after the period of ten business days beginning with the date on which the notice of intention to appoint is filed under paragraph 27(1).

General note—The words in para 28(1) that 'an appointment may not be made' suggest that a purported appointment made under para 22 in the absence of compliance with paras 26 and 27 will be void ab initio and, it is submitted, as such will be incapable of cure under para 104.

Consent in writing of person given notice under para 26(1)—There is no form prescribed for the giving of consent in writing, although Form 2.8B envisages consent being endorsed on the form before being returned to the company or its directors.

The position where no person is entitled to notice under para 26(1)—Paragraph 30 provides that para 28 has no application where there is no person entitled to notice of intention to appoint under para 26(1). In *Hill v Stokes plc* [2010] EWHC 3726, [2011] BCC 473, it was held that the reference in para 28(1) to 'Paragraph 26' should be read as a reference to 'Paragraph 26(1)'.It would follow that the ten business days time limit imposed by para 28(2) will not apply where any person is entitled to notice of intention to appoint under para 26(2), but not under para 26(1).

The effect of the expiry of the relevant period—In *Re Cornercare Ltd* [2010] EWHC 893 (Ch), [2010] BCC 592, HHJ Purle QC held that para 28(2) does not prevent a fresh notice of intention to appoint from being served and filed, resulting in a fresh 10-day appointment window. However, the court has the power to prevent this where it would amount to an abuse of process (see the notes to para 26 above).

Moreover, an appointment of an administrator made after the expiry of the prescribed period in para 28(2) does not automatically invalidate the appointment but should be treated as a curable irregularity under IR 1986, r 7.55: *Re Euromaster Limited* [2012] EWHC 2356 (Ch), [2012] BCC 754.

29 Notice of appointment

(1) A person who appoints an administrator of a company under paragraph 22 shall file with the court—

    (a)   a notice of appointment, and
    (b)   such other documents as may be prescribed.

(2) The notice of appointment must include a statutory declaration by or on behalf of the person who makes the appointment—

    (a)   that the person is entitled to make an appointment under paragraph 22,
    (b)   that the appointment is in accordance with this Schedule, and
    (c)   that, so far as the person making the statement is able to ascertain, the statements made and information given in the statutory declaration filed with the notice of intention to appoint remain accurate.

(3) The notice of appointment must identify the administrator and must be accompanied by a statement by the administrator—

    (a)   that he consents to the appointment,
    (b)   that in his opinion the purpose of administration is reasonably likely to be achieved, and
    (c)   giving such other information and opinions as may be prescribed.

(4) For the purpose of a statement under sub-paragraph (3) an administrator may rely on information supplied by directors of the company (unless he has reason to doubt its accuracy).

(5) The notice of appointment and any document accompanying it must be in the prescribed form.

(6) A statutory declaration under sub-paragraph (2) must be made during the prescribed period.

(7) A person commits an offence if in a statutory declaration under sub-paragraph (2) he makes a statement—

    (a)   which is false, and
    (b)   which he does not reasonably believe to be true.

General note—Compliance with these provisions is of more than administrative importance, in that an appointment under para 22 will not take effect by virtue of para 33(a) if an administration order or an appointment under para 14 is made before the requirements of para 29 are satisfied. Paragraph 31 provides that the appointment of an administrator under para 22 only takes effect when the requirements of para 29 are satisfied.

These provisions correspond with those in para 18 which apply in a para 14 appointment case, although there is no facility for an out-of-court business hours appointment to be made under para 22.

Paragraph 29(1) and (2)

Documents for filing with the court—The prescribed form of the notice of appointment will vary according to the circumstances. Form 2.9B must be used where a written notice of intention to appoint has been given to any person under para 26(1), but not, as appears from para 8 of the form, where such notice is only given to any person within para 26(2). Form 2.10B must be used where there is no person entitled to notice of intention to appoint under para 26(1). Rule 2.25 provides that Form 2.10B, but not Form 2.9B, must be accompanied by the documents prescribed in IR 1986, r 2.22. For para 29(6) purposes the period prescribed by r 2.24 is not more than five business days before the notice of appointment is filed with the court.

Forms 2.9B and 2.10B each incorporate a statutory declaration which must be completed for para 29(2) purposes. The contents of the statutory declaration are varied by para 30 in a Form 2.10B case.

The administrator's statement for para 29(3) purposes must be in Form 2.2B, as prescribed by r 2.23(2)(a), in relation to which the administrator is afforded the protection of para 29(4).

Procedure—Rule 2.27 governs notification and advertisement of an administrator's appointment and prescribes Form 2.11B for the form of advertisement and Form 2.12B as the form of notice.

Paragraph 29(7)

Penalties—The penalties prescribed by s 430 and Sch 10 are also provided for in s 5 of the Perjury Act 1911.

Paragraph 29(5)

Effect of failure to use prescribed form—In *Re Kaupthing Capital Partners II Master LP Inc (in administration); Pillar Securitisation SARL v Spicer* [2010] EWHC 836 (Ch), [2011] BCC 338, Proudman J held that the use of the wrong prescribed form (Form 2.10B instead of Form 1B) rendered the appointment invalid and was not capable of cure under IR 1986, r 7.55.

30

In a case in which no person is entitled to notice of intention to appoint under paragraph 26(1) (and paragraph 28 therefore does not apply)—

    (a)   the statutory declaration accompanying the notice of appointment must include the statements and information required under paragraph 27(2), and

    (b)   paragraph 29(2)(c) shall not apply.

General note—These provisions are triggered where no person is entitled to notice of intention to appoint under para 26(1). That position is unchanged where any person is entitled to notice under para 26(2) for the reasons set out in the notes to para 28.

31 Commencement of appointment

The appointment of an administrator under paragraph 22 takes effect when the requirements of paragraph 29 are satisfied.

General note—This provision predicates the effectiveness of a para 22 appointment on satisfaction of the requirements in para 29. This is an event of some moment, since it is at this point, and no sooner, that the administrator becomes entitled to exercise those statutory powers identified in the note to para 60.

The reference in para 31 is to 'paragraph 29', and not merely para 18(1), as a consequence of which it would appear that an appointment is not effective unless there is strict compliance with para 29(2), (3), (5) and (6). Despite any such defects in his appointments, however, para 104 would operate to render valid any act on the part of the administrator, although that provision does not operate to validate the defective appointment itself, which might be remedied either through the administrative step necessary to secure compliance with para 29 or, in an appropriate case, through an application to court for an appropriate direction under para 63. It is also arguable that a defective appointment might be capable of being cured under IR 1986, r 7.55, since out-of-court appointments seem likely to constitute 'insolvency proceedings' for the purpose of that provision, given that such appointments are attributed a case number, title and court file and, by virtue of para 5, out-of-court appointees are officers of the court.

The effectiveness of a para 22 appointment is unaffected by any non-compliance with para 32(a).

On the timing of the commencement of the appointment of the administrator see the notes to the analogous para 19 and r 2.16.

32

A person who appoints an administrator under paragraph 22—

    (a)   shall notify the administrator and such other persons as may be prescribed as soon as is reasonably practicable after the requirements of paragraph 29 are satisfied, and

    (b)   commits an offence if he fails without reasonable excuse to comply with paragraph (a).

General note—This provision imposes notice obligations on the person appointing an administrator under para 22. Notice obligations are also imposed by para 46(2) on the administrator himself following appointment. Rule 2.26(2) requires that the administrator's appointor must send a copy of the sealed order to the administrator as soon as reasonably practicable. No 'other persons' have been prescribed for the purposes of para 32(a).

Non-compliance with para 32(a) will not affect the validity of the appointment of an administrator or his standing to act as such, the sanction for default lying in the criminal penalties under para 32(b), on which see s 430, Sch 10 and the daily default fine imposed by para 106(2)(b).

33

If before the requirements of paragraph 29 are satisfied the company enters administration by virtue of an administration order or an appointment under paragraph 14—

    (a)   the appointment under paragraph 22 shall not take effect, and

    (b)   paragraph 32 shall not apply.

General note—This provision should be read in conjunction with the general note to para 29. As defined in para 1(2)(b) a company 'enters administration' when the appointment of an administrator takes effect, on which see para 13 in the case of an administration order and para 19 in the case of a para 14 appointment.

34 Invalid appointment: indemnity

(1) This paragraph applies where—

    (a)   a person purports to appoint an administrator under paragraph 22, and

    (b)   the appointment is discovered to be invalid.

(2) The court may order the person who purported to make the appointment to indemnify the person appointed against liability which arises solely by reason of the appointment's invalidity.

General note—This provision bears a very close resemblance, and is identical in substance, to that in s 34 which provides for an indemnity by court order where the appointment of a receiver and manager appointed out-of-court is discovered to be invalid. The commentary to the identical para 21 (which applies to an out-of-court appointment by a qualifying floating charge holder) will apply equally to para 34.

ADMINISTRATION APPLICATION – SPECIAL CASES

35 Application by holder of floating charge

(1) This paragraph applies where an administration application in respect of a company—

    (a)   is made by the holder of a qualifying floating charge in respect of the company's property, and

    (b)   includes a statement that the application is made in reliance on this paragraph.

(2) The court may make an administration order—

    (a)   whether or not satisfied that the company is or is likely to become unable to pay its debts, but

    (b)   only if satisfied that the applicant could appoint an administrator under paragraph 14.

General note—This provision allows the holder of a qualifying floating charge to make application for an administration order without the requirement of proof that the company is or is likely to become unable to pay its debts otherwise required by para 11(a). Subject to the application including a statement that it is made in reliance on para 35, the court will only make an order if satisfied that the applicant could appoint out-of-court under para 14: see paras 14–17 and the notes to those provisions.

If the holder of a floating charge is unable to satisfy the court, for the purposes of para 35(2)(b), of its standing to appoint under para 14, then the charge holder would remain entitled to pursue an administration order, conceivably in the same application, as a creditor under para 12(1)(c), but subject to meeting both conditions in para 11.

In *Barclays Bank Plc v Choicezone Ltd* [2011] EWHC 1303 (Ch), [2012] BCC 767, Newey J held that the fact that a company had cross-claims against the floating chargeholder which exceeded the amount of the debt owed by the company could not detract from the enforceability of the charge.

In *Re St John Spencer Estates & Development Ltd; AIB Group (UK) plc v St John Spencer Estates & Development Ltd* [2012] EWHC 2317 (Ch), [2013] 1 BCLC 718, Robert Ham QC (sitting as a deputy High Court judge) noted that the purpose of the para 35 procedure was to provide secured lenders with a simple and assured route to realise their security where the company was in default, and to enable any doubts as to the enforceability of the security to be determined in advance without the administrators being exposed to any risk that an appointment out of court was invalid.

36 Intervention by holder of floating charge

(1) This paragraph applies where—

    (a) an administration application in respect of a company is made by a person who is not the holder of a qualifying floating charge in respect of the company's property, and

    (b) the holder of a qualifying floating charge in respect of the company's property applies to the court to have a specified person appointed as administrator (and not the person specified by the administration applicant).

(2) The court shall grant an application under sub-paragraph (1)(b) unless the court thinks it right to refuse the application because of the particular circumstances of the case.

General note—This provision serves to confer a level of priority on the holder of a qualifying floating charge by allowing the charge holder to nominate its own administrator on the hearing of an administration application. The provision is particularly relevant to institutional charge holders, which commonly operate a panel of preferred appointees. The wording in para 36(1)(b) does not require the charge-holder to be represented at the hearing, although this will be preferable to both the charge holder and the court, where the alternative proposed appointee is opposed by the applicant.

The use of the word 'shall' in para 36(2) requires the court to give effect to the alternative appointment proposed by the holder of a qualifying floating charge unless the court thinks it right to confirm the applicant's proposed appointment 'because of the particular circumstances of the case'. Those circumstances might include proof of a previous professional relationship giving rise to a conflict of interests or the applicant establishing to the court's satisfaction that its proposed appointee has engaged in significant work prior to the application so as to be far more readily familiar with the company's affairs – a point most obviously demonstrated by reference to the preparation of the affidavit and/or report in support of the application – in comparison with the charge holder's proposed appointee whose appointment might be shown to involve an avoidable duplication of such work and associated professional costs.

The fact of an administration application does not affect the standing of the holder of a qualifying floating charge effecting an out-of-court appointment of its chosen appointee under para 14.

Procedure—For the documents and evidence required of the holder of a qualifying floating charge on an application under para 36(1)(b) see IR 1986, r 2.10 which also provides that the costs of the applicant for the administration order and the applicant charge holder under para 36(1)(b) shall ordinarily be paid as an expense of the administration.

'... the court thinks ...'—Paragraph 36(2) is the first use in Sch B1 of the term 'the court thinks'. The same words also appear in paras 39(1)(b)–(d) and 68(3)(c) and (d). The proper interpretation of the verb 'thinks' is not clear. Unless what is intended is nothing more than what might be thought by the draftsman to be plain, unambiguous language with no real change in substance from earlier formulations, it appears more likely that what is intended is something other than the court being 'satisfied' of something, since that term is used in paras 11 and 95(a) where the word 'thinks' might otherwise have been employed. The key distinction, it is submitted, between the word 'thinks' and the court being 'satisfied' lies in the former term requiring an exercise of mind in the formation of a view or opinion without any requirement for that view or opinion being conclusive. The term 'satisfied', on the other hand, calls for a determinative judgment to be made on a balance of probabilities. This approach would square with the use of 'thinks' in paras 36(2) and 68(3)(c) and (d) which each involve the court in an exercise of discretion dependent on the circumstances of any case without, it seems, any strict need for findings of fact to be made. The same approach to para 39(1)(b)–(d) would also avoid the obvious difficulty, by what might otherwise quite properly be regarded as a determination for the purposes of any of the transaction avoidance provisions mentioned within those subparagraphs, which might otherwise arise if reference to the court being 'satisfied' had been utilised by the draftsman. The term 'thinks', therefore, it is suggested, should be interpreted as shorthand for 'has considered and is of the view that, without necessarily reaching a final determination on any issue of fact and/or law' whereas the term 'satisfied' is a convenient substitute for 'satisfied on a balance of probabilities'.

37 Application where company in liquidation

(1) This paragraph applies where the holder of a qualifying floating charge in respect of a company's property could appoint an administrator under paragraph 14 but for paragraph 8(1)(b).

(2) The holder of the qualifying floating charge may make an administration application.

(3) If the court makes an administration order on hearing an application made by virtue of sub-paragraph (2)—

    (a)   the court shall discharge the winding-up order,

    (b)   the court shall make provision for such matters as may be prescribed,

    (c)   the court may make other consequential provision,

    (d)   the court shall specify which of the powers under this Schedule are to be exercisable by the administrator, and

    (e)   this Schedule shall have effect with such modifications as the court may specify.

General note—Where the holder of a qualifying floating charge is precluded from effecting an out-of-court appointment under para 14 by virtue of the company being in compulsory liquidation (to which para 8(1)(b) refers) this provision allows the charge holder to make an administration application which, if successful, has the consequence of requiring the court to discharge the winding-up order and to comply with those matters in para 37(3)(b) and (d).

For no obviously good reason there is no provision by which the holder of a qualifying floating charge might seek an administration order where a company is in voluntary liquidation, although a liquidator might pursue such an order, irrespective of whether the company is in voluntary or compulsory liquidation, under para 38.

In a voluntary liquidation there is no good reason why the holder of a qualifying floating charge should not present a winding-up petition, having waived its security to the extent of the petition debt, with a view to obtaining a winding-up order so as to facilitate the appointment of an administrator under para 37. The court may not, however, be inclined to make a winding-up order in the face of such a tactical ploy.

Cases in which an order might be made under para 37—Although liquidation is a terminal procedure, the fact of liquidation is not necessarily inconsistent with the court being satisfied, for para 11(b) purposes, that the making of an administration order is reasonably likely to achieve the purpose of administration. The 'purpose of administration', of course, is made up of the hierarchy of the three objectives or sub-purposes in para 3(1). In the vast majority of liquidations the business of a company is not carried on as a going concern, although this can arise in a voluntary liquidation where the carrying on of business can be shown to be for the benefit of the winding up. The objective in para 3(1)(a) is, therefore, unlikely to feature in a para 37 application, although this possibility cannot be discounted, subject to the proviso that there will usually be a need to act with some speed so as to avoid the loss of goodwill or the adverse reaction of third parties to a winding up. Far more likely in a para 37 application is the charge holder's assertion that the achievement of either of the objectives in para 3(1)(b) or (c) is reasonably practicable although, particularly where the business of the company is incapable of being continued or wound down as a going concern, the burden on the applicant will be in substantiating why either objective should produce a more advantageous outcome than would otherwise arise in the liquidation, taking account of the likely cost of each alternative procedure, which should always be provided so as to facilitate an informed comparative assessment by the court. An order might also be made under para 37 where a qualifying floating charge holder has appointed an administrative receiver whose agency for the company is terminated upon the making of a winding-up order.

It should also be noted that some judges will not automatically accept an unsubstantiated assertion, even one advanced by an experienced and qualified valuer, as can arise in practice, to the effect that the estimated realisation value of a particular asset, on either an open market or forced sale basis, is necessarily higher in administration than in liquidation.

Paragraph 37(3)(a)

The discharge of a winding-up order is not the same as rescission and means only that for the future the order shall cease to have effect; as a consequence, any disposition between the presentation of the winding-up order and its discharge under para 37(3)(a) will be void in the absence of a validating order for the purposes of s 127: *Re Albany Building Ltd* [2007] BCC 591 at [5] and [6] (HHJ Norris QC sitting as a judge of the High Court; validating order made on application of joint administrators).

Paragraph 37(3)(b)

'the court shall make provision for such matters as may be prescribed'—This is a reference to those matters set out in r 2.13(a)–(g) which the court shall 'include' (ie non-exhaustively) in its order.

Procedure—The application will be by way of ordinary application with an affidavit or witness statement in support containing those matters set out in r 2.11 together with any other information which the applicant considers will be necessary to assist the court in reaching its determination.

See rr 2.11 and 2.13.

38

(1) The liquidator of a company may make an administration application.

(2) If the court makes an administration order on hearing an application made by virtue of sub-paragraph (1)—

(a)   the court shall discharge any winding-up order in respect of the company,

(b)   the court shall make provision for such matters as may be prescribed,

(c)   the court may make other consequential provision,

(d)   the court shall specify which of the powers under this Schedule are to be exercisable by the administrator, and

(e)   this Schedule shall have effect with such modifications as the court may specify.

General note—This provision is very similar to para 37, save that it allows a liquidator – in either a voluntary or compulsory liquidation – to make an administration application. The commentary and procedure outlined in the notes to para 37 apply equally here.

It is understood that an administration order on the application of a liquidator was granted by Hart J on 25 September 2003 in an unreported case, albeit in rather unusual circumstances. The case involved a winding-up order which was made many months after the presentation of a petition by the Inland Revenue. The directors had caused the company to make payments to the Revenue following presentation of the petition in the belief that a winding-up order would not be made. The directors were oblivious to the order as, apparently, was the company's bank, which had not frozen the company's account. On informing the directors that the company was in liquidation the official receiver identified that the company was solvent on its balance sheet and that it retained a strong order book. Within two weeks of the speedy appointment of an insolvency practitioner as liquidator by the Secretary of State the administration order was obtained.

Consequential provisions in a voluntary liquidation case—In contrast to a compulsory winding up, there is no provision for the court to discharge a voluntary winding up. Given that administration and liquidation must, by the nature of each, be seen as mutually exclusive, practical necessity and good order would dictate the making of an order by the court under s 147(1) staying a voluntary winding up from the time of the making of the administration order.

Procedure—See rr 2.11 and 2.13.

39 Effect of administrative receivership

(1) Where there is an administrative receiver of a company the court must dismiss an administration application in respect of the company unless—

(a)   the person by or on behalf of whom the receiver was appointed consents to the making of the administration order,

(b)   the court thinks that the security by virtue of which the receiver was appointed would be liable to be released or discharged under sections 238 to 240 (transaction at undervalue and preference) if an administration order were made,

(c)   the court thinks that the security by virtue of which the receiver was appointed would be avoided under section 245 (avoidance of floating charge) if an administration order were made, or

(d)   the court thinks that the security by virtue of which the receiver was appointed would be challengeable under section 242 (gratuitous alienations) or 243 (unfair preferences) or under any rule of law in Scotland.

(2) Sub-paragraph (1) applies whether the administrative receiver is appointed before or after the making of the administration application.

General note—Administrative receivership and administration are mutually exclusive regimes. The starting point is in the requirement that the court must dismiss an administration application where an administrative receiver is in office unless one of the four conditions in para 39(1)(a)–(d) is met. The status or former status of the company as a private or public company is irrelevant: *Chesterton International Group plc v Deka Immobilien Inv Gmbh* [2005] BPIR 1103. For the purposes of para 39(1)(a) there will usually be no incentive for the appointor of an administrative receiver to consent to the making of an administration order. By virtue of the words 'the court thinks' – on which see the note under that heading to para 36 – para 39(1)(b)–(d) do not require the court to come to a final determination under any of the transaction avoidance provisions mentioned therein.

It is irrelevant whether an administrative receiver was appointed prior to or following the issue of the administration application: para 39(2). An administrative receiver – as defined in para 111(1) by reference to s 251 – may be appointed pursuant to floating charge security satisfying s 29(2)(a) which was created prior to 15 September 2003 or in any of the seven exceptional cases identified in ss 72B to 72GA.

For the effect of the making of an administration order on an administrative receiver or a non-administrative or LPA receiver see para 41.

EFFECT OF ADMINISTRATION

40 Dismissal of pending winding-up petition

(1) A petition for the winding up of a company—

    (a)   shall be dismissed on the making of an administration order in respect of the company, and

    (b)   shall be suspended while the company is in administration following an appointment under paragraph 14.

(2) Sub-paragraph (1)(b) does not apply to a petition presented under—

    (a)   section 124A (public interest),

    (aa)   section 124B (SEs), or

    (b)   section 367 of the Financial Services and Markets Act 2000 (petition by Financial Services Authority).

(3) Where an administrator becomes aware that a petition was presented under a provision referred to in sub-paragraph (2) before his appointment, he shall apply to the court for directions under paragraph 63.

General note—This provision is concerned only with a winding-up petition which is extant on the making of an administration order or at the time of the appointment of an administrator by a qualifying floating charge holder under para 14. Paragraph 25(1) prohibits an out-of-court appointment of an administrator by a company or its directors under para 22 where a winding-up petition has been presented but is not yet disposed of.

Paragraph 40(1)

'**A petition ... (a) shall be dismissed ...**'—The dismissal of a winding-up petition takes effect automatically by virtue of para 40(1)(a). Nevertheless, it is useful to record the fact of the dismissal within the body of the administration order. The court will also usually be prepared to order that the costs of the winding-up petition shall rank as an expense in the administration, although any costs order must necessarily turn on the facts of any particular case.

Paragraph 40(1)(b)

'**A petition ... (b) shall be suspended ...**'—The suspension of a winding-up petition is a new and innovative concept. Suspension, as opposed to dismissal, appears designed to retain a petition before the court so as to guard against the scope for abuse of the moratorium provisions through the tactical appointment of an administrator by a qualifying floating charge holder. Given the express disapplication of s 127 identified under the next heading below, it appears implicit that a suspended petition remains live or effective, so as not to require revival or awakening, notwithstanding its suspension. Suspension also provides a benefit to creditors in any ensuing liquidation by fixing the starting point for the periods in which transactions might be challenged by a liquidator under ss 238 and 239 at the earliest possible time: see ss 129(2) and 240(3)(e).

Paragraph 55(2)(d) specifically empowers the court to make an order on a suspended winding-up petition where an administrator reports to the court that creditors have failed to approve proposals or revised proposals.

Is a validation order under s 127 necessary where a winding-up petition is suspended under para 40(1)(b)?—Section 127, as amended by para 15 of Sch 17 to the Enterprise Act 2002, is disapplied in respect of anything done by an administrator whilst a winding-up petition is suspended. The effect of the amendment appears to have been overlooked in *Re J Smiths Haulage Ltd* [2007] BCC 135 at [5] (HHJ Norris QC, sitting as a judge of the High Court), though the same conclusion was reached as provided for in the amendment. The amendment does not, however, affect the period between the presentation of a winding-up petition and the appointment of an administrator such that dispositions of company property during that period will continue to require validation by the court.

Paragraph 40(2)

Public interest and Financial Services Authority winding-up petitions—Either variety of winding-up petition identified in para 40(2) is unaffected by the making of an administration order or the appointment of an administrator by a qualifying floating charge holder under para 14. A winding-up order may also be made in respect of either petition where a company is in administration: see para 42(3) and the notes thereto.

The requirement in para 40(3) that an administrator makes an application for directions is mandatory. Any hearing on such an application should take account of the possible orders available to the court on a winding-up order being made under para 82(3) and (4).

41 Dismissal of administrative or other receiver

(1) When an administration order takes effect in respect of a company any administrative receiver of the company shall vacate office.

(2) Where a company is in administration, any receiver of part of the company's property shall vacate office if the administrator requires him to.

(3) Where an administrative receiver or receiver vacates office under sub-paragraph (1) or (2)—

    (a)   his remuneration shall be charged on and paid out of any property of the company which was in his custody or under his control immediately before he vacated office, and

    (b)   he need not take any further steps under section 40 or 59.

(4) In the application of sub-paragraph (3)(a)—

    (a)   'remuneration' includes expenses properly incurred and any indemnity to which the administrative receiver or receiver is entitled out of the assets of the company,

    (b)   the charge imposed takes priority over security held by the person by whom or on whose behalf the administrative receiver or receiver was appointed, and

    (c)   the provision for payment is subject to paragraph 43.

General note—Paragraph 41(1) applies only where an administration order 'takes effect' and requires the vacation of office of any administrative receiver. That provision applies only to administration orders, since the fact of an administrative receiver holding office is a bar to any out-of-court appointment by virtue of paras 17(b) and 25(c).

No form of administration affects the appointment of a receiver of part of the company's property – that is, any receiver appointed out of court who does not meet the criteria in s 29(2)(a) – unless the administrator requires the receiver to vacate office under para 41(2). In practice, an administrator will usually require such a receiver to vacate office other than, for example, where the receiver's task is all but complete and the remaining conduct of the receivership is unlikely to affect the administration of the company and is to be carried out expeditiously and on clearly defined terms.

On vacation of office a receiver should surrender property in his custody or under his control to the administrator; the receiver may also consider it appropriate to seek an acknowledgement of the existence and extent of the statutory charge in his favour under para 41(3)(a).

Paragraph 41(3)(a) and (4)

The charge in favour of the receiver—The statutory charge created by para 41(3)(a) bites only on property within that provision. The sum secured will, by virtue of the definition of 'remuneration' in para 41(4)(a), extend not only to fees properly due to the receiver but also disbursements and expenses properly incurred, such as fees due to solicitors and agents.

Paragraph 41(4)(c)

'The provision for payment is subject to paragraph 43'—There is some ambiguity here. Paragraph 43 is concerned with the imposition of a general bar against various forms of legal process. The draftsman's approach in casting para 41(4)(c) appears to be predicated upon the assumption that any payment due to a former receiver must impliedly involve the enforcement of the statutory charge created under para 41(3)(a). It is suggested that that assumption is open to question since the payment of a secured debt need not involve the enforcement of the underlying security. Caution, at least, dictates that an outgoing receiver should not draw 'remuneration' due to him without the consent of the administrator or the permission of the court under para 43(2).

42 Moratorium on insolvency proceedings

(1) This paragraph applies to a company in administration.

(2) No resolution may be passed for the winding up of the company.

(3) No order may be made for the winding up of the company.

(4) Sub-paragraph (3) does not apply to an order made on a petition presented under—

    (a)   section 124A (public interest), or
    (aa) section 124B (SEs),
    (b)   section 367 of the Financial Services and Markets Act 2000 (petition by Financial Services Authority).

(5) If a petition presented under a provision referred to in sub-paragraph (4) comes to the attention of the administrator, he shall apply to the court for directions under paragraph 63.

General note—This provision, which should be read in conjunction with para 40, provides that, save in the exceptional case of an order made under a winding-up petition within para 42(4), a company in administration, as defined in para 1(2)(a), may not be placed into voluntary or compulsory liquidation. Paragraph 42 does nothing, however, to prevent the *presentation* of a winding-up petition. Any resolution for voluntary winding up in contravention of para 42(2) will be a nullity and of no effect.

Orders made on a public interest or Financial Services Authority winding-up petition— Paragraph 82 enables the court either to order that the appointment of the administrator shall cease to have effect or that the appointment shall continue subject to the court specifying the powers and role of the administrator.

Paragraph 42(5)—The application for directions by the administrator in the specified circumstances is a mandatory requirement.

43 Moratorium on other legal process

(1) This paragraph applies to a company in administration.

(2) No step may be taken to enforce security over the company's property except—

    (a)   with the consent of the administrator, or

    (b)   with the permission of the court.

(3) No step may be taken to repossess goods in the company's possession under a hire-purchase agreement except—

    (a)   with the consent of the administrator, or

    (b)   with the permission of the court.

(4) A landlord may not exercise a right of forfeiture by peaceable re-entry in relation to premises let to the company except—

    (a)   with the consent of the administrator, or

    (b)   with the permission of the court.

(5) In Scotland, a landlord may not exercise a right of irritancy in relation to premises let to the company except—

    (a)   with the consent of the administrator, or

    (b)   with the permission of the court.

(6) No legal process (including legal proceedings, execution, distress and diligence) may be instituted or continued against the company or property of the company except—

    (a)   with the consent of the administrator, or

    (b)   with the permission of the court.

(6A) An administrative receiver of the company may not be appointed.

(7) Where the court gives permission for a transaction under this paragraph it may impose a condition on or a requirement in connection with the transaction.

(8) In this paragraph 'landlord' includes a person to whom rent is payable.

General note—The various forms of protection within this provision very closely resemble those made available previously under ss 10(1) and 11(3) in Part II. Given that the purpose of both moratoria is the same in facilitating the achievement of the purpose or purposes of administration, the commentary below draws on authorities decided under the previous regime which are of continued relevance. As previously, there is nothing within the provisions to suggest that Parliament's intention was the statutory interference with the substantive rights or interests of creditors or third parties; rather the moratorium protects against the exercise or enforcement of such rights.

Paragraph 43(1) makes clear that the provisions are only effective on a company being 'in administration', a term defined in para 1(2) by reference to the appointment of an administrator.

The Financial Collateral Arrangements (No 2) Regulations 2003—These Regulations (SI 2003/3226) came into effect on 26 December 2003 and operate by way of disapplying certain domestic insolvency legislation as would otherwise apply to financial collateral arrangements so as to give effect to EU Directive 2002/47. The Regulations are of potentially far reaching consequences in that they afford priority to close-out netting provisions under such arrangements in place of the automatic set-off provisions in r 2.85 (which is broadly analogous to r 4.90 in winding-up). Whilst not of any great significance to traditional security taking under English law, the Regulations are of some relevance in administration in that they will preclude the operation of the statutory moratorium where, in an applicable arrangement, A takes fixed security over cash (or cash equivalent) held by B when B goes into administration and A wishes to enforce its security.

Paragraph 43(2)

'No step ...'—In *Bristol Airport plc v Powdrill* [1990] BCC 130 at 151E–151F Browne-Wilkinson V-C held that, at least in the case of an ordinary possessory lien, the assertion by the lien holder of a right to retain the property constituted the taking of a 'step' to enforce security which would, therefore, in the absence of the administrator's agreement, require the leave of the court. More generally, what appears to be required in the taking of a 'step' is an unqualified assertion of the barred rights, but not a mere threat or hypothesis which of itself will not breach the statutory moratorium.

'No step may be taken to enforce security ...'—The term 'security' is defined very broadly in s 248(b) in non-exhaustive terms as 'any mortgage, charge, lien or other security'.

Paragraph 43(3)

'No step ...'—See the note to para 43(2) above.

'... to repossess goods in the company's possession under a hire-purchase agreement ...'—As under the previous provisions, reference to a 'hire-purchase agreement' includes a conditional sale agreement, a chattel leasing agreement and a retention of title agreement: see para 111(1).

Since the protection in para 43(3) is expressly dependent on the relevant goods being 'in the company's possession' the burden rests on the office-holder not only in ensuring that the company has possession, but also that such possession can be evidenced. Note here that para 67 imposes a general duty on an administrator on his appointment to take custody or control of all property to which he thinks the company is entitled.

Paragraph 43(4)

'A landlord may not exercise ...'—Paragraph 43(8) provides that the term 'landlord' includes a person to whom rent is payable, and so the term must be read as including any subsequent assignee entitled to receive rent.

'... a right of forfeiture by peaceable re-entry in relation to premises let to the company ...'—Subject to the leave of the court, this provision protects against the exercise of any right of forfeiture by peaceable re-entry. The protection is restricted to premises which are let to the company, but not necessarily occupied by it. The protection afforded by the subparagraph applies generally and draws no distinction between the grounds giving rise to the exercise of the right of forfeiture such that it will be immaterial whether the right arises on breach of a covenant for payment of rent or any other covenant which, but for the moratorium, would give rise to such relief.

Paragraph 43(6)

'No legal process (including legal proceedings, execution, distress and diligence) may be instituted or continued against the company or property of the company'—This form of words is the one for which the draftsman has opted to replace the words 'no other proceedings and no execution or other legal process' which had appeared in ss 10(1)(c) and 11(3)(d) and which remain in s 252(2)(b) in the case of an IVA interim order. The change in wording is not necessarily problematic, however, since the term 'legal process' plainly now includes 'legal proceedings' and must, it is submitted, be taken as a more precise term than 'proceedings' (to use the former terminology) which had been held to extend to either legal proceedings or quasi-legal proceedings. Certainly it is inconceivable that Parliament might have intended to reduce substantially the protection offered by the moratorium in the new administration regime through the use of the term 'legal proceedings'. One potential problem, however, in the terms used in para 43(6) lies in the use of the word 'legal process' as a generic term, which is apparently wider than, but encompasses, the term 'legal proceedings'. The difficulty lies in the fact that the term 'legal process' had previously been held by Millett J in *Re Olympia & York Canary Wharf Ltd* [1993] BCLC 453 at 457A, relatively restrictively, as meaning a process which requires the assistance of the court. Given the breadth of the term 'legal proceedings' – identified in the next section below by reference to the term 'proceedings' under Part II – it is difficult to see how that narrow interpretation of 'legal process' can survive the implementation of Sch B1. It is suggested that the term requires a purposive interpretation by the court so as to catch all forms of legal and quasi-legal proceedings and enforcements and any other form of process in which the court or court procedures play a necessary part, on which see the commentary attaching to s 130.

In *Re Frankice (Golders Green) Ltd (in administration) and others* [2010] EWHC 1229 (Ch), [2010] Bus LR 1608, Norris J held that a proposed review hearing before a regulatory panel of the Gambling Commission to consider whether to to revoke or suspend the operating licences of three companies in administration fell within the description of 'legal process'.

'legal proceedings'—As suggested above, the term 'legal proceedings' should be attributed the meaning formerly attributed to the term 'proceedings' under Part II. The term 'proceedings' is a more compendious expression than the word 'action' which had been used previously in s 9 of the Bankruptcy Act 1914. The term 'proceedings' is apt to denote any legal or quasi-legal proceedings and has been held to extend to arbitration proceedings (*Bristol Airport plc v Powdrill* [1990] Ch 744 (Browne-Wilkinson V-C)), proceedings before an industrial tribunal (*Carr v British International Helicopters Ltd (in administration)* [1994] 2 BCLC 474 (EAT)), a statutory adjudication process under s 108 of the Housing Grants, Construction and Regeneration Act 1996 and under cl 41A of the standard form JCT 80 building contract (*A Straume (UK) Ltd v Bradlor Developments Ltd* [2000] BCC 333 (His Honour Judge Behrens)), criminal prosecution under the Environmental Protection Act 1990 (*Environment Agency v Clark* [2000] BCC 653 (Robert Walker and Henry LJJ and Scott-Baker J)) and, but not without some degree of doubt given the diametrically opposed views of Sir Andrew Morritt V-C and Lord Woolf (with whom Waller and Robert Walker LJJ agreed), an application by a special freight train operator for a replacement access contract under s 17 of the Railways Act 1993 in *Winsor v Special Railway Administrators of Railtrack plc* [2002] 2 BCLC 308. On the other hand, it is doubtful that the service of a counter-notice under Part II of the Landlord and Tenant Act 1954 for a fresh tenancy constitutes 'proceedings': *Bristol Airport plc v Powdrill* [1990] Ch 744 at 766 (Browne-Wilkinson V-C). The conclusion of the Scottish Court of Session in *Air Ecosse Ltd v Civil Aviation Authority* [1987] 3 BCC 492 to the effect that the words 'other proceedings ... against the company' in the former s 11(3)(d) were confined to the activities of creditors and did not extend to actions which might be open to persons who were not creditors, such as competitors asserting rights under different statutes, is now extremely doubtful given the later authorities which construe the term far more broadly.

In *Re Olympia & York Canary Wharf Ltd* [1993] BCLC 453 at 457A Millett J identified that the words 'legal process' refer to a process which requires the assistance of the court and which would not, therefore, extend to the service of a contractual notice, whether or not the service of such a notice was a pre-condition to the bringing of legal proceedings. This interpretation may, however, require revision for the purposes of Sch B1 for the reasons set out above, on which see the commentary attaching to s 130.

A simple money claim will fall within the scope of the term 'legal proceedings'.

Territorial limitations of the moratorium—The prohibition on legal process in para 43(6) does not have extraterritorial effect (i.e. it does not extend to proceedings brought in foreign courts): *Bloom and others v Harms Offshore AHT 'Taurus' GmbH & Co KG and another* [2009] EWCA Civ 632, [2010] Ch 187. However, the court has jurisdiction to prevent a creditor from taking advantage of a foreign attachment by granting an anti-suit injunction, although the comity owed by the courts of different jurisdictions to each other will normally make it inappropriate for the court to grant injunctive relief affecting procedures in a court of foreign jurisdiction.

The permission of the court—In *Metro Nominees (Wandsworth) (No 1) Limited v Rayment* [2008] BCC 40, HHJ Norris QC held that general rule in the normal case for permission for peaceable re-entry or to commence legal proceedings was that if a creditor sought to exercise a proprietary right that was unlikely to impede the achievement of the purpose for which the administration was being pursued, then leave should normally be given. Where that was not the case (so that there was a likelihood that the proprietary right would impede the achievement of the purpose) then the court has to carry out a balancing exercise, balancing the legitimate interest of the lessor and the legitimate interests of the other creditors. In carrying out that balancing exercise, great importance or weight was normally given to the proprietary interests of the lessor (the underlying principle being that an administration for the benefit of unsecured creditors should not be conducted at the expense of those who have proprietary rights, save to the extent that this was unavoidable).

In *Magical Marking Ltd v Phillips* [2008] EWHC 1640 (Pat), [2008] FSR 36, Norris J granted permission to the claimant to continue a breach of copyright claim.

In *Somerfield Stores Ltd v Spring (Sutton Coldfield) Ltd* [2009] EWHC 2384 (Ch), [2010] 2 BCLC 452, where a landlord company opposed the tenant's application for a new tenancy under Part II of the Landlord and Tenant Act 1954 on the ground that it intended to redevelop the property but was unable to do so by reason of subsequently being put into administration, and the administrators required 6–12 months to put in place a viable scheme for redevelopment for the benefit of the sole secured creditor, HHJ Purle QC (sitting as a High Court judge) granted permission to the tenant under para 43(6) to continue the application for a new tenancy.

In *Innovate Logistics Ltd v Sunberry Properties Ltd* [2008] EWHC 2450 (Ch), [2009] BCC 164, the Court of Appeal refused to grant permission to a landlord to seek repossession of premises which were necessary for the continuation of the company's business during the administration.

In *Re Nortel Networks UK Ltd: Unite The Union v Nortel Networks UK Ltd* [2010] EWHC 826 (Ch), [2010] BPIR 1003, Norris J refused permission to employees of a company in administration and a trade union for permission under para 43(6) to institute legal proceedings against the company in relation to the termination of employment contracts by the administrators. Paragraph 43(6) imposed a general rule that those with monetary claims against the company may not pursue them. The employees and the trade union could not demonstrate that their case was exceptional.

The court has jurisdiction to grant retrospective permission for the commencement of legal proceedings under para 43(6): *Bank of Ireland v Colliers International UK Plc* [2012] EWHC 2942 (Ch), [2013] Ch 422. In addition, the court has jurisdiction to grant permission once administration had ended in an appropriate case, although it will be rarely exercised: *Gaardsoe v Optimal Wealth Management Ltd (in liquidation)* [2012] EWHC 3266 (Ch), [2013] Ch 298.

Paragraph 43(6A)

Scope of provision—In contrast with the position under para 41(1) where an incumbent administrative receiver must vacate office on the making of an administration order, the fact of a company being in administration operates as an absolute bar against such an appointment being made. For the term 'administrative receiver' see s 29(2) and the general prohibition and excepted cases in ss 72A–72GA.

Paragraph 43(7)

When will leave be granted by the court, on conditions or otherwise?—The decision by a third party to seek leave of the court should ordinarily follow the third party's confirmation that the administrator is not prepared to consent to the particular enforcement, repossession, exercise of right etc. An administrator should, however, take care to ensure that his refusal of consent is justifiable, and certainly in practice he should give reasons for his refusing consent, since the guidance set out below indicates that a costs consequence may follow if such consent is unreasonably withheld. In *Re Atlantic Computer Systems plc* [1992] Ch 505 Nicholls LJ, as he then was, in giving the judgment of the court also comprising Neill and Staughton LJJ, albeit with some reluctance, acceded to an invitation by the parties to give guidance on the principles to be applied on an application for the grant of leave under the former s 11. Those principles formed the cornerstone of many subsequent applications in which leave was sought, not only on the issue of leave but also the more subtle question of the imposition of conditions, most commonly the requirement that an administrator makes a rental payment in respect of any particular item as an expense of the administration for the period of its use. There is no reason to suppose that the new administration regime should involve differing principles on the question of leave. What follows therefore is the relevant extract of Nicholls LJ's judgment in full (at 542–544) which concerned claims to repossess computer equipment and enforce the security constituted by the assignment of the benefit of subleases but which should be read as conveying general observations regarding cases where leave is sought to exercise existing proprietary rights, including security rights, against the company in administration:

'(1) It is in every case for the person who seeks leave to make out a case for him to be given leave.

(2) The prohibition in section 11(3)(c) and (d) is intended to assist the company, under the management of the administrator, to achieve the purpose for which the administration order was made. If granting leave to a lessor of land or the hirer of goods (a "lessor") to exercise his proprietary rights and repossess his land or goods is unlikely to impede the achievement of that purpose, leave should normally be given.

(3) In other cases where a lessor seeks possession the court has to carry out a balancing exercise, balancing the legitimate interests of the lessor and the legitimate interests of the other creditors of the company: see *per* Peter Gibson J in *Royal Trust Bank v Buchler* [1989] BCLC 130, 135. The metaphor employed here, for want of a better term, is that of scales and weights. Lord Wilberforce averted to the limitations of this metaphor in *Science Research Council v Nassé* [1980] AC 1028, 1067. It must be kept in mind that the exercise under section 11 is not a mechanical one; each case calls for an exercise in judicial judgment, in which the court seeks to give effect to the purpose of the statutory provisions, having regard to the parties' interests and all the circumstances of the case. As already noted, the purpose of the prohibition is to enable or assist the company to achieve the object for which the administration order was made. The purpose of the power to give leave is to enable the court to relax the prohibition where it would be inequitable for the prohibition to apply.

(4) In carrying out the balancing exercise great importance, or weight, is normally to be given to the proprietary interests of the lessor. Sir Nicholas Browne-Wilkinson V-C observed in *Bristol Airport Plc v Powdrill* [1990] Ch 744, 767D–767E that, so far as possible, the administration procedure should not be used to prejudice those who were secured creditors when the administration order was made in lieu of a winding-up order. The same is true regarding the proprietary interests of a lessor. The underlying principle here is that an administration for the benefit of unsecured creditors should not be conducted at the expense of those who have proprietary rights which they are seeking to exercise, save to the extent that this may be unavoidable and even then this will usually be acceptable only to a strictly limited extent.

(5) Thus it will normally be a sufficient ground for the grant of leave if significant loss would be caused to the lessor by a refusal. For this purpose loss comprises any kind of financial loss, direct or indirect, including loss by reason of delay, and may extend to loss which is not financial. But if substantially greater loss would be caused to others by the grant of leave, or loss which is out of all proportion to

751

the benefit which leave would confer on the lessor, that may outweigh the loss to the lessor caused by a refusal. Our formulation was criticised in the course of the argument, and we certainly do not claim for it the status of a rule in those terms. At present we say only that it appears to us the nearest we can get to a formulation of what Parliament had in mind.

(6) In assessing these respective losses the court will have regard to matters such as the financial position of the company, its ability to pay the rental arrears and the continuing rentals, the administrator's proposals, the period for which the administration order has already been in force and is expected to remain in force, the effect on the administration if leave were given, the effect on the applicant if leave were refused, the end result sought to be achieved by the administration, the prospects of that result being achieved, and the history of the administration so far.

(7) In considering these matters it will often be necessary to assess how probable the suggested consequences are. Thus if loss to the applicant is virtually certain if leave is refused, and loss to others a remote possibility if leave is granted, that will be a powerful factor in favour of granting leave.

(8) This is not an exhaustive list. For example, the conduct of the parties may also be a material consideration in a particular case, as it was in the *Bristol Airport* case. There leave was refused on the ground that the applicants had accepted benefits under the administration, and had only sought to enforce their security at a later stage: indeed, they have only acquired their security as a result of the operations of the administrators. It behoves a lessor to make his position clear to the administrator at the outset of the administration and, if it should become necessary, to apply to the court promptly.

(9) The above considerations may be relevant not only to the decision whether leave should be granted or refused, but also to a decision to impose terms if leave is granted.

(10) The above considerations will also apply to a decision on whether to impose terms as a condition for refusing leave. Section 11(3)(c) and (d) makes no provision for terms being imposed if leave is refused, but the court has power to achieve that result. It may do so directly, by giving directions to the administrator; for instance, under section 17, or in response to an application by the administrator under section 14(3), or in exercise of its control over an administrator as an officer of the court. Or it may do so indirectly, by ordering that the applicant shall have leave unless the administrator is prepared to take this or that step in the conduct of the administration. Cases where leave is refused but terms are imposed can be expected to arise frequently. For example, the permanent loss to a lessor flowing from his inability to recover his property will normally be small if the administrator is required to pay the current rent. In most cases this should be possible, since if the administration order has been rightly made the business should generally be sufficiently viable to hold down current outgoings. Such a term may therefore be a normal term to impose.

(11) The above observations are directed at a case such as the present where a lessor of land or the owner of goods is seeking to repossess his land or goods because of non-payment of rentals. A broadly similar approach will be applicable on many applications to enforce a security: for instance, an application by a mortgagee for possession of land. On such applications an important consideration will often be whether the applicant is fully secured. If he is, delay in enforcement is likely to be less prejudicial than in cases where his security is insufficient.

(12) In some cases there will be a dispute over the existence, validity or nature of the security which the applicant is seeking leave to enforce. It is not for the court on the leave application to seek to adjudicate upon that issue, unless (as in the present case, on the fixed or floating charge point) the issue raises a short point of law which it is convenient to determine without further ado. Otherwise the court needs to be satisfied only that the applicant has a seriously arguable case.'

Cases for leave to enforce proprietary rights will necessarily turn on their own facts and require the court to identify the relevant facts and to weigh those matters in the balance; for examples see *Re Neesam Investments Ltd* [1988] 4 BCC 788 (fixed charge over office building where charge-holder concerned that amount of debt secured by charge would exceed value of security in course of administration); *Bristol Airport plc v Powdrill* [1990] Ch 744 (court refused leave to airport authorities to exercise statutory right of detention on aircraft under s 88 of the Civil Aviation Act 1982 in respect of airport costs due); *Re David Meek Plant Ltd* [1994] 1 BCLC 680 (leave to possess goods on hire purchase refused to a number of finance companies but granted to two companies which had sought to repossess the day before presentation of the administration petition); *Re Divine Solutions UK Ltd* [2003] EWHC 1931 (Ch), [2004] 1 BCLC 373 (application for leave to proceed with proceedings before employment tribunal dismissed where administration order made for period of only one year and where little evidence adduced by applicant to substantiate claim of unfair dismissal); and *Metro Nominees (Wandsworth) Ltd (No.1) v Rayment* [2008] BCC 40 (permission to enforce terms of lease by proceedings but not immediate physical re-entry notwithstanding service of 'unimpleachable' notice under s 146 of the Law of Property Act 1925 and offer to pay rent by administrators).

Permission to commence a simple money claim, rather than allow an administration to run its course, will be granted only in the most exceptional of cases: *AES Barry Ltd v TXU Europe Energy Trading Ltd* [2005] 2 BCLC 22 at [24] (Patten J). In *Fashoff (UK) Ltd v Linton* [2008] 2 BCLC 362 at [97]–[108] HHJ Toulmin QC, sitting as a judge of the High Court, held that, in light of the creditor's obligation to act promptly in seeking leave (by virtue of guideline (8) above), a creditor with proprietary rights under a retention of title clause which had delayed by some eight months in applying to court following an administrator's refusal to consent to the recovery of goods would be refused leave where the creditor's conduct had prevented and continued to prevent a distribution to creditors in the administration.

In *The Funding Corp Block Discounting Ltd v Lexi Holdings plc (in administration)* [2008] 2 BCLC 596 at [5] and [6] Briggs J equated the task of the court under guideline 12 above with that in proceedings against a company not in administration where that company made an application for defendant's summary judgment under CPR Pt 24.

Creditor and third party self-help remedies which are not protected against by the statutory moratorium in administration—Nothing within the moratorium provisions suggests that the statutory protection afforded to a debtor is intended as depriving a creditor or third party from utilising any self-help remedies against the debtor company, even where the effect of such remedies is harmful to the financial interests or standing of the company in administration.

These self-help remedies would include repudiation for breach of contract, service of a contractual notice (such as one making time of the essence, as in *Re Olympia & York Canary Wharf Ltd* [1993] BCLC 453 (Millett J, as he then was)) or forfeiture (though not by peaceable re-entry) of a lease. Neither would the protection of the moratorium appear to catch a combination of accounts, most obviously by a bank or trading customer, or an application for an extension of time for the registration of a charge over the company's property, as in *Re Barrow Borough Transport Ltd* [1990] Ch 227. It is suggested that the filing and service of a defence to a claim commenced by a company under the protection of the moratorium would amount to the legitimate exercise of a self-help remedy, whereas the filing and service of a counterclaim with the defence would contravene para 43(6), but not to the extent that the counterclaim was relied on solely for the purpose of a defence by way of set-off, on which see CPR, r 16.6.

Since the exercise of a right of set-off cannot be characterised as constituting proceedings, execution or other legal process, such a right – whether legal equitable, contractual or otherwise – will, other than where the set-off falls within the scope of r 2.85, remain available to a third party, for which proposition see *Electromagnetic (S) Ltd v Development Bank of Singapore* [1994] SLR 734, a decision of the High Court of Singapore in which jurisdiction the administration regime had been modelled on the former English provisions in Part II.

It is further suggested that the service of a demand, say for the return of goods, constitutes no more than self-help and will not fall within the scope of para 43(6) (on which see *Barclays Mercantile Business Finance Ltd v Sibec Developments Ltd* [1992] 1 WLR 1253), although it is arguable that the position is different where the service of such a demand or other notice is a contractual pre-condition for the taking of any step protected against by s 43(2)–(6A), on which see *Re Olympia & York Canary Wharf Ltd* [1993] BCLC 453 at 454G–454H.

'transaction'—See the very broad and non-exhaustive definition in s 436 which identifies a 'transaction' as extending to something less than contractual agreement.

44 Interim moratorium

(1) This paragraph applies where an administration application in respect of a company has been made and—

    (a)   the application has not yet been granted or dismissed, or

    (b)   the application has been granted but the administration order has not yet taken effect.

(2) This paragraph also applies from the time when a copy of notice of intention to appoint an administrator under paragraph 14 is filed with the court until—

    (a)   the appointment of the administrator takes effect, or

    (b)   the period of five business days beginning with the date of filing expires without an administrator having been appointed.

(3) Sub-paragraph (2) has effect in relation to a notice of intention to appoint only if it is in the prescribed form.

(4) This paragraph also applies from the time when a copy of notice of intention to appoint an administrator is filed with the court under paragraph 27(1) until—

    (a)   the appointment of the administrator takes effect, or

    (b)   the period specified in paragraph 28(2) expires without an administrator having been appointed.

(5) The provisions of paragraphs 42 and 43 shall apply (ignoring any reference to the consent of the administrator).

(6) If there is an administrative receiver of the company when the administration application is made, the provisions of paragraphs 42 and 43 shall not begin to apply by virtue of this paragraph until the person by or on behalf of whom the receiver was appointed consents to the making of the administration order.

(7) This paragraph does not prevent or require the permission of the court for—

    (a)   the presentation of a petition for the winding up of the company under a provision mentioned in paragraph 42(4),

    (b)   the appointment of an administrator under paragraph 14,

    (c)   the appointment of an administrative receiver of the company, or

    (d)   the carrying out by an administrative receiver (whenever appointed) of his functions.

General note—The interim moratorium, which is provided for in all court and out-of-court appointments, is very similar in substance to, but quite distinct from, the moratorium protection in paras 42 and 43 which is triggered only on a company being 'in administration'.

The period for which the interim moratorium takes effect—In the case of an administration application the interim protection is triggered once the application 'has been made': para 44(1). In the absence of any express stipulation for the filing of the application and all supporting documents – on which see IR 1986, r 2.5(1) – the interim moratorium protection is obtained automatically at the moment at which the application itself is filed with the court. In certain cases it might be thought appropriate to give notice and provide evidence of the operation of the moratorium to a pressing creditor.

In the case of an out-of-court appointment under paras 14 or 22 the interim moratorium is obtained from the time at which a copy of the notice of intention to appoint is filed with the court. In a para 14 case, however, para 44(3) provides that the triggering of the moratorium is conditional on the copy notice being in Form 2.5B, as is provided for in r 2.15. Although r 2.20 provides that a notice of intention to appoint in a para 22 case 'shall be in Form 2.8B', the interim moratorium will trigger in such a case even if the copy notice filed with the court is not in the prescribed form.

In the case of an administration application the interim moratorium endures until the application has been dismissed or, alternatively, until an administration order is made, in which case there is a seamless triggering of the moratorium under paras 42 and 43. As a further alternative, the interim moratorium will continue under para 44(1) where the court has made an interim order under para 13(1)(d) or some other order under para 13(1)(f) which accedes to the application but which amounts in substance to something less than the making of an administration order: see the notes to para 13(1).

In a para 14 case the interim protection will automatically end after the five business days period stipulated in para 44(2)(b) in the absence of an appointment having been effected. The same rule applies in a para 22 case in which the relevant period is ten business days: see the reference to para 28(2) in para 44(4)(b).

If no person is entitled to service of a notice of intention to appoint under para 15(1) (in a para 14 case) or under para 26(1) (in a para 22 case) then, subject to compliance with the pre-conditions applicable to either case, the holder of a qualifying floating charge, or the company or its directors, may proceed to an immediate appointment so as to render the interim moratorium irrelevant. This remains the position notwithstanding the fact that certain persons prescribed by r 2.20(2) are entitled to notice of intention to appoint in Form 2.8B in a para 22 case, since the purpose of such notice is not in allowing for a challenge to the proposed appointment but, rather, to avoid an inadvertent breach and contempt of court on the part of any such third party of the terms of the moratorium under paras 42 and 43 on the appointment taking effect. Where there is any delay in the period between the filing of the copy notice of intention and the appointment of an administrator in a para 22 case in circumstances where the only persons entitled to notice are those prescribed in r 2.20(2) for para 26(2) purposes, the filing of the copy notice will trigger the interim moratorium for up to ten days: para 44(4)(b).

Paragraph 44(5)–(7)

The protective nature of the interim moratorium—The effect of para 44(5) is, in effect, to replicate paras 42 and 43 for the purpose of defining the scope of the interim moratorium save, of course, that there will be no administrator in office who might consent to those steps otherwise prevented by paras 43(2)–(6). One effect of the application of paras 42 and 43 is that, during the period of the interim moratorium, the court may give permission for what is termed 'a transaction' which would otherwise be prohibited by para 43, subject to any condition or other requirement which the court might impose.

Paragraph 44(6) only applies where an administrative receiver is in office at the time of the making of an administration order, although the provision has no application in a para 14 or para 22 case. Save where the court thinks the security pursuant to which an administrative receiver has been appointed is susceptible under the statutory provisions identified in para 39(1)(b)–(d) the court may not make an administration order where an administrative receiver is in office other than in the scenario where the receiver's appointor consents to the making of an administration order under para 39(1)(a). In the absence of such consent the interim moratorium, by way of its application of paras 42 and 43, has no application. Even where such consent is given, para 44(7)(d) allows for the continued carrying out by the administrative receiver of his functions pending the making of an administration order.

In contrast with the prohibitions imposed by para 43, para 44(7) allows for the presentation of a winding-up petition – but not the making of a winding-up order – on the grounds in para 42(4), the appointment of an administrator by the holder of a qualifying floating charge under para 14, the appointment of an administrative receiver and the carrying out by an administrative receiver of his functions.

45 Publicity

(1) While a company is in administration, every business document issued by or on behalf of the company or the administrator, and all the company's websites, must state –

    (a)   the name of the administrator, and

    (b)   that the affairs, business and property of the company are being managed by the administrator.

(2) Any of the following persons commits an offence if without reasonable excuse the person authorises or permits a contravention of sub-paragraph (1) –

    (a)   the administrator,

    (b)   an officer of the company, and

    (c)   the company.

(3) In sub-paragraph (1) 'business document' means –

    (a)   an invoice,

    (b)   an order for goods or services,

    (c)   a business letter, and

    (d)   an order form,

whether in hard copy, electronic or any other form.

Amendments—SI 2008/1897.

General note—The substance of these publicity requirements is common to those under the former administration regime under s 12, receivership under s 39 and liquidation under s 188.

  It is common practice and advisable for an administrator to include on all business documents an express statement to the effect that the administrator contracts as agent of the company only and without personal liability, notwithstanding the fact that a provision to that effect appears in any case in para 69.

PROCESS OF ADMINISTRATION

46 Announcement of administrator's appointment

(1) This paragraph applies where a person becomes the administrator of a company.

(2) As soon as is reasonably practicable the administrator shall—

    (a)   send a notice of his appointment to the company, and

    (b)   publish a notice of his appointment in the prescribed manner.

(3) As soon as is reasonably practicable the administrator shall—

    (a)   obtain a list of the company's creditors, and

    (b)   send a notice of his appointment to each creditor of whose claim and address he is aware.

(4) The administrator shall send a notice of his appointment to the registrar of companies before the end of the period of 7 days beginning with the date specified in sub-paragraph (6).

(5) The administrator shall send a notice of his appointment to such persons as may be prescribed before the end of the prescribed period beginning with the date specified in sub-paragraph (6).

(6) The date for the purpose of sub-paragraphs (4) and (5) is—

(a) in the case of an administrator appointed by administration order, the date of the order,

(b) in the case of an administrator appointed under paragraph 14, the date on which he receives notice under paragraph 20, and

(c) in the case of an administrator appointed under paragraph 22, the date on which he receives notice under paragraph 32.

(7) The court may direct that sub-paragraph (3)(b) or (5)—

(a) shall not apply, or

(b) shall apply with the substitution of a different period.

(8) A notice under this paragraph must—

(a) contain the prescribed information, and

(b) be in the prescribed form.

(9) An administrator commits an offence if he fails without reasonable excuse to comply with a requirement of this paragraph.

General note—This provision, as with paras 47 and 48, applies to all administrations and provides the procedural steps by which the process of administration is commenced.

Although the rules here are administrative in nature, they are nonetheless of practical importance so far as concerns the giving of notice to third parties such that non-compliance without reasonable excuse constitutes an offence under para 46(9).

In *Re Advent Computer Training Ltd* [2010] EWHC 459 (Ch), [2011] BCC 44 HHJ Purle QC (sitting as a judge of the High Court) held that notice of appointment and statement of proposals could be sent to creditors by e-mail. The earlier decision in *Re Sporting Options plc* [2005] BPIR 435 (in which Mann J was not prepared to direct that those documents be sent by e-mail to the creditors of a company which carried on a gaming business on the internet and where confirmation of bets (but not the placing of bets) was notified by e-mail) was distinguished on its facts, the court noting that e-mail communication had moved on in the five years since that decision.

Paragraph 46(2)

Scope of provision—The notice of appointment is as in Form 2.11B, an amended version of which appears in the Schedule to the Insolvency (Amendment) Rules 2004 (SI 2004/584). The 'prescribed manner' for publication of the notice is provided for in r 2.27(1). In addition to advertisement in the London Gazette, it may be appropriate to advertise in one or more local newspapers if, for example, a significant number of creditors are located in one geographical area.

Paragraph 46(3)

Scope of provision—The notice of the administrator's appointment is in Form 2.12B, as provided for in r 2.27(3). The court may consider disapplying the sending out of a notice if, say, the company's creditors comprise a very large number of persons to whom small amounts are owed, with the consequence that the sending out of notices would be disproportionately expensive. In those circumstances the court might require the placing of one or more additional advertisements to those required under r 2.27(1).

Paragraph 46(4)

Scope of provision—The notice is in Form 2.12B, as prescribed by r 2.27(3).

Paragraph 46(5)

Scope of provision—The persons prescribed are those in r 2.27(2), as applicable. Notice must be given 'as soon as reasonably practicable' after the relevant date in para 46(6).

Penalties—See s 430 and Sch 10 and the daily default fine under para 106(2)(c).

47 Statement of company's affairs

(1) As soon as is reasonably practicable after appointment the administrator of a company shall by notice in the prescribed form require one or more relevant persons to provide the administrator with a statement of the affairs of the company.

(2) The statement must—

    (a)   be verified by a statement of truth in accordance with Civil Procedure Rules,

    (b)   be in the prescribed form,

    (c)   give particulars of the company's property, debts and liabilities,

    (d)   give the names and addresses of the company's creditors,

    (e)   specify the security held by each creditor,

    (f)   give the date on which each security was granted, and

    (g)   contain such other information as may be prescribed.

(3) In sub-paragraph (1) 'relevant person' means—

    (a)   a person who is or has been an officer of the company,

    (b)   a person who took part in the formation of the company during the period of one year ending with the date on which the company enters administration,

    (c)   a person employed by the company during that period, and

    (d)   a person who is or has been during that period an officer or employee of a company which is or has been during that year an officer of the company.

(4) For the purpose of sub-paragraph (3) a reference to employment is a reference to employment through a contract of employment or a contract for services.

(5) In Scotland, a statement of affairs under sub-paragraph (1) must be a statutory declaration made in accordance with the Statutory Declarations Act 1835 (and sub-paragraph (2)(a) shall not apply).

General note—This provision applies in all administrations.

The statement of affairs is a key document, which will be of fundamental importance to the formulation of the administrator's proposals for para 49 purposes. In producing the statement, the 'relevant persons' (see below), and those advising them, should bear in mind that the statement must be verified by a statement of truth (compliant with Part 22 of the CPR) and that a copy of the document is, subject to IR 1986, r 2.30, sent by the administrator to the Registrar of Companies and filed by him with the court under r 2.29(7).

In practice, an administrator will frequently have had some insight prior to his appointment into those matters set out in the statement of affairs. The veracity of what is presented to the office-holder should not in any case be taken at face value without consideration or relevant and obvious inquiry. Neither should the administrator be accepting of any reticence on the part of any relevant person in producing or submitting the statement of affairs, given the statutory obligation to do so under paras 47 and 48. An administrator has specific standing under r 7.20(2)(a) to make application to court for an order enforcing para 47 together with an order for costs. Failure to comply with a requirement by an administrator under para 47(1) constitutes an offence under para 48(4), on which see s 430, Sch 10 and the daily default fine under para 106(2)(d).

Paragraph 47(1)

Scope of provision—The administrator's notice is in Form 2.13B, on which see r 2.28.

Paragraph 47(2)

Scope of provision—The statement of affairs shall be in Form 2.14B and must comply with r 2.29(1). The administrator may also require any relevant person to submit a statement of concurrence in Form 2.15B stating that he concurs with the statement of affairs: r 2.29(2). A statement of concurrence may be considered appropriate where, for example, the administrator has doubts or concerns as to the information set out in the statement of affairs where the individual from whom the statement of concurrence is required is properly able, given the information to which that individual has access or the level of knowledge attributed to that individual, to concur or otherwise comment on the contents of the statement of affairs.

Limited disclosure—Rule 2.30 specifically provides for an application by the administrator to court for an order for limited disclosure in respect of the statement of affairs on the grounds that the disclosure of the whole or part of the statement of affairs would prejudice the conduct of the administration. The reference in r 2.30(1) to 'prejudice the conduct of the administration' should, it is submitted, be interpreted as meaning 'would be likely to cause financial harm to those with an interest in the administration'. Mere administrative inconvenience which might arise from the disclosure of whole or part of the statement of affairs should not justify limited disclosure, given the rights of third parties to inspect the company's file at Companies House over and above the right to inspect the court file conferred under r 7.31. Perhaps the best and most common example of circumstances which can be shown to prejudice the conduct of the administration arise where the statement of affairs includes price-sensitive information from which competitors or any prospective purchaser might derive a commercial advantage, an observation consistent with r 2.33(3), which allows for the non-disclosure in a statement of an administrator's proposals of information 'which could seriously prejudice the commercial interests of the company'.

'relevant person'—For the scope of the term 'officer' in para 47(3)(a) see the definition in s 1121 of the Companies Act 2006 which extends to a director, manager or secretary of the company, and see also the notes to s 206(3). The reference in para 47(4) to a contract for services means that, subject to evidence of such a contract, those providing services to the company, most obviously its solicitors, accountants or auditors, might be called on to submit a statement of affairs or a statement of concurrence. Such requests are, however, very rare in practice.

Procedure—In addition to the above, see also r 2.32 (expenses of statement of affairs).

48

(1) A person required to submit a statement of affairs must do so before the end of the period of 11 days beginning with the day on which he receives notice of the requirement.

(2) The administrator may—

    (a)   revoke a requirement under paragraph 47(1), or

    (b)   extend the period specified in sub-paragraph (1) (whether before or after expiry).

(3) If the administrator refuses a request to act under sub-paragraph (2)—

> (a) the person whose request is refused may apply to the court, and
> (b) the court may take action of a kind specified in sub-paragraph (2).

(4) A person commits an offence if he fails without reasonable excuse to comply with a requirement under paragraph 47(1).

General note—This provision applies in all administrations.

The standing of a person to apply to court under para 48(3) is conditional on the administrator refusing a request to act under para 48(2).

Procedure—A release from duty to submit a statement of affairs might be granted or be sought by a relevant person in the event of genuine illness and disability or, possibly, say, through a prolonged and unavoidable absence overseas which precludes access to the company's books and records.

49 Administrator's proposals

(1) The administrator of a company shall make a statement setting out proposals for achieving the purpose of administration.

(2) A statement under sub-paragraph (1) must, in particular—

> (a) deal with such matters as may be prescribed, and
> (b) where applicable, explain why the administrator thinks that the objective mentioned in paragraph 3(1)(a) or (b) cannot be achieved.

(3) Proposals under this paragraph may include—

> (a) a proposal for a voluntary arrangement under Part I of this Act (although this paragraph is without prejudice to section 4(3));
> (b) a proposal for a compromise or arrangement to be sanctioned under Part 26 of the Companies Act 2006 (arrangements and reconstructions).

(4) The administrator shall send a copy of the statement of his proposals—

> (a) to the registrar of companies,
> (b) to every creditor of the company of whose claim and address he is aware, and
> (c) to every member of the company of whose address he is aware.

(5) The administrator shall comply with sub-paragraph (4)—

> (a) as soon as is reasonably practicable after the company enters administration, and
> (b) in any event, before the end of the period of eight weeks beginning with the day on which the company enters administration.

(6) The administrator shall be taken to comply with sub-paragraph (4)(c) if he publishes in the prescribed manner a notice undertaking to provide a copy of the statement of proposals free of charge to any member of the company who applies in writing to a specified address.

(7) An administrator commits an offence if he fails without reasonable excuse to comply with sub-paragraph (5).

(8) A period specified in this paragraph may be varied in accordance with paragraph 107.

Amendments—SI 2008/948.

General note—The statement of the administrator's proposals is produced for consideration by creditors at the initial creditors' meeting under para 51 or para 52(2). There is no prescribed form for the statement itself, although the statement must be attached to Form 2.17B, by virtue of IR 1986, r 2.33(1), on being sent to the Registrar of Companies in compliance with para 49(4)(a).

In *Re Advent Computer Training Ltd* [2010] EWHC 459 (Ch), [2011] BCC 44 HHJ Purle QC (sitting as a judge of the High Court) held that notice of appointment and statement of proposals could be sent to creditors by e-mail. The earlier decision in *Re Sporting Options plc* [2005] BPIR 435 (in which Mann J was not prepared to direct that those documents be sent by e-mail to the creditors of a company which carried on a gaming business on the internet and where confirmation of bets (but not the placing of bets) was notified by e-mail) was distinguished on its facts, the court noting that e-mail communication had moved on in the five years since that decision.

Paragraph 49(2)

Contents of the statement of the administrator's proposals—The word 'must' in the opening to para 49(2) requires that the statement must include those matters prescribed in r 2.33(2) and para 49(2)(b). The words 'in particular', however, indicate that an administrator should not proceed in formulating his proposals with slavish adherence to those prescribed matters, but should also include in his statement any additional matter or matters which he deems necessary in the circumstances so as to enable a reasonable creditor to make an informed assessment of his proposals for achieving the purpose of administration under para 49(1). An administrator may also consider it prudent to provide an explanation of any discrepancy between the financial information upon which his proposals are based and the financial position put in evidence in support of any administration application to the court.

The altered approach under Sch B1 to the formulation of the administrator's proposals—The former Part II made no specific stipulation as to the contents of the statement of an administrator's proposals under s 23(1). Rule 2.33(2), read together with para 49(2) and the scope of that provision as identified above, represents a marked shift from that position. Under the former law it was not uncommon, particularly in the case of an administration instituted hastily, to find that an administrator's proposals were cast in the most general of terms, which would often not extend beyond proposing that creditors simply approve the continued management of the affairs of the company for the purpose or purposes for which the order was granted and that the administrator be authorised to market or sell the assets of the company on receiving a suitable offer, together with equally general proposals as to reporting to creditors. That former practice, it is submitted, is inconsistent with the new provisions which, amongst other specific matters, impose a positive duty on the administrator under r 2.33(2)(m) to set out how it is envisaged that the purpose of the administration will be achieved and how it is proposed, in specific terms, that the administration shall end. On the other hand, it is, in practical terms, something of a counsel of perfection to expect that all administrators in all cases will be in a position to map out with unfailing accuracy how the conduct of the administration is to evolve. This necessitates some sense of commercial balance. What should be expected, it is submitted, is the administrator's best assessment of the way forward. It should also be borne in mind here that, despite the requirement for a relative degree of precision, para 54(1) specifically allows for the revision of an administrator's proposals but does not apparently require creditors' approval for such revision other than where, as para 54(1)(c) provides, 'the administrator thinks that the proposed revision is substantial'. This point is discussed further in the notes to para 52.

The administrator's proposals will, of necessity, have to take into account the purpose of administration in para 3(1). In particular, para 49(2)(b) reinforces the point made in the commentary to para 3(1) to the effect that the administrator must be able to present cogent and objectively sound reasons as to why the sub-purposes in either para 3(1)(a) and/or (b) cannot be achieved.

Further limitations on the administrator's proposals—Paragraph 73(1) provides that an administrator's statement of proposals – which, by virtue of para 73(3), includes a revised or modified statement – may not include any action which affects the right of a secured creditor of the company to enforce its security, would result in a preferential debt being paid otherwise than in priority to a non-preferential debt, or would result in one preferential creditor being paid a smaller proportion of his debt than another. Those limitations do not apply in the circumstances set out in para 73(2), namely where the relevant secured creditor consents in the case of a CVA under Part 1 (subject, again, to the relevant secured creditor consenting to any variation of his secured rights) or on a proposal for sanction for a compromise or arrangement under Part 26 of the Companies Act 2006.

Paragraph 49(3)

Proposals including a CVA proposal or a proposal under Part 26 of the Companies Act 2006—A CVA or a scheme of arrangement will commonly provide the mechanism by which an administrator seeks to rescue a company as a going concern by way of creditors agreeing to accept less than full payment of their debts. In the case of a CVA, s 4(3) protects the right of a secured creditor to enforce his security other than where the creditor consents to any variation of such rights. In the case of a scheme of arrangement, the protection of secured (and preferential) rights will be achieved by the obligation under ss 895-901 of the Companies Act 2006 to place such creditors in a separate class or classes for voting purposes.

The sending out of copies of the administrator's statement of proposals—In keeping with the increased emphasis in Sch B1 on administration being as speedy a process as practicably possible, para 49(5) should be read as imposing a requirement for compliance 'as soon as is reasonably practicable'. The period of eight weeks mentioned in para 49(5)(b) is not to be read as the ordinary rule in all cases and, indeed, is only relevant if it is not reasonably practicable to send out the statement within that period. Paragraph 107 allows for the extension of the eight-week time period by the court on the application of the administrator, more than once and retrospectively, although the court will ordinarily require a clear explanation in evidence as to the reasons for any such application being made to it. An extension is also possible with the consent of creditors under para 108, albeit in more limited circumstances. In the event of a time extension for para 49(5) purposes the administrator must notify all those persons set out in para 49(4) of the court order in Form 2.18B as soon as reasonably practicable.

Paragraph 49(7)

Penalties—See s 430, Sch 10 and the daily default fine in para 106(2)(e).

50 Creditors' meeting

(1) In this Schedule 'creditors' meeting' means a meeting of creditors of a company summoned by the administrator—

    (a)   in the prescribed manner, and

    (b)   giving the prescribed period of notice to every creditor of the company of whose claim and address he is aware.

(2) A period prescribed under sub-paragraph (1)(b) may be varied in accordance with paragraph 107.

(3) A creditors' meeting shall be conducted in accordance with the rules.

General note—The procedure governing creditors' meetings is as set out in IR 1986, rr 2.34–2.48.

    Paragraph 58 allows for the business of any creditors' meeting to be done by correspondence between the administrator and creditors. Further commentary is provided in the notes to that provision. The term 'correspondence' is defined in para 111(1) as including correspondence by telephone or other electronic means, most obviously e-mail and fax communications.

Paragraph 50(1)(b)

'... the prescribed period of notice ...'—Rule 2.35(4) provides that at least 14 days' notice must be given to creditors within the scope of that provision, subject to the possibility of an adjournment as provided for in r 2.35(6) and (7). The notice of any meeting within r 2.35(1) shall be in Form 2.20B: r 2.35(2). The mandatory form of proxy is in Form 8.2.

Meetings of members—There is no requirement under any provision in Sch B1 for the convening of a meeting of the members of a company, although the administrator may consider such a meeting to be appropriate in a specific case. Rule 2.49 governs the venue and conduct of company meetings in administration, although a proposal for a CVA by an administrator will be governed by rr 1.13–1.16.

51 Requirement for initial creditors' meeting

(1) Each copy of an administrator's statement of proposals sent to a creditor under paragraph 49(4)(b) must be accompanied by an invitation to a creditors' meeting (an 'initial creditors' meeting').

(2) The date set for an initial creditors' meeting must be—

    (a)   as soon as is reasonably practicable after the company enters administration, and

    (b)   in any event, within the period of ten weeks beginning with the date on which the company enters administration.

(3) An administrator shall present a copy of his statement of proposals to an initial creditors' meeting.

(4) A period specified in this paragraph may be varied in accordance with paragraph 107.

(5) An administrator commits an offence if he fails without reasonable excuse to comply with a requirement of this paragraph.

General note—Paragraph 53(1) provides that the business of what is defined here as the 'initial creditors' meeting' is the approval or rejection by creditors of the administrator's proposals or, alternatively, approval of the proposals with modifications to which the administrator consents. Literally construed, para 53(1) does not actually provide for the rejection of proposals, although para 55(1)(a) plainly envisages such rejection or, rather, as it is put, a failure to approve, which must be read into para 53(1).

    It is not possible for the creditors to approve modifications upon which they insist but to which the administrator is not prepared to give his consent.

Options where the administrator's proposals are not approved—If the administrator's proposals are not approved at the initial meeting, then the administrator must report the matter to the court (and others) under para 53(2) and may then proceed in one of four ways. If the administrator considers that approval might be obtained to revised proposals then, consequent on para 55(1)(a), he might invite the court to direct the summoning of a further creditors' meeting under para 55(2)(e) (or para 56(1)(b)), together with appropriate consequential provisions which, it is suggested, would include a direction consistent with para 49 for the circulation of the revised proposals. Alternatively, the administrator might invite the court to make an order under para 55(2)(a) terminating his appointment with any other appropriate order within the scope of para 55(2)(b)–(e). The administrator's third alternative is to proceed without the court's involvement where he considers that revised proposals are capable of obtaining approval. Although not expressly anticipated by Sch B1, savings in time and cost and the commercial need for the administrator to be able to act with such autonomy, it is submitted, dictate that the administrator would have power under para 62 to call a meeting of creditors to consider revised proposals, subject to compliance with the rules governing creditors' meetings in IR 1986, rr 2.34–2.44. As a further alternative, in an appropriate case the administrator may consider adjourning the initial creditors' meeting for a period of up to 14 days, as provided for in IR 1986, r 2.35(6), most obviously where the level of creditor support necessary to approve the proposals is marginal and is considered by the administrator to be capable of being bridged after further representations or reflection or where the administrator wishes to consider modifications upon which the creditors are insistent as a condition to approval. The same four alternatives would apply under para 55(1)(b) in the event that a further creditors' meeting fails to improve revised proposals.

Cases in which there is no requirement for an initial creditors' meeting—Whilst mandatory in all other cases, an administrator may dispense with an initial creditors' meeting where he intends to apply to the court or file a notice under para 80(2) for the administration to cease at a time before he has sent a statement of his proposals to creditors, in which case he must comply with the procedure in r 2.33(6). Neither will the obligation to convene the initial meeting arise where the administrator sends a notice under para 84(1) to the Registrar of Companies, with the consequence that the company moves from administration to dissolution under that provision. Furthermore, no initial meeting is required where the administrator's statement of proposals fulfils the criteria in para 52(1) other than where at least 10% of the creditors request the summoning of such a meeting under para 52(2).

Time limit for the initial creditors' meeting—The ten-week period referred to in para 51(2)(b) refers to the date of the meeting itself, and not the date by which the administrator's proposals are to be sent to creditors. Furthermore, para 51(2)(a) raises a rebuttable presumption that it will be reasonably practicable in all cases to hold the initial meeting within ten weeks. Very often it will be reasonably practicable to hold the meeting sooner, and sometimes very much sooner.

Paragraphs 107 and 108 allow for the extension of the ten-week period by the court or creditors, subject to the limitations therein.

Is it possible to hold a 'further creditors' meeting' prior to an 'initial creditors' meeting'?—The limit on the scope of the business conducted at the initial creditors' meeting as imposed by para 53(1) is apparently predicated upon the assumption that a first meeting of creditors will only ever be required to consider the administrator's proposals. Whilst in practice this is usually the case, it is submitted that there is no good reason why in appropriate circumstances a meeting should not be summoned if requested or directed under para 56(1) (despite that provision being headed 'Further creditors' meetings') or by the administrator himself under para 62 prior to the initial creditors' meeting. This might conceivably arise in a case of urgency or one in which the weighing up of creditors' views at an early stage and on a formal basis is deemed necessary by the administrator to assess the viability of the administration.

Procedure and forms—Rule 2.34(1) requires notice of an initial creditors' meeting to be given in the newspaper in which the administrator's appointment was advertised and, if the administrator considers it appropriate, in any other newspaper, so as to ensure that the notice comes to the attention of the company's creditors. There is no prescribed form for the advertisement. Under r 2.34(2) the administrator may give notice in Form 2.19B to any past or present director or officer of the company – on which terms see s 1173(1) of the Companies Act 2006 and the notes to s 206(3) – whose presence at the meeting is, in the administrator's opinion, required.

If an extension to the ten-week period in s 51(2)(b) is obtained by court order, then r 2.34(3) requires a notice in Form 2.18B to be sent to each person entitled to notice under para 49(4).

Penalties—On penalties see s 430, Sch 10 and the daily default fine provided for in para 106(2)(f).

    (c)   the administrator thinks that the proposed revision is substantial.

(2) The administrator shall—

    (a)   summon a creditors' meeting,

    (b)   send a statement in the prescribed form of the proposed revision with the notice of the meeting sent to each creditor,

    (c)   send a copy of the statement, within the prescribed period, to each member of the company of whose address he is aware, and

    (d)   present a copy of the statement to the meeting.

(3) The administrator shall be taken to have complied with sub-paragraph (2)(c) if he publishes a notice undertaking to provide a copy of the statement free of charge to any member of the company who applies in writing to a specified address.

(4) A notice under sub-paragraph (3) must be published—

    (a)   in the prescribed manner, and

    (b)   within the prescribed period.

(5) A creditors' meeting to which a proposed revision is presented shall consider it and may—

    (a)   approve it without modification, or

    (b)   approve it with modification to which the administrator consents.

(6) After the conclusion of a creditors' meeting the administrator shall as soon as is reasonably practicable report any decision taken to—

    (a)   the court,

    (b)   the registrar of companies, and

    (c)   such other persons as may be prescribed.

(7) An administrator commits an offence if he fails without reasonable excuse to comply with sub-paragraph (6).

General note—This provision only operates where the administrator's proposals have been approved, with or without modification, at an initial creditors' meeting and the administrator proposes a revision to the proposals and 'thinks' – a term discussed in the notes to para 3(3) – that the proposed revision is substantial. Once that view is formed the procedure in para 54(2)–(6) is triggered.

    The approval of revised proposals, or the insubstantial revision of proposals, binds the administrator by virtue of para 68(1), subject to para 68(2).

'... the proposed revision is substantial'—What is 'substantial' will inevitably vary from case to case. However, since insolvency procedures, and certainly administration, are mechanisms in which creditor interests are central, and given that those interests are essentially measured in financial terms, it is submitted that a revision will be 'substantial' if, measured in financial terms, the likely consequence for creditors generally would be regarded by an honest and reasonable hypothetical creditor as being substantial. Alternatively, a revision might be regarded as substantial if the methodology or strategy to be employed in the conduct of the administration differs significantly from that originally approved, even where the likely outcome for creditors in financial terms is no different or not substantially different from that contained in the original proposal.

Alternatives to the para 54 procedure—The timescales involved in the convening of a meeting under para 54 may render that procedure unworkable in a time-critical or urgent case. In those circumstances it is open to the administrator to make an application to court for directions sanctioning the proposed revision under para 68(2) on the grounds set out in para 68(3)(c). Alternatively, approved proposals now frequently contain a standard-form provision which, as approved at the initial creditors' meeting, allows the administrator to implement revisions either at his own discretion or, for example, with the permission of any creditors' committee, a practice approved of by Neuberger J, as he then was, in *Re Dana (UK) Ltd* [1999] 2 BCLC 239.

Revisions in a para 52 case—Where the administrator's proposals contain a statement in accordance with any of the three grounds in para 52(1), then there is no requirement for an initial creditors' meeting to consider the proposals under paras 51 and 53 unless at least 10% in value of the creditors of the company request such a meeting under para 52(2). If no such initial meeting is requested, then the administration simply proceeds in accordance with the administrator's statement of proposals. If the administrator then proposes a substantial revision to those proposals, the mechanism in para 54(2)–(6) and rr 2.45 and 2.46 would not appear to trigger since there could not be said to have been administrator's proposals which had been 'approved (with or without modification) at an initial creditors' meeting' for the purposes of para 54(1)(a). This is unlikely to be problematic where the original proposals contained a statement for the purposes of either para 52(1)(b) or (c) since in neither case would unsecured creditors have had any legitimate expectation of financial participation in the administration. A difficulty might arise, however, in a para 52(1)(a) case where the original proposals anticipated all creditors being paid in full but where, on account of the revision to the proposals, unsecured creditors are to receive less, even substantially less, than payment in full. It would be odd indeed if in those circumstances the administrator was not under any obligation to seek the approval of unsecured creditors. It is suggested that in the event of a proposed substantial revision to proposals in a para 52(1)(a) case the administrator should either convene a meeting of creditors of his own volition under para 62 or, at the very least, in keeping with the approach apparent in para 52(2), notify creditors of the position and propose summoning a creditors' meeting should at least 10% in value of creditors so request.

Procedure—The provisions in rr 2.35–2.48 which apply to all creditors' meetings will apply to a meeting summoned under para 54, although rr 2.45 and 2.46 provide specifically for such an event. The statement of proposed revisions, compliant with r 2.45(2), must be attached to Form 2.22B which is sent with a notice of the meeting to each creditor under para 54(2). The result of the meeting is notified to all creditors and the court under r 2.46 using Form 2.23B.

Paragraph 54(6)

Scope of provision—The Financial Services Authority is also entitled to notice in an appropriate case by virtue of s 362(3) of the Financial Services and Markets Act 2000.

55 Failure to obtain approval of administrator's proposals

(1) This paragraph applies where an administrator reports to the court that—

    (a)   an initial creditors' meeting has failed to approve the administrator's proposals presented to it, or

    (b)   a creditors' meeting has failed to approve a revision of the administrator's proposals presented to it.

(2) The court may—

    (a)   provide that the appointment of an administrator shall cease to have effect from a specified time;

    (b)   adjourn the hearing conditionally or unconditionally;

    (c)   make an interim order;

(d)   make an order on a petition for winding up suspended by virtue of paragraph 40(1)(b);

(e)   make any other order (including an order making consequential provision) that the court thinks appropriate.

General note—This provision applies where the administrator's report to the court under para 53(2)(a) or para 54(6)(a) confirms those matters in para 55(1)(a) and (b) respectively. No report will be necessary in the event of an adjournment of any creditors' meeting at which no decision is made as to the administrator's proposals or revised proposals.

In *Re BTR (UK) Ltd; Lavin v Swindell* [2012] EWHC 2398 (Ch), [2012] BCC 864, HHJ Behrens (sitting as a judge of the High Court) held that it was implicit from the language of para 55(2) that where para 55(1) applies an application must be made to the court for directions. That application should ordinarily be made by the administrator, but if he does not make the application, it can be made by a creditor.

Action by the court on receipt of a report—Although para 55(2) appears to envisage the court exercising its discretion of its own volition without the need for any application before it, in *Re ML Design Group Ltd* [2006] EWHC 2224, [2006] All ER (D) 75 Richard Sheldon QC, sitting as a deputy High Court judge, held that, where an initial meeting had failed to approve proposals within para 55(1)(a), the administrators should be required to comply with r 2.114(1) and (3) by way of a procedure analogous to that under para 79. Accordingly, a progress report should be attached to an application for termination and creditors given notice of the application. The administrators were also directed to notify creditors that an application for the fixing of remuneration would be made to the court.

Nothing in para 55(2) can be read as precluding an administrator from formulating and presenting revised or further revised proposals to creditors, although it would be prudent to appraise the court of that position on the filing of the administrator's report. In an appropriate, albeit exceptional, case the court retains a discretion, as it did under the former law, to make an order under para 55(2)(e) that proposals which have not been approved by creditors are nevertheless carried into effect: *Re Maxwell Communication Corp plc* [1992] BCLC 465 at 467G–467I (Hoffmann J, as he then was) and *Re Structures & Computers Ltd* [1998] 1 BCLC 292 at 297G–298C (Neuberger J, as he then was): compare *SCL Building Services* [1990] BCLC 98 (Peter Gibson J, as he then was), and *Re Land and Property Trust Co plc (No 2)* [1991] BCLC 849 (Harman J). The key point demonstrated by the first mentioned of these authorities is that even a majority creditor does not have a right of veto on the implementation of an administrator's proposals, although the fact of such opposition will invariably weight as a factor in the exercise of the court's discretion: *Re DKLL Solicitors* [2008] 1 BCLC 112 at [17]–[20] (Andrew Simmonds QC sitting as a deputy High Court judge; partnership administration order made in respect of firm of solicitors notwithstanding opposition of Revenue with £1.7m debt of total £2.4m liabilities).

56 Further creditors' meetings

(1) The administrator of a company shall summon a creditors' meeting if—

(a)   it is requested in the prescribed manner by creditors of the company whose debts amount to at least 10% of the total debts of the company, or

(b)   he is directed by the court to summon a creditors' meeting.

(2) An administrator commits an offence if he fails without reasonable excuse to summon a creditors' meeting as required by this paragraph.

General note—Although an administrator may call a meeting of members or creditors under para 62, he may be required to summon a meeting of creditors either by the requisite level of creditors or at the court's direction. As noted in the commentary to para 51 there is no good reason why in an appropriate case such a meeting should not be summoned prior to the initial creditors' meeting.

Procedure where meeting requisitioned by creditors—The procedure is as set out in IR 1986, r 2.37. The administrator is not, however, required to summon the meeting unless a sum covering the expenses of summoning and holding the meeting, as determined by the administrator, is deposited with him by the creditor or creditors requisitioning the meeting: see r 2.37(3)–(6).

Penalties—See s 430, Sch 10 and the daily default fine in para 106(2)(j).

57 Creditors' committee

(1) A creditors' meeting may establish a creditors' committee.

(2) A creditors' committee shall carry out functions conferred on it by or under this Act.

(3) A creditors' committee may require the administrator—

(a)   to attend on the committee at any reasonable time of which he is given at least seven days' notice, and

(b)   to provide the committee with information about the exercise of his functions.

General note—The formation of a creditors' committee is at the option of any creditors' meeting, but usually the initial creditors' meeting. Although r 2.52(1) provides that in the discharge of its function the creditors' committee 'shall assist the administrator in discharging his functions, and act in relation to him in such manner as may be agreed from time to time', there is no requirement that the committee should concur or acquiesce in the administrator's conduct. On the contrary, the creditors' committee may, and often does, act as a brake or monitor on the administrator on behalf of creditors generally and to that end may call the administrator to account under para 57(3). The administrator should also place an appropriate degree of weight on the views of the creditors' committee, whether expressed informally or by way of a vote, subject to his retaining sole responsibility for the discharge of his functions in the management of the affairs, business and property of the company; whilst bearing in mind that the court will only authorise an administrator to act contrary to a resolution of a creditors' committee in 'very exceptional circumstances': *Re CE King Ltd* [2000] 2 BCLC 297 at 306B–306C (Neuberger J, as he then was).

Paragraph 57(2)

'**... functions conferred on it by or under this Act**'—As well as the function identified in r 2.52(1) the following matters also fall to the creditors' committee. The committee may apply to court under para 91(1)(a) in an administration order case for the replacement of an administrator on a vacancy arising under para 90. In an out-of-court appointment case the committee may also resolve on the time from which an administrator is discharged (previously released under s 20) from liability under para 98(2)(b). The division of unsold assets in specie under r 2.71 is subject to the permission of the creditors' committee, which is also responsible under r 2.106(3) for the fixing of the basis for the administrator's remuneration and is entitled to notice under r 2.108(2) of any application by the administrator to the court for an increase in the amount or rate of his remuneration as fixed. The committee is also subject to a duty under r 12.8(2)(a) to review the adequacy of an administrator's security for the proper performance of his functions.

Procedure—The procedure for the formation and conduct of a creditors' committee appears in rr 2.50–2.65. For the purposes of r 2.50(1) the creditors' committee should comprise those five creditors attracting the largest number of votes in value where there are more than five candidates for appointment: *Re Polly Peck International plc* [1991] BCC 503 at 508D–508G (Morritt J, as he then was). Although r 2.61 allows for resolutions of the creditors' committee to be passed by 'post', that term could and, it is submitted, should be read subject to the broad definition of 'correspondence' in para 111(1) so as to allow resolutions to be passed by fax or e-mail.

(a)   has not been presented against the debtor at any time before the determination date;

(b)   has been so presented, but proceedings on the petition have been finally disposed of before that date; or

(c)   has been so presented and proceedings in relation to the petition remain before the court at that date, but the person who presented the petition has consented to the making of an application for a debt relief order.

5

A debt relief order has not been made in relation to the debtor in the period of six years ending with the determination date.

6 Limit on debtor's overall indebtedness

(1) The total amount of the debtor's debts on the determination date, other than unliquidated debts and excluded debts, does not exceed the prescribed amount.

(2) For this purpose an unliquidated debt is a debt that is not for a liquidated sum payable to a creditor either immediately or at some future certain time.

7 Limit on debtor's monthly surplus income

(1) The debtor's monthly surplus income (if any) on the determination date does not exceed the prescribed amount.

(2) For this purpose 'monthly surplus income' is the amount by which a person's monthly income exceeds the amount necessary for the reasonable domestic needs of himself and his family.

(3) The rules may—

(a)   make provision as to how the debtor's monthly surplus income is to be determined;

(b)   provide that particular descriptions of income are to be excluded for the purposes of this paragraph.

8 Limit on value of debtor's property

(1) The total value of the debtor's property on the determination date does not exceed the prescribed amount.

(2) The rules may—

(a)   make provision as to how the value of a person's property is to be determined;

(b)   provide that particular descriptions of property are to be excluded for the purposes of this paragraph.

Amendments—Inserted by Tribunals, Courts and Enforcement Act 2007, s 108(1), Sch 18.

PART 2
OTHER CONDITIONS

9

(1) The debtor has not entered into a transaction with any person at an undervalue during the period between—

    (a)   the start of the period of two years ending with the application date; and

    (b)   the determination date.

(2) For this purpose a debtor enters into a transaction with a person at an undervalue if—

    (a)   he makes a gift to that person or he otherwise enters into a transaction with that person on terms that provide for him to receive no consideration;

    (b)   he enters into a transaction with that person in consideration of marriage or the formation of a civil partnership; or

    (c)   he enters into a transaction with that person for a consideration the value of which, in money or money's worth, is significantly less than the value, in money or money's worth, of the consideration provided by the individual.

10

(1) The debtor has not given a preference to any person during the period between—

    (a)   the start of the period of two years ending with the application date; and

    (b)   the determination date.

(2) For this purpose a debtor gives a preference to a person if—

    (a)   that person is one of the debtor's creditors to whom a qualifying debt is owed or is a surety or guarantor for any such debt, and

    (b)   the debtor does anything or suffers anything to be done which (in either case) has the effect of putting that person into a position which, in the event that a debt relief order is made in relation to the debtor, will be better than the position he would have been in if that thing had not been done.]

Amendments—Inserted by Tribunals, Courts and Enforcement Act 2007, s 108(1), Sch 18.

SCHEDULE 4ZB
DEBT RELIEF RESTRICTIONS ORDERS AND UNDERTAKINGS

Amendments—Inserted by Tribunals, Courts and Enforcement Act 2007, s 108(1), Sch 18.

1 Debt relief restrictions order

(1) A debt relief restrictions order may be made by the court in relation to a person in respect of whom a debt relief order has been made.

58 Correspondence instead of creditors' meeting

(1) Anything which is required or permitted by or under this Schedule to be done at a creditors' meeting may be done by correspondence between the administrator and creditors—

    (a)   in accordance with the rules, and
    (b)   subject to any prescribed condition.

(2) A reference in this Schedule to anything done at a creditors' meeting includes a reference to anything done in the course of correspondence in reliance on sub-paragraph (1).

(3) A requirement to hold a creditors' meeting is satisfied by conducting correspondence in accordance with this paragraph.

General note—This provision is new and should be read in conjunction with IR 1986, r 2.48. Subject to conducting correspondence in accordance with para 58(1) and (2) the requirement to convene any creditors' meeting within the meaning of para 50 is discharged with an inevitable saving in time and cost. Although the procedure is available at the option of the administrator, at least 10% in value of the creditors of the company may require the administrator to summon a meeting under r 2.48(7) in accordance with r 2.37. Furthermore, if an administrator's proposals or revised proposals are rejected by creditors by conducting correspondence under para 58 in place of holding a creditors' meeting, the administrator retains a discretion under r 2.48(8) to call a meeting to consider the proposals or revised proposals.

    The para 58 procedure will be inappropriate, and will almost certainly lead to a waste of time and money, if what is proposed is plainly controversial or likely to be challenged by one or more creditors holding at least 10% in value of the company's debt.

Procedure—The relevant procedure appears in r 2.48. An amended version of Form 2.25B appeared in the Schedule to the Insolvency (Amendment) Rules 2004 (SI 2004/584). The procedure is invalid under para 58 if the correct form is not used. If the administrator does not receive at least one valid Form 2.25B by the closing date for votes fixed by him, then he is obliged to call a meeting of creditors under r 2.48(6).

FUNCTIONS OF ADMINISTRATOR

59 General powers

(1) The administrator of a company may do anything necessary or expedient for the management of the affairs, business and property of the company.

(2) A provision of this Schedule which expressly permits the administrator to do a specified thing is without prejudice to the generality of sub-paragraph (1).

(3) A person who deals with the administrator of a company in good faith and for value need not inquire whether the administrator is acting within his powers.

General note—Paragraph 59(1) and (2), which correspond with the former s 14(1)(a) and (b), should be read in the context of the administrator's powers, which are considered in the commentary to para 60 below. The general power to do anything within the scope of para 59(1) is deemed by para 111(3) to include inaction. The implication from the use of the word 'or' in para 59(1) is that action by an administrator need be 'necessary', but not necessarily 'expedient', and vice versa. The use of the word 'or' might also have been more appropriate in place of the word 'and' in para 59(1), since the reference to 'the management of the affairs, business and property' must be a reference to any or all of those matters.

Disclaimer—An administrator has no statutory powers to disclaim onerous or leasehold property analogous to those available to a liquidator under ss 178 and 179. Given the specific terms in which the powers identified in the commentary to para 60 are cast, there is no basis for reading such a power of disclaimer into Sch B1.

Paragraph 59(3)

Third parties dealing with the administrator—Paragraph 59(3) corresponds with the former s 14(6) which referred to 'a person dealing with the administrator' who was 'not concerned to inquire' whether the administrator was acting within his powers. Nothing turns on the minor linguistic changes in the new provision which is itself almost certainly superfluous in any case, given the protection afforded to such a third party by s 39 of the Companies Act 2006 and the general law of agency. A third party need not inquire whether the administrator is acting within his powers and will also be unaffected by any constructive knowledge of a breach of any fiduciary duty on the part of an administrator.

60

The administrator of a company has the powers specified in Schedule 1 to this Act.

General note—The powers in Sch 1 are extremely broad and comprise 22 specific powers and a twenty-third general power enabling the office-holder 'to do all other things incidental to the exercise of the foregoing powers.' As identified in the note to para 69, however, the powers of an administrator as agent of the company cannot extend beyond those of the company as principal. Conversely, the scope of Sch 1 means that an administrator may exercise any power which would have been available to the directors prior to the appointment of the administrator: *Denny v Yeldon* [1995] 1 BCLC 560 at 564A–564F (Jacob J, as he then was, permitting an administrator to procure the amendment of a company's pension scheme trust deed).

The exercise of any power under Sch 1 must be within the scope of para 59(1) as 'anything necessary or expedient for the management of the affairs, business and property of the company', an observation consistent with para 59(2).

An administrator also has powers to remove or appoint a director under para 61, to call meetings of members or creditors under para 62, to apply to the court for directions under paras 63 and 68(2), to make a distribution to a creditor under para 65(1) and to make payments under para 66 other than in accordance with para 65 or para 13 of Sch 1.

61

The administrator of a company—

    (a)   may remove a director of the company, and
    (b)   may appoint a director of the company (whether or not to fill a vacancy).

General note—The power to remove a director under para 61(a) is most likely to be of use where, despite the limitation on the exercise of management power by a company in administration or any officer under para 64, a director purports to exercise such management power or otherwise interferes in the conduct of the administration. The removal of a director in breach of any contract under which he holds office will give rise to a claim in damages against the company, but not the administrator, for loss arising as a foreseeable consequence of the breach, irrespective of the fact that the removal was effected under a statutory power: *Southern Foundries (1926) Ltd v Shirlaw* [1940] AC 701 and *Shindler v Northern Raincoat Co Ltd* [1960] 1 WLR 1038.

The appointment of a director under para 61(b) is unlikely other than where the appointment serves the interests of the administration, as discussed in the notes to para 64 below, or possibly where the appointment is necessary to ensure compliance with the company's articles of association.

62

The administrator of a company may call a meeting of members or creditors of the company.

General note—The administrator's power to call a meeting of members or creditors is unlimited. It is submitted, however, that this power may only be exercised properly if incidental or pursuant to the general power in para 59(1).

For creditors' meetings see para 50 and the notes thereto; for members' meetings see IR 1986, r 2.49.

63

The administrator of a company may apply to the court for directions in connection with his functions.

General note—As an officer of the court – on which see para 5 and the notes thereto – an administrator would have standing to make an application to the court for directions even in the absence of this provision. Although the wording in this provision is less specific than the former s 14(3) which allowed for an application 'in relation to any particular matter arising in connection with the carrying out of [the administrator's] functions', its substance is the same. Paragraph 63 should be read in conjunction with para 68(2) under which the court may give directions in connection with any aspect of the management of the company's affairs, business or property, but, in the case of the latter provision, only in any of the four circumstances identified therein. The scope of the words 'in connection with his functions' is extremely broad and, in practice, will catch an almost endless range of circumstances, depending on the facts of any particular case. Obvious examples include directions as to whether pre-administration payments were susceptible as preferences, as in *Re Lewis's of Leicester* [1995] BCC 514, directions as to the enforceability of a contract, or, arguably, a direction for the removal of a delinquent co-appointee under para 88 and his replacement under para 91.

Any application for directions should not put the court in a difficult or embarrassing position by failing to raise a particular and clear issue or issues. The application should set out the directions sought and, if possible, the alternatives, even though the court may ultimately grant relief other than the relief or the alternatives put forward: *Re Synthetic Technology Ltd* [1990] BCLC 378 at 380F–380H (Harman J). Neither should an administrator employ an application for directions as a means of avoiding what amounts in substance to a matter of commercial judgment by seeking to place the burden of such a decision on the court. As Neuberger J (as he then was) observed in *Re T & D Industries plc* [2000] 333 at 344J, '… a person appointed to act as an administrator may be called upon to make important and urgent decisions. He has a responsible and potentially demanding role. Commercial and administrative decisions are for him and the court is not there to act as a sort of bomb shelter for him.' His Lordship later held that, as a matter of principle, the court will not interfere with a commercial decision on the part of an administrator unless what was proposed was a course based on a wrong application of the law and/or was conspicuously unfair to a particular creditor, although the court would not second guess an issue which an administrator was far better placed to resolve: *Re CE King Ltd (in administration)* [2000] 2 BCLC 297 at 306C–306G: see also *MTI Trading Systems Ltd v Winter* [1998] BCC 581. Inappropriate applications to the court will almost inevitably be met with hostile orders for costs: *Re CE King Ltd* at 303E. Accordingly, the court may, in an appropriate case, decline to give directions on all or part of the matters before it, particularly where the evidence before the court is incomplete and not all parties with an interest in the matter in issue are before the court, as in *Re NS Distribution Ltd* [1990] BCLC 169 at

171E–171F (Harman J, refusal to sanction sale of single asset at good price: 'It is not in my view right for the court to be asked to bless all such steps. If it were, the court would be inundated with applications of this sort').

An administrator appointed under Sch B1 may sell the assets of a company without the need for the approval of the court under para 63 or para 68: *Re Transbus International Ltd (in administration)* [2004] EWHC 932 (Ch), [2004] BCLC 550 (Lawrence Collins J, expressly adopting in relation to Sch B1 administrations the principles identified in *Re T & D Industries* (above)).

Time for the making of an application for directions—An administrator may seek directions at any time during the course of his office or on the hearing of the administration application, at which time directions may be given under para 13(1)(f).

Applications for directions by parties other than the administrator—Although para 63 only envisages an application by an administrator for directions it is suggested that the position under Sch B1 will remain as it did under Part II such that the court retains an inherent power to give directions, albeit not under para 63, to an administrator as an officer of the court on the application of a third party capable of demonstrating a genuine and legitimate interest in the directions sought. Such an application is capable of being made by a creditor, as in *Re Mirror Group (Holdings) Ltd* [1992] BCC 972 at 976G–976H (Sir Donald Nicholls V-C, as he then was) or by a third party, say as to the terms upon which an administrator might continue to make use of the third party's goods for the benefit of the administration, as in *Barclays Mercantile Business Finance Ltd* [1992] 1 WLR 1253 at 1259D–1259G (Millett J, as he then was).

Where the court is prepared to give directions, say in directing that an administrator could dispose of company assets without the leave of the court prior to a meeting of the company's creditors, as in the *T & D Industries* case (above), the court's direction in approving any particular course of action is not to be taken as absolving an administration of any liability if the proposed course turns out to have been negligent in some way: ibid at 346B–346C. Under the new provisions a creditor or member might pursue such a complaint under para 74.

64

(1) A company in administration or an officer of a company in administration may not exercise a management power without the consent of the administrator.

(2) For the purpose of sub-paragraph (1)—

    (a)   'management power' means a power which could be exercised so as to interfere with the exercise of the administrator's powers,

    (b)   it is immaterial whether the power is conferred by an enactment or an instrument, and

    (c)   consent may be general or specific.

General note—The appointment of an administrator does not of itself affect the status of a director as such. The powers of the directors, however, are curtailed on the administrator's appointment. In contrast to the position in receivership, which is discussed in the notes to s 42, para 64(1) prohibits the exercise of a 'management power' without the consent of the administrator. It is submitted that the hypothesis introduced by the use of the words 'could be' in the definition of the term 'management power' in para 64(2)(a), together with the express powers conferred on the administrator under Sch 1 and the provisions in paras 59(1) and (2) and 68(1), effectively precludes the exercise of any power whatsoever by the directors or any of them without the consent of the administrator. An errant director runs the risk of being removed under para 61(a).

The appointment of an administrator has no bearing on the statutory duties of the directors to convene an annual general meeting and to file accounts and an annual return with the Registrar of Companies. This, at least, is the theory. In fact, directors rarely comply with such obligations, in the main, it is thought, because they are oblivious to the continuance of their duty to do so. As a matter of practice, neither does the Registrar of Companies enforce such obligations in any case.

An administrator will not ordinarily consent in either general or specific terms to the exercise of a management power by a company or its officers. In an appropriate case, however, the administrator may consider it appropriate, expedient or even necessary to consent, invariably subject to agreed terms, to the continued management role, in whole or part, of some or all of the directors. This all assumes, of course, the continuing co-operation and willingness to act on the part of any one or more of the directors. Perhaps the most obvious example of a director engaging in management in administration will arise in a trading administration where the nature of the company's business is idiosyncratic, as in the case of a football club, or otherwise highly specialist in nature. The administrator must bear in mind in all cases that what is termed his 'consent' in para 64 will usually amount to a delegation of his responsibilities and that responsibility for the conduct of the administration rests with him alone, given the provisions mentioned in the opening paragraph above. Furthermore, for both the purposes of third party perception and the need for ongoing, pro-active monitoring, the administrator will also have to be mindful that those to whom he chooses to delegate may well have held office during the financial demise leading to the company's administration such that it will usually be prudent for an appropriate member of the administrator's staff, at the very least, to be in situ during the period of the administrator's consent.

Although an administrator might consider the making of an application for directions as to the extent of his delegation of management powers, it is submitted that, in all but the most exceptional of cases, the court is likely to view such a decision as commercial or administrative in nature so as to remain a matter for the administrator alone: see para 63 and the notes thereto.

65 Distribution

(1) The administrator of a company may make a distribution to a creditor of the company.

(2) Section 175 shall apply in relation to a distribution under this paragraph as it applies in relation to a winding up.

(3) A payment may not be made by way of distribution under this paragraph to a creditor of the company who is neither secured nor preferential unless the court gives permission.

General note—Paragraph 65 finds no equivalent in the former Part II provisions. Although there appear to have been a number of unreported cases under the former law in which the court was prepared to sanction the making of a distribution to pre-administration unsecured creditors, in *Re The Designer Room Ltd* [2004] EWHC 720 Rimer J held the general rule to be that in an ordinary case an administrator had no power to make such a distribution since, in the absence of an express provision, such action could not be construed as necessary or incidental to the functions of the administrator, even where the making of a distribution would have been cheaper and more convenient that on a liquidation. Rimer J took account of and accepted that in *Re WBSL Realisations (1992) Ltd* [1995] 2 BCLC 576 Knox J had permitted payments to be made under para 13 of Sch 1 on being satisfied that those payments were necessary to preserve the goodwill of the company's business in the course of the administrators seeking to achieve a survival of the company and its business as a going concern, but only on terms that any distribution was brought into account on any subsequent liquidation so as to achieve parity between all creditors. That decision, however, and that of Pumfrey J in *Rolph v AY Bank Ltd* [2002] BPIR 1231 which followed it, in similar circumstances, were decided on very unusual facts and, as such, were capable of being distinguished from the general rule in *Designer Room*.

The absence of a power to distribute in an ordinary Part II case meant that the only way of effecting a distribution to creditors was to discharge the administration order under s 18 and to place the company into liquidation, thereby incurring the DTI levy applicable in a compulsory liquidation or, alternatively, by engaging the cumbersome requirements associated with placing the company into voluntary liquidation following *Re Mark One*

(Oxford St) plc [1999] 1 WLR 1445. Paragraph 65 overcomes that practical difficulty and radically alters the complexion of administration by allowing distribution to all species of pre-administration creditor, subject to the court's permission in the case of an unsecured creditor: see *Re Lune Metal Products* [2007] 2 BCLC 746 at [6] (Neuberger LJ, as he then was). The new position is not only justifiable on account of savings in time and expense but also because Sch B1 now envisages the possibility of an administration being conducted, in effect, as a form of quasi-liquidation, given the machinery for the proving of debts etc in rr 2.68–2.105 and the specific provision in para 84 for the seamless movement from administration to dissolution without an intervening liquidation.

Paragraph 65(1)

'**... a distribution to a creditor of the company**'—The term 'creditor' can only refer to pre-administration creditors, given r 2.69. A post-administration creditor is only capable of being eligible for the making of a payment – as opposed to a 'distribution' – under para 66. As regards pre-administration creditors r 13.12(5) provides that the term 'creditor' has the widest possible scope by reference to the definitions of the terms 'debt' and 'liability' in r 13.12(1) and (4) and the qualifications thereto. The term 'creditor' will, of course, also extend to preferential and secured creditors as at the date on which the company entered into administration, on which see s 387(3A) on preferential debts. The position of unsecured creditors is considered in the notes to para 66(3) below.

Paragraph 65(2)

The effect of s 175—The effect of para 65(2) is to impose on an administrator a statutory duty, akin to that imposed on a receiver by s 40, to pay preferential creditors, as defined in s 386(1) and Sch 6 and assessed in accordance with s 387(3A), in priority to the holder of any floating charge or unsecured creditors to whom a distribution would otherwise be made.

The holder of a valid fixed charge retains priority over preferential claims. In addition, by virtue of s 175(2)(a) the expenses of an administration rank ahead of preferential claims.

The claim of a floating charge holder caught by para 70, and, therefore, unsecured claims, is also subject to an administrator's claim for remuneration and expenses under para 99(3) and debts or liabilities arising out of any contract entered into by an administrator under para 99(4).

Paragraph 99(3)(b) affords the administrator's claims priority over the claims of the floating charge holder and which finds no equivalent in liquidation. Whilst s 175(2)(b) (applicable in liquidation) is framed in terms of property comprised in or subject to a floating charge, para 99(3)(b) creates a specific statutory charge which is distinct from and ranks in priority to any floating charge under para 70. It is the operation of that statutory charge which effectively removes the assets subject to it from the scope of any floating charge.

In *Re Collins & Aikman Europe SA* [2007] 1 BCLC 182 at [27] Lindsay J identified that the words 'under this paragraph' in para 65(2) refer to a distribution under either para 65(2) or para 65(3) and appear to require that any such distribution 'shall be subject to those creditors characterised under *English* law as preferential creditors being paid (or at least with such provision for them that their payment could be expected would not be jeopardized, either in amount of at all, by the proposed distribution before the distribution under para 65 is made.' It is plain, however, from para [29] of the judgment that Lindsay J was not reaching any final determination on the point, particularly given his Lordship's reference to the judgment of HHJ Norris QC (sitting, as he then was, as a judge of the High Court) in *Re MG Rover Belux SA/NV* [2006] EWHC 3618 (Ch) where, as appears from the report of that case, the judge was prepared to give permission for a distribution under para 65(3) on being satisfied that preferential creditors under local law (ie Belgian law) were provided for without enquiry into the position of English preferential creditors. There is much, it is submitted, to be said for Lindsay J's preliminary view since the words 'under this paragraph' (and not 'under this sub-paragraph') in para 65(2) must be a reference to para 65 generally, and not to any sub-paragraph thereof, which cannot avoid the reference to s 175 which itself (in s 175(1)) makes specific reference to 'preferential debts' within the meaning of s 386.

The notes to ss 40, 107 and 175 include commentary on the consequences of a breach of the statutory duty to preferential creditors now imposed on an administrator under para 65.

The court's permission under para 65(3) for a distribution to a creditor of the company—The legislation gives no guidance as to when permission might be granted by the court under para 65(3). It is suggested, however, at least as a starting point, that only in very exceptional circumstances will the court be prepared to detract from the pari passu principle embodied in r 2.69. Nevertheless, it remains that para 65 contains no express bar on a distribution which involves an inequality of treatment as between the same class of creditors. Neither is there any compelling reason why there should be. Support for this analysis appears in the judgment of HHJ Norris QC, sitting as a judge of the High Court, in *Re HPJ UK Ltd (in administration)* [2007] BCC 284 in which the court was asked to sanction a distribution to unsecured creditors which involved a payment of £2.25m to HMRC in respect of an undisputed claim of £1.2m in respect of PAYE, NIC, corporation tax and VAT and in full and final settlement of an assessed claim for £7.2m for corporation tax in respect of a US agency together with an interim distribution of between 62p and 81p (subject to the conclusion of the administration) in the pound to the remaining 1.2% of unsecured creditors. In granting permission for the distribution his Lordship observed (at [11]):

> 'In my judgment paragraph 65 is sufficiently flexible to enable administrators to make a distribution in respect of a compromised claim of exactly the type which has been negotiated in the present circumstances. The plain words of the paragraph are sufficiently broad to encompass the proposal in the present case. I do not think it can be said that "a distribution" must of necessity be a rateable payment. There is no policy reason why the court should obstruct a carefully negotiated compromise achieved between parties of equal power, the outcome of which has received the unanimous approval of the creditors.'

In *Re GHE Realisations Ltd* [2006] BCC 139 at [7] and [8] Rimer J identified four specific factors as being material, but not necessarily conclusive, on the issue of whether the court should grant permission for a distribution under para 65. First, does the administrator have sufficient funds to make the distribution proposed? Secondly, the administrator should not propose to exit the administration by moving to creditors' voluntary liquidation under para 83 (in which a distribution to creditors would be possible). Thirdly, do the administrator's proposals, as approved by creditors, include a proposal to make a distribution of the sort proposed? Fourthly, is the proposed distribution consistent with the administrator's functions and duties and any actual or intended proposals to creditors? Having adopted the guidance in *GHE Realisations*, and having observed that, given the width of the discretion in para 65(3), it is doubtful that it is possible to draw up a definitive list of considerations relevant to all cases, in *Re MG Rover Belux SA/NV (in administration)* [2007] BCC 446 at [7] and [8] HHJ Norris QC, sitting as a judge of the High Court, identified the following considerations as relevant to the facts of that case (which, it is suggested, in whole or part, are capable of have some general significance to other cases):

'(a) The matter is to be judged at the time when permission is sought;

(b) the court must at that time be satisfied that the proposed distribution is conducive to the achievement of the then current objectives of the administration;

(c) the court must be satisfied that the distribution is in the interests of the company's creditors as a whole (because para 3(2) of Sch B1 says that the administrator must perform his functions in that manner);

(d) the court must be satisfied that proper provision has been made for secured and preferential creditors (for the requirement to obtain the permission of the court seems to be directed at their protection);

(e) the court must consider what are the realistic alternatives to the proposed distribution sought by the administrators, consider the merits and demerits of adopting a course other than that proposed by the administrators and assess whether the proposed distribution adversely affects the entitlement of others (when compared with their entitlement if one of the other realistic alternatives were to be adopted);

(f) the court must take into account the basis on which the administration has been conducted so far as the creditors are concerned (under the original proposals, any modification to those original proposals, or any indications given in any reports to creditors), and in particular whether the creditors have approved (or not objected to) any proposal concerning the relevant distribution;

(g) the court must consider the nature and terms of the distribution; and

(h) the court must consider the impact of the distribution upon any proposed exit route from the administration.'

To all of these considerations, it is suggested, the following two considerations might be added. First, the court should exercise its discretion on the basis of evidence as to the likely level of distribution or distributions to be made, and the source thereof, mindful that any recipient might seek to rely on the court's order as a defence to a claim for overpayment. Secondly, any permission should be specific, so far as practicable, as to the level of any distribution, as opposed to a general, non-specific form of permission.

Unsecured claims will not be relevant in a para 3(1)(c) case. The most likely scenario in which para 65(3) will be relevant is in avoiding the time and expense of a liquidation where the only practical purpose of the liquidation would be the distribution of assets by way of dividend to unsecured creditors. Where there are no assets remaining for distribution to creditors in the administration the duty in para 84(1) (moving from administration to dissolution) will be engaged, subject to disapplication under para 84(2). If assets do remain for distribution to unsecured creditors then para 83 becomes available.

Procedure—Rules 2.68–2.105 provide a self-contained mechanism for the making of distributions in administration.

66

The administrator of a company may make a payment otherwise than in accordance with paragraph 65 or paragraph 13 of Schedule 1 if he thinks it likely to assist achievement of the purpose of administration.

General note—Paragraph 13 of Sch 1 confers a power on an administrator 'to make any payment which is necessary or incidental to the performance of his functions', a phrase broad enough to extend to either pre- or post-administration liabilities or a payment to a party who is not a creditor but who requires payment as a pre-condition of providing a supply of goods or services. Paragraph 66 finds no counterpart in the former Part II and amounts to a power to make a payment which is not within para 13 of Sch 1, or para 65, but which the administrator 'thinks is likely to assist achievement of the purpose of administration'. (The word 'thinks' is discussed in the notes to para 3(3) and, it is submitted, envisages a subjective view subject to objective reasonableness). The quandary as to how a payment might fall outside para 13 of Sch 1 but still be likely to assist achievement of the purpose of administration may be one with no satisfactory solution. Neither do the DTI's Explanatory Notes cast any light on the matter. All that may be gleaned from para 66 is that Parliament intended to confer the widest possible power on an administrator in making payments so as to assist in the achievement of the purpose of administration. Certainly para 66 contains none of the limits relating to the payment of secured or preferential creditors as appear in para 65(2) and (3): *Re Collins v Aikman Europe SA* [2007] 1 BCLC 182 at [30] (Lindsay J). Whether exercised under para 66 or para 13 of Sch 1 an administrator would, therefore, be entitled to discharge pre-administration liabilities, say to a key employee or an essential supplier where there is a real risk of discontinued service or supply on non-payment, or a party with whom a liability has been incurred in the course of the administration, whether or not entitled to such payments under English law. Any such payment would remain possible, certainly under para 66, even if it contravened the strict ranking of claims in administration, provided the administrator 'thinks' that the payment is likely to assist achievement of the broader purpose of administration: *Re MG Rover Espana* [2005] BPIR 1162 at [13] (HHJ Norris QC sitting as a High Court judge).

An administrator should always consider making an application to court for directions under para 63 so as to sanction any payment. The judgment of Peter Smith J in *Re TXU UK Ltd* [2003] 2 BCLC 341 at [18]–[19] contains a useful discussion of the proper approach to payments made under para 13 of Sch 1, where such payments can be said to be for the overall benefit of the administration, and suggests that 'administrators would be unwise to make such a decision (as to payment) without applying to the court because they may face retrospective challenge.' Those guidelines, it is submitted, will apply equally to para 66. The court may also direct that a payment ranks as an expense of the administration: see *Re Atlantic Computer Systems plc* [1992] Ch 505 at 528 (Nicholls LJ); see also r 2.67(1).

67 General duties

The administrator of a company shall on his appointment take custody or control of all the property to which he thinks the company is entitled.

General note—This provision imposes an unqualified obligation on an administrator which resembles that found previously in s 17(1). However, the reference in para 67 is now to property 'to which [the administrator] thinks the company is entitled', and not property 'to which the company is or appears to be entitled', as previously.

The term 'thinks' is new (and is discussed in the notes to para 3(3)) with the consequence that the present provision relies on the administrator's subjective view with the proviso that that view must be objectively reasonable.

68

(1) Subject to sub-paragraph (2), the administrator of a company shall manage its affairs, business and property in accordance with—

(a) any proposals approved under paragraph 53,

(b) any revision of those proposals which is made by him and which he does not consider substantial, and

(c) any revision of those proposals approved under paragraph 54.

(2) If the court gives directions to the administrator of a company in connection with any aspect of his management of the company's affairs, business or property, the administrator shall comply with the directions.

(3) The court may give directions under sub-paragraph (2) only if—

(a) no proposals have been approved under paragraph 53,

(b) the directions are consistent with any proposals or revision approved under paragraph 53 or 54,

(c) the court thinks the directions are required in order to reflect a change in circumstances since the approval of proposals or a revision under paragraph 53 or 54, or

(d) the court thinks the directions are desirable because of a misunderstanding about proposals or a revision approved under paragraph 53 or 54.

General note—The powers of an administrator under Sch 1 and as identified in the note to para 60 arise automatically on his appointment. Under the former provisions – on which see *Re Charnley Davies Ltd* [1990] BCC 605 (Vinelott J); *NS Distribution Ltd* [1990] BCLC 169 (Harman J); *Re Consumer & Industrial Press Ltd (No 2)* (1988) 4 BCC 72 (Peter Gibson J, as he then was); *Re Montin Ltd* [1999] 1 BCLC 663; *Re Osmosis Group Ltd* [1999] 2 BCLC 329; *Re PD Fuels Ltd* [1999] BCC 450; and *Re Harris Bus Co Ltd* [2000] BCC 1, 151 (Rattee J) – there was a divergence of opinion as to whether an administrator could not exercise his statutory powers prior to the approval of his proposals under s 23 without a direction from the court under s 17(2)(a). In *Re T & D Industries plc* [2000] BCC 956 Neuberger J, as he then was, engaged in an extensive review of the authorities and held that the exercise of powers under s 14 was not subject to a direction under s 17(2)(a). As such, the administrator was entitled to exercise his statutory powers to sell the company's assets prior to the approval of his proposals by creditors. Neuberger J's conclusion was subject to a number of provisos. First, an administrator should never act for the purpose of avoiding consideration of his proposals. Secondly, if circumstances allow, the administrator should formulate his proposals and either call the creditors' meeting as soon as reasonably practicable or seek a direction from the court for the summoning of a meeting on short notice. Thirdly, in very urgent cases, where such steps were not possible, the administrator should at least seek to consult with the major creditors of the company prior to completing any sale.

Paragraph 68, it is submitted, does not alter the position from that identified above. As such, an administrator is at liberty to exercise all of his statutory powers immediately following his appointment and in the absence of the approval of his proposals under paras 53 or 54. Indeed, consistent with that view, IR 1986, r 2.33(6) specifically envisages an application by an administrator for the cessation of the administration prior to his having sent a statement of his proposals to creditors in accordance with para 49. Furthermore, there is nothing in the wording in para 68 to suggest that the exercise of any statutory power prior to the approval of the administrator's proposals is conditional upon a direction from the court under para 68(2). The administrator remains, however, under the obligation in para 49(5)(a) to send out his statement of proposals 'as soon as is reasonably practicable after the company enters administration.' The guidance provided by Neuberger J in the *T & D* case as to regard being had to an application to court, the convening of a creditors' meeting on short notice or at least liaison with major creditors, will also remain relevant. As discussed in the notes to para 63, the court will also have little enthusiasm for what amounts to a commercial decision which falls to the administrator alone or a hearing which is of little practical use in the absence of third parties who might reasonably be expected to advance arguments contrary to the administrator's proposed course of action. Conversely, there is an inherent risk in employing administration as a convenient device for the effecting of a so-called 'pre-pack' sale, particularly one entered into with the former owners or directors of the company in administration, other than where the administrator can be confident on reasonable, objective grounds that the sale could be said to be in the best interests of the creditors as a whole. In some cases, however, such a sale is either the only viable way forward or is genuinely the most effective course for maximising realisations for the benefit of creditors. Schedule B1 does nothing to intrude on an administrator's standing to opt for such a course.

Nothing in para 68 imposes a requirement for the approval of the court where an administrator proposes selling the assets of a company prior to the meeting of creditors under para 53 to consider the administrator's proposals: *Re Transbus Ltd (in administration)* [2004] EWHC 932 (Ch), [2004] 2 BCLC 550. The position therefore remains as it was held to be under the former Part II, on which see the commentary to para 63 and, in particular, the responsibility of the administrator for such a decision to sell.

Paragraph 68(3)

The grounds for the provision of directions under para 68(2)—Ground (a) is most likely to arise in a case of urgency, typically where an administrator seeks sanction for a sale of the company's business and assets or seeks a direction for the convening of a creditors' meeting on short notice to that end. Even where no proposals have been approved the court may wish to consider the basis of and the evidence supporting any administration application on which an administration order was made under para 13(1)(a).

The significance of ground (b) is that the court has no jurisdiction to give directions which are inconsistent with any proposals or revised proposals which have been approved by creditors other than in the limited circumstances in grounds (c) and (d). This represents a marked shift from the position under the former law where such jurisdiction, albeit one exercised only in exceptional cases, did exist: see *Re Smallman Construction Ltd* [1989] BCLC 420 (Knox J). Given the terms of para 68(3)(b), it is submitted that no jurisdiction can exist under para 68 by which the court might give directions which are inconsistent with any proposals or revised proposals approved by creditors.

Although the words 'only if' appear in the opening to para 68(3), the wording in para 68(2) is itself positive in nature and does not prescribe that no directions may be given by the court other than in relation to the company's affairs, business or property such that an inherent jurisdiction in the court survives: *Re Collins & Aikman Europe SA* [2007] 1 BCLC 82 at [37] (Lindsay J).

Eligible applicants—Unlike para 63, para 68 makes no reference to the parties eligible to make application for directions under para 68(2). It is suggested that the eligible class of persons would extend beyond the administrator himself so as to catch third parties, and most obviously creditors, with a genuine and legitimate interest in the directions sought: see further the notes to para 63.

Paragraph 68(3)(c) and (d)

'… **the court thinks** …'—See the commentary on this term in the notes to para 3(3).

Time for the making of an application for directions—An administrator may seek directions at any time during the course of his office, even if simultaneous with or on the hearing of the administration application under para 13(1)(f).

69 Administrator as agent of company

In exercising his functions under this Schedule the administrator of a company acts as its agent.

General note—This provision repeats the substance of the former s 14(5).

The scope of the administrator's power as agent—The status of an administrator as agent means that, irrespective of the considerable breadth of the powers in Sch 1, an administrator can have no greater power than the company itself as principal under the scope of the company's objects clause provisions in its memorandum of association: *Re Home Treat Ltd* [1991] BCLC 705 at 706I–707B (Harman J). Should such an issue arise, s 39 of the Companies Act 2006 may be of assistance to a bona fide third party. Paragraph 59(3) also provides that a person who deals with an administrator in good faith and for value need not enquire whether the administrator is acting within his powers.

Contracts entered into by the administrator as agent—Other than in the unlikely event of express agreement to the contrary, any contract entered into by the administrator as agent will be binding on the company, but not on the administrator personally: *Re Atlantic Computer Systems plc* [1992] Ch 505 at 526D–526E (Nicholls LJ).

Paragraph 99(4) creates a statutory charge in respect of a debt or liability arising out of a contract entered into by an administrator.

Contracts adopted by an administrator—The term 'adopted' is discussed in the commentary to s 44, which will apply equally here. The statutory charge under para 99(4) extends, by virtue of para 99(5), to liability under a contract of employment adopted by an administrator.

Tax liability—With effect from 15 September 2003 the appointment of an administrator closes an old accounting period and starts a new accounting period by virtue of s 12(7ZA) of the Income and Corporation Taxes Act 1988 as amended by para 1 of Part V, Sch 41 of the Finance Act 2003. As the proper officer for the company for tax purposes the administrator is required to pay tax on account as required and to give notification and make returns to the Inland Revenue in respect of taxable income or capital gains. The status of the administrator as agent of the company, however, means that the administrator cannot be assessed for corporation tax personally, which post-administration liability remains the liability of the company. Certainly this analysis accords with the Inland Revenue's practice as notified previously in the ICAEW Technical Release 799 of June 1990. Rule 2.67(1)(j) makes express provision for corporation tax on chargeable gains accruing on the realisation of any asset of the company as an expense of the administration.

Neither does an administrator have any liability for pre-administration corporation tax. If an administrator refuses to discharge such liability as an expense of the administration, then the Inland Revenue may have no alternative but to make application to the court under para 43(6)(b) for permission to levy distress. Alternatively, it might be possible to obtain a direction from the court under para 68(2) that the liability be discharged as an expense of the administration, on which jurisdiction see *Re Atlantic Computer Systems plc* [1992] Ch 505 at 528C–528G (Nicholls LJ).

Tort liability—In *John Smith & Co (Edinburgh) Ltd v Hill* [2010] EWHC 1016 (Ch), [2010] 2 BCLC 556, Briggs J dismissed an administrator's application for summary judgment in a claim against him by a reversioner on the basis that on the basis that the administrator's decision to allow scaffolding to remain around a building leased by the company constituted a breach of the covenant of quiet enjoyment and was interfering with its attempts to assign the sublease.

70 Charged property: floating charge

(1) The administrator of a company may dispose of or take action relating to property which is subject to a floating charge as if it were not subject to the charge.

(2) Where property is disposed of in reliance on sub-paragraph (1) the holder of the floating charge shall have the same priority in respect of acquired property as he had in respect of the property disposed of.

(3) In sub-paragraph (2) 'acquired property' means property of the company which directly or indirectly represents the property disposed of.

General note—This provision relates only to property which is subject to a floating charge, as defined in para 111(1), and, by para 70(1), allows the administrator to deal with such property irrespective of the security rights of the holder of the charge, which will almost certainly have crystallised. Paragraph 70(1) will not, however, permit such dealing where the property in question is subject to a valid fixed charge, in which case the administrator may consider an application to court under para 71(1).

The effect of para 70(2)—Any floating charge property which is disposed of by an administrator other than with the express consent of the floating charge-holder must, it is submitted, be disposed of in reliance on para 70(1). In those circumstances the security rights of the floating charge holder are deemed to attach to what is termed the 'acquired property' (see below). The security rights of the charge holder in respect of the acquired property will be the same as those which attached to the property disposed of by the administrator under para 70(1). Those rights will, however, remain subject to the statutory charge created under para 99(3) in relation to a former administrator's remuneration and expenses, and any debt or liability falling within para 99(4).

It should also be noted that the holder of a floating charge is in a weaker position than the holder of non-floating security, not only because of the autonomy granted in favour of the administrator by para 70(1) but also because para 70 contains nothing equivalent to para 71(3) which, in effect, provides the holder of non-floating security with a statutory right to the value of any property disposed of by an administrator as would be realised on a hypothetical sale of the property at market value.

'acquired property'—The most obvious example of 'acquired property' directly representing floating charge property will be the proceeds of sale or other consideration representing the price of that property. Property will indirectly represent the property disposed of if the proceeds of sale, or other consideration provided on the disposal of the floating charge property, is then converted into some other property to which the floating charge holder's security rights will apply under para 70(2).

Market contracts etc—This provision does not apply to market contracts and the like by virtue of para 47 of Sch 17 to the Enterprise Act 2002.

71 Charged property: non-floating charge

(1) The court may by order enable the administrator of a company to dispose of property which is subject to a security (other than a floating charge) as if it were not subject to the security.

(2) An order under sub-paragraph (1) may be made only—

    (a)   on the application of the administrator, and

(b) where the court thinks that disposal of the property would be likely to promote the purpose of administration in respect of the company.

(3) An order under this paragraph is subject to the condition that there be applied towards discharging the sums secured by the security—

(a) the net proceeds of disposal of the property, and

(b) any additional money required to be added to the net proceeds so as to produce the amount determined by the court as the net amount which would be realised on a sale of the property at market value.

(4) If an order under this paragraph relates to more than one security, application of money under sub-paragraph (3) shall be in the order of the priorities of the securities.

(5) An administrator who makes a successful application for an order under this paragraph shall send a copy of the order to the registrar of companies before the end of the period of 14 days starting with the date of the order.

(6) An administrator commits an offence if he fails to comply with sub-paragraph (5) without reasonable excuse.

General note—The substance of this provision is mutually exclusive with para 70 and is similar to the provisions in the former s 15 and s 43. Reference should be made to the commentary on the latter provision, which will apply here, in addition to the following.

In *Re Capitol Films Ltd, Rubin v Cobalt Pictures Limited* [2010] EWHC 3223 (Ch), [2011] BPIR 334, Richard Snowden QC held that conduct of the administrators of a film company in administration had been unreasonable to such an extent that it was appropriate to make an order for them to pay the costs of their application under the para 71 personally and on the indemnity basis.

Paragraph 71(1)

'... **property which is subject to a security (other than a floating charge)** ...'— The term 'security' is not defined in Sch B1, but is defined in s 248(b)(i), albeit for the purpose of the First Group of Parts in ss 1–251, as meaning 'any mortgage, charge, lien or other security'. The distinction between the enforcement of security under para 43(2) and the reference to the exercise by a landlord of a right of forfeiture by peaceable re-entry in para 43(4) suggests, in keeping with the decision of Lightman J in *Razzaq v Pala* [1998] BCC 66, that the latter form of right does not constitute a security. Furthermore, it is apparent from r 2.66(1) that the reference to security is to be distinguished from goods in the possession of a company under a hire-purchase agreement. The term 'hire-purchase agreement' is defined in para 111(1) as including a conditional sale agreement, a chattel leasing agreement and a retention of title agreement. Hire purchase property is addressed specifically by para 72. For present purposes the term 'security' must, therefore, refer not only, and most obviously, to a valid fixed charge but also, it is submitted, to a lien and also any other security rights precluding dealings in the underlying property by an administrator other than rights arising under a hire-purchase agreement.

Paragraph 71(2)(b)

'... **where the court thinks** ...'—See the commentary in the notes to para 36.

'... **would be likely** ...'—This term, it is submitted, must be taken as meaning 'more likely than not'.

Procedure—See r 2.66.

Paragraph 71(3)(b)

'Market value'—This term is defined in para 111(1) as 'the amount which would be realised on a sale of property in the open market by a willing vendor'. It is submitted, however, that, in context, that definition can only mean the amount which would be raised in the open market by a willing vendor *administrator* in the particular circumstances of the case since a contrary, literal reading would potentially entitle the security holder under para 71 to a windfall since the amount to which the security holder would be entitled on a true, administration-free market could well exceed, perhaps significantly, the market price obtainable by an administrator.

Whilst an application should be supported by appropriate valuation evidence the court may adjourn an application to allow for an inquiry where there is a dispute or difficulty in fixing valuation: *Re ARV Aviation Ltd* (1988) BCC 708 (Knox J, a decision on the similarly worded s 15). Where the court is presented with two conflicting valuations it is inappropriate for the court to determine valuation by splitting the difference between the two: *Stanley J Holmes & Sons Ltd v Davenham Trust plc* [2006] EWCA Civ 1568, [2007] BCC 485 (Tuckey, Arden, Lloyd LJJ).

Market contracts etc—This provision does not apply to market contracts and the like by virtue of para 47 of Sch 17 to the Enterprise Act 2002.

Penalties—See s 430, Sch 10 and the daily default find in para 106(2)(j).

72 Hire-purchase property

(1) The court may by order enable the administrator of a company to dispose of goods which are in the possession of the company under a hire-purchase agreement as if all the rights of the owner under the agreement were vested in the company.

(2) An order under sub-paragraph (1) may be made only—

    (a)   on the application of the administrator, and

    (b)   where the court thinks that disposal of the goods would be likely to promote the purpose of administration in respect of the company.

(3) An order under this paragraph is subject to the condition that there be applied towards discharging the sums payable under the hire-purchase agreement—

    (a)   the net proceeds of disposal of the goods, and

    (b)   any additional money required to be added to the net proceeds so as to produce the amount determined by the court as the net amount which would be realised on a sale of the goods at market value.

(4) An administrator who makes a successful application for an order under this paragraph shall send a copy of the order to the registrar of companies before the end of the period of 14 days starting with the date of the order.

(5) An administrator commits an offence if he fails without reasonable excuse to comply with sub-paragraph (4).

General note—See the notes to para 71 above.

73 Protection for secured or preferential creditor

(1) An administrator's statement of proposals under paragraph 49 may not include any action which—

(a) affects the right of a secured creditor of the company to enforce his security,

(b) would result in a preferential debt of the company being paid otherwise than in priority to its non-preferential debts, or

(c) would result in one preferential creditor of the company being paid a smaller proportion of his debt than another.

(2) Sub-paragraph (1) does not apply to—

(a) action to which the relevant creditor consents,

(b) a proposal for a voluntary arrangement under Part I of this Act (although this sub-paragraph is without prejudice to section 4(3)),

(c) a proposal for a compromise or arrangement to be sanctioned under Part 26 of the Companies Act 2006 (arrangements and reconstructions) or

(d) a proposal for a cross-border merger within the meaning or regulation 2 of the Companies (Cross-Border Mergers) Regulations 2007

(3) The reference to a statement of proposals in sub-paragraph (1) includes a reference to a statement as revised or modified.

Amendments—SI 2007/2974; SI 2008/948.

General note—These provisions should be read in the context of para 49, on which see the commentary thereto. Further commentary also appears in the notes to s 4(3) and (4), which apply equally here.

For the purposes of paras 73(1)(a) and 73(2)(a) the term 'secured creditor' is not defined in Sch B1, but is defined in s 248(a), but only for the purposes of ss 1–251, as a creditor who holds in respect of his debt a security over property of the company. A landlord does not constitute a secured creditor by virtue of a right of forfeiture by peaceable re-entry, on which see the distinction drawn between para 43(2) and (4) and the decision of Lightman J in *Razzaq v Pala* [1998] BCC 66.

74 Challenge to administrator's conduct of company

(1) A creditor or member of a company in administration may apply to the court claiming that—

(a) the administrator is acting or has acted so as unfairly to harm the interests of the applicant (whether alone or in common with some or all other members or creditors), or

(b) the administrator proposes to act in a way which would unfairly harm the interests of the applicant (whether alone or in common with some or all other members or creditors).

(2) A creditor or member of a company in administration may apply to the court claiming that the administrator is not performing his functions as quickly or as efficiently as is reasonably practicable.

(3) The court may—

(a)   grant relief;
(b)   dismiss the application;
(c)   adjourn the hearing conditionally or unconditionally;
(d)   make an interim order;
(e)   make any other order it thinks appropriate.

(4) In particular, an order under this paragraph may—

(a)   regulate the administrator's exercise of his functions;
(b)   require the administrator to do or not do a specified thing;
(c)   require a creditors' meeting to be held for a specified purpose;
(d)   provide for the appointment of an administrator to cease to have effect;
(e)   make consequential provision.

(5) An order may be made on a claim under sub-paragraph (1) whether or not the action complained of—

(a)   is within the administrator's powers under this Schedule;
(b)   was taken in reliance on an order under paragraph 71 or 72.

(6) An order may not be made under this paragraph if it would impede or prevent the implementation of—

(a)   a voluntary arrangement approved under Part I,
(b)   a compromise or arrangement sanctioned under Part 26 of the Companies Act 2006 (arrangements and reconstructions),
(ba)   a cross border merger within the meaning of regulation 2 of the Companies (Cross-Border Mergers) Regulations 2007, or
(c)   proposals or a revision approved under paragraph 53 or 54 more than 28 days before the day on which the application for the order under this paragraph is made.

Amendments—SI 2007/2974; SI 2008/948.

General note—This provision is new, but bears some resemblance to the former s 27 which did not play a significant part in advancing the interests of creditors or members in administration, at least by reference to the reported authorities. The new provision might initially be read as being extremely broad in scope. Certainly it has been suggested that para 74(1) and (2) permits the court to make an order providing for the appointment of an administrator to cease to have effect (on which see para 88): *SISU Capital Fund Ltd v Tucker* [2006] BPIR 154 at [88] (Warren J). Paragraph 74 remains, however, subject to a number of limitations identified below.

Eligible applicants—Paragraph 74 is only available to 'a creditor or member of a company in administration ...'. Such application may be brought after the administration has come to an end: Re Coniston Hotel (Kent) LLP [2013] EWHC 93 (Ch).
   Irrespective of para 74(1), the Financial Services Authority has standing to make an application by virtue of s 362(4) of the Financial Services and Markets Act 2000, as does a Member State liquidator, whose standing is equivalent to that of a creditor, by virtue of Art 32(3) of the EC Regulation on Insolvency Proceedings.

Paragraph 74(1)

'... **unfairly harm the interests of the applicant** ...'—Paragraph 74(1) envisages an application in relation to past, present or proposed conduct. It is, however, necessary, in the case of an application by any person under that provision, that the applicant is able to establish that the conduct complained of has, is or will cause 'harm' to the interests of that applicant, whether alone or with others. It must follow, therefore, in accordance with the well established principles on just and equitable winding-up petitions (now under s 122(1)(g), on which see the notes thereto) and unfair prejudice petitions (under s 994 of the Companies Act 2006), that an applicant must initially discharge the burden of establishing a tangible interest – that is, in financial terms – in the relief sought in the application. This is far more than an exercise in semantics and would require either a member or any class of creditor to establish that the outcome of his application, if successful, would mark either a participation or an improved participation in the administration, or any ensuing liquidation, on his part. For the same reason, a secured creditor who is fully secured for his indebtedness will not have standing to proceed with a claim other than where the conduct complained of can be shown as being capable of reducing the status of that creditor to less than fully secured.

In *Cheshire West and Chester BC, Petitioners* [2010] CSOH 115, [2011] BCC 174, the Court of Session (Outer House) held that administrators had caused unfair harm to the council as landlord to the company by the non-payment of rent after the appointment of the administrators.

'... **harm** ...'—The term 'harm' is discussed in the notes to para 3(4)(b) and, by reference to the Parliamentary debates on the terms of the Enterprise Act 2002 mentioned therein, must be understood as meaning 'prejudice'. It is clear, however, from para 74(1) that mere harm is insufficient in that the applicant must establish unfair harm (or prejudice) in the sense that the conduct or proposed conduct of the administrator is not only harmful but is unfairly harmful to the applicant, whether alone or in common with some or, apparently, all other members or creditors. It is submitted that it is doubtful that the conduct of an administrator can be unfairly harmful to the entirety of a company's members or creditors if unfairness is to be judged by the standard of comparing the applicant to the position of some or all of the other members or creditors of the company. That analysis certainly finds support in the cases under s 459: see *Re Saul D Harrison & Sons plc* [1995] 1 BCLC 14 at 31C (Neill LJ); *Nicholas v Soundcraft Electronics Ltd* [1993] BCLC 360 at 366H and 372I (Ralph Gibson LJ).

'... **unfairly** ...'—In order to succeed in such application, it will be necessary for the applicant to demonstrate both that the action complained of is or will be causative of harm to its interests and that that harm is unfair; harm alone is not enough: *Re Lehman Brothers International (Europe) (in admin); Four Private Investment Funds v Lomas* [2008] EWHC 2869 (Ch), [2009] BCC 632).

Action taken by administrators in the interests of the creditors as a whole is not open to challenge simply because it affects an individual creditor differently: *Re Zegna III Holdings Inc* [2009] EWHC 2994 (Ch), [2010] BPIR 277.

Paragraph 74(2)

Scope of provision—Paragraph 74(2) should be read in conjunction with paras 4 and 76 and the notes thereto. The provision envisages a claim on the basis of either a failure in terms of speed or efficiency on the part of the administrator by reference to what is 'reasonably practicable'. In practice, it is very doubtful that the court will be sympathetic to an application which amounts in substance to nothing more than a difference of opinion between the applicant and the administrator as to the past, present or proposed conduct of the administration. On the other hand, the court will always be alive to properly evidenced complaints where an administrator can be shown to be lacking in speed or efficiency by reference to the objective benchmark of what is 'reasonably practicable'. It is submitted that, whilst an applicant under para 74(2) need not establish as a prerequisite any actual or prospective harm to the applicant in terms of his financial participation in the administration (or, it is submitted, any ensuing liquidation), it is doubtful that the court will be receptive to an application where the applicant has no prospect of a financial participation in the administration.

Alternative courses of action—Before embarking on a claim under para 74 a creditor should also consider the possibility of seeking relief by way of permission to take action otherwise prevented by the moratoria and related provisions in paras 40–43. Certainly, para 74(5)(b) anticipates an application by the holder of fixed or other non-floating security or the owner of goods under a hire-purchase agreement. Other possibilities are also mentioned in the next section.

Paragraph 74(3) and (4)

Relief available—Subject to the limitations imposed by para 74(6), the scope of the relief open to the court is cast in the broadest possible terms. There is, it is submitted, a danger in drawing analogies between para 74 and the relief granted by the court in petitions brought under s 994 of the Companies Act 2006. In cases where the substance of what is alleged is nothing short of professional misconduct or negligence, consideration should be given to the making of an application by a creditor under para 81 for an order ending the administration or an application under para 88 removing the administrator from office, or an action in misfeasance proceedings under para 75.

75 Misfeasance

(1) The court may examine the conduct of a person who—

    (a)   is or purports to be the administrator of a company, or

    (b)   has been or has purported to be the administrator of a company.

(2) An examination under this paragraph may be held only on the application of—

    (a)   the official receiver,

    (b)   the administrator of the company,

    (c)   the liquidator of the company,

    (d)   a creditor of the company, or

    (e)   a contributory of the company.

(3) An application under sub-paragraph (2) must allege that the administrator—

    (a)   has misapplied or retained money or other property of the company,

    (b)   has become accountable for money or other property of the company,

    (c)   has breached a fiduciary or other duty in relation to the company, or

    (d)   has been guilty of misfeasance.

(4) On an examination under this paragraph into a person's conduct the court may order him—

    (a)   to repay, restore or account for money or property;

    (b)   to pay interest;

    (c)   to contribute a sum to the company's property by way of compensation for breach of duty or misfeasance.

(5) In sub-paragraph (3) 'administrator' includes a person who purports or has purported to be a company's administrator.

(6) An application under sub-paragraph (2) may be made in respect of an administrator who has been discharged under paragraph 98 only with the permission of the court.

General note—With effect from 15 September 2003 all references to administrators were removed from s 212 (summary remedy against delinquent directors and office-holders) by virtue of para 18 of Sch 17 to the Enterprise Act 2002. Paragraph 75 is dedicated specifically to any so-called misfeasance claim against an administrator appointed under Sch B1.

Although the notes to s 212 will be of continuing relevance to claims pursued under the new procedure in para 75, three specific changes should also be considered. First, para 75 is not dependent on a company being in liquidation. Secondly, para 75(1) now extends not only to an administrator or a former administrator but also to the conduct of a person who 'has purported to be the administrator of a company' – words also used in para 75(5) – which would catch an individual whose appointment was actually invalid or void. Thirdly, by virtue of para 75(3), there is now a specific procedural requirement for the specifics of the allegation or allegations.

The reference to 'an administrator who has been discharged under para 98' in para 75(6) equates to the *release* of an administrator under the former s 20.

In *Re Coniston Hotel (Kent) LLP* [2013] EWHC 93 (Ch), Norris J held that the court could not order a wrongdoing administrator to pay equitable compensation for breach of fiduciary duty to an individual creditor. If there was a deficiency in the insolvency then the payment was for the benefit of the creditors as a class.

In *Charalambous v B&C Associates* [2009] EWHC 2601 (Ch), [2009] 43 EG 105 (CS), Michael Furness QC granted the administrators' application to strike out a claim against them pursuant to para 75 on the basis that absent some special relationship, an administrator owed no general common law duty of care to specific unsecured creditors in relation to the conduct of the administration.

ENDING ADMINISTRATION

76 Automatic end of administration

(1) The appointment of an administrator shall cease to have effect at the end of the period of one year beginning with the date on which it takes effect.

(2) But—

   (a) on the application of an administrator the court may by order extend his term of office for a specified period, and

   (b) an administrator's term of office may be extended for a specified period not exceeding six months by consent.

General note—Paragraph 76 applies to all administrations under Sch B1 and raises a rebuttable presumption in all cases that an administration will be conducted to its conclusion within the period of 1 year beginning with the date on which the company enters administration, as defined in para 1(2)(b) and ending one year thereafter. In *Re Property Professionals + Limited* [2013] EWHC 1903 (Ch) HHJ Purle QC (sitting as a High Court judge) held that this period should be calculated from the precise time at which the administration order was made. Accordingly, where administrators were appointed at 2.13pm on 3 February 2010, their term of office terminated just before 2.13pm on 3 February 2011.

In *Re Taylor Made Foods plc* (unreported, 28 February 2010), where the administrators' term of office had terminated at a weekend, Henderson J allowd an application for an extension to be made on the next day that the Court Office was open.

The 1-year period significantly exceeds the unworkable 3-month period originally proposed, but still represents a marked shift from the position under the former Part II which imposed no such time limit, with the consequence that, in some cases at least, there was no real incentive for the administrator to conduct the administration with the degree of vigour which might otherwise have been the case, or to apply for a discharge of the order in accordance with the duty in s 18(2) in a timely fashion. The imposition of a time limit, albeit one capable of extension, also squares with the administrator's duty under para 4 to perform his functions as quickly and efficiently as is reasonably practicable.

Under the former law the practice adopted by judges in the Chancery Division varied on the making of an administration order as regards the perceived need to monitor the conduct of an administration. It was common enough that an administration order was made for a fixed period of time, at the expiry of which the matter would come back to court, particularly where the petition was advanced on grounds that a sale of the company's business and/or assets might be achieved within a stipulated period. Less commonly, an order would require that an administrator should make an application for directions within a fixed period for the further conduct of the administration. In cases where such an order was not made, there would be no reason why the matter should come back before the court at any time prior to the application for discharge under s 18, in the absence of an application by the administrator for directions or a contentious application in the administration by a third party. Despite the imposition of the one-year period in para 76(1) there will continue to be cases under Sch B1 where the court may wish to review the continuance of the order within a far shorter timescale and to impose any such consequential order as is considered appropriate under para 13(1)(f), although there is no mechanism for such an order in an out-of-court appointment case under paras 14 or 22. Further, there is no good reason why in an appropriate out-of-court appointment case an aggrieved creditor should not make an application to court for directions under para 68(2) or on the basis identified in the notes to para 63, where it is alleged that the administrator is in breach of his duty under para 4, even though that duty is only likely to be owed to the company itself.

Extending the one-year period in para 76(1)—The presumption identified in the general note above is capable of rebuttal so as to allow for the extension of the administrator's term of office either by the court for an unlimited but specified period under para 76(2)(a) or with the consent of the company's creditors, as defined and qualified in para 78(1)–(3), for a period not exceeding six months under para 76(2). In practice, the administrator may have to do very little to procure the consent of creditors. It is curious that, close on to ten years since the first one-year periods of administration would have fallen to expire or require extension under the new Sch B1 regime, there is no reported authority which deals squarely with the test applicable to an application to extend the period of administration. In an article by Philip Ridgeway and Ryan Beckwith (Insolv Int 2005, 18(2), 25-28) reference is made to an unreported decision called *Re Trident Fashions (No 3) (in administration)* in which the High Court apparently accepted that the appropriate test is whether the extension of the administration is reasonably likely to achieve the purpose of administration, the authors noting that, in grating the one-year extension sought, the court considered it unlikely that creditors would suffer prejudice as a result of the extension and that the secured creditor, shareholder and key funders had consented to the extension sought. It is respectfully suggested here that the test so identified in *Trident* is correct but that factors such as the unlikelihood of prejudice to creditors and the consent or support of any interested party (as with opposition by such a party) can only be factors relevant to the exercise of the court's discretion in granting or refusing an extension, but not of themselves determinative. Further, given that an extension constitutes a derogation from the statutory one-year (maximum) period of administration, and the statutory duty imposed on an administrator by para 4 of Sch B1 to, the evidential burden must rest with the applicant administrators in establishing to the court's satisfaction that there is a reasonable likelihood that the purpose of the particular administration before the court will be achieved. It is one thing for administrators to assert that proposition, but another for the administrators to discharge the test identified above in evidence, especially (as often arises in practice) where the extension is sought on the basis of pursuing further a single activity such as pursuit of a claim in litigation, the sale of a property or properties or the collection of book debts. The projected costs of extending the administration will often be key here. The evidence in support of the extension application will usually require the administrators to set out the likely cost of extending the administration (which the court may want to consider in light of the costs to date) and the anticipated benefit of those costs being expended together with a comparison of the administration not being extended, most obviously by the company being placed into liquidation.

Paragraph 10.1 of the *Practice Direction: Insolvency Proceedings* provides that In the absence of special circumstances, an application for the extension of an administration should be made not less than one month before the end of the administration. The evidence in support of any later application must explain why the application is being made late. The court will consider whether any part of the costs should be disallowed where an application is made less than one month before the end of the administration.

Circumstances in which an extension of the period of administration may not be obtained—Paragraph 78(4) provides that an extension by consent of creditors may only be obtained once, whether for 6 months or less, and not after any extension by order of the court. There is no limitation on the number of times that an extension may be granted by order of the court, irrespective of the fact of any previous extension by consent of creditors, by virtue of para 77(1)(a).

Once expired, whether at the end of the statutory one-year period or any extended period, paras 77(1)(b) and 78(4)(c) expressly provide that an administrator's term of office is incapable of being extended retrospectively by the court or with creditor consent. Schedule B1 provides no solution to this problem, which dictates that an administrator must be resolute in monitoring the period of his term of office, given his potential personal liability for trespass to or inference with the company's property and/or a claim for breach of duty in misfeasance proceedings under para 75 arising out of his failure to conduct the administration appropriately where he fails to apprehend the end of his term of office and to seek any extension necessary.

In an appropriate case where an administration is in its later stages the administrator might couple an application for extension to court with an application for permission under para 65(3) to make a distribution to unsecured creditors.

Following expiry of the term of an administration the former administrator will have no standing to exercise any of the powers under paras 59–64, including the power to apply to the court for directions, or to discharge those duties referred to in paras 67 and 68, although the former administrator's remuneration and expenses would remain protected by the statutory charge created by para 99(3). Further, it is suggested that on expiry of the term of the administration the control and management of the assets of the company must revert to the company acting by its directors and that the former administrator is under a duty to give actual notice of that position, and the circumstances giving rise to it, to the directors and all creditors of the company.

The position where an application for extension is filed with the court before the end of the one year period, but only comes on for hearing after its expiry, was considered by HHJ Norris QC, sitting as a High Court judge, in *Re TT Industries Ltd* [2006] BCC 373. Identifying the problem as one of jurisdiction, as opposed to procedure, the judge took the view that any lapse of time after the end of the statutory one-year period could not be cured under para 107 of Sch B1, s 376 of IA 1986, r 12.9(2) of IR 1986 or CPR r 40.7 (at [6]). Despite the wording in para 77(1) the judge took the view (at [14]) that that provision does not deprive the court of standing to make an extending order where: (a) the application is made after the administrator's term of office has expired; and (b) there is a real possibility that the court itself had contributed to the matter not coming on for hearing before expiry of the term (as the judge found to be the case), since the court's jurisdiction allowed it to extend an order on the ground that unavoidable delays in the administration of justice should not interfere with the rights of parties: see *Re Keystone Knitting Mill's Trade Mark* [1929] 1 Ch 92. Given that this issue had not apparently come before the court previously the judge went on to draw attention to the proper procedure available in some courts (the *TT Industries* case proceeded in the Birmingham District Registry of the High Court, Chancery Division) in which it was apparent to court staff that an administration order was about to lapse, the matter would be placed before the judge for immediate consideration on paper (and for the judge to grant a short extension pending a hearing if there was insufficient time for a proper consideration of the matter); to issue strong guidance to practitioners to draw attention (on the face of the application and a covering letter) to the fact that an order was required by a specified date; to remind practitioners that a Chancery (Section 9 or High Court) judge may not be immediately available to consider cases (even on paper); and to give a clear warning that applications lodged within the last few days of a current administration (where no satisfactory reason was given for the lateness) and with which the court could not deal during the currency of the administration were likely to be treated as cases where the order has not been obtained through the default of the administrator.

Procedure—See rr 2.110–2.112. Rule 2.111(1) prescribed Form 2.30B for filing with the court on the automatic end of an administration together with a final progress report compliant with IR 1986, r 2.47.

Form 2.31B is prescribed by r 2.112(3) for the purpose of the notification to the Registrar of Companies under para 77(2) of an extension or an extension by court order. The same form is also used for para 78(5) purposes following an extension by consent of creditors. No provision is made for the notification of either form of extension to creditors themselves, although this would be common practice and usually conveyed in correspondence. In the case of a court application for extension, r 2.47(4) would appear to require the sending of a copy of the progress report filed with the court under r 2.112(1) to be sent to creditors, attached to Form 2.24B, within 1 month of the end of the period covered by the report.

77

(1) An order of the court under paragraph 76—

(a)   may be made in respect of an administrator whose term of office has already been extended by order or by consent, but

(b)   may not be made after the expiry of the administrator's term of office.

(2) Where an order is made under paragraph 76 the administrator shall as soon as is reasonably practicable notify the registrar of companies.

(3) An administrator who fails without reasonable excuse to comply with sub-paragraph (2) commits an offence.

General note—These provisions should be read in conjunction with para 76, on which see the notes thereto.

Penalties—See s 430, Sch 10 and the daily default fine in para 106(2)(l).

78

(1) In paragraph 76(2)(b) 'consent' means consent of—

(a)   each secured creditor of the company, and

(b)   if the company has unsecured debts, creditors whose debts amount to more than 50% of the company's unsecured debts, disregarding debts of any creditor who does not respond to an invitation to give or withhold consent.

(2) But where the administrator has made a statement under paragraph 52(1)(b) 'consent' means—

(a)   consent of each secured creditor of the company, or

(b)   if the administrator thinks that a distribution may be made to preferential creditors, consent of—

    (i)   each secured creditor of the company, and

    (ii)   preferential creditors whose debts amount to more than 50% of the preferential debts of the company, disregarding debts of any creditor who does not respond to an invitation to give or withhold consent.

(3) Consent for the purposes of paragraph 76(2)(b) may be—

(a)   written, or

(b)   signified at a creditors' meeting.

(4) An administrator's term of office—

(a)   may be extended by consent only once,

(b)   may not be extended by consent after extension by order of the court, and

(c)   may not be extended by consent after expiry.

(5) Where an administrator's term of office is extended by consent he shall as soon as is reasonably practicable—

    (a)   file notice of the extension with the court, and

    (b)   notify the registrar of companies.

(6) An administrator who fails without reasonable excuse to comply with sub-paragraph (5) commits an offence.

General note—For the relevance of 'consent' see para 76(2)(b). An extension of an administrator's term of office through the consent of creditors may only be effected once. It is not, therefore, open to an administrator to seek a further extension where a first extension by creditors was for a period of less than 6 months.

The three alternative meanings of 'consent'—'Consent' means either:

(a)   the consent of those creditors identified in para 78(1)(a) and (b). The wording employed in both paras 78(1)(b) and 78(2)(b)(ii) means that consent depends on the consent of more than 50% of the particular class of creditor who respond to an invitation to give or withhold consent. Since the exclusion of votes under para 78(1)(b) is dependent on a non-response to an invitation, it would follow that a response conveying an abstention should be taken into account; or

(b)   if the administrator has made a para 52(1)(b) statement (ie in his statement of proposals to the effect that the company has insufficient property to enable a distribution to be made to unsecured creditors other than by virtue of the 'prescribed part' provisions in s 176A(2)(a)) the consent of each secured creditor of the company; or

(c)   if the administrator has made a para 52(1)(b) statement, and the administrator thinks that a distribution may be made to preferential creditors, the consent of each secured creditor of the company and those preferential creditors identified in para 78(2)(b)(ii).

Consent under para 78(3)—Written consent may involve a saving of the cost involved in the convening of a creditors' meeting although, as a matter of good practice, an administrator may consider this a false economy if he perceives some obvious level of dissent between a significant number of creditors in value despite written consent apparently being obtainable. Written consent may include such consent in electronic form by virtue of para 111(2).

Extension of administrator's term of office—See paras 76 and 77 and the notes to para 76.

Penalties—See s 430, Sch 10 and para 106(2)(m).

79 Court ending administration on application of administrator

(1) On the application of the administrator of a company the court may provide for the appointment of an administrator of the company to cease to have effect from a specified time.

(2) The administrator of a company shall make an application under this paragraph if—

    (a)   he thinks the purpose of administration cannot be achieved in relation to the company,

    (b)   he thinks the company should not have entered administration, or

    (c)   a creditors' meeting requires him to make an application under this paragraph.

(3) The administrator of a company shall make an application under this paragraph if—

> (a)   the administration is pursuant to an administration order, and
> (b)   the administrator thinks that the purpose of administration has been sufficiently achieved in relation to the company.

(4) On an application under this paragraph the court may—

> (a)   adjourn the hearing conditionally or unconditionally;
> (b)   dismiss the application;
> (c)   make an interim order;
> (d)   make any order it thinks appropriate (whether in addition to, in consequence of or instead of the order applied for).

General note—Paragraph 79(1) applies in all administrations. Paragraphs 79(2) and 79(3) prescribe circumstances in which an application under para 79(1) is mandatory. Whilst paras 79(2) and 79(3) subject the administrator to an obligation to make an application under para 89(1) in those circumstances, the administrator is not precluded from making such an application in other circumstances: *Re TM Kingdom Ltd (in administration)* [2007] BCC 480 at [16] (HHJ Norris QC, sitting as a judge of the High Court; para 79(1) application approved to allow company to be placed into CVL to avoid ad valorem charges on compulsory winding up and unoccupied business rates then ranking as an expense of an administration but not of a liquidation). Although para 79(2) applies to all administrations (most obviously under para 79(2)(b) where the administrator becomes aware of something which fundamentally alters his perception of the basis upon which the company was put into administration), para 79(3) is restricted to those cases in which an administration order has been made, given that an out-of-court appointee may file a notice under para 80(2) where he thinks that the purpose of administration has been sufficiently achieved.

Paragraph 79(1)

Administrator's appointment ceasing to take effect—A company is no longer in administration once an administrator's appointment ceases to take effect: see para 1(2)(a) and (c) and the notes to para 1.

Paragraph 79(2)

'he thinks ...'—For commentary on the meaning of the term 'thinks' see the notes to para 3(3).

The court's discretion under para 79(4)—It is apparent from para 79(4)(d) that the court need not grant the specific relief sought in a para 79(1) application. The fact that proposals under para 49 have not been sent out to creditors does not inhibit the exercise of the court's discretion, although the procedures identified below provide for the provision of information to creditors in such a case.

Under Sch B1, as with the former Part II, an administrator is not obliged to seek the winding up of a company at the end of his term of office. Under the former provisions it was very common for an administrator to couple an application for discharge of an administration order under s 18 with a petition for winding up, or for the court to accept undertakings pursuant to which the company was placed into voluntary liquidation. A similar practice should be adopted by office-holders and by the court under the new provisions in light of the approval of the Court of Appeal (Chadwick, Rix and Arden LJJ) in *Oakley Smith v Greenberg* [2003] EWCA Civ 1217, [2003] BPIR 709 at [31] and of the view expressed by Millett J, as he then was, in *Re Barrow Borough Transport Ltd* [1990] Ch 227, to the effect that the court should not sanction the cessation of an administration in the absence of proposals for the realisation and distribution of the assets of the company, which could include moving the company into a CVL under para 83, other than where it is intended to return control of the company and its assets to the company's directors.

The wording of para 79(4)(d), it is suggested, is sufficiently broad to allow the court to make a winding-up order and an order for the appointment of a liquidator notwithstanding the absence of a winding-up petition or, it seems, where there is already an extant winding-up petition which is not before the court at that time. If the court makes an order under para 79(1) providing for the appointment of an administrator to cease to have effect, then the court is obliged to discharge any administration order under para 85(2).

Procedure—The procedural requirements appear in IR 1986, rr 2.114 and 2.116 which require notification of an order ending administration to be given to the Registrar of Companies in Form 2.33B, attaching a copy of the court order and a copy of the final progress report produced under IR 1986, r 2.110.

Where the administrator intends to apply to the court before he has sent out his proposals under para 49, then he must follow the procedure in r 2.33(6).

Where the administrator seeks a winding-up order, then the petition is treated as a contributories' petition by virtue of r 4.7(9), thereby bringing rr 4.22 and 4.23 into operation together with r 4.7(7), (8) and (10). It is doubtful that the court has power to make a winding-up order in the absence of a winding-up petition: *Re Synthetic Technology Ltd* [1990] BCLC 378 at 382C–382H (Harman J), and see now the reference to 'a petition under s 124' in r 2.114(4). The decision of Neuberger J, as he then was, in *Lancefield v Lancefield* [2002] BPIR 1108 at 1111C–1112D (an insolvent partnership case) to the contrary effect is, with respect, doubtful in the absence of reference to the *Synthetic Technology* case, although *Lancefield* was a case decided on its own very exceptional facts. The court has no standing to appoint any person other than an outgoing administrator as liquidator under s 140: *Re Exchange Travel (Holdings) Ltd* [1992] BCC 954 at 958H–959A (Edward Evans-Lombe QC, sitting as a deputy High Court judge).

Applications for discharge of an administration order under the former s 18 were invariably combined with applications for release under s 20. As remains the case with an application under para 79(1), the former provisions did not require notice to be given of an application for release. As a consequence, some judges in the Chancery Division adopted a practice of only granting release on being satisfied that notice had been given to creditors of the release application. It is submitted that there are very good grounds for the adoption of that practice in relation to para 79 since creditors might otherwise be denied the opportunity of raising with the court legitimate grievances against an administrator prior to what equates to his release from liability by virtue of para 98(1). Notice in this sense means notice of the time, date and place at which the administrator's application for release is to be heard: the giving of a general notice that release will be sought at some unspecified point in the future in the body of the administrator's proposals under para 49 is insufficient for these purposes.

Paragraph 86 applies where a court order provides for the appointment of an administrator to cease to have effect.

80 Termination of administration where objective achieved

(1) This paragraph applies where an administrator of a company is appointed under paragraph 14 or 22.

(2) If the administrator thinks that the purpose of administration has been sufficiently achieved in relation to the company he may file a notice in the prescribed form—

    (a)   with the court, and
    (b)   with the registrar of companies.

(3) The administrator's appointment shall cease to have effect when the requirements of sub-paragraph (2) are satisfied.

(4) Where the administrator files a notice he shall within the prescribed period send a copy to every creditor of the company of whose claim and address he is aware.

(5) The rules may provide that the administrator is taken to have complied with sub-paragraph (4) if before the end of the prescribed period he publishes in the prescribed manner a notice undertaking to provide a copy

of the notice under sub-paragraph (2) to any creditor of the company who applies in writing to a specified address.

(6) An administrator who fails without reasonable excuse to comply with sub-paragraph (4) commits an offence.

General note—The termination of the administrator's office under this provision is permitted only on the single ground in para 80(2). An administrator in such a case remains obliged to make an application to court under para 79(2) in any of the three circumstances mentioned therein and, furthermore, may make an application under para 79(1) in any other circumstances.

Paragraph 80(2)

'if the administrator thinks ...'—For commentary on the term 'thinks' see the notes to para 3(3).

Paragraph 80(3)

Administrator's appointment ceasing to take effect—A company is no longer in administration once an administrator's appointment ceases to take effect: see para 1(2)(a) and (c) and the notes to para 1.

The termination of the administrator's appointment under para 80(3) is expressly stated as being subject to satisfaction of the requirements in para 80(2) which requires the appropriate notice to be served on only the court and the Registrar of Companies, but not creditors for whom notice is afforded in r 2.113(4). Creditors, therefore, are not guaranteed any effective means of preventing termination under para 80(2). Furthermore, neither para 80 nor, indeed, Sch B1 or the Rules provide any mechanism for the prevention or undoing of a termination effected of the administrator's own volition. The termination will not, however, affect the administrator's personal liability, which will remain subject to para 98(2).

Where an administrator proposes invoking the procedure under para 80, then he should remain mindful of the practice approved of by the Court of Appeal in *Oakley-Smith v Greenberg* [2003] EWCA Civ 1217, [2003] BPIR 709 at [31], as noted in the commentary to para 79.

The discharge from liability – equivalent to what was formerly termed 'release' from liability under s 20 – of an administrator whose office is terminated under para 80 is determined in accordance with para 98(2).

Procedure—Rule 2.113(1) requires that the notice given under para 80(2) is in Form 2.32B and is accompanied by a final progress report compliant with r 2.110. Further notification and advertisement requirements, including the giving of notice to creditors, appear in r 2.113(2)–(6).

Penalties—See s 430, Sch 10 and the daily default fine in para 106(2)(n).

81 Court ending administration on application of creditor

(1) On the application of a creditor of a company the court may provide for the appointment of an administrator of the company to cease to have effect at a specified time.

(2) An application under this paragraph must allege an improper motive—

    (a)   in the case of an administrator appointed by administration order, on the part of the applicant for the order, or

    (b)   in any other case, on the part of the person who appointed the administrator.

(3) On an application under this paragraph the court may—

(a)　　adjourn the hearing conditionally or unconditionally;
(b)　　dismiss the application;
(c)　　make an interim order;
(d)　　make any order it thinks appropriate (whether in addition to, in consequence of or instead of the order applied for).

General note—Save to the extent that under the former s 19(1) the court retained a general power to remove an administrator from office 'at any time', this provision is new so far as it confers standing specifically on a creditor to apply for the cessation of the appointment of an administrator on the grounds of 'improper motive' in the appointment of the administrator in para 81(2).

The specific terms of this new provision are necessary so as to allow a creditor without notice of an out-of-court appointment to challenge the appointment in an appropriate case. It is clear from para 81(2), however, that the provision applies to both out-of-court and court appointments since, whilst in theory a creditor might appear and be heard at the hearing of the administration application, in practice any unsecured creditor is not entitled to notice of the application and may therefore only be in a position to raise a challenge to the court appointment after the event.

If nothing else, the drafting of para 81 is curious. Although para 81(2) requires an allegation of improper motive by the applicant creditor it is by no means clear from the wording of the provision that an order under para 81(1) is conditional upon a finding as to such improper motive. The view taken here is that a substantive order under para 81(1) must be taken as being so conditional since otherwise the requirement for the applicant's allegation of improper motive would be rendered meaningless. It is further suggested that an order is capable of being made under para 81(1) where a finding of improper motive is made without that finding necessarily relating to the particular improper motive alleged. It is also clear enough, it is suggested, that an order under para 81(3), in contrast to para 81(2), is conditional upon neither an allegation nor a finding of improper motive.

Paragraph 81(1)

'**... the court may provide for the appointment of an administrator of the company to cease to have effect ....**'—This wording reflects the formula provided for in para 1(2)(a) whereby a company is 'in administration' while the appointment of an administrator of the company has effect. This would suggest that a successful application under para 81(1) would result in a company no longer being 'in administration'. However, it is submitted that there is no good reason why, in an appropriate case, the court should not make a consequential order under para 81(3)(d) for the appointment of a replacement administrator. Such a replacement appointment would suppose that the court had reached a finding of 'improper motive' for the purposes of para 81(2) but nonetheless considered it justifiable, most likely but not necessarily with the support of the applicant creditor, to continue the administration under the control of a replacement office-holder. Equally, it is conceivable that the court could reach a finding of improper motive for para 81(2) purposes and yet decline both to terminate the administration and to replace the incumbent office-holder, most likely on the grounds of economy and/or the wishes and/or the interests of creditors.

Paragraph 81(2)

'**improper motive**'—This is a new term and one which does not appear elsewhere in the legislation. It is submitted that the proper approach on the part of the court to the term involves a two-stage process. First, that the court should be concerned in establishing, as a matter of fact, the motive on the part of the applicant for an administration order or the appointor in an out-of-court appointment; secondly, it falls to the court to consider whether, in the particular circumstances of a case, that motive is improper.

It is doubtful that the fact of the court or an out-of-court appointee having formed the view that the purpose of administration in para 3(1) is reasonably practicably capable of achievement will be of any real assistance in establishing improper motive. This is because the allegation of improper motive in appointment must, by definition, refer to the period pre-appointment and, in particular, the conduct of the administration order applicant or out-of-court appointee. The fact of any improper motive need not relate to or have any influence on the achievability of the administration purpose or, indeed, the conduct of the administration itself. Accordingly, it is submitted that, at least in the usual course, the court will not ordinarily be concerned with the conduct of the administration on a para 81(2) application although, for the purposes of its investigation into the allegation of improper motive, the court may well be assisted by evidence on the part of the administrator as to the circumstances leading up to his appointment. It is further submitted that, in reaching a finding of improper motive, the court is not concerned with a detailed investigation into the mind of the applicant or out-of-court appointor in effecting the appointment but is properly entitled to draw inferences from the surrounding facts of the case.

Although para 81(2) imposes a requirement for an allegation of improper motive, a bare allegation in isolation is unlikely to be of assistance to the court. What the provision should be read as calling for is an allegation of improper motive which is supported by particulars in support of the allegation, whether in evidence or points of claim, depending on the form of the application and any directions given by the court. An application which fails to allege improper motive in contravention of para 81(2), and, arguably, an application which fails to give proper particulars of that allegation, is defective and may be susceptible to being struck out by the court under any of the grounds in CPR, r 3.4(2) or under CPR, r 24(2) (summary judgment), on which see IR 1986, r 7.51 and the notes to rr 7.1 and 7.2.

See also the note headed 'Procedure' below.

Paragraph 81(3)

Further orders—The scope of the orders available to the court under this provision is unfettered, particularly given para 81(3)(d). Such orders may be tailored to the particular circumstances of the case, most obviously where the court is minded on the initial return date of the application to give directions for the filing of further evidence and where there is a need to regulate or limit the scope of the administration pending the matter coming back before the court. Unlike para 81(2) the making of an order under para 81(3) is not subject to the requirement for the establishment of improper motive, as discussed in the General Note above.

Procedure—Although r 2.115, which specifically addresses the procedure applicable to applications under para 81(1), envisages the hearing of an application on notice following the giving of five clear business days' notice to a respondent (subject to abridgment of time under r 12.9), the requirement for an evidential finding of improper motive will (and certainly where the application is opposed) usually preclude a trial of the application without the opportunity for the filing of evidence and cross-examination for which an order may be made under r 7.7(1). In certain exceptional cases, however, the court may be satisfied that the allegation of improper motive is so plainly made out, or is plainly capable of being inferred from the surrounding facts, that an order may safely be made under para 81(1) without further investigation and cross-examination.

Paragraph 86 applies where a court order provides for the appointment of an administrator to cease to have effect.

Costs—The fact that para 81 application is rendered otiose by an administrator making an application for his appointment to cease and for a winding-up order prior to the para 81 application coming on for hearing does not prevent the court from ordering the costs of the para 81 application against the administrator if the circumstances justify: *Coyne v DRC Distribution Ltd* [2008] BCC 612 (Ward, Jacob and Rimer LJJ: costs order by judge justified where creditor made para 81 application following administrator's failure to take steps to recover assets transferred away pre-administration).

82 Public interest winding-up

(1) This paragraph applies where a winding-up order is made for the winding up of a company in administration on a petition presented under—

    (a)   section 124A (public interest), or
    (aa) section 124B (SEs),

(b) section 367 of the Financial Services and Markets Act 2000 (petition by Financial Services Authority).

(2) This paragraph also applies where a provisional liquidator of a company in administration is appointed following the presentation of a petition under any of the provisions listed in sub-paragraph (1).

(3) The court shall order—

(a) that the appointment of the administrator shall cease to have effect, or

(b) that the appointment of the administrator shall continue to have effect.

(4) If the court makes an order under sub-paragraph (3)(b) it may also—

(a) specify which of the powers under this Schedule are to be exercisable by the administrator, and

(b) order that this Schedule shall have effect in relation to the administrator with specified modifications.

General note—Paragraph 42(2) and (3) imposes a general bar on the placing of a company into liquidation where that company is in administration. That general bar is subject to the making of a winding-up order on a public interest or Financial Services Authority petition by virtue of para 42(4) or the appointment of a provisional liquidator following presentation of such a petition by virtue of para 82(2).

On the making of a permitted winding-up order – paras 40(3) and 42(5) envisaging an application for directions by the administrator under para 63 in the interim – the court must decide whether the appointment of the administrator should cease or continue. In the latter case, the wording employed in para 82(4) suggests that, whilst both the administrator and the liquidator are each to hold office contemporaneously, it is the scope of the administration which should be restricted so as to allow for the proper conduct of the winding-up petition.

Paragraph 82(3)

Scope of provision—A company is no longer in administration once an administrator's appointment ceases to take effect: see para 1(2)(a) and (c) and the notes to para 1.

Procedure—Paragraph 86 applies where a court order provides for the appointment of an administrator to cease to have effect.

83 Moving from administration to creditors' voluntary liquidation

(1) This paragraph applies in England and Wales where the administrator of a company thinks—

(a) that the total amount which each secured creditor of the company is likely to receive has been paid to him or set aside for him, and

(b) that a distribution will be made to unsecured creditors of the company (if there are any).

(2) This paragraph applies in Scotland where the administrator of a company thinks—

(a) that each secured creditor of the company will receive payment in respect of his debt, and

799

(b)   that a distribution will be made to unsecured creditors (if there are any).

(3) The administrator may send to the registrar of companies a notice that this paragraph applies.

(4) On receipt of a notice under sub-paragraph (3) the registrar shall register it.

(5) If an administrator sends a notice under sub-paragraph (3) he shall as soon as is reasonably practicable—

(a)   file a copy of the notice with the court, and
(b)   send a copy of the notice to each creditor of whose claim and address he is aware.

(6) On the registration of a notice under sub-paragraph (3)—

(a)   the appointment of an administrator in respect of the company shall cease to have effect, and
(b)   the company shall be wound up as if a resolution for voluntary winding up under section 84 were passed on the day on which the notice is registered.

(7) The liquidator for the purposes of the winding up shall be—

(a)   a person nominated by the creditors of the company in the prescribed manner and within the prescribed period, or
(b)   if no person is nominated under paragraph (a), the administrator.

(8) In the application of Part IV to a winding up by virtue of this paragraph—

(a)   section 85 shall not apply,
(b)   section 86 shall apply as if the reference to the time of the passing of the resolution for voluntary winding up were a reference to the beginning of the date of registration of the notice under sub-paragraph (3),
(c)   section 89 does not apply,
(d)   sections 98, 99 and 100 shall not apply,
(e)   section 129 shall apply as if the reference to the time of the passing of the resolution for voluntary winding up were a reference to the beginning of the date of registration of the notice under sub-paragraph (3), and
(f)   any creditors' committee which is in existence immediately before the company ceases to be in administration shall continue in existence after that time as if appointed as a liquidation committee under section 101.

General note—This provision finds no equivalent in the former Part II and enables an administrator to procure a seamless transition from administration to creditors' voluntary liquidation without the need for meetings of members and creditors as envisaged by s 98(1). There is no provision for a move from administration to a members' voluntary liquidation. The para 83 procedure is not dependent upon the method of appointment of the administrator seeking to invoke it; nor does para 83 require the making of an order under paras 79 or 85: *Re Ballast plc (in administration)* [2005] BCLC 446 at [21] (Blackburne J).

The variations to the provisions ordinarily applicable to a creditors' voluntary liquidation effected by para 83(8) should be read in conjunction with IR 1986, r 4.1(6) which applies to the conduct of the liquidation.

One practical advantage of a CVL over a compulsory liquidation is the saving of the DTI ad valorem levy, which applies in the latter case only.

Where a CVL is envisaged as the exit route from an administration, there is a requirement under r 2.33(2)(m) for the administrator's proposals under para 49 to include a statement of the proposed liquidator and a statement in accordance with para 83(7) and r 2.117(3). Where, however, the move to a CVL is only considered subsequent to the initial creditors' meeting which approved the administrator's proposals under para 53(1), it will be necessary to put the matter to creditors as a revision to the administrator's proposals under para 54(1) since r 2.33(2)(m), it is submitted, deems that move to be something substantial. On the other hand, it will not be necessary to put the matter to creditors as a substantial revision where the original statement of proposals includes a statement under para 52(1)(b), since in those circumstances para 54 is inoperative in the absence of an initial creditors' meeting under para 54(1)(a). It would appear that where a para 52(1)(b) statement has been made, but grounds subsequently arise which cause the administrator to think that a distribution will be made to unsecured creditors, so as to bring the administration within para 83(1)(b), it will be unnecessary for the administrator to put the proposed move to a CVL to creditors since para 54 will not apply in the absence of an initial creditors' meeting under para 54(1)(a). If that analysis is correct, then it gives rise to a further anomaly identified in the note on procedure below.

Other than in a case where a company is to be handed back into the control of its directors, an administrator is obliged, on the grounds identified in the notes to para 79, to make provision for the distribution of free assets following the termination of his term of office.

In a case where there are no assets for distribution to creditors, whether or not following a distribution under para 65, the duty in para 84(1) will trigger subject to disapplication under para 84(2): *Re GHE Realisations Ltd* [2006] BCC 139 at [24] (where the approach of the administrators was to realise the company's assets, to pay preferential creditors in full, to make a distribution to unsecured creditors without first placing the company into voluntary liquidation).

The only means of challenging the procedure under para 83 is by an application under para 74 which will require a causative link between the action challenged as being unfair – which, it is submitted, might bring in the issue of what the administrator 'thinks' and the basis for such thinking – and the alleged harm to creditors' interests: *Unidare plc v Cohen and Power* [2005] BPIR 1472 at [65]–[66] (Lewison J).

Paragraph 83(1) and (2)

'... **the administrator ... thinks**'—The term 'thinks' is considered in the notes to para 3(3).

Paragraph 83(3)–(6)

Scope of provision—It is the registration by the Registrar of Companies of the notice sent to him by the administrator which triggers the move from administration to voluntary liquidation under para 83(6). Rule 2.117(1) provides that Form 2.34B must be used under para 83(3). The word 'may' in that provision, however, makes clear that the para 83 procedure remains optional in all cases within the scope of para 83(1).

Provided that the notice under para 83(3) is sent to the Registrar whilst he remains in office, it is immaterial to the operation of para 83(6)(a) that the administrator's term of office has lapsed before registration of the notice by the Registrar, as where an out of court appointment was effected on 31 January 2005, a para 83(3) notice was stamped as received by the Registrar on 28 January 2006 but the notice was not registered until 1 February 2006: *Re E-Squared Ltd* [2006] BCC 379 (David Richards J). In such a case the company is wound up at the date of the registration and the former administrator takes office as liquidator.

A notice under para 83(3) takes effect only on its registration by the Registrar of Companies, not on the date when the registrar receives it. An administrator's term of office is by implication from the words of para 83(6) extended by filing a conversion notice, from the date on which it would otherwise expire by effluxion of time until para 83(6) comes into effect on registration of the notice, unless in the interim he resigns, dies, is removed from office or ceases to be qualified to act: *Re Globespan Airways Ltd; Cartwright and another v Registrar of Companies* [2012] EWCA Civ 1159, [2013] 1 WLR 1122; *Re Property Professionals + Limited* [2013] EWHC 1903 (Ch).

If an administrator or his staff erroneously files Form 2.34B in a case to which para 83(1) applies, then the subsequent commencement of a CVL under para 83(6) is irreversible, even on an application to the court, and is not in any way dependent on or affected by the state of mind or intention of the administrator.

Paragraph 83(6)

Administrator's appointment ceasing to take effect—A company is no longer in administration once an administrator's appointment ceases to take effect: see para 1(2)(a) and (c) and the notes to para 1.

Preferential creditors—In a para 83 case s 387(3)(ba) preserves the position of preferential creditors by fixing the relevant date for determining the existence and amount of preferential debts as that on which the company entered administration.

Time limits applicable to transaction-at-undervalue and preference claims in liquidation—The 'relevant time' under ss 238 and 239 is fixed by s 240(3)(d) in a para 83 case as the date on which the company entered administration.

Procedure—See r 2.117. Form 2.34B, as prescribed by r 2.117(1), must have attached to it a final progress report compliant with r 2.110 and r 2.117(1) itself on being sent to the Registrar of Companies.

Rules 2.33(2)(m) and 2.45(2)(g) impose requirements in relation to an administrator's proposals or revised proposals respectively.

Rule 2.117(3) provides that the appointment of the liquidator nominated in the administrator's proposals or revised proposals 'takes effect by the creditors' approval, with or without modification, of the administrator's proposals or revised proposals.' As identified above, in circumstances where a statement has been made in accordance with para 52(1)(b), but the administrator subsequently thinks that a distribution to unsecured creditors is likely, there appears to be no requirement for approval of revised proposals in which a r 2.45(2)(g) statement would be included. The only solution here would appear to be for the administrator to make an application for directions under para 63, or possibly para 68(2), for the convening of a creditors' meeting for the purpose of approving the revised proposals.

Paragraph 86 applies where a court order provides for the appointment of an administrator to cease to have effect.

84 Moving from administration to dissolution

(1) If the administrator of a company thinks that the company has no property which might permit a distribution to its creditors, he shall send a notice to that effect to the registrar of companies.

(2) The court may on the application of the administrator of a company disapply sub-paragraph (1) in respect of the company.

(3) On receipt of a notice under sub-paragraph (1) the registrar shall register it.

(4) On the registration of a notice in respect of a company under sub-paragraph (1) the appointment of an administrator of the company shall cease to have effect.

(5) If an administrator sends a notice under sub-paragraph (1) he shall as soon as is reasonably practicable—

    (a)   file a copy of the notice with the court, and

(b) send a copy of the notice to each creditor of whose claim and address he is aware.

(6) At the end of the period of three months beginning with the date of registration of a notice in respect of a company under sub-paragraph (1) the company is deemed to be dissolved.

(7) On an application in respect of a company by the administrator or another interested person the court may—

(a) extend the period specified in sub-paragraph (6),
(b) suspend that period, or
(c) disapply sub-paragraph (6).

(8) Where an order is made under sub-paragraph (7) in respect of a company the administrator shall as soon as is reasonably practicable notify the registrar of companies.

(9) An administrator commits an offence if he fails without reasonable excuse to comply with sub-paragraph (5).

General note—These provisions find no counterpart in the former Part II, although they find an equivalent in ss 202 and 203 which provide for early dissolution in company liquidation in similar circumstances.

The duty imposed on an administrator by para 84(1) by the use of the word 'shall', and the consequent duty imposed on the Registrar of Companies under para 84(3), are only triggered where the administrator 'thinks that the company has no property which might permit a distribution to its creditors'. The reference to 'creditors' is not limited to unsecured creditors. Consequently, para 84 can have no application where the administrator thinks that there might be even the smallest distribution to any class of creditor. The provision in para 84(1) will, therefore, be triggered either where the administrator forms the view that the company has no property for distribution to creditors or where no such property remains following a distribution under para 65. Accordingly, para 84 provides a convenient and straightforward enough procedure for bringing the existence of a company to an end through dissolution where an intervening winding up would serve no useful purpose. The mandatory application of the scheme in the circumstances prescribed in para 84(1), however, is capable of disapplication by the court, but only on the application of the administrator, under para 84(2), perhaps most obviously where a winding-up might serve a useful purpose by way of investigations undertaken by a liquidator, regardless, it is submitted, of whether those investigations might lead to the recovery of property for the benefit of the company.

Paragraph 84(1)

'If the administrator … thinks …'—For commentary on the meaning of the term 'thinks ' see the notes to para 3(3). The requirement is for the administrator to form the requisite view only at the time para 84(1) applies: *Re GHE Realisations Ltd* [2006] BCC 139 at [24] (Rimer J).

'… that the company has no property which might permit a distribution to the creditors …'—This condition is met once the administrator forms the view that there are no assets remaining which allow for a distribution: *Re Preston & Duckworth Ltd* [2006] BCC 133 (Mr Recorder Hodge QC sitting as a deputy High Court judge). The contrary view, expressed obiter, by Blackburne J in *Re Ballast plc (in administration)* [2005] 1 WLR 1928 at [20], to the effect that para 84(1) only applies where the company in administration has no property at any time during the administration which might permit a distribution, is wrong and should not be followed: *Re GHE Realisations Ltd* [2006] BCC 139 at [23] (Rimer J). Although a company with no assets will not usually be eligible for administration, this might arise where an individual company with no assets enters administration with the other members of a group of companies.

The effects of para 84(1) being triggered—The wording in para 84(2) allows for the disapplication of para 84(1) on an application by an administrator prior to the sending of a notice under para 84(1). On receipt of the notice the Registrar is under an unconditional obligation to register it under para 84(3), which gives rise to the termination of the administrator's appointment as such. (Despite the cessation of his appointment the administrator will, however, only be discharged from liability – being the equivalent of release under the former s 20 – under para 98(2) which operates quite independently of para 84.) The dissolution of the company follows automatically under para 84(6), subject to para 84(7), on the expiration of the three-month period commencing with registration of the para 84(1) notice. Paragraph 84(5) is administrative in nature and does not affect the consequences of termination of appointment and dissolution under para 84(4) and (6), although an administrator will face liability for default under para 84(9).

A move from administration to dissolution does not require the obtaining of an order under paras 79 or 85: *Re Ballast (in administration)* [2005] 1 WLR 1928 at [21] (Blackburne J), followed in *Re GHE Realisations Ltd* [2006] BCC 139 at [25] (Rimer J).

Possible action following dissolution—Once para 84(4) takes effect, para 84 provides the court with no power to restore the administration, although para 84(7) does allow for the suspension or total disapplication of the subsequent dissolution under para 84(6).

However, s 1029(1)(b) of the Companies Act 2006 expressly provides that an pplication may be made to the court to restore to the register a company that is deemed to have been dissolved under para 84(6).

Although s 1029(2) does not specifically list an administrator in the list of persons who may make such application (in contrast s 1029(2)(j) expressly refers to 'any former liquidator of the company'), it is submitted that an administrator will constitute 'a person appearing to the court to have an interest in the matter' Applications under s 1029 are commonly made where it transpires that a company was, in fact, legally or beneficially entitled to property at the date of dissolution or for the purpose of facilitating a claim against the company's insurers under the Third Parties (Right Against Insurers) Act 1999.

Deemed dissolution under para 84(6) does not affect the jurisdiction of the appropriate court to determine director disqualification proceedings: *Secretary of State for Trade and Industry v Arnold* [2008] BCC 119 (HHJ Pelling QC, sitting as a judge of the High Court).

Paragraph 84(4)

The effect of the registration of a notice under para 84(4) is the cessation of the appointment of an administrator. By reference to the definition in para 1(2)(a) the company would thereafter no longer be 'in administration'. It would follow, therefore, that in the period between registration of the notice and the end of the 3-month period provided for in para 84(6), or any extended period under para 84(7), the company would be neither in administration nor in dissolution. It would, it is submitted, be quite extraordinary in these circumstances if the company was to revert to the control of its directors in this interim period, and it seems most unlikely that this is what Parliament could have intended. It is suggested that during such an interim period, and despite the fact that the company is no longer in administration, by virtue of the appointment of the administrators ceasing to have effect, the company must remain subject to the powers of the administrator on a residual basis pending dissolution, rather than reverting to the control of its directors (who would not have been removed as such merely by the fact of the company being in administration) or existing in some other undefined state of limbo.

Procedure—See IR 1986, r 2.118. The administrator's notice under para 84(1) must be in Form 2.35B and have attached to it a final progress report compliant with r 2.110. Any notice given to the Registrar of Companies under para 84(8) must be in Form 2.36B.

Penalties—See s 430, Sch 10 and the daily default fine in para 106(o).

85 Discharge of administration order where administration ends

(1) This paragraph applies where—

(a)   the court makes an order under this Schedule providing for the appointment of an administrator of a company to cease to have effect, and

(b)   the administrator was appointed by administration order.

(2) The court shall discharge the administration order.

General note—This provision applies only to cases in which an administration order is made and should be read in conjunction with para 79(1), (3) and (4) and the notes thereto. Discharge under para 85 equates to discharge of an administration order under the former s 18(1). Discharge now follows mandatorily from an order under para 79(1). The cessation of an administrator's term of office as administrator does not, however, automatically release him from liability, which remains subject to para 98(2).

86 Notice to Companies Registrar where administration ends

(1) This paragraph applies where the court makes an order under this Schedule providing for the appointment of an administrator to cease to have effect.

(2) The administrator shall send a copy of the order to the registrar of companies within the period of 14 days beginning with the date of the order.

(3) An administrator who fails without reasonable excuse to comply with sub-paragraph (2) commits an offence.

General note—This is an administrative provision which applies in all cases where the court makes an order under Sch B1 terminating the appointment of an administrator, a class of cases not necessarily limited to those in which an administration order is made by the court. Paragraph 86 will therefore apply to paras 79(1), 81(1), 82(3) and 83(6) and any order made under any other provision in Sch B1 by which the appointment of an administrator ceases to have effect, but the wording in para 86(1) makes clear that the provision will not apply to any such order made under any provision other than those in Sch B1.

Procedure—See r 2.116. The Registrar of Companies is notified in Form 2.33B, to which a copy of the court order and a copy of the administrator's final progress report under r 2.110 must be attached.

Penalties—See s 430, Sch 10 and the daily default fine in para 106(2)(p).

REPLACING ADMINISTRATOR

87 Resignation of administrator

(1) An administrator may resign only in prescribed circumstances.

(2) Where an administrator may resign he may do so only—

(a)   in the case of an administrator appointed by administration order, by notice in writing to the court,

(b)   in the case of an administrator appointed under paragraph 14, by notice in writing to the holder of the floating charge by virtue of which the appointment was made,

(c) in the case of an administrator appointed under paragraph 22(1), by notice in writing to the company, or

(d) in the case of an administrator appointed under paragraph 22(2), by notice in writing to the directors of the company.

General note—This provision should be read in conjunction with paras 90–95 which deal with the appointment of a new administrator where there is a vacancy in office. The 'prescribed circumstances' referred to in para 87(1) are those listed in IR 1986, r 2.119(1), being that the administrator may resign on grounds of ill health or because he intends ceasing to be in practice as an insolvency practitioner or there is some conflict of interest, or change of personal circumstances, which precludes or makes impracticable the further discharge by the administrator of his duties as such. In *Re Alt Landscapes Ltd* [1999] BPIR 459 at 461D–461H Lloyd J, as he then was, held that the term 'impracticable', in the context of the analogous r 6.126(3) in bankruptcy, connoted something more than inexpedient and undesirable and came to something not far short of impossible. An administrator may also resign on grounds other than those just mentioned, but only with the permission of the court under r 2.119(2).

In any case where an administrator may resign he may do so only subject to compliance with the giving of notice in writing in the circumstances prescribed in para 87(2).

Paragraph 1(2)(b) provides that a company does not cease to be in administration merely because an administrator vacates or is removed from office without being replaced. As a matter of professional conduct an outgoing administrator should satisfy himself as to arrangements for his replacement before vacating office.

Procedure—In addition to the above, an administrator is also subject to the formalities in r 2.120 (notice of intention to resign), which must be in Form 2.37B, and r 2.121 (notice of resignation), which must be in Form 2.38B.

The duties of an administrator on vacating office appear in r 2.129.

Costs—The fact that an application is rendered otiose by an administrator making an application for his appointment to cease and for a winding-up order does not prevent the court from ordering the costs of the application against the administrator if the circumstances justify: *Coyne v DRC Distribution Ltd* [2008] BCC 612 (Ward, Jacob and Rimer LJJ: costs order by judge justified where the creditor made para 81 application following administrator's failure to take steps to recover assets transferred away pre-administration).

88 Removal of administrator from office

The court may by order remove an administrator from office.

General note—Paragraph 88 should be read in conjunction with paras 90–95. Although the provision imposes no requirement for removal of an administrator by the court from office being conditional on 'cause shown', as is expressly provided for in s 108(2) and implied, on the authorities, into s 172(2) in liquidation. In *SISU Capital Fund Ltd v Tucker* [2006] BPIR 154 at [88] Warren J considered that, like Nourse LJ addressing s 172(2) in *Re Edennote Ltd* [1996] 2 BCLC 389 at 397H–397I and 398F, 'it is not easy to think of any circumstances (that is to say, I cannot at present think of any circumstances) in which the court would remove a liquidator under para 88 [*Editorial Note:* presumably, his Lordship intended to refer to an administrator] without cause being shown'.

In *Clydesdale Financial Services Ltd v Smailes* [2009] EWHC 1745 (Ch), [2009] BCC 810, David Richards J granted an application to remove the administrators of an insolvent solicitors' practice where they and their firm had been so closely involved in negotiations for the sale of the firm's business immediately prior to their appointment that they could not be expected to conduct an independent review of the transaction. It was noted that on such application, the court will have regard to, but will certainly not be bound by, the wishes of the majority of creditors.

Where an application to remove an office-holder is forced by that office-holder's refusal to resign voluntarily where the circumstances would justify such resignation, the court may make a costs order of the application against the outgoing office-holder on the indemnity basis: *Shepheard v Lamey* [2001] BPIR 939 (Jacob J, as he then was, a liquidation case).

In *Re St Georges Property Services (London) Ltd, Finnerty v Clark* [2010] EWHC 2538 (Ch), [2011] BPIR 242 the two shareholders of a company (who were also substantial unsecured creditors) applied under para 88 for the removal of administrators who were unwilling to seek to challenge the default rate of interest charged by the company's secured lenders pursuant to s 244 as an extortionate credit transaction. The Chancellor held that if an administrator is unbiased and entitled on the material before him to reach a relevant conclusion his decision should be respected unless and until the court concludes otherwise. The fact that another mind might reach a different conclusion may be a reason to challenge the administrator's decision but cannot be a good reason to remove him altogether. The decision was upheld by the Court of Appeal ([2011] EWCA Civ 858, [2011] BPIR 1514).

On block transfer orders see para 1.6 of the *Practice Direction: Insolvency Proceedings* and Form PDIP4 (multiple appointments of office-holders).

A company continues to be in administration notwithstanding the removal from office of an administrator: see para 1(2)(d).

Eligible applicants—No provision is made for the class of persons eligible to make an application under para 88. Other than in a block transfer-type case, where the applicant and respondent are, very commonly, partners or co-office-holders with the outgoing individual, the court will, it is submitted, require an applicant to establish a genuine and legitimate interest in the discontinuance of the administrator's term of office. In an ordinary case this will not extend to a creditor with no prospect of receiving a distribution in the administration or any subsequent liquidation or a third party seeking to interfere in the administration for personal reasons: *Deloitte & Touche AG v Johnson* [2000] 1 BCLC 485, PC.

Procedure—See IR 1986, r 2.122 which prescribes Form 2.39B for the giving of notice of an order removing an administrator to the Registrar of Companies.

The duties of an administrator on vacating office appear in r 2.129.

Costs—The fact that an application is rendered otiose by an administrator making an application for his appointment to cease and for a winding-up order does not prevent the court from ordering the costs of the application against the administrator if the circumstances justify: *Coyne v DRC Distribution Ltd* [2008] BCC 612 (Ward, Jacob and Rimer LJJ: costs order by judge justified where the creditor made para 81 application following administrator's failure to take steps to recover assets transferred away pre-administration.

89 Administrator ceasing to be qualified

(1) The administrator of a company shall vacate office if he ceases to be qualified to act as an insolvency practitioner in relation to the company.

(2) Where an administrator vacates office by virtue of sub-paragraph (1) he shall give notice in writing—

    (a) in the case of an administrator appointed by administration order, to the court,

    (b) in the case of an administrator appointed under paragraph 14, to the holder of the floating charge by virtue of which the appointment was made,

    (c) in the case of an administrator appointed under paragraph 22(1), to the company, or

(d) in the case of an administrator appointed under paragraph 22(2), to the directors of the company.

(3) An administrator who fails without reasonable excuse to comply with
sub-paragraph (2) commits an offence.

General note—The vacation of office under para 89(1) is automatic and requires no further
action such that there is no requirement for an application under para 88(1): *Re Stella
Metals Ltd* [1997] BCC 626 (Knox J).

Procedure—In addition to para 89(2) see IR 1986, r 2.123 which requires notice of vacation
of office to be given to the Registrar of Companies in Form 2.39B.

Penalties—See s 430, Sch 10 and the daily default fine in para 106(2)(q).

90 Supplying vacancy in office of administrator

Paragraphs 91 to 95 apply where an administrator—

(a) dies,
(b) resigns,
(c) is removed from office under paragraph 88, or
(d) vacates office under paragraph 89.

General note—Paragraphs 91–95 apply only to the filling of a vacancy in office which arises
in any of the four circumstances identified therein. Paragraphs 96 and 97, on the other hand,
allow for the substitution of a replacement administrator in the circumstances prescribed
therein. Paragraphs 100–103 allow for the appointment of an additional administrator or
administrators and the joint and concurrent status of appointees.

As a general rule, the approach taken in paras 91–95 is to confer on the person responsible
for the administrator's appointment primary responsibility for his replacement subject, in
the cases of paras 93 and 94, to the prior rights of a qualifying floating charge holder in the
case of an out-of-court appointment and, in the cases covered by paras 93–95, any order of
the court.

Procedure—See rr 2.125 and 2.128. An application to appoint a replacement administrator
must be accompanied by a written statement in Form 2.2B which confirms the consent of
that person so to act. Notice of the appointment of a replacement or additional
administrator to the Registrar of Companies must be in Form 2.40B. For the procedure on
block transfer orders see also para 1.6 of the *Practice Direction: Insolvency Proceedings* and
Form PDIP4.

91

(1) Where the administrator was appointed by administration order, the
court may replace the administrator on an application under this
sub-paragraph made by—

(a) a creditors' committee of the company,
(b) the company,
(c) the directors of the company,
(d) one or more creditors of the company, or
(e) where more than one person was appointed to act jointly or
concurrently as the administrator, any of those persons who
remains in office.

(2) But an application may be made in reliance on sub-paragraph (1)(b) to (d) only where—

    (a)   there is no creditors' committee of the company,

    (b)   the court is satisfied that the creditors' committee or a remaining administrator is not taking reasonable steps to make a replacement, or

    (c)   the court is satisfied that for another reason it is right for the application to be made.

General note—This provision only applies where the administrator was appointed by court order. An application may only be made by any of those persons listed in paras 91(1)(b)–(d) where any of the three circumstances in para 91(2) arise. Paragraphs 91(2)(b) or (c) might apply where the court can be provided with credible evidence that a creditors' committee is dilatory in replacing a sole appointee or where a remaining administrator is guilty of such conduct in replacing an outgoing co-appointee subject, in the latter case, to the court being satisfied that the appointment of a replacement co-appointee is appropriate.

In contrast to paras 92–94 cases, para 95 does not provide a fall back position to those persons listed in para 91(1) in a para 91 case, since para 95 applies only to out-of-court appointment cases under paras 92–94, whereas para 91 is concerned only with cases where an administrator is appointed by court order.

Applications by an outgoing administrator or his partners—Paragraph 91(1)(e) is insufficiently broad in scope to catch an outgoing administrator. Neither will that provision extend to an outgoing administrator's partners save to the extent that any such partner remains in office as co-administrator. Whilst it must be doubtful that the reference in para 1.6(3)(i) of the *Practice Direction: Insolvency Proceedings* to an outgoing office-holder having standing to make an application for a transfer is capable of overriding the limited scope of para 91(1), applications by outgoing office-holders do arise in practice, invariably in non-contentious cases. The court could in any case regard an application by an outgoing administrator as being made under para 63 which, it is submitted, is sufficiently broad so as to allow for the appointment of a replacement administrator, but only where the application by the outgoing office-holder was made prior to the termination of his office as such.

Procedure—See the note on procedure in para 90. For block transfer cases see *Re A & C Supplies Ltd* [1998] 1 BCLC 603 (Blackburne J), *Re Equity Nominees Ltd* [2000] BCC 84 (Neuberger J, as he then was); *HM Customs & Excise v Allen* [2003] BPIR 830; and the commentary on such orders under the heading 'resign' to s 172.

92

Where the administrator was appointed under paragraph 14 the holder of the floating charge by virtue of which the appointment was made may replace the administrator.

General note—This provision is only exercisable in the circumstances listed in para 90. No limitation is imposed on the holder of the floating charge by virtue of which the appointment was made in effecting the appointment of a replacement. Neither is there any bar to the replacement being effected by an assignee of the floating charge pursuant to which the original appointment was made. Given the breadth of the provision and the commercial self-interest in the holder of a floating charge effecting a replacement speedily, it is very difficult to envisage circumstances in which the court might engage its power under para 95(b).

Procedure—See the note on procedure to para 90 and see r 2.133(5). No form for the appointment of a replacement administrator is prescribed.

93

(1) Where the administrator was appointed under paragraph 22(1) by the company it may replace the administrator.

(2) A replacement under this paragraph may be made only—

    (a)   with the consent of each person who is the holder of a qualifying floating charge in respect of the company's property, or

    (b)   where consent is withheld, with the permission of the court.

General note—Paragraph 93 can only operate in the circumstances listed in para 90. In such circumstances a company has an unfettered power in replacing a vacancy in office subject to the consent of any person who is a holder of a qualifying floating charge, as defined in para 14. Even where such consent is withheld, the court has power under para 93(2)(b) to give permission for the company's proposed replacement. It is submitted that the court will grant such permission where the consent of any holder of a qualifying floating charge is, objectively construed, unreasonably withheld in the circumstances of the case.

Procedure—See the note on procedure to para 90 and see IR 1986, r 2.133(5). No form for the appointment of a replacement administrator is prescribed.

The court is unlikely to consider an application where the relevant charge holder or holders have not been served with the application.

94

(1) Where the administrator was appointed under paragraph 22(2) the directors of the company may replace the administrator.

(2) A replacement under this paragraph may be made only—

    (a)   with the consent of each person who is the holder of a qualifying floating charge in respect of the company's property, or

    (b)   where consent is withheld, with the permission of the court.

General note—The commentary to para 93 above is equally applicable where the outgoing administrator was appointed by the directors of the company under para 22.

95

The court may replace an administrator on the application of a person listed in paragraph 91(1) if the court—

    (a)   is satisfied that a person who is entitled to replace the administrator under any of paragraphs 92 to 94 is not taking reasonable steps to make a replacement, or

    (b)   that for another reason it is right for the court to make the replacement.

General note—The power of the court is only exercisable in cases under paras 92–94, although eligible applicants are defined by reference to those persons listed in para 91(1) to which para 95 is otherwise inapplicable.

The provision will only operate where a vacancy in office arises in those circumstances listed in para 90 and is most likely to be of practical use where either the person entitled to appoint a replacement under the relevant provision is dilatory in making an appointment (as in para 95(a)) or proposes or appoints a replacement who is manifestly unsuitable to act in the best interests of the administrator (as in para 95(b)).

Procedure—See IR 1986, rr 2.125–2.129 and the notes on procedure to paras 90–94.

96 Substitution of administrator: competing floating charge-holder

(1) This paragraph applies where an administrator of a company is appointed under paragraph 14 by the holder of a qualifying floating charge in respect of the company's property.

(2) The holder of a prior qualifying floating charge in respect of the company's property may apply to the court for the administrator to be replaced by an administrator nominated by the holder of the prior floating charge.

(3) One floating charge is prior to another for the purposes of this paragraph if—

    (a)   it was created first, or

    (b)   it is to be treated as having priority in accordance with an agreement to which the holder of each floating charge was party.

(4) Sub-paragraph (3) shall have effect in relation to Scotland as if the following were substituted for paragraph (a)—

    '(a)   it has priority of ranking in accordance with section 464(4)(b) of the Companies Act 1985,'.

General note—This provision is not concerned with a replacement in office where a vacancy arises, as in the circumstances listed in para 90, but allows for the holder of a prior ranking qualifying floating charge, as defined in para 96(3), to apply to the court to replace an administrator appointed by the holder of a junior ranking floating charge.

The approach of the court to a para 96 application—It is submitted that the court should adopt a two-stage approach to a para 96 application. First, the court will be concerned with the enforceability of the prior ranking qualifying floating charge under paras 14, 16 and 17, on which see the notes thereto. The question of enforceability should be assessed as at the time of the application, since nothing in para 96(2) suggests that the prior ranking charge need have been enforceable at the time of the original appointment under the junior ranking security. If satisfied as to enforceability the court should then go on to consider the merits of the application. Despite the prior ranking of the applicant's security, the court may require some persuasion in acceding to a substitution where the prior ranking charge holder was given notice of the earlier appointment and consented to it in writing under para 15, the more so where the substitution would lead to the administration bearing an additional and avoidable level of expense and delay where the conduct of the administration has been progressed in some real way. At the other extreme, the court is likely to have considerable sympathy with an application made at a very early stage where it can be evidenced that the prior ranking charge holder was not given notice under para 15 and reacted expeditiously on becoming aware of the position.

Procedure—See rr 2.125–2.129 and the general commentary on procedure to paras 90–95.

97 Substitution of administrator appointed by company or directors: creditors' meeting

(1) This paragraph applies where—

- (a) an administrator of a company is appointed by a company or directors under paragraph 22, and
- (b) there is no holder of a qualifying floating charge in respect of the company's property.

(2) A creditors' meeting may replace the administrator.

(3) A creditors' meeting may act under sub-paragraph (2) only if the new administrator's written consent to act is presented to the meeting before the replacement is made.

General note—As with para 96, this provision is concerned with the substitution of an administrator for another in the prescribed circumstances, and not with the filling of a vacancy arising under the circumstances listed in para 90. In contrast to para 96, however, para 97 does not involve the court and allows a creditors' meeting to substitute its choice of administrator for one appointed by a company or its directors under para 22, but only where there is no holder of a qualifying floating charge as defined in para 14. The standing of the creditors' meeting to replace the company or directors' choice of administrator is unqualified and reflects the priority status afforded to the wishes of creditors by the provisions, irrespective of the bona fide status and intentions of the incumbent administrator and his appointor.

Procedure—See rr 2.125–2.129 and the general commentary on procedure in the notes to paras 90–95.

98 Vacation of office: discharge from liability

(1) Where a person ceases to be the administrator of a company (whether because he vacates office by reason of resignation, death or otherwise, because he is removed from office or because his appointment ceases to have effect) he is discharged from liability in respect of any action of his as administrator.

(2) The discharge provided by sub-paragraph (1) takes effect—

- (a) in the case of an administrator who dies, on the filing with the court of notice of his death,
- (b) in the case of an administrator appointed under paragraph 14 or 22, at a time appointed by resolution of the creditors' committee or, if there is no committee, by resolution of the creditors, or
- (c) in any case, at a time specified by the court.

(3) For the purpose of the application of sub-paragraph (2)(b) in a case where the administrator has made a statement under paragraph 52(1)(b), a resolution shall be taken as passed if (and only if) passed with the approval of—

- (a) each secured creditor of the company, or
- (b) if the administrator has made a distribution to preferential creditors or thinks that a distribution may be made to preferential creditors—
  - (i) each secured creditor of the company, and
  - (ii) preferential creditors whose debts amount to more than

50% of the preferential debts of the company, disregarding debts of any creditor who does not respond to an
invitation to give or withhold approval.

(4) Discharge—

(a) applies to liability accrued before the discharge takes effect, and
(b) does not prevent the exercise of the court's powers under
paragraph 75.

General note—Broadly speaking, para 98 finds its former equivalent in s 20. The former
provision provided for the 'release' of an administrator, a term which meant, by virtue of
s 20(2) and (3), that a former administrator was thereafter discharged from all liability both
in respect of his acts or omissions in the administration and otherwise in relation to his
conduct as administrator save to the extent of any order of the court under s 212 in
misfeasance proceedings. There is an avoidable confusion in para 98 referring not to release
but to 'discharge', given that the draftsman has also employed the term 'discharge' in
relation to the wholly different matter of the discharge of an administration order under
para 85. It is also clear from Sch B1 that a discharge from liability under para 98 is
something quite distinct from the appointment of an administrator ceasing to have effect
under paras 76, 79–81, 83 or 84 or the provisions on replacement, disqualification or
substitution under paras 87–97. A cessation in office will, of itself, do nothing to discharge
an administrator from personal liability from what is termed in para 98(1) 'any action of his
as administrator', a phrase which will also extend to inaction by virtue of para 111(3).

The time for discharge under para 98(2)—Paragraph 98(2)(a) is self-explanatory. In a para 14
or para 22 case, then, unless a resolution can be obtained from any creditors' committee or
the creditors – subject to the strict requirements of para 98(3) in a para 52(1)(b) case – it will
be necessary to obtain discharge by order of the court under para 98(2)(c). Discharge from
liability is only available from the court under that provision in an administration order case.

The words 'in any case' in para 98(2)(c) indicate that the jurisdiction of the court arises in
all administrations in providing for the time at which discharge takes effect or, perhaps more
importantly, in preventing discharge as it would otherwise arise under para 98(2)(a) or (b),
most obviously where a creditor or creditors object to such discharge by making an
application to the court. Thus, as under the former s 20, the court is empowered to suspend
discharge for a sufficient period as to allow for an appropriate level of investigation into the
conduct of an administrator against whom legitimate complaint is raised, or even to allow
for the institution of proceedings against an administrator, although in the latter case the
court will no doubt wish to take into account the new provision in para 98(4)(a), which finds
no counterpart in s 20, and which preserves any pre-discharge liability in any case. Although
decisions such as that of Edward Evans-Lombe QC, sitting as he then was as a Deputy High
Court judge, in *Re Exchange Travel (Holdings) Ltd* [1992] BCC 954 (in which release was
suspended for three months so as to allow for investigation of the administrator's conduct)
provide an example of the exercise of the court's discretion, each case will ultimately rest on
its own facts and the court's perception of the level of compulsion, as opposed to genuine
but misplaced sense of grievance, in a complainant's case.

The scope of the administrator's discharge—As noted above, para 98(4) is new and leaves
pre-discharge liability unaffected by the operation of para 98(2). Neither does discharge
affect any power exercised by the court in misfeasance proceedings under para 75. Although
para 75, like s 212, is procedural in the sense that those provisions provide a convenient and
workable procedural gateway for substantive claims against office-holders, it is plain enough
from the reference in para 98(4)(b) to 'the exercise of the court's powers' that discharge does
not exonerate a former administrator from liability arising on an order of the court which is
itself only capable of being made on a *substantive* cause of action.

99 Vacation of office: charges and liabilities

(1) This paragraph applies where a person ceases to be the administrator of
a company (whether because he vacates office by reason of resignation,
death or otherwise, because he is removed from office or because his
appointment ceases to have effect).

(2) In this paragraph—

'the former administrator' means the person referred to in sub-paragraph (1), and
'cessation' means the time when he ceases to be the company's administrator.

(3) The former administrator's remuneration and expenses shall be—

(a) charged on and payable out of property of which he had custody or control immediately before cessation, and
(b) payable in priority to any security to which paragraph 70 applies.

(4) A sum payable in respect of a debt or liability arising out of a contract entered into by the former administrator or a predecessor before cessation shall be—

(a) charged on and payable out of property of which the former administrator had custody or control immediately before cessation, and
(b) payable in priority to any charge arising under sub-paragraph (3).

(5) Sub-paragraph (4) shall apply to a liability arising under a contract of employment which was adopted by the former administrator or a predecessor before cessation; and for that purpose—

(a) action taken within the period of 14 days after an administrator's appointment shall not be taken to amount or contribute to the adoption of a contract,
(b) no account shall be taken of a liability which arises, or in so far as it arises, by reference to anything which is done or which occurs before the adoption of the contract of employment, and
(c) no account shall be taken of a liability to make a payment other than wages or salary.

(6) In sub-paragraph (5)(c) 'wages or salary' includes—

(a) a sum payable in respect of a period of holiday (for which purpose the sum shall be treated as relating to the period by reference to which the entitlement to holiday accrued),
(b) a sum payable in respect of a period of absence through illness or other good cause,
(c) a sum payable in lieu of holiday,
(d) in respect of a period, a sum which would be treated as earnings for that period for the purposes of an enactment about social security, and
(e) a contribution to an occupational pension scheme.

General note—The scheme of this provision is similar in substance to the former s 19. Although s 19 was frequently referred to as creating a statutory charge in favour of an administrator, the former provision, as now with para 99(3) and (4), actually envisaged two specific statutory charges, each in favour of what is termed 'the former administrator', of which that in para 99(4) takes priority over that under para 99(3). The scope of those charges is considered below. Furthermore, whilst the heading to para 99 and the use of the term 'the former administrator' might suggest that the remuneration and expenses and sums payable under para 99(3) and (4) respectively are only payable on an administrator vacating office so as to trigger the creation of the statutory charges therein, it was held under s 19, and, it is submitted, remains the case under para 99, that those items are payable in the course of an administration such that the statutory charges only trigger so as to secure any such sums which remain outstanding on an administrator vacating office. This point is also considered below.

The circumstances in which para 99 operates—In addition to any of those circumstances in which an administrator vacates office under paras 87–89 or 91–97, para 99 will also apply where the appointment of an administrator ceases to have effect under paras 79–81 or 83 or 84. The operative parts of the provision are in para 99(3) and (4), which apply automatically on a person ceasing to be the administrator of a company.

Paragraph 99(3)

Scope of the charge—Paragraph 99(3) very closely resembles the former s 19(4). The term 'remuneration' refers to that remuneration to which an administrator is properly entitled under rr 2.106–2.108. Although r 2.67(1) lays down an order of priority in respect of the expenses of an administration, that provision, which found no counterpart under the former Part II, is useful here in that it appears to incorporate all those classes of costs, disbursements, allowances etc which are each individually capable of amounting to 'expenses'. As regards the payment and remuneration of such expenses, Blackburne J observed in *Re Salmet International Ltd* [2001] BCC 796 at 803B–803D, in relation to the analogous s 19(4) and by reference to an extract from the judgment of Dillon LJ in *Re Paramount Airways Ltd (No 3), Powdrill v Watson* [1994] BCC 172 at 180G–180H, noted below, that:

'... the sub-section is not to be understood as empowering the administrator to draw his remuneration and discharge any expenses properly incurred by him only at the time he ceases to be administrator. The sub-section does not prohibit payment of remuneration or expenses during the course of the administration. Many an administration would be quite impossible if expenses could only be discharged out of the company's property at the time that the administrator ceases to act. In my view, its purpose is to make clear that when the administrator leaves office he will be entitled to deduct his (undrawn) remuneration and pay any expenses properly incurred by him (but not hitherto provided for) out of any property of the company in his custody or under his control in priority to the floating charge holder's rights. It is necessary so to provide because a person may cease to be an administrator before his remuneration has been drawn and any expenses properly incurred by him have been paid.'

It is submitted that precisely the same analysis as above will apply to para 99(3).

The reference to para 70 in para 99(3)(b) is to a floating charge, as defined in para 111(1).

The statutory charge created under para 99(3) is subject to any charge under para 99(4), an order of priority which is incapable of variation given the unqualified words relating to payment pursuant to such security in para 99(4)(b). As regards payment of any debt or liability otherwise secured by the para 99(4) charge, Dillon LJ observed in *Powdrill v Watson* (see above) in connection with the former but analogous s 19(5) that:

'Although strictly sums payable are, under s 19(5), only payable when the administrator vacates office, it is well understood that administrators will, in the ordinary way, pay expenses of the administration including salaries and other payments to employees as they arise during the continuance of the administration. There is no need to wait until the end, and it would be impossible as a practical matter to do that. What is picked up at the end are those matters which fall within the phrase, but have not been paid.'

Given the resemblance between these provisions it is again submitted that the above reasoning will continue to apply in relation to para 99(4).

The fact that an administrator has the benefit of security under para 99(3) does not preclude the administrator from presenting a petition for winding-up: *Re Lafayette Electronics Europe Ltd* [2007] BCC 890 (HHJ Norris QC, sitting as a judge of the High Court).

The operation of the charge created by para 99(3), subject to that provided for in para 99(4), survives liquidation and the handing over of assets to a liquidator: *Re Sheridan Securities Ltd* (1988) 4 BCC 200 at 203 (Mervyn Davies J).

Paragraph 99(4)

Scope of the charge—Paragraph 99(4) applies to contracts entered into by 'the former administrator', or his predecessor, and extends to any contract of employment adopted by such an office-holder, as qualified in para 99(5) and (6). The term 'adopted' here should be understood by reference to the commentary to s 44 on administrative receivership, which applies equally to an administrator.

Where administrators had incurred liabilities caught by para 99(4), had made part-payment of those liabilities and had subsequently been replaced, those part-payments did not form part of the company's estate and were not to be taken into account for the purposes of pari passu distribution as between all creditors entitled to the benefit of the para 99(4) charge; in addition, the new administrators were also entitled to a reasonable sum in respect of their costs of administering that fund on the basis of *Re Berkeley Applegate (Investment Consultants) Ltd* (1988) 4 BCC 279: *Re Sports Betting Media Ltd (in administration)* [2008] BCC 177 (Briggs J).

Whether a debt or liability 'arises out of a contract' is fact specific: see, for example, *Centre Reinsurance International Co v Freakley* [2006] UKHL 45, [2007] 1 BCLC 85 (claims-handling expenses not liabilities within the meaning of the former but analogous s 19(5)).

In *Re Nortel Companies* [2013] UKSC 52, the Supreme Court held that a financial support direction issued by the Pensions Regulator to a company after it had entered insolvent administration was to be treated as a provable debt and would rank pari passu with other unsecured debts.

Paragraph 99(5) and (6)

'Wages or salary', protective awards, payments in lieu and redundancy payments—A protective award does not fall within the ambit of para 99(6)(d) and is therefore outside of the scope of para 99(5)(c) and the super-priority status conferred by para 99(5); likewise, payments in lieu, as categorised by Lord Browne-Wilkinson in *Delaney v Staples* [1992] 1 AC 687 at 692D–692H, do not fall within para 99(5): *Re Huddersfield Fine Worsteds Ltd* [2005] EWCA Civ 1072, [2005] BCC 916 (Neuberger, Clarke and Jacob LJJ), reversing a decision of Peter Smith J and affirming a decision of Etherton J below to the effect that 'wages or salary' are conferred a 'super priority' status as part of the rescue culture encouraged by the new administration regime. That decision confirms the position as it was understood to be prior to the implementation of Sch B1. In *Re Allders Department Stores Ltd* [2005] EWHC 172 (Ch), [2005] BCC 289 Lawrence Collins J (as he then was) held that both statutory redundancy payments and claims for unfair dismissal were each outside of the scope of para 99(5). Neither were such payments within the scope of necessary disbursements under r 2.67(1)(f). This decision also reflects the pre-Sch B1 position as it was understood in practice. In *Re Leeds United Association Football Club Ltd (in administration)* [2008] BCC 11 Pumfrey J again identified that the words 'wages or salary' in paras 99(5) and (6) were to be attributed their normal meaning (in accordance with *Delaney v Staples*) as consideration for work done or to be done under a contract of employment. Accordingly, following the decision in *Huddersfield Fine Worsteds*, a payment by an employer for wrongful dismissal following termination by the employer in respect of a period following termination was not a payment of wages since the employee was not under an obligation to render services during that period. An administrator could therefore adopt a contract of employment but subsequently dismiss the employee without the damages payable as a consequence of the dismissal ranking as 'wages or salary'. Following the decision in *Allders Department Stores*, with which David Richards J had also agreed in *Exeter City Council v Bairstow* [2007] BCC 236 at [77], Pumfrey J further rejected a submission that liabilities for wrongful dismissal could rank as necessary disbursements for the purposes of r 2.67(1)(f).

GENERAL

100 Joint and concurrent administrators

(1) In this Schedule—

(a)　a reference to the appointment of an administrator of a company includes a reference to the appointment of a number of persons to act jointly or concurrently as the administrator of a company, and

(b)　a reference to the appointment of a person as administrator of a company includes a reference to the appointment of a person as one of a number of persons to act jointly or concurrently as the administrator of a company.

(2) The appointment of a number of persons to act as administrator of a company must specify—

(a)　which functions (if any) are to be exercised by the persons appointed acting jointly, and

(b)　which functions (if any) are to be exercised by any or all of the persons appointed.

General note—This provision is cast more elaborately than s 231 which governed joint appointments under Part II. Paragraph 100(1) sets up para 100(2) by providing a default rule that the reference to the appointment of any two or more persons as administrators of a company is to be taken as meaning that any or all may act jointly or concurrently as administrator. Paragraph 100(2) then requires the appointment to specify which functions (if any) are to be exercised by the appointees acting jointly and those to be exercised by any or all (which might include some but not all) of those persons. The practical implication of para 100(2) is the requirement for a statement of the position, be it in an administration order or a statement attached to a notice of appointment.

Paragraphs 101 and 102 provide further and rather lengthy definitions and dealing provisions on joint and concurrent appointments. Paragraph 103 governs the procedure on the appointment of an additional office-holder following administration, subject to the overriding consent of the person or persons then acting: see para 103(6).

On the notice and advertisement of joint appointments see IR 1986, rr 2.127 and 128.

101

(1) This paragraph applies where two or more persons are appointed to act jointly as the administrator of a company.

(2) A reference to the administrator of the company is a reference to those persons acting jointly.

(3) But a reference to the administrator of a company in paragraphs 87 to 99 of this Schedule is a reference to any or all of the persons appointed to act jointly.

(4) Where an offence of omission is committed by the administrator, each of the persons appointed to act jointly—

(a)　commits the offence, and

(b)　may be proceeded against and punished individually.

(5) The reference in paragraph 45(1)(a) to the name of the administrator is a reference to the name of each of the persons appointed to act jointly.

(6) Where persons are appointed to act jointly in respect of only some of the functions of the administrator of a company, this paragraph applies only in relation to those functions.

102

(1) This paragraph applies where two or more persons are appointed to act concurrently as the administrator of a company.

(2) A reference to the administrator of a company in this Schedule is a reference to any of the persons appointed (or any combination of them).

103

(1) Where a company is in administration, a person may be appointed to act as administrator jointly or concurrently with the person or persons acting as the administrator of the company.

(2) Where a company entered administration by administration order, an appointment under sub-paragraph (1) must be made by the court on the application of—

    (a)   a person or group listed in paragraph 12(1)(a) to (e), or
    (b)   the person or persons acting as the administrator of the company.

(3) Where a company entered administration by virtue of an appointment under paragraph 14, an appointment under sub-paragraph (1) must be made by—

    (a)   the holder of the floating charge by virtue of which the appointment was made, or
    (b)   the court on the application of the person or persons acting as the administrator of the company.

(4) Where a company entered administration by virtue of an appointment under paragraph 22(1), an appointment under sub-paragraph (1) above must be made either by the court on the application of the person or persons acting as the administrator of the company or—

    (a)   by the company, and
    (b)   with the consent of each person who is the holder of a qualifying floating charge in respect of the company's property or, where consent is withheld, with the permission of the court.

(5) Where a company entered administration by virtue of an appointment under paragraph 22(2), an appointment under sub-paragraph (1) must be made either by the court on the application of the person or persons acting as the administrator of the company or—

    (a)   by the directors of the company, and
    (b)   with the consent of each person who is the holder of a qualifying floating charge in respect of the company's property or, where consent is withheld, with the permission of the court.

(6) An appointment under sub-paragraph (1) may be made only with the consent of the person or persons acting as the administrator of the company.

General note—Although the former legislation included no express power to appoint an additional administrator, the court had been prepared to make such an appointment on the basis of its inherent jurisdiction: see, for example, *Clements v Udal* [2002] 2 BCLC 606 (Neuberger J, as he then was). The power to appoint an additional administrator is now put in express terms.

For commentary on each of the circumstances in para 103(2)–(5) see the commentary to paras 91, 96 and 97.

104 Presumption of validity

An act of the administrator of a company is valid in spite of a defect in his appointment or qualification.

General note—Although the reference to an administrator in s 232 was removed by para 21 of Sch 17 to the Enterprise Act 2002 in anticipation of the implementation of Sch B1, the substance of para 104 remains as under the previous provision, on which see the notes thereto.

Defective Administration Appointments—In *Re Blights Builders* [2008] 1 BCLC 245, administrators were (invalidly) appointed under para 22 when there was an extant winding up petition against the company. HHJ Norris QC (as he then was) held that the appointment was incapable of cure under IR 1986, r 7.55 (at the time of the hearing, the decision of Hart J in *Re G-Tech Construction Limited* [2007] BPIR 1275, in which it was held that the court had the power to make a retrospective administration order, had not been reported). Accordingly, he made a fresh administration order and declared that pursuant to para 104, their acts as joint administrators were to be treated as valid in spite of the defect in their appointment.

However, in *Re Kaupthing Capital Partners II Master LP Inc (in administration); Pillar Securitisation SARL v Spicer* [2010] EWHC 836 (Ch), [2011] BCC 338, Proudman J held that the use of the wrong prescribed form (Form 2.10B instead of Form 1B) was a fundamental flaw going to the validity of the appointment itself and was not capable of cure under para 104.

In *Re Care Matters Partnership Ltd* [2011] BCC 957, Norris J, in considering whether or not the actions of an administrator could be validated under para 104 distinguished between cases where there was simply no power to appoint because, for example, there was no valid charge in respect of which the power under para 14 could be exercised, or the persons purporting to appoint an administrator under para 22 were not directors at all, and a case where there is power to make an appointment but the power has been defectively exercised through some irregularity in procedure. He ruled that in the latter case para 104 was available.

105 Majority decision of directors

A reference in this Schedule to something done by the directors of a company includes a reference to the same thing done by a majority of the directors of a company.

General note—This provision is of significant practical utility. Previously it was common practice to exhibit to an affidavit or witness statement in support of an administration petition a resolution of the board confirming the decision to seek an administration order and related matters. Difficulties could arise from time to time where it was impractical to convene a board meeting. All that is now required for 'something done by the directors' – being a reference to the decision of the directors – is a majority decision for which evidence – most obviously in writing – will be required without the need for a formal board meeting, unanimity amongst the directors, or even a formal board resolution. This new approach is not without its potential difficulties, however, in that the validity of a majority decision for the purposes of this provision might be capable of challenge, notwithstanding para 105, where the wishes of that majority in number are outweighed either by the express wishes of a dissenting director or directors, or directors with weighted board voting rights.

Para 105 does not apply to para 22: *Minmar (929) Ltd v Khalastchi* [2011] EWHC 1159 (Ch), [2011] BCC 485.

106 Penalties

(1) A person who is guilty of an offence under this Schedule is liable to a fine (in accordance with section 430 and Schedule 10).

(2) A person who is guilty of an offence under any of the following paragraphs of this Schedule is liable to a daily default fine (in accordance with section 430 and Schedule 10)—

    (a)   paragraph 20,
    (b)   paragraph 32,
    (c)   paragraph 46,
    (d)   paragraph 48,
    (e)   paragraph 49,
    (f)   paragraph 51,
    (g)   paragraph 53,
    (h)   paragraph 54,
    (i)   paragraph 56,
    (j)   paragraph 71,
    (k)   paragraph 72,
    (l)   paragraph 77,
    (m) paragraph 78,
    (n)   paragraph 80,
    (o)   paragraph 84,
    (p)   paragraph 86, and
    (q)   paragraph 89.

General note—The amount of any daily default fine is as provided for in Sch 10.

107 Extension of time limit

(1) Where a provision of this Schedule provides that a period may be varied in accordance with this paragraph, the period may be varied in respect of a company—

    (a)   by the court, and
    (b)   on the application of the administrator.

(2) A time period may be extended in respect of a company under this paragraph—

    (a)   more than once, and
    (b)   after expiry.

General note—The reference to any provision which 'provides that a period may be varied in accordance with this paragraph' is to para 49(8) (administrator's proposals), para 50(2) (notice of creditors' meeting) and para 51(4) (time for initial creditors' meeting). The draftsman appears to have made specific provision for the extension of the time limits within those provisions on the application of the administrator alone by reference to para 107 on account of the central procedural importance in administration of the giving of notice and convening of the creditors' meeting, default in relation to two of the provisions giving rise to potential criminal liability. That approach should not be seen as implying that other time limits within Sch B1 are of any lesser importance, only that the court may vary such other time limits as empowered under particular paragraphs or by way of consequential order.

In *Re Advent Computer Training Ltd* [2010] EWHC 459 (Ch), [2011] BCC 44, HHJ Purle QC held that the power in paras 49(8) and 107 of to vary the period can properly be construed as empowering the court to vary the period in relation to some only of the prescribed matters.

Rule 12.9 (time limits) has no application to the provisions within Sch B1 on account of being limited to the extension or variation of time limits prescribed by the Insolvency Rules (as amended).

108

(1) A period specified in paragraph 49(5), 50(1)(b) or 51(2) may be varied in respect of a company by the administrator with consent.

(2) In sub-paragraph (1) 'consent' means consent of—

    (a)   each secured creditor of the company, and

    (b)   if the company has unsecured debts, creditors whose debts amount to more than 50% of the company's unsecured debts, disregarding debts of any creditor who does not respond to an invitation to give or withhold consent.

(3) But where the administrator has made a statement under paragraph 52(1)(b) 'consent' means—

    (a)   consent of each secured creditor of the company, or

    (b)   if the administrator thinks that a distribution may be made to preferential creditors, consent of—

        (i)   each secured creditor of the company, and

        (ii)   preferential creditors whose debts amount to more than 50% of the total preferential debts of the company, disregarding debts of any creditor who does not respond to an invitation to give or withhold consent.

(4) Consent for the purposes of sub-paragraph (1) may be—

    (a)   written, or

    (b)   signified at a creditors' meeting.

(5) The power to extend under sub-paragraph (1)—

    (a)   may be exercised in respect of a period only once,

    (b)   may not be used to extend a period by more than 28 days,

    (c)   may not be used to extend a period which has been extended by the court, and

    (d)   may not be used to extend a period after expiry.

General note—The references to the periods in para 108(1) are to the eight-week period for the sending by an administrator of the statement of his proposals (para 49(5)), the 14-day period prescribed by IR 1986, r 2.35(4) for the giving of notice to every creditor of a creditors' meeting (para 50(1)(b)) and the 10-week period for the holding of the initial creditors' meeting (para 51(2)(b)).

The key point here is that the above periods may only be varied – invariably, in practice, meaning extended – by the administrator with the consent of those creditors identified in para 108(2) or, where the administrator has made a statement that the company has insufficient property to enable a distribution to be made to unsecured creditors other than by virtue of s 176A(2)(a) (prescribed part for unsecured debts), as identified in para 108(3).

By virtue of s 436B, a written conent may be by electronic communication for the purposes of para 108(1).

Paragraph 108(5) imposes relatively stringent limits on the extension of the prescribed periods. An extension is permissible only once, and then by not more than 28 days, but not where a period has already been extended by the court, even, it seems, where the court's extension was for a period of less than 28 days. Retrospective extension is not permissible.

Paragraph 108(4)(a)

'written'—For the extension of the scope of 'a thing in writing' to a thing in electronic form – most obviously e-mail – see para 111(2).

109

Where a period is extended under paragraph 107 or 108, a reference to the period shall be taken as a reference to the period as extended.

110 Amendment of provision about time

(1) The Secretary of State may by order amend a provision of this Schedule which—

    (a)   requires anything to be done within a specified period of time,

    (b)   prevents anything from being done after a specified time, or

    (c)   requires a specified minimum period of notice to be given.

(2) An order under this paragraph—

    (a)   must be made by statutory instrument, and

    (b)   shall be subject to annulment in pursuance of a resolution of either House of Parliament.

General note—To date no order has been made by the Secretary of State under this provision.

111 Interpretation

(1) In this Schedule—

'administrative receiver' has the meaning given by section 251,

'administrator' has the meaning given by paragraph 1 and, where the context requires, includes a reference to a former administrator,

'correspondence' includes correspondence by telephonic or other electronic means,

'creditors' meeting' has the meaning given by paragraph 50,

'enters administration' has the meaning given by paragraph 1,

'floating charge' means a charge which is a floating charge on its creation,

'in administration' has the meaning given by paragraph 1,

'hire-purchase agreement' includes a conditional sale agreement, a chattel leasing agreement and a retention of title agreement,

'holder of a qualifying floating charge' in respect of a company's property has the meaning given by paragraph 14,

'market value' means the amount which would be realised on a sale of property in the open market by a willing vendor,

'the purpose of administration' means an objective specified in paragraph 3, and 'unable to pay its debts' has the meaning given by section 123.

(1A) In this Schedule, 'company' means—

(a) a company registered under the Companies Act 2006 in England and Wales or Scotland,
(b) a company incorporated in an EEA State other than the United Kingdom, or
(c) a company not incorporated in an EEA State but having its centre of main interests in a member State other than Denmark.

(1B) In sub-paragraph (1A), in relation to a company, 'centre of main interests' has the same meaning as in the EC Regulation and, in the absence of proof to the contrary, is presumed to be the place of its registered office (within the meaning of that Regulation).

(3) In this Schedule a reference to action includes a reference to inaction.

Amendments—SI 2009/1941; SI 2010/18.

'company'—See para 111A and the note to EC Regulation, Art 3.

The decision in *Re The Salvage Association* [2003] BCC 504 to the effect that a company incorporated by Royal Charter may be placed into administration gave rise to some confusion as to whether the EC Regulation permitted an unincorporated entity to enter administration or a company voluntary arrangement. The effect of that decision was effectively reversed by statute with effect from 13 April 2005 by way of the Insolvency Act 1986 (Amendment) Regulations 2005 (SI 2005/879) which amends ss 1(4) and 436 and para 111 and inserts para 111A so as to provide that only companies as defined in s 735(1) of the Companies Act 1985 (now s 1(1) of the Companies Act 2006) and certain companies formed or incorporated outside the United Kingdom which may enter administration or a CVA.

In *Re Hellas Telecommunications (Luxembourg) II SCA* [2009] EWHC 3199 (Ch), [2010] BCC 295, Lewison J held that an entity that was a combination of a joint stock company and a limited partnership registered in Luxembourg, with a separate legal personality, a constitution and shareholders, was within the definition of a 'company'.

In *Re Dairy Farmers of Britain Limited* [2009] EWHC 1389 (Ch), [2010] Ch 63, Henderson J held that an industrial and provident society was not a 'company' within the meaning of para 111(1A).

Similarly, in *Pantner v Rowellian Football Social Club* [2011] EWHC 1301 (Ch), [2012] Ch 125, HHJ Behrens QC held that an unassociated football and social club was not a 'company'. Since the club's rules contained provisions for election, a management committee, subscriptions and expulsion, the club was a members' club and not an 'association' within s 220. The club had none of the usual attributes of a company and, given that it was not susceptible to compulsory winding up, there was no reason why Parliament should have intended it to be subject to the administration regime.

A Northern Irish company may no longer apply for an administration order in England and Wales: for commentary see Moss 'Jurisdiction over Northern Ireland Company – the Comi in England Heresy' (2005) 18(7) Insolv Int 107–108.

'correspondence'—This term will extend to fax or other electronic communication, most obviously e-mail.

'floating charge'—The definition of this term here has no different meaning from that in s 251. For a comparison of the nature of a floating charge over a fluctuating body of assets and a legal possessory lien created by contract over stock coupled with a right to sell and use proceeds see *Re Hamlet International plc (in administration)* [1999] 2 BCLC 506 (Mummery LJ, Chadwick and Henry LJJ agreeing).

111A Non-UK companies

A company incorporated outside the United Kingdom that has a principal place of business in Northern Ireland may not enter administration under this Schedule unless it also has a principal place of business in England and Wales or Scotland (or both in England and Wales and in Scotland).

General note—See the note under the heading 'company' to para 111 above.

112 Scotland

In the application of this Schedule to Scotland—

    (a) a reference to filing with the court is a reference to lodging in court, and

    (b) a reference to a charge is a reference to a right in security.

113

Where property in Scotland is disposed of under paragraph 70 or 71, the administrator shall grant to the disponee an appropriate document of transfer or conveyance of the property, and—

    (a) that document, or

    (b) recording, intimation or registration of that document (where recording, intimation or registration of the document is a legal requirement for completion of title to the property),

has the effect of disencumbering the property of or, as the case may be, freeing the property from, the security.

114

In Scotland, where goods in the possession of a company under a hire-purchase agreement are disposed of under paragraph 72, the disposal has the effect of extinguishing as against the disponee all rights of the owner of the goods under the agreement.

115

(1) In Scotland, the administrator of a company may make, in or towards the satisfaction of the debt secured by the floating charge, a payment to the holder of a floating charge which has attached to the property subject to the charge.

(2) In Scotland, where the administrator thinks that the company has insufficient property to enable a distribution to be made to unsecured creditors other than by virtue of section 176A(2)(a), he may file a notice to that effect with the registrar of companies.

(3) On delivery of the notice to the registrar of companies, any floating charge granted by the company shall, unless it has already so attached,

attach to the property which is subject to the charge and that attachment shall have effect as if each floating charge is a fixed security over the property to which it has attached.

116

In Scotland, the administrator in making any payment in accordance with paragraph 115 shall make such payment subject to the rights of any of the following categories of persons (which rights shall, except to the extent provided in any instrument, have the following order of priority)—

(a) the holder of any fixed security which is over property subject to the floating charge and which ranks prior to, or pari passu with, the floating charge,

(b) creditors in respect of all liabilities and expenses incurred by or on behalf of the administrator,

(c) the administrator in respect of his liabilities, expenses and remuneration and any indemnity to which he is entitled out of the property of the company,

(d) the preferential creditors entitled to payment in accordance with paragraph 65,

(e) the holder of the floating charge in accordance with the priority of that charge in relation to any other floating charge which has attached, and

(f) the holder of a fixed security, other than one referred to in paragraph (a), which is over property subject to the floating charge.

Amendments—Inserted by Enterprise Act 2002, s 248(2), Sch 16. Amended by Enterprise Act 2002, s 248(2), Sch 16; SI 2003/2096; SI 2004/2326; SI 2005/879.

SCHEDULE 1
POWERS OF ADMINISTRATOR OR ADMINISTRATIVE
RECEIVER

Sections 14, 42

1

Power to take possession of, collect and get in the property of the company and, for that purpose, to take such proceedings as may seem to him expedient.

2

Power to sell or otherwise dispose of the property of the company by public auction or private contract or, in Scotland, to sell, hire out or otherwise dispose of the property of the company by public group or private bargain.

3

Power to raise or borrow money and grant security therefor over the property of the company.

4

Power to appoint a solicitor or accountant or other professionally qualified person to assist him in the performance of his functions.

5

Power to bring or defend any action or other legal proceedings in the name and on behalf of the company.

6

Power to refer to arbitration any question affecting the company.

7

Power to effect and maintain insurances in respect of the business and property of the company.

8

Power to use the company's seal.

9

Power to do all acts and to execute in the name and on behalf of the company any deed, receipt or other document.

10

Power to draw, accept, make and endorse any bill of exchange or promissory note in the name and on behalf of the company.

11

Power to appoint any agent to do any business which he is unable to do himself or which can more conveniently be done by an agent and power to employ and dismiss employees.

12

Power to do all such things (including the carrying out of works) as may be necessary for the realisation of the property of the company.

13

Power to make any payment which is necessary or incidental to the performance of his functions.

14

Power to carry on the business of the company.

15

Power to establish subsidiaries of the company.

16

Power to transfer to subsidiaries of the company the whole or any part of the business and property of the company.

17

Power to grant or accept a surrender of a lease or tenancy of any of the property of the company, and to take a lease or tenancy of any property required or convenient for the business of the company.

18

Power to make any arrangement or compromise on behalf of the company.

19

Power to call up any uncalled capital of the company.

20

Power to rank and claim in the bankruptcy, insolvency, sequestration or liquidation of any person indebted to the company and to receive dividends, and to accede to trust deeds for the creditors of any such person.

21

Power to present or defend a petition for the winding up of the company.

22

Power to change the situation of the company's registered office.

23

Power to do all other things incidental to the exercise of the foregoing powers.

Amendments—Abolition of Feudal Tenure etc (Scotland) Act 2000, s 76(2), Sch 13, Pt 1.

General note—These powers should be read against s 42 (administrative receivers), para 60 of Sch B1 (administrators) and the notes thereto.

SCHEDULE 2
POWERS OF A SCOTTISH RECEIVER (ADDITIONAL TO THOSE CONFERRED ON HIM BY THE INSTRUMENT OF CHARGE)

Section 55

1

Power to take possession of, collect and get in the property from the company or a liquidator thereof or any other person, and for that purpose, to take such proceedings as may seem to him expedient.

2

Power to sell, hire out or otherwise dispose of the property by public roup or private bargain and with or without advertisement.

3

Power to raise or borrow money and grant security therefor over the property.

4

Power to appoint a solicitor or accountant or other professionally qualified person to assist him in the performance of his functions.

5

Power to bring or defend any action or other legal proceedings in the name and on behalf of the company.

6

Power to refer to arbitration all questions affecting the company.

7

Power to effect and maintain insurances in respect of the business and property of the company.

8

Power to use the company's seal.

9

Power to do all acts and to execute in the name and on behalf of the company any deed, receipt or other document.

10

Power to draw, accept, make and endorse any bill of exchange or promissory note in the name and on behalf of the company.

11

Power to appoint any agent to do any business which he is unable to do himself or which can more conveniently be done by an agent, and power to employ and dismiss employees.

12

Power to do all such things (including the carrying out of works), as may be necessary for the realisation of the property.

13

Power to make any payment which is necessary or incidental to the performance of his functions.

14

Power to carry on the business of the company or any part of it.

15

Power to grant or accept a surrender of a lease or tenancy of any of the property, and to take a lease or tenancy of any property required or convenient for the business of the company.

16

Power to make any arrangement or compromise on behalf of the company.

17

Power to call up any uncalled capital of the company.

18

Power to establish subsidiaries of the company.

19

Power to transfer to subsidiaries of the company the business of the company or any part of it and any of the property.

20

Power to rank and claim in the bankruptcy, insolvency, sequestration or liquidation of any person or company indebted to the company and to receive dividends, and to accede to trust deeds for creditors of any such person.

21

Power to present or defend a petition for the winding up of the company.

22

Power to change the situation of the company's registered office.

23

Power to do all other things incidental to the exercise of the powers mentioned in section 55(1) of this Act or above in this Schedule.

Amendments—Abolition of Feudal Tenure etc (Scotland) Act 2000, s 76(2), Sch 13, Pt 1.

SCHEDULE 2A
EXCEPTIONS TO PROHIBITION ON APPOINTMENT OF ADMINISTRATIVE RECEIVER: SUPPLEMENTARY PROVISIONS

Section 72H(1)

1 Capital market arrangement

(1) For the purposes of section 72B an arrangement is a capital market arrangement if—

    (a)   it involves a grant of security to a person holding it as trustee for a person who holds a capital market investment issued by a party to the arrangement, or

    (aa)   it involves a grant of security to—

        (i)   a party to the arrangement who issues a capital market investment, or

        (ii)   a person who holds the security as trustee for a party to the arrangement in connection with the issue of a capital market investment, or

    (ab)   it involves a grant of security to a person who holds the security as trustee for a party to the arrangement who agrees to provide finance to another party, or

    (b)   at least one party guarantees the performance of obligations of another party, or

    (c)   at least one party provides security in respect of the performance of obligations of another party, or

    (d)   the arrangement involves an investment of a kind described in articles 83 to 85 of the Financial Services and Markets Act 2000

(Regulated Activities) Order 2001 (SI 2001/544) (options, futures and contracts for differences).

(2) For the purposes of sub-paragraph (1)—

(a) a reference to holding as trustee includes a reference to holding as nominee or agent,

(b) a reference to holding for a person who holds a capital market investment includes a reference to holding for a number of persons at least one of whom holds a capital market investment, and

(c) a person holds a capital market investment if he has a legal or beneficial interest in it; and

(d) the reference to the provision of finance includes the provision of an indemnity.

(3) In section 72B(1) and this paragraph 'party' to an arrangement includes a party to an agreement which—

(a) forms part of the arrangement,

(b) provides for the raising of finance as part of the arrangement, or

(c) is necessary for the purposes of implementing the arrangement.

2 Capital market investment

(1) For the purposes of section 72B an investment is a capital market investment if it—

(a) is within article 77 or 77A of the Financial Services and Markets Act 2000 (Regulated Activities) Order 2001 (SI 2001/544) (debt instruments), and

(b) is rated, listed or traded or designed to be rated, listed or traded.

(2) In sub-paragraph (1)—

'rated' means rated for the purposes of investment by an internationally recognised rating agency,

'listed' means admitted to the official list within the meaning given by section 103(1) of the Financial Services and Markets Act 2000 (interpretation), and

'traded' means admitted to trading on a market established under the rules of a recognised investment exchange or on a foreign market.

(3) In sub-paragraph (2)—

'recognised investment exchange' has the meaning given by section 285 of the Financial Services and Markets Act 2000 (recognised investment exchange), and

'foreign market' has the same meaning as 'relevant market' in article 67(2) of the Financial Services and Markets Act 2000 (Financial Promotion) Order 2001 (SI 2001/1335) (foreign markets).

Amendments—SI 2010/86.

3

(1) An investment is also a capital market investment for the purposes of section 72B if it consists of a bond or commercial paper issued to one or more of the following—

    (a)   an investment professional within the meaning of article 19(5) of the Financial Services and Markets Act 2000 (Financial Promotion) Order 2001,

    (b)   a person who is, when the agreement mentioned in section 72B(1) is entered into, a certified high net worth individual in relation to a communication within the meaning of article 48(2) of that order,

    (c)   a person to whom article 49(2) of that order applies (high net worth company, etc),

    (d)   a person who is, when the agreement mentioned in section 72B(1) is entered into, a certified sophisticated investor in relation to a communication within the meaning of article 50(1) of that order, and

    (e)   a person in a State other than the United Kingdom who under the law of that State is not prohibited from investing in bonds or commercial paper.

(2) In sub-paragraph (1)—

'bond' shall be construed in accordance with article 77 of the Financial Services and Markets Act 2000 (Regulated Activities) Order 2001 (SI 2001/544), and includes any instrument falling within article 77A of that Order, and
'commercial paper' has the meaning given by article 9(3) of that order.

(3) For the purposes of sub-paragraph (1)—

    (a)   in applying article 19(5) of the Financial Promotion Order for the purposes of sub-paragraph (1)(a)—
        (i)   in article 19(5)(b), ignore the words after 'exempt person',
        (ii)   in article 19(5)(c)(i), for the words from 'the controlled activity' to the end substitute 'a controlled activity', and
        (iii)   in article 19(5)(e) ignore the words from 'where the communication' to the end, and

    (b)   in applying article 49(2) of that order for the purposes of sub-paragraph (1)(c), ignore article 49(2)(e).

Amendments—SI 2010/86.

4 'Agreement'

For the purposes of sections 72B and 72E and this Schedule 'agreement' includes an agreement or undertaking effected by—

    (a)   contract,
    (b)   deed, or
    (c)   any other instrument intended to have effect in accordance with the law of England and Wales, Scotland or another jurisdiction.

5 Debt

The debt of at least £50 million referred to in section 72B(1)(a) or 72E(2)(a)—

    (a)   may be incurred at any time during the life of the capital market arrangement or financed project, and

    (b)   may be expressed wholly or partly in foreign currency (in which case the sterling equivalent shall be calculated as at the time when the arrangement is entered into or the project begins).

6 Step-in rights

(1) For the purposes of sections 72C to 72E a project has 'step-in rights' if a person who provides finance in connection with the project has a conditional entitlement under an agreement to—

    (a)   assume sole or principal responsibility under an agreement for carrying out all or part of the project, or

    (b)   make arrangements for carrying out all or part of the project.

(2) In sub-paragraph (1) a reference to the provision of finance includes a reference to the provision of an indemnity.

7 Project company

(1) For the purposes of sections 72C to 72E a company is a 'project company' of a project if—

    (a)   it holds property for the purpose of the project,

    (b)   it has sole or principal responsibility under an agreement for carrying out all or part of the project,

    (c)   it is one of a number of companies which together carry out the project,

    (d)   it has the purpose of supplying finance to enable the project to be carried out, or

    (e)   it is the holding company of a company within any of paragraphs (a) to (d).

(2) But a company is not a 'project company' of a project if—

    (a)   it performs a function within sub-paragraph (1)(a) to (d) or is within sub-paragraph (1)(e), but

    (b)   it also performs a function which is not—

        (i)   within sub-paragraph (1)(a) to (d),

        (ii)   related to a function within sub-paragraph (1)(a) to (d), or

        (iii)   related to the project.

(3) For the purposes of this paragraph a company carries out all or part of a project whether or not it acts wholly or partly through agents.

8 'Resources'

In section 72C 'resources' includes—

  (a) funds (including payment for the provision of services or facilities),
  (b) assets,
  (c) professional skill,
  (d) the grant of a concession or franchise, and
  (e) any other commercial resource.

9 'Public body'

(1) In section 72C 'public body' means—

  (a) a body which exercises public functions,
  (b) a body specified for the purposes of this paragraph by the Secretary of State, and
  (c) a body within a class specified for the purposes of this paragraph by the Secretary of State.

(2) A specification under sub-paragraph (1) may be—

  (a) general, or
  (b) for the purpose of the application of section 72C to a specified case.

10 Regulated business

(1) For the purposes of section 72D a business is regulated if it is carried on—

  (a) (*repealed*)
  (b) in reliance on a licence under section 7, 7A or 7B of the Gas Act 1986 (transport and supply of gas),
  (c) in reliance on a licence granted by virtue of section 41C of that Act (power to prescribe additional licensable activity),
  (d) in reliance on a licence under section 6 of the Electricity Act 1989 (supply of electricity),
  (e) by a water undertaker,
  (f) by a sewerage undertaker,
  (g) by a universal service provider within the meaning of Part 3 of the Postal Services Act 2011,
  (h) by a Post Office company within the meaning of Part 1 of that Act,
  (i) (*repealed*)
  (j) in reliance on a licence under section 8 of the Railways Act 1993 (railway services),
  (k) in reliance on a licence exemption under section 7 of that Act (subject to sub-paragraph (2) below),
  (l) by the operator of a system of transport which is deemed to be a railway for a purpose of Part I of that Act by virtue of section 81(2) of that Act (tramways, etc),
  (m) by the operator of a vehicle carried on flanged wheels along a system within paragraph (l) or
  (n) in reliance on a European licence granted pursuant to a provision contained in any instrument made for the purpose of

implementing Council Directive 1995/18/EC dated 19th June 1995 on the licensing of railway undertakings, as amended by Directive 2001/13/EC dated 26th February 2001 and Directive 2004/49/EC dated 29th April 2004, both of the European Parliament and of the Council, or pursuant to any action taken by an EEA State for that purpose.

(2) Sub-paragraph (1)(k) does not apply to the operator of a railway asset on a railway unless on some part of the railway there is a permitted line speed exceeding 40 kilometres per hour.

(2A) For the purposes of section 72D a business is also regulated to the extent that it consists in the provision of a public electronic communications network or a public electronic communications service.

(2B) In sub-paragraph (1)(n), an 'EEA State' means a member State, Norway, Iceland or Liechtenstein.

11 'Person'

A reference to a person in this Schedule includes a reference to a partnership or another unincorporated group of persons.

Amendments—Inserted by Enterprise Act 2002, s 250(2), Sch 18. Amended by Communications Act 2003, s 406(1), (7), Sch 17, para 82(1), (4), Sch 19(1); SI 2003/1468; SI 2005/3050; Postal Services Act 2011, s 91(1), (2), Sch 12, Pt 3, paras 124, 126; SI 2012/2400.

General note—See the note on ss 72A–72H in the introductory note to receivership preceding s 28.

SCHEDULE 3
ORDERS IN COURSE OF WINDING UP PRONOUNCED IN VACATION (SCOTLAND)

Section 162

PART I
ORDERS WHICH ARE TO BE FINAL

Orders under section 153, as to the time for proving debts and claims.

Orders under section 195 as to meetings for ascertaining wishes of creditors or contributories.

Orders under section 198, as to the examination of witnesses in regard to the property or affairs of a company.

PART II
ORDERS WHICH ARE TO TAKE EFFECT UNTIL MATTER DISPOSED OF BY INNER HOUSE

Orders under section 126(1), 130(2) or (3), 147, 227 or 228, restraining or permitting the commencement or the continuance of legal proceedings.

Orders under section 135(5), limiting the powers of provisional liquidators.

Orders under section 108, appointing a liquidator to fill a vacancy.

Orders under section 167 or 169, sanctioning the exercise of any powers by a liquidator, other than the powers specified in paragraphs 1, 2 and 3 of Schedule 4 to this Act.

Orders under section 158, as to the arrest and detention of an absconding contributory and his property.

SCHEDULE 4
POWERS OF LIQUIDATOR IN A WINDING UP

Sections 165, 167

General comment on Schedule 4—This Schedule deals with the powers that are given to liquidators of companies. The powers are not exhaustive of those given to liquidators. Particular reference should be had to s 168 where supplementary powers for liquidators are mentioned. Liquidators of voluntary liquidations are given powers in ss 165 and 166. Other provisions in the Act, such as s 236 (power to apply for examinations), set out specific powers given to liquidators. The Schedule does not apply to provisional liquidators, but courts have the power, in their discretion, to grant provisional liquidators particular powers when appointing them. See the notes accompanying s 135.

Generally on liquidator powers, see A Keay *McPherson's Law of Company Liquidation* (3rd edn, Sweet and Maxwell, 2013) at 517-541.

PART I
POWERS EXERCISABLE WITH SANCTION

General comment on Part 1—The powers in this Part must have the sanction of the court or the liquidation committee in a court winding up (s 167(1)). This is also the case in relation to creditors' voluntary liquidations, save that if there is no committee the sanction of a creditors' meeting suffices (s 165(2)(b)). If a liquidator goes to the liquidation committee for approval and it fails to give that approval, the liquidator could apply to the court and its decision is paramount: *Re North Eastern Insurance Co Ltd* (1915) 113 LT 989.

In members' voluntary liquidations, the sanction of an extraordinary meeting of the company is required (s 165(2)(a)).

1

Power to pay any class of creditors in full.

2

Power to make any compromise or arrangement with creditors or persons claiming to be creditors, or having or alleging themselves to have any claim (present or future, certain or contingent, ascertained or sounding only in damages) against the company, or whereby the company may be rendered liable.

General note—The power to effect compromises is wide, and wide enough to permit the liquidator to enter into any compromise arrangement with creditors that might have been entered into by the company itself: *Re Bank of Credit and Commerce International SA (No 2)* [1992] BCC 715, [1993] BCLC 1490.

According to Australian authority, the role of the court is not to evaluate whether a proposal is commercially sound, as that is the function of the liquidator. The court will only interfere where there is some lack of good faith, error in law or principle, or some real and substantive ground for questioning the proposal: *State Bank of New South Wales v Turner Corporation Ltd* (1994) 14 ACSR 480 at 483. If a party alleges a lack of good faith etc, then the burden that is on that party is not light, as the liquidator is regarded as being generally in the best position to assess whether a proposal is in the best interests of the creditors: *Re Geelong Building Society* (1996) 14 ACLC 334 at 338.

The main concern for a court, in deciding whether or not to sanction a compromise in relation to an insolvent company, is whether the compromise benefits and serves the interest of the creditors in the funds of the company: *Re Edennote Ltd (No 2)* [1997] 2 BCLC 89; *Re Greenhaven Motors Ltd* [1999] BCC 463, [1999] 1 BCLC 635, CA. It has been held that just because the liquidator might benefit personally from a compromise, namely relief from liability in costs, a compromise will not be refused: *Re Greenhaven Motors Ltd* [1999] BCC 463, [1999] 1 BCLC 635, CA.

Courts, when hearing applications seeking the sanction for a compromise, will not consider all of the issues considered by the liquidator in coming to his or her decision about the compromise proposal. Rather, the court's function is to review the proposal, consider the liquidator's commercial judgment and knowledge of the liquidation, and ensure that it is satisfied that the liquidator has not committed an error of law or that there is any ground for suspecting bad faith or impropriety: *Corporate Affairs Commission v ASC Timber Pty Ltd* (1998) 16 ACLC 1642 at 1650. The English courts have taken a similar approach. While the court is not bound by the views of the liquidator it should not conduct a mini-trial of the merits of the issues that relate to the claim that is being compromised:*Rubin v Coote* [2009] EWHC 2266 (Ch), [2010] BPIR 262 (appeal dismissed: [2011] EWCA Civ 106, [2011] BCC 596).

In considering whether to sanction a compromise, it has been said in the Australian case of *Re S & D International Pty Ltd (in liquidation) (No 7)* [2012] VSC 551 that the following questions should be considered: Is the compromise of debt proposed by the liquidator in the best interests of creditors? Has the liquidator made a proper assessment of prospects and recovery of the debt? Are there any concerns about future claims by creditors against the liquidators in relation to the debt? Is the proposed compromise in good faith and for a proper purpose? Has there been full and frank disclosure to the Court/creditors of all matters relevant to the debt and the proposed compromise?

A compromise can be sanctioned retrospectively by the court: *Re Associated Travel Leisure* [1978] 1 WLR 547; *Re A Debtor* [1984] 3 All ER 995.

3

In the case of a winding up in Scotland, power to compromise, on such terms as may be agreed—

    (a)   all calls and liabilities to calls, all debts and liabilities capable of resulting in debts, and all claims (present or future, certain or contingent, ascertained or sounding only in damages) subsisting or supposed to subsist between the company and a contributory or alleged contributory or other debtor or person apprehending liability to the company, and

    (b)   all questions in any way relating to or affecting the assets or the winding up of the company,

and take any security for the discharge of any such call, debt, liability or claim and give a complete discharge in respect of it.

Amendments—SI 2010/18.

3A

Power to bring legal proceedings under section 213, 214, 238, 239, 242, 243 or 423.

Amendments—Enterprise Act 2002, s 253.

General note—This was introduced by the Enterprise Act 2002 so as to require liquidators to obtain sanction before initiating proceedings under the relevant sections mentioned in the paragraph. Until recently, the costs of such proceedings could not be claimed by liquidators from the company's assets (*Re Floor Fourteen Ltd*, sub nom *Lewis v IRC* [2001] 3 All ER 499, [2002] BCC 198, CA), but that has been overruled now by a change to r 4.218(1) (see the notes under that rule). Paragraph 3A ensures that liquidators do not embark on potentially costly proceedings without sanction from the required body.

It has been held that retrospective sanctioning of proceedings by the courts is permissible. But prospective sanctioning cannot be seen as also giving retrospective sanctioning: *Gresham International Ltd v Moonie* [2009] EWHC 1093 (Ch), [2010] BPIR 122, [2009] 2 BCLC 256. Retrospective sanctioning was not given in this case. Peter Smith J said that if it was a matter of mere inadvertence on the part of the liquidator in obtaining sanction, then sanction would have been granted retrospectively as part of the court's supervisory jurisdiction, but that was not the situation in this case.

The absence of sanction does not render proceedings a nullity, but it does prevent the liquidator recovering his or her own costs up to the time of the sanctioning: *Gresham* ibid.

PART II
POWERS EXERCISABLE WITHOUT SANCTION IN VOLUNTARY WINDING UP, WITH SANCTION IN WINDING UP BY THE COURT

4

Power to bring or defend any action or other legal proceeding in the name and on behalf of the company.

General note—While the liquidator has to obtain the sanction of the court to bring proceedings in the name of the company, the liquidator is able to bring or defend proceedings in his or her own name without sanction: *Re Silver Valley Mines* (1882) 21 Ch D 381. Liquidators might be reluctant to do so as they may well be liable for any costs. If proceedings are commenced in the name of the company without sanction, the liquidator may ratify and then continue the proceedings in his or her name without the need for court approval: *Alexander Ward & Co Ltd v Samyang Navigation Co Ltd* [1975] 1 WLR 673, HL. Many actions that a liquidator might want to bring will have to be in his or her own name, such as preference proceedings under s 239, as the actions are given to the liquidator on liquidation, and were not available to the company prior to winding up. On the question of costs, even if proceedings are brought in the name of the company, a liquidator might be held personally liable for costs under s 51(1) and (3) of the Supreme Court Act 1981, which gives the courts the power to order costs against non-parties: *Aiden Shipping Co Ltd v Interbulk Ltd* [1986] AC 965, HL; *Globe Equities Ltd v Globe Legal Services Ltd* (1999) BLR 232; (1999) *The Times*, April 14, CA.

5

Power to carry on the business of the company so far as may be necessary for its beneficial winding up.

General note—A voluntary liquidator, who does not get leave to carry on business, must be aware that he or she needs to have reasonable grounds for believing that carrying on the business is beneficial or else he or she may be held personally liable for any loss sustained: *Re Centralcast Engineering Ltd* [2000] BCC 727.

While in *Re Wreck Recovery & Salvage Co* (1880) 15 Ch D 353 at 362) Thesiger LJ said that the liquidator's statutory authority to carry on business is to be construed liberally, the power is only to be exercised where it is clearly necessary and will benefit the winding up, and it does not cover activity that involves speculation with the assets in the hope of making a profit for the benefit of the creditors or shareholders. In this context 'necessary' means something more than beneficial, and it will be determined by the court, having regard to all the circumstances of the case: *Re Wreck Recovery & Salvage Co* at 360. The power confines a liquidator to acts relating to the business of the company as it existed when the winding up commenced: *Re Crouch* [2007] NSWSC 1055, (2007) 214 FLR 244 at [23].

Courts will not decide on whether a liquidator acted improperly in carrying on a business by making a judgment from hindsight; a court will not chastise a liquidator who, at the relevant time, acted bona fide, and reasonably formed the opinion that it was necessary to carry on the business for the benefit of winding up or disposal of the company's business: *Re Great Eastern Electric Co* [1941] Ch 241.

The liquidator is permitted to carry on the business so that it can be sold as a going concern at a higher price than would be received for the assets in a liquidation sale: *Re Skay Fashions Pty Ltd (in liq)* (1986) 10 ACLR 743; *Warne v GDK Financial Solutions Pty Ltd* [2006] NSWSC 464, (2006) 233 ALR 181 at [49].

PART III
POWERS EXERCISABLE WITHOUT SANCTION IN ANY WINDING UP

6

Power to sell any of the company's property by public auction or private contract with power to transfer the whole of it to any person or to sell the same in parcels.

General note—'Property' here includes causes of action vested in the company at the time of the liquidation (*Seear v Lawson* (1880) 15 Ch D 426 at 432–433; *Grovewood Holdings plc v James Capel & Co Ltd* [1995] BCC 760). So, a sale of a bare cause of action is permissible, as is a transfer of a half beneficial interest or other share in recoveries in return for financing the action (*Grovewood* ay 764; *Ruttle Plant Ltd v Secretary of State for the Environment, Food and Rural Affairs* [2008] EWHC 238 (TCC) at [25]). An assignment together with the power to manage proceedings to the assignor is permissible where the action is one that is vested in the company: *Rawnsley v Weatherall Green & Smith North Ltd* [2009] EWHC 2482 (Ch), [2010] 1 BCLC 658, [2010] BPIR 449, [2010] BCC 406. But an assignment by the liquidator to a third party of the fruits of proceedings with the power to initiate or continue legal proceedings brought to enforce a cause of action, is not permissible as it is champertous if the right to bring the action is vested in the liquidator, such as under s 214: *Grovewood Holdings* at 765; *Ruttle Plant* at [43]). A liquidator cannot surrender his or fiduciary power to control proceedings commenced in the name of the company *(Ruttle Plant* at [43]). Liquidators are not permitted to assign actions that are granted to them as liquidators, such as under s 214 or s 239, because they are actions given by statute to them personally in the position of liquidator: *Re Oasis Merchandising Services Ltd* [1995] BCC 911, affirmed on appeal [1997] 1 All ER 1009, [1997] BCC 282, CA.

It has been held by the New South Wales Court of Appeal that where the company, before liquidation, had agreed that particular property was incapable of being assigned, the power in this paragraph does not enable the liquidator to assign the property provided that the agreement not to assign was valid in law: *Owners of Strata Plan 5290 v CGS & Co Pty Ltd* [2011] NSWCA 168 at [64].

Where a liquidator is considering making an assignment of a cause of action, he or she, if not a lawyer, should not proceed on the basis of his or her own valuation: *Ultraframe*

(UK) Ltd v Rigby [2005] EWCA Civ 276 at [52]. Furthermore, according to the Court of Appeal in *Ultraframe* (at [52]), it is desirable for the liquidator to follow the procedure laid out in *Stein v Blake* [1996] AC 243 at 260 by Lord Hoffmann, namely to agree the assignment on the basis that a right to a percentage of the proceeds of the action is reserved for the liquidator on behalf of the company.

The power to disclaim is able to be covered by this paragraph: *Re Business Dream Ltd* [2011] EWHC 2860 (Ch), [2012] BCC 115 at [36].

6A

In the case of a winding up in England and Wales, power to compromise, on such terms as may be agreed—

> (a) all calls and liabilities to calls, all debts and liabilities capable of resulting in debts, and all claims (present or future, certain or contingent, ascertained or sounding only in damages) subsisting or supposed to subsist between the company and a contributory or alleged contributory or other debtor or person apprehending liability to the company, and
>
> (b) subject to paragraph 2 in Part 1 of this Schedule, all questions in any way relating to or affecting the assets or the winding up of the company,

and take any security for the discharge of any such call, debt, liability or claim and give a complete discharge in respect of it.

Amendments—Inserted by SI 2010/18.

General note—Prior to the enactment of this provision liquidators had to secure the sanction of the court.

7

Power to do all acts and execute, in the name and on behalf of the company, all deeds, receipts and other documents and for that purpose to use, when necessary, the company's seal.

General note—If liquidators enter into contracts on behalf of the company, they do not become liable if they make it clear to the other parties that they are acting on behalf of the company: *Stead Hazel & Co v Cooper* [1933] 1 KB 840.

8

Power to prove, rank and claim in the bankruptcy, insolvency or sequestration of any contributory for any balance against his estate, and to receive dividends in the bankruptcy, insolvency or sequestration in respect of that balance, as a separate debt due from the bankrupt or insolvent, and rateably with the other separate creditors.

9

Power to draw, accept, make and indorse any bill of exchange or promissory note in the name and on behalf of the company, with the same effect with respect to the company's liability as if the bill or note had been drawn, accepted, made or indorsed by or on behalf of the company in the course of its business.

General note—When exercising this power a liquidator should sign as the liquidator as well as for and on behalf of the company in order to avoid personal liability on the cheque or other instrument involved: *Rolfe Lubell & Co v Keith* [1979] 1 All ER 860.

10

Power to raise on the security of the assets of the company any money requisite.

General note—If a liquidator raises money as against company property, which is used as security, the security granted is subject to the rights of existing secured creditors whose rights are fixed: *Re Regent's Canal Ironworks Co* (1875) 3 Ch D 411.

11

Power to take out in his official name letters of administration to any deceased contributory, and to do in his official name any other act necessary for obtaining payment of any money due from a contributory or his estate which cannot conveniently be done in the name of the company.

In all such cases the money due is deemed, for the purpose of enabling the liquidator to take out the letters of administration or recover the money, to be due to the liquidator himself.

12

Power to appoint an agent to do any business which the liquidator is unable to do himself.

13

Power to do all such other things as may be necessary for winding up the company's affairs and distributing its assets.

General note—This is known as the incidental power, or even a 'mopping-up provision' (*Re Phoenix Oil and Transport Co Ltd (No 2)* [1958] Ch 565, [1958] 1 All ER 158). The power is extremely broad (*Re Cambrian Mining Co* (1882) 48 LT 114 at 116), and relies on the professionalism and competence of the liquidator. It permits the liquidator to do anything which may be thought expedient with reference to the property of the company (*Re Cambrian Mining Co* at 116). Australian authorities have provided that the power allows a liquidator to lease company property (*Re Premier Permanent Building Society* (1890) 16 VLR 643) or purchase property for the purpose of resale: *Re Bairnsdale Food Products Ltd* [1948] VLR 624.

The power cannot be invoked to permit the liquidator to do something which is specifically covered by another paragraph in Sch 4 and that can only be exercised with approval (*Re Phoenix Oil and Transport Co Ltd (No 2)*).

The power to disclaim is able to be covered by this paragraph: *Re Business Dream Ltd* [2011] EWHC 2860 (Ch), [2012] BCC 115 at [36].

SCHEDULE 4ZA
CONDITIONS FOR MAKING A DEBT RELIEF ORDER

Amendments—Inserted by Tribunals, Courts and Enforcement Act 2007, s 108(1), Sch 18.

PART 1
CONDITIONS WHICH MUST BE MET

1 Connection with England and Wales

(1) The debtor—

- (a) is domiciled in England and Wales on the application date; or
- (b) at any time during the period of three years ending with that date—
- (i) was ordinarily resident, or had a place of residence, in England and Wales; or
- (ii) carried on business in England and Wales.

(2) The reference in sub-paragraph (1)(b)(ii) to the debtor carrying on business includes—

- (a) the carrying on of business by a firm or partnership of which he is a member;
- (b) the carrying on of business by an agent or manager for him or for such a firm or partnership.

2 Debtor's previous insolvency history

The debtor is not, on the determination date—

- (a) an undischarged bankrupt;
- (b) subject to an interim order or voluntary arrangement under Part 8; or
- (c) subject to a bankruptcy restrictions order or a debt relief restrictions order.

3

A debtor's petition for the debtor's bankruptcy under Part 9—

- (a) has not been presented by the debtor before the determination date;
- (b) has been so presented, but proceedings on the petition have been finally disposed of before that date; or
- (c) has been so presented and proceedings in relation to the petition remain before the court at that date, but the court has referred the debtor under section 274A(2) for the purposes of making an application for a debt relief order.

4

A creditor's petition for the debtor's bankruptcy under Part 9—

(2) An order may be made only on the application of—

    (a)   the Secretary of State, or

    (b)   the official receiver acting on a direction of the Secretary of State.

2 Grounds for making order

(1) The court shall grant an application for a debt relief restrictions order if it thinks it appropriate to do so having regard to the conduct of the debtor (whether before or after the making of the debt relief order).

(2) The court shall, in particular, take into account any of the following kinds of behaviour on the part of the debtor—

    (a)   failing to keep records which account for a loss of property by the debtor, or by a business carried on by him, where the loss occurred in the period beginning two years before the application date for the debt relief order and ending with the date of the application for the debt relief restrictions order;

    (b)   failing to produce records of that kind on demand by the official receiver;

    (c)   entering into a transaction at an undervalue in the period beginning two years before the application date for the debt relief order and ending with the date of the determination of that application;

    (d)   giving a preference in the period beginning two years before the application date for the debt relief order and ending with the date of the determination of that application;

    (e)   making an excessive pension contribution;

    (f)   a failure to supply goods or services that were wholly or partly paid for;

    (g)   trading at a time, before the date of the determination of the application for the debt relief order, when the debtor knew or ought to have known that he was himself to be unable to pay his debts;

    (h)   incurring, before the date of the determination of the application for the debt relief order, a debt which the debtor had no reasonable expectation of being able to pay;

    (i)   failing to account satisfactorily to the court or the official receiver for a loss of property or for an insufficiency of property to meet his debts;

    (j)   carrying on any gambling, rash and hazardous speculation or unreasonable extravagance which may have materially contributed to or increased the extent of his inability to pay his debts before the application date for the debt relief order or which took place between that date and the date of the determination of the application for the debt relief order;

    (k)   neglect of business affairs of a kind which may have materially contributed to or increased the extent of his inability to pay his debts;

    (l)   fraud or fraudulent breach of trust;

    (m) failing to co-operate with the official receiver.

(3) The court shall also, in particular, consider whether the debtor was an undischarged bankrupt at some time during the period of six years ending with the date of the application for the debt relief order.

(4) For the purposes of sub-paragraph (2)—

'excessive pension contribution' shall be construed in accordance with section 342A;
'preference' shall be construed in accordance with paragraph 10(2) of Schedule 4ZA;
'undervalue' shall be construed in accordance with paragraph 9(2) of that Schedule.

3 Timing of application for order

An application for a debt relief restrictions order in respect of a debtor may be made—

(a)   at any time during the moratorium period relating to the debt relief order in question, or

(b)   after the end of that period, but only with the permission of the court.

4 Duration of order

(1) A debt relief restrictions order—

(a)   comes into force when it is made, and

(b)   ceases to have effect at the end of a date specified in the order.

(2) The date specified in a debt relief restrictions order under sub-paragraph (1)(b) must not be—

(a)   before the end of the period of two years beginning with the date on which the order is made, or

(b)   after the end of the period of 15 years beginning with that date.

5 Interim debt relief restrictions order

(1) This paragraph applies at any time between—

(a)   the institution of an application for a debt relief restrictions order, and

(b)   the determination of the application.

(2) The court may make an interim debt relief restrictions order if the court thinks that—

(a)   there are prima facie grounds to suggest that the application for the debt relief restrictions order will be successful, and

(b)   it is in the public interest to make an interim debt relief restrictions order.

(3) An interim debt relief restrictions order may only be made on the application of—

    (a)   the Secretary of State, or

    (b)   the official receiver acting on a direction of the Secretary of State.

(4) An interim debt relief restrictions order—

    (a)   has the same effect as a debt relief restrictions order, and

    (b)   comes into force when it is made.

(5) An interim debt relief restrictions order ceases to have effect—

    (a)   on the determination of the application for the debt relief restrictions order,

    (b)   on the acceptance of a debt relief restrictions undertaking made by the debtor, or

    (c)   if the court discharges the interim debt relief restrictions order on the application of the person who applied for it or of the debtor.

6

(1) This paragraph applies to a case in which both an interim debt relief restrictions order and a debt relief restrictions order are made.

(2) Paragraph 4(2) has effect in relation to the debt relief restrictions order as if a reference to the date of that order were a reference to the date of the interim debt relief restrictions order.

7 Debt relief restrictions undertaking

(1) A debtor may offer a debt relief restrictions undertaking to the Secretary of State.

(2) In determining whether to accept a debt relief restrictions undertaking the Secretary of State shall have regard to the matters specified in paragraph 2(2) and (3).

8

A reference in an enactment to a person in respect of whom a debt relief restrictions order has effect (or who is 'the subject of' a debt relief restrictions order) includes a reference to a person in respect of whom a debt relief restrictions undertaking has effect.

9

(1) A debt relief restrictions undertaking—

    (a)   comes into force on being accepted by the Secretary of State, and

    (b)   ceases to have effect at the end of a date specified in the undertaking.

(2) The date specified under sub-paragraph (1)(b) must not be—

(a) before the end of the period of two years beginning with the date on which the undertaking is accepted, or

(b) after the end of the period of 15 years beginning with that date.

(3) On an application by the debtor the court may—

(a) annul a debt relief restrictions undertaking;

(b) provide for a debt relief restrictions undertaking to cease to have effect before the date specified under sub-paragraph (1)(b).

10 Effect of revocation of debt relief order

Unless the court directs otherwise, the revocation at any time of a debt relief order does not—

(a) affect the validity of any debt relief restrictions order, interim debt relief restrictions order or debt relief restrictions undertaking which is in force in respect of the debtor;

(b) prevent the determination of any application for a debt relief restrictions order, or an interim debt relief restrictions order, in relation to the debtor that was instituted before that time;

(c) prevent the acceptance of a debt relief restrictions undertaking that was offered before that time; or

(d) prevent the institution of an application for a debt relief restrictions order or interim debt relief restrictions order in respect of the debtor, or the offer or acceptance of a debt relief restrictions undertaking by the debtor, after that time.

Amendments—Inserted by Tribunals, Courts and Enforcement Act 2007, s 108(1), Sch 18.

SCHEDULE 4A
BANKRUPTCY RESTRICTIONS ORDER AND UNDERTAKING

Section 281A

1 Bankruptcy restrictions order

(1) A bankruptcy restrictions order may be made by the court.

(2) An order may be made only on the application of—

(a) the Secretary of State, or

(b) the official receiver acting on a direction of the Secretary of State.

2 Grounds for making order

(1) The court shall grant an application for a bankruptcy restrictions order if it thinks it appropriate having regard to the conduct of the bankrupt (whether before or after the making of the bankruptcy order).

(2) The court shall, in particular, take into account any of the following kinds of behaviour on the part of the bankrupt—

(a) failing to keep records which account for a loss of property by the bankrupt, or by a business carried on by him, where the loss occurred in the period beginning 2 years before petition and ending with the date of the application;

(b)   failing to produce records of that kind on demand by the official receiver or the trustee;

(c)   entering into a transaction at an undervalue;

(d)   giving a preference;

(e)   making an excessive pension contribution;

(f)   a failure to supply goods or services which were wholly or partly paid for which gave rise to a claim provable in the bankruptcy;

(g)   trading at a time before commencement of the bankruptcy when the bankrupt knew or ought to have known that he was himself to be unable to pay his debts;

(h)   incurring, before commencement of the bankruptcy, a debt which the bankrupt had no reasonable expectation of being able to pay;

(i)   failing to account satisfactorily to the court, the official receiver or the trustee for a loss of property or for an insufficiency of property to meet bankruptcy debts;

(j)   carrying on any gambling, rash and hazardous speculation or unreasonable extravagance which may have materially contributed to or increased the extent of the bankruptcy or which took place between presentation of the petition and commencement of the bankruptcy;

(k)   neglect of business affairs of a kind which may have materially contributed to or increased the extent of the bankruptcy;

(l)   fraud or fraudulent breach of trust;

(m)   failing to cooperate with the official receiver or the trustee.

(3) The court shall also, in particular, consider whether the bankrupt was an undischarged bankrupt at some time during the period of six years ending with the date of the bankruptcy to which the application relates.

(4) For the purpose of sub-paragraph (2)—

'before petition' shall be construed in accordance with section 351(c),
'excessive pension contribution' shall be construed in accordance with section 342A,
'preference' shall be construed in accordance with section 340, and
'undervalue' shall be construed in accordance with section 339.

3 Timing of application for order

(1) An application for a bankruptcy restrictions order in respect of a bankrupt must be made—

(a)   before the end of the period of one year beginning with the date on which the bankruptcy commences, or

(b)   with the permission of the court.

(2) The period specified in sub-paragraph (1)(a) shall cease to run in respect of a bankrupt while the period set for his discharge is suspended under section 279(3).

4 Duration of order

(1) A bankruptcy restrictions order—

    (a)   shall come into force when it is made, and

    (b)   shall cease to have effect at the end of a date specified in the order.

(2) The date specified in a bankruptcy restrictions order under sub-paragraph (1)(b) must not be—

    (a)   before the end of the period of two years beginning with the date on which the order is made, or

    (b)   after the end of the period of 15 years beginning with that date.

5 Interim bankruptcy restrictions order

(1) This paragraph applies at any time between—

    (a)   the institution of an application for a bankruptcy restrictions order, and

    (b)   the determination of the application.

(2) The court may make an interim bankruptcy restrictions order if the court thinks that—

    (a)   there are prima facie grounds to suggest that the application for the bankruptcy restrictions order will be successful, and

    (b)   it is in the public interest to make an interim order.

(3) An interim order may be made only on the application of—

    (a)   the Secretary of State, or

    (b)   the official receiver acting on a direction of the Secretary of State.

(4) An interim order—

    (a)   shall have the same effect as a bankruptcy restrictions order, and

    (b)   shall come into force when it is made.

(5) An interim order shall cease to have effect—

    (a)   on the determination of the application for the bankruptcy restrictions order,

    (b)   on the acceptance of a bankruptcy restrictions undertaking made by the bankrupt, or

    (c)   if the court discharges the interim order on the application of the person who applied for it or of the bankrupt.

6

(1) This paragraph applies to a case in which both an interim bankruptcy restrictions order and a bankruptcy restrictions order are made.

(2) Paragraph 4(2) shall have effect in relation to the bankruptcy restrictions order as if a reference to the date of that order were a reference to the date of the interim order.

7 Bankruptcy restrictions undertaking

(1) A bankrupt may offer a bankruptcy restrictions undertaking to the Secretary of State.

(2) In determining whether to accept a bankruptcy restrictions undertaking the Secretary of State shall have regard to the matters specified in paragraph 2(2) and (3).

8

A reference in an enactment to a person in respect of whom a bankruptcy restrictions order has effect (or who is 'the subject of' a bankruptcy restrictions order) includes a reference to a person in respect of whom a bankruptcy restrictions undertaking has effect.

9

(1) A bankruptcy restrictions undertaking—

(a) shall come into force on being accepted by the Secretary of State, and

(b) shall cease to have effect at the end of a date specified in the undertaking.

(2) The date specified under sub-paragraph (1)(b) must not be—

(a) before the end of the period of two years beginning with the date on which the undertaking is accepted, or

(b) after the end of the period of 15 years beginning with that date.

(3) On an application by the bankrupt the court may—

(a) annul a bankruptcy restrictions undertaking;

(b) provide for a bankruptcy restrictions undertaking to cease to have effect before the date specified under sub-paragraph (1)(b).

10 Effect of annulment of bankruptcy order

Where a bankruptcy order is annulled under section 282(1)(a) or (2)—

(a) any bankruptcy restrictions order, interim order or undertaking which is in force in respect of the bankrupt shall be annulled,

(b) no new bankruptcy restrictions order or interim order may be made in respect of the bankrupt, and

(c) no new bankruptcy restrictions undertaking by the bankrupt may be accepted.

11

Where a bankruptcy order is annulled under section 261, 263D or 282(1)(b)—

(a) the annulment shall not affect any bankruptcy restrictions order, interim order or undertaking in respect of the bankrupt,

(b) the court may make a bankruptcy restrictions order in relation to the bankrupt on an application instituted before the annulment,

(c) the Secretary of State may accept a bankruptcy restrictions undertaking offered before the annulment, and

(d) an application for a bankruptcy restrictions order or interim order in respect of the bankrupt may not be instituted after the annulment.

12 Registration

The Secretary of State shall maintain a register of—

(a) bankruptcy restrictions orders,

(b) interim bankruptcy restrictions orders, and

(c) bankruptcy restrictions undertakings.

Amendments—Inserted by the Enterprise Act 2002, s 257(2), Sch 20.

General note—See s 281A and the notes thereto.

SCHEDULE 5
POWERS OF TRUSTEE IN BANKRUPTCY

Section 314

General note—For commentary on the exercise of powers with and without sanction in winding up see the notes to Sch 4 above.

PART I
POWERS EXERCISABLE WITH SANCTION

1

Power to carry on any business of the bankrupt so far as may be necessary for winding it up beneficially and so far as the trustee is able to do so without contravening any requirement imposed by or under any enactment.

2

Power to bring, institute or defend any action or legal proceedings relating to the property comprised in the bankrupt's estate.

2A

Power to bring legal proceedings under section 339, 340 or 423.

3

Power to accept as the consideration for the sale of any property comprised in the bankrupt's estate a sum of money payable at a future time subject to such stipulations as to security or otherwise as the creditors' committee or the court thinks fit.

4

Power to mortgage or pledge any part of the property comprised in the bankrupt's estate for the purpose of raising money for the payment of his debts.

5

Power, where any right, option or other power forms part of the bankrupt's estate, to make payments or incur liabilities with a view to obtaining, for the benefit of the creditors, any property which is the subject of the right, option or power.

7

Power to make such compromise or other arrangement as may be thought expedient with creditors, or persons claiming to be creditors, in respect of bankruptcy debts.

8

Power to make such compromise or other arrangement as may be thought expedient with respect to any claim arising out of or incidental to the bankrupt's estate made or capable of being made on the trustee by any person.

PART II
GENERAL POWERS

9

Power to sell any part of the property for the time being comprised in the bankrupt's estate, including the goodwill and book debts of any business.

9A

Power to refer to arbitration, or compromise on such terms as may be agreed, any debts, claims or liabilities subsisting or supposed to subsist between the bankrupt and any person who may have incurred any liability to the bankrupt.

9B

Power to make such compromise or other arrangement as may be thought expedient with respect to any claim arising out of or incidental to the bankrupt's estate made or capable of being made by the trustee on any person.

10

Power to give receipts for any money received by him, being receipts which effectually discharge the person paying the money from all responsibility in respect of its application.

11

Power to prove, rank, claim and draw a dividend in respect of such debts due to the bankrupt as are comprised in his estate.

12

Power to exercise in relation to any property comprised in the bankrupt's estate any powers the capacity to exercise which is vested in him under Parts VIII to XI of this Act.

13

Power to deal with any property comprised in the estate to which the bankrupt is beneficially entitled as tenant in tail in the same manner as the bankrupt might have dealt with it.

PART III
ANCILLARY POWERS

14

For the purposes of, or in connection with, the exercise of any of his powers under Parts VIII to XI of this Act, the trustee may, by his official name—

    (a)   hold property of every description,
    (b)   make contracts,
    (c)   sue and be sued,
    (d)   enter into engagements binding on himself and, in respect of the bankrupt's estate, on his successors in office,
    (e)   employ an agent,
    (f)   execute any power of attorney, deed or other instrument;

and he may do any other act which is necessary or expedient for the purposes of or in connection with the exercise of those powers.

Amendments—Enterprise Act 2002, s 262; SI 2010/18.

General note—See s 314 and the notes thereto.

SCHEDULE 6
THE CATEGORIES OF PREFERENTIAL DEBTS

Section 386

General comment on Schedule 6—This was changed in a significant way by the Enterprise Act 2002, in order to accommodate the abolition of the Crown's right to be counted as a preferential creditor. This strategy is part of the Government's attempt to promote corporate rescue and the use of administration as the formal way of dealing with an insolvent company's financial problems. As a result of the commencement of the corporate insolvency provisions in the Enterprise Act, the number of categories of preferential debts was reduced significantly. Hitherto, the majority of provisions in Sch 6 related to debts owed to the Crown, and notably tax deducted from employees' income and not remitted to the revenue authorities, and Value Added Tax due to HM Customs (formerly paras 1 and 3). The abolition of the Crown preference brings the UK into line with such countries as Germany, Austria and Australia, although many other countries, such as Spain, Italy and South Africa, retain a priority for the tax authorities.

The main priority that is provided for under Sch 6 is benefits for company employees (paras 9–13).

The Schedule applies to all insolvency regimes. Notwithstanding the fact that the Schedule appears to establish some sort of hierarchy, with those debts mentioned early on receiving a priority status over debts occurring later in the Schedule, this is not the case, as all preferential debts are equal, and if there are insufficient finds to pay all preferential debts, then they abate in equal proportions (s 176(2)(a)).

There are several references to 'the relevant date' in the Schedule. This expression is explained in s 387. See the notes accompanying that section.

1–7 Category 1: Debts due to Inland Revenue   (*Repealed*)

8 Category 4: Contributions to occupational pension schemes etc

Any sum which is owed by the debtor and is a sum to which Schedule 4 to the Pension Schemes Act 1993 applies (contributions to occupational pension schemes and state scheme premiums).

9 Category 5: Remuneration etc of employees

So much of any amount which—

(a)   is owed by the debtor to a person who is or has been an employee of the debtor, and

(b)   is payable by way of remuneration in respect of the whole or any part of the period of 4 months next before the relevant date,

as does not exceed so much as may be prescribed by order made by the Secretary of State.

10

An amount owed by way of accrued holiday remuneration, in respect of any period of employment before the relevant date, to a person whose employment by the debtor has been terminated, whether before, on or after that date.

11

So much of any sum owed in respect of money advanced for the purpose as has been applied for the payment of a debt which, if it had not been paid, would have been a debt falling within paragraph 9 or 10.

12

So much of any amount which—

(a) is ordered (whether before or after the relevant date) to be paid by the debtor under the Reserve Forces (Safeguard of Employment) Act 1985, and

(b) is so ordered in respect of a default made by the debtor before that date in the discharge of his obligations under that Act, as does not exceed such amount as may be prescribed by order made by the Secretary of State.

13 Interpretation for Category 5

(1) For the purposes of paragraphs 9 to 12, a sum is payable by the debtor to a person by way of remuneration in respect of any period if—

(a) it is paid as wages or salary (whether payable for time or for piece work or earned wholly or partly by way of commission) in respect of services rendered to the debtor in that period, or

(b) it is an amount falling within the following sub-paragraph and is payable by the debtor in respect of that period.

(2) An amount falls within this sub-paragraph if it is—

(a) a guarantee payment under Part III of the Employment Rights Act 1996 (employee without work to do);

(b) any payment for time off under section 53 (time off to look for work or arrange training) or section 56 (time off for ante-natal care) of that Act or under section 169 of the Trade Union and Labour Relations (Consolidation) Act 1992 (time of for carrying out trade union duties etc);

(c) remuneration on suspension on medical grounds, or on maternity grounds, under Part VII of the Employment Rights Act 1996; or

(d) remuneration under a protective award under section 189 of the Trade Union and Labour Relations (Consolidation) Act 1992 (redundancy dismissal with compensation).

14

(1) This paragraph relates to a case in which a person's employment has been terminated by or in consequence of his employer going into liquidation or being adjudged bankrupt or (his employer being a company not in liquidation) by or in consequence of—

(a) a receiver being appointed as mentioned in section 40 of this Act (debenture-holders secured by floating charge), or

(b) the appointment of a receiver under section 53(6) or 54(5) of this Act (Scottish company with property subject to floating charge), or

(c) the taking of possession by debenture-holders (so secured), as mentioned in section 754 of the Companies Act 2006.

(2) For the purposes of paragraphs 9 to 12, holiday remuneration is deemed to have accrued to that person in respect of any period of employment if, by virtue of his contract of employment or of any enactment that remuneration would have accrued in respect of that period if his employment had continued until he became entitled to be allowed the holiday.

(3) The reference in sub-paragraph (2) to any enactment includes an order or direction made under an enactment.

15

Without prejudice to paragraphs 13 and 14—

(a) any remuneration payable by the debtor to a person in respect of a period of holiday or of absence from work through sickness or other good cause is deemed to be wages or (as the case may be) salary in respect of services rendered to the debtor in that period, and

(b) references here and in those paragraphs to remuneration in respect of a period of holiday include any sums which, if they had been paid, would have been treated for the purposes of the enactments relating to social security as earnings in respect of that period.

Amendments—SI 2008/948.

General comment on Category 5—This is now the main category in the Schedule and one that will have to be taken into account in most insolvencies. The primary focus is on paras 9 and 10, which relate to the remuneration and holiday pay of employees of the insolvent.

Who is an employee for the purposes of this category has been a vexed issue, and the case law is difficult to synthesise. The fact that a director is the majority shareholder of a company does not of itself prevent a contract of employment arising (*Clark v Clark Construction Initiatives Ltd* [2008] ICR 635, [2008] IRLR 364, [2008] All ER (D) (Feb) (EAT) (involving a claim against dismissal from a solvent company) (an appeal to the Court of Appeal was dismissed ([2008] EWCA Civ 1446). The Court of Appeal in *Secretary of State for Employment v Bottrill* [1999] BCC 177, [1999] ICR 592, [1999] IRLR 326 said that the fact that a director holds a controlling interest in the company was only one factor in the equation, albeit probably a significant factor. The leading case on the subject is now *Secretary of State for Business Enterprise and Regulatory Reform v Neufeld* [2009] EWCA Civ 280. The judgment of the Court was that there was no reason in principle why a person who was the controlling shareholder and a director of a company could not be an employee. Rimer LJ said that in the situation where the contract is a valid one, was in writing and sufficiently explicit to establish its content, he could not see the relevance of the power of the shareholder/director in making a determination as to whether the director was or was not an employee. His Lordship said that if: 'the contract was not in writing, or was expressed only in short form, so that it is necessary to examine the conduct of the parties in order to deduce the content of the contract, the position of the individual and manner in which the company's affairs were conducted provide the factual setting for the inquiry.' (at [61]). The Court said that there are two issues that have to be considered by a court. First, whether the contract is a genuine contract or a sham. Second, if the contract is genuine, does it amount to a contract of employment ([81]). In considering the second issue various matters might be of relevance including the fact of the director's control of the company. But it would not go against a director merely because he or she had capital invested in the company.

Paragraphs 9, 10 and 12 enable employees to claim: remuneration in respect of the whole or any part of the four months before the relevant date, not exceeding the prescribed amount (at present this is £800); accrued holiday pay for the period of employment before the relevant date (this is also payable to former employees and those whose employment was terminated at or after the relevant date); any amount which is ordered to be paid by the company under the Reserve Forces (Safeguard of Employment) Act 1985, and it is ordered in respect of a default by the company in respect of the employee's obligations under the said Act, not exceeding the prescribed sum (at present it is £800).

The monetary limits mentioned above are prescribed by order of the Secretary of State and at present they are set out in Insolvency Proceedings (Monetary Limits) Order 1986 (SI 1986/1996).

To safeguard employees, because they could be waiting a significant amount of time before they receive their entitlements in an insolvent estate, there is a scheme provided under the Employment Rights Act 1996. Pursuant to this scheme, payments are made to employees by the Secretary of State out of the National Insurance Fund, according to the entitlements that employees have. The Secretary of State is then subrogated to the employees' rights to the extent that the payments made are in respect of the insolvent employers' liabilities, which have preferential status under the Act.

Paragraph 11 covers the situation where a third party advances money to the company for the payment of remuneration or holiday pay of employees. If this is done the third party is entitled to be subrogated to the rights which would be given to the employees. But the right under this paragraph does not exist where an advance is made for general purposes, or the person advancing the money does not specify that it be used for the payment of employees.

See Keay and Walton 'The Preferential Debts' Regime in Liquidation Law: In the Public Interest?' (1999) 3 *Company Financial and Insolvency Law Review* 84; A Keay *McPherson's Law of Company Liquidation* (3rd edn, Sweet and Maxwell, 2013) at 890–903.

15A Category 6: Levies on coal and steel production

Any sums due at the relevant date from the debtor in respect of—

(a) the levies on the production of coal and steel referred to in Articles 49 and 50 of the ECSC Treaty, or

(b) any surcharge for delay provided for in Article 50(3) of that Treaty and Article 6 of Decision 3/52 of the High Authority of the Coal and Steel Community.

16 Orders

An order under paragraph 9 or 12—

(a) may contain such transitional provisions as may appear to the Secretary of State necessary or expedient;

(b) shall be made by statutory instrument subject to annulment in pursuance of a resolution of either House of Parliament.

Amendments—SI 1987/2093; Pension Schemes Act 1993, s 190, Sch 8, para 18; Employment Rights Act 1996, s 240, Sch 1, para 29; Enterprise Act 2002, ss 251(1), 278(2), Sch 26.

SCHEDULE 7
INSOLVENCY PRACTITIONERS TRIBUNAL

Section 396

1 Panels of members

(1) The Secretary of State shall draw up and from time to time revise—